FIGHTING THE GREAT WAR AT SEA

FIGHTING THE GREAT WAR AT SEA

STRATEGY, TACTICS AND TECHNOLOGY

NORMAN FRIEDMAN

FOREWORD BY ADMIRAL SIR GEORGE ZAMBELLAS KCB DSC ADC DL
FIRST SEA LORD AND CHIEF OF NAVAL STAFF

Seaforth
PUBLISHING

FRONTISPIECE: In 1914 it seemed that big-gun capital ships were the ultimate arbiters of naval warfare. The battlecruiser HMS *Princess Royal* is shown. (Naval Institute collection)

This paperback edition first published in Great Britain in 2019 by
Seaforth Publishing,
A division of Pen & Sword Books Ltd,
47 Church Street,
Barnsley S70 2AS

www.seaforthpublishing.com

British Library Cataloguing in Publication Data
A catalogue record for this book is available from the British Library

ISBN 978 1 5267 6549 9 (PAPERBACK)
ISBN 978 1 4738 4936 5 (EPUB)
ISBN 978 1 4738 4953 2 (KINDLE)

Pen & Sword Books Limited incorporates the imprints of Atlas, Archaeology, Aviation, Discovery, Family History, Fiction, History, Maritime, Military, Military Classics, Politics, Select, Transport, True Crime, Air World, Frontline Publishing, Leo Cooper, Remember When, Seaforth Publishing, The Praetorian Press, Wharncliffe Local History, Wharncliffe Transport, Wharncliffe True Crime and White Owl

Typeset and designed by Ian Hughes, Mousemat Design Limited
Printed and bound in China by 1010 Printing International Ltd

Contents

Foreword

2014 marks the centenary of the start of the First World War – the first truly global conflict. So, notwithstanding the deserving spotlight on the mud, barbed wire and trenches of the Western Front, this authoritative book, by an internationally respected naval historian and strategist, is a timely reminder that this war was fought across a much wider front – at sea, as well as on land – spanning the entire globe.

This new study also provides a showcase for Dr Friedman's rare ability to understand and explain not just strategy but also technology, and the interaction between both. Let's not forget: this was the first war in which the maritime battle-space became three dimensional, as aircraft and submarines emerged to trigger the start of a revolution in strategy, operations, tactics and technology, both at sea and from the sea.

In examining the scope and complexity of naval warfare in the First World War, Dr Friedman is also careful to relate his analysis to enduring naval strategy and contemporary maritime operations. In addition to explaining the pre-eminent global authority and performance of the Royal Navy, he helps the reader to understand that, in strategic terms, Kaiser's Germany was gradually brought to its knees by the combined effect of Allied military and naval operations. This was a prelude to the strategic success of multinational and joint operations seen in many subsequent conflicts, through to the present day.

Of particular note, Dr Friedman also focuses on the nascent strategic partnership formed between the United Kingdom and the United States of America during the First World War. The sustained US Navy and Royal Navy cooperation between 1917 and the Armistice was the first practical manifestation of the "Special Relationship." In the following century, the maritime foundations of our strategic TransAtlantic relationship have been very deeply established.

More broadly, Dr Friedman stresses how victory in 1918 was heavily contingent on the continuing ability of Allied nations to connect and trade across the world's oceans, an opportunity which Allied seapower simultaneously denied to Kaiser's Germany. In 1914, the United Kingdom was one of the most globalised powers, with an intimate linkage between the City and the Royal Navy underpinning both national prosperity and security. In this new century, London is still the global capital of maritime business, and the oceans remain our commercial superhighways, with 90% of the world's trade (by volume) being carried by sea. And the White Ensign still flies around the world, in support of the United Kingdom's national ambition – helping to protect our vital economic, diplomatic and security interests and, alongside our partners, helping to maintain stability in the international system at sea.

So, as well as providing a comprehensive, compelling and convincing historical analysis of the First World War at sea, this book has a contemporary relevance too. That is as it should be, because the United Kingdom, and indeed the world beyond, remains as dependent on the sea today as 100 years ago.

George Zambellas

Admiral Sir George Zambellas KCB DSC ADC DL
First Sea Lord and Chief of Naval Staff

June 2014

Acknowledgements

MANY FRIENDS HELPED ME with this project, whose origins extend back many years to research on various types of warships and on First World War naval tactics, strategy and technology (some of which is reflected in earlier books). The germ of my understanding of First World War British strategy (and particularly of opportunities offered by British sea power) was a discussion many years ago with Captain Peter Swartz USN in which he characterised the US Navy's Maritime Strategy as the classic way sea powers confront land powers. He and I were working at the time for US Secretary of the Navy John Lehman, and I had occasion to advocate and explain the Maritime Strategy for various audiences, including at the US Naval War College and in the United Kingdom. I already felt that NATO strategy for the war which might have broken out in Europe might easily lead to something like the First World War stalemate on the Western Front. I was much attracted to the Maritime Strategy as an alternative to such a disaster. I wondered whether some analogue of the Maritime Strategy might have been a better way for Britain to have fought the First World War. What stuck in my mind then, and since, was that Captain Swartz's description was perfectly apt for Britain in the Napoleonic Wars and in the Second World War – but not at all for the First World War. That made me ask why; what was different about Britain in the First World War? It is possible that the answer is that in the Napoleonic Wars and in the Second World War the fact that a single individual was the problem (Napoleon and later Hitler) made it possible to concentrate on the objective of destroying that individual and his power base. In 1914 it was not so obvious what the British war aim should have been, partly because it was not so obvious why the war had broken out. I am grateful to Dr David Stevens (chief historian of the Royal Australian Navy's Seapower Centre-Australia [SPC-A]) for the opportunity to describe my approach to the First World War as keynote speaker at the 2013 King-Hall Conference, and to the audience (and the other speakers) for valuable comments. Similarly, I am grateful to audiences in New York and in Washington for their reactions to my approach, including my characterisation of the Imperial German Navy before 1914 and the wartime consequences of its pre-war nature. I have benefited greatly from discussions with Dr Jon Sumida, with Dr Nicholas Lambert, with Dr David Stevens, with Dr Thomas Hone, with Captain Chris Page RN (former head of the Royal Navy Historical Branch), with Stephen Prince (current head of the Royal Navy Historical Branch), with David Isby, with Christopher C Wright (editor of *Warship International*), with Dr Josef Strazcek (currently probably the pre-eminent historian of naval signals intelligence in the First World War), with A D Baker III, with Commander David Hobbs RN (ret), with Chris Carlson, and with Alexandre Sheldon-Dupleix of the French naval historical section. Others whose assistance I much appreciate were Ian Buxton, Raymond Cheung, Dr Steve Roberts (who, among other things, maintains a unique Shipscribe website which includes the only really detailed account of ships built for the US Emergency Shipping Board during the First World War), and Alan Raven.

As with my earlier publications, this book is based mainly on archival sources. For access to them, I would particularly like to thank Jenny Wraight, the Admiralty Librarian (and others at the Royal Navy Historical Branch); Jeremy Michel and Andrew Choong of the Brass Foundry outstation of the National Maritime Museum; and the staffs of the Public Record Office (now called The National Archive, but still the PRO to veterans), of the US National Archives (both downtown and at College Park), of the French Ministry of Defence archive at Vincennes, and of the Royal Australian Navy's Seapower Centre-Australia (in effect the RAN Historical Branch). Dr Evelyn Cherpak very kindly helped me at her unique archive at the US Naval War College. I am also grateful to the staff of the US Navy Department Library. Dr David Stevens very generously provided me with copies of documents he had copied during research in the United Kingdom and the United States in connection with his own history of the Royal Australian Navy during the First World War.

For photographs my main institutional sources were the still photo collection at Archives II (College Park), the collection of the US Navy Historical and Heritage Center (I am particularly grateful to Chuck Haberlein, its curator emeritus), the photo library of the US Naval Institute (I would particularly like to thank its curator Janis Jorgensen), the Royal Australian Navy's Seapower Centre-Australia, and the State Library of Victoria in Australia. I would also like to thank Dr David Stevens, A D Baker III, Chris Cavas, Christopher C Wright, Dr Maurizio Brescia, Dr Raymond Cheung, Philip Jarrett, Miles McLaughlin and Alan Raven.

I hope that the result justifies the assistance of all those who have helped. Everyone involved helped make this a better book. I remain responsible for the views expressed and for any errors I have made.

I could never have undertaken this project without the sustained loving support of my wife Rhea. Her encouragement has made my work possible. For the current project I greatly benefitted from her comments, based on her historical training, on my views as represented in this book, particularly on the run-up to war in 1914.

Introduction

THIS BOOK IS ABOUT how the naval part of the First World War was fought – about what the navies (and their governments) expected, about what limited them and about the many surprises they encountered. It is not a full operational history, but instead it explores various themes in the naval history of the war, many of them technological and tactical. Without such exploration, much of what happened during the war does not make sense. For example, the quick destruction of three British battlecruisers at Jutland might seem to prove that the battlecruiser concept was fatally flawed or that German shells were disastrously superior to British – except that it could be traced to extraordinarily dangerous British practices adopted after the same German guns and shells proved ineffective at the earlier battle of Dogger Bank. Moreover, contemporary British documents show that the Royal Navy came to exactly that conclusion at the time. The conclusion is not that, had the battlecruisers been handled better, the Royal Navy would have won, but more that the battle should have been even more of a draw than it was. German documentation gives some indication of the impact of the battle on their fleet, which was not quite what is usually assumed. A better understanding of war planning and tactical development on both sides illuminates the actions that the two navies took, both at the beginning of the war and later on.

Above all the naval part of the First World War involved new technology. The most recent experience of modern naval war, the Russo-Japanese War of 1904–5, was only a decade old, yet in the intervening period navies had been revolutionised. Although fire control was primitive at best, both Russian and Japanese heavy guns hit at unprecedented ranges and some of those hits seemed decisive. This experience was used to justify the new 'dreadnoughts' in the Royal Navy and the US Navy. Alongside the guns was extensive use of sea mines, one of which sank a Russian battleship in 1904 and killed the best Russian naval commander, Admiral Makarov. Wartime use of sea mines so impressed both the British and the Americans that they converted existing cruisers into specialised minelayers.

Alongside mines were torpedoes, mainly surface-launched. Although torpedoes did not live up to their advertising during the war, they were generally classed alongside mines as devastating weapons, capable of sinking a capital ship with a single hit. By 1904 torpedo range and accuracy were beginning a dramatic rise which helped create the dreadnought revolution (greater gun ranges to keep battleships out of mutual torpedo range). By 1904 torpedo threats in narrow seas such as the English Channel and parts of the Mediterranean had already much affected British naval thinking.

The advent of dreadnought battleships (the first of which was completed only eight years before the outbreak of the war) dramatically changed the way in which fleet power was calculated. In 1904 even minor powers had large battle fleets, built up over a long era of more or less stable technology. On that basis it was unlikely that a single battle could change the balance of naval power as understood by the major powers. In 1914 the fleets of the minor powers were entirely obsolete; even major powers like France and Russia were only beginning to commission dreadnoughts. The number of such ships was so limited that it was possible to imagine a single decisive battle in which a dreadnought fleet might be wiped out. It would take so much effort to replace such a fleet that for the loser the naval war might effectively be over. This possibility of decision at sea contrasted with the changing reality of war ashore, in which national resources in terms of men and materiel were so vast that no single battle or campaign was likely to be decisive. Given the possibility that a big battle would destroy the core of a fleet, governments and naval commanders were understandably cautious. It was not only Admiral Jellicoe who could 'lose the war in an afternoon'. The result was that the massively expensive battle fleets generally were not risked, so that there was only a single battle between the British and German fleets – battlecruisers and lesser types fought on a far more frequent basis, because their loss would not have been catastrophic.

On the other hand, in their large pre-dreadnought fleet the British (and, to a lesser extent, the French) had a considerable number of more or less expendable capital ships. Losses of such

Dreadnoughts changed the calculus of sea power, making the vast majority of battleships suddenly obsolete – and available for secondary operations. HMS *St Vincent*, a first-generation dreadnought, is shown in May 1910.

ships would be regrettable, but they would not tip the balance of seapower calculated in terms of dreadnoughts and their successors. The mass of pre-dreadnoughts made it possible for the British to distribute seapower along their coast (to counter a possible invasion threat) at a limited direct cost to the Grand Fleet. They also made Gallipoli a reasonable gamble. Modern destroyers were a different proposition: never available in sufficient numbers and needed even when dreadnoughts were not present.

Alongside the new battleships were modern long-range submarines, which had not existed at all during the Russo-Japanese struggle. Although both sides in that earlier war had submarines, they were effectively limited to harbour defence. By 1914 it was widely accepted that sea-going submarines could change the balance of seapower, but it was not widely expected that they would be effective commerce raiders. That was not a matter of naiveté; it was inherent in the accepted rules of trade warfare. The First World War demonstrated what could happen if the rules were jettisoned.

A perhaps subtler new technology was radio, generally in the form of wireless telegraphy (W/T: Morse code) rather than voice radio (radio telephony, or R/T). W/T made for effective scouting before the crucial battle of Tsushima in 1905, but its potential for global command and control had not yet been realised. In 1914 the Royal Navy had a truly global communications system and both the British and the Germans conducted operations intended specifically to cripple their opponents' command and control systems. During and probably also before the war, the British used signals intelligence to create, in effect, an ocean surveillance system with enormous operational implications.

Aircraft were another new technology. In 1904 the only effective aircraft were big airships, but no navy yet operated them. In 1914 the German navy had Zeppelins and the British thought they had effective sea-based torpedo bombers. Although the promise of naval aircraft was not quite realised during the war, the Zeppelins' scouting capability certainly affected operations in the North Sea.

The new technologies brought forth new tactics and new concepts of fleet operation. After the war many British naval officers claimed that their navy had been obsessed with materiel rather than with tactics, but enough pre-war documents have survived to show that this was not the case. It was essentially an excuse for tactical failure, particularly at Jutland. It does not appear that the Imperial German Navy spent nearly as much effort developing its own tactics.

The sheer speed with which some technologies were developed and fielded is astonishing. The most striking examples are aircraft and anti-submarine sensors and weapons, with submarines not too far behind. The United States entered the war in April 1917 – and by the end of the year its listening devices, not even conceived before that, were in widespread service.

Pre-war naval intelligence badly lagged behind the new technologies. The British seem to have succeeded in keeping the nature of HMS *Dreadnought* secret until she was deliberately unveiled and also the nature of the first battlecruisers. More importantly, they concealed the development of their war plans, as they moved towards a distant blockade of Germany. The Germans managed to prevent the British from discovering much about ships under construction. There is some evidence that British tactical intelligence was so poor that the Royal Navy came to depend on French sources – which seem to have been flawed – for their accounts of German exercises, the main evidence of their tactical thinking. Intelligence failure led to gross British overestimates of German capabilities and to serious mis-estimation of German wartime naval intentions, the British clearly massively mirror-imaging.

All of the major combatants invested heavily in their navies, but the British and the Germans stood apart from the others in the size of their fleets and in the extent of their efforts. This book therefore concentrates on their North Sea experience, which seems to have attracted most of the post-war naval attention around the world. For example, the historical papers written at the French naval war college between the two world wars are overwhelmingly concerned with the war in the North Sea between the two largest navies, rather

The pre-dreadnought HMS *Magnificent* is shown disarmed as a troop transport for the Dardanelles (in 1915), with a 9.2in gun monitor alongside. She and three sisters (*Illustrious*, *Mars* and *Victorious*) lost their 12in guns to *Lord Clive* class monitors. (Dr David Stevens, SPC-A)

Only a few years separated *Princess Royal* from the armoured cruiser *Duke of Edinburgh*, which in theory had had much the same function. Shown in 1912, *Duke of Edinburgh* had about half the displacement of the new battlecruiser *Princess Royal* and far less powerful armament (9.2in rather than 13.5in guns).

than with French naval operations or with those of the Italians (their most likely future enemy) or the Austrians.

This book is based largely on British official records.[1] Unfortunately the British pre-1914 record is spotty at best, many important documents having been discarded. Although post-1914 records were systematically preserved, there are still problems. The Admiralty underwent a major reorganisation in 1917. It is not at all clear that this reorganisation had fundamental effects on the working of the Admiralty, but it dramatically changed the way in which records were assembled and retained. For example, detailed Admiralty Board Minutes and Memoranda began to be kept.[2] Pre-1917 Board Minutes amount to no more than recording that the Board met on a given day; they give no hint of what was discussed. The volumes of wartime records dated from the autumn of 1917 onwards are far more revealing than earlier ones – which does not necessarily mean that what happened was very different. Many pre-1917 British handbooks have survived because they were provided to the US Navy soon after the United States entered the war in April 1917.

British official documents were originally classified under a fifty-year rule, so that many bear markings like 'closed until 1967'.[3] As a consequence, any account written before about 1970 is likely not to incorporate much or any material taken from the records of the Royal Navy. Many officers did speak out and in many cases their papers became available to particular authors well before 1970. In effect they were a commentary on documents which did not become available until later, if ever.[4]

Many of the published and private accounts amount to self-justification and are difficult to evaluate without access to contemporary documents. I have, however, made extensive use of two published sources. One is Lord Hankey's two-volume work *The Supreme Command*, which draws heavily on his diaries. Hankey was Secretary to the pre-war Committee on Imperial Defence and to the wartime War Council and War Cabinet. The point of his book, which was written in the late 1930s but not published until 1961, was the need the war revealed for a command structure over the two fighting services, capable of evaluating their conflicting views. Hankey's book is particularly revealing of the issues surrounding

Gallipoli. As an observer rather than a prime mover, Hankey is likely to be less biased than other writers. The other published source is the extraordinary collection of letters from Prime Minister Asquith to his mistress Venetia Stanley. Asquith wrote about policy and about Cabinet and War Council sessions, revealing a considerable amount of highly classified information. He seems not to have been concerned with security, merely noting that some items in the letters should be considered *most private* (his italics). In the absence of a Cabinet secretary, these letters are probably the best contemporary source for decisions taken and for their logic. Unfortunately for historians, in the spring of 1915 Venetia Stanley decided to marry and Asquith ceased to write to her. Both Hankey's account and the Asquith letters indicate that the story of Gallipoli was far more complicated than the widely accepted one that it was simply Winston Churchill's folly.

The account of German operations is based largely on the German official history, *Der Krieg zur See 1914-1918*. It was based on German internal records, but it was very much a political document intended to justify the heavy – and ultimately ineffective – German investment in naval forces before the war and also to deal with the bitterness associated with the High Seas Fleet mutiny of 1918.[5] Much wartime German practice is reflected in tactical documents captured and translated by the Royal Navy during and immediately after the war.

The US Navy was a very interested observer of the war before April 1917 and then a major participant, particularly in the anti-submarine war. Its massive surviving records include observations of the Royal Navy (and, to a lesser extent, the Imperial German Navy) and also accounts of its own rapid wartime development, particularly in anti-submarine devices and weapons.

An important point for those not versed in British politics of the period is that the label 'Liberal' applies to a party, not to liberal ideology. The Liberals won the 1906 election (against the Conservatives [Tories]) and remained in power until a National (all-party) government took over late in 1916. Until after the war the Labour Party had little influence. As Labour power grew after 1918, the Liberals collapsed to become the small third British party, later merged with a splinter group from Labour to be renamed the Liberal Democrats. The current (2014) British Government is a Conservative-Liberal Democrat coalition opposed by Labour.

By 1918, some saw submarines as the future of sea power. Every navy asked what lessons the German submarine campaign had taught. Surrendered U-boats are shown at Parkestone Quay, Harwich.

CHAPTER 1
A Maritime War

THE FIRST WORLD WAR was above all a maritime war, not in the sense that most of the action was at sea, but rather in the sense that maritime realities shaped it. That was inevitable: one of the main protagonists, the United Kingdom, was the core of a maritime empire. Britain was the first truly globalised country, relying on imports for essential resources which could be produced less expensively abroad. Those imports included much of the British food supply. Before the war, Admiral 'Jacky' Fisher pointed out that, for the British, the consequence of a naval defeat would be starvation.

Britain and Deterrence

Before the First World War Britain was above all the foremost trading nation in the world. Not only did she import and export vast amounts, but she also had by far the largest merchant fleet in the world and the largest shipbuilding industry to support it. These merchant ships handled much of the world's maritime trade, not only the trade between the world and the British Empire. This reality was associated with support of free trade (i.e., minimal tariffs), which in turn helped fuel the explosive growth the world enjoyed during much of the nineteenth century. The vast development of British maritime trade during that century was bound up with the development of a financial empire centred on the City of London. In 1914 the City was the hub of world trade,

the dominant factor in world finance. It made most world trade possible, because goods bought in one place could be paid for in another with bills discounted or cashed in London. To make that possible, the banks involved borrowed money from the major British merchant banks, which in turn invested heavily abroad. London was the place to go to raise money – for a railway or for a new battleship. By the decade before the war Britain was running a net imbalance of visible trade, but that was balanced by 'invisible' exports produced by the City's financial services and by income derived from foreign investments.

During the pre-war era, most governments who needed large loans floated them in London. For example, the South American dreadnoughts were paid for in this way. The major British ship-builders were associated with particular London banks. Because they were also associated with the world's largest naval programme, the same builders were more efficient than their foreign competitors.[1] In 1914 the great bulk of the naval export market was centred on Britain. That export market financed expansion of a naval shipbuilding industry beyond what the Royal Navy needed, giving Britain a valuable surplus wartime capacity. On the outbreak of war the Germans rightly assumed that the balance of naval power could only worsen, simply because the British could and would grossly outbuild them. This was quite apart from the capacity to build the mass of minor warships needed to fight the war, thanks to the dominance of British builders of commercial ships.

Before 1914, battleships were the visible side of seapower. Grand Fleet flagship HMS *Iron Duke* is shown as completed. She was one of four sisters, the last British battleships completed before war broke out.

That the City was a central part of the British economy as a whole had enormous implications for the British government as it contemplated a political crisis in Europe in the years leading up to 1914. These implications are not obvious from contemporary documents, because there was no particular spokesman for the City in government, no one whose views were recorded or challenged or acceded to. Yet the importance of the City must have been so obvious that it was almost never written about, just as almost no one making military policy in the Cold War United States wrote about the economic impact of decisions. It is for the historian, writing in a very different world, to understand what the interaction had to mean.

Before 1914 the balance between the British Government and capital (represented by both the City and industry) was very different from that we now take for granted. Government was smaller and weaker and in Britain and the United States its power to take property (including taxing power) was much more circumscribed.[2] The idea that the proper role of government was to guarantee national prosperity and that prosperity was best guaranteed by limiting government intervention, took hold in the mid-nineteenth century. Its greatest symbol was probably the elimination of tariffs on cereals. The British situation was radically different from that on the Continent, but it is not clear that British Governments appreciated what that meant. They were certainly aware that economic pressure *on them* could have massive political consequences.

In the years leading up to 1914, the City surely found the prospect of war unacceptable, even unthinkable. Everyone in the City was well aware that countries were increasingly linked by trade, to the point where it seemed that almost none of them could do without it. Financial panics, such as one which shook the United States in 1907, were clearly bad enough. Everyone probably suspected that a war would cause a much worse crash. Moreover, governments generally felt somewhat insecure. A crash would starve, hence enrage, workers, who were regarded everywhere as a potential revolutionary army. In effect the default view of anyone in the Government outside the fighting services was presumably that war was most unlikely.[3] Books on the impossibility (or more accurately, the impracticality) of war in an interlinked world sold well.[4] The City's views were surely well represented in the Cabinet, particularly in the Treasury and in the Foreign Office. That is presumably why the growing British commitment to France was never presented to the Cabinet, many of whose members would have found it unacceptable.

The ruling Liberal Party itself considered war unlikely and it resisted military (which largely meant naval) expenditures, much preferring social investment. Maurice Hankey, the long-time secretary of the Committee on Imperial Defence (CID), wrote long after the war that Prime Minister Asquith and his Foreign Secretary Sir Edward Grey

rightly treated war as something to be avoided by every possible means. They were not so foolish as to close their eyes to the menacing attitude of Germany, but they always believed that with patience, honesty and frankness the international difficulties with Germany might be surmounted as they had been with France and Russia . . . [hopefully] the rise of Germany as a commercial power would gradually lead to an increase in the

Effective seapower required massed capital ships. As numbers increased, fleet tactics became more difficult to implement. The Grand Fleet is shown at sea. Note the funnel smoke these coal-burning ships generated. It made the fleet more visible from beyond the horizon, but it also obscured a fleet commander's view of his own ships. Note also the cruising formation in columns, which was not the line-ahead formation adopted for battle. Determining proper deployment into battle formation might decide a battle. At Jutland, Admiral Sir John Jellicoe successfully deployed the Grand Fleet battle line across the 'T' of the German High Seas Fleet, thanks in part to much better situational awareness achieved by maintaining a tactical plot. (Dr David Stevens, SPC-A)

sobering influence of men of affairs and that in time, with the growth of democratic institutions, the German people would see that their real interests and their prosperity depended on the maintenance of peace . . . [until then] nothing must be done which would tend to precipitate the catastrophe it was so intensely desired to avoid.[5]

As Hankey recalled it, in Asquith's view, the navy was not provocative, but the conscription urged by some in the army certainly was.

To the Liberals, the immediate threat was not war but a social explosion. They therefore wanted to shift from military to social spending. The most obvious potential cause of a social explosion would be hunger: in 1911 the Liberal Government mobilised 30,000 troops to protect food supplies against industrial action.[6] Asquith, who became Prime Minister in 1908, initially hoped to stop building heavy warships altogether. A large radical element of the Liberal backbench strongly supported arms control. They looked forward to the 1907 Hague Peace Conference, called in 1906.

Asquith was caught in a dilemma familiar to many American strategists of the Cold War. There was a deterrent (even a form of

The sea unites. In 1914 Britain was the most globalised country on Earth, the one most dependent on foreign resources. As the German Navy rose to present a mortal challenge, the Royal Navy also had to maintain power overseas. HMAS *Australia* represents one attempt to do so, by convincing Dominions on the Pacific to finance 'fleet units' which could run down commerce raiders or, alternatively, form a Pacific Fleet. They had to reckon with a powerful German squadron based at Tsingtao in China (Graf Spee's force) and also with a potential Japanese threat. Despite the alliance with Britain, Japan took some weeks to declare war on Germany and at least some Germans were surprised that Japan went to war against them. In 1917 the German Zimmermann Telegram posited a German-Japanese alliance (with Mexico) against the United States (the Japanese used the German offer to extract concessions from the Allies). After the war the British remembered Japanese wartime action against the Empire, such as support for nationalists (subversives) in India. HMAS *Australia* is shown before Jutland, with turret-top rangefinders and also with torpedo net booms.

mutually assured destruction, since a war would badly damage both Britain and Germany). How far should he go to develop the means of war-fighting, for use if the deterrent broke down? To what extent would assembling those means reduce deterrence? The words were not used at the time, but the problem was certainly understood. Preparation for economic warfare, including but not limited to blockade, offered the possibility of devastating effect if activated, without creating peacetime provocation which might, in Asquith's view, trigger a war. It was probably the only such alternative available to him.

The Liberals won the 1906 and 1910 elections, the latter fought on the basis of Lloyd George's 'People's Budget', which entailed increased taxes. In 1914 the Liberals expected to face another election in 1915 and again there was considerable pressure to reduce naval spending. The Liberals pointed to the growth of the Social Democratic Party (SDP) to dominance of the Reichstag in Germany as evidence that the Germans would be unable to make war, unaware that the growth of an anti-military party might be propelling the conservative rulers of Germany *into* war for fear that their window of opportunity was closing. An important consequence of Liberal Party orientation was that few in the party spent much time thinking through the implications of a war. Once war began, the Cabinet had little basis for decision, yet key decisions were normally made on a Cabinet-wide basis. Prime Minister Asquith found himself convening a War Committee dominated by his military ministers.

During the period between 1905 and 1914 the Conservative Party, which tended to emphasise defence, was continuously in opposition. It says a great deal about the strength of British public feeling about the Royal Navy that the Liberals' attempts to cut the naval budget generally failed, even though the navy itself might complain about what amounted to belt-tightening. The Germans did not understand as much. During the build-up of the German fleet, its architect Admiral Tirpitz once mused that he feared that if he went too fast the British would return the Conservatives to power and that they would spend enough to overwhelm him. In fact the Liberals themselves proved quite willing to outspend and outbuild him.

A century later, we see the pre-1914 world as peaceful, even idyllic, because we know what came next. At the time, governments throughout Europe were haunted by various kinds of subversion. Many feared growing Socialist movements, which were clearly hostile to the status quo. There was a terrorist fringe, most prominent in Russia. Anarchists were active in every European country. Like modern terrorists, they created vast anxiety, even though there were relatively few attacks. The British Government faced increasing pressure for Irish Home Rule – and the real possibility that the army, which had a substantial Irish element, would refuse to support it if Ireland exploded into civil war. That was aside from other movements considered subversive, such as the growing Suffragette movement. In 1914 a British government which considered it most unlikely that Europe would explode into war faced the immediate threat of a civil war in Ireland. It is not surprising which engaged its attention.

Looking back, we can see what the British Government of 1911 (and 1914) did not. No country on the Continent had a government influenced by economics the way the British were; there was no equivalent of the City to enforce such influence. There were certainly many bankers and industrialists who saw the world the way the City saw it, but they did not run their governments. Those who did saw national life in much older ways. National power and prestige were connected directly with territory. Perhaps worst of all, neither Asquith nor anyone else in the British Government seems ever to have appreciated the extent to which the German army (or rather its General Staff), rather than German business, ruled Germany – people jokingly said that Germany was an army with a country attached, but they did not take it seriously. Connected with the dominance of the army and the Prussian minor aristocracy was the peculiar sensitivity of German rulers to the security of eastern Prussia – a major opportunity foregone once war broke out. That is, Asquith and everyone else in power mirror-imaged, a sin for which no one has found an effective antidote.

Consideration of war against Germany began at about the same time the expensive and unsatisfactory Boer War ended (at the outset, Germany was hardly the only potential enemy Britain faced, the Franco-Russian alliance being more threatening). The end of the war left serious financial problems, so it prompted a defence review, ordered in December 1902. The defence budget (largely the naval budget) was already expanding more rapidly than the governments of the day thought affordable, due in large part to the need for large numbers of armoured cruisers, each as large (and as expensive) as a battleship, both for trade protection and for fleet operations. Going into the review, the navy wanted to keep its budget intact. The army needed a new role, because the Boer War had soured interest in any new colonial conflict. The army argued that it was an essential defence against invasion. The only other justification for a substantial army was the need for an expeditionary force in the new context of the German threat.

Since home defence was also a naval role, anyone trying to cut defence could seek cuts there. The Cabinet formed a Defence Committee (ultimately reconstituted as the Committee on Imperial Defence). The navy argued successfully that it could preclude an enemy landing (or reinforcing or supplying whatever enemy troops managed to get ashore). The navy argued successfully that its new submarines were a better coast defence than the army's minefields, which might endanger ships approaching British ports. One of the navy's leading advocates was Admiral Sir John ('Jacky') Fisher, who had recently returned from command of the Mediterranean Fleet. While there he had faced the first French submarines capable of moving beyond the French coast, in addition to the large French force of surface torpedo craft. He began to develop the idea that the North Sea could be made impassable by submarines and other torpedo craft ('flotilla defence') and that capital ships could operate only outside its confined waters.

Having been badly defeated in the review, the army sought an alternative role in the context of the new anxiety about Germany. Nascent British war plans against Germany emphasised traditional themes: blockade, both to strangle the Germans and to protect British trade. The army was already aware that it could not justify itself on the basis of seizure of the enemy colonies themselves, which were considered to be of limited value. What would the army's role be in a European war against Germany? If the British were working in coalition with the French, what could they do from the sea which would have an immediate effect on the war ashore; meaning, which would impress the French?

When the British thought they would have to fight the Russians in 1885, their plans included naval penetration of the Baltic and landing troops there. With the rise of torpedo craft and mines, landings became increasingly dangerous. However, about 1905 the German fleet was still weak enough that British losses in such operations would not have tipped the balance of naval power, so the Royal Navy could propose dangerous landings on, for example, the German Baltic coast both for their strategic impact and as a way of using dominant British seapower to demonstrate support for France.

Initially the army was interested, but its leaders soon realised just how risky such operations could be; a force landed in the Baltic might find itself marooned there. By about 1906 the British army general staff had fixed on direct support of the French army as its single best option. In France the army would have the benefit of good sea communications back to Britain. The Royal Navy soon concluded that no landing on the German coast would be decisive. Blockade was another thing. The more closely the Royal Navy examined the German economy, the more dependent it seemed on foreign trade. Blockade (later, a wider form of anti-trade warfare) might well be a decisive weapon, so much so that the army need not be deployed in any numbers.[7]

The army was naturally not amused. It fought hard against a strategy which did not require any large expeditionary effort.[8] It found an ally in the Foreign Office, which disliked the entire idea of blockade. The Foreign Office was interested in deterrence. It was also affected by the widespread view within the Liberal Party that private property, any more than private citizens, should not be subject to attack in wartime. The Foreign Office seems also to have considered the entente with France so important an achievement that it was worth reinforcing with military promises. British reliance on blockade might limit any ties to France. As it sought to promote a Continental commitment in a future war, the army general staff did its best to disprove the navy's contention that blockade or some stronger form of economic warfare could achieve a rapid decision. Army leaders argued to the British Government that theirs was the only supportive operation the French would take seriously. Arguments between army and navy leaders played out before Prime Minister Asquith during acute European crises, particularly in 1908 and in 1911.

Both argued that the Germans could evade any attack on their trade by using neutral ports, particularly Rotterdam and Antwerp, in wartime.[9] Admiralty analysts showed that both ports had limited capacity. In 1908 German Chief of the General Staff von Moltke wrote that it was essential to maintain a neutral Holland as the conduit for essential goods, the 'windpipe through which we can breathe'. However, in 1914 the Germans contemplated crossing through the Dutch Limburg Appendix if they failed to smash the Belgian frontier fortifications. The Admiralty did not take account of Scandinavian ports, which could feed goods to Germany through the more or less German-controlled Skaggerak, as they actually did during the war.

It did not help that the Admiralty did not have a formal and widely articulated war plan. The First Sea Lord Admiral Fisher was fond of saying that he had the war plan in his head and that it was too secret to disclose. He created a war planning cell, but its product was not widely disseminated and naval exercises and practices did not necessarily reflect Fisher's ideas.[10] Fisher actively opposed the creation of a formal war staff with a corporate memory of previous war planning (in fact the Naval Intelligence Department of the Admiralty did perform planning staff functions). War plans, to the extent that they were formalised, were embodied in brief war instructions provided to the commanders of the deployed fleets, to be opened only upon the outbreak of war. Because Fisher did not disclose his own favoured war plan, any later First Sea Lord could develop his own plan without much or any reference to past efforts. It is therefore impossible to say, for example, that the Royal Navy abandoned close blockade in 1907 or in 1912 any more than that it expected to carry out a close blockade at those or earlier times.

Unlike a Continental power, which had to concentrate on the armies on its borders, the British could envisage a wide range of possibilities: the sea could connect them and the Empire with a wide range of countries. To an army, that kind of range of possibilities was inconceivable. Armies require detailed planning because even the smallest operation demands enormous logistical preparation. The war plans prepared by various armies before 1914 were largely about logistics: about how to move masses of troops and how to keep supplying them as they moved forward. Contact with the enemy was a relatively minor – tactical – part of overall planning. When Director of Military Operations General Henry Wilson explained his war plan to the CID in 1911, his map showed how the army would deploy and what French roads it would block against the oncoming Germans. Famously, he demonstrated how detailed his staff work had been by including in his schedule a ten-minute stop for coffee.

Logistics obviously also affects naval operations, but in a much less pervasive way. Ships carry their own fuel and other supplies; troops carry very little of theirs. The logistical consequences of deploying a fleet one way or another are relatively minor, but those of deploying a mass army are enormous. Even changing the port supplying that army has vast implications, which became evident when the war of movement in 1914 threatened the Channel ports on which the British army depended. To change ports meant changing the entire structure which moved goods from port to troops (much the same might be said of any considerable relocation of troops). Armies emphasise staff work because the main role of the staff is to translate broad concepts of operation into details, many of them logistical. Logistics is why the outbreak of the First World War was so closely bound up with railway timetables: trains moved both masses of troops and their supplies and in 1914 there was no alternative on land.[11]

Naval technology was changing much more rapidly than that ashore, with important possible implications. In 1907 Fisher strongly advocated flotilla defence of Britain: he thought that surface torpedo craft and submarines could make the North Sea impassable for battle fleets. In that case close blockade was impossible. Fisher was unable to convince everyone, which is one reason why the Royal Navy kept building battleships.

In the 1911 crisis, a particularly bellicose and inept presentation by First Sea Lord (from 1910, after Fisher) Admiral A K Wilson before the CID prompted Prime Minister Asquith to rein him in. Like Fisher, Wilson rejected the creation of an Admiralty War Staff. Asquith was impressed by his Secretary of State for War, Richard Haldane, who was important in his Liberal Party. Haldane could point to the army's recovery from its Boer War failures. The symbol of revival was the army's new general staff, which promised a modern scientific approach to soldiering. No one in the army would concoct a war plan too secret for the general staff, as Wilson had concocted his own plan, which involved a form of close blockade, without informing anyone in the fleet (several senior admirals refused to implement his war orders). Wilson's predecessor Admiral Fisher had made much the same claims about his own war plan, that it was too secret to discuss within the fleet. He had been compelled to provide the CID with a dossier of

As the Royal Navy strained to overmatch the Germans in the North Sea, it also had to reckon with growing Italian and Austro-Hungarian fleets in the Mediterranean. Before the war Italy was part of the Triple Alliance. An agreement with France helped, but it did not completely solve the problem. Once Italy entered the war on the Allied side, her battle fleet more than counterbalanced the Austrian fleet. The newly-completed Austro-Hungarian *Viribus Unitis* is shown.

alternative war plans, without disclosing which one he planned to execute, as proof that he had been sponsoring formal war planning. This time the claim of secrecy was sufficient to make Wilson anathema. It does seem that Wilson had made no attempt to consult previous war plans or planners, but Fisher wrote a strong letter defending him.

The 1911 meeting is usually taken as the formal origin of the British army commitment to France, but Prime Minister Asquith felt compelled by his Cabinet to agree a few months later to bar any further staff talks, which certainly suggests the opposite. This makes sense if the 1911 meeting is taken simply as an attempt by the army general staff to secure backing for its plan, rather than as Asquith's comparison of army and navy war plans.

Haldane seems to have hoped that by pointing to the Admiralty's lack of an effective staff he would promote himself into the First Lord's seat, on the grounds that what he had done for the army he could do for the navy. Asquith could not lightly dismiss his First Lord, but he could switch him with Home Secretary Winston Churchill. Asquith seems to have considered Churchill a better spokesman than Haldane for the large budgets the navy required. Haldane's importance to the Liberals carried him only so far.

Churchill promptly fired Wilson, which may have been his main function from Asquith's point of view. Given that Wilson had apparently shown no ability to develop viable war plans, Churchill's task was clearly to create a naval war staff. The lack of a staff was something of an illusion. The Royal Navy already had a small staff in the form of its Naval Intelligence Department (NID), supplemented by fleet staffs. Churchill's War Staff turned out largely to be a renamed and slightly reorganised NID.

How all of this is to be interpreted depends on how seriously Asquith took the threat of war compared to other threats. The possibility of some explosion in Ireland, as almost happened in 1914, was much more immediate than a European war. In this context the visible strength of the Royal Navy was a valuable deterrent backing up the logical argument against war. As the largest single item in the budget, the Royal Navy also limited social expenditures. Selling that budget was important, but so was controlling its growth. The Liberals knew that there was enough public awareness of the importance of the fleet that if they slacked off the rival Conservatives might push them out of office at the next election.

In 1914 the Germans had a force in the Mediterranean, the battlecruiser *Goeben* and the light cruiser *Breslau*. They sought refuge in Turkey when war broke out. Although nominally transferred to the Ottoman Navy, the ships remained under German control. They brought Turkey into the war by shelling Sevastopol without Turkish consent. *Goeben* survived as the Turkish *Yavuz*, the last remaining operational dreadnought. She was photographed on 10 May 1947 during a US fleet visit.

The rise of armoured cruisers badly strained British naval finances, because these ships had to be dealt with both within a battle fleet and as commerce raiders: in 1904 the British wanted a 2:1 ratio of armoured cruisers over those of the combined fleets of the next two European powers. At the same time the British felt they had to match the battleship strengths of the next two powers (with a 10 per cent margin). The French *Amiral Aube* is shown. She was completed in 1904, just as British naval attention began to shift from the Franco-Russian alliance to a new German threat. This cruiser was named after the prime exponent of the *jeune école*, a form of naval warfare based on commerce raiding by such ships. This doctrine assumed that French torpedo boats would prevent the British from bottling up the cruisers in their ports (they would also raid commerce in the Channel).

During the 1911 crisis, then, Asquith probably assumed that war would not break out (the outcome of the crisis presumably confirmed for him that he was right). For political reasons he could not afford to infuriate Haldane. He saw no point in angering the army, key to stability in Ireland. Asquith had been trained as a lawyer; his wartime behaviour displayed the lawyer's preference for conciliation over hard choices. Given a belief in economic mutual deterrence, he probably thought much as many in the US government did in the 1970s. Even if a crisis led to war, surely it could be contained and wound down. No irreversible steps should be taken at the outset. Haldane's French commitment fell into that category. Wilson's planned instant attack on German torpedo craft did not. Governments bent on deterrence do not like fire-eaters. In the 1960s intense interest in how to limit the risk of war was reflected in discussions of escalation, crisis bargaining and, later, limited nuclear options. Before 1914 no one wrote about the 'escalation ladders' which fascinated nuclear strategists half a century later, but the idea that initial steps in war should be limited, controllable and reversible was surely present in many minds.

As Home Secretary Churchill had been at the centre of anti-subversive efforts, in effect the guarantor of the part of national security Asquith considered most urgent. His transfer to the Admiralty was seen at the time as something of a step down. It was a real step down if Asquith regarded war as most unlikely but subversion as a current threat. Churchill was full of strategic ideas

– some of them expressed during the 1911 crisis – but they did not really matter as long as war was never going to break out.[12] Asquith may also have felt safer with Churchill out of the Home Office, where he had presided over some rather violent incidents.[13]

British official behaviour in the years leading up to the war is redolent of the way governments in the West behaved under the mutual deterrence understood to be in force half a century later during the Cold War. In this context numbers are more important than effectiveness. Appearances matter: whether or not the weapons are ever to be used, the other side cannot be allowed to imagine that he can gain superiority. In the British case, it appears that the point of building the *Queen Elizabeth* class battleships was to demonstrate to the Germans that their innovation of building fast battleships rather than British-style battlecruisers could be overmatched. In that light it does not seem strange that First Lord Winston Churchill chose to offer the Germans a 'building holiday', a suspension of the battleship-building race, in 1912, once the *Queen Elizabeth* class was in train. Such attempts at arms control were a familiar fixture of the deterrent world of the 1970s: if war was unthinkable there was no point in building weapons to the point of bankruptcy.

Acts, such as signing treaties or allocating forces, are symbolic, intended not for tactical purposes but rather to achieve diplomatic ends. The possible consequences of agreements tend not to be thought through – if war is literally unthinkable, then why think in terms of what might happen if it broke out? Those who find this somewhat absurd may ponder the US government's enthusiastic post-Cold War policy of guaranteeing the security of former Soviet republics in order to convince them to turn their nuclear weapons over to Russia, the idea being that mutual deterrence limited to two (actually three) superpowers was much safer than a fragmented nuclear world. No one in the US government seems to have asked whether the blank cheques being passed around would ever have to be honoured.

Although the effect of deterrence thinking seems obvious in British national policies of 1910–14, it would be misleading to imagine that the Royal Navy (or for that matter the army) had abandoned efforts to be ready to fight. Churchill might govern available resources and make choices favouring numbers over readiness, but the Royal Navy did not necessarily accept the deterrent idea. While deterrence might be preferred, it had to be ready to fight. That included developing war plans. Anyone who remembers the Cold War and deterrent thinking will recognise exactly this kind of schizophrenia.

When war broke out despite expectation, Asquith and others in the British Government seem to have expected a stalemate in the West. Russia was the only virtually limitless source of military manpower. It seemed that if the French managed to stop the initial German offensive, the Russian 'steamroller' might well destroy Germany, or at the least force it to sue for peace. Asquith initially resisted the despatch of the expeditionary force to France, on the grounds that it would be useless. Perhaps surprisingly, its commander Field Marshal Sir John French agreed. The force was sent only after those resisting its despatch failed to produce any alternative plan by means of which the British could display support for France. Even then the Cabinet assumed that the key British contribution to the war would be seapower and associated economic attack against Germany.

Germany and Tirpitz

In 1914 Germany was the greatest power in Continental Europe. The Kaiser considered himself monarch by divine right and he considered the Prussian Army the most important element of his state. Germany was often described as 'an army with a country attached'. In 1848, when a temporary German legislature offered the Kaiser's grandfather the crown of a unified Germany, he rejected it because he refused to accept the authority of a 'rabble'.[14] Unification came out of a successful war with France in 1870 – which the Kaiser's Chancellor Otto von Bismarck instigated but enticed the French Emperor Napoleon III to declare. The new German Empire (Reich) that emerged from the war was ruled by the Kaiser and his largely Prussian army.

The new government was by no means a parliamentary democracy. The upper house of parliament (Bundesrat) consisted of the kings of the states comprising the German Empire; in theory it was the German imperial government. Prussia had an effective veto because it had sufficient votes and the Prussian King was Kaiser. The Kaiser chose (and dismissed) not only the Chancellor but also the State Secretaries of the various departments, although in theory they were appointed by the Chancellor.

The elected component was the Reichstag, elected by universal male suffrage through a secret ballot. The Kaiser had the power to dissolve the Reichstag and call new elections (there was no equivalent to the British practice of dissolving the House of Commons and calling new elections in the event of a vote of no confidence). The Reichstag could not initiate legislation (which was proposed by the Kaiser's Chancellor), but laws – including the annual budget – could not be enacted without its vote. Once approved and signed, the Reichstag could not rescind laws, a point of great importance as Admiral Tirpitz grew his fleet through successive Navy Laws.

Like other Western European countries, Germany was affected by the wave of industrialisation of the nineteenth century, which

It took a battleship-size armoured cruiser to match an enemy armoured cruiser; hence the fiscal crisis Admiral Sir John Fisher was brought in to solve. When *Minotaur* was completed, she was of roughly battleship size. Her very tall topmasts gave her long wireless receiving range, so that she could be integrated into a global command-and-control system. It sought to track commerce raiders by analysing their attacks. This intelligence-based system was very different from the more or less random hunting which critics attributed to the Admiralty. In August 1914, *Minotaur* was flagship on the China Station, supported by the considerably smaller armoured cruiser *Hampshire*, the light cruiser *Yarmouth* and the pre-dreadnought *Triumph*. As the 1914 crisis escalated, the British China Fleet was ordered to concentrate with other Far Eastern ships at Hong Kong. Since the Germans had already left their base at Tsingtao (for a peacetime cruise) when war broke out in August, it was impossible to bottle them up there. The fleet concentration further south was intended to protect vital trade against whatever attacks the German Asiatic Squadron might mount. This photograph was obtained by the US Office of Naval Intelligence on 5 August 1908.

swept people out of the countryside and into the cities – and from supporting conservative parties whose votes were dominated by landowners to the socialist parties. It was generally assumed that major landowners could compel their labourers to vote as they wished, but such control vanished as people moved into the cities. The shift from countryside to cities affected all the industrialising countries, probably the United Kingdom more than the others. However, the Kaiser and his supporters found it particularly threatening because the Reichstag was in effect the only brake on them. The sense of threat was so bad that in the 1890s there was some sentiment among the Kaiser's supporters to curb industrialisation to limit the growth of the working (city) class. Bismarck had tried to buy off the emerging working class by providing social benefits, but once he was gone the Kaiser and his advisors were more and more afraid of a rising proletariat. Electoral boundaries in Germany were never altered to reflect the shift of population, so it took time for the socialists to convert their large majorities (in elections from 1890 on) into power in the Reichstag, but by 1912 they finally had enough votes to form a centre-left coalition.

There was a long history of conflict between Kaiser and Reichstag, the Kaiser and his advisers often considering a military coup to restore an absolute monarchy. There was even a German term for such a coup: 'Staatsstreich'. Even before German unification, the Kaiser (of Prussia) had problems with his parliament: in 1860 it rejected funding for the army. Bismarck, who was then Chancellor, dissolved the Diet (the Prussian equivalent to the Reichstag) but did not call new elections. He ruled without it, meanwhile seeking to increase conservative votes. He instigated a war against Austria in 1866, apparently largely in order to excite patriotic emotions which would sweep the conservatives into office.[15]

The Kaiser saw the army as his main bulwark against a rising population moving to the left. That made the army at least as important for preserving the Kaiser and the state as for foreign operations.[16] Conversely, it made for an army general staff which did not clearly distinguish between its foreign and domestic roles. For example, war could be attractive as a way of turning German politics sharply to the right, towards whatever policy the Kaiser and the establishment favoured. That had certainly happened in 1870. With the centre-left victory in 1912, the latent problems of the German state came very much into focus.

Late in 1913 a junior German army officer in Alsace beat a civilian who had insulted him.[17] A civilian court convicted the officer, but it was overruled by a military court. Chancellor Bethmann-Hollweg, representing the Kaiser, supported the officer and, by extension, the army. The Reichstag majority passed a vote of no confidence in him, many deputies talking about how the incident symbolised the unacceptable power of the army. Bethmann-Hollweg refused to resign; he was responsible only to the Kaiser. The Reichstag deputies were unwilling to push further, for example to reject that year's budget, possibly for fear of a Staatsreich.

However, it was clear that the Reichstag was becoming more assertive and the Kaiser and the General Staff (and others in the German Establishment) considered that unacceptable. They became somewhat panicky. There is considerable evidence that early in the twentieth century the General Staff (and the associated establishment) came to see a successful war as a way out of deepening internal political problems.[18] Such a war had to be presented to the Reichstag as defensive and success had to bring dividends which would make it appear well worthwhile. The object was not the gains in territorial or other terms, but a more docile Reichstag. If this explanation is correct, the First World War was ignited by domestic German politics. It was an extroverted German civil war – just as the 1870 war against France had actually been about creating national unity. The seizure of Alsace and Lorraine (and a huge war indemnity from France) were incidentals which demonstrated that the war had been worthwhile.

The prime mover in 1914 was not the German military as such, but the army General Staff, which had led the Prussian army to victory in 1870. The expensive German navy was not involved. For example, no naval operation figured in the war plan activated in August 1914. The army's view was that victory over the French army would force France to surrender whatever was wanted later on. Army planners do not seem to have taken the possibility of a protracted war with naval implications at all seriously.

The German General Staff was positioned very differently from its counterparts in most countries. In peacetime they were all planning staffs – not, at least in theory, political planners. Such staffs and their naval counterparts are trained to examine conditions objectively and to produce plans for all possible circumstances. For example, between the two World Wars both British and US naval planners developed plans to fight each other, even though that was very nearly politically impossible. The difference between most countries and Germany was that in those countries it was clearly understood that the civilian authority would decide whether war plans were relevant; the civilians decided who was and who was not an enemy. What made the primacy of the General Staff so important and had such devastating effects, was that the General Staff evaluation of which neighbouring countries *might*, if they wished, cause damage translated, in minds like the Kaiser's, into the belief that exactly those countries *would* attack Germany. Very sadly, it is possible that no one in the German General Staff or in the Kaiser's government realised that their way of thinking was not the standard everywhere.

Given Germany's lack of natural borders, General Staff thinking translated into ideas of pre-emptive attack, even though the countries involved, France and Russia, had no real intention of attacking Germany. Russian modernisation after the Russo-Japanese War became a threat which had to be countered before it gave the Russians a chance of attacking Germany – even though there was no evidence that the Russians had any such intent in the years leading up to 1914.

In theory, the Kaiser, not the General Staff, ran Germany. He often acted as a moderating force (though sometimes the opposite, as when he vowed 'revenge' against anyone who displeased him). The Kaiser was famously mercurial and he must have been a considerable trial to all of those who ran the German government on a day-to-day basis. British Foreign Secretary Sir Edward Grey once described him as a powerful battleship, all screws turning, entirely without a rudder, which one day would collide with something with terrible consequences. In 1908 the Kaiser gave an embarrassingly frank interview to the British *Daily Telegraph*, after which his power was considerably reduced.

The Kaiser spent much of the 1914 crisis on his yacht, visiting Norway with the German fleet. The German official naval history took his absence from Berlin as proof that Germany was innocent of the charge that it had deliberately triggered the war. Later a

German historian found evidence that the General Staff had deliberately kept the Kaiser 'with his pacifist ideas' out of Berlin during the critical period.[19] If this analysis is correct, had the crisis of 1914 (and possible crises in the next few years) been averted, the Reichstag might have gained so much power that there would have been no German internal political problem to turn into a world war.

The most bizarre feature of the German pre-1914 political landscape was that the German navy accounted for so much of the military budget but that at the same time it had no role whatever in deciding German policy, particularly in the choice for or against war. There was no attempt whatever to co-ordinate army and navy war planning; indeed, there was no coherent naval war plan to execute in 1914. This anomaly makes it difficult to explain the rise of the German navy, particularly since that rise was accompanied by a shift towards enmity against the United Kingdom, the one country the German army could not touch. The German effort to build a navy specifically to deal with the Royal Navy effectively guaranteed that the United Kingdom would ally with France and enter the war in 1914, neither of which helped the Germans at all.

The German war plan developed before 1914 by the (army) General Staff was designed to defeat both Continental enemies, France and Russia. The General Staff did not envisage a situation in which one would fight without the other and the assumption seems to have been that to deal with only one of the two would expose Germany to defeat by the other. Because France was still so much more powerful than Russia, at least at the outset of a war, the General Staff naturally envisaged an initial attack against France while a smaller force in the East held back the Russians. Once the French were dealt with, the bulk of the army could be moved east via the efficient German railway system.

The Kaiser was far more interested in the potential enemy to the East, Russia. He and his junker (minor nobility) officers and government officials were particularly sensitive about the security of eastern Prussia, because that is where they had estates and where they normally lived. He feared that, despite their defeat by the Japanese in 1904–5 and their debilitating 1905 revolution, the Russians were successfully modernising. In 1912 the Kaiser talked to his officers in a panicky mood about prospects for Russian modernisation by 1916. It seems likely that those seeking a military solution to the Reichstag were playing on his fears. When war broke out in 1914, the Kaiser asked plaintively why Germany was throwing most of her troops against France, even though Russia was the immediate problem. His War Minister von Moltke famously said that 11,000 train timetables could not be changed – and the Kaiser told him that he was not the man his uncle, the victor in 1870, had been. After 1918 the German general responsible for railways stated that he could in fact have done what the Kaiser wanted. It was the General Staff which refused to divorce the Russian problem from the potential French threat. Similarly, when the crisis came in 1914, the Kaiser wanted to concentrate his fleet in the Baltic to attack Russia. To a German Navy which had spent its life planning for war against Britain, this was an impossible idea. Tremendous effort was expended to reverse the Kaiser's order.

The German war plan envisaged only a land war: the army would envelop the French armies, to which end it would execute a vast encircling movement. There was not enough space on French soil, so the German General Staff solved this tactical or operational problem by having some of its armies march through neutral Belgium, ignoring its political implication. There is no indication that naval considerations affected the General Staff planners: their strategy for quickly defeating France focussed on the French army. The General Staff did not take the British into account, because it counted only the strength of the small British army, not the effect of British seapower. The Prussian aristocrats who ran the army almost certainly assumed that their army could win a land war so quickly that any financial catastrophe would not matter. That had, after all, been achieved in the last big German war, the one against France in 1870. Moreover, after 1870 the Germans extracted a large war indemnity which solved their financial problems. This time all potential combatants had so much strategic depth and such large armies, that a single decisive battle was virtually impossible.[20] Any war, even one confined to the Continent, would inevitably be drawn-out.[21] The German General Staff seems not to have had the slightest interest in this possibility, or in the way that it would make economic power count.

By 1911 the British were aware that the Germans were planning to march through Belgium and their army planners thought that such an advance would trigger British intervention.[22] The British had pledged to uphold Belgian neutrality; they saw Belgium as the part of the European coast from which an invasion could most easily be launched. It was probably far more significant that the German naval building programme had convinced many in Britain that the Germans were their sworn enemies. The British Government was probably the element in British society *least* hostile to Germany, because it thought it had a war-stopping deterrent. It may even have imagined, at the outset, that a Continental war could be limited and that it would end quickly after some posturing. The German invasion of Belgium showed that the Germans were in earnest; the British deterrent had failed altogether.

Many in Germany were aware that a drawn-out war might be difficult; there was considerable popular pre-war interest in economic self-defence. The only pre-war answer offered by the German government was that Germany had enough on hand to survive a nine-month war. As the country industrialised, like Britain it came to depend on imports for some of its food. Its cereals were supplied from Russia and Romania, generally by ship through the Black Sea. In a protracted struggle, with Russia cut off, Germany might have to rely heavily on overseas supplies – but the British could cut them off. It does not seem that anyone on the German General Staff took this potential problem very seriously.

In all of these terms, the most bizarre feature of the pre-1914 European landscape was the rapid rise of the German Navy under the leadership of Grand Admiral Alfred von Tirpitz. It is not at all clear that, at least at the outset, most Germans understood what naval expansion would mean for their relationship with the British. Tirpitz seems to have been a careerist who concentrated on bringing his navy larger and larger resources, with little interest in what he would do with them. It appears that there are so many explanations for the rise of Tirpitz' navy because there was no single consistent explanation: Tirpitz fastened on whatever rationale would work, with whoever found that rationale attractive. He found an ally in Kaiser Wilhelm II, who liked warships and envied the British their large fleet and their Empire.[23] Tirpitz' concentration on the British was probably inevitable, in that he wanted to justify building a fleet about the size of the Royal Navy. At the end of the nineteenth century the French fleet was declining, as the

French found it difficult to finance both a large fleet and a large enough army (to face the Germans), so they were not a useful justification for a naval programme. Tirpitz may have been inspired by the rapid rise of the US Navy after 1883. It must have seemed that good public relations had managed to convince not only the US public but also the Congress that the country needed a large fleet. By about 1906 the US Navy was the second largest in the world. Presumably Tirpitz omitted to notice that the arguments for a more powerful US Navy had something to do with US national strategy and with the fact that the country could be attacked from abroad only by sea.

Tirpitz offered a variety of justifications, most famously a form of deterrence theory (or 'risk theory'). He claimed that it was necessary to keep the British from intervening in a future European war. The British relied on their dominant sea power. Germany could build a fleet so powerful that even in defeating it the British would lose their naval dominance. This argument protected Tirpitz from the natural criticism that Germany could not possibly afford a British-size fleet (there is evidence that Tirpitz hoped ultimately to out-build the British). The 'risk theory' also imbued in many German seamen the idea that they would probably die in a fight against the Royal Navy, but that their deaths would be worthwhile

as a means of breaking British naval power. Just why that would be worthwhile once war began, with the British allied to the other major European naval powers, is not clear.

The risk theory can be taken at face value, though it is difficult to understand why keeping the small British army out of a general European war was so vital. No one pushed back very hard because the Kaiser backed Tirpitz (although he himself preferred a fleet of cruisers, for trade warfare). Later it was often said that heavy expenditure on the navy reduced the strength of the German army just enough that it failed to envelop the French in 1914.

Another argument was connected with the somewhat ramshackle character of the German Empire. Tirpitz pointed out that naval construction provided good jobs and work for important industries, hence supported the conservative (pro-Kaiser) government. Krupp, which certainly stood to benefit heavily from the naval programme, backed the German Navy League, which in turn helped shape public opinion. The navy was also connected with a push for colonies, which was said to add national prestige (but attracted little popular support). In effect Tirpitz' political arguments collapsed in the 1912 Reichstag elections. To convince Germans to back him, Tirpitz built a very effective propaganda machine around the News Bureau in his Navy Department – an

The battlecruiser was part of a solution to the armoured cruiser problem. Instead of being stationed in a focal area waiting for an enemy raider to appear, the fast battlecruiser would be vectored out to run down a raider. HMS *Invincible* is shown as built, with tall topmasts to give her long wireless receiving range. Note the anti-torpedo (boat) guns atop 'A' turret, where they had excellent command but were useless while the turret guns were firing. Their position reflected the assumption, which the British held in varying degrees down to about 1913, that destroyers would always operate separately from the battle fleet and would never participate in a day gunnery action.

organisation equivalent to more conventional navy departments such as that concerned with ship design and construction.

The permanent character of Reichstag laws was of enormous benefit to Tirpitz. He was indignant that he had to go before the Reichstag every year to justify what he wanted, subject to Deputies' whims. He was probably acutely aware that he was playing to the Kaiser's distaste for the legislative process, particularly when it touched the ships he personally liked. A fixed establishment, which the army already had, was called an 'aeternat', an 'eternal' arrangement (it was said to have been 'eternalised'). The army had already exploited this system, its establishment subject to review only every five (later seven) years. Tirpitz sought an 'aeternat' in the form of the 1897 Navy Law. That set a lower limit on the size of the fleet. The centre-left understood the 1897 law as an assault on Reichstag powers, just as the Kaiser saw Tirpitz' laws as a way of giving him more direct power over the size and shape of the fleet. Tirpitz probably came to realise that the Kaiser could be quite as difficult a customer as the Reichstag, but he got his fleet. The 1898 Navy Law set the size of the fleet: by 1908 there should be two modern battle squadrons (eight ships each) and a fleet flagship, plus two ships as a material reserve, all supported by a large cruiser force (in the 1897 Navy Law, sixteen large and thirty small cruisers). The key word was 'modern': capital ships had to be replaced when they were twenty-five years old. On this basis automatic replacement would be completed in 1923. Further Navy Laws were passed in 1900, 1902, 1906, 1908 and 1912. Since Tirpitz wanted to build a considerably larger fleet, in the 1902 Navy Law he added a provision for a steady building rate of three ships per year, including replacements. That replacement was automatic explains why, for example, the battleship laid down as *Ersatz Wörth* (and launched as *Baden*) replaced the old battleship *Wörth*. On the other hand Battleship T (*Bayern*) was an addition to the overall size of the fleet.

The 1902 Navy Law set a building tempo: three battleships and one large cruiser each year. In 1898 Tirpitz became interested in a second six-year programme, to provide a third battle squadron, perhaps to be followed by a third law, which would add another battle squadron. Tirpitz described the Navy Law and its successors as the 'Iron Budget' which guaranteed desired construction. The 'Iron Budget' was why the navy accounted for over half the German defence budget in 1912. It was also why the German defence budget, which was 90 per cent of the total Imperial budget, roughly doubled between 1890 and 1912.

The fleet plan was based on Tirpitz' experience as head of the Naval Staff (Oberkommando der Marine, or OK) abolished by the Kaiser in 1899. Before he left in 1895, he conceived a long-range fleet programme, which the OK began to promote.[24] The stated rationale was that Germany must have 30 per cent superiority over the most powerful of the northern fleets (Russia and the French Northern Fleet). Ultimately Tirpitz sold the Kaiser the idea of a large, prestigious and above all visible battle fleet: capital ships. That explains why Tirpitz was uninterested in either submarines or airships. Submarines in particular could not then (and cannot now) contribute very much to peacetime naval presence. Because he was not very interested in war-fighting, Tirpitz saw U-boats as a drain on scarce resources. Later it was said that he had refrained from buying U-boats until they were fully reliable. It seems fairer to say that Tirpitz wanted battleships and that he could not afford much else.

Tirpitz benefitted considerably from the army's role as bulwark of the regime.[25] Memories of 1848 and the 1870 Paris Commune remained fresh. To the Kaiser and his circle, the guarantee of army loyalty was that its officers were all members of the minor Prussian (mainly Junker) nobility. The number of acceptable officers set the size of the army. The bourgeoisie was not considered reliable. The army did not begin to expand in earnest (with non-aristocratic junior officers) until the war scares of 1910–11. There was also some fear that to enlarge the army would require enlistment of more working-class men, whose socialist leanings might make them subversive. The removal of these brakes on army expansion from 1912 on explain why the navy fraction of the German national defence budget declined after peaking at 52 per cent in 1912.

Tirpitz' problem was that the unit prices of capital ships kept rising inexorably (and rapidly) from about 1905 onwards. At times, however, he had to promise the Reichstag that his estimates for expenditure some years in the future were correct. The Kaiser sometimes told him simply to disregard fiscal constraints, but that could not work very well. Had the number to be built each year not been fixed, the Germans could have traded off numbers against costs; but that was not possible. Even worse, when he pushed through the 1906 Navy Law, Tirpitz offered the Reichstag a long-range fiscal plan (and promised that no new consumption taxes would be needed to finance it). As the financial squeeze worsened, he was obliged to find cuts elsewhere in his budget. For example, the German navy was chronically short of mines and torpedoes, with, for example, consequences for wartime doctrine as to how torpedoes were to be used. It was later argued that the German fleet was also undermanned with specialists in peacetime, again to cut its cost.

By building his navy and by proclaiming that it was designed specifically to fight the British, Tirpitz effectively guaranteed that if a big European war began, the British would feel compelled to participate. They could not possibly ignore a mortal threat. Moreover, British public opinion would strongly support participation in such a war, because for about thirty years the Royal Navy and its friends had driven home the point that dominance of the sea kept Britain alive. That had been true since Britain had become dependent on foreign sources of food, but few British civilians – or politicians – understood that before the 1880s. In 1881 a British naval strategist, Captain Colomb, told the Royal United Services Institute that most people concentrated on the militia as their defence against invasion, not realising that invasion was beside the point. Defeat at sea would bring starvation. Colomb and other naval officers were painfully aware that neither major political party was much interested in modernising the Royal Navy to match growing foreign fleets. The Liberal Prime Minister William Gladstone was particularly hostile to naval spending, which he considered a drag on the British economy.

In 1884 the senior Royal Navy operational officer, Admiral Phipps-Hornby, mounted an attack through the press. One of his officers, then-Captain 'Jacky' Fisher, leaked information to a friendly journalist W T Stead, who published a series of articles called 'The Truth About the Navy'.[26] The British public, or at least the political public, became acutely aware of what British seapower meant to them and the pressure for modernisation became irresistible. The result was several increases in appropriations, crowned by the Naval Defence Act of 1889. Among other things, the British Government felt compelled to accept a two-power standard: the

The torpedo was an important factor in British strategy. Because it made destroyers into giant-killers, the torpedo made possible a surprise mass destroyer attack on an enemy base – which the Japanese tried at Port Arthur in February 1904. Ultimately it was torpedo bombers, rather than surface attackers, which realised this possibility, but the potential for surprise attack determined where the British battle fleet would be when war broke out. The German destroyer *S-125* is shown. She was built by Schichau and commissioned on 4 April 1905. She was considerably smaller than contemporary British destroyers (355 tons designed), but had a more powerful torpedo battery of three 45cm tubes (the British typically had two in larger boats). The tube in a well forward of the bridge was a standard design feature until well into the First World War and many British officers thought it made for better seakeeping (it did not). Gun armament was three 5cm guns; at this time the British typically had 7.6cm (3in or 12pdr) guns.

British fleet should be more than equal to the next two. Since the next two were France and Russia, who would soon be allies hostile to the British, this was not at all irrational. A second campaign, in which Captain Charles Beresford MP took Fisher's place, led to a second Act in 1893, which filled gaps in the first Act. At about the same time the Admiralty defined naval adequacy in terms of modern ships, defining 'modern' in terms of ages at which ships should be replaced (Tirpitz adopted this practice in his Navy Laws; it is not clear to what extent he realised that the Admiralty was using this practice).

For historians the Naval Defence Act is usually the end of the story: the Royal Navy won its place at the heart of British defence thinking and it retained its supremacy up to 1914. In fact, however, the Act was the beginning. The key message, that naval supremacy meant survival, was learned and accepted both by politicians and by the public. It made sense because it was true; Britain benefitted hugely from globalisation, but she also depended more and more on seaborne supply.

Inevitably any massive increase in the Imperial German Navy would be seen as an attack on the United Kingdom. The bulk of the German Navy seemed to have no purpose *except* to threaten the Royal Navy and with it the lifeblood on which the British depended. Tirpitz' efforts were probably largely responsible for the growing British entente with France from 1904 onwards and they were certainly responsible for British fleet concentration in the North Sea.

It was not that the British accepted that Germany was their sole likely enemy, but rather that Germany was expanding her fleet (and announcing that it was directed against Britain) at the same time that the other traditional enemy, France, was feeling compelled to shift spending more and more from navy to army. The British argued that German naval spending was a luxury rather than a necessity. That increased the sense of threat. It was inconceivable to them that the German fleet did not figure in German war planning. For example, in 1909 the Germans announced that they were improving the Kiel Canal so that it could accommodate the new dreadnought battleships. Fisher promptly predicted that the Germans would fight in July or August 1914, when the enlarged Canal was opened. It seemed that a usable Canal was a prerequisite for war.

War certainly did come in August 1914, but it seems unlikely that Tirpitz or the Kiel Canal had much to do with its timing. It is just possible that the Germans relied on an imagined naval deterrent when they presented the Austrians with their blank cheque, but it seems far likelier that the German 1912 elections were crucial. As became evident after the war, German naval war planning in 1914 was nearly non-existent and certainly grossly unrealistic. Tirpitz had concentrated on advertising deterrence and he was taken badly aback when it failed. His diary entries and equivalent correspondence by Chief of the Admiralty Staff Admiral von Pohl were published soon after the war.[27] Tirpitz and von Pohl spent the months at headquarters after war broke out arguing over whether the fleet should be preserved as a post-war bargaining chip or whether it had to fight a big battle so that whatever was left was not discarded after the war. Each assured the other that the fleet would have important wartime roles – but they were never discussed. This was particularly odd given that von Pohl was the chief war planner.

Because the Kaiser's navy had little or nothing to do with German security needs, German General Staff (army) war planning took no account of naval considerations or of the potential offered by naval forces. The war plan did not envisage any special effort to seize the French Channel ports, when that might have been possible in 1914. At times during the early part of the war, the Chief of the German General Staff needled senior naval officers with the comment that the sailors might be employed more usefully as troops. Tirpitz appears to have formed a naval unit (to fight in Flanders) as a way of demonstrating naval participation in the war, though later it was explained in terms of planning to fight based on the Belgian coast. In discussions of war aims, Tirpitz did press for seizure of the Belgian coast as a vital asset for a further war against Britain which he and other Germans assumed would follow a truce once France and Russia had been defeated on land.

After the war, many Germans viewed their expensive navy with considerable bitterness. An American naval officer, assigned immediately after the war to the Allied Control Commission assigned to enforcing the terms of the peace, remarked that German naval officers in Berlin felt compelled to wear civilian clothes lest they be attacked in the street. A popular pamphlet was titled 'Tirpitz, Grave-Digger of Germany'.[28] A prominent German naval commentator, retired Captain Ludwig Persius, wrote soon after the war that Tirpitz' pursuit of a 'prestige' fleet had been suicidal, for exactly the reasons laid out above.[29]

The British might have been hostile to Germany whether or not Tirpitz had built his fleet. British policy had long been to maintain a balance of power in Europe, on the theory that if any one Continental Power became dominant it might be able to crush Britain by building up both a great army *and* a great navy. That was far too abstract to create the strong popular animosity towards Germany which developed during the early twentieth century. It took the mortal challenge of an expanding German fleet to do that. If anything, the challenge was underlined by the fact that there was no obvious rationale for a powerful German fleet. In 1902, when the first major Navy Law was passed, significant voices in the Royal Navy were arguing that the challenge from Germany was at least as important as the traditional challenge posed by the French and the Russians.

Ultimately Germany was unable to win a protracted war against an enemy with access to the world's resources. The great German failure was to ensure that the British, with their access to the world, entered the war. Moreover, increasingly desperate German attempts to break the Allied connection with the rest of the world, via the sea, ultimately brought the United States into the war. The United States held the balance of resources in 1917–18; the Germans did not have the resources to deal with the huge army it could and did generate. That army in turn could not have reached the battlefields of Western Europe had the Allied navies not held the German U-boats at bay.

Austria-Hungary

Interacting tensions *could* have led to a world war at any time before 1914. Each time all concerned held back. They were well aware of the cost of a war. Something different happened in 1914. The particular crisis in 1914 began when a Serbian nationalist killed the Austrian crown prince, the Archduke Franz Ferdinand, during his visit to Sarajevo in Bosnia-Herzegovina. It was widely suspected that the Serbian government was more or less responsible and Austria was expected to demand punishment. The war began when Austria demanded terms so harsh that they practically required Serbia to fight. She then prosecuted the war in such a way that Austria's ally Russia apparently had to join in.

The Austrians certainly wanted to crush Serbia, which they considered a mortal threat because of its support of subversion in their Slavic domains. Unlike Germany, Austria-Hungary was a collection of eleven main ethnic groups and in 1914 they were

beginning to demand a degree of independence. The Slavs in the south seemed particularly restive. They were supported by Serbians across the border and the Serbians enjoyed some support from the Russians. This combination linked the kind of subversion every government in Europe feared to classic international tensions.

Normally the Austrians would have curbed their desire to crush Serbia, because war against Serbia risked intervention by Russia. This time they felt free to act because the Kaiser assured the Austro-Hungarian Emperor that he would back whatever they did – the 'blank cheque'. It is often suggested that the Kaiser acted this way because of a personal connection to the assassinated Archduke. However, the General Staff assumed that the Kaiser, who they considered too pacifistic, would pull back and he was deliberately allowed to go on a planned fleet cruise to Norway as the crisis developed.[30] Chancellor Bethmann-Hollweg seems to have thought that the crisis would be limited to the Balkans and to have had no inkling that something much larger was imminent.

Was the 1914 crisis over the assassination different in quality from the string of earlier crises, each of which was advertised as a possible trigger for war, or was something else happening in 1914? Any of the major crises of the period before 1914 might have become the pretext for a war.[31] Details were not really important *if* one of the governments involved really wanted to fight. The Germans who wanted war considered it essential to present the conflict as defensive so as to ensure Reichstag and popular support.[32]

Both Austria-Hungary and Italy were allied to Germany under the Triple Alliance. However, they were sufficiently hostile to each other that plans for joint naval action against France (in the event of war) were never developed to a useful extent. Much of Italy as it existed in 1914 had been wrested from Austria in 1866 and in 1914 Austria still held considerable territory that Italians regarded as theirs. The Germans seem to have assumed that Italy would leave the Triple Alliance. In 1914 the country remained neutral; it joined the Allies in 1915. That manoeuvre made the Adriatic sea between Austria-Hungary and Italy a naval theatre of war. However, once at war both countries concentrated most of their energy on land operations.

The Other European Powers

France was the other great modern European power. Its great fear was that Germany could overwhelm France yet again, thanks to its much larger population (which supported a much larger and better-equipped army).[33] The only solution to French problems was an alliance which could cancel out German strength. The French found it in Russia. The Franco-Russian alliance was concluded in 1894.

France was unusual in that she depended on sea control at the moment of mobilisation for war, because her Algerian army across the Mediterranean was so significant a part of her overall army strength, helping balance the greater manpower Germany could wield. Thus the initial wartime role of the French Navy was to guarantee the passage of the army from Algeria to France. It was assumed in the Admiralty that the main mission of the German warships in the Mediterranean, the battlecruiser *Goeben* and the light cruiser *Breslau*, was to interdict this traffic. *Goeben* went to Turkey, ultimately with immense consequences, after the German Admiral commanding the Mediterranean Division was informed by W/T that an alliance with Turkey was being concluded.[34] Once the African army had been transported successfully to metropolitan France, the French fleet became available for other operations, including the Dardanelles and the blockade of Austria. France was normally nearly self-sufficient (at least in food), to the point that British nineteenth-century naval war planners did not consider blockade an effective means of attacking her. Much of what she did import came from the Mediterranean, which made Austria and Italy potential naval problems.

During the late nineteenth century, there was considerable friction between Germany and Russia, not least because the Russians thought that their long-time enemies the British were likely to be in league with the Germans. Germany and Russia shared a divided Poland. Having lived through a Polish revolt in 1863 and also through Muslim revolts in Southern Russia, the Tsarist government feared that the loss of its half of Poland would ignite nationalist sentiments elsewhere in the Empire. Many slavophiles also saw Germany as a dangerous modernising force which would destroy the Russian Empire. They had considerable influence on many Tsars. The Russians came to see France as an enemy which tied Germany down. In 1875 the French enlarged their army and Bismarck used the German press to threaten war (neither side was apparently particularly eager to fight). He was enraged when the Russians told him that they could not tolerate the destruction of France: they were determined to preserve the balance of European power.

As the putative protectors of the Slavs, the Russians were also locked into hostility against Austria-Hungary, with its own expansion into the Balkans. For a time any such considerations were overshadowed by the need to protect autocracy from the forces of democracy in Europe, so Germany, Russia and Austria formed the 'Three Emperors' League'. Russian troops backed the Austrians by putting down the Hungarian rising in 1849–50. By the 1870s the situation had changed and in 1879 Bismarck signed a treaty with Austria-Hungary. Its secret military clauses bound each to defend the other in the event of a Russian attack (the Russians thought they also bound the two together offensively). That year's German military plan called for a pre-emptive attack on Russia. To head off Russian suspicions, Bismarck recreated the

Three-Emperors' League, but it did not last. The three-year Reinsurance Treaty (1887) bound Germany to defend Russia in the event of an attack by a third party. The Russians were unenthusiastic, but in the early 1880s they were too weak to risk Prussian enmity. In 1890 the Kaiser decided that Russia was not to be trusted and he decided not to renew Bismarck's earlier 'reinsurance' treaty binding Germany to Russia. There was a brief attempt to mend fences about 1904, but it came to nothing. The Russians built an alliance with France from 1894 onwards.

In 1914 Russia was modernising with French financial and industrial help. She was also the main playground for subversives, the birthplace of anarchist philosophy. In 1905 failure in the Russo-Japanese War nearly brought down the Tsarist system. By 1914, it seemed that the Russian Empire was prospering and that the problems of the past had been buried. The celebration of the 300th anniversary of the Romanov Dynasty in 1913 had been a great success. Recovery from the disaster of 1905 left the Russians free to contemplate longer-term goals. However, in 1914 those at the top of the Russian government agreed that the empire needed peace above all in order to recover from its many remaining problems.

Probably the most sensitive Russian national interest lay not in central Europe but in the south. About 47 per cent of Russian trade, much of it wheat exports, passed through the Turkish Straits. Russia was a great exporter of wheat and other grains, much of it grown in the rich 'black soil' of the Ukraine. Unfortunately the Russians did not control the mouth of the Black Sea – Turkey did (and still does). Their great foreign policy objective was to gain control of the Dardanelles, the route out of the Black Sea. In support of that objective the Russians hoped eventually to control the Balkans – which, in 1914, the Austrians partly ruled. It should not be surprising that the Russians were supporting anti-Austrian subversives in the Balkans, or that Russia was allied to Serbia, the base for such action. The Russians had been involved in the 1903 coup in Serbia which created a nationalist government sympathetic to Serbs determined to oust the Austrians from the Balkans. To some extent the Russian association with the Balkans was connected to the idea that Russia was and should be the leader of all the Slavic nationalities, hence

Scapa Flow was chosen as the wartime Grand Fleet base because it was far enough from the Heligoland Bight to preclude a surprise mass German destroyer attack, but at the same time close enough that the Grand Fleet could operate freely in the North Sea without having its own destroyers run quickly out of fuel (British destroyer endurance considerably exceeded German, thanks to the adoption of oil fuel). There was no infrastructure at Scapa Flow, so ships had to go some distance for maintenance work such as docking to scrape and paint their hulls. This was a particular problem early in the war, when many ships were sidelined with condenser problems whose solution required docking. (G05580 (c) National Maritime Museum, London)

natural allies of the Serbs and others under both Austrian and Turkish domination.

Control of the Dardanelles became even more urgent as the Russian government focussed on creating a prosperous peasant class as a bulwark against revolution. These peasants depended on income from grain exports through the Black Sea. Grain was, moreover, the principal Russian export product and 90 per cent of it went through the Dardanelles. That was apart from the fact that revenue from these exports financed Russian industry. During the Balkan War, it became clear that the king ('Tsar') of Russia's nominal ally Bulgaria wanted control of the Dardanelles. The Russians discovered that they had no real allies when it came to this vital interest. This conclusion made it impossible for them to accept a proposed Greek role in the Dardanelles in 1915.

Russian economic dependence on the Dardanelles was demonstrated when the Turks briefly closed them during their war with Italy in the summer of 1912, the grain-exporting season. Russian exports through the Black Sea fell by a third and revenue by about 30 per cent (from about £77 million to about £57 million).[35]

In 1914 the Germans were dabbling in the politics of the Dardanelles, threatening a vital Russian interest. Beginning in 1903, they convinced the Turkish sultan to allow them to build a railway from Berlin to Baghdad. Those supporting the project told the Kaiser that that it was the key threat to the British Empire, because it provided direct land access to the East (the British saw Baghdad in German hands as a direct threat to their rule in India).[36] The British shifted between seeing the railway project as a threat and accepting it as a normal commercial undertaking. To the Germans, the railway was associated with an alliance with Turkey, which in turn might provide them with influence over the hundreds of millions of Muslims in the British Empire.[37] Other steps included transferring obsolete warships. In 1913 General Liman von Sanders was appointed head of a German military mission to Turkey intended to modernise the Turkish army after its failures during the Balkan Wars of 1912–13. In 1914 von Sanders took command of the key Turkish division outside Constantinople; the Russians told the Germans that such a step amounted to intolerable meddling with their own sensitive interest in the Dardanelles. Von Sanders was then made inspector of the entire Turkish army, in which capacity he reinforced the defences of the Dardanelles once war broke out. The von Sanders affair helped bring a relatively irresponsible War Minister to power in Russia.

Facing the Germans as possible enemies, the Russians had to reckon with the possibility of a sudden German naval stroke against their capital, St Petersburg, which lies on an inlet of the Baltic. In 1914 the Russian fleet was greatly inferior to that of the Germans and the Russians expected to rely mainly on a combination of mines and light torpedo craft to defend their capital. Perhaps their own memory of the Crimean War, when the British created just such a threat, made them sensitive to this danger.

From the Russian point of view, British entry into the war made an enormous difference. However superior it might be, the German fleet was unlikely to be released for a major operation in the Baltic. Pinning it down there, or even suffering significant losses there, the fleet would be unable to face its main enemy, the Royal Navy. This point arose several times when, at the outset of the war, the Kaiser demanded an all-out naval demonstration against Russia.

British Naval Strategy

The Navy Laws accelerated German naval construction just as warships became considerably more expensive. In the 1880s, the British had faced a Franco-Russian alliance and they announced (in line with the 1889 Act) that they would maintain a fleet enjoying an edge over those of the next two powers – because those next two powers might well be allied against them. Once the British reached accommodations with France and Russia, the growing German fleet became the standard against which the Royal Navy was measured: the British sought 60 per cent superiority over the Germans.

Developments from about 1903 on complicate evaluation of any such yardstick. During the 1903 defence review and possibly as early as 1900, Admiral Fisher and others became convinced that in wartime torpedo craft, particularly submarines, would make it impossible for large warships to survive in narrow seas such as the North Sea. Under those circumstances it was no longer clear what role battleships would play. In the past, their role as capital ships had rested on the assumption that no lesser ships could destroy them: it took a battleship to deal with another battleship. Lesser ships could operate only under the protection, or by evading the threat of, battleships. Torpedoes, which could be launched by small craft and by submarines, could sink battleships. What then was the role of battleships in narrow waters? Once he became First Sea Lord in 1904, Admiral Fisher began to press for a radical change in British naval strategy, in which the North Sea would be given over to sea-denial forces, perhaps a hundred destroyers and a similar number of submarines. Outside the North Sea, the most important capital ship role would be to run down enemy commerce raiders. There was no reason to imagine that an enemy battle fleet would ever emerge from the North Sea, given the underwater menace.

There were two quite distinct objections, one tactical and the other political. The tactical objection was that submarines might find it difficult to find and engage fast capital ships. Unless they patrolled immediately outside the enemy's ports, they might well fail to find his ships and they were not so fast that they could contact ships detected at a distance (their detection range was limited, too). It is not clear how much these problems were appreciated before the war. However, once Fisher left office in January 1910, his successors were far less confident that torpedo craft could keep the enemy's fleet in harbour. Wartime experience shows that they were right. Fisher (and apparently everyone else) grossly down-played the difficulty submarines and other torpedo craft would find in actually finding an enemy's surface ships. That said, the Germans certainly took the threat of British submarines in the North Sea seriously.

The political objection had to do with deterrence. A *visible* battle fleet had political weight, whether or not it was likely to be effective in wartime. In a world ruled by deterrence, what is visible counts heavily. In reality, submarines might make the North Sea impassable to the German battle fleet, but the pre-war Admiralty and the pre-war British government were both well aware that they needed a visible form of seapower. Admiral Fisher was less interested in the expensive visible side of seapower because when he took office he confronted a severe financial crisis. He may also have hoped that his battlecruisers would have the same political weight as battleships. On the German side, Admiral Tirpitz seems to have been even more interested in the visible side of seapower, hence much less interested in submarines. Moreover, had Tirpitz

One major wartime surprise was the great endurance of submarines. German destroyers might be unable to reach Scapa Flow, but U-boats could, even in 1914. Once that was obvious, the fleet had to be withdrawn until sufficient anti-submarine nets had been set up, with facilities to support the small craft tending them. Here an *Invincible* class battlecruiser enters Scapa Flow through the nets guarding it in 1917.

accepted Fisher's concept of sea denial in the North Sea, he would never have been able to claim that his growing battle fleet would exert leverage over the Royal Navy.

In 1912 the British and the French reached an agreement: the British would take responsibility for the North Sea, the French for the Mediterranean. The British did not quite quit the Mediterranean, but they gave up any attempt to match the potentially hostile force there (Austria-Hungary plus Italy). In theory such an agreement might have proven very embarrassing if France but not the United Kingdom went to war, leaving much of the French coast exposed to German naval attack. The 1912 arrangement was much closer to alliance than the British had previously accepted.

This is not to say that before 1914 the British concentrated on the threat from Germany to the exclusion of all other possibilities. Britain followed a policy of non-alignment until it allied with Japan and until well into the twentieth century the British faced a serious Russian challenge in India and in the Far East. Russian defeat in the Russo-Japanese War greatly reduced that threat and, consequently, emphasised the developing German threat. As late as 1909 the Admiralty was promoting a plan for the major Dominions (and India) to build fleet units for Pacific operations. They would have been directed both at the detached German cruisers in the Far East and at a rising Japan which was already showing an appetite for

Western colonial possessions. Surviving British pre-war instructions for overseas fleets reflect the possible variety of crises; they are not specifically directed at Germany.

Once Britain was drawn into a European war, the facts of maritime life came into play. Despite numerous pre-war scares, it was extremely unlikely that the British Isles could be successfully invaded, so long as the Royal Navy existed. An enemy might put some troops ashore, but they would soon be cut off from reinforcements and supplies and they would be unlikely to survive for long. That in turn meant that no war involving the United Kingdom could be ended quickly by any victory the Germans might achieve on land. Any big Continental war would inevitably be protracted. It would become a test not only of national capability but also of the inherent strength of the societies involved. Access to resources would count more and more as the war continued.

It seems unlikely that the Germans ever seriously contemplated invading the United Kingdom. Once their armies had been halted in France, they lacked surplus troops for so risky an enterprise and no one in the German naval leadership was ever a particularly enthusiastic risk-taker. Nor did the German naval leadership have sufficient prestige within Germany to affect military decisions. The British were never sure of that and throughout the war they continued to develop anti-invasion and anti-raid plans. It is not clear to what extent this planning was a reaction to the British army's demands to maintain troops in the United Kingdom. Before the war, the army had used the threat of invasion as a force builder. All of this having been said, pre-war exercises demonstrated that there were serious gaps in British ocean surveillance which could have permitted a small invasion force to get to the British coast.

As long as Britain enjoyed naval supremacy, she could draw on the resources not only of her Empire but also of an informal empire consisting of the countries in which she had important commercial interests, countries bound to Britain by important common interests. For example, although the United States broke out of the formal empire in 1783, in 1914 it was very much part of the informal empire. That was aside from the sentimental tie that many Americans of British descent retained; some went so far as to include their country in 'Greater Britain' (many others disagreed vehemently). That the City of London was the centre of world finance reinforced this connection to the rest of the world.

In wartime, as long as the Royal Navy retained command of the world ocean, Britain could draw on the immense strength of her two empires. Outside the war zone, these places could produce unhampered by the enemy. Other countries obviously enjoyed somewhat analogous ties to the world, but the British had the ability to interdict their connections to those countries. In particular the Royal Navy could and did block trade access to Germany. The British Government faced a dilemma. It drew considerable strength from a friendly if neutral United States – which also had strong trade relations with Germany. Until the United States entered the war in 1917, the blockade of Germany had to be limited to avoid US enmity. Even so, it deeply affected the Germans. For example, German exports essentially ceased. Germany lacked financial resources to match Britain's.

Thinking about war-fighting

Because Britain headed a maritime empire, her government was more likely than that of any of the other Great Powers to think about how land and sea forces should be integrated in wartime. Admiral Fisher was fond of saying that 'the British Army is the projectile fired by the Navy', but the army took that as an insult and there is no evidence that anyone in the British government took the statement to a logical conclusion and thought about where the projectile should be fired in the event of a European war.[38]

When initial war plans were being drawn up in the event of a war against Germany in 1905–6, Fisher proposed landing troops on the German Baltic coast where, among other things, they might be within striking range of Berlin (the Germans ridiculed the idea, saying that the hundred thousand or so troops would simply be arrested). Fisher was later fond of pointing out that during an Eighteenth Century war against Russia Prussian King Frederick the Great lost his nerve (and asked for a bottle of poison) only when the Russians were poised to land on the Pomeranian coast near Berlin. The idea died when, among other things, the army pointed out that operations in the Baltic during the Crimean War had achieved nothing. That was very much the agreed view in 1914. Ironically, more recent review suggests that successful Baltic naval operations, particularly against the fortress of Sveaborg, brought the Russians to the bargaining table, because they pointed to a possible naval success against the Russian capital of St Petersburg.

To the extent that Germany was governed by an army led by Junkers, small landholders from eastern Prussia, on the border with Russia, that area was the most sensitive part of the country. Fisher's abortive war plan was the closest the British came to exploiting that fact (Fisher may merely have been thinking of proximity to Berlin). After about 1906 the two services planned nearly independently, the main point of contact being the understanding that the Royal Navy would ensure safe delivery of British divisions to France. No one in the British Cabinet ever seems to have asked whether the expeditionary force constituted a blank cheque tying the British to France. That may have been the fault of British deterrent thinking. Fisher was unable to derail the army plan in favour his own for a landing on the German Baltic coast.[39] By this time the CID was becoming interested in the Admiralty's favoured plan of economic attack against Germany. It is not clear to what extent the CID or the Prime Minister believed that economic attack could crush Germany so rapidly that no other war plan would have to be executed.

German naval planners seem to have taken the Baltic possibility seriously. They focussed on a decisive battle against the Royal Navy, the object of which would have been to exercise their deterrent. The post-war German official history *Krieg zur See* strongly criticised the pre-war and wartime German navy for not having taken into account the other roles of seapower, such as trade protection, which were so clearly understood by the Royal Navy. Focussing exclusively, at least at first, on a fleet versus fleet battle was a gross simplification of Mahan's teachings (the Imperial Japanese Navy of the Second World War can be similarly criticised). Until about 1912 the expected locus of the battle was the Skaggerak, the strait leading into the Baltic. In these narrow waters torpedo boats and mines could be expected to sink British capital ships. After 1912 the focus shifted to an expected early British attack on Wilhelmshaven, the German fleet base.[40] When war broke out, the German fleet was in its fortified base and there seems to have been every expectation that the British would attack, to be destroyed by a combination of shore defences and underwater weapons. In effect the Germans were thinking of their own fleet as bait. It is not entirely clear why German strategists shifted focus, but it may be that in 1912 the Germans found out that the British planned to commit their army expeditionary force to France, hence were unlikely to pursue a Baltic strategy. It is not at all clear why they imagined that the British were so foolish as to commit naval suicide to meet German expectations. The usual explanation is that they imagined that British 'offensive spirit' would not have accepted anything less than an early frontal attack.

One of the weirder aspects of British thinking during the run-up to 1914 was that no one seems to have looked back at the previous great war, the one against Napoleon, for strategic lessons. As fought, the First World War certainly differed greatly from the Napoleonic Wars, not least because the protagonists could and did support much larger armies, to the point where the sort of decisive victories Napoleon gained became impossible. However, in outline the wars were not so different. In both cases, the key fact was that nothing done on land could eliminate one of the protagonists, the United Kingdom. That left the land power locked in a struggle of exhaustion, while the sea power had access to all the resources of the world – as long as it maintained command of the sea. Moreover, the sea power could strike at will around the periphery of the land power's domains. Even if a strike failed utterly, that would not end the war, because troops could be withdrawn to strike again elsewhere. As long as the sea power remained intact, it could keep creating coalitions to attack the land power, and also the land power might well overreach in its attempts to knock out the sea power without invading.

Napoleon found himself waging economic war against the United Kingdom, whose economy was based largely on seaborne trade with Europe. He tried and failed to impose a self-blockade (embargo) of the Continent. Ultimately he invaded Russia because the Russians had refused to join his embargo against British goods. That in turn proved his downfall. In connection with the Maritime Strategy espoused by the US Navy in the 1980s, an American strategist described British policy against Napoleon as the 'Mr. Micawber strategy', holding on in the belief that 'something will turn up'. That is not the worst analogy. As long as the British were safe and were gaining economically, Napoleon had to keep looking for some way to deal with them. Ultimately he triggered a land war he could not win, against the Russians. During the First World War, the Germans found themselves compelled to deal with the fact that the British had access to overseas resources, hence to attack both British seaborne trade and the United States, as a source of British strength. Attacks on the United States included covert attacks on munitions plants (such as Black Tom in New York Harbor in 1916) and then the attempt to bring Mexico into the war to neutralise the possible American threat (via the Zimmermann Telegram of 1917). The latter attempt levered the United States into the war.

That Napoleon could not invade the British Isles made it possible for British strategists to undertake high-risk/high-payoff land operations; even the loss of much of the army could not be fatal. In the British view, Trafalgar gained sea supremacy and after that it was possible to land an army on the periphery of Europe.

The first such operation, a landing at Walcheren on the Scheldt estuary, was unsuccessful; the army had to be withdrawn. The second such operation was Wellington's protracted campaign on the Iberian Peninsula. Wellington alone was certainly not enough to destroy Napoleon, but he represented a serious strain building on the disaster in Russia. When Napoleon could not destroy Wellington, he felt compelled to retreat back across the French border, ultimately to defeat.

Perhaps the greatest lesson of the Napoleonic Wars was that the British could and did survive any number of disasters visited on their Continental allies. What counted was their ability to keep fighting, coupled with their ability to back each alliance financially, thanks to their wealth (and their sophisticated financial structure, which enabled the British Government to keep raising money while its rivals went broke). The lesson that alliances were expendable so long as the United Kingdom remained intact seems to have been lost on the British Governments of 1914 and beyond. They often tried to reduce their commitment on the Continent, but they considered the defeat of France an unacceptable catastrophe. The experience of the Second World War suggests that the British realised, correctly, that was not the case.

Looking back, one must wonder whether anyone in the British Government asked how much sacrifice it was worth to keep France

Admiral von Tirpitz conceived his Navy Laws at a time when battleship design, hence unit cost, had stabilised. He could therefore tell the Reichstag what a long-range plan would cost. *Wittelsbach* class pre-dreadnought battleships are shown on manoeuvres in 1912. Within a few years, continuing escalation in unit cost made any kind of long-term planning unrealistic. (Naval Institute collection)

in the war. The British Government proved guilty of one of the worst strategic sins: it never decided what its objective was. Was it to knock Germany out? To keep France intact? Something else? As long as the question was not asked, there was no need to develop a national (as opposed to single-service) strategy which would have built on Fisher's observation that the British Army was best seen as a striking arm wielded by sea power.

The British Government may have had some fear of invasion, should the Germans defeat France and so gain a large surplus army. Invasion was a staple of pre-1914 future-war fiction, the most famous example being Erskine Childers' *Riddle of the Sands*. Pre-war advocates of national conscription (to create a Continental-size army) argued that it was needed to deal with exactly that threat.[41] The Royal Navy often pointed out that although it might be possible to land a few troops in the United Kingdom, they could not be supported, because any follow-up force would be annihilated at sea. A British submarine officer asked whether those fearing invasion were aware that, at the press of a button, he could sink a troopship with thousands of soldiers on board.

It is difficult to say how seriously the threat was taken during the war, although effort was certainly devoted to planning against it. Without ocean surveillance, it was impossible to be sure that the Germans would not come.[42] As most of the trained troops in the United Kingdom were sent to France, fear of invasion increased. Thus in November 1914 Churchill warned Jellicoe that the Germans might use the mass of shipping caught in their ports by the blockade and troops freed by a deadlock on the Western Front to attack England.[43] The main German problem would be to land the artillery on which their army seemed to depend so heavily and for that they would have to seize an undefended British port. Elaborate preparations were therefore ordered to render such ports unusable in the event of an attack. There is no evidence that the Germans ever came close to imagining such an operation, although they certainly took the possibility of British amphibious operations seriously.

The invasion bogey seems to be connected with the pre-war fight over how the British army should have been used. Had the possibility of an assault on the German coast been taken seriously,

the army staff would have been compelled to work out its requirements in detail. It would have discovered what was clear later on, that even a small amphibious operation was difficult at best. Moving a quarter-million man army from Germany to the British coast over 350nm away would have been an extraordinary operation, requiring years of visible preparation – not merely taking over immobilised merchant ships. When a detailed account of the much smaller operation the Germans mounted against the Russian Åland Islands in 1917, the British were surprised by how elaborate their arrangements were.[44]

The 1916 disaster on the Somme forced the British to confront the likelihood that they could not win the war outright; they might have to accept a negotiated settlement. It is interesting to see just what that meant. For a Continental power like France, disaster meant national defeat and perhaps dismemberment. For the British it meant having to accept a peace something like the one they accepted from Napoleon in 1801: a truce until one side or the other decided to try again. Now British strategists did have to think about wider possibilities and they soon focussed on the East – the Middle East and the Caucasus. In fact the British were not compelled to withdraw from the war and the French front held, but throughout 1917–18 British resources were increasingly invested in eastern areas which offered new strategic possibilities. Sea power and the

The dreadnought revolution raised the unit cost of battleships, but the 'iron budget' Tirpitz had created did not allow him to trade off unit quality against numbers: his Navy Laws locked in the number of battleships. Tirpitz concealed the ongoing fiscal crisis partly by cutting back on personnel and on procurement, for example of mines and torpedoes, with consequences for wartime operations. He also tried to hold back unit costs by, for example, limiting the calibre of battleship guns. *Westfalen*, photographed by Ulrich Shreier, is shown. She was one of the first group of German dreadnoughts, the *Nassau* class. To hold down size (hence cost), they had 11in guns rather than the 12in of contemporary British and other foreign battleships. Tirpitz had seriously considered an all-big-gun armament of smaller guns, but he rejected it on the ground that gunnery range was growing and that at greater ranges they would be useless. (Naval Institute collection)

unique maritime position of the United Kingdom, made that a real option. There was a reason for all the effort put into defeating the Ottoman Empire in 1917–18.

Admittedly, in the most recent large war, in the Crimea more than half a century earlier, the British Cabinet had proved ill-adapted to making strategy of this type. Once any land force had been committed, the Cabinet concentrated on fighting that land war, however peripheral it might be. The Crimean War began as the Great Russian War, the Crimea having been selected for an initial attack because it seemed to be an ideal place to mount a large amphibious raid. Once the British and the French were deeply embroiled there, the British Cabinet came to imagine that victory in the Crimea would be overall victory. There was never much chance of that. The Crimea had virtually no strategic significance to the Tsar; it was a pit into which his enemies poured their energy, while he merely expended a few of his numerous troops. Unsurprisingly, the fall of the Crimea had no further repercussions, at least for the war. Operations in the Baltic seem to have been much more effective; a successful attack on Sveaborg foreshadowed a likely attack against the Russian capital of St Petersburg. At the end of the Russian War there was widespread awareness that the naval threat to St Petersburg had been decisive. It really did promote the strategic objective of the war, which was to force the Russians back from expansion through both the Black Sea and Europe. For example, the Russians had to accept a settlement barring them from maintaining a fleet in the Black Sea, which would have threatened Turkey. The British remembered, so that their reaction to a crisis against Russia in 1885 was to form a Baltic Fleet. By 1914 they had apparently forgotten the lesson.

During the run-up to 1914, closer observation of German politics might have revealed the special sensitivity of eastern Prussia. A British fleet operating in the Baltic might have moved troops, either British or Russian, around the German defensive position in East Prussia, turning it. It might be argued that the Germans would have found it impossible to trade gains in France for serious losses in eastern Prussia. They would have had to move large units East, so relieving pressure on the French. Anyone who finds the actual course of the war horrific might find such a strategy at least interesting; it will be discussed in a later chapter.

It happened that the British had something closer to the necessary organisation than any other country, in the form of the Committee on Imperial Defence (CID) created out of the Cabinet Defence Committee. Unfortunately the CID was created more to examine ways of defending the Empire than ways of dealing with a European problem. A pre-war proposal to make the CID a kind of joint staff or a staff supervising both Admiralty and War Office failed. The closest the British Government seems to have come to adjudicating between the very different Admiralty and War Office concepts of future war came in the context of crises between 1906 and 1911, when the Prime Minister and the CID reviewed war planning. It is not clear how serious these reviews were. The army certainly argued its case for the commitment to France. The navy position was less straightforward. For example, it never seems to have argued blockade vs presence on the Continent and it certainly never argued its case for an economic attack. That suggests that the meetings were not about adjudication at all, but rather about the army's attempt to sell its own policy in a context in which blockade or economic warfare was the default assumption.

A century after the Great War broke out, we have a better idea of what a major war in Europe might look like. In effect the Second World War was what would have happened in the First World War had the Germans succeeded in overrunning France. In that sense 1940 – that the fall of France did not defeat Britain – was a demonstration that the blank cheque the British offered the French may have been somewhat excessive. Note that this blank cheque, unlike the one the Kaiser offered the Austrians just before the war (which was probably decisive in making the war as terrible as it was) has received no great attention, yet it too was decisive in shaping the war.

In the 1980s the US Navy took this lesson into account when it offered a maritime – not a naval – strategy for a potential European war set off by the Soviet Union. The Navy's argument was that seapower offered unique possibilities, first for deterrence and then both for slowing a Soviet advance through Western Europe (by attacking the Soviet flanks) and for winning even if the Soviets reached the Channel. The great deterrent point was that the Soviets could not count on victory if they reached the Channel; defeating the NATO armies on the Central Front would not be enough. The Navy also emphasised the effect on the Soviets of the threat of a second, eastern, front – China, supported by the Seventh Fleet. The threat of flank attacks, even of an attack through the Baltic on Leningrad, might well reduce the power of a Soviet land attack by demanding that forces be held back. A careful reading of First World War experience shows examples of all of these possibilities. Not surprisingly, the US Army was less than enthusiastic and no one ever decided whether the Maritime Strategy would become US policy. Fortunately no one ever found out how well it would have worked. From our present point of view, what matters is to understand that some of the actors in that terrible drama did have different options. It is important to ask why they were not really examined – and whether we can or would do better.

The British deterrent failed in 1914 and the army plan intended to support deterrence had to be activated. British stiffening for France came in two categories: the agreement to protect the French North Sea coast so that the French Navy could transport African troops in an emergency and the plan to land the British Expeditionary Force (BEF) in northern France, near the Belgian border. The naval agreement with France had been initiated in 1912. Although as late as 3 August the British refused to commit troops to France, under the agreement they had to provide naval cover as soon as the French went to war. Initially the French 2nd Cruiser Squadron (Admiral Rouyer) patrolled the Straits of Dover – though under British orders beginning on 27 July. Once war broke out, the Dover and Channel Patrols took up their war stations.

The troop commitment turned out to have enormous naval implications. Initially the Royal Navy had to cover the movement of troops to France, mainly to Le Havre, but also to Rouen and to Boulogne to reduce railway congestion inside France. The troopships were not convoyed. Instead, they sailed independently as soon as they were full, exploiting the favourable geography of the Channel. Light forces protected both ends of the route, the Grand Fleet blocking any attempt by the High Seas Fleet to intervene. The strait itself was patrolled by the Channel Squadron, the destroyers and submarines of the Dover Patrol and by French destroyers and submarines. A line of twelve British submarines operated north of the Dover Patrol destroyers, to intercept enemy surface ships which might try to intervene.

The continuing British troop presence in northern France

created a vital sea lane of communication across the Channel, which the Royal Navy was constrained to defend. Also, once the BEF, which represented the bulk of the active British army, was in France, the possibility of invasion attracted more attention, at least by the army (the 6th Division was brought over from Ireland and concentrated at Cambridge instead of going to France). British naval forces were concentrated in the North Sea between the German fleet and the British coast and two British submarines were stationed just off the Jade and Weser estuaries to report any German movements. These latter were the beginning of the British use of their long-range submarines for a close observational blockade of Germany.

Once landed, the BEF moved north, ultimately into Belgium to face the oncoming Germans. That moved its supply line north as well, making the Belgian ports of Ostend and Zeebrugge on the coast and Antwerp well inland up the Scheldt, more and more important. At the outbreak of war the British mined their approaches and concentrated on protecting ports further south, but soon they had to reverse, recover the mines sown off the Belgian ports and use them.

The British created an independent Southern Force specifically to protect the Belgian coast, keeping the Scheldt (the route to the largest port, Antwerp) open and to provide early warning of any German attempt to attack the sea lane in the Channel. Events on land now dramatically changed the naval geography. The German army war plan envisaged a movement around the flank of the French army, incidentally cutting it off from the French Channel ports. During the initial movement through Belgium, the Germans seized Brussels. The British troops which had advanced into Belgium (and the Belgian government) withdrew to the inland port of Antwerp. A further German advance threatened to cut the Channel link supplying the British troops, so the 6th Division, the last in the United Kingdom, was sent over to support the British troops already in place.

When the Belgians evacuated Ostend, the British army wanted it left intact, as they hoped to move back. They knew they would have to depend on it for supplies. When it seemed that the Germans were about to seize Ostend, the Southern Force was ordered to shell the area, but specifically to concentrate on German troops and to avoid damaging the town. That was impossible, because the roads inland were masked by sand dunes. As the Germans advanced rapidly in their flanking movement around the French army, not only Ostend but also the French Channel ports were endangered; the Admiralty had to consider evacuating stores from Boulogne and Le Havre to Cherbourg. However, it was unwilling to cede these ports to the enemy and it pressed the French to help defend Dunkirk, Calais and Boulogne. Admiral Jellicoe was compelled to consider moving his fleet south in the event the easterly Channel ports fell.

Some of the other naval implications of the German war plan became evident. The German General Staff apparently thought of the sea as a protected flank. The Admiralty saw the German movement as an opportunity, so it moved the three available battalions of Royal Marines into Ostend, on the Germans' flank and not as yet in German hands because it was not the army's objective. At this time the Belgian army command was considering mounting an offensive from Antwerp and the small force in Ostend offered a promising reinforcement. Moreover, the fleet offered supporting heavy artillery, in the form of the guns of three new

monitors bought from Brazil, for which they had been completing on the outbreak of war (*Severn*, *Humber* and *Mersey*).

There had been no pre-war planning for such an operation, probably because there had never been much co-ordination between the Admiralty and the War Office. Moreover, the British did not believe that the German offensive would be so successful. The high dunes around Ostend precluded fire support by the monitors. The Royal Marine force was thrown together on an emergency basis; the Marines were not well prepared for land combat. They were intended to hold Ostend while 16,000 Belgians, who had retreated into France, were brought up from Le Havre. Although some of them were landed at Ostend, it was soon evident that the Belgians were too exhausted to defend the port.

It was hoped that the landing at Ostend – a flank attack against the German army – would relieve the crushing pressure on the retreating BEF. This particular British operation collapsed because of further events on land (Ostend played an important role in a later British-French-Belgian attempt to hold parts of Belgium). Although the advancing Germans made no attempt to seize the French Channel ports (as feared), the advance of their flanking army cut or at least threatened the lines from those ports to the army inland and the line of supply had to be shifted much further south, to St Nazaire. To cover the new line of supply, the Channel Fleet had to shift further south and it could no longer support the force at Ostend, which had to be withdrawn on 30/31 August.[45]

To shield the landing against possible German attack, the Admiralty ordered a demonstration in the Heligoland Bight, which developed into the battle described below. The Germans thought that the British were trying to entice the High Seas Fleet to sea, within striking distance of British submarines. That interpretation reflected the considerable German fear of British submarines at this time.

When the French stopped the German advance, the situation reversed, both armies racing to the sea. A flanking attack from the sea might cut German communications and force the Germans to withdraw. Initially the planned naval demonstration was to have been mounted at Ostend, but then it was shifted to Dunkirk and Calais and once again the Royal Marines were the planned force, to be backed by aircraft and armoured cars. This time they were to give the impression that they were the advance guard of a much larger force. That might include colonial troops which had now been brought home. The force covering the transports going to Dunkirk included the armoured cruisers *Cressy*, *Hogue* and *Aboukir*; it was on this duty that they were sunk by *U 9*.[46] The attack dramatised the threat posed by submarines to the Grand Fleet itself (and to all armoured ships in confined waters) and drove Admiral Jellicoe to propose direct attacks on submarine bases (initially by mining them shut, using trawlers). Despite Weddingen's exploit, the troopships continued to operate freely. The U-boat operation was undertaken to assist the army and it seems clear that the German naval authorities did not see the troopships as a source of leverage which might have forced the Grand Fleet to come within range of their mines and torpedoes.[47]

German War Planning and Early Experience

At the outset, German naval planning seems to have focussed on an initial decisive fleet battle. Until 1912, the Germans generally thought in terms of a battle in the Skaggerak, the strait leading from the North Sea to the Baltic. They had a large force of torpedo boats and they had a well-developed mine warfare capability. Some in the Imperial Navy saw both as equalisers which might even the odds even though the German battle fleet was considerably weaker than the British. Presumably the Germans imagined that in wartime the British would decide to attack their valuable Baltic coast. A British fleet trying to force the straits could be damaged by mines and by torpedo boats, particularly if the Germans gained control of the Danish coast through invasion.[48] The small German battle fleet operating in the North Sea would suffice to deal with whatever survived.

After considerable debate, the November 1912 German tactical orders envisaged combat in the Heligoland Bight, i.e., just off the German coast and the naval base of Wilhelmshaven. The fleet would take the strategic defensive, but it would seek to damage the British by frequent energetic sorties. The idea of using coastal weapons (mines and torpedo boats) as equalisers must have remained attractive. German strategic exercises showed that minefields could damage an approaching British fleet. When war broke out in 1914 the German fleet retreated to base, under the cover of minefields and fully-manned coastal guns. Their leadership disregarded intelligence which showed that the British would stay well offshore in the event of war.[49]

The German orientation downplayed wide-area surveillance of any kind; it seemed to be enough to maintain patrols of the Heligoland Bight and perhaps of the area of the German Bight just outside it. Even when they became aware that the British had abandoned any idea of close blockade, the Germans imagined that the British fleet would come close to Heligoland.[50] The Germans never seem to have conducted pre-war exercises which would have taught them the importance of ocean surveillance, as the British 1912 and 1913 manoeuvres demonstrated to the Royal Navy. Until 1916 they did not exploit the potential of their Zeppelins, generally limiting them to probes of particular areas in which they expected to operate. *Krieg zur See* refers again and again to operations undertaken or cancelled on the basis of fragmentary information provided by a few agents. U-boats observed British forces from time to time, but they were never deployed as pickets specifically to provide a full picture of British naval activity. After the war the Germans found from the British official history that again and again in 1914 parts of the Grand Fleet had been much closer to their base area in the German Bight than they had imagined. They had missed several opportunities to destroy elements of the British fleet.

Because the British expected to operate much further offshore, they needed some form of ocean surveillance to detect and track any sortie by the High Seas Fleet. They found that they could not rely on lines of cruisers in the North Sea. In 1912 their chief war planner suggested using submarines in German waters, but at the outbreak of war they did not yet have enough and their W/T did not offer sufficient range. The important point was that the British understood what they needed to make their strategy work. Their pre-war efforts prepared them to exploit wartime ocean surveillance information obtained by code-breaking. It is also possible that the Royal Navy was already using signals intelligence for what amounted to ocean surveillance pre-war. Ocean surveillance was remarkably absent from published British and US accounts of war experience, including internal classified ones.

According to the German official history, at the outset of war

the only important difference between the German and British fleets was the balance of numbers favouring the British.[51] From this point of view the object of German war planning should be to improve the odds before risking a battle. The Germans' equaliser was underwater weapons, wielded largely by destroyers and submarines in operations they called 'kleinkrieg' (small war, as opposed to the 'large war' fought by capital ships). Before the war Tirpitz regarded kleinkrieg as a threat to his fleet-building plan.[52] Kleinkrieg had been the main defence of the German coast; Tirpitz started his career as a torpedo – kleinkrieg – specialist. Fisher's flotilla defence – sea denial making the North Sea impassable to capital ships – was a much-expanded version of kleinkrieg in a narrow sea. It may be that by insisting that torpedo boats (destroyers) be amalgamated with the fleet, the German naval authorities (and probably particularly Tirpitz) avoided the political danger that someone might see a defensive kleinkrieg as a preferable alternative to an offensively-oriented battle fleet. This is aside from the reality that in 1914 (and even much later) kleinkrieg was not quite enough to deny the North Sea to a large fleet.[53]

As an indication of German pre-war thinking, the last war game played by the Admiralstab in the winter of 1913/14 began with a German fleet movement to the English coast.[54] As the fleet returned to Germany, it had to fight an action about a third of the way back, about 200 miles from Wilhelmshaven. The German officer playing the British commander demonstrated in his report that the British main fleet would have to be based at Scapa Flow, using it as the base of the chief line of blockade. By this time many in the Admiralstab realised that the British would adopt (as they did) a strategy of distant blockade, but, according to the British official history, they failed to draw the proper conclusions, imagining that the British would never adopt this kind of strategic defensive. Moreover, in German pre-war manoeuvres, the war had always been purely military, without regard for political limitations. Tactical considerations had been put before strategic ones.[55]

Much worse, the Germans became obsessed with the idea that the British would attack the Heligoland Bight, to the exclusion of any other possibility. At the outset both the Admiralstab and the staff of the High Seas Fleet expected that the British would take the strategic offensive; many even expected that the British fleet would deliver a sudden annihilating blow (which had been advocated by many British naval writers before the war). Surely British public opinion would demand some kind of attack within the area the Germans wanted to use, the German Bight. Until that happened, fleet commander Admiral von Ingenohl and the Admiralstab both argued that Germany should resort to naval guerrilla warfare, which meant mainly mines and U-boats.

The last big German peacetime manoeuvres (May 1914) demonstrated how effectively submarines could attack a fleet.[56] For the first time the U-boats carried out offensive operations against a (presumed) enemy. According to von Ingenohl, writing in 1918, the experience was 'almost a revelation' to all senior and commanding officers, as they showed that the inner Heligoland Bight was an ideal submarine operating area due to the favourably sited deeps, the nature of the bottom and the ease with which submarines could fix their positions from Heligoland. On the first day nearly every ship which appeared was 'sunk' by the U-boats. The U-boats also inflicted heavy damage on the fleet anchoring off the bar in the Jade, proceeding to sea at dusk and at sea north of Heligoland. The conditions were considered realistic. All involved concluded that with enemy submarines lying in wait off the estuaries, the German fleet would find it difficult to sortie. The U-boat officers claimed that even a strong destroyer screen would only hamper enemy submarines and certainly would not be a complete defence.[57] Given this experience, the Germans were perhaps unduly impressed when British submarines were seen in the Heligoland Bight early in the war.[58]

On 30 July Admiralstab chief Admiral von Pohl sent fleet commander von Ingenohl an operations order: he should try to damage the British fleet by attacking any reconnaissance or blockading forces in the Heligoland (German) Bight and by a mine and U-boat offensive (*i.e.*, kleinkrieg) near the German coast. Once the odds had evened, the fleet could seek a decisive battle.[59] This order also called for a war on commerce under the prize rules. Ships allocated for commerce warfare were to proceed to foreign areas as soon as possible. The Admiralstab had no executive power over von Ingenohl, so the operations order was only a suggestion. It had only recently come to see Kleinkrieg as a useful equaliser. On 6 August the fleet was ordered to avoid battle while conducting the torpedo and mine offensive. Von Pohl told Tirpitz that Chancellor Bethmann-Hollweg wanted to preserve the fleet as a bargaining chip at the end of the war. The Admiralstab war order assumed that the British would attempt a close blockade, based partly on what was known of British dispositions during the period of strained relations in 1911.[60]

The Germans correctly assumed that the heavy units of the first (active) fleet would concentrate on the east coast of Scotland (they assumed they would use the Firth of Forth and the Moray Firth), which were centrally located relative to both the German Bight and the Skaggerak. Lighter squadrons might concentrate either on the Scottish coast or further south, on the Thames, where they would be in a flanking position. That would also reduce the load on the Scottish bases and reassure the British public. That is a fair prediction of the basing of Grand Fleet destroyer flotillas at Harwich, near Dover. The Germans also fairly correctly guessed that the old battleships would concentrate in the eastern Channel ports (Dover, Portsmouth, perhaps also the Thames). The Germans also imagined that when war seemed probable, British light forces would take up positions near German waters (the British had been interested in setting up a destroyer blockade of the German coast, but had abandoned that idea).

Although at one time British manoeuvres showed that they planned a close blockade, the Admiralstab wrote that 'the manoeuvres of the last few years and a number of weighty arguments indicate that Great Britain will adopt a distant blockade as the basis of her plan of campaign'. The Germans thought the British would frequently alternate the two types of blockade, even though they realised that a close blockade was more difficult for blockader than blockaded, due in part to the threat of torpedo attack. Thus German planners described a possible British close blockade plan in considerable detail, based on observations of earlier British naval exercises. That entailed patrols not only of the entrances to the North Sea but also of the Skaggerak (North Sea to Baltic), to cripple German trade. The Admiralstab argued that the British would have to watch the Skaggerak to protect their northern blockade line from a surprise attack, but that seems to have referred to observation of the 1912–13 manoeuvres in which one blockade line extended from the Danish coast to the middle of the English coast. Finally, the Germans expected the British to employ mines

and submarines in the Heligoland Bight. Despite reasonably good analysis, the Germans assumed that the British would do what they (the Germans) wanted them to do: steam directly into the Helgoland Bight to fight Tirpitz' decisive battle.

The Germans also overrated British reconnaissance: they felt under constant observation not by surface warships, but by submarines, neutral fishing craft and what the Germans assumed was an excellent espionage service in Holland and Denmark. They cited the insular position of Britain and the neutrals' dread of coercive measures against their trade, as explanations for their own lack of information as to British movements. The British would benefit from air reconnaissance, presumably launched from ships; ironically, the British denigrated this capability but thought the Germans would benefit hugely from their Zeppelin force.

Above all, the Germans believed that they should reserve their fleet solely for the destruction of the British fleet. That led them into a bizarre kind of justification for inactivity. Without firm knowledge of the movements of the British fleet (which the Germans lacked), their fleet might not accomplish anything if it sortied. However, it might be whittled down by British submarines in the Bight – in effect, the Germans turned their kleinkrieg idea on themselves. The Germans told themselves they could not afford any losses at all. An attack on British transports opened the possibility that the Grand Fleet, operating as distant cover, could cut off the retreat of the High Seas Fleet – a consistent theme in German thinking. The Germans did not have enough scouts to surprise the British (and they did not yet have enough airships to substitute). The need for scouts had been understood before the war, but construction had been delayed due to the priority Tirpitz gave battleships (and to the fact that, unlike the British, he was never willing to lump battleships and battlecruisers together as capital ships). Thus the supplement to the 1906 Fleet Law provided six cruisers beyond replacements (Cruisers E through L [there was no Cruiser I]), but battleships overdue from the 1900 law replaced the cruiser planned for 1910 and the 1910 and 1911 cruisers were each postponed a year. The problem worsened when battleship lifetime was reduced in 1908 from twenty-five to twenty years, postponing two cruisers until 1917. The authors of *Krieg zur See* were not at all satisfied with these excuses. Tirpitz wrote that the balance of forces would never be as favourable as at the outset, because the British were clearly outbuilding the Germans (they had ten battleships, all armed with 15in guns, under construction).

Not risking the main fleet left few forces for the initial phase, naval guerrilla warfare by mine and U-boat. For example, although light cruisers and destroyers were fitted to lay mines, they were considered integral to the High Seas Fleet and therefore could not be used. High Seas Fleet U-boats were a different matter. The fleet command would release only these units to attack the transports bringing the BEF to France.[61] When the Kaiser personally ordered the submarines to attack the transports, only four were available. The submarine command considered the area east of the entrance to the Channel (where the transports were) considerably less favourable than the open North Sea. Problems cited included the absence of sea-marks, the number of shallows and the strong and difficult tides. The U-boats had had no training for offensive operations. They had not even been supplied with chronometers (for navigation). The U-boats were to attack the (assumed) covering force so as to force transports to run for port (the author

Tirpitz's great nightmare came in two closely-spaced stages. First came the advent of semi-dreadnoughts. They had heavy intermediate-calibre guns. The next stage, the full dreadnought revolution, replaced the intermediate guns with more maximum-calibre guns, so that the ship had a uniform battery of heavy guns. This second stage followed the first so closely that the impact of the first is often forgotten. The Germans designed but did not build semi-dreadnoughts. In effect their first dreadnought designs substituted single 11in turrets for projected twin 8.2in turrets. At the same time the 17cm intermediate calibre guns of earlier German battleships were replaced by 15cm (5.9in) guns. The semi-dreadnought HMS *Lord Nelson* shows twin 9.2in broadside turrets and twin 12in main-calibre turrets at her ends. Like HMS *Dreadnought*, she dispensed with the earlier secondary battery of 6in guns; the only weapons below intermediate calibre were light anti-torpedo (boat) guns.

of *Krieg zur See* asks why anything short of attacking the transports would have worked). Nothing was achieved. Since no heavy covering force was sighted, the German naval command concluded that perhaps the British had not yet begun to land troops in France.[62]

U-boat operations off the British coast would provide information to support a later mining campaign. The U-boat operation was also justified on the ground that it would inflict losses which would induce the enemy to come out. This was not as odd an idea as might be imagined. In the absence of effective anti-submarine measures, the only effective way to deal with submarines was to attack them at source – at their base. To do that the British would have to get past the German fleet. All of this required that the U-boats make their presence known, so they were ordered to attack British destroyers. In this sense the initial logic of U-boat operations directly supported the German goal of triggering a decisive fleet action in home waters. In this particular case, the three long-range (diesel) U-boats found no attack opportunities, but they did perform useful reconnaissance. The usually pessimistic fleet command concluded from the absence of targets that the British main fleet was probably so far from Germany that

it was beyond the capacity of the U-boats to find. Harbours serving to replenish its supplies (the Moray Firth) were too strongly guarded to penetrate and submarines operating from Germany did not have the endurance to operate outside for long periods to await the enemy. U-boat operations against the enemy's main fleet would have to be abandoned for the present. On the other hand, the three U-boats had demonstrated that submarines were a safe means of reconnaissance in enemy-controlled waters.

It was soon clear that the British had not closely blockaded the Heligoland Bight; German surface warships were free to sortie. One of the U-boats discovered large British forces in the Hoofden and the eastern entrance to the Channel, covered by a line of destroyers. C-in-C High Seas Fleet planned to place two light cruisers (*Strassburg* and *Stralsund*), a little south of the position of the most northerly line of British destroyers presumed to be protecting these ships. At the same time two U-boats were to take up positions further north, to attack enemy ships attempting to follow the two cruisers as they retired. The cruiser *Kolberg* was in distant support and three battlecruisers in Terschelling Roads were ordered to have steam up. This was a miniature version of the way in which submarines were intended to support a surface fleet at this time. The Germans were well aware of the risk that cruisers and U-boats would become confused, so the cruisers were assigned to escort the submarines to their positions. This was the first offensive German operation of the war. That it was mounted by only two light cruisers reflects the caution of the High Seas Fleet command. It was much impressed by the threat of British submarines in the Bight and it used the initial war order, which mandated that the High Seas Fleet remain a fleet in being, to justify not using heavy ships.

The two cruisers encountered some British submarines and destroyers and may have damaged some of them, but none was sunk. While shelling the destroyers, the Germans observed that they were evading fire by rapid changes in course and speed. To them this was apparently a new idea, which they decided to adopt. The Germans also found that at a distance the British destroyers so resembled their own that they sometimes ceased fire. They concluded that destroyers had to make recognition signals frequently when approaching their own forces and that the system of recognition signals needed further development.

The German official history, which described this indecisive action in considerable detail, mentioned that the High Seas Fleet staff followed it with great interest by means of the cruisers' W/T signals. To the Germans, the main W/T lesson was that their system was superior to that of the British: none of the British ships had been able to jam the German signals. Despite British attempts, according to the account in *Krieg zur See*, the high clear German note could always be distinguished above the jamming noise. The British were not yet in a position to exploit the German predilection for using W/T, but the Germans did not appreciate that W/T was inherently dangerous. To the Germans, the operation showed that by using their W/T separated groups of their ships could work together. However, *Stralsund* was unable to communicate to the other cruisers or to the U-boats her position relative to the enemy, or the course on which the action was being fought accurately enough for them to come to her assistance. However, neither submarine managed to attack, even though one of them was in an exceptionally favourable position. The Germans were also impressed that the British had refused action and that they had failed to hit the German ships. The Germans found it remarkable that the British were transmitting their call for assistance in plain language.

Given the apparent success of this first operation, the High Seas Fleet planned a follow-on attack against British shipping off the Dogger Bank. There they expected to find many trawlers as well as protecting warships. This time the attacking force was to consist of two light cruisers (*Rostock* and *Strassburg*) and a destroyer flotilla. Three submarines were sent out to support them and this time they did not accompany the cruisers. The operation against the trawlers was to be conducted under the Prize Rules, so the cruisers carried a German naval reservist trawler captain who was expected to distinguish British boats. The two cruisers were to be preceded by a reconnaissance, to be conducted by the cruisers *Cöln*, *Stuttgart* and *Danzig* plus two destroyer flotillas. Another five destroyers were to search for enemy submarines in a sector north of the planned operation. In the event, *Rostock* narrowly escaped being torpedoed by a British submarine and nothing was found on the Dogger Bank. Two destroyer flotillas and two aircraft were sent out to engage reported British submarines and any destroyers which might be following them. A light cruiser (*Mainz*) went out in support and the two available battlecruisers (*Von der Tann* was in dock) were ordered into Schillig Roads to be ready for sea if needed in distant support. Given the danger of submarine attack, the planned battlecruiser sortie was cancelled. The old cruiser *Hamburg*, which had escorted the three U-boats into position, did manage to find and sink three British trawlers and two of the destroyers working with *Rostock* sank six more. The Germans were reinforced in their belief that trawlers in the North Sea were watching their movements, or perhaps even supporting British submarines.

Gross navigational inaccuracy was an unpleasant surprise. It would have been difficult or impossible for widely-separated units to close to support each other. No shore marks were visible for 18 hours, so the ships had to dead-reckon. When land was sighted, it turned out that *Rostock*'s estimated position was 10 miles off. This was despite frequent exchange of positions by W/T.

An operation on 6 August typified reconnaissance and surveillance as then understood by the Germans. The intelligence centre of Westellenbogen on Sylt reported seeing several columns of smoke off Esbjerg: coal-burning ships could not help making smoke visible beyond the horizon. The Germans sent out an aircraft and at dawn they sent out the cruiser *Mainz* and destroyers, which got as far as Esbjerg. They saw no indications of an enemy operation.

To the Germans, the two cruiser operations demonstrated that their pre-war training and doctrine were satisfactory. The next operation was minelaying in the Humber and the Tyne by two forces, each consisting of a minelayer, a light cruiser and a half-flotilla of destroyers. The Germans had previously decided not to risk their specially-built minelayers until the longer nights of the fall, but according to their official history the more important reason was that minefields might endanger the U-boats sent to reconnoitre the British coast. The minelaying was unopposed.

The Germans were so concerned to keep the estuaries leading out of Wilhelmshaven open that they kept sweeping the offshore area. Light cruisers and destroyers covered the sweepers.[63] These operations ended when the British demonstrated their own effectiveness off Heligoland on 28 August 1914. The Germans had

expected them since the outbreak of war and on several occasions they thought British forces were approaching. The battle began when a British submarine fired two torpedoes at the German destroyer *G.194*, on station about 16nm NW of Heligoland. By this time it was standard procedure to activate anti-submarine measures about an hour later. An hour after that a British cruiser appeared. Further ships from both sides joined in. The Germans lost three cruisers (*Cöln*, *Mainz* and the older *Ariadne*) and the destroyer *V.186*. Once the Germans appeared in sufficient force to wipe out the initial light British attack force, British battlecruisers appeared to cover their retirement.

The British treated this battle of Heligoland Bight as a minor if successful action. For the Germans the battle was traumatic. They suffered their first combat losses. There was great anger against Tirpitz, the losses being blamed on his policy of using smaller-calibre guns: 4.1in for cruisers against the British 6in, 3.4in for destroyers against the British 4in.[64] The heavier British guns could fire effectively at greater range. The battle seemed to reveal problems with shells.[65] British destroyers were not only faster, they could accelerate more rapidly to high speed thanks to their oil-burning boilers. On a tactical level, the battle showed that it would take more than a single cruiser to fully protect a destroyer flotilla.[66] The Kaiser was furious that his ships had been surprised and sunk. He wanted to bar all future operations in which similar surprises were possible. Tirpitz and head of the Admiralstab Admiral von Pohl barely managed to convince him not to sign a restrictive new order; the orders in force, they said, were enough. In the fleet, there was a feeling that the British had shown much greater offensive spirit. The German official history reported a tendency to overrate German losses and underrate British ones.

The Germans thought the point of the British operation off Heligoland was to lure out the German battleships, exposing them to the British submarines offshore. The German official history argues that the heavy ships were restrained by the standing order emphasizing the need to preserve them for the decisive battle (it was probably more significant that they could not get over the bar until the tide was right). The idea that light forces would retreat specifically to lure ships over torpedoes (and, sometimes, mines) seems to have fascinated both the Germans *and* the British.

Heligoland Bight was followed by an additional misfortune, the torpedoing of the old light cruiser *Hela* – only the fourth light cruiser as yet lost – by a British submarine in a fleet exercise area on 13 September 1914. Fleet commander von Ingenohl decided that he could not afford to carry on such exercises in open waters, or to conduct further demonstrations with cruisers or other ships. In effect he was accepting the Kaiser's demand that he immobilise his force.

The British found the inactivity of the High Seas Fleet inexplicable. Surely it was being held back for some particular operation. Perhaps it would be used against the deployed trade protection squadrons. As the 1913 manoeuvres had demonstrated, it was impossible to guarantee that the German fleet cloaked in North Sea mist and fog could not break out. Admiralty studies of trade protection showed that a raider – or, better, a raiding fleet – would need above all to coal and it would probably try to seize coal stockpiled at a British base. That was the logic of sending battlecruisers to the Falklands in 1914. Graf Spee went to the Falklands specifically to seize the fuel he needed.

In 1914 the threat of a breakout led to the deployment of older

British battleships at various colonies which might be subject to attack. Clearly one such ship could not defeat a German fleet, but it could inflict sufficient damage on ships very far from home to preclude their safe return, even to slow the enemy fleet enough for the Grand Fleet to catch up.[67] The possibility of a German breakout exercised Allied minds as late as 1918, when the US Navy's London Planning Group asked what would happen if German battlecruisers broke out into the Atlantic specifically to attack trade.[68] By that time it seemed that attack on trade was the single objective of German naval operations and that the Germans were surely seeking some antidote to convoy. That was hardly impossible, as Scheer proved when he sent cruisers to attack a Scandinavian convoy late in 1917 and brought the High Seas Fleet out for a larger attack on such a convoy in the spring of 1918 (remarkably, neither figured in the Planning Group papers). As early as September 1917 the US planners argued that battlecruisers were the most likely threat, given their speed and armament and supposed long endurance. A battlecruiser might be sent out accompanied by a fast liner loaded with coal, which could be transferred either at sea or at a secluded anchorage. Even if caught while coaling the battlecruiser would probably be able to beat off any attackers short of capital ships. This was not far from the

Germans' Second World War battleship operations against British trade, though during the First World War the Germans seem not to have thought about it.

The only alternatives were either to hunt down the battlecruiser or provide sufficient escorts to beat it off. Given the limited British battlecruiser force, the only Allied hunting or intercepting force was four Japanese battlecruisers, which Admiral Jellicoe had failed to obtain in 1917 (they could best be based at Portland). That left dreadnoughts (of which the Allies had a considerable superiority) as necessary convoy escorts. On the other hand, the battlecruiser had to find the convoy in the first place and the most likely means of doing so would be a scouting line of U-boats. To work with them the battlecruiser would have to use her W/T, so the US planners proposed building radio D/F stations in the Azores.

As in 1917, the Japanese showed no interest in stationing their battlecruisers in European waters; it took a major concession to get them to deploy destroyers in the Mediterranean.[69] The British were sceptical, but ultimately the US Navy based two battleships, which were not associated with the Grand Fleet, at Berehaven specifically to deal with the problem and the two navies agreed procedures to take in the event of a German battlecruiser raid.

Tirpitz's other nightmare was that armoured cruisers, which were explicitly included in his Navy Law plans, would rise to battleship size (and cost). In the period before the First World War, he kept trying to keep battleship and large cruiser (battlecruiser) categories separate, in the face of the Kaiser's insistence that they should be merged. In retrospect it seems that Tirpitz's battlecruisers were far closer to fast battleships than their British contemporaries, but Tirpitz's policy helps account for his determination not to allow German battlecruiser gun calibre to rise. The pre-dreadnought armoured cruiser *Scharnhorst* is shown. She was the first German armoured cruiser with a uniform-calibre main battery, in this case eight 21cm guns. In 1914 she was part of the East Asia Squadron (under Rear Admiral Graf Spee), having been on that station since 1911. Graf Spee's Cruiser Squadron consisted of the two sister armoured cruisers *Scharnhorst* and *Gniesenau* and the light cruisers *Emden* and *Leipzig*. When war broke out Graf Spee's two armoured cruisers were already cruising in the south seas (they left at the end of June, before the crisis escalated and were to have returned to Tsingtao in September 1914) and his cruiser *Nürnberg* was on the Mexican coast (about to be relieved by *Leipzig*). Once war began, Graf Spee left the area. *Scharnhorst* is shown in a Renard photo received by the US Navy's Office of Naval Intelligence on 7 May 1908.

Two Norwegian coast defence ships building in 1914 were taken over as *Glatton* and *Gorgon*. Initially completion had high priority, but both ships were suspended in May 1915 so that *Courageous* and *Furious* could be completed more quickly. They were resumed to a modified design incorporating deep anti-torpedo bulges. Elevation of the main guns was increased to 40°; with a special shell, they achieved the extraordinary range of 39,000 yds. *Gorgon* (ex-*Nidaros*) is shown leaving the Tyne on completion in May 1918. Although resale to Norway was proposed in 1919 and sale to Argentina, Peru or Romania was discussed in 1920, she was disarmed in 1921 and used as a bomb and shell target beginning in 1922.

CHAPTER 2

Resources

THE FIRST WORLD WAR became a war of resources as soon as the Germans failed to achieve a quick victory by defeating the French army during its first weeks. For the Allies the key to victory was access to the world's resources via the seas, largely thanks to the dominant position of the Royal Navy. Access by sea made it possible for countries such as France to survive even after so many men went into the army. Resources included manpower. For example, on the Western Front the Allies benefitted from hundreds of thousands of Chinese labourers. Without access by sea, they could never have reached Western Europe. Physical access was not enough. As in the Second World War, because the resources were overseas in other countries, the Allies needed the finance to buy what they needed. It mattered, for example, that at the outset Chancellor of the Exchequer Lloyd George assumed that Britain was so wealthy that he did not have to raise taxes to pay for the war; he could rely on loans.[1] Later in the war the British found themselves seizing foreign securities so that they could be sold to finance the war and also raising large loans on Wall Street. In the past, Britain had held alliances together with her financial resources; this time their demands far exceeded those of the past.

The Need for Money

The City would be key to any war Britain would fight. In the last world war, against Napoleon, the crucial British advantage was financial: Britain alone had developed a banking system which could sustain war by creating, in effect, a revolving line of credit for the government (the public view of how well the British were doing was reflected in the rates of interest on Government bonds, or 'consols'). In 1914 Britain was still the pre-eminent world centre of finance. Inevitably the City would provide much of the capital needed by allies to sustain a war. That role would be stretched further if the war badly interrupted the Allies' own trade, *i.e.*, their own means of earning income. The British had been the paymasters of various coalitions during the Napoleonic Wars, but the First World War was vastly more expensive. Huge armies required vast numbers of weapons and they expended ammunition on a lavish scale. Replacements included ammunition (and some weapons) bought from abroad, particularly in the United States. That in turn required an ocean of cash, much of it provided by the City (and much of it in loans provided by Wall Street).

In the autumn of 1914 newly appointed Secretary of State for War Field Marshal Kitchener was raising a vast 'New Army' to supplement the pre-war volunteer army. It was not immediately clear what employment he had in mind for it. Whenever he was asked what he planned to do with the 'New Army', Kitchener replied that he was keeping his plans secret; he would tell the Cabinet about them only if they divorced their wives, i.e., if they could avoid leaking what they knew.[2] There is some evidence that initially the Government saw mass recruitment as a means of stabilising the British economy in the face of mass unemployment due to the economic crash caused by the outbreak of war.[3] The men Kitchener recruited came out of the British workforce and thus damaged the economy supporting, among other things, the army. A J Balfour, a former Prime Minister now in the Cabinet,

circulated a paper, 'The Limits of Enlistment', which pointed to the economic effects of raising Kitchener's army. Exports had fallen about 40 per cent compared to the previous year. Balfour pointed out that the only alternatives to rebuilding exports would be borrowing abroad or selling securities, neither of which was desirable. Even the British ports felt the effect of Kitchener's recruiting drive, as they lost stevedores and other personnel.

Given Kitchener's enormous personal prestige (and supposed military expertise) and Asquith's consensus rule, no one could challenge his creation of the massive 'New Army' or even limit its growth as it went beyond what amounted to a public works project and sucked men from vital industries. As Kitchener's 'New Army' formed, it became the subject of proposals for maritime attacks around the periphery of Germany. Up to early 1915 it was by no means clear that these new units would end up in France. That seems to have become inevitable only with the crisis caused by the German 1915 offensive on the Western Front. However, without the mass army, the British would not have had the option of concentrating on France and the Western Front.

The direct and indirect costs of Kitchener's manpower were bad enough, but on land the First World War was very much a war of artillery and guns and shells were expensive. Initially Chancellor of the Exchequer Lloyd George, who was much impressed by his country's wealth, sought to finance the war entirely by borrowing. That might have made sense if the war had ended quickly, but after First Ypres and Gallipoli it was clear that it would be protracted and that it would require large-scale British land operations. The September 1915 budget raised income tax and added a large surcharge for high incomes, but even so only a quarter of wartime expenditure was paid for by taxes. In 1915 the British Treasury began to raise money on the New York market. Heavy borrowing made for inflation which reduced the value of the pound by two-thirds over six years. One scholar speculated that without US intervention, the British would have been unable to continue beyond 1917.[4]

It was unfortunate for Britain at war that its main pre-war

In 1914, Britain had the world's largest naval industry, hence was building most of the ships – naval and merchant – that countries were buying. Ships under construction became available once war broke out. HMS *Erin* was the ex-Turkish *Reshadieh*. She is shown late in the war, with a kite balloon (but without flying-off platforms on her superfiring turrets). Late-war features included searchlights concentrated around her after funnel (so that it would be difficult to estimate her course at night) and bearing markings on her superfiring turrets (to make it easier for ships in company to concentrate with her on a single target). Another ship (*Fatih*) was laid down by Vickers on 11 June 1914. She was never completed, the material being cleared from the slip in August.

trading partner had been Germany. Before the outbreak of war the British Government contemplated an economic attack against Germany (as described in the later chapter on blockade), but its proponents do not seem to have considered in detail the impact of such an attack on Britain itself – for example, the loss of the export trade, which other countries could pick up. That made sense if the British Government was convinced that a powerful economic attack would swiftly overcome Germany, but it did not count the ability of many in Britain to convince the Government to relax economic measures once they were applied and once they were clearly damaging the British economy.

Resources included food. Before 1914 many governments accepted that their societies were unstable and that bread shortages leading to riots might well undermine them. Turkish entry into the war in October 1914 cut off Russian access to the Mediterranean via the Dardanelles. At that time the Ukraine contributed heavily to world cereal (e.g., wheat) production. The 1914 Australian wheat crop failed, leaving the United States with the only available surplus. India had a bumper harvest, but profiteers exporting too much of it threatened famine, so the Government of India limited exports. The price of wheat in Britain rose 72 per cent. Asquith remarked in January 1915 that it was 'cheaper to storm the Dardanelles' than to impose price controls on bread.[5]

The Royal Navy also took over the Turkish *Sultan Osman I*, which became HMS *Agincourt*, shown here late in the war. (Abrahams photo via Dr David Stevens, SPC-A)

The Royal Navy bought the Chilean battleship *Almirante Latorre*, which became HMS *Canada*. Unlike the two ex-Turkish ships, she was returned after the war, surviving until 1959. She is shown entering Malta in 1919 with relief crews on board. Note the flying-off platforms on 'B' and 'X' turrets, the bearing markings on 'A' turret and the splinter mattresses still in place on her bridges. (Dr David Stevens, SPC-A)

Shipbuilding

In 1914 the United Kingdom was still heir to the Industrial Revolution and it had by far the strongest shipbuilding industry in the world. Firms building large merchant ships (particularly liners) also built warships, but most firms specialised in either warships or merchant ships. Decades of export orders had created a powerful arms industry, albeit oriented more towards naval than towards army requirements. At the outbreak of war, British shipyards had export orders which could be turned to British requirements, adding to British naval strength: battleships for Turkey and Chile, cruisers for Greece and destroyers for Chile and Greece. British seizure of two Turkish battleships, crews for which had already arrived to take them home, outraged Turkish opinion, but it now seems clear that the Turks had already come to terms with the Germans and they even offered to hand over the battleships to Germany.

Britain had considerable productive resources, but they were finite and as the war continued the question of allocation, particularly between the navy, the growing army and the civilian economy became more and more acute (allocation of course also much affected the Germans). Before 1914, the Royal Navy was by far the largest buyer of heavy guns in the United Kingdom. As Kitchener formed his 'New Army', however, it had to be equipped with heavy guns.[6] Moreover, as the war developed, heavy artillery and vast numbers of shells were needed on land. As a consequence, the three major armaments firms had to share their capacity between the navy and the army.

Once war broke out, the Admiralty commandeered British shipbuilding resources, drastically slowing not only construction but also the repair of merchant ships. The scale of merchant ship losses made that acceptable in 1915 and through much of 1916,

but by the end of 1916 – before the Germans began their unrestricted U-boat campaign – losses were such that the new coalition government led by Lloyd George appointed a Shipping Controller. He was to make more efficient use of existing shipping and also to fight for further construction. That led to cuts in the Admiralty's 1917 and 1918 programmes (*i.e.*, ships already on order and those to be ordered from May 1917 on, during the 1917–18 fiscal year). On 8 March 1917 the War Cabinet decided, for example, to suspend work on three of the four *Hood* class battlecruisers ordered the previous year. That was partly due to a serious manpower squeeze and partly to the determination to shift effort to merchant ship repair and new construction. The navy tried to claw these ships back, arguing that the Germans were building enough battlecruisers to gain superiority in the North Sea. In fact the Germans kept building capital ships even after Jutland – though they never completed any after *Hindenburg*.

In September 1917, First Sea Lord Jellicoe prepared a memorandum showing the relative strengths of the British and German fleets up to 1 January 1921. He particularly wanted to expedite one or more battlecruisers.[7] The Operations Committee of the Admiralty decided that it was impossible to expedite any battlecruiser other than *Hood*. No decision on *Hood* could be taken until it was clear how much progress had been made with the ship's armour and armament, whether additional ships would have to be sacrificed, how much more labour would be needed (and how it would be obtained) and one detailed question answered: could the ship be finished without filling her bulges with tubes, which must have been a very laborious proposition. Three weeks later DCDS explained that *Hood* could not be accelerated by more than three months and then only by postponing delivery of five destroyers for six months and stopping work altogether on an oiler and two

At the lower end of the scale, the Royal Navy picked up three river monitors being built for Brazil. Although completed by February 1914, they were laid up in August because the Brazilians had decided not to pay for them. The Royal Navy arranged to buy them to keep them out of enemy hands and they were formally taken over on 3 August 1914. This is HMS *Humber* (ex-*Javary*), just completed. She soon served on the Belgian coast and then in the Mediterranean. Her two sisters sank the German cruiser *Königsberg* in the Rufiji River in East Africa (6–11 July 1915), using indirect fire supported by air spotting.

The Royal Navy obtained two cruisers building for Greece. This is HMS *Chester* (ex *Landros Katsonis*). She and her sister *Birkenhead* introduced the 5.5in calibre to the Royal Navy; it was adopted for the battlecruiser *Hood*, the carrier/cruiser *Furious* and the carrier *Hermes*. Its 85lb shell was lighter than that of the 6in (so the gun could fire faster), but it had nearly the same penetration and range. Initially the ships were not taken over, as the British hoped that Greece would join the Allies. When that had not happened (and the Greek government was increasingly pro-German), they were taken over. These ships were part of a larger programme under a French contract, the British part of which was the two light cruisers and four destroyers. Presumably the 5.5in gun was adopted because it was the same calibre the French used as a secondary battery (the programme included a *Bretagne* class battleship).

standard cargo ships. That ended the attempt to expedite *Hood*, but it left the Naval Staff very unhappy with the expected dire state of the British battlecruiser fleet – a problem, in the end, of resources stretched too thin.

The next chance for the Naval Staff was the 1919 programme discussed early in January 1918. It became interested in reviving HMS *Anson*, a sister to HMS *Hood*, which had been stopped the previous year. If the work proceeded uninterrupted, the ship could be completed in October 1920. The cost would be omitting projected 1919 ships to be built by the same yard (Armstrong Whitworth): one light cruiser and eight submarines and possibly a delay to the carrier *Hermes*. The Operations Committee decided to go ahead with *Anson*. Other conventional combatants in the proposed 1919 programme were eight light cruisers (allowing for one which would have been built by Armstrong: three 'E' class and five *Danae* class), sixty destroyers (six leaders and fifty-four 'S'

class) and twenty-two submarines (not including the eight sacrificed for *Anson*). The submarine type was not determined (either 'H' or 'R' class). There was some question of possibly obtaining submarines from Canada or the United States, but neither seemed likely. The destroyer part of the programme was considered particularly urgent, given the need for destroyers as escorts. In March 1918 the Operations Committee decided that the twenty-two submarines should be seventeen *L 50* class and five 'K' class.[8]

The 1919 programme was too ambitious. As the massive US programme gathered momentum, it became possible to cut British warship building in order to reduce the demand on scarce manpower in shipyards. Admiral Sims was invited to attend the 27 August 1918 meeting of the Operations Committee, so that he could discuss the American programme (he was told that nothing he said would be considered binding on the United States). The Committee was reluctant to kill the three suspended *Hood*s outright. Although that would release considerable manpower, it was referred to the War Cabinet. The Royal Navy was well enough equipped with light cruisers to accept some delays; similarly with submarines. The main question was whether the United States could be relied upon to allocate 128 destroyers to supplement its force in European waters by August 1919. If it did so, cuts in the British programme were possible.[9]

The need was huge: another 154 destroyers. Average destroyer casualties were not fewer than twenty-four per year and were expected to rise, so it was safe to allow for thirty per year. That made twenty for the eight months ending 1 September 1919. Obsolete types also had to be replaced (sixty of the '30-knotter' class and twenty-eight 'Rivers'). Of these ships, fourteen were

being relieved in 1918, another six might be retained for subsidiary purposes, but the other forty needed replacing.[10]

In addition to these sixty replacements, it was desirable that to fight the ASW war the destroyer force should grow by another ninety-four ships. Of these, the first priority was to add thirty-six of them to begin a system of hunting flotillas for which few destroyers had previously been available without dangerously weakening the Grand Fleet. 'With the institution of these forces, it is hoped to operate on the lines of communication of the enemy submarines and to render their ingress and egress more dangerous.' The projected distribution was ten at Buncrana (Ireland), four at Falmouth, four at Gibraltar and eighteen for the North Sea.

Another thirty were wanted to augment escort flotillas 'which at present are worked almost beyond the limit of their capacity'. Initially one escort unit (eleven ships) was provided per convoy; of the eleven, three would be resting and refitting, the unit being at sea about six days and a convoy being taken in or brought out every eight days. When the system began, convoys dispersed at the approaches to the Irish Sea and the Channel, but the U-boats began hunting in exactly those areas, so that convoys had to be escorted all the way to port. As U-boat range increased, convoy operations had to be extended over longer distances. The arrival of the US Army in Europe greatly increased activity (by two convoys every eight days and to 6000 troops every night across the Channel). By the autumn of 1918 additional convoys were supporting the Archangel Expeditionary Force. Monster transports (large liners) needed separate escorts. Armed merchant cruisers had to be escorted to their own home ports after leaving their convoys. All oilers had to be convoyed. Cable ships and special ships also had to be escorted. Projected allocation was six for Portsmouth cross-Channel escorts and twelve each for the Mediterranean and Devonport escorts.

The Admiralty was also interested in a specialised destroyer-like escort, in effect a destroyer with depth charges instead of torpedo tubes and perhaps with less power so that she had a longer radius of action. It should also be suitable as a hunter, with listening gear. On this basis the Admiralty proposed that some of the US destroyers be built on these lines. There was also a design for a specialised escort, which would be less expensive than a destroyer,

HMS *Talisman* was one of twelve large destroyers Turkey ordered in 1914, six in France and six from an Armstrong-Vickers syndicate (subcontracted to Hawthorn Leslie; two would have been built in Turkey). Only the four British units appear to have been laid down. They became the *Talisman* class destroyers. They had more firepower per ton than British ships: five 4in guns and three sets of torpedo tubes, one right aft. The Royal Navy retained all the guns (two of which were mounted side by side on the forecastle), but eliminated the extra set of tubes. The parallel Greek 1914 programme included four modified 'M' class destroyers, which the Royal Navy took over.

with a smaller complement. Any US ships of this type should be in excess of their destroyer requirement.[11]

Another twelve were wanted to reinforce Grand Fleet flotillas so that each might be maintained at a strength of four divisions, the division being the tactical unit (eight would complete the 3rd Flotilla and four would complete other Grand Fleet flotillas). Ten were needed to augment flotillas in the Mediterranean and six for the Halifax ASW patrol and escort, not previously possible while more urgent needs were being met.

Of the desired 154, it was proposed to ask the United States to provide 128 (at the rate of 16 per month). The British planned to produce thirty-two destroyers (four per month) in the same period, for a total of 160 by 1 September 1919. The US destroyers would operate together and in co-operation with their own forces, relieving entire British units (initially the 2nd and 4th British Escort Flotillas at Buncrana and Devonport and the British destroyers on the Otranto Barrage and forming a small unit at Halifax). At this point the Devonport flotilla was fifty-six ships, the Buncrana flotilla was thirty and thirty were needed for Otranto (to form a mixed force).

The desired figure of 128 US destroyers was to complete the necessary establishment in British and Mediterranean waters by 31 August 1919; it was not expected that any US destroyers would be available to relieve the British building programme before 1 January 1919, as American output up to that date was already allocated for specific US requirements.

The US Navy was also being asked to produce trawlers and minesweepers.[12] The United States was also asked to build, to British design, two or three fast minelayers, a proposal to be taken

Bethlehem Steel offered quick production of twenty submarines based on the US Navy's 'H'-class design. They were assembled in Montreal so as not to run afoul of US neutrality. In British service they were designated the 'H' class. Two of them were retained for Canadian service: *CH-14* and *CH-15*, shown here. (RCN)

up with Assistant Secretary of the Navy Franklin D Roosevelt. The 1919 British small-ship programme comprised 140 standard trawlers, fifty fast trawlers ('Kil' class), 160 drifters, thirty-six minesweepers, thirty boom defence vessels and three mooring vessels.[13]

There were also offensive minelayers, of which the British were currently converting two ships. Except for the converted liner *Princess Margaret* and some destroyers, none of the British minelayers could operate near enemy bases. Construction of three ships of suitable design in the United States would provide the desired force of six such ships. The British were then developing a design for a fast minelayer which emerged after the war as HMS *Adventure*.

The British manpower situation was so desperate in the autumn of 1918 that the War Cabinet decided to assume that the United States would agree to these requests and on that basis shift yards from naval to merchant ship work.[14] The Admiralty would have preferred to wait for formal American agreement. That impacted the 1919 programme. For example, *Anson* was not restarted. The general clear-out of British men of military age to reinforce the army in France had subtler destructive effects on the Royal Navy. For example, the programme to arm merchant ships was delayed by six months. A programme to provide the Grand Fleet with 25ft rangefinders (which the Germans had) had been put back so that it would not be completed until May 1920.

Keeping the Royal Navy at Sea

Whatever warships the Admiralty had or built had to be kept operational. In the First World War that meant frequent drydocking (docking) to be scraped and repainted. Ships also often required machinery repairs, such as repairs to condensers (early in the war several Grand Fleet capital ships were out of action for weeks at a time due to 'condenseritis').[15] More frequent and sustained steaming exacerbated the situation. Jellicoe often pointed out that

the Germans could emerge at their chosen moment (presumably with all their capital ships serviceable) while he would have to make do with his average strength. In wartime ships needed fuel and stores on a much larger scale than in peacetime, not least because ships were operating far more intensively. This was aside from the need to mobilise personnel on an unprecedented scale.[16] When it decided to base the Grand Fleet at Scapa Flow, the Admiralty further complicated its task, because Scapa was undeveloped and, worse, lacked any railway connection to the mainland. As a consequence, the Grand Fleet needed a large supporting fleet of specialised merchant ships loaded with coal, food and ammunition. Temporarily moving the fleet from Scapa to a more secure anchorage meant moving all of those ships as well.

Docking was a particular problem. The Royal Navy's bases (with their docks) had been built to deal with France: Devonport, Portsmouth, Plymouth and Chatham. The shift to a North Sea orientation was too quick and other calls on the naval budget too drastic, to develop a second set of bases with full maintenance facilities. Neither of the two main planned North Sea bases, Rosyth and Scapa Flow, had docking or repair facilities. Rosyth was approved by the Conservative Government (which fell in 1906), but the successor Liberal Government decided to slow work and as pre-war Controller Jellicoe doubted that a drydock would be completed until 1917 (it was actually completed by 1916).[17] Visiting Germany for the Kiel regatta, Jellicoe passed through Hamburg and was much impressed by the floating drydocks in use there. Two, capable of taking the largest British battleships, were ordered, for the Medway and for Portsmouth. One was later towed to Invergordon, making it possible to dock Grand Fleet capital ships without a long trip to the nearest dock at Plymouth.[18] The two northern bases were not developed pre-war because they could not really be used in peacetime. The Royal Navy was a volunteer service, so a fleet base had to have ready access to entertainment and to families. It also needed considerable infrastructure and the ability to support a large workforce. Scapa Flow could not possibly meet such requirements, but from a strategic point of view it was ideal. Rosyth had to be developed to the point where it could accommodate the whole Grand Fleet. The infrastructure and personnel issues were also significant after the war, when the Royal Navy shifted its emphasis to the Far East. A proposal to base a fleet at Singapore failed for these reasons.

Fortunately for the Royal Navy, most of its ships burned coal mined in South Wales, so its fuel supply was relatively immune to German attack. Welsh steaming coal was the best in the world both for its energy content and for the lack of smoke (presumably because more of the coal than usual was consumed when it burned). Although the German navy had built up reserves of this coal pre-war, in wartime it had to depend more on inferior domestic supplies and that in turn reduced the performance of its ships. The unfortunate aspect of coal fuel was that it was relatively slow and difficult to transfer onto a ship. The Royal Navy began to shift to oil fuel, with its much higher energy content, with its destroyers and the fast *Queen Elizabeth* class battleships burned only oil fuel (other battleships burned a mixture of coal and oil). Pre-war policy was to build up sufficient storage for six months of war operation and that was nearly in place in 1914. The use of oil had an important tactical advantage: destroyers had limited endurance, but they could be fuelled at sea by battleships.[19]

Unfortunately, all supplies of oil fuel were overseas, hence were

In 1914 Britain was the world's largest commercial shipbuilder. With the outbreak of war, many ships were suspended. They became available for conversion to naval use. Probably the most spectacular example was the carrier *Argus* – the first full-deck carrier in the world – converted from incomplete hull of the Italian liner *Conte Rosso*. Laid down in June 1914, the ship was bought in August 1916. She was completed in September 1918, her first aircraft eighteen Sopwith Cuckoo torpedo bombers, embarked that October. (Abrahams via Dr David Stevens, SPC-A).

British sea control made weapons ordered by German firms undeliverable once war broke out. They included four twin 14in guns (with mountings) ordered from Bethlehem Steel in the United States to arm the Greek battle-cruiser *Salamis*, under construction by Blohm & Voss in Hamburg. Bethlehem Steel offered them to the Admiralty, which used them to arm four *Abercrombie* class monitors (the name ship is shown).

subject to interruption by the U-boat offensive.[20] Casualties to tankers caused the fleet oil reserve to fall from 5.1 months' worth in February 1917 to 2.9 months' worth in May 1917. Oil-burning Grand Fleet ships had to limit their speeds. That was why the British government asked in 1917 that the US Navy send only coal-burning battleships to support the Grand Fleet (the US Navy had adopted an oil-fuel only policy at about the same time as the Royal Navy and this order prevented it from sending its most powerful ships). Because coal rather than oil was the predominant fuel in 1914, the world tanker fleet was relatively small, hence unusually vulnerable to attack. Because there was no native source of oil and because transportation might fail, there was agitation in the mid-1930s for a return to coal fuel, an entirely impractical step because of the difference in energy content between coal and oil.

That destroyer endurance was far less than that of the capital ships of the Grand Fleet simplified rapid deployment of the Grand Fleet as it responded to intelligence of a German sortie. Only the destroyers had to be filled with fuel and that was a quick process because they burned oil. Even then their endurance was only about three days. Even a quarter-fill of a capital ship was good for about twice that and most capital ships were always at least this full of coal. However, to coal the whole fleet for an extended deployment required at least four days. In 1915 the Grand Fleet typically burned 800 to 1000 tons per hour.[21] The need to conserve coal affected operational procedure. Initially the Grand Fleet kept all boilers continuously lit so that it could instantly get to sea. Once it became clear that signals intelligence would warn it of a German sortie, readiness could be reduced and coal consumption somewhat reduced.

Without permanent shore facilities to store and load it, coal at Scapa meant a mass of colliers, each of which could coal only one ship at a time. Before the war, it was estimated that the battle fleet alone would need about 200 colliers, but as mobilised the Royal Navy had only sixty-five of its own. As of 1 October, the Grand Fleet had 163. Another eighteen were at other bases or in reserve and 124 were abroad. Lack of coal, due to lack of colliers, made it necessary for two of its twenty dreadnoughts to miss a sortie on 13 August 1914.[22]

The United States

In 1914 the United States was already the most powerful industrial country in the world and the only one to have mastered mass production, mainly in the form of the car industry in Detroit. The success of the car industry foreshadowed the possible contribution of American production to the Allies, particularly after the United States entered the war. Even before that, the United States provided seaplanes, munitions, small arms and some warships: 'H'-class submarines (assembled in Canada from US components) and 550 motor launches. All of these went to the Allies rather than to the Germans because they could never have been slipped through the British blockade of Germany. Once the United States entered the war, it began mass-producing destroyers, sub-chasers and submarines, all of which were important contributions to the anti-submarine war. It also mass-produced the anti-submarine mines which formed the bulk of the North Sea Mine Barrage. Had the war continued, US-built warships would probably have been transferred in considerable numbers to the Allied navies, including the Royal Navy. The war did cut the United States off from some specialty industrial products, such as high-quality optics and machine tools, which in the past had come largely from Germany. The US Navy, for example, found itself encouraging home industry to fill these gaps.

The United States was also a leading agricultural country in 1914. In contrast to Europe, the United States had been able both to industrialise and to expand agricultural production for export; during the war its government urged farmers to grow crops to feed the world (much the same thing happened in the Second World War). The combination of industrial and agricultural strength limited the impact of U-boat warfare on the United States. Before the United States entered the war, it continued to export agricultural products to Germany via European neutrals. The British government had to balance its need to impose economic pressure on Germany against its need to avoid a break with the United States, which was a key wartime source of munitions and a

Resources included people. British sea control made it possible for the empire – and the informal empire – to contribute directly to the British war effort. This is the Canadian troop convoy, October 1914. Less well known was the Chinese contribution of hundreds of thousands of labourers who worked on the Western Front. (Dr David Stevens, SPC-A)

German shipbuilding was not nearly so robust as British in 1914, but Germany did export destroyers and submarines. This large (1160-ton) *G 101* class destroyer was laid down for Argentina. This photograph probably shows her on trials, with both pairs of twin 50cm torpedo tubes in place (but without the two single tubes just abaft the break of the forecastle); and four 8.8cm guns (bow, stern and forward of the after deckhouse). The ships had been designed for 4in Bethlehem Steel guns and 21in torpedo tubes, but these weapons were undeliverable once war began.. The ships were completed with standard German navy weapons. All four of this class were completed in 1915 and all survived the war. (Naval Historical and Heritage Command photo courtesy of MSSGT Donald R Shake USAF)

potential ally. The situation was further complicated in that a major source of agricultural exports was the Midwest, where pro-German sentiment was strongest.

In 1917–18 an entirely new resource became available in the form of US industrial capacity (in addition to US warships and personnel). The Royal Navy planned to cut its own destroyer and minesweeper production in the expectation that US-built ships would become available. It is not entirely clear whether the additional ships would have been transferred to the Royal Navy, as US-built ships were transferred during the Second World War. The United States did transfer sub-chasers to both France and Italy. This was in addition to mass production of merchant ships by the US government's Emergency Shipbuilding Corporation described in a later chapter.

In September 1917 the Admiralty War Staff compiled a list of hoped-for American assistance:[23]

1. Four coal-burning dreadnoughts for the Grand Fleet to release three or four Grand Fleet dreadnoughts for foreign service to relieve pre-dreadnoughts. The US ships became the 6th Battle Squadron of the Grand Fleet. The Royal Navy was paying off old capital ships to man destroyers. The situation would continue to worsen as the navy had to find officers and crews over the next eighteen months for nineteen light cruisers, twelve flotilla leaders and 119 destroyers under construction.

2. More destroyers (some had long since arrived) to expand the convoy system and increase protection for each convoy. 'The United States destroyers are more suitable for convoy work on the western approaches to Great Britain than British destroyers, owing to their size and greater radius of action. Any increase possible in this direction would enable more British destroyers to be used in the North Sea to operate offensively against enemy submarines'.

3. More convoy cruisers, to make it possible to run more convoys, or to split convoys into smaller groups.

4. More patrol craft, tugs, etc for patrol work (twelve tugs had already been supplied; the War Staff wanted twenty more).

5. Rapid merchant ship construction (which was already under-way).

6. Supply of a large number of mines for the Northern Barrage and assistance in laying them. The barrage would also require a large number of patrol vessels, which the United States might help supply. Note that the Eagle Boats, which were soon ordered, were apparently not intended to support the Northern Barrage.

Each of the ship items represented a major theme that continued after 1917. For example, when new First Lord Sir Eric Geddes compiled a paper on ASW requirements for the War Cabinet in January 1918, it included a list of ships desired from the United States by 15 March of that year: forty-eight destroyers or sloops, 128 trawlers or similar craft and eighty motor launches (actually 110ft sub-chasers).[24]

The Germans planned to use their big, fast liners as raiders, considering ships of under 17 knots useless as auxiliary cruisers. Auxiliary cruisers leaving German ports should make at least 20 knots to have a good chance of breaking through the British fleet. In 1914 only four liners (cruisers A through D) fit those requirements, although nine fast new ships were about to enter service. Despite their great size and value they were to carry only light armament (they were not stiffened, for example, for 5.9in guns). Since their silhouettes were very distinctive, they needed high speed for their safety. Although no faster than most cruisers, the liners could maintain high speed for much longer. However, their operational lifetime was limited because they could not replenish without being brought to battle and quickly sunk, or else interned in neutral ports. The German liner *Kronprinz Wilhelm* won the 'Blue Riband' (the Atlantic speed record) in 1902. She displaced 24,900 tons (14,908 GRT). About 1903 some in the Admiralty thought that the German government had subsidised such fast ships specifically to create wartime raiders. On that basis the British subsidised the turbine liners *Mauretania* and *Lusitania*, which were stiffened for the very heavy gun armament of twelve 6in. When war broke out *Kronprinz Wilhelm* was in New York. At sea she was armed by the cruiser *Karlsruhe* with two 12cm and two 8.8cm guns (she had ammunition only for the 8.8cm). Commissioned on 6 August, she captured fifteen ships (total 60,522 GRT) before having to intern herself at Newport News on 26 April 1915. She was seized once the United States entered the war, becoming the troopship *Von Steuben*, named after a German who fought in the Revolution. *Kaiser Wilhelm der Grosse* was a near-sister, better armed (six 10.5cm and two 37mm guns) but much less successful (three ships, 10,683 GRT). *Kronprinz Wilhelm* is shown under tow in New York in 1916. (Harris & Ewing via Library of Congress)

CHAPTER 3
Blockade, Trade Warfare and Economic Attack

THE ULTIMATE WEAPON WIELDED by the Royal Navy was economic. In past wars that meant blockade, the seizure of any enemy's ships and cargoes. From 1870 on, the world economy grew dramatically, due to the development of the London credit market and also to the collapse of shipping costs as ships improved dramatically. Where in the past economic warfare had meant blockade, now it had a wider meaning, because even the internal trade of countries depended so heavily on the London credit market. Expansion was possible because the banks in London which handled commercial credit began to finance their operations not only via the Bank of England but also via the new joint-stock ('high street') banks such as Barclays. Typically a quarter of their capital was in 'London bills' of exchange related to trade.[1] Credit was vulnerable to financial panic. In 1907 a US financial panic temporarily wiped out US trade. The effect of the panic was overcome by a banking syndicate assembled by J P Morgan. The outbreak of war would clearly create a much worse panic. Could the British exacerbate its effect on Germany, using the international credit system to destroy the German economy? Before 1914 British advocates of economic attack (including blockade) against Germany argued that this weapon alone could quickly end a war.

Conversely, the need for a powerful Royal Navy to guarantee British trade against foreign attack had been the central theme of the naval revival of the 1880s; Admiral Fisher often wrote that the effect of naval defeat would be starvation. During the 1880s French naval offices of the *Jeune École* advocated a direct attack against British trade, a forerunner of the German unrestricted U-boat campaign of the First World War. Like some Germans, they argued not that they could starve Britain out, but that the loss of sufficient shipping would cause a panic which would compel a British Government to sue for peace. A later idea was that losses would drive up insurance costs to the point at which the British merchant fleet would be immobilised (this approach was sometimes called 'guerre industrielle'). The fact that the Royal Navy had to defend against such attacks doubtless made it more sensitive to the possibility that it could destroy a modern enemy by imposing its own economic attack.

A century later, one might doubt that a quick economic catastrophe would collapse an enemy society; the First World War and later horrors showed that societies are far more resilient than had been imagined. Typically the effect of economic attack, for example sanctions, is to give the target government more rather than less support, both because the public is furious to be attacked and also because the target government tends to become nearly the sole source of valuable goods (no sanction or blockade is fully effective). Thus Saddam Hussein's power in Iraq was strengthened by the economic sanctions imposed on him (but he did find it

The northern part of the British blockade was enforced by the 10th Cruiser Squadron (initially Cruiser Force B, or the Northern Patrol Force), which operated between the coast of Scotland and the coast of Norway. It had to patrol two entrances to the North Sea, the 40-mile stretch between the Shetlands and Orkneys and the 150 miles between the Shetlands and a point in Norway north of the islands which might shield a ship further south. The two passages divided the force into two divisions. Initially the force consisted of the eight elderly *Edgar* class protected cruisers, the oldest on the Navy List, supplemented by the torpedo gunboat *Dryad*. This force was intended to intercept German merchant vessels (and neutrals trading with German ports carrying contraband) and to take and destroy armed merchant ships or men of war passing into or out of the North Sea. The force was based at Scapa Flow. Initial operations were complicated by a series of false reports of a German base somewhere on the Norwegian coast. While the cruiser force investigated one such report, the German raider *Kaiser Wilhelm der Grosse* managed to break out into the Atlantic (she was sunk on 26 August by HMS *Highflyer* in the Rio de Oro, Spanish West Africa). Armed merchant cruisers soon joined the patrol, the first (HMS *Alsatian*) arriving on 18 August. For the British, the great surprise was that on the outbreak of war the Germans had ordered all merchant ships in neutral ports to stay there, in effect abandoning trade (this was the opposite of British orders). The patrol was therefore wound down, the Norwegian patrol being scrapped. The Shetlands end was to be taken up by armed merchant cruisers, the *Edgars* working in a new patrol area near Buchan Ness (based on Cromarty) until October 1914. Their main task was to prevent the Germans from mining the exits from Scapa Flow (minefields off the Tyne and the Humber were discovered on 26 August). *Hawke* was torpedoed by *U 9* (15 October 1914). Admiral Jellicoe then withdrew his fleet from the North Sea, leaving the 10th Cruiser Squadron and the newer ships of the 3rd Cruiser Squadron to patrol the blockade line (initially with the old battleships of the 3rd Battle Squadron in support, but those ships soon left for Lough Swilly). A chase of a suspected German minelayer (which turned out to be the Norwegian liner *Bergensfjord*) demonstrated that the *Edgars'* engines were increasingly unreliable. An 11 November gale showed their lack of seaworthiness and their unsuitability for winter work. Plans soon called for refitting half the class at a time in Clyde yards. Meanwhile Jellicoe was becoming disenchanted with the blockade, as nearly all detained ships were soon released, even if they were carrying cargoes such as copper and petroleum consigned to Germany. He wanted to discontinue boarding altogether, but the Admiralty pointed out that agreements with neutrals not to re-export goods to Germany could not have been reached had their ships not been boarded and detained. The Admiralty therefore decided to replace the *Edgars* with a force of twenty-four armed merchant cruisers, the *Edgars* to be paid off as they became available. On 20 November the *Edgars* were ordered paid off. Four were soon bulged and sent to the Mediterranean: *Edgar, Endymion, Grafton* and *Theseus*. The other three (*Crescent, Gibraltar* and *Royal Arthur*) became depot ships. The cruisers were replaced by armed merchant cruisers late in 1914 (in January 1915 the 10th Cruiser Squadron consisted of twenty-three armed merchant cruisers). HMS *Royal Arthur* is shown in Victorian livery, as built. In 1914 she was the only one of the class which had not undergone a major refit and rearmament.

difficult to keep his military supplied with spares, with disastrous results when he went to war). It might be argued that in 1914 Germany was so vulnerable to British economic attack that the impact would have been too sudden to allow for much resilience.

Those advocating blockade in 1914 were encouraged by the apparent success of the US Navy against the Confederates during the American Civil War, a success much promoted by Mahan, who had been a Union naval officer on blockade duty. The Confederacy was a particularly good example of a country dependent on external supply, in its case of manufactured goods, not least guns and powder. Claims of blockade success may have been enhanced by the reluctance of Confederate army officers to admit that they had lost in the field; modern analyses suggest that the blockade had limited effect. The blockade did run up the cost of goods in the

Confederacy and that had serious social consequences. It did not help that the Confederate states did a poor job of distributing what they did get, due in part to bad internal communications, which in turn were a consequence of a limited rail network, material for any extension of which had to come mainly from outside the Confederacy.[2] Problems of internal distribution affected First World War Germany, too. On the other hand, it had been British ships which ran the Union blockade and many in Britain were aware that they had been quite successful.

British economic attack against Germany faced two different challenges. First, Germany was Britain's main pre-war trading partner. Destroying the German economy would badly damage the British. It was difficult to unwind British dependence on German

trade once the war began. The necessary compromises were so embarrassing that the official blockade history completed in 1937 was not published for twenty years. The British also had to reckon with the effect of their measures, particularly blockade and its relatives, on relations with the United States. Allowances for the United States drastically reduced the impact of the blockade on Germany, but once the United States entered the war the situation changed dramatically.

One important factor was not appreciated before the war. Modern experience has shown that embargoes and blockades, even if theoretically devastating, can generally be evaded to a limited extent. However, even a relatively ineffective interdiction operation bites hard once its victim is fighting, because then the victim needs

HMS *Alsatian* was the first armed merchant cruiser to join the 10th Cruiser Squadron and she became its flagship. Even though no subsidies had been arranged for the purpose, *Alsatian* had built-in stiffening for guns and had ten bulkheads. Because she was turbine-powered, she enjoyed some inherent immunity from shellfire, as they were below her waterline. Her steering gear was also below the waterline. She was the first North Atlantic liner with a cruiser stern. Launched on 22 March 1912, she measured 18,481 GRT (deep displacement 22,150 tons with 5700 tons of coal on board). She sailed on her maiden voyage for the Allen Line on 17 January 1914 (her first transatlantic voyage began on 22 May 1914). She and her sister *Calgarian* were taken over on 7 August 1914 as part of the first group of thirteen armed merchant cruisers and converted at Liverpool along with the three big Cunarders and Canadian Pacific Railway's *Empress of India*. She was initially armed with eight 4.7in guns. After becoming flagship of 10th Cruiser Squadron she had eight 6in and two 6pdrs. Conversion included adapting lower cargo spaces as additional coal bunkers, increasing her coal stowage from 3500 to 7000 tons and her endurance to 11,500nm. She was rated at 19.5 knots (one report has her capable of 22 knots). *Alsatian* was the first Royal Navy ship to be dazzle-painted; she was also one of the first ships with wireless D/F (the only other armed merchant cruiser so fitted was *Orvieto*). In November 1917 the 10th Cruiser Squadron was disbanded in favour of a much smaller 2nd Cruiser Squadron consisting of the armoured cruisers *Minotaur* and *Shannon*; the armed merchant cruisers *Alsatian*, *Orvieto* and *Teutonic*; and the armed boarding steamers *Amsterdam* and *Duke of Cornwall*. A proposal to convert the three armed merchant cruisers into aircraft carriers was rejected. *Alsatian* was returned to Canadian Pacific Ocean Services (which had absorbed the Allan Line) and renamed *Empress of France*; she continued to operate until 1931 and was broken up in 1934. *Alsatian* is shown late in the war. Her sister *Calgarian* was sunk by a U-boat on 1 March 1918. (By courtesy of Ian Johnston)

HMS *Ambrose* (formerly of the Booth Line) served with the 10th Cruiser Squadron , but later became a submarine depot ship, as shown here, with 'L' class submarines alongside. She was taken over on 20 November 1914 and then purchased outright (to become a depot ship) on 20 October 1915. As an armed merchant cruiser, she was armed with eight 4.7in guns and two 6pdrs; built in 1903, she measured 4595 GRT. She was rated at 15 knots. *Ambrose* was taken over as part of a greatly-enlarged Northern Patrol conceived after HMS *Audacious* was sunk by a mine on 27 October. The Admiralty thought the mines had been laid by merchant ships flying neutral flags. To ensure that they would not pass through its net, on 2 November it declared the whole North Sea a military area, the idea being that every ship entering the North Sea should be subject to some kind of examination. To that end, the Admiralty announced that all ships passing a line from the northern point of the Hebrides through the Faeroes to Iceland did so at their own peril, as the Germans were laying mines outside British territorial limits. Ships trading with Scandinavia should use a safe route via the Straits of Dover. In theory that would have limited the North Sea to suspect ships. In fact shipping companies protested. They were given safe routes provided that ships inbound to Europe put into Kirkwall for examination. There were already seven armed merchant cruisers in the 10th Cruiser Squadron. Another seventeen were urgently needed. They would put the blockade into place as soon as possible, if only, in the words of the Staff History, 'in order that passing vessels might report it to be at work'. Ships of fair speed and moderate size were preferred, but in the end what mattered was that the ships be in port or be available soon. All were officially requisitioned on 23 November. Admiral de Chair hoisted his flag on board *Alsatian* on 4 December. The area patrolled was not the same as that of the original Northern Patrol and it was moved so that the enemy was less likely to mount a cruiser raid. It was initially split into four areas: between the Faeroes and Iceland; north of the Shetlands; south of the Faeroes; and west of the Hebrides. The 10th Cruiser Squadron became more vital after an 11 March 1915 Order in Council declared that no ship would be allowed to proceed to a German port and any from a German port would have to hand over all goods embarked there; any vessel proceeding to an enemy port after declaring for a neutral one would be seized. All ships intercepted at sea now had to be searched. In all, forty-one liners served with the 10th Cruiser Squadron at various times, before it was paid off on 7 December 1917 because transatlantic trade was effectively controlled at source once the United States was in the war. In addition to armed merchant cruisers, in 1917 the Admiralty took up eleven (later twelve) smaller merchant ships as commissioned convoy escorts (and convoy flagships), each to be armed with either three 6in or two 6in and two 4in guns. Eventually they also had a pair of 11in ASW howitzers. They were slower (10 to 12 knots) and less expensive to operate than armed merchant cruises. (Abrahams via Dr David Stevens, SPC-A)

much more material support than in peacetime. In the limited form actually practiced during the First World War, blockade and a wider economic attack gradually strangled Germany, though it never by itself brought that country down. The Germans came to realise that in future they might have to fight an extended war without access to overseas resources. The German seizure of vast stretches of Russian territory in 1918 was intended largely as a way to escape the effects of blockade. In a 1930 history of the blockade, a French naval officer observed that the Germans would probably invade the Soviet Union in any future European war specifically to evade the effects of a blockade.

Blockade literally meant sealing off an enemy's ports (*i.e.,* blocking them). The word was applied loosely both to attempts to bottle up the enemy's fleet and to an attack on his seaborne trade. That did not limit the attack on an enemy's seaborne trade, which could be mounted wherever it was found. For example, during the Napoleonic Wars the Royal Navy blockaded the French coast, but its frigates also hunted down French merchant ships at sea, taking them as prizes. The French hunted British merchant ships at sea; they called this kind of warfare *guerre de course*, meaning hunting (coursing) warfare. Similarly, during the American Civil War, the US Navy blockaded Confederate ports. The Confederates commis-

HMS *Changuinola* was another 10th Cruiser Squadron armed merchant cruiser. She is shown in 1918. Taken over on 21 November 1914, she measured 5978 GRT (deep displacement 10,625 tons, with 1680 tons of coal on board). Completed in 1912, she was armed with six 6in guns and two 3pdrs. She was rated at 15.5 knots.

sioned commerce raiders to hunt down US ships. Before the First World War the Royal Navy paid considerable attention to the requirements of protection against such cruiser warfare.

As understood before 1914, trade warfare, whether in the open ocean or in a blockade, was an attack on enemy property, not on enemy non-combatants. A raider or blockader had to stop a ship so that her papers could be examined to determine whether she was a legitimate prize. If she was, she could be seized and taken into port as a prize. If that was impossible, she could be sunk at sea. In either case the attacker had to ensure the safety of the non-combatants on board. This idea of trade warfare was illustrated in a pre-war French book on naval warfare: the deck of a liner is shown, with two ladies reclining on deck chairs under a parasol while two officers from a cruiser on the horizon climb an accommodation ladder to the deck. It is all entirely civilised. Only warships or troopships could be sunk on sight (in some formulations of international law, ships in convoy could also be sunk on sight).

When the Royal Navy practiced trade warfare in some of its annual manoeuvres, its cruisers were enjoined to obey the prize rules. In at least one case, the post-exercise report criticised a cruiser commander for claiming too many prizes off a port, on the ground that he could not possibly have visited all of them in the time allowed. When Admiral Fisher became First Lord he argued that an enemy might be considerably more ruthless. In 1906 he ordered an exercise in which surface raiders notionally sank merchant ships on sight, but there was insufficient co-operation from ship owners to provide realistic numbers of targets. The exercise was not repeated. However, in 1911 Fisher, by then retired

and a strong advocate of submarines, predicted that in wartime they would be compelled to execute unrestricted submarine warfare: they would sink any ship they found. He was ridiculed at the time. Although his opponents might have been considered grossly unrealistic, they could reasonably argue that any policy that brutal would have repercussions among neutrals.

It was one thing to attack an enemy's merchant fleet. In wartime trade would surely shift to neutrals. Because one neutral, the United States, held so much of the balance of power after war broke out, the question of just how neutral shipping should be handled became crucial to both sides. The British elected to weaken their economic attack against Germany partly in order to keep the United States friendly. They had to reckon with a large pro-German segment of the US population, well represented in Washington. The Germans had not thought much about economic warfare before 1914. Once they imposed their form of blockade, via submarines, they also had to take US views into account. Until late 1916 Chancellor Bethmann-Hollweg successfully argued that Germany, too, could not afford a break with the United States. When he lost that argument and Germany opted for unrestricted submarine warfare, the United States was tipped into joining the Allies.

This history had important post-war consequences. Even though the world was less globalised after 1918 than it had been before 1914, economic attack was still a valuable weapon. Some countries, such as Japan, were clearly more vulnerable to blockade than others. When US and British naval war planners thought about a possible war with Japan (which both navies considered the most likely future enemy), they understood that blockade would ultimately be decisive. The question was how to gain a position from which a successful tight blockade could be mounted. In conventional terms, that required the defeat of the Japanese fleet. The Germans had, however, demonstrated an alternative: even before the Japanese fleet had been faced, let alone defeated, submarines might well be able to sink the Japanese economy. For both the

Mauretania, shown here as hospital ship, was financed partly by the Admiralty as a fast armed merchant cruiser capable of running down the new German liners which could outrun all British ships. The idea of maintaining a fleet of subsidised merchant ships against wartime requirements was not new. Moreover, the Admiralty maintained a list of suitable ships, selected gun positions and other necessary modifications and maintained files of what work would have to be done in wartime. Only some of the ships involved attracted subsidies. By 1903, when the agreement to build *Mauretania* and her sister-ship *Lusitania* was reached, the Admiralty was unhappy with the results subsidies had achieved, as shipowners had been unwilling to build really fast (meaning uneconomical) ships despite them. From 1887 on, the Admiralty subsidised particular fast liners, whose owners agreed that they would be specially fitted for quick conversion. In June 1897, for example, the subsidised Cunarder *Teutonic* was converted in 24 hours. The subsidised ships were carried on the Navy List and allowed to fly the Blue (rather than Red) Ensign. Further unsubsidised ships were listed for wartime conversion, some being held available. The subsidy agreements were allowed to lapse in 1905–6, but the Admiralty arranged loans to build the large fast liners *Lusitania* and *Mauretania* and to fit them for wartime conversion, with twelve 6in guns. At the time, they were described as ideal armed merchant cruisers. They were intended specifically to compete with fast new German liners, which it was assumed had been subsidised specifically for wartime use as commerce raiders (it is not clear that this was the case, but the Germans certainly had their own list of liners to convert in an emergency). Security for the loans was the Cunard fleet, which was not to be allowed to fall into foreign hands (management and shares of Cunard were not allowed to fall into foreign hands, either). Despite the end of subsidies, several companies continued to build ships to Admiralty requirements. The Admiralty maintained a list of potential armed merchant cruisers of British registry, plus a reserve of guns and necessary fittings (it happened that when war broke out, ships were fitted out without much reference to pre-war plans). The subsidy issue had no impact on Admiralty plans to take over and convert suitable liners in the 1914 emergency. A secret advance notice was sent to some shipowners on 31 July 1914 that certain of their ships might be required as armed merchant cruisers. First Lord Winston Churchill had already informed the Superintendent of Contract Work on 28 July. Both *Mauretania* and *Lusitania* were taken over briefly in 1914, but then released back into merchant service as unsuitable (meaning mainly that they were too large to be sufficiently manageable). The larger *Aquitania* was also taken up under the Cunard agreement. She actually sailed as an armed merchant cruiser, armed with the standard battery of eight 4.7in guns (the two other big Cunarders were never used). After about two weeks *Aquitania* collided with the Leyland Liner *Canadian*. It was decided that given her enormous running cost and the greater suitability of smaller ships (i.e., their handiness), she should be returned to passenger service. Initial conversions of thirteen ships were begun at Liverpool, Tilbury and Southampton.

British and the Americans, the experience of the First World War was cautionary. The necessary unrestricted submarine campaign would inevitably include attacks on neutral shipping. In a British war against Japan, that would mean US ships and it might bring the United States into the war against the British. For Americans, the fear was that British merchant ships would be sunk and that the British would enter the war against the United States. The great irony was that both navies were looking at the same prospective enemy and that they would more likely be allies than anything else. That was an important reason why, after Pearl Harbor, the US submarine force received the order to execute unrestricted submarine warfare against Japan.

Before the Declaration of Paris (1856) the rules of trade warfare were not codified. It was generally understood that in war all enemy ships could be captured. Goods supporting the enemy military could be declared contraband and seized even if they were on board neutral ships. Such seizures could occur anywhere on the high seas; they constituted legitimate trade warfare. The status of

neutral ships was not widely agreed. When the British and the French fought the Russians from 1854 on, their practices differed. Based on the 'ancient rights' of seapower, British practice was to seize enemy cargoes on board neutral ships. The French did not do so. At the outset of the war the British announced that they would abide by French practice, although in future they might revert to their earlier practice. Blockade was a special case. A distinction was drawn between a 'paper' blockade which was declared but not strongly enforced and an 'effective' blockade which caught nearly all ships seeking to get through.[3] An 'effective' blockade of a particular enemy port made all ships, enemy or neutral, going in or out subject to seizure, whatever they were carrying.

The 1856 Paris conference which ended the Crimean War codified the law of trade warfare at sea. The British accepted the change they had already made in practice. To many British naval officers, abandonment of the 'ancient rights of seapower' had rendered blockade, their main weapon, ineffective. Now a neutral flag covered all goods except contraband (goods which would

HMS *Marmora* was an armed merchant cruiser, taken over on 3 August 1914. She was armed with eight 4.7in guns, one of a pair of which is evident forward of her foremast. Built in 1903, she measured 10,509 GRT. *Marmora* was sunk by *UB 64* south of Ireland on 23 July 1918. She was serving as a convoy ocean escort at the time (for a convoy from Cardiff to Dakar), having previously served in the Central Atlantic and off West Africa. In addition to their cruiser role, armed merchant cruisers escorting convoys carried cargo, to help boost overall British capacity. DNC had to issue special instructions on permissible loading consistent with armed merchant cruiser employment. In March 1918 DNC issued new rules intended to increase cargo capacity. Armed merchant cruisers normally carried coal – topweight – unusually high up to provide protection against shellfire. They were also required to maintain greater stiffness than would be normal in cargo ships. Ships were therefore given considerable permanent ballast and sometimes were also required to carry considerable water ballast. In one case (*City of London*) cargo was considered more important than protective coal, so DNC was able to approve removing 1500 of her 2300 tons of permanent ballast (and admitted that all of it could be removed if less stringent stability requirements were imposed).

support the enemy's war effort). Even neutral goods on board enemy ships could not be seized at sea unless they were contraband. If neutral ships were inherently safe, then on the outbreak of war a country could re-flag most of her merchant ships to protect them. The definition of contraband could be made so tight that few goods could be seized. The United States wanted a general agreement that goods, whatever their owner, on board neutral ships (like its own) were not to be seized at sea. What goods should be designated as the enemy's? Goods ultimately intended for an enemy might be transshipped at some neutral port. Could they be seized before they made their final journey into enemy hands? The British adopted a doctrine of 'continuous voyage', in which it was assumed for purposes of seizure that any goods ultimately intended for an enemy port could be seized wherever they were found. Ironically, they fell victim to just this doctrine during the American Civil War, when ships and goods *en route* to British islands in the Caribbean before going on board fast blockade-runners were sometimes seized by US warships. As for blockade, it was not entirely clear what 'effective' meant. Did the blockading ships have to remain off the blockaded port, or could the blockade be enforced by a cruising squadron offshore? During the American Civil War, the British disputed the interpretation the US government placed on 'effective'.

The British downplayed blockade when France and Russia seemed to be the most likely enemies, because both were self-sufficient in food and also in other things. Until about 1905 British strategists had to confront the possibility that their country would be neutral in a war between Germany and Austria-Hungary on one side and France and Russia on the other. Under those circumstances they wanted the most restrictive international rules to protect their shipping and to keep it operating. As attention turned to Germany as a likely enemy, the situation changed. Now the emphasis was on cutting off German trade in wartime. This transition affected different departments of the British government at different times – there was no pre-war moment when a Prime Minister circulated a paper declaring that all British policies should be directed against Germany. At one point Admiral Fisher remarked that any rules adopted to protect neutral shipping would be abandoned once a war began, hence the Foreign Office could make any agreements it liked. However, the reality after 1914 was that the neutrals, particularly the United States, had leverage to enforce rules. That leverage would have been ineffective only if, as some hoped, an economic attack on Germany proved almost instantly effective.

The most important change in British perception was that Germany was potentially vulnerable in a way that France was not. Appointed Deputy DNI and head of the Trade Division in 1901, Captain Edward Inglefield discovered that the United Kingdom was not, as many imagined, uniquely vulnerable to disruption. Germany was also now vulnerable, in a way France was not.[4] The earliest British naval war plan against Germany (1902) envisaged a crippling attack against German trade in hopes that German commercial interests would stop the war at minimum cost to the United Kingdom. This seems to have been the beginning of the Royal Navy idea that Germany was vulnerable to economic pressure. A 1904 presentation to the CID offered a combination of attacks on German overseas trade and attacks on her colonies.[5] In 1905 DNI Captain Charles Ottley (later Secretary to the CID) assured new First Sea Lord Admiral Fisher that out of the 1903 total, fully 60 per cent of German trade was seaborne, hence vulnerable to naval attack. To impose a blockade would be 'to sever an artery, essential it seems to me, to the financial existence of Germany'. The Royal Navy began planning in earnest for economic warfare just as an effort was mounted to codify and therefore potentially to restrict, the wartime rules on blockade.

In 1906 a second Hague Peace Conference was announced to continue the work of codifying the rules of war begun at the 1899 Conference. A major subject was the law of trade warfare. Fisher knew that 168 of 397 Liberal MPs had signed a petition supporting a Cabinet proposal to extend immunity to all shipping in wartime – to preclude trade warfare altogether. This vote coincided with a formal study of war plans against Germany, initiated by Fisher. His planners hoped to interdict German trade, exploiting the blocking position of the United Kingdom at the mouth of the North Sea. The interdiction forces in the Channel and north of Scotland would be covered by the British fleet. Unlike earlier blockade plans, this one took account of modern developments in underwater warfare, which Fisher in particular thought precluded classical blockade of a port. A close blockade, which was no longer viable, would have permitted the seizure of all ships going into or out of German ports, no matter what they carried. The preferred distant blockade, which did not have any legal status, would be limited to German-flagged ships and to neutrals carrying contraband.

The conference convened at The Hague in 1907. Fisher wrote that the Liberals wanted to abandon the 'special anti-German weapon of smashing an enemy's commerce'. He managed to have his Director of Naval Intelligence Captain Ottley sent to the conference as part of the British delegation, but its head was a Labour lord who favoured the petition. Ottley told the other members of the delegation that of all possible enemies Germany was most vulnerable to trade disruption. The Admiralty gained a limited success in tightening the rules on reflagging ships. It could also benefit from an Italian proposal which would have made the proposed distant blockade fully legal. However, no final agreement was possible and the conference was reconvened in London in 1909.

With the help of Lloyd's, the Naval Intelligence Department discovered an alternative to blockade. The law of trade warfare concentrated on cargoes, not ships. It turned out that the British controlled 55 per cent of world shipping. The nominal figure for Germany was 10 per cent and even that was probably an over-estimate. Neutral tonnage was insufficient to carry enough to feed Germany, whoever supplied the goods. There was nothing in international law to preclude British government control of British-flag ships, which could be forbidden to trade with the enemy.

Late in 1906, on the eve of the 1907 conference, there was a serious crisis over Morocco. Fisher doubted that there would be a war, but if it came he urged Asquith to rely entirely on economic pressure against Germany. He considered the planned Expeditionary Force too small to make a difference and argued that the Germans would be best advised to contain the French while annihilating the British.[6] Asquith accepted Fisher's argument that the small British Expeditionary Force was unlikely to make a difference. When war broke out its despatch to France was delayed while he and other members of the War Council sought some viable alternative.[7]

In response to Asquith's request for details of its economic strategy, the Admiralty submitted a paper in December 1908. It admitted that not all German trade could be stopped at sea, but it added the argument that the outbreak of war would cause a panic. German dependence on British credit gave the British another effective weapon: the credit system would transmit the blow throughout Germany. The British could deliberately increase the

impact of the credit panic which would occur anyway. Some alarmists thought the Germans could exert financial pressure against Britain, but their arguments were dismissed. Even without military back-up an economic attack might be sufficient support for France.

In the spring of 1909 the Military Needs of the Empire sub-committee of the CID reported that 'a Power possessing command of the sea against Germany can by blockading her ports bring great economic pressure to bear against her . . . the longer the duration of the war, the more serious the situation . . . [But] naval pressure as could be exerted by naval means alone would [not] be felt sufficiently soon to save France in the event of that country being attacked in overwhelming force'.[8]

Meanwhile the revived Hague Conference met in London.[9] It established three lists of goods. 'Absolute contraband' could be intercepted even on board a neutral ship. 'Conditional contraband' could be intercepted only if consigned to an enemy's armed forces. 'Free' goods could not be stopped except by an 'effective' blockade. The Conference ended the doctrine of continuous voyage: 'conditional' goods could not be seized at sea on the basis of intelligence indicating their ultimate destination. Food was placed on the conditional list rather than on the free list.

Hankey considered surrender of continuous voyage disastrous. The CID had concluded that 'one of the most effectual means by which this country could strike at Germany . . . would be by putting pressure upon the masses of the German people through the seizure of German oversea supplies'.[10] Because German merchant ships would soon be driven from the sea, the question would be how to strangle neutral sources of supply. The British could either impose a close blockade of the German coast (which was impracticable due to underwater weapons) or they could extend the definition of absolute contraband so widely as to deny the Germans everything that their complex industrial system and their population needed. In that case it would be legal to seize any neutral ship headed for a German port.

The Admiralty had, moreover, informed the CID that it could not operate a fleet in the Baltic. That in itself made a blockade of the whole German coast impossible; neutral ships headed for German Baltic ports could not be seized. That left only Hankey's second choice – but the definitions of absolute and conditional contraband in the Declaration of London left too many important items on the 'free list'. Moreover, conditional contraband could be seized only if it was destined for the armed forces of the enemy. Although that was already British practice, it was not yet part of international law. Hankey argued that in a war against Germany Great Britain might well revive the practices towards neutrals she had used during the Napoleonic Wars, even at the risk of again infuriating neutrals like the United States. He also recognised that the British could not afford to announce their position at the outbreak of war without risking war with many neutrals. In effect he would eliminate the special status of contraband of any kind. That is exactly what happened during the war. Hankey's fear of neutral reaction proved well-founded.[11]

Ten years after the war Hankey wrote that 'to the best of my knowledge, every single person who was concerned either in drawing up the Declaration or in trying to put it through Parliament lived to regret that instrument'. That nearly all food had been placed on the conditional list could also be considered unacceptable, since given the presence of defence forces in nearly all

The armed merchant cruiser *Carmania*, a former Cunarder, fought a celebrated action against the new German liner *Cap Trafalgar* on 14 September 1914 off Trinidad, sinking her. She had been built in 1905 and was armed with eight 4.7in guns. She measured 19,524 GRT and was rated at 18 knots. She was taken up from trade on 8 August 1914. *Cap Trafalgar* was about the same size (18,710 GRT, displacing 23,640 tons) and about as fast, but far more lightly armed (two 10.5cm and four 37mm guns). Neither ship was capable of hitting at long range, so they closed and hammered each other. *Carmania* made sufficient waterline hits on her enemy to sink her. She took seventy-nine hits, but lost only nine killed. Her coal protection prevented one 10.5cm shell from penetrating the top of her engine room and thin armour added around her boilers protected them. She presumably gained some protection from the fact that she was turbine-powered, so she did not have the high cylinder heads of ships with piston engines. Her bridge and most deck machinery were wrecked and she was gutted by fire. Repairs and a refit took until late November 1914, after which the ship was employed on the 'Tagus Patrol', examining merchant ships arriving at and departing from the River Tagus (Lisbon). She was later employed on the Canary Islands Patrol and spent some time at the Dardanelles (mainly at Mudros). *Carmania* was returned to her owners on 6 July 1916 and then employed as a troopship. As built, *Carmania* was one of the two largest Cunarders and a test ship for turbines vs. quadruple-expansion engines (installed in her sister-ship *Caronia*). She survived as a passenger ship until 1932. (Dr David Stevens, SPC-A)

British ports, any food sent to them could be construed as for their use. There were two successes at London. The Germans and the Dutch failed to block the kind of distant blockade the British now planned.[12] The Declaration also made it difficult to reflag ships.

That mattered, because there were not enough neutral ships to carry German trade. For the Admiralty, the single most objectionable aspect of the Declaration of London was its association with the establishment of an International Prize Court which would regulate blockade operations.

Not surprisingly, the Liberals supported the Declaration. Arms-control agreements were valued as symbols of a civilised approach to international relations. To anyone who spent time in government during the era of US reliance on deterrence, in the 1970s, this attitude will be eerily familiar. Arms-control agreements themselves were seen as major achievements, whatever their details and their implications. That became clear in the later debates when the United States withdrew from the ABM Treaty and when the Senate failed to ratify the Complete Test Ban Treaty. The Declaration of London fell into this category, probably particularly because it could be seen as a British gesture throwing off the belligerent rights which others considered outrageous. Looking back at the Napoleonic Wars, Foreign Secretary Grey argued that interference with neutral trade at the time had cost 'world-wide hostility and an extension of the field of war', presumably meaning the War of 1812 with the United States.

The Admiralty initially accepted the Declaration as the best that could be achieved, but then turned against it, stalling it. One argument against the Declaration, probably part of the Admiralty campaign, was that it failed to prohibit conversion of fast merchant ships into warships on the outbreak of war. It is difficult to see why this was a crucial issue, since it was widely expected that all the powers, including the United Kingdom, would arm fast liners in wartime as auxiliary cruisers.[13]

The armed merchant cruiser *Otranto* helped destroy the German light cruiser *Dresden* in March 1915. She was armed with eight 4.7in (later, eight 6in) guns and was rated at 18 knots (12,128 GRT). Fitting out was simple and took only nine days. It entailed installation of guns and mountings (four with shields), some superstructure being removed to improve fields of fire. Simple magazines and shellrooms were built and a rangefinder placed atop the bridge. Protection amounted to 0.5in plating around the steering engine and bags of coal stowed abreast the tops of the cylinders; there were also flooding arrangements for the fore and aft holds. Signalling arrangements included the usual bridge semaphores and signal lights. *Otranto* and the cruiser *Glasgow* survived the Battle of Coronel, *Otranto* having been bracketed by the German cruiser *Gniesenau*. (Dr David Stevens, SPC-A)

For some years some British naval officers had claimed that the Germans planned to arm their merchant ships on the high seas as soon as war broke out and that many German merchant ships carried weapons and ammunition for just that purpose. Both at the Hague and at London the British had sought to solve this problem by limiting the arming of merchant ships to a country's ports, an unprecedented step. Those who assumed the Germans were planning a surprise attack on British trade using freshly-armed merchant ships saw German resistance to the British proposal as proof of such a plan. For their part the Germans were supported by the French and the Russians – the Russians had long planned to arm their 'volunteer fleet' abroad in the event of war and the French backed up their allies. There was no hard evidence and the Germans had no such plans. However, the purported German plan fitted with suspicion that the Germans were subsidising fast liners specifically for wartime use, a theme raised in the Admiralty as early as 1901.

Because the Declaration of London made food contraband, it could be argued that the supposed German merchant raider threat would be particularly directed against British food ships. The British already took the threat of fast armed German liners seriously. The supposed new threat was a swarm of converted merchant ships fast enough to catch British freighters and too numerous to hunt down very quickly. Churchill was sceptical. In September 1913 he wrote to Prime Minister Asquith that

> *the whole of this threat is very shadowy. Whether the German vessels have their guns on board is extremely doubtful. Not a scrap of evidence has been forthcoming during the last year and a half in spite of every effort to procure it. How are they to be converted on the high seas? Where are they to get rid of their passengers? Are they to take hundreds of non-combatants with them on what the stronger naval Power may well treat as a piratical enterprise? Where are they to coal?*[14]

He was presumably responding to calls for new trade protection cruisers, which resulted in an abortive design study that year. His own solution was simply 'to arm a similar number of British merchant ships of the right speed and make arrangements to commission these for their own defence and that of other British ships in their neighbourhood and on their route'. These ships would form a deterrent. Because the German armed merchant ships would not be particularly survivable, even inferior armament on board merchant ships would deter them; they would not be able to survive long passages after being damaged.

This programme was entirely apart from the Admiralty's long-standing plan to take up liners on the outbreak of war and convert them into armed merchant cruisers (thirteen ships were taken up immediately after war was declared). Pre-war issues of *Jane's Fighting Ships* included with the warship silhouettes those of large fast liners which might be armed in wartime. The Germans were said to have guns on board their large liners, to be installed upon the outbreak of war. That was not true; some liners in foreign waters were, however, armed by gunboats which met them. The armament in question was substantially less impressive than had been imagined by the British before the war, partly because resources were thin and partly because, contrary to British expec-tations, ships seem not to have been built with armament in mind.

Churchill had already established an Admiralty committee to consider arming British merchant ships in December 1911.[15] The committee reported in May 1912. Ships would be armed purely defensively, each with two 4.7in guns placed to fire only aft. At this time the Admiralty had 152 such guns in storage. Churchill publicly announced the arming policy on 26 March 1913. The ships involved were meat and grain ships from Canada, Australia and South America. There was some question as to whether ships could carry ammunition in peacetime, the decision being to mount the guns but not to carry ammunition to foreign ports. It would be

Built in 1913, the armed merchant cruiser *Andes* was rated at 16 knots (15,620 GRT; deep displacement was 22,710 tons, with 3800 tons of coal on board). She was taken over on 22 March 1915. She and the armed merchant cruiser *Alcantara* fought the German *Greif* on 29 February 1916, both *Alcantara* and *Greif* being sunk. The German ship was known to have been armed with 5.9in guns and as a result of the action it was decided that all armed merchant cruisers should have at least one or two 6in, to avoid being outranged by the new German merchant ship raiders. Ultimately the standard armed merchant cruiser armament was two 6in BL forward, six 6in QF, two 11in howitzers, two 6pdr or other anti-aircraft guns and four Type D depth charges. Outfits became more elaborate, with features such as powered ammunition hoists, improved fire control, improved W/T, paravanes and better watertight subdivision; instead of the eight days required in 1914, conversion of the last of the armed merchant cruisers (*Naldera*) took three months. In April 1918 she was armed with eight 6in, two 6pdr and two 11in ASW howitzers. On 26 January 1918 *Andes* and *Orotova* were ordered fitted to carry a Short 184 float plane for convoy escort duty. These ships covered convoys from Dakar, which might be attacked by long-range (cruiser) U-boats. Orders to fit *Morea*, *Moldovia*, *Almanzora* and *Kildonan Castle* were all cancelled. The armed merchant cruiser *Mantua* embarked a Short 184 at Plymouth on 29 September 1918. None of these extemporised seaplane carriers had any special protection for their aircraft (which were to be replaced for each voyage), but at the end of the war a member of the Admiralty Board commented that an aircraft on board an armed merchant cruiser might be a good solution to the problem of an attack on a convoy by two or more cruiser submarines, more economical than provision of several fast armed escort ships. The idea was revived during the Second World War, when several armed merchant cruisers were provided with catapults and floatplanes. All floatplanes on board armed merchant cruisers were ordered disembarked on 20 November 1918.

supplied in British ports when relations with Germany became strained and war seemed likely. The first armed ship to sail was apparently ss *Aragon* of the Royal Mail Line (sailed 25 April 1913). The first to fire her guns was the White Star liner *Ceramic*, building at Belfast, which had her two guns fitted before completion. She sailed with guns on board on 5 July 1913.[16] By September 1913 the Admiralty was preparing to supply 4.7in guns to fifty or sixty ships. As of June 1914, thirty-nine ships of nine shipping lines had been armed, with more planned. These ships were called Defensively Armed Merchantmen (DAM).

The DAM ships were mostly abroad when war broke out, hence had guns but no ammunition. Thus on 7 October 1914 the German auxiliary cruiser (armed liner) *Kronprinz Wilhelm* encountered the freighter *La Correntina*. The British ship outgunned her, but that did not matter; she had no ammunition. She had to surrender. No other DAM ships encountered German raiders.

The German reaction to the British programme was to decide in the spring of 1914 to do exactly what the British feared: they would place guns (but not ammunition) in the holds of some fast merchant ships.[17] War broke out before anything could be done. Similarly, instead of the mass of fast specially-designed liners the British had feared, in 1914 the Germans had only four suitable ships which they prepared to arm at Cuxhaven and Geestemunde. They were only beginning to enlarge this force, having made arrange-

ments with the North German Lloyd and Hamburg-America lines that their new mail boats and liners should be built as far as possible with a view towards employment as auxiliary cruisers. That affected speed, endurance, number of propellers, steering gear, watertight subdivision, seaworthiness, protection of machinery by bunkers, positions for gun mountings, magazines, searchlight platforms, hospitals, cooking arrangements, W/T, coaling and towing gear, etc. The German West Africa Line offered to prepare positions for two small guns in their newest steamers. Some mail boats and fast liners did have fixed positions for 4.1in guns and others were stiffened. None of these ships could have mounted the 5.9in cruiser guns the British had long feared, however.

Soon after the outbreak of war (8 August 1914) Churchill asked for a list of the best fifty ships to arm for National Supply purposes. It could include the best ten DAM whose armaments should be reinforced. All ships on the list were to be compulsorily armed before setting out on their next voyage. The total of armed merchantmen of all classes would then be forty-six DAM (ten of which might have reinforced armament), fifty new DAM and twenty-five armed merchant cruisers (fifteen to be armed in the UK, four in India, four in Hong Kong and two in Australia). Note that another seven DAM had just been armed. DNO prepared a list of twenty-five suitable ships, of which ten were each to be armed with four 6in guns.

Then the situation changed dramatically. The US Government declared that it would intern any armed ship in a US port. The British did not want to disarm their merchant ships, partly because they feared that South American and possibly other governments would follow suit, but on the other hand the US action made it impossible for the Germans to arm numerous ships in US ports. A ship scheduled to be armed, *Kronprinzessin Cecilie*, was interned in New York. Two of the four liners armed in 1914 were later interned in the United States (*Prinz Eitel Friedrich* and *Kronprinz Wilhelm*). Work on the ten additional armed merchant ships was reversed or suspended and three of the existing ships disarmed.[18] It is not clear from the official history how many ships were still armed as of September 1914. The armament issue returned when the Germans announced their first campaign of unrestricted U-boat warfare in February 1915 (see Chapter 12).

Given the Liberals' majority, it was inevitable that the House of Commons passed the Declaration when it came to a vote in 1911.[19] The House of Lords rejected it. DNI Rear Admiral Alexander Bethell wrote in October 1911 that the distant blockade could be considered effective (legal) and that therefore in wartime the Royal Navy could search all neutral ships passing through a blockade zone for German cargoes and for goods ultimately destined for Germany. This was the 'Bethell Interpretation' of the Declaration. First Sea Lord Admiral A K Wilson agreed: any neutral veering off the straight track to her supposed neutral destination could be seized for blockade running. If a neutral discharged at a German port, she could be seized on her outbound voyage. Despite the failure to ratify it, much of the Declaration was incorporated in the British *Prize Manual* in use in 1914. The British were not surprised that the US Government, which had ratified the Declaration, asked soon after war broke out whether the German and British Governments would abide by it

Meanwhile the British Government developed policy for a wider economic attack on Germany in the event of war. In January 1911 Asquith approved formation of a CID subcommittee on Trade with the Enemy in Time of War. It was to find further measures which would damage the German economy and starve the German population. Lord Esher, an important figure in pre-war British defence policy, pointed to the deterrent effect of economic attack and to its ability to end a war quickly. In a 1911 memo Hankey, who wrote the committee's report, claimed that the

HMS *Duke of Clarence* was an armed boarding steamer taken over from the Lancashire and Yorkshire Railway Co. on 6 November 1915 and returned to civilian use on 11 February 1920. She was built in 1892 and measured 1635 GRT (312 x 36ft); she could make 18 knots. Initial armament was one 4in and two 12pdrs. She is shown on 21 May 1918 at Rosyth. Armed boarding steamers were crucial to the British blockade, because under the rules as understood pre-war ships had to be stopped, visited (to determine where they were going and what they were carrying) and then sent into port. Blockade emphatically did not entail sinking ships on sight; the safety of crew and passengers had to be assured. The armed boarding steamer programme began with a 28 September 1914 telegram from Admiral Jellicoe, who pointed out that he did not have enough destroyers for the required work and that the weather was too severe for them. He did not, apparently, mention that the recent loss of the cruisers *Cressy*, *Hogue* and *Aboukir* showed that big cruisers, auxiliary or not, were endangered when they stopped to examine merchant ships. After their loss, only in areas regarded as safe from submarines were cruisers and older battleships allowed to stop and lower boarding boats when smaller ships were not available (even then they were to keep moving while their boats were in the water). Twelve ships were requested. Requirements were a speed of 12–14 knots, coal for at least five days' steaming, W/T, suitable boats, two 3pdrs (later considerably increased) and a naval officer in command. The most suitable ships were cross-channel passenger ships with considerable cargo space; the first twelve were taken up in October 1914 and completed about the middle or end of November. A second group of eight was taken up for the Western Patrol and the Fastnet Patrol etc. Eventually there were about thirty, all 250 to 300ft long.

United Kingdom, together with her likely allies France and Russia 'undoubtedly possesses the means of exercising such enormous and fatal pressure upon Germany . . . that I for my part can hardly conceive that Germany, except for an act of madness, would embark upon a war under such conditions'.

Completed in December 1912, the committee's report emphasised the importance of controlling British shipping. Without those ships, goods could not flow into Germany at the rates required to sustain that country. Control could be backed by a prohibition against trade with the enemy, although it was difficult to say where any particular transaction began or ended. The attempt to deny credit to the Germans collapsed when the banks argued that any attempt to do so would ruin them and the country. They did not answer when asked whether the British could hold out any longer than the Germans. The report therefore omitted banking altogether. It also omitted the difficult question of how to control trade in British ships between neutrals, which might include goods destined for Germany. How could a neutral be prevented from re-exporting goods it legitimately acquired? The report emphasised the need to keep the controversial distant blockade concept secret. That presumably fed into German fantasies that at the outbreak of war the Grand Fleet would steam into the Heligoland Bight to attack it, as a prerequisite for a classic close blockade. Asquith predelegated the imposition of controls to be applied at the outbreak of war. A CID 'War Book' enumerated them.

There were also defensive economic arrangements. The most prominent was war risk insurance, which Hankey thought was Churchill's most important contribution as First Lord. Without it, the British merchant fleet would have been completely immobilised in 1914. On the other hand, the British Government seems not to have worked out specific measures to combat the inevitable financial panic which set in as the July 1914 crisis deepened.

When war broke out, the British War Council considered the Royal Navy the decisive arm and it understood that economic attack was its strategy. Jack Pease, a minister, wrote his brother that 'we decided that we could win through by holding the sea, maintaining our credit, keeping our people employed & our own industry going – by economic pressure, destroying Germany's trade, cutting off her supplies – we would gradually secure victory . . . Our Navy, finance & trade was our life's blood & we must see to it that these are maintained'.[20]

The Germans were aware that they would face economic attack in the event of war; in 1912 they created a standing commission to prepare to meet it.[21] Despite creating a substantial and gloomy literature on their economic vulnerability, the Germans apparently made little provision to resist. However, in the winter of 1914 many German officials stated that their economic situation was desperate. In a remarkable parallel to contemporary British thinking, Tirpitz was the first German minister of state to question the earlier assumption that the country was immune to blockade. Early in 1906 he raised the question of what would happen if Germany were at the same time embroiled in a war against both Continental powers and an overwhelming seapower. Tirpitz questioned the earlier assumption that it would always be possible to obtain supplies indirectly through neutrals; he assumed that the British would impose restraints on Dutch, Belgian and Danish commerce. Even if neutral harbours remained open, they would become badly congested and it was not certain that railway capacity was sufficient to substitute Rotterdam and Copenhagen for Hamburg. The army, which was then developing its offensive plan, was not very interested. Other departments agreed that, although imported food and forage had become essential, supplies on hand would suffice for nine months: Germany could survive a short war.[22]

Tirpitz asked what would happen in an eighteen-month war. Studies by his experts showed that it would be difficult to distribute imports if they had to come through the neutral harbours. The industrial centre of the Rhineland was already supplied by rail from Rotterdam and Antwerp, so it was now assumed that they could take the additional load imposed if German ports were closed. The mobilised army would need far more, not less, food and forage and rolling stock would be diverted to military use. Under an agreement with Germany, her ally Austria-Hungary had agreed to ban export of the Hungarian wheat crop so that it could be diverted to Eastern Germany; but once there, it had to be shipped elsewhere.[23]

The studies to date had not even touched on availability of metal and textiles, both of which would be vital in wartime. That work was not undertaken until 1911.[24] This time the situation was gloomier. Although agricultural production had increased, it had not kept pace with imports. Some products were exported, but keeping them in the country would not provide more bread. There was a growing understanding in Germany that in the event of war the British would be part of the enemy alliance and that imports might be cut off. Although government discussions of wartime economics had been kept secret, public discussion (which began in 1907) created pressure on the German government. The government yielded late in 1912, convening a standing commission. Its recommendations were technical, for example to compile better statistics and to allocate rolling stock for proper internal distribution in wartime. The official British historian of the blockade credits the commission for the preparation which enabled the Germans to resist the economic attack the British mounted, despite the loss of a quarter of its foodstuffs and even more of some of its raw materials (more recent accounts of the blockade also credit inefficiency on the British side, at least up to 1916).[25]

On the eve of war in 1914 the economic commission concluded that Germany would find it difficult to survive a long war cut off from all imports. She needed both a short war and unimpeded trade with both Scandinavia and the United States. By the autumn of 1914 it was clear that the war would be protracted. It seemed that imports from the United States would be cut off. At that point the British though that they had imposed all the restraints on trade that they could, but the Germans thought they had only begun. A British declaration on minelaying (November 1914), which was actually a reaction to German mining, was interpreted as a declaration of unlimited economic war. There was a sense of desperation in the German high command, which led directly to the German decision to declare unrestricted submarine war early the following year.[26] German military strategy created a self-imposed problem. In 1914 Germany imported much of its wheat from Russia (via shipping through the Black Sea) and Romania. By attacking Russia in 1914, Germany thus eliminated a major source of supply. Romania also shipped through the Black Sea and thus was subject to the British blockade.

The rub was that so much of the British economy depended on trade with Germany. The Board of Trade, in effect representing the economy, fought against economic warfare of any sort. It also pointed out that the neutrals would hardly accept British government control of shipping. For example, the US view might be that the British, who carried most American goods to Europe, were seeking to seize American markets. The Board of Trade also argued that trade control was irrational because the Germans could obtain most of what they needed through neutrals (it had originally produced the necessary data for the War Office, in its struggle against the Admiralty). British trade would be crippled without crippling the Germans. The Treasury tended to agree. Board of Trade objections and obstruction persisted through about May 1915.

Shipping control was an example. Despite the Admiralty's plans to gain control of all British merchant ships, about 200 were reflagged in 1914 and the British government also allowed some reflagging of German merchant ships.[27] As the Admiralty had feared before the war, British ships carried British goods to Germany, financed by British banks. These failures of pre-war policy was so embarrassing that the official history of the blockade was not released for many years. How could the British have provided the means for the Germans to kill British troops and seamen? It might be pointed out that British taxes on the same trade paid for the British troops in the first place, so that the Germans were in effect paying for the British to kill their troops. No one in 1914 understood what total war meant. In all past wars trading with the enemy had been the rule, not the exception. In effect it took time for globalisation to unwind sufficiently that economic warfare was not more or less suicidal.

Not having been subjected to emergency war regulation, the banks were instead subject to persuasion. A Cornhill Committee was formed to deal with cases in which banks or their foreign subsidiaries continued to provide credit to the enemy. By mutual agreement of the banks and the Government, its papers were destroyed at the end of the war. It seems clear that at first the Germans continued to use credit supplied by British banks. The British Government may have considered the credit issue covered at least partially by an order prohibiting any payment to anyone living in enemy territory, but bankers could get around it by making payments to accounts in neutral countries.

It also turned out that the pre-war economic warfare advocates had not imagined the level of staff work required to make their programme work. For example, it was one thing to demand that, say, Holland import no more wheat than she needed, but quite another to know how much that was. Banning trade with the enemy came to mean demanding licenses for all export transactions, but the system was soon swamped because priorities were not established. No one developing pre-war policy had set up the specialised organisations needed to make, let alone enforce, wartime policy. This gap was not filled until 1916. It might be pointed out that the British, who had certainly thought through their war plan as much as anyone else, were also caught badly short on staffing in the Admiralty and, for that matter, the War Office. In each case, short staffing meant poor co-ordination between high policy and what was or could actually be done. The staffing problem suggests that even had there been no resistance to economic attack, it could not have achieved the quick results its advocates claimed for it.

On 6 August, two days after war broke out, the US Government asked both Germany and the United Kingdom whether they planned to abide by the Declaration of London. Initially the Germans posed several unacceptable conditions. They also claimed the right (banned under the Declaration) to mine open waters off British bases. The British initially pointed out that they had never ratified the Declaration, but on 20 August they announced that they would abide by it, subject to additions and modifications intended to limit supply to the German army and to German munitions factories. The 'additions and modifications' included a new contraband list, revival of the doctrine of continuous voyage and a provision that prize courts could condemn ships and cargoes 'on any sufficient evidence'.[28] Continuous voyage soon had to be abandoned because it was too difficult to check the supposedly neutral consignees. Instead, under an Order in Council of 29 October 1914 when it became apparent that any neutral port had become a transshipment point for conditional contraband for the enemy, all ships sailing to it could be seized. Initially little came of this because data on national consumption of various commodities was spotty. Later the British concluded rationing agreements with neutrals such as Norway and Holland, under which they would receive amounts roughly equal to their pre-war imports of various products. The British Government finally abandoned the Declaration of London altogether by an Order in Council of 7 July 1916. That had only a marginal effect, because very few cargo cases ever went to court.

The great problem in all of this was the United States, which was also a major German trading partner. It was also a major potential source of munitions to the Allies and a potential ally in any protracted war. President Woodrow Wilson had, moreover, hopes of mediating a settlement through his close associate Colonel Edward House, who for a time shuttled between London and Berlin. The stated US view was 'free ships, free goods', meaning that a neutral flag (theirs) should protect whatever a ship was carrying.

Foreign Secretary Grey was particularly determined not to alienate the Americans, who periodically threatened to place an embargo on munitions. Such threats were credible because the large segment of the American population, mostly in the Midwest, sympathetic to the Germans was well represented in Congress. The Germans' own clumsy approach to trade warfare, which is discussed below, helped the British enormously. In 1915, after the Germans announced their first round of unrestricted submarine warfare, Colonel House told Grey that the Germans would abandon the submarine campaign if the British abandoned their blockade. The sinking of the *Lusitania* killed this initiative, but only after Grey privately told House that he supported it.

Once the Germans started mining international waters (a violation of the Hague convention), the British stated that they felt free to impose stiffer blockade rules.[29] They announced that since there was reason to believe that the German government had taken over control of all foodstuffs in that country, this form of conditional contraband could be seized on the ground that it might be used by the German military. The British also announced that, as the North Sea was not entirely safe (due to German minefields), merchant ships should use the swept channel along the British coast and should put into Dover for clearance. They typically anchored in the Downs for clearance. In 1915 traffic in the Downs amounted to 80 to 120 ships per day, half of them British.

Initially the British formed a cruiser force (10th Cruiser Squadron) to enforce the distant blockade north of Scotland. Enforcement entailed prior knowledge of the routes of ships passing through the area. Given the means of gathering shipping intelligence the Admiralty had already assembled (largely to protect British shipping), this was not too difficult. The cruisers intercepted both eastbound and westbound ships. During 1915 they stopped 3098 ships, of which 1130 were neutral merchant ships allowed to pass after having been boarded or, in some cases, simply identified at sea. Another 743 were sent into Kirkwall or Lerwick for examination. A cruiser hove-to to launch a boat to examine a merchant ship made a tempting U-boat target, so the cruisers were soon used only to force merchant ships to stop. Smaller merchant ships commissioned as Armed Boarding Steamers actually stopped for searches. The cruisers themselves proved ill-suited to lengthy patrols in rough water, so they were replaced by armed merchant cruisers.

Despite its limitations, the blockade tightened, but during 1916 it did not cripple Germany in any noticeable way. The British had hoped that some particular shortages would be decisive. For example, their experts thought that the Germans would exhaust their supply of manganese, which was necessary to harden guns, in 1915. German metallurgists found an effective substitute.[30] Similarly, nitrates were needed both for agriculture and to make high explosives. Before the war they came mainly from guano in Chile and that source was cut off by the blockade. Again, German chemists found an alternative way of fixing nitrogen. By some estimates this success prolonged the war by two years. But the new method of nitrate production was expensive and output did not match pre-war needs, so German farms lacked fertiliser and their production declined. Other products could not be replaced. Rubber was an example. In 1918 the German army and the German economy rolled mainly on wooden tyres. Imported materials were also essential to the manufacture of machine tools; without them, tools wore out much more quickly and that in turn affected production of everything the German military needed.

A subtler effect of the blockade was to reduce sharply German army mobility by the end of the war. There was no question of obtaining enough petrol to create a motorised army (only the British approached that), so the Germans depended on horses. Without access to most of the world, they could not easily make up for horse casualties in the army and of course horses in army service could not contribute to farming or to transportation within the country. By way of contrast, the Allies had access to all the world's horses outside Europe and they never suffered shortages. In 1918 the German army was noticeably short, for example, of horses to pull its field artillery, with real tactical consequences.[31] It is also often claimed that the 1918 German offensive was slowed as soldiers stopped to loot Allied food supplies, both for their own use and to send them back home to make up for drastic shortages.

During 1916 the Germans were able to feed and clothe their army in the field, but their civilian population suffered badly. At the beginning of 1916 bread, meat and fats were all rationed and textile, leather, metal and other material were made available only after

HMS *Snaefell* was an armed boarding steamer taken over from the Isle of Man Steam Packet Co. on 24 November 1914. She was armed with two 12pdrs and one 2pdr pom-pom. Built in 1910, she measured 1368 GRT (270 x 42ft) and was rated at 18 knots. *Snaefell* was one of the second group of eight taken up. She was sunk in the Mediterranean on 5 June 1918 by *UB 105*. (Dr David Stevens, SPC-A)

government requirements had been met. A family with middling income would have enough for one meal a day and that only if the official rations were supplemented by vegetables and potatoes. By this time bread was unpalatable because it had so much corn and barley in it. The system, moreover, was unable to spread the burden evenly, so that the industrial towns in the west did far worse than the countryside and Kiel and Hamburg were particularly badly off. The towns in the Rhineland and the maritime cities had always in the past relied heavily on overseas supplies. Moreover, rising prices widened the gap between rich and poor and thus created future social problems. During the first months of 1916 there were food disorders in Hamburg, Kiel, Magdeburg and Cologne.[32]

The 1916 potato crop was less than half as much as usual (23.5 vs 52 million tons), so the population which could not afford potatoes at inflated prices had to make do with turnips. The grain and sugar harvests fell by a total of about eight million tons. Black market prices for most foods were about ten times pre-war figures. Conditions sharply deteriorated in July and August and there were clothing shortages. In normal times imports would have made up for any domestic problems, but now the blockade had cut them back. A lack of lubricants made it necessary to cut back railway operations, so there were severe coal shortages in Berlin, Leipzig, Kiel, Hamburg, Hanover, Dresden and Vienna. Thus the winter of 1916–17, which the Germans called the 'Turnip Winter', was particularly grim. Even when food rations were available in sufficient quantities, civilians had to wait for hours in food queues, exposed to the bad weather of a German winter after which they could return to unheated homes. In contrast to pre-war predictions, such privation did not bring down the German government; the population was more than willing to make sacrifices for victory. As in 1914, they wanted some magic way of breaking the blockade that was clearly slowly strangling them. That made for a strong popular demand for unrestricted submarine warfare. The German population was encouraged by the victory over Romania in the late autumn of 1916, which placed one of the great granaries of Europe in German hands. Even so, the German high command was painfully aware that the economic attack was becoming more and more effective. German domestic production, which had been declining since 1914, recovered in 1917.

Evaluation of the blockade is difficult because of its politics. The Germans argued that the 'hunger blockade' created deserved bitterness towards the Allies, hence helped justify their post-war attitude. They later published tables of deaths they attributed to the blockade, including a considerable increase in deaths due to tuberculosis in 1917–18. They also claimed that their troops continued to be well fed and well equipped, albeit sometimes insufficiently supplied with food and spirits at the front. It appears, however, that shortages were evident among those not in front-line combat service, such as enlisted men of the High Seas Fleet. Their rations were much more like those of civilians than like those of officers and the gap between the two helped inflame the mutinies of 1917 and 1918.

There was also a subtler factor: the blockade disheartened Germans from early 1917 on. The failure of the submarine campaign created a contagious sense of hopelessness and anger against authority.[33] This was evident, for example, when Chancellor Bethmann-Hollweg felt compelled to make the electoral laws of Prussia more equitable (as announced in the Kaiser's Easter Message). He said that national unity would be endangered if this and similar reforms were not granted. Bethmann-Hollweg later wrote that he had felt the effects of the beginning of the Russian Revolution. The proposal provoked enough discord that it was evident that the problem was deep-seated. The Reichstag took up the issue and one recommendation was that it should be consulted on appointments of ministers of state. This amounted to the sort of revolution the General Staff and the German establishment had sought to suppress in 1914. It was, moreover, understood as revolution; the word began to appear on walls. The Reichstag was careful to say that the revolution contemplated would not touch the Kaiser, but anyone aware of the course of the French Revolution would see that it was likely to go much further.

Up to 1917, supplies of bread and meat were typically lowest just before the harvest, in April, May and June. There were often strikes, but the ones in 1917 were different because they were political. In mid-April metal workers in Berlin, Leipzig, Magdeburg and some other industrial towns struck for several days, demanding political reforms rather than (as before) only better rations. They also demanded that the government announce that it was ready to make peace without annexing any enemy territory. This was unheard-of in disciplined Germany and the political strikes spread. Censors were ordered to suppress news of these strikes. When the Reichstag convened in the autumn to vote credits, the socialists began to manoeuvre away from the government. The socialist deputies apparently decided that they could no longer maintain their positions with their supporters unless they accepted the new revolutionary politics.

At this juncture a Centrum Deputy, Erzberger, proposed that the Reichstag consider whether the submarine campaign would knock Britain out of the war. He had made himself familiar with the navy's logic and had discovered that far from a certainty, the submarine campaign – which had brought the United States into the war – was justified by rather loose logic and by hopes. He pointed to the gaping holes in the arguments, showing that if existing merchant tonnage was used more efficiently the campaign could not win for many years, if at all. The magic German weapon, which his own party had promoted energetically the previous autumn, was probably yet another official lie. The government was asking for vast credits without any credible war plan. Surely the proper objective was a peace conference at which Germany would not try to annex any territory. Erzberger's resolution passed by a large majority on 17 July 1917. Many Germans later said that Erzberger had created a discouragement which later became decisive. When he attacked the navy's claim that it could win in six months, Erzberger was showing that the German authority which had brought the country into the war was open to question.

The politics of the Reichstag spread to many sailors of the relatively inactive High Seas Fleet. In April 1917 Admiral von Capelle told the Reichstag that there was friction between officers and enlisted men. Nothing was done beyond punishing disobedient seamen. On 6 June a watch aboard the *Prinzregent Luitpold* refused rations. As in the workshops, this was not simply a demonstration against bad food; the officers considered the men almost dangerous. For a time it was settled by giving out more flour, but there was too little food – thanks to the blockade – to do that very often. The trouble began again on board the fleet flagship on 5 July, the watch on deck protesting. It spread to other ships and when Captain Thorbecke of the *König Albert* died after falling out of a pinnace, it was rumoured that he had been murdered (British intel-

ligence picked up the rumour). The problem, which included meetings demanding peace without annexation, subsided only at the end of August 1917. The fleet was pacified and two men shot, but it remained restive and it was described as brutally indisciplined during the Finnish operation in the autumn.

German public opinion calmed in the autumn of 1917 because even though the submarine campaign was not succeeding, there was other good news: the defeat of Italian armies in October and the final collapse of Russia. It no longer seemed so obvious that Germany had to sue for peace. However, the blockade continued to demoralise the population. Germans broke up the meetings of the new Vaterland party, which had been formed by nobles, wealthy men and landlords (i.e., the establishment) to reignite German patriotism. Tirpitz often appeared at its rallies. The party achieved exactly the opposite: the Vaterland Party polarised Germans. It gave many of them a symbol to hate without directly attacking the Kaiser.

Although the Germans later claimed that the blockade tightened appreciably after the United States entered the war, in fact their economic situation improved after March 1917. The winter of 1917–18 was not as terrible as that of 1916–17. German victory over Romania had more than balanced the loss due to the accession of the United States to the Allies. The blockade had already tightened almost as much as it could by late 1916.[34] However, the improvements over the situation in 1916 were too small to lift the dispiriting effect of the blockade. The conquest of Ukraine in the early months of 1918 brought little relief, because that country was already being torn up by the Russian Civil War.

Although it seemed that the political disorder of the previous year had died down, in January 1918 a massive strike spread through German Austria and Germany, initially for food, but then (as in 1917) about politics. On 26–27 January nearly a quarter of a million men were on strike in greater Berlin. These strikes were not called by the unions, which could not control them. They died out early in February, the men being driven back to work by hunger. This too was a symptom of the blockade: the strikers could not amass enough to live on if they stayed out of work. The calm that returned was widely considered illusory. The British historian of the blockade sees the January strikes as the beginning of a new radical phase of German workers' politics, the unions and the socialists having been largely discredited. He argues that this was the politics which soon infected the army and the fleet.

Ludendorff felt firmly enough in control to try another 'last card', the great Western Front offensive. It stalled on 18 July. Five days later the generals told the Kaiser that the armies could not win the war. However, in August, September and October the same generals told the Kaiser that the army could still hold out and that the Allies might well become weary enough to accept terms. It was not the Reichstag but the Kaiser who made Prince Max Chancellor in hopes that he would be acceptable to President Wilson, as terms were to be negotiated.

Then everything collapsed. The first sign was that Krupp workers at Essen hissed the Kaiser when he addressed them on 13 September. The explosion began with a High Seas Fleet mutiny, but it soon spread to the German cities, making it impossible for the army to continue the war. The revolutionary movement echoed earlier discontent, evident during the 1917 fleet mutiny: that the war was being fought for the rich and that the workers (and troops) were mere slaves. To the British official historian of the blockade, the driving force was fury at the suffering all of them had endured – due to the blockade. There is some indication that the explosion was touched off when Ludendorff decided suddenly that the war was lost, which meant that all the privation suffered under the blockade had been for nothing.

In November 1918 the Allies were aware that the blockade was both their most powerful and their most usable weapon. Unlike their armies, which could have pressed on into Germany, it did not cost Allied lives. The Allies treated the Armistice as what it was, in theory – a cease-fire – rather than what it became, the effective end of the war. The war would not really end until the Germans came to terms. As an enforcer, the blockade was continued and extended to the Baltic. For many Germans, the continued blockade was a source of anger justifying revenge. For the Allies, extension was a natural consequence of the character of the Armistice, which was not a surrender (some Germans talked of a break, after which the war would be renewed).

If this history is accepted, then the blockade slowly sapped the Germans' will, to the point where a reverse at some point would break them. That particular reverse was the failure of the 1918 Ludendorff offensive. In purely military terms, the shortened German lines in the West might have held. The internal collapse ended any hope on the part of the German army that the war might be protracted into 1919 and that the Allies' war-weariness might be exploited. Had the spring offensive succeeded, the bitterness at home might well have receded and it would not be apparent that the blockade had been so important a factor in the war. This is a psychological or social argument. The blockade wiped out German exports, hence an important source of German revenue. Once the

initial 'war chest' had been expended, the Germans, like the British, borrowed to pay for the war. Inflation raised the cost of living by 48.7 per cent in the first year of the war. As a measure of inflation, the ratio of gold to notes fell from 76.2 per cent in 1914 to 29.9 per cent in 1917.[35]

The blockade also struck at Austria-Hungary and as early as April 1917 Emperor Karl appealed to the Germans to seek peace because he feared revolution, 'which is finding a powerful ally in the general famine'.[36] In 1917–18 the food-producing areas of Hungary and Croatia defied the central authorities and hoarded food. Similarly, the main German food-producing area of Bavaria was radicalised. Presumably in both cases food producers did not want to give up what they had. These areas may have been more troublesome than the hungry cities.

Ludendorff and Tirpitz both emphasised the impact of blockade in their post-war memoirs. That may have been partly political: it reduced any blame on the army for German defeat. Much the same can be said of post-war German emphasis on the civilian lives lost due to the blockade (the death rate among the groups most exposed to shortages was said to have increased by 37 per cent between 1913 and 1918). The Germans were also interested in claiming that the impact of the Allied blockade on their civilians justified their own campaign of unrestricted submarine warfare.

The blockade continued after the Armistice as a means of pressuring Germany to accept peace terms. It is not clear how effective it was. Paradoxically, it may have helped undermine the German government which accepted the Armistice and negotiated at Versailles, since the German army and the General Staff kept

At the outset the Germans had no hope of blockading British trade, but they could hunt it in the open ocean, using cruisers (including converted merchant ships). There was a real difference. Blockade was intended to close down maritime access to the target country, whereas commerce raiding could only affect a fraction of the enemy's ships. The German cruiser *Emden* was the best-known of the small raiding cruisers the Germans used early in the war. After a massive hunt, she was run down by HMAS *Sydney*. She had anchored so that some of her crew could destroy a wireless station – part of a network which passed intelligence (including indications of her position) to the hunters. One lesson of the cruise of the *Emden* was how a single evasive surface ship could tie down massive naval forces. This idea led to the construction of the British 'County' class after the war and, indirectly, to the deployment of HMS *Prince of Wales* and HMS *Repulse* to the South China Sea in 1941. (US Naval Institute collection)

claiming – falsely – that the German army had not been defeated in the field.

It seems clear in retrospect that without an attack via the commercial credit system, there was no way that an economic attack from outside could quickly destroy Germany. Moreover, because Germany was Britain's largest trading partner, cutting the German economy off from Britain's had to do considerable damage to the British economy as well, making it more difficult to prosecute the war on land. Over the longer term, the impact of blockade was considerable, though probably not as decisive as many imagined after the First World War.

Submarine Blockade

In the autumn of 1914 the German navy was not proving very effective against the Grand Fleet. Captain Bauer, who commanded the U-boat force, argued that the mine barrier the British had just laid across the Straits of Dover (which threatened his boats) was illegal and that in retaliation U-boats should operate against British merchant ships. Not long afterwards High Seas Fleet commander von Ingenohl was informed that the initial war orders, under which the fleet could not be risked, would not be changed. On 7 November 1914 he wrote that 'from a purely military point of view' a submarine campaign against British trade 'will strike the enemy on his weakest spot and will make it evident, both to him and his allies, that his power at sea is . . . insufficient to protect his imports'.[37] He thought that a few losses would cause the British to stop all east coast traffic and that the British would be unable to retaliate because there was already very little German traffic. Von Ingenohl sent his proposal up the Admiralstab. He added that he was in no position to judge the effect of his proposal on higher policy and on neutral opinion.

Correspondence published after 1918 shows that many in the German government took a very exaggerated view of the British attack on German trade, particularly after the list of contraband was extended by a 2 November 1914 Order in Council.[38] The Germans were already nervous. The initial offensive had stalled and their own pre-war studies showed that if the war lasted very long they were vulnerable to economic attack. The German economy was suffering badly (it would recover in 1915). It seemed that any counter-attack was justified by the perceived British violation of the spirit of the Declaration of London. The Kaiser and Chancellor Bethmann-Hollweg both resisted the call for an unrestricted submarine campaign: it was even more contrary to international law to sink merchant ships on sight, as Bauer and von Ingenohl were proposing. Bethmann-Hollweg feared the effect on neutral states, presumably both those re-exporting food and other materiel to Germany and on the United States. For example, the Americans might impose a commercial boycott. Late in 1914 Italy presented further problems, as that country shifted from neutrality towards the Entente. Bethmann-Hollweg could also point to increased irritation among the neutrals as the British tightened the blockade.

Admiralstab chief Admiral von Pohl proposed the formula the Germans adopted: Great Britain should be declared blockaded and neutral governments warned that, since the blockade would be executed by submarines, their ships might be sunk without warning if they tried to break the blockade. This was unrestricted submarine warfare – unrestricted in the sense that the submarine could attack any ship in sight, without any attempt to distinguish enemy from neutral.

Von Pohl submitted this paper before his staff analysed the problem, deciding that at least ten blockade stations would have to be occupied. Only if the campaign lasted a long time and proved very destructive (and terrifying) would it keep neutral shipping out of British harbours. The staff did point out that the Germans were not in any position to do such damage that the British would suffer hunger. German diplomats thought that neutral protests would be inversely proportional to the success of the plan: it was essential that the submarines stop all traffic to England for a week at a time. It would therefore be best to wait until more submarines were available. Tirpitz said that, since submarines were the last and most effective means of coercing the British, no campaign should be mounted until enough were ready.[39] The Kaiser disliked submarine warfare, so on 25 November he told von Pohl that he rejected the idea. Von Pohl did not give up. On 7 January the Kaiser reiterated his order against any fleet action and he also indicated that von Pohl, who was very adverse to such action, would soon replace von Ingenohl as fleet commander. Under these circumstances a submarine campaign was about the only naval option open to Germany in the North Sea. The Admiralstab abandoned its opposition.

In November 1914 Tirpitz went so far as to give an interview to an American journalist in which he pressed for a submarine campaign against trade. It was published in Germany in mid-December. He pointed out that the United States had not protested the closing of the North Sea to neutral shipping. How could Americans protest an equivalent counter-blockade by the Germans? To the reporter's question as to whether such a blockade was planned, Tirpitz replied that the British were already trying to starve Germany and that the Germans would be justified to do the same to the British. The interview had particular impact because, although Tirpitz had enjoined the reporter to submit it for clearance, that had not been done. The British blockade was biting; foodstuffs were becoming scarce and industry was still dislocated by the initial shock of war. Many Germans read the interview as an announcement that their government had found a way to break the British blockade.[40] That created intense pressure on the Chancellor, which von Pohl exploited.[41]

Bethmann-Hollweg and the Kaiser resisted for a time; when von Pohl again proposed the submarine campaign on 7 January, the Kaiser told him that for the time being the campaign would be postponed, to be reviewed later. The Germans had paid no attention before the war to the requirements of economic attack against the British and no one on the Admiralstab had any experience with submarines. Thus there was no one to refute or even criticise whatever von Pohl said. At a 1 February meeting he overcame Bethmann-Hollweg's misgivings by claiming that it was possible for submarine commanders to distinguish neutral from enemy ships, so that only enemy ships would be sunk.[42] At the same time von Pohl claimed that Germany had enough submarines to inflict sufficient damage on Britain to force her to terms in a short time. Bethmann-Hollweg agreed to the submarine blockade the next day. Given von Pohl's assurance, when he inspected the fleet on 4 February the Kaiser signed the order for the submarine campaign when von Pohl suddenly produced it.

The US Government warned of serious consequences should any American ship be sunk, or any American citizens killed. It would hold Germany responsible for any damage to American interests. Admiral von Tirpitz seems to have been genuinely surprised that the neutrals, particularly the Americans, protested vigorously. The Germans replied that they had sufficiently warned neutrals to avoid being sunk by delineating the war zone. The most famous example of this declaration was the advertisement the German consul in New York ran for several days before the liner *Lusitania* sailed, warning Americans that they were taking the ship at their own risk.

Despite disclaimers to the United States, confidential orders issued on 20 February 1915 enjoined U-boat commanders from sinking American and Italian ships (Italy was wavering between remaining neutral and entering the war on the Allied side). However, there was no instruction to avoid sinking British passenger liners. When the *Lusitania* was sunk on 7 May 1915, 1198 passengers, including 120 Americans, were killed. The US government was outraged. Not only were the Germans risking retaliation, they also inadvertently cancelled an American attempt to curb the British blockade. Although the Germans rejected the American protest, in June U-boat commanders were ordered not to sink passenger liners.

It might be logical that a submarine torpedoing a merchant ship could not possibly attend to the safety of passengers and crew, but in 1915 legitimate trade warfare was still understood to require that effort. No one at the top of the German government seems to have realised that no one outside Germany would equate torpedo attack without warning to the conventional practice of stopping and examining ships. At the beginning of 1915 the US government was involved in a furious debate with the British over cotton exports. In effect the U-boat campaign trumped any such argument. Once the *Lusitania* was sunk by a U-boat, a US Senator pointed out that he could never equate a life taken by the Germans to a bale of cotton seized by the British. It did the Germans no good to argue that the British blockade was starving them.

The US government demanded that U-boats abide by the internationally-understood duties of examination (to determine that a particular merchant ship was either an enemy vessel or carrying contraband) and of safeguarding the life of passengers and crew. The German protest that U-boats could not carry out the expected examinations in the face of decoy ships (Q-ships) and armed merchantmen did not carry much weight with the Americans. The Germans understood that U-boats were unable to maintain the kind of blockade the Americans and other neutrals considered legitimate. The question, from mid-1915 on, was how to balance the Americans' threat against the value of pressure exerted against the British. During the summer of 1915 Chief of the General Staff von Falkenhayn said Germany must absolutely avoid bringing the United States into the war.

This issue was argued between the political and military authorities of the German Supreme War Council, the hope being to find a form of U-boat warfare which would not bring the United States into the war on the Allied side. On 19 August 1915 a fresh crisis arose when the liner *Arabic* was sunk, again with Americans on board. The Germans had to reveal to the Americans their new instructions to U-boat commanders not to sink large liners. The incident apparently delayed Bulgarian accession to the Central

Some senior Royal Navy officers believed that the Germans planned to arm numerous merchant ships as raiders and that to that end they routinely carried dismounted guns and ammunition. Their best evidence was German resistance to British proposals, both at The Hague in 1907 and in London in 1909, to prohibit conversion of merchant ships to auxiliary warships on the high seas. In fact the Germans never had such ambitious plans. Their post-war history of cruiser operations argued that they should have made exactly such preparations. Because the Germans had failed to place guns and ammunition on board in peacetime (due in part to resistance on the part of shipping companies), they had to rely on ships in home waters at the outbreak of war and on ships which could be armed by warships on the high seas. On 26 March 1913 Winston Churchill announced that the British were arming food ships for self-defence, each with two 4.7in guns in the stern. The Germans protested that such defensive armament made the ships warships or else illegal, but the British defended their practice. On the outbreak of war thirty-nine ships of nine shipping lines had guns on board, one being the freighter *Argyllshire* of Turnbull, Martin Co., shown here at the end of the war. She made her first voyage as an armed merchant ship on the Australasian trade in November 1913. In 1915, when it became urgent to arm more merchant ships, those which still had their two guns aft surrendered one of them. Hence *Argyllshire* shows only a single gun aft. (Allan C Green via State Library of Victoria)

Powers, which had been expected in August 1915. Bethmann-Hollweg renewed his opposition to unrestricted submarine warfare, opposing both Admiral von Tirpitz and new Admiralstab chief Admiral Bachmann. Bachmann was forced out of the Admiralstab, replaced by Admiral von Holtzendorff. The Kaiser rejected Tirpitz' resignation but felt compelled to order him not to become involved in any naval matter touching on foreign policy. The Kaiser also extended the order sparing large passenger ships to one sparing all passenger ships from attack without warning (30 August 1915).

Between February and September 1915 the Germans sank about 570,000 tons of shipping, a monthly average of about 80,000 tons. That had been achieved by about thirty-five submarines (the Germans were adding about four per month). Given a substantial building programme, the Germans could expect to double their force in the near future and that would probably sink about 160,000 tons per month. Since the newer U-boats were of better design, they could probably sink even more. In a year, the Germans might expect to sink about two million tons of shipping. They knew that the Admiralty had taken over a large fraction of the British merchant fleet (over 1000 ships) and that another large fraction was taken up by the carrying trade to the allies. Due to the expansion of naval construction, British shipbuilding was down to about 650,000 tons per year. U-boats could sink ships faster than they could be built.

In mid-September von Holtzendorff extended the Kaiser's order: to avoid any possible infraction, submarines were to cease attacks on commerce on the West Coast of England and the Channel. In the North Sea they were to abide by the Prize Regulations. Von Holtzendorff held out the possibility that the submarines thus released might be used to attack naval targets. The unrestricted submarine campaign would continue in the Mediterranean, where it was unlikely to encounter Americans (the Italian liner *Ancona* was sunk on 23 November 1915, but American protests were avoided because the U-boat was flying the Austro-Hungarian flag). High Seas Fleet commander von Pohl and Flanders commander von Schröder abandoned submarine attacks on commerce in the North Sea as impractical. The U-boats turned instead to minelaying, which no one now protested.

None of this indicated general agreement with Bethmann-Hollweg and, by implication, von Falkenhayn. Towards the end of 1915 von Falkenhayn became less pessimistic. Bulgaria had joined the Central Powers and Serbia had been occupied by the Austrians, so there was now a secure land connection between Germany and Turkey. It seemed to von Falkenhayn that the Central Powers could win even if the United States entered the war. However, he doubted that the land forces could end the war in 1916. Could unrestricted submarine warfare defeat England that year? On 30 December 1915 von Holtzendorff said yes. A submarine offensive begun after the end of the winter – *i.e.*, under suitable weather conditions – could break the British in, at most, half a year. During that half-year American reinforcements would have little effect. Moreover, a U-boat offensive was the only effective weapon left to Germany. Tirpitz strongly concurred.

The Supreme War Council debated the issue in January and February 1916. Before any decision could be reached, a fleet proposal was received: armed merchant ships (but not passenger liners) should be attacked without warning. On 4 March 1916 the Kaiser decided that the general unrestricted submarine warfare demanded by army and navy was still to be postponed, but that

enemy merchant ships in the war zone could be sunk on sight; armed enemy merchant ships outside the war zone could be sunk on sight; but enemy passenger ships should not be attacked. Tirpitz regarded this solution as impractical; it placed too great a burden on a submarine commander. This time (12 March 1916) the Kaiser accepted his resignation.

As might be imagined, the rules were easier to write than to follow. On 24 March *UB 29* torpedoed the unarmed French passenger ship *Sussex*, having mistaken her for an armed auxiliary. American citizens were again killed and the US government again threatened to break relations. The new submarine campaign was suspended by a 24 April 1916 order. U-boats were now released to support the High Seas Fleet directly. Neither High Seas Fleet commander Scheer nor Flanders commander Schröder considered it worthwhile to employ U-boats in stop-and-examine commerce warfare. The only real advantage of abandoning unrestricted submarine warfare was that US President Wilson was now likely to focus instead on the British conduct of their own blockade.

After Jutland, High Seas Fleet commander Admiral Scheer became a strong advocate of unrestricted submarine warfare. His August 1916 sortie convinced him further of the capabilities of his U-boats, so he pressed his case. Scheer's advocacy bore odd fruit. On 6 October Admiralstab chief Admiral von Holzendorff issued an order in the Kaiser's name: the U-boats were to be concentrated against trade, but were to follow the Prize Rules.[43] In the North Sea, the trade war was to be supported, as far as possible, by surface craft. Any purely military role for the U-boats, either in support of the High Seas Fleet or independently, was to be subordinated to the war against trade. By this time Scheer believed that his submarines were a more and more important part of his fleet's combat power, so losing them was most unwelcome. Scheer considered the Prize Rules suicidal for U-boats (it happened that the Flanders U-boats operated successfully under them). He could countenance the loss of his submarines only if they were to be devoted to unrestricted submarine warfare. The Admiralstab was holding back in view of the threat of US intervention – as perceived by Chancellor Bethmann-Hollweg.

By August 1916 the Chancellor admitted that no doubt an unrestricted submarine campaign was coming, but not yet. The neutrals in question this time were the Danes and the Dutch, not the Americans. The Germans needed a new force to deal with Romania, which had just joined the Allies. To assemble it they had to drain the forces guarding the borders with the two European neutrals.[44] The new army leadership (Hindenburg and Ludendorff) did not take maritime or economic issues into account. In August they were focussed on the immediate crisis in the land war, the Russians and Italians advancing and the new threat posed by Romania. By early October the situation was improving. The fall of the Romanian capital Bucharest (6 December) brought considerable relief. By that time, too, the German General Staff was working to push Russia out of the war by inserting revolutionaries (notably Lenin) into the country. On the other hand, there was no real prospect of breaking the deadlock in the West. In December 1916 the Germans offered peace terms, which they imagined the Allies might accept as a way of dealing with the deadlock. They were rejected as unacceptable.

By late 1916 conditions in Germany favoured renewal of unrestricted submarine warfare. For some time the Admiralstab had claimed that the submarines could put Britain out of the war in six to eight months.[45] The Reichstag parties enthusiastically supported the supposedly magic weapon. In October the Centrum Party announced that it would keep supporting the Chancellor only if he accepted unrestricted submarine warfare.[46] The final decision to undertake unrestricted submarine warfare was taken without the protracted debate surrounding the earlier decisions. Ludendorff wrote to Bethmann-Hollweg in December 1916 that the success of a French counter-attack at Verdun convinced him that the war could no longer be decided on land. The only remaining card was unrestricted submarine warfare.

On 8 January 1917 a conference of German naval and military leaders formally decided on the campaign, but presumably Ludendorff's decision and the politics of the Reichstag made that a forgone conclusion. Scheer was an enthusiastic supporter, but he and his staff were careful not to claim that the campaign would end the war within a set time. They only estimated that 500,000 tons per month would be sunk.[47] When he arrived the next day, Bethmann-Hollweg pointed out that the United States would now enter the war. Could the U-boats sink the transports bringing American troops to Europe? Scheer's operations officer said that they would sink whatever ships they encountered.[48] Bethmann-Hollweg did not resist and the Kaiser approved resumption of unrestricted submarine warfare, to begin on 1 February. Scheer turned out to be right: the U-boats really could sink about 500,000 tons each month.

By October 1916 the British were aware that a massive new U-boat campaign was coming. They took measures to use shipping more efficiently (a Ministry of Shipping was created in December 1916), to reduce consumption and to produce more food at home. Rationing was introduced before the campaign began. They amassed whatever reserve of wheat they could before the attack began. For example, the American harvest was expected to be poor, so the British contracted for additional wheat from Australia, despite the increased shipping load it imposed. The week before 1 February showed the greatest weekly import of wheat. Efforts were also made to boost home production of food.[49] The most important short-term measure seems to have been rationing.

The German campaign panicked shipowners, to the point that neutral ships were unwilling to sail until the British Ministry of Blockade refused clearances to leave British ports until it received assurances that equivalent tonnage of the same registry had cleared for Britain from foreign ports.[50] By putting all North Sea shipping at risk, the U-boats dramatically cut shipments into Denmark, the Netherlands, Norway and Sweden: 313 ships between February and April 1917, compared to 1070 between February and April 1915. Heavy losses to British shipping made it more and more difficult to support operations around the periphery of Europe; Jellicoe demanded reductions in the Anglo-French force in Salonika (only limited withdrawals were made). A French proposal to invade Greece so as to attack Austria-Hungary had to be rejected for lack of supporting shipping. To a limited extent the British benefitted when the North American harvest turned out better than expected, as it required far less shipping (in ship-time terms) than the Australian.

The German campaign failed. It is not clear how close it ever came to success. Shipping losses peaked in April 1917 at 869,103 tons, but with the introduction of convoy they began to decline in May. Shipping production and, at least as importantly, repair were considerably increased (unrepaired damage reduced ship capacity by 10 per cent from February to June 1917). Although Allied shipping losses during the first six months of the campaign more than met Scheer's promises, the British did not come close to collapse at the time.

The German reaction to the British declaration that the North Sea was a military area was unrestricted submarine warfare. They turned the declaration that neutrals were taking their chances (actually against German mines) in the North Sea into a declaration that when they entered a zone around the British Isles they were taking their chances of being torpedoed without warning. This was actually a form of commerce raiding rather than blockade, the new feature being indiscriminate attack. It was feasible because in 1915 U-boats were nearly impossible to detect or attack. At the time U-boats were the only German warships essentially immune to the British naval blockade, except that they could run afoul of mines. Here a U-boat surrenders at Harwich in 1918; the Royal Navy officer on deck is examining her papers.

HMS *Theseus* is shown bulged for bombardment duty. The centreline 9.2in guns were replaced by 6in, the ships retaining their earlier broadside battery of ten 6in (in April 1918 *Edgar* and *Grafton* each had only one centreline 6in). Work began in December 1914. At least *Theseus* was completed the next March (the April 1915 armament list shows her as the only rearmed ship in the class). In addition to bulges, the ships were given timber stiffening (very visible on the side of *Theseus*) and prominent bow gallows for bow protection against mines. The ships lost 4 knots of speed but seakeeping and handling were reportedly not changed. Thus modified, *Grafton* survived a torpedo on 11 June 1917 and *Edgar* survived an April 1918 hit. All four served in the Dardanelles and then in the Mediterranean.

CHAPTER 4
Expectations versus Reality

I T IS OFTEN SUGGESTED that most naval officers of the pre-1914 generation were obsessed with the new technology and hence neglected to think about how it would be used. Much the same was later said of US nuclear submarine officers. It certainly took considerable effort to master the technical aspects of new ships and weapons. However, there was lively interest in the tactical implications of the new technology. If anything, there seems to have been too much appreciation of where the technology might lead and too little of its current limitations. In

Britain Admiral Fisher seems to have been the leading example of the problem. He could see the tactical implications of such new technologies as torpedoes and long-range wireless, but he grossly down-played current limitations. He seems to have had little or no interest in promoting exercises which might have highlighted steps needed to achieve what he expected the new technology to deliver. That is particularly obvious in hindsight in his approach to naval strategy using ocean surveillance via radio intelligence.

Lessons of the Russo-Japanese War

The most recent naval war, the Russo-Japanese War, was largely a fleet-on-fleet fight. Neither side had so many battleships that it could afford many losses and neither had any hope of adding them in wartime (the Russians tried but failed to buy several ships). Merchant shipping and blockade hardly figured in the war, but naval supremacy certainly did. At the outset, the Japanese considered the large Russian Pacific Fleet based in Port Arthur the single great obstacle to moving an invasion force across the Sea of Japan to Manchuria, the prize they sought. The Russians also had Baltic and Black Sea Fleets, which they could deploy (albeit laboriously) to reinforce the Port Arthur force. They could move troops, again somewhat laboriously, from European Russia to the Far East via the Trans-Siberian Railway.

In February 1904 Japanese destroyers successfully penetrated Port Arthur in an attempt to solve the problem at the outset. This attack was not very successful; torpedoes did not match their advertising. The idea of a surprise attack made a considerable impression on other navies and the Port Arthur attack may have inspired the attack on Pearl Harbor a quarter-century later. An initial fleet-on-fleet battle was also indecisive. Afterwards a Japanese

mine sank the Russian Pacific Fleet flagship, killing its charismatic leader Admiral Makarov. His successor was a lot less aggressive, perhaps fearing that the Japanese had closed the mouth of Port Arthur with mines. The Japanese thus gained sufficient sea control to land their army. It seized enough ground to emplace heavy mortars on the heights above Port Arthur. They sank most of the ships inside the base during a lengthy siege. The Russians sought to lift the siege by bringing their more powerful Baltic Fleet halfway around the world into the Sea of Japan. By the time it arrived, Port Arthur had fallen. The Japanese destroyed the Baltic Fleet at the battle of Tsushima, which helped shape expectations for fleet battle in the next war.

The role of heavy guns was changing dramatically as the war was fought. Until very recently they had fired very slowly, the faster medium-calibre guns being considered decisive (the heavy guns were reserved to deal with the heaviest armour). Advances in turret design also made the heaviest guns far more usable. Experience at Tsushima in effect ratified a growing opinion that the heaviest guns were the weapons of the future. An increasing rate of fire was crucial, because it was assumed that the effect of shellfire would be cumulative. To disable or sink an opponent, a ship had to pour in a considerable volume of fire. That might mean fire by a numerous battery of large-calibre guns on a sustained basis. This perception was an important basis for the dreadnought revolution in capital ship design.

By way of contrast, it was understood that an underwater weapon – a torpedo or mine – could disable or sink a ship with a single hit. However, the chance of a hit by a slow-moving torpedo was considerably less than that with a fast-firing gun. In 1904 torpedo range was beginning to increase dramatically with the introduction of heaters, a simple form of internal combustion. At least in the Royal Navy, an important reason for extending heavy gun range was to keep British battleships out of torpedo range of enemy battleships. At least in theory, the art of successful naval battle was to combine guns and underwater weapons using new tactics.

Although torpedoes were relatively ineffective during the war, mines were quite the opposite. Their success led both the Royal Navy and the US Navy to convert cruisers to specialised minelayers (the Germans already had them). The Japanese revealed to the British that at Tsushima one of their destroyers sank a

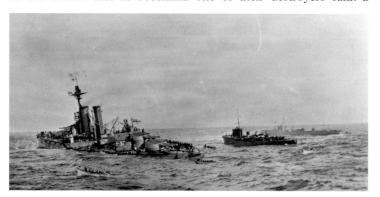

For naval thinkers in 1914, the great question was how to use guns and torpedoes in action. It was assumed that even a single underwater hit could be fatal – as when a single German mine sank the new dreadnought HMS *Audacious* in the Irish Sea on 27 October 1914. In fact it turned out that such ships could often survive multiple underwater hits. (Abrahams via Dr David Stevens, SPC-A)

Russian battleship by laying a pair of connected floating mines in her path. By 1909 the floating-mine attack was a standard Japanese tactic. Destroyers passing 1000 to 2000m ahead of the enemy, on the same course, would drop mines, then steam away at maximum speed. Although analysis showed that such mines were not particularly effective, the idea made a considerable impact on Director of Naval Ordnance John Jellicoe. It almost certainly explains Jellicoe's repeated wartime statements that the Germans planned to lay mines in the path of his fleet. Many German destroyers were fitted for minelaying, but of a more conventional sort. The floating-mine report appeared at about the same time the Royal Navy became interested in re-integrating destroyers into its battle fleet. On 24 April 1913 First Sea Lord ordered that all destroyers of 'River' and later classes should carry four mines each on the upper deck (each with 120lbs of TNT), the mines normally to be drifting but suitable for mooring. Little came of this idea, because the mines were never developed. However, 'L' class destroyers carried mine rails until 1915.

The Japanese experience at Tsushima did not address other important questions. The most difficult was how to find the enemy at the outset. In the past, it was assumed that at the outset one fleet would blockade the other in its port. When the enemy tried to get to sea, the blockading fleet would attack and destroy it. During the late nineteenth century, that became less and less attractive because a blockading fleet made a good torpedo target. Initially that meant that the attacking fleet could not penetrate the enemy's harbour, because it might be infested with small torpedo craft. Soon the torpedo boats grew to the point where they could operate well offshore and the area within sight of the enemy port became too hot to occupy. It might still be possible to station fast cruisers within sight of the enemy port. By 1904 early forms of radio had made it possible for such ships to provide an offshore fleet with sufficient warning. However, the trend was not good and the advent of seagoing submarines would make traditional forms of blockade altogether impossible.

At Tsushima the situation was simplified. The Russian fleet had to pass through a narrow strait (which gave its name to the battle). Japanese cruisers in the strait gave Admiral Togo sufficient indication of the approach path of the Russians for him to deploy appropriately. Once guns began to fire and coal-burning ships were steaming at high speed, no Admiral on his bridge could easily see (or communicate with) most of his fleet. Increasing gun range expanded the battle space, making it even more difficult for the Admiral even to visualise what was happening. No one said as much in 1904, but increasing numbers of ships also made it nearly impossible for an Admiral to maintain a mental picture of what was happening around him.

At Tsushima, Togo split his fleet into two squadrons because he doubted that a single officer could control more than eight ships. Later the choice was between such 'divisional tactics' and the tactics of a single concentrated fleet. Tsushima demonstrated both the potential of divisional tactics and their dangers. In theory one squadron was to support the other, but in fact the force split up. Togo was fortunate that one squadron did not fire on the other (it may have helped that the two fleets were very differently painted). The split offered the Russians valuable opportunities, which fortunately for Togo they wasted. In more modern terms, the issue was how to maintain both control and situational awareness on the part of the fleet commander.

Seapower and Seaborne Trade

In the popular mind, seapower in 1914 meant capital ships, or perhaps large cruisers standing in for them. Naval supremacy would be decided by a fight between the two opposing fleets. In fact the maritime prize was free use of the sea coupled with the ability to deny free use to the enemy. The capital ship fight was expected to determine who could use lesser warships to block enemy trade and to protect friendly trade. For example, it took large numbers of ships to stop numerous merchant ships. They could not possibly survive in the face of enemy capital ships. As a covering force, the Grand Fleet had to be able to fight and win a battle against the concentrated German High Seas Fleet, because if the High Seas Fleet broke out it could wipe out British shipping and also the British ships enforcing the blockade against Germany. Naval warfare was always about who could and who could not freely use the sea.

Despite much post-war talk to the contrary, the demands of trade protection shaped British naval policy – and even foreign policy – for decades prior to the war. The great charge against the Admiralty is that by the First World War it had lightly abandoned the successful trade protection policy of the past, convoy. Convoy Acts forced merchant ship owners to submit to Royal Navy orders and to join convoys with escorts. It was argued after the war that convoy had been abandoned because as a defensive strategy it was inferior to a more offensive form of protection, hunting down U-boats. The reality was considerably more complex.

Prior to the unrestricted U-boat campaign, the threat was cruisers, which combined high performance with endurance and firepower. With the advent of large fast liners, there was considerable pre-war speculation that they might represent a new kind of threat, but in practice armed liners were ineffective.[1] In 1915 the Germans commissioned a new kind of auxiliary cruiser, a merchant ship operating in disguise (it was called an auxiliary cruiser ['Hilfskreuzer']). Similar ships were used during the next war. In neither case did they contribute seriously to commerce destruction.

Convoy died by the 1870s because with the advent of steam the Royal Navy had fewer and fewer ships which could match modern merchant ship performance (endurance at speed).[2] Late nineteenth-century British war plans envisaged attacking French convoys and Russian outposts, at which commerce-raiding cruisers would be based. Troopships sent out for this purpose would be convoyed, but there was no hope of providing enough fast long-range cruisers to convoy most merchant ships. The only option was somehow to hunt raiding cruisers down. In December 1874 First Naval Lord Admiral Milne wrote an analysis of trade protection which shaped future policy. He argued that a commerce raider would be drawn into the areas where the great sea routes were concentrated – what were later called focal areas. Raiders would find themselves drawn into the focal areas, where they would meet British cruisers which would destroy them. Milne identified eighteen such areas. Even a focal area defence required numerous cruisers, which the British built.

It happened that the British enjoyed an important advantage. By far the best steaming coal in the world came from Wales and was controlled by British companies. Protecting overseas stores of this coal, which were mainly in British-controlled harbours, would go a long way towards immobilising raiders. In this sense the direct defence of British colonial harbours was a means of trade protection.

The focal area strategy was never made public, because

Pre-dreadnoughts were much more vulnerable to underwater damage. HMS *King Edward VII* sinks after being mined off Cape Wrath on 6 January 1916. In much the same way, the German pre-dreadnought *Pommern* was lost to a single torpedo hit the night after Jutland, but German dreadnoughts survived multiple torpedoes. (SPC-A)

implicit in it was acceptance of heavy early losses in exchange for the destruction of the enemy raiders. The problem would be solved in the first months of the war. This may seem bizarre. In fact in 1960 the US Navy's position on trade protection was that it would be compelled to accept losses of about 100 merchant ships per month for the first three months of a naval war against the Soviet submarine force, during which time the Soviet force would be destroyed. The US strategy involved some convoying, but it was assumed that convoy would be ineffective against modern submarines. The emphasis was on blocking choke points and hunting using long-range detection. This was very much reminiscent of pre-First World War thinking about trade protection.

Unfortunately an attacker did not have to match the Royal Navy's numbers; it could build a few cruisers which could overmatch the focal-point ships. In the 1890s new lightweight steels made it possible to build fast armoured cruisers. Focal-point cruisers had to deal with whatever came their way. Armoured cruisers had other roles, too, such as fleet scouts and screens, but probably trade protection was the most punishing financially for the Royal Navy. By 1904 the British policy of maintaining a sufficient edge over the next two naval powers (France and Russia) meant maintaining a 2 to 1 advantage in armoured cruisers, presumably meaning roughly equal numbers as fleet scouts and as trade protection ships. To fill the focal areas the Royal Navy needed about as many armoured cruisers as it had battleships. Unfortunately a big armoured cruiser cost about as much as a battleship.

The Royal Navy was the single largest item in the British budget and the budget exploded with the rise of armoured cruisers. In 1896–7, before the British began building such ships, the British national budget was £101.5 million, of which £23.8 million (23.4 per cent) went to the Royal Navy. In 1904–5 it was £142 million, of which £41 million (28.8 per cent) went to the Royal Navy.[3] The 1904–5 figure was worse than it looked, because the total budget was still swollen by increased army expenses related to the Boer War. The British sought an ally for the first time in their peacetime history at just this time, surely to balance off part of the Franco-

Russian cruiser threat to British trade, the lifeblood of the Empire. The British first approached the Germans (as a counter to France), but found their terms unacceptable.[4] The alternative was Japan, which could neutralise the Russians in the Far East. The Russian Far East threat was not so much to important British possessions (mainly Australia and New Zealand at this time), but to Far Eastern, including Indian, trade using large long-range cruisers.

Even with the Japanese alliance, the British faced a large French cruiser force, which could be based outside European waters the Admiralty might hope to control. The financial crisis was not quite as bad, but it still loomed. 'Jacky' Fisher was brought to the Admiralty in 1904 to solve it. He realised that if there could never be enough cruisers to fill out the focal areas, then enemy raiders would have to be hunted down. However, if the Admiralty kept track of British trade it would also be keeping track of losses to enemy cruisers. On that basis it could direct cruisers to hunt down the raiders. The new W/T technology would make direction more efficient. Fisher reorganised the Trade Division formed in 1901 as a trade tracking centre, the forerunner of a related ocean surveillance operation. These initiatives built on Fisher's experience as Mediterranean C-in-C, using code-breaking to predict the movements of the French and Russian fleets he faced.

As long as the Germans relied on cruisers (including armed merchant cruisers), the policy Fisher had developed worked. It took enormous effort to hunt down some of the cruisers, but they did not last long. The Germans later enjoyed some success with disguised armed merchant cruisers like SMS *Moewe*, because even when spotted they could not necessarily be identified as warships by the cruisers hunting them. As an immediate defence while the German cruisers were hunted down, the naval war college recommended dispersal, as raiders relied on known trade routes to find their quarry. Dispersal might be the best protection. When war broke out in 1914, among the first Admiralty instructions to merchant ship owners was to shift away from the established routes.[5]

The great surprise of the First World War was that a particular kind of raider, the submarine, could pass right through any barrier created by surface forces. For U-boats, British supremacy on the surface of the sea was irrelevant – unless, as at Zeebrugge, it translated into an ability to destroy the submarines in their base. At the outset submarines were not counted as viable commerce raiders because they could not be used effectively without violating internationally-understood rules of war.

It proved possible to protect a ship against underwater damage by bulging, building protective structures outside her hull. Four *Edgar* class cruisers were the first British warships to be blistered (they were the only cruisers so modified). This is the bulge built onto HMS *Endymion*. The bowsprit was part of a bow protection device against mines, a predecessor of the paravane. The four modified *Edgars* went to the Dardanelles, where they were considerably more survivable than the pre-dreadnoughts previously sent there. None of the pre-dreadnoughts were bulged and the shipyard effort involved was too great to allow installation on board existing Grand Fleet capital ships. However, in May 1915 permission was given to bulge the incomplete *Ramillies*. Her sister-ships *Revenge* and *Resolution* were later fitted (in, respectively, October 1917 – February 1918 and late 1917 – May 1918). Surprisingly, the bulges in these ships did not cost speed. The *Renowns* and the 'large light cruisers' were all built with 'internal' bulges which did not cost speed.

Tactics: Gun and Torpedo

In the 1890s tactics often meant fleet manoeuvring in elaborate patterns (a well-known photograph of the time showed the British Mediterranean Fleet battleships executing the 'gridiron', in which lines of ships passed through other lines). By 1914 tactics meant how to manoeuvre a fleet so as to destroy or evade another fleet. The large numbers of the past had given way to smaller numbers of individually much more powerful ships.

Gun and torpedo ranges both expanded enormously during the pre-war decade. Fleets spread out. As a result, the battle space expanded to the point where an Admiral on his bridge could no longer easily see or understand what was happening. Even if he could have seen all of his ships under good conditions, in combat his vision was badly compromised by the combination of funnel smoke (inevitable for coal-burning warships) and gunsmoke. That combination was first really experienced at Tsushima in 1904.

In 1914 only the Royal Navy had the slightest idea of how to solve the problem. Commanding the Grand Fleet, Admiral Jellicoe adopted a suggestion by his fleet gunnery officer Captain Frederic Dreyer that he use a plot to visualise the positions of his own and enemy ships. In effect it was a small-scale equivalent to the strategic plot being developed at the Admiralty, first to visualise trade patterns (and find raiders) and then to control a fleet operating in the North Sea.[6] Plotting had an unsuspected consequence. It was impossible to reproduce the flagship's plot precisely, even if all the ships in the fleet were maintaining their own plots. Only the fleet commander, looking at his plot, could draw the implications needed for command. The plot did make it possible for the commander to assign, for example, a fast division where it might be needed, but it did not provide for him to devolve command to divisional commanders – who would not have sufficient plots of their own. The plot, moreover, made the C-in-C hostage to the accuracy of the information provided by his ships, which acted as his sensors.

Successful plotting involved not simply the location (at some particular time) of an enemy force, but its course and speed, so that it could be projected ahead and appropriate action taken. At Jutland, as Beatty's Battlecruiser Fleet fell back on the supporting Grand Fleet, Jelicoe's signalman asked for the enemy's course and speed. Beatty, who seems not to have understood how important that might be, could signal only the direction to the enemy, which did not really help. Jellicoe managed to learn enough, probably from the smoke of the German fleet on the horizon, to estimate their course and speed and his simple plot made it possible for him to deploy his fleet on the appropriate course. The achievement was not only that he crossed the enemy's T, but also that he avoided the entirely possible head-on approach which would have been so dangerous, at least in his eyes.

Jellicoe certainly realised that plotting required that his ships, particularly his scouts, report regularly and that they give the positions of the enemy ships they spotted. His wartime orders emphasise the need for including their own positions when reporting. However, plotting as a tactical information system appears not to have been tested before Jutland. Jellicoe seems not to have understood how much testing tactical plotting demanded. Perhaps the great surprise was that without precise navigation plotting could not be effective. As early as 1906 a British cruiser admiral pointed out that using W/T for scouting (i.e., abandoning chains of ships repeating back to the flagship) carried risks because

reported positions might well be several miles off. That might not matter too much, because in a coal-burning era all ships smoked (though the Royal Navy's Welsh steaming coal smoked less than most), hence could be seen beyond the horizon. However, ultimately what mattered was a series of reports on the same enemy ships by different scouts. The plot made it possible to combine such data to deduce the course and speed of the enemy. The results made sense only if enemy positions were indicated consistently. Otherwise the plotter would deduce an altogether wrong course and speed. Unfortunately the point of the plot was to predict where the enemy was going, which depended on his course and speed. The most famous aspect of Jellicoe's plot at Jutland was its use to estimate the threat posed by enemy torpedoes. Several officers were detailed specifically to plot torpedo tracks and Jellicoe kept their plot within sight. Later it was suggested that errors in plotting made him overestimate the threat.

Failure always teaches more than success and Jellicoe learned a great deal from the failure of the attempt to intercept the German fleet after their Scarborough Raid in November 1914. The British light cruisers – the fleet's scouts – made contact but failed to report it properly. Cruiser commander Commodore Goodenough disengaged due to a poorly-drafted signal sent by Admiral Beatty, who wanted to detach one of his cruisers to screen him against German destroyers he might encounter. Scarborough was the first success of British signals intelligence and Jellicoe, Beatty and Churchill thought it might well be the single golden opportunity to destroy the German fleet. Jellicoe and Beatty fastened on the cruiser failure, because had the cruisers held contact the battleships could have followed up. In one way the problem was the peacetime assumption that the force commander knew all and had to be obeyed. In another it was poor understanding of the full role of a scout, the most important part of which was full reporting of the enemy's position, course, speed and composition. Commanding the British battlecruisers, Admiral Beatty was all for dismissing cruiser commander Commodore Goodenough in favour of one of his battlecruiser captains. Fortunately Goodenough survived to render excellent scouting service at Jutland. His failure at Scarborough explains numerous injunctions in Jellicoe's fleet orders demanding reliable reporting by scouts.

Before Jutland, Admiral Jellicoe did his best to ensure that his scouting captains would report enemy positions and courses, so that he could form a full tactical picture. All Grand Fleet warships were required to maintain plots, on the basis of which they could (and should) report. However, the system was apparently not tested during fleet exercises, so Jellicoe was unaware of the dramatic effects serious navigational errors could have. Given bad data, the plot on his flagship could easily show ships doing impossible things – appearing to make 60 knots, say, or no more than 3 knots. Jellicoe may have suffered particularly badly from slapdash navigation on the part of ships of the Battlecruiser Fleet. After Jutland ships were required to maintain plots in terms of distance and bearing from the flagship, rather than in absolute terms of position. The use of relative positions largely solved the problem, except for ships, such as distant scouts, reporting from beyond the horizon.

Contemporary documents reveal no discussion of plotting or its profound implications and historians of Jutland have mentioned it only in passing. However, the Grand Fleet analyses of fleet exercises in 1918 always included a section on Navigation and Plotting, evaluating ships' performance in this vital subject. For all the navies allied to the British, tactical plotting must have been a revelation. All of them adopted plotting post-war and it proved key to the night battle tactics used successfully by the British and the Japanese during the Second World War.[7] The Germans had no equivalent. A neglected aspect of the battle of Jutland was that German commander Admiral Scheer continuously felt confused as he tried to extricate his fleet from the British. He had, it appears, very little sense of where ships were.

British wargame rules indicate what heavy guns were expected to do. British officers were familiar with them because they were used to evaluate success in frequent tactical (PZ) exercises. As of 1912 British exercise rules (quoted in instructions Admiral Jellicoe issued for tactical experiments) assumed that at 10,000 yds it would take 75 minutes for a modern battleship (like HMS *Hercules*) to disable another such ship. At 15,000 yds, it would take 300 minutes – five hours, an unimaginably long time. Yet 10,000 yds was the sort of range sought to keep battleships out of torpedo range of each other. It is no surprise that the Royal Navy became interested in concentrating the fire of several ships. Admiral Jellicoe credited torpedoes with 10,000 yds range at 30 knots – a distance they would cover in ten minutes. It must have seemed impossible that any battleship, or even any pair of battleships, could deal with her opposite in line that quickly. These figures are enough to explain why the Royal Navy adopted heavier guns. Official wargame rules issued in July 1913 took 12,000 yds as the maximum range for 12in and 13.5in guns.[8] According to these rules it would take about 20 minutes for one *King George V* to neutralise another at 7000 yds and about 26.5 minutes at 10,000 yds. These rules reflected what British naval officers thought would happen in battle. The rules imply that even at 7000 yds it would take a long time to destroy an enemy battleship. The great wartime surprise, particularly at Jutland, was that gunfire did not have to be cumulative to be effective. The destruction of three British battle-cruisers by what appeared to be single hits shocked not only the British but also the Germans. Later it turned out that horribly flawed British magazine practices had made these hits as effective as they were.

During the period after 1904, the Royal Navy sought longer and longer gun ranges so that its battleships could fight outside the range of torpedoes fired by enemy battleships. Ultimately North Sea weather limited gun range most of the time, but torpedoes kept improving. Trials in 1908 showed that a lengthened 21in torpedo could reach 10,000 yds at 30 knots and Jellicoe assumed this performance in tactical trials he conducted in 1912. The 21in Mk II which equipped British battleships in 1914 had a range of 10,000 yds at 28 knots. The German G7 was credited with 10,000m at 27 knots.

It proved difficult to keep increasing gunnery range whatever the weather. British fleet performance in 1911 was so disappoint-ing that a special gunnery conference was called. In 1912 Battle Practice range was decreased from 9000 to 8000 yds. No explanation was given, but shorter ranges would have been consistent with the belief that North Sea conditions would make longer ones irrelevant. Partly as a result of reducing range, the eight best ships made better than 30 per cent hits in 1912, whereas in 1909 the fleet average had been about 20 per cent. Apparently existing gunnery techniques had reached their limit. It would take considerable investment in new technology to maintain the hitting rate while much raising Battle Practice range – which measured the

fleet's capability. The fleet would usually fight at or inside typical Battle Practice ranges. That was not to deny that, under good visibility, it might open fire at greater ranges.

One of the great wartime surprises was that the battles were fought at long ranges because fleets were unlikely to get into contact *except* when visibility was excellent. The failure to engage after the Scarborough Raid is a case in point: contact was lost partly due to poor weather (and partly, it should be added, due to a gross signalling blunder on Admiral Beatty's part). That ships could and would engage at great ranges particularly surprised the Germans, who had justified a policy of using smaller-calibre higher-velocity guns on the basis of expected short North Sea ranges.

The 1911 Admiralty conference did not mention it, but by that time the Royal Navy was developing a new kind of analogue computer fire control under contract to Anthony Hungerford Pollen. Pollen's Argo Clock modelled the firing situation to predict the range and bearing to which shells should be fired. Although Pollen had a monopoly contract, the Admiralty was also supporting an analogous system under development by its rangefinder firm, Barr & Stroud. Gunnery officer Frederic Dreyer was promoting a much simpler device which used a geometric approximation to predict range, without any modelling. In 1912 plans called for comparative trials of the Argo Clock and the Dreyer Table, but they were never carried out. Instead, the simpler and far less expensive Dreyer Table equipped most British ships during the First World War. It was a variation on the device most navies used to predict range: a 'clock' fed with the measured or estimated rate at which the range was changing. If the rate itself did not change very rapidly, using a constant rate was not too bad an approximation. The more sophisticated analogue computer was more flexible and it could allow for manoeuvres by the firing ship. During the war the US Navy adopted the modelling technique in the form of the Ford Rangekeeper, which seems to have been derived from the Argo Clock. The Germans used a simpler range clock fed with an estimated range rate.

Jellicoe seems to have opted for longer range despite reduced effectiveness. As commander of the Second Division of the Home Fleet in 1910–12, he issued war orders: if weather permitted he would open fire at 15,000 yds and develop maximum fire at 12,000 to 13,000 yds. He expressly cautioned against going inside 7000 yds, for fear of torpedoes. Apart from his 13.5in superdread-noughts, Jellicoe's fleet could not achieve much very rapidly at 10,000 yds.[9]

In October 1913 Home Fleet commander Admiral Sir George A Callaghan issued war orders envisaging opening fire at 15,000 yds (if weather permitted), closing to a 'decisive range' of 8000 to 10,000 yds where superiority of fire might be established.[10] Ships might press home attacks at shorter ranges. No one had yet tried really long-range firing. Callaghan called for experiments to determine maximum effective range. The only ones he was able to run before the war were at about 14,000 yds. This figure is interesting because explicit war orders seem to have assumed that the fleet could fight at much greater ranges – as in fact it did during the war.

Both Callaghan and his successor Jellicoe planned to open fire at a range beyond that it which many shells would hit in order to establish 'fire supremacy'. Having done that, they would close in to fire at a more practicable range. It would take a storm of shells to have the desired effect at that range. In order to allow for the wasted long-range shots, ships had to carry much more ammunition. To be able to fire steadily at long range, in 1913 Admiral Callaghan ordered ammunition added well beyond the usual eighty rounds per gun. In half an hour a gun might well fire sixty rounds and enough had to be left for the short-range action. Once war began, this likelihood that shells would be expended before ships closed to effective range became worrisome: surviving orders issued in 1914–15 explicitly warn against such waste. It must have been difficult both to urge gunners to open fire *and* not to waste. Yet there was no way to expand magazines.

Overloading magazines made for congestion at the bottoms of ammunition hoists. Extra cordite would crowd the spaces at the bottoms of the powder hoists. Supply to the guns would be anything but fast enough. Comments by German survivors of the Falklands battle must have encouraged attempts to fire faster. They said that slow British fire had made their gunnery easier. If a German ship was smothered in splashes, her gunlayers might well fail to hit altogether. Thus rapid fire was both an offensive *and* a defensive measure. Experience at Dogger Bank reinforced this view. Orders issued early in 1915 emphasised the need for rapid fire. Admiral Beatty sanctioned attempts to overcome congestion by drastically relaxing safety measures, with horrific effects at Jutland.

All of this left open the question of what to do if visibility precluded long-range firing. In that case the battleships would be within torpedo range and they would have only a few minutes of firing time until enemy torpedoes reached them. A battle line in close order was a perfect target for long-range torpedoes, because the ships in it filled so much of the line. These were 'browning' tactics. On land long-range guns fired, not at individuals, but 'into the brown', meaning into the mass of enemy troops. An enemy battle line could be imagined as an extended target. In order to concentrate its fire, its ships had to steam fairly close together – much closer than modern naval officers would consider safe. Perhaps 30 per cent of the total length of the battle line consisted of ships, which suggested that 30 per cent of 'browning' shots by long-range torpedoes would hit. Unlike shells, individual torpedo hits were expected to sink ships. 'Browning' shots figured in British destroyer instructions drafted in 1913.[11]

In *The World Crisis* Winston Churchill remembered that in November 1912 Second Sea Lord Admiral Lord Louis Battenberg warned of the threat of 'browning' shots from the German battle line. About a year later the danger had apparently receded.[12] In Vol III of his history (1927) Churchill summarised what he remembered of pre-war expectations: first the British would smash the German fleet, then they would evade any torpedoes the Germans had launched. Evasion meant following a standardised signal, a blue pennant which ordered each ship to turn away from the enemy line. Ships' fire-control solutions would inevitably be ruined by so radical a turn. Whatever damage they would do would have to be done during the ten minutes or less between coming into torpedo range and turning away.

Churchill's account probably reflects what he was told when serving as First Lord before the war. Smashing means neutralisation. Even at 10,000 yd range, it would take a German torpedo only about ten minutes to reach the British line. Churchill associated the tactics he described with a half-hour engagement. The half hour could well mean a battle opening at much longer range, including an approach phase lasting as much as twenty minutes. During that

time the British would try to achieve the 'fire superiority' Jellicoe sought. However, they would not begin to do devastating damage until the Germans came much closer. To do that they had to fire far more rapidly and more effectively than in the past, which suggests that they expected to use some new technique. A section hurriedly inserted in the wartime edition of the official *Gunnery Manual* describes a new means of rapid-fire control for medium ranges.[13] It was not discussed after the war, as war experience emphasised long-range fire.[14] An exercise Jellicoe conducted in October 1916 shows that by that time he was well aware of the battleship-to-battleship torpedo problem and that he did not consider it solved. The reason was the advent of really long-range torpedoes (15,000 yds or beyond).

When war broke out, the British lacked any proven capability to control guns at long range. That placed Jellicoe in a very different position when he took over the Grand Fleet. The fleet had been trained to fight at 8000 yds or less, well within torpedo range. Effective rapid fire at medium ranges was a future rather than a current proposition. In his initial Grand Fleet Battle Orders Jellicoe told the fleet that it would fight at long range. The British had long (correctly) believed that the Germans wanted to fight at much shorter ranges, where their heavy secondary batteries would be effective. Short range would also favour their favourite manoeuvre of passing torpedo craft through their line to attack the enemy during a gun engagement, not least to break up the enemy line. After the war it seemed that Jellicoe had concluded that since the Germans wanted to fight a close action, it would be advantageous to fight at longer-range, to 'develop and practise the game of long bowls'. It also seemed that Jellicoe had decided to concentrate completely on gunnery.[15] Jellicoe's avoidance of torpedo range made sense. His pre-war experience as DNO and then Third and Second Sea Lords made him painfully aware of the failure of British attempts to develop underwater protection. He believed, again correctly, that the Germans had done much better. His only superiority over the Germans was in long-range heavy gunnery. He was also aware that gunnery, particularly at long range, could not give decisive results in the time available.

Jellicoe had no particular reason to imagine that ships and materiel which had struggled to hit targets at 9000 yds could suddenly hit at 50 per cent greater ranges. His August 1914 draft tactical orders envisaged deploying at 16,000 yds, but opening

The blister could be badly torn up without endangering the ship. This is damage to HMS *Endymion*.

Torpedoes armed many kinds of ships, from capital ships down. Pre-war tacticians had to take into account both torpedo fire from an enemy battle line and possible torpedo fire from enemy destroyers and light cruisers. This is the torpedo room of HMAS *Australia*. (Josef Straczek)

range was dropped from Callaghan's 15,000 yds to 9000–12,000 yds (which he described as long range).[16] Jellicoe expected to benefit heavily from British gunnery superiority at such ranges. These orders suggest that Callaghan's longer-range test firings were less than successful and, moreover, that Jellicoe expected decisive range to be something like 6000 to 8000 yds (no decisive range was cited in the draft orders). A few weeks later Jellicoe issued a radically different Addendum No. 1 to Grand Fleet Battle Orders envisaging opening with 13.5in guns at 15,000 yds and with 12in guns at 13,000 and at even greater ranges should the enemy fire first. Ships would shift to rapid fire at about 10,000 yds. The orders were extraordinary. Almost nothing had been done to practice such firing.

Jellicoe did not intend to open fire beyond 18,000 yds unless the enemy did so, or the conditions required it – as in a chase, which occurred at Dogger Bank. Ships must always be *ready* to fight at extreme ranges. Jellicoe's April 1915 gunnery orders show that to do that he relied on the pre-war technique of bracketing to find the range, which meant not firing the next salvo until the first had splashed and been spotted. Thus at 18,000 yds a 13.5in ship could fire salvos at 50-second intervals (at 12,000 yds, 40 seconds). Once the range had been found, ships would shift to 'rapid salvos', the next salvo being fired as soon as guns were ready. Any spotting corrections would be applied to a later salvo. Heavy guns could fire at least two such salvos each minute. Jellicoe's April 1915 instructions envisaged accelerating to a salvo every 20 seconds once spotting could be discounted (as in rangefinder control). The maximum range envisaged was at least twice pre-war range. Except for directors, nothing had been added to improve performance. Jellicoe later wrote about how hard he had worked the fleet to improve its long-range performance. He was fortunate in having the Moray Firth in which to fire (Beatty's battlecruisers had no such practice area). In 1915 they fired at least twice at 16,000 to 17,000 yds.

Jellicoe's most significant change to Callaghan's battle orders was to assign the two leading pairs of British battleships to concentrate on the two leading German ships (if the fleets were on opposite courses, the two rear pairs would attack the German van). The idea that concentrated fire could break up the German formation became more important after Jutland and was an important post-war theme in British naval tactics. It backfired to some extent at Dogger Bank, when the captain of HMS *Tiger* interpreted it to mean that he should fire on the leading German ship instead of on the ship opposite him. Post-Jutland British fire-control developers accepted that hits would be few and involved new types of salvo firing and spotting designed to make the most of whatever opportunities arose. Pre-war concepts involving rate measurement were abandoned.

After the war many British naval officers expressed their disappointment in Jellicoe's performance at Jutland: why had he failed to come to grips with the Germans? Surely he could have achieved more at shorter ranges. In fact it did not much matter what ranges Jellicoe wanted to adopt. He fired as soon as he could, as the Germans approached and his fleet did not have all that long to fire before the Germans tried to disengage. Jellicoe could have chosen the range only if he had much faster ships.

Soon after war broke out, Jellicoe wrote in his battle orders that he sought action on parallel courses because he thought it would give the most decisive results and because it would avoid the danger of German minelaying: the Germans would not run their own fleet (alongside the British) into a minefield they had laid.[17] This was striking because the object of deployment as developed as early as 1901 (and as practised by Jellicoe at Jutland) was to lay the fleet athwart the path of the enemy fleet, crossing his 'T'. Jellicoe's preference for parallel courses may have been tied to his fire-control capability. The closer the enemy course paralleled his, the lower (and less variable) the range rate and the simpler the fire-control problem. Jellicoe almost certainly associated a low range rate with a high hitting rate. One of the nightmares considered by his officers just before the war was a German reversal of course, which would greatly increase the range rate.[18] Not only that but a fleet on the opposite course would enjoy greater effective torpedo range, because the opposing fleet would be running towards its torpedoes as they ran through the water.

The Germans apparently expected to fight at much shorter ranges. It was generally understood that the Germans considered their gunnery most effective at medium range, about 6000 yds. Evidence included the fact that they had retained medium-calibre (5.9in) guns on board their dreadnoughts, at a cost in weight (for armour or for main-battery guns), on the theory that the smaller faster-firing guns could contribute usefully in a fleet action. As if to confirm British guesses, in his 1915 tactical orders (which the British obtained) German fleet commander von Ingenohl announced that he expected to fight at 6600 to 8800 yds (presumably a translation of 6000 to 8000m).

The Germans had to get to their preferred battle range while the British shelled them from greater ranges. They adopted a tactic of evasive action (zig-zagging) while closing the range, on the theory that it would defeat any British attempt at measuring rates. German comments on British tactics strongly suggest that they were aware of British reliance on plotting to measure rates Because their rate estimates did not involve sustained plotting, the Germans could still exercise effective fire control while manoeuvring Zig-zagging frustrated British fire control, particularly at Jutland and after that battle the British changed their fire-control practices to deal with it. Ironically, a British officer proposing tactics pre-war had suggested exactly this technique, pointing out that fire control would still be possible from a ship moderately zig-zagging, whereas her manoeuvres would frustrate conventional fire control used against her.[19]

Torpedoes could turn a small ship into a giant-killer. Before the war, that meant destroyers and submarines. During the war, the advent of powerful aircraft engines made it possible to build very fast torpedo boats. The first were built in Austria-Hungary, but the British CMBs (Coastal Motor Boats) saw much more action. *CMB 3*, a 40-footer of the initial batch, runs trials. Her hard-chine hull form was based on that of pre-war racing boats. (Dr David Stevens, SPC-A)

Until about 1911 the Germans seem to have thought that by adopting high range rates as they approached the British, they could avoid almost all damage. Then they realised that might not be sufficient protection. If they could fire on the way in, while the range was changing, they might make British fire control ineffective. Observing the Germans, in 1914 the Russians noted that the Germans emphasised radical changes of course and high range rates in their exercises. After Jutland, the Germans told the Austrian Naval Attaché that in their exercises they had always worked with big and rapid alterations of range and exercise firing while turning. They thought the British relied too much on range clocks and hence on measured range rates, which required that they maintain a steady course. In the autumn of 1914 British naval intelligence published the secret German report of gunnery practice for 1912–13.[20] The Germans had recently begun practicing long-range firing under 'difficult conditions', at ranges of 11,000 yds and above. The longest range for any of the capital ships was 15,000 yds. For example, the recent battleship SMS *Kaiser* had fired at 14,000 yds down to 13,500 yds at a closing rate of 43 yds/min. Typical results for heavy ships were 9.2 per cent hits at 12,000 yds.

It is not clear why, without a much higher speed than the British, the Germans thought they could ever close the range, whatever damage the British could or could not do. During the inter-war period, the Royal Navy considered medium range (about 15,000 yds) best and had to solve the Germans' problem, of how to survive while closing an enemy which could hit at much greater range. Among other things, it hoped to use mass destroyer torpedo attacks to help force an enemy into position. The one problem it could not solve was that its battle line was significantly slower than that of its most likely enemy, Japan (this particular problem was unsuspected, as the British did not realise that the Japanese had greatly increased the speeds of their battleships during reconstruction).

Once war broke out, the Germans concentrated on the tactics they had developed to minimise their chances of being hit; their mind-set was fundamentally defensive. They employed the tactics they had designed to get them into fighting range without being destroyed on the way, then stopped closing well before getting there. Thus battle ranges were almost always much longer than the Royal Navy had practiced before the war. The Germans had never expected to achieve much *en route* to decisive range. The destruction they wrought at Jutland was a surprise as much to them as to the British.

The torpedo was radically different from the gun. Each shot was much more lethal, but at long range hitting was far less likely, because the torpedo took so long to reach its target. The navies of the First World War dealt with two dramatic changes in the torpedo. One was the gyro, which ensured that a long-range torpedo would run more or less straight. The gyro could also be set to turn the torpedo away onto a pre-set angled course. Navies differed as to how valuable this feature was, because it required more sophisticated fire control and also because it might make for reduced reliability. The other was the 'heater', a form of internal combustion which dramatically increased torpedo range. By 1914 'heaters' had boosted maximum range from perhaps 1000 yds (1900) to about 10,000 yds or more. Even well before 1910 navies were taking the torpedo seriously as a complement to or even an alternative to guns. The US and Russian Navies and possibly others, seriously considered capital ships whose main batteries would be large numbers of torpedoes. Some British ordnance experts suggested that now the torpedo might be used alongside the gun in a fleet action. It was, however, generally accepted that even a gyro torpedo had limited accuracy at full range.

The torpedo turned a destroyer or even a motor boat into a giant-killer – as the Italians demonstrated when they sank the Austrian battleship *Szent Istvan* in 1918. During the run-up to 1914 admirals had to take into account torpedoes on board both battleships and destroyers (designated torpedo boats in the German navy). The British Mediterranean Fleet integrated torpedo-firing destroyers into its formations beginning about 1900, but as First Sea Lord Admiral Fisher (who had originated the Mediterranean tactics) argued that destroyers should be used independently to dominate the narrow North Sea. The British imagined, wrongly, that the Germans planned to use their destroyers similarly.

Pre-1914 navies treated destroyers not too differently from the way later navies treated aircraft. Discussing fleet torpedo boat tactics, a US Admiral later wrote that of course any battleship which spotted an approaching torpedo boat (or destroyer) would open fire. Waiting for a positive identification would be too dangerous. The surface torpedo firing zone grew rapidly in the years between 1904 and 1914, making the identification problem less and less tractable.

The situation changed after Fisher left the Admiralty and

reports that the Germans were integrating their destroyers into the Grand Fleet gained currency. The Germans practiced a showy manoeuvre in which destroyers on the unengaged side of their battle line passed between their battleships to attack the enemy battle line during the gun action between the two lines. Initially the British reaction was derisory. It would be far more efficient to attach destroyers to the van or the rear of the fleet, to disrupt the enemy line by concentrated attacks on his van or rear. Destroyers venturing into the space between the two fleets would make few hits and would probably be wiped out. However, the German attacks could disrupt the British formation, ruining its gunnery: the German torpedo tactic could be read as a tactical gunnery counter-measure. Until this point, the British saw destroyers as a threat entirely separate from a day gun battle, so their capital ships had their anti-destroyer guns atop their turrets. They switched to protected positions and new capital ships, beginning with the *Iron Duke* class battleships and their battlecruiser equivalent, HMS *Tiger*, had more powerful anti-destroyer guns.

To see what the Royal Navy should do, in 1909–10 Home Fleet commander Admiral William H May conducted exercises.[21] As in the past, he was interested mainly in using destroyers to finish off enemy ships crippled during a gun action, as Admiral Togo had planned to use his own destroyers at Tsushima. Only if weather was misty (visibility less than 8000 yds) could they get close enough to an undamaged and unengaged enemy fleet to attack it before the gun action. However, May did take account of the new long-range torpedoes, which could be used in 'browning' shots against the enemy line rather than against individual ships. In his exercises, destroyers suddenly emerging from the mist made 'browning' shots at 3000 yds.

An exercise seems to have demonstrated the value of 'browning' rather than close-range aimed attacks. White's destroyers emerged from the mist and attacked as Black's fleet began to form battle line out of cruising columns. During that manoeuvre the enemy fleet could not turn away to evade 'browning' shots by the attackers. He would have to rely either on counter-attack by his own destroyers or on his battleships' fire – in which case the battleships might be unable to engage the opposing British battleships. At the least, dreadnoughts would have to assign one turret to anti-destroyer fire, reducing their effective broadsides.

The destroyers could have made a successful 'browning' attack, but in order to hit particular ships they came too close to Black's ships. Black would have been unable to form his battle line unless he had light cruisers to beat off this attack. There would be no time to call the cruisers forward if they were not already present on the wings of the battle fleet. May concluded that in misty weather the destroyers should be well up on both wings of the battle fleet.

If a fleet had already formed, its battleships could turn away together – but that might well lead to great confusion. Once the fleets were engaged, the enemy battleships would be concentrating their efforts on the British battle line. Small ships might not even be too visible in a haze of gun and funnel smoke. Running at maximum speed, destroyers might well survive until they fired. Again, May envisaged 'browning' rather than short-range aimed shots. To avoid being sunk (wasting their torpedoes), destroyers should be able to fire as soon as they came under enemy fire.

Once the battle had begun, destroyers approaching the enemy fleet had to pass through a danger zone extending from 1000 yds in front of the British line to 2000 yds beyond it, but they would be

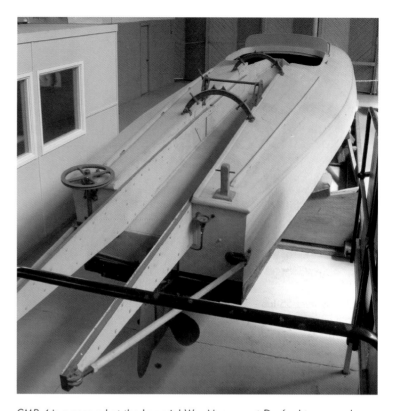

CMB 4 is preserved at the Imperial War Museum at Duxford to remember the great successes CMBs achieved in the Baltic during the British intervention against the Bolsheviks in 1919. The single 18in torpedo was stowed in the trough, head first. A piston, which has not survived, pushed it into the water tail first to launch it. The boat swerved out of the way of the accelerating torpedo. This arrangement made it possible to aim the torpedo (by aiming the boat). Although the cockpit appears to be nearly in the bow, it was actually well astern (abaft the step of the hull) and there was a machine gun position forward. The boat had a single aircraft-type engine driving one propeller. In February 1919 the British Secret Service asked Lieutenant Augustus Agar RN to run agents into St Petersburg. In June, Agar made the small harbour of Terrioki, three miles from the Russo-Finnish border, his base. It was 35 miles from St Petersburg. His two 40-footers were towed from Abo, Finland to Terrioki by the destroyer HMS Voyager. As Agar was setting up his base, the fortress of Krasnaya Gorka rebelled against the Bolsheviks and Agar decided to attack the Bolshevik cruiser Oleg. His CMB 4 sank the cruiser on the night of 17/18 June after having to stop for twenty minutes to replace the torpedo-launching cartridge. This was much the kind of attack the Harwich Force planned against the German fleet from 1916 on. Between 10 June and 26 August 1919, Agar made nine trips to St Petersburg to insert or pick up agents. Of his two boats, CMB 7 was seriously damaged on the last trip and had to be scuttled. Agar's success led Baltic commander Rear Admiral Sir Walter Cowan to ask for more CMBs to attack the two battleships and one submarine depot ship in St. Petersburg. He received a small flotilla of 55-footers. On the night of 17/18 August Agar in CMB 4 led six 55-footers through the forts to the entrance to Kronstadt. They were preceded by an air attack intended to distract the defenders. Two of the boats were lost to enemy fire and a third to a collision, but the others destroyed the enemy fleet, sinking the battleships Petropavlovsk (hit by three torpedoes from CMB 31 and CMB 88) and Andrei Pervosvenni (one torpedo from CMB 88). Petropavlovsk was later raised and returned to service, but Andrei Pervosvenni saw no further service. In a further operation in September, CMB 4 and two 55-foot CMBs laid mines in the channel leading to the naval base of Kronstadt. Agar received the VC and the DSO. (Dr Raymond Cheung)

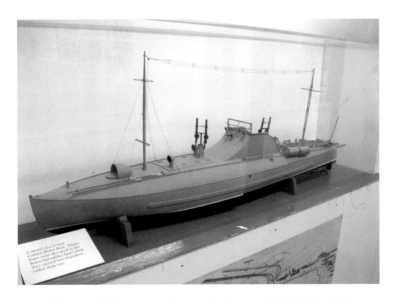

Most CMBs were 55-footers, as depicted by this model. Only the 40-footers could be transported on the davits of a light cruiser. A 55-footer could deliver two 18in torpedoes (or, in theory, one 21in) and it had a substantial anti-aircraft battery of two twin Lewis guns. This model also shows four depth charges. Note the twin rudders and twin propellers and the hard-chine hull form. Not visible is the step under the steering position. (Dr Raymond Cheung)

fairly safe from attacks by enemy light cruisers. A run from the end of the British line would place destroyers in the danger zone for longer (nine minutes in the worst case), but it would hamper the British line far less than the pass-through.

In wartime, given their limited endurance, destroyers could operate with the fleet if they returned to base every two or three days or if action were imminent. The limit would be strain on their crews. Destroyers could be replenished at sea, particularly with oil in ordinary weather.

The great problem was identification: because destroyers were potentially so deadly, battleship doctrine was usually to fire at any that were not positively identified as friendly. The only effective means of identification was to confine them to a no-fire sector. In cruising formation that might be the rear of the fleet. With action imminent, a squadron of destroyers could be stationed on either flank of the battleships (beam or quarter), with orders not to hamper the main fleet when it changed from cruising to battle formation. The best position would depend on whether the commander wanted an early or late attack, based on weather. To reserve destroyers for attacks once the action was fully developed, destroyers should occupy unexposed positions, for example on the unengaged side of the battle line, 2000 yds off. May envisaged them passing through gaps between divisions (the Germans passed between ships) or they might attack from the head or tail of the British line. In the latter case a well-placed cruiser at one end of the enemy line could pour fire into the destroyers as they approached.

Given the new heaters, battleship torpedo range now roughly equalled effective gun range. May wondered whether it would be worthwhile to risk destroyers in a day action when the battleships themselves offered more torpedo firepower. He concluded that the role of destroyers working with a fleet was first to attack with torpedoes and only then to frustrate enemy destroyer attacks. Cruisers and scouts were better anti-destroyer weapons in a fleet context. Given long torpedo range, destroyers should never fire towards their own fleet. Once separated, they should not close the British fleet, as the battleships would fire at them. They should return to their bases after attacking. Destroyers should never stay with the battleships after dark, as the battleships would fire indiscriminately.

It followed that destroyers operating with the fleet needed heavier torpedo armament, at the least twin tubes rather than single tubes plus single stowed torpedoes. It could even be argued that guns should be traded for more torpedoes. May's successor Admiral Callaghan argued that torpedo attack supporting the fleet was the single most important destroyer mission, hence that torpedo armament should be emphasised over guns. Like May, he considered light cruisers his best defence against enemy torpedo attack. The Board initially swatted him down. In line with earlier thinking, it held that the primary British destroyer role was to kill enemy destroyers in the North Sea while operating independently off German destroyer bases. The German fleet might take some short-endurance destroyers to sea with it, but they would have to return to port quite soon for reliefs. British destroyers off the German coast would pick them off as they came and went, much as, four decades later, NATO envisaged submarines in choke points picking off Soviet submarines as they returned to their bases for fuel and torpedoes.

Callaghan was unconvinced. In the 1913 manoeuvres destroyers were unable to find each other at night; the entire concept of hunting in the North Sea was disproved. Thus Callaghan's 1913 fleet orders envisaged deploying his fleet destroyers on the unengaged side of his line, half ahead on the beam and other half astern on the quarter. Whichever way the enemy line approached, half would be in position to attack. For Callaghan, light cruisers were the antidote to enemy torpedo attack. Destroyers should be used against the enemy's battle line.[22] New destroyers should be armed more heavily with torpedoes, their designs placing less emphasis on guns. This position was controversial for a time, but the destroyers planned for the 1914–15 programme would have had a heavier torpedo armament and lighter guns (because of the outbreak of war, the previous year's more conventional class was repeated).

It was generally agreed that at sea light cruisers were the best antidotes to destroyers. The original torpedo-boat destroyers had been stationed off French ports in hopes that they could sight emerging enemy torpedo boats and run them down, all the while firing at them. Although they were poor gun platforms, they were the only warships which could stay long enough with a fast target to disable it. By way of contrast, any ship opposing an enemy torpedo attack would have only a brief chance to do so. A light cruiser was a far better gun platform than a lively destroyer. That is why Jellicoe's predecessor Admiral Callaghan preferred to emphasise the offensive role of his destroyers. Jellicoe understood why, but he never felt that he had enough light cruisers. He therefore used his destroyers, which were very much second-best as defensive assets, to make up the numbers and his tactics did not involve mass destroyer attacks against the German battle line.

Battleships could also fire 'browning' shots, but the British emphasised attacks by other craft within a battle fleet. The same gunnery personnel were used either for gun fire control or for torpedo control on board capital ships. During his tenure with the Grand Fleet, Jellicoe pressed for increased torpedo range, mainly in hopes of giving his battleships a better 'browning shot' weapon. In the spring of 1916 the British provided battleships with a 15,000 yd setting. Until the end of 1915 the settings were 10,000 yds at 28 knots and 4000 at 44 knots. Readjustment responded to reports of longer German torpedo ranges (at Jutland, however, British torpedoes considerably outranged German ones).

Pre-1914 British knowledge of evolving German tactics was limited at best; the British tended to mirror-image. As the British developed the 'browning' concept, they assumed the Germans would do the same. The German tactical publications which fell into British hands after the outbreak of war showed, among other things, that the Germans regarded torpedoes as far too valuable to waste in 'browning' shots. Presumably that was because pre-war German naval economics, shaped by the Navy Laws, had precluded providing them in great quantities.

In practice torpedoes were much less accurate and reliable than they seemed to be in pre-war exercises. The theory of 'browning' shots was still valid, but it took many more torpedoes to execute them. 'Browning-shot' tactics were never used, although they were still destroyer attack doctrine in both the Royal Navy and the US Navy at the end of the war. The British never provided enough torpedoes on board their destroyers and cruisers to make effective browning shots. A major wartime surprise was that at long ranges torpedoes were so ineffective.

Torpedoes had other unsuspected limitations. Before the war it was assumed, at least by the Royal Navy, that submarines would close to 500 yds to fire, so as to be sure of hitting. In pre-war exercises, torpedoes were set to run somewhat deep so as pass under their targets. That hid the reality that a torpedo launched by a submarine submerged to periscope depth had to climb to reach its set depth and the climb took some time, hence distance. To hit a shallow-draught ship such as a destroyer, a submarine had to back off to something more like 1000 yds. The faster the target, the better the chance that she would miss at that range. Much the same might be said of a British submarine lying in wait to torpedo a surfaced submarine passing at fairly high speed.

Capital ships turned out to be tougher than expected. A pre-dreadnought might well sink after a single torpedo hit. Dreadnoughts and their successors were more difficult to sink. The Royal Navy lost a single such ship, HMS *Audacious*, to an underwater hit and she took a long time to sink – so long that it seems likely that better damage control and some minor improvements would have saved her. HMS *Marlborough* survived a torpedo at Jutland, although it can be argued that she was lucky in where it struck. German ships proved remarkably resistant to underwater damage. Multiple torpedoes eventually did sink the battlecruiser *Lützow*, but she had been pounded so badly that they were only part of the problem. During the war, DNC discovered a way of protecting ships against torpedo hits by blistering, but no Grand Fleet capital ship could be taken out of service long enough for that and the speed penalty due to blistering would have been unacceptable in a battlecruiser. The only Grand Fleet capital ships properly protected against torpedo hits were the two *Renown*s.

As the British built more and more battleships, a key question was how to use them *en masse*. By the 1890s they expected to fight in line ahead, so they devoted much attention to the problem of deploying from cruising formation (columns) into the line best oriented to the enemy – preferably athwart his course (crossing his 'T'). When the President of the US Naval War College visited his British equivalent in 1909, he observed that this was the main problem addressed in its tactical game.[23] The normal fleet cruising formation was three columns, the C-in-C heading the centre column. Cruisers were normally thrown out well ahead and on the flanks and the rear. A key factor was visibility range, which in 1909 at the War College was taken as about four miles (8000 yds) by day under average North Sea and Channel conditions, about ten miles in West Indies by day and two miles at night.

Fleet manoeuvre required extensive signalling and by 1900 the Royal Navy had a very elaborate signal book. In effect it was the vocabulary an Admiral could use to manoeuvre his fleet. The role of the Admiral's flag lieutenant was to translate his commands into the language of the signal book. There was internal debate as to whether even the best signalmen could help an Admiral control a fleet in combat. In the 1880s Admiral Tryon argued that the fleet could not effectively fight because its signalling system would fail when stressed. He pressed for a radically simpler system which amounted to 'follow the leader' manoeuvres. The Admiral would simply indicate whether or not the fleet was to conform to his movements. It did not help that Tryon died when his flagship HMS *Victoria* was rammed while the Mediterranean Fleet manoeuvred to anchor in 1893. Contrary to his teaching, Tryon was attempting a particularly elaborate, if elegant, manoeuvre and he seems to have miscalculated the distance between columns of ships. Jellicoe, at that time a Commander, narrowly avoided drowning as *Victoria* sank. Presumably he was being given a particularly graphic lesson in the dangers of complex manoeuvring.

The British came to understand that the simpler the formation, the better the chance that it would work – in more modern terms, 'keep it simple, stupid'. The simplest and most supple formation, it turned out, was line ahead, because maintaining it required little signalling. Although the Signal Book remained as elaborate as ever, line ahead was very much the kind of tactic Tryon envisaged. Line ahead had a long history under sail, but with the advent of steam navies tried many alternatives, including line abreast and line of bearing. Under sail, line ahead made for simplicity, but given short gun range it was impossible to concentrate fire on any one enemy ship. Each side in a line-ahead battle would deliver roughly the same weight of fire. Nelson broke the enemy line at Trafalgar specifically so that he could concentrate fire on particular enemy ships, breaking up their formation. He accepted the risk that they might be cut off and overwhelmed by an alert enemy. Was there a battleship-age equivalent to Nelson's tactic?

Having tried alternatives, by the 1890s the Royal Navy

In 1914 the heavy gun was the dominant weapon, but it was assumed that its effect would be cumulative. Gunfire would pound ships but only rarely sink them. The British liked Lyddite shells because it appeared that the fumes they generated would incapacitate crews. No one imagined sudden explosions like those which sank three British battlecruisers at Jutland. Slow destruction, as of Graf Spee's big cruisers at Coronel, or *Blücher* at Dogger Bank, conformed much more closely to expectation. Thus fleet tactics envisaged night attacks by destroyers after a day gunnery action, largely to finish off cripples. This fleet battle practice target gives some idea of the area over which shells were expected to hit (shells falling outside were not counted as hits). At about 8000 yds the Royal Navy expected better than 50 per cent hits and even then it did not expect to knock out modern battleships very quickly. This target was photographed on 29 September 1912. (Dr David Stevens, SPC-A).

returned to line-ahead close-order tactics, a position not shared by some other major navies. The British found that line-ahead tactics much simplified station-keeping and the line was less liable to be thrown into disorder. In any other formation, course could not safely be altered without any signal – at a time when signalling was likely to be slow and uncertain, if not impossible. Perhaps as importantly, a line-ahead formation seemed to solve the problem of distinguishing friend from foe. Anyone in line was a friend, anyone outside a foe. Problems would arise only if the line kinked (as during the night action off Guadalcanal in 1942), so that some captains thought they were watching an enemy breaking through. That was unlikely in daylight.

This was logic, not fetishistic devotion to the traditions of the age of sail. When he conducted tactical experiments in 1910–11, Admiral May sought an alternative to line ahead, which he considered basically defensive. In his view a fleet in rigid line-ahead formation could not readily counter-attack. The alternative divisional organisation was inherently flexible and, it seemed, relatively easy to command. May saw it as inherently offensive. Also, it was far easier to exploit ships' speeds when they were organised in divisions (no more than eight ships, preferably four). From a theoretical point of view (Admiral May's phrase) divisional tactics were extremely attractive.[24]

The rub was what Togo had found at Tsushima: individual divisions had to be kept under sufficient control that they reinforced each other but did not accidentally fire at each other. The fleet C-in-C had to know a lot more about what was happening in the battle in order to do that. Devolving control to the commanders of the divisions was risky in a world filled with smoke. Jellicoe's experience of tactical experiments in 1912 seems to have convinced him that it was too easy for the divisions to tangle and even to engage each other instead of the enemy. These exercises

revealed another problem as well. The British believed that a modern battleship could survive under fire for a considerable time. In the 1912 manoeuvres enemy ships were not exposed to fire for long enough. The fleet needed some way of laying down sustained fire for much longer. To do that it had to remain in formation, shelling an enemy fleet which would presumably also remain in formation.

Jellicoe, and probably other British officers, came to see rigid control as insurance against a dangerous melee punctuated by torpedo hits. When he came to write his Grand Fleet Battle Orders, Jellicoe abandoned his earlier acceptance of decentralised command once battle began. He sought to maintain control throughout. Divisional tactics might be the best way to concentrate fire on parts of the enemy's fleet, hence to achieve results in a reasonable length of time. Jellicoe later said that he would have adopted divisional tactics if he could have, but that he did not have enough time to train his fleet in them.

Divisional tactics were not quite the same as accepting that once battle began a C-in-C might no longer be able to exert full control and much would have to be done by those commanding the fleet's divisions. That begged a question. Who would control fleet resources such as massed destroyers? Who would direct them so that they attacked only the enemy's fleet and not a hapless division of one's own fleet?

Deploying across the enemy's path was the best possibility. The worst, which seemed entirely possible, was that the British and German fleets would approach head-on, both fleets being in line ahead. In that case the battle might well open with a salvo of German torpedoes fired towards the British fleet. Because the British would be running towards the torpedoes, their effective range would be increased considerably. A quick run past the Germans on parallel courses would never provide enough time for gunfire to be effective. Jellicoe believed that it also presented dangers. He wanted to get onto a parallel course steaming in the same direction, because only then would he have enough time to pour enough shells into the German ships. Having run past the Germans, he could turn behind them and pass through their wake. However, Jellicoe was aware of the Japanese use of floating mines and he had sponsored its British equivalent. What if the Germans had the same idea? The wake of the German fleet was the last place he wanted to be. What sort of manoeuvre would bring his battle line onto the desired parallel course, in the same direction, without exposing it to floating mines?

Jellicoe's predecessor Admiral Callaghan, who championed offensive destroyer operations in a fleet context, wrote in his March 1914 battle orders that the tactics of a fleet consisting of three or more battle squadrons plus battlecruisers and many other ships were fundamentally different from those of a fleet of one or two battle squadrons.[25] Probably a single officer could command the smaller fleet for much longer than a larger one. Surely the larger the fleet, the greater the need to decentralise. Callaghan thought that he could control approach and deployment, but once firing began he would have to devolve to squadron commanders, subject to general instructions. He hoped to be able to deploy quickly enough to establish superiority of fire. The objective would normally be the enemy's rear, a departure from the earlier idea of deploying across the enemy's 'T'. Callaghan cautioned against ships being drawn off by an enemy fast division, which could break up his line. Presumably he had the German battlecruisers in mind.

Overall, the British tactical problem was simple to state but difficult to solve. If the British fleet were far more numerous than its German enemy, how could its apparently crushing *numerical* superiority be translated into *tactical* superiority? How could targets in the enemy battle line be designated so that all were covered and how could multiple ships concentrate their fire on the enemy? The more numerous the fleet, the longer the line. A very long line steaming more or less parallel to a shorter enemy line would overlap it, the ships at the end too far from the enemy to fire. British experiments in longer-range fire may have been intended specifically to solve the tactical problem presented by the ships at the ends of the British line. Breaking up the fleet into mutually supporting units ('divisional tactics') could solve the geometric problem, but not the tactical one.

The Germans also planned to fight in line ahead, but with important differences from British practice.[26] Draft tactical orders the British obtained in 1914 included the 'Gefechtswendung' (Action [Battle] turn) of the whole battle line through 16 points (180°). It was the first item described under the category 'turning together in action', alternatives being available if it was impracticable (as stated in the book).[27] The parallel Tactical Order No. 1 (Hints for Battle) included first the injunction that the enemy might turn together to escape; 'it would be *unfavourable* for us to pursue him, as we should then run into the area commanded by the enemy's torpedoes, without being able ourselves to make use of them'. The Germans would have to use the same manoeuvre to extricate themselves, even if that took them out of range. The manoeuvre might have to be repeated until the German fleet was once more in range. 'It would be advantageous for *us, if we could make the enemy follow us, so as to get him into the area commanded by our torpedoes*' (italics in the original). Using this manoeuvre, a German fleet being pursued by the British could suddenly turn on its pursuer at a high speed of approach. The resulting high range rates would make gunnery difficult for both fleets, but the Germans could also fire a salvo of torpedoes towards the approaching German fleet. Effective torpedo range would be considerably increased, because the British would be running into the German torpedoes.

A British captain raised exactly this problem in May 1914, before the British had the German manoeuvring orders. It later turned out that the British Naval War College had become interested in exactly this kind of manoeuvre, as a way of subjecting the British fleet to mines and U-boats. At the end of the war the British were still trying to find a tactical solution. A British fleet pursuing the fleeing Germans would find itself running towards German torpedoes, whereas the Germans would be opening the range British torpedoes would have to cover.

The 1914 German orders emphasised the lack of modern light cruisers for scouting. In cruising formation, the light cruisers, perhaps supplemented by destroyers, would form an arc of a circle about 25 miles ahead of the main body, a distance chosen so that the enemy could not get around the scouting line but also far enough away that the enemy outside the scouting line could not see the main German fleet. The German battlecruisers of the 1st Scouting Group would be concentrated between the main fleet and the scouts, about 10 miles back, so that they could back up the scouts. The orders allowed for the possibility that the position and direction of the enemy's scouting line could be determined by aerial reconnaissance, in which case cruisers could be concentrated to penetrate it.

Once the enemy had been found, the battlecruisers would fall back to a position at the head of the German line formed out of the cruising columns of battleships. Its two tasks, presumably in order of importance, were to fire torpedoes at the head of the enemy line and to deal with the enemy's fast division (his battlecruisers) at the head of his line. When the fleet formed up, the battlecruisers would constitute its fast division operating semi-independently. To avoid being surrounded, it was to manoeuvre at high speed; an action between the fast divisions on both sides might develop. It was accepted that it would be very difficult for the fast division to reach the assigned position. It needed the earliest possible information as to the direction in which the main fleet was to deploy. In another departure from British practice, the 4th Battle Squadron (*Wittelsbach* class pre-dreadnoughts) would form about 5000 to 6000 m on the disengaged beam of the battle line (consisting of the other three squadrons), available to reinforce it as needed.[28] This was a sort of divisional tactics.

If there were no doubt as to the direction in which the action would develop, all flotillas would try to steam ahead as far as possible. If they could do so without obviously manoeuvring to attack, the foremost destroyers should attack with long-range torpedoes. The main destroyer role during a day battle would be massed attack on the van and line of the enemy. Where the British were interested in attacks which would spoil enemy deployment, the Germans wanted their destroyers to wait until the two battle lines had formed and were punishing each other. Where the British feared that the Germans would attack specifically to ruin their fire control, the German instructions emphasised the way in which fire control requirements would prevent an enemy from manoeuvring to avoid torpedoes. If the enemy refused to maintain formation in the face of torpedo attack, at the least the destroyers would be reducing the weight of fire on their battleships. Perhaps the key phrase was that '*every officer in command of a destroyer must remember that his torpedoes must put at least one of the enemy's ships out of action . . .the probability of a hit* is the only thing to justify the expenditure of a torpedo. A destroyer which has fired all its torpedoes without obtaining a hit has not fulfilled its purpose in the action'. Torpedoes should not be fired at excessive range, a safety margin of at least 25 to 30 per cent of range being allowed. The instructions cautioned that '*great care* and *exact knowledge* about the *positions of our own ships*' (my italics) was a prerequisite for angled shots.

There was no reason to open fire beyond 12,000m (13,200 yds) unless the enemy forced that. Nor was there any reason to concentrate fire, as 'the advantage of engaging *all* the ships of the enemy is out of all proportion to the loss of effective fire through its dispersion'. Given the 'destructive effect of underwater hits at very great ranges with [HE] shell . . . these should be used as soon as the range is found, as well as AP'. As in the Royal Navy, there was a severe injunction against wasting ammunition, the implication being that if the enemy kept the range wide, the medium-calibre guns might not be used at all.

As the British watched the Germans and as they obtained German documents, they began to feel some insight into German thinking. In October 1914 Admiral Jellicoe circulated a German report of gunnery practice by the 1st Battle Squadron of the High Seas Fleet. He particularly noted that the Germans intended to develop a high rate of fire when they found the range, that they were achieving a very small spread with their heavy guns and

Dreadnought battleships were conceived by the Royal Navy as a way of using guns effectively at greater ranges, initially outside the torpedo ranges of battleships. This is the forward superstructure of HMS *Colossus* as built. The external sign of increasing gunnery sophistication is the big spotting top. When *Colossus* was being designed, fleet commander Vice Admiral Sir Francis Bridgman argued that masts themselves were a danger. It would be better to use an armoured position near the conning tower. DNO Captain Reginald Bacon replied that aloft control would be particularly important during the approach phase of an action. Once the action became general rangefinding and formal control would no longer be very important. It followed that a single aloft position would be vital, but that there was not much point in providing a second such position aft, where it would be smoked out. Since they did not need long radio receiving range, battleships did not need a mainmast to support high antennas (battlecruisers did). HMS *Colossus* therefore revived the single-mast arrangement of HMS *Dreadnought*, which had been discarded. A single mast also had the virtue that it made determination of the ship's course by an enemy more difficult. The single mast was placed abaft the forefunnel so that its vertical member cold support the heavy boat crane (ships with two masts used the vertical member of the mainmast). Unfortunately the spotting top, which clearly suffered from smoke interference, became more rather than less important as range rapidly increased. The *Orion* and *Lion* classes were designed with similar masts before *Colossus* went to sea and demonstrated the smoke problem; the *Lion*s had to be rebuilt at considerable cost. (Author's collection)

finally that, as he thought, they expected to fight at limited range – since the secondary battery (5.9in guns) took part, it seemed that they would fight within 8000 yds. In at least two cases visibility was low. He was relieved that there was no sign of a director system.[29]

On 30 October Jellicoe sent the Admiralty his understanding of how he would have to fight, based on what he had learned so far about the Germans.[30] He felt that the Germans had shown that they planned to rely heavily on submarines, mines and torpedoes,

presumably based on German submarine and mining operations to date. Surely they would use the same weapons in a fleet action, 'especially since they possess an actual superiority over us in these particular directions'. It seemed to him that the Germans could not be sure of having all of their submarines and minelayers with them unless they could choose where to fight, probably in the southern North Sea where they could also have air support. He therefore planned to fight in the northern North Sea, which incidentally was closer to his own base, giving his wounded ships a better chance of getting home. That was also where he could be sure of concentrating his own short-legged destroyers with his cruisers. Given the need to concentrate torpedo craft, the Germans would not come out except at a moment of their choice, when all these craft were ready. He, on the other hand, always had to be ready and his cruisers were often using up their coal. Yet he needed a large cruiser force to scout and to screen his battle force, 'so that the latter may be manoeuvred into any desired position behind the cruiser screen'. That also favoured the northern North Sea.

Jellicoe was sure the Germans would use their submarines with their battle fleet. The cruisers might lead them into position so that the High Seas Fleet could lead him over them. The basic safeguard was to manoeuvre the Grand Fleet at high speed so as to upset essentially fixed U-boat dispositions. Given their limited underwater endurance and speed, the submarines could not follow unless they surfaced; after an interval of high-speed manoeuvring, Jellicoe felt that he could safely close the High Seas Fleet. The situation was grim: German underwater weapons might disable half his fleet before he could open fire 'if a false move is made'. He might have to refuse to follow a turn-away by the High Seas Fleet and he was anxious that the Admiralty understand the situation and not see a turn-away on his part as refusal to fight, which would rightly be condemned.

Information from a German lieutenant captured at Heligoland seemed to confirm Jellicoe's belief that the Germans would mass their torpedo craft in the closest possible formation to 'brown' the British. If they went to sea,

they would take with them the largest possible number of torpedo craft, which would attack from between their ships in threes or as many as possible in close formation, pushing their attacks to within two or three thousand yards. They are quite sure that our torpedo craft bunched at the head of the line will not stop them, nor will the fire of our ships, as they say it takes many hits to sink a torpedo boat destroyer (which seems proved). Apparently they place so much importance on this that they will not now risk their new boats and officers and men are instructed to push their attack home or die. They believe that their big destroyer attack in a fleet action will put half our ships at least hors de combat.[31]

In the wake of Jutland, Jellicoe modified his battle orders. Where he had initially assumed that the Germans wanted to fight at short range, now he believed that they would keep their heavy ships either out of range or at long range, relying on their torpedo craft (destroyers), He thought that such tactics were facilitated by the high speed of some of the German battleships.[32] This was a grossly inaccurate reading of the battle, in which the only mass torpedo attacks were mounted as part of Scheer's effort to extricate his fleet. It shows just how obsessed Jellicoe was with the underwater threat.

During the war the basic battle hints were supplemented by other tactical orders, so that by the end of the war the list had grown to twenty-four and the original hints had been replaced by a report of methods of screening the fleet dated 9 April 1918.[33] The most striking feature of this instruction was that, instead of concentrating on the area ahead of the fleet, the screen should normally completely surround the fleet. The pre-war idea had been that the German fleet would have the initiative, steaming towards an oncoming enemy. War experience showed that the enemy might well be able to get around to the fleet's rear. As ASW screens, destroyers had to cover both the front of the fleet and both its flanks. Again, this was very different from pre-war thinking.

After Jutland, it was generally agreed that the Germans had invested much more effort in night fighting, which meant much better techniques for recognition signals. Remarkably, their 18 October 1915 tactical orders for such signals were still in force at the end of the war.[34] In theory all such systems relied on a challenge and answer, but by this time the Germans had learned that challenges by a force or ship approaching one already in action were often unanswered. At the discretion of the CO, each ship would, without waiting to be challenged, continually show the new challenge as long as he was burning his searchlights or firing. The 'challenge number' would be shown using the forward NSA (Night Signal Apparatus – a designation which suggests an IR device). If an approaching force was unable to make out the NSA before joining the action, it might make the signal FSL ('make recognition signal by searchlight or Morse lamp'). Other emergency signals were FTB (show the 'new challenge' continuously) and FTC (show the 'new challenge' until further orders). There was also an emergency signal using a searchlight pointed up, in case a ship was being fired on by friendly forces.

As fleets grew larger, an important issue was how to concentrate the firepower of multiple ships against single enemy ships. To do that, ships needed some means of passing range data. The Royal Navy introduced range drums, as shown here on board the battlecruiser HMS *Inflexible*, visiting New York in 1910. The drum is the horizontal cylinder visible on the fore side of the foretop. These drums were widely distributed in the pre-war Royal Navy.

The corresponding British night recognition signal was two green lights 2m apart horizontally on the starboard yardarm and two red lights on the port yardarm. There was also a two- (later three-) letter recognition signal made by searchlight or flashing lamp, changing at midnight local time, as ordered at the end of March 1915 (the Germans concluded that to deceive the British they should use a badly-manipulated searchlight sending out a two-letter challenge in hopes that no special care would be taken to make sure it was the right challenge). By 1917 typical night recognition lights were red and white horizontal lights on the foremast. By day ships relied on flags. For example by order of 16 November 1914, to avoid confusion due to the similarity between British and German naval ensigns, British ships were also to show at least one red ensign in a conspicuous position. Destroyers and torpedo boats generally flew the Red Ensign at the yardarm in such a place as not to interfere with signal flags.

The Radio Revolution[35]

Looming over the visible changes to navies was a subtler but perhaps even more important one: wireless (radio), in both strategic and tactical aspects. Radio systems were described as either wireless telegraphy (dot-and-dash transmission of individual letters and numbers: W/T) or radio telephony (voice: R/T). Radio was first demonstrated (over a very short distance) by the German physicist Heinrich Hertz in 1887. Navies quickly understood its potential: for the first time it might be possible for ships to communicate beyond the horizon. Wireless was also the only way for a command centre ashore to communicate instantly with ships at sea. Underwater (acoustic) signals, which many navies adopted about 1906–7, was a short-range competitor, but only wireless offered really long range. By 1901 the Royal Navy was testing short-range tactical sets on board ships.

Already very interested, the Royal Navy learned what wireless could do when it was used to gather destroyers in fog during the 1904 Torpedo Manoeuvres. Wireless was vital to Admiral Togo at Tsushima in 1905. His deployment was keyed to the Russian choice of which side of the Straits through which to pass – which was transmitted to him by W/T from a Japanese scout cruiser. On the other hand, wireless did not help Togo maintain control of his two-division fleet once the battle began.

Togo's use of wireless exemplified a radical change in scouting. Now a scouting screen could be maintained without the large numbers of repeating ships formerly needed to transmit what the scouts saw back to the main body of the fleet. Once scouts could report back from beyond the horizon, there was a different issue. They had to know (and to report) where they were, so that the command to which they reported could turn their information into something useful. That was not the case for a scout reporting visually, since those on board a flagship could see where the scout was. Incomplete reporting (no position) was such a problem during the action off Scarborough in December 1914 that Admiral Jellicoe had to send his fleet a message emphasizing the need for position reports.

During the early part of the twentieth century the Royal Navy, the largest in the world, led the world's navies in W/T installations and technology, although the German navy and the US Navy were rapidly catching up.[36] During the war, German sets (using tubes) were considered superior technically, but it appears that the British approach to wireless within the fleet was substantially more sophisticated, having been developed through years of large-scale fleet exercises. Moreover, W/T was integral to the new concept of centrally-controlled fleet operations developed by Admiral Fisher. When he took office in 1904 the British already controlled much of the world telegraph network. Fisher realised that by adding long-range radio stations to key telegraph stations he could produce just

Inflexible is shown at full speed, her coal-fired boilers pouring out smoke which makes her after spotting top nearly useless. During the battle of the Falklands, her spotters suffered from vibration despite the support offered by the heavy tripod masts, and at times they were badly smoked. Note the director on the platform below the foretop, and the spiral surrounding the fore topmast. It was an anti-rangefinding measure, intended to break up the visible vertical mark represented by that mast. The British were unaware that such measures were useless against the stereo rangefinders the Germans used. Although often captioned as a photo of the ship at the Falklands, features such as the extended bridge and the director indicate that it was taken later.

the global command net he wanted. It took cables and telegraph to send a message halfway around the world to a distant station, after which long-range radio could take over.

Among Fisher's first investments as First Sea Lord was a Navy-owned shore wireless network, whose main stations (Cleethorpes and Horsea in England and Malta and Gibraltar in the Mediterranean) could transmit to ships 500 miles out at sea. All were connected to the Admiralty by cable. Wireless was so important that, despite this investment, Fisher bought new stations in 1908. Cleethorpes and Horsea were upgraded to a range of over 1000 miles. A powerful station was installed at the Admiralty. New transmitters were ordered for British warships. The meaning of this combination was not lost on the Germans. In 1914 the German cruiser *Emden* was destroyed while her crew tried to disable a British wireless and cable station in the Pacific. Conversely, British attacks on German cables drastically reduced the ability of the German Admiralty to contact distant forces – such as Admiral von Spee's Asiatic Squadron, once it left the German base at Tsingtao in China. Radio was also developed for use within a fleet, although visual signalling was preferred. To that end the Royal Navy developed techniques it hoped would limit the reach of tactical sets. By 1914 it had a considerable variety of sets in service.[37]

Having gained considerable experience with radio, the Royal Navy was well aware of the potential advantages of an enemy intercepting its signals. One recommendation after a major fleet exercise testing radio jamming was that the navy should adopt multiple special wartime frequencies, not to be used or disclosed in peacetime, as well as a system of wartime call signs, again not to be used in peacetime.[38] A special radio frequency (tune) was assigned to the Red Fleet in the major exercise later in 1906. By 1907 planned W/T watches were one to operate the set in the silent cabinet, the other to cipher/decipher. All ciphering was by book code, but the Royal Navy was seeking a mechanical device.[39]

Wartime W/T organisation placed the Admiralty at the head of the entire shore system of the British Isles and the Mediterranean, with each deployed fleet focussed on the Admiral afloat.[40] At least in theory, the Admiralty transmitted to the Admirals, who commanded their fleets; there was no option for the Admiralty to transmit direct to any subordinate. That created a problem in with the Grand Fleet, as Admiral Jellicoe was C-in-C Home Fleet*s*, commanding widely-dispersed forces. After Beatty's battlecruisers were moved to Rosyth, Beatty was given, in effect, a separate line from the Admiralty. Separated ships would not normally communicate with each other directly. Instead, a ship would normally communicate with the nearest low or medium-power shore station, which in turn would communicate with the shore station nearest the addressee. A fleet had a designated W/T guardship intended to listen for Admiralty messages addressed to the fleet commander. Within a fleet, there was also a dedicated Destroyer Wave. It might be used directly, or the depot ship or flotilla cruiser (later, leader) could use the Destroyer Wave to transmit messages on the Admiral's wave. For example, flotilla cruisers (leaders) would listen on the Admiral's wave for five minutes at a time at quarter past and quarter to every hour.

The Admiral of a fleet or squadron was assigned his own frequency, which was 'guarded' (listened for) by the senior officer of each group. It was also guarded by the Second in Command. The main scouting group would keep watch on (and use) the Admiral's wave. Ships within the Admiral's force were broken down into groups, each with its own senior officer (plus not more than eight ships). That included all but the most important cruisers. Principal Grand Fleet squadrons all functioned as groups in this sense. Each group kept a guard on the Admiral's (or other senior officer's) frequency, retransmitting on the group's own frequency (which designated the group, frequencies being identified by letter). An Inter-Group Guard ship kept watch on the Group Wave

Photographed in 1918, *Inflexible* shows how pre-war gunnery ideas played out in wartime. The most dramatic visible change was greatly increased range, which explains the big rangefinder atop her foretop. The platform below the top, which before the war accommodated a searchlight, now carries a cylindrical director to co-ordinate the fire of the ship's turrets. Concentration fire, abandoned in 1914, returned in 1917. The front face of the foretop carries a range clock, which displays the range at which the ship is firing (in effect it replaced the earlier range drum). The ship's foreturret carries bearing markings so that other ships can fire at the same target. The smaller rangefinder atop the bridge is for plotting and also for long-range torpedo control. The structure below the open bridge is a charthouse and plot. Another wartime feature is the big life raft carried abaft the bridge structure. Such rafts could float off a sinking ship, saving lives even if boats could not be launched (or did not survive a battle). The 4in anti-destroyer guns initially atop 'A' turret were moved into the superstructure when it became clear that destroyers would join in a day action. Late in the war that made the top of 'A' turret available for the anti-aircraft gun shown. The tripod foremast of the light cruiser in the background shows multiple range clocks, because other cruisers co-operating with her might not be in line ahead, hence might not be able to see a clock oriented fore and aft.

(group frequency) and collected messages from ships in her group intended for the senior officer and for ships in other groups, retransmitting as required. A separate Group Repeating Ship read all messages sent by the Group Guard and kept track of any failures to answer the Group Guard's messages. Whenever possible, communication between Senior Officer and Group Duty ships should be by auxiliary (low-power) radio, to limit the enemy's ability to intercept signals. The point of the entire scheme was that there were so few available frequencies, as the spark transmitters in use were fairly broad-band.

Special provision was made for radio silence. The *Wireless Instructions* referred to the possibility that the distance to a ship could be estimated from the strength of her signals, but the issue was the more general possibility of interception (it turned out that signal strength could be deceptive). A fleet commander could order all of his ships to continue W/T watch but would not answer any messages.

Wireless works because a fraction of any varying electrical signal coupled to an antenna will radiate into space, generally in all directions. The lower the frequency, the further it goes, with some qualifications (at particular high frequencies signals bounce off the ionosphere and can travel around the world). Frequency means wavelength: the lower the frequency, the longer the wavelength. How much of the signal goes out into space depends on the antenna (gain), which in turn depends on the size of the antenna in

The Germans did not initially use spotting tops, because they assumed gun range would be short. The top (with a more rigid tubular foremast) was fitted to *Friedrich der Grosse* in 1918; she is shown at Scapa Flow after the German fleet surrender. The *Königs* were similarly fitted in 1918 (but *Kronprinz Wilhelm* may have had a tubular foremast and gun control top on commissioning in 1914 and some battlecruisers had foremast spotting tops in 1914). The upper top, with rangefinder, was for main battery control. Below it was a spacious torpedo control level. German director control was simpler than British because the Germans relied on gyros at the guns to fire them at the right time in the ship's roll. Their director was really a pointer which co-ordinated the bearings of the guns. That suggests no interest in counteracting the pronounced effect of roll on gun bearing, particularly on bearings near dead ahead and astern. After the ship was surrendered, her officers said that the foremast vibrated, even at anchor in harbour. It is not clear why tripod legs were not added. The main battery was usually controlled from a position above and abaft the conning tower. In contrast to the British, the Germans had no interest in trying to conceal a ship's course either in day (by using a single mast) or at night (by concentrating search-lights more or less amidships with remote control). (Naval Institute collection)

wavelengths. That is why the US Navy needed tens of miles of antenna to transmit the extremely low frequency (ELF) signals it used to communicate with submarines in the 1980s. Before the First World War signals were usually designated by wavelength, typical Royal Navy waves being 400ft or 1025ft or 2760ft or 4250ft long (in modern terms 2.5 MHz, 950 kHz 350 kHz and 280 kHz meaning thousands of cycles per second).[41] These frequencies were chosen because they were the lowest that could be picked up by shipboard antennas of reasonable size, it being difficult to generate high-frequency signals.

Like its wired equivalent, wireless started with a signal, a long (dash) or short (dot) pulse or, in a more sophisticated version, a voice signal. None of these signals worked at the kind of frequencies a shipboard antenna could transmit. The antenna sent, for example, a short burst of high-enough frequency electrical noise. To create that, a shipboard wireless set had to turn on a source of such noise for a short time (equivalent to a dash or dot). In early systems that was created by a series of sparks. Each spark mixed components with a wide variety of frequencies.[42] The sending antenna filtered out most of them; to a limited extent it was tuned. As might be imagined, most of the energy involved was at the wrong frequencies; it was wasted. It took a lot of spark to create a relatively weak signal. The signal was, moreover, mixed with background noise. At radio frequencies the world is not at all silent. The signal spreads out from the sending antenna, so that only a small fraction reaches the receiving antenna. Like the sending antenna, the receiving antenna chokes out all but a narrow range of frequencies. It too has a gain.[43]

The Royal Navy continued to use spark radios during the war. They were robust and durable, easily repaired and their broadband signals could force through interference. Against that, they were inefficient, their broadband signals caused serious interference (which was particularly evident at Jutland, when many ships attempted to transmit more or less simultaneously) and they and their antennas required considerable insulation. A late-war account of submarine W/T transmission, for example, mentions that if the insulation on a mast was ruined, the spark could not go up the mast into the aerial.

The alternative to a spark transmitter was a means of creating a continuous wave at a more or less pure frequency.[44] The first such device used by the Royal Navy was the Poulsen Arc, which offered by far the longest-range performance before and during the First World War. The alternative way to produce a continuous wave was a vacuum tube transmitter. Because its signal was a clear tone, the Poulsen could not be heard by a conventional receiver; it needed a special device.[45] In 1914 the Royal Navy installed Poulsen sets on board several cruisers, to function as linking ships between long-range stations at home and deployed ships with shorter-range spark radios.[46]

By 1907 the Poulsen Arc had largely been perfected and many US battleships had it. It produced a narrow-band continuous-wave signal, which could be applied directly to an aerial. Dots and dashes were applied to the continuous wave as a series of tones (which could not be heard as such in First World War receivers).[47] Arc transmitters were also liked for their robustness and durability and they could easily be built to produce very powerful signals. However, they were slow to start, as the arc had to form. The transmitter had to be monitored to keep to the desired frequency. Maximum frequency was limited (to 250 kHz). The transmitter produced not only the desired frequency but also harmonics (multiples of the basic frequency). Arc transmitters were considered unsuitable for fleet use because it was impossible to 'listen through' to hear the Admiral's signal.

Vacuum tubes were introduced for a variety of roles, beginning with diode detectors, but the most important type was the triode, the basis for amplifiers and for transmitters.[48] Tubes started quickly and they were easier to key than an arc transmitter. Against that, they were fragile and it was more difficult to trouble-shoot vacuum tube sets. The British tested their first tube in 1908, but as of 1914 they had not adopted tubes.[49] The Germans adopted tube radios, which offered much cleaner (less interfering) signals than wartime British spark transmitters. After the war the British adopted tube radios,[50] while during it they used vacuum tube amplifiers to detect German radio signals at long range.[51]

Typical shipboard antennas were vertical wires connected at one end to a ground (such as the metal in a ship) and at the other to a horizontal element, in either a T- or an inverted-L or an inverted V-pattern. Performance depended on how long the vertical and horizontal elements were. Typically the horizontal part consisted of parallel wires whose total length was a larger fraction of the wavelength to be used. British practice was to create a cylinder of parallel wires, each insulated from the others. Other navies used multiple wires side by side. Relatively low (by later standards) frequencies made for either long wires or inefficient antennas coupled to higher-powered or more efficient transmitters. The first British battlecruisers had pairs of high masts specifically to attain the highest possible wireless performance, in this case reception rather than transmission. That had tactical consequences. High masts could be seen further beyond the horizon. Paired masts gave away a ship's inclination, the angle between her course and an enemy's. During the First World War, the Royal Navy found itself cutting down topmasts and wherever possible eliminating one of the earlier pair of masts altogether.[52]

Whatever fraction of the original signal which survives the filters represented by the sending and receiving antennas and dissipation due to distance has to be recognised against the noisy background. That means converting something varying thousands of times a second into a dot or dash (or, later, voice) which an operator could use. That was called rectification (stripping away the radio-frequency oscillation). The earliest device to do that was the coherer, a glass tube with metal filings inside. When a signal passed through it, the filings lined up visibly. The lined-up filings of the coherer reduced the wireless signal to a current which could be detected.[53] Later more reliable rectifiers were fed into earphones. Thus the dot or dash in the signal became a sound which an operator could use the same way a telegraph operator used the tap of the key. Better rectifiers were soon invented (the coherer had to be tapped to recover after each signal, which seriously limited it). Rectification was not perfect, however, so the same earphones picked up the noise ('atmospherics') accompanying the radio signal. Often the brain of the operator was the key component which could pick dots and dashes out of the whistles of static. Much the same could later be said of underwater sound.

During the war the Royal Navy continued to rely on wireless for longer-range messages, but to a considerable extent on flags within fleets and formations.[54] Flag hoists offered a considerable command vocabulary and answering hoists made it clear that signals had been received. The system placed signallers (officers) in an important position: they generally decided how to convey a commander's message. To do that, a signal lieutenant had to have some idea of what sorts of commands would be sent and therefore an education in fleet tactics. Conversely, a signal lieutenant who did not have the full vocabulary at his command could not express his commander's intentions properly. That seems to have been the case with Admiral Beatty's flag lieutenant Ralph Seymour in several battles. The standard signal book included a discussion of how a fleet should function in battle; there is some question as to whether it was updated as British tactics changed radically in the run-up to 1914. The Germans never produced so elaborate a vocabulary.

After Jutland, among the many fleet committees formed to report the lessons of the battle were a W/T Committee and a separate committee intended specifically to evaluate interference from German ships and the potential of radio direction-finding at sea.[55] Given accounts of widespread self-interference ('pandemonium' in some accounts), it is interesting that the committee report mentioned none at all; it was concerned more with ensuring that aerials survived in battle. Early in the action the Germans tried to jam British signals, but 'not the slightest difficulty was experienced, the interference being almost completely cut out by slight alteration in tuning'. Attempts to jam Type 3 sets failed because the German jamming note was so high that loud signals from ships in company could easily be read through by an experienced operator. Admiral Jellicoe summarised the report: he wanted ships rigged for dual (frequency) reception by their main radio stations, instead of being limited to a single frequency. Priority should go to all flagships and then to the W/T Guard Ships in the battle squadrons. A few flagships were

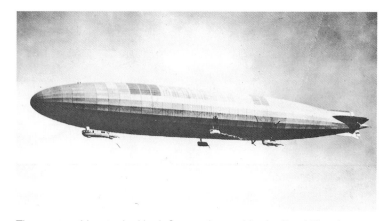

The great problem in the North Sea, understood by the Royal Navy but not by the German navy, was ocean surveillance: knowing when the enemy fleet was at sea and where it was. On the eve of war, the Germans had by far the greatest potential to solve the problem in the form of their airships (mainly Zeppelins), but they considered airships essentially tactical scouts tied to their fleet, substitutes for the light cruisers they lacked. There was no systematic search of the North Sea. Perhaps because it lacked effective airships, the Royal Navy was acutely aware of the need for ocean surveillance, in its case mainly achieved by exploiting German wireless messages. L 30 was the first of a class of ten delivered in 1916. They were 643ft long and 78–75ft in maximum diameter, powered by six 220hp Maybach engines, the exhaust from one of which is visible. They drove two pusher propellers and two propellers on 'wings' built out from the airship's body. Full speed was 60mph and maximum altitude was 14,000ft. Four cars were suspended under the envelope, the forward one being divided in two. Payload was 27 tons, far beyond anything possible with a contemporary aircraft. (Philip Jarrett)

already fitted. The fleet flagship *Iron Duke* had three separate W/T (silent) cabinets (each with a receiving operator) and typically maintained lookouts in two of them, thus avoiding considerable use of auxiliary W/T and providing the Admiral with information on two or three lines without delays entailed by re-transmission from Guard Ships.

The most interesting innovation on the British side was the prototype radio direction-finder in HMS *Lion*, which had not yet been calibrated properly. Its operator, a Royal Marine lieutenant, was confident that once calibrated properly it could be used to plot the bearings of major enemy units. This D/F set was the first effective naval over-the-horizon sensor in the world. This device employed vacuum tubes for sensitivity and for precise tuning. Performance apparently depended very much on the operator's skill. Work was ongoing to reduce interference from British auxiliary sets, which operated at much the frequency of the German ones. The final report to the Admiralty pressed for a D/F set capable of receiving at ranges up to 50 miles, with an aerial which could be used without interference from the main battery and with a particularly sensitive receiver for wavelengths between 2000 and 3500ft. It would be 'of extreme value in locating the enemy and also our own ships in thick weather or at night'. All D/F gear tried so far required an aerial so large that it could not be kept up once guns began to fire. The second D/F system was fitted on board HMS *Princess Royal* during her post-battle refit (the post-Jutland file includes a report of initial operations dated 12 October 1916: average bearing error was 15° on Q wave). An extemporised set was installed on board HMAS *Australia* (completed November 1916). In December, Admiral Beatty asked for similar sets on board *Barham* and *Warspite*, having found the *Princess Royal* set extremely useful (he soon added his new flagship *Queen Elizabeth*). He also endorsed a request by 2nd Cruiser Squadron for a set on board HMS *Minotaur* for test purposes. In the latter case, the set was valued both for detecting and fixing enemy ships and for navigation using German shore stations. When the United States entered the war, the US Navy developed its own much more compact shipboard radio direction-finder, which was used against U-boats (the US Navy seems to have been unaware of the British capital ship set; the British thought it impractical to build a destroyer radio direction-finder).[56]

In 1903 the Germans formed Telefunken, which made their wartime W/T sets.[57] Telefunken used alternators to produce distinctive high notes as its dots and dashes and during the war British operators reportedly considered its signals much cleaner than their own. It is not clear why this was so. The British considered German transmitters much better than their own and the Germans achieved remarkable ranges for the time.[58] They were also much more willing to use low-powered tactical transmitters, as at Jutland. In general the Germans seem to have been unaware of the potential for interception, so they used wireless far more freely than the Royal Navy.[59] The Germans used both flags and radio within their formations. The argument in favour of wireless was that flags might not be very visible in a smoky battle environment. The argument against wireless was that it might be difficult to distinguish near-simultaneous signals from many different ships.

The best indication of German surface combatant practice at the end of the war was what the British found on board the High Seas Fleet ships interned at Scapa Flow.[60] The caveat is that the Germans stripped the ships of all fire-control equipment before steaming to Scapa and there was reason to think they had done the same with their latest radio equipment. Against that, examination of the larger ships showed no large empty spaces and one German remarked that the British would find nothing of interest. Transmitting offices all had a clock with an electric attachment to a box showing wavelengths, presumably to indicate when they should be used.

The standard installation for larger German warships (above light cruiser size) was three separate W/T offices: main (with separate spaces for transmission and reception), auxiliary and after-action. There was no separate British-style silent cabinet, but the whole receiving room was lagged for silence. The transmitters were a CW unit (equivalent, presumably to a Poulsen) and a quenched-spark unit. The sets were served by three parallel three-wire units, which could be used in different combinations covering the range from 350 to 600m (857 down to 500 kHz). The auxiliary office contained a spark set (130 to 600m) and the after-action office contained a portable set and a receiver (160 to 2000m) plus a small petrol generator like that in British ships.

There was no trace of tube transmission, radio direction-finding, separate fire-control sets, supersonic signalling (presumably a cover for sonar), or ultra-violent light receivers, all of which the Allies were trying out. The cruiser *Emden* did have a tube receiver and the cruiser *Nürnberg* had a heterodyne (tube) receiver. Several ships had two-tube amplifiers.

British Signals Intelligence

Radio (wireless) had important implications for any navy using it. Signals were generally transmitted in all directions, not only towards the intended recipient, so radio was always a potential source of intelligence. To some extent the sender could be identified: until well after 1945 most radio messages were sent by

A fleet relying on air reconnaissance needed some way for its airmen to distinguish its ships from the enemy's. Beginning in 1917, the Germans painted large white circles on battleship turrets (typically at least the superfiring or highest turret forward, but often turrets forward and aft, as here). Smaller ships had circles on their foredecks. The fleet flagship *Baden* is shown. Her near-sister *Bayern* could be distinguished by her considerably less elaborate bridge, which did not incorporate facilities for a fleet commander. (Naval Institute collection)

hand. Each of the few radiomen aboard a ship had a characteristic 'fist', which a skilled intercept operator could identify (during the Second World War this process was automated to some extent). Even without code-breaking, wireless offered some intelligence. Ships, both merchant and naval, use unique call signs (as addresses for radio messages). Because messages had to be addressed specifically, call-sign tracking and traffic analysis can continue even if enemy codes cannot be read. Range could be estimated, albeit crudely and not entirely reliably, by signal strength. In 1904 it was discovered that the direction to the transmitter could be measured (radio DF, or direction-finding).

The First World War inaugurated a new kind of intelligence exploiting wireless. In the past, intelligence was generally strategic because of the considerable delay between receiving information and providing it to ships at sea. As C-in-C of the British Mediterranean Fleet from 1899 to 1902, Fisher began the transformation to operational intelligence by exploiting the telegraph link through Malta. He still could not command the fleet from Malta once it left harbour. Within a few years, wireless changed the situation. A commander at the centre of an intelligence web could command a fleet in more or less real time, steering it towards contact with an unseen enemy. The British practiced exactly such tactics at least as early as 1913 and Fisher was writing obliquely about them as early as 1908.

Fisher's account concentrated on the use of wireless to command forces. It referred to the mass of information accumulated by the Admiralty, without reference to sources. In 1908 the Royal Navy was very much interested in running down enemy commerce-destroying cruisers and the Admiralty was well-placed to use merchant shipping data, such as that collected by Lloyd's, to estimate where such cruisers were operating. Admiral Fisher's 1908 memo refers to the deliberate choice to give battle-cruisers the highest possible masts so that their wireless antennas would be well placed to operate at maximum range. It was clear that Fisher appreciated the value of strategic wireless; he invested heavily in it.

In his memo Fisher made no reference to intercepting or decrypting foreign naval messages so as to keep track of foreign fleets. Nor does it seem that the pre-1914 Royal Navy built up a system of radio direction finders to track foreign message traffic. However, manoeuvre instructions do mention the common practice of decrypting messages (in one case the practice is forbidden, because the manoeuvre is intended to test the ability to intercept the enemy fleet *without* such information). Fisher himself later wrote about 'listening to what all the Captains of warships at sea were saying', which implies systematic wireless interception. A letter from a Royal Navy captain, offered for sale to the National Maritime Museum (and not bought) mentioned how, on the eve of war, the ship was listening to German naval messages to find out when war would break out. The implication was that this was standard procedure.

Well before 1914 the Royal Navy leadership realised that by monitoring and decoding German naval wireless messages, the British could achieve a degree of ocean surveillance, which in turn could be exploited.[61] That the Germans enthusiastically used radio tactically helped. Instructions for the 1909 manoeuvre cautioned that officers should refrain from the popular pastime of code-breaking to predict enemy movements, since 'in actual war the difficulties to be solved would be much enhanced by the lack of

acquaintance with the enemy's methods'. The British dilemma was to continue to pass vital information by wireless without offering too much to an enemy which might exploit British signals. Exploitation might include traffic analysis as well as code breaking. When war came, moreover, the Royal Navy expanded explosively, and many new-entry officers found it difficult or impossible to cope with coding and decoding aboard small warships. Messages were often sent in clear rather than in code, and the Germans could and did exploit this opportunity. The difference between British and German wartime practices was primarily that the British exploited code-breaking to deduce German intentions, whereas the Germans did not.

The British certainly were aware of the vulnerabilities W/T entailed. They invented a broadcast technique specifically to defeat traffic analysis, and they became interested in the deception opportunities presented by W/T. Grand Fleet W/T orders included several deceptive techniques.[62] The Royal Navy also introduced W/T direction-finding, both ashore and at sea, as a way of tracking the German fleet. For their part, the Germans liked their radios and used them enthusiastically, both in port and at sea. Their dispersed anchorage at Wilhelmshaven practically required radio communication between ships. The Germans seem to have been unaware that even when they transmitted at much-reduced power, their messages could be (and were) intercepted at a considerable distance.

It is not clear to what extent the pre-1914 Admiralty relied on code-breaking and radio direction-finding. When the British finally released records of pre-Second World War signals intelligence, it appeared that they had introduced radio direction-finding in 1914. The British were certainly lucky to obtain all three of the German naval code books before the end of 1914, but they were also well aware of how to exploit that good fortune. Of the three, the German merchant fleet code (HVB), which was also used within the High Seas Fleet, was seized in Australia on 11 August, although the Australian Naval Board did not inform the Admiralty of its success until 9 September. The most secret code book (SKM) was obtained by the Russians from the sunken *Magdeburg* (lost on 26 August 1914) and then passed them to the British, who received it on 13 October. However, the copy in the PRO shows no sign of water immersion.[63] The Germans suspected that the British had simply broken their code, which was apparently both cumbersome and poorly constructed.[64] Very soon after the SKM was received, the British code-breakers intercepted signals indicating a German destroyer operation, which a British force was ordered to intercept. It sank the destroyers and in December a British trawler came up with the third of the German code books, the VB (to Room 40, the 'miraculous draught of fishes'). The VB was apparently to have been used to communicate with the German army in Flanders. It was normally used by flag officers.[65]

The Germans seem to have assumed that their messages were secure because they re-enciphered (super-enciphered) their codes. That is, once a message had been rendered in code, each group was altered in a way determined by an additional key, which could be changed periodically. The great secret of Room 40 was not that the British had the code books, but that they learned to break super-encipherment so quickly that they could exploit German messages operationally.

Given their confidence in super-encipherment, the Germans

In 1917–18 the Royal Navy took fighters to sea specifically to deal with Zeppelins and thus to blind the Germans. Existing aircraft could be launched from turret tops or from lighters towed at high speed by destroyers. In both cases, the aircraft ditched, its air bags keeping it afloat while the pilot was rescued and the aircraft salvaged (mainly to recover its engine). This fighter was on board HMS *Tiger*. (RAN via Dr David Stevens, SPC-A)

used their three codes far too widely. The HVB was intended for merchant ships and so was widely distributed pre-war. It was also widely used within the Imperial Navy, both by minor units and, crucially, by U-boats and Zeppelins. The Germans never seem to have realised that a good operational intelligence organisation could piece together hints, for example minesweeping orders, to deduce fleet operations. Moreover, because U-boats stayed at sea for long periods, they were often still using an old key when a new one came into force, offering the golden opportunity of reading the same message in two keys.

Probably the greatest lesson of wartime British signals intelligence was that code-breaking was not enough. Messages were hints of what was happening and it took someone knowledgeable, with a light touch, to turn them into usable intelligence. Despite the October success against the destroyers, the new code-breaking organisation failed to predict the German battlecruiser raid on Yarmouth in November 1914. Commander Herbert Hope proved brilliantly capable of understanding what the Germans were doing.[66] Hope's first success was the Scarborough Raid in December 1914. Others in the Royal Navy seem to have sensed the potential of signals intelligence. Admiral Jellicoe argued that it was

worthwhile to mine the Heligoland Bight because the Germans would reveal their intention to sortie by sweeping an exit path.[67] This warning would be made even if an operation were planned very secretly. On several occasions the Germans discovered that their efforts at security had failed and they typically imagined that they either had a traitor in a senior position or that officers were gossiping much too freely. On other occasions they imagined that fleet movements had been betrayed by North Sea trawlers secretly in British pay. When the Germans came to compile their own operational history, after the British official history had been published, they found out that between December 1914 and December 1916 the Grand Fleet had come out nearly *every time* the High Seas Fleet sortied. That was the most graphic measure of success of the British signals intelligence organisation. Early in 1917 Hope was promoted to Captain and sent to sea as captain of the cruiser HMS *Dartmouth* in the Adriatic; he was promoted to Rear Admiral after the war. By that time it must have seemed that the war he had brilliantly fought against the High Seas Fleet was more or less over; the great priority was the U-boats.

The other great success was in the U-boat war. U-boats used their radios far too freely and their messages could be deciphered and their positions revealed by radio direction-finding. That made evasion possible. It was also the basis for hunting tactics and the success of Room 40 may explain why the Admiralty considered hunting a viable alternative to convoy operations as late as it did (that is different from hunting as a valuable adjunct to convoy, in 1917–18, particularly after improved acoustic sensors entered service).

The Germans gradually changed their codes, beginning with the HVB used by minor units – and, unfortunately for them, by U-boats – early in 1916. It was used by and carried, by Zeppelins, so copies were recovered from crashed ones. However, before any had been recovered, Room 40 had reconstructed most of the codebook.[68] In May 1917 the Germans finally changed their main codebook, replacing it with an entirely new one called the FFB.[69] The VB was replaced by a new code which Room 40 called Nordo and this time it was restricted to flag officers. At the same time they changed all their call signs and Admiral Scheer drastically curtailed signalling. However, the Germans continued to use the AFB, the replacement for the HVB. The British could still tell, at least in theory, that the High Seas Fleet was preparing to come out through a freshly-swept channel, but Scheer's improved security made prediction of what would come next a much more delicate proposition. Room 40 suffered three considerable failures. It failed to detect the attack by the two German cruisers against the Scandinavian convoy in October 1917 and, it appears, the German destroyer raid against a later convoy on 12 December.[70] Worse, Room 40 failed to detect the major if ultimately abortive German sortie of April 1918, against a Scandinavian convoy.[71] Ironically, this operation failed because of faulty German intelligence, which failed to inform Admiral Scheer that the British had changed convoy schedules.

The British were always acutely aware that the Germans could wreck signals intelligence, so during the war they sought back-ups. Since surface scouts could not work near the German coast, they used submarines. The surveillance role was considered so important that standing orders prohibited patrolling submarines from attacking any ships they saw until after they had radioed sighting reports.

For radio intelligence to work, the enemy has to co-operate. If he uses radio indiscriminately, he can be tracked, but if he realises how much he is giving away, even that valuable source of intelligence can disappear. It appears that before 1914 many naval officers were aware of the danger that their codes might be broken, but few seem to have realised that simply transmitting radio signals would allow their ships to be tracked. When the US Navy entered the war in April 1917, it used its tactical radios enthusiastically and indiscriminately. The British had to educate the Americans in the use of radio intelligence in order to convince them, successfully, to cut down on tactical radio. After the war, the British revealed that they had been reading German codes, an admission which led the Germans to adopt the 'Enigma' machine code they used during the Second World War. For their part the British seem to have concluded that since codes had been shown to be so breakable, no one would be foolish enough to use radio extensively in a future war. That led them to grossly underestimate the number of messages they would be sending, which in turn led them to adopt coding methods which proved insecure.

German Signals Intelligence

The Germans were listening to British signals, but in 1914 they were making no systematic attempt to exploit British W/T. According to their official history, in December 1914 British W/T was being intercepted mainly by designated ships (during the Scarborough Raid, for example, the battlecruiser *Moltke* was W/T intercept ship). Typically several ships in a force had their receivers tuned to a particular British frequency ('wave'). The Navy Office furnished keys it thought the British were using, but decoding was said to be slow and clumsy and there is no indication in the official history that at this time it had any impact on operations. Messages could not be decoded quickly enough for the C-in-C to use tactically, whereas, unknown to the Germans, their messages were being turned around instantly, even in December 1914.

The first German successes were by a Bavarian army unit at an intercept station set up in November 1914 near Roubaix on the Franco-Belgian frontier.[72] This was not a naval operation, but most of what Roubaix intercepted was British naval traffic, so it worked on that material. Although not trained in cryptology, the officers at Roubaix broke a simple British naval cipher at the end of December 1914. They mainly recovered reports on merchant ships stopped and checked for contraband at Dover, but they also broke messages to and from British submarines at sea. On 31 January Roubaix broke the British message advising all British merchant ships approaching home waters to fly neutral (or no) flags; the Germans used this information as part of their justification for the order to sink all shipping in the new 'war zone' they soon declared around the British Isles.[73] In May 1915 Roubaix was routinely solving messages from all British coastal patrols, from Channel patrols and in the British Merchant Navy Code.

The following month Roubaix broke the Allied Naval Code used between British and French ships in the Channel. In a few cases Roubaix profited by British errors, such as a request to repeat a message in an earlier code because the message in the current code was unreadable. That brought information on the activities of the Grand Fleet (but this information is not reflected in *Krieg zur See*). In mid-July a naval officer was detached to Roubaix to arrange co-operation with the Imperial Navy. From the end of July

1915 decrypts were sent directly to the command of the High Seas Fleet, Naval Forces Baltic, MarineKorps Flandern, the Admiralstab, naval stations Kiel and Wilhelmshaven and the commander of U-boats. On 30 October 1915 High Seas Fleet commander Admiral von Pohl formally thanked Roubaix for its bimonthly bulletins, which gave a nearly complete picture of enemy patrol and home defence forces (but not, significantly, of the Grand Fleet). That in turn was very helpful to the U-boats and Zeppelins.

Given these successes, the Imperial Navy set up its own intercept and evaluation operation (Entzifferungsdienst) at Neumünster, with an outstation at Bruges.[74] To operate it the navy withdrew its liaison officer from Roubaix in February 1916 so that it could exploit the techniques developed there. Roubaix continued to intercept and attack British codes. Late in February Neumünster read a British message passing intelligence that three raiders disguised as Danish merchant ships were breaking out (this seems to have referred only to *Greif* and *Wolf*).[75] During the 1916 Lowestoft raid Bruges reported the messages recalling ships off the Belgian coast. However, the system operated sluggishly. The report from British submarine *E 23* that she had torpedoed the battleship *Westfalen* during the August 1916 fleet sortie was promptly intercepted and broken by Bruges, but it waited five hours to send it on to Neümunster and the signal was further delayed *en route* to higher headquarters. Moreover, given the fragmented German naval command, it is not clear who could have made full use of such information.

Most of what was obtained was low-level information including minefield data.[76] For example, Roubaix broke a series of British messages sent in 1917 indicating which German minefields had been swept. Earlier messages confirmed the German belief that British submarines were patrolling the Heligoland Bight and the North Sea. It helped that, like the Germans, the British did not change their two most-frequently used codebooks, one of which was for the Auxiliary Force.

The Germans also tried traffic analysis, which was useful because the Royal Navy was so huge that it had to send numerous operational messages. The German official history refers again and again to the use of the volume of British wireless traffic as an indicator of whether the British were aware of a German operation. For example, in April 1915 the High Seas Fleet sortied to lay mines on the Dogger and Swarte Banks. Until some hours after that British wireless volume remained normal, which suggested that the British were not yet aware of the operation. The Germans also tried to estimate range from the strength of wireless transmissions, but soon learned (in 1915) that this technique was useless.

In the first half of 1917, the British were becoming more aware of German decryption and were adopting new techniques which complicated analysis. Even so, Roubaix continued to forward large numbers of reports and it was successful enough for a second surveillance command to be set up.[77] In the autumn of 1917 all German army signals intelligence was unified as a new signals intelligence service and Roubaix shifted mainly to army work. Presumably this fed into the build-up to the April 1918 army offensive. By that time Neumünster and the Imperial Navy's signals intelligence arm were well established.

It seems clear that the Germans never made much use of what they obtained. They did not, for example, use W/T to find convoys. Probably most importantly, they did not have a Commander Hope or other analysts who understood naval operations well enough to

use apparently low-level intelligence sent in breakable ciphers to deduce Grand Fleet operations. Again and again, the official German history refers to operations premised on vague agent reports from neutral capitals and on rumours in the British press. These were not covers for hard intelligence; the official history is quite willing to cite signals intelligence information.

Neumünster turned out to be very much a double-edged sword, because it used radio to broadcast its own successes, alerting the British and the Russians of their own code failures. The worst example came in 1917 when Neumünster sent out its solutions of the current British fleet code in German code, each British solution followed by its German coded equivalent. In effect it was giving the British the current German FPB code.[78]

It is not clear to what extent the Germans were aware of British signals intelligence. The author of *Krieg zur See* (Nordsee) indicates both that they were unaware and that, on the eve of Jutland, the Germans were using special phrases to deceive any listeners. For example, U-boats watching the British coast were to be told that the High Seas Fleet was at sea by the phrase 'take into account that enemy's forces may be putting to sea', and other phrases were to be used by the U-boat reconnoitring the target area, Sunderland.

The Aircraft Revolution

In 1914 navies generally agreed that aircraft had changed sea power, but they apparently over-rated what they could do. By 1918 aircraft technology had advanced to the point that expectations were being realised. Where in 1914 the British had seaplanes that could barely lift torpedoes from calm water, in 1918 they had carrier-based torpedo bombers which offered a credible way of attacking the High Seas Fleet in harbour (something proposed in 1914). The great surprise for a modern reader is how overrated (not by any means under-rated) aircraft were during the war. Their operations and their potential were described in much the way they might have been during the Second World War. For example, when a 1915 British raid on Zeebrugge damaged a U-boat there, the Germans concluded that the base was unsafe until it had been provided with massive anti-aircraft defence. In 1917–18 there was a massive fight to control the air near Zeebrugge, as though the base might be bombed out otherwise. The Germans built massive U-boat shelters similar to those at European U-boat bases during the Second World War, even though the bombs they faced were

pathetic by later standards and bomb-aiming grossly inaccurate. For that matter, in 1917–18 the US Navy made air attacks on German submarine bases a key element of its strategy. The only reason that is not obvious nearly a century later is that the war did not last long enough for it to go into effect.

As understood before the war, the most striking aircraft role was reconnaissance. The pre-war Royal Navy was so impressed by German airship progress that in 1912 it decided that it was no longer possible for it to use uninhabited islands off the North German coast as temporary destroyer bases supporting an inshore squadron. At the time, the Germans did not yet have Zeppelins in naval service, but they were about to acquire some.[79] The British found the potential of airships so impressive that the cruiser *Hermes* was converted into a seaplane carrier for the 1913 Manoeuvres specifically so that her aircraft could simulate the Zeppelins the Imperial Navy was about to commission. For their part the Germans were impressed by the demonstrated British ability to operate aircraft from ships. The British, not the Germans, conducted the first naval air raid, against Cuxhaven at Christmas 1914.[80] Even the most primitive seaplane carriers gave the British deployable naval aircraft, so HMS *Ark Royal* was able to provide reconnaissance and spotting support at the Dardanelles in 1915. Later the Royal Navy used air spotting to support monitors shelling Zeebrugge and Ostend.

From about 1915 on, the High Seas Fleet frequently took a few floatplanes to sea on board cruisers, which could hoist them out for launching. At this time the British were doing the same on board dedicated carriers, but until 1916 these ships were not integral with the Grand Fleet. The German official account suggests that the aircraft on board the cruisers were rarely if ever launched at sea, no great surprise in the rough North Sea. Only at the end of the war did the Germans plan to convert cruisers into seaplane carriers.[81] By that time the British had a large carrier force and they were deploying a large force of wheeled – higher performance – seaborne aircraft.

Given the failure of British wartime attempts to develop viable airships comparable to the German Zeppelins, the Grand Fleet sought alternatives. One was reconnaissance aircraft launched from the take-off decks of carriers such as the converted liner HMS *Campania*. She demonstrated that wheeled aircraft could take off from a deck and she was rebuilt as shown to lengthen the deck so that she could fly off two-seat reconnaissance aircraft. Typically they were seaplanes on wheeled trolleys, not land planes which might ditch alongside on their return. On that basis she could accommodate ten large aircraft. In 1917 *Campania* was credited with seven deck-launched reconnaissance aircraft (*Furious* had four). The next ship to have that capacity was the modified 'large light cruiser' *Furious*. Due to her age and poor performance, *Campania* was not included in the Grand Fleet carrier force in 1918. *Campania* is shown on 5 April 1916. (Author's collection)

On the eve of war the Royal Navy saw the Zeppelins as the eyes of the German fleet, but it seems to have taken some time for the Germans to appreciate what they had. The German navy became interested in Zeppelins due to the success of the first German Zeppelin airline, Deutsche Luftfahrt (DELAG) and after the army bought some.[82] Admiral Tirpitz initially resisted the idea.[83] As C-in-C High Seas Fleet, Admiral von Ingenohl did not use airships to support the fleet, but his successor Admiral von Pohl did so for the first time on 29 March 1915.[84] On 4 June he explicitly recommended airships as cruiser replacements, something the British thought the Germans had already done.[85] He pressed for considerable enlargement of the airship force and for a corresponding increase in bases (big sheds [hangars] were necessary to shelter the huge airships from the wind). Among the results was a programme to build six two-airship sheds. The official German history of the war at sea commented that in fine weather an airship might be considered equivalent to two light cruisers (as a scout, as it would not have anything like their firepower).[86] Before the war the Germans expected the British to come to them, into the Heligoland Bight. They wanted intensive reconnaissance of the Bight, which was practicable using airships and some aircraft. They had far less interest in what the British were doing further out to sea, with one important exception. When they went to sea, they needed reconnaissance around the path it would take. It appears that Admiral Scheer was the first to seek wider-area reconnaissance by the navy's airships. By 1916 the British saw German airships as Scheer's insurance against engaging the Grand Fleet and they were increasingly interested in destroying them, using either anti-aircraft guns (an airship was not so very much faster than a destroyer) or shipboard fighters.

Initially the Germans were unlucky. Their first airship *L 1* crashed into the sea near Heligoland in September 1913. Their second (*L 2*) burned at Fuhlsbüttel on 17 October 1913, killing nearly their whole naval aeronautics staff. With only *L 3* in service at the outbreak of war and both the North Sea and the Baltic to cover, the German navy had to press a non-rigid (Parseval type)

into service.[87] However, it reached an agreement with the army that the navy would receive every second Zeppelin and also some Schütte-Lanz airships. Bases, nearly all with anti-aircraft weapons, were built at Tondern and at Haage in East Frisia and at Seddin in Pomerania. A network of meteorological stations was set up, communicating with a central station at Wilhelmshaven. During the summer of 1917, with the navy regularly bombing Britain with airships, the army turned over its remaining Zeppelins (*LZ 111, LZ 113* and *LZ 120*) to the navy.

By the end of 1914 the navy had four operational airships of the improved *L 3* class and two named training airships. As an indication of what airships could already do, these ships, which were considered small by later standards, had a payload (including fuel) of 8700kg, at a time when aircraft payloads were in the low hundreds of kilogrammes. Proposals to raid England with Zeppelins were made by the Admiralstab as early as 20 August 1914, but its chief Admiral von Pohl resisted on the grounds that they were desperately needed as High Seas Fleet scouts. Only with the appearance of the fourth Zeppelin (*L 6*) in October 1914 could one be spared for raiding, which began in 1915. The initial Zeppelin attacks on London, executed by naval airships, were allied to the new campaign of unrestricted submarine warfare.[88] In both cases, the hope was not so much that the British would be knocked out of the war (as the Germans hoped in 1917), but that they would find their vulnerability, both to bombs and to torpedoes directed at merchant ships, so shocking that they would elect to come to terms. From a German fleet point of view, the raids on London seriously detracted from the air reconnaissance on which the High Seas Fleet depended. Dogger Bank was another milestone: for the first and only time during the war, an airship (*L 5*) was present above the German fleet during a battle.[89]

As an indication of how quickly Zeppelins were pressed into service, *L 20* was commissioned at the end of 1915, *L 39* at the end of 1916 and *L 60* at the end of 1917. The total acquired by the Imperial Navy was sixty-five Zeppelins, nine Schütte-Lanz airships (which had wooden rather than metal structure), three Parseval semi-rigids and one M-ship. Deducting special and training ships, seventy-two of the seventy-eight were operational, for reconnaissance and attacks. On average each performed sixteen reconnaissance missions and three attacks. In the North Sea, seventy airships performed 926 reconnaissance flights and 159 attacks. In the Baltic, twenty-four airships performed 220 reconnaissance flights and delivered forty-one attacks. The first thirty attacks were carried out in 1915, followed by 107 in 1916, forty-six in 1917 and seventeen in 1918. All were against fixed targets; an attempt to develop a remote-controlled anti-ship weapon for use from airships failed. The elements and the explosive potential of the hydrogen in the hull destroyed about as many airships as the enemy. Losses to explosion amounted to two in 1915, four in 1916 and six in 1918. Losses to weather: four in 1915, four in 1916, five in 1917 and one1 in 1918. Losses to enemy action: four in 1915, eight in 1916, nine in 1917, five in 1918.

A July 1918 German tactical instruction describing airships gives some idea of their capabilities and limitations as understood after four years of war.[90] At this time the main operational type was the *L 50* and a new high-capacity *L 70* was about to enter service. An *L 50* had five high-efficiency 260hp engines with 'super compression' (*i.e.*, superchargers for high altitude) driving four propellers (the two rear engines were coupled to one propeller). It was 664ft 8in long (beam 78ft 5in) and could reach 67mph. An *L 70* had seven such engines and six propellers; it was 693ft 10in long with a beam of 78ft 5in and it could reach 78mph. A typical crew was twenty-one (twenty-five in *L 70* and later ships), including two elevation and two directional helmsmen. Armament was two machine guns plus a 20mm cannon (being introduced) and bombs weighing up to 300kg (660lbs). W/T range using a 1.2 kW Telefunken set was 500–600nm (300nm for the emergency set). The set used a 100m antenna hung below the ship. However, the W/T could be used only when the gas bags were full. When hydrogen was released, it could form an explosive mixture under the airship. 'In the majority of cases the ship will not be able to inform the station with which it is in W/T communication that she dare not transmit any further', e.g. might not be able to acknowledge a long message. In that case she could still receive. Airships typically carried both the AFB and FFB code books with transposition table for the FFB, but if flying over neutral or enemy territory they were limited to the AFB with the current transposition table and that for the next day.

At about 200m visibility was about 30nm; at about 4000m it was about 60nm. Ceiling depended on weather, but the North Sea fighting airships could generally reach 6000m (19,685ft) during an attack. The Germans considered an airship safe from anti-aircraft fire at a range of 4–5nm and an altitude of 3000m. Endurance was normally twenty-four to forty-eight hours, but with special preparation it could be extended to 100 hours. Over the sea, airships fixed their positions by using dead-reckoning and directional W/T. Procedure as given in September 1918 was for an airship in contact with an enemy force to transmit every 15 minutes so that her absence could be noted. Only the shadowing airship was to signal. Ships could not be berthed or brought out of their sheds with wind blowing at more than Force 3 (5m/sec). Head winds of Force 4–5 halved the speed.

The Royal Navy also wanted airships, but it was much less successful developing them. It seemed to have had a much clearer idea of the potential value of airship reconnaissance for naval forces. That led it both to an extensive airship programme and to take fighters to sea specifically to deal with enemy air reconnaissance. DNO Captain H S Bacon made the first proposal to build a British airship on 21 July 1908; on 7 May 1909 Vickers received a contract to build an airship using Zeppelin technology as part of the 1909–10 programme. At this point the Royal Navy was interested mainly in airships as fleet scouts and a January 1909 CID report it favoured rigids over non-rigids due partly to their higher speed (hence better resistance to wind).[91] A rigid was easier to moor and it was considered easier to navigate, as a crew member could climb to the top of the hull to take navigational fixes. The Germans had not yet integrated airships into their fleet, but the CID reported evidence that they planned to do so. It compared a £35,000 airship with an £80,000 destroyer and a £400,000 light cruiser. This was HM Airship 1, *Mayfly*. Unfortunately she was wrecked on 24 September 1911 by ground wind before she could fly (she was broken in two). Admiral Sir A K Wilson headed the inquiry and he became convinced that aircraft were much better; First Lord Winston Churchill backed the airships.

In December 1911, however, the naval and military attaches in Berlin submitted an alarming report of German airship progress. Based on what German airships had already done, it seemed that they could reconnoitre the whole North Sea

except in foggy or stormy weather, it is probable that no British war vessels or torpedo craft will be able to approach within many miles of the German coast without their presence being discovered and reported . . . Unless we had obtained the command of the air, any idea that our torpedo craft could seek shelter among the Frisian Islands and remain there undetected must be abandoned . . . It is difficult to exaggerate the value of this advantage to Germany.[92]

Hence the urgent need to simulate a Zeppelin on reconnaissance duties in the 1913 Manoeuvres. The CID also noted the potential for a Zeppelin bombing raid on the United Kingdom, as Zeppelins had already flown the equivalent of the distance from Germany to England. The clearest evidence of a purely naval role for Zeppelins was the erection of the necessary protective sheds (hangars) at Hamburg and Kiel. At this stage the army had much more experience with airships, but the CID pointed out that they were much less suited to expeditionary operations, so in October 1913 the Royal Navy took over all British airship operations, including the army's stock of airships.[93]

The *Mayfly* disaster showed how difficult it was to handle airships on the ground, so in June 1913 the Admiralty proposed that it begin with smaller non-rigids, to gain experience.[94] Bids were requested and Vickers offered one rigid airship based on Zeppelin technology and four Parseval-type non-rigids (it had a licensing agreement with Parseval).[95] Other major shipbuilding firms were also approached. Armstrong (Elswick) reached a licensing deal with the other major non-rigid firm, Forlani (Italian). Vickers received a contract for the Zeppelin and three Parsevals under the 1913–14 Estimates and Armstrong one for three Forlanis (one to be deferred) under the 1914–15 Estimates, the navy deciding not to buy a rigid airship (presumably of Schütte-Lanz design). A second *Astra Torres* was also ordered. Rigid development proved difficult, the first successful one (Vickers' *HMA 9*) not leaving her shed until 16 November 1916. As a result, the Grand Fleet never enjoyed the advantage of airship reconnaissance it believed the High Seas Fleet had.[96]

To post-war navies, the German successes outweighed wartime British failures. It seemed that airships were the ideal long-range scouts of the future, limited only in that fighters could shoot them down. Airships could lift so much weight, however, that they could carry fighters for self-defence. The British tried this idea even before the end of the war and the US Navy later built and deployed the airship-borne F9C Sparrowhawk, on board its two airship 'aircraft carriers' *Akron* and *Macon*. Despite their loss, as late as 1940 the US Navy was still interested in huge airships for scouting. It shared the Royal Navy's need for strategic scouts capable of watching an enemy fleet sortie. Like the Royal Navy, the inter-war US Navy made up for the lack of such scouts by investing heavily in an entirely different surveillance technology, signals intelligence. Unlike the Royal Navy, the US Navy discovered to its great misfortune what would happen when the enemy suddenly changed codes and ruined its electronic surveillance system – Pearl Harbor.

Although the Royal Navy could not obtain the ocean surveillance it sought in the form of airships, it went much further than the Germans in taking aircraft to sea. The key development, demonstrated on board the carrier *Campania* in August and November 1915, was that a wheeled aircraft could take off from a flat deck on shipboard. Initially that was a short inclined deck forward of the ship's bridge, which sufficed for a Sopwith Schneider floatplane riding a wheeled trolley. There was no attempt to recover the floatplane on deck; it had to land on the water.[97] The deck was too short for the desired W/T-equipped two-seat reconnaissance aircraft, but it was extended sufficiently by modifying the ship. In this form *Campania* barely missed Jutland, not having sailed in time and being recalled because she was not sufficiently screened against submarine attack. Given the success of this project, two fast merchant ships were converted into carries with take-off decks (*Vindex* [commissioned 26 March 1915, conversion completed October 1915] and *Manxman* [commissioned 17 April 1916, but conversion not completed until December 1916]). *Vindex* was the first ship ever to launch a landplane (3 November 1915). She was assigned to the Harwich Force. *Manxman* was assigned to the Battlecruiser Fleet rather than the Harwich Force, but transferred to the Mediterranean in October 1917. She first operated the Sopwith Pup, which became the standard fleet fighter.

The first experiments with arrester gear were conducted about February 1916, leading ultimately to the decision to complete a suspended liner, laid down for Italy, as the full flush-deck carrier HMS *Argus*. Captain Sueter of the Air Department pressed for a 27-knot cruiser-carrier, for which a design was completed, but given the urgency of other projects, it was not laid down during 1916. In contrast to other naval officers writing at this time about carrier requirements, Sueter included among their functions attacks against both land targets and ships at sea.[98] Sueter wanted three carriers. Director of Air Services agreed that Sueter's ships would be well worth while, particularly to counter both Zeppelin reconnaissance and the threat that Zeppelins might bomb the fleet in the latter stages of a battle. Third Sea Lord referred to a design offered to Sueter in 1915. Consideration had been suspended while

In the spring of 1918, Grand Fleet air requirements cantered on reconnaissance: to find the High Seas Fleet and to deny it Zeppelin reconnaissance using organic fighters. The converted cruiser *Cavendish* (*Vindictive*) could operate six reconnaissance aircraft. At that time the projected Grand Fleet carrier force consisted of *Cavendish*, *Furious* and *Argus*, with fighters also launched by the 'large light cruisers' *Courageous* and *Glorious* and the cruiser *Caledon*: a total of twenty-five deck-launched reconnaissance aircraft and thirty fighters. In fact many battleships and cruisers also carried fighters atop their turrets, so the fleet fighter figure was considerably higher. Note that at this point the fleet air requirement did *not* include torpedo bombers (*Argus* was credited with fifteen reconnaissance aircraft and ten fighters). *Cavendish* was renamed *Vindictive* to remember the cruiser which fought heroically at Zeebrugge in April 1918. Note her separate flying-off and flying-on decks. *Vindictive* was completed on 21 September 1918 (commissioned 1 October). She was used only for trials (on 1 November a Sopwith Pup was successfully landed on her after deck). After the war she ferried aircraft to North Russia, but they operated only from ashore, perhaps because she grounded almost immediately after arriving. (Author's collection)

experiments in landing-on were conducted, but it was revived in February 1916. A modified design was submitted and now it was estimated that such a ship would take 15 to 18 months to build. Third Sea Lord wanted to wait for practical trials by *Campania* and in that case trade some speed for bulges and a serious gun battery (5.5in guns). The initial result of all of this discussion was to take over a suspended liner and order her completed as a carrier (*Argus* was purchased in August 1916). After that the landing-on experiments resumed. Completion was forecast in about a year.

In October 1916 Admiral Jellicoe complained that he still had far too few aircraft, his only carriers being *Campania* and *Engadine*, which had been taken over as a seaplane carrier in 1914. As an interim solution, two more merchant ships were taken over while building and completed as carriers with flying-off platforms: *Nairana* and *Pegasus*. They were completed on 14 August and 25 August 1917 respectively. By this time there were effective torpedo bombers and Sueter was trying to raise interest in operations (see the chapter below on the fleet in battle).

In October 1916 Jellicoe was superseded by Admiral Beatty, who shared his urgent need for air services for the fleet.[99] In January 1917 Beatty wrote to the Admiralty that he badly needed more aircraft to deal not only with the Zeppelins but with German seaplanes carried, he claimed, by six seaplane carriers (which did not actually exist). He had only three carriers, of which *Engadine* had no flying-off platform, hence was useless in anything but the calmest weather, *Manxman* was too slow and short-legged and only *Campania*, which was very old and hence unreliable, was at all what he needed. He hoped the new seaplane carrier (presumably *Argus*) would help, but he had no idea of her capabilities or of her likely date of completion. In February the Board answered that in addition to his own ships, the long-range bomber wing of the RNAS, which was attacking blast furnaces and munitions plants in Alsace-Lorraine, would also be hitting Zeppelin bases. *Argus* was described with an air group of eight reconnaissance aircraft, six anti-Zeppelin aircraft (i.e., fighters) and, if necessary four torpedo bombers. It was hoped that the reconnaissance aircraft could land on; experiments were most encouraging. *Argus* should be ready in November.

Beatty had convened a Grand Fleet Committee on Aircraft Requirements, which reported on 5 February.[100] It stated two requirements for aircraft to work with the fleet: reconnaissance and

The 'large light cruiser' *Furious* was modified while under construction, her forward single 18in gun replaced by a hangar and flat flying-off deck. Admiral Beatty approved reconstruction because the loss of a single slow-firing gun would mean little to the firepower of his fleet. He rejected similar conversion of her half-sisters *Courageous* and *Glorious* on the grounds that losing a twin 15in turret was a very different matter. They were given the usual turret flying-off platforms for fighters. Aircraft were lifted from the hangar by crane. *Furious* is shown as initially completed. (Author's collection)

After a successful landing onto the flight deck on 2 August 1917, Admiral Beatty recommended replacement of the after 18in gun by a landing-on deck. Work was simplified by duplicating the deck and hangar already designed for HMS *Vindictive*. In addition, the forward hangar was given a hydraulic lift. This work was considered urgent; it was completed in March 1918. The flying-on deck proved useless due to turbulence created by the ship's superstructure. In this form HMS *Furious* raided the German Zeppelin base at Tondern on 19 July 1918 – an attack at source to blind the German fleet – using seven Camel fighter-bombers. Two airships (*L 54* and *L 60*) were destroyed in their sheds. This was the first carrier air strike in history. *Furious* is shown as completed in March 1918, with a flying-on deck aft and a net to act as back-up arrester gear. (Dr David Stevens, SPC-A)

anti-Zeppelin. Shipboard reconnaissance would mesh with long-range reconnaissance conducted by seaplanes based ashore (the Royal Navy was taking delivery of new 'Porte Boats' and 'Large Americas'). By this time arrangements had been made to carry two seaplanes and a portable flying-off platform on board the large light cruiser *Furious*, still under construction; in March it was decided simply to replace the ship's single forward 18in turret with a flying-off deck and hangar. There may have been proposals to convert some light cruisers (Beatty opposed them, but he may have referred to a garbled version of the *Furious* proposal).

An Admiralty Air Policy was laid down early in 1917. The existing seaplane carriers would be maintained and *Furious* modified. Work on *Argus* would proceed, but the hope of completing her by November 1917 would be abandoned. Four new carriers, two large and two small, would be built (the two smaller ships were *Nairana* and *Pegasus*).[101] By September, plans for one of the seagoing carriers had been abandoned, but it had been approved for the cruiser *Cavendish* (later *Vindictive*) to be completed as a carrier and the two cruisers *Cassandra* and *Yarmouth* had been provided with flying-off platforms for single aircraft (fighters). At a meeting in September, Beatty asked for aircraft arrangements in the 'large light cruisers' *Glorious* and *Courageous* and in the cruisers *Caledon* and *Dublin*. The question was whether these ships provided enough reconnaissance and fighter aircraft to give the Grand Fleet superiority over German aircraft. At this time the Grand Fleet was credited with the carriers *Nairana*, *Furious*, *Engadine* and *Pegasus* and the air-capable cruisers *Cassandra*, *Dublin* and *Yarmouth*. Only *Furious* could fly off her four reconnaissance aircraft from her deck; the other three carriers had to fly theirs off from the water. *Campania* had seven deck-launched reconnaissance aircraft, but was much slower than the others. *Furious* had four fighters, *Nairana* three and *Pegasus* five, all flying off decks. None of these ships was credited with torpedo bombers. In the spring of 1918 the carriers *Cavendish* (six reconnaissance aircraft) and *Argus* (fifteen reconnaissance and ten fighters) would be added. *Courageous* and *Glorious* would each be able to fly off two fighters and the cruiser *Caledon* would add

another, for a total of twenty-five deck-launched reconnaissance aircraft and thirty fighters.

Grand Fleet Battle Orders envisaged keeping five reconnaissance aircraft continuously airborne during the approach and in action. Allowing ten for the approach and fifteen for the battle, the numbers available were just sufficient. However, the thirty fighters might well not be sufficient, so the Admiralty proposed fitting flying-off decks to as many more light cruisers as possible, pending Beatty's approval. 'As for his claims about the Germans, it is not known to what extent seaplanes or aeroplanes are being carried with the High Seas Fleet.'

As of September, it was proposed to fit an after landing-on deck and additional hangar to *Furious* and to convert *Courageous* and *Glorious* with forward decks and hangars as in *Furious* as already converted. The Admiralty analysis pointed out that even the largest carrier could launch only one aircraft at a time and each time it turned into the wind to do so it lost position in the fleet formation. On that basis it was by no means clear that adding aircraft capacity would also add to the number which could usefully be launched. Converting two more 'large light cruisers' would triple the number launched at one time and would add ten to twelve reconnaissance aircraft. This was by far the quickest way to gain more carrier capacity, as conversion would take no more than three or four months. The sacrifice of forward turrets was acceptable given the crushing superiority of Allied battleship gun power over the High Seas Fleet. Given the additional reconnaissance aircraft, it might be possible to release the new *Argus* from that role and devote her completely to carrying torpedo bombers. Her hangar could accommodate more than twenty of them and three or four reconnaissance aircraft could be lashed to her flight deck for pre-strike reconnaissance. In that case *Argus* could be employed on special operations against the enemy's ships in harbour or in support of the battle fleet. Given her comparatively low speed, *Argus* would find it difficult to remain in position in the fleet as she flew off many reconnaissance aircraft, so she might be particularly suited to torpedo attack.

By the end of the war, carriers and their aircraft were firmly embedded in British naval thinking, to the extent that it was the British delegation to the Washington Naval Conference (1921) which ensured a rather large tonnage (*i.e.*, potentially a large number) of carriers in the Royal Navy and the US Navy. Aircraft were also key to the Allied ASW campaign.

Smaller wartime carriers could launch only small single-seaters. This is HMS *Nairana* in 1918. She carried three fighters forward and four seaplanes aft, serviced by the massive gantry. (Allan C. Green collection via State Library of Victoria)

Navies favoured line-ahead formation because of its simplicity. Unlike all other formations, line ahead required virtually no signalling, as each captain could tell what he had to do by looking at the ship ahead of him. Conversely, if a line-ahead formation was disrupted, ships might easily be thrown into disorder. The German fleet is shown in line ahead before the war, with pre-dreadnoughts in the foreground. The Germans sought to organise their fleet in homogeneous eight-ship squadrons. (Naval Institute Collection, photo by Brown Bros., New York)

CHAPTER 5
The Fleets

THE MAIN COMPONENTS OF a 1914 fleet were capital ships (battleships and battlecruisers), cruisers and destroyers. Every navy was trying to add submarines, because they could ambush an enemy fleet. The most extreme version of such integration was probably the Royal Italian Navy, whose main tactic, as related to a US Naval Attaché, was to lead an enemy over mines and submarines. When the Germans drafted their war orders in January 1914, their fleet commander Admiral von Ingenohl warned specifically that the British might turn away to lead them over mines and submarines. Admiral Jellicoe later attributed exactly that motive to the Germans at Jutland, when they turned away.

The core of the fleet was its battleships, which alone were considered capable of fighting it out with other battleships. They were expected to fight in tight formation, because if they dispersed an enemy might concentrate his fire on part of the battle force. A battle force would normally fight in line ahead, because in that formation it could concentrate its fire (and avoid identification errors). However, line ahead was an unwieldy cruising formation.

The British at least expected to cruise in multiple columns. Among other things, that would minimise the target presented to a submarine. As the British fleet approached an enemy force, its commander had to deploy from columns into line ahead. He had to know the strength and course and position of the enemy so as to make the correct deployment. Since about 1901, the Royal Navy had known that if it knew the enemy's course and speed it could deploy across the enemy's path – it could 'cross his T'.

The fleet therefore needed scouts. An enemy would screen his fleet with cruisers, the intent being to hide his own course and strength. Numerous exercises showed that it took powerful cruisers to smash through to gain this kind of information. In 1914 the ships suited to this task were battlecruisers, in effect fast but lightly-armoured battleships, supported by light cruisers. The Germans had their own battlecruisers, but their choice had been to sacrifice firepower rather than armour for speed. On paper the German ships were as fast as their British counterparts, but British naval intelligence thought that their operational performance would be

much lower. They burned coal without the oil which supplemented coal in the British ships and German coal was generally considerably worse than the Welsh steaming coal used by the Royal Navy. On this basis the oil-burning *Queen Elizabeth* class battleships were credited with performance broadly equivalent to the German ships, but with far more powerful armament. This judgement changed during the war.

Destroyers were essentially ocean-going torpedo boats. The British originally called them torpedo-boat destroyers because they had been conceived partly as an antidote to French torpedo boats. They were fast enough to run such craft down, spraying them with fire as they did so. That was exactly what was wanted in a blockading destroyer, but the situation in a fleet action was rather different. In such an action, the enemy destroyers would approach at high closing speeds and they would not be exposed to defensive fire for long. Destroyers were poor gun platforms. In the blockade mode, they would have enough time to inflict sufficient damage. In a fleet, they probably would not. Under these circumstances, cruisers operating with the battleships would be far more effective destroyer-killers. Admiral Jellicoe saw his destroyers mainly as an anti-destroyer arm only because he felt had too few cruisers for that role. His predecessor Admiral Callaghan wanted to abandon the anti-destroyer role and build destroyers with heavier torpedo batteries.

The great question in 1914 was whether and how, submarines could or should be integrated into a battle fleet. It was widely understood that a submerged submarine could sink any warship, but submarines were relatively immobile. By 1914 the major navies were all interested in the possibility of building submarines which could keep up with a battle fleet, submerging in order to create an ambush for an enemy. Unfortunately diesel engines, the typical submarine surface powerplants, were not nearly powerful enough to provide a submarine with fleet speed. The British sought to solve the problem during the war by using steam power in their 'K' class.

Battleships were the core of pre-1914 fleets. The Grand Fleet battle line is shown at sea in 1918. The battleship is HMS *Orion*; the destroyer is HMS *Oak*, tender to the fleet flagship. Tactics were designed to bring such a fleet into position to deal with an enemy fleet and then to concentrate its firepower. Without such concentration, a fleet-on-fleet engagement was most unlikely to be decisive. Hence the importance of devices such as concentration and crossing the 'T'. (Dr David Stevens, SPC-A)

The German approach to the same problem was to deploy submarines in advance of a planned fleet operation. Both navies much underestimated the associated problems of navigation and communication. However, the fleet submarine idea survived the First World War in many navies. It died with the advent of fast battleships, but it revived many years later in the form of nuclear attack submarines in direct support of surface forces (an idea which also died due to communications and identification problems).

The Admiralty

The Royal Navy of 1914 was run by the Board of Admiralty, in effect a committee of admirals (plus some civilians) most of whom had specific responsibilities. The Board had both a civilian and a naval side, the civilian side being headed by the First Lord of the Admiralty. He was a member of the Cabinet and in effect the connection between the navy and the Government. The First Lord might be considered broadly equivalent to a US Secretary of the Navy. Usually his role was to defend the navy's requirements within the Cabinet. However, personalities could be important. Prime Minister Asquith appointed Winston Churchill to the post specifically in order to shape the navy's policies to his own requirements. Churchill in turn was far more activist than previous First Lords, as is evident not only in the printed Minutes which survive but also in documents such as the Ships' Covers of classes designed under

Fleets normally cruised in parallel columns, a compact formation which minimised size and hence detectability, but which was unsuited to combat. The British in particular made careful pre-war studies of how to deploy from cruising to combat (line-ahead) formation. Here the Grand Fleet cruises in columns. (Knight Album at NHB via Dr David Stevens, SPC-A)

his watch. His claim of responsibility for the *Queen Elizabeth* class battleships is a case in point (albeit one in which the documentary record is thin). Churchill had had no previous naval experience and the letters he received from retired First Sea Lord Admiral Sir John Fisher suggest that Fisher saw him as his own representative on the Board.

The professional head of the navy was the First Sea Lord. His colleagues tempered his decisions to some extent; how much depended on personalities. In theory decisions were collective and only the most minimal Minutes were kept. Thus although Third Sea Lord (Controller) was responsible for materiel (such as ships and weaponry), the decision to accept a particular design or even a particular set of requirements was a Board responsibility. Again, how much that was true depended on personalities. Before commanding the Grand Fleet, Admiral Jellicoe was successively Director of Naval Ordnance and Third and then Second Sea Lord, which made him unusually well aware of the limitations of his ships and weapons – and of innovative weapons and tactics devised by the pre-war Royal Navy.

The great weakness of the nineteenth-century Admiralty was its resistance to the creation of a supporting staff. After a series of disasters connected with mobilisation against Russia (at the time the most likely enemy) a small Naval Intelligence Department (NID) was created in 1887. It took on various staff functions. For example, it sometimes made tactical studies, for example of the value of speed in battleships. The great bulk of its surviving products are descriptions of foreign navies and their exercises (it also published classified accounts of British naval exercises). In the case of Fisher's revolution, a more formal staff might have forced him to explain *to the Royal Navy* what he was doing in such a way that others might have contributed to it and perhaps extended it. This sort of explanation would presumably have made for much more effective use of Fisher's intelligence-based operational concept.

Winston Churchill was appointed First Lord of the Admiralty in 1911 specifically to create a War Staff for the Admiralty, in theory parallel to the new army general staff introduced after the failures of the Boer War. In fact he slightly enlarged the existing NID, renaming it the War Staff and establishing formal sections (divisions) for war planning, intelligence and mobilisation. In wartime an operations division would be added. In retrospect it appears that the main effect of Churchill's changes was to formalise staff functions which were already being carried out. These functions were further formalised when the Admiralty was again reorganised in 1917. Because the documentary record is organised by originating organisation, it gives the impression of much greater changes than actually occurred.

War Planning

The 1905–6 Moroccan crisis led to serious discussion of possible war plans against Germany. In 1904–5 the previous British Government had faced the possibility that it would be drawn into the Russo-Japanese War, partly due to the alliance with Japan and then into a war against France due to the Franco-Russian alliance. War orders issued in 1905 and 1906 were probably the last designed to deal with a possible war against France and Russia.[1] The new crisis broke not long after the Russo-Japanese War. This time the British defused it by backing the French. They had to face the possibility that they might be fighting Germany in support of France. Admiral Fisher advocated a Baltic amphibious operation.[2] Later Fisher claimed that Royal Navy manoeuvres in the Baltic had helped defuse the 1906 crisis, and that the Baltic was the sensitive spot the Royal Navy could most usefully threaten.

While on leave after the 1906 crisis abated, Admiral Fisher decided that he needed a formal war plan against Germany. About November 1906 he created a small committee headed by Captain G A Ballard.[3] It considered a Baltic operation, but in the end it favoured a very different option, which ultimately became the basis for the navy's First World War strategy. That was to mount a distant blockade of the North Sea (conducted from its southern and northern entrances) backed by a battle fleet based in the northern part of the British Isles. The base was to be chosen so that the Germans could never mount a surprise destroyer attack like the one the Japanese had executed at Port Arthur in 1904.[4]

The fleet would make periodic sweeps of the North Sea to demonstrate its presence. For Ballard, the point of the plan was that the Germans would feel compelled to break the blockade. They would have bring their battle fleet out to fight the British battle fleet, preferably on the far side of the North Sea (from Germany), where they would not benefit from their considerable investment in mines and torpedo craft. In this view the blockade was an indirect means of freeing up British sea power (by causing the decisive battle) rather than a long-term means of crushing German society. Others viewed blockade as the key means of attacking Germany.

Ballard could reasonably assume that the Germans would find blockade intolerable. He did not reckon with the disconnect in Germany between the fleet building programme and the role of seapower; Tirpitz made the fleet itself the object of the exercise. *Krieg zur See* roundly criticised this concentration, as did German Vice Admiral Wolfgang Wegener in his 1929 book on German wartime strategy.[5] During the war, the British could never understand why the Germans did not come out to break the blockade choking them.

The rub in any such plan for distant operations was the need to maintain close observation of the German fleet at the same time that the threat of mines and torpedoes kept the main British fleet on the other side of the North Sea. German destroyers presented another problem. Given their torpedoes, they were considered a major threat to any large ship operating in the North Sea. Long experience in facing French torpedo boats in the Channel had convinced the Royal Navy that, once out to sea, such craft could not be contained. The only viable counter was to station destroyers off their bases. When the enemy craft emerged, they could be run down. Thus the British solution to the German destroyer problem was to maintain a considerable destroyer force off the German coast; British destroyers periodically practiced this operation. In the

This is the view across the 'T' of the 4th Battle Squadron, led by HMS *Hercules* (followed by *Collingwood, Neptune, St Vincent, Colossus, Bellerophon, Superb* and *Temeraire*). In theory, a fleet steaming across this scene at right angles to the course of the battle squadron could pour fire onto the leading ship. However, to make fire effective ranges and bearings had to be corrected continuously. For a ship on a course at right angles to the observer, the range changed at a maximum rate, meaning that correction had to be very fast. Against that, the enemy presented a long target (extended in the direction of range, hence easier to hit). Also, because the target bearing changes slowly, the range rate changes slowly. As the angle between crosser and crossed opened, the range rate decreased, but the rate at which it changed increased – this changing rate was more difficult to handle than a constant if high rate. It was entirely beyond the capacity of fire-control systems which attempted to measure a fixed range rate and use it to calculate future range. The prime example of such a system was the British Dreyer Table and the simpler German system suffered much the same limitation. Only the later synthetic fire control systems (the first of which were the British Argo Clock and its offspring the US Ford Rangekeeper), which modelled target motion and did not use rates explicitly, could handle this sort of problem. (Photo by Abrahams of Devonport via Dr David Stevens, SPC-A)

To cross the enemy's 'T' an Admiral had to know the enemy's course and speed (and range) – and he also had to conceal his own. Each fleet operated behind a cruiser screen. Each also used cruisers as scouts. They had to fight through the enemy's cruiser screen to obtain key information. The screening cruisers did not necessarily have to be as fast as the enemy's scouts. That is why, in 1914–16, the Grand Fleet still employed a mass of armoured cruisers about as fast as its battleships. The Grand Fleet's big cruisers are shown in 1914–15. Two *Monmouth* class cruisers are in the foreground, with three *Warriors* in the distance. One virtue of battlecruisers was that they could smash through such screens. (Dr David Stevens, SPC-A)

context of the Ballard plan, the destroyers would also provide warning if the German fleet came out. However, there was always the question of how long destroyers could be maintained off the German coast in wartime. That inevitably brought up the possibility that a forward operating base would have to be seized – a difficult operation, made more and more difficult as the Germans built a submarine force.

Admiral Fisher tightly controlled war planning. He liked to say that he had the navy's war plans locked in his head, although he did have to issue basic war orders to be executed once war broke out. He seems to have planned to execute Ballard's plan, but that cannot be certain. In any case, when he left office his successor had the same prerogatives. Admiral A K Wilson was certainly aware of Ballard's ideas, but the situation had changed dramatically since 1907 because the Germans were building a substantial submarine force. Wilson shared Fisher's awareness of the dramatic potential of submarines. He had witnessed submarine operations during the 1904 Torpedo Manoeuvres and had noticed that submarines seemed to be ineffective in shoal water.[6] On that basis (certainly no longer the case in 1911) he apparently thought that a fleet would be safe from submarine attack only when close inshore on the German side of the North Sea. Wilson may also have thought that the new anti-submarine sweeps then under development gave the fleet a reasonable chance of survival against submarines operating under difficult conditions.

Wilson never published his war plan, but some of his comments at a fatal August 1911 CID meeting suggest what he had in mind. If a destroyer force could not be maintained for long on the German coast, the only option was to kill the German destroyer force on the outbreak of war. Once that had been done, the distant blockade could be maintained. As Wilson described his plan to Prime Minister Asquith, British destroyers would rush up the German rivers (in which the German fleet was based) to sink the

enemy destroyer force at the outbreak of war. Asquith had never heard anything so aggressive or so dangerous; Wilson admitted that his own destroyers would take heavy losses in the process. Wilson's new war orders, issued in January 1911, provided for a strengthened inshore force to operate at the outbreak of war: four armoured cruisers, two destroyer flotillas and two sections of submarines, plus three minelayers. A third destroyer flotilla might be released from patrolling the English and Scottish coasts (which would be mined upon mobilisation) to reinforce or relieve the other two. As many destroyers as possible would be massed on the German coast at the outbreak of war, even if many would soon have to be withdrawn to fuel. The plans did not envisage the seizure of a forward base, presumably because the destroyer issue would be decided very quickly. Wilson was too inarticulate to explain what he proposed to do and the most important effect of his discussion was to convince Asquith that he had to go. Asquith moved Winston Churchill from the Home Office to the Admiralty specifically to quash what he saw as Wilson's over-aggressive plan. Asquith was thinking in deterrent, not war-fighting, terms.

Unsurprisingly, the Admiralty issued new War Orders in April 1912. It was assumed that war would probably break out suddenly, with no more than 48 hours' warning. The Germans would strike because they had 'some great enterprise [i.e., invasion] in mind which will be launched almost simultaneously' with the outbreak of war. The war orders allowed for two possibilities, war against Germany without allies and war in alliance with France. In the latter case the passage of the expeditionary force across the Straits of Dover would be covered.

The first priority would be to prevent the Germans from making a surprise attack (probably using destroyers) which would tip the balance of naval power. Thus the British fleet had to be positioned beyond German destroyer striking range, yet still in position to intercept a German fleet sortie. The 1912 plan split the fleet into a modern component (four battle squadrons) at Scapa, Rosyth, or Cromarty or at sea and a southern component (two older battle squadrons) assembled at Spithead or Portland – which was much the way the British arranged their force in 1914. All cruisers and destroyers on the East Coast would form a protective cordon while the northern and southern fleets formed and deployed.

The earlier close destroyer blockade of the German North Sea coast was cancelled. Neither Wilson's plan nor Fisher's earlier one had envisaged a close commercial blockade of the German coast, but now some sort of mid-North Sea line was needed. The War

Plan envisaged a line 470 miles long across the North Sea, covered by 105 ships (cruisers and destroyers).

This was Ballard's concept of operations. The long line across the North Sea was expensive and inefficient, but it was the least bad of three alternatives. One, close observation of the German coast, had just been dropped. The threat was invasion anywhere along the British coast. To meet it, the Admiralty would have to disperse significant forces along the coast. Apparently no one considered Fisher's flotillas adequate. Dispersing heavy ships was the most expensive plan of all, so it too was dropped apart from the old battle squadrons.

Back at the Admiralty as Director of Operations Division of the new War Staff in 1912, Ballard knew that the 470-mile line was unlikely to work. Ships would be too far apart to be certain of seeing the oncoming German fleet or invasion transports.[7] The most efficient way to detect a German sortie was the earlier close-in line of watchers and the only watchers who could survive in the face of German defences were long-endurance submarines. For the future, Ballard looked to a new generation of submarines which could keep the sea for ten days or more at a time. The 'D' and 'E' classes were usable, though not ideal and as yet there were not enough of them. Another problem, which Ballard did not mention, was that they had only short-range W/T. They therefore needed nearby surface ships to act as links to shore across the North Sea.[8]

With too few submarines, Ballard asked how the observation line could be shortened to something workable. Large-scale mining might limit the path the Germans could take.[9] This possibility had not received Admiralty attention, because until 1912 'the Board had adhered – although recently not without misgivings – to the policy of a close watch on the German coast, in which mines would be rather a source of danger to ourselves than otherwise'. This did *not* mean a traditional close blockade, but rather the destroyer operation. Hence no wartime role had yet been assigned to the existing stock of more than 9000 mines – which could fill a line 160 miles long with mines 100ft apart. A line could block the northern North Sea as well as access to Dutch ports. In 1912 the latter were considered the major potential gap in any blockade of Germany, as her needs might be met by shipments through Rotterdam. Ballard's minefield would solve that problem. The huge minefield could be announced as a deterrent to merchant traffic. There might not be

Typically a line-ahead formation turned one ship at a time. That could subject the ship at the turn to concentrated enemy fire. Yet it was the only way to turn the formation without signalling and risking collision between tightly-packed ships. At Jutland, for example, the 5th Battle Squadron (*Queen Elizabeth* class) turned away from the German fleet in this way, subjecting *Warspite* in particular to concentrated fire. Here the Grand Fleet turns 16 points (180°), ship by ship. In the German 'battle turn' at Jutland, all the ships turned 16 points simultaneously, rapidly reversing the direction of the line; it was remarkable that none of them collided in the process. (Abrahams of Devonport photo via Dr David Stevens, SPC-A)

enough money for mines, but there was enough for 50,000 warning leaflets, a bluff which might work at the outbreak of war.

The mine barrier would cut the line to be watched by nearly two-thirds, to a much more workable 170 miles. Before any such policy could be adopted, the enemy's ability to defeat it by minesweeping had to be evaluated and the British minelaying force built up: the seven existing converted cruisers would need a month to lay the 160-mile barrier. Some cruisers might be converted temporarily for that role. This minelaying policy had not been adopted by the time war broke out.

The 1912 and 1913 manoeuvres revealed exactly what Ballard feared: the line across the North Sea was the weak point. Watching ships missed the attacking force in misty North Sea weather. On the other hand, once it reached the British coast a German force would reveal itself for counter-attack. Surely the Germans would not attack the British coast unless their operation offered the greatest payoff, a successful invasion. In both the 1912 and 1913 manoeuvres, therefore, the object of Red was invasion.[10] In both cases he succeeded. Blue was unable to prevent raids and landings and could never quite bring Red to action. The British fleet commander commented that to draw the natural conclusion, that the primary role of the fleet was to prevent invasion, would have been a disastrous surrender of the initiative at sea.

In 1913 Admiral John Jellicoe, leading the nominal German fleet (the Red fleet), evaded detection and landed nominal troops on the British coast.[11] The manoeuvres also suggested that it would be best for the British fleet to operate well away from the coast, where enemy submarines would probably loiter. Danger areas were places the fleet was likely to pass or to approach: the Forth, near the Dogger Bank, between Swaarte Back and Terschelling Light and in and near the Moray Firth. These places figured prominently in First World War naval combat. In the 1913 manoeuvres, a British inshore squadron (off Flamborough Head) was 'perpetually troubled by submarines'. Such operations 'need special consideration owing to increased liability to such attack'.

The 1913 manoeuvres also finally killed the idea of independent destroyer operations in the Royal Navy. It turned out that groups of destroyers could not find the enemy fleet at night, partly because without effective ocean surveillance no one knew where to send them.[12] Both exercise C-in-Cs kept their destroyers with their battleships to use in the expected fleet action. 'As we have strong reasons to believe that this is the German plan, no doubt a British C-in-C would do the same in war . . . would always wish to have at least one flotilla with him – hence at least *two* flotillas must be attached to the Battle Fleet'. Results were limited because systematic training of destroyers to work with the battle fleet had only recently begun. Given their limited endurance, destroyers had to be based on the coast, to which they could return to fuel without losing too much time before reaching the fleet cruising offshore. Unfortunately all the likely bases – Harwich, Immingham, the Tyne, Rosyth, Aberdeen, Invergordon and Scapa Flow – were undefended. Given the new requirement to integrate destroyers more closely with the battle fleet, the Admiralty War Staff pointed out that much larger destroyers (more like the big new leaders) should become the standard. Nothing was done because once war broke out the only way to get many more destroyers was to continue to build the existing type.

In the wake of the manoeuvres a conference was held at Cromarty in October 1913. New war orders were sent to Home Fleet commander Admiral Callaghan in May 1914.[13] Upon the outbreak of war he would take command of all naval forces in the North Sea other than Local Defence Flotillas. That is why Admiral Callaghan's successor Admiral Jellicoe was C-in-C Home Flee*ts*. General instructors mirrored Ballard's 1907 plan: the strategy was

> to cut off all German shipping from oceanic trade and to secure the British coasts from any serious military enterprise and incidentally but effectually to over the transport across the Channel of an Expeditionary Force to France should the Government decide upon such an operation . . . It is believed that the prolongation of a distant blockade will inflict injury upon German interests, credit and prestige sufficient to cause serious economic consequence . . . Provided that the entrances of the North Sea from the westward and the northward are closed to all shipping under the German Flag, a close commercial blockade is unnecessary.

The northern blockade would be enforced by lines of cruisers and light cruisers from the Shetlands to the coast of Norway in the east and to the Orkneys in the west. Although under the orders of C-in-C Grand Fleet, these ships 'should not be withdrawn except upon a pressing emergency, as the duty entrusted to them is an essential feature of the general war policy'. Similarly, a line of light cruisers would be stationed in the western approaches to the Channel. The Straits of Dover would be patrolled by destroyer flotillas and submarines. Arrangements would be made to control all shipping in the southern theatre (English Channel west of and including the Straits of Dover).[14]

There was a legal problem: the planned blockades were not

Before the outbreak of war, the role of battlecruisers was under very active discussion within the Royal Navy. Should they be spread out as scouts, stiffening groups of smaller cruisers? Should they be concentrated in squadrons, to punch through an enemy's screens and later to reinforce the battle line as a fast division? In April 1913, newly promoted to command the battlecruisers, Rear Admiral Beatty listed their functions, beginning with supporting rapid reconnaissance of an enemy coast, supporting a blockading force; forming a support between armoured cruisers and the battle fleet when cruising and only as the fourth and fifth out of five, forming the support of a cruiser force watching the enemy's fleet at sea and (last) forming the fast division of a battle fleet in a general action. However, his confidential battle orders (17 July 1913) covered only three cases: engagement with enemy battle or armoured cruisers; engagement of the rear of an enemy fleet with a view to slowing it so that the British fleet could catch the enemy; and forming a fast division of the battle fleet in a general action. In the last case, the battlecruisers would concentrate against the enemy's van or rear. If the van, 'one of our chief objects will be to pour in a steady fire with long-range torpedoes'. In either case, the battlecruisers would concentrate on the enemy's flank, pressing in to short (decisive) range while the enemy was already engaged by British battleships. An analysis of gunnery aspects of the fast division (October 1913) included the comment that the ships of the battlecruiser group were particularly vulnerable; if they lost their speed they were inferior to battleships and could be cut off and destroyed, as were *Princess Royal* and *Indefatigable* in a War College exercise on 10 October 1913. The great problem of a fast division was that the enemy's gun range was unknown. Ideally the fast division could use its speed to manoeuvre outside the enemy's gun range until it got to an advantageous position, but if it was caught, it would not enjoy the support of the rest of the fleet. Jellicoe chose instead to place his fast division at the head of his line, to be used once the two fleets were engaged. Once action began, the fast division could haul ahead, always staying within about two miles of the head of the line. Just how well that would work depended, among many other things, on whether the high-speed manoeuvres of the battlecruisers made for range rates so high (and changing so rapidly) that gunnery became ineffective. British battlecruisers are shown at Scapa Flow, 6 August 1916. Their flagship HMS *Lion* still has no 'Q' turret, as hers was demolished during the battle of Jutland. (Dr David Stevens, SPC-A)

really blockades, in that the term meant that the blockading force was trying to stop all traffic trying to pass through to an enemy via blockaded ports, treating all neutrals equally. Neutral ports could not legally be blockaded. The projected lines of blockade were actually lines of patrol to intercept German ships or neutrals carrying contraband. They could not stop neutrals engaged in ordinary trade, even if bound for a German port. Legally, blockade should fall equally on all neutrals, but this one would not. For

example, countries outside the lines of blockade would be cut off, but those inside would be unaffected. Moreover, it would be difficult or impossible to deal with goods destined ultimately for Germany via a neutral port (the doctrine of 'continuous voyage' was more and more difficult to enforce). To war planner Ballard, these difficulties could be met by his earlier proposal to create mine barriers in the North Sea, using what he thought was a large stock of British mines. The British could avoid humanitarian objections by announcing the mined area. He proposed to begin with mines across the Straits of Dover and also to announce mining of areas of the North Sea outside territorial waters (to the south and east of a line from the East Goodwin Bay to a point just outside Danish waters). The latter field would be a bluff, intended to convince ships approaching Danish and German ports from the west that they were in as much danger as any approaching through the Straits of Dover.

Seen here in 1918, Battle Cruiser Force flagship HMS *Lion* shows typical wartime modifications, most noticeably the flying-off platform atop 'X' turret and the searchlights concentrated around her third funnel. The wires visible between the second and third funnels were part of the ship's wireless direction-finder array, the first in any British warship. Her torpedo net booms were landed after Jutland.

Upon a warning telegram being sent, the Grand Fleet would deploy in northern waters and the Channel Fleet (2nd Fleet, meaning older ships) in the English Channel. The third independent commander was Admiral of Patrols. Cruiser squadrons of the Grand Fleet, except for those on the Northern Blockade, would initially be used as an observation force to sweep and patrol the North Sea. This was the remnant of the earlier patrol line down the middle of the North Sea. Some time soon after the orders were written, the words 'observation duty in the North Sea'

Until 1910 the British assumed that the German fleet would go to sea without its short-legged destroyers, mainly because they mirror-imaged their own practice of using destroyers as independent strike forces. The Germans had long maintained that their destroyers were integral with their fleet and their manoeuvres featured a showy evolution, shown here, in which the destroyers passed through their battle line during a day action. Ironically, as CinC Mediterranean, Admiral Fisher had tried exactly the same manoeuvre in his own fleet. He certainly expected that he would take his destroyers with him. The shift when he moved to the Admiralty reflected his growing belief that destroyers and then submarines would make the narrower waters of the North Sea impassable to capital ships. Manoeuvres later showed that Fisher had grossly underestimated the problem destroyer groups would encounter trying to find their targets in the open sea. The battleships are *Wittelsbach* class pre-dreadnoughts; the destroyers are of the then-new *V 1* class completed from 1911 onwards. (Naval Institute collection)

applied to the cruiser squadrons were crossed out; they were needed too badly for other tasks.[15] C-in-C Grand Fleet could operate his battlecruisers either with the Grand Fleet or to support its cruisers. 'It may, however, become necessary to detach them to pursue and fight enemy's ships of similar classes which may leave the North Sea for commerce destruction.'

Of five Grand Fleet destroyer flotillas, only one would be attached directly to the fleet. Two would operate from the Humber and two from Harwich, all being under the C-in-C Grand Fleet. When the War Orders were revised in June 1914, two destroyer flotillas were permanently assigned directly to the Grand Fleet and Admiral Jellicoe frequently argued that he should also have one of the two Harwich flotillas. The June 1914 War Orders envisaged the other two flotillas as a swing force which might join the Grand Fleet or the Channel Fleet as required, but otherwise under the orders of Commodore (T) at Harwich to sweep part of the North Sea supported, when it was ready, by a cruiser force (Force C).

'D' class and later oversea submarines would 'as opportunity serves, be employed offensively towards the German North Sea coast in the Heligoland Bight, so as to maintain a close watch of the entrances to the enemy's harbours and to attack any outgoing ships'. This was Ballard's submarine operation. The June 1914 War Orders added that, as the number of oversea submarines grew, the ultimate object would be to establish and maintain a close watch on all enemy ports.

Upon the outbreak of war Callaghan was to take his fleet towards the enemy coast in a 'reconnaissance in force' before returning to his assigned war station. He would repeat such sweeps at intervals (over different ground each time) to demonstrate to the Germans how hazardous it would be for them to send a raiding expedition or other relatively weak fleet detachment across the North Sea towards the British coast. The fleet should cruise in such a way that its precise position was screened effectively by flotillas and cruisers spread ahead of it over a broad front – which might well intercept any German ships *en route* to 'execute some special mission'. Thus *German* uncertainty as to the position of the British fleet might be an effective deterrent. The responsibilities of the Admiral of Patrols included trawler sweeping of all mines laid off the East Coast. The June 1914 version of the War Plans included projected co-operation with the French navy: patrols off parts of the French Channel coast by three submarine flotillas (one working with a torpedo-boat flotilla) and with French cruisers supporting the British force in the western end of the Channel.

The strategy had two great flaws. First, the Germans would be utterly unaware of whatever the fleet did, unless it ran directly into the Heligoland Bight. That is evident from the post-war German official history of North Sea operations. Grand Fleet sweeps might be (and were) essential to maintain morale and effectiveness, but they did not increase the deterrent value of the Grand Fleet. Second, even had there been enough cruisers to cover the North Sea, they would not have spotted a German operation conducted in foggy weather. That was demonstrated when the Germans shelled Yarmouth in November 1914. It also turned out that Fisher's flotilla defence was not enough: the units, including a submarine, near the scene of the bombardment were unable to engage the enemy or to hold him long enough for the Grand Fleet to arrive. In 1914 the British did have submarines capable of operating in the Heligoland Bight, but they were not yet equipped (or, it seems, trained) to act as an inshore observational blockade. Even in 1918, when the

Once it was accepted that the Germans would use their destroyers in a day action, the British had to solve several problems. Until this point they had assumed that destroyers would attack only either before or after the day action, so that the best place for anti-destroyer guns was atop turrets, where they would have the best vantage. Now capital ships had to be rebuilt, their anti-destroyer gun crews shielded from the blast of their own guns. The fleet had to be provided with fast cruisers specifically to beat off destroyer attacks. If British destroyers were to be used against the enemy's battle fleet, they had to beat off the enemy's defending cruisers. It was also soon obvious that the only viable tactics were massed 'browning' attacks against an entire enemy battle squadron or battle line. Ideally British destroyers needed a lot more torpedo tubes. The outbreak of war coincided roughly with this last realisation and it was impossible to change destroyer designs when the main demand was for sheer numbers. This is one of the new breed of fast light cruisers intended to work with and against destroyers: HMS *Aurora* is shown as built. She had a mixed battery: 6in guns to deal with enemy cruisers, 4in guns on her broadside to deal with destroyers. (Author's collection)

submarines were conceived as a vital scouting line, they had serious limitations, as the last High Seas Fleet sortie that April showed.

Ballard's strategy was essentially (and reasonably) reactive. The Grand Fleet had no business risking attack by U-boats and damage from mines unless some worthwhile payoff was likely. That meant coming out whenever the High Seas Fleet came to sea. What made Ballard's strategy a success was British signal intelligence – not only decoding or decrypting, but also interpretation. It was the difference between the entirely unopposed November raid and a substantial, if ineffective, reaction to the December raid.

Ballard's strategy apparently did not commend itself to First Lord Winston Churchill, who wanted a more active offensive approach. Through the War Staff, he asked for a range of alternatives, including both the fleet sweep (Plan M) and a close blockade of the German Bight by strongly supported flotillas for four or five days to close the Elbe (Plan L.a without any local base and Plan L.b with a base seized from the Germans), as well as a plan to establish a cruiser-destroyer base near Stavanger, Norway to control the exits from the Skaw (*i.e.*, from the Baltic: Plan T). Jellicoe rejected the close blockades as far too costly. Callaghan's flag secretary, Roger Backhouse, complained in a memo that the war planners gave the fleet far too many disparate objectives (including covering the expeditionary force). In the end, it was Ballard's plan that the Royal Navy followed.

The Royal Navy and its Public

The Royal Navy of 1914 had benefitted from thirty years of intense public interest. In 1914 it received by far the largest fraction of overall British defence spending, as befitted the key service of a maritime empire. Many in Britain assumed that the war would open with a Trafalgar-style victory. They were unaware of changed realities or, for that matter, of how long it took for Nelson to work up to the point of fighting the battle of Trafalgar. The Royal Navy had no institutional interest in explaining the war at sea to the British public, as was illustrated by the remarkably inept way in which the news of Jutland was disseminated. Individual officers, such as Grand Fleet C-in-C Admiral Jellicoe, did give speeches explaining the lack of action during the winter of 1915–16, but there seems to have been no attempt whatever to create a unified public picture of the navy and its rationale. That had unfortunate post-war consequences for the Royal Navy.

The lack of attention to the public may have been a symptom of a wider disease. It seems clear in retrospect that Admiral Fisher fully understood the way in which British seapower could be used to fight German land power. He and his successors seem to have been unable to articulate the potential offered by seapower and the British Cabinet seems not to have been able to ask the right questions. The story of Gallipoli seems to show as much. Gallipoli is usually presented as Winston Churchill's bizarre attempt to give the Royal Navy a role in a largely land war. In fact the operation was approved by the entire Cabinet and its most important rationale seems to have been to relieve financial pressure on the Russians. When the operation failed, its proponents naturally submerged. As the most junior member of the Cabinet, Churchill was left as scapegoat and he never complained. Churchill (and Fisher) left the Admiralty in May 1915 (he remained in the Cabinet for six months as Chancellor of the Duchy of Lancaster). He then fought for a time in France as a battalion commander. It seems clear that he was still well-regarded, because he returned to the Cabinet in July 1917 as Minister of Munitions, an important post in which his energy was much needed. After the war he was made

Secretary of State for Air and then Chancellor of the Exchequer at an unusually early age. In effect he was rewarded for his willingness to carry the onus of the failed operation, not punished for having pushed it through. Gallipoli had been a classic high-risk, high-gain operation in the mould of Walcheren during the Napoleonic Wars. The difference was that the Cabinet did not realise that it could redeploy to match Wellington's Peninsula campaign. The Royal Navy's leaders failed to understand or to articulate that possibility.

In theory the Royal Navy created the postgraduate (war college) element of the Royal Naval College about 1900 specifically to institutionalise the study of tactics and strategy. It might have had a considerable influence had the war been fought in, say, 1920, but it is also possible that explicit discussion of grand strategy in peacetime ran against the grain of British military culture. No other country did any better; the Germans lost the war because they concentrated on the operational rather than the grand strategic level of war.

The British Tactical Revolution[16]

In 1914 the Royal Navy was in the throes of a tactical revolution, begun by 'Jacky' Fisher, based on the use of naval intelligence and wireless. As C-in-C Mediterranean in 1899–1902, Fisher had complained bitterly to the Admiralty that he had insufficient forces. He had to contend with no fewer than three potential enemy fleets: the French Mediterranean Fleet, the French Channel Fleet and the Russian Black Sea Fleet. His Mediterranean Fleet was clearly superior to any one of the three, but if they joined, he would be in

Not until 1916 did Admiral Jellicoe realise that in beating back German destroyer attacks his own light cruisers might well reach positions from which they could deliver effective torpedo attacks of their own. He therefore asked for much heavier torpedo armament for his light cruisers, resulting in twelve- and even sixteen-tube batteries. HMS *Danae* is shown in 1930, little altered since the war, with two of her four triple torpedo tubes visible. (Author's collection).

Admiral Jellicoe never felt that he had enough cruisers to beat off mass German destroyer attacks, so he chose to use his own destroyers mainly for that purpose. The mass German attacks did not materialise at Jutland and it can be argued that he would have been better advised to use his own destroyers more offensively during the day action. The 11th Destroyer Flotilla is shown screening the Grand Fleet in 1916–17. (Dr David Stevens, SPC-A)

trouble. In addition, he had to contend with French torpedo boat stations both on the French coast and on the coast of French North Africa (Algeria). The Admiralty firmly rejected his requests for more destroyers to watch these bases. He had to find a new way of fighting his fleet.

Fisher noticed that the telegraph line between France and Russia passed through Malta, where his fleet was based. Malta repeated the telegrams to boost transmitting power. Fisher persuaded the manager of the telegraph company, which was British, to provide him with copies. He set up an informal decryption office. Soon he was reading the operational traffic between Toulon and the Russian fleet base at Sevastopol. In the absence of wireless, any rendezvous between the French Mediterranean Fleet and the Black Sea Fleet had to be arranged by telegram. Fisher set up a plot at Admiralty House, his Malta head-quarters. Given the projected courses and speeds of the two enemy fleets, he could send out his own fleet to intercept them in turn.

This was a new way to deal with an enemy fleet and Fisher thought through its implications. One of them was that the British Fleet had to be fast enough to make the best use of the intelligence. Fisher was particularly proud that he convinced his fleet engineers to provide him with reliable high speed, an extraordinary achievement in an era of reciprocating steam engines which so often shook themselves to pieces at speed. Successive interception of enemy fleets required that Fisher's own fleet destroy them rapidly; otherwise it would be tied down and would not be able to hit the other enemy fleet before it arrived at a set rendezvous. This requirement seems to have interested Fisher in volume of fire. His first approach to an all-big-gun ship was to arm her with sixteen 10in guns, the largest weapons which he thought could fire rapidly.

Interception at sea demanded scouts fast enough to get well ahead of the British battle fleet and to range far enough out to find an enemy fleet even if it was well off its predicted (from intelligence) course. Once there, they had to be able to penetrate any cruiser screen it had thrown up, so that the British fleet could manoeuvre into position. This would seem to have been the origin of the battlecruiser idea: an unusually fast armoured cruiser with heavy enough guns to deal with battleships. It was not the only origin and in fact by 1899 the British were already building big armoured cruisers whose designers considered them fast battleships. However, it is easy to see the need for battlecruisers in

Fisher's new kind of intelligence-based naval warfare.

There was also a subtler revolutionary idea. In the past, it had been obvious that a fleet should be commanded by the Admiral on board it. Governments might meddle (a French Admiral in the Crimea was outraged to be commanded 'at the end of a telegraph line'), but only the fleet commander on board his flagship could see what was happening. Now, however, it might be argued that authority should be split between the Admiral at sea and whoever sat at the centre of the intelligence web. That plot at Admiralty House was now a vital command tool. It did not quite portend remote command, but whoever sat at Admiralty House had a measure of operational command, at least until the fleets came into contact.

For their part, the Germans thought they did not have nearly enough light cruisers to scout ahead while dealing with the threat of destroyer attack. The light cruiser Strassburg was designed in 1908–9 and built in 1910–12, a member of the Magdeburg class. Unlike contemporary British light cruisers, she was armed entirely with twelve 10.5cm (4.1in) guns. In 1915 she was rearmed with seven 15cm guns and two 8.8cm. Cruisers like this were intermediate between the British 'Town' class (scouts and trade protection) and fast destroyer-support cruisers like the Arethusas and their 'C' and 'D' class successors. Strassburg was designed for 27 knots and made 28.2 on trials, making her faster than a 'Town' but slower than an Arethusa. She survived the war and became an Italian prize (she was renamed Taranto). Subsequent German cruisers were based on this design, though later ships had three rather than four funnels. (US Naval Historical and Heritage Command, courtesy of MSGT Donald L R Shake USAF)

Fisher brought his ideas with him to the Admiralty when he took office as First Sea Lord in October 1904. The visible ones were the new kinds of capital ship. The new kind of command structure was much less obvious (because it was much more secret), but it was also more significant. In Fisher's mind, naval intelligence should be converted from a compiler of data on foreign navies to an operational system maintaining a picture of foreign naval movements and intentions, largely as culled from signals. Analogous techniques could be applied to merchant shipping. Among other things, data on merchant ships (and their disappearances) could be used to deduce the positions of enemy raiders. That could change the way in which the Royal Navy protected trade. Fisher's thinking translated into the creation of a plot showing the positions and courses of enemy warships or formations, on the basis of which the Royal Navy could be deployed. Although the plot would exploit signals intelligence, it could also benefit from many other sources of information, such as lines of scouts stretched across the North Sea.

The First Sea Lord at the Admiralty, the centre of the intelligence web, would become an operational commander rather than a policy-maker. At times Fisher waxed poetic: First Sea Lord and the main fleet commander would have to have a deep understanding of each other, so that they could work in unison. As in many other things, Fisher's understanding of what *could* be in the distant future much exceeded what could actually be done in the pre-1914 world. To make Fisher's vision a reality required a degree of ocean surveillance which was impossible in the pre-aircraft, pre-radar era and difficult even them. Even so, it gave the Royal Navy of the First World War enormous advantages and it made possible the distant blockade strategy it adopted.

It is not clear what Fisher expected his source of intelligence to be. He may well have had wireless in mind, because in his memoirs he wrote about how he knew what every Captain off the shores of Europe was saying (by wireless) and that he had the key telegrams (wireless messages) before foreign Admiralties had them. Once war broke out in 1914, the British relied heavily on wireless and code-breaking. This source of data was soon joined by radio direction-finding (surviving documents all date this technique to after the outbreak of war, but that may not be true).

Fisher's concept of shore operational control of a battle fleet seems to have been tested for the first time during the summer 1909 manoeuvres. The ashore headquarters (Naval Centres) of two of the three fleets involved (Red and Blue) had operational control, communicating with its fleet via designated radio (W/T) sending and receiving ships acting as the Admiralty radio station (the Red fleet used the shore station at Cleethorpes for transmission). Each fleet had a string of War Signal Stations.

The 1913 manoeuvres revealed a serious problem. Local commanders imagined that the War Room in the Admiralty had a clearer picture of the situation than they had. They surrendered initiative: surely they should await War Room orders. This problem was repeated throughout the war. One striking form was an inability of light forces, such as destroyers and cruisers, to report frequently enough. Apparently junior commanders did not realise that the picture in the War Room consisted at least partly of what they reported. Much the same applied to the fleet plot which Admiral Jellicoe introduced.

The Red Fleet used the Naval Centre at Sheerness, which would have controlled North Sea flotillas in wartime, as its headquarters 'for the distribution of intelligence on the Red side'. The 1913 exercises seem to have shown that it could not handle its communications load. Captain George Ballard, recalled from retirement to solve the coastal patrol problem, wanted to decentralise, creating six local command centres, each with its own war

Given British interest in 'browning' attacks, it is remarkable that it took until 1917 for the British to deploy triple torpedo tubes, increasing the broadsides of their destroyers by 50 per cent. The British designed a quadruple tube during the war, but it did not enter service until afterwards. HMAS *Vampire* shows her two triple tubes. (Allan C Green via State Library of Victoria)

The US Navy adopted the British 'browning' idea pre-war. It showed what that could mean. US destroyers had pairs of triple tubes on each side. Gyro angling made it possible for all the torpedoes to converge at a point ahead of the destroyers, giving a single destroyer a twelve-torpedo punch (a few US destroyers built during the inter-war period had sixteen tubes). Despite the close contact between the two navies in 1917–18, the British were never aware of the US innovation (which, to be fair, was exercised only after the war, though conceived before it); British accounts explain the sided arrangement of American torpedo tubes as a matter of providing spares, firing one broadside and then the other. British light cruisers had a similar torpedo battery, but the Royal Navy never seems to have been interested in curved ahead fire. USS *Dent* (DD 116) shows her port side pair of triple torpedo tubes in this wartime photograph.

room. How these war rooms would have co-ordinated with that in the Admiralty was never clear.

Red orders for 1913 stated that 'it is to be taken as an axiom that the fewest possible signals should be made by W/T. . . W/T signals are constantly of help to an opponent. . .On the other hand, instances have occurred of important information not being sent. . .' The solution was broadcast. Instead of signalling back and forth, ships copied signals included in fleet broadcasts, the messages being transmitted under coded or otherwise concealed headings. Broadcasting drastically reduced the value of traffic analysis, making it much more difficult to deduce the structure of the force at sea. It also became more difficult to deduce operations by noting which transmitters spoke to which other transmitters at any given time. The US Navy adopted a similar broadcast system in the 1920s (initially called the 'no receipt' system because no ship acknowledged receiving a message). Without receipts, a ship might never know that the intended recipient had missed a message. The US solution was to number all messages; each ship guarded (received) all Fleet Broadcast messages. US Navy called this the Fox broadcast, after the old phonetic letter for F.

A New Way to Protect Trade

Before 1914 the Royal Navy accepted that an enemy would strike at British seaborne trade, the lifeblood of the Empire. It was assumed that he would use surface raiders, mainly cruisers. The question was how to destroy them. Fisher was brought to the Admiralty in October 1904 because the sheer cost of providing enough cruisers, largely (but not entirely) for trade protection, was

breaking the Admiralty budget. His new intelligence-driven concept of warfare offered an alternative.

Fisher's experience in the Mediterranean told him that it might be possible to use the mass of available information to deduce where raiders were operating. For example, Lloyd's kept track of planned voyages. If ships did not arrive as expected, it might be assumed that they had been attacked *en route*. Collating sufficient information would indicate where a raider might be operating. Once merchant ships had radios, they could indicate that they were under attack (the 'RRR' signals of the Second World War were used in this way). Fisher created a Trade Division at the Admiralty both to track seaborne trade and to design wartime blockade. If the Admiralty had a good indication of where a raider was operating, it could use the new technology of W/T to direct powerful cruisers to that spot. This kind of direction required high speed (information would become stale) and long wireless reception range. The new battlecruisers offered both (they had unusually high masts specifically for better reception). Like their armoured cruiser forebears, they also had other vital functions, such as fleet scouting and screening. For a time, Fisher thought that they could replace battleships altogether, offering more capabilities.

In his manifesto, *Naval Necessities*, describing his 'system', Fisher wrote several times that enemy cruisers had to be hunted down. That meant his new way of warfare, as the accepted alternative was to place cruisers in focal areas into which raiders would inevitably be drawn. Hunting was the only way to cut the number of British cruisers. At least initially, it entailed a change in British dispositions. The fastest and most powerful cruisers would be concentrated in home waters, from which they could be despatched most efficiently.

The Grand Fleet needed a huge destroyer force, both to screen it against submarine attack and for the earlier functions of attack and anti-torpedo defence. This is one of its destroyer pens, late in the war (note the 'V&W' class destroyers with triple tubes).

This departure from earlier practices has often been misunderstood. It seemed that under Fisher the Royal Navy was being compelled to call its forces home from abroad because it could not afford both to maintain dispersed fleets and to build a powerful force in home waters. In fact Fisher probably saw it very differently, as a way of using a limited number of much faster and more powerful cruisers against raiders anywhere in the world.

Battlecruisers in home waters could easily reach out into the Atlantic or the Mediterranean, but they could not quickly reach the Pacific. The new concept of trade protection required that the big cruisers be instantly available both in home waters and in the Pacific. At the 1909 Imperial Conference, Fisher lobbied the major Dominion governments to develop the necessary naval forces. He wanted each to build a 'fleet unit' consisting of a battlecruiser and several modern light cruisers. These ships, like the battlecruisers in

Destroyers had such limited endurance that they in effect defined the radius of action of the Grand Fleet. Fortunately for the Royal Navy, its destroyers burned oil, hence could be fuelled at sea. Nearly all Grand Fleet capital ships burned a combination of oil and coal, hence could fuel destroyers. The procedure, in which a capital ship towed a destroyer and also passed a fuel hose aft, was slow but effective.

home waters, could run down raiders. Alternatively, the fleet units could combine into a Pacific Fleet capable to meeting a hostile fleet. In the event, only the Australian Government was willing to buy a fleet unit, built around the battlecruiser *Australia*. The New Zealand government bought a battlecruiser (HMS *New Zealand*) for the Royal Navy, but could not buy a full fleet unit, nor could it afford to operate one. India and Canada turned Fisher down. At the time, Fisher was interested in deploying some British battlecruisers in the Pacific to fill out the trade protection force there. That proved impossible as the fleet concentrated in home waters to face the Germans. The deployment of three battlecruisers to the Mediterranean in 1914 also seems to have been intended to provide a force within range of potential raiders.

The new system worked, but it took time to run down raiders based on shipping data. By mid-1915 all German cruisers abroad at the outbreak of war had been sunk by British cruisers intercepting them. That the system worked so well against surface raiders may explain why the Admiralty kept trying it against U-boats, the rub being that the hunters could not see the U-boats and could not detect them even at close range until hydrophones had been perfected.

British Deployments

The Royal Navy spanned the globe, its ships distributed among fleets and stations. Deployments reflected changing threats. When Fisher commanded it in 1899–1902, the Mediterranean Fleet was the most important in the Royal Navy, because it faced the main strength of the two most likely enemy navies, the French and the Russian. It also defended the most important British trade route, through the Mediterranean and Suez to India. By far the next most important fleet was the Channel Fleet, which faced the French bases along the Channel.

Fisher was made First Sea Lord to solve the problem of rising naval costs. The Royal Navy had a large reserve fleet, but not the reserve to man it in wartime. It also had to deal with changing threats. In the autumn of 1904 First Lord Selborne convened a committee to rethink deployments. It began with a new analysis of the threat. The likeliest was a war against Germany in combination with Russia, the next likeliest a war against the older threat of a Franco-Russian combination. Selborne added that the worst threat was German intervention in an ongoing war against France and Russia.[17]

For European waters, the question was how to maintain sufficient strength both in the Mediterranean and in the North Sea. Given the variety of threats and the possibility Selborne mentioned, neither the North Sea nor the Mediterranean could be left uncovered. A 'swing' fleet was created which could reinforce either theatre. At this time the Royal Navy had a Home Fleet and a Channel Fleet. The Channel Fleet was renamed the Atlantic Fleet and based in Gibraltar as the 'swing' fleet. The Home Fleet was renamed the Channel Fleet and oriented towards the North Sea. Given the Russian threat, the Royal Navy had to maintain a powerful Eastern Fleet. Unlike Europe, the Far East required dispersed peacetime dispositions to maintain order. The Eastern Fleet (or Group) was therefore normally split into a China Station, an Australia Station and an East Indies Station, the ships of which would be united in wartime. The United States, which had figured in previous planning, was considered friendly, so the North

Nearly all First World War capital ships and most other warships, burned coal. Fuelling was laborious and nearly impossible at sea (although navies worked hard to solve that problem and the US Navy built large colliers for the purpose). Here a capital ship is coaled, the collier alongside placing sacks of coal on deck. The men waiting on deck will move it to hatches, by means of which it was taken below. Coaling was an all-hands evolution which might take a day or more. Coal produced dense smoke which revealed the position of a fleet beyond the horizon and it generated ashes (clinker) which had to be cleared periodically from boilers. Because boilers were stoked by hand, their size was limited and ship designers had to provide sufficient stoking space in front of furnaces, plus access to the coal itself. Although in theory coal in bunkers added protection, it also required scuttles which limited a ship's watertight integrity. One of the surprises of the wartime and post-war eras was that a liquid layer of oil outboard of a ship's vital areas was an effective means of protecting against torpedo hits. Oil fuel was attractive for other reasons, such as its much greater energy content and the fact that an oil-fired ship could accelerate much faster. From a British naval point of view, the main drawback was that oil had to be brought to the United Kingdom over a great distance, the tankers turning out to be vulnerable to attack. By way of contrast, the US Navy adopted oil fuel largely because the United States had such generous supplies. (Photo from Knight Album NHB via Dr David Stevens, SPC-A).

America and West Indies Station need not be maintained as a wartime fleet. Instead, it was made the peacetime training squadron. Parallel to this reorganisation was reorganisation of ships in reserve. Obsolete ships were discarded. The rest were given nucleus crews on a sliding scale, the more modern ships having the most complete crews.

By mid-1906 the international situation had changed further. The crisis over Morocco, which nearly caused war, focussed British attention on Germany and the North Sea. It was the occasion for Admiral Fisher's request for war plans, which produced the strategy the Royal Navy actually used during the First World War. In October 1906 it created a new Home Fleet, formed from modern reserve ships taken from the Channel and Mediterranean Fleets (four battleships from the Channel Fleet, two from the

Mediterranean) and from the 1st and 2nd Cruiser Squadrons.[18] Although created from reserve ships, the Home Fleet was envisaged as semi-operational, carrying out, for example, battle practices not normally conducted by Reserve Divisions. Its primary object would be seagoing efficiency, so it would cruise as often as possible. The cruisers would operate from time to time with those of the other fleets for instructional and tactical exercises. The Home Fleet would include all flotilla craft, under a new Admiral (D); they would be detached to the Channel and Atlantic Fleets as expedient from time to time. C-in-C The Nore (at the mouth of the Thames) would retain his independent responsibility for local defence.

Fisher stated that he planned to build the Home Fleet into a force 'at once so efficient and so near at hand that it can guarantee the security of the country even in the absence of other Fleets on the high seas or in comparatively distant waters'.[19] Critics called the Home Fleet a training fleet, but Fisher pointed out that all fleets had a large proportion of new officers and men; in 1904 the Channel Fleet changed from one-third to one-half its complements every year. The best ships for training were those near Home Ports, which now meant the Home Fleet and the 4th Cruiser Squadron. The fully-manned ships of the Home Fleet (twelve capital ships [including armoured cruisers] and forty-eight destroyers) were absolutely ready for war and the remaining torpedo craft, with four-fifths of their crews on board, were 'ready according to any but the severest standard'. Meanwhile the Channel Fleet had been considerably strengthened by adding newer battleships.[20]

The creation of the Home Fleet coincided roughly with the appointment of Admiral Sir Charles Beresford, Fisher's long-time opponent, to command the Channel Fleet. Beresford saw the new fleet as a direct slap, charging that his own command had been cut to create it. Fisher's reply was that the Channel Fleet was already superior to the German fleet and that the Home Fleet was in effect a complete reserve against any German attempt to wear down a British fleet facing it. Both it and the Atlantic Fleet could join the Channel Fleet in wartime. In March 1909 the Home Fleet absorbed the Channel Fleet, which became its First and Second Divisions (each with an eight-ship battle squadron). The former Home Fleet was the third and fourth divisions, a reserve force assigned to the major home naval commands. The dreadnoughts were in the 1st Battle Squadron of the First Division, Home Fleet. The battlecruisers were in the attached 1st Cruiser Squadron.[21] The Atlantic Fleet survived as a 'swing' force which might reinforce the dwindling Mediterranean Fleet in an emergency, or might combine with the Home Fleet.

Fisher's assignment of all flotilla craft to an Admiral (D) was associated partly with his idea that ultimately the North Sea should be barred to the German fleet mainly by powerful flotillas of sea-going destroyers (later supplemented by long-range ['oversea'] submarines). To the extent that the threat of invasion was taken seriously, it would be dealt with by groups of coastal torpedo boats and submarines led by cruisers. This idea seems to have largely died by the time Fisher left the Admiralty in 1910.[22]

By 1910 plans for war against German called for merging the Atlantic and Home Fleets in wartime. Although the Atlantic Fleet was still considered a 'swing' fleet in 1912, by that time its base had moved from Gibraltar and Berehaven (for exercises) to Dover and Berehaven. Its ships continued to be repaired at Gibraltar, not least to keep that dockyard alive. Fleet organisation was again reviewed in 1912, in the context of both a growing German threat and the growth of the Italian and Austrian fleets, both part of the Triple Alliance with Germany, hence both potentially hostile.[23] Both were now on the point of commissioning dreadnoughts, so the previous British Mediterranean force of four *Duncan*s and *Swiftsure* and *Triumph*, all pre-dreadnoughts, would soon be completely outclassed. They were now, in First Lord Churchill's words, 'merely a useless and expensive symbol of power'.[24] To maintain a credible force in the Mediterranean would entail drawing down the force in Home waters, which would be increasingly dangerous as the Germans continued to build up.

The issue was critical because it demanded more of an Admiralty running very hard to maintain the desired edge over the Germans. In February 1912 First Lord Churchill wrote the Chief of the War Staff that it might necessary to carry the principle of

concentrating the fleet to its logical end, meaning bringing the battleships home.[25] It seemed to Churchill that German diplomacy had been brilliant: instead of building against each other, Italy and Austria were both building together against Great Britain. The Italians were clearly reluctant allies of the Austrians and they might well come over to the British (as in fact they did) 'if it were reasonably certain that with the assistance of our Fleet they could hope to recover from Austria "Italia irredenta" they would renounce the Triple Alliance, take their chance in a land campaign and become our effective ally'. There would also be effects on Black Sea, Levant and Far Eastern trade. Nor could effects on the Empire and on Egypt be disregarded. In Malta 'we can[not] disregard a possible enhancement of a disloyalty that is always slumbering'. Overall, withdrawal would be seen 'as a direct result of successful German policy', expulsion from the Mediterranean. Surely it would confirm the value of the sacrifices the Germans were making to build their immense fleet.

Without a fleet at Gibraltar, it would be impossible to close the Straits. Partial control could be exercised by a flotilla of destroyers and submarines, which could make passage hazardous enough that an enemy would not try to get through without strong strategic reasons. Adding a few small cruisers would also disrupt enemy trade trying to get through. Flotillas would also have to be used to cover the Canal and mask the Dardanelles. Chief of War Staff pointed out that without a strong fortified base, flotillas were useless against an enemy with undisputed command of the sea. Even then at best they could only delay attack. An enemy might well try to eject the British from Egypt. The Dardanelles could be masked only by a battle fleet; flotillas were inadequate. 'Generally speaking, flotillas left in the eastern basin of the Mediterranean on the withdrawal of our Battle Fleet would soon fall an easy prey to a Mediterranean enemy'.

Austrian and Italian policy was fluid enough that nothing could be predicted beyond 1915. Current plans envisaged eight Italian and four Austrian dreadnoughts, all of which would probably be in commission by the end of 1915; Italy would also have eight fairly good pre-dreadnoughts, contemporary with the *King Edward VII* class. It would take a force of at least twenty modern battleships, plus armoured cruisers and destroyers, to handle a combined Austrian and Italian fleet. A lesser force (twelve battleships or so) could operate effectively defensively from Malta. That was impossible. On 15 February Churchill wrote that the naval situation disclosed by the new German Navy Law

renders the formation of an additional Battle Squadron in Home Waters necessary. We cannot afford to keep fully commissioned battleships abroad during these years of tension. The first ten days and especially the first five days of war would require the maximum immediate deployment of naval power in the North Sea and the Channel. Once our mobilisation has been effected and even before any naval decision has been obtained, it should be possible to detach a Battle Squadron for the Mediterranean. But the greatly increased striking force which Germany is organising, against which we must always maintain sufficient margins, makes it necessary that all fully commissioned battleships, whether eventually destined for the Mediterranean or not, should be retained in the main theatre of operations until our mobilisation is complete, or the enemy's fleet beaten.

The destroyer *S-132* was typical of German practice. She was handed over to the US Navy as a war prize. The view from astern shows her at Norfolk Navy Yard on 12 October 1920. Before handing her over, the Germans removed all fire-control equipment, including rangefinders. She was part of the 1916 Mobilisation class of standard destroyers. Unlike earlier German ships, she had no well deck forward of her bridge structure. The chute on her side aft was for one of two depth charges, the centreline structure being for minelaying (she could carry twenty-four mines). Among Admiral Jellicoe's chief concerns was his fear that if he crossed the wake of the German fleet, destroyers would lay mines in his path. He was certainly right that most German cruisers and destroyers were fitted to lay mines, but wrong that the Germans planned to do so tactically.

The CID Secretariat played down the spectre of combined Italian and Austrian action; there were grounds to believe that the Triple Alliance did not cover conflicts arising out of Mediterranean considerations, as on several occasions Italy had claimed freedom of action and the Germans had accepted that. It appeared that Italy remained in the alliance mainly because it offered collective insurance against an Austrian attack she could not meet. Austria wanted the alliance limited to common defence in the event of overwhelming danger. Both countries appeared to resist any attempt by the Germans to direct their foreign policy (the Germans tried to push the idea that, as the predominant partner in the alliance, they should dictate its policy).[26]

Italy was a particular problem, because she might try to seize Malta, which was regarded as part of 'Italia Irredenta'. It was clear that the Italians would be deterred if they knew that the French were definitely to be allied with the British, but the French could not make any such commitment unless the British could promise that they would cover the French Atlantic coast in the event of war against Germany. Without a French commitment, the Spanish might react to British withdrawal by reverting to her preferred former anti-French policy. Spain was deterred by fear of France and of French designs on Spanish Morocco. The situation was complicated in that England was co-guarantor of this particular arrangement. It seemed that the Spanish relied on British pressure – on a physical British naval presence – to hold back the French. Without it, they would revert to the Triple Alliance and thus help make the Mediterranean impassable to British shipping. Nor was it possible to overrate 'the importance of the part which the sea power outwardly and visibly exercised by Great Britain in those waters has played in creating the position which she holds in Constantinople'. The British position in Turkey, then, was a direct consequence of her overwhelming strength in the Mediterranean. A retreat would tip the scales towards Germany and the Turks would probably become interested in the reconquest of Egypt, still in theory an Ottoman province. The mere possibility of a Turkish descent would inflame the Egyptian population.

We hold Egypt and control her administration at present not by the actual number of British bayonets assembled in the Nile valley, but in virtue of the political authority attaching to our position as commanding the sea . . . the British occupation of Egypt is so intimately bound up with the control of the maritime communications, that it seems superfluous to set out an elaborate argument to prove that the evacuation of the Mediterranean by the British naval forces must materially affect the situation.

Overall, the CID Secretariat concluded, 'it will be enough to say generally that the disappearance of the British fleet from the Mediterranean would encourage and strengthen all the elements that make for disorder and war'.

The nightmare, in 1912 and during the First World War, was that the British fleet at its average strength had to face the Germans at their selected moment. It was generally accepted that German policy was to act aggressively without warning (it is not clear when that had been done). Thus the navy wanted a sufficient North Sea force that even if the Germans destroyed one of the Home Fleet squadrons by surprise, there would still be enough force left to contain them. At a July 1912 CID meeting Lloyd George said he found it inconceivable that the Germans would arrange far ahead to make preparations and then manufacture a crisis. Foreign Secretary Sir Edward Grey, certainly not the most belligerent of men, said that 'he was afraid that there was no difficulty about that. A diplomatic crisis could easily be created in twenty-four hours and there were always unsettled questions – two or three at the present moment – which could be made the pretext for an ultimatum'.[27]

The problem in 1912 was not so much ships as trained men. Churchill argued that it was a waste of very limited resources to provide full complements for six inferior ships of the Mediterranean Fleet. To keep these ships in full commission, he had been laying up much stronger ships with nucleus crews at home. The fleet had a third squadron of the *King Edward VII* class and these ships would have to be laid up one by one to man the new ships coming into service. The alternative was to bring the Atlantic Fleet home (as had been done), move the Malta battleships into its place at Gibraltar and make certain adjustments. The gain from bringing home the six old battleships would be twofold: all of the best ships could be put into the highest state of readiness and all could be concentrated in the decisive theatre. Once the Italians and the Austrians had their dreadnoughts, the six old battleships would be useless anyway. The only way to maintain local superiority in the Mediterranean would be to build and man an entirely new battle squadron, which would be unnecessary and extravagant. There was, moreover, no time to build these ships even if Parliament voted the money. Not only could they not be built in time, but the men to operate them could not be readied. Churchill argued that in the Mediterranean the British had to act like the weaker power they were and rely on the torpedo. Enough armoured and protected cruisers would remain at Malta to fulfil all diplomatic functions. Malta would be provided with a strong flotilla of submarines and the destroyers already there would be reinforced. A new submarine and torpedo station would be established at Alexandria, with another submarine flotilla with sufficient radius of action to threaten the Dardanelles.

Churchill proposed, and the Government accepted, that the ideal solution was to rely on the French, contributing British bases and torpedo craft to an Anglo-French fleet. The arrangement would be activated only if the two countries were allies in war; it would not commit them to any alliance. In 1912 France was more powerful than the combined Austro-Italian fleet, but in 1913–14 she would drop back, not recovering until October 1915 – and even then she might be frustrated by additional Austrian construction. Therefore the British had to contribute a naval force which would secure effective superiority. Peacetime calculations would doubtless be made in terms of dreadnoughts. The Admiralty calculated that it could best spare two battlecruisers. No one in the Mediterranean had such ships and their great speed and power gave them the ability to look after themselves in any situation. Basing them at Malta would maintain British prestige far better than a larger number of weak ships. 'Their speed, their armour, their armament are all great assets, even their appearance has a sobering effect.' The Admiralty therefore proposed to base HMS *Indomitable* and *Invincible* at Malta.[28] In exchange, the six old battleships would go home. Churchill's understanding was that both battlecruisers would be replaced by new ones for the Home Fleet.

The French had already agreed to Churchill's arrangements in secret staff talks, which had begun in 1908. These discussions broadly paralleled the army staff talks. Nothing was committed to writing at the time.[29] Talks were revived in 1911. This time it was agreed that in case of war the Admiralty would have general direction of naval operations, each navy having a well-defined zone of action. The French agreed to concentrate their home fleets in the Mediterranean. There they would engage and destroy the Austrian and Italian fleets and to deal with both if they entered the war as allies of the Germans. The French zone at the outset would be the western basin of the Mediterranean, but operations might extend as far as the southeast extremity of Italy – but not the Adriatic. The French would engage the Austrians if they left the Adriatic. In the autumn of 1911, a more confident French navy convinced Wilson that it could handle the Austrians and the Italians throughout the Mediterranean. Commerce protection and the protection of the entrance to the Suez Canal was left to the British. Fisher had asked

the French to take over the entire defence of the Straits of Dover, with free use of the port of Dover. Wilson opted instead for a considerable British force in the Straits, the French torpedo boat and submarine flotillas withdrawing from the Straits in wartime, so that the defence and blockade of the Straits would be entirely British. The line of separation between British and French forces would be the line from Dieppe to Beachy Head. The French area was about two-thirds of the Channel from the French coast.

In January 1913 the French naval C-in-C sketched a plan for the outbreak of war.[30] His main task was to ensure the safe passage of the Algerian Army Corps to France. Although he felt that he commanded the Mediterranean with his twelve battleships and six armoured cruisers, he could not do that unless he also had the six older battleships normally held in northern waters – in other words, until he knew the British would protect the northern French coast. When, or if possible before, war broke out, he planned to close the east-west passages of the Mediterranean: that between Sardinia and Cape Bon, the Straits of Bonifacio and that between the north of Corsica and the French coast, all by torpedo craft. If British battleships were available, they would be assigned to close the outlet of the Adriatic (the Straits of Otranto), while the French concentrated on preventing the juncture of isolated parts of the Italian fleet and also between any parts of the Italian and Austrian fleets. Reality was better than might have been expected. Because the Italians remained neutral and a threat to their coast, the Austrians could not steam out of the Adriatic into the Mediterranean. The French never had to deal with the larger Italian fleet, leaving them with surplus forces which were used to support the attack on the Dardanelles. Given the decision to withdraw the battleships, the Atlantic Fleet merged with the Home Fleet. Three battlecruisers were assigned to the Mediterranean rather than the two Churchill envisaged; when war broke out they were HMS *Inflexible*, *Indomitable* and *Indefatigable*. They were the only capital ships in that sea which could catch the German *Goeben*, assigned to the Mediterranean as flagship of the German Mediterranean Division.

Fleets in home waters were redesignated the Home Fleets (plural), of which the First Fleet was the active one. The First Fleet now included four Battle Squadrons (no Divisions), each consisting of six to eight ships, with a separate fleet flagship (at that time, HMS *Neptune*). By December 1913, the First (Home) Fleet had two squadrons of dreadnoughts (one of super-dreadnoughts), one of *King Edward VII* class semi-dreadnoughts and a fourth consisting of *Dreadnought* herself, the two *Lord Nelson*s and HMS *Cornwallis*, an earlier battleship. Each battle squadron had one to three attached cruisers and there were four separate armoured cruiser squadrons (of which the first was the 1st Battlecruiser Squadron). There were also attached minesweepers and four twenty-ship destroyer flotillas. Once war began the Home Fleet was renamed the Grand Fleet, although its documents were still designated HF, for Home Fleet.

The partly-manned older ships were now organised as the Second and Third Fleets, so that they could be activated as tactical units in wartime. All had nucleus crews, the Second Fleet being more fully-manned. Ships operated periodically to maintain readiness and a test mobilisation was conducted in 1913. When the crisis broke in July 1914, the Royal Navy had just completed a test mobilisation of its full strength. Also in home waters were the separate Patrol Flotillas of older destroyers and torpedo boats plus submarines of the 'A' to 'E' classes.

German torpedo tube practice was markedly different from British or American. *S-132* had two pairs of revolving tubes, the tubes being set at an angle from each other. The midships view shows one of her two fixed tubes, mounted at the break of the forecastle. For all that might be said about German emphasis on torpedo attack, this was not a particularly impressive battery and it was substantially less versatile than that on board a late-war British destroyer with six tubes.

The fleet commanders communicated with each other via the Admiralty. As long as each commander was supreme in his fleet, he could and would promulgate his own tactical ideas. A few of the relevant memoranda from the Mediterranean Fleet have survived. By about 1910 the Admiralty was beginning to standardise practice; it was considering issuing a tactical handbook (in fact it held back). By this time there was only a single major British fleet – the Home (later Grand) Fleet. It was the main beneficiary of the new kind of command and control. Very little seems to have been written about what was changing, perhaps because the very few senior officers who might command that fleet would have informal understanding of how Fisher's system and its successors were supposed to work.

In addition to the fleets, the Royal Navy operated groups of cruisers and lesser ships on designated foreign stations. They showed the flag in peacetime and could deal with enemy raiders in wartime. In effect their presence was a declaration of British power and interest to the countries of the informal empire. Anyone trying to attack one of Britain's friends would have to deal with ships on that station and thus risk war with Britain. This connection was never explicit, but it was probably widely understood. Forces on the stations were also available to the authorities in nearby British colonies; thus lists of cruiser employment before the First World War often include references to various colonial wars.

In August 1914 the most powerful overseas force other than a full fleet was the Royal Australian Navy (RAN), successor to the Australia Station. It was the only one built around a capital ship, the battlecruiser HMAS *Australia*, its structure a remnant of a 1909 Admiralty project for 'fleet units' to be built by the major Dominions. The 'fleet units' could merge to form a new Empire Pacific Fleet. Once war began, the RAN seized German colonies in the South Pacific and in East Africa, all of which were potential bases for raiding cruisers (or for radio stations which would control those cruisers).

The overseas stations were Atlantic and West Indies (with one cruiser assigned to the South Atlantic), Cape and West Africa, East Indies and New Zealand (the RNZN was not formed until 1943). The East Indies station was responsible for East Africa. Stations changed as the war continued. Although the basic fleet structure did not change during the war, that did not apply to the stations. In addition, the British formed the 10th Cruiser Squadron specifically to enforce the blockade around the north of Scotland. By January 1915 it consisted of twenty-three armed merchant cruisers backed by boarding steamers rather than conventional cruisers.

The Imperial German Navy

The Imperial German Navy was organised very differently from the Royal Navy. The Kaiser was the head of state and of the armed services. He exerted his power through Civil, Military and Naval Cabinets, each of which was responsible for all senior appointments in its sphere. The Kaiser's power over the army was limited, the General Staff appointing Chiefs of Staff to the commanders appointed by the Kaiser. The General Staff also had executive authority over army operations. There was a reason the Kaiser could not change the war plan in 1914 and concentrate on Russia; he was not really army chief. The General Staff had executive power because the Kaiser accepted that in the event of a land war, failure would be fatal: an enemy army would overrun Germany, which had no natural boundaries on which to base a defence. War planning was a vital state function and in effect the war planners defined the sort of war for which Germany was prepared. There was apparently little or no contact between the General Staff and the navy; the General Staff did not think in terms of the sort of protracted war the navy might have to fight.

The Imperial Navy was a different proposition. In important ways it was the Kaiser's toy. He saw no point in relinquishing power over it.[31] Nor, for that matter, does it appear that the navy had much to do with decisions for war or peace or with the kind of national strategy the General Staff was developing.[32] Once war broke out, unexpectedly for the navy, two its most senior officers, Admirals Tirpitz and von Pohl (chief of the naval staff) spent their time debating what the navy should do to ensure a post-war future for itself.[33] Both of them saw a real possibility that the navy was no more than a bargaining chip at the ultimate peace table. Neither showed much interest in what naval operations might ensure victory (although each assured the other that the navy would fulfil an as-yet undefined valuable role in the war). These conversations do not suggest much in the way of war planning. It is no great surprise that the Kaiser had to personally approve each operations order for the High Seas Fleet and often he added a demand that the fleet commander take care not to lose ships. Thus the outcome of the initial battle of the naval war, Heligoland Bight, exerted an unusually strong influence on the Germans because the Kaiser was so angry that his ships had been surprised and some of them sunk. It was only with some difficulty that Tirpitz and von Pohl convinced the Kaiser not to issue entirely crippling orders intended to preclude future surprises at sea.

Once war began, the Kaiser set up his own General Headquarters (GHQ), where he was attended by Tirpitz and the chief of the Admiralstab as well as chief of the naval cabinet Admiral von Müller – and from which he did not of course have much communication with the High Seas Fleet command or, for that matter, with the Admiralstab itself in Berlin.[34] In the absence of a unified naval command, the Kaiser assumed authority and he was easily swayed by his advisors.

Alongside the Naval Cabinet were the Navy Department (Reichs Marine Amt: Imperial Navy Office) and the Admiralty Staff (Admiralstab) created in 1899. The Admiralstab were war planners equivalent in theory to the General Staff, but until 1918 they had no executive power. Nor did these planners have any impact on the shape of the fleet and its ships. That was the remit of the Navy Department presided over by Admiral von Tirpitz. Tirpitz, who had set up the navy's building programme, was personally responsible for the characteristics of German warships. Once war broke out, he was blamed for their failings, particularly for their smaller-calibre guns (as compared to their British equivalents) and for the choice not to adopt oil fuel (because Germany lacked oil reserves). Tirpitz was often criticised for his obsession with numbers of ships rather than with their capabilities. For example, he thought that the early pre-dreadnoughts should be included in the battle fleet, to make up its numbers, despite their inferior capabilities.

In principle the German organisation broadly resembled that of the contemporary US Navy, with its Secretary, its Bureaus and its war-planning General Board. It was organised around a central naval bureau (Z) and an administrative department (V). The materiel departments or (in US parlance) bureaus were ship design and construction (K) and weapons (W); in contrast to the US Navy and the Royal Navy, there was no separate machinery department. There were a general department (A: intelligence and hydropgraphics), an estimates (budget: E) department and justice,

personnel and medical departments. There was also a large news bureau (N) unlike anything the US Navy or the Royal Navy possessed. It was Tirpitz' personal propaganda arm, intended to convince a land-minded German population that it badly needed a large expensive fleet.

A key difference between the German organisation and its US counterpart was that, whereas the US Secretary of the Navy was generally a civilian unversed in naval warfare, the German State Secretary was an Admiral with strong views. He therefore saw no need of a staff to mediate between him and his bureaus. For that matter, he saw little need to accept the advice of his war-planning Admiralstab, whereas the US Navy's General Board was created precisely to advise the Secretary of the Navy. It soon expanded into applying its war-planning expertise to the US Navy's building programme. Tirpitz considered himself his own expert staff in such matters. On the other hand, he had to deal with an interventionist Kaiser, whereas the US Navy only rarely faced a President with strong naval views (both Roosevelts were the main cases in point). Although the Kaiser's views generally did not prevail, they had to be taken into account and carefully dealt with. That dramatically slowed the German programmes, a case in point being the relatively slow adoption of the 15in (38cm) gun, compared to its progress in the Royal Navy.

The need to promote the navy merely in order to insure its survival made the Imperial Navy much more political, in the sense of involving itself in domestic politics, than other contemporary navies. Attention paid to convincing the Reichstag to keep appropriating money detracted from any kind of tactical or war planning, to the extent that in 1909 the US Attaché described the German navy as less mature (presumably tactically) than any other he had seen.

Because the Admiralstab lacked any power comparable to that of the army's General Staff, the Kaiser in effect exerted direct control over operational commanders, the most important being the commander of the High Seas Fleet, the Baltic commander (the Kaiser's brother Prince Heinrich) and the commander of the East Asian Squadron (Admiral von Spee). There was no single senior naval commander – equivalent to the British First Sea Lord – who could deal with the chief of the army general staff on anything like an equal basis. Tirpitz had ensured as much by convincing the Kaiser that only the Kaiser could decide on great offensives and thus co-ordinate army and navy, probably as part of his 1899 campaign of flattery to ensure passage of the Navy Laws. That was why the commander of the High Seas Fleet did not answer to the Admiralstab, only to the Kaiser. This fragmentation also insured that, in theory, only the Kaiser could decide how to allocate naval forces between, say, the High Seas Fleet and the Baltic. In reality it ensured that all such decisions would be negotiated by various parties including, in 1914, the chief of the Admiralstab and Tirpitz, because they had direct access to the Kaiser.

When war broke out, nearly the whole of German naval power was concentrated in the High Seas Fleet. It comprised a main body plus the 1st Scouting Group of battlecruisers supported by light cruisers and destroyers. The High Seas Fleet also included the long-range U-boats and the naval Zeppelins, the latter being in effect its long-range scouting element. Ships could be transferred as required to the Baltic command. In addition to the High Seas Fleet, Germany maintained a Mediterranean Squadron consisting of the battlecruiser *Goeben* and the light cruiser *Breslau*.

Like all other major navies, the Germans had minor forces stationed abroad to protect their interests, but these forces paled in comparison to those of the British and even the French. The Germans did have potential foreign bases in their colonies, but the only important one was Tsingtao in China, a prize Germany received after participating in the suppression of the Boxer Rebellion in 1900. Tsingtao was the base of a strong East Asian Squadron commanded by Graf von Spee, the only really powerful German naval force outside European waters.

No one in Britain seems to have realised how disconnected the Imperial Navy was from German national war planning. Surely anything which could absorb such resources had to be integrated with the army. Similarly, surely the Germans were aware that they had made the British their enemies by building a navy whose announced purpose was to develop so serious a threat that the British would stay out of a European war. At least some German naval officers were embarrassed by what was happening. For example, a letter from a German friend of Admiral Jellicoe's survives. He writes that German needs a large navy so that it will be taken seriously; surely Jellicoe should realise that Germany cannot afford a fleet large enough to threaten the Royal Navy. The two countries should be allies, not enemies. This sort of naiveté had no real impact on British opinion. Once the war began, Jellicoe and the Admiralty spent their time thinking about what the Germans could and should do with their fleet.

There seems to have been a general assumption that the Germans would act suddenly, 'as was their custom' (it is not clear what pre-war German operations that reflected). Thus in 1914 the British feared a sudden destroyer raid on their fleet, as the Japanese had tried to conduct against the Russians in Port Arthur in 1904. The 1914 mobilisation was guarded by destroyers stationed at harbour entrances specifically to deal with this possibility.

A second possibility was invasion. The British had a small standing army and in 1914 much of it was despatched to France. Invasion had been a staple of British future-war literature for years; one of the most popular examples was Erskine Childers' classic *The Riddle of the Sands*. In it the Germans secretly assemble shallow-draught fishing craft in coastal areas. As the British army recovered from the Boer War, it used the possibility of invasion as a justification for growth. The Territorial Army (reservists) was formed specifically as an anti-invasion force. The Royal Navy resisted claims that invasion was a real possibility, Fisher and his successor Wilson both arguing that the real threat was starvation rather than invasion. The army was effective enough in debate to keep its side of the argument alive. There is no evidence that the Germans ever contemplated invasion: they were far too cautious to risk their fleet, let alone a large ground force.

Above all, the British expected the Germans to act aggressively at sea as they had on land. From 1914 on they paid particular attention to long moonless winter nights, which might conceal a fleet advance across the North Sea. Painfully aware of reductions in strength due to such necessities as boiler cleaning and condenser repair, Admiral Jellicoe assumed that the Germans would choose a moment of maximum strength. It seems never to have occurred to him that a German operation might be timed by other factors, such as the Kaiser's reluctant agreement to let his fleet go to sea. This assumption applied particularly to destroyers, by far the most delicate ships in the High Seas Fleet. Jellicoe consistently over-rated the number the Germans could take to sea at any one time. Given

The forward 10.5cm/45 gun on board *S-132* shows no British-style shield. That might not be very important in a long-range battle, but it would certainly matter in a close-range battle. This was the same type of gun as in U-boats (it was designated a UTOF, a U-boat/torpedo boat gun). The device on deck transmitted range data to the gun via the cable.

the potential for torpedo and (he thought) mine attack, the German destroyer force seemed to be an effective equaliser, making up for superior British capital ship numbers. We now know that the Germans did not see things in anything like this light.

Particularly after Jutland, the British came to see the German battlecruisers as the likely antagonists in the North Sea. As in 1914–16, they could steam quickly across the North Sea if not encumbered by the mass of the High Seas Fleet. Given poor intelligence of German shipbuilding, the British accepted unrealistic claims that new ships were being built, hence that their own force was on the point of being outnumbered. The most extreme consequence was a failed 1917 attempt to lease the four Japanese *Kongo* class battlecruisers (that the Admiralty did not want their crews must have been a grave insult to the Japanese). In fact the Germans *did* launch a battlecruiser raid on a convoy in 1918. It failed only because of poor German intelligence. However, by that time work on German capital ships had long been abandoned in favour of U-boat construction.

Naval industry

In 1914 Germany's great industrial strengths were steel, chemicals and electrical equipment. The latter advantage explains why the Imperial Navy had excellent fire-control equipment, such as the first operational synchros. Gyros were apparently better and more plentiful than in the United Kingdom, so they were provided at the guns rather than (as in the Royal Navy) only at a centralised director. Germany also had the world's best diesels, an advantage of considerable significance in submarines. German policy barred companies from exporting the weapons or other sensitive materiel that they were producing for the Imperial Navy. They had to separate production for the Imperial Navy from export production to bar foreigners from German secrets. US naval intelligence officers reported considerable disinformation, a particularly sensitive point being the effective lifetime of guns.

Tirpitz' ships were expensive compared to those bought by the Royal Navy. Although there were several builders, including navy yards, there was only one source of guns, mountings and armour: Krupp. Tirpitz was willing to pay a high premium for what Krupp offered. Krupp was also very nearly the only source of artillery for the Germany army, so Tirpitz had to compete with it. Krupp did have some export business to spread its overhead costs, but as its prices rose that declined rapidly. In 1914 only the Netherlands was closely tied to Krupp as sole supplier.

In the important case of the only capital ship the Germans sold abroad during the immediate pre-war period, the Greek *Salamis*, the builder had to go abroad, to Bethlehem in the United States, for weapons. As a consequence, unlike the British, the German navy could not take over the incomplete battlecruiser once war broke out. Presumably her structure was incompatible with German weapons and also presumably she was considered grossly inferior to ships designed for the Imperial Navy. The British blockade insured that her American-made guns and mountings would never be delivered. They were soon resold to the British and mounted on board monitors which shelled German positions on land. *Salamis* was never completed.

The policy for guns applied similarly to another key new technology: Diesels. In 1914 MAN was the most advanced diesel maker in the world, producing four-stroke submarine engines and trying unsuccessfully to build big engines for German capital ships. German policy barred exports of the type of engines sold to the Imperial Navy. Thus the company sold the US Navy two-stroke engines, which proved unreliable. After the war the US Navy copied the four-stroke MAN engines on board the U-boats it obtained, since they were far better than anything it had.

High unit costs made the building race with the British more ruinous than it might otherwise have been. The financial squeeze must also have limited the more hideable operational expenses, such as purchases of expendables like torpedoes. This kind of effect shows in subtleties such as the exhortation, in German torpedo orders, not to fire these expensive weapons unless hits were very likely – the Germans did not adopt British-style 'browning shot' tactics. This squeeze probably crowded out investment in personnel. It may also have limited pre-war exercises – sheer cost certainly affected the Royal Navy that way.

Personnel

The German navy differed from the Royal Navy in another important way. Like the Germany armies, the enlisted arm of the Imperial Navy was a conscript force, its personnel taken largely from the maritime part of the country. In this sense the navy competed directly with the army for personnel and it was somewhat undermanned. It also lacked the long-service non-commissioned officer force built up by the Royal Navy; in this sense it was far more like the Cold War Soviet Navy than the Cold War US or Royal Navy. A weak non-commissioned officer force placed greater burdens on the professional officer corps. Cold War experience suggests that the conscript force could not build up the level of seamanship developed in a long-service navy. Merely going to sea was a much greater ordeal for the German fleet than for the Royal Navy.

German capital ships were said to be far less habitable than their British counterparts. That was partly because German warship designers apparently had little interest in habitability and partly because, given the emphasis on survivability, ships were much more minutely compartmented than their British equivalents. The British found German capital ships so uncomfortable that they assumed, incorrectly, that German crews lived in barracks ashore whenever their ships were in port.

This was entirely apart from the fact that the German navy had expanded so rapidly, hence that so many of its officers were relatively inexperienced. In 1911 a US officer described the German navy as a 'smooth water' force, based on what he saw of it. He felt that the German enlisted force was not as competent as might have been desired.[35] The 1913 German manoeuvres were said to have demonstrated that the navy had come of age and that it was a fully seagoing force, but it seems significant that the first major overseas voyage by German capital ships came only in 1912 (a cruise to South America). One consequence was that on the eve

of war the Germans were concentrating far more on relatively simple manoeuvring orders than on overall fleet tactics, as seems to be reflected in their draft war instructions issued at that time.

There were apparently serious social problems, which facilitated the mutinies which destroyed the High Seas Fleet in 1918.[36] Although most German naval officers were middle class, they seem to have wanted to emulate the aristocratic army officers, with their disdain for enlisted men. The effect of the wartime blockade was felt strongly by the enlisted men, who watched officers continuing to enjoy various benefits, such as lavish food and liquor. The social gulf between officers and enlisted men in both army and navy was reflected in severe punishments for relatively minor offenses (the German army was similar; for example it shot many times as many men on the Western Front as did the British army). After the war, a former senior warrant officer (then the head of the warrant officers' association) contrasted the situation in his own navy with the much closer bond between officers and enlisted men in the Royal Navy, as reported by the wartime Russian naval attaché.

It did not help that many of the junior officers with the best leadership skills were siphoned off into small units outside the fleet, such as destroyers on detached duty, submarines and minesweepers. These units did not suffer mutinies in 1918; it was the crews of the capital ships and some cruisers who refused to go into battle. They were the ones who decided that the insane officers wanted to go on a 'death ride' for the sake of their honour, when the country was already collapsing.

By 1914 all major navies were interested in using submarines to support surface fleets, preferably by laying ambushes for enemy ships. The British began work on fast 'oceanic' submarines in 1913, the outcome being the steam-powered 'K' class. *K-6* is shown, probably at Scapa Flow.

Scapa Flow was chosen as the wartime Grand Fleet base. It was large enough to accommodate the fleet, yet its entrances could be closed against submarines. It was far enough from the Heligoland Bight to be safe against a surprise destroyer attack. Grand Fleet battleships are shown at anchor there in 1917. There was no infrastructure to support the fleet. For example, because there was no coaling pier and no coal storage, the fleet was supported by numerous colliers. A supporting merchant ship is visible beyond the light cruiser to the left. (Naval Institute collection)

CHAPTER 6
The Chessboard – Naval Geography

IN THE FIRST WORLD WAR, as in centuries past, the single key fact of European naval geography was that Great Britain lies across the throat of the North Sea. Any ship trading with Germany or her neighbours had to steam either around the north of Scotland or through the Channel and the Royal Navy could control both. Similarly, no German surface fleet could gain access to the world's oceans – and to the seaborne resources which supported the United Kingdom – without passing through either the Channel or the sea north of Scotland. The clearest proof that German national strategy did not take the maritime facts of life into account was that the Germans made no attempt to secure territory outside the bottleneck, either on the French coast outside the Channel or in Norway.

British geography was well suited both to the past antagonism against France and to the new struggle with the Germans. However, in 1914 the British base structure still reflected the earlier emphasis on France, with bases placed to command the Channel:

Portsmouth and Plymouth. The money spent on increasingly expensive ships during the pre-war decade precluded investment in facilities further north. Candidate fleet bases were, from south to north, Harwich, Rosyth on the Fifth of Forth, Cromarty and the new fleet anchorage at Scapa Flow in the Orkneys. Of these Harwich could not accommodate heavy ships. Neither Rosyth nor Cromarty was large enough to accommodate the whole Grand Fleet. Scapa was remote from the British rail network and therefore from the massive resources the fleet needed on a daily basis. Moreover, existing facilities, particularly graving docks, had not been enlarged since they had been built for pre-dreadnoughts. That limited the beam and hence the survivability (against underwater damage) of the new capital ships. In an unpublished memoir, Admiral Jellicoe recalled his success, as Controller, in buying floating drydocks which enabled him to dock his ships as far north as Rosyth, rather than having to send them periodically much further south.[1]

Favourable geography offered the British two alternative ways to deal with the Germans. The classic approach would have been a close blockade of German ports. That became more and more dangerous in an era of underwater weapons. By about 1910 it was freely admitted that submarines would make coastal waters far too dangerous to occupy on a continuous basis. For a time there was some question as to whether submarines could operate submerged in shallow waters, hence some hope that a fleet operating really close to shore could be immune to them, but within a few years any such optimism was gone.

The great question raised before 1914 was whether Britain could be invaded. During the pre-war years the army used the possibility of invasion as a force-builder, always arguing that the Germans could put a substantial force ashore. The Royal Navy generally argued that invasion was impossible, but during the 1913 Manoeuvres Admiral Jellicoe, representing the Germans, managed

Scapa Flow late in the war, with US battleships of the 6th Battle Squadron at left. The ship in the foreground is probably USS *Wyoming*. Note the anti-rangefinding baffles on her forefunnel and what appears to be a false bow wave.

to evade North Sea patrols. It had to be admitted that a small force could be put ashore, but that any substantial reinforcement would be impossible. That justified a limited British home army force. Once the Germans occupied ports in Belgium, which were much closer to the British coast, the invasion issue revived.

For the Royal Navy the key realisation was that although it was no longer possible to keep the German fleet in its harbour through a classic blockade, a blockade could be enforced at a considerable distance, from northern waters and from the Channel. Instead of waiting in its base for the Royal Navy, the Germans would have to come out and fight in order to break the distant blockade. The

Right: The North Sea was the principal theatre of war for the Royal Navy and the Imperial German Navy, although both were engaged in many other areas. The wartime British fleet base at Scapa Flow was chosen specifically to preclude any German knockout blow (using destroyers) at the outbreak of war. Unfortunately the high cost of new ships precluded creation of new bases in the northeast; on the outbreak of war Rosyth was only partly finished. The massive shipbuilding industry on the Tyne did not solve the problem. Portsmouth and Plymouth had been built up for the expected war against France, but after 1904 (and particularly 1906) the British focus shifted to Germany. From a strategic point of view, the great surprise was not merely the effectiveness of submarines, but their long cruising range, which made the Irish Sea a theatre of operations even early in 1915, when the liner *Lusitania* was sunk there. Berehaven, which had been considered a very secondary base, became important. US battleships were based there in 1918 to deal with a possible German surface break-out around the north of Scotland – a possibility made real by surface attacks on convoys in the autumn of 1917 and by the abortive German sortie in the spring of 1918.

The German side of this geography was much affected by Tirpitz's fleet rationale, which featured a decisive surface battle. Until 1912 the expected venue was the Skaggerak, the theory being that in wartime the British would try to pass through the Danish Straits *en route* to the Baltic. Fisher said that he had deterred war in 1906 by conducting fleet exercises there; he always emphasised the sensitivity (to the Prussians) of their Baltic coast. In 1912, however, Tirpitz shifted the venue to the German Bight. He and other Germans convinced themselves that, given the spirit of Nelson, the British would be unable to resist the urge to settle matters at the outset of a war by attacking the Germans at Wilhelmshaven. To that end the German fleet remained in its protected harbour at the beginning of the war. The British, who had a less romantic idea of sea power, refused to come. For their part, they could not understand how the Germans could tolerate a distant blockade, enforced mainly at the northern mouth of the North Sea, choking off their trade (nor could they understand why the Germans initially made such feeble attempts to destroy British trade). The Germans remained sensitive to possible threats to their Baltic coast via the Skaggerak and the Kattegat, which is probably why they called the Battle of Jutland the Battle of the Skaggerak – they assumed the Grand Fleet was probing the route to the Baltic.

Note how close Nieuport, which remained in Allied hands through the war, was to the German Flanders bases of Ostende and Zeebrugge. Bruges, Ostende and Zeebrugge constituted the German 'triangle', which supported U-boat warfare in the southern English Channel and the Thames Estuary. It was entirely realistic for Admiral Richard Bacon to propose, in 1916–17, a big amphibious operation in conjunction with a land offensive towards these bases – but the conditions of war in 1916–17 made an advance of even a few miles difficult or impossible. The heroic attacks of April 1918 were designed to neutralise Zeebrugge and Ostende, but without any hope of seizing and occupying them. Both places were so close to Allied territory that they were extensively bombed; by 1918 that was becoming effective.

HMS *Barham* at Scapa Flow about 1917. She displays the initial post-Jutland improvement of centralised remotely-controlled searchlights (abaft her after funnel) and anti-rangefinding baffles, but not the somewhat later range dials and bearing markings. Her main topmast has been landed, to make it impossible to determine her course while she is hull-down on the horizon, at the cost of reduced wireless range. She has a director atop her spotting top forward and an armoured rangefinder-director atop her conning tower.

The Grand Fleet's light cruisers at Scapa Flow, 1917. The 'Town' class ships in the foreground (with four funnels) were the fleet's scouts, stiffened by the battlecruisers. Note their high topmasts, to give better wireless performance. They were retained even as the topmasts of the other ships were cut down so as to make them more difficult to see beyond the horizon. High paired topmasts also made it easier to determine a ship's course. The smaller fast cruisers (*Arethusa* and 'C' and 'D' classes) were intended to work with and against destroyers. (NMRN via Dr David Stevens, SPC-A)

When war broke out, Scapa had been designated as fleet base but no anti-submarine defence was in place. Here the boom is opened so that ships can pass through. (Naval Institute collection)

Local defence, including boom defence, involved large numbers of trawlers and drifters, which had little means of dealing with submarines or destroyers which might suddenly appear. The drifters were armed with 14in torpedoes in the dropping gear developed for ships' boats. Here a torpedo is being prepared.

further from its bases it had to fight, the worse its chances. It is not clear whether the British realised as much, but Tirpitz had built his fleet to fight within 100 miles of its base. He had assumed that it would be badly punished in any battle with the Royal Navy. The superior survivability of German capital ships would count only if they did not have a long trip home. Given Tirpitz' thinking, German destroyers were designed without the endurance to cross the North Sea to reach British waters (in fact, however, the High Seas Fleet was able to take its destroyers with it when it steamed towards British waters).[2]

Britain might be essentially impossible to invade, but she did depend on imports in order to live. Moreover, despite the excellent British railway network, London in particular depended on coastal shipping into the Thames Estuary. Imports might go into West Coast ports such as Liverpool and Glasgow, but much of what was delivered then had to go to London via coastal shipping. Thus, although the big West Coast ports might be relatively difficult for

the Germans to attack, the supply to London became vulnerable once the Germans established themselves in the Belgian coastal ports of Ostend and Zeebrugge.

For the British, geography embraced all the oceans of the world, because Britain drew her strength not only from her overseas empire but also from distant trading partners. The most obvious example was the United States: as long as the Royal Navy could ensure passage between the United States and the United Kingdom and as long as the British could afford to keep buying US products, US industrial strength had to be added to the considerable industrial strength of the United Kingdom. Even before the United States entered the war, British strength included that contributed by the overseas Empire, particularly by Australia, Canada, India and New Zealand. This maritime element of British power is often forgotten, so that it seems that in 1914 Britain was a small collection of offshore islands facing German industrial superpower. Much the same can be said of the British situation in 1940: the British Empire and Commonwealth was very much a superpower.

Once the war began, it was British seapower which knit together the Entente. The pre-war Entente of France and Russia could co-ordinate operations, but once at war those two countries were separated by the masses of Germany and Austria-Hungary. French seapower was not sufficient to overcome German and so to reach Russian European harbours. British seapower made an enormous difference. Although the attempt to open the great passage through the Dardanelles failed, throughout the war the British could always get through to Russian Arctic ports such as Archangel. British (and to an extent French) seapower ensured that troops and resources could cross the Channel, making a physical connection between Britain and France. Had the British not been at war and had they not held the Channel, it would not have mattered how willing the British and others were to resupply France. The same maritime power made it possible for the Allies to mount peripheral attacks, for example to maintain a force at Salonika from 1915 on.

It was always a lot easier to move masses of materiel by water than by land, although in the years leading up to 1914 British geographer Harold Mackinder maintained that railways were evening the imbalance. In his view power was passing from the

Scapa was so far from Heligoland that a fleet based there was poorly placed to intercept a German raid. After Scarborough, the battlecruisers were moved to Rosyth. That made them a separate command and the Battlecruiser Force soon became the Battlecruiser Fleet. The 2nd Battlecruiser Squadron is shown at Rosyth, with the Forth Bridge in the background, at about 9pm in June 1915. (Dr David Stevens, SPC-A)

The Grand Fleet did not immediately move to Rosyth because the port did not have a sufficient area protected against submarines. By late in the war Rosyth was the main base of the Grand Fleet. These capital ships include the US 6th Battle Squadron, with its distinctive cage masts, at left. Battlecruisers are anchored at right. (Dr David Stevens, SPC-A)

Bases had infrastructure. Without it, ships had to leave their bases for protracted periods of maintenance, including drydocking to clean and paint their hulls. With the shift from the Channel (the French threat) to the North Sea (the German threat), the Royal Navy had to create new bases. That meant, among other things, digging new graving docks. Large floating drydocks helped provide the needed capacity, so that ships did not have to steam all the way to the south coast. A *Warrior* class armoured cruiser is shown during the First World War, presumably at Rosyth.

The Dover Barrage and other anti-submarine booms were covered by unpowered boom defence vessels like these. Some of them, like *B.D. 33*, lacked searchlights and had only a single gun forward. (Author's collection)

periphery of the world to the centre (the 'heartland'). For Germans, Mackinder was saying that the future lay with them and their contiguous ally, Austria-Hungary; that was why the two were called the Central Powers. The rub, again and again, was that the ocean was unmarked; ships could go anywhere there was enough water under their keels. It took enormous effort to build and maintain a railway. If none existed, trade and troops had to go around some other way. As noted, in Germany itself, there was insufficient rail capacity to carry enough food from the farming areas in the east to the industrial cities in the west: a net German balance of food could equate to famine under blockade conditions.

To the Germans, this geography had another aspect. They had only one base on the North Sea coast, Wilhelmshaven, in the funnel represented by the Heligoland Bight.[3] British forces could be based anywhere along the east coast of the British Isles. A German force coming from Wilhelmshaven could be flanked by a British force, but the British had only to watch Wilhelmshaven. Moreover, a German sortie against the British coast ran the risk of being cut off from north or south or both. The British would know that the Germans had to steam back to Wilhelmshaven.[4] Wilhelmshaven itself was limited. It lay on the estuary of the Jade. Jade Bay, where the fleet typically moored, silted badly and had to be dredged continuously. Typically it took two high tides for the fleet to sortie past the sandbars and shoals in the Jade outside the harbour. Thus the fleet could not instantly respond to any surprise in the Heligoland Bight outside the Jade. The fleet also used the nearby Ems, Weser and Elbe rivers, which also emptied into the Heligoland Bight (the Weser served Bremerhaven, the Elbe Cuxhaven and Hamburg). If the British gained control of islands off the river mouths, they could block access to the sea by the High Seas Fleet. Borkum, a favoured objective early in the war, lay in the mouth of the Ems.

The original base of the Imperial Navy was Kiel, on the Baltic. For the Germans the Kiel Canal linking Kiel and Wilhelmshaven (via the Elbe and the Ems) had something of the significance the Panama Canal had for the US Navy: it converted a two-fleet situation into one in which a single strong fleet could transit back and forth between its two main operating areas, in this case the North Sea and the Baltic.

The German army's success in Belgium altered naval geography by providing the Germans with a base on the North Sea coast within reach of the rich shipping of the Downs and the Thames Estuary (and much closer as an invasion base). Before the war a German naval planner imagined seizing Antwerp and holding it until the army could link up. Once war broke out in 1914, Tirpitz pushed for the seizure of the Belgian coastal ports (Ostend and Zeebrugge, both linked to Bruges by canal). He called the trio of ports 'the Triangle', and he imagined developing them to the point where they could support his battle fleet. As it was, the 'Triangle' became a base for destroyers and submarines which could attack the dense British shipping near the mouth of the Thames. Zeebrugge was only 70 miles from the Thames Estuary, so destroyers based there could reach their targets in less than four hours – which often meant that they could make a round trip entirely under cover of darkness. It took about four times as long for destroyers from the Elbe. Only under cover of darkness could the destroyers operate without fear of interception by heavy British ships.

German occupation of the Belgian ports changed the significance of Dover. At the outbreak of war, the force based at Dover was a means of controlling merchant traffic through the Channel. Once the Germans were in Zeebrugge and Ostend, it was the base for the force intended to neutralise the German bases, initially through bombardment. It was also the base for the mine and net barrage intended to close the Channel exit from the North Sea to German submarines. Destroyers based both at Dover and at Harwich fought the German destroyer force based at Zeebrugge.

Geography affected the prospects for a German invasion of the United Kingdom, a possibility which exercised the British from time to time. The sheer distance from Germany to the British coast made it unlikely that an invasion could succeed, because either the invasion shipping or the necessary reinforcement shipping would almost certainly be detected and intercepted. The Belgian coast was a different proposition, which was one reason the British

RUSSIA

AUSTRIA-
HUNGARY

Odessa

Venice

Pola

Sevastopol

Adriatic Sea

ROMANIA

*Black
Sea*

SERBIA

BULGARIA

MONTENEGRO

Cattaro

ITALY

Constantinople

Taranto

ALBANIA

Salonika

Strait of Otranto

Gallipoli

GREECE

Mudros

OTTOMAN
EMPIRE

Corfu

*Aegean
Sea*

Sicily

Malta

Crete

Cyprus

SYRIA

Mediterranean Sea

Alexandria

Suez
Canal

ARABIA

EGYPT

Dardanelles Detail

T
U
R
K
E
Y

*Aegean
Sea*

Gallipoli

Chardak

The Narrows

Imbros

Maidos

Kilid Bahr

Charnak

Sedd el Bahr

Karentina

Cape Helles

Dardanelles

Kum Kale

⚓ Fleet bases

guaranteed Belgian neutrality. The possibility of invasion was a British concern through the war, although to some extent it was also a way for the British to justify keeping a large ground force in the United Kingdom rather than moving it to France.

When they contemplated surface action in the North Sea, both navies were well aware of its misty weather, which often limited visibility to a few miles. For example, in pre-war debates on the value of gun range, British officers sometimes argued that anything beyond 10,000 yds was useless because such visibility was so rare. Poor visibility made scouting difficult in the 1913 British manoeuvres, allowing Admiral Jellicoe's 'invasion' force to slip through the cordon of light cruisers stretched across the North Sea. The great surprise of the Dogger Bank action was that visibility was sometimes so good that pre-war ideas of gun range had to be discarded. At Jutland, good visibility alternated with bad, ships appearing and disappearing suddenly. Neither side had any sensor which could overcome the weather, although during the war German U-boats were fitted with hydrophones with which they could locate ships at some distance. After Jutland the British had radio direction-finders on board some ships and when the US Navy deployed to Europe from 1917 on it also had shipboard radio direction-finders.

Geography also affected the war against the U-boats. The southern end of the North Sea could be blocked by a barrage across the Straits of Dover. Throughout the war the British sought to make this barrier more and more impenetrable, using mines, nets and patrols. At the very least, the barrier across the Straits forced U-boats seeking to operate in the Irish Sea or further West to go the long way around the British Isles. Every hour a U-boat spent in transit was an hour she could not spend on profitable operations.

For most of the war there was no hope of blocking the broad northern exit from the North Sea against passage by submarines.

In 1912 the Royal Navy and the French navy agreed that in wartime the British would be responsible for the Channel and the French would be largely (but not completely) responsible for the Mediterranean, the British commanding in the Channel and the French in the Mediterranean. However, the British contributed the bulk of the force at the Dardanelles and commanded the operation. Command relationships turned out to be so tangled that in January 1918 the Royal Navy told the War Cabinet that they had been responsible for the far greater loss rate of merchant ships in the Mediterranean, compared to the waters around the United Kingdom (this problem had just been resolved). As an example of the tangle, this 1918 photo shows the British-built Greek destroyer *Aetos* under French control (the French seized control of the Greek navy in December 1916), with a British *Bellerophon*-class battleship (*Superb* or *Temeraire*) in the right background and a French *Danton*-class battleship on the left.

Left: Although in retrospect the Eastern Mediterranean might seem to be a very secondary theatre of war, in fact it carried important possibilities. In 1914–15 the only way to supply Russia on a large scale was via the Dardanelles and the Black Sea to Sevastopol and nearby Odessa. Opening that route and thus increasing pressure on the Germans in the East, was the motive for the Gallipoli campaign. In effect the argument between First Lord Winston Churchill and First Sea Lord Admiral Fisher was over which of two routes to the East the Allies should follow: the Baltic, which Fisher favoured, or the Dardanelles, which Churchill favoured and the Cabinet ultimately approved. Fisher was particularly furious because the fleet of specialised ships he had assembled for the Baltic was largely expended in the Dardanelles. As the Dardanelles operation collapsed, few if any wanted to remember the logic involved – which might have justified continued and even much-expanded efforts.

The remains of the southern approach to the war was the Anglo-French position at Salonika in Greece. Compared to Gallipoli, it had the advantage that its presence was unopposed; but it did not offer access to Russia. It was a jumping-off place for an offensive into southern Germany once Austria-Hungary left the war. Those who see the Salonika operation as vital point out that by 1918 the Germans lacked the troops necessary to resist any push to the north and that they knew it and consequently saw the Austrian collapse as a disaster.

At the outbreak of war, Italy and Austria-Hungary were nominally allied Central Powers. The British and French had to reckon with the possibility that their navies would join together to dominate the Eastern Mediterranean and possibly the whole sea. Both countries had begun a burst of battleship-building which neither the British (tied to the North Sea) nor the French could completely match. We now know that co-operation between the two hereditary enemies was never likely. The Austrians had no safe route into the Mediterranean and throughout the war the Allies tried to block the Straits of Otranto to Austrian-based submarines. Fast Austrian cruisers periodically raided the Italian coast; the Italian bases were far enough away that reaction forces usually could not appear in time. For their part the Italians sought to destroy the Austrian fleet at its main base of Pola, mainly using fast motor boats and special attack craft.

From a British perspective, the prize in the Eastern Mediterranean was the Suez Canal. Suez was the key to using the strength of the Empire – from places like Australia and India – to reinforce the position in Europe. Once Turkey was at war, the British faced the possibility that a Turkish force would cross the desert from Syria to attack. That nearly happened, but the Turks were defeated. This possibility led to British interest in an attack against the Turkish line of communication running down the Syrian coast, particularly at Alexandretta. The value of such an attack paled in comparison with the value attached to opening the route to Russia. Although the British sent aid through the White Sea to Murmansk and Archangel, those places lacked the sort of developed rail system to be found in the south. Even in the Second World War, when rail communications were much better, the Allies found themselves bringing much of the aid to the Soviet Union through the south, in this case through Iran. Iran does not seem to have been a viable alternative to the Dardanelles in the First World War.

The small cruiser *Diamond* is shown at Venice about 1920. The three pairs of prominent davits on each side were installed specifically to handle CMBs, *Diamond* becoming, in effect, a CMB carrier intended to support raids on enemy bases. She transferred to the Mediterranean Fleet from the Harwich Force during 1918.

The *Beagle* class destroyer *Basilisk* is shown in the Mediterranean about 1915; note the projections right aft, which were probably supports for a mine sweep (in co-operation with another destroyer). She and her sisters were the last British coal-burning destroyers. In 1914 the sixteen ships of this class were the only British destroyers in the Mediterranean. In January 1918, by way of contrast, the Mediterranean Fleet included eight *Acorn* ('H') class, all sixteen *Beagle*s and 10 old 'D' class (30-knotter) destroyers, plus eighteen torpedo boats, all mainly for anti-submarine work. There were also ships attached directly to the Italian fleet (including four destroyers) and a force in Egyptian waters. These fleets included twelve pre-dreadnought battleships (but no dreadnoughts, which were all assigned to the Grand Fleet). (Dr David Stevens, SPC-A)

British dominance of the sea made the First World War a global maritime war. In 1914 the British concentrated troops from their whole Empire. The threat of German attack brought remote naval forces such as that on the Cape Station into play. In their area of responsibility, which stretched from East Africa around the Cape to the West, the Germans had a large colony (which became Kenya and Tanganyika) and the fairly modern cruiser *Königsberg*. The three-cruiser British force had to protect British trade in the western Indian Ocean, ideally by bottling up the German cruiser. Through the area passed the large Indian troop convoy from the east (to proceed via Suez) and a convoy from South Africa (carrying the Imperial garrison normally stationed there) to the west, via St Helena. Initially there was no interest in neutralising the German threat by seizing the colony, but that changed as the Germans threatened the vital Uganda Railway (in British East Africa). At the outbreak of war, the British flagship was the old cruiser *Hyacinth*. (RAN)

When the United States entered the war, the US Navy sought some way of leveraging the country's immense productive ability to deal with the single largest problem, the U-boat war. One such project was a Northern Barrage of special deep-water anti-submarine mines. The navy's experts found a mine mechanism which could be effective against a submarine at various depths and US industry was able to mass-produce the new mines. All of this was in addition to mass production of anti-submarine warships and their weapons. The two mine barriers worked in conjunction with mines and submarines in the Heligoland Bight, blocking the path between German naval bases and the North Sea. By 1918 mining was a major British and Allied anti-submarine weapon.

As First Sea Lord, Admiral Sir John Fisher liked to say that the British had the 'keys which lock up the world'. He meant that world trade inevitably flowed through choke points the Royal Navy either did or easily could control: the Channel and the northern approach to the North Sea; Gibraltar and Suez at the ends of the Mediterranean (plus Aden on the Red Sea); the Cape of Good Hope at the southern tip of Africa; Cape Horn at the southern tip of South America (thanks to the Falklands); and the Malacca Straits in the East, between the Indian Ocean and the South China Sea. Once the Panama Canal opened, the British islands in the Caribbean would become bases for ships controlling traffic through it. Control over these choke points could never be total, so the Germans or other enemies could always slip a few ships through; but they certainly could be used to choke off seaborne trade to any target country.

Locking up the entrances to the Mediterranean was not quite enough to protect British trade passing through that sea. Germany was allied to Austria-Hungary, which had a substantial fleet, including submarines. Germany was also allied to Italy and in

theory Italy and Austria-Hungary planned mutual naval action against France. In fact the two countries were rivals and the Germans doubted (correctly) that Italy would enter the war on their side. Had these two countries not in effect neutralised each other, the Austrian fleet would have been a major factor in the Mediterranean. As it was, Austrian (and Austrian-based German) submarines much affected trade through the Mediterranean.

The key geographical fact of the Mediterranean was that the Austrian fleet lay behind a choke point at the southern end of the Adriatic Sea, the Straits of Otranto. At the end of the war the Allies made considerable efforts to block it, particularly against submarines. The last major Austrian naval operations were intended to break that blockade.

In 1914 the Germans were pursuing an alliance with Turkey. Although not primarily a naval alliance, it offered serious naval implications. Through Palestine, Turkey had a land route (at least in theory) to attack the Suez Canal, one of the keys to the world and a crucial passage for British trade with the East. Turkey also ruled Arabia, which meant that at least in theory it could control the Red Sea and the entrance to the Gulf. In theory Egypt, which the British ruled indirectly, was part of the Turkish Empire. All of this was quite aside from German hopes that by entering into alliance with them the Turkish Caliph, in theory the ruler of the world's Sunni Muslims, could touch off a rebellion in the British Empire. Turkey also controlled the exit from the Black Sea, through which much of Russia's foreign trade passed. In any protracted war, the viability of the Russian economy depended in part on this trade.

In addition to territory in their own hands, in 1914 the British were allied to Japan through their first peacetime alliance, which was concluded in 1902.[5] If Japan honoured her treaty obligations, she might also be counted on to neutralise German bases in the Far East – as she did in 1914. However, the British also had to reckon with Japan's own ambitions in the Far East, which became evident during the war.

One great surprise of the First World War was the extent to which submarines could subvert geography, because generally they could not be spotted and engaged on the surface. Even if a submarine had to spend most of her time on the surface, she could usually spot a surface ship before being spotted and thus could dive before the surface ship could attack. Another surprise was the sheer endurance demonstrated by submarines, hence the distances they could cover. For example, the Germans were unpleasantly surprised that British submarines could make the passage through

The hunt for *Königsberg* began in earnest after she sank the old cruiser *Pegasus* on 20 September 1914 off Zanzibar. (RAN)

Above and right: The German cruiser *Königsberg* began the war raiding British commerce in the western Indian Ocean, but she then retreated into the delta of the Rufiji River, where a powerful British force bottled her up beginning in October 1914. It soon included the pre-dreadnought battleship HMS *Goliath*. She had covered the landing of the Royal Marines at Ostend at the beginning of the war and then had been transferred to the East Indies Station in September 1914 to help cover vital troop convoys. When the East Indies Station took over action against the *Königsberg*, she participated (November 1914). In April 1915, after the three river monitors arrived, *Goliath* went to the Dardanelles, where she was damaged on 25 April and 2 May 1915. On the night of 13 May she was torpedoed and sunk by the Turkish torpedo boat *Muavenet*. Note the anti-aircraft guns mounted on 'A' turret and her quarterdeck and the crow's-nest built atop her foretop spotting position. (RAN)

the Baltic to Russian bases such as Libau. By 1916 the Germans had submarines which could cross the Atlantic after a run around the north of Scotland and in 1918 related long-range cruiser submarines carried the U-boat war all the way to Canada and the United States.

In the late nineteenth century the European rush to seize colonies complicated British maritime geography. From a British point of view, it was essential to maintain free sea communication with the East (including Australasia) and with the Americas. As long as Britain itself blocked most access by possible European enemies to the world's ocean, the classic British strategy of blockading possible enemy bases was viable. Matters became considerably more complicated once potential enemies had bases outside the blockable area. During this period, the most likely maritime enemies facing the British were the French and the Russians, with the Americans a distant third. The United States could be blockaded, but only using massive forces and at a high cost. Once the United States began to build a substantial fleet, naval war in the Western Atlantic became too difficult to contemplate seriously. The British settled their differences with the United States and cultivated American leaders, expressing the idea that the two countries shared far too much to be other than friendly cousins. The United States was more and more important as a trading partner and also as an area of British investment. Much the same could be said of Germany at this time. Moreover, in an era of

openly racial reasoning, it was often pointed out that the British were Anglo-Saxons – the British arm of a German race (the Saxons). Such talk died as the Germans built a fleet expressly to rival theirs (the rising US Navy caused no such pre-1914 anxiety, because it was never directed aggressively at the British).

As long as their bases were all in Europe, the French and the Russians were containable naval threats. Once they expanded outside Europe, they gained bases which might be difficult to blockade, hence which could support a devastating cruiser campaign against British commerce. That applied particularly to the Far East, where the French had Cam Ranh Bay in Vietnam and the Russians had Vladivostok and, after 1895, Port Arthur in China. For this reason the standard naval war plan against France envisaged the formation of convoys taking troops to seize the French overseas bases. That had nothing to do with a desire to expand the British Empire, but everything to do with stopping French commerce warfare at source. Up to 1914, the Franco-Russian threat faded in comparison to the rising German threat. Like the French, the Germans had overseas bases, such as Tsingtao in China (the home of the German Asiatic Squadron). As in previous war plans, it was essential to neutralise these bases as a prerequisite for running down the cruisers based in them.

Just as the German army had to solve a two-front problem (France and Russia), the Imperial Navy had to deal with two possible fronts, one in the North Sea (against the Royal Navy) and

The armed merchant cruiser *Kinfauns Castle* carried the seaplane which first spotted the *Königsberg* trapped up the Rufiji River. HMS *Goliath* is in the background. The German cruiser had previously been blocked in by sinking a collier across the river entrance, but she was so far up-river that none of the British ships could hit her. *Kinfauns Castle* was a Union Castle liner taken up with *Armadale Castle* at Southampton, among the first thirteen armed merchant cruiser conversions. She measured 9664 GRT (rated at 17.5 knots) and had been built in 1899. She was armed with eight 4.7in guns. In July 1918 she was taken up for conversion to a minelayer, but the project was cancelled at the end of the war. (RAN)

one in the Baltic (against Russia). Its fleet could not be in two places at once. In the army's case, the planned solution was to concentrate against the more powerful enemy (France), while holding off the weaker Russians. Once France had been defeated, the highly-developed German railway system could move the bulk of the army to the East to deal with the Russians. That was the content of the national war plan. In reality, it was impossible to defeat the French quickly enough and the Germans had to fight on two (actually more) fronts on land.

The Imperial Navy relied even more heavily on an internal line of communication to make up for the fact that it had to face in two directions simultaneously. In its case that was the Kiel Canal, connecting the Baltic to the North Sea. The Canal was opened in 1895 and then reopened in 1914 after having been enlarged to take modern capital ships. In retrospect it is understandable that many in the Royal Navy thought that the Germans would strike once the Canal had been rebuilt, as it was a prerequisite for successful two-front naval operation. In retrospect it seems that the German Government – the Kaiser and, more importantly, the General Staff, had other things in mind.

Several times during the war British naval officers proposed Baltic operations. The existence of the Kiel Canal provided a powerful counterargument. A Baltic operation would, at the least, split the British fleet. Each portion might be inferior to the concentrated German fleet, which could transit the Canal, destroy one of the British units, then transit back to fight the other. There were few other circumstances in which the Germans could achieve gross superiority over the British.

Germany occupied a somewhat similar position to Britain with respect to European Russia (although it was actually Denmark, a neutral, which blocked the exit from the Baltic). Moreover, the Russian capital, St Petersburg, lay on the Baltic, in theory within the reach of the superior Imperial German Navy. This position justified a huge Russian investment in both local naval forces and in coast defence. Even so, the Russians feared the huge German fleet. The German naval view of the situation saved them. Just as the German army General Staff concentrated on the problem of a two-front land war (France and Russia), in which France was a much more important target than Russia, the German naval staff

balanced the Royal Navy against the Imperial Russian Navy. When the crisis came in 1914, the Kaiser demanded an immediate concentration in the Baltic; he saw Russia as the problem. His naval advisors laboured successfully to dissuade him, because in their eyes the war was about the threat of the Royal Navy. Any losses in a Baltic adventure would make the fleet even weaker when it had to confront its real enemy. Early German losses in the Baltic reinforced this view.

The German situation was further complicated by the significance in their thinking of eastern Prussia, which lies along the Baltic. The Imperial Navy drew its officers from all over the Empire, though mainly from coastal areas. The army was not imperial: its core was Prussian. Its officers came overwhelmingly from the minor nobility – the Junkers – of eastern Prussia. To the extent that the Kaiser identified with the army, he naturally saw a threat to Prussia (from Russia) as mortal. That explained his rather panicky reaction to Russian modernisation and also his demands, at the outbreak of war, both for abandonment of the Schlieffen Plan in favour of a one-front attack on the Russians and for a naval thrust into the Baltic with all available forces. In both cases the military's reaction was that concentrating on one front would open Germany to defeat in the rear. The French would not fail to take advantage of a gap in the West to seize Alsace and Lorraine and surely the British would attack by sea if the German fleet was otherwise occupied. These reactions can also be understood if the General Staff view was that Germany had to win a quick decisive war for political purposes. For example, France might well fail to exploit an opening in the West, but German forces tied down in the East could not quickly deal with her.

Furthermore, the German navy was aware that blocking the Baltic would not quite cut Russia off the way blocking the North Sea blocked Germany. The Russians had ports on the White Sea outside the Baltic, such as Archangel and thus could receive supplies from Britain whether or not the Germans dominated the Baltic. Moreover, Russia had two other coasts, on the Black Sea and on the Pacific. In 1914 nearly half of all Russian foreign income came from exports via the Black Sea. German naval strategists seem to have considered it essential to shut down that opening to the world, so they made special efforts to bring Turkey into the war. The Germans had no leverage in the Far East, but the capacity of the one railway connection, the Trans-Siberian, was limited. During the war the Russians did receive munitions via the Far East, but quantities were limited.

The ex-Brazilian river monitors, supported by air spotting, combined the necessary firepower and shallow draught to sink the *Konigsberg*. This is HMS *Mersey*. (RAN)

HMS *Iron Duke* was Grand Fleet flagship from 1914 to 1916, including at the Battle of Jutland (she succeeded HMS *Neptune*). She is shown in July 1914, newly fitted with a director (the cylinder atop her foretop), in standard British dark grey livery.

CHAPTER 7

Fleets in Battle

CAPITAL SHIPS AND THEIR consorts were the most expensive and the most visible elements of sea power in 1914. As in the past, the dominant fleet could shield the lesser warships which would enforce sea control, driving the enemy's trade from the seas and shielding one's own trade. It was often said, before and after the First World War, that capital ships maintained sea control, but cruisers (and their lesser cousins) exercised it. Because the battle fleets were the focus of so much attention, it is unfortunately easy to reduce naval warfare to a clash between them. The British certainly understood as much in 1914. The object of their naval strategy was to draw out the German battle fleet so that it could be destroyed. Once that had been done, the British would be free to use their command of the sea for riskier projects on the periphery of the German-controlled part of Europe.

The Germans did not see naval power the same way. Although their shipping was swept from the sea at the outbreak of war, they never showed much interest in seeking a naval battle to break the British block on traffic through the North Sea – a lapse bitterly criticised in the post-war official German naval history. Instead, the Germans emphasised fleet on fleet battle, preferably near the Heligoland Bight and their bases, assuming that the British would come to them. That probably went back to the defective rationale Tirpitz developed for the German fleet, that its sole object was to break British naval superiority. Tirpitz fully expected that his own fleet would be badly, probably fatally, damaged in the process. The British never fully appreciated the character of German naval strategy. They could not believe that so much had been invested in the High Seas Fleet to gain so little. Thus they spent much of the war waiting for a German sortie which came only a very few times. Because the Germans had the strategic initiative (there could be a major action only if they decided to come out), what follows is based largely on the accounts of German reasoning and practice in the German post-war official history of the war in the North Sea.

Prior to the outbreak of war, the Royal Navy saw the gun as the weapon of the superior fleet. Several ships could concentrate fire on one. The torpedo was seen as the weaker side's equaliser: a smaller fleet could fire enough to sink a more numerous one. The British expected the Germans to emphasise the torpedo. Tirpitz had begun as a torpedo specialist. The Germans mounted more torpedo tubes on their battleships and they pioneered tactics in which destroyers directly supported the battle fleet. To the surprise of the wartime Royal Navy, the Germans relied mainly on gunnery. That may have been because they chose to (or were compelled to) fight at much longer ranges than they had envisaged pre-war. It turned out that British ideas of torpedo tactics were considerably more sophisticated than those of the Germans.

It took months for German fleet C-in-C Admiral von Ingenohl to decide not to abide completely by the injunction to limit himself to naval guerrilla warfare and so to make major-unit battle possible in the North Sea. Commander of Scouting Forces (including battlecruisers) Rear Admiral Hipper proposed a battlecruiser attack which would improve fleet morale without violating the injunction against risking the fleet. Von Ingenohl agreed and he submitted it to the Kaiser on 9 September.[1] The Kaiser agreed to restore the battlecruisers to complete readiness, so that two or three of them could be sent against British patrol (blockade) lines in the northern part of the North Sea. At the same time the auxiliary minelayer *Berlin* would mine the west coast of England, a plan that the Admiralstab had prepared at the end of August. Airship reconnaissance and U-boats would protect the cruisers from the kind of surprise the Kaiser abhorred after Heligoland.[2]

The plan grew more complicated as it was elaborated by the Admiralstab in Berlin, temporarily headed by Rear Admiral Behncke.[3] Information was limited, so Behncke had to guess. He assumed the main patrol line was the one between the Shetlands and Norway, with a second line between Scotland and Norway. The bulk of the Grand Fleet was assumed to be either at sea or at a base, probably the Moray Firth, with the battlecruisers at sea during the day to reconnoitre. Under these assumptions the attacking battlecruisers might be engaged by the British battlecruisers either *en route* to the target or on their return, so they should be backed by something heavier, preferably the four *Kaiser* class battleships. Behncke also doubted that airship reconnaissance was good enough, so he wanted four fast cruisers both to screen the battlecruisers and to scout for them, backed by two destroyer flotillas. Moreover, since the main body of the Grand Fleet might come out to attack the German force, the main body of the High Seas Fleet should come out to a supporting position. A line of submarines plus mines might deal with British ships as they emerged from harbour. In other words, even a small operation would quickly turn into exactly the operation the Kaiser had forbidden, in which the entire fleet had to participate. Chief of the Admiralstab Admiral von Pohl (now absent at the Kaiser's headquarters) adhered to the original idea of limiting the operation to three battlecruisers operating alone. Von Pohl well understood that Behncke's ideas, however militarily sound, would kill any operation.

Von Pohl argued that the loss of the *Kaiser*s in action would so reduce German naval strength that the German fleet would no longer be an effective threat against the British; it would cease to be the desired strong 'fleet in being'. He argued that the battlecruisers could certainly outrun British battleships and that they would face only the four British battlecruisers, against which their superior armour-piercing shell and torpedoes and their superior survivability would tell.[4] Behncke clearly welcomed an action, in which he hoped the Germans could take advantage of minefields and U-boats. Von Pohl clearly doubted that an action would be worthwhile and he quoted the war order the Kaiser had signed to that effect.[5] The context was that von Pohl was at the Kaiser's General Headquarters, where he frequently saw both the Kaiser and Chancellor Bethmann-Hollweg. Despite the failure of the initial offensive, it must still have seemed that the war might soon end in some kind of negotiated peace. To Bethmann-Hollweg, an intact fleet was a valuable bargaining chip at that point – and it was not at all clear that a somewhat ambiguous naval victory would be nearly as useful.

Fleet commander von Ingenohl showed interest in Behncke's plan, but wanted not to send his fleet out until the day of the battlecruisers' return, to avoid running the risk of submarine attack and for fear of tipping off the enemy. He thought the best time would be heavy weather, in which the light cruisers and destroyers could not operate. As modified by von Ingenohl, the operation consisted of a sortie by three battlecruisers, which would reach the British picket line at dawn and roll it up, steaming back to reach the German Bight during the night or at dawn. In effect they would be bait for the British fleet; submarines would be placed on the approach routes to the Humber and Harwich and the entrance to the Moray Firth would be mined (by the minelayer *Kaiser*), so that ships emerging to pursue the battlecruisers would be caught. German destroyers were to be held in readiness for night attacks, presumably on British ships pursuing the Germans and the force would be supported by airship and aircraft reconnaissance. The minelayer *Berlin* would also be involved, sailing before the battlecruisers. In any case von Ingenohl's options were limited; the Kaiser had to sign off on the operations order. Von Pohl was much closer and notoriously the Kaiser tended to listen to whoever last reached him.

This operation actually began, with U-boats sailing (the minelayer *Berlin* had to turn back). The battlecruisers were anchored outside the bar of the Jade when the Admiralstab reported enough British naval activity in the North Sea that it seemed unlikely that they could reach the target area uncontested. The main effect of the U-boat operation was to show that the British were not using the Firth of Forth as a naval base.

The Yarmouth Raid

This abortive operation is interesting because ultimately it led to the operation the Germans actually carried out, the November 1914 raid on Yarmouth, the first capital ship operation they attempted. Von Ingenohl used the abandonment of the September raid to ask for re-evaluation of the initial war order restricting fleet operations.[6] He wanted greater freedom of action. General Headquarters replied restricting him further; von Pohl wrote him that the Kaiser 'feared that the Fleet might encounter a superior force just as the light cruisers [at Heligoland] had done'. The Kaiser wanted Von Ingenohl specifically to ask his permission before fighting a decisive action. Von Pohl managed to fend that off, but he still enjoined von Ingenohl to inform the Kaiser (or himself) as early as possible before taking action. Chancellor Bethmann-Hollweg also considered it essential to preserve the fleet. Von Pohl held out the hope that the British might yet attack the Heligoland Bight 'because a strong agitation for a naval offensive has been set on foot in Great Britain'. He also felt that the battle of Heligoland Bight showed that the British were willing to risk their capital ships to attack by U-boats: the British fleet would expose itself at Heligoland, as the German had always imagined. Until it did so, there was no opportunity for decisive action as defined in the war order.[7]

Von Pohl was still badly spooked by the threat of British submarines off the estuaries from which German ships would emerge into the Heligoland Bight. However, he proposed allowing the High Seas Fleet to cruise outside the Heligoland Bight, arguing that he might find himself facing only part of the British Fleet. Acting Admiralstab chief Admiral Behncke soon commented that if such operations were properly planned, their success might force

With his battlecruisers typically some distance ahead of him, Admiral Jellicoe relied on his 'Town' class light cruisers as his scouts. They served him well at Jutland. The 2nd Cruiser Squadron attached to the Grand Fleet called itself 'Sir John Jellicoe's Light Cavalry'. This is HMS *Gloucester*. At the time of Jutland, she was part of the 3rd Light Cruiser Squadron. (Author's collection)

the British to leave their bases to keep closer watch on the German Bight, exposing them to U-boat and destroyer attack (i.e., to kleinkrieg).

It is not clear that von Ingenohl was so very intent on action. He described the possibility of a battle in the Skaggerak, but argued that if he was damaged, British light forces could further damage his force as it retired. This argument played to the Kaiser's fear of losing the fleet. Von Ingenohl wanted a specific order not to go to sea, but all the Admiralstab would give him was an expansion of the limits set by the war order. Behncke was not going to help: he wrote that von Ingenohl had always been free to act, as the war order allowed him to seize favourable opportunities even before the odds had been evened. Behncke went further, suggesting the value of carefully-planned limited operations and stressing the deterioration of the fleet as it was confined to harbour, a loss he considered outweighed any political reason to preserve the fleet. Asked about the battlecruiser operation, Tirpitz had much the same view. He did stress that any fleet action should be no more than 100 miles from Heligoland. Tirpitz was particularly insistent that the fleet not be preserved as a bargaining chip: 'when we make peace after such a terrible war as this without the Fleet having shed its blood and achieved something, we shall never get anything more for the Navy. All available monies that can be scraped together will go to the Army and the great efforts of His Majesty the Kaiser to raise Germany to a Sea Power will have been made in vain.'[8] *Krieg zur See* argued that this was more than simply an attempt to help the navy after the war. Both von Pohl and von Müller (chief of the Naval Cabinet) were urging the Kaiser to see the current war (with its minimal naval involvement) as a stepping-stone toward the

complete development of Germany as a seapower, in which connection they and Chancellor Bethmann-Hollweg often analogised it to the first (of two) Punic Wars, the second of which would defeat the ultimate enemy, Britain.

Tirpitz in particular thought that the German destroyer force had not yet been used, whereas at Heligoland Bight the British destroyers had shown 'that they don't know how to attack'. He was beginning to develop the idea that it was not necessary to deploy the fleet, but that kleinkrieg offered major opportunities. Presumably this thinking led Tirpitz to realise just what a kleinkrieg force at Zeebrugge and Ostend could achieve.

Through Admiral von Pohl, the Kaiser told von Ingenohl that he could not allow the fleet to be risked until the military situation on land stabilised and until a decided advantage had been gained on at least one front. However, he would approve offensive action by cruisers and destroyers, particularly by the battlecruisers. He said he would accept losses in such operations. The fleet could not be risked to support the battlecruisers if they were sent out.[9] Ultimately the Kaiser approved a new order: the fleet should fight, but avoid losses.[10] Von Ingenohl concluded that he had to hold back his main body, because action seemed impossible without risking serious losses.

By October, weather had shut down German air reconnaissance of the North Sea, so von Ingenohl had very fragmentary information. Based on frequent reports of British ships in the Skaggerak, he imagined a substantial British fleet operating there, with the two other British fleets (Second and Third) operating, respectively, between Scotland and Norway and in the Channel or off the Dogger Bank. He imagined that the British wanted to lure him to attack one of these formations, in which case the other fleets would cut off his retreat. An attack on any one of the three formations would require his whole fleet and would incur serious losses, so it had to be rejected in view of the Kaiser's order. The best he could do was to renew mining attacks against the British bases on the east and west coasts of Scotland, supported at a distance by the battlecruisers, which would steam as far as the Dogger Bank. It was during this operation that *Berlin* laid the mine which sank the new British battleship *Audacious*. The main German response to reports of British activity was U-boat deployment, both to search for reported British forces and to attack wherever possible.

For their part the British had concentrated the Grand Fleet specifically to cover the transport of troops to (and their withdrawal from) Ostend. The British also had to cover the Canadian convoy carrying troops to Boulogne. Among the ships detailed to escort the convoy was the battlecruiser *Princess Royal*. Direct cover was needed because the cruiser *Karlsruhe* might be active in the Atlantic and also because the Germans had armed several liners as auxiliary cruisers. Among other things, the Grand Fleet was responsible for ensuring that additional cruisers did not break out of the German Bight.

Once the Germans had occupied Bruges and Ostend, von Ingenohl saw them as a port of refuge for any force he sent into the North Sea. He was therefore encouraged to send out four destroyers to mine the Downs or at least the Thames Estuary or some other place near the coast. Like others in the German navy, he was aware that without the shipping in the Downs, London would be unable to exist.[11] All four of the elderly destroyers involved were sunk.[12]

Von Ingenohl became convinced that no major fleet operation

would result in an engagement with the British fleet until the latter took the offensive; the only result would be losses to British submarines, which were thought to infest the German Bight. On that basis he had cancelled fleet exercises of any kind in the Bight. Von Ingenohl thought that he could safely despatch his battle squadrons one by one through the Kiel Canal to exercise off Kiel, so as to remain effective. When the General Staff urged that the navy relieve pressure on land, he assigned U-boats to attack British transports. Admiral von Pohl urged further minelaying operations for the next new moon, but von Ingenohl cited the recent disaster as proof that the British could ambush any such operation. For a minelaying operation to succeed, it had to have heavy support.

This thinking led to the first major German surface operation of the war, the Yarmouth Raid. The initial plan was to use the battlecruisers to cover a minelaying operation by light cruisers, which would mine the area between Smiths Knoll Lightship and Lowestoft to attack traffic between the East Coast of England and the Channel as well as to interrupt fishing. The use of the battlecruisers in effect violated the Kaiser's recent order. Von Ingenohl justified it on the ground that they desperately needed war training at sea. The fleet had been at maximum effectiveness when war broke out and its idleness was affecting it.

For security, the cruisers had to leave the Jade at night, but in that case they would reach the minelaying areas in daylight. To give them a good chance to lay their mines unopposed, von Ingenohl planned a diversion: the battlecruisers would shell Great Yarmouth.[13] The battlecruisers were preceded by two light cruisers as scouts. Plans for a destroyer screen were abandoned due to heavy weather. A U-boat line was set up off Terschelling to attack any British force pursuing the minelayers and battlecruisers back across the North Sea.[14] The German main body went to sea as distant cover. The operation required the Kaiser's personal sanction and thus considerable correspondence which threatened to ruin secrecy. The Kaiser added that he expected reconnaissance, specifically including air reconnaissance, to be mounted north of the raiders' course to prevent them from being cut off as they retired.[15] Bad weather delayed the operation to 5 November, by which time the fighting in Flanders, which might have benefitted from the minelaying, was over. The Germans apparently achieved complete surprise, encountering only a torpedo gunboat (which radioed an alarm) and two destroyers (which they failed to hit).[16] As they bombarded Yarmouth, they zig-zagged at high speed to preclude attacks by any submarines which might be present. Shore batteries fired back. After the operation, Hipper reported faulty W/T practice, which he attributed to the long period of idleness after the outbreak of war.

For their part, the British assumed that the bombardment was the beginning of a major operation. Once fighting stalemated in France, they came to imagine that the Germans would have surplus forces which might be used for an invasion. Admiral Beatty was ordered to steam to Heligoland to cut Hipper off and the Grand Fleet sortied from Lough Swilly to concentrate on Scapa. Tyrwhitt was ordered back to port so that he could not be cut off by the superior German force. It was also possible that the Germans were headed for the Channel. The battlecruisers could not get there in time, so the Channel Fleet was moved south to block Hipper and any follow-on force. A trawler discovered the new German minefield.

Although it had achieved little in concrete terms, the raid was considered a valuable boost to the fleet's morale. At least one of the German captains thought that the raid had shown that the British were thinly stretched: otherwise they would surely have found and dealt with the raiders. For him it followed that further raids might weaken the British fleet to the point of evening the odds.[17] It is not clear that anyone higher up shared this opinion. Von Ingenohl was still very cautious.

When the British fleet approached the German Bight a few weeks later, von Ingenohl decided not to come out for fear that British submarines had been deployed outside his harbours to attack his ships.[18] The British operation began as a sweep covering a planned attack on the Nordholz Hangars, which the author of *Krieg zur See* dismisses as unimportant given the force involved. However, the British saw the Zeppelins at Nordholz as the eyes of the High Seas Fleet and on that basis they were well worth destroying. The Admiralty cancelled the air attack on the ground that a German force superior to the British force (detached to conduct the air attack) was at sea. This report was false; it must have been one of the last which was not based on code-breaking. Jellicoe pressed on, the Germans assuming that he wanted a rerun of the battle of Heligoland in August. Von Ingenohl deduced that if the British were setting up a battle they must have deployed submarines in advance.[19]

The Scarborough Raid

Given the success off Yarmouth, Hipper proposed to attack commerce in the Skaggerak, on the theory that such an operation would draw the British out into an unfavourable battle area. Von Ingenohl considered a direct attack on the British coast a more likely draw, particularly since forces had surely been stationed on the coast specifically to deal with a new raid. He proposed to send out his battlecruisers (1st Scouting Group), his modern light cruisers (2nd Scouting Group) and his two fastest destroyer flotillas. All would be in position off the British coast at daybreak, after which they would separate, groups of two or three battlecruisers proceeding to shell Hartlepool and Scarborough. U-boats would be stationed off Harwich and the Humber to attack ships coming out to deal with the bombardment. The battleships, the 3rd and 4th Scouting Groups (older cruisers) and the rest of the destroyer flotillas would be held back in distant support 130 miles away, returning to the German Bight that evening. Von Ingenohl doubted that the Kaiser would approve the operation unless he made it explicit that he was holding his main body back. On 19 November 1914 the Kaiser approved the plan. The operation was postponed for a few days because British newspaper reports seemed to indicate leaks.[20] Hipper decided to begin it on the night of 14/15 December because he wanted to take advantage of the new moon.

These plans were laid soon after Graf Spee's cruiser squadron wiped out a British force at Coronel on 1 November. The Germans knew that British capital ships were being sent to the South Atlantic to deal with Graf Spee and therefore that the Grand Fleet had been weakened. It was possible that battleships as well as battlecruisers were going. When the operation was planned, one objective was to threaten the British Isles so as to deter the British from sending more ships, relieving some of the pressure on Graf Spee. When his force was wiped out on 8 December this part of the logic of the operation died. The detachment of British battlecruisers became no

SMS *Frankfurt* was typical of later German light cruisers. She was one of two 1912 ships, the numbers being limited because of the rising cost of capital ships. Completion was delayed to August 1915 due to the higher priority of other work when war broke out. Unlike earlier German cruisers, these two ships were armed with eight 5.9in (15cm) guns: two side by side on the forecastle, two each side on the main deck behind breakwaters and two on the centreline aft. This arrangement was continued in all later German light cruisers. There were also two 8.8cm (3.4in) anti-aircraft guns, visible abaft the after funnel and two twin 50cm torpedo tubes. The Germans never adopted the heavy torpedo batteries of British wartime light cruisers (the final series of German light cruisers did, however, have 60cm rather than 50cm tubes). Light cruisers seem not to have enjoyed a high priority. The 1913 programme consisted of four repeat units, which were given the names of commerce-raiding cruisers sunk early in the war, such as *Emden*. Once war began, ten more cruisers were ordered, but only five were launched and only two completed. *Frankfurt*'s sister *Wiesbaden* torpedoed the British battleship *Marlborough* while disabled at Jutland. *Frankfurt* was handed over to the US Navy after the war (hence the US flag) and sunk in a bombing experiment. (US Naval Historical and Heritage Command)

more than an element tipping the balance slightly in favour of the Germans.

This was essentially a repeat of the Yarmouth Raid, including minelaying (this time by the cruiser *Kolberg*), except that this time British signals intelligence detected the raid in time for the raiders to be intercepted. This may have been the first tactical use of British signals intelligence. The German official history remarks that instead of distributing ships along the coast for defence, the British concentrated their fleet and planned to intercept the Germans. That strongly suggests that they expected to gain sufficient information via signals intelligence to do so, as without such intelligence interception would be impossible. The Admiralty clearly saw its intelligence of the raid as a golden opportunity, quite possibly never to be repeated, since the Germans would surely realise that their signals were being read. The sense of a golden opportunity made the failure to intercept and destroy Hipper's force particularly bitter; the British did not realise how durable their intelligence advantage would be. British signals intelligence apparently *did not* show that the High Seas Fleet was at sea as a distant covering force for Hipper, who would fall back on it if pursued.

Krieg zur See claims that the British were steering for a rendezvous only 30 miles from the point the High Seas Fleet expected to reach at about the same time. The British interception force consisted of the 2nd Battle Squadron (six super-dreadnoughts) under Admiral Warrender. His scouting force consisted of Admiral Beatty's battlecruisers and associated light cruisers and destroyers under Commodore Goodenough. The Germans had four battlecruisers (plus the semi-battlecruiser *Blücher*), four light cruisers and two destroyer flotillas.

For his part, von Ingenohl was acutely aware that if he actually joined his battleships to his battlecruisers he would be directly violating the Kaiser's order that the High Seas Fleet should be preserved to fight a decisive naval battle. Ironically, had the British force, which was only part of the Grand Fleet, pressed onwards, it would have offered the Germans exactly the battle they wanted to fight on very favourable terms. The British became aware of that only after the skirmishing which followed the Scarborough Raid; they realised how close the 2nd Battle Squadron had come to disaster. The possibility of a similar disaster in the future affected their thinking about how the battlecruisers and the Grand Fleet battleships should operate.

The Germans had no idea that the British were reading their signals. Von Ingenohl imagined that they had a vast trawler organisation in the North Sea reporting German movements.[21] It was known that the British were offering large rewards for information about German fleet movements. During the night after leaving port, his screening destroyers were struck by the large numbers of trawlers, nearly all of Dutch registry. Most had insufficient papers, but there was no time to deal with them. On its return through the same area, the fleet saw no trawlers at all. Von Ingenohl had to admit, however, that no one saw any sign of a W/T set on any of the trawlers. Von Ingenohl himself considered monitoring British W/T his best means of detecting British activity. His fleet was not, however, making any attempt to read coded British messages. After going to sea on 15 December he heard no unusual activity.

Once he was at sea, one of von Ingenohl's cruisers reported six enemy destroyers and took off in pursuit. Von Ingenohl was painfully aware that his own fleet created a dense column of smoke, visible from a great distance, when it ran at 'utmost speed'. His battlecruisers having been detached to conduct the bombardment, he was left with a weak cruiser scouting force (3rd and 4th Scouting Groups), which could not screen his fleet from enemy cruisers. He was sure that the British knew exactly what he was doing and that they would be sending destroyers into the Heligoland Bight to intercept him on his way back, probably in a night attack.

The German battle squadrons formed into line ahead, presumably to deal with any possible encounter with a British battle fleet, but von Ingenohl had no intention of offering battle. He knew that under normal circumstances he would have met the battlecruisers 250 miles from the Jade. If he then turned around, at an average cruising speed (15 knots) he would be back in the Jade at 7 o'clock the next morning – he would be exposed to destroyer torpedo attack most of the night. After his two screening cruisers each reported a submarine contact, von Ingenohl decided to turn back towards home. At about the same time the scouting force commander responsible for the raid itself, Admiral Hipper, signalled that he was detaching his light forces, which would fall back on the main body. That would leave him only the battlecruisers and the minelaying cruiser *Kolberg*. Von Ingenohl could not see why; his ships were steaming in good weather. Hipper reported later that not far away he was in such bad weather that he had to detach his lighter ships. As it steamed home, the German main body saw numerous floating mines; von Ingenohl thought the British had purposely laid them in hopes that they would drift into the German Bight and thus hamper German movements (he admitted that they might be British mines whose moorings had broken – as was the case).

The closest contact between the two fleets came when von Ingenohl's light forces, detached from his battlecruisers, were falling back on the fleet and came upon Warrender's battleships. The two light cruisers present pushed between destroyers and battleships, but the British battleships withdrew. The Germans thought they were avoiding the risk of a night destroyer torpedo attack. More importantly, the radioed reports from the two cruisers made it possible for the German Scouting Force (battlecruisers) to avoid contact with Warrender's battleships as they withdrew after bombarding Scarborough.

The Germans found themselves explaining why their destroyers had not stayed in touch with Warrender's force to deliver a night torpedo attack. Von Ingenohl blamed insufficient destroyer endurance remaining after 35 hours of high-speed running. Later he learned that the sea was running against the destroyers. They were too far from Warrender's ships and would have had to steam too far against that head sea, between enemy forces (light cruisers and battleships). They would have been sunk by the battleships while working sufficiently far ahead of them to deliver an attack. All of the officers commanding flotillas and half-flotillas apparently considered making immediate attacks but held off because the risks were not balanced by the slim chance of success. They had too little fuel, it turned out, to stay in touch until nightfall. Von Ingenohl wrote specifically that the destroyer commanders' decisions met with his approval. The senior flotilla officers made their own statement that initially they were on an opposite course to the British fleet, hence could not fire without working around to a favourable position. Most of the destroyers would have had to readjust their torpedoes to night range (4400 and 4900 yds), although some, which could not change settings in the tubes, already had their torpedoes set for this range. Von Ingenohl reported that he had encountered an unusually large number of British submarines, which he suspected had been positioned in his path.

Contact having been lost, Beatty still hoped to bring Hipper to action. He steered for the centre of the gap between the North Sea minefields. At that point Warrender signalled that he had sighted enemy cruisers and destroyers and was chasing them. Beatty had to turn so as to cut them off. Visibility was so poor that the ships could not be recognised definitely. They used British recognition signals, but that turned out to be a ruse allowing these German ships to escape. For his part, Warrender narrowly avoided running into a large German destroyer force which could have launched a massive salvo. He tried but failed to overhaul the German cruisers, largely because some of his attached cruisers (*Devonshire* class) were too slow. The only thing he learned before the mist closed in was that there were no battlecruisers among the German ships; Hipper was somewhere else and Warrender had to guess where. He was receiving signals from the Admiral of Patrols, whose ships were reporting the positions of the German ships off the British coast. The Admiralty received and decoded (and then transmitted) a signal from the German battlecruisers giving their position in relation to the gap in the Dogger Bank minefields through which they had to pass.[22] This signal also gave their course and speed. Beatty thought the course incorrect, as it passed over part of the Dogger Bank itself. Based on his interpretation of the possibilities, he sought to place himself between Hipper and his base at Wilhelmshaven. Receiving the same signal, Warrender read it differently. He had not found Hipper to the south of the gap, so he steered north, his cruisers forming a scouting screen ahead of him. Neither contacted the other and their lack of co-operation helped Hipper escape.

Up to this point von Ingenohl had not signalled Hipper. When Hipper reported that he had completed his bombardment and was headed home, von Ingenohl signalled his own position, course and speed: he was headed home at maximum speed and he was 150 miles away. This was presumably the first that British signals intelligence received to realise that von Ingenohl had been at sea in the first place, but it was also clear that Warrender was not in any immediate danger.[23] For their part the German cruisers scouting for Hipper confused him into thinking that he was facing two separate enemy battle forces including no fewer than eleven battleships. He sought to avoid action, but even so, for a considerable time he and Beatty were no more than 25 miles apart. The Admiralty kept intercepting, reading and re-transmitting the signals from Hipper and his scouts. For his part, Hipper was hearing considerable British W/T traffic, but he was unable to read any of it. He deduced that the British were keeping in touch either in preparation for a mass destroyer torpedo attack or to lay mines on the route he had to take back to Germany. The strength of some of the British signals led him to believe that they were quite close; he was also able to sense the point at which the British decided to break off.

Because it knew so much of the story in the form of intercepted and decoded German signals, the Admiralty could see just how close Warrender and Beatty had come to engaging Hipper. The opportunity had been golden, it had been squandered and it might well never recur. Beatty was fortunate not to have been blamed, because his inept (and foolish) signal had caused Goodenough to lose critical contact.[24]

German accounts show that several times British destroyers found themselves near (and aware of) submerged U-boats, but that they were unable to attack; the anti-submarine sweeps developed before the war apparently were not used. The depth charges issued the following year would have converted these opportunities into attacks. U-boats were also reported inside some harbours and the Grand Fleet felt compelled to leave its base at Scapa Flow for Lough Swilly in Ireland until its anti-submarine defences (nets and booms) had been installed. The Germans were entirely unaware of this development.[25]

There was considerable criticism of von Ingenohl, who had squandered his own chance to destroy part of the British fleet. When the raid was reported to the Kaiser, he reversed himself: 'the desire to preserve intact the Fleet or parts of the Fleet should in no circumstances be carried so far as to forfeit good chances of success because losses might possibly be incurred. If the probable results appear to be worth the risk, an advantageous situation must be made the most of, without any regard to secondary considerations.'[26]

For the British, the main lessons of the battle were failures of scouting and of initiative. An unlearned lesson was that Hipper escaped largely because the battlecruisers and battleships were poorly co-ordinated, due in part to inept signalling on the part of Beatty's force. Goodenough contacted a German cruiser and destroyers and ordered his cruisers to concentrate while signalling Beatty that he was in action. Beatty could hardly see Goodenough's flagship; he concluded that the enemy ships were the screen behind which Hipper's battlecruisers were. He guessed the enemy course and instead of simply reinforcing Goodenough he turned to what he thought would be a course to intercept Hipper and hold him until Warrender's battleships appeared. He had no cruisers with him, so he decided to take one of Goodenough's to deal with possible German destroyer attacks. Not knowing which unengaged cruiser he saw, Beatty ordered a general signal to disengage and accompany him. Goodenough received the signal and disengaged. He was obeying an order he assumed was backed by the greater knowledge held by his fleet commander. After the battle, Beatty complained bitterly: Goodenough should be relieved. Jellicoe realised that the inept signal had been the problem and fortunately retained Goodenough, who performed brilliantly at Jutland. Goodenough apparently thought Beatty was simply clearing the line of fire for

his ships. It would have seemed bizarre for Beatty to have withdrawn one of a group of light cruisers engaged with the enemy. It was left for Jellicoe to write forcefully later that no ship in contact with the enemy should obey an order to break off, because the more senior officer giving the order might well not be aware of just what was happening. It also followed that scouts had to report in greater detail and more frequently, a point driven home again and again in subsequent Grand Fleet orders.

For the Germans, the most important lesson of the operation was that it now seemed possible to entice parts of the British fleet into action on unequal terms. The old concept of waiting for an advantageous moment near the German coast could be replaced by a new one in which a raid on the British coast might be turned into the opportunity needed to even the odds.[27]

Originally the Scarborough raid was to have included minelaying in the Moray Firth, but during the raid the Germans found many British mines in that area, so von Ingenohl opted to wait until the weather had cleared sufficiently for him to send in a fast destroyer flotilla for reconnaissance. He assumed incorrectly that the British were using trawlers to lay their minefields, which meant in practice that he grossly inflated British minelaying capacity. He also had indications of a major pending British operation. It was rumoured that 200 ships had been preparing early in December for a blocking operation and that some had been transformed to resemble warships. It was not clear whether the blocking operation was to be against French ports which might come into German hands, or whether the British planned to block the North Sea estuaries (it was, however, unlikely that both the Jade and the Elbe could be blocked at the same time).[28] The reports may have been distortions of early reports of Admiral Fisher's Baltic project, or of the redistribution of the British fleet. In fact the British operation was the air raid against the Zeppelin sheds at Cuxhaven on 25 December 1914, the first carrier operation in history. The Germans were aware of the timing of the operation, but not of its nature. A U-boat stationed offshore actually saw the British carriers as they steamed past her. However, no German surface ships came out to intercept the British carrier force, which had heavier units in distant support, even though it was within 30 miles of the German coast for four hours. The only German

HMS *Lion* was flagship of the British battlecruisers throughout the war. She is shown after Jutland (note the absence of torpedo nets) but before major modification. Her searchlights are centralised around her third funnel, but they are not yet remote-controlled and she does not yet have a flying-off platform on 'X' turret. Note the director on a platform below her foretop. Originally *Lion* had a reversed tripod mast, as in an *Orion* class battleship, but the spotting top was badly affected by funnel smoke and a pole in front of the funnel was substituted. Later tripod legs were added to help support the weight of the spotting top shown.

response was seaplane attacks against the British force. This was considerably less impressive than the British response to the Scarborough raid, probably because German intelligence was far less effective than British.

Just as the British assumed that the battlecruisers shelling Scarborough were part of a larger operation, the Germans assumed that the few British seaplanes were part of something larger, perhaps a probe to entice their capital ships onto waiting British submarines. Although their battlecruisers were briefly readied to sail, they were held back.

For the British, the two raids called into question the pre-war decision to base the Grand Fleet at Scapa Flow, from which it could not react quickly enough. The fear of invasion remained real. It was argued that the pre-dreadnoughts on the southern English coast were inadequate protection.[29] Initially it was proposed that the entire Grand Fleet be moved south, Sheerness and the Humber being candidate bases. Neither the Admiralty nor Admiral Jellicoe considered the East Coast a good base for the entire fleet, but Beatty suggested Rosyth, which was further north, as a base for his battlecruisers. The second German raid made it impossible to resist some reinforcement of the southern area and Beatty's proposal was accepted. It had the important consequence of making Beatty's effectively an independent command (soon renamed the Battlecruiser Fleet rather than the Battlecruiser Squadron). In December 1914, Beatty had been subordinate to Admiral Warrender, who in effect represented Jellicoe. He had received Admiralty intelligence information from Warrender. Now Admiralty signals went directly to Beatty as well as to Jellicoe. In a future action, Beatty's fleet would rendezvous with the Grand Fleet at sea. Moreover, operating practices and doctrines in the two organisations would begin to diverge. Beatty's effective independence would protect him from searching criticism of his poor signalling.

To their surprise, the British found that the Germans did not change their codes or their W/T practices after the Scarborough raid; they were utterly unaware of their vulnerability. Given the ability to read and interpret German signals, the Grand Fleet could spend more time in harbour, as it could be called out in time to deal with any German raid. That proved fortunate, because in January 1915 an unusually large portion of the battle fleet was suffering from 'condenseritis' and other machinery problems.

The Battle of the Falklands

Meanwhile the first heavy-gun action of the war was fought: the battle of the Falklands on 8 December 1914. The two British battlecruisers *Invincible* and *Inflexible* destroyed von Spee's Asiatic Squadron, which had recently wiped out a British squadron at Coronel. Visibility was excellent, falling at the end only to 15,000 yds. The British were surprised that instead of maintaining a steady course for good gunnery, von Spee's ships zig-zagged to make British gunnery more difficult. German survivors remarked that British fire was slow. Both British ships found their fire control hampered by funnel smoke: HMS *Invincible* found her foretop smoked in and only her 'A' turret and her conning tower could see the enemy continuously. Rangefinding was difficult at the very long range and enemy zig-zagging worsened matters considerably. The British used up most of their ammunition: one 12in gun on board *Inflexible* fired 109 rounds (she was designed

to carry eighty per gun). By this time the British ships were carrying many more rounds per gun than magazines had been designed to take and congestion around the bottoms of ammunition hoists may explain the low rate of fire noticed by the Germans. Zig-zagging seems to have been a standard German gunnery countermeasure, as the British encountered it whenever they met German capital ships. The gunnery range far exceeded what had been practiced pre-war and it may have confirmed to the British that Admiral Jellicoe's instructions to open at long range were practicable. His ships had been trying to reach the desired ranges and the results were not particularly good.[30] The British were impressed by the effect of plunging shells at long ranges and by the blast effect of German fire.

The Battle of Dogger Bank

At the end of December 1914 the Kaiser asked the Admiralstab for a memorandum on future plans for naval operations, taking into account the experience both of the Scarborough raid and of the British Christmas carrier air raid.[31] In transmitting the Kaiser's request his Chief of Naval Cabinet added that Chancellor Bethmann-Hollweg's views on the political situation should be taken into account. It seemed clear that neither minelaying nor U-boat attacks had created sufficient pressure to bring British heavy units into the German Bight. Neither of the cruiser raids had accomplished much, except for considerable political gains. The British would not risk their fleet without compelling cause. To do that the German fleet would have to come out. To do that successfully it needed much better reconnaissance, by air and by U-boat. As for the danger from British submarines, the more the High Seas Fleet went to sea, the less it would be endangered by British submarines lying close off the estuaries. The fleet should always operate in concentrated form and U-boats should co-operate tactically with it. The Kaiser's new order that risks could and should be taken seems to have energised the Admiralstab, which had previously found all sorts of reasons why even a small operation required the whole fleet, hence could not be mounted. For his part, Bethmann-Hollweg considered fleet employment a wholly military issue, though he had some doubts as to the proposed employment of airships and submarines with the fleet.

The Kaiser authorised C-in-C High Seas Fleet to make frequent sorties into the North Sea on his own initiative, 'with the object of cutting off advanced enemy forces or of attacking them with superior strength'. However, 'as far as possible the C-in-C is to avoid encounters with superior enemy forces, as in the present circumstances the High Seas Fleet has the added importance of being a valuable political instrument in the hands of the Kaiser; an unfavourable outcome of a naval action would therefore be a particularly serious matter'. All proposed operations taking the fleet as far as the British coast were to be reported beforehand to the Kaiser. This was not at all what the writers of the memo had had in mind; it was less cautious than the previous year's policy, but not the full-blooded offensive the Admiralstab wanted. As long as preservation of the fleet was to guide the C-in-C, he could always make excuses not to act. Admiral von Ingenohl wrote that it would be almost impossible to gain successes against parts of the British fleet and he doubted that any German operation would induce the British to take the risks the Germans wanted. German operations on the far (British) side of the North Sea were exactly what the

Lion at Invergordon, 1915, in the livery used at Jutland. Note the anti-aircraft gun superfiring over 'X' turret. This was the ship's appearance at the time of Dogger Bank.

British wanted. However, once the winter storms were over, the fleet could and would make much more frequent sorties.

Von Ingenohl had consistently argued that he should not take his fleet beyond the radius of action of his destroyers, which he considered essential to success in a major engagement (Jellicoe regarded the German destroyer force as an equaliser).[32] He saw the two raids as great minelaying successes. He was therefore interested in a third repetition, this time to mine the entrance to the Humber; another operation would mine the entrance to the Firth of Forth (it had to be abandoned due to bad weather).[33] The British having laid a large minefield in the Heligoland Bight, von Ingenohl was reluctant to risk heavy ships in it; he sent out two cruisers and a destroyer flotilla, retaining his fleet in its base to deal with the British blocking operation of which he had been warned (as noted above).[34] The two raids had certainly raised Admiralty awareness of the possibility of invasion, so through January it was particularly sensitive to reports of major movements by German capital ships. At about the same time von Ingenohl hit upon the idea of circulating a report that German ships were about to bombard the Humber coast, in hopes of luring the British fleet into the German Bight.

When the weather improved, von Ingenohl's Chief of Staff suggested a cruiser-destroyer sortie to the Dogger Bank. Trawlers, which the Germans believed were providing the British with key operational intelligence, could be cleared away and perhaps the British patrol forces could be attacked. Having (the Germans thought) operated in the German Bight a few days earlier, the British fleet had presumably retired to coal. The Germans assumed that the British battlecruisers were at Scapa to prevent German commerce raiders from breaking through into the Atlantic and the heavy ships divided between the Firth of Forth and the Thames. On this basis a quick battlecruiser operation seemed feasible, even without support by the German main body. It was even argued that by not moving the main body to sea, the Germans were making it

less likely that the British would learn about the operation. Hipper was ordered simply to reconnoitre the Dogger Bank, arriving at dawn. Although the new guidelines envisaged bringing the fleet along with the battlecruisers, that was currently impossible, as von Ingenohl had authorised refits and repairs to prepare the fleet for a possible later operation.

As at Scarborough, British signals intelligence worked; it reported that Hipper was about to sail for the Dogger Bank. The Admiralty ordered the battlecruisers from the Firth of Forth and the light cruisers and destroyers from Rosyth to rendezvous with the Harwich force. As during the Scarborough raid, Beatty had the 1st Light Cruiser Squadron (Goodenough) as scouts and screen, plus destroyers. The British battleships were ordered out in distant support of Beatty's battlecruisers. Von Ingenohl imagined they were out of action because they were coaling, but the Admiralty telegram giving details of the German operation stopped that. Beatty caught Hipper's force, in the first capital ship on capital ship action of the war.

Hipper had only four battlecruisers and he believed (correctly) that Beatty had five.[35] He therefore included in his force the large armoured cruiser *Blucher*, in effect a semi-battlecruiser armed with armoured cruiser guns (8.2in). He had to match Beatty's numbers because if he had fewer ships, two of Beatty's ships would concentrate fire on one of his. As it happened, Grand Fleet Battle Orders emphasised the need to concentrate on the leading ship of an enemy line, so as to throw the line into confusion. Otherwise, normal practice was for each ship to fire at the opposite ship in the enemy line. The captain of HMS *Tiger* took his orders to mean that although he was second in line, he should concentrate with the leading British ship on the leading German ship – leaving the second German ship not engaged at all. That this lapse was *not* disastrous seems to have made a considerable impression on Admiral Beatty. Jellicoe pointed out that the standing orders were intended for the special case of crossing the enemy's 'T' in a mass engagement, not a fight by a few battlecruisers, but Beatty protected *Tiger*'s captain.

Visibility was excellent, so ships opened fire at ranges well beyond what had been imagined before the war. Beatty's flagship

Lion opened fire on *Blücher* at 21,000 yds and hit at 19,000 yds. The German battlecruisers *Seydlitz* and *Derfflinger* were hit at or beyond 17,000 yds. *Lion* straddled her targets within five to ten minutes. That was far better than the Germans did. The British performance convinced Beatty that his ships could hit at up to 22,000 yds (existing orders envisaged 15,000 yds as extreme range). That required modifications to fire control instruments. For example, the automatic range transmitter on the main (Argo) rangefinder was limited to 16,000 yds. Sights in *Princess Royal* (and probably the others) were calibrated out to 20,200 yds (elevation 15° 21"), even though the guns could elevate to 20°. As in the Falklands, British rangefinders were not very useful at such ranges, so fire control was mainly by spotting.

Beatty's ships fired single guns to test the range, shifting to salvos only after their single shots had crossed the target. That made for slow initial fire. As in the Falklands, the Germans zig-zagged to ruin British fire control, which assumed the enemy was steaming on a steady path. That made it necessary to make bold corrections (*Princess Royal* needed a 1000 yd up correction at 16,000 yds) and it also made for few hits. Inspired by the German tactics, Beatty suggested a moderate zig-zag (2 point turn, return to course after three minutes) as a way of avoiding further damage once the Germans found the range.

The battlecruisers' fire tore *Blücher* apart.[36] As in the Falklands, even though her magazines must have been penetrated, she did not explode; she sank due to massive cumulative damage (the newspaper photograph of her turning turtle was immensely popular). On the other hand, there was no reason to think that German ships were immune to magazine damage. *Seydlitz* lost both of her after turrets.[37] This damage did not sink the ship and she was even able to keep firing her other turrets. The Germans were extremely impressed by the damage, which was attributed to a single 13.5in hit.[38]

In the stern chase which developed, gunlayers in forward turrets found themselves badly hampered by spray and unable to distinguish parts of the German ships because of dense smoke. Hipper had destroyers with him and Beatty was unable to close him at one point in the action because he would have had to follow in their wake – and he accepted Jellicoe's contention that they might well drop mines in their wake.

German shellfire damaged HMS *Lion* badly enough to immobilise her, but she did not seem to be in any danger of sinking. In contrast to what happened at Jutland, a shell which exploded in the handling room of 'A' turret (and set it afire) did not destroy the

A painting of the battle of Heligoland Bight, 28 November 1914, shows Admiral Beatty's battlecruisers and his destroyers coming to the rescue of the Harwich Force light cruisers and destroyers, which had swept into the Heligoland Bight. The operation was proposed by submarine commander (Commodore (S)) Roger Keyes as a way of dealing with German destroyer patrols which were hampering British submarine operations in the Bight. Supported by Harwich Force commander Commodore Reginald Tyrwhitt, it was approved by the Admiralty without early notification to Grand Fleet commander Admiral Jellicoe. The plan originally called for two battlecruisers in distant support. When he was informed, Jellicoe offered Grand Fleet support, but was told that three more of Beatty's battlecruisers (plus light cruisers) would suffice. Tyrwhitt and Keyes never received word that Beatty's ships were to support them and the sudden appearance of his light cruisers caused some confusion. Keyes' submarines had been told that any cruiser other than the two leading Tyrwhitt's two destroyer flotillas should be presumed hostile (HMS *Southampton* was nearly attacked). Beatty's appearance turned out to be fortunate. The lesson for the British was that there had to be better co-ordination between the distributed elements of the Grand Fleet. Tyrwhitt was lucky that the German fleet could not quickly cross the bar between it and the action. (Painting by W L Wyllie, PW1231 © National Maritime Museum, London)

ship (the turret was flooded in time). Other shells penetrated the ship's belt armour. Ultimately *Lion* was forced out of line and left dead in the water, with Beatty able to contact the other battlecruisers only by signal flags. However, Beatty never seems to have thought that she was in danger of sinking. *Tiger* was slightly damaged, but not put out of action.[39] Beatty concluded that German shellfire was ineffective: 'their 11in is no good, seldom burst and the effect when they do very local. The 12in is serious, but not to be compared to our 13.5in. Their guns are good, calibration too close, gun laying excellent, but the projectile no good and I am sure we can stand a lot of it . . .'[40]

Beatty was convinced that, had his ships fired faster, they would have sunk more of the German force. That was reasonable; the German battlecruiser *Seydlitz* was badly burned out and further damage might have proven fatal. Beatty blamed the slow fire of his ships on earlier admonitions not to waste ammunition. More likely it can be traced to the much earlier decision to overload magazines. Even after the British ships shifted from ranging shots to rapid salvos, their fire slowed as gunlayers found it more difficult to spot their own splashes amid the splashes from enemy 'shorts'. Without director control, fire eventually had to stop even if all turrets were intact. The official British statement of lessons learned emphasised the need for rapid fire, as the enemy would be sure to take advantage of the respite offered by slower fire. Beatty's belief in faster fire was almost certainly responsible for the explosions at Jutland. Beatty also failed to realise that his ships' gunnery was poor and therefore he made no effort to improve it. That too would be obvious at Jutland.

Beatty ignored a serious signalling failure. His Flag Lieutenant Ralph Seymour failed to transmit Beatty's instruction, sent after *Lion* was disabled, that the other battlecruisers should pursue the escaping German ships rather than continue to pour fire into the doomed *Blücher*. That error saved Hipper.[41] Earlier in the battle he had tried to use the threat of torpedoes fired by his destroyers to force the British to turn away. As the destroyers formed up to attack, the British ships did turn away, though not for long and apparently not because they understood that they faced a torpedo attack. The incident is interesting mainly as an illustration of the way in which the threat of destroyer torpedoes could be used.

There seemed to be no reason to doubt the pre-war idea that gun damage would be cumulative. HMS *Lion* was hit fifteen times with little lasting effect. It might be most profitable to tear up the less heavily armoured parts of the target, as the Japanese had done at Tsushima. The Admiralty suggested that, given its anti-personnel effects, Lyddite (HE) non-AP shell was so useful that it should be used in equal proportions to AP. Moreover, Lyddite made much more visible explosions when it hit, so it made for much better spotting (powder common shells made the best splashes). Thus it might be wise to fire Lyddite first, then AP. The Germans relied entirely on AP. Beatty remarked that 'for armour penetration the [German] shell seem very good, but in general destructive and incendiary effect they are not equal to our Lyddite, which have proved so effective in every action of the war. Only one small fire was caused in our ships by German shell, whilst three out of the four German ships were heavily on fire at various times'.[42] The German airship *L 5* observed the final stages of the action, including the British turn-away, which was radioed to Hipper on board the badly damaged *Seydlitz*.

As the German ships returned home, many on board thought that HMS *Tiger* had been sunk, in which case they had made a worthwhile exchange for *Blücher*.[43] The Germans broadcast this news and it took some time for the truth to come out. Dogger Bank showed that the German navy could not hope to even the odds in small battles. Less than a month later Admiral von Pohl wrote that the entire operations showed a lack of foresight and prudence; the disaster on 28 August 1914 at Heligoland could be traced to the

same source and only by chance had the two coastal raids succeeded. Whether or not this criticism was fair, von Ingenohl was finished and on the Kaiser's orders he hauled down his flag on 2 February. Von Pohl relieved him.

German Options

Tirpitz had just handed von Pohl a memo on the future of the naval war, arguing for a radical change of course. For him, the war had been caused by the British attempt to overcome her main Continental rival: the City of London (i.e., the financial centre) had caused the war. It followed that the whole German effort should have been directed against the British economy. Tirpitz' navy was of course the only weapon Germany could wield against that enemy. Experience to date made it unlikely that the fleet could whittle down the Royal Navy to the point where the odds would favour it in a general engagement. Tirpitz argued that the odds were really tipping the other way: during the winter of 1915–16 the Royal Navy would receive strong reinforcements whereas the German building programmes had petered out.

Tirpitz offered four possibilities. One was a continued air offensive aimed at the docks and the City warehouses, because they were central to the British economy. The second was a submarine blockade; Tirpitz realised that political considerations might limit it. The third was energetic prosecution of a submarine and destroyer campaign against Channel shipping, based on Tirpitz' 'Triangle' in Belgium (although prospects for destroyer attacks would decline as the nights became shorter). The fourth was cruiser warfare in the Atlantic against British food imports. Cruiser warfare might force the British to withdraw ships from the Grand Fleet and thus to even the odds against the High Seas Fleet. Until this point the German navy had concentrated on the expected fleet engagement, war against trade being a strictly subsidiary affair conducted by cruisers (supported to some extent by minelayers).

The new fleet commander, von Pohl, planned a further minelaying operation, to be covered by the fleet, during the new moon period in March 1915. He considered it almost the only practical means of inflicting direct damage on the enemy, as opposed to the indirect effect of the submarine blockade. Initially he was unable to carry out his planned operation due to bad weather and on 17 March the Admiralstab informed him that the General Staff badly wanted naval support in the Baltic, as the Russians were attacking with large forces. There were already High Seas Fleet units in the Baltic for exercises and von Pohl offered them as well as a battle squadron of pre-dreadnoughts plus lighter forces. He would be left with one battle squadron in the North Sea. By this time the four Russian dreadnoughts were complete and there was some question as to whether the Russians might gain control of the Baltic as their fleet grew. One of the battle squadron commanders went so far as to write, in February 1915, that the proper place for the High Seas Fleet was the Baltic; a decisive or even a serious battle in the North Sea should be avoided altogether, because it would probably weaken the German fleet to the point where it could not keep the British out of the Baltic. This was Tirpitz' risk theory in reverse.[44] The Admiralstab thought otherwise: the North Sea was central. Von Pohl was told to lend only limited forces to the Baltic command, as otherwise he would be unable to exploit whatever opportunities arose in the North Sea. Von Pohl thought the Admiralstab was grossly over-optimistic,

imagining that the Grand Fleet had been weakened by transfers to the Mediterranean for the Gallipoli campaign. He knew that nearly all the British ships involved had been of secondary importance.

The Admiralstab kept pressing for some operation which would draw part of the British fleet into the Heligoland Bight, but von Pohl could not imagine any reason for the British to be so stupid. He also complained that he never had his whole fleet together, due to the constant need for alterations and refits, many of which should have been completed pre-war. Moreover, given the experience at Dogger Bank, von Pohl was determined that his battlecruisers never go out without the direct support of the whole fleet. Even within a radius of 70 miles of Heligoland, a sortie might turn into a major fleet action. Von Pohl also emphasised the inadequacy of his reconnaissance forces. He had practically no information as to the position of the British fleet and invariably reports were so late that they could not be used as the basis for a fleet sortie. Cruiser reconnaissance was useless outside the Heligoland Bight. Air reconnaissance depended on weather (there were few clear and calm days) and there were too few airships. Yet good reconnaissance was essential if the fleet was not to encounter, or be cut off by, superior enemy forces. Nor, in von Pohl's view, did his fleet enjoy the speed advantage it would need to break off action if it was outnumbered.[45]

At the end of March von Pohl decided on a very short sortie.[46] For the first time, airship reconnaissance was in place (despite frequent snowstorms). This sortie differed from past ones in that the fleet left port in battle formation, the scouting force directly ahead of the main body. The battlecruisers (1st Scouting Group) and their attendant light cruisers took station 12 miles ahead of the battleships. All of the dreadnoughts (1st and 3rd Battle Squadrons) except for *Nassau* and *Westfalen* took part. Two light cruiser Scouting Groups screened the battleships against destroyer attack. Each of the two main formations had its own destroyer anti-submarine screen, consisting of two flotillas (in vee formation) for the battlecruisers and three (vee with line abreast between its arms) for the battleships. The airships scouted directly ahead of the fleet. Thus they did not discover that, warned by signals intelligence, the Grand Fleet had left harbour roughly simultaneously with the High Seas Fleet. It turned back as soon as it became obvious that the German sortie was harmless. Von Pohl was criticised for pointlessly risking his fleet to mine and submarine attack.

By this time the Kaiser was again maintaining that in future neither the fleet nor even single capital ships were to leave harbour without his express orders and that he would issue such orders only in connection with a definite objective, such as forcing the Firth of Forth. He seems to have been motivated by an unfortunate visit by a junior officer, Prince Adalbert, to his GHQ. Because of his position in the nobility, Adalbert could not be kept out of GHQ by his naval superiors. His vivid descriptions of the problems the fleet encountered in the North Sea convinced the Kaiser that action was dangerous; Bachmann (now Admiralstab chief) wrote that the Kaiser saw the fleet as a bargaining chip to be preserved and used at the end of the war.[47] He had become convinced that even without action, mines and submarines in the North Sea might impose great, even decisive, losses. Thus the Kaiser wanted exercises limited to the Baltic. He also complained that too many detailed orders, even for things like laying mines in the Jade, were coming before him because of differences of opinion in the fleet. Surely he should rule only on basic policy – but he was the only authority who could rule between, for example, von Pohl and the North Sea station commander on the mine issue. At the least, he wanted no more dissension within the fleet as to offensive operations.

It proved difficult to move the Kaiser, the ultimate argument being that, should the fleet not come into action for the rest of the war, responsibility should rest on the fleet commander and not the Kaiser. The 29 March sortie showed that von Pohl did not want to stay at anchor and that made it easier to move the Kaiser. On 30 March the Kaiser offered von Pohl complete freedom of action though 'it is of course to be understood that . . . engagements must be broken off whenever circumstances become unfavourable'. This order also freed von Pohl from any instructions issued by the Admiralstab. It helped that von Pohl kept saying that he did not want to become involved with superior enemy forces. against the Kaiser's instructions. Air reconnaissance promised to make that possible. Von Pohl contrasted his policy with his predecessor's: 'Admiral von Ingenohl always sent out only weak forces . . . I always take the whole fleet. This may lead to success, but may also lead to heavy losses.' All involved were impressed that Bachmann and von Pohl had achieved so much. Bachmann concluded that the Kaiser could be swayed by being shown only carefully selected information, for example information about enemy dispositions and appreciations on the general situation.

For the April New Moon (11 to 18 April) von Pohl wanted to revive his earlier minelaying project on the Dogger Bank and Swarte Bank. Airship reconnaissance revealed large numbers of fishing trawlers, which the Germans assumed were a reconnaissance screen, as they would normally not be fishing so far to seaward of Heligoland. They also seemed to be signalling. As the date of the operation approached, airships sighted large numbers of British destroyers and some cruisers in the area and it seemed likely that they were part of the Grand Fleet. Von Pohl decided not to risk his fleet. As it happened, the Grand Fleet was cruising in the central part of the North Sea and the Harwich Force was approaching the Heligoland Bight from the west (the airships detected only the latter). It became clear after the war that the British had been alerted (the Germans also noted, when they read the British official history after the war, that every time in March that von Pohl had readied his fleet to go out, the Grand Fleet had come out). The Germans also encountered some British submarines in the Bight. They became convinced that the submarines had to be driven off before von Pohl's minelaying sortie could be carried out.

Von Pohl's staff decided that the British had planned to draw von Pohl away to the west or the north, then place a large force in his rear to cut him off. On this basis von Pohl decided that by 18 April the British must no longer be in position, so the minelaying operation, supported by the fleet, could go ahead. Only after the war did the Germans discover that the Grand Fleet had been at sea, at one point no more than 200 miles from von Pohl.

By this time the Germans were well into their first U-boat offensive. When the U-boats were ordered on 19 April to avoid attacking neutral ships, it seemed that the High Seas Fleet might become more active to compensate. However, on 20 April von Pohl told his admirals that a naval battle had to be avoided at all costs for the present, owing to the general political situation. His operations officer asked what the point of any operation would be. The recent sortie had shown again that the fleet had to exercise as a whole. For example, deployment from cruising to battle (line ahead) formation

The Germans lost the light cruisers *Mainz*, *Ariadne* and *Cöln* at Heligoland Bight, plus the destroyer *V 187*. The losses proved profoundly disheartening, the Germans concluding that British ships were superior to theirs in firepower and in performance (the latter due to the use of oil fuel). This painting shows a British destroyer rescuing survivors of the sinking cruiser *Mainz*. (Painting by W L Wyllie, PV3448 © National Maritime Museum, London)

had not been practiced in a long time. However, such exercises could hardly justify North Sea operations and it was unthinkable to transfer the whole fleet into the Baltic for fleet exercises. Von Pohl felt compelled to say that he would sortie as necessary to attack weak parts of the enemy fleet and to deny British assertions that the Germans were effectively blockaded in their harbours. His chief of staff warned that he was running a great risk of destroying the fleet's morale: was the fleet seeking or avoiding battle? It seemed that von Pohl wanted to fight only in that part of the North Sea in which he fully controlled the situation and it was time to define that part and to stay in it.

Von Pohl decided at this time to sortie his fleet to the north, to drive off enemy forces believed to be near the Dogger Bank. He decided not to combine the operation with further minelaying on the Dogger Bank. Airships accompanied the fleet. The Germans much valued the experience they gained in tactical co-operation between airships and the fleet. However, the airships had hardly gone further ahead of the fleet than light cruisers might have done. They did not, for example, detect the fact that the Grand Fleet had also sortied. The Grand Fleet was moving into position to cut off the High Seas Fleet had it continued on course. If that had happened, the airship on the northern wing of the cruiser screen would probably have sighted the British fleet.[48]

As of early May 1915 Von Pohl thought that he still could not defeat the Grand Fleet in battle. With his submarines mostly employed against British shipping, his only means of wearing down the Grand Fleet was minelaying. He did not want to risk unescorted minelayers.[49] However, to escort minelayers with the whole of the High Seas Fleet would be to risk exactly the sort of battle he thought he could not win 'in view of the present disparity of forces'. Von Pohl was particularly unwilling to go as far as the Firth of Forth and the Moray Firth. That left him the option of minelaying closer to home, for example on the Dogger Bank. He thought that he might be able to use his fleet to lead the Grand Fleet onto such minefields. The fine late spring weather would make airship reconnaissance more effective, so that he could avoid contact with the whole Grand Fleet. He began with a fleet sortie to cover mines laid on the eastern edge of the Dogger Bank on the routes from the Firth of Forth and the Moray Firth to the German Bight, as he had long planned to do.

This may have been one of the earliest cases in which the Germans benefitted from intercepted British W/T, in this case an order for all auxiliary patrol craft to return urgently to port.[50] Von Pohl assumed that exactly these craft would have been deployed to detect him. Why would they have been withdrawn? To him, it was clear that if the order had anything to do with his operation, they had been replaced by fast, powerful ships. Unfortunately, by the time he received this message, his airships had already gone home and none of his ships could launch their own seaplanes. He had no idea of what awaited him on the far side of the Dogger Bank. As von Pohl manoeuvred his fleet for exercises, one of his cruisers struck a mine. He had no sweepers with him and his cruisers spotted many floating mines. He assumed that the British knew he was coming out and had mined his return path. That they had done so without German knowledge suggested that the German patrols of the Bight were grossly inadequate. It soon became obvious, moreover, that the British were aware of von Pohl's minelaying plans and they soon had minesweepers on the Dogger Bank. The Germans now realised that they needed some form of fleet sweeper.[51] They used 'barrage breakers' (sperrbrechers), a group of which typically preceded the High Seas Fleet through the potentially mined areas of the North Sea. That made W/T orders to a sperrbrecher group an excellent indication that the High Seas Fleet was coming out.[52]

Well before von Pohl left harbour on 29 May, the Admiralstab informed him that the British were aware that that an operation was in view, but that seems to have been based on nothing more than press reports.[53] Because no firm basis was given, von Pohl sortied anyway. The operation was supported by five airships, one of which had to abort due to engine trouble. Seaplanes were also launched. As the weather worsened, the other airships had to turn back. Without his aerial scouts, von Pohl decided to turn back. The operation did cover the departure of the auxiliary cruiser *Meteor*, which mined the approaches to Archangel, through which the Russians hoped to receive considerable amounts of munitions.

This was von Pohl's fifth sortie. In June he wrote that his objective had been to induce the enemy to meet him under advantageous conditions. In order to preserve his strength, he had to avoid losses to enemy night torpedo attacks and to mines. It was therefore necessary to search the planned route thoroughly before proceeding. Given his inferior cruiser strength, successful manoeuvre near the enemy required air reconnaissance. That in turn made weather crucial, hence it had been possible to make only one sortie in the worse months (February–March) and four in the more favourable months. That the airships spotted no British forces

British destroyers were damaged at Heligoland Bight, but they survived. The Germans were impressed by the performance of their 4in guns; their own destroyers had 8.8cm (3.4in) weapons. Damage to the destroyer HMS *Laurel* from a salvo from the cruiser *Mainz* is shown. Both the Royal Navy and the Imperial German Navy considered cruisers rather than destroyers the only really effective anti-destroyer ships. (US Naval Historical and Heritage Command)

H.M.S. LAUREL.

seemed to show that the Grand Fleet was unwilling to come out; but the sorties had covered only a very limited area, never beyond the Dogger Bank. After the war it became clear that had the German fleet gone only slightly further it would have met the Grand Fleet. The official German naval historian saw no reason for von Pohl to have avoided action, given the relative strengths of the fleets at this time and also given the urgent need to provide support for the political and strategic effects of the submarine war on commerce which had recently begun.

Von Pohl also argued that to avoid enemy torpedo boat (destroyer) attacks he had to limit any sortie to a day and a night, which in turn defined the area he could cover. He thought that he could not tempt the Grand Fleet into battle without going much further, into the extreme northern or southern part of the North Sea. That was unacceptable unless the odds already favoured the High Seas Fleet; von Pohl assumed they did not. According to the official German history, von Pohl considered that a failure would jeopardise the outcome of the war, not only at sea but also on land. In retrospect this might seem to have been a bizarre echo of the argument that Admiral Jellicoe, who commanded the Grand Fleet, was the only man who could lose the war in an afternoon. However, it can be argued that, had the High Seas Fleet been annihilated, the British would have been freed to undertake exactly the sort of risky coastal operations that were proposed and rejected. In particular they might well have felt free to operate in the Baltic, turning the flank of the German army there.

Given this reasoning, von Pohl argued that he had to resort to submarines and minelayers rather than to capital ships. He pointed out that U-boats operating off the British East Coast had encountered few merchant ships of clearly British nationality, hence that U-boats might better be used off the British fleet bases; he wanted two or three sent into positions off the Firth of Forth.[54] The war against commerce on the East Coast would be carried out to the extent that the main object (the attack on the Grand Fleet) did not suffer. Meanwhile fleet sorties would be suspended, not least because it was not clear to what extent the German Bight had been mined (several floating mines were encountered during the 29–30 May sortie). The period of inactivity would be used to refit the fleet.[55]

Von Pohl fastened on a cruiser-destroyer commerce raid off the Skaggerak, to intercept Swedish shipping from Gothenburg carrying contraband to the United Kingdom. *Krieg zur See* reveals a long period of debate and dither: a simple idea soon became quite complex. Initially the German force was to have steamed north from the Heligoland Bight, operated near Gothenburg and returned to Germany via the Baltic (hence via the Sound). The Germans had forced the Danes to mine their side of the passage through the straits, but they had been unable to persuade the Swedes to mine their own territorial waters on the other side of the straits. Their object had been to keep the Royal Navy out of the Baltic. Once heavy ships were added, the question of a deep-draught passage arose and it seemed that the ships would have to return via Danish territorial waters (it is not clear why they could not pass through unmined Swedish waters). Von Pohl stressed the value of the Skaggerak-Kattegat route as a second sally port for the German fleet, in addition to the route out of the Heligoland Bight. He pointed out that the British minefields in the Bight limited egress routes and the cleared corridors through the minefields appeared to be watched by British submarines. The Admiralstab

feared that if the German battle fleet used the straits, the British might do the same.

British light cruisers had been reported in the Skaggerak, so the cruiser-destroyer force should be supported by the battlecruisers. Like other proposed German operations, this one soon involved the distant support of the whole High Seas Fleet. It may have been the first time that von Pohl accepted the possibility of fighting a fleet action outside the German Bight, as far away as the Skaggerak. The operation was delayed about two weeks because several important German ships, including the battlecruisers *Derfflinger* and *Seydlitz*, were out of action due to machinery problems. Also, for a time weather precluded airship reconnaissance. Von Pohl also had to reckon with a demand that by early August key parts of his force be detached for an urgent operation in the Baltic, against Riga. Within a few days the operation in the North Sea had to be cancelled, as the situation in the Baltic became more urgent. Without any equivalent to the British First Sea Lord, the Germans had no one knowledgeable who could decide whether forces were better deployed to the North Sea or to the Baltic. The Admiralstab lacked the power to do so.

Once the fleet returned from the Baltic in September, von Pohl could plan a new operation, this time minelaying beyond the Dogger Bank. He deployed five U-boats beyond the area to be mined and the minelaying cruisers were supported directly by light cruisers, with the battlecruisers and the main body in distant support. Airships were also deployed. After the war it turned out that, had the airships ventured further, they would have seen substantial but weaker British forces not too far away (this time it appeared that the Grand Fleet had *not* been forewarned of the German operation). However, the British were laying fresh minefields in the Heligoland Bight and the High Seas Fleet nearly ran across them as it returned to port. The Germans spotted numerous floating British mines and one of their torpedo boats was mined (but did not sink).

The British minefield was the beginning of an attempt to make the German Bight impassable, a project Admiral Jellicoe had long advocated. It would be limited only by the number of mines available. As First Lord, Winston Churchill had strongly opposed it, on the grounds that the Germans would always be able to sweep their way out. Churchill also argued that extensive mining would limit the movements both of the Grand Fleet and of British submarines in the North Sea. With his departure, the mining offensive became possible, although it was limited by the number of mines available to the Royal Navy and also by their poor quality. The German official historian also argued that the Admiralty was also convinced of the value of offensive mining by the operations of U-boat minelayers in the North Sea and also of the minelayer *Meteor*. Perhaps the most important effect of extensive British mining at this stage was that the Germans were forced to conduct minesweeping ahead of any High Seas Fleet sortie – and for that they had to make arrangements by W/T, which the British intercepted and decrypted. For their part the Germans had to sweep over increasing distances and therefore required airship escort, so that they could not be surprised by superior British forces. That in turn limited them to conditions under which airships could operate freely. For their part the Germans commented after the war that extensive mining of the Heligoland Bight was profitable because it was so narrow.

In mid-October the C-in-C Baltic asked for a torpedo-boat

flotilla and several patrol boats to deal with British submarines operating there. Von Pohl was reluctant; despite the number of torpedo boats he had on paper, he did not have enough ready for service to provide sufficient anti-submarine screens.[56] He was most impressed by the threat of British submarines in the North Sea and the German Bight. On the other hand, the British submarines in the Baltic were interrupting trade (particularly in Swedish iron ore) absolutely essential to the German war effort. Von Pohl ended up acceding to a later Baltic request for two light cruisers and two flotillas, but he hoped to retain them long enough for one further fleet operation. He had put off any such operation both to complete refits and on the ground that persistent east winds would make airship reconnaissance difficult and also interfere with gunnery (a leeward position was preferable). Now he planned a full fleet sortie as far as the Horns Reef in hopes of capturing enemy scouts frequently reported there and also to disturb traffic between Newcastle and the Skaggerak. The call for transfers to the Baltic by 25 October at the latest limited von Pohl to a sortie on 23–24 October 1915. He planned to go beyond Horn Reef only if supported by airship reconnaissance, which would insure against meeting a superior enemy force. Plans initially included two U-boats on the flanks of the fleet, but they had to turn back due to a heavy ground swell. Five airships were assigned to reconnaissance, but they had to turn back due to wind.[57] That left von Pohl with only cruiser reconnaissance, which he considered insufficient to avoid running into the Grand Fleet under unfavourable conditions (no submarines and wind which would put him in the windward position). He therefore broke off the operation, having in mind also the order to detach the flotillas to the Baltic (further forces were soon ordered to prepare for transfer if wanted). British submarines tried but failed to attack von Pohl on the way home, when evasive manoeuvres might well have placed his ships in the minefields.[58] That the Grand Fleet was not at sea suggests that for once von Pohl was enjoying good W/T security. For the remainder of 1915 von Pohl was reduced to destroyer sweeps of Scandinavian shipping *en route* to England, the results of which were meagre.

Jellicoe's Responses

Nothing that happened at Dogger Bank had changed Jellicoe's image of German tactics and during 1915–16 he practiced against them with his fleet.[59] Jellicoe's first tactical exercise (PZ 1) was ordered in a 6 June 1915 memo. The opposing fleets would be Red (Jellicoe) and Blue (enemy). Blue tactics should include (a) an endeavour to manoeuvre for position before the action began; (b) an attempt to close the range; (c) a turn-away in succession to either (i) induce Red to follow and thus to place Blue in a position favouring a Red torpedo attack (by his battle line or his destroyers) or (ii) luring Red over a minefield. The Blue light cruisers representing minelayers might also represent torpedo flotillas attacking the Red van. A second exercise was practice for the battlecruisers, cruisers, light cruisers and destroyers in taking up battle stations shortly before or after the fleet formed battle line.

A further tactical exercise (July 1915) was designed to gain information on the use of submarines when accompanying a battle fleet and how the British fleet could best counter the submarine threat in the early stages of a fleet action; and also to test scouting and battle tactics in bad visibility, when the two fleets would first sight each other at medium or close range. The scenario was a

German fleet returning from a raid on the Tyne, with submarines in company. This seems to have been a much more elaborate exercise. The probable tactics of the enemy were again to try to draw Red over a submarine trap, or into a minefield laid when the position of the Red battle fleet had been established. Enemy submarines would probably be in close touch with his battlefield during the night and minelayers at some distance astern, 'as their chance of success depends on their being able to lay their mines hidden without being sighted by any of our ships provided the mines can be laid in the right place'.

After a June 1915 exercise testing what Jellicoe understood of German tactics, Jellicoe commented that the geographical position of Heligoland governed deployment, as it probably would.[60] However, if the Germans were favourably placed to reach their base, they might first deploy away from it to give minelayers and submarines a chance to get into position unobserved, so that the High Seas Fleet could draw the Grand Fleet over them. The Germans probably would not want to lay mines ahead of themselves, as the minelayers would have to work out of touch with the battle fleet. As the British screen would probably be wider than the German, they would run a considerable risk of discovery. The exercise showed that the British cruisers could abort a German minelaying operation, although in this case the cruisers did not press their attack home, so the minelayers got further towards the van of the Red fleet than was desirable. Jellicoe's experiment with a fast division (*Queen Elizabeth* and *Warspite*) engaging the enemy rear had not been entirely successful, particularly bearing in mind that the enemy would be using 10,000 yd gyro torpedoes capable of angling and perhaps even fired from trainable tubes. The ships might also be threatened by enemy destroyers in his rear. In a subsequent deployment exercise, the question was raised of how close heavy cruisers should be to the light cruisers, keeping in mind that the Germans were very weak in numbers of heavy cruisers and that theirs were slow.

A 'most interesting fact' brought out by the war game was that the German battlecruisers could move from the rear of their fleet to the van, while the fleets were in sight but not yet within 20,000 yd range (the Germans were steaming at 15 knots, which was a practical limit if their pre-dreadnoughts remained in their fleet). Jellicoe noted that the difference of three knots in speed 'might have made all the difference between bringing the German battle fleet to action and letting it escape'. He was particularly concerned that the destroyers' modified sweep, which he suspected was useless when near the enemy fleet, was limiting his mobility.

In February 1916 Jellicoe tried another exercise, in which he had 'certain information' – as he normally did from signals intelligence – of the position of the Blue fleet and he wanted his battle-cruisers to engage and delay the enemy until the main Red fleet could turn up.[61] Blue received information that Red was nearby to the southeast and he spread his cruisers, minelayers and imaginary submarines to cover his withdrawal to Heligoland. Submarines had to dive before being sighted by Red cruisers.

Meanwhile Jellicoe had to deal with Beatty's demands for more ships, specifically the fast *Queen Elizabeth*s. About the beginning of February 1916 the Admiralty circulated an updated list of the German fleet, showing three new battlecruisers (*Derfflinger*, *Lützow* and *Hindenburg*) completed, with two more building.[62] No one had seen these ships and it was feared that instead of the planned eight 12in guns they had six 15in (and 13in side armour, as in the *Queen*

*Elizabeth*s). Rear Admiral Pakenham, commanding Beatty's 2nd Battlecruiser Squadron, wrote to his chief to warn him that without more ships the battlecruisers would be outclassed, in which case 'it is probable that Germany would then have gained a position whence she could dictate terms of peace to this Empire'. Up to this time the British preponderance in fast ships had confined the Germans to the southern part of the North Sea. At the very least, the battlecruisers could no longer act as a detached fast division or rapid-reaction force of the Grand Fleet. To Pakenham the obvious solution was to add the fast *Queen Elizabeth*s to the Battlecruiser Fleet. He may have been affected by exaggerated rumours of their speed. No one involved seems to have had the slightest idea of how much additional power each extra knot required. However, a real effort was made to see whether the supposed 15in armament of the new German battlecruisers was a realistic proposition.[63]

Beatty took up the idea enthusiastically. He proposed that the *Queen Elizabeth*s (5th Battle Squadron) replace the 3rd Battle Squadron (pre-dreadnoughts) at his base at Rosyth, giving him superiority over anything short of the High Seas Fleet itself. Jellicoe saw these ships as an invaluable fast division of the Grand Fleet, so he was unenthusiastic.[64] He pointed out that the *Queen Elizabeth*s were considerably slower (23.5 knots with fuel on board) than the battlecruisers. They were certainly not fast enough to do anything about *Lützow* and *Hindenburg* when they joined the German battle-cruiser force. Even if the Germans had 15in rather than 12in guns, the British force would have more guns, many of them 13.5in. Beatty would not give up. Surely if they carried much less fuel (which would be appropriate in the narrow North Sea) the *Queen Elizabeth*s could make their 25-knot design speed, which was also the speed of his slower first-generation battlecruisers. Even if not, past experience showed that the battleships could keep up with his battlecruisers until they sighted the enemy. Even after a three-hour chase, the *Queen Elizabeth*s at 23.5 knots would be only $4\frac{1}{2}$ miles astern of the battlecruisers; Beatty 'could imagine no better or more valuable support'. He thought it likely that the High Seas Fleet would turn up; he thought that von Ingenohl had been fired after Dogger Bank precisely because he had not brought the High Seas Fleet to support the German battlecruisers. If the High Seas Fleet did appear, the *Queen Elizabeth*s would be an invaluable rear guard. Beatty likened the organisation he wanted to that at Scarborough in December 1914, when a battle squadron had backed up his ships. This time, of course, both battleships and battlecruisers would be under his own control.

Jellicoe argued that adding the *Queen Elizabeth*s could not possibly be enough for Beatty, since they could not hold off the whole High Seas Fleet. Beatty would want more battleships at Rosyth and soon the Grand Fleet would be split in two, each part inferior to the High Seas Fleet. Beatty realised that Jellicoe would never give him the ships he wanted, so he wrote directly to the Admiralty. Jellicoe was frosty: 'I should prefer that any future discussion of proposals regarding the strategical distribution of vessels of the Grand Fleet other than those under your immediate orders, should be addressed only to the C-in-C, unless the matter is one of such urgency as to render direct communication with the Admiralty a necessity.'

Beatty did not get his desired *Queen Elizabeth*s. He was probably lucky, because Jellicoe was much more insistent on gunnery training than he was. When the *Queen Elizabeth*s did support Beatty's battlecruisers at Jutland (because of a

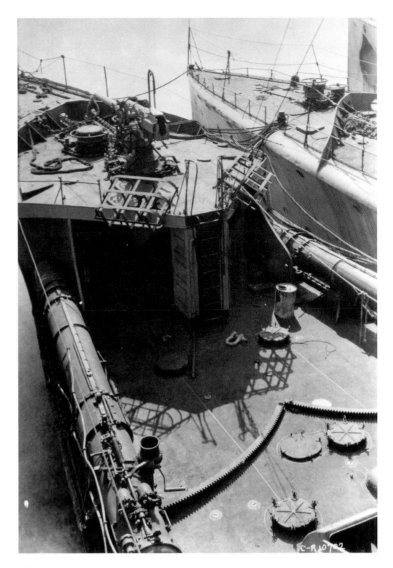

The British assumed that the German navy emphasised the torpedo attack role for its destroyers, with considerable consequences for its own battle tactics. German destroyers were typically armed with six tubes, compared to the two or four of their British contemporaries (two single tubes up to the *Acasta* class of the 1911–12 programme, then two twins). The Germans gained two tubes by mounting single trainable tubes in a well forward of the bridge; British officers tended to disregard the degree to which a rough sea would make these tubes unusable. Ships typically had one gun on the short forecastle forward of the tubes. These two forward tubes were aboard the destroyer *V 43* (second flotilla of Mobilisation destroyers, ordered 1914), launched in 1915 and surrendered to the United States at the end of the war. She was photographed at Norfolk Navy Yard on 11 October 1920. (US Navy)

coincidence), it turned out that they had enormously better gunnery – as Beatty's German counterpart Admiral Hipper wrote after the battle.[65] As for the *Derfflinger*s, the puzzle of their gun calibre was cleared up only after the German raid on Lowestoft in April 1916, when a shell from that ship was found on board the Harwich Force cruiser.

Admiral Scheer Replaces Von Pohl

On 9 January von Pohl had to be hospitalised for a severe internal problem, which turned out to be terminal cancer (he died on 23

Bow gun and torpedo tubes of *V 43*. The bow gun is as far aft as the forecastle reaches, leaving insufficient space for a twin torpedo tube in the well forward of the ship's bridge. That limited the broadside to five rather than six tubes. (US Navy)

the British had many vulnerable points to defend. The key point was that all available naval forces had to be integrated: submarines to attack commerce, mining, war against Scandinavian trade, aerial attack and the High Seas Fleet itself. In particular, mining, the war against trade and sweeps by the High Seas Fleet should be co-ordinated. As a preliminary, the German Bight out to the Horns Reef had to be kept clear of enemy forces by standing patrols, minefields and frequent sweeps by light forces. Activity should be continuous, including fleet sweeps (supported by airships and aircraft) as far as the Hoofden, the Dogger Bank and the Skaggerak. Airship raids on England were in future always to be mounted in conjunction with torpedo boat sweeps exploiting the reconnaissance performed by the airships as they flew to their targets.[66] There was some hope that airship raids on England would cause the British to send out ships which the Germans could snap up.[67] Scheer recognised that the most powerful provocation of all would be bombardment of a British town, assuming he had sufficient air reconnaissance to avoid being trapped by a superior force. When he visited Wilhelmshaven on 23 February, the Kaiser approved Scheer's programme. For his part, Scheer was spurred on by the government decision not to resume unrestricted submarine warfare.

While Scheer was formulating his offensive plans, the British were rethinking their own. The Russians, as represented by their Naval Attaché Captain von Schoultz, pressed for an operation in the Baltic which would open their supply line to Sweden, the source of iron ore, machine tools and railway equipment and rails. The Admiralty pointed out that no such operation was practicable as long as the High Seas Fleet survived; no Baltic operation, then, was compatible with the relatively passive policy adopted by Admiral Jellicoe, who allowed the Germans to remain as a 'fleet in being'. Jellicoe became interested in a more active policy which would draw the Germans out, just as Scheer imagined that he had to draw the British (albeit not the whole Grand Fleet) out. Jellicoe attended a 17 February 1916 meeting of the Cabinet's War Council, at which First Lord A J Balfour pointed out that maintaining the Grand Fleet so far north opened the British southern coast to raids such as those carried out in 1914. He decided to move the Grand Fleet south, to Rosyth and the Humber. Although work was proceeding to enlarge both, it was not yet complete.

As a first step, it was proposed that the 5th Battle Squadron (*Queen Elizabeth* class fast battleships) would be shifted from Scapa Flow to Rosyth, where it would be attached to Beatty's Battlecruiser Fleet. Jellicoe was unenthusiastic (see above) and for the moment, Jellicoe's objection was upheld and reorganisation of the Grand Fleet was deferred pending completion of the new *Royal Sovereign* class battleships. By 15 April these ships were available and reorganisation was imminent. The German raid on Lowestoft (see below) made such proposals more urgent.[68]

Scheer's first major fleet operation was scheduled for 3–4 March: the battlecruisers and fast scout cruisers plus two torpedo-boat flotillas were to steam into the Hoofden, towards England, in conjunction with an air raid on England, with the main body of the High Seas Fleet in support. Co-ordinated with this sortie, the Zeebrugge U-boats were to mine the exit from Dover, the northern exit from the Downs, two Thames channels and the exits from Harwich (they laid all the planned fields except that in the Downs). Other Zeebrugge submarines took station off the British coast. This operation was delayed by fog and then by the need to escort the

February 1916). He was succeeded by Vice Admiral Reinhard Scheer, who commanded the High Seas Fleet through its great battle at Jutland. By that time the fleet had lost its confidence in von Pohl, who had been unable to achieve visible results. Even had von Pohl not fallen ill, it was time for new naval leadership.

Scheer wanted to make the fleet more offensive-minded. At the beginning of February he promulgated new 'Principles Covering the Conduct of the Naval Campaign in the North Sea'. He affirmed that he could not seek a decisive battle and that therefore he had to prevent the British from forcing one on him. However, systematic and consistent pressure on the enemy would force him to abandon his policy of waiting for the High Seas Fleet to come out and instead to send out smaller forces. These attacks would wear down any British sense of such superiority that the Grand Fleet could hope to bring the Germans to action as it chose. To Scheer, his own advantages were that he had the initiative and that raider *Moewe* home from a cruise in the North and South Atlantic. *Moewe* was met by the battlecruisers which otherwise would have steamed to the Hoofden. The operation was finally carried out a few days later, despite weather which greatly limited airship operations. The Germans intercepted a British signal recalling all patrol units, which they interpreted to mean that the British were aware of the operation. In a departure from previous German practice, a strong torpedo boat force was sent out towards the Firth of Forth as the High Seas Fleet turned home, in hopes that British heavy units might be enticed to sea by the fleet sortie. The torpedo boat operation was timed for a night battle, should the British come out. According to the German official history, the British were initially unaware of this fleet sortie, but once the Germans were spotted near Terschelling on the Dutch coast, the Grand Fleet came out. The British were still out of interception range when they deciphered German signals indicating that the High Seas Fleet was returning to its base, upon which units of the Grand Fleet began to turn back. The German torpedo boats found nothing – as the British had discovered in their 1913 manoeuvres, even a narrow sea like the North Sea was much too broad for groups of destroyers to find their targets at night. The main achievement was to demonstrate to the Germans that they could indeed steam much further out into the North Sea than they had under von Pohl. For various reasons it was about a month before Scheer was ready to try again.

On 25 March a British carrier force built around the Harwich Force raided the Zeppelin sheds at Tondern, in an attempt to neutralise the airships then attacking England.[69] Much of Scheer's fleet had passed into the Baltic after the earlier fleet operation, but the ships were now just back; Scheer had a powerful force to throw against the relatively small British carrier attack force. On the debit side, his own airships were grounded (which was why the British air attack was such a surprise), so he lacked the scouting capability he needed. He was also crippled by delays in passing the relevant messages about the British attack. The British picked up and decrypted the German messages ordering the High Seas Fleet out to attack the carrier force. As the day wore on, Scheer decided that he had no chance of engaging the retiring British force, but that his destroyers might make a night attack.[70] The night attack turned into a confused action and the next day the whole High Seas Fleet went out in search of the British force, its operation based in part on a decoded British message referring to the destroyer *Medusa*, which had been disabled by collision. Beatty wanted to make a sweep to the east in company with the Harwich Force, but the Admiralty rejected his idea in view of information that Scheer was likely to come out again. It considered the advanced force so endangered that it ordered Jellicoe out with the Grand Fleet. At dawn the Grand Fleet was steaming directly towards the High Seas Fleet and a fleet action seemed imminent. Both fleets were steaming towards the wreck of the *Medusa* in a heavy sea. The Germans now found themselves in difficulty; their torpedo boats could not use their weapons in the heavy sea and the battlecruisers found seas breaking over their bows. They could not use their secondary batteries. Visibility was poor. As the enemy was not in sight, the Germans turned back. Scheer received some W/T intelligence suggesting that the British had not turned back, but he did not consider it conclusive. The weather precluded any form of air reconnaissance. Without it, he was unwilling to risk action. On the way back, his battlecruisers narrowly escaped attack by British submarines (a torpedo passed 80–100m astern of *Lützow*).

Scheer had missed a major opportunity: his fleet could have attacked Beatty's battlecruisers well before Jellicoe's battleships could have joined them. On the other hand, with the advantage of British W/T intelligence, Beatty knew where the High Seas Fleet was and could easily evade it. During the operation, a German torpedo boat was apparently mined outside the known British minefields, so before Scheer could go out again the extent of any new British minefield had to be determined. The Germans soon discovered that the British were using submarines to lay mines in the Bight. That increased the minesweeping load on the fleet, but there was no way to enlarge its sweeper force.

Scheer now realised that the British would not chase German airships with their surface ships, so airship raids could not tempt British forces into his sights. He fell back on the idea of a massive fleet sweep up to the Skaggerak. Cruisers and torpedo boats steaming ahead of the main body would threaten Scandinavian trade with the United Kingdom, hence should draw out British light forces to retaliate. Submarines from Zeebrugge would be stationed off the southeast British coast, with larger High Seas Fleet submarines further north. The plan, set for early April, had to be abandoned due to weather precluding airship reconnaissance during the darkest part of April. Meanwhile the Russians asked for a British naval demonstration in the North Sea to hold the High Seas Fleet there and preclude major transfers to the Baltic while they renewed their minefields off the Gulf of Finland after the ice broke.

Scheer now had to consider the possibility of a British surprise fleet attack on the Heligoland Bight. As the battle there two years earlier had shown, High Seas Fleet ships in the estuaries could not quickly get to sea because they had to wait for the tide. British submarines made it too dangerous to keep the whole fleet at sea in the Bight. The compromise was to maintain an outpost force, including two battlecruisers and one battle squadron, in the Jade. Scheer had to hope that this rather limited force would be enough to spoil a British fleet attack, forcing a withdrawal. Given the view that even the whole High Seas Fleet was insufficient to face the Grand Fleet, Scheer's hopes for the outpost force seem less than realistic.[71] His rationale was that a surprise attack would most likely be a raid, for example the bombardment of the offshore islands in the Heligoland Bight.

The Lowestoft Raid

Scheer estimated that the British would attack between 13 and 20 April. He decided to make a spoiling attack with his whole fleet. The British did not, however, appear as expected. The High Seas Fleet, which had gone to sea, was recalled for a new operation scheduled for 23 April. This time it would be the Germans demonstrating to support their own allies, in this case Irish rebels. The Irish planned a rising for Easter Sunday 1916 and the Germans provided guns (which the British captured). The Irish leaders asked for a vigorous demonstration by the High Seas Fleet and by its airships against the East Coast of England. For their part the Germans hoped that British troops otherwise available for the Western Front would be tied down in Ireland.

Before the Germans could mount their demonstration, they learned via code-breaking that the Grand Fleet was at sea (21 April), presumably preparing for the attack Scheer had predicted. He immediately sent the High Seas Fleet to sea. This movement in turn generated W/T messages which the British decoded. The messages made it clear that the fleet was going to sea, but not its intention. The British fleet had gone to sea to support a sweep by light forces into the Kattegat. By this time the British had a set procedure for dealing with possible German attacks on their own coast: the main body was to be 100nm north of Aberdeen with the battlecruisers 40nm ahead and the 3rd Battle Squadron and 3rd Cruiser Squadron in the rear as reinforcements. Scheer recalled his fleet after one of his cruisers was mined and two enemy submarines were sighted. German W/T messages told Admiral Jellicoe that Scheer had turned back. Jellicoe therefore returned to his previous operation in the Skaggerak, the naval demonstration the Russians wanted. After dense fog set in, the fleet suffered several collisions and Jellicoe decided to withdraw from the Danish coast.

Now it was time for the German demonstration bombardment of Lowestoft and Great Yarmouth. Originally scheduled for 24 April, it was delayed by the abortive sortie against the British fleet. According to the German official account, Scheer thought of this operation as far more than the desired demonstration. He thought that the elements of the Grand Fleet operated separately, so that the opportunity existed to catch some without the others. Moreover, while the British might not respond to some of his feints, they could not fail to respond to a coastal raid. Quite aside from the spur to the Grand Fleet, Lowestoft was a minelayer base and Yarmouth was the base used by British submarines operating in the German Bight. Neutralising both offered considerable advantages.[72]

In support of the operation, the Zeebrugge force planned to send seven of its small U-boats to mine Harwich and the channels at the mouth of the Thames the evening before the bombardment, in hopes that they would catch the Harwich Force on its way out to meet the Germans. Torpedo-armed U-boats (UB-boats) from Zeebrugge would also be sent out (two of them would act as navigational aids for the German force as it approached the minefield laid during the November 1914 bombardment of Yarmouth). These submarines went out on the 24th and were unaware that the operation had been postponed. *En route* to the British coast the battlecruiser *Seydlitz* was mined, generating W/T traffic between the Scouting Group and the German flagship and in the process alerting the British (if they were not already aware of it) that an operation was underway. For their part the Germans monitoring British W/T were aware that the British had been alerted. One such message recalled all patrol vessels to harbour. The Germans thought they had been spotted by British submarines, but in fact as usual the British were reacting to signals intelligence. The Germans thought the British would try to cut off their retreat, touching off a battle off the Dutch Islands, in waters they considered advantageous. For its part the Admiralty considered it likely that the Germans would mount a naval demonstration, most likely a coastal raid, in support of the Irish rising. Upon being told, Admiral Jellicoe put the set measures into force. The Harwich Force was recalled to refuel, Admiral Beatty made ready for sea and the Grand Fleet battleships completed fuelling. Jellicoe was informed when the High Seas Fleet sailed and he was also informed that *Seydlitz* had been mined. Decoded German signals made to change course after the mining gave Jellicoe considerable insight into German intentions. Although the precise intentions of the German operation were not revealed, the Admiralty accurately deduced that this would be a repeat of the 3 November 1914 raid on Yarmouth.

Admiral Beatty was ordered to sea, Two of his battlecruisers, *Australia* and *New Zealand*, had collided in fog during the previous operation, but they were more than replaced by the *Queen Elizabeth* class fast battleships of the 5th Battle Squadron, ordered to sea in his wake. Beatty was ordered not to accept battle with superior forces (the main body of the High Seas Fleet) until the main fleet was in position to support him. The older ships of the 3rd Battle Squadron (*King Edward* class) and the 3rd Cruiser Squadron were placed to guard the Tyne. Coastal patrols were called in and replaced by torpedo boats and submarines, the flotilla defence. Air reconnaissance was ordered. The Admiralty considered the situation particularly dangerous because the Germans might push into the Channel under the protection of the High Seas Fleet, attacking the lines of communication supporting the British army in France. The British also feared the destruction of the mass of merchant shipping in the Downs and possibly also attacks on the key French coastal harbours. Finally, it was possible that the German operation covered an invasion, a contingency taken seriously by the British army if not the Admiralty. Any German attack on or near the Channel exploited the position of the Grand Fleet so far to the north, hence so many hours from contact. The British therefore planned to station destroyers and submarines in the Hoofden so that they could attack the High Seas Fleet as it came towards the British coast. In this particular case Tyrwhitt was told to place his cruisers and destroyers between the submarines and the Bight, so that they might attract the Germans onto the submarines. Any damage inflicted would slow the High Seas Fleet and give the Grand Fleet more time to come into position. Given the (accurate) Admiralty assessment of German intentions, the Admiralty ordered additional submarines into positions an attacker shelling Yarmouth would probably occupy. As further information was obtained, the Dover Patrol was ordered to cease operations off the Flanders coast and concentrate on the English coast.

As in 1914, the German battlecruisers were assigned to conduct the bombardment, the main body of the High Seas Fleet following 50 miles behind. Airships preceded the German fleet. Their attack on the British coast proved ineffective and the British showed no interest in chasing them out to sea. Instead they concentrated on the approaching German ships. It turned out that the British submarines were not in position to attack the Germans. However, Commodore Tyrwhitt correctly placed his small force of three cruisers plus destroyers in the path of the German battlecruisers. The German force brushed him aside. Later he managed to engage the German battlecruisers, but his destroyers were unable to get into torpedo range. The submarines off Yarmouth were unable to attack, in some cases because British aircraft assigned to attack the Germans attacked them by mistake, forcing them to dive. Since the Germans had not been slowed during their approach, there was no hope that the Grand Fleet could catch them as they retired. On the other hand, Tyrwhitt managed to shadow the retiring German force and British submarines tried to work into position for an attack. The submarines proved poorly placed and the Admiralty recalled Tyrwhitt because the Grand Fleet was in no position to exploit his efforts.

Even so, on its way home the German battlecruiser force came within 45 miles of the British battlecruisers. Had the British battlecruisers had any way of exploiting German W/T, they might have closed with the Germans. Not too long afterwards a shipboard D/F (direction-finding) set was installed on board Beatty's flagship *Lion*, though it was not calibrated until after Jutland. Given two such installations far enough apart, it might have been possible to deduce the position of the German force.

At the closest approach of Beatty's force, the German main body was only 40 miles from the German battlecruisers and Beatty's nearest reinforcement, the 5th Battle Squadron, was 100 miles away. Jellicoe was considerably further away, only 100 miles from the Firth of Forth. The author of the official German history assumes that, given its intelligence-derived insight into the situation, the Admiralty was aware that it would have been dangerous to allow Beatty to continue towards the Germans. He was recalled well before he could have sighted the Germans and the fleet returned home.

Scheer was unaware of Tyrwhitt's efforts because an airship supporting him had not gone quite far enough to spot the British force. Unaware that Tyrwhitt's efforts had been systematic, but aware of the sudden withdrawal of the Dover Patrol force off the Belgian coast, Scheer concluded that the British had been surprised and that they might seek retaliation the next day. To be ready for that he had to put his cruisers and torpedo boats into port to refuel.

Once more the Germans had missed the point of the British operation, which was intelligence-driven. It was extremely embarrassing that the British arrangements had failed, but they had been intelligent and they had been possible because the British had excellent signals intelligence. Scheer was disappointed that he had not cut off any part of the British fleet, but he thought he had

taught the British that they had to detach a strong force to protect their coast against any future raid. Moreover, the raid had aborted a British operation to lay nets and mines to seal off the Zeebrugge submarine base. At the least, Scheer could imagine that the British would have to assign a strong force to cover any future operation of this type and that he could destroy it in a future raid.

The Lowestoft raid demonstrated to the British that, despite excellent intelligence, they could not count on intercepting the High Seas Fleet if it came out to attack their coast. Early in May Jellicoe mounted an operation designed to entice Scheer out, so that he could be destroyed. A larger-scale air attack on the Zeppelin sheds at Tondern was to be combined with minelaying in the swept channels of the German Bight. Nine submarines were to be deployed, three along the Dutch coast and six off the Horn Reefs. The Grand Fleet would take position 60 miles off the Danish coast. The idea was that the High Seas Fleet would emerge to snap up the carrier force. In doing so it would be led over mines and submarines and then into the Grand Fleet (including Beatty's

The British were impressed by the potential minelaying capability of German destroyers. Minelaying ramps are visible on board two surrendered destroyers at the Norfolk Navy Yard, 1920, but note that the third (G 102, designed for Argentina) lacks any such facility. Mine rails had all been removed before the ships were handed over, but the ramps were associated with minelaying rather than with depth charges. (US Navy)

force) offshore. Unfortunately, out of nine aircraft lowered into the water by the two carriers, only two managed to take off and one crashed into a screening destroyer.[73] The Germans hardly noticed an attack by a single aircraft, so they failed to take the bait. Eventually a U-boat reported the presence of the British force. Ironically, the Germans already believed, from agent reports (perhaps spread by the British in preparation for the trap), that a major British operation against the German Bight was likely, but they did not associate it with either the single aircraft or the U-boat report. The weather precluded airship reconnaissance. Instead, submarines were ordered to sea to investigate further and the German fleet was ordered to be ready for sea at short notice. Admiral Jellicoe, who had waited for news of an enemy sortie, decided to retire and the operation ended. However, the idea of enticing the High Seas Fleet out and also of luring it over a mine and submarine trap, survived. Post-war analysis showed that later German air reconnaissance had been less than successful: it failed to detect Beatty's battlecruisers only 35 miles from Horn Reefs. Without better information, e.g. from code-breaking, Scheer never realised how little he could depend on his aircraft and airships. Nor did submarine scouts ever fulfil his expectations.

Jutland

Early in April 1916 the German government decided to suspend its campaign of unrestricted submarine warfare, which had been resumed the previous month. That freed U-boats to work with the High Seas Fleet in any sortie towards the Skaggerak. Scheer decided that from 17 May onward he wanted all of his forces ready for an offensive operation supported by the large force of newly-available U-boats (the operation was somewhat delayed by condenser problems in some of the battleships and then by the need to complete repairs to the battlecruiser *Seydlitz*, mined on the previous sortie). He had already despatched all available torpedo-carrying U-boats to stations off the main British naval bases. Scheer's plan was to draw the British fleet over the U-boats using the High Seas Fleet as bait.[74] U-boat endurance affected any decision Scheer made: all would have to leave their stations on 1 June. Scheer thought that the British force was spread over several East Coast ports, so that a bombardment (in this case of Sunderland) would draw them out piecemeal. Some airships would operate directly with the battlecruisers assigned to shell Sunderland; others would scout towards the Firth of Forth, the Humber, the Hoofden and the Skaggerak. Scheer considered air reconnaissance essential to any operation near the British coast, as it would protect him from any engagement with the whole Grand Fleet. If the weather precluded or much limited it, he considered an operation into the Skaggerak as an alternative. He would be protected from the British fleet to some extent by distance and to some extent by the Danish coast to one side. On 26 May Scheer issued orders describing the alternative operation; by 30 May he would decide which to execute.

With winds blowing the wrong way on 30 May, but with his whole fleet ready (*Seydlitz* joined on 29 May), Scheer decided to execute the Skaggerak option. His hope was that with the appearance of German cruisers in the Skaggerak the British would have to protect their commerce with Scandinavia by countering them. The trigger was to be the visible presence of Hipper's battlecruisers off the Norwegian coast. Scheer changed his plans in two

important ways. He decided to operate as close to Hipper as possible, on the theory that without air reconnaissance the full fleet should be concentrated. However, when the engagement began, Hipper was 50 to 60 miles ahead of Scheer's main body.

Scheer agreed to take with him the pre-dreadnought squadron (2nd Battle Squadron) which might otherwise have been left behind to guard the German Bight. German accounts, such as that in *Krieg zur See*, make much of the determination of the squadron's commander to join in the battle regardless of the vulnerability of his ships and of Scheer's reluctant agreement to take him along. In many previous operations, however, this squadron had been integral with the battle fleet. Moreover, the tactics of the time envisaged fire distribution in which each ship engaged the one opposite. A more numerous fleet engaging a shorter line would concentrate its fire. Adding the pre-dreadnoughts slowed the German battle line, but also extended it so that British fire would be more diluted. This seems a more rational explanation for Scheer's decision.

At the end of May Admiral Jellicoe was again interested in an operation to draw out the High Seas Fleet and, incidentally, to draw it over a new minefield (to be laid by HMS *Abdiel*) near the Horn Reefs, the line of retreat of any German fleet sortie.[75] Objectives listed in the Operation Order were (i) to mine the probable course of the German fleet outside the northern end of the Arum channel and also at the seaward end of the southern channel leading out of the German Bight; (ii) to attack the Zeppelin sheds at Tondern with twelve to fourteen aircraft (which would finally be enough to destroy them); and (iii) to draw the ships of the German High Seas Fleet over the minefields 'and if possible to bring them to action'.

Jellicoe still rejected Beatty's proposal that the *Queen Elizabeth*s be attached to the Battlecruiser Fleet, but when the 3rd Battlecruiser Squadron (*Invincible*, *Inflexible* and *Indomitable*) was sent to Scapa for exercises, Jellicoe detached the *Queen Elizabeth*s to Beatty on a temporary basis. He would later argue that losing his fast division had badly upset his tactical arrangements. Beatty could argue that, as he had written a few months earlier, the *Queen Elizabeth*s had turned out to be an invaluable rear guard when the whole High Seas Fleet turned up.

Jellicoe's plan was to put two light cruiser squadrons, with a battlecruiser squadron in support, off Skagen at dawn on 2 June. They would enter the Danish Straits via the Kattegat; in the past all such operations had drawn German forces. The Battlecruiser Fleet and the Grand Fleet would operate in support, shielded from German airship reconnaissance by a carrier force built around HMS *Engadine*. The minefield to be laid by HMS *Abdiel* was west of those she had laid earlier in May. Three of the Harwich submarines were to lie in wait north of the minefield. Other submarines would be deployed east of the Dogger Bank. Jellicoe's plan was not executed because the Germans acted first, but HMS *Abdiel* did lay her minefield.

The Admiralty was already aware that the Germans were planning an operation. That was suggested first by the lull in German activity after Jellicoe's first abortive operation, by the distribution of U-boats off British ports and then by indications that the High Seas Fleet was assembling outside the river estuaries at Wilhelmshaven. Jellicoe sailed before the High Seas Fleet did, but without knowing much about German plans.[76] It was soon clear that the High Seas Fleet squadrons had received an important operations order, but that signal did not indicate what it was.

Amidships torpedo tubes and 10.5cm (4.1in) gun, *V 43*. (US Navy)

Jellicoe was therefore ordered to take up his position in the North Sea, as in previous operations, about 100 miles east of Aberdeen. The known positions of the U-boats suggested that the High Seas Fleet would be steaming northwest, but the Admiralty feared that this might be only a feint to cover another raid or other operation in the south. Among other southern forces, the Harwich Force of light cruisers and a few destroyers was therefore held back.[77]

The battle of Jutland which followed was a major triumph of British signals intelligence: Jellicoe and Beatty intercepted Scheer on the far side of the North Sea, a place Scheer considered reasonably safe despite his lack of air reconnaissance. Beatty encountered the German scouting force before reaching the agreed rendezvous with Jellicoe. It began with an encounter between the British battlecruisers and their German equivalents – in effect a rerun of Dogger Bank, but with very different consequences. Two British battlecruisers, *Indefatigable* and *Queen Mary*, exploded and instantly sank when hit in or near their turrets (*Invincible* later sank the same way). What had gone wrong? The main change between Dogger Bank and Jutland was a change in British magazine practices. The other change was that the Germans realised that they had to fight at greater ranges, hence increased the elevation of their guns. The British later blamed the explosions on plunging fire. The theory was that German shells easily penetrated British deck armour and then went on to explode in magazines. The problem with the theory is that there were no hits on British machinery spaces, which accounted for a far greater proportion of a ship's deck area than magazines. Director of Naval Construction d'Eyncourt made exactly this point soon after the battle, but it was ignored.

The key was Beatty's interpretation of Dogger Bank. He believed that his ships would have sunk the Germans had they only fired more rapidly.[78] He also considered the German shells ineffective. Fire was slowed by congestion in the ammunition hoists due to the earlier practice of overloading magazines. The choice both to overload magazines *and* to seek high rates of fire made sense given the North Sea visibility problem and a choice not to invest in whatever would be needed to achieve high hitting rates at longer ranges. If the Royal Navy thought it had what was needed to hit at high rates at very long ranges, it would not have worried about wasting ammunition at those ranges and it would also have worried less about evading German torpedoes, because it would have fought mainly outside torpedo range. Congestion (hence slow fire) was inescapable as long as the standard safety measure, keeping cordite charges in special fireproof cases (Clarkson's cases) until they were loaded into the guns, was followed. The cases had to be carried up the hoists and then down again and they were temporarily stowed at the bottoms of the hoists. Once magazines were filled beyond capacity, there were many more cases at the bottoms of the hoists. After Dogger Bank the fleet's solution was largely to turn a blind eye to magazine regulations. Visits by divers to the wreck of the *Queen Mary* confirmed that bare cartridges were strewn about her turrets, in direct violation of magazine regulations.[79]

Bare charges were placed in the turrets, in the working chambers, in the handling rooms below the turrets (placed there to break up the direct path between turret and magazine) and at the bottoms of the hoists.[80] In effect the working chambers and handling rooms became ready-use magazines carrying unprotected charges. This was certainly done in the battlecruisers and apparently also on board some battleships. At least in some ships, doors between magazines and handling rooms were removed so that ships could fire more rapidly. Not long after the battle, Admiral Jellicoe wrote that he supposed that if this was done, any penetration of a turret would probably cause a fatal magazine explosion. Anyone aware of the dangerous magazine practices the British had adopted would have concluded that, had the British ships' magazines been operated properly, turret hits would not have sunk them. DNO concluded as much immediately after the battle.[81]

DNC d'Eyncourt stoutly defended the construction of the British ships, which Beatty also blamed for the disasters.[82] Having had considerable pre-war experience of other navies as Armstrong's warship salesman, he pointed out that navies did not differ much in warship technology and that, being a new navy, the Germans were not likely to be very innovative (as had practically been confirmed in Reichstag debates). None of the British battleships had been sunk and some of the battlecruisers had survived considerable damage. The German ships were not declared ready for battle until the end of September. In DNC's view it was clear that German ships had been at least as badly damaged as their British counterparts.

Later DNC felt compelled to answer the fleet's understanding that the battlecruisers had been sunk by enemy shells penetrating their magazines or exploding so close to them as to ignite the contents.[83] The only case which came close was a shell which burst near *Barham*'s 6in magazine, creating splinters which penetrated the crown of the magazine (and had no further effect). There were, moreover, few cases in which fragments penetrated protective decks over machinery spaces, which occupied a much larger part of the ship than the magazines, were amidships (hence more likely to be hit) and were also not better protected. He used diagrams of the ships to show that enemy shells could not penetrate the lower protective decks of modern battlecruisers and battleships before they exploded, nor that they could burst so far beyond the point of entry as to explode close to the magazines. The effect of the fiction that German shells had burst in magazines was to create demands for much more armour, pushing up ship size and cost without proportionate increase in armament. That would mean abandoning the fundamental maxim of British warship design, in d'Eyncourt's view, that the best defence was superior offense – which he thought had been vindicated at Jutland. British battlecruisers had survived action against German battleships, but the more heavily protected German ships had been badly mauled.

Immediately after the action, Beatty wrote that experience in *Lion* showed that open magazine doors in turrets were very dangerous. 'Present safety arrangements of flash doors are ineffective when turret armour is penetrated. Flash from shell may reach cordite in main cages and thence to handling rooms. This occurred in *Lion* when turret roof was penetrated but magazine doors being closed at once saved magazine from catching fire.' In distributing Beatty's warning, Jellicoe ordered immediate action. 'If any ship has removed the flash doors in the working chambers of her turret, they are to be replaced. The turret trunk in handling rooms is to be made as flash tight as possible by closing inspection holes etc. The lid of a cordite case in the magazine is only to be removed immediately prior to the cordite being removed from that case for use.'[84]

Beatty's position soon changed. He began to say that the problem was German shells penetrating magazines, an evasion of the charge of allowing fatally bad magazine practices. DNC pointed out that the only documented case of shell splinters penetrating to a magazine was in *Barham* (see above). On this basis not much was to be gained by Beatty's idea of lowering the magazine by placing shell rooms on top. That would, moreover, bring magazines closer to potential underwater damage. DNC agreed that the Germans had provided heavier deck protection, at the expense of other fighting qualities, such as heavier guns. For him the appropriate lesson was that battlecruiser turret protection should match that of battleships. In another letter in the package, DNC d'Eyncourt pointed out that, apart from the ships which blew up, some of the battlecruisers survived considerable damage. Even relatively light internal protection could stop the splinters from German shells, which tended to burst 10–15ft inboard and better magazine practices and flash protection were not difficult to apply. On that basis he thought that the *Renown* and *Repulse* and even the *Courageous* class would prove successful. This comment in particular (which was part of a package given to the US Navy in September 1917) must have been most encouraging to a US Navy planning six large and very lightly-armoured battlecruisers of the *Lexington* class.

Both Jellicoe and Beatty were to have been reprimanded for reversing magazine regulations (several wartime orders repeated that cordite was not to be stowed outside magazines). However, when Jellicoe was promoted to First Sea Lord and Beatty to Grand Fleet commander, the reprimands were cancelled. Third Sea Lord Rear Admiral Frederick Tudor, responsible for the investigation, was sent to command the China Station. Captain C V Usborne mentioned casually at Greenwich in 1923 that, due to better magazine arrangements, ships were no longer tinderboxes, as they had been at Jutland. He did not distinguish between battleships and battlecruisers. The British did admit that flash had been a problem. Their interest in protection against flash is visible in later British attention to magazine regulations (which were extended to the closed hangars of British carriers) and to the anti-flash clothing adopted by the Royal Navy. Flash experiments were conducted on board the pre-dreadnought *Prince of Wales* in 1917. The battle did not really disprove Beatty's perceptions of Dogger Bank. Apart from ships destroyed by magazine explosions, none of the British ships suffered very badly. That reinforces the argument that more was wrong with British magazine practices than right about German shells. Although the Germans later boasted about the superior performance of their shells, at the time they felt that they had made a mistake in adopting smaller-calibre higher-velocity guns. After Jutland they wanted ships armed with heavier guns.

Since 1916 many explanations have been given for the 'scandal' of Jutland – for the failure of the superior British fleet to mangle the smaller German fleet. For example, it has been argued that British fire control was inferior, because before the war the Admiralty adopted the Dreyer Table rather than the much more advanced Pollen Argo Clock.[85] Another explanation is that British shells were defective; they could not penetrate German armour in condition to explode.[86] Another, made post-war by the Germans, is that British fire control was grossly defective, the Germans scoring hits at a much higher rate.[87] Much has also been made of defective tactics. All of these explanations have some merit, but none rises to the level of scandal. After the war, Jutland was wildly controversial, the argument turning on exactly what Beatty did after he encountered the German battlecruisers and then the German fleet. As post-war First Sea Lord, he went so far as to rewrite the official history and even to demand changes in the official track charts.

However, whatever tactical charges can be made against Beatty pale in the face of the scandal of disastrous magazine practices, which was covered up quite successfully.[88] That success is evident in the widespread belief that Jutland proved that battlecruisers were death-traps, the question *not* asked being why the US Navy continued to plan to build six of them in full knowledge of British experience at Jutland.

The fleet could not be told that its efforts to fire rapidly had been fatal. Nor could Jellicoe and Beatty admit that they had fatally failed to enforce magazine regulations. Instead, both Jellicoe and Beatty pressed the excuse that deck armour was too thin was to blame (the fleet did, however, tighten up magazine procedure). As First Sea Lord, Jellicoe demanded that the new battlecruisers of the *Hood* class be redesigned with extra deck armour, over Tudor's objections. Changes so delayed the class that three of the four were cancelled. Given the claim that plunging fire was suddenly significant, the British equated heavy deck armour with 'post Jutland' design. It was actually more properly equated with an expectation that ships would fight at even longer ranges than at Jutland – which is why the US Navy had introduced heavy decks in its *Nevada* class in 1911.

Admiral Beatty failed to catch the German battlecruiser force after the Scarborough Raid, largely through his poor signalling. At Dogger Bank, when he did catch the Germans, he failed to destroy much of their force, again through poor signalling. His errors caused his ships to concentrate on the fast armoured cruiser *Blücher*, which was not a true battlecruiser, hence whose loss had only limited impact. After the losses at Jutland, Admiral Beatty wanted to know why ships like *Blücher* succumbed only to cumulative damage, whereas his battlecruisers blew up.

The battlecruiser fight revealed the same command problems as at Dogger Bank. One of the German ships was never engaged at all. Also, Beatty was unable to gain immediate support from the squadron of fast *Queen Elizabeth* class battleships temporarily attached to his force. It did not help that he had made no attempt to discuss his tactics with Rear Admiral Evan-Thomas, commanding the fast division, even though he had been pressing to have it permanently attached to his command. His force badly damaged and his faith in it badly shaken, Beatty retired towards the distant Grand Fleet, with the German battlecruisers and the German battle fleet following. His fast battleships followed, having been badly handled (without disaster) by the main German fleet. That was Beatty's role: to find the enemy and then to lead them into collision with the Grand Fleet. For his part, Scheer did not much benefit from scouting, due to his decision to concentrate his force. Had he not done so, Hipper would have collided with the Grand Fleet in enough time to have warned Scheer off.

Jellicoe was able to deduce enough of what was happening to deploy his fleet across the path of the oncoming Germans, so that his battleships crossed their 'T'. Scheer had never wanted to confront the whole British fleet, so he spent the balance of the battle trying to wriggle out of the trap Jellicoe had sprung. It says a great deal for Jellicoe's understanding of what was happening (situational awareness), supported by plotting, that he managed to manoeuvre his battle line across Scheer's path two more times. In the process he lost another battlecruiser (*Indefatigable*) and the big armoured cruiser *Defence* (a second armoured cruiser, *Warrior*, foundered on the way home). None of the German ships exploded, but *Seydlitz* almost sank again and the new battlecruiser *Lützow* was sunk by cumulative gun and torpedo damage. Magazine or turret hits by

13.5in or 15in shells tended to burn out German turrets. There was no evidence then or later that the Germans had taken precautions after nearly losing *Seydlitz* at Dogger Bank.

As Scheer sought to disengage, Jellicoe thought that he might be trying to draw the Grand Fleet into a mine-submarine trap. As DNO and then Controller, Jellicoe had become painfully aware of how vulnerable his ships were to underwater attack. That was reinforced when the new battleship *Audacious* foundered after striking a mine on 27 October 1914. Jellicoe first raised this possibility in an October 1914 letter to the Admiralty. In response, a 1 December 1914 Admiralty Confidential Order stated that the Germans might invite pursuit specifically to draw the British fleet into such a trap and that they had practiced this tactic (it is not clear whether there was any evidence of this). Jellicoe further emphasised this possibility in a December 1915 addition to his Grand Fleet Battle Orders. Exercises both at sea and on the game board had shown that a German turn-away covered by torpedo fire would be difficult to counter, because it would force Jellicoe to choose between losing contact and losing effective firepower (as his ships turned individually to evade torpedoes) until he could reform his line. Jellicoe seems to have decided that he too could effectively use mine-submarine traps, since they were part of both of his May 1916 plans to draw out and destroy the High Seas Fleet.

The expected mass German torpedo attacks never happened. Only one British battleship, HMS *Marlborough*, was hit – not by the mass of torpedo craft – and she survived.[89] In 1916 DNC argued that she had stood up very well to this damage, her performance being considered satisfactory in comparison with that of smaller and older ships sunk by torpedoes. *Marlborough* was fortunate that she had not been hit in the worst place and also that she had just been provided with a hundred-ton submersible pump. Flooding caused an 8° list, which was not enough to force her CO to counterflood (partly because he had to reckon with the possibility of another hit). Jellicoe could reasonably argue that she had been rather lucky, because a similar amount of explosive sank her near-sister *Audacious* two years earlier.[90]

Like many other battles, Jutland proved that eye-witnesses are often mistaken. On 7 June Jellicoe distributed a list of ships he believed his fleet had sunk, based on eye-witnesses: three capital ships (including a *Kaiser* class battleship), five light cruisers, six destroyers and a submarine. 'All of the above vessels were actually seen to sink. It is probable, but not certain, that two more battleships or battle-cruisers sank'.[91] The reality was much less impressive, beginning with one battlecruiser (*Lützow*) and the pre-dreadnought *Pommern*.[92]

Jutland in effect both proved that Beatty had reason to want the *Queen Elizabeth*s to back him up and that he had no business so far from the support of the Grand Fleet. Jellicoe met with the Sea Lords after the battle (probably on 25–27 June) to draw immediate lessons.[93] All concluded that, if the initiative were with the British, the battlecruisers would not be advanced as far ahead as in the past; the fleet would always be closer by. The 5th Battle Squadron would be considered mainly as a fast wing of the battle fleet, never as part of the battlecruiser force. It might be detached to reinforce the battlecruisers, but only at Jellicoe's discretion; it should never be considered integral with the battlecruiser force. The extent to which the *Queen Elizabeth*s could or should support the battlecruisers would depend on measured-mile trials scheduled for HMS *Barham*.

The battlecruisers would operate alone only in the event of a raid on the English coast and the Admiralty would decide how far they could go and the extent to which they might be permitted to seriously engage the enemy without the support of the battle fleet. The decision would depend both on the urgency of the situation and on the strength of the enemy force. Beatty continued to fight for the *Queen Elizabeth*s at least up to late August 1916.[94]

At the same time, arrangements to move the Grand Fleet south to Rosyth were to be pressed forward. Once that was done, the battlecruisers would always be near the main fleet, so the question of sending them out without such support would no longer arise. However, rebasing depended on the supply of paravanes to the light cruisers and destroyers, since one battle squadron (the 4th: 12in-gun dreadnoughts) would continue to be based at Scapa, hence minesweepers also had to stay there. The 3rd Battle Squadron (*Dreadnought* and seven *King Edward VII* class pre-dreadnoughts) would stay in the Medway and it was recognised that it was unlikely to participate in any fleet action unless it was fought south of the Dogger Bank. This conference also approved initial steps to improve ships' protection.[95]

Torpedoes were clearly more important than had been imagined. Jellicoe wanted the rate of fire increased by doubling the underwater torpedo batteries (from two to four) of the new battlecruisers, on the ground that they more than other capital ships were likely to get into position to fire torpedoes. DNC pointed out that there was not enough space; the best that could be done was to increase the rate of fire, partly by placing each tube in its own compartment.

The experience of Jutland emphasised the need for effective scouting near the German coast. The British had long known that their submarines could survive there, but their W/T range seldom exceeded 60 miles, whereas U-boats could communicate reliably at, it was thought, 400 miles. The only solution was Poulsen sets, previously thought too massive for submarine installation. This time the need was so obvious that it was pushed through as a matter of urgency.[96]

For Jellicoe and the Royal Navy, the great surprise of Jutland was that Scheer did not want to stand and fight. It was one thing that their battlecruisers fled at Dogger Bank. It was another that, having come out (why?), the Germans were interested mainly in avoiding damage and getting clear. British pre-war strategy had been premised on convincing the Germans that they had to come out, then sinking them. The British never realised during the war the extent to which the Kaiser had hobbled the German battle fleet by demanding that it avoid losses. Even the aggressive Scheer had never had any intention of risking his fleet against the whole Grand Fleet.

Jellicoe's pre-battle correspondence reveals that he did not feel that he enjoyed the crushing superiority which the Germans saw. He assumed that the Germans would come out only to fight him and thus to gain sea control. Surely the Germans would time any operation so that they would be at maximum strength, whereas he would always have to fight at average strength. He knew that the Germans had fewer capital ships, but he assumed they were superior to his own. Jellicoe seems to have considered the German destroyer force an equaliser, given his own doubts about his ships' survivability in the face of underwater hits. Each German destroyer had more torpedo tubes than his own and he still imagined that the Germans might lay mines in his path. Jellicoe never felt that he had enough light cruisers to deal with the expected mass German

Jutland: the 'Run to the South'. the British battlecruisers engage the German battlecruiser force commanded by Admiral Hipper. Hipper was operating in advance of the German main body and upon engaging Beatty's battlecruisers he led them back (south) towards it. This painting was based on a photograph showing HMS *Queen Mary* last in line; she was blown up during this action. Note that she lacks the dark grey panel she and other battlecruisers had in earlier photographs. A May 1916 photograph of the three *Lion*s does not show it. (Painting by W L Wyllie, PW0914 © National Maritime Museum, London)

destroyer attacks, hence he saw his own destroyers as defensive rather than offensive. He systematically overestimated German destroyer strength. Scheer certainly did not employ his destroyer force aggressively. Neither Scheer nor his predecessors considered the odds anything like even in a battle against the whole Grand Fleet, whatever their destroyer strength. Torpedo boats seem to have played a far smaller role in the German High Seas Fleet than the British imagined. The one torpedo hit the Grand Fleet suffered was from a disabled German light cruiser, not a destroyer. Post-war critics thought that at Jutland Jellicoe's plotters, who provided much of his situational awareness, had grossly overestimated the German torpedo threat, which in turn had made Jellicoe even more cautious than he might otherwise have been.

The most important single fact of the battle may have been Scheer's lack of situational awareness, due to the fact that he had no plot. For Scheer it was a terrible surprise when Jellicoe first appeared athwart his course, crossing his 'T'.[97] His one object was surely to disengage so that he could escape. The German signal-book (which the British had) included a 'battle turn', in which all of his ships turned 180° (16 points) simultaneously, their retreat to be covered by smoke and by a destroyer torpedo attack (at Jutland, by one flotilla). This was exactly the German manoeuvre Jellicoe had feared. If the Germans fired torpedoes to cover their retreat, an onrushing Grand Fleet would run into the approaching torpedoes, whereas its own torpedoes would be outrun.

Jellicoe assumed Scheer was heading straight for Heligoland, so he manoeuvred the Grand Fleet into a position across Scheer's assumed line of retreat. Jellicoe's light cruisers gained touch with the High Seas Fleet and once more the Grand Fleet crossed Scheer's 'T'. This time Scheer ordered his battlecruisers to charge at the Grand Fleet (presumably to attract its fire) and he covered a 'battle turn' with a mass destroyer attack. Only two of the flotillas attacked, firing thirty-one of their fifty-eight torpedoes, only twenty-one of which reached the British battle line. None hit. The attack was frustrated by a light cruiser squadron, a destroyer flotilla

and battleship fire. In about eleven cases ships had to evade torpedoes, which were running very slowly by that time. Scheer did succeed in disengaging, as Jellicoe felt compelled by the torpedo threat to turn away.[98] The torpedo threat was actually localised (to the rear of the Grand Fleet), but Jellicoe probably feared that the torpedo attack was the beginning of a general attack by High Seas Fleet torpedo boats. It did not help that Jellicoe did not see the battle turn executed by the High Seas Fleet battleships. Once clear, Jellicoe again formed a battle line and steered it across Scheer's path back to Heligoland. Scheer was again trapped and again he had to disengage. This time falling darkness saved Scheer, although his badly damaged battlecruisers were engaged by Beatty's and further punished. When darkness fell, the leading ships of the two lines were six miles apart, on converging courses.

To Jellicoe, Scheer was making it obvious that he did not want to fight the Grand Fleet. Any future opportunity to fight the High Seas Fleet would be fleeting. As in earlier actions, the Germans zig-zagged to ruin British fire control. The British concluded that to rely on cumulative damage by shellfire was pointless. They would not get many hits while the Germans zig-zagged. Moreover, firing opportunities were fleeting, targets emerging suddenly from the mist. Often there was time for only a few rangefinder readings. Those hits had to count, or at the least they had to stop German ships. The most important post-Jutland project was a new armour-piercing shell, one hit from which in a machinery space would immobilise a German battleship. As the post-war summary of wartime gunnery progress put it, 'theoretically no number of hits with old-type shells could cause destruction of the modern German battleship, whereas one hit *in a suitable position* with the new projectile will immobilise her'.[99] Initially it seemed that the key to better shell performance was a superior German fuze, but the Admiralty's Shell Committee soon decided that entirely new shells were needed.[100] They were tested against mock-ups of the German battleship *Kaiser* and the new British battlecruiser *Hood*, then under construction. By 1918 the British thought the shell problem had been solved, so that any repeat Jutland would be fatal for the Germans. Post-war tests against the surrendered German battleship *Baden* seemed to prove the point. There was no expectation that a magazine hit would destroy a German battleship. Note, however, that when the Royal Navy used the new-type shells to sink *Bismarck* and *Scharnhorst* during the Second World War, damage was cumulatively fatal, rather than instantly disabling. It seems that the failure to do fatal or at least disabling damage with single hits was due to the sheer difficulty of disabling a very large, well-designed ship.

The single most difficult post-Jutland tactical question was how to deal with a German attempt to escape by turning away. The Grand Fleet could not simply pursue, because it had to reckon with the possibility that the Germans would cover their retreat with a mass torpedo attack. In that case pursuing British ships might be running into the German torpedoes. On the other hand, once the British line opened so that the ships could rush forward, they would present small torpedo targets and few if any would be hit. Then the question would be whether the Germans were leading them over a mine-submarine trap. Jellicoe had previously argued that if the Germans were forced into sustained high-speed manoeuvres, they would probably no longer be anywhere near a trap they had set up. Their submarines were not fast enough to move with the High Seas Fleet, whereas the new 'K'-boats about to join the Grand Fleet could move with it.

Jellicoe himself certainly did not want to keep in touch to fight a night action. His nightmare was a confused action in which the larger fleet would suffer the worse losses. The whole point of rigid line-ahead tactics was to avoid the sort of chaotic blue-on-blue fighting implicit in a night action. Jellicoe was, moreover, well aware that his fleet was poorly equipped for night action, with a clumsy system of recognition (IFF) signals and with poorly-situated searchlights which might well give away not only the presence of his ships but also their courses. After Jutland the Grand Fleet formed a Searchlight Committee. Enormous attention was given to concentrating searchlights amidships, so that they would not be so revealing, with remote controls allowing them to be used more effectively. The fleet gunnery committee called for tests of German-style coloured recognition lights.

Even though relatively few German ships were visible to any one British ship at any one time, it proved remarkably difficult to keep spotter, director and Dumaresq on the same target. The fleet committee on gunnery lessons called for installation of more precision target designators (Eversheds). Elliott Bros. was already producing a device which designated the target to the spotter and helped him keep his glasses on it; the committee wanted production accelerated on an urgent basis. Main and secondary batteries had to practice rapidly opening fire and quickly switching targets. That demanded quick target recognition; the committee stated that familiarity with the silhouettes of German ships was essential. An unstated point was that reluctance to open fire on individual targets was due at least as much to uncertainty as to their identity as to lack of initiative.

One vital point was not discussed, at least not in the fleet's post-Jutland papers. Jellicoe had benefitted enormously from his tactical plot, but many of the reports fed into it had been badly misleading, due to navigational errors on the part of the reporting ships. It might also be argued that reporting had often been insufficient: no one understood that the deployed ships, not just the scouts, were

Jellicoe's key sensors. British practice had been to minimise W/T, partly to avoid mutual jamming of sets on very few separate frequencies. To that end, a ship's CO had to approve each signal sent and COs often had other vital concerns as they fought their ships. Ships conducted frequent enemy-reporting exercises when in harbour, but they were to learn *how to report once the ship's Captain ordered them to do so*. Captains did not attend; the message that it was essential to report what was seen was not impressed on them.[101] One vital post-Jutland development was to express all reports in terms of distance from and bearing to the flagship, so that the flagship could maintain a consistent plot representing the true tactical situation.

The battle and its aftermath revealed an apparent lack of initiative in the Grand Fleet. For example, individual British captains who saw German ships, including capital ships, nearby the night after the battle failed to fire. No one reported the presence of German ships astern of the Grand Fleet. The later explanation was almost invariably that surely the fleet commander would have known and would have ordered ships to fire.[102] Jellicoe certainly understood after the battle: he told the Tactical School in 1934 'never imagine that your C-in-C sees what you see'. Once the Germans succeeded in disengaging, no attempt was made to put out scouts to keep touch with them. It is possible that Jellicoe had been so well served by signals intelligence in the past that he assumed he could be brought back into touch at daybreak.[103]

The problem may have been the sheer size of the Grand Fleet, which was more like a tightly-packed army than a small manageable fleet. In an army, the great danger is that troops will accidentally fire at each other, particularly if units get out ahead of the mass of troops. Initiative can often be extremely dangerous. It was better for a ship not to fire at a supposed enemy than to mistakenly sink a British ship. Accounts of Jutland, moreover, suggest that the fleet's confidence in its ability to recognise German ships was limited. The utmost requirement for Jellicoe was to preserve his superiority. As long as the Germans knew that he had the stronger fleet, they would be unable to use the High Seas Fleet until they had defeated the Grand Fleet.

A small, flexible fleet is an entirely different proposition. Jellicoe's dilemma, that individual initiative and aggressiveness might lead to a fatal melee, was resolved by the arms-control treaties, which ensured that nothing as massive as the Grand Fleet would ever fight in close order again. The post-war Royal Navy successfully nurtured the initiative and aggressiveness which served it so well during the Second World War. It is sobering that the post-war US Fleet, with its twelve battleships, seemed to mirror Jellicoe's experience of limiting initiative in order to maintain a cohesive and hence tactically effective force. To the extent that the realities of a mass fleet shaped Jellicoe's practices, that the post-war US Fleet showed similar limitations is a strong argument against claims that the Grand Fleet was unduly shaped by an excessively deferential and stratified British society, in which it was impossible to question High Authority.

In an 11 September 1916 (*i.e.*, post-Jutland) revision of *Grand Fleet Battle Orders*, Jellicoe observed that the German 1st and 3rd Battle Squadrons 'alone have probably a higher speed than the British battle fleet as a whole' and this will add to the difficulty of turning away especially if as [at Jutland] these tactics are accompanied by torpedo attack on the centre and rear of our fleet. If the rear, or centre and rear only, are threatened by torpedo attack

Shells falling around the battlecruisers during the 'Run to the South', 4pm on 31 May 1916. From left to right the ships are *Indefatigable*, *New Zealand*, *Tiger*, *Queen Mary*, *Princess Royal* and *Lion*; they are steaming to the right. (Dr David Stevens, SPC-A)

the flag officer leading the van of the main battle fleet should use to his utmost the speed of his squadrons in order to keep within effective gun range of the enemy'.[104] This was radical in that it posited decentralised command of the three elements of the fleet.

> *The experience of the battle of Jutland when the enemy escaped serious punishment by turning away covered by smoke screens and destroyer attacks showed the desirability of considering methods of reducing the torpedo menace other than that of turning the fleet away by the Preparative [signal], especially if in low visibility this turn takes the fleet out of gun range and allows the enemy to execute the turn away when not under gunfire.*

In the wake of Jutland, Jellicoe emphasised divisional tactics, which

had always been buried in his *Grand Fleet Battle Orders*.[105] He would form the battle line en echelon in squadrons or divisions, the van pressing on the enemy van in a strong position for both gun and torpedo attacks, while the centre and particularly the rear were further back so that while within effective gun range they were less vulnerable to enemy torpedoes. If visibility was less than 10,000 yds, the only alternative to accepting the danger from torpedoes was to refuse action altogether or to engage with only the van. The van would consist of the *Queen Elizabeth*s and a reconstituted 1st Battle Squadron. It would enjoy a speed advantage over the rest of the battle fleet, allowing them to manoeuvre. New signals were added to the standard fleet book.

In an October 1916 exercise testing these ideas, the van of the Red fleet was placed so that the 5th Battle Squadron was within 14,000 yds of the enemy van, close enough to hit but far enough away to be safe from Blue's torpedoes. However, torpedoes fired by the Blue line could hit the rest of the British line. The situation was what might occur if the two fleets met and Blue made turns to get closer and also to get into a good torpedo position, hence ready to fight. The torpedoes enjoyed long range but only medium speed,

HMS *Lion* straddled during the battlecruiser engagement, with destroyers ahead of her, photographed by Lieutenant Fawcett, HMS *Lydiard*. (Author's collection)

HMS *Lion*, with enemy shots falling short, during the battlecruiser action, photographed by Lieutenant Fawcett, HMS *Lydiard*. The enemy is on the far side of the photograph. (Author's collection)

hence could not hit the Red van. If the centre and rear of Red turned away to avoid the torpedoes, they would also open to nearly the limit for 12in fire, 18,000 yds. This was not desirable, so the only alternative was to dispose the fleet so as to minimise the torpedo risk while holding the enemy under effective gun fire. That applied particularly to the rear of the British fleet. It would be both at the worst gun range and facing the greatest torpedo risk (remember that both torpedo and ships were moving, so what counted was the actual running range of the torpedo, not the range of the ships when it was fired).

Jellicoe's understanding of Jutland showed in his comments on what to do. He could either hold good gun range while taking some precautions, or he could turn away and break off. Now he would contemplate turning away 'only if the torpedo losses are serious and if the strategic situation renders such action possible'. Until the new shells became available, Jellicoe and later his successor Beatty had to reckon with the possibility that in a fleet action they might have to rely more on torpedoes than on shellfire. However, Jellicoe continued to see his destroyers primarily as defensive assets, at least until the enemy had been shaken by gunfire. Instead, he emphasised the value of torpedo firing by his cruisers and battleships. Thus in contrast to Jutland, in the October 1916 exercise Red's battleships fired their torpedoes at maximum range. His battleships fired 148 torpedoes, of which fifty-three would have crossed the enemy's track, fifty-five of the lost shots being due to Blue's two 16-point (180°) turns. Other lost shots were due to director errors and insufficient margin of running range. The large number of hits were possible only because the ships were (notionally) armed with new very long range torpedoes capable of 18,000 yds at 19 knots or 15,000 yds at 25 knots, rather than the current 10,000 yds at 22 knots. Jellicoe also expected his light cruisers and destroyers to direct heavy torpedo fire at his enemy's van. His battleships would concentrate on the enemy's centre and rear, partly to avoid firing at his own light cruisers and destroyers approaching the enemy's van. This was not at all what he had done at Jutland. There was a reason that, through his tenure at the Grand Fleet, Jellicoe had constantly pushed for development of longer-range torpedoes. Now they were in sight and he knew exactly what they could do.

Before the battle, Scheer was well aware of the general belief that the numerically inferior German fleet could not stand up to the Grand Fleet. The need to match numbers had been the rationale for Tirpitz' progression of fleet plans and for his plea in 1912 not to start a war because the navy was not yet ready. Scheer's great discovery was that he had survived the battle while somewhat evening the odds, the British having lost three battlecruisers to his one. Later the German official history trumpeted the survival of several badly-damaged German capital ships, notably *Seydlitz*, as proof that Tirpitz had been right to emphasise survivability (a somewhat questionable claim, given his endless attempts to cap growth in capital ship size). It certainly helped that, thanks to British signals intelligence, the battle was fought much closer to the German than to the British coast. To Scheer, survival at Jutland meant that he could take chances, because the penalties of failure – of meeting the Grand Fleet – were acceptable. The German official history presents Scheer seeking battle in August 1916, frustrated only by inept Zeppelin reconnaissance. To the British, Scheer turned away because the same reconnaissance warned him that he was running towards the Grand Fleet. The German official history

was intended to show the Imperial Navy in the best possible light and also to encourage offensive-mindedness, so this particular point must be open to question.

Scheer never admitted that he had been surprised and nearly destroyed and that he had concentrated on extricating his fleet. After the battle he claimed that the second encounter was a deliberate attack by his fleet against the Grand Fleet, despite his turn away and his covering destroyer attack. It is difficult to see his performance as a great demonstration of tactics and the failure is surely at least partly traceable to Scheer's lack of situational awareness. That neither Scheer nor his predecessors had made special efforts to gain such awareness of a battle space extending beyond their view may be traced to the rapid growth of the German Navy, which did not give senior officers much of a chance to understand the problems inherent in controlling a massive fleet. Afterwards some British officers were much impressed by what appeared to be German divisional tactics and the sort of decentralisation Jellicoe stoutly resisted. It is probably fairer to see a failure to understand, as Jellicoe did, the perils of decentralisation without situational awareness.

The Germans professed themselves satisfied with their performance at Jutland. For example, they told the Austrian naval attaché that, amazingly, a C-in-C who had not previously commanded a fleet and admirals who had not previously manoeuvred their battle squadrons succeeded in following all their instructions perfectly.[106] That did not explain Scheer's tactical failure to avoid having his 'T' crossed twice.[107] *Krieg zur See* pointed out that if Scheer had not been so anxious to press on during the early part of the battle, he might have realised that he was heading directly towards the British battle line. He would have proceeded at slower speed in cruising (column) formation, from which he could have deployed into a battle line more or less parallel to the British, instead of exposing his van to concentrated British fire.[108] Scheer's first definite information that the entire British fleet was present seems to have been a wireless message from one of his destroyers reporting statements from prisoners from the sunken British destroyer *Nomad*. Just as he was digesting this news, the horizon ahead of him lit up with the gun flashes of the Grand Fleet battleships.

The author of the post-war German account of Jutland was at pains to present Scheer's turn-away as something other than a standard manoeuvre frequently practiced to extricate the fleet from a dangerous situation.[109] He stated that German tactics were actually similar to British, envisaging deployment from columns into line ahead, with the enemy bearing if possible abaft the beam.[110] That was impossible when Scheer confronted the Grand Fleet crossing his 'T', so he selected one of his repertoire of possible manoeuvres, the 16-point turn, which the British later characterised as the 'battle turn-away'. The German author maintained that Scheer was not trying to break away, but rather to take up the engagement again on better terms. That was a way of explaining Scheer's subsequent charge towards the British line (the second time his T was crossed) as other than a total blunder.

The German official historian claimed that Jellicoe had been reluctant to follow Scheer's 16-point battle turn partly because his own destroyers, which would have protected him against Scheer's torpedo flotillas, were not in place to do so. Jellicoe had always, it seemed, concluded that only 'sufficient time and superior speed' could solve the problem presented by a turn-away and that it was too late in the day for that. Jellicoe also had to avoid a course which would have brought him into a position bearing abaft the beam of the German battle line. The German historian thought that the only solution for Jellicoe would have been to divide his fleet, having his van or his rear engage and hold the German van or rear, so that the Germans could not turn as they desired. That level of co-operation was impractical in poor visibility (and very much against Jellicoe's insistence that only by remaining together could his fleet avoid blue-on-blue). Jellicoe therefore placed his fleet athwart Scheer's expected line of retreat – and once again crossed Scheer's 'T'. The German official historian ascribed Scheer's second attack to excessively optimistic reports of British losses, to a reluctance to retreat and to his determination to support a mass torpedo attack. None of this was particularly convincing and all of it reflected Scheer's post-battle effort to explain a potentially disastrous manoeuvre. It seems fairest to say that Scheer had too little situational awareness.

After three days in Wilhelmshaven, the Austrian attaché reported that the German fleet was intoxicated with what it considered its victory; 'they know themselves to be superior to the enemy as regards tactics . . . they know that their gunfire was more effective than that of the enemy and that they can rely implicitly on their flotillas which had always been looked upon in the Imperial Navy as one of the chief factors in an action. Finally, they know that their largest ships can stand heavy fire and serious damage.' All of this must have been heartening to Germany's sole ally. However, the Germans admitted that they were impressed by British fire control 'and the enormous piercing power of their heavy shell at great distances . . . They do not deny that they were extraordinarily fortunate and that if the action had been prosecuted with energy on the British side . . . things might have gone very badly for Germany, especially as the British still had an intact Battle Squadron of 12 units at their disposal which had not yet taken part in the action'.

Prior to the battle, he Germans had no idea that the Grand Fleet was at sea; the attaché stated that as the German fleet steamed north, it intercepted a few corrupted W/T messages which seemed to refer to small British formations. It seemed, too, that submarine arrangements had gone badly awry. The U-boats stationed off the British coast, which were to have attacked returning damaged ships, were to return home on 1 June and to be relieved by a smaller force. Why, then, did Scheer sail on 31 May, knowing that they would not be in place on 2 June, when damaged ships might be returning? Why, too, did Scheer steam out when one of his most powerful ships (*König Albert*) was refitting and just a few weeks before his 15in battleship *Bayern* was ready? This was hardly the attack the Royal Navy expected, at the High Seas Fleet's best moment and the Grand Fleet's average moment. Given these oddities and the absence of the air reconnaissance on which the Germans set such store, the attaché thought the account he had been given was dubious, that the Germans had steamed out in the knowledge that the Grand Fleet was at sea and the moment favourable for an attack. Perhaps they knew only that Beatty was at sea and hoped to trap him. That this was not so makes the oddities stranger.

The attaché also reported that in Berlin there was much talk in military circles of British intent to push into the Baltic; it was known that Kitchener was going to Russia (he died shortly after Jutland when the cruiser *Hampshire* was mined) and that suggested

some connection. The attaché rightly dismissed the idea: 'I consider this senseless, for it cannot be presumed that the British Fleet would leave their shores unprotected and do the Germans the favour of operating in the Baltic, which would certainly be a most advantageous area for the German Fleet'.

According to the attaché, the Germans considered British gunnery superior to theirs.

Their salvoes fell most astoundingly close together and aroused admiration on all sides. Some people affirm that they fell too close together and that it was consequently difficult to cover a sufficiently large danger space. . . In the König, *3 rounds out of a salvo of 4 hit between the capstan and the bridge. This is attributed to careful calibration, which the British have studied for a long time and which, as is well known, was abandoned by the German navy after a few trials . . . The British rangefinders are superior to the German and the construction of their turrets enables them to shoot at ranges impossible for German guns. The question of range appears to be immaterial to the British, who fire at any range as long as visibility permits.*

The Germans are fully convinced of the great superiority of 15in guns over all others . . .

In one respect the British seem behindhand as compared with the Germans; namely that they cannot alter range quickly enough and are too dependent on the range clock. The British rely on steady fire at long range and they adapt their tactics to this and avoid alterations of course and range most assiduously.

The German ships' turn onto an opposite course (while engaged with the main British fleet) was too radical for them to maintain fire, but that did not much matter, because the German ships were already unable to find targets, because the light was too bad for them. However, the Germans thought that it helped because it also prevented the British from hitting. Their salvoes fell close to ships, but tended not to hit. The British rate of fire was described as fair, but not excessive (some said it was very moderate).

The Germans told the attaché that British shells 'had great penetrating power and from all reasonable distances the main armour was generally pierced clean through'. Recovered shell splinters showed that the British were using both AP and common (HE) shells, the former generally not bursting after penetrating. AP shell broke into large splinters once it penetrated, which 'pierced everything in their course and often went right through the whole ship, unless they struck an armoured part. Several intact bodies were found, with and without caps and also entire bases'. The Germans concluded correctly that the British did not have an effective delayed-action fuze for shells with bursters. They told themselves that their superior shells made up to some extent for their smaller-calibre guns and their inferior gunnery. The Germans guessed that the British magazine explosions were due to their closed powder containers not being flash-tight enough; they could not imagine that the British had abandoned such containers altogether in some ships. Given the greater apparent power of their own shells, the Germans thought that, had the British 15in shells been of German type, the battlecruisers *Seydlitz* and *Derfflinger* would both have been sunk.

Before the war, the British expected the fumes from their Lyddite HE shells to disable enemy crews. As it happened, before the battle many of the German ships were supplied plentifully with gas masks. The German officers all told the Austrian attaché that the masks not only saved many lives but also enabled men to carry on in parts of the ship from which they would otherwise have been forced. Gas from shells, mines and torpedoes penetrate 'in an incredible manner through ventilators, telephone leads, etc. to compartments far away from the point of impact'. In one case gas masks made it possible to keep operating a main engine compartment until it could be ventilated.

The Germans professed themselves very satisfied with their torpedo attacks, but the attaché noted dramatic changes in tactics. For the future, in order to concentrate attacks, flotilla leaders would be put under the orders of a leader riding a light cruiser. At Jutland there were two such leader ships, the cruisers *Rostock* (two flotillas) and *Regensburg* (three flotillas), with another flotilla allocated to the battlecruisers and another to the main fleet. Accounts in *Krieg zur See* indicate that the two individual flotillas were intended mainly as anti-submarine screens.

Jellicoe thought the German ships were faster than his, but the Austrian attaché wrote that 'the advantage of speed lay entirely with the British, not only as regards the main fleet on account of the *Deutschland* class [pre-dreadnoughts], but also as regards the battlecruisers [which] have proven considerably faster than the German battlecruisers, an unpleasant experience which had already been made on 25 January 1915 [Dogger Bank]'. The Germans used the supposed superior speed of the British ships to dismiss British claims that their own fleet fled the battle area. They told the Austrian attaché that due to the moderate depth of German harbours, German designers found it difficult to attain high speeds even with great power, the speed of later battlecruisers (*Seydlitz* and *Derfflinger*) being a disappointment.

At Jutland the German ships all still had torpedo nets, which endangered them. The after nets of the battlecruiser *Derfflinger* were hanging in the water and would have fouled her propeller had they not been held by a single lashing. She had had to stop during the action to secure her nets and the Germans felt that they might easily have caused her loss. All nets were unshipped from all ships immediately after the action. They would not be carried again, except possibly in the Baltic.

The High Seas Fleet Sorties

After the battle, Admiral Scheer wrote the Kaiser that although the battle had shown the world that the High Seas Fleet was the equal of the Royal Navy, no victory at sea could compel the British to come to terms, given the geographical disadvantage of Germany and the vast material superiority of the enemy. Only an attack on British trade could win the war.[111] It was only two months since the Supreme War Council had abandoned a modified form of unrestricted submarine war against commerce for fear of bringing the United States into the war and it would be six months before a new U-boat war against commerce was approved. Given the limits the Germans had accepted, they had to find other ways to attack enemy commerce. In 1916 they were already using U-boats effectively in the Mediterranean, where American passengers and ships were unlikely to be found. The Admiralstab was looking for other methods applicable to British waters.

Scheer had to admit that the battle had not changed the balance of forces in any important way. At best the outcome was equivocal; as an American wrote at the time, 'the prisoner has assaulted his jailer, but he remains in jail'. The question of success or failure for Jellicoe is more complex. He had certainly kept the blockade, which was slowly affecting Germany, intact. On the other hand, unless he could destroy the High Seas Fleet, it was impossible for the British to undertake riskier operations such as opening the Baltic to Russian resupply. Without that resupply, the Russian armies were starved of heavy guns and ammunition and ultimately they could not defeat the Germans. Even in 1916, it could be argued that the Germans could not be defeated in the West, because they had no vital interests there. Defeat in the East would have been a very different proposition.

According to Scheer, the battle showed that his ships were more survivable, that his guns were surprisingly effective and his tactical mobility unsurpassed. He could point to the success of his battlecruisers, despite their numerical inferiority. To Scheer, the main fleet action showed that he could win if the odds were even nearly equal. He had also shown that he could break off the action if the odds against him were too great. All of that meant that the previous instructions, with their emphasis on avoiding risk, could be revised, because the High Seas Fleet had done well even without adequate air reconnaissance or submarine support. Moreover, several of the fears felt before Jutland could be forgotten: the British would not be opening the Baltic or reinforcing their Mediterranean Fleet against Turkey, because they could not afford to underestimate the High Seas Fleet. Scheer also argued that he had badly damaged the prestige of the Royal Navy and that in turn might have reduced the British will to continue the war. Scheer could not, however, deny that the battle had not broken the British blockade; indeed, the Grand Fleet remained in the North Sea while Scheer had to run back to port. It is not clear from the official German history to what extent he had to accept that he still could not run great risks.[112]

According to the official German history, the perceived success raised the question of how else German naval forces could contribute to the war effort. That was particularly important given the failure of the German offensive at Verdun, the initial success of the Russian offensive in the East (the Brusilov Offensive) and the shock of Romanian entry into the war. Moreover, by 1916 the British blockade was beginning to make itself felt. Thus the Germans finally considered what the British had long sought: a naval battle intended specifically to break the blockade. The alternative was renewed war against British and Allied seaborne trade. Both carried risks. If fleet action failed and enough of the High Seas Fleet was destroyed, the British could take their fleet into the Baltic and revive the Russians. Given stiff US protests which had caused the Germans to break off unrestricted submarine warfare in the past, resuming it would risk bringing the United States into the war, with its massive resources. There was also a subtler risk. In order to avoid enraging the Americans, the British had let American goods, including food, through their blockade. Romania had also been a major source of some foods. Now Romania was at war with Germany and war with the United States would stop food shipments.

By the end of June 1916 all but Scheer's worst-damaged ships were ready; the last of the badly-damaged ships, *Seydlitz*, was ready on 27 September.[113] Scheer decided to undertake a major operation in August and also to transfer a torpedo-boat flotilla to the Flanders command.[114] The August operation was a repeat of the raid on Sunderland originally planned for May. Submarines were again deployed in support and this time the weather permitted airship support. As in May, Scheer hoped that the British would react to a bombardment and that he could snap up portions of the Grand Fleet reacting to this direct threat. He went to sea on 18 August. Two of his battlecruisers were still under repair, but the battleship *Bayern* had joined the High Seas Fleet. This time Scheer left the slow pre-dreadnoughts at home. He needed all the mobility he could get. Hipper's Scouting Group, which was to conduct the bombardment, was reinforced by the battleships *Bayern*, *Markgraf* and *Grosser Kurfürst* in place of the two battlecruisers still being repaired. The U-boats were deployed in the open sea, along the probable route the British ships would take. Their group commander was embarked on board the battleship *Prinzregent Luitpold*, from which he could control them directly by wireless, based on information received. In contrast to the earlier fleet sortie, the submarines were placed in position only just prior to the fleet sortie. As before, the Flanders submarines co-operated with the High Seas Fleet submarines.

This time the Germans were particularly sensitive to the possibility that the British would learn of the operation by intercepting their W/T, so they tried to avoid sending messages before making contact with the enemy. That did not work: the British still intercepted enough to be aware that the High Seas Fleet was going to sea.[115] British signals intelligence also indicated the presence of Scheer's U-boats, though not exactly where they were. The British had no indication of Scheer's objective, but they considered the situation reminiscent of the build-up to Jutland, including the extensive use of U-boats. The Grand Fleet was alerted and it was soon at sea. The Admiralty also alerted the battle squadron at Sheerness and the Harwich Force. As before, Scheer was entirely unaware that the British had been alerted; he thought their first opportunity would be reports by submarines in the Heligoland Bight. As the German fleet steamed out, a British submarine torpedoed the battleship *Westfalen*, which had to turn back. She reported the incident by W/T, breaking the wireless silence Scheer had ordered. Moreover, the British were able to D/F this signal, giving them the position of the High Seas Fleet. Scheer continued on his way. Almost four hours after *Westfalen* was torpedoed, Scheer's own signal intelligence organisation was able to tell him that enemy forces were at sea, some of them from the Firth of Forth.

As Jellicoe's fleet steamed south through the North Sea, one of his cruisers, HMS *Nottingham*, was torpedoed and sunk while zig-zagging at 20 knots.[116] Jellicoe seems to have decided that he was being led into the submarine-mine trap he always feared and a few minutes after he received the report that the cruiser had sunk, he ordered the fleet to pull back. To the author of *Krieg zur See*, Jellicoe's withdrawal showed that he was not really seeking action. Given the earlier known position of the High Seas Fleet (due to D/F when *Westfalen* was mined), Jellicoe should have known that he was steaming away from his enemy. This was, after all, one of the longest days of the year and the Grand Fleet had been forced to break away at Jutland only due to nightfall. Had Jellicoe not turned back, his southerly course would have crossed the westerly course of Scheer's fleet at about 1pm. Jellicoe seems to have understood correctly that Scheer was planning to attack the British coast and he moved into a blocking position. Other British forces were sent to sea to co-operate with him. In the early afternoon, Jellicoe received a D/F report correctly giving the position of the German flagship 40 miles from him (an hour and a half previously). He cleared for action, his cruisers took up battle positions and he began to manoeuvre his fleet (but not yet to deploy). Tyrwhitt's Harwich Force was placed in position to attack the High Seas Fleet as it retired after the expected battle. It seemed that the High Seas Fleet was coming; some of the Grand Fleet ships spotted the airships

HMS *Indefatigable*, a first-generation battlecruiser, is shown before the war. She was blown up at Jutland. The great question was whether the losses during the battle should be attributed to a basic flaw in the battlecruiser concept, or to fatally bad magazine practices without much relevance to the concept. It appears that the problem was Admiral Beatty's flawed interpretation of his ships' performances at Dogger Bank. (Abrahams via Naval Institute collection)

usually associated with it. In fact the airships were only trying to keep touch with the Grand Fleet and none of them was sure of what it was seeing.

Scheer thought that only parts of the Grand Fleet were at sea, so he continued on course for the British coast. At 1pm, not long before Jellicoe received the D/F report, he was 70 miles from the coast. At this point he received a report from one of his airships that a strong British force was headed towards him. Scheer decided to abandon his raid on Sunderland and head for the reported force. He thought the British were unaware of his presence, hence that he could snap up part of the British fleet. A further clarifying report stated that the reported force included large cruisers (the German phrase for battlecruisers) and battleships, as well as about sixteen destroyers and small cruisers. He closed up with his scouting force. Scheer also benefitted from submarine reconnaissance, the reports of which were, in theory, transmitted directly to his U-boat commander on board the battleship *Prinzregent Luitpold*.[117] During the afternoon, Scheer decided that his quarry lay to the east, so he turned in that direction. His own signals intelligence reported a British light cruiser well north of him. He thought she was part of the group reported by the airship and this report indicated to him that the airship report had been unreliable. He was in no position to engage the British fleet in daylight, nor was he any longer in position to shell Sunderland. Scheer considered a night torpedo attack on the reported British force, but his destroyers were already short of fuel. By this time Scheer no longer believed any of the reports of the positions of British forces, particularly as he continued to receive confusing reports from his airships. He suspected that the British force to the north consisted of destroyers and that, should he continue, his own fleet would be subject to a night attack. Having suffered such an attack at Jutland, he was reluctant to risk another. He turned home.

The British interpretation of what happened was different. It was that, once Scheer knew that the Grand Fleet was nearby (due to the errors made by the airship tracking the Harwich Force), he decided to retire, because he had no desire to repeat his close shave at Jutland. The timing of events can fit either explanation; naturally Scheer would not write in his War Diary (the source for *Krieg zur See*) that he retired on realising just what he faced.[118] It was one thing to snap up a limited British force and quite another to fight the whole fleet. Scheer might write that he had proven that his force could stand off the more powerful Grand Fleet, but it seems unlikely that he really thought so. In retrospect his odds this time were even worse than before Jutland.[119] As Scheer retired, he was shadowed by the Harwich Force. Tyrwhitt broke off when Jellicoe informed him that the Grand Fleet was too far away. He calculated that no torpedo attack he could deliver would have delayed the High Seas Fleet for long enough for Jellicoe to catch up. *Krieg zur See* commented that Tyrwhitt's decision, which was soon confirmed by Jellicoe, was exactly opposite to German ideas about the employment and independent attack of torpedo boat forces such as his.

On the way back to Scapa Flow, Jellicoe lost a second cruiser, HMS *Falmouth*, to submarine attack, while zig-zagging at 23 knots – while she should have been safe. He was already aware that many U-boats were present, some having been sighted by his ships. The two 'Town' class cruisers he lost were essential scouts. Signals intelligence might bring the Grand Fleet close to its quarry, but it took scouts to find the High Seas Fleet so that the Grand Fleet could

engage it. Jellicoe's scouting force was limited and he could not afford to have it wiped out. For him the main lesson of the 18–19 August operation was that the scout cruisers needed their own destroyer screens against submarine attack. He asked the Admiralty for more destroyers, since he considered the destroyer force already attached to the Grand Fleet and to the Battlecruiser Fleet the minimum acceptable.[120] The Admiralty pointed out that submarine attacks on light cruisers were nothing new and not a reasonable pretext for demanding more scarce destroyers; there was little hope of building them more quickly. It did not help that the force Jellicoe now considered inadequate was roughly the one he had requested the previous year. His fleet was being moved south to give it longer effective endurance, based largely on the need to economise on destroyer steaming time. Destroyers were in demand for other duties.[121]

Jellicoe answered that, except in an emergency, he could not take the Grand Fleet very far south and risk further losses to his essential scouts. If the Germans tried to raid the British coast south of Sunderland (*i.e.*, south of the Tyne) again, they would contend only with local defence forces: the Humber and Harwich Forces and the 3rd Battle Squadron of pre-dreadnoughts. The Admiralty approved Jellicoe's decision: better to risk a coastal raid than to risk the superiority of the Grand Fleet.[122]

Scheer's scouting commander Hipper observed that the airship and U-boat reports had been inconsistent, denying Scheer any clear idea of what enemy forces he faced or where they were. The raid showed that full airship reconnaissance of the North Sea was impossible both due to the limited number of airships and to varied weather conditions, which in some cases had prevented airships from seeing surface forces. On the other hand, this was the first attempt to use U-boats and airships together on a large scale (the senior airship officer, who had been embarked on board *L 32* for the operation, thought that twelve rather than eight airships should have been used). It became clear that defective navigation often caused airships to send misleading reports. At least one German concluded that the British were not eager to fight.[123] Scheer was impressed by the way in which U-boats had worked with his fleet.[124] Scheer realised that the British submarines in the Heligoland Bight were intended particularly to watch for his fleet, hence that it would be best to get to sea under cover of darkness, or at the least to use torpedo boats, aircraft and airships to force them down as his fleet passed. Scheer was also impressed by airship reconnaissance, describing this operation as the first time 'copious' strategic airship reconnaissance had been mounted. He did agree with Hipper that a broad scouting line of airships was useful only if observation was uninterrupted (it was not clear how that could be achieved). Scheer also pointed to the need for precise navigation by the airships, again something not easily achieved. Scheer blamed his failure to achieve anything on a combination of failed reconnaissance and the 'elusive' policy of the British.

Overall, Scheer recognised more than ever that he could not win the war with a surface action, even if he could force one (and survive it). His experience in August impressed him more and more with the capabilities of the U-boats, hence with their potential to force a decision through unrestricted submarine warfare. He pressed the Kaiser with this idea, but during the autumn of 1916 his argument was rejected.

Scheer's idea of combining airship raids on England with sweeps by surface forces led to an operation on the night of 25/26 September by fleet torpedo forces into the Hoofden backed by the Outpost force (battlecruisers and one battle squadron). The main body of the High Seas Fleet was in distant support. As before, the Germans used their W/T freely and surely gave away the operation, but Jellicoe had already decided not to come so far south. For their part the Germans knew that a British convoy was coming from Holland, but their torpedo flotilla commander decided not to engage it.[125]

As far as another fleet operation was concerned, Scheer felt that he could wait until he had all of his units back from repairs and refits and from exercises in the Baltic. The August operation was the first time the High Seas Fleet had been concentrated since Jutland. Afterwards, the torpedoed *Westfalen* was not ready for sea until 26 September and *Seydlitz* and *Derfflinger*, badly damaged at Jutland, also were not ready until that month. Scheer planned a fleet operation for 18 September, but had to postpone it several times and finally cancel it due to weather. The detachment of a battle squadron to the Baltic made it impossible to carry out a major operation until mid-October.

Initially Scheer envisaged a sweep to a point east of the Dogger Bank, with the object of luring a British force over lines of U-boats. When his submarines were assigned instead to the war against seaborne trade (on 6 October), he had to modify his plan into a search of trade routes in the area between Horns Reef and Terschelling, with provision for an associated night attack by his torpedo-boat flotillas. For reconnaissance, Scheer had airships (over an arc of a 180-mile circle) but no submarines. The High Seas Fleet sailed at about midnight on 18/19 October, a relatively bright night. As early as the afternoon of 18 October, the Admiralty was aware that a sortie was imminent and Jellicoe was ordered to keep his fleet at short notice. Local defence forces, including the Harwich Force, were ordered to assemble in the event Scheer attacked the coast. Jellicoe speculated that the German operation was a diversion intended to help auxiliary cruisers break out into the Atlantic, so the patrol in the north was reinforced. At 9.30am on 19 October the Admiralty had correctly located Scheer's force and determined its course; he was then 55nm northeast of Ameland. The next news of Scheer's location was that he was homeward bound, about 90nm northwest of Heligoland at 6pm. The British forces stood down. On this occasion the German signals intelligence centre at Neumünster correctly located British submarines positioned off the British coast and also indicated that the Humber Patrol had been recalled. Scheer concluded that the British were aware of his operation. Overall, Scheer had achieved nothing (one of his cruisers had been torpedoed on the way out). He had no idea that Jellicoe had decided to stay out of the area in which he had operated. However, he guessed that the British fleet would not be risked lightly.

The November High Seas Fleet Sortie

The High Seas Fleet sortied again early in November 1916 to cover the recovery of *U 20*, which had gone aground north of Bobjerg. This time the battleships *Grosser Kurfürst* and *Kronprinz* were both torpedoed by the British submarine *J 1* at the unusually long range of 4000 yds (two hits for four torpedoes fired). Both ships managed to remain in formation, but needed extensive repairs.[126] Until this time Scheer and Hipper were not in awe of British submarines to the extent Jellicoe was of German. With two of his destroyer flotillas detached to Flanders, Scheer could not put up

much of an anti-submarine screen for his battleships. The battleship captains proposed what might seem obvious anti-submarine measures: ships should steam at greater intervals, at higher speed and they should zig-zag with a varying mean course.[127] The Kaiser asked why the whole fleet had been risked to salvage a single submarine, which could have been saved by a single half-flotilla of torpedo boats.

In November two more battleships were due to refit and the question was whether the fleet should sortie or whether the time required to repair the two torpedoed battleships should be used to repair the rest of the fleet. Scheer decided on repairs and he despatched his battlecruisers to the Baltic for exercises. *Von der Tann* suffered a turbine problem and was not ready again until the end of December. As repairs were completed, Scheer could again consider an operation between 10 and 23 December. A planned sweep to the Skaggerak (10 December) was abandoned when *Moltke* had to drop out due to a damaged propeller shaft. Scheer also thought that Jellicoe's replacement by Admiral Beatty as Grand Fleet commander might indicate a more aggressive policy, probably involving attacks on Zeebrugge but possibly also a direct attack on the Heligoland Bight. He did not want to risk an engagement when several of his own capital ships were unavailable. Scheer was also aware of increasing British minelaying in the Bight. One of his battle squadrons returned from exercises in the Baltic during the night of 29/30 January 1917. Scheer concentrated his force in the Jade against an expected British operation against Flanders or in the Heligoland Bight.

Meanwhile the military situation in the East continued to improve, which in German eyes made it less dangerous to begin unrestricted submarine warfare. On 9 January 1917 the Kaiser approved a new campaign, to begin on 1 February. It was considered essential that raids by High Seas Fleet airships against England continue, at least in part because the air defence of the United Kingdom tied up major British resources. Since, at least in theory, operations by the High Seas Fleet tied up British naval forces which might otherwise have been devoted to ASW, Scheer could justify continuing his past operations. Now the primary roles of the High Seas Fleet were to protect U-boat transit from the Heligoland Bight; to weaken British ASW; and to attack enemy merchant shipping without warning. However, resources were required to escort U-boats out of the Bight past British submarines patrolling there. The U-boat campaign coincided roughly with the advent of effective British mines (mainly H-2s). Deliveries began in July 1917. Now Scheer had to support an intensified minesweeping programme.

In support of the war against British trade, Scheer initially planned light cruiser sweeps into the Hoofden, but they had to be called off during February due to unusually cold foggy weather. The cruisers required visibility, so instead Scheer ordered a torpedo-boat sweep (21–22 February) – which netted nothing. Another sweep had to be cancelled due to fog.

An Abortive Convoy Raid

Scheer continued to exercise his fleet in hopes that it could be employed. That had its costs: early in March the battleships *Kronprinz* and *Grosser Kurfürst* collided in the Heligoland Bight and they were not ready again until 14 May and 27 April respectively,. Despite their absence, Scheer planned a fleet sortie into the

Hoofden to attack the convoys between Holland and England. Submarines were not considered a good option because the convoys were escorted by destroyers; at this time they and the French coal convoys were the only trade convoys the Admiralty was running.[128] Scheer planned to use his battlecruisers and other scouting forces supported by two and half torpedo boat (destroyer) flotillas. They would emerge at night, sweep into the Hoofden and then as far as Lowestoft. The main body would provide distant cover. The operation would attack merchant ships (which could now be sunk on sight rather than stopped, examined and then perhaps sunk) and the fleet would then shell a British coastal town. Airship reconnaissance and also reconnaissance by aircraft from Flanders would support the fleet, but if necessary the airship element could be abandoned.[129] Scheer sent his proposed Operations Order to the Admiralstab at the end of February. Admiral von Holtzendorff was enthusiastic; neither the Flanders destroyers nor the submarines had been able to attack the Holland to England convoys.

Von Holtzendorff nonetheless felt compelled to seek the Kaiser's approval, as without air reconnaissance there might be some increased risk. Further study by the Admiralstab was not encouraging: if the Grand Fleet got word in time, it could corner the High Seas Fleet west of Terchelling, on the Dutch coast.[130] Without air reconnaissance, Scheer might well be trapped. In contrast to Jutland, there would not be any lines of submarines waiting to trap the Grand Fleet. The naval disaster the Admiralstab feared would encourage neutrals – the United States – to join the Allies. Scheer would not be permitted to come out unless he had air reconnaissance to save him from any trap. For the moment, the operation died. Visibility (the moon) limited it to the period before 12 March and Scheer was unwilling to accept the requirement for air reconnaissance, particularly since he had done well without it at Jutland. He wanted (and thought he had) absolute freedom of action. He also thought that British actions had clearly demonstrated that the Grand Fleet would not fight inside Terschelling and that given the Grand Fleet's dispersal, it could not easily concentrate in the waters involved. The Kaiser was unmoved. Since Jutland the Kaiser had often insisted on avoiding another fleet action under unfavourable conditions. Whatever Scheer might say about Jutland, the Kaiser did not consider it an unalloyed success.

Scheer suspected that von Holtzendorff and the Admiralstab now agreed with Bethmann-Hollweg and the Kaiser that the fleet should be preserved as a bargaining chip to be used during a peace conference. Alternatively, it might be saved to deal with the possibility that the British would force the Danish Straits and so enter the Baltic.[131] Scheer also feared the corrosive effect on his fleet of enforced inactivity. As for the airships, at Jutland he had done well without them, but on 19 August they had led him astray. As it was, the operation had to be abandoned because weather conditions on 11 and 12 March, the last days on which it was possible, were unfavourable to airships. Scheer sent the fleet into the Baltic for exercises. He detached a second torpedo-boat flotilla to Flanders. The exercises (and the refits of the two battleships which had collided) split up the High Seas Fleet so that it could not contemplate another fleet operation for some time.

Scheer did intend to bring the High Seas Fleet out in the event of a British attack on Flanders. In May 1917 he received credible information that British, French and American surface ships were to attack Flanders.[132] This may have been a distorted version of the plans then being made by the Dover Patrol for a landing on the Flemish coast as a prelude to an attack on Zeebrugge and Ostend. In that event Scheer planned to steam up the Dutch coast, using a swept channel he planned. He would be supported by eight airships. He would seek action at dusk in the northern exit from the Hoofden, followed by a night torpedo attack by his destroyers. The Kaiser approved, subject to Scheer being able to break off should he face superior enemy forces. 'Such ultimate hazarding of my Fleet remains subject to my own command according to the general military situation.' Nothing happened because the landing operation (described in another chapter) was never carried out and the Grand Fleet never steamed into Scheer's arms.

Meanwhile the British minelaying offensive into the Heligoland Bight intensified. Because navigation could not be precise, minelayers refreshing the field could not simply lay mines where mines had previously been laid; they had to operate just outside the earlier minefields. The mined area gradually extended out into the German Bight, further and further from Wilhelmshaven. As the minesweepers were working further and further out, groups of light cruisers had to be assigned to cover then, supported by airships and aircraft. Any High Seas Fleet operation would have required that the cruisers and airships be withdrawn (to work with the fleet). That in turn would have stopped minesweeping, which was essential if the High Seas Fleet U-boats were to proceed from their base to the sea. The Royal Navy laid only 1679 mines in the German Bight during 1916, but during 1917 it laid 15,686 of them. This was only a fraction of the field Grand Fleet commander Admiral Beatty proposed early in 1917. He wanted 60,000 mines laid over a line 157 miles long to close the entire mouth of the Heligoland Bight. This monster minefield was to be watched by destroyer and light cruiser patrols. As it was, mines were concentrated on the northern and southern exit routes from the Bight, which were used by U-boats. Scheer laid his own minefields to try to close some of these approach routes to British minelayers.

During the summer of 1917, Scheer exercised his units in the Baltic. As the British laid their minefields further and further from Heligoland, Scheer felt compelled to cover his minesweepers. On 15 September he formed a special force, with the battlecruiser *Moltke* as flagship, including two battle squadrons, to carry out mine clearance near the entrance to the Heligoland Bight.[133] Meanwhile, on 6 October most of the fleet departed for the Baltic for the seizure of the Åland Islands.

A Convoy Raid: October 1917

Scheer ordered a surface attack on a convoy to add to the U-boat war against British trade. He chose the convoy then being run to Norway and assigned the two fast minelaying cruisers *Bremse* and *Brummer* to carry out an attack between Bergen and the Shetlands. Afterwards the cruiser *Bremse* was to continue on to attack shipping west of Great Britain. If the two cruisers could not reach the convoy, they were to attack enemy surface forces in the central North Sea. The two cruisers were camouflaged to some extent by painting them in the grey used by the Royal Navy. The 17 October 1917 attack on the convoy was entirely successful; the cruisers wiped out both convoy and escort. It demonstrated that surface ships were potentially more effective than U-boats against a convoy, because they could keep up with the convoy and keep destroying it and its escort. A single U-boat could not attack more than one or two of the ships and the escort would soon drive it off. The cruisers sank the escorting destroyers; the convoy had no cruiser escort, presumably because it was not considered likely that it would encounter major German surface ships.

As usual, British signals intelligence picked up the operation and during the night of 16/17 October the cruisers intercepted British signals, mostly in clear language (one group was encrypted). They were able to deduce that the convoy was escorted by one and perhaps two, destroyers. During the attack, *Brummer* intercepted a weak wireless signal, either from a steamer in the convoy or from the destroyer *Mary Rose*. It seemed likely that British shore stations could determine the location and that the Admiralty would arrange pursuit, but initially monitoring of British signals on board the cruisers revealed nothing out of the ordinary. *Bremse* did not carry out the planned further attack due to insufficient fuel.[134]

The Minefield Battle: November 1917

Operations in the Baltic were completed at the end of October, leaving Scheer free to plan another fleet operation in the North Sea. He began with a 2–3 November mine-clearance support operation out to Horns Reef.[135] This force did not encounter the British, but a second sortie, ordered on 15 November, did. This time the German force was supported by airship reconnaissance. The minesweepers were supported by three light cruisers with destroyers and two battleships were in distant support. This time the Admiralty was aware of the operation. It decided to intercept. The Grand Fleet sent out a battlecruiser-cruiser force, with battleships in distant support (50 miles back).[136] The cruisers, including *Courageous* and *Glorious*, engaged. The fast battlecruiser *Repulse* soon arrived to support the British cruisers. She and the British cruisers broke off when the German battleships appeared. The rest of the British force never joined the battle. Later Admiral Beatty had to admit that the failure to snap up the German force was yet another disaster due to inept command and control. He claimed that his flag lieutenant Ralph Seymour had cost him victory in all four of his battles: Scarborough, Dogger Bank, Jutland and the November 1917 action. Beatty did not get a fifth opportunity. In January two of Scheer's battleships covered another mine-clearance operation, but Beatty did not pounce.

Renewed Convoy Raids

For his part, Scheer considered another cruiser raid on a convoy, but plans to carry it out between 10 and 18 December were cancelled due to weather. High Seas Fleet operations against shipping were limited to destroyer sweeps, one of which caught and destroyed a convoy. The Admiralty reinforced the escorts of the Scandinavian convoys to the point where cruiser raids became impractical. With the accession of the US Navy, the Grand Fleet now enjoyed such crushing superiority that battleships could be detached in support of the convoys. In March and April, however, Scheer mounted cruiser-destroyer raids on Scandinavian shipping, as he had in the past. They were not particularly productive.

At the beginning of 1918 the Admiralstab called for a combined effort by Scheer and by the force in Flanders to support the projected Spring 1918 offensive, which the Germans hoped would decide the war before many US troops arrived in Europe to tip the balance

HMS *Indefatigable* shortly before Jutland. Note the absence of torpedo net booms, but also of life rafts. The most obvious change since before the war is that her tall masts have been cut down to make it more difficult to distinguish her beyond the horizon. Her overall light grey paint scheme was ordered for all ships in home waters except torpedo craft on 19 November 1914, the grey to be 1 part black to 20 parts white by weight (destroyers remained dead black). This shade was chosen after experiments off Malta. The grey panel along her side was intended to suggest a ship stopped alongside, which in turn would suggest that the battlecruiser was also stopped. In effect it was the opposite of a painted bow wave. It seems to have been standard in the Battle Cruiser Force during 1915, but ships were all-grey at Jutland. Ships were ordered to paint on false bow waves on 6 April 1915, but the practice was ordered abandoned on 1 June.

against Germany. The staff did not envisage a fleet action in the Channel, but rather a battle in the Hoofden. This was what Scheer had envisaged the previous year. Scheer was already interested in using the High Seas Fleet against shipping, in this case a convoy in northern waters. If that succeeded, the fleet might also attack shipping to the west, between Ireland and England. As earlier, he envisaged an attack by his battlecruisers, with his battleships in distant support. The Flanders U-boats were to attack British transports bringing reinforcements to the planned battle in France, which began in April 1918. This time Scheer had a newly-completed seaplane carrier to provide him with organic air reconnaissance. He planned a fleet attack on the Norwegian convoy for 24 April.

This time Scheer appears to have maintained secrecy; the Admiralty was apparently unaware that he was coming out.[137] This seems to have been the first German fleet operation which British signals intelligence missed. However, the British had stationed four submarines in the Heligoland Bight specifically to warn that the High Seas Fleet was coming out. *J* 6 was particularly well placed and she spotted the ships. Unfortunately her captain did not recognise them as German; he thought the destroyers and light cruisers were British ships returning from laying mines. When he spotted the German battlecruisers he dismissed them as yet another support operation for minesweeping. Scheer seemed to be in luck. The weather even favoured airship reconnaissance. Then things went wrong. The battlecruiser *Moltke* suffered such serious machinery damage that she had to be towed home. Her starboard inner turbine exploded and she took on 2000 tons of water. Initially her captain tried to maintain secrecy by signalling only by searchlight. However, salvage arrangements had to be made by wireless – which Scheer had to assume the British had intercepted. However, for a time he remained on course.

The German signals intelligence organisation told him that the target Norway convoy of thirty (actually thirty-four) lightly-escorted ships was to have left for England on the previous day, but then that was corrected to the 24th. Scheer still had his whole fleet, except for *Moltke* and the battleship *Oldenburg*, which was towing her home. However, he did not want to loiter until the convoy turned up; he turned back for home. *J 6* saw part of his fleet return to base. *Moltke* herself was torpedoed by another British submarine as she approached port.

The signals from *Moltke* seem to have been the first clear indication to the Admiralty, hence to the Grand Fleet, that the High Seas Fleet was at sea and the Admiralty reacted instantly, particularly to the threat to shipping in the northern part of the North Sea. Scheer could argue that this reaction alone would have kept the target convoy in port.

On 11 August Scheer replaced Admiral von Holtzendorff as chief of the Admiralstab. Slightly later the Admiralstab was given the executive authority it had lacked from the outset. In theory the Imperial Navy finally had a unified command and Scheer could finally make the U-boat war the clear priority of the entire service. Scheer's scouting commander Admiral Hipper took over as commander of the High Seas Fleet. Through October most High Seas Fleet activities in the North Sea were sorties in support of mine clearance. There was no attempt to interfere with the laying of the North Sea Barrage.

The Grand Fleet After Jutland

After Jutland the Royal Navy energetically addressed the issues Jutland raised. For gunnery the key problem was that opportunities would likely be fleeting, part of the solution being an entirely new way of firing, spotting and correcting the fall of shot. Another part was much greater effort devoted to concentration fire, so that more ships would make use of such fleeting opportunities. The visible marks of this effort were bearing markings on turrets and range dials on masts, so that ships in a group could match the bearing and range used by one ship which could see the target. An invisible element was a new Type 31 wireless set intended specifically to handle gunnery concentration information. Given few opportunities, each hit had to do much more damage, so an enormous effort was mounted to improve armour-piercing shells. These shells were intended to immobilise German battleships so that fire could be poured onto them.

Pending development of the new shells and improved gunnery technique, the experience of Jutland suggested that the balance between gun and torpedo should change. Jellicoe's first post-Jutland Grand Fleet Battle Orders drew attention to 'the vital importance of seizing every possible opportunity for firing torpedoes from our own ships (battleships to light cruisers inclusive). When in line ahead, alterations of course of not more than a point may be made by ships to enable torpedoes to be fired, speed being increased to keep the ship abreast of her station in line and to allow her to resume it without hampering her next astern'.[138] The new emphasis on torpedo attacks by the fleet shows in the change in British light cruiser armament to massive torpedo batteries (typically twelve above-water tubes). Similar language appeared in the revised Battlecruiser Orders.

Note that Jellicoe was not reversing his position that he needed his destroyers mainly to beat off German destroyer attacks.

However, in destroyer instructions issued in November 1916, he wrote that the best counter to mass German destroyer attacks was for the British destroyer force to attack the German battlefleet with torpedoes first, so the British flotillas should attack as soon as the heavy ships were engaged. They should not attack first, because they would be driven off by the gunfire of the German heavy ships and cruisers. Once those ships were engaged by the British battle line, they would be unable to devote much attention to the attacking British destroyers.[139]

A key assumption in 1916–17 was that the Germans had 15,000 yd torpedoes, which defined the area the British fleet should try to avoid (in fact their long-range setting for standard [50cm] torpedoes was about 11,000 yds at 28.5 knots).[140] Beginning in 1916, a few German ships had 60cm torpedoes which could reach 15,000m (16,400 yds) at 28 knots. Beginning in 1915, Admiral Jellicoe had pressed for longer torpedo range and in 1916 a 15,000 yd setting was introduced. In 1917 the 21in Mk IV* torpedo had an 18,000 yd setting (21 knots). A new Mk V was conceived as a 15,000 yd weapon (29 knots), although the speed had to be reduced when air flask pressure was reduced. A further Mk VI torpedo was intended to reach 18,000 yds at 29 knots, but to achieve that performance it had to be lengthened, hence could not fit existing tubes. It failed its trials, but work proceeded on longer-range weapons. In 1918 a requirement was approved for a weapon which could reach 20,000 yds at 30 knots. To reduce resistance in the water, it had to be fatter (relatively shorter than a conventional torpedo). The new weapon emerged as the 24.5in torpedo on board the *Nelson*s. The need for really long range led the British to investigate an oxygen cycle after the war – and it inspired the Japanese in their own development of the 'Long Lance' of the Second World War.

As C-in-C Grand Fleet, Beatty issued new Grand Fleet Battle Instructions in January 1918.[141] He wanted to deploy athwart the course of the enemy, a return to earlier principles from Jellicoe's stated desire to deploy on parallel course, but what Jellicoe had actually done at Jutland. He also stated explicitly that he wanted to bring his weight to bear on part of the enemy fleet, to destroy it and thus throw the rest into confusion. This intent fitted the extensive work on concentration of fire. Range should be within 12in gun range but outside the danger range defined by enemy 15,000 yd torpedoes. Although the goal was to annihilate the whole enemy fleet, that might be impossible due, for example, to failing light (as at Jutland) or the vicinity of minefields. In that case it would be better to concentrate fire on part of the enemy's line, such as his rear, rather than to dilute it and let the enemy escape. Some of the enemy ships would have to be left unengaged.

Beatty's version of decentralisation was to retain control over the general movement of the fleet. Upon joining action, flag officers commanding battle squadrons and divisions were given full power to manoeuvre 'whilst conforming generally to the movements of the C-in-C'. In the event they did not receive his instructions, the commanders of the battlecruiser force and the 5th Battle Squadron in the van would have to decide on which flank of the battle fleet to proceed to as the fleet deployed, guided by the requirement that they always stay within mutual supporting range and within supporting distance of the main body, 'and should not come under the fire of the enemy battle fleet before it is fully engaged by our battlefleet'. That reflected Beatty's own experience at the outset of Jutland, when the *Queen Elizabeth*s were within supporting range of

'Windy Corner' at Jutland, the 5th Battle Squadron (*Queen Elizabeth* class battleships) turning one by one to run north with the battlecruisers back towards the Grand Fleet. This was the conclusion of the 'run south', in which Admiral Beatty's force chased the German battlecruisers back to the German High Seas Fleet. Remarkably, the *Queen Elizabeth*s survived, even though for a time *Warspite* had her steering disabled and simply circled in front of the German battle fleet. To support Beatty as he ran north towards the Grand Fleet, Admiral Jellicoe detached his own fast division (Admiral Hood's 3rd Battlecruiser Squadron, substituting in his fleet for the *Queen Elizabeth*s). Hood's appearance screened Jellicoe's deployment. He also forced the German 3rd Battle Squadron towards the east, preventing it from possibly crossing Jellicoe's 'T' (though no one was aware of that possibility at the time). Both before and after the battle, Beatty tried in vain to have the *Queen Elizabeth*s transferred to his own battlecruiser force. (Painting by W L Wyllie, PW2238 © National Maritime Museum, London)

his own ships, but they and the battlecruisers were very much under the full fire of the High Seas Fleet without any direct support from the British main body, still far away.

In striking contrast to Jellicoe, Beatty wrote that although he would try to stay out of German torpedo range, he would close in if that cost him gunfire effectiveness and he would turn towards a retiring enemy. Whatever happened, the Germans had to kept under fire. If that put them in position to fire torpedoes, ships would evade (torpedo tracks had proven quite visible) and then resume firing. They would generally turn towards the enemy rather than away (as at Jutland) to avoid running out of gun range. Flag officers of divisions under torpedo threat should always seek to stay within gun range, so they could keep up the pressure on the Germans. Beatty made explicit reference to a possible signal ordering 'engage the enemy more closely' (the signal he wanted to make at Dogger Bank, but could not), in which case 'the torpedo menace is to be disregarded and every effort made to close to decisive gun range'. Beatty hoped that light cruisers and destroyers in the van of the fleet (and the fleet's own anti-destroyer guns) could beat off German destroyer attacks, but if the German destroyers did reach launch positions, ships should evade (turn towards) and keep firing at the German battle line.

As in Jellicoe's instructions, British destroyers were to attack once the Germans were firing, hence could not concentrate on them. They had to be placed so that, in attacking, they did not open the British line to German torpedo attacks. That placed them in the van of the British fleet, turning in the direction of the British van (which should parallel the German) when firing their browning shots. If the Germans attacked first, the British destroyers would beat them off and then proceed to make their own torpedo attacks.

The Final Operation

As the German military position deteriorated in the autumn of 1918, High Seas Fleet chief of staff Rear Admiral von Trotha proposed a final operation.[142] What should the fleet do if the U-boat campaign were stopped? Up to this point, the vital role of the fleet had been to support the U-boats, largely by keeping their paths through the Heligoland Bight clear. If the enemy could operate freely in the German Bight or in the Belt; or if the U-boat war had to be abandoned; or if the British succeeded in mastering the U-boats; or if the fleet faced a shameful end (*i.e.*, surrender), the fleet should fight a final and fatal battle as its highest goal, so that it could justify itself to the nation after the war. Only in that case could a new fleet arise in the future. Von Trotha and Scheer's former fleet operations officer Captain von Levetzow worked out details in Berlin beginning on 16 October and the plan had been elaborated by 20 October. That day the German government acceded to President Wilson's demand that U-boat attacks on passenger ships cease. On 22 October Scheer told General Ludendorff, who at that point was in effect the German government, that it was essential that the fleet act before becoming a bargaining chip in any peace settlement. The U-boats had all been released from the war against shipping and an armistice was imminent. The fleet must above all prove its value to the German nation. Operating in conjunction with U-boats, it might reverse the situation in home waters.[143]

The plan envisaged a sortie into the English Channel.[144] Hipper agreed that its goal was a final battle against the Grand Fleet. He expected to fight off Terschelling on the Dutch coast. Preparations included laying (by U-boat) a large minefield intended to close off Scapa Flow (the British detected and swept it). The operations order was issued on 27 October, to begin on 29 October (later 30 October). The fleet was to steam out of the German Bight out of sight of the Dutch coast during the day. It would pass through the Hoofden to attack the Flanders coast and the mouth of the Thames as the second stage of the operation.[145] These operations were calculated to draw out the Grand Fleet. Upon their completion, the High Seas Fleet would turn back towards Terschelling. Meanwhile mines would be laid in the path the Grand Fleet would likely take. Hopefully the pursuing Grand Fleet could be caught in a night action allowing extensive torpedo boat attacks. In addition, six lines of U-boats were arranged so that the Grand Fleet would be forced to cross them.

This final operation was never executed. When it was time to sail on 30 October, crews mutinied; eventually nearly the whole of the High Seas Fleet was affected. The mutineers charged that their officers were intent on committing suicide (and killing them in the process) to save their honour. After the war, a German officer described the plan as nothing more than a limited attempt to help the army in Flanders. By that time the mutiny had spread and it must have seemed that the German civil war which had loomed in 1914 had broken out. The plan above, from the post-Second World War final volume of the German official history, can hardly be described as an attempt to help the German army in Flanders, but it is also more than an attempt at a spectacular naval suicide.

An Alternative: Attack at Source

Because they could be delivered by small agile craft (motor boats or aircraft), torpedoes offered the Royal Navy the possibility of destroying the High Seas Fleet at its base. In July 1915, three junior officers of the Harwich Force suggested that a fast lightweight boat carrying a torpedo could be taken near its target on a cruiser's davits.[146] Commodore Tyrwhitt considered the difficulties of transporting the boats to the vicinity of an enemy harbour considerably less than those of convoying seaplane carriers. Each light cruiser could carry at least two in her davits, which would not have to be modified. In Tyrwhitt's view 'there seems to be enormous scope for vessels of really high speed such as those mentioned, whose draught is practically nil and whose speed is 30 knots and upwards and if these are manned by resolute and determined officers there

appears to be no reason why the enemy's innermost harbours should not be penetrated and their ships sunk at their moorings'. The idea was inspired by the exploits of ships' picket boats in the Dardanelles, which could get remarkably close to their objectives despite heavy defensive fire and their low speed. The proposal was to employ not the two boats used in the Dardanelles, but twenty, with more than twice the speed of the picket boats. Given their very shallow draught, speedboats could pass over mudbanks along the German coast, which were not defended because they were considered impassable.

The Admiralty had received earlier proposals, which it had rejected on the ground that on releasing so great a weight as a torpedo, the lightweight boat would become unstable; the flimsiness of the boat might also be a problem. However, the Admiralty was open to the idea and in September 1915 it asked for a more detailed proposal. The three officers wrote back in September, offering a rough design. They estimated that a 28ft boat could carry one 14in torpedo, a 33ft boat one 18in and a 40–50ft boat one 21in or two 14in. They recognised that firing the torpedo was the great problem, as it could not go over the bow rising steeply out of the water at high speed. They originated the idea of launching the torpedo tail-first, so that the boat would not have to swerve before firing.

The most senior of the three, Lt C C B Hampden (HMS *Lookout*), made private arrangements with Thornycroft to conduct experiments. The Admiralty was sufficiently impressed that in mid-November he was told to communicate directly with HMS *Vernon*, the torpedo development establishment, so that one of its representatives could witness them. At this point Thornycroft considered 32ft the minimum length of a boat carrying an 18in torpedo. As 30ft was the maximum length of a boat which could be carried inboard by a light cruiser, such boats would have to be carried outboard. That was no problem, as the operation had to be conducted in fine weather. Initially (November 1915) it seemed that a Thornycroft 34ft design would be very satisfactory. Anson carried out what amounted to a proof-of-concept trial on 8

Targets moved in and out of the mist during the battle of Jutland, prompting post-battle interest in ways of communicating target data from ship to ship. HMS *Royal Oak* and HMS *Hercules* are shown, with other ships barely visible on the horizon.

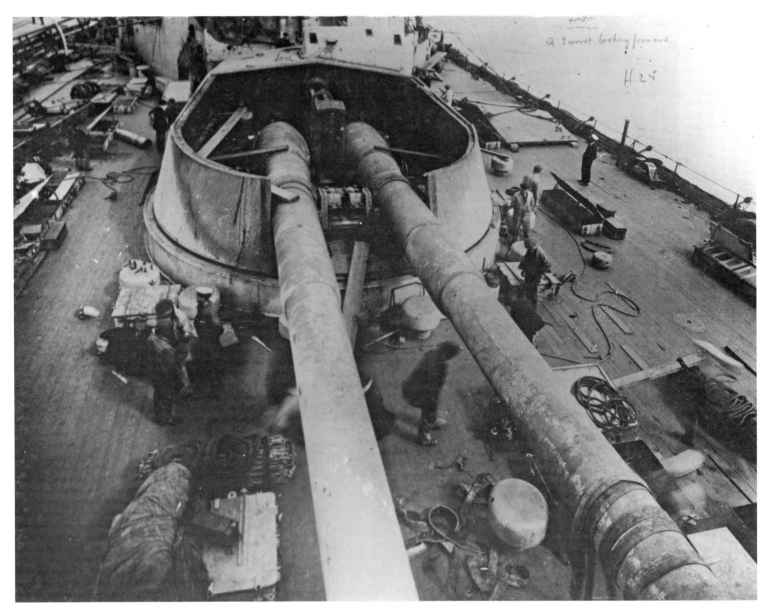

Some British battlecruisers survived considerable damage at Jutland. 'Q' turret of HMS *Lion* had its roof blown off but its magazine saved by timely flooding. In effect this was proof that ships which did not engage in suicidal magazine practices were difficult to destroy. The effect of flash on a turret containing too many charges would have been far too quick for any sort of counteraction to work. (RAN)

November and described his scheme in detail to the Fourth Sea Lord. The main objection at the time was that the boat could not make full speed carrying the weight of an 18in torpedo; Lt Hampden showed that it could by loading down the 28ft Thornycroft hydroplane *Carsena* with the weight of a 14in torpedo. She managed 25 knots. The Admiralty agreed to a test with a Thornycroft 34ft boat; the firm offered either the privately-owned *Crusader* or a new 34ft test boat. Hampden was immediately transferred to *Vernon* for special duties, to conduct the test and develop the new weapon. Initial trials (reported 3 January 1916) were conducted using a 12-knot motor boat from the air department. Hampden thought that with so slow a boat the torpedo would not take its depth properly, but the experiment was more successful than expected (depth-taking was crucial, because if the torpedo initially dove too deeply it would probably bury itself in

harbour-bottom mud). Thornycroft was prepared to guarantee 30 knots with the full expected load, including the single torpedo.

As of the beginning of January 1916, Thornycroft already had a boat of the type proposed in hand; the firm expected that it would be ready in eight to ten weeks, although the engine might take longer. To solve that problem, Hampden proposed to borrow a 250hp Green engine from the Royal Navy Air Department. Tyrwhitt urged approval of the project. The Admiralty asked Tyrwhitt to discuss the project, noting that Hampden had pointed to advantages over the alternative of dropping torpedoes from seaplanes. First Sea Lord had qualms; he wrote that he saw many weak points in the project. However, at a 25 January 1916 conference it was decided that twelve Hydroplanes (to be called 'submarine vedettes') should be based near the Blackwater River for Hampden's operation.

Thornycroft began the prototype boat (*CMB 1*) as a private venture, but the Admiralty soon bought and ordered the other eleven well before the prototype had been completed.[147] Thornycroft seems to have been responsible for the method of launching a torpedo at high speed: ramming it backwards down a stern trough. The torpedo took a short time to accelerate to full speed, giving the boat time to clear it.

The twelve boats were ready by August 1916 and Tyrwhitt prepared a plan for Operation 'MB'.[148] The chief requirements were fine weather (so that the boats could operate) and the turn of the tide to be within two hours, so there was enough water in the Schillig Roads. The force would arrive at the jump-off point (Position Y) $4^1/2$ hours before sunrise; the CMBs would take three hours to get to the scene of the attack and another half hour to carry it out. They would then run 65 miles to the pick-up point (Position X), where the light cruisers would recover them an hour after sunrise. The plan allowed for a fall-back recovery position in the event the CMBs arrived before the light cruisers. If enemy action made the post-attack runs impossible, the CMBs would make for either Denmark or Holland, both neutral and intern themselves if they did not encounter British ships on the way.

A copy of the operation order was forwarded to Admiral Jellicoe for his comments. He concurred generally, but wanted a strong submarine force to cover the retirement of the CMBs and of the Harwich Force, as he could not provide a strong covering force from the Grand Fleet. Among other things, he cautioned that the enemy was generally aware when his fleet left harbour, hence its use would break the secrecy essential to the operation. Tyrwhitt issued a revised operation order on 2 September and further refinements on 15 October. Meanwhile Tyrwhitt had asked for permission to carry out a rehearsal on 9 September. The Admiralty formally approved the operation on 17 October. The only missing element was air reconnaissance, to indicate which ships were in the Schillig Roads and where they were.[149] Not long after Scheer's October 1916 sortie, on the night of 21/22 October, the Force convoyed the seaplane carrier *Vindex* into position for exactly this purpose.

The Germans saw a single British aircraft overhead. They were unable to find and attack the British carrier force, even though their airships spotted some of its ships. It happened that thick fog precluded effective air reconnaissance, so the carrier operation was in vain (one of the British seaplanes landed on the water off Heligoland in hopes of seeing something). There was no further air reconnaissance and for the time being the CMB project died. The Germans assumed that the air operation was another attack on the airship sheds, as part of a counter to Zeppelin raids on England.

This failure did not kill the project, which had to be postponed until fine weather returned the next year. In the interim, the CMBs were reassigned to the Dover Patrol, four of them to Dunkirk. In April 1917, CMBs were waiting outside Zeebrugge when it was bombed to force the German destroyers out. They claimed two German destroyers.[150] After that the force at Dunkirk was doubled and regular night patrols begun up the coast as far as Zeebrugge. CMBs torpedoed other German ships over the next few months, but did not sink any. By May, thirteen boats were assigned to the Dover Patrol, based at Queensborough (and then Dover) and at Dunkirk.[151] Their duties included minelaying off Zeebrugge and Ostend. A larger 55-footer, which could not be carried by a cruiser, was developed specifically to operate in the North Sea.[152]

A Coastal Motor Boat Committee reported on 1 September 1917. It divided roles into (A) base raiding, the original function; (B) minelaying; and (C) ASW. Of these, (B) meant laying mines near Zeebrugge and Ostend and other German bases. (C) meant sprint-and-drift ASW using directional hydrophones, in co-operation with trawlers. To get to their targets, boats conducting (A) operations had to be carried on board larger ships. Light cruisers could carry 40-footers. Fast merchant ships (or specially-

The German battlecruiser *Seydlitz* was nearly sunk both at Dogger Bank and at Jutland; she is shown at Wilhelmshaven on 6 June 1916, the guns of her burned-out 'A' turret having been removed. German magazine practices apparently ensured that, while a turret might be burned out by a hit, the magazine below would not explode. Several ships suffered such damage at Jutland. There is no evidence that magazine practices were changed to reflect the experience at Dogger Bank, except perhaps for the decision to issue gas masks to crews. (Naval Institute collection)

built CMB carriers) might carry the more formidable 55-footers, which could be armed with two rather than one 18in torpedoes. To raid the Belgian coast, a boat should carry either a torpedo and a depth charge or two submarine-type (S4) mines or 'O' type floating mines. That was a 55-footer. Similarly, ASW demanded a 55-footer, which could carry either a torpedo and four D type depth charges, or six Type D, or two mines. Ultimately the 55-footers with the most powerful engines went to the Dover Patrol, boats with less powerful engines being reserved for ASW.

The Committee decided that all twelve 40ft boats in the Dover Patrol should be allocated to Harwich for overseas (*i.e.*, Heligoland Bight) strike operations. The 40-footers in the Dover Patrol would be relieved by 55-footers. That brought up the question of a permanent CMB carrier, as opposed to the Harwich cruisers, which could carry CMBs for particular operations. The cruiser *Diamond* (or a similar ship) could be modified to carry six CMBs (she was soon modified). However, a specially-designed carrier might also support 55ft CMBs, which were much more formidable than the 40-footers. She would be a fast merchant ship not suitable for cargo-carrying (*i.e.*, not desperately needed to make up for tonnage being lost to U-boats). As for the 40-footers, they had seen considerable service during 1917 and needed thorough overhauls. They could not therefore be used offensively before undergoing at least a month's refit, by which time the weather would prohibit operations. Thus any Harwich CMB raids would be deferred until 1918.

The final gun action of the war was second Heligoland (15 November 1917), in which a British cruiser force attacked German minesweepers and was itself intercepted by increasingly powerful German ships. HMS *Calypso* is shown. (Painting by W L Wyllie, PW1812 © National Maritime Museum, London)

The larger 55ft boats would be used in the North Sea, both to deal with submarines, to raid the Belgian coast and to lay mines there: twenty-four for the Dover Patrol (Dover and Dunkirk), twenty at Portland and eight at a sub-base at Portsmouth (with other sub-bases at Torquay and Newlyn). The Dover boats would attack Zeebrugge and Ostend and ships using those bases; lay mines off those bases; and protect the Downs and Dunkirk Roads from any enemy CMBs when they might appear. All of these boats had to be fast (38 knots minimum). There was no immediate need for more 55-footers, but higher-powered engines were under consideration.

There was also an urgent requirement for remote-controlled explosive boats for experimentation (Distant Controlled Boats, DCBs), the Germans already having employed such craft on the Belgian coast. CMBs were wanted only because they offered the requisite speed. The 40-footer was preferred because, already having seen considerable service, it was considered expendable. They also cost less than half as much as a 55-footer. Overall, a CMB was not considered suitable because a DCB would be loaded with explosive in her bow, weighing it down; the only compensating weight in a CMB was the engine, which would have to be moved aft. Four 40-footers were ordered converted, to be replaced at once by new boats so that Harwich could have a full raiding complement of twelve.[153]

C-in-C Mediterranean asked for twelve boats immediately and the Committee agreed that they would be of considerable value, but it wanted them thoroughly tried in Home Waters before going abroad and it also thought it preferable to build any Mediterranean boats abroad. Thornycroft was willing to suggest suitable builders. The Committee recommended revisiting this question in six weeks.

At about the same time Plans Division estimated numbers which might be available to raid the Heligoland Bight.[154] By the end of 1917 twelve 55-footers would have relieved the 40-footers at Dover, eight of which would have been thoroughly overhauled. If Dover were denuded, twenty boats would be available. By March, all twenty-four 55-footers would have been delivered, so thirty-two boats in all would be available (this omitted the four to be converted into DCBs). Plans Division assumed that suitable carriers could be found for 55-footers, each ideally carrying no more than six boats. By March four such ships would be needed. Alternatively, the lighters designed to carry Large America seaplanes might be adapted to carry 55-footers instead.

Possible North Sea objectives would be Zeebrugge and Ostend (easily raided, but targets were mostly inside the locks); Emden (probably mostly inside, but near England); Heligoland (numerous submarines, torpedo craft, etc always in the outer and inner war harbours and torpedoes could be fired into the harbour through the entrance); Kiel (too far away), Cuxhaven (submarines), the Lister Deep (submarines and destroyers), Hamburg (too far up the Elbe), Bremerhaven (unlikely that ships would be found there), Wilhelmshaven (the duty ships of the High Seas Fleet were believed to lie in Schillig Roads). Mediterranean objectives were Cattaro (difficult due to the long narrow entrance) and Pola (ships in the outer anchorage, which might include Austrian battleships). In Home Waters Wilhelmshaven was the best target, with Heligoland also attractive. Plans Division proposed an attack by the end of the year.

Now that he was to get his CMBs back, in the autumn of 1917 Tyrwhitt revived the idea of a CMB strike, this time by six CMBs aboard three light cruisers (later reduced to two, as only four CMBs were available), escorted by a division of destroyers.[155] This time the target was the German light cruisers anchored off the Ems. This operation was not carried out, but in January 1918 the Admiralty held a conference on possible CMB attacks. In May 1918 Tyrwhitt reminded the Admiralty that enemy ships constantly cruised near and sometimes anchored in positions accessible to his cruiser-borne CMBs. He must have been somewhat frustrated when Plans Division asked which of his cruisers could carry CMBs, as he had pointed out on several previous occasions that all them could do so, two per ship. In June, Plans Division proposed that the raid on the Schillig Roads be Tyrwhitt's first priority and that it be co-ordinated with Grand Fleet and submarine action. It estimated that the earliest time, counting training time and numbers available, would be 5 August. Among other things, it suggested that CMB officers acquire experience by operating off the Belgian coast. By this time, a total of eight modern light cruisers had been fitted to carry CMBs in place of their boats.[156]

Plans Division had little influence on the Admiralty. Tyrwhitt executed Operation 'CMB 1' on 30 June 1918, a sweep into the Heligoland Bight. Another element was added: Large America seaplanes towed by destroyers on fast lighters incorporating slipways.[157] They could be used, at Tyrwhitt's discretion, either to locate the enemy or to assist in recovery of the CMBs at the end of the operation. Six CMBs were used. The CMBs spotted a U-boat, which dived before it could be attacked. They attacked two German minesweepers, torpedoing one. They also sighted three German destroyers, but could not attack due to daylight (the destroyers would have evaded their torpedoes) and to a shortage of fuel. All returned safely. Of the three Large Americas, one partially carried out the planned patrol, but was lost when one of its engines failed while it was flying at low altitude. The other two failed to take off; one sank and the other was shipped back onto its barge. Tyrwhitt reported that the weather had been ideal and he thought the only mistake had been in starting too close to sunrise. By this time it was at least as important to attack U-boats as German surface ships, so he suggested that in future CMBs be paired, one armed with a torpedo and the other with four depth charges. That would deal with the submarine which dived. The CMBs performed excellently, but the seaplanes were a let-down. They had apparently been overloaded.

Tyrwhitt executed Operation 'CMB 2' (four rather than six CMBs) on 7/8 July. This time they saw nothing. The sea was again too rough for the seaplanes. Operation 'CMB 3' was carried out on the night of 17/18 July, but one of the four CMBs was lost in unexpectedly rough weather. No enemy ship was seen due to poor visibility. Operation 'CMB 4' (six CMBs, two with depth charges) was mounted on 1 August 1918, beginning at 6.15am rather than before dawn. This time the seaplanes were able to take off. A Zeppelin spotted the force and dropped bombs near some of the ships. Although no enemy ships were encountered, the commander of one pair of CMBs concluded that 'CMBs have a much more interesting time in daylight and, as long as modern enemy craft are not encountered in numbers, should have a good chance of bringing off a successful attack'.

This was encouraging, so on 11 August the Harwich Force conducted Operation 'CMB 5', the object of which was to attack enemy sweepers and other surface craft. The attack on the sweepers was important as a way of maintaining the mine barrage of the Heligoland Bight. This operation was considerably less successful, all six boats being lost. The force included three destroyers each towing a seaplane lighter and two each towing a Camel fighter on a lighter. Weather was ideal, but without any wind the seaplanes were unable to take off. Tyrwhitt considered that acceptable because seaplanes from Yarmouth were due over his force. They failed to intercept four German seaplanes and did not understand Tyrwhitt's signal that they should meet the returning CMBs. One of the Camels shot down a Zeppelin which turned up. Its pilot homed on frequent smoke screens made by the cruisers and both he and his aircraft were picked up.[158] Visibility from the surface was remarkable (the Zeppelin was seen 50 miles away), but from the air it was very poor (the Camel did not see the force until it was two miles away).

The CMBs were less successful. The first indication of trouble was that they failed to turn up at the rendezvous. Tyrwhitt sent out cruiser-destroyer groups to search for them and he tried to get the seaplanes off. He then reported to the Admiralty and asked for seaplanes from Yarmouth. He was unable to tell them about the five seaplanes he saw, which frequently attacked his force, 'confirming my opinion that the means of communication between seaplanes and ships leaves a lot to be desired'. The Admiralty took the problem quite seriously and asked both for an air-sea communication exercise over Harwich and for the RAF to provide an explanation of its failure. Had the seaplanes covered the CMBs, they would have survived.

German aircraft broke up the operation. The CMB commanders suspected that the Germans had spotted the wash (wake) of the CMBs. First, three German bombers were seen right astern (running up the wakes), followed by three more on the port bow and then by two more. The CMBs took up a pre-arranged anti-aircraft formation (close order, to concentrate fire). Initially the boats' machine guns kept the aircraft out of effective machine gun range (bombs could be dodged) and they kept on course in hopes of finding enemy ships. However, more enemy aircraft appeared, ammunition ran out and guns jammed. At that point the boats ran for the Dutch coast, to be destroyed before their crews went ashore (the Dutch seized *CMB 41*, *CMB 44* and *CMB 48*). The Germans showed their contempt for Dutch neutrality by strafing one of the boats for a quarter-hour after she had been beached on Dutch soil.

Operation 'CMB 6' was proposed in September 1918 but considerably modified. Possibly because it now involved the separate

Once the United States entered the war, its large fleet (the second most powerful in the world as recently as 1906, before the rise of the German fleet) joined the British. Here the US 6th Battle Squadron, led by USS *New York*, arrives at Scapa Flow on 7 December 1917 (as photographed from the fleet flagship *Queen Elizabeth*). Note that the US battleship already has British-style anti-rangefinding baffles on her cage masts and a false bow wave intended to make it difficult for a U-boat commander to estimate her speed. The baffles were soon eliminated; they do not appear in photos of the ships on patrol in the North Sea. With the arrival of these ships, the Royal Navy was able to transfer the two dreadnoughts *Superb* and *Temeraire* to the Mediterranean. At the end of the war the 6th Battle Squadron consisted of USS *New York* (flagship), *Arkansas*, *Florida*, *Texas* and *Wyoming*. Three more US battleships were based at Berehaven in Ireland to counter possible German battlecruiser raids into the Atlantic: USS *Utah*, *Nevada* and *Oklahoma*.

RAF, it became more and more elaborate. Thus the initial six CMBs became eight (two spares). The three towed seaplane lighters became four, three for F2A seaplanes detached from Felixstowe, one to recover an F2A from a co-operating group of four to six F2As from Yarmouth (and to provide fuel for Yarmouth seaplanes). An additional flight of six F2As from Felixstowe was added. The two Camel lighters became three and then four. Two of the Camels might be used to support the seaplanes. Plans included deliberately breaking W/T silence to draw out hostile aircraft so the Camels could destroy them. A final Operation Order was submitted on 15 October and immediately approved by the Admiralty. Tyrwhitt went to sea on 18 October, but the weather was unsuitable and he returned to port. Only the air reconnaissance was carried out. No further CMB operations were proposed before the war ended, but note that the air attack which ended CMB 5 did not end interest in such attacks. In addition to the 40- and 55-footers, a 70-footer was designed specifically for minelaying off the Belgian coast, as an ASW measure.[159]

The CMBs were conceived as an alternative to torpedo-carrying seaplanes. When war broke out in 1914, Commodore Murray Sueter, heading the Royal Naval Air Service, proposed an air strike against the High Seas Fleet. He asked for (and received) three fast Channel packets for conversion into seaplane carriers. Sueter proposed first to reconnoitre Kiel and Wilhelmshaven to be sure of where the High Seas Fleet was and then to strike it. Unfortunately existing seaplanes could not lift even small torpedoes from the sea. When a British seaplane finally did torpedo a ship (in the Dardanelles in 1915), the seaplane did so after it

landed. There was a good reason why CMBs seemed a far better bet in 1915.

What changed for aircraft was the advent of a flying-off platform on the Grand Fleet carrier *Campania*. A seaplane on a wheeled dolly could roll down it to take off, even though weather conditions would have prevented it from lifting from the sea. By late 1916 there was an improved seaplane capable of delivering a new lightweight 18in torpedo. There was also a design for a landplane torpedo bomber which could fly off a carrier.[160] Captain Sueter finally had the weapon he had envisaged in 1914. He argued that the two obvious targets for these aircraft were the High Seas Fleet and the Austrian Fleet. A practice run against HMS *Dreadnought* showed that a properly-handled torpedo bomber was difficult to hit. Sueter imagined that both his targets could be attacked during the summer of 1917, presumably by seaplanes. He pointed out that at Gallipoli a makeshift Short torpedo bomber had successfully torpedoed two ships and that the officer who had accomplished that was now in his department.

This was rather ambitious; in December 1916 only ten torpedo seaplanes were on order and the torpedo land plane had not yet flown. Director of Air Services doubted that it would be so very easy to attack Wilhelmshaven with slow (66-knot) torpedo seaplanes; the Austrians at Pola might be an easier proposition. Ultimately Sueter was offered command of a torpedo force in the Adriatic, which would operate from the Italian coast. The difficulties of transporting a large seaplane force to within striking distance of Wilhelmshaven made that attack impossible.

The Wilhelmshaven option came back to life when the landplane torpedo bomber, the Sopwith Cuckoo, became available. Production was ordered in August 1917. At this stage the point was that such an aircraft could reliably deliver a torpedo, not whether it could be recovered after attacking. The first proposal for a torpedo bomber strike from a carrier seems to have been made by Captain A V Vyvyan (Director of Air Services) to Fifth Sea Lord on 30 August 1917, responding to Admiral Beatty's complaint earlier in the month that there was no definite air policy, including no torpedo bomber policy.[161] The Germans were already attacking ships in the North Sea with seaplane torpedo bombers; surely at some point the Grand Fleet would have to face them.[162]

'At the close of an engagement, in the failing light, an attack delivered by, say, 24 such craft approaching from the East would be very effective and would be hard to counter.' So would an attack mounted by the Grand Fleet: 'an attack at dawn on ships at anchor in Cuxhaven, Schillig Roads, or other enemy bases could hardly fail to have results'. The new *Argus* had the desired capacity, but she was too slow to work with battlecruisers. Vyvyan proposed that she be armed only with torpedo bombers and to hold her both for strikes and as a landing platform for the fleet's fighters, which otherwise were one-shot aircraft. *Argus* might open or close action using her torpedo bombers.

Beatty was clearly impressed, but he took Vyvyan's ideas a step further. On 11 September he submitted a paper to the Admiralty describing a torpedo bomber strike against the High Seas Fleet.[163] It says a great deal for how quickly this kind of technology could be developed that Beatty hoped to carry out his attack by the spring of 1918. By this time 100 Cuckoos were on order, with delivery expected to begin in April 1918 and to continue at the rate of ten per week. In addition, 200 torpedoes had been ordered. Their 170lb warhead (weight limited by the carrying capacity of the Cuckoo) was unlikely to inflict mortal damage on a capital ship.

Beatty saw his attack as a vital step in the anti-submarine war. All attempts to block the U-boat bases in the Heligoland Bight were futile as long as the Germans could remove whatever obstacles, such as mines, the British placed. That in turn was possible only because the High Seas Fleet stood behind the minesweepers and other craft keeping the exits from the bases open. Destroy the High Seas Fleet and the U-boat bases could be blocked permanently. A mass torpedo bomber attack could do just that. As Beatty envisaged it, the attack should be made by waves of forty bombers each (total force at least 121 bombers), launched from a point an hour's flying time from Wilhelmshaven. He understood that the new torpedo bomber could fly at 90 mph, with an endurance of $3^{1}/_{2}$ to 4 hours. Each bomber could carry a gun in addition to its torpedo if flown by a lightweight pilot. Having dropped its torpedoes, each wave would defend the next against enemy aircraft. The returning aircraft would fly to a set rendezvous in the lee of the Dutch coast, where they would meet the carriers. The torpedo bomber strike would be co-ordinated with an attack by H.12 (Small America) seaplanes armed with 230lb bombs, which could hit floating docks, engine houses, mine storage and submarines lying in the basin (hence presenting a mass target suitable for bombing). The flying boats would refuel from destroyers.

For Beatty the point of a really massive attack was that no single hit by the small torpedo a Cuckoo could carry was likely to sink a German capital ship. He therefore wanted each five-plane flight to concentrate on a single ship. His strike was sized to deal with a fleet of twenty-four German ships. If that was too small, he needed more aircraft (at one point in his proposal he called for a 25 per cent margin in carrier numbers and at least a 60 per cent margin in torpedo bombers).

The key was the simplicity of carriers. An ordinary merchant ship could be given a flying-off deck sufficient for seventeen torpedo bombers plus two fighters, for a total of eight carriers. The fighters were needed, not to escort the bombers, but rather to deal with Zeppelin scouts. Each carrier should be able to fly off five torpedo bombers in quick succession, to contribute to the forty-bomber wave. The carriers should be converted from the fastest merchant ships available (Beatty calculated that 12 knots would be enough to get them from the Wash to a suitable take-off point in darkness). They would have to be blistered against torpedoes and given paravanes to protect them from mines.

In September 1917 there was no experience of recovering wheeled aircraft at sea, although a Sopwith Pup did land success-fully on board HMS *Furious*. Beatty did not say as much, but the returning torpedo bomber force would have ditched near the carriers. A few of the bombers might have been pulled from the sea, their engines salvaged. Beatty therefore wanted a minimum of 60 per cent spare aircraft for later attacks. It also occurred to Beatty that, if the initial attack succeeded, the Germans might withdraw surviving ships into the Kiel Canal. He therefore wanted a simulta-neous attack to block the canal.

Beatty's seems to have been the first proposal since Sueter's for a mass air attack on the German fleet. British naval air policy up to that point concentrated on providing reconnaissance aircraft and fighters (to defeat German air reconnaissance). Torpedo bombers were under development and the carrier *Argus* (under construc-tion) could accommodate them, but there does not seem to have been a coherent air strike plan.[164]

The Admiralty pointed out that the project could not be carried out as simply or as quickly as Beatty imagined.[165] Fast (20-knot) ships had to be selected, as aircraft could not take off from slow ones. As the U-boat offensive continued, they became more and more valuable and less and less available. Conversion was not so simple as Beatty imagined and it would delay the operation well beyond the summer of 1918. Specially-built ships would take even longer, not less than eighteen months (Beatty noted in the margin of the Admiralty reply that surely the big armed merchant cruisers of the 10th Cruiser Squadron, redundant now that the United

US battleships *en route* to Scapa Flow, 1917. Note the disruptive camouflage on the funnels of the ship in the foreground, which is almost certainly USS *Florida*. (Naval Institute collection)

States was in the war, could be spared). Beatty also noted that the US Navy was using catapults to launch aircraft from armoured cruisers, hence it might be possible to use similar devices for the torpedo bombers. Finally, the Admiralty pointed out that 'there is considerable uncertainty as to whether so many torpedo carrying aeroplanes and torpedoes can be obtained before the latter part of 1918'. That was not least because the Cuckoo had to compete with fighters for its powerful engine.

Beatty fought hard for his planned attack, but in October the Admiralty definitely quashed the project. The torpedo was small and of short range and to gain any success would require extended practice. Suitable ships just were not available. Unable to get his special carrier strike group, later in September Beatty revised his fleet aircraft requirements to fifteen reconnaissance, thirty torpedo bombers and fifty fighters.[166] Beatty remained intently interested in a larger torpedo bomber force and he repeatedly asked the Admiralty when he would receive his aircraft. In February 1918 he was given a delivery schedule showing a total of 200 between April and November. Then the situation deteriorated, possibly in part because after the RAF was formed the new Air Ministry began cutting back naval requirements.[167] In July 1918 Beatty was told that he could expect twelve aircraft that month (compared to an earlier promise of forty-five) and twenty-eight (vs. forty-three) in August. As of February he had been promised a total of 100 by the end of July, then twelve – and in fact he had three. As late as 18 July he had been promised thirty-six trained pilots, but there were none.

Later it appeared that production delay was due in part to problems with the Sunbeam Arab engine which had replaced the original Hispano. In September the Air Ministry promised that a first squadron would be ready for HMS *Argus* later in the month.

Once the torpedo planes were available, work proceeded on plans for a strike at the High Seas Fleet, albeit on a much smaller scale than Beatty had imagined the previous year. How close the attack came to execution is evident in the 1918 Christmas card sent by officers of the torpedo bomber unit. It showed the High Seas Fleet *en route* to surrender, with the words 'Oh, that we might have met'.[168] The idea was incorporated in the war plans the Mediterranean Fleet drew up during the confrontation with Italy in 1935 and the operation was executed very successfully at Taranto in November 1940. Many have suggested that it was the inspiration for Pearl Harbor.

Because the High Seas Fleet did not come out to chance battle, the British became increasingly interested in attacking it in its base, a concept later often called 'attack at source'. The two mechanisms tried during the First World War were CMBs and torpedo bombers. At the end of the war the carrier *Argus* was nearly ready to launch a torpedo strike. A Sopwith Cuckoo, which could operate from a carrier, is shown dropping its torpedo. (Philip Jarrett)

Although the revolution in battleship design is usually associated with HMS *Dreadnought*, the British initially spent a great deal more on three battle-cruisers. That was natural: in 1905–6 their great problem was overmatching the armoured cruisers of their likely wartime enemies. HMS *Inflexible* is shown as built. Note the 4in anti-destroyer guns on 'A' turret and also the two semaphores extending above her forebridge.

WARTIME LESSONS CAN BE read from changes in the capital ship programmes of the various navies, particularly the Royal Navy and the German Navy.

The Royal Navy[1]

In 1914 the Royal Navy had completed about a decade in the throes of a series of revolutions in capital ship design, during which the displacement (and cost) of battleships and battlecruisers rose by more than 60 per cent, with no sign of levelling off. The more or less steady design development of the 1890s suddenly gave way to what were later called semi-dreadnoughts, with intermediate-calibre guns to supplement their main batteries and their secondary batteries. These weapons were adopted because it was increasingly possible to fire them as rapidly as the secondary guns; the semi-dreadnoughts were abandoned partly because within a few years main-battery guns could be fired more quickly and with far greater effect. The Royal Navy led the world in these developments, suddenly producing the fast battleship HMS *Dreadnought* in 1906. British security was effective, to the point that the rival German navy took a considerable time to produce an inferior rival in its *Nassau* class.

The revolution in the Royal Navy was touched off in part by a financial disaster, that in the face of foreign armoured cruisers the Royal Navy had to produce its own battleship-sized armoured cruisers, often in greater size and certainly in greater numbers. That was necessary both for trade protection (the ships would occupy focal areas around the world into which raiding cruisers would find themselves drawn) and to scout effectively for the battle fleet, against foreign fleets which might be screened by armoured cruisers. In 1889 the Royal Navy convinced the government of the day (and, as importantly, the British political public) that the survival of British command of the sea depended on maintaining a strength equal to that of the next two navies. In 1889 these happened to be those of France and Russia, which were joining in an alliance. Thus the 'two-power standard' amounted to parity (plus an edge) compared to the likely enemy coalition. The disaster was that with the advent of armoured cruisers the Royal Navy found itself having to build an additional considerable fleet of battleship-size ships, which had not been envisaged in the financing of the 1889 Naval Defence Act. Worse, the number of armoured cruisers was tied not only to numbers in foreign navies but also to the need to occupy a series of stations around the world. As an example of what that meant, in November 1904, in connection with

plans to redistribute the fleet, the stated standard was a 10 per cent margin in battleships and a *2:1 margin* in battleship-size armoured cruisers.[2]

Within the fleet, the armoured cruisers were essential because, in the face of enemy armoured cruisers, only they could press home reconnaissance to locate the enemy's battleships and to determine their course and speed, so that a British fleet could deploy across their path. Similarly, only armoured cruisers could block an enemy's reconnaissance. Since the British had introduced modern armoured cruisers with the *Cressy* class, moreover, they had regarded such ships as fast second-class battleships, suitable to fight all but the best of the enemy's battleships.[3] The main limitation of these ships as battleships was not, as might be imagined, armour, but rather their weak main armament, 9.2in rather than 12in guns.

For example, late in 1904, when the 1905–6 programme was being sketched, it seemed that British battleship numbers were such that the next year's programme could be cut from the planned three battleships to one, which became HMS *Dreadnought*. However, it also seemed that the next year's programme would include no fewer than five armoured cruisers, of an as-yet undetermined type. This figure was cut to four and then to three, the *Invincible* class. By this time money was tight and the situation was worsening, because there was no new source of British government income in sight.

Something had to be done to eliminate the 2:1 requirement for battleship-size armoured cruisers. As First Sea Lord, Sir John Fisher's solution was to pay a bit more per cruiser to provide battleship guns, so that he could consider both his battleships and his armoured cruisers as capital ships. That solution was justified by his new form of command and control, which dramatically decreased the number of such cruisers needed for trade protection (an important reason for the 2:1 ratio; fleet requirements would have justified nothing more than a 10 per cent ratio). His innovation would free cruiser-killers from the need to occupy particular foreign stations: they would be vectored to attack their prey. They could therefore be concentrated with the fleets. The navy still needed them as fleet scouts, but that did not entail anything like the number of ships trade protection had involved.

In 1905 Fisher could reasonably argue that at the increased gun ranges now possible, armoured cruiser protection was no less effective than that of any battleship. At 4000 yds, which in 1905 was long range, even current battleship armour could be penetrated by existing guns. It did not really make much difference whether armour was thick or thin. Moreover, the faster the target, the more difficult it would be to hit (Fisher's dictum was 'speed is armour'). Shell damage was considered cumulatively effective: an enemy had to make many hits to disable a ship. A few hits would be ineffective and if speed and manoeuvre rendered fire control ineffective, speed would indeed be a form of protection. The more we learn about fire control in that era, the better this argument becomes. One might add that battlecruisers hit at Jutland but not blown up due to suicidal magazine practices did indeed continue in action quite effectively.

The protection situation changed as effective battle ranges increased. At 8000 yds, the thin side armour of the first battlecruisers could still be penetrated, but it paid to put thick armour on a battleship. The Royal Navy understood as much; its second-generation battlecruisers (*Lion* class) had 50 per cent thicker side

HMS *Dreadnought* might be seen either as a super-fast battleship or as a slow battlecruiser. Within a few years of her construction, the British were lumping battleships and battlecruisers together as capital ships and they were measuring their strength against that of the Germans in terms of numbers of capital ships rather than numbers of battleships. British tactical planning assumed that, once the scouting function had been fulfilled, the battlecruisers would fall back on the main body as a fast division – as Beatty's battlecruisers did at Jutland.

armour. Later programmes emphasised battleships; Fisher got only one battlecruiser in the 1906–7 Estimates and none in 1907–8.[4] Battlecruiser construction stopped with the five *Queen Elizabeths*. In a Minute on the 1913–14 programme, First Lord Winston Churchill remarked that the *Queen Elizabeths* had been conceived as an overwhelming counter to the German battlecruisers, which the British correctly understood were fast battleships.[5] Churchill therefore stopped building battlecruisers as such, a choice bitterly resented once war broke out. Both Beatty (commanding the battlecruisers) and his superior Jellicoe kept asking for more battlecruisers to deal with the Germans. On the eve of war Churchill seems to have realised that the *Queen Elizabeths* were not as fast as battlecruisers; he wanted the 1914–15 ship redesigned.[6]

When war broke out, the British were completing the five *Queen Elizabeth* class battleships of the 1912–13 and were working on five *Royal Sovereign* class battleships ordered under the 1913–14 programme; all ten were armed with the new 15in gun, which had been ordered on a crash basis. The initial expectation explains why the *Queen Elizabeths* were so often seen as heavy battlecruisers, their speed grossly overstated as 26 or even 27 knots (they failed to make their design speed of 25 knots). The British also assumed that the sustained sea speed of the German battlecruisers was quite limited, presumably partly by the low-quality coal the Germans were forced to use.[7] In connection with the proposed construction of further fast battleships, fleet commander Admiral Jellicoe remarked early in 1916 that his attempts to use the *Queen Elizabeths* as a fast wing division had failed because 'their excess of speed over the Battle Fleet proper is so small that it is always questionable whether they will be able to get to the head of the line on deployment without blanketing the battle line'. A wing division needed a much larger speed margin over the battleships. Jellicoe recalled that he had said as much when serving as Controller at the time of the *Queen Elizabeth* design. These considerations explain why Jellicoe was particularly impressed by the apparently high speed shown by some German battleships at Jutland.[8]

Another important factor in 1912 was a drastic change in the German Navy Law.[9] Churchill circulated to the Cabinet a translation of the new law and an intelligence assessment. The main feature, in his view, was a dramatic increase in the striking force in all classes due to a planned increase in German personnel. Prior to 1912 the Royal Navy reckoned with an active battle fleet of seventeen battleships, four battlecruisers and twelve small cruisers, demobilised to a great extent during the winter. With the additional personnel, the Germans would keep most of their fleet continuously in commission and they were building towards a fleet of twenty-five battleships, twelve battlecruisers and eighteen small cruisers. Instead of keeping half their torpedo boats (destroyers) in full commission, they would maintain nearly all of their 115 in that status, working up to a total of 144. There was also a considerable increase in submarine funding (the Admiralty knew nothing of the rate of construction implied). Churchill argued that because the Germans had a conscript navy, personnel money would go much further than in the United Kingdom.

At this time Churchill was arguing that the Royal Navy could not maintain its previous one-power standard in the Mediterranean while maintaining the 60 per cent edge over the Germans which the Committee on Imperial Defence had recently endorsed.[10] He claimed that a viable battle fleet could be restored to the Mediterranean only if the building programme was considerably boosted. In 1912 he hoped that a large Canadian contribution would solve the problem. The alternative was to accept an arrangement with France (which Churchill and presumably the Prime Minister, favoured). It seems likely that Churchill saw the *Queen Elizabeth*s as a qualitative jump comparable to that represented by HMS *Dreadnought*, a way of changing the balance with Germany at one step.

The last British pre-war programme (Estimates for 1914–15, submitted in March 1914) included four battleships: three of the *Royal Sovereign* class and one more *Queen Elizabeth*. There were no battlecruisers, as indeed there had been none in the 1912–13 and 1913–14 programmes.[11] It appears that the programme had originally called for three *Queen Elizabeth*s and one *Royal Sovereign* and had been recast to save construction time by replacing two of the more complicated *Queen Elizabeth*s with simpler (but slower) *Royal Sovereign*s. There is no evidence that anyone involved regarded the *Queen Elizabeth*s as too slow; the problem was that a planned Canadian contribution to the Admiralty programme was collapsing. Admiralty papers on the financial situation in 1914 show that the Treasury was pushing hard to reduce that year's programme to two battleships. Winston Churchill's Minutes as First Lord show interest in replacing battleships with torpedo craft, either surface or submerged, in hopes of solving the problem.[12]

In March 1914 the Admiralty had just been frustrated, finally, in its hopes that the Canadians would pay for one or more battleships to supplement the British budget and there was not enough money to buy further ships to offset the growing strength of the two potentially hostile Mediterranean navies, those of Italy and Austria-Hungary (which ultimately offset each other).[13]

The four 1914–15 battleships were all cancelled on 26 August 1914.[14] Admiralty policy was not to proceed with any ships which could not be completed before the end of 1915. The Royal Navy had just seized two battleships being completed for Turkey (which became HMS *Agincourt* and HMS *Erin*) and also had access to two being built for Chile (which became HMS *Canada* and the carrier HMS *Eagle*). None of them offered either the firepower of the 1914–15 ships (all of which would have mounted 15in guns) or the speed of the planned *Queen Elizabeth* (which would have been HMS *Agincourt*), but they were more immediately available than the planned ships.

Having returned to the Admiralty at the end of October 1914, Fisher decided to re-order some of the 1914–15 ships as shallow-draught 32-knot battlecruisers, initially called 'Rhadamanthus', which he hoped could be completed before the end of 1915 (later he accepted that they would not be ready until April 1916, which was still extraordinary). He wrote to Churchill that, aside from HMS *Tiger*, they would be the only British ships fast enough to catch the newest German battlecruiser *Lützow*; he wanted three of them. He also wrote to Jellicoe (on 21 December) in connection with the recent Scarborough Raid (by German battlecruisers) that the only new capital ships the Royal Navy needed were battlecruisers.[15] Churchill approved the project on 28 December. It is not clear to what extent Fisher associated these and other ships he was then advocating with his Baltic project, but on 27 December he wrote Controller that it was vital 'for strategic reasons' that deep draught be limited to 26ft. Work on the new battlecruisers began very quickly. Apparently the first keel plates for *Repulse* were laid *before* design work began.[16]

By March 1915 every effort was being made to complete the two fast battlecruisers in an unprecedented 16 months after having been ordered at the end of 1914. That raised an unpleasant question: what if the Germans were making similar efforts to complete the battlecruisers on order in 1914? Late in March 1915 Third Sea Lord Rear Admiral Tudor circulated a table showing what the Germans could have if they could complete ships 18 months after laying them down.[17] That might be impossible, so he also constructed a table for completion after 24 months. It had taken 27 months to complete the battleship *Queen Elizabeth*, of

It took some time for the Royal Navy to adopt superfiring turrets, which economised on weight while retaining the same broadside. HMS *Colossus* is shown at Scapa Flow, with a *Bellerophon* class battleship in the near background. She displays the important post-Jutland modification of remote-controlled searchlights grouped amidships so that their light would not give away the ship's course. Note the absence of any sort of funnel cap to reduce smoke in the spotting top.

The British continued to build both battleships and battlecruisers, the last pre-war battlecruiser being HMS *Tiger*. She is shown late in the war, with a hangar to shield the fighter carried atop her raised 'X' turret. (US Navy Historical and Heritage Command)

which 22 months were under normal and only five under accelerated conditions. That the British situation would not be very happy in either case allowed Tudor to make his key point, that work on the ships closest to completion, *Canada*, *Barham*, *Valiant* and *Malaya*, could not be allowed to lag. Given his own unhappy experience trying to accelerate completions, Churchill was properly sceptical – and he was proved more than correct.[18]

It is also not clear to what (if any) extent the two full battle-cruisers were connected to the project for three 'large light cruisers' of the *Courageous* class, undertaken at roughly the same time. It has often been suggested that the 'large light cruiser' designation was adopted because the Treasury was unwilling to sanction capital ships, whereas cruisers were acceptable. Once stated, the requirement for shallow draught seems to have survived the end of Fisher's regime at the Admiralty. Unfortunately surviving Constructors' Notebooks do not include design work on the 'large light cruisers', and the Cover does not give any clear indication of their parentage. A sketch design was complete by the end of March 1915.[19] *Furious*, the third 'large light cruiser', was not included in the first order for such ships. She seems to have been intended from the outset as a platform for the single 18in gun, but the Cover does not contain the relevant correspondence (the project may have been considered too secret).[20]

Both Jellicoe and his deputy Beatty proved all too willing to believe vague intelligence showing that the Germans were rapidly closing (or had already closed) the gap with the Grand Fleet and their beliefs helped drive the wartime capital ship programme. The fundamental problem was that the British never grasped just how little influence the German navy had on national policy. It was inconceivable that (as was the reality) a government which at times had devoted more than half its defence budget to the navy did not consider the navy a significant factor and did not prioritise warship construction in any way. Yet that is clearly the implication of the record available after the war.

About October 1914 the French naval attaché in London reported that a wide variety of sources indicated that the Germans were improving their battleship firepower.[21] The British ambassador to Romania heard 'from a reliable informant' that the Romanian representative of Ehrhardt (the firm responsible for German medium-calibre field guns), 'who has just returned from Germany tells him that Germans are replacing guns on their capital ships with guns which carry 2km further than any English gun'. The French attaché thought that this report might explain his own

information. Churchill wrote in red on the message 'I presume that I am right in thinking that this is physically impossible'. His DNO agreed; all the Germans might do was rearm their new battleships with guns five calibres longer (50 rather than 45 calibre guns). DNC pointed out that even this modification would affect the balance of the turrets and the necessary modification to loading arrangements made the change unlikely. There was also speculation that the Germans had changed their heavy HE shells to the 'compartment system', which gave them more powerful bursting charges.

DNO and DNC should have ended the speculation about heavier guns, but the Admiralty did not trust its own information about the Germans. Churchill found himself asked to sign a letter to Jellicoe and Beatty informing them that there was 'considerable evidence' to the effect that the 12in guns of certain German battleships were being replaced by 14in guns. 'Although this substitution appears at first sight intrinsically improbable', it was plausible if the Germans had found their 12in gun unsuccessful and had worked out a scheme of rearmament months or even years before. It was also plausible that Krupp was secretly making 14in guns, as 'the capacity of their works is notoriously very great in all departments'. The 12in barbettes might be large enough to accommodate 14in guns, 'the effect on stability being accepted in view of the width of the German ships'.

For all the impulsiveness with which Churchill was later credited, he did not trust this sort of panicky conclusion. He formed what amounted to a technical intelligence committee, headed by Third Sea Lord (Controller), to evaluate the possibility of the claimed rearmament. The other members were the heads of the relevant departments: Director Intelligence Division (Captain H F Oliver), Director of Naval Ordnance (Captain Morgan Singer), Director of Naval Construction (E H T d'Eyncourt) and the previous DNC, Sir Philip Watts. The committee met on 14 October.

The committee considered rearmament plausible because Watts recalled that the *Orion*s, the first British super-dreadnoughts (with 13.5in guns), had originally been designed for 12in guns. The decision to shift to 13.5in had been taken in secret and the turrets redesigned. Changing turrets on board an existing ship would be a far more difficult proposition, but it was possible *if* a decision had already been taken and material prepared. The *Kaiser* class were known to have 12in guns. Longer 12in guns could be substituted, with counterweights to balance them, but that would not buy much. The ships could be refitted with 14in (but not larger) guns, but that would entail complete reconstruction of the turrets, erection alone requiring at least six months. The newer *Königs* were a more interesting proposition, because although all reference books credited them with 12in guns, there was no direct ('ocular') evidence of their gun calibre. References had been made in the Reichstag to their inferior calibre. Meanwhile Krupp was offering guns of up to 16in calibre and it appeared that large-calibre guns had been tested.

It was reported in mid-1912 that both 14in guns and mountings had failed their tests,

and were reported on adversely by the German naval authorities. At the time the Koenig *[sic] class were commenced it is certain that much consideration was being given to a gun larger than 12in and if at that time they had possessed a successful design of gun and mechanism, it is considered extremely probable that such a gun would have been arranged for rather than the 12in. It therefore occurs to the Committee that the Germans may have looked ahead and made their turrets and mountings for the ships of the* Koenig *class, so that they would take a 14in gun when it was found possible to mount a gun of that size which could be accepted. It is therefore considered quite possible that in the meantime the difficulties have been surmounted and the 14in guns made in sufficient numbers to be placed in the completed vessels (three) of this class.*

The committee agreed that the British would find great difficulties in such an operation as regards ammunition, but the Germans might not, because they apparently already used the 14in gun for coast defence. There seemed to be no valid reason not to imagine that the *Königs* completing at the outbreak of war had been rearmed. It was much less likely that the *Kaisers* were involved, because when the first of them were laid down the Germans had only just placed their 12in gun in service.

All of this was a misreading of what was happening in Germany. No one in the Royal Navy realised how long it took the Germans to get from concept to completed ship. The more powerful armament under consideration in 1910 applied not to the *Königs* but to the class which would follow them, the 15in gun *Badens*. The Germans did indeed hope to overtake the British with a new gun – but it was a 15in chosen before the British decided to arm the *Queen Elizabeths* with a gun of that calibre. British naval industry, and the Royal Navy technical establishment, were far more agile than the Germans. Krupp's secretiveness hid the fact that it moved ponderously. The 14in gun was planned for a new class of battlecruisers. What *could* be done was not what would be done.

In January 1915 Beatty's battlecruisers fought their German counterparts at Dogger Bank. This action demonstrated that battle ranges had been badly underestimated before the war and it led Admiral Jellicoe to demand 30° gun elevation in any new ships. British knowledge of new German ships was so thin at this time that a report by an interned Englishman of a conversation with the

'master gunner' of the *Blücher* (sunk at Dogger Bank) caused a considerable stir in the Grand Fleet, to the extent that it apparently influenced Jellicoe's views of what he might be facing.[22] The Englishman said that he had been detailed specifically to translate for prisoners on board the German cruiser. He described details he had been given of the latest German 11in and 12in guns and the 'master gunner' then mentioned incidentally the 38cm guns of the battlecruiser *Lützow* and those following her.

Jellicoe, ever the pessimist, accepted the Englishman's claims as though he was an ordnance expert. Jellicoe knew that the German 1913 battleships would be armed with 15in guns (*Bayern* class). He also took the 'could' of October 1914 as definite information. On this basis he argued that it was 'most improbable' that the Germans would have adopted such a gun for only four ships, whilst intending to go to a 15in gun immediately afterwards (as was known to have been the case in their 1913 battleships). Although he had been Controller at the time the *Queen Elizabeths* were being designed, Jellicoe seems not to have appreciated that a 15in gun was far more massive than a 14in. He concluded that it was almost certain that the *Königs* had really been rearmed with 15in guns. If that was true, Jellicoe faced four German ships armed with 15in guns while his own ships with similar weapons were not yet in service. Moreover, all of the British ships were, in Jellicoe's view, less well protected than their German counterparts.

The German 'master gunner' also claimed, incorrectly, that the Germans guns outranged their British equivalents: their 12in were sighted to about 23,500 yds and their 11in to 21,500 yds. The British equivalent ranges were 19,000 yds for the 13.5in gun and

The *Queen Elizabeth* class fast battleships were intended specifically to supplant both conventional battleships *and* battlecruisers, but in 1914 there was interest in building a new super-*Tiger* armed with 15in guns. First Lord Winston Churchill wrote early in 1914 that these ships had been conceived specifically to prevent the German battlecruisers from turning the British battle line by threatening to cross its 'T' (in his post-war book *The World Crisis* this was inverted, so that the ships were supposed to have been given sufficient speed to cross the German 'T'). In effect this ship materialised as HMS *Hood*, although no document connects the two projects. *Queen Elizabeth* is shown post-Jutland at Scapa Flow with initial improvements. Her torpedo nets are gone, as are the four low (hence wet) stern 6in secondary guns. She has the new searchlight controls on her after funnel, but they are not yet in final form. Note too the anti-rangefinding baffles on her masts, but not on her funnels. *Queen Elizabeth* became fleet flagship when Admiral Beatty took over the Grand Fleet from Admiral Jellicoe.

the 12in Mk XI and 15,750 to 18,500 yds for 12in Mk X, depending on projectile. In fact the opposite was true: the British greatly outranged the Germans. In Jellicoe's eyes, the fact that ships had fought successfully at 18,000 yds or more at Dogger Bank reinforced the looming German superiority. He reiterated to the Admiralty his view that his margin of superiority was too thin and that it could vanish altogether if the Germans chose their moment properly. Moreover, at their selected moment, the Germans would enjoy massive superiority in torpedo craft and the High Seas Fleet would also surely incorporate 12 pre-dreadnoughts, 'whereas we can rarely count on more than 7 ships of the 3rd Battle Squadron (*King Edward VII* class) to place against them'. All of this led up to his demand that the *Queen Elizabeth* be brought home from Gallipoli and the completion of her sisters rushed. That may have been the point all along.

Whether or not Jellicoe believed what he wrote, it was taken seriously. The Admiralty committee was convened anew.[23] It pointed out that persistent reports from better sources were often misleading. Before the war *Blücher* herself had often been reported rearmed with 12in guns, but it was obvious at Dogger Bank that nothing like that had been done. Even so, one of her survivors repeated the 12in gun claim. The first of the *König* class had been laid down in May 1911, so her design must have been settled much earlier, well before the first British 13.5in ship had been completed and before the 15in decision had even been made in the Admiralty. Reportedly the Germans had had great trouble with their 14in gun, so it seemed unlikely that they would soon jump to a 15in gun. As for the source, a 'master gunner' in the Imperial Navy was not quite a warrant officer, more like a British turret gunlayer, so 'he might, therefore, not be in a position to know facts concerning calibre of guns of battleships under construction or just completed'. DNO added that he thought the 'master gunner' was being purposely misleading.

Churchill was unfazed: 'this is a very alarmist letter and twists all the facts into the most unfavourable position'. It was absurd for Jellicoe to imagine that six new ships armed with 15in guns would join the German fleet before a single British so armed became available. Whether the *König*s had been rearmed was 'searchingly investigated' by an Admiralty committee the previous October. There was no evidence that the ships had been laid up long enough

HMS *Warspite* is shown late in the war, with fighters atop 'B' and 'X' turrets. Note the range dials on the side of the searchlight housing. Ships had one rather than two high topmasts, varying in whether it was the fore or main topmast. By the time of this photograph, anti-rangefinding baffles had been abandoned.

for such reconstruction; 'they have been doing their practices and moving about quite regularly'. The committee had found that 14in guns were just feasible; 15in guns would be quite another matter. Nor was there any solid evidence for 15in guns on the *Lützow*. Given British experience, it was ludicrous to imagine that the new German battleships with 15in guns were anywhere near ready – as indeed they were not. Moreover, British experience was that gun mountings, exactly what was supposed to be changed in the *König*s, were the most difficult to produce.

Third Sea Lord Tudor agreed with his committee, but he added that even though it was improbable that the *König*s were armed with 15in guns, Jellicoe was right to take that possibility into consideration. He pointed out that the Germans had four 15in battleships on order and surely they were 'accelerating [them] for all they are worth'. No one in the Royal Navy could imagine that the Imperial German Navy was not so central to the German war effort that it would enjoy the sort of priority accorded the Royal Navy. In fact labour had drained from the German shipbuilding industry as the army mobilised and the two 1913 ships were completed only in 1916, after Jutland. The other pair were never completed.

Jellicoe's call for urgent completion of 15in gun battleships may have led the Board to plan one or more new capital ships for the 1915–16 programme.[24] In the autumn of 1915, with Fisher and Churchill (and Fisher's concentration on battlecruisers) gone from the Admiralty, DNC ordered work on a new battleship design. It might be imagined as an updated *Queen Elizabeth*.[25] In December 1915 or early January 1916 DNC offered Controller two alternative battleship designs (A and B). Controller Rear Admiral Tudor asked for two more alternatives, both of 22-knot speed.[26] In January the Board asked for details of a modified design with *Queen Elizabeth* class speed and Jellicoe was asked for his views.

In fact by early 1916 Jellicoe considered British superiority in battleships so great that further construction was unnecessary.[27]

However, he considered his margin in battlecruisers too thin; the Germans were building at least three very fast powerful battlecruisers, *Hindenburg*, *Ersatz Victoria Luise* and *Ersatz Freya*, in addition to the *Lützow*.[28] He was almost certain that they would approach 30 knots, at least for a few hours and that would make them faster than any British battlecruiser. He was also almost certain that at least the last three German battlecruisers would be armed with guns of about 15.2in. Hence any new large British armoured ships should be battlecruisers 'and the need for them is great'.

In Jellicoe's view, the new *Glorious* class was unable to compete with German battlecruisers due to their inadequate protection and the same might be said of the forthcoming *Repulse*. 'They will not be capable of tackling a Battle Cruiser, although they may be faster'. Jellicoe rejected battleships of 'intermediate speed' (25 to 27 knots) which was of little value; 'either they should be Battle Cruisers of 30 knots or Battleships of 21 knots'.

If something more powerful than the 15in gun had been designed, it should go into any new ship. If not, it should be considered at once. A new ship should have no fewer than eight guns. The new 5in gun seemed powerful enough as an anti-torpedo (boat) weapon; the ship should have no fewer than twelve. Jellicoe considered DNC's favoured placement on the forecastle (with consequent omission of gun ports) a great advantage, even though it risked blast damage to the smaller guns when the main battery was firing.

Any new ship should also have more protection above the main belt. Jellicoe also felt that his battlecruisers had inadequate deck armour compared to the latest German ships. One deck, preferably the lowest armoured deck, should be at least $2^{1}/2$in thick. Jellicoe seems to have accepted that any battlecruiser would have to have long unarmoured ends. He felt that considerable protection against shells had been accepted as the price of anti-torpedo protection (bulge and crushing tubes) and wondered whether improved compartmentation and better pumping facilities would be a viable alternative. He did not see any advantage in holding draught to less than 26ft; surely 30ft could be accepted if that made a reduction in length possible (but length was probably essential for a battlecruiser).

The last pre-war British battleship design, the Royal Sovereign *class, reverted to slower speed. Presumably battlecruiser construction would have been resumed in 1915 had the war not intervened.* HMS Revenge *is shown in 1918, with a kite balloon (note the observer's basket).*

Given Jellicoe's comments, DNC soon ordered work begun on a new battlecruiser. Alternative armaments included the '15in B' gun, which was actually the 18in gun planned for HMS *Furious*.[29] However, DNC was also pursuing the earlier fast battleship designs, any of which could have six 15in B guns instead of eight 15in.[30] Since Jellicoe clearly wanted higher speed, an attempt was made to estimate the cost of going to 35 knots (about 225,000shp in *Repulse*). The name *Hood* seems to have been chosen almost immediately for the new battlecruiser.[31] A 32-knot design with eight 15in guns was chosen for development.[32] Ultimately four ships were ordered: *Hood*, *Howe*, *Rodney* and *Anson*.

Third Sea Lord met with Jellicoe aboard the Grand Fleet flagship on 12 October 1916, by which time the fleet had absorbed the experience of Jutland.[33] As might be imagined, Jellicoe began with a call for increased above-water protection of the new battlecruisers 'at all costs' because he considered them no match for the Germans. Third Sea Lord told him that they were being given 12in belts. Jellicoe also pointed out that, given their great lengths, the *Repulse* and *Courageous* class ships had to run at high speed to avoid submarine attack and therefore he wanted suitable screening destroyers. Third Sea Lord told him that the new 'V' class destroyers to be delivered during 1917 would be much better seakeepers than their predecessors and also longer-legged given their 25 per cent greater fuel capacity. *Hood* was modified with considerably stronger protection after Jutland. In August 1918 further additional protection was planned for the other three ships, which had been suspended the previous year, but they were never completed.

The Imperial German Navy

During the pre-war period, British information about German shipbuilding was spotty at best. Through access to German budget documents, the British were well aware that each ship cost the Germans much more per ton than their own, but they assumed the Germans could build much faster than they could and that they could maintain a much higher degree of secrecy while doing so. The British seem to have been particularly unaware of the extent to which the fragmented German command system delayed warship design and construction. The Kaiser's personal intervention considerably complicated matters, since he could and did choose among design options.[34]

The Navy Laws made it impossible for the Germans to trade off numbers for the increased cost of new battleships once HMS *Dreadnought* appeared. Tirpitz was particularly embarrassed that he sold his long-term programme to the Reichstag partly on the basis of estimates showing that it was affordable – with the unstated assumption that he would keep building roughly the same kind of ships. This problem seems particularly to have shaped the German 1909–10 ships (*Kaiser* class). The advent of battlecruisers costing even more than battleships did not help, as previously Tirpitz saved money on his large cruisers. Tirpitz found himself trying to hold back the steady growth of ships, which was also a steady growth in costs. For example, to hold battlecruiser displacement to something like the displacement of the same year's battleships, he had to trade off gun calibre for speed.

On the other hand, because the Germans were building their facilities as they built their new navy, they could invest in wider-beam docks, particularly floating drydocks, which made it possible for them to adopt wider beams, for better survivability, in their capital ships. Tirpitz backed survivability in his dreadnoughts on the theory that he wanted them to get home after the big battle, which he hoped would be within a hundred miles of their Wilhelmshaven base. In this sense he was vindicated by the survival of the battlecruiser *Seydlitz* after she suffered terrible damage both at Dogger Bank and at Jutland. On the other hand, he was cursed after Jutland because except for the three British battlecruisers his guns did not disable any of the British ships. German officers demanded heavier guns for any later ships.

Abortive German plans for semi-dreadnoughts are usually lumped with plans for dreadnoughts, but it seems better to see the two as two successive unhappy shocks. It did not help that in November 1902 the Kaiser became enamoured of the big armoured cruiser as the standard type for the German fleet, fore-shadowing his later romance with the fast battleship as a single standard type. In October 1903 the Kaiser went so far as to ask whether the ships of the 1906 Navy Law should be battleships or armoured cruisers. Had the Germans built semi-dreadnoughts, their intermediate-calibre gun would have been the 21cm (8.2in) weapon of their armoured cruisers.

In December 1903 the Kaiser sent the Navy Office (RMA) a proposal for a 13,800 ton battleship with semi-dreadnought armament (four 28cm, eight 21cm), a cruiser-like coal supply (2000 tons) and a speed of 18 knots. Not too long afterwards he was calling for an 'Overseas Battleship' with a speed of 20 to 23 knots. At the end of January 1904 the construction office (K bureau)

The only battlecruisers the Royal Navy acquired during the war were the two lightly-protected but very fast and heavily armed *Renowns*. Reportedly First Sea Lord Admiral Fisher managed to extract them from the Treasury by threatening to resign unless they were approved. HMS *Repulse* is shown post-war, after receiving 9in belt armour from the ex-Chilean battleship *Almirante Cochrane*, which was converted into the carrier *Eagle*. She had been the first ship to be fitted with a flying-off platform (visible on 'B' turret), Sqdn Commander Rutland making the first flight in a Sopwith Pup on 1 October 1917.

offered three projects to the Kaiser: 5A, 5B and 6. They began with his demand for higher speed, which was taken as 21 knots and with a semi-dreadnought battery including 21cm (8.2in) guns. Thus 5A had them in four single mounts plus single casemates, 5B in four twin turrets. Design 6 added another two. The existing *Deutschland* design and its predecessor *Braunschweig* class had a mixed battery of four 28cm and fourteen 17cm guns plus 8.8cm anti-torpedo (boat) guns. The new designs offered higher command for the 21cm guns than for the 17cm guns on the earlier ships, hence better seagoing battle performance. The constructors (K) favoured 5B, which offered the best firing arcs. New designs were appropriate because ships built in 1906 would begin a new battle squadron, which Tirpitz hoped would be homogeneous.

These ships seemed to be well in line with foreign semi-dreadnoughts. In the spring of 1904 the general (naval intelligence) office suggested an alternative single-calibre ship: 14,500 to 15,000 tons, sixteen 21cm guns. The constructors (K) pointed out that with the improvement in heavy-gun range, there was no point in mounting anything but 28cm guns – much as Admiral Fisher concluded and as Cuniberti pointed out in a celebrated (but probably not influential) article in the 1903 issue of *Jane's Fighting Ships*. A year before Fisher and the Committee on Designs, the constructors proposed a ship armed with ten to twelve 30.5cm guns, displacing 16,000 to 18,000 tons and capable of 18.5 knots. They offered alternatives armed with eight 28cm, or with six 28cm and four 24cm (an older German battleship calibre), or with four 28cm and eight 24cm, all displacing 14,000 tons. The ordnance office and the general office proposed ships armed with sixteen or twelve 21cm guns, which could be expected to fire more rapidly than the 28cm. Tirpitz saw two proposals in April 1904: a 14,000-ton ship with twelve 21cm costing 27–28 million Marks and a 15,000 ton ship with sixteen 21cm guns costing 30–31 million Marks. *Deutschland* cost about 24.5 million.

Tirpitz considered the jump to 15,000 tons too radical, because its cost could wipe out his building programme. The difference between complete squadrons of the two types could pay for four torpedo boat divisions. Tirpitz also pointed out that the bigger ship was too beamy, at 23.2m, to pass through the Kiel Canal. By December, Tirpitz was also pointing out that the British were rapidly extending battle range. At the earlier close ranges, a powerful 21cm battery might batter down an opponent, but longer range would be different, the ships of the next 10–15 years should have 28cm guns. The German fleet had been planned for close-in battle, but that would have to change. That revived the mixed-calibre semi-dreadnought. On the basis of a 25 April 1904 instruction, the designers developed two mixed-calibre designs, Projects 1A and 1B, each of 14,100 tons, 128m long, with a 19,000ihp powerplant (*Deutschland*: 16,000ihp). Design 1B carried its 21cm guns in casemates; 1B had them in single turrets. Design 1A was offered to the Kaiser, who asked for some modifications, including better casemate protection; displacement rose to 14,400 tons. He formally approved the design on 7 January 1905. It was expected to cost 29.5 million Marks. The Kaiser had already (on 27 February 1904) asked for a design with eight 24cm guns, leading to further design studies (10A-F). Tirpitz had to head them off.

Tirpitz received his first hints of disaster from his attaché in London; in January and February 1905 he reported that the *Lord Nelson*s were to be armed with ten 10in (25.4cm) guns on a displacement of 18,000 tons.[35] On 20 February the German Navy Department received a report that the next British battleship would displace over 18,000 tons. Tirpitz, who had just rejected the proposed 15,000-tonner as far too large, cannot have been amused. He was occupied convincing the Reichstag that his 1906 Navy Law was affordable and that depended on a low estimate of future battleship prices. He also thought that he would lose a year's construction if he had to adopt a single-calibre main battery. To buy larger battleships he would have to economise on cruisers, which were carried as a separate category in the Navy Laws.

Many in European navies still preferred a faster-firing heavy gun to the standard battleship main battery calibre (12in in the UK, 11in in Germany). Thus at first Admiral Fisher preferred an all-10in (500lb rather than 850lb shell) for greater volume of fire; he had to be persuaded that the smashing effect of a 12in shell was so much greater that there was no point in the smaller gun. In Germany the equivalent argument favoured the 21cm (8.2in) gun over the 28cm (11in). The 21cm/45 offered a 108kg (238lb) shell at a muzzle velocity of 900m/sec (2953ft/sec), which compared to 302kg (672lb) and 855m/sec (2805ft/sec) for the 28cm/45 on board German *Nassau* class dreadnoughts. The 28cm gun offered about 2.5 times the muzzle energy (which might be taken as a measure of armour penetration at short range) and its advantage would be greater at longer ranges. However, if both guns could penetrate, then the higher firing rate of the 21cm gun might make a considerable difference. Tirpitz dismissed the all-21cm ship because it would become less and less effective as gun ranges increased. That was demonstrated in the two battles German 21cm cruisers fought against British ships with heavier guns, the Falklands and Dogger Bank.

Early in 1905, based on attaché reports, Tirpitz ordered a new series of studies of ships with more than the usual four 28cm guns, but still with powerful batteries of the intermediate guns of earlier German battleships. Where he had previously rejected 15,000 tons

as a ruinous leap, now he had to accept that almost as a minimum. Worse, these studies became the basis for what he was offering the Reichstag in estimates connected with the 1906 Navy Law – as projections for the future.[36] The situation only worsened as the actual characteristics of HMS *Dreadnought* leaked out. In May and June 1905 the naval attaché in London reported, more or less correctly, that she would be armed with ten 30.5cm guns and would displace 18,000 tons and that she would have a speed of 21 knots (with 23,000shp turbines). The Kaiser was furious; his constructors had known about Cuniberti's article for two years and they had had the attaché's report in February, yet they were offering him far inferior ships.

To make matters worse, on a Mediterranean tour the Kaiser saw the new Italian *Regina Elena* class battleships. They seemed to match his idea that battleship and armoured cruiser should merge. He proposed, in effect, a *Regina Elena* rearmed with six to eight 28cm/45 (the Italian ship had two 30.5cm and twelve 20cm guns). Italian Admiral Bettolo had told the Kaiser that he had a plan for a new battleship armed with eight 30.5cm guns, with a high speed which offered great tactical advantage. Always an advocate of high speed, the Kaiser said on his return in May 1905 that nothing short of 22 knots (as in the Italian ships) would be acceptable in future. The future fleet should be built around armoured cruisers and torpedo craft. The Kaiser's modified *Regina Elena* might or might not be practical, but it the sketches Tirpitz displayed seem rather tame.

The constructors offered an all-21cm ship, which became project a (six double turrets); more elaborate versions were designated projects b and b2. Other studies were made of ships with eight 28cm guns (the usual two twins plus two single turrets on either beam) and six to eight 17cm in casemates. Of these, Project d, with six 17cm, was expected to cost 34.5 million Marks. Another version ordered by Tirpitz on 17 March (e) had the eight

HMS *Hood* was the culmination of British First World War capital ship thinking. Although always listed as a battlecruiser, she was described at the end of the war as a perfect blend of battleship and battlecruiser. Her protection approximated that of a *Queen Elizabeth* or *Royal Sovereign* class battleship, to the extent that when she was sunk the Admiralty signalled commanders of such ships that they were just as vulnerable. She is shown in the 1930s. (Naval Institute collection)

28cm plus ten 15cm (possible within a limit of 33 million). On 18 March Tirpitz showed the Kaiser Projects a (18.75 knots, 14,600 tons, 31 million), b1 (15,300 tons, 32 million, with 21cm intermediate-calibre battery), c (14,400 tons, 18.5 knots, 33 million, eight 28cm and eight 17cm) and e (15,400 tons, 18.5 knots, 33 million). The Kaiser chose c. It was much like the later German dreadnoughts except that the Germans soon shifted back to 15cm guns as their secondary battery.

By the end of September problems with the design were leading inexorably to a German dreadnought. Project c was developed in several versions with more power and higher speed (A and B with 19,000ihp for 19 knots and in August c1 with 20,000ihp for the same speed). Towing tests showed that a longer hull (132m x 24m) was needed and protection and stability had to be corrected. To improve draught and also to increase deck space, the two funnels of the original design were replaced by three. Displacement rose to 15,800 tons (31 million). The price of the planned 1906 Navy Law had to be recalculated at the end of March 1905, as the projected unit price was now 34.5 million rather than the earlier maximum figure of 31 million.

Tirpitz began to give way. Initially he accepted the leap to 16,000 tons, then to 17,000 – 18,000 was too much. Soon 17,000 tons was a minimum, not a maximum. Early in September 1905 he asked the chief of his construction office for a new version of project c (16,000 tons) with twin 28cm turrets instead of the single turrets, but retaining the eight 17cm guns. Speed should be 18.25 knots. Tirpitz was willing to spend another three million. It proved impossible to hold displacement to 17,000 tons, as Tirpitz hoped. To make matters worse, the larger ship would not go through the Kiel Canal, so a project to enlarge the canal also had to be undertaken, preferably without admitting it was yet another charge on the navy budget (the project was justified partly by its value to trade). A series of design studies forced Tirpitz up to 18,000 tons – now he was going in a single year from a 13,000-ton predreadnought to an 18,000-ton dreadnought – and also forced him to give up the heavy secondary gun he clearly liked.[37]

In September 1905 Tirpitz finally declared the designs with eight 28cm dead. At the same time he decided to substitute twelve 15cm for the ten 17cm. The calibres are deceptive, because shell weight and guns size are proportional to the cube of calibre, a factor of about 1.45 – the 17cm gun and shell would weigh about 45 per cent more than the 15cm. He realised that the number and rate of fire of the 17cm guns was not enough and that other navies considered the 15cm (5.9in) powerful enough to supplement heavy guns. The price per ship was now 36.5 million, about 50 per cent more than for the previous *Deutschland*.

On 21 June 1906 Tirpitz ordered a series of further sketch designs designated G. This 18,400 ton design was shown to the Kaiser; it had the 15cm guns in place of the earlier 17cm. He approved it on 4 October. Further versions were drawn up to the end of January 1907. The main improvements were replacement of the 15cm/40 by a new 15cm/45 secondary gun plus about 100 tons of additional armour. The final sketch design was designated G7b. It differed from the *Nassau* class as built mainly in that it had three funnels, the foremost forward of its foremast. As completed, *Nassau* had two funnels, the foremost abaft the foremast. The arrangement of 8.8cm guns was also different.

Even then Tirpitz had to accept that his ship was armed with much less powerful guns than *Dreadnought*, 28cm rather than 30.5cm (11in rather than 12in). He did not have much choice, since as yet there was no German 30.5cm gun available. German writers later claimed that in North Sea conditions a high-velocity gun firing a light shell was preferable, as it would have greater energy at the relatively short ranges possible under misty conditions. It is not clear to what extent that was a rationalisation. Tirpitz also could not match the British jump to turbines. Without them, the tall cylinders of reciprocating engines took up centreline space that might otherwise have gone into centreline turrets like those of HMS *Dreadnought*: the new German battleship could have had the same broadside with fewer turrets, on a smaller displacement. Tirpitz built two each of this *Nassau* class under his 1906 and 1907 programmes – but the design was not really ready until well into 1907. It did not help Tirpitz that in selling his Navy Law to the Reichstag he had promised to match other powers, yet his new ships, the *Nassau* class, were clearly inferior both in firepower and in speed.

Tirpitz also had to deal with Fisher's jump in armoured cruiser design. He had no interest in the British idea of using armoured cruisers as a fast wing of the battle fleet.[38] Instead he saw them mainly as scouts, capable of breaking through the enemy's fleet screen and of shielding lighter forces. He also feared that if his armoured cruisers were counted as capital ships, he would be unable to build the battleships he wanted. Moreover, really powerful cruisers would cost as much as battleships and would be lumped with them for budgetary reasons.[39] That in turn limited the number of large cruisers he felt he needed. However, the heavier uniform battery of 21cm guns in the *Scharnhorst*s opened the question of whether they, like the British armoured cruisers, were suitable to lie in the line with battleships, what the Germans called the 'Typenfrage', the question of exactly what relationship there should be between types of heavy warships.

The 1906 programme included two battleships (the first two *Nassau*s) and armoured cruiser E. Tirpitz initially asked for two alternatives, a modified *Scharnhorst* and a larger ship with twelve rather than eight 21cm guns.[40] As the Cruiser E design developed, the argument for a single type of capital ship kept recurring. Tirpitz tried to answer it by saying that only a cruiser, never a slower battleship, could defeat another cruiser. A cruiser with heavy guns and weaker armour was affordable, but a battleship-cruiser was not. It was very much in Tirpitz' interest to hold cruiser main armament down to 21cm guns. He did allow an alternative with 24cm guns, the old German battleship main armament, in place of 21cm.[41]

To appease the Kaiser, in May 1905 Tirpitz asked his designers for a fast battleship, but it was not a serious project. Meanwhile he was receiving the reports from London (about HMS *Dreadnought* but apparently not about *Invincible*) which were forcing up the prices of his battleships. Given a more or less fixed total budget (and the ongoing debate over the 1906 Navy Law), he had to hold down the cost of the accompanying armoured cruiser, E.[42] On 13 May he asked the constructors to sketch a modified *Scharnhorst* with 21cm/45 main battery and with eight 17cm/45 instead of the earlier 15cm/40s. The result was not very encouraging, as other requirements, such as speed, forced up size and cost. By June Tirpitz was imposing an upper limit of 24 million, which was roughly the cost of the previous-generation battleship *Deutschland*. By this time Tirpitz wanted more speed, which once more would force up size and cost, whatever the armament of the ships.

Throughout his career as head of the Navy Office, Admiral von Tirpitz was haunted by the Kaiser's strong preference for a merged battleship-armoured cruiser. When he visited Italy, the Kaiser thought he saw exactly what he wanted in the *Regina Elena* class; the Italians refused to differenti-ate between battleships and armoured cruisers. On his return to Germany, the Kaiser asked Tirpitz to design (in effect) a *Regina Elena* with a uniform 28cm (11in) gun battery. Although Tirpitz refused, he felt compelled to order larger battleship designs featuring uniform gun batteries. This is *Regina Elena*.

By September, the new *Nassau* class battleship design was clearly beyond what the Kiel Canal could accommodate and Tirpitz could consider a more powerful cruiser. He still did not want a cruiser larger than the battleship, because locks at in the Kiel Canal were still a limiting factor on such ships. He also did not want a jump in cruiser size and cost like that he felt obliged to take in battleship design, on tactical, political and policy grounds. He wanted to retain a qualitative difference between cruisers and battleships, not least to avoid the threat (to his policy of building numbers of ships) of the advent of a single very expensive type of fast capital ship. That left Tirpitz falling back on the earlier idea of an armoured cruiser with six twin 21cm turrets in the same hexagonal arrangement as the new battleship, but with higher speed and thinner main armour. In September, Tirpitz imposed a new cost limit of 27.5 million (the latest sketch design, E11, was expected to cost 26.25 million).[43] The developed version of the design, E15, was shown to the Kaiser on 4 October 1905. In preparation, Tirpitz asked his designers for a parallel series of designs armed with 24cm guns.[44] Work on this series continued up to March 1906. It had no real future, given its greater cost. The final twelve-gun design was elaborated, its form improved for slightly higher speed (24 knots). There seems to have been no interest in using turbines to achieve higher speed.

British security seems to have kept the details of the new *Invincible* class battlecruisers from Tirpitz; he received details from his attaché in London only about a week after the meeting at which he approved the new armoured cruiser design, at the end of May 1906. The ship was built as SMS *Blücher*. There was nothing Tirpitz could do as he read the report from London. He had already used up his reserve funds to pay for what (to him) was a gross jump in cruiser size and capability. He had to reckon with a furious Kaiser, who read the same report he had received. There is, incidentally, no

evidence that Tirpitz was fooled either by British disinformation (that the *Invincible*s would have 9.2in guns) or by his own belief that the British would merely improve their previous armoured cruiser design.[45] The Germans seem not to have had the slightest intelligence, correct or otherwise, bearing on this point.

When the Kaiser received the report that the *Invincible*s would have 12in guns, he wrote that they would therefore be battleships – exactly the fast battleships he espoused.[46] Tirpitz told the naval attaché that his report had to be wrong. Cruiser E armed with 24cm guns would hardly have effectively countered ships armed with 12in (30.5cm) guns. By the time Tirpitz found out that the *Invincible*s really did have battleship guns, his 1906 design was much too far along to be changed. The story about misleading intelligence was probably spread as self-justification.

A 29/30 June 1906 memo prepared by the naval intelligence department for Tirpitz (but apparently not read) characterised the *Invincible*s as 15,000 to 16,000 ton ships armed (correctly) with eight 12in guns but (incorrectly) with a speed of 23 knots.[47] The naval intelligence department suggested that a suitable 1907 cruiser would cost 32 million, a figure obtained by adding 4.5 million to the cost of the 1906 armoured cruiser *Blücher*. Based on the information from London, the naval intelligence office suggested building a ship armed with six to eight 28cm guns (in twin turrets or in two twin and four single turrets), eight 15cm/45 in casemates or in twin turrets, the usual twenty 8.8cm anti-torpedo boat guns and four torpedo tubes; armour to be 10 to 20 per cent thinner than in a battleship (but with the same thickness for the conning tower) and a speed of 23 knots. For the time being, Tirpitz calmed the Kaiser by telling him that the British ships displaced no more than 15,000 tons and delaying the attaché report about their 12in guns (which he doubted).

Cruiser F (*Von der Tann*) was planned for the 1907 programme alongside the second pair of *Nassau*s. The Kaiser was so impressed with early reports of the new British ships that he proposed a competition, with a prize of 40,000 Marks, for the design of a fast battleship at least 3 knots faster than foreign battleships (23.5 knots) armed with at least four 28cm guns. It should not exceed the displacement of the latest battleships (19,000 tons). Proposals due on 1 January 1907 were invited from the naval shipyards at Kiel, Wilhelmshaven and Danzig as well as from the construction department of the Navy Department. There were apparently no invitations to private builders, but even allowing competition between the navy yards and the departmental design organisation would have considerably weakened Tirpitz and the construction office which served him.[48]

Tirpitz had to head this off, because a unified capital ship would be far more expensive than a slow battleship. The Reichstag might approve ships as they gradually became more expensive, but it would not accept a sudden jump in size and cost. On holiday in July 1906, Tirpitz wrote that if the British were actually building much more powerful ships, the next German battleship should have twelve 30.5cm guns and twelve 15cm, the next cruiser eight 30.5cm, eight 15cm and turbines. He asked for sketch designs.[49] Tirpitz soon decided that he would repeat the 1906 design (*Nassau*) in 1907 to obtain a uniform battleship division which could operate together tactically; the more powerful battleship design was deferred to the 1908 programme. Once he had accepted that the 1907 cruiser would have battleship guns, Tirpitz opted for 28cm rather than 30.5cm, as he certainly could not afford to offer a cruiser more powerful than his battleship. This was effectively the end of Tirpitz' attempt to hold down costs by clearly separating his armoured cruisers from his capital ships. He was building the Kaiser's favoured fast battleship, but not as a standard type; nearly all of his ships would still be battleships.

On 4 September 1906 Tirpitz gave the cruiser project to the constructors: eight 28cm guns (compared to 30.5cm in the battleship). The key decisions came so late in the usual design cycle that work must have been rushed through; it must have helped that the constructors did not have to develop a parallel battleship design. By this time designs with single turrets had been abandoned, so the 28cm guns were all to be in twin turrets. The medium battery would be eight 15cm, the light battery as in the previous year's cruiser, displacement not to exceed that of the new battleships and the cost to be lower than that of those ships. Speed should be about that of the 1906 cruiser and armour also as in that ship (but strengthened if possible). If the ship should have turbines. *Nassau*, the 1906 battleship, cost more than 36 million Marks, but in 1906 estimated cost was somewhat lower, probably about 34 million.

Tirpitz was accepting a cruiser larger and more expensive than his battleships, yet less powerful and slower than the British *Invincibles*. His ship was also much more heavily armoured and much more survivable against underwater damage, but much of that advantage was invisible (except for the greater displacement of the German ship). It is not clear to what extent Tirpitz or the constructors were aware of the armour thickness of the *Invincible* class. The constructors delivered their first four sketch designs, all derived from the 1906 cruiser (*Blücher*) and all with triple-expansion engines, on 15 September.[50] On 28 September the Kaiser chose one of the developed versions for further development. Turbines were not introduced into the design until November 1906.

Tirpitz jumped to the next calibre, 30.5cm (12in) beginning with the 1908 battleships of the *Helgoland* class, which were effectively *Nassau*s with more powerful guns and better protection – at a considerable price – because at the end of May 1906 German Naval Attaché in London Captain Carl Coerper reported that the Admiralty had ordered a prototype 13.5in gun. In June he reported that it would be mounted on board the next year's battleships (1906–7 Estimates). Tirpitz discounted the report because the British had announced the tonnage of the new ships; the reported

Tirpitz tried utterly unsuccessfully to hold down unit battleship cost, because his 'iron' Navy Laws specified the *number* of ships he had to build. At the same time he had to sell a budget – a total sum of money – to the Reichstag. That was one reason his first dreadnoughts were armed with 11in rather than 12in guns. These ships and their immediate successors were also affected by the gap in German steam turbine technology. Their reciprocating steam engines occupied a considerable height near the centreline, so there was no space for centreline turrets such as that on board HMS *Dreadnought*. The hexagonal arrangement adopted was essentially that of the abortive German semi-dreadnought designs. It was sometimes rationalised as a means of providing firepower on both sides in a melee, but that was wisdom after the fact. Had the bulk of the High Seas Fleet not been scuttled in June 1919, these *Nassau* class ships would probably have been permitted to the post-war German navy. *Westfalen* is shown as completed, before installation of torpedo nets. (A Renard of Kiel photo via US Navy Historical and Heritage Command)

600-ton increase over the original *Dreadnought* was not enough. In fact the gun design was requested only on 28 October 1908, the first '12in A' being delivered in November 1909 and test-fired on 19 November. The British did introduce a better gun in the 1907–8 ships (*St Vincent* class), but it was the 12in/50 Mk XI. Its design had been requested on 21 June 1906. This was probably the gun to which Coerper referred.

Coerper's report mattered because it arrived in Berlin as the 1908 Navy Law was being framed. Tirpitz decided to enlarge the battleship and cruiser of his 1908 programme (equivalent to the British 1908–9 programme), adopting a new 12in/45 gun for the battleship. He had to fend off the Kaiser's budget-breaking preference for a single type of fast battleship, which would have been an enlarged version of the 1907 cruiser (*Von der Tann*). The increase in main battery calibre and a slight thickening of armour (by 20 to 30mm) cost 4000 tons (compared to the previous *Nassau* class), which was enough to confirm to Tirpitz that he had been right about the British: 600 tons would not buy nearly enough ship to mount much more powerful guns.

Although simply enlarging the *Nassau* class might have been the simplest thing to do, Tirpitz was unhappy with the cost and he called for alternatives. He seems to have been impressed by the US superfiring gun arrangements as in the *Michigan* and *Delaware* classes. He was shown a series of four alternative arrangements at a 28 February 1907 meeting.[51] As built, the *Helgoland*s were armed with 12in/45s. Compared to the protracted evolution of the *Nassau* class, this design effort must have been a considerable relief. The British also tried some radical alternatives, but they made up their minds much more quickly and they did not have to contend with budget-breaking proposals from someone who could not be rejected out of hand.

Parallel to the *Helgoland*s was the 1908 Cruiser G (*Moltke*) This time Tirpitz accepted that he would have to pay a great deal more per ship; he planned to spend 44 million on the new cruiser, compared to 47 million for a *Helgoland*. For once he managed to control costs (Cruiser F cost 44.08 million), but at the expense of the characteristics he wanted. The general (naval intelligence) department, aware of foreign developments, pushed for ten 30.5cm guns in a modified *Dreadnought* arrangement, if possible with the two after guns superfiring to save length, some weight being saved by reducing the medium-calibre battery from ten to eight 15cm guns. Armour should match that of the previous year's cruiser and speed should be not less than 24.5 knots. The construction department warned that adding one turret to Cruiser F would add 1000 to 1400 tons. It proposed an arrangement similar to that of HMS *Dreadnought*, but with the wing turrets *en echelon* (the arrangement used in the *Kaiser* class battleships the following year).

It is not clear whether a design was completed with the heavier guns, but on 17 May 1907 a meeting at the Navy Department ratified the 28cm ship. The ship ended up with a new 50-calibre 28cm gun to parallel the 50-calibre 30.5cm guns of the new battleships, a choice apparently made by the construction branch rather than by Tirpitz himself.[52] She had an additional (superfiring) turret aft. The ship was to have a maximum displacement of 22,000 tons (like the new *Helgoland* class battleships) and a speed of 24 to 24.5 knots. Work proceeded rapidly and a sketch design was presented to the Kaiser on 28 May.[53] Perhaps predictably, the Kaiser asked for an alternative with eight 30.5cm guns, like the *Invincible*s, but it seems to have gone nowhere.

The superfiring guns aft required a forecastle, on which the forward turret was mounted. That added considerable armour weight. There was some interest in sacrificing one turret as compensation for improved protection.[54] Ultimately Cruiser G displaced 3600 tons more than Cruiser F. Designed power was increased to 42,000shp (47,000shp on trial) and as built the ship was rated at 47,000shp. Rated speed was then 25.25 knots. From the point of view of general arrangement, Cruiser G foreshadowed the 1909 battleship design (*Kaiser* class). Tirpitz hoped that Cruiser H (1909 programme: *Goeben*) would be more heavily armed and generally superior to the 1908 ship but he accepted a repeat *Moltke*: Blohm & Voss, which had built both the 1907 and 1908 ships, offered favourable terms for a repeat 1908 ship.[55]

That left Cruiser J (*Seydlitz*), which was part of the 1910 programme which produced the later *Kaiser*s. The project began with a March 1909 memo by Tirpitz asking for necessary and desirable improvements to Cruiser G/H. The general (naval intelligence) department revived the idea of trading off one turret for more armour. It argued that the *Invincible*s were really fast battleships, hence that future armoured cruisers should have something closer to battleship characteristics. This argument may seem bizarre; all the German battlecruisers had thicker armour than their British counterparts. However, it makes sense if the Germans believed that they had to fight at short range, where they needed thicker armour to survive. Thinner British armour might

The *Helgoland*s which succeeded the *Nassau*s were 12in gun versions. *Ostfriesland* is shown on her arrival at New York, 9 August 1920, as a prize. Note the turret-top rangefinders installed well after completion.

then be associated with greater battle range. This possibility fits the German decision to retain a powerful medium-calibre battery of 15cm or even 17cm guns, rather than the all-big-gun battery adopted by the Royal Navy. Moreover, it took more armour to resist British 12in fire than for the British ships to resist German 11in fire.

As before, Tirpitz was necessarily determined to hold down the cost of the new ship; he wanted minimum changes to Cruiser G/H. At a Navy Department meeting late in August 1909, before meeting the Kaiser, he said that he would accept thicker belt armour (280mm rather than 250mm) and better deck armour, which was expected to add 0.75 to 1 million to the price of the ship. He would not give the new ship the same armament as the battleships (five twin 30.5cm turrets), but he considered an earlier proposal to substitute four twin 30.5cm for the five twin 28cm of the earlier ships. There was some interest in gaining machinery space and triple turrets were suggested for this reason. The first sketch designs were presented to Tirpitz on 25 September 1909. He chose an improved G/H with a forecastle for further development. Note that there had not yet been seagoing experience with any of the German dreadnoughts or battlecruisers, so the forecastle did not reflect sea experience of any kind. The forecastle seems to have been adopted entirely to increase the command of the forward guns, but its buoyancy is credited with having saved *Seydlitz* after Jutland. The most important further developments were even thicker armour over the machinery (300mm) and a different boiler arrangement.[56]

The British introduced the 13.5in gun in the *Orion* class,

bought under the 'We Want Eight' programme (1909–10 Estimates). It raised the cost of the ship by 23 per cent, but for his own 1909–10 ship Tirpitz felt compelled to keep cost roughly constant. He asked for the new design in a 15 May 1908 memo. It should have the same armour and boiler room length as the previous class, but it should be turbine-powered, with her 15cm secondary guns mounted higher. The new ship would have the same number of 12in turrets as her predecessor, but Tirpitz left open their arrangement. Tirpitz was interested in the 'American' arrangement (superfiring turrets) which had been proposed but not adopted the previous year. Tirpitz recalled the previous year's Scheme 14, which had two after superfiring turrets forward, two wing turrets and two turrets further aft on the centreline. His constructors turned that into a new Scheme 1, with the two centreline turrets also superfiring. This was the arrangement the French adopted for their first dreadnoughts of the *Paris* class and the Brazilians in their *Sao Paolo*. Wing turrets were wanted both as a lee-reserve and for better performance in a melee.[57]

The result was far too expensive, but early in July 1908 Tirpitz' battleship designer Buerkner proposed a way out. Sacrificing one heavy turret would save 1600 tons (and 4.4 million Marks). More money and tonnage could be saved by eliminating cruising turbines. Tirpitz waited until January 1909 to tell the Kaiser that the newest ships would have two fewer 12in guns because the alternative was unaffordable. A series of alternative armament arrangements was sketched.[58] Of these sketches, one offered the same broadside as the earlier unaffordable Scheme 1. It had only one turret forward, but the two amidships turrets were spread out so that either could fire on the opposite beam. That in turn required rearrangement of the boilers into two sets of rooms; the ship had two rather than the three funnels of the *Helgoland* class. Tests against the target ship *Jupiter* (the former casemate ship *Deutschland*) at medium range (about 4000m) showed that the planned 300mm belt with its coal backing could be penetrated by 28cm shells, so it was replaced by a 340mm belt (350mm as the ships were completed) which was expected to resist the new British 13.5in (34.3cm) shells. The Kaiser approved the design on 27 January 1909, his fifty-sixth birthday. The result was a compromise and various improvements ate up all the tonnage saved by omitting the turret. It did not help Tirpitz that the British *Neptune* and her half-sisters, which had much the same arrangement, displaced about 4500 tons less. Five ships of this *Kaiser* class were built under the 1909 and 1910 programmes.

Turbines offered limited endurance, so there was interest in

The first German battlecruiser *Von der Tann* was Tirpitz's signal failure: for the first time he was unable to control total fleet cost by holding down the cost of armoured cruisers. Compared to her British contemporaries, she had much better protection at the cost of much less powerful guns; in some sense the lack of protection of the British ships was balanced by the limited long-range power of German guns and vice versa for more powerful British guns and better German protection. On the other hand, the broader beams and much more minute compartmentation of German capital ships gave them far better resistance to underwater hits.

diesel power for capital ships, manifested as early as *Moltke* (1908). Diesels would save space and weight, but their main attraction was greatly extended cruising radius. Just why that was worthwhile (diesels cost about $4^2/3$ times as much per horsepower) is not clear, since the High Seas Fleet was designed to operate near the German coast. Tirpitz may have wanted to show that, like Fisher, he could initiate a maritime revolution. He knew that in Britain Vickers was building inferior MAN diesels under license to power British submarines. In 1909 MAN said that its engines were far enough along to be suitable; in January 1910 diesel power was proposed for the fifth ship of the *Kaiser* class, *Prinzregent Luitpold* (*Ersatz Odin*). MAN designed a six-cylinder 12,000bhp diesel for the battleship and built a three-cylinder test rig. The other German diesel builder, Germania, built its own test rig. Plans called for the MAN diesel on board *Prinzregent Luitpold* and a comparable Germania diesel on board a ship of the next series, *Kronprinz* (*Ersatz Brandenburg*). The schedule was overoptimistic and once war broke out MAN was fully occupied building submarine diesels. The big MAN diesel was not completed until April 1917, but the Germania test engine was completed for trials in January 1915. *Prinzregent Luitpold* was completed with an empty centreline machinery space. Because the diesel would not have been used at full speed, she was given larger turbines on her two shafts, so that she made about the same speed as her three-shaft sisters. Later ships were also to have had diesel power, but despite some claims it seems unlikely that any did.

There was also interest in a fully-centreline main battery arrangement. At a 15 January 1910 meeting Tirpitz ordered the next class modelled on the previous one, but with all five turrets on the centreline. Presumably that reflected abandonment of melee tactics. Aside from the rearrangement, the new ships were to be as close as possible to their predecessors, to save design and construction time. Underwater protection was improved. Tirpitz wanted the diesel pushed as hard as possible.

The weapons bureau (W) wanted a more powerful 32cm

(12.6in) gun for the 1911 and 1912 ships, in view of the increase in British (to 13.5in) and US (to 14in) calibres. It would penetrate better at 8000 to 10,000m.[59] Tirpitz doubted that battleships would fight at ranges beyond 10,000m. His tactical concepts, which included melee, did not admit greater ranges. Costs also had to be considered. Tirpitz left open the possibility that the 1912 ships would be given more powerful guns. Note that the British later thought that the Germans had decided to do exactly what W wanted – and Tirpitz rejected in 1911. In May 1910, looking towards the 1912 programme, Tirpitz asked whether it was necessary to increase calibre and, if so, whether it was necessary to retain five turrets. The weapons bureau renewed its call for a more powerful gun, this time of 32.3cm (12.7in) calibre. A ship so armed would, it was estimated, displace 26,000 tons and cost 54 million Marks compared to about 47.5 for the previous class. Some weight might be saved by reducing the medium battery from 15cm to 12cm (4.7in) calibre, taking the ship closer to the British ideal of the 'all big gun' ship. Tirpitz favoured reducing the number of such guns. He seriously considered a four-turret ship with more powerful guns – which later materialised as the *Baden* class. For the present, Tirpitz considered the more powerful ship unaffordable. He also wanted to build homogeneous squadrons.

The 1911 programme (Cruiser K, *Derfflinger*) was a new opportunity to bring battlecruisers up to battleship main battery standard, the 30.5cm gun of the 1908–12 battleships. Discussions began in May 1912. Near-term new technology included a triple turret being designed by Krupp and the big MAN and Krupp-Germania diesels planned for battleships. The naval intelligence department considered the 30.5cm (12in) gun a minimum in the face of British 13.5in guns on board the new battlecruisers *Lion* and *Princess Royal*. It could point to the all-centreline gun arrangement offered but rejected the previous year for Cruiser J (*Seydlitz*). The weapons department compared recent trials data for 28cm, 30.5cm and 32cm guns. Assumed battle range was 8000 to 10,000m and the target was the 250mm belt armour assumed for the latest British battlecruisers. The 28cm gun could not penetrate effectively, but at the minimal cost of 36 tons (weapons and ammunition) a battery of eight 30.5cm rather than ten 28cm could penetrate. The superiority of the 30.5cm battery would increase at greater ranges.

Ever determined to avoid cost escalation, Tirpitz resisted; the ship designed for long-range fire was a luxury he said he could not afford. He seems to have come around to the 30.5cm battery reluctantly, but it was the only one incorporated in the sketch designs. They began with the *en echelon* battery offered for *Seydlitz* and then quickly shifted to an all-superfiring arrangement.[60] At a 1 September Tirpitz meeting asked how much an additional turret would cost. The answer apparently convinced him to accept the four-turret designs. Tirpitz expected to show a design to the Kaiser on 26 September; to provide him alternatives the construction department delivered its three sketch designs with a 22 September memo. The two after turrets were somewhat more widely separated to reduce the effect of a lucky hit and also to improve fire on bearings near dead ahead. Armour matched that of *Seydlitz*. Scheme 4, a slightly modified Scheme 3, went to the Kaiser on 26 September 1910 and was approved. The ship was expected to cost a quarter to three-quarters of a million more than J. In fact Cruiser K (*Derfflinger*) cost 46.65 million: Tirpitz' nightmare series of battlecruiser cost escalations was effectively over. This *Derfflinger* was the last German battlecruiser design to result in a completed ship.

For 1912 another battlecruiser was planned, the first to replace an earlier armoured cruiser directly: *Ersatz Kaiserin Augusta* (*Lützow*). Given that the 1912 battleship repeated the 1911 design (*König* class), it was no great surprise that the 1912 battlecruiser was essentially a repeat 1911 ship. Design work coincided with the first overseas cruise by a new German capital ship, the South American cruise by *Von der Tann*. That seems to have been the first real experience of heavy weather. That emphasised the value of freeboard forward. There was interest in oil-fired boilers, which offered advantages such as smoke-free steaming, greater efficiency and easier fuelling. The Imperial Navy had experimented with oil firing a decade earlier and its coal boilers could have oil sprayed on

Once the Germans adopted turbines, they also adopted superfiring guns (which they thought of as an American innovation, as in USS *Michigan*). *Moltke* was a cruiser equivalent of the *Kaiser* class battleship, with thinner armour and 11in rather than 12in guns. She survived serious damage at Jutland and her sister-ship *Goeben* survived five mines in Mediterranean (nominally Turkish, actually German) service. She is shown surrendering at Scapa Flow in 1918.

them. The constructors argued that coal itself was an important part of the ship's underwater protection (at times the British constructors made similar arguments). As built, both the 1911 and 1912 ships had eight coal-fired boilers replaced by four oil-fired boilers.

Tirpitz exploited the forced German backdown in the second Moroccan crisis (1911) to help him pass his final pre-war Navy Law the next year.[61] It reduced the building tempo of German battleships to two per year in 1913. There was speculation that it could be the basis of a deal offered to the British under which they would accept a 3:2 ratio of strength over the German fleet. It is not clear to what extent the offer was merely a tactical one to make the Navy Law more attractive to the Reichstag. More important to the British was the increase in personnel and readiness. For Tirpitz the most important gain was probably enough money to build larger ships. Each of the two 1913 ships cost 57.56 million Marks, a jump of 8 million Marks over the 1912 ships of the *König* class. The money made it possible for Tirpitz to jump up in calibre to 15in.

In June 1911 Admiralstab chief Vice Admiral August von Heeringen, formerly chief of the general (intelligence) department, pointed out that not only the British but also the French were using more powerful guns, in their case 34cm (13.4in) guns in the *Bretagne* class. In August Tirpitz asked for alternatives: 35cm (13.8in), 38cm (15in) and 40cm (15.7in). This time he was willing to leapfrog the other sea powers. Adopting the 35cm would mean following the other sea powers (in particular the Americans); to Tirpitz the 38cm or 40cm gun would place Germany ahead, as he knew that no foreign gun of such calibre existed (the British had not yet chosen this calibre for the *Queen Elizabeth*s).

Tirpitz feared that the 35cm gun might only be a way station to the 40cm (16in gun). He preferred to jump as far as possible in one step because he wanted to avoid building another mixed-calibre squadron; Pushing the heavier gun, the W bureau argued for the prestige the jump in calibres would bring. Krupp told Tirpitz that 40cm was the limit for British-style wire-wound gun construction, so he would not be facing more powerful weapons within a few years. In fact the British built 18in (45.7cm) guns of this type during the First World War.

In September 1911 Tirpitz was offered two alternatives: ten 35cm and eight 40cm, in each case in twin turrets. W favoured the heavier gun, which could penetrate all known armour and would not fire any more slowly than the lighter gun. Tirpitz had to balance the greater hitting probability of 25 per cent more guns against the greater effect of each 40cm shell. His battleship designer preferred a four-turret design was better from a design point of view. On this basis Tirpitz asked for a four-turret design with twin and triple 35cm turrets. By this time several navies had already adopted triple turrets. This request probably explains published German arguments against the triple turret. Early estimates showed that a four-turret eight-gun 35cm ship would probably displace about 2000 to 3000 tons less than the eight 40cm ship. Tirpitz was also unhappy to do no more than match British super-dreadnoughts with ten 13.5in guns. It helped that the chief of the naval intelligence office (general office) told him that foreign navies were already looking toward heavier calibres. The German navy would have to do the same at some point. It might as well lead the pack. The Kaiser was first shown design data for a 40cm gun ship on 26 September 1911: Study D1a, with eight 40cm guns, fourteen 15cm and ten 8.8cm on 28,250 tons (177m long), with 1000 tons of coal and a diesel on the centreline, plus active roll damping.[62] In January

1912 Tirpitz received design data for the two alternative ships: one with ten 34.7cm (13.7in, nominally 35cm), displacing 29,000 tons and costing 59.7 million Marks; one with eight 40cm/45, which would cost over 60 million at 29,000 tons.

The 40cm design was elaborated between January and June 1912 and Tirpitz showed it to the Kaiser during Kiel Week at the end of June 1912, in the form of a 1:200 sketch. By that time displacement had grown to 28,500 tons. Tirpitz was able to reduce the estimated cost to 58 million by recalculating the cost of the heavy armament (21.4 vs 22 million), but that was too close to the edge of what was available. Eliminating the diesel would save another 1.7 million. The machinery section of the construction department argued that it was important to press ahead with this development in the interest of maintaining MAN and Germania; the work should be pressed ahead rather than slowed. Tirpitz chose to kill the diesel, accepting the loss of half a knot (nominal speed was 21.5 knots rather than 22 knots). Based on previous trials, he believed the ship would actually make 23 knots. Other important changes were additional 15cm guns (sixteen rather than fourteen) and modification of some of the 8.8cm anti-torpedo guns as anti-aircraft guns (at that time termed anti-balloon guns).

This ship was too expensive. As an affordable alternative, the constructors (K department) offered a ship with eight 38cm guns displacing 28,100 tons and costing about 57.5 million. Tirpitz chose the 38cm option on 6 January 1912. This was before the Royal Navy ordered its 15in (38cm) prototype. Design development of this *Baden* class was formally completed on 11 September 1912. This was the last battleship design completed for the Imperial Navy. One battleship each was planned for the 1914 and 1915 programmes.[63] They were conceived as somewhat modified repeat versions of the 1913 ships, to maintain squadron homogeneity. Plans called for further ships in 1916 and in 1917, but they were never ordered.

The Kaiser still badly wanted to merge battleship and battle-cruiser into a single fast battleship type, but Tirpitz continued to fend him off.[64] Cruiser 1913 (*Ersatz Hertha*: Hindenburg) was essentially a repeat Cruiser 1912 with the same 30.5cm guns, not the 38cm guns of the 1913 battleship.[65] Tirpitz could not afford a much larger ship.

Meanwhile, the British actually were building the fast *Queen Elizabeth* class battleships. Their security was good, so information about them reached the Germans only gradually. In November 1912 the German naval attaché in London reported correctly that the new ships would burn oil fuel only. Further information was obtained in 1913, the last bits from Winston Churchill's 26 March speech offering a building holiday. It became clear that they would constitute a fast division of battleships, more powerfully armed than battlecruisers. At the end of October 1913 there were, moreover, incorrect reports that the British were to build battleships with ten 15in guns as 'answers' to the two latest German ships.[66]

As insurance against that possibility, the intelligence (general) bureau called for a sketch design of a Battleship 1916 with ten 38cm guns and also a study to compare twin turrets with the triple and quadruple turrets being adopted abroad. The bureau considered five turrets better than fewer because they offered a greater reserve against the loss of a turret. An alternative showed two quadruple and two twin turrets, for a total of twelve guns. This project seems to have petered out in the summer of 1914.

Cruiser 1914 was *Ersatz Victoria Louise* (*Mackensen*). As of 1914 plans called for one cruiser and one battleship in each of the 1914, 1915 and 1916 programmes and one cruiser and two battleships in 1917. The projected sister cruisers were *Ersatz Freya* (*Prinz Eitel Friedrich*), *Ersatz Blücher* (*Graf Spee*) and *Ersatz Friedrich Carl* (A: possibly to have been named *Fürst Bismarck*). *Ersatz Freya* was the 1915 cruiser. The 1916 ship was laid down that year and the projected 1917 ship brought forward a year using war funding. All but *Mackensen* were financed partly by war budgets. Later in 1916 three ships of a revised *Ersatz Yorck* design (see below) were laid down. Only the first two ships were launched and they were stopped in 1917 while far short of completion. The third ship was launched in 1921 to clear her slip and the fourth was broken up on the slip, little advanced.

Although normally the design would not have been taken up until the spring of 1913, the apparent inferiority of Cruiser 1912 (*Hindenburg*) brought the project forward to the summer of 1912. As might be imagined, by that time the Kaiser was furious that in his 1913 battlecruiser Tirpitz did not match the heavy guns of the 1913 battleships, as he had been personally involved in the decision to adopt those guns. He believed that Tirpitz and his Navy Office felt free to short-change the 'front' (operational fleet) in their own reactionary interest. He compared Tirpitz' failure to the Prussian army's 1870 failure to adopt rapid-fire cartridge rifles (which the French had). This lapse was blamed for the catastrophe at St. Privat (which was actually due to attacking an enemy in close order). The Kaiser told Tirpitz that he was setting up the Imperial Navy for a similar disaster. Tirpitz could not evade the Kaiser altogether, so on 13 August 1912 he ordered his constructors to design a new battle-cruiser armed with four twin 35cm guns. Choosing a gun short of the 38cm battleship gun might hold down the size and cost of the next (1914) battlecruiser.[67] Tirpitz apparently considered 30,000 tons a financial and psychological limit, partly because he had just promised the Reichstag that his next ship would be no more than 1500 tons larger than the last (the 1913 battleship: 28,500 tons). It was bad enough that the 1913 battlecruiser would be so much larger than the 1913 battleship.

The constructors tried a variety of guns: 34cm/45, 35cm/45 and 35.5cm/50. In hopes of cutting size, design speed was cut half a knot to 27 knots and belt armour was cut from 300mm to 270mm. A new feature was a tripod foremast with a fire-control top, a feature which would be adopted by the *Derfflinger* class and other German capital ships in wartime. The addition of the raised fire-control position in the tripod suggest interest in greater battle ranges. At such ranges thinner side armour might suffice.

On 9 September Tirpitz was offered seven sketch designs. Even with the smallest of the three guns, trying to match the other characteristics of Cruiser K (*Derfflinger*) boosted a ship over the 30,000-ton limit, to 31,000 tons or even 31,500 tons. The designs fell into two series: A (34cm guns) and B (35cm guns). With speed cut to 27 knots and belt protection to 270mm, they were not far from Tirpitz' 30,000-ton limit: 28,200 to 28,400 tons for A and 28,700 to 29,800 for B. Variations relaxed the reductions. Thus A1 and B1 restored the earlier 300mm belts; A1 would displace 29,000 tons, B1 29,500 tons. To restore speed without adding power, A2 and B2 were lengthened (to, respectively, 222m and 224m; the previous ship had been 212.5m long). That cost about 1300 tons and breached the 30,000-ton limit. B2 was expected to cost 57.1 million. Scheme C was armed with 35.5cm guns and was even less

Reflecting Tirpitz's demand to avoid expensive new design features, *Seydlitz* was essentially a *Moltke* with a forecastle – which saved her after Jutland, when it was the only part of the ship above water at the bow.

affordable. Ten days after seeing the five sketch designs, Tirpitz chose A2 for development. The resulting A3 (31,500 tons, 18 September 1912) confirmed that he was in trouble: it displaced 4300 tons more than the latest design, for *Ersatz Hertha* (*Hindenburg*) and was expected to cost nearly a quarter more. This ship would cost 58 million Marks, about 11 million more than the 1913 battlecruiser and exactly what Tirpitz feared. Meanwhile another South American cruise, this time by *Moltke* (11 May – 24 June 1912) confirmed that greater freeboard at the bow was essential and that further boosted size.

At about this time the Kaiser became enamoured of the concept of a torpedo battleship, so the next sketch designs showed increased torpedo armament, with twenty-six and then thirty 60cm torpedoes rather than the original twenty-two. Moreover, the torpedo battleship idea required rapid torpedo fire, which in turn meant some means of rapidly reloading the tubes. Both increased quantity and fast reloading required considerable internal volume. Tirpitz had his constructors see what they could do in a ship limited to 29,000 tons, in effect a mixture of A3 and Cruiser K (*Derfflinger*) features. These ships were armed with the 30.5cm guns of Cruiser K rather than with the more powerful weapons now desired. Schemes 8, 9 and 10 were produced in September 1912, of which Scheme 8 had twenty-six torpedoes, the others having thirty each. All had the same battery of six submerged 60cm torpedo tubes. Cruiser K had had only four underwater torpedo tubes (in *Hindenburg*, 60cm with sixteen torpedoes). It was possible to enlarge boilers so as to maintain the 27.5 knots of Cruiser K. Armour matched that of Cruiser K. On this basis Scheme 8 was cut back to 219m. Cost was cut to 51.9 million, *i.e.*, with less than half the increase over Cruiser K that A3 had represented. Scheme 9 was cut back even further, to 215 m by eliminating two boilers. They and the reduced length cost a quarter-knot; she would have cost 52.9 million. Scheme 10 was lengthened for speed and internal volume (for torpedoes), to 220m (29,500 to 29,600 tons, 53.1 million).

Of this series, Scheme 9 was shown to the Kaiser on 30 September 1912. Meanwhile there was interest in upgunning Cruiser K, the constructors offering at least 35cm to match the new British *Tiger* and the new Japanese *Kongo* class. Improvement would have been effected after completion. The British may have been aware of this project, because once war broke out they thought, wrongly, that the *Derfflinger*s had been upgunned. The 30.5cm gun now seemed too weak. There were also further discussions of triple and even quadruple turrets. Given the requirement that battlecruisers enjoy a speed advantage over battleships, the advent of the 25-knot *Queen Elizabeth*s made it difficult to reduce speed to make the new ships affordable. The British were trying to negotiate a pause in the capital ship building competition with the Germans and the Germans suspected they were planning further fast battleships, capable of 25–26 knots and armed with eight or nine 38cm guns. Tirpitz correctly doubted this report; the next British battleships were the slow *Royal Sovereign* class.

At a 2 May 1913 audience the Kaiser demanded a more powerful armament, which meant the full battleship calibre, 38cm. The constructors offered ships with three twin 38cm turrets, D9 and D10, on the short hull previously tried with four 30.5cm turrets. The torpedo battery was increased to eight tubes (thirty torpedoes). D9 (29,200 tons) had much the same hull as Scheme 9, with slightly greater beam (29.5m rather than 29.3m) to preserve stability. She would have cost 55.6 million. The alternative D10 (28,500 tons) was not as beamy (29m) and was slightly slower (27.25 knots); she would have cost 54.7 million. D9 had a conventional main battery arrangement, but D10 had a single turret forward and two superfiring turrets aft. This sketch design is sometimes erroneously represented as the next German battlecruiser design (*Ersatz Yorck*). The constructors also cut back A3 as a new A16, with the same armament but a slightly shorter hull (223m, 30,000 to 30,500 tons, 27.25 knots (56.6 to 57.2 million). It combined the armament of A3 with the speed, protection and torpedo battery of Scheme 9. These sketch designs were submitted in March 1913 and further six-gun designs were submitted in June 1913. Of these, D48a was presented to the Kaiser on 28 June 1913.

W considered eight 35cm equivalent to six 38cm, so there was a parallel series of 35cm sketch designs: D47, D48, D48a, D50, D51 and D52. of which only D47 had two turrets forward. D52 had superfiring turrets at both ends, a twin superfiring over a single turret, the idea presumably being that the single turret could be accommodated more easily in a narrow part of the hull (for the same reason, the US *Salt Lake City* class cruisers had triple 8in mounts superfiring over twins). All of these designs came roughly within Tirpitz' tonnage limit and all had 300mm belt armour amidships. D48a differed from the others in having sixteen rather than fourteen 15cm guns. Speed was 29.5 knots. D51 differed from the others in having casemates on two decks; two of its forward 15cm were in the hull below the superstructure deck. D48a was presented to the Kaiser: 29,600 tons, 218.5 x 29.5 x 8.4m, turbines for 27.5 knots, price 55.3 million.

Tirpitz liked the 35cm gun because adopting it would preserve the clear distinction between battleship and battlecruiser, which was key to his plans to produce numerous more or less affordable battleship rather than a smaller number of much more expensive fast battleships. The Royal Navy had apparently ceased battlecruiser construction with HMS *Tiger* (13.5in guns) and the 35cm gun was certainly comparable. Tirpitz also preferred eight guns to six. Against that, he had to accept that the 38cm gun existed, but the 35cm still had to be developed and produced. He wavered. At the

end of October 1913 the naval attaché in London reported that on policy and financial grounds the British were tending towards smaller-calibre guns (34cm and 35cm) which could be mounted in greater numbers. The Kaiser was dubious. Tirpitz chose the ship with eight 35cm guns on a minimum displacement.

By this time it seemed clear that the Royal Navy had given up on battlecruisers. A ship with eight 30.5cm guns might be powerful enough. The idea died both because the smaller-calibre gun would be less and less effective at greater ranges and because it seemed clear that battlecruisers might find themselves fighting battleships. On 22 November Tirpitz offered the Kaiser Design 58, with eight 35cm guns, to displace 31,000 tons. Even then he was still considering ships with 34cm or even 30.5cm guns. A more detailed design was completed in March 1914, reflecting some minor weight reductions. The most important improvement was a small bulbous bow, adopted to improve hull lines which had been compromised when the superstructure was pushed forward to allow for expanded torpedo spaces aft. The final Design 60 was shown to the Kaiser on 23 May 1914. Changes included elimination of the stern torpedo tube of earlier German designs (torpedo capacity was reduced from thirty to twenty-eight). Speed was brought up to 27.5 knots (0.3 knots more than in Design 58). *Mackensen* was ordered on 14 August 1914, two weeks after the outbreak of war. Through 1916 the design was slightly altered to improve protection.

As laid down, Cruiser 1914 differed from all earlier German battlecruisers in having four rather than three shafts. She incorporated a major forward step for the Imperial Navy, a means of coupling turbines more efficiently to propellers. All previous ships had their turbines coupled directly to the propellers. Unfortunately propellers are most efficient at low speed, but turbines are most efficient at high speed. All major navies sought a means of coupling high-speed turbines to low-speed propellers. That is one reason why the US Navy adopted electric drive (it also offered much better subdivision). The alternatives were reduction gearing and the Föttinger hydraulic transmission, the latter unique to the German Navy. Design D48 originally envisaged the usual pair of direct-coupled turbines, but in later designs for *Ersatz Victoria Louise* (*Mackensen*), the 1914 cruiser, two cruising turbines were geared to the inner shafts. The desired solution using a Föttinger 'transformer' appeared in Design D48. These couplings were planned for this class.[68]

In March 1914 the constructors pointed out that without much change in dimensions or speed or hull weight, the same ship could mount four twin 38cm instead of twin 35cm guns. Displacement and therefore draught would increase somewhat. Tirpitz was uninterested, because at this time he was deeply concerned with the need to keep battlecruisers separate from battleships.

By the end of January 1915 the Imperial Navy had lost five armoured cruisers: *Yorck* on 4 November 1914, *Friedrich Carl* on 17 November, *Scharnhorst* and *Gniesenau* on 8 December and *Blücher* at Dogger Bank on 24 January 1915. Almost immediately planning began on direct replacements – new battlecruisers (*Ersatz Yorck* to *Ersatz Blücher*). Initially all were to have been repeat *Mackensen*s. In April 1915 thoughts turned to new designs for at least some of them. The project gained urgency with the loss of the armoured cruiser *Prinz Adalbert* on 13 October 1915. At that point only two of the pre-war armoured (rather than battle) cruisers were left, *Prince Heinrich* and *Roon*. Initially the Kaiser agreed with

Tirpitz to build one more *Mackensen*, which became *Ersatz Blücher*, the third ship of the class. *Blücher* had been the only one of the lost armoured cruisers at all comparable to battlecruisers; she had been a unit of the High Seas Fleet Scouting Force. The Kaiser did not see any immediate need for more new ships; surely new construction could be left until after the war. He also revived his earlier pressure to build his favourite type of ship, a single standard type of fast battleship rather than the previous combination of battle-cruisers and slow battleships. Unless that was done, he rejected any improved version of an existing design.

It did not help that the Reichstag saw little naval activity to justify further capital ship construction for an inactive 'fleet in being' of expensive capital ships. It was reluctant to vote further credits. By this time ship cost was noticeably escalating, due partly to wartime inflation. *Mackensen* was expected to cost 66 million, nearly half again as much as *Hindenburg*. Later the other four replacement ships were ordered under the war programme.

When Tirpitz resigned in March 1916, he was replaced by Admiral Eduard von Capelle, who make no attempt to exercise similar dictatorial power over the Navy Department. Tirpitz had been losing power since mid-1915. About the time he resigned, *Ersatz Prinz Adalbert*, the sixth replacement ship, was chosen as the first of the new class of 'Grosskampfschiffe' (large combat ships). The idea of a unified ship, which the Kaiser had always strongly favoured, may have been advanced at this time by Vice Admiral Hebbinghaus, chief of the general (naval intelligence) bureau, which often proposed ship characteristics. He considered it a compromise between the Kaiser's wishes, the realities of the Navy Law plan and the extreme requirements levied by new fleet commander Admiral Scheer. The cost of the war and the requirements of long-range battle (as demonstrated at Dogger Bank) and also of the new 'kleinkampf' being waged in the Channel from Zeebrugge meant that two separate lines of capital ship development were no longer affordable (as the Kaiser certainly felt).

The final pre-war battleship class to be completed was the *König* class, in which superfiring was finally accepted fore and aft to increase the broadside (with the same number of turrets) by a fifth. This is probably *Kronprinz Wilhelm*, the last of the class, which was completed with a heavy tubular foremast supporting a fire control top.

The new ship would be built under the 1916–17 programme (later the 1917 programme) rather than under war emergency programmes. To support this project, on 19 April 1916 the constructors offered three designs each for a unified ship (Grosskampfschiffe – GK) and for a battleship (Linienschiffe): GK 1, GK 2 and GK 3 and L1, L2 and L3. All would have been armed with 38cm guns. The GK series was based on earlier battle-cruisers. GK 1 would have displaced 34,000 tons and was rated at 29.25 knots (110,000shp); armament was eight 38cm, sixteen 15cm and the same five 60cm torpedo tubes as *Mackensen*. This design was an enlarged *Mackensen* with similar protection. GK 2 and GK 3 were somewhat larger (GK 2 was 38,000 tons, 120,000shp, 29.5 knots) but had the same armament and similar protection. GK 3 (38,000 tons, 115,000shp for 29 knots) had a raised stern for better seakeeping at high speed. Not surprisingly, the Kaiser liked what he saw. It seems to have been clear that the GK series met the fleet's demands for speed, protection and firepower.

The L series were fast *Queen Elizabeth*-style battleships with 350mm sides amidships and with the same armament as the GK series. L1 would have needed 65,000shp to reach 26 knots (34,000 tons); L3 was somewhat larger (38,000 tons, with greater coal capacity and a 95,000shp powerplant). As described by Griessmer, L2 offered ten 38cm guns, but it seems likelier that this was the battery planned for the larger L3. L1 was described as an enlarged *Baden*. All of these ships had a mix of coal- and oil-firing boilers, the constructors and Tirpitz' successor von Capelle rejecting an all-oil ship on the ground that coal offered valuable protection. An

Admiralstab memo dated 26 September 1916 mentioned two earlier draft battleship designs (not designated), a 34,000-tonner with 24 knot (presumably sustained) speed and eight 38cm and 38,000-tonner with 23.5 knot speed and ten 15in guns. Scheer favoured GK 2 and L3, which offered maximum speed and range.

In August 1916 the Germans assumed for planning purposes that the war against England would end in 36 months (in fact it ended in 27). Construction of a *Mackensen* was expected to take 36 months. Von Capelle did not want the navy to end the war with obsolescent ships, so he stopped construction of three of the planned battlecruisers: *Ersatz Yorck*, *Ersatz Scharnhorst* and *Ersatz Gniesenau* (and, if possible, *Ersatz Freidrich Carl*). He ordered a new design. Because all of these ships were being paid for with war credits, they would have to be laid down before the end of the war. Their design would be based on the GK series, which came closest to what the fleet (in the person of Admiral Scheer) wanted.

By this time work on improved versions of the GK series was already underway. It seemed possible to accept an additional 2500 tons of displacement (compared to GK 1, 34,000 tons) in order to buy stronger armour, above all an upper armour deck at least 50mm thick (as in GK 3). A reduction to 28 knots seemed acceptable. The resulting 36,500-ton design (GK 6) was submitted on 22 July, after Jutland. At this point it became clear that German harbours might limit the size of a ship, for example the locks at Wilhelmshaven. Scheer was unhappy with the reduced speed (28 knots). At this point Germany was building or planning seven replacement armoured cruisers of the *Mackensen* type and two more *Baden* class battleships. On 24 August von Capelle proposed that all of them be replaced by a homogenous four-ship battleship division.

When von Capelle joined in the correspondence on 24 September, he was clearly thinking about post-war construction, assuming that initially he could build four capital ships, either battleships or battlecruisers, making either three battle squadrons or two battlecruiser squadrons. He had come down in favour of battleships on the basis of (a) a memo by the General bureau on the relative value of speed and fighting power, (b) because eight cruisers but only two battleships were then under construction and (c) because it was possible to design a balanced battleship but not a balanced battlecruiser under the current limitations (the Kaiser asked whether this would always be the case). Von Capelle's four-battleship division would make a homogeneous squadron with the four *Baden*s. The dreadnought fleet would then consist of twenty-five battleships (four *Nassau*s, four *Helgoland*s, four *Kaiser*s, five *König*s, eight *Baden*s and later) and twelve battlecruisers (*Von der Tann*, *Moltke*, *Seydlitz*, two *Derfflinger*s and seven *Mackensen*s, not counting *Goeben*). To the Admiralstab this was an ill-balanced fleet.

The great question was speed. It was clearly an offensive characteristic, but how was it to be evaluated? To von Capelle's staff, it might be overrated. It would be most valuable if an enemy was sighted beyond fighting range or when a scout reported him – but North Sea weather was poor and the Germans had too few scouts. A faster ship could refuse action, but to do that she had to be much faster than her enemy and retreat was 'unpleasantly suggestive of flight'. A more powerful fleet might want speed to bring its enemy to action, but the Germans would likely be outnumbered. Surely what mattered was what happened in battle, when initial speed superiority might easily be lost. A slower but more survivable ship would be far more valuable.

Von Capelle concluded that the Germans should be building fast battleships, which should be designated 'grosser Kampfschiffe' (large fighting ships: capital ships) rather than battleships or battlecruisers (in German parlance, armoured cruisers). Unfortunately German warship designers were limited by German ports and waterways. Specific limits were set out in a 14 September 1916 memo on future warships. The locks of the Third Entrance at Wilhelmshaven limited ships to 771 x 101.7 x 31.1ft (the depth was actually 32ft 2in, but a margin of 1ft had to be allowed). To allow for larger ships, a fourth lock would have to be built. Other limits were imposed by the dimensions of the basins at Wilhelmshaven; difficulties connected with the Oste-bank; and that larger ships would be unable to proceed into the Jade and the Elbe except for a few hours before and after high tide. Maximum displacement of a battlecruiser within the stated limits (even with 32ft draught) was 37,000 tons. With her fuller form, a battleship might displace up to 41,000 tons.

After the war, German naval documents became available describing the discussion of further capital ship construction from the autumn of 1916 onwards, which meant the perceived lessons of Jutland.[69] The discussion began with a 3 September 1916 request from Tirpitz' successor Admiral von Capelle for characteristics of a post-Jutland capital ship. The fleet had been most impressed by the British 15in guns, so it wanted something more powerful, a 42cm (16.5in) gun. It offered much greater range (33,900 yds) and much greater effect per hit; the fleet wanted eight such guns. The Admiralstab pointed out that Krupp was fully occupied, so that supply might take far longer than the fleet imagined. It offered instead ten 15in. The 15in gun had already been tested (on land) under war conditions and it fired much more rapidly, hence had a much better chance of hitting.

For Scheer, long gun range had another consequence. German capital ships had 5.9in (15cm) guns not as anti-destroyer (anti-torpedo) weapons, as in the Royal Navy, but as rapid-fire supplements to the heavy guns; that was why there had been interest in mounting 17cm guns. The anti-destroyer weapon was the 8.8cm (3.4in) gun. With longer gun ranges, the 15cm gun seemed less and less useful. When Scheer sought weight savings so that he could get desired improvements, the 15cm gun and its ammunition became candidates. Two such guns were eliminated from battlecruisers under construction and Scheer wanted the ammunition supply of the rest cut by two-thirds, to fifty rounds per gun. At the same time the 8.8cm guns seemed less and less useful against destroyers and their numbers were drastically cut (the surviving ones were remounted as anti-aircraft guns).[70]

Scheer rejected von Capelle's idea of a single type of capital ship as too compromised. His most immediate need was for four battlecruisers. His had not been fast enough at Jutland. Something had to be done at once. Just as the British overestimated German ship performance, the Germans overestimated British performance. They believed that *Tiger* and the *Lions* had made 28.5 knots in action. They knew that the Admiralty had claimed 32 knots for the *Furious* class. If that was trial speed on the measured mile, it would correspond to a sustained (six-hour) speed of 29.5 to 30 knots, 4 knots faster than the *Mackensen* class. Had these ships had all-oil fuel, they would have gained at most 1.5 knots. The GK 6 design already used oil more than previous German ships; shifting to all-oil would buy only a knot. The Germans thought that eliminating coal would make the ship more vulnerable. Oil would

The battlecruiser parallel to the *König* was *Derfflinger*, which traded a turret and some protection for higher speed. The name ship of the class is shown at Scapa Flow after the war. During the war, Admiral Fisher and Admiral Beatty both pushed for more battlecruisers on the grounds that this ship was faster and more heavily armed than theirs; in fact she was neither.

have to be stowed either near boilers and magazines or above water, so as not to reduce radius of action.

Given the limit imposed by the waterways, Scheer could not have it all ways: he would have to trade off speed, protection and firepower.[71] Having sacrificed everything for speed, the British were now adding protection. The Germans thought the British were not limited in dimensions (they seem to have been unaware of the limits set by British docks), but even they faced financial limits. However, it could be assumed that the British would succeed in improving the performance of their armour-piercing shells and that would make protection even more important for the Germans (the Kaiser agreed in a marginal note).

As for speed, in a very long-range action, a slower ship could compensate by turning away slightly (the Kaiser queried this and added an exclamation point). Jutland did not seem to prove the value of speed: the German battlecruisers had been ordered to close the enemy (so that the German main body could escape), exposing themselves to the 'risk of being surrounded', even though they were not much slower than the enemy. On this basis the sustained (six-hour) 26-knot speed of the *Mackensen*s seemed sufficient. The Kaiser was sceptical of the Admiralstab proposal for a ten-gun ship; eliminating one turret would buy back the desired speed and it had by no means been demonstrated that, as the Admiralstab claimed, the five-gun salvo of the ten-gun ship offered much better spotting than a four-gun salvo. If the British improved their own protection, surely the Germans would have to adopt the more powerful gun.

Scheer pointed out that of the eight battlecruisers which had been laid down, not one offered the speed and gun power of the latest British ones (presumably *Renown* and *Repulse*). He therefore considered battlecruisers 'of the most powerful type', the first necessity. He wanted deck protection improved to resist the heaviest British guns, main armour extended almost to the ends of the ship (*Lützow* had flooded at the ends due to riddling), barbettes and turrets strengthened and conning towers enlarged and strengthened. Compartmentation was to be improved and pumping power increased.

'Hindrances' such as delays in building guns and in enlarging locks should be removed, not taken as fixed. Tirpitz' successor von Capelle pointed out that British harbours and channels were less limiting than German ones. Given her much larger naval industry, Britain could be much more agile in improving ships, for example in response to new technical developments. Germany also suffered from inferior coal: for a given horsepower they needed more or larger boilers, requiring more space and weight. Inferior coal had less thermal content and it also produced more ash, which required more frequent cleaning of each fire and reduced sustained speed. It appears that the Germans were not yet aware that the new British capital ships burned only oil, which created no ash at all. Finally, for the same gun calibre the Germans required more space and weight. For the same tonnage, a German ship could devote less of it to protection.

Adding up what Scheer wanted, von Capelle estimated it amounted to 20,000 tons when compared with the existing *Mackensen* design: 5000 to 6000 tons for increased speed, 7000 tons for heavier armament, 6000 to 7000 tons for extra armour and 1000 tons for other improvements. It is not clear whether these figures took into account growth in the ship due to added weight, as there is a considerable multiplier effect. Against this added weight, Scheer was willing to sacrifice only two broadside torpedo tubes, net protection and two 15cm guns and eight anti-aircraft guns, which might amount to 1000 tons. The upper limit on a battlecruiser was, as noted, 37,000 tons (because a fuller-form battleship (hull of *Bayern* form) might displace 4000 tons more, von Capelle suggested that it might be the better platform for the 16.5in gun). Von Capelle concluded that GK 6 was about the best that could be done. Sustained speed (six hours, bunkers three-quarters full) would be 25.75 knots. Scheer was willing to sacrifice torpedo nets, two of the usual five underwater torpedo tubes and some of his secondary guns, which amounted to 1000 more tons. The only hope for a powerful-enough battlecruiser was a fourth lock at Wilhelmshaven.[72]

Not surprisingly, Scheer considered GK 6 a bad bargain because it differed so little from the battlecruisers already laid down. If the obstacles to greater size could not be removed, it would be best to limit the next programme to battleships armed with 16.5in guns. The Admiralstab agreed with Scheer: it might be that only in a battleship could a useful advance be gained within the limits, but battlecruiser construction could not be abandoned until a new fourth lock was built at Wilhelmshaven, a project that would require many years of effort. Perhaps there was some other way to reconcile the fleet's demands within the 37,000-ton limit. To do that, the Admiralstab interpreted Scheer's demands as eight 15in guns, a service (sustained) speed of 27 knots, two armour decks, good internal protection, improved conning tower and barbette protection and bow armour at least 4in thick. Casemate armour might be dispensed with and side armour should be of the same extent as in GK 6, but thinner.[73] A marginal note indicated that speed and armament did *not* realise the fleet's aims.

All of this referred to a fleet designed for the expected future war against England. By this time many in Britain thought, after the Somme, that the war could not be won on land. Some sort of compromise peace would be agreed, after which there would be a pause and then the war would break out anew, the basic issues not having been decided. That was much what had happened during the Napoleonic Wars, the temporary peace having been the Peace of Amiens in 1801. The September 1916 German Admiralstab paper reflected much the same sort of thinking, presumably because of the failure of the attempt to bleed the French army white at Verdun.

The German fleet had been built, as far as the Admiralstab could see, to fight a decisive fleet action. Now there was another view current in the fleet, that no military means would suffice to overthrown England. The sole effective weapon was economic exhaustion by cutting trade and overseas communication. This view would soon triumph in the resumption of unrestricted submarine warfare. The Admiralstab saw formations of battlecruisers as essential complements to submarines, 'to hold open the gates of egress for attacking forces, to roll up the blockade line, to fight with isolated formations in their own territory and to support the war on commerce on the oceans'. Without choosing one view or the other (since the war would show which was correct), the Admiralstab observed that both possibilities required cruisers, so it would be no mistake to continue building them.

In October plans were announced to build the fourth lock at Wilhelmshaven, which would lift the displacement limit. On that basis the Admiralstab proposed to postpone battlecruiser building for the next two years or more and to concentrate for the moment on battleships. For the moment, the building programme included the replacements for the sunken cruisers, which had already been authorised. The last three were modified to take four 38cm rather than 35cm turrets; they became a new *Ersatz Yorck* class. This was essentially the 38cm *Mackensen* that the constructors had mentioned in 1914. It seemed possible that the first ship could be completed in the summer of 1919, the second and third in the autumn. In a 13 February 1917 letter to Scheer describing changes in the capital ships, von Capelle explained why and how he had ordered changes to *Ersatz Yorck* and the two later ships. Construction of the ships and their armour (and, presumably, armament) had been so badly delayed by overburdening of yards and factories with more pressing orders for war materiel that completion to a new design would not be postponed by more than about four months. The new design offered more firepower (38cm guns) and stronger armour. Work on the engines was so advanced that von Capelle had decided against altering them. Draught would increase by about a foot, length by about 14.7ft and displacement by 2400 tons. Given the same power, the ships would sacrifice about half a knot of speed. As in the other ships, two 5.9in guns would be sacrificed. The two broadside torpedo rooms in the forward and after parts of the ship would be replaced by a single room with two rather than four tubes, the torpedo load being reduced from twenty to sixteen or eighteen. Armour would be strengthened beyond what was then planned for *Ersatz A*, the last *Mackensen*, particularly in the armour deck, barbettes, turrets and conning towers. At the ends of the ship armour would be carried higher.

Improvements were also ordered for battleships under construction. Von Capelle listed them in his letter to Scheer. The *Baden*-class battleship *Sachsen* was already overweight, so the only improvement was an increase of 70 per cent in the floor area of its after conning tower. In *Württemburg*, the armoured deck over the magazines and central transmitting station was thickened by 20mm to a total of 50mm and the after conning tower enlarged as in *Sachsen*. In the first three *Mackensen*s, 1.2in (30mm) plating was added to bring the deck over the magazines and central transmitting station to 2.4in, the armour deck abaft the citadel to 3.2in (flat) and in parts to 4.3in and the lowest parts of the barbettes were thickened to 3.5 in. The floor area of the after conning tower was enlarged by 80 per cent. As partial weight compensation two 5.9in guns were removed. In the fourth ship, *Ersatz A*, which was not as advanced, it was possible to thicken the protective deck and the barbettes using single thicknesses of new plates, which would be stronger than the combinations of plates in the other ships. In addition, the armoured deck above the magazines and transmitting station was made 2in rather than 1.2in thick, the armoured deck abaft the citadel, including its slopes, was made 2.7in and 3.9in rather than 2in and 3.1in and the middle parts of the barbettes were made 5.9in instead of 4.7in thick. The after conning tower was enlarged as in the others and two 5.9in were removed.

The Germans were apparently unaware that British wartime programmes were going in very much the opposite direction, towards high speed and thin armour. *Ersatz Yorck* bears comparison with HMS *Hood*, which had been designed a few months earlier. As initially designed, *Hood* had much the same armament but a much higher speed (32 knots rather than 27.25 knots), with more than 50 per cent more power. She also had a much thinner belt (8in rather than nearly 12in). In this form *Hood* would have displaced about 36,500 tons, about 3000 more than the German ship. As redesigned with thicker armour, presumably comparable to that in the German ship, *Hood* displaced 41,500 tons. To reach her designed speed, *Hood* had to be far longer than the German ship and that made a considerable difference in displacement.[74]

Design work on the *Ersatz Yorck* class delayed plans for new battleships. They would not be begun before the end of the war. The alternatives were four 42cm turrets (22 knots), five 38cm turrets (22 knots) and four 38cm turrets (25 knots). In June 1918 the general (A2) bureau of the Navy Department weighed in with a memo arguing on gunnery grounds for more guns per ship, not least to make for more shots per salvo.[75] It argued that at long range hitting was a matter of probability: the more guns, the better the chance of hitting. There was an upper limit to salvo numbers: it was difficult to spot for more than a four- or five-shell salvo, with four shots easier to spot than five. At this time (and later) the US Navy preferred to fire full-battery salvos of up to twelve shots at a time and that apparently did not present problems. A2 argued that more than four shots would be a desirable salvo once guns were on the target and accurate observation could be dispensed with for a few salvos. Moreover, a four-shot salvo should be considered the lower limit because from time to time one gun might not fire due, for example, to mechanical problems.

A2 also argued that mounting two guns per turret was an unsatisfactory solution; he favoured four-gun turrets. A ship might have one four-gun and two two-gun turrets. Weight saved in this way might go into speed or into heavier guns. It was known that four triple 12in compared top six twin 12in offered a saving of about 1200 tons (these figures were presumably based on the Austrian battleships). A2 also replied to a 6 February 1918 memo arguing for a reduction in the number of guns to gain calibre. In this 9 February memo he argued that given the great variation in heavy gun performance, anything short of a four-gun salvo gave a disproportionately poor chance of hitting; with only six guns 'the prospect is practically nil'. The memo apparently argued that number of guns should be sacrificed for higher speed. A2 preferred to adopt three- or four-gun turrets.

In January 1918 the constructors offered von Capelle two alternative battleship designs to be offered to the Kaiser. In an earlier memo (18 May 1917) von Capelle had reported to the Kaiser that it was impossible to submit sketches because fundamental questions had not been answered, for example the decision as to whether torpedoes should be at the ends or amidships (or omitted) and what the speed of the ship should be. Now the constructors offered two alternatives, L20 alpha and L24 alpha, of which the former (44,500 tons) had submerged torpedo tubes and the latter (45,000 tons) had above-water tubes. Length had to be increased to 780.8 and 787.4ft respectively and to retain the metacentric height of the *Bayern* class beam had to be increased to 115ft. The constructors claimed that these were the extreme measurements possible for a ship using the Wilhelmshaven New Lock, presumably the Fourth Lock then under construction. Given the limits on size, it was possible to mount the desired eight 42cm

guns and to achieve the desired increased speed only by holding down all other requirements. For L20 alpha it was possible to increase speed by about 3.5 knots (under service conditions, to about 24.5 knots); on trial the ship might make as much as 26 knots. Compared to previous plans, the double-ended oil-burning boilers had been replaced by single-ended ones, improving arrangement. The longer L24 alpha might gain another 1.5 knots.

Negotiations with Krupp for the design of a twin 42cm turret were ongoing. Their outcome would determine the sub-division of the lowest part of the ship, including the machinery arrangement. As in the battlecruisers, the 15cm armament had been cut to twelve guns. The anti-aircraft battery would be 3.4in or 4.1in guns, as it had proven impossible to design a suitable 5.9in anti-aircraft gun. The torpedo would be the new J9, which was longer than the H8 in the *Bayern* class. That would make for a torpedo flat 9.8ft longer than in *Bayern* (the ship would have to be at least 6.6ft longer and that would cost 600 tons). The above-water alternative had been suggested by the general bureau (A). Abandoning torpedo armament altogether would save 200 to 300 tons and add welcome personnel space. There was increasing question as to whether torpedo development had been allowed to go too far.[76]

Armour thicknesses would match those of *Bayern*, the armoured deck being above the designed waterline. The constructors also tried designs with an armoured deck higher up, as in the

The last pre-war battleship design incorporated a new 15in gun. Although the decision to adopt the new weapon considerably preceded the British decision on the *Queen Elizabeth* class, the German ships took far longer to design and build. All five *Queen Elizabeth*s as well as *Revenge* and *Royal Oak* of the subsequent 15in gun class fought at Jutland, but the first of the two German 15in ships, *Bayern*, was not commissioned until July 1916. Her sister the fleet flagship *Baden* is shown at Scapa Flow in 1919 after salvage, having been scuttled in shallow water. She was used for tests by the Royal Navy. Among other things, they showed that the new armour-piercing shells adopted in 1918 would have been fully effective. (US Naval Institute collection)

battlecruisers, since that offered advantages in magazine, torpedo room and auxiliary engine room arrangement. However, that placed the armoured deck in an unfavourable position from the point of view of hits and armour thickness had to be reduced due to the greater armoured area. Two armoured decks were carried through the whole length of the belt. The lower armoured deck was strengthened above the magazines, engine and boiler rooms and transmitting stations. Compared to *Bayern*, heavy side armour was extended over the whole length of the ship except for the unarmoured extreme ends. In the fore part of the ship it was carried up to the battery deck. The barbettes and turret decks (presumably roofs) were strengthened. Both conning towers were considerably enlarged. The torpedo bulkheads were strengthened over the magazines, engine rooms and transmitting stations. At this point the thicknesses shown on the sketches were only provisional.

The Kaiser was shown the plans on 22 January.[77] They were accompanied by a memo by Admiralstab chief von Holtzendorff. The key question, as it had been for some time, was how much speed was worth; how much should other ship qualities, such as armament and protection, be sacrificed to gain it? Was the war to be decided by a large-scale battle, in which battlecruisers had to work with battleships? Or would it be decided by a U-boat campaign involving surface raiders? If the latter, the old type of battleship was superfluous. Surface warships supporting the submarines had to be fast enough to choose whether or not to accept battle. No decision would be possible until after the war. For the moment, a key point was that the Germans built more slowly than the British, hence had to have a margin of speed at the outset (since it would be eaten up by quick British replies). High speed had to be maintained for a protracted period. Oil fuel only would be best, but it would not be easy enough to obtain in foreign waters. The Kaiser had already recommended abolition of casemate batteries amidships to make it easier to replenish oil fuel at sea (the guns would be mounted instead in turrets). It became clear that the High Seas Fleet considered its battleships too slow; had they been faster they would have enjoyed valuable opportunities. Longer endurance (and better ability to keep the sea) would have made it possible to carry on the war at sea far from a home base. The existing 35cm gun had sufficient range and penetrating power; the choice between 35cm and 38cm guns should depend on which gave the heavier broadside in a long battle. Should triple turrets be adopted? Triples would give better bow and stern fire, but they were not 50 per cent more powerful than twins. The Austrians should be consulted on their experience. Ten 15cm guns would be a sufficient medium battery.

The meeting also considered cruisers for foreign waters. The number of bases would decide the type. In a cruiser design, the ability to remain at sea was the most important. Ships had to be fast enough to stop and examine merchant ships as well as to evade the enemy. They had to be protected only enough to survive 6in fire by merchant ships. On this basis, speed should be 28–29 knots for short periods and 25 knots for several hours, with economic running at medium speed and rapid acceleration. Armament should be uniform, with eight guns in midships twin turrets (either 6.7in or 7.5in). Displacement would probably be well over 12,000 tons (the Kaiser thought 14,000 tons).

At the meeting, the Kaiser revived his familiar theme: the Empire could not afford the luxury of two separate types of capital ship. Nor could the Empire afford to expand ship size indefinitely.

Some compromise type must be found. Admiral Scheer considered neither sketch design fast enough. If a certain number of fast capital ships should be built as 'advanced guards' for the fleet, then the appropriate sacrifices were the underwater tubes and perhaps one heavy gun turret.[78] Chief Constructor Dr Bürkner estimated that he could trade one turret and the submerged tubes for more than 3 knots. The best turret to sacrifice would be No. 2 rather than No. 3, because that would save more weight and it would also make for a better hull form. The Kaiser decided that, in addition to the submerged-tube type he had been offered, plans should be drawn for a faster type without submerged tubes and with three rather than four turrets. This should be the first ship laid down.

More generally, the Kaiser took the occasion to berate his constructors and his Navy Department for having produced inferior ships. On about the same tonnage, the British had produced *Valiant*, which had about the same tonnage and armament as *Bayern*, but an endurance of 20,000nm – surely that was a step towards what was wanted. All that the Navy Department could produce at about the same time was a 31,000-ton battlecruiser (*Mackensen*). Proposals made in the autumn of 1913 for six 38cm guns had been rejected by the fleet, who demanded, in the Kaiser's memory, eight 42cm guns; the Navy Department rejected that as impossible. In consequence it proved only a 35cm gun and only eight instead of ten or twelve. 'The English have shown in the *Valiant* that the Navy's demand can be satisfied with a smaller tonnage combined with much better armour protection.' This was in the Kaiser's own hand. The charges were a gross misrepresentation of the way the choices had been made, not to mention a gross exaggeration of the qualities of HMS *Valiant*.

A table of current ships showed that, apart from the British and the Germans, battleship calibres were generally 30 to 35cm, so it seemed to the Kaiser that ten 35cm guns would be enough for a modern capital ship. *Valiant* seemed to him to be a step in the right direction as far as fuel supply, speed and endurance were concerned. The ideal ship would displace about 31,000 to 32,000 tons, with 80,000shp engines for 27–28 knots, armed with ten 35cm/45, twenty 15cm and ten–twelve anti-aircraft guns plus eight twin torpedo tubes. With 5000–6000 tons of oil she should have an endurance of 20,000nm. The Kaiser added that she should have 11.8in (30cm) waterline armour, 20cm sides, 15cm elsewhere, 27cm turrets and a 35cm conning tower. The Kaiser also appears to have produced a sketch of a 12,000-ton light cruiser: two–four 21cm and twenty–twenty-four 15cm guns plus six torpedo tubes, making 28 to 30 knots on 50,000 to 60,000shp (this figure may have been provided by the constructors), with 2500 tons of coal and 800 tons of oil (or all oil) to achieve 14,000nm at 13 knots. None of this was terribly realistic. German files contained engineering evaluations of both the Kaiser's brainchildren. For the larger ship, the Kaiser's estimates of horsepower and range were wildly off. At 29,345 tons *Lützow* only made 26.43 knots on 80,988shp. Endurance at 13 knots would be 8300 to 8500nm. A more realistic figure for the cruiser's endurance would have been 5700 to 6000nm.

After the meeting Scheer wrote to von Capelle: he had always wanted a 30-knot battleship and he wondered whether the solution might be triple or quadruple main battery turrets. The possibility that such turrets would solve the speed vs. guns problem delayed further design work to the summer of 1918. In May 1918 the Kaiser asked what had become of the battleship plans and was told they were suspended pending the study. Von Capelle wrote to von Holtzendorff (Admiralstab) on 11 June 1918 with the results. Compared with four twin 42cm turrets, two quadruple turrets would save about 803 tons, three (rather than four) twins would save about 1322 tons and two triples would save about 1552 tons. If barbette weight was taken into account, the savings would be, respectively, 2377, 2337 and 3238 tons. However, quadruple and triple turrets should be given greater protection, given the effect of knocking one out; that would consume the saving in barbette weight. Barbette diameter would increase from 36.75ft (twin) to 40.7ft (triple) or 44.6ft (quadruple) and so would space required for ammunition hoists. Ammunition could no longer be stowed at the sides of the hoist rooms if torpedo bulkhead spacing were to be preserved. It would also be difficult to place triple or quadruple turrets near the ends of ships whose hulls were narrow enough to give the desired speed. Even twin turrets near the ends made for hull forms requiring enormous power. Ammunition supply would be worse in triple or quadruple turrets, as on technical grounds it would be impossible to match the rate of a twin turret. The firing rate per gun per minute would decrease from the 1.75 of a twin turret to 1.2 for a triple or quadruple, the salvo interval increasing from 17 to 25 seconds. A quadruple turret would fire two guns per salvo, a triple alternating one and two rounds per salvo. The total number of rounds per minute would be 14 for four twin mounts, 10.5 for three twins, 9.6 for two quadruples and 7.2 for two triples.

Having shown to his own satisfaction that neither triple nor quadruple mounts were worthwhile, von Capelle planned to offer two designs. One would be a powerful battleship with four twin 42cm guns (ninety rounds/gun) capable of 24.5 knots under war conditions (26 knots on the measured mile). The other would be the promised fast battleship with three twin 42cm (120 rounds/gun), about 27 knots under war conditions (28 knots on the measured mile). Both would have similar armour and three underwater torpedo tubes. If the tubes were omitted, each would gain about a knot. Von Holtzendorff replied that the plans for the fast battleship should be worked out, but he also said that he would recommend neither for construction: the 'powerful' battleship was too slow and the 'fast' battleship was not fast enough and had insufficient gun-power. Given war conditions, a new capital ship could not be finished before the new Fourth Entrance to Wilhelmshaven, which was already under construction. He therefore recommended that work on the locks should be pushed so that considerations of docking would no longer interfere with capital ship design. By this time the Kaiser had concluded that his beloved single type was impossible. He agreed that L20 alpha should be built, as well as a new fast battlecruiser. He reserved to himself the decision as to which would come first. The war ended before that could happen.

Given Tirpitz's determination to hold down the cost (size) of 'armoured cruisers' (battlecruisers), the German 1913 battlecruiser was essentially a repeat *Derfflinger* with 12in rather than 15in guns (*Mackensen*, the next year's battlecruiser, had 14in guns, but was never finished). *Hindenburg* was the last German capital ship completed during the war, in October 1917.

For his planned Baltic operation, Admiral Fisher ordered the world's first self-propelled landing craft, the X-lighter. They were plated against small-arms fire. Typical capacity was 350 men or 50 horses, although the X-lighter was sometimes credited with 500-man capacity. The X-lighter was too late for Gallipoli, seeing its first service during the Suvla Bay landings in the Dardanelles. Their use during the evacuation contributed to its success (no casualties). This one is shown at Mudros, probably in 1916, with a crated Farman aircraft aboard (the girders on deck are part of the aircraft). Wide wooden stairs led from the bow into the boat's hold, emerging on deck at the fore end of the line of bulwarks visible under the fore end of the crate. The bulwarks ran close to the centreline; part is visible under the crate. The derricks for the ramp are visible at her bow (at right) and the steering position, protected by portable plating, is visible just to the left of and behind the man standing atop the end of the framing section, presumably part of the aircraft. The box near the stern is the engine room casing over the engine room in the hull. At its fore end is the vertical silencer for the engine exhaust (the tube forward of it is the flue for the crew's stove). These boats had gun platforms, but were delivered unarmed. The base of the gun position is probably the dark mass visible behind the girder to the left of the crate (a gun screen could be erected over its fore side). Note the rubbing strake. The dark area abaft the boat's stern is the above-water part of her rudder. There was no kedge anchor to help the boat retract from a beach, only a towing bridle aft. The boats were called 'beetles' because of their profile (with the ramp-supporting horns forward) and because they were painted black. 'Beetles' had spoon bows to take a shelving shore. In effect they were self-propelled relatives of Thames barges, powered by a variety of diesel engines, for a speed of 5 to 7 knots. Those used at the Dardanelles were towed by freighters and colliers from the United Kingdom to Mudros (the tow from Devonport took 25 days), one of them being lost when the towing freighter (*Burrsfield*) was sunk by *U 33*. On delivery at Mudros, they received local pennant numbers: K for troop carriers (which made them 'K-boats') and L for fourteen boats converted into water carriers. At Suvla the 'beetles' proved underpowered: strong currents carried them past the planned beaching positions. Some beetles came close enough to shore that their ramps dropped down onto dry land, but others grounded well offshore, their troops having to wade ashore. Although the landing was conducted at night and was to some extent a surprise, many troops were killed because they were too tightly concentrated – they marched ashore in platoons. One platoon was wiped out by a single high-explosive burst. Nine 'beetles' were lost during the Dardanelles campaign. Later analysis by the US Marine Corps emphasised the concentrated targets the 'beetles' presented. X-lighters were also used during the North Russian campaign just after the war (twenty-seven were employed, of which three were lost). In 1916, nine X-lighters were converted to water carriers and five to fuel carriers for use in the United Kingdom; all were named. After the war, X-lighters were sold to France, Egypt, Greece and Spain (twenty-six boats). The Spanish boats, each carrying 300 troops, ammunition and stores, were used to land troops at Cebadilla Beach during the Rif War (1925). During the Rif War landing none of the boats got close enough to the shore and some Spanish troops waded out neck-deep. The landing succeeded because the beach was undefended. Five of the lighters converted for United Kingdom use served at Dunkirk. (L7192-043 © National Maritime Museum, London)

CHAPTER 9
Inshore Operations and an Inshore Fleet

BEFORE 1914 THE GREAT question was whether the Royal Navy should conduct an inshore operation in addition to its distant blockade. The possibility of reverting to a close blockade, or at least of setting up an advance base on the German side of the North Sea, seems to have arisen initially in the context of the possibility of German invasion of the United Kingdom, a staple of pre-1914 army thinking. It was taken seriously throughout the war, albeit usually in the form of a limited raid likely to be cut off. Perhaps because a German invasion from 350 miles away seemed conceivable, the British considered a long-range seaborne operation perfectly feasible. They had, moreover, an example in view: in 1914 the Japanese overran the German colony of Tsingtao in China, beginning with a landing on a nearby beach.[1]

Tsingtao fitted the expected pattern of an amphibious assault. Troops and their materiel were landed on an undefended beach, after which the troops conducted a conventional operation.[2] Getting the troops to the beach was a purely naval operation. It could be argued that even a defended place generally offered some undefended landing option. When Rear Admiral Lewis Bayly surveyed past British landings in 1913, he found that they were often conducted against places considered so impossible (as at Montreal) that they were not defended. What was different both at Gallipoli and in the German landings in the Baltic in 1917 was that the landing places were, at least in theory, defended and had to be overrun. After the war British amphibious doctrine emphasised undefended beaches, exploiting the mobility of seapower. The US Marines were concerned with defended beaches because there were no undefended spots on the islands they had to overrun. When they contemplated such operations late in the Cold War, however, the Marines also emphasised the undefended-beach option. When the British considered the possibility of a German assault on them, early in the war, they assumed that the Germans would have to seize a port to land their heavy equipment, particularly the artillery on which they seemed to depend, so the major

anti-invasion measure was to arrange to disable the East Coast ports as quickly as possible.[3]

On 31 January 1913 Admiral Bayly, who was about to strike his flag in HMS *Lion*, was instructed, presumably by Churchill (via the Admiralty Secretary) to report on the possibility of seizing an advanced flotilla base on the Dutch, Danish or Scandinavian coasts on the outbreak of war with Germany.[4] This was much the base required for the destroyer blockade which had previously been studied. The study was to begin on 3 March. Bayly pointed out that no base would be needed if the Germans sought early action. If they did not, the seizure of a base might draw them out: the existence of the base would be intolerable but, because it would be covered by the Grand Fleet, the Germans could not eliminate it without accepting a fleet action. Bayly ruled out earlier ideas of using an advanced base to support a close blockade, remarking in an interim report that the losses to be incurred would probably be greater than if the close blockade were carried out without the base. He also felt that simply sending the BEF across the Channel would most likely draw out the German Fleet in response.[5] On the whole, Bayly did not consider seizure a good step for the outbreak of war, although it might be useful later on.

This analysis was headed 'invasion question', and on that score Bayly wrote that it would be impossible to maintain a sufficient observation force to be certain of intercepting German transports without a forward base. The 1913 manoeuvres soon showed that he was right: a German force could slip through conventional patrols in the North Sea. Only near the German coast could patrols be made so dense that it would inevitably be caught. The conventional response was that raids could not be caught, but that anything larger was unlikely to slip through; it would surely be seen at some point. To Bayly, the certainty of catching a German invasion force was well worth the cost of acquiring and maintaining a forward base. There was, however, a further problem. It would be one thing to maintain a force off Wilhelmshaven, but quite another to deal

To execute his Baltic landing, Admiral Fisher needed expendable fire support ships. He ordered them in the form of the monitors, which were deployed to both the North Sea (as part of the Dover Patrol) and the Mediterranean. HMS *Raglan*, shown in the Eastern Mediterranean, was one of the first four, armed with twin 14in guns ordered from Bethlehem Steel for the German-built Greek battlecruiser *Salamis*, but undeliverable due to the outbreak of war. The upper deck abaft the funnel (which had been raised) was originally left open to accommodate a floatplane, but it was almost never carried. The aircraft was to have been handled by cranes on a pair of kingposts; only the port kingpost had survived by this time. The ship shows a single 12pdr at the after end of her extended forecastle. In 1916 it was moved abeam the turret and a single 6in in a shield mounted abaft the funnel (this gun was also mounted in the other Mediterranean monitor, *Abercrombie*). *Raglan* was sunk by *Goeben* and *Breslau* during their 20 January 1918 sortie, when both German ships struck mines and *Breslau* was sunk. (Dr David Stevens, SPC-A)

with an invasion fleet coming out of Kiel and through the Danish Straits (Denmark being assumed neutral and trying to avoid German hostility). A force from Kiel could also pass through the Kiel Canal and out past Wilhelmshaven. The Germans might also leave from major commercial ports, such as Hamburg. In any case the Germans could choose their moment, waiting until misty rainy weather set in. According to the *North Sea Pilot*, an attacking force could count, on average, on fifty-four days of fog each year.

Bayly's key point was that seizure of a base would have a great moral effect in England: 'victory is more often gained by offensive than by defensive action'. Instead of thinking about invading England, the Germans would have to concentrate on the threat posed by the British advanced base. The two possibilities were Borkum (245 miles from the Humber) and the Lister Deep (320 miles from the Humber). Borkum was by far the better of the two, with deep water on two sides. The Germans realised as much and had fortified it. Bayly used a series of historical examples to show that in the past the British had often carried out such attacks without ensuring full command of the sea, but had been content to cover any enemy ships which might contest the operation, so that they had to fight before doing so. The operation thus became a way of drawing out the High Seas Fleet if (as actually happened) it did not seek an early fleet action. 'Lastly, why are we to fear a German raid or invasion if we, with a superior Navy, are afraid to do the same?'[6]

Slightly later Churchill asked Bayly to consider how large a force the Germans could land in England either as a surprise attack or with the British fleet mobilised.[7] The study was designated 'oversea attack'. An 18 April 1913 memo from Churchill suggested three scenarios: (1) surprise attack ('bolt from the blue') to prevent despatch of an expeditionary force; (2) attack after the expeditionary force had gone far overseas (e.g. to India) and forces at home mobilised, but relaxed ('bolt from the grey') to overwhelm the United Kingdom; (3) minor raids after war began, e.g. to seize bases for flotilla action, with threats to invade in force so as to force a fleet action.[8] Scenario (3) could of course be turned around as a raid on the *German* coast to force a fleet action. All of this effort was fed into the Admiralty's contribution to a CID study of the possible scale of a German invasion: could the Germans land more than 70,000 men in England? That scale in turn would determine how much of a ground force had to be maintained in England if an expeditionary force were sent overseas. The Admiralty position was that as long as the Royal Navy remained predominant, an organised invasion by a European army of about 60,000 to 70,000, with all of its cavalry, artillery and transport, could not evade the fleet.

Bayly analysed past assaults from the sea and concluded that the keys were deception and sufficient force. Deception meant choosing the one place an enemy would consider impossible (due for example to rocks and surf) and also making at least one feint attack. It might be impossible to hide preparations, but false reports could still deceive an enemy as to the target. The largest possible force should be concentrated offshore ready to attack as signalled. Bayly was also struck by repeated references to special landing craft (flat boats during the age of sail). The Royal Navy already had ramped horse boats (suitable for guns of up to 4.7in calibre) which were typically towed towards a beach by destroyers or other ships, then released near the shore. Bayly's lessons were much the ideas applied to successful amphibious operations during the Second World War. At the time, Bayly was roundly criticised for basing his analysis on operations no later than 1801; surely the advent of steam, submarines, mines, wireless, machine guns near a beach and long-range guns further inland had changed the situation.

Bayly now applied his analysis to a British seizure of an advanced base within range of the German fleet at Wilhelmshaven. He concluded that British destroyers might be based in a variety of neutral harbours without any need to land an expeditionary force.[9] It was not of course clear why any of the neutrals would happily accommodate the Royal Navy. The next step was to consider Borkum. Bayly assumed that the fleet covering the operation would protect it from the German fleet, so he limited himself to what would be needed to overrun the island. His ideas included running some ships ashore to act as temporary fixed batteries, based on the Russo-Japanese War experience of the Russian *Retvizan*, which served that purpose while temporarily grounded. He added a detailed analyses of the seizures of Sylt and Esbjerg (in Denmark), and also produced a hand-written analysis of a raid on the Elbe to destroy the locks at the entrance to the Kiel Canal, thereby making it impossible to transfer ships rapidly between the Baltic and the North Sea. In effect Bayly produced a feasibility study which encouraged further consideration of such operations. Among other things, he produced sketches of the landing craft he expected to need and these sketches may have had something to do with the later decision to order such craft in numbers (unfortunately the surviving report does not include either the sketches or the characteristics envisaged).[10]

To the War Staff, Bayly had proved that the seizure of Borkum or Sylt would be a very serious operation (his numbers exceeded those estimated by the Operations Division). The attack force would undoubtedly suffer considerable losses. In fact intelligence as to the defences of these islands was spotty, so the projects were clearly gambles. In July 1913 the chief of the Operations Division

A series of shallow-draught 'Insect' class 'China gunboats' were built, reportedly to operate on the Danube once the Dardanelles operation had succeeded. They were ordered in February 1915. They were sometimes described as 'river monitors'. Given Admiral Fisher's much greater interest in the Baltic at this time and the fact that the Dardanelles operation was intended more to open the Black Sea route to Russia than to attack Austria-Hungary directly, it seems more likely that these ships were conceived to support a force launched from the Baltic as it proceeded south towards Berlin. The parallel but much smaller 'Fly' class were intended for the Tigris. HMS *Scarab* is shown as built, armed with two 6in and two 12pdrs. In many units the shields were later removed.

wrote to the Chief of Staff that, although gambles in war might be justified if the payoff were sufficient, in this case that would not be the case. Both islands were within range of heavy German guns, hence untenable by flotilla craft in daylight. They would probably also be attacked by small German torpedo craft. Bayly's plan was shelved as a useful reference, though probably not a guide to future operations. The underlying argument that seizing a base would force the German fleet out was not addressed. The Admiralty Operations Division produced a parallel report.[11]

Surprisingly, the project did not die. The file includes a set of detailed corrections, based on fresh intelligence, dated 19 November 1913. It in turn included questions to be settled by DNI (with his answers), suggesting that to at least someone in the Admiralty one of Bayly's operations was a real possibility should war break out. Probably the important effect of Bayly's study was to provide some idea of what a modern amphibious operation would entail. That affected all the early wartime amphibious proposals, both Fisher's Baltic concept and the Dardanelles operation. An early effect of the plan was that the Admiralty acquired three gunboats (monitors) which were being completed for Brazil. They were almost immediately used off the Belgian coast.[12]

On the eve of war alternative plans for a close blockade of the Heligoland Bight and for the seizure of Borkum or Sylt were circulated as Plans L(a) and L(b).[13] Jellicoe was unimpressed by either. He considered (a), which might be undertaken to catch a German invasion force, nothing more than an appearance of offensive action and as for (b) he considered a direct attack on a German naval base more useful. Churchill was undeterred by Jellicoe's remarks, however. On 1 August 1914 he sent a Most Secret letter to Prime Minister Asquith raising the issue and enclosing some of the reports; he wanted two army officers detailed to work out their side of a plan. That day a plan to seize the Borne Deep (Ameland Gat) in Holland as an advanced flotilla base was sent to the First Sea Lord, together with some important objections (the Dutch had considerable resources on the ground to resist this breach of their neutrality). Work on the plan to attack Sylt continued through early December 1914. DNC was asked whether the draught of specific old battleships and cruisers could be reduced as necessary. By this time the argument was not that the existence of a forward base would bring the High Seas Fleet to action, but that forward-based submarines and destroyers could inflict significant damage on it. The Sylt and Borkum projects were both brought into question in December 1914 because neither seemed to be far enough from other German territory to be immune to bombardment from the shore (later it seemed that Borkum was far enough off). Churchill remained interested. Late in December Bayly was made commander of the Channel Fleet, which included the elderly battleships needed to carry out the attack. It could be argued that the greatest flaw in his detailed planning was inattention to the possibility of underwater attack. On 1 January 1915 one of Bayly's battleships, HMS *Formidable*, was torpedoed and sunk while he steamed his ships in line ahead at low speed despite submarine warnings.[14] Bayly was removed from command and moved to Queenstown as C-in-C there – ironically, to be deeply involved in ASW, including the origin of Q-Ships. The Sylt project survived. With it survived the need for special craft for a landing operation.

On 3 January 1915 Churchill wrote to Admiral A K Wilson, who he had brought back to the Admiralty as part of his War Group, that all preparations should be made at once for the attack; all the necessary craft and appliances should be ordered at once.[15] They included:

1. Monitors for shallow water bombardment and subsequent defence of the base.
2. Gratings to protect vulnerable parts of the decks of the bombardment force against howitzer fire.
3. Transports for 12,000 men made invulnerable by nets and blisters, with facilities for getting quickly into boats.
4. Flat-bottomed craft for landing infantry, plated against rifle fire.
5. Shields for attacking enemy defences.
6. Arrangements for making smoke.
7. Indicator nets and mines to protect against German submarines.
8. Towing charges and modified sweeps for destroyers to protect against submarines.

The 'river monitor' HMS *Cicala* in her element, on the Dvina River in North Russia in 1919, fighting the Bolsheviks. (Dr David Stevens, SPC-A)

Small monitors were extemporized as 9.2in and 6in guns became available. Most were sent directly to the Dardanelles, where many participated in the August 1915 landing at Suvla Bay. *M 21* was one of a class of ten armed with Mk VI guns from *Edgar* class cruisers. The after gun was a 12pdr 18 cwt, the high-angle gun a 6pdr Hotchkiss on an improvised high-angle mounting. She is shown newly completed, still flying the Red Ensign.

Plans should be drawn up for attack on either 1 March or 15 April, a comparison between the two showing whether it was worth waiting until everything was ready. Bombardment would be supported by air spotting. Troops would be landed on the second day of bombardment. The High Seas Fleet would be prevented from interfering by forty British submarines of 'B' and later classes and by about sixty destroyers. The Grand Fleet would operate in distant support. The file on the Borkum plan includes a typed memo (probably from Jellicoe, but undated) arguing that the plan

Inshore operations were inherently risky (at one point Admiral Fisher stated that twelve battleships would have to be sacrificed at the Dardanelles). They were possible because in 1914 the Royal Navy had an enormous force of pre-dreadnoughts, at least some of which could be considered surplus. The old battleship HMS *Prince George* is shown at Salonika in December 1915, rigged as a specialist bombardment ship, with anti-mine bow protection forward. She had been sent to the Dardanelles as a 'mine bumper', suffering severe damage from Turkish guns during the 1915 bombardments. She was repaired at Malta and participated in the evacuation from the Dardanelles in 1916. She was hit by a torpedo which failed to explode. Early in 1916 she was paid off at Chatham and disarmed for such uses as auxiliary sickbay and destroyer depot ship.

might be worthwhile if the High Seas Fleet came out, but that the Germans would probably be content with inflicting heavy losses (as part of their plan to wear down the Royal Navy) during the operation; there was no reason the High Seas Fleet would have to come out. Churchill replied that he thought of the operation as the first step in an aggressive plan 'which would cow the enemy, beat him into his ports and mine and wire him in these'.[16] Surely the Germans would feel compelled to retake Sylt and in doing so they would expose themselves to the British submarines defending it. The file on the proposed attacks includes the first report of the attack on the forts at the Dardanelles, in November 1914.[17]

When he returned on 30 October 1914 as First Sea Lord, Fisher began to promote another amphibious operation, this time on the German Baltic coast in Pomerania. He had long maintained that a stretch of coast about 10 miles long was particularly sensitive to the Germans and that the navy could land a large Russian army there. It could entrench itself and tie down a vast number of Germans, relieving pressure on both the Western and the Eastern Fronts. In 1914 the only substantial British naval force capable of bringing that Russian army into place was the Grand Fleet. The question was whether, once it was in the Baltic, the High Seas Fleet would be freed for offensive action. Fisher's immediate answer was that he could lay sufficient mines to hold the Germans back long enough, but his own planner, Julian Corbett, felt compelled to ask why the same mining argument could not apply to the Grand Fleet itself in the shallow Baltic.[18] At the outbreak of war, the Germans tried to block the Danish Straits, the entrance from the North Sea to the Baltic. They forced the Danes to mine their own waters, but they failed to convince the Swedes. The Swedish refusal to mine their own offshore waters left a wide clear (if shallow) path into the Baltic. At this time Fisher was also interested in an army attack up the Flanders coast to throw the Germans out of their new base at Zeebrugge. That soon had to be abandoned as impractical.[19]

In December 1914 and again early in January 1915 Fisher backed Churchill's Borkum plan in the War Council. He said that once the Borkum operation had destroyed the High Seas Fleet or mined and netted it into its harbour, a further operation could be

Fisher needed an expendable covering force for any Baltic operation. This requirement seems to explain the otherwise bizarre 'large light cruisers' *Glorious* and *Courageous*. Fisher's theory seems to have been that they could deal with the German pre-dreadnoughts in the Baltic as long as the German dreadnoughts were pinned down by the threat of the Grand Fleet in the North Sea. Fire-control limitations would make it difficult for a German pre-dreadnought to take on a 32-knot 'large light cruiser'. If the Germans rose to the bait, in theory the Grand Fleet could support attacks, for example on the locks of the Kiel Canal, which would make it impossible for them to return to their base in the North Sea. As an adherent of the 'do not complain, do not explain' school, Fisher never explained his reasoning, so his 'Baltic Scheme' has been subject to ridicule. Without the scheme, it is difficult to justify the 'large light cruisers', and they were converted into carriers immediately after the war. HMS *Glorious* is shown late in the war, with aircraft atop both of her turrets. In 1917 both she and her sister-ship *Courageous* were given heavy additional torpedo batteries: six twin tubes, one each side abreast the mainmast and two each side around the after turret. In the spring of 1917 *Courageous* had mine rails installed on her quarterdeck, but she never laid any mines.

mounted in the Baltic, culminating in an army landing on the Pomeranian coast near Berlin. A blockade in the Baltic would have cut Germany off from Swedish iron ore, paralysing its arms industry.[20] By this time Fisher was ordering large numbers of new warships, which he later wrote were all associated with his Baltic plan. Most of them were not necessarily intended for the Baltic, but the monitors and the landing craft were useful only for inshore amphibious work.

The background of the monitors is obscure.[21] Until late 1914 bombardment meant using obsolete battleships, as HMS *Revenge* (later renamed *Redoubtable*) was used during the autumn of 1914 on the Flanders coast. Once Admiral Fisher rejoined the Admiralty at the end of October 1914 it was probably clear that some amphibious operation was likely. Churchill had already acquired the three Brazilian river monitors. On 3 November 1914 Charles S Schwab, President of the US Bethlehem Steel Corporation, visited the Admiralty seeking contracts. He offered to build twenty 'H' class submarines. He also offered the four twin 14in turrets ordered to arm the Greek battlecruiser *Salamis*, then under construction in Germany – and undeliverable due to the British blockade. At the time heavy guns were relatively easy to obtain, but not full gun mountings including turrets. Schwab's four mountings were uniquely valuable. Fisher could have decided to incorporate them in a British ship (the Chilean battleship *Almirante Cochrane*, taken over as HMS *Canada*, had similar twin 14in guns), but instead he had his

Third Sea Lord (Controller) immediately ask his Director of Naval Construction (Tennyson d'Eyncourt) to design two armoured monitors, to be completed in four months, each to be armed with two 14in guns or equivalent. Since there were four turrets in all, four ships were ordered. Churchill called them the 'Styx' class and he soon wanted more. The remaining sources of complete heavy gun mountings were obsolete *Majestic* class battleships with two turrets each (gun elevation could be increased to 30° to give them the desired range) and turrets ordered for the battleships *Repulse* and *Renown*, which became surplus when the ships were reordered late in November 1914 as three-turret battlecruisers. Four *Majestics* were disarmed to produce eight 12in gun monitors, giving a total of fourteen battleship-calibre monitors. Smaller-calibre guns from cruisers armed fourteen 9.2in gun monitors and battleship 6in guns removed from mountings that turned out to be too wet armed another five monitors. The monitors would have provided any landing force with artillery support until its own guns and their transport were landed. Whether they represented any such plan and whether the variety of capabilities involved (from heavy guns down to the sort armies typically moved with them) is not clear. Some of the guns just happened to be available, but it is also possible that they were sought out.

In addition to the monitors were twelve 'China gunboats' slightly larger than the 6in coastal monitors and armed with two 6in guns each ('Insect' class) which Fisher called river monitors in one of his lists of ships ordered under his leadership. They were said to be for service on the Danube and thus were later associated, at least publicly, with the Gallipoli operation. However, in 1914–15 the Royal Navy was using cover designations for operations. Thus the projected assault on Borkum became first an assault on the nearby island of Sylt and then, in the same file, an assault on Danzig. On this basis the 'China' designation and the 'Danube' designation may both have been covers for the use of a gunboat on a river leading from the North Sea, the idea being that it would provide mobile artillery support for an advancing army. There were also twelve smaller 'Fly' class river gunboats (one 4in each) built in sections and erected (after Fisher left office) in Mesopotamia; four more were ordered after Fisher left the Admiralty. They too might be seen as potential supporting units for an advance south from the Pomeranian coast. Nothing tied either to a particular place and both proved useful later. In the absence of detailed records, it is impossible to say whether they were conceived for Fisher's project.

The landing craft seem to have derived from Bayly's 1913 proposal. Fisher ordered them about 20 February 1915 for 'Home Expeditions'.[22] Fisher's new construction programme included 200 large and ninety smaller barges, the former carrying 500 men or horses, the latter 250 men each. The large barges were diesel-powered and protected against small-arms fire. The 200 large barges were all ordered in February 1915, designated *X.1* to *X.200*. Nearly all had been delivered by August 1915. Another twenty-five were ordered in February 1916 (*X.201* to *X.225*), plus twenty-five unpowered ('dumb') versions (*DX.1* to *DX.25*) to be towed by X-lighters. The smaller *Y.1* to *Y.60* were ordered in February 1915, followed by *Y.61* to *Y.90* slightly later. All were either unpowered or propelled by outboard engines. The landing craft fleet is usually described as capable of landing 50,000 men on a beach, with their horses and other equipment.

The monitors and the landing craft were clearly intended to support an amphibious operation, although it also turned out that the monitors could very usefully bombard the Flanders coast and even act as minor capital ships for the Dover Patrol. The landing craft are easier to tie to Fisher's project. They were ordered in February 1915 on an urgent basis, at a time when the Dardanelles was still conceived as a naval operation without troop support. 'Home Expeditions' was clearly a cover.

Fisher also ordered the two large fast shallow-draught battle-cruisers *Renown* and *Repulse* and three large-gun 'large light cruisers' (*Courageous*, *Glorious* and *Furious*). As was his frequent practice, Fisher did not provide any consistent justification. There was opposition to both projects, so he asked Jellicoe to write him an informal letter explaining why fast new battlecruisers were essential for his fleet (Fisher's argument was that nothing except the 29-knot *Tiger* could catch the new German battlecruiser *Lützow*). However, when he gave evidence before the Dardanelles Committee, he made much of the shallow draught of all five ships. Instructions to DNC for the *Repulse* class demanded shallow draught 'for strategical reasons'. Supposedly the 'large light cruisers' were ordered as such because sanction had been given for additional cruisers and there might have been problems with additional capital ships.[23] Fisher wanted all five ships completed within a year, which would have meant by the end of 1915. That was impossible, but even so construction was extremely fast.

Despite his claims, Fisher did not order any single integrated programme on 3 November 1914 or any other day; the story of the monitors alone shows otherwise.[24] The 3 November meeting was specifically about accelerating the submarine programme, with some reference to later projects. Nor can his programmes be associated unambiguously with the Baltic, as Fisher claimed in 1916; most of the ships could be seen either as essential counters to the new German threats of mines and submarines, or as a continuation of pre-war designs to make up for wartime losses and to fill unexpected gaps. The latter particularly applied to destroyers and submarines.

However, parts of Fisher's large new fleet might well have changed the character of a Baltic operation, because they constituted a new inshore fleet which might have been sent into the Baltic instead of the Grand Fleet. In effect many of the new ships formed an expendable second fleet. The German Baltic fleet was weak, because the bulk of the German fleet had to retained in the North Sea to face the Grand Fleet. If the Germans did not shift forces into the Baltic, the weak force there would have been overwhelmed by Fisher's five special capital ships (at least in pre-Jutland thinking, in which lightly-armoured fast capital ships were considered survivable).

The Gallipoli landing was hurriedly arranged and the shipping extemporised. The most impressive improvisation was the 6000-ton collier *River Clyde*, which was rigged, in effect, as an infantry landing ship, with four sally ports for troops along her sides. Her conversion was proposed by Commander Edward Unwin RN, who had been Grand Fleet Coaling Officer and was placed in charge of lighters at Mudros, during the run-up to the landing at Gallipoli. Unwin made his suggestion at a meeting to discuss details of the landing from boats. Unwin argued that since the beaches were defended, it would be fatal to land from open boats. Upon grounding, boats would become targets, filled with men without cover. Instead, troops should ride ashore on board an old steel merchant ship with a hole cut in her bow, from which a ramp could carry them ashore after she grounded. She could also bring in ammunition and serve as a water distilling plant. Such a ship would be destroyed by enemy artillery – but the Turks had only machine guns at the beaches. The chairman of the meeting, Captain G P W Hope, rejected the idea (because it would create too lucrative a target), but it was rescued by Rear Admiral Rossyln Weymss, commander at Mudros. The collier was fitted out by the repair ship *Reliance*. Instead of a long bow ramp, Unwin chose a self-propelled hopper barge, which would be towed alongside the collier. Any gap between her and the collier would be filled by lighters. Instead of a hole in the bow, holes were cut in the ship's sides and wooden staging built so that troops could run down to the lighters at the bow. Twelve machine guns were mounted amid sandbags in the ship's bow and the ship's bridge was armoured with two thicknesses of half-inch plating. Unwin commanded the collier, which was allocated to V Beach. She carried about 2000 troops. What happened next demonstrated how difficult an amphibious operation can be. *River Clyde* carried back-up troops, but she got to the beach before the initial assault troops and the army officers on board wanted Unwin to wait. That was difficult, as with the hopper lashed alongside he could not go astern. He managed to circle and then go back towards the beach, but he grounded further out than expected due to an unknown reef. It did not help that the Turkish machine guns were protected by stone and sand-bags, hence immune to machine gun fire from the ship; they cut troops down as they ran down the causeway of lighters. Had the ship had even a small gun, such as a 12pdr, she would have been able to deal with these defences. Even so, the ship protected a large number of troops, who went ashore in reasonable safety after night fell. To the US Marines who looked to Gallipoli for lessons applicable to their own plans for the Pacific, Unwin's idea was brilliant but incomplete. His ship was the best vantage point of all for seeing what the troops needed in the way of fire support, but he had no way of communicating to the battleships offshore, or to the flagship. Even so, one Marine officer argued that, had similar ships been used at all three beaches, the landing force would have succeeded. It was most unfortunate that Unwin's brilliant innovation was considered an experiment and not fully supported. (D3126-A, © National Maritime Museum, London)

River Clyde approaching the beach, with the steam hopper lashed alongside and wooden staging visible on her side. The ship's momentum was to have carried the steam hopper forward to act as a bridge between the ship and lighters forming a causeway to the beach. Amid the din of shellfire, the engine-room crew of the hopper panicked and she reversed. Commander Unwin improvised a causeway of lighters, held together by a taut line – the shore end of which he wound around himself. Note the sandbagged machine gun position in the bow of the *River Clyde*. This painting by W L Wyllie was based on a sketch by a naval officer who was present at the landings. (PW2078, © National Maritime Museum, London)

Troops disembarking on W Beach (Gallipoli), showing the ships' boats in which troops approached the beach. Boats were towed in strings (usually of four) to within a few hundred yards of the beach. To right of centre a steam picket boat from HMS *Agamemnon* has slipped her tow, skeleton crews from the ships rowing the boats the last few hundred yards to the beach. There were no self-propelled landing craft. This mode of approach was far more rapid than by single oared boats, but it also created concentrated targets for the defenders. Typically a cutter carried about thirty-two troops. Later analysis by the US Marine Corps, which was very much interested in amphibious attacks on defended beaches, emphasised the narrowness of the beaches, a total frontage of 900 yds on X, W and Y beaches, to which eighteen tows were directed. This crowding demanded particularly good seamanship. The Anzac force landed 1500 men at night on 1000 yds of beach (Anzac Cove) – which turned out not to be the intended objective, but, fortunately, was undefended. That involved twelve tows (forty-eight cutters). The same boats landed 12,000 men in less than eight hours. The Marines concluded that the landing force had to move as quickly as possible towards the beach, to minimise the effect of enemy fire (hence had to be in powered boats) and that the targets it represented had to be multiplied as far as possible. That is why US (and British) infantry landing craft of the Second World War typically carried only about forty men each. This painting by W L Wyllie was again based on a sketch by a naval officer present at the landing. (PV1023, © National Maritime Museum, London)

Fisher planned to delay any move by the High Seas Fleet by simultaneously mounting attacks on the German North Sea islands backed by the Grand Fleet (the battle of Heligoland Bight had shown that it could survive there). He expected that before long the force of German public opinion (actually, the force of German army and elite opinion) would compel the Germans to put the High Seas Fleet into the Baltic, opening the German North Sea coast to attack. Not only could the British mine the approaches from Wilhelmshaven (and destroy the German minesweeping force), they could probably destroy the locks of the Kiel Canal. That would prevent the High Seas Fleet from moving back into the North Sea. Both the mining and the lock destruction projects had been discussed in 1914.

In the Baltic, moreover, the High Seas Fleet would be subject to attack by the mass of submarines and destroyers which would have accompanied the British assault force. By early 1915 the British already had submarines operating successfully from Russian bases in the Baltic. The German official history provides considerable evidence that the presence of British submarines always worried the German fleet command, whose ASW was even less effective than that of the Royal Navy. It might be inferred that to Fisher the large new submarine force he ordered late in 1914 was part of his Baltic enterprise. The fleet in the Baltic would have been supported by the Russians at Riga and it would have supported a mass Russian landing in Fisher's favoured place on the Pomeranian coast, well behind the German front in the East. Fisher wrote that 'it is the Russians we want to enter Berlin, not the French or English'.

Fisher's building programme did not include transports, but plans for Bayly's Borkum project generally included obsolete battleships and cruisers carrying assault boats. At this stage of the war there would not have been any specific programme for troop carriers, because merchant ships were plentiful and they could easily have been modified (as at Gallipoli). Fisher's programme also included sweepers (sloops), although they seem to have been intended mainly to support the Grand Fleet.

Fisher's friend and biographer Admiral Bacon argued that the Baltic project had been unjustly condemned.[25] By the time he was writing, Bacon had planned an abortive mass landing on the Belgian coast (in 1917). He was convinced that if the location of the landing beach could be kept secret, a landing in the Baltic would have been perfectly feasible. Given Fisher's mass of landing craft (assuming they would have been successful), two divisions could have been delivered in half an hour and two more every day for several days. The Russians would have dug in. Although the idea seemed bizarre at the time, given the failure of amphibious attack at Gallipoli, it was very much in accord with later amphibious thinking. As long as an enemy cannot predict where the blow will fall, it is impossible for him to mass sufficient forces at the point of attack.[26] A ten-mile (or longer) stretch of beach on the Baltic was very different from narrow beaches at Gallipoli under cliffs dominated by an alert Turkish army. Presumably Fisher doubted that the Germans would have mined their own coast.

The scene from *River Clyde* gives some idea of the sheer variety of shallow-draught craft used for the landing. None was powered; all had to be rowed or towed into place. A few horse boats, like the one on the right in the foreground, could be unloaded over ramps. This one is being used as part of a causeway leading ashore, mainly for horses. (Dr David Stevens, SPC-A)

Fisher may have thought that even a credible threat of an operation, backed by a construction programme, would be decisive. During the Crimean (Great Russian, in the terminology then used) War, the British Baltic Fleet successfully bombarded a Russian naval fortress at Sveaborg. That showed that assault on such fortresses was feasible and the British began a massive (and well-publicised) programme to build the inshore attack force which would be needed to strike at the Russian capital of St Petersburg. The credible threat of such an attack, which was never carried out, seems to have been a decisive factor in convincing the Russians to end the war. Fisher joined the Royal Navy in 1854, before these events, of which he was doubtless well aware. Later he was part of the mobilisation of a new Baltic Fleet against Russia in 1885.

When Fisher was first selling his Baltic offensive at the end of 1914, he had neither the expendable fleet nor even its monitors and landing craft. Any Baltic operation would have risked the Grand Fleet – or, it might be said, would be impossible until the Grand Fleet dealt with the High Seas Fleet. Fisher finessed the problem with talk about mining in the High Seas Fleet, but that was probably not serious.[27] Chief of Staff Admiral H F Oliver later recalled wondering how the Grand Fleet, proceeding into the Baltic in single file behind its minesweepers, would deal with an attack by the High Seas Fleet, perhaps directly across its 'T'. Fisher was extremely devious, so it is difficult to be sure of his motives. At the end of 1914 and early 1915 the War Council had by no means decided to keep reinforcing the army in France; it was quite interested in alternatives – which eventually meant Gallipoli. There also seems to have been a widespread view that the only decisive front was in the East, that nothing done in the West could compel the Germans to make peace.

In these circumstances, Fisher had to keep the idea of a war-winning Baltic operation alive, even if it was not yet at all practical.

Conversely, Churchill had to prevent Fisher from killing his own favourite project, the Dardanelles. Fisher's biographer Ruddock Mackay argues that Churchill approved the first two of Fisher's three freak cruisers (for the Baltic) as a way of placating Fisher during a crucial discussion of the Dardanelles project (this may have been about Borkum, not the Dardanelles). Presumably Fisher believed that the Dardanelles project would disappear, leaving the Baltic project alive. Both Fisher and Churchill liked the monitor programme, because each considered it valuable for his own favoured project. Chief of Staff Admiral Oliver pointed out that even if they were taken, Borkum or Emden could not be held without surplus troops which did not exist. Oliver thought that Fisher had pressed the impractical Baltic project specifically to kill Churchill's suicidal Borkum project.[28]

At the end of 1914, Fisher could look forward to both monitors and landing craft becoming available within the next six months. Six months later he expected to have the shallow-draught battlecruisers and a mass of new destroyers and submarines, both of which were needed for his Baltic fleet. He was also buying anti-submarine ships and minesweepers and he may have seen the rationales for both as a way of obtaining what he needed for the larger operation. All of this is necessarily speculative. Fisher was given to grand claims and he did not leave a detailed campaign plan. The one sketched here is necessarily surmise based on Bacon's account; Bacon had access both to Fisher and to papers now lost. It does seem fair to say that in order for the Baltic operation to be carried out, Fisher had to protect his new fleet from being frittered away during 1915. His complaint, as expressed by Bacon, was that much of the fleet was 'diverted and perverted to the damned Dardanelles'. By the time the ships actually were ready, Fisher had resigned in disgust. It is not clear whether he hoped, as with previous attempted resignations, to gain sufficient control to hold things together through early 1916, when the Baltic fleet would have been ready.

When Fisher joined the Admiralty on 30 October 1914, an initial war programme of repeat orders for existing designs had already been approved the previous September: two repeat *Calliope* class cruisers, twelve destroyers and eight submarines. Fisher's new programme amounted to:[29]

– Five shallow-draught battlecruisers.
– Two light cruisers (*Centaur* class, ordered December 1914).
– Five flotilla leaders (three ordered November 1914, two more February 1915).
– Fifty-six destroyers (but total orders between November 1914 and May 1915 amounted to seventy-six ships: thirty-one 'M' class ordered in November 1914, sixteen 'M' class ordered February 1915, sixteen 'M' class ordered May 1915, one Yarrow 'M' class ordered November 1914 and two in February 1915, two Thornycroft M class ordered November 1914 and two in February 1915, four *Talisman* class ordered November 1914 and two Admiralty 'R' class ordered in February 1915).[30]
– Sixty-four submarines (all ordered in November 1914: *E 19–E 56* [thirty-seven boats: *E 28* cancelled], *G 8–G 14* [seven boats], twenty 'H' class [ordered from Bethlehem Steel in the United States]).[31]
– Thirty-seven monitors (including the three ex-Brazilian units bought earlier and the two *Glatton*s built for Norway).
– Twenty-four light gunboats (twelve 'Fly' class and twelve 'Insect' class, all ordered February 1915).

– Nineteen whaling steamers (fifteen 'Z-Whalers' plus four purchased whalers).

– Twenty-four submarine destroyers (P-boats ordered in May 1915).

– Fifty seagoing patrol boats (the first of the motor launches built by Electric Boat in the United States, ordered in April 1915).

– Two hundred motor barges with oil engines (X-lighters, ordered February 1915).

– Ninety smaller barges (Y-lighters, ordered February 1915).

– Thirty-six sloops ('Flower' class).

– Total: 612

That the letters X, Y and Z were applied to the landing craft and to the whalers suggests that they formed part of a single project. Note that Fisher did *not* include trawlers or drifters in the fleet he said he bought for the Baltic.

The numbers of destroyers and submarines ordered probably do not reflect Fisher's Baltic schemes, as they were determined largely by available building capacity, the idea being to produce destroyers (and probably also submarines) as quickly as possible. That said, Fisher's new Baltic fleet certainly required a large destroyer force to protect it against submarine attack. The sloops were justified as a substitute for destroyers and were not associated with any special operation. Similarly, the P-boats were conceived specifically to release destroyers from duty escorting the Grand Fleet to sea, so that they could work tactically with the fleet at sea.

When the War Council met on 7 January, three possibilities were on the table: Borkum, the advance up the coast towards Zeebrugge and some operation in the Near East. Other theatres, including the Baltic, were ruled out, at least for the time being. British field commander Sir John French liked the attack up the coast; he argued that it was time to attack, before the Germans fielded large fresh forces. The War Council gave him a chilly reception; it already seemed unlikely any army on the Western Front could advance very far. The War Council was left with the Borkum project, which it approved and a growing interest in some sort of operation against Turkey. Proposals for an attack on the Dardanelles (the Turkish Straits leading to the Black Sea) had been raised almost as soon as the German battlecruiser *Goeben* and its companion light cruiser *Breslau* gained refuge in Turkish waters in August 1914.

The Dardanelles and Gallipoli

At the outset, the British envisaged war against Turkey as a continuation of the Balkan Wars of 1912–13. In the first, the Balkan League of ex-Turkish states (Greece, Bulgaria, Serbia and Montenegro) took almost all remaining Turkish territory in the Balkans. In the second, a dissatisfied Bulgaria attacked its former allies Greece and Serbia and Turkey and Romania together attacked Bulgaria, which lost most of its gains from the previous war. Prime Minister Asquith could reasonably expect that at least some of the Balkan states would join enthusiastically in any attack against Turkey, supplying troops for an operation in which the British would provide the sea power. However, he seems not to have understood that Bulgaria was hardly likely to co-operate with Greece and Serbia, whatever the promised prize in further Turkish territory (Bulgaria joined the Central Powers).[32] The situation was

Turkish shore batteries at Gallipoli were effective. Here the destroyer HMS *Raccoon* has been hit. The battleship in the background is HMS *Agamemnon*. (Dr David Stevens, SPC-A)

further complicated by the French desire for a sphere of influence in the Levant (Syria and Lebanon), perhaps broadly equivalent to the British control of Egypt: both the Levant and Egypt were nominally parts of the Turkish empire. It was well understood that the Russians wanted guaranteed access to the Mediterranean, but as the war continued through 1914 they wanted more: possession of Constantinople. That also complicated the situation, since early British plans envisaged a Greek land attack combined with a naval operation: the Russians absolutely rejected Greek involvement.

The British attitude towards Turkey was tied up with their relationship with Russia. As long as the Russians were a threat (mainly to British India), they were anxious to support Turkey and to maintain their own access to the Black Sea via the Dardanelles. The British wanted to keep the Russians out of the Mediterranean because once there they might seek access to India. Moreover, the Russian push into Central Asia seemed to be aimed at Persia (Iran) and the warm waters of the Gulf – access to India by sea, rather than the difficult overland access the British already feared via Afghanistan. Support for Turkey against Russia did not preclude British occupation of Egypt, which was nominally part of the Turkish (Ottoman) Empire, though effectively independent. In 1914 the situation was complicated. The British had reached an understanding with the Russians, so they were inclined to support free Russian access to the Mediterranean through the Dardanelles, the Russians having renounced any threat to India. On the other hand, the Turkish empire bordered Egypt, so a hostile Turkey would threaten the vital Suez Canal.

All of this meant that the Royal Navy had long acquaintance with the Dardanelles. There had been major naval war scares in 1878 and in 1885. During the 1878 crisis the battleships of the Mediterranean Fleet ascended the Dardanelles in a snowstorm to support the Turks. With the entente with Russia, the situation reversed. In 1907 the British Committee on Imperial Defence investigated the problem of forcing the Dardanelles. Landing an expeditionary force on or near the Gallipoli Peninsula 'would involve great risk and should not be undertaken if other means of bringing pressure to bear on Turkey were available'.[33] The study envisaged a quick rush past the forts, not the gradual reduction by bombardment later proposed by the Mediterranean fleet commander Vice Admiral Carden. The army General Staff seems to have been responsible for the conclusion; DNI, 'though concurring generally, thought that the General Staff had underrated the value of naval co-operation and that, if such an operation were forced on us by arrogance or outrage on the part of the Turkish Government, there was no reason to despair of success, though at the expense, in all likelihood, of heavy casualties'.

For decades Turkey had been considered the 'sick man of Europe'. Various governments had taken most of her European territory. Many in the British government personally disliked the Turks, not least for their treatment of Christian minorities in their empire and they seem to have regretted the earlier British policy of supporting Turkey. Prime Minister Asquith wrote with some enthusiasm about the possibility of ejecting Turkey from her few remaining European possessions. There was hope of Greek assistance.[34]

Initially the British hoped that the Turks could be induced to intern the German ships and to remain neutral, or even to come over to the Allied side, even though Turkey had signed a defensive treaty of alliance with Germany on 2 August.[35] Turkish forces had performed poorly in the recent Balkan wars and there was some expectation that the mere appearance of British ships might bring down the government. In 1914 there was a widespread belief within the British government that the current Turkish government was weak and the population heavily pro-British. Their very poor showing when HMS *Doris* turned up on the Syrian coast in the December 1914 contributed to the idea that they would perform poorly this time, even though the Dardanelles were the key to Constantinople. That the Turks had fought well to protect Constantinople despite an otherwise poor showing in the Balkan Wars was apparently disregarded.

Frustrated by Turkish unwillingness to enter the war, the Germans on board the two warships (battlecruiser *Goeben* and light cruiser *Breslau*) nominally interned in Constantinople acted. With the consent of a few members of the Turkish government, on 29 October they entered the Black Sea and shelled Sevastopol and Odessa. The Russian ambassador left the next day. The British ambassador presented an ultimatum: the Turkish government should dissociate itself from the bombardment and carry out its repeated promise to remove the crews of the German ships. The Turkish cabinet reasserted its neutrality but it also refused to seize the ships.

The next day Admiral Carden was ordered to shell the forts at the mouth of the Dardanelles. Carden attacked on 3 November, doing considerable damage, but also making it clear that the British might later be interested in forcing the Straits. It was never clear who issued the bombardment order; the telegram describing the damage done was bound into the file on the plan to seize Borkum. Presumably this report was considered relevant as an example of what modern naval gunfire could do to forts. There may well have been a hope that the pro-German Turkish government would collapse due to the bombardment. To Admiral Souchon, the commander of the German (nominally Turkish) naval force in Constantinople, the straits were an opening which had to be closed if he was to operate freely in the Black Sea. Not long after he arrived Souchon cabled home for mining and coast defence experts.[36] Thus it is not clear how important Carden's warning was in the later fight in the Straits. War was not declared until 5 November.

Once at war, Turkey threatened the Suez Canal, because her empire included the vast swath of territory to the north, abutting Egypt. That was an urgent issue. At the first War Council meeting (1 December 1914) Churchill proposed an attack on the Gallipoli Peninsula as the ideal defence of the Canal. Opening the straits there would open the Turkish capital Constantinople to attack. So crucial a threat would preclude a Turkish attack elsewhere.[37] That would, however, require a large ground force. Churchill's alternative was a feint at Gallipoli to cover an attack on Haifa or on the Syrian coast, probably at Alexandretta. He recalled that in pre-war CID studies the standard riposte to a Turkish attack on Egypt was a landing on the Palestine coast, to cut the Turkish line of communications. Kitchener felt that there was no need to worry about Egypt.[38] The amateurishness of the Turkish attack on the Canal, which was easily defeated, must have seemed to confirm the belief that the Turks could not fight.

As December wore on, another factor emerged. No one had really expected a decision in France; Russia was likely to be the decisive theatre. However, with bad news coming from Russia, there was pressure for a diversion which might relieve pressure. By the end of 1914 the Russian army was in considerable trouble. It was hard-pressed by the Turks in the Caucasus and was barely holding Poland against the Germans. At the beginning of January 1915 the Russians asked Kitchener to arrange a military or naval demonstration against the Turks which could relieve pressure on the Caucasus. Kitchener replied that something would be done, but that he could not promise relief. This turned out to be a temporary problem, but by this time the British were becoming aware that the Russians were suffering partly because they were badly short of shells. They lacked the industrial capacity to produce enough. The only path to supply both shells and the machinery to make enough of them was the Dardanelles. British command of the sea made it possible to ship via Archangel in the Arctic, but rail capacity from there to anywhere else in Russia was very limited. Kitchener doubted that the deadlock on the Western Front could be broken, so he was open to some alternative operation.[39] Others in the War Council were also looking.

At the end of December War Council Secretary Maurice Hankey suggested that the most effective operation would be an attack on Turkey 'to demonstrate that alliance with Germany against a great sea power is a fatal error'. He envisaged a campaign in combination with the same Balkan states which had recently fought that country. Lloyd George was also interested in using seapower for a peripheral attack, since he saw no prospect of a decision in France. His alternatives were a direct attack against Austria via either Salonika or the Adriatic coast, or an attack against Turkey in Syria, to cut any communication with Egypt and hence any threat to the Canal.[40] Once the Dardanelles were open, Hankey envisaged the attack on Austria proposed by Lloyd George, in combination with Russia, Romania and Serbia. The minor problem with this plan was that most of the countries assigned to carry out the overland attacks were still neutral.

France presented another problem.[41] The naval agreement signed in 1912 had given France precedence in the Mediterranean in exchange for British protection in the North Sea and the French were intent to protect their interest in the Levant (Syria and what is now Lebanon). Initially they demanded that a French admiral command whatever operation was mounted. Dealing with their

Horses debark from a 'beetle' at Suvla Bay. Note the open hatch providing access from the hold. (Dr David Stevens, SPC-A)

Petrograd was incomplete and the Russians depended heavily on the Trans-Siberian Railway, with its very limited capacity (in summer they could obtain munitions via Archangel on the White Sea).[44]

Troops were not available. Churchill had been exchanging telegrams with Admiral Carden, who had been encouraged by his November bombardment of the Gallipoli forts. He envisaged a step by step attack, beginning with the destruction of the forts at the entrance to the Straits. To deal with the more modern forts he wanted three modern capital ships backed by twelve pre-dreadnoughts. He already had two battlecruisers and the battleship *Queen Elizabeth* was going to Gibraltar for gun trials. Churchill pointed out that they could just as well be conducted by shelling the forts. Churchill introduced his plan for a bombardment without using troops at the 13 January War Council.

The War Council was immediately impressed by Churchill's plan. The Zeebrugge operation was still on the table, so in mid-January it decided that (1) the Flanders (Zeebrugge) plan should be worked out so that a decision could be made early in February; (2) the Admiralty should develop a plan for action in the Adriatic to influence Italy; (3) the Admiralty should also prepare for a naval bombardment and seizure of the Gallipoli forts; and (4) if the Western Front was still stalemated in the spring, plans would be developed to send British troops elsewhere.

By the time the War Council met again on 28 January, the Flanders option was dead because the French had reduced their own army between the British and the sea. Their commander Marshal Joffre considered the operation too risky and he wanted to concentrate his own troops for a spring offensive. The Adriatic operation was stillborn; the Admiralty concentrated on Gallipoli. The Russians supported the idea enthusiastically and the French navy promised to co-operate.

Before the 28 January War Council meeting, Asquith was aware that Fisher disliked the proposed Dardanelles operation as well as Churchill's Zeebrugge operation; in hindsight it seems clear that he wanted to keep the Baltic option alive. No one on the War Council was in a position to evaluate the options and to force decisions; that did not come until the institution of a War Cabinet, whose members were free to concentrate on military issues, in 1917. The War Council was therefore a means of reaching compromise decisions. In this case, Asquith managed to smooth relations between Churchill and Fisher by convincing Churchill to give up plans to shell Zeebrugge while Fisher approved the Dardanelles operation.[45] At the meeting, Fisher 'maintained an obstinate and ominous silence', but Churchill's operation was warmly supported by Kitchener and Foreign Secretary Grey and enthusiastically by Balfour.[46] As Secretary, Hankey did not bring up his belief that the operation was doomed without the support of ground troops.[47] He did circulate an account of the forcing of the Dardanelles by a British squadron in 1807. The ships got through successfully, but they were badly mauled on the way back because no British army had occupied the straits. Hankey took that to mean that unless the forts and the straits were secured by troops, any ships which got through to Constantinople would be trapped there. The French contributed ships to the bombardment fleet.

Given the vital need both to provide the Russians with the material and financial means of continuing the war and to bring out their wheat, it was inevitable that the War Council would support an attack on the Dardanelles as the most promising of the options

demands stopped the Dardanelles project for a time at the end of December 1914. The project resumed when the French agreed to British command with French support and a French Rear Admiral as second-in-command of the naval force. That is why the initial attack included four French battleships.

Soon after receiving the plea from the Russians, Kitchener wrote to Churchill that the naval advantages of possession of Constantinople and of getting the Russian wheat from the Black Sea were so overwhelming that he much favoured Hankey's plan for the Turkish operation. A successful attack would reopen communication with Russia, settle the Near Eastern Question (i.e., dismember Turkey) and open the Danube to bring British seapower into the heart of Europe. Fisher was also coming around to favouring action in the Near East. The tentative plan was to withdraw 75,000 seasoned troops from the British force in France, replacing them with Territorials. They would land at Besika Bay near Gallipoli after troops from Egypt feinted at Haifa and Alexandretta. Simultaneously the Bulgarians would be induced to attack Constantinople and the Greeks to attack Gallipoli overland. The navy would force the Dardanelles using old battleships, the bombardment force earlier earmarked for Borkum. The operation would be co-ordinated with a Russian, Serbian and Romanian attack on Austria-Hungary.[42] Kitchener later wrote Churchill that analysis by the War Office had concluded that the Dardanelles would be the most suitable place to attack and that 150,000 men would be needed.[43]

Looking back after the war, the Germans apparently agreed that success at the Dardanelles would have had enormous impact. In his memoir, Hankey quoted German supreme commander Erich Ludendorff: had the Allies gained control of the straits, the Russians would have received enough munitions to make the fight in the East – the most sensitive place in the German Empire – a much more serious matter. The railway line from Murmansk to on offer. It could, however, be argued that with better information it would not have sanctioned an attack without troop support. Ironically, from Fisher's point of view troop support would have consumed exactly the resources he was amassing for a Baltic operation, hence would have made a Dardanelles attack more rather than less threatening to his plans. Churchill did try to obtain troops, but without success.[48]

A technique for using indirect fire against inland targets using map references was tested a few days after the initial bombardment of the forts.[49] It was particularly well adapted to air spotting and the attack was supported by aircraft from the seaplane tender *Ark Royal*. Success was incomplete: when firing ended due to nightfall, the forts on the European side of the straits had been silenced, but one on the other side was still firing. Even so, at first the attack seemed to be a success and as such it brought immediate dividends. The Bulgarians became so friendly that they were asked their conditions for entering the war on the Allied side. The Greeks offered to place three of their divisions on the Gallipoli peninsula. Italian entry into the war seemed imminent. With success apparently within sight, problems appeared. The Russians suddenly demanded not free passage, but possession of Constantinople. Even though they could not contribute troops (they offered their fleet for later Black Sea operations), they insisted that the Greeks not be allowed into Constantinople. In response, the Greek General Staff announced that the moment for intervention had passed and Venezelos' offer of assistance died. King Constantine forced his resignation and appointed a pro-German prime minister in his place.[50]

The bombardment began on 19 February under the command of Admiral Carden. He estimated that, given two weeks of good weather, he could break into the Sea of Marmara beyond the Straits. In addition to their guns, the Turks mined both the approaches to the Narrows and the Narrows itself. Sweepers had to declare the approaches clear before battleships could begin shelling from outside the Strait. The only available sweepers were trawlers

with civilian crews.[51] Because of the shore batteries, all sweeping attempts were made at night. The draught of the trawlers used exceeded the mooring depth of the mines. It was not understood that the strong current flowing out of the Narrows caused the mines to dip, bringing them below trawler draught. The same strong current which saved the trawlers slowed them badly. They had to steam up into the Narrows and then sweep back at low speed under heavy fire. Sweep wires often did not cut mooring cables, so that sweepers dragged mines out of the straits, where special dumping areas were set up. The need to clear sweeps periodically by dumping considerably slowed sweeping.

It was often said that minefields were nearly useless unless they were patrolled or otherwise protected and that was certainly the case with the Turkish minefields. The ten lines of contact mines in the straits were defended not only by forts in known locations, but also by mobile field artillery, which was difficult or impossible to knock out. Even at night, sweepers could be caught by searchlights ashore. It did not help that weather often precluded air reconnaissance and spotting, a prerequisite for indirect fire. Night sweeping under fire made it difficult or impossible for the sweepers to be sure of where they had or had not swept.

Carden's successor Admiral de Robeck tried a daylight attack on 18 March, losing three old battleships (HMS *Ocean* and *Irresistible* and the French *Bouvet*) to mines. A fourth, the French *Gaulois*, was badly damaged and had to be beached.[52] However, the bombardment also substantially damaged the forts. The minefield involved had been laid beyond the main fields on 8 March, after the battle had begun. The sweep force now included destroyers of the *Beagle* and 'River' classes had been fitted with sweeps.[53] The eight auxiliary minesweepers previously assigned to the Grand Fleet were on their way from the United Kingdom, as were more fast trawlers. Given reinforcements, sweeping resumed at the end of March. This time it was carried out in daylight, supported by battleships. At the end of the war the scale of the necessary mine clearance operation became clearer.[54] It must have been clear that

The Dardanelles was a land-sea operation, not only in the sense that the fleet supported troops ashore, but also in the sense that the navy sought to isolate the battle area by cutting Turkish seaborne communications. Several British and Australian submarines penetrated the Turkish minefields protecting the Sea of Marmora and Turkish transports supplying the army in the Dardanelles. The Australian *AE 2* had to be scuttled on 30 April 1915 after suffering severe damage by the Turkish torpedo boat *Sultan Hissar*. *AE 2* is shown arriving at Portsmouth, on 17 February 1914, before going out to Australia. Note that she had no deck gun. (Allan C Green via State Library of Victoria)

an attack from landward could have silenced the forts which covered the minefields in the Narrows.[55] Ironically, from the outset Churchill had planned to use Royal Marines to capture shore-mounted torpedo tubes near the mouth of the straits. Kitchener remarked that if he needed troops at the outset, he would need more later.

Based on Churchill's report of this action, the War Council approved further operations. By this time General Ian Hamilton had arrived to command the ground force *en route* to the Dardanelles.[56] On 22 March he and de Robeck decided that there would be no further major naval attack until the army was ready to land.[57] The army staff view was that although a landing would be very difficult against troops well supplied with ammunition, the Turks were probably short of it. Moreover, they had performed poorly in the recent Balkan Wars. The peninsula would be blockaded by British submarines and the only access road commanded by naval gunfire. To the staff, then, the operation was to some extent a gamble on the short supplies and poor fighting quality of the Turks, neither of which was close enough to reality.[58]

While he waited for the army, de Robeck strengthened his minesweeping force, but his attention was fixed on the landings. It is now known that by the evening of 18 March the guns commanding the straits were short of ammunition and the Turks were badly short of mines.[59] On this basis de Robeck might have tried again, although it is by no means obvious that the ships would have made it through on the second (or later) try. Encouraging a further naval attack in August, Churchill wrote that De Robeck originally planned to resume his purely naval attack 'as soon as the minesweeping service was re-energised with naval ratings and protection by an anti-mine net could be afforded to the battleships engaging the forts'. He had changed his mind when he was assured that the army could take the end of the Gallipoli peninsula without undue loss, the fleet and the army then advancing 'side by side'.[60] By August, with the land campaign stalemated, the army assurances were a bad joke and the army was asking for many more troops it could not hope to obtain. The naval option was all that was left.

The earliest date for a landing was set for 14 April; in fact the landing was on 25 April. On the same day the Russian Black Sea Fleet attacked the Bosporus forts (at the other end of the straits) as a feint and diversion. It had already shelled the forts on 3 April. Attention turned from the Narrows to pre-landing sweeps. By the end of April the destroyers had brought the swept area up to 8000 yds of the Narrows forts, having accounted for about seven mines. Although they had sustained few casualties, the crews were badly strained by sweeping all day under fire and then patrolling all night. On this basis it was decided to suspend sweeping until the army had advanced sufficiently that the fleet could support the sweepers through the Straits.

Very little attention seems to have been paid to the choice of landing beaches, or to the preparation of the assault force (for example, the transports were not combat-loaded, creating serious confusion at the beaches). Assault objectives were poorly defined and many of the assault units did not know what they were supposed to attack. The assault boats had to be towed to the beaches, with the exception of the modified steamer *River Clyde*, beached as a forebear of Second World War assault ships. The Turks were unable to mine the landing beaches, but that was not known to the assault force. The landing itself, which Hankey feared was

The Dardanelles campaign included the first aerial torpedo attack. This Short 184 (designated by its individual serial number) from HMS *Ben-my-Chree* hit a Turkish transport on 12 August 1915 with a 14in weapon. Maximum dropping height was 15ft, so the aircraft landed and then attacked from 300 yds. This aircraft was also known as the 225 from the rating of its engine. It was conceived specifically as a torpedo bomber, but was used mainly for reconnaissance. It remained in production throughout the First World War. The seaplane success in the Dardanelles led directly to the development of the Sopwith Cuckoo and to plans for a British torpedo attack against the German High Seas Fleet in 1917 and then in 1918.

too dangerous to attempt at once, was successful, but the troops found themselves pinned down by Turkish fire from the heights above.[61] Initially Kitchener was relieved that the troops had landed successfully, thinking the landing the most difficult part of the operation; but the troops were soon bogged down and they and the Turks found themselves fighting trench warfare much like that on the Western Front.

One justification for a seaborne operation was that it could easily be reversed in the event it did not succeed. That had been done with the most famous failed British amphibious operation of the past, the attack on Walcheren during the Napoleonic Wars (the next operation was the support of Wellington on the Peninsula). This time withdrawal was more difficult, because it would affect British prestige not only in the Balkans but also in vital parts of the Empire – Egypt and India. A Turkish success might revive the threat to the Suez Canal and it also might help the Germans in their project to encourage Muslims in the Empire – the largest Muslim entity on earth – to rebel. To the extent that the British thought their chance of success hinged on Turkish munition shortage, the passage of time brought the possibility that the Germans would gain a land link to Turkey via Serbia and Bulgaria, which was considering joining the Central Powers. Within a few months the reality was that the army was five times as large as originally envisaged (fourteen divisions) and that its commander still considered it inadequate. It had taken 110,000 casualties. The claims of the army in France ruled out ammunition for a sustained offensive.

In May, after the troops had been reduced to Western Front style yard-by-yard warfare, de Robeck cautioned the Admiralty that the entire operation might not deliver what was sought: 'the temper of the Turkish Army on the peninsula indicates that the forcing of the Dardanelles and subsequent appearance of the Fleet off Constantinople will not, of itself, prove decisive'.[62] Moreover, even if the fleet got into the Sea of Marmara beyond the Narrows, the forts behind it would preclude resupply. That would not matter if the army took the forts quickly enough.

The Dardanelles were not the Western Front in a very important way: the sea was a manoeuvre space and it was also a major supply route for both sides. Although the Turks had a road through Bulair, much of what they used came via the Sea of Marmara. The manoeuvre aspect was reflected in a further series of landings on 6 August, using the new landing craft Fisher had ordered in February. Again there were serious problems due not only to factors such as the fast currents but also to excessive secrecy about troops' objectives. It is not entirely clear whether the new landings could have carried the day.[63] They certainly did create an invaluable element of surprise.

The attack on Turkish seaborne supply was another important, though often neglected, part of the story. Despite mines, nets and dangerous currents, British and Australian and a few French submarines managed to operate in the Sea of Marmara beyond the Narrows in the Dardanelles, through which Turkish supplies had to come. It is not clear to what extent they and their threat, choked off Turkish seaborne resupply, or to what degree the Turks could not subsist on the Bulair road alone. One of the arguments made in August 1915 in support of a renewed naval attack was that without the Bulair road the Turkish land force in the Dardanelles could not hold out at all. The Turks could support a smaller force, but it would not be enough to hold off the large British and ANZAC force. A naval surface force in the Marmara could shell the road and thus close it. Modern experience of interdiction shows that it is most effective when the force whose supplies are being interdicted is under pressure due to its own intense operations. There is no indication that the connection between the submarine campaign and the state of the Turkish forces was ever taken into account in shaping the British land campaign.[64]

The Germans also had submarines in the Eastern Mediterranean, where they could attack the Allied force, particularly the battleships.[65] However, the U-boats almost certainly could not sink the monitors, which were heavily bulged. Their shallow draught might also protect them from contact mines in the Straits. They also had deck armour against the plunging fire of the shore batteries. The monitors could cut the Bulair road.

Once the operation bogged down, the War Council had to choose whether to withdraw. The alternatives were another attempt at a rapid advance, a siege, or reinforcement in hopes that the situation could change (for example, that the submarine campaign in the Sea of Marmara would succeed). There was no support for immediate withdrawal. Any rapid push would require reinforcements, some of which were on the way. A siege would require too much support. The prestige issue was still very relevant. For example, in a Cabinet debate, Lord Curzon, who had served as Viceroy of India, strongly opposed withdrawal.

Looking back about twenty years later, Hankey admitted that it was nearly inevitable that a Gallipoli operation would be carried out, given the urgent need both to open the route to Russia and to deal with the collapse of Balkan policy. The weather probably precluded any landing before the late April date ultimately chosen.

The War Council had to choose between a naval bombardment and inaction at a time when inaction carried high costs. The required naval force not only was available, but it would not have been usable anywhere else. Hankey hated the operation, but it did retrieve the position in the Balkans and that provided later benefits (it made the operation mounted in Salonika possible). Once the naval attack had been mounted, the only choices were either to feed in troops or to give up all operations in the East. Kitchener, who was considered the greatest authority on Oriental psychology, would not contemplate withdrawal. For him, at least initially it was unthinkable to lose the advantages gained by the fall of the outer forts. Abandonment would be shattering to Russia, particularly after the British agreed that she could occupy Constantinople. It would seem so shabby a trick that the Russians might begin to seek a separate peace, a devastating development for the war as a whole. Moreover, if the attack were abandoned, the British could not simply leave the region; they would have to keep large forces in Egypt and in Mesopotamia.[66] The only other possible naval objectives in the area were Alexandretta (Iskenderun) and Haifa, the fall of neither of which would have any wider impact. An attack on Alexandretta would have relieved the Russians in the Caucasus, but it was ruled out by the French, who insisted on their primacy in Syria.

Eventually withdrawal was ordered despite its costs. In the autumn of 1915 the War Council gave way to a Dardanelles Committee designed to find a way ahead; soon this committee became the War Committee. The bright hopes of January 1915 had clearly gone. There was some talk of retaining one of the beachheads, but even that was given up. The only major voice pressing for one more naval attempt were Commodore Roger Keyes, de Robeck's Chief of Staff and Captain Godfrey RMLI. They argued that the gun defences had been drawn down to fight the land battle and that the mines had been neglected and thus might no longer be so serious a threat.[67] De Robeck allowed Keyes to carry his plan back to England in October 1915 specifically to argue it before the Admiralty (despite de Robeck's opposition). Keyes believed it gained some support from First Lord Balfour and from First Sea Lord Admiral Sir Henry B Jackson. Neither was as committed to the operation as Churchill had been. De Robeck also went back to England temporarily and his stand-in Admiral Weymss (otherwise SNO Mudros) told Keyes (who had returned) to prepare a detailed plan. In Weymss' view, with the Allies beaten in Serbia and outmanoeuvred by the Greeks, evacuation was daunting and attack was the only policy left. Late in November or early in December 1915 he wrote that 'a success now would mean everything to us all over the world and the more I contemplate the matter the more confident do I feel that we have enough chance of success to justify our attempt'.[68] Apparently Admiralty support for Keyes' plan evaporated after he left London to return to the Dardanelles.

Gallipoli could be read in two opposite ways. One was that it was idiocy for ships to fight forts: opposed landings and perhaps all amphibious operations, should be avoided. The opposite was to note how close the operation, particularly the August landings, had come to success despite an incredible series of mistakes: modern amphibious warfare had a real future. That was how the Royal Navy and the US Navy read the situation post-war and the problems at Gallipoli certainly did not deter the Germans from an opposed landing in the Gulf of Riga in 1917, Operation 'Albion'.

For that matter, the Dover Patrol planned a big amphibious operation on the Flanders coast in 1916 and again in 1917. It was aborted only because of the failure of the army advance with which it was supposed to link up.

By showing the British how complicated an amphibious operation could be, the experience at Gallipoli modified expectations of what the Germans could do if they tried to invade Britain.[69] By November 1915 the focus had turned to measures to be taken in the event of an invasion or raid, particularly fleet dispositions. With the fleet at Scapa and Rosyth, it was entirely possible that a transport force might reach the British coast undetected, but the Germans would be aware that two of the three raids mounted before January 1916 were intercepted, one of them resulting in the battle of Dogger Bank. A large fleet of transports would do a lot worse than the fast cruiser forces the Germans employed. The Admiralty emphasised that, given British command of the sea, nothing more than the smallest German force could hope to return home before the end of the war.

In January 1916 a joint Admiralty-War Office conference examined what the Germans were likely to do. Their report never mentioned Gallipoli, but instead it referred to recent experience.[70] The attack force would consist of merchant ships plus a covering

fleet. The merchant ships would not have steam boats suited to transport troops to even a welcoming beach. In all previous large-scale operations (presumably Tsingtao and Gallipoli) the covering force had provided steamboats to tow the rowing boats, officers for supervision, working parties and numerous boats. This time the covering force would be under constant submarine threat, hence the transports would have to provide their own means of landing troops and supporting equipment. Steamboats and other landing craft would have to be supplied to the merchant ships, along with special derricks (and crew) to handle them. Each transport might possibly tow one lighter, but towing would limit the speed of the force to 8 knots, making it far more vulnerable. This was not a bad summary of the situation a quarter-century later, except that it was recognised that specialised boats were needed. No instance was known in which more than infantry with their first-line transport and a few guns were landed on the first day, suggesting that an alerted defence would have a considerable advantage – as at Gallipoli.

The sheer size of the assault force would make it vulnerable. The scale envisaged (135,000 or 170,000 men) would require 200 transports, a line 40 miles long if in single file. Anchored in three or four lines they would require 10 to 13 miles of beach. The force would hardly be invisible once the sun rose and it would need a long time to unload. Although local defence forces might be unable to get at the transports in daylight, they were well armed with torpedoes and they could expect to penetrate effectively at night. The Grand Fleet would probably arrive by the next dawn and quickly end the operation. That would give the transports no more than 24 to 28 hours before it was attacked. At Gallipoli, 29,000 men with seven days' supplies had been disembarked in $12\frac{1}{2}$ hours, but it helped enormously that the Mediterranean is tideless; on the other hand, the landing had been opposed fiercely.[71] The Germans had the laid-up merchant ships, but it was not clear where they would get the crews. With the ships idling since August 1914, their crews had dispersed, many into the navy. Estimates of the invasion threat mentioned this issue, but no one was willing to rely on manpower limits to preclude invasion – which was the one way the Germans might knock the British out of the war, if they could seize and hold London.

When a second conference met on 9 August 1916, the Admiralty pointed out that German experience at Jutland would probably diminish their appetite for invasion. For the moment the High Seas Fleet was unlikely to move without the badly-damaged battlecruisers (a bad guess, given the German sortie on 18-19 August). As importantly, the growth of the fleet had made it possible to bring the 3rd Battle Squadron (*Dreadnought* and six *King Edward VII*s) south, making a landing anywhere near the Thames Estuary – probably the primary target area – more difficult, though still possible, as the enemy fleet would be an overwhelming force. More importantly, the Germans had no surplus force, because they were tied down at Verdun and on the Somme and the Eastern Front (which for the moment was not going their way). When and if the situation changed, the August conference concluded that the enemy might try landing 160,000 men.

The Germans conducted their own major amphibious operation in 1917, against the Russians in the Åland Islands in the Baltic. These ramped craft carrying field guns are unpowered cattle boats, the ramps forming their sterns. (Captain G von Koblinski via Naval Institute Photo Collection)

The 'battleships' of the Dover Patrol were 12in gun monitors. *General Craufurd* was one of eight ships armed with 12in turrets from disarmed *Majestic* class battleships (with elevation increased from 13.5° to 30°). Two of them went to the Mediterranean, the other six becoming the 'capital ships' of the Dover Patrol. They were conceived to support land operations as part of Admiral Fisher's Baltic plan, but they proved useful at the Dardanelles and of course off the Flanders coast. Unlike valuable battleships, they were effectively expendable. Moreover, they were heavily blistered against underwater attack and were difficult to sink. Construction depended on the availability of surplus guns and mountings.

CHAPTER 10
The Battle of the Narrow Seas

ALTHOUGH THE BATTLES BETWEEN the Grand Fleet and the High Seas Fleet have attracted the greatest attention since the First World War, much of the naval action in the North Sea was fought in its narrow southern neck, between German destroyers based at Zeebrugge and Ostend and the Harwich Force and the Dover Patrol. The Germans' targets were the shipping in the Downs off the British coast and the Dover Barrage which prevented U-boats from passing out of the North Sea by the shortest possible route. For its part the Dover Patrol supported the bombardment not only of Zeebrugge/Ostend but also of the seaward flank of the German army in Flanders.

For the Germans, Zeebrugge turned out to be an enormously productive investment, hence a major British target. In 1917 it was an objective of the abortive British land offensive in Flanders. The Dover Patrol planned a large-scale amphibious operation to place three British divisions behind the flank of the German army which this land offensive was supposed to force back into Flanders, the entire operation being intended to seize Zeebrugge and hence to reduce German submarine effectiveness. Aside from Gallipoli, the abortive Flanders landing seems to have been the only wartime example of a land operation with an expressly naval objective.

After the war, the fight in the southern North Sea must have seemed particularly interesting to the French and the Italians, who were operating in the fairly narrow seas of the Mediterranean. The French relied heavily on Mediterranean sea lines of communication and after 1918 the Italians were their most likely enemy. They assumed that the Italians, like the Germans during the war, would use fast surface forces to attack their convoys. That seemed, to them, to explain why the Italians were building large destroyers with heavy gun armament. At least initially, the French conceived their super-destroyers (contre-torpilleurs) specifically to intercept and destroy the Italian striking force. Neither navy invested heavily in modernising its battleships during the 1920s. Each probably concluded that, as in the North Sea, battle fleets would function mainly as 'fleets in being', neutralising each other. Fast light forces would battle each other. For these navies, the new 10,000-ton 'Treaty' cruisers were the equivalents of the wartime battlecruisers, whose construction was prohibited under the Washington Treaty. Fast smaller cruisers and destroyers would attack and defend trade. Perceptions changed only in the late 1920s, when the Germans suddenly threatened French Atlantic trade with their 'pocket battleships', and the French therefore suddenly needed fast capital ships to run them down. Since such ships could also run down the 'Treaty' cruisers, it was time for the Italians to obtain fast capital ships of their own, initially completely rebuilt battleships and then entirely new ones of the *Littorio* class.

At the outbreak of war, Admiral von Tirpitz became interested in the possibilities of what he called the 'Triangle', the Belgian ports of Ostend and Zeebrugge, which were linked by canal to Bruges.[1] In mid-August 1914 Tirpitz tried to convince the army to change the planned path of advance through Belgium specifically to seize these ports. The army was unwilling to do so (and probably could not do so, because of the sheer logistical effort of supporting it). At this stage Tirpitz thought that the French had already been defeated. He wanted the Belgian and French harbours seized before they could be destroyed, because he wanted to move the base from which the High Seas Fleet operated as far west as possible in order to operate more effectively against Britain.[2] He

For the British, the German bases on the Flanders coast mattered because they brought even the smallest U-boat within range of the southern North Sea and the massive concentration of shipping there. The Germans developed extremely small U-boats specifically for this role. *UB 1*, seen here as the Austrian *U 10*, was the prototype. She was shipped in sections by rail from Germany to the Austrian naval base at Pola. Armament was limited to two torpedoes in the two bow tubes and the powerplant was a diesel engine which normally powered a barge. Surfaced displacement was only 127 tons. Of the seventeen *UB I* class submarines, four were transferred to Austria-Hungary, one was used for training and the remaining twelve served in Flanders. The Dover Patrol sought to neutralise the submarines at Zeebrugge and Ostend by maintaining a net and mine barrier off the ports and also by shelling and bombing them. For their part the Germans saw the surface ships based at Zeebrugge and Ostend primarily as a means of supporting the U-boats rather than as an independent means of attacking the mass of shipping in the North Sea. Thus the Zeebrugge destroyers raided the Dover Barrage blocking U-boat access to the North Sea rather than the shipping in the Downs. (International Naval Research Organisation Gogg Collection via US Naval Historical and Heritage Command).

particularly wanted the army to seize Ostend. When it refused, he decided to form his own land force, which ultimately became MarineKorps (Navy Corps) Flandern.[3]

The 'Triangle' enjoyed important advantages. Although the coast could be mined, its conditions favoured minesweeping and strong currents and a sandy bottom made it difficult to moor mines securely.[4] Except for the harbours, the coast was not suited to large-scale landings because the beach shelved gradually and there was a strong current running along it. Even flat-bottomed boats would ground some way out to sea, troops having to wade ashore through machine-gun fire. However, the Germans reckoned with the possibility of a surprise landing at Ostend or Zeebrugge. Their defences included heavy guns (which the German army sometimes took back to support operations on land).

Initially Tirpitz probably was at least as interested in showing that the navy was actively participating in the land war. Given the army's initially victorious sweep through Belgium and France, there was considerable fear that it might be too late to see action. It was impossible to provide sufficient training for mobile warfare, so it was assumed that the MarineDivision (later the MarineKorps) was to be employed in static occupation of part of the Belgian coast (once it arrived, it was thrown piecemeal into mobile warfare in the 'race for the sea' after the French victory on the Marne). The Kaiser issued a formal order creating the MarineDivision on 29 August 1914. It initially placed the division under army command,

to be used at the outset as a besieging and occupying force to relieve part of the field army then occupying Belgium. 'At the same time all possible preparations are to be made for guerrilla warfare [*i.e.*, kleinkrieg] against England from the coasts of Belgium and Northern France'.

Thus initial equipment of the MarineDivision included seventy torpedo tubes and torpedoes to arm small steamers which might already be available in Belgium, six portable W/T stations and an airship hangar (to be ready in October). The radios were apparently intended to control U-boats and other light units operating in the Channel and the southern North Sea based on reconnaissance reports by aircraft operating from Flanders.[5] Three 11in guns ordered by Belgium but lying in Krupp's factory were considered as possible defences of the base in Belgium.

As a member of the Admiralstab, the commander of the new organisation, Admiral von Schröder, had studied the Dutch and Belgian coasts extensively and he immediately proposed to make Bruges and Zeebrugge the central points of his command. The inclusion of Bruges turned out to be important, as was the exclusion of many other places in Belgium so that effort could be concentrated on Tirpitz' 'Triangle'. As the 'race for the sea' continued, the British had to evacuate Ostend, as they and the Belgians had previously evacuated Antwerp. All three harbours in the 'Triangle' were in German hands by 21 October 1914. To the Germans' surprise, unlike previously-evacuated Antwerp, all three were intact. That due both to limited time and also to the British army's insistence that the ports be left intact so that they could be used when they turned the Germans' flank and expelled them from Belgium.[6] Once the harbours were in German hands, the MarineDivision could carry out Tirpitz' plans.

When the battleships *Renown* and *Repulse* were reordered as three-turret battlecruisers, two twin 15in turrets became surplus. They soon became the basis for the monitors *Marshal Ney* and *Marshal Soult*. Both were diesel-powered, using engines ordered for a pair of small tankers. Both monitors were assigned to the Dover Patrol, but *Marshal Ney* suffered from unreliable (German-built) engines and was reassigned as guard ship in the Downs, armed with 6in guns. She is shown as built.

Initially the MarineDivision had no naval component, but in October 1914 the Admiralstab examined the possible use of submarines, torpedo boats and aircraft from the newly-captured 'Triangle'. It concluded that submarines were the best option. The shadow of Heligoland still loomed: it seemed that German torpedo boats could not operate effectively in the face of British destroyers. If they were assigned to the 'Triangle', they would need light cruiser support and that in turn would mean drawing down the already inadequate cruiser strength of the High Seas Fleet.[7]

A second MarineDivision was raised by cutting the naval fortresses to skeleton garrisons and by taking men from older warships, the two forming the MarineKorps Flandern in November 1914. The Kaiser formally changed the role of the MarineKorps to Tirpitz' kleinkrieg. For his part, MarineKorps commander Admiral von Schröder pressed for the transfer of seagoing U-boats and torpedo boats (destroyers). High Seas Fleet commander Admiral von Ingenohl was willing to transfer submarines to the 'Triangle', but only if they remained under his command, hence could be withdrawn as needed to support fleet operations. He adamantly opposed a request for a half-flotilla of torpedo boats (destroyers). Admiralstab chief von Pohl promised Schröder half-flotillas of both submarines and destroyers, but he did not have the power to provide them. For his part, Schröder argued that he should have not only destroyers but also a light cruiser, which could do far more from Zeebrugge than from the Bight.[8] Once the Germans had decided on unrestricted submarine warfare for 1915, Tirpitz' Navy Office proposed a much larger force.[9]

Initially Zeebrugge was a stopping point for High Seas Fleet submarines, increasing their operating radius. They could not be permanently based there, because there was no infrastructure to carry out their frequent refits. There were also too few High Seas Fleet U-boats: a total of eighteen, of which on average nine were available. As long as the Germans entertained the possibility that the British would attack the German Bight, at least four were required to defend Heligoland and another two for the Ems, leaving only three for all other High Seas Fleet functions. However, small submarines (UB- and UC-boats) and surface minelayers ('A' class) were designed specifically for coastal operation.[10] As early as December 1914 it had been decided to base half a flotilla of U-boats (five boats) at Zeebrugge for coast defence. These craft were sent in sections by rail and assembled by Cockerill in Antwerp, going up to Bruges and then to Ostend and Zeebrugge by canal.[11]

The submarine force at Zeebrugge was not increased to the desired half-flotilla until objections to the use of U-boats against the line of communications from Britain to the Continent had been resolved. That came on 15 January, when the Chief of the Admiralstab wired the MarineKorps and the High Seas Fleet that all large steamers observed approaching Le Havre, Dunkirk, Boulogne, or Cherbourg at night could be sunk without warning.[12] This was the beginning of unrestricted U-boat warfare and also of Zeebrugge as a real rather than as a potential problem for the Royal Navy.

The first of the small submarines (UB 10) arrived in Bruges on 27 March 1915 and on 29 March the Flanders Submarine Flotilla was commissioned. By that time their mission had shifted from defence to attacking British trade in the North Sea, unrestricted submarine warfare having been announced by the Germans. The 'A' class torpedo boats were used mainly to maintain a standing

Erebus was a second-generation 15in gun monitor reflecting experience with the earlier ships. She had better propulsion for considerably higher speed. Initially her secondary battery was a pair of 6in guns, later increased to four. They in turn were replaced by four (later eight) single 4in. The two guns forward of the turret are 12pdrs. The twelve-sided barbette was intended to simplify construction. This photograph shows the ship after her 1918 refit, with four 4in secondary guns.

patrol off Zeebrugge and Ostend, the submarines being the offensive weapon. From air and submarine reconnaissance the Germans knew that British shipping was often concentrated around the North Hinder lightship, only 34 miles from Zeebrugge, hence easily within range of the UB-boats. *UB 4* torpedoed the first ship there on 10 April 1915. Ultimately the MarineKorps accounted for roughly a quarter of the German submarine force and was responsible for a proportionate fraction of sinkings (23 per cent).[13]

Until the U-boats and torpedo boats arrived, the MarineKorps' only offensive weapons were a few seaplanes (the first seaplane station had been set up on 5 December 1914). These aircraft were initially intended as the eyes of the U-boats and torpedo boats of the MarineKorps, but they had communication problems.[14] The seaplanes soon attacked Dover and Sheerness, but without much effect. However, they did show that they could observe the shipping in the Downs and in the Thames Estuary, so that they could support the submarines and torpedo boats when the latter became available. They could observe British minelaying operations off the Flanders coast and at times they could spot for the heavy guns emplaced by the MarineKorps.[15] Plans to base airships in Flanders were abandoned.

If the Germans did not realise the potential the 'Triangle' offered, the Admiralty did. At the end of 1914 and into early 1915 it pressed for an offensive in Flanders to seize them.[16] The British were already shelling the Flanders coast, having begun in an effort to slow the German advance which took Ostend and Zeebrugge.[17] Sir John French, commanding the British army in northern France, produced a memorandum laying out his requirements for such an attack.[18] The Flanders attack was an alternative to Fisher's Baltic project and to the Dardanelles project. French cautioned that no victory in Flanders would be decisive. He considered the Russian front far more important, although he also considered a French defeat a disaster to be avoided. The War Council of the Cabinet

When HMS *Furious* had her 18in guns removed for her carrier conversion, three of the Dover Patrol monitors were designated to receive them (*Prince Eugene* was never refitted). This is HMS *Lord Clive*. The gun was mounted athwartships and had limited traverse.

chose Gallipoli as the most promising of the three.[19] When it approved the Dardanelles operation on 8 January 1915, the Cabinet decided to defer consideration of a combined attack on Zeebrugge and an advance through Flanders (to Zeebrugge) to February 1915, but Gallipoli soon absorbed so many resources that the Flanders plan was shelved.

When the armies on the Western Front deadlocked in 1914, the Admiralty became interested in an attack from the sea, which might tip the odds. Initial proposals were made by Channel Fleet commander Admiral Lewis Bayley, who had been a pre-war proponent of amphibious operations on the German North Sea coast, to seize the islands of Sylt and Borkum. He took over the Channel Fleet two days after the Scarborough Raid and immediately proposed an attack against the Flanders coast. For the moment not enough destroyers and minesweepers were available, but that would soon change. Bayley's fleet had already been reinforced with more old battleships. The Admiralty planners emphasised the need to take the new U-boat base the Germans were creating in the 'Triangle'. The British army agreed to mount an overland offensive before the Germans moved in more troops. The French agreed to threaten the German rear in order to choke off reinforcements. At this juncture *U 24* demonstrated how serious the submarine threat in the Channel was. While the British concentrated forces to ferry an entire division to France, *U 24* managed to torpedo and sink the pre-dreadnought *Formidable* (1 January 1915). The Royal Navy immediately assigned submarines to patrol off Zeebrugge (one was lost to a mine) and laid a new minefield offshore.

The advent of specially-built monitors in mid-1915 made it possible to shell Zeebrugge and Ostend on a systematic basis. In effect these ships constituted a new shore bombardment fleet, which could be risked without loss to the Grand Fleet or even to the battleships guarding the southern part of the North Sea. Prior to completion of the monitors, the only surplus heavy bombardment ship available to the Royal Navy was the modified pre-dreadnought battleship HMS *Revenge*, her 13.5in guns lined down to 12in. She had been scheduled for scrapping but was brought back at the outbreak of war. Later she was bulged and renamed *Redoubtable*, her original name having been taken by a new *Royal Sovereign* class

battleship. Because they had very shallow draught, the monitors could operate in shallow water surrounded by sandbanks, hence immune to submarine attack.

Once Germany declared unrestricted submarine war against British and allied shipping in 1915, the Flanders bases became more important, because so much British shipping was always concentrated in the southern North Sea. The MarineKorps soon asked for a half-flotilla of the most modern torpedo boats (destroyers). By this time the British were attacking Zeebrugge with aircraft. On 12 February 1915 they managed to damage *U 14*, putting her out of action for several months. The new High Seas Fleet commander von Pohl did not want to lose forces to the MarineKorps, so he reversed his earlier advocacy and argued that Zeebrugge and Bruges were inadequately protected against air attack and that surely the enemy would mount an effective attack against the bases.[20]

Without any central naval authority, only the Kaiser could adjudicate between von Pohl and Tirpitz' MarineKorps commander.[21] The MarineKorps commander argued much as Tirpitz had for cruiser warfare: that the British would have to detach elements of the Grand Fleet to counter any substantial German surface force based in Flanders, hence would improve the odds for the High Seas Fleet. The British would find themselves pushing patrols into the Hoofden and they would have to be backed by the Grand Fleet.

Von Pohl argued that he always had to be prepared for a major battle. Even though the present time was not suitable for a sortie into the North Sea, he had to develop and maintain readiness; he could not afford to lose anything to a peripheral operation like the one in Flanders. Von Pohl's trump card was that the High Seas Fleet was not yet completely ready for a fleet battle, hence had to be held together to train. No one else, particularly not the Admiralstab, could question his judgement on that point. Surely the British would react to the German submarine blockade with a North Sea

The Germans emplaced heavy guns to protect their Flanders bases. Firing from within the range of these guns, the monitors relied heavily on smoke screens like this one. Dover Patrol Commander Rear Admiral Bacon considered smoke so effective that he planned to rely on it to shield his force during an amphibious assault on the Flanders coast in 1917. The craft in the foreground is a motor launch. (US Naval Historical and Heritage Command)

By 1916 Admiral Bacon concluded that the best solution to the Flanders base problem was an amphibious assault. Although extensive preparations were made in 1917, the operation was scrapped because the army was unable to advance far enough in Flanders to link up with the force to be landed. The idea that the bases had to be destroyed by a landing force survived and the attempt was made in April 1918. The old cruiser HMS *Vindictive* was modified to act as command and assault ship. Note the machine-gun position built as a fighting top above her bridge, the extensive use of blast mattresses and the disembarking gangways. (Painting by W L Wyllie, PW1864, © National Maritime Museum, London)

offensive (presumably to attack the U-boats at their bases). That did not happen, but von Pohl was unmoved. Bachmann pointed out to him that the Kaiser had agreed to transfer the half-flotilla and that he attached great importance to it on political as well as military grounds.

Von Schröder wanted the destroyers to attack enemy patrols attempting to keep his submarines out of the North Sea and to keep his harbours clear for High Seas Fleet submarines. The destroyers might mine the British coast and they might also carry out night attacks against merchant shipping on the south and east coasts of England. He wanted a full flotilla to compensate for the more powerful armament of British destroyers which would oppose his. A single flotilla at Zeebrugge would probably tie down two or three British flotillas.[22] At this time German destroyers (torpedo boats) were organised into eleven-boat flotillas, so von Schröder was being promised five boats. He actually received three and that only after a struggle over providing sufficient crews (the High Seas Fleet claimed that it was short of personnel). That was after a fight off Flanders demonstrated clearly that the small 'A' boats were no match for the Dover Patrol destroyers. Early in August the Admiralstab told von Schröder that he might expect his destroyers that October, but they did not arrive until 3 March 1916.[23]

Throughout, the German naval high command seems to have seen Flanders primarily as a submarine base, with a supporting surface force. As the initial unrestricted submarine campaign was curtailed, the Germans turned to minelaying and Flanders seemed well placed to support it. Thus from 1916 to 1917 the Flanders submarine flotilla changed character, from eleven torpedo and five

minelaying U-boats in June 1916 to fourteen torpedo (UB) and twenty-four minelaying (UC) boats in January 1917. None of these submarines was suitable to work directly with the High Seas Fleet, but all of them could reach important British base areas and thus support High Seas Fleet operations, such as that against Lowestoft in April 1916. Between June and September 1916 six UB-boats mined French ports to attack the troop traffic supporting the Somme offensive (three were lost)

Von Schröder's argument that he needed a more powerful surface force was based on the needs of the submarines. In the spring of 1916 the British increasingly deployed mines and fixed nets to close the submarine base in Flanders. They were laid outside the range of the guns emplaced ashore, but initially the barrage was not defended, so the German surface force on the coast could clear it. British aircraft spotted the clearance effort and the Dover Patrol brought in monitors and destroyers to stop it. Now it took the torpedo boats (destroyers) of the Flanders force to protect the clearance effort and there were hardly enough of them.[24] The British, moreover, could see what had been cleared and could replace it. Von Schröder complained in May that he could not clear away anything like the amount the British could add to the barrage.[25] To some extent British activities were complicated because the dividing line between the areas of responsibility of the Dover Patrol and the Harwich Force lay on the barrage set up off the Flanders coast.[26]

At the same time Admiral Scheer seems to have recognised that the Flanders force should be part of his offensive operation against the Royal Navy. He may have seen destroyers in Flanders as a way to tie down British destroyers which would otherwise be assigned to the Grand Fleet and in that way weakening it.[27] Jellicoe certainly saw matters that way. Once von Schröder had a significant destroyer force, the important merchant traffic from Holland to England had to be convoyed against it.[28] This convoy operation began in the summer of 1916. The destroyers to do so had to come from the Grand Fleet; at times Jellicoe went so far as to argue that the fleet would be immobilised by such a demand. This was convoy

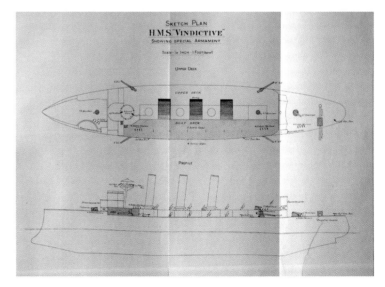

Modifications to HMS *Vindictive* as assault ship are shown in a drawing included in the after-action report. The 6in BL were her old cruiser guns. The howitzers were presumably anti-submarine projectors. Flammenwerfers were flame throwers. Stokes mortars were standard trench weapons. Not shown on the sketch are the assault ramps for the troops.

against surface attack, not submarine attack, but Jellicoe's fear of losing his destroyers to convoy presaged his later objection that convoy against U-boats would have the same effect.

A vital but unrecognised virtue of destroyers in Flanders was that their operations did not entail the sort of W/T traffic typical in High Seas Fleet sorties. The corresponding accounts of major fleet actions always begin with Admiralty signals (based on code-breaking) prior to the sailing of the High Seas Fleet. Enough traffic was usually generated to indicate that something was about to happen in the southern North Sea, but without detail and distances were so short that there were no additional signals to indicate where the Flanders destroyers were headed. Too, the command in Flanders could often use telephones where the High Seas Fleet needed radio, for example to order a channel swept before an operation. The Germans generally maintained radio silence once an operation was underway.[29] Thus the Dover Patrol and the Harwich Force lacked the kind of advance warning the Grand Fleet habitually enjoyed. On the other hand, if Zeebrugge was under attack, German ships normally based there took refuge in Bruges, where they were visible to British aircraft and were far enough from the sea that their progress back to Zeebrugge could be monitored in daylight to provide warning of an impending operation.

Under these conditions defence against the Zeebrugge destroyers was complicated, because they had several possible targets. They could (and did) attack the forces monitoring the anti-submarine barrage across the Dover Straits. They could also attack the harbours used to support the vital cross-Channel traffic, which supported the British army in France and they could also attack shipping concentrations, such as that in the Downs off the Thames. Without specific information, Vice Admiral Bacon, who commanded the Dover Patrol, had to cover multiple possibilities.

Moreover, surface raids from Zeebrugge caught the Royal Navy where it was weakest operationally, in night fighting. With large numbers of ships at sea in separate formations, the British were concerned to avoid friendly fire. As Jellicoe observed in the Grand Fleet, any sort of melee favoured the weaker force over the stronger. British ships had to depend on recognition signals, standard practice being to flash a challenge and not to fire until the wrong reply had been received. Simply flashing the challenge often indicated to a German ship that it had come upon a target and destroyers could not absorb German fire while deciding to shoot back. For their part the Germans divided the operational area into sectors, assigning one to each small group of destroyers. Thus any ship one of their groups encountered could be assumed hostile and immediately engaged (the Germans adopted a similar practice with U-boats operating off the British coast).

Von Schroder was told in May that he would be getting a full High Seas Fleet destroyer flotilla and it moved to Flanders on the night of 7/8 June 1916. To cover the transfer, von Schröder sent his half-flotilla to attack the British trawlers supporting the ASW barrage off Zeebrugge. As with other High Seas Fleet operations, the British were well aware of the movement of the flotilla, but they were not aware of the half-flotilla operation. Von Schröder hoped to use his half-flotilla to drive the British ships patrolling the barrage off Zeebrugge into the oncoming full flotilla of German destroyers.[30] The operation turned out badly because the full flotilla did not notify the Flanders force of a change in course. British destroyers caught the half-flotilla and nearly sank one of the ships before the full flotilla could arrive to end the battle. The full flotilla

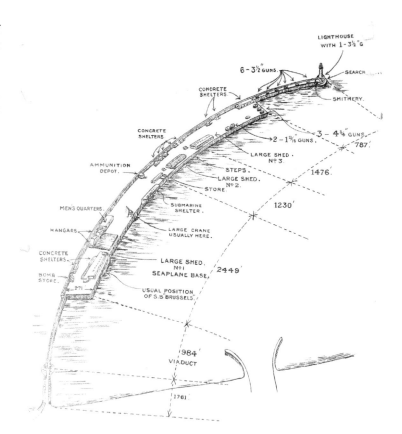

The target: the mole at Zeebrugge, as sketched for the after-action report.

did mount some small raids on shipping and it did lay one minefield, but it had only limited value and it was withdrawn on 30 July. The timing suggests that it was wanted to support the sortie Admiral Scheer planned for August. Von Schröder continued to press for more destroyers on a permanent basis, but on 21 June he was told that due to losses at Jutland he could not expect any.

The Admiralstab still favoured a more powerful force for Flanders, so early in September its chief proposed to Tirpitz' successor that the half-flotilla be built up to a full one.[31] That did not happen, but Scheer was sympathetic. Not long afterward and before the abortive mid-October High Seas Fleet sortie, Scheer agreed to transfer two full destroyer flotillas (twenty destroyers) to Flanders. Like the flotilla provided earlier, this was a temporary addition to the strength of the MarineKorps Flandern. The destroyers sailed on the night of 23/24 October specifically to support the submarines there, by attacking the Dover and Harwich Forces, countering British anti-submarine forces off Zeebrugge.[32]

As with Scheer's fleet sorties, before the flotillas left the Admiralty knew that something was about to happen and it correctly deduced that it had to do with Flanders. Tyrwhitt was ordered to assemble his force, but it happened that the British and German light forces never sighted each other – at night even the narrow neck of the North Sea was wide enough for that. This was much the lesson the Royal Navy had learned in 1913, when night destroyer attacks just did not happen because the destroyers never found their targets.

Von Schröder was also interested in raids on British shipping, although he knew that the Dover Patrol was strong enough to preclude regular attacks.[33] Moreover, any German torpedo boats operating in the Straits had to be back off their bases before daylight to avoid being snapped up by British cruisers. That made

HMS *Vindictive* managed to return from Zeebrugge to Dover under her own power. (Painting by W L Wyllie, PW1862, © National Maritime Museum, London)

any proposed sweep south through the Straits of Dover particularly difficult. It was also particularly promising and von Schröder hoped that an initial surprise attack would be possible, before the British became aware that his force had been augmented. He tried at once, on the night of 26/27 October, with his total of twenty-four torpedo boats (destroyers), the primary target being transports *en route* to France. Dover Patrol commander Vice Admiral Bacon was already aware that von Schröder had his additional ships and that he would have to attack at night, so he stopped night transport runs. He was not, however, aware of the particular attack Von Schröder had planned, so he did not reinforce the patrols effectively. They suffered badly. Bacon's counter-attack was unsuccessful, partly due to garbled orders and partly to unwillingness of British destroyers to attack in the dark before they were sure their targets were hostile. It did not help that the patrol had become complacent, because it had not yet been attacked, hence it did not immediately sound a warning. In the aftermath of the attack, the Admiralty considerably reinforced Bacon's force. The Germans had no idea that the Admiralty was aware that the Zeebrugge force had been reinforced and had carried out the attack.[34] A Court of Inquiry, with whose findings the Admiralty concurred, decided that at night it was more important to keep forces concentrated (to avoid the risk of friendly fire) than to get small forces into place as quickly as possible.

Von Schröder considered the attack successful, because none of his destroyers had suffered, but apparently it did not occur to him that there was a reason the transports had not been present. Apparently the British became aware of an operation early in November, which had largely to be broken off because they seemed to be setting up a trap. On 3 November one of the two flotillas was returned to the High Seas Fleet. The British may have been aware of another planned attack, this time by the single remaining flotilla, because they cleared the Downs of shipping (however, they did not intercept the German destroyers).[35] Von Schröder's other High Seas Fleet flotilla went home on the night of 30 November. It is not clear whether the British were aware of this operation, but they did not intercept it (it is also not clear that they realised that von Schröder's force had been so largely drawn down).

Probably the most important effect of the successful German surprise attack was to convince both the British and the French governments that as long as they held Zeebrugge the Germans had

the initiative in the Channel and therefore that they could disrupt the vital traffic supporting the British army in France. Jellicoe, who was now First Sea Lord, joined with Bacon and Field Marshal Haig, the British commander in France, in urging a land attack to seize or at least disrupt the German Flanders bases.[36] Jellicoe seems to have been far more impressed by the threat of German destroyers than by the submarines in Flanders, which were actually far more productive. In March 1917 he went so far as to write that, unless Flanders was neutralised, the British could not continue the war in 1918, because too many destroyers would be drawn into the North Sea and the Grand Fleet would be immobilised.[37]

A further High Seas Fleet destroyer flotilla was transferred to Von Schröder on 22 January 1917. The Admiralty seems to have been well aware of this plan, because as First Sea Lord Admiral Jellicoe redistributed forces to deal with it. The Harwich Force intercepted the flotilla and inflicted considerable damage, but it failed to sink any of the German destroyers. By this time the Germans considered Flanders a very likely Allied target area, because surely the destruction of the Zeebrugge base would become urgent once they began the planned unrestricted submarine warfare campaign. They also feared that any Allied advance up through Flanders would open Zeebrugge to sufficient heavy gunfire to neutralise it as a base. With the six fresh destroyers, von Schroder had nearly a full flotilla. In mid-February he mounted an operation which was intended as part of Scheer's High Seas Fleet sortie into the Hoofden, but the High Seas Fleet element was aborted due to weather. In accord with Scheer's emphasis on supporting the U-boat offensive, the main object of the operation was to attack the patrol in the Straits so that U-boats could pass through it. Although von Schröder's destroyers achieved nothing on this particular night, he considered it successful: the British failed to catch any of his ships and he was tying down forces which might otherwise have been used against the U-boats.

A second flotilla arrived on 23 March, but on 29 March the flotilla already in Flanders returned to Germany.[38] However, von Schröder received a full flotilla in exchange, this time on a permanent basis (unless it had to be returned to make up losses in the High Seas Fleet). With the half-flotilla built up to full strength, late in March the Flanders force had two full destroyer flotillas. It also began offensive operations with the smaller 'A' class torpedo boats, used up to that point only to patrol off Zeebrugge. For example, they shelled Dunkirk and they sank a French torpedo boat in a night raid. The German destroyers shelled Calais. On one of the night attacks, they were engaged by a British force; famously, HMS *Broke* rammed and sank the German destroyer *G-42* after a hand-to-hand fight while the two ships were locked together (Evans of the *Broke* became a British hero).

Vindictive was scuttled as a blockship during a second attack, at Ostend.

The Germans built a few Luftschiffmotoren-Boote (LM-Boats), the designation indicating that they were powered by airship engines (typically three of them). The German programme was begun in the summer of 1916 by the Flanders command, specifically to fend off British destroyers while the nets blocking Zeebrugge were cut (some adapted motor boats were promising but unsuccessful). A newly-built Lürssen LM-boat is shown. (Christopher C Wright)

The need to beat off British forces attacking the German Flanders bases led the Germans to develop light craft comparable to the British CMBs: LM-Boote (Luftschiffmotoren-Boote) powered by airship (Luftschiff) engines.[39] In the summer of 1916 the Flanders command requested fast motorboats. Initially it was offered five adapted civilian boats, of which only one (*Boncourt*) was fast (36 knots). None was satisfactory, so new boats had to be built. The main problem was to find a suitable engine, the solution being the 210 HP (metric) Maybach airship engine (three per boat). The Flanders command asked for four boats each armed with a 3.7cm machine cannon and another two each with a 45cm torpedo tube and a machine gun. The first four were ordered from Lurssen and Naglo, the last from Oertz. These boats were somewhat larger than CMBs, with a complement of seven or eight. Required speed was 31 to 32 knots. In the autumn of 1916 the Baltic command asked for six to eight fast motor boats to operate in the Irben Straits. The Flanders command also wanted more boats, so a total of thirteen were ordered in May/June 1917, with one more in each of August and October. Two more were ordered in June/July 1918 to replace the first two, which had been sunk and then another ten (*LM 24–33*) in August 1918 (most were not completed). Some boats were ordered from a fourth builder, Roland (*LM 17–20* and *31–33*). After the initial series, both Lurssen (*LM 7–10, 21–26*) and Naglo (*LM 11–13*) produced torpedo boats; Oertz produced *LM 14–16*. Roland's *LM 17–20* and *LM 31–33* were similar to the Oertz boats. *LM 1–13* were all planing boats, but those from *LM 14* on had round-bilge displacement hulls. In the late summer of 1918 the Austrians requested LM-boats for an attack against the Allied blocking force in the Straits of Otranto.

The Germans also became interested in small (6-ton) remote-controlled explosive boats (FL-boote: Fernlenk Boote) specifically to attack the monitors bombarding their Flanders bases. Lurssen built seventeen of them. They were conceived pre-war by Dr W von Siemens of Siemens-Schukert on the basis of a remote-controlled torpedo. Trials began as early as 1906. Work was suspended because there was no suitable engine, but it was resumed on the outbreak of war. Tests were completed in September 1915, twelve

boats being ordered. Of these, eight were immediately assigned to Flanders. Soon other commands, including those on Norderney and in Kurland, wanted boats, so five more were ordered. Six were assigned to the Baltic, to operate from Libau. By the end of 1916 there were FL-stations at Zeebrugge, Ostend, Libau and North Kurland. Boats were command-guided by wire, the controller watching the boat and its target. The first boats were delivered to Flanders in the second half of November 1915. They were declared operational on 28 December. For trials using the lighthouse at Kiel, the operator's eye was 27m above the water, giving a range of vision of 15km (the operator at Zeebrugge was 30m above water, giving a range of vision of 20 to 25km). The torpedo boat *T 146* was fitted as a control ship. To increase effective range, the Germans soon adopted a floatplane with a wireless, which could observe the boat and signal the controller ashore. This arrangement proved difficult, partly because control was crude (the only signals were to steer port or starboard or to keep going). As a consequence, boats zig-zagged. In co-operation with Telefunken, Siemens began work on direct radio (wireless) control by an aircraft. Six boats were modified for wireless control (*FL 4, 13, 14, 15, 16* and *17*). The boats were not particularly successful. *FL 3* destroyed itself on 24 April 1916 due to a control problem. *FL 4* was sunk by destroyer shellfire off Ostend on 3 November 1917 while closing with a monitor 5000m away. *FL 5* was destroyed by an engine fire due to an attack on 25 September 1916 off the Flanders coast. *FL 7* destroyed 50m of the mole at Nieuport on 1 March 1917. *FL 8* was sunk by a British monitor while 300m from its target on 6 September 1917. *FL 10* was lost during an attack under air control on 28 May 1918. *FL 12* hit but failed to damage the monitor *Erebus* in a 28 October 1917 attack. The fates of *FL 13* and *FL 16* are unknown. Despite the relative failure of the FL-boats, they enormously impressed the Royal Navy, which rushed to develop its equivalent DCB (Distant Controlled Boat) and which decided that DCBs would be a major threat in future. The likely DCB threat (and, presumably, a motor torpedo boat threat) justified development and then retention of the multiple 2pdr pom-pom.

As von Schröder had imagined, the British considered Zeebrugge a vital target. By 1917 bombers were considerably more effective than they had previously been. Von Schröder began moving his destroyers to the Zeebrugge mole, where anti-aircraft guns gave them better cover. British aircraft spotted them there and on 8 April a CMB attack was co-ordinated with an air raid. One of

Some LM-boats, like this one, had a single forward-firing 45cm torpedo tube in the bow. (Christopher C Wright)

the CMBs torpedoed a destroyer alongside the mole (the Germans initially thought the damage had been done by a submarine). Von Schröder moved his destroyers back behind the mole, frustrating further British CMB raids. CMBs encountered German destroyers at sea, but without effect.

The air and CMB raid was the beginning of attempts to neutralise von Schröder's force at source rather than at sea. Compared to grander attempts of this kind against the High Seas Fleet U-boat force, Dover Patrol commander Vice Admiral Bacon had the advantage that his force was ultimately expendable: unlike Jellicoe or Beatty, he could not lose the war at one blow. The problem had two components. One was Zeebrugge itself, heavily defended but ultimately exposed. The other was Bruges, the essential repair base for the small U-boats operating out of Zeebrugge. If the locks in the canal connecting the two could be destroyed, the problem of the Zeebrugge force would be considerably reduced.

Bacon's initial attack was made by three 15in gun monitors on 12 May. Due to dense fog, the Germans initially did not realise that the monitors were present. The monitors failed to hit the locks in the canal to Bruges, but they did destroy the rail line connecting Zeebrugge to the mainland. Bacon now developed a more ambitious plan, in which monitors with collapsible bow extensions would ram themselves into the mole at Zeebrugge. Troops on board would rush across bridges extended from the monitors to destroy the German guns and also any torpedo boats alongside. Another monitor would tie up alongside and shell the locks leading to Bruges. Once the guns on the mole had been neutralised, the monitors would withdraw while blockships were sunk in the harbour. The operation would be covered by a smoke screen and by destroyers.

Bombardment of Zeebrugge, Ostend and the canal continued, but the monitors were unable to hit the crucial locks leading to Bruges. During a 4 June 1917 operation the Germans lost one destroyer at sea and another badly damaged and a third was serious damaged in drydock at Ostend; the Germans concluded that they had to develop Ghent as a replacement base. The Admiralstab and Scheer agreed to strengthen the Flanders force with more destroyers.[40]

The various attacks convinced von Schröder to give up offensive surface operations in May in favour of defensive ones. The British seem to have been unaware of this shift and although the Flanders destroyers had achieved very little, they feared that at some point the Germans would realise just how effective they could be. The Royal Navy apparently had no way to deal with destroyer raids, however much it reinforced the Harwich Force and the Dover Patrol. Worse, the various transfers from the High Seas Fleet proved that the Germans could build up the force in Flanders at will, as long as they were willing to immobilise the High Seas Fleet temporarily. The British could not afford to immobilise the Grand Fleet, because at any time the High Seas Fleet might come out. There was, then, a limit to the strength available to the Harwich Force and the Dover Patrol. The as-yet unrealised potential of the Flanders force was enough to justify a massive attack up the Flanders coast. Even if the army failed to seize the port, it could gain ground on which heavy guns commanding the port could be emplaced.[41] This was exactly what von Schröder and the Admiralstab feared the British would do.

Bacon had been promoting an amphibious operation since the

The Royal Navy was fascinated by the possibility of remote control. When the Germans deployed their first FL-boats, the British assumed that the aircraft overhead was controlling them directly by wireless and they began a crash programme to develop an equivalent, which they called a DCB. The craft shown (in 1918) was built by Thornycroft as a '40ft Fast Motor Pinnace', actually a modified 40ft CMB hull driven by a single V12 engine. A sketch plan is included in the Thornycroft Collection at the Brass Foundry outstation of the National Maritime Museum. Although the number on the bow is 3 (i.e., *DCB 3*), other records show that the Thornycroft boat (Admiralty designation *MB 1143*) was *DCB 4*. Thornycroft also described the boat as 'Mr Tom Thornycroft's new design 40ft hard-chine boat'. Presumably the yacht-like cabin was camouflage, as there was very little space under it. A one-ton explosive charge could be carried in the bow. Note the symbol painted on deck to make it easier for a controlling aircraft to see where the boat was headed. With only a single engine, this boat was slower than a CMB; on trials she made 23.39 knots. She and two sisters were ordered on 16 June 1917, *MB 1142* going to the RAF. *MB 1143* was sent to HMS *Vernon* for trials. She was delivered on 12 April 1918. At least one converted CMB apparently had a simpler steering shelter aft, where the second crewman is shown here.

autumn of 1915.[42] At that time only one German battery (the 11in Tirpitz Battery) outranged his monitors. He proposed to rush the port, landing troops behind the batteries and taking the town, then joining up with troops from Nieuport down the coast.[43] He would have landed troops at daybreak, shielded by a smoke screen. The naval part of the operation, which Bacon thought feasible, would have been to lay enough ships alongside the quays to project a force powerful enough to seize the town and docks and destroy the batteries, then to land a follow-on force within 48 hours. His initial force would take sufficient ground for it to hold safely as a base for further operations. The force would be carried in ninety trawlers (100 men each) in divisions of six, using gang-planks to get troops onto the mole. The trawlers would be supported by six 12in and one 9.2in monitor, each of the 12in monitors carrying 300 men, who could walk ashore. The monitors would also carry additional guns, field guns and armoured cars. The six monitors would enter Ostend harbour between two lines of towed smoke boats, then berth alongside the jetties, or as close to it as possible. Each would have sixteen to twenty trawlers in company. The German guns would be destroyed in reverse. The operation would be undertaken in conjunction with an Allied attack from Ypres (British) and

The Dover Patrol covered the Dover Barrage, a mass of nets and mines intended to prevent U-boats from entering the Channel from the North Sea. A large force of small ships, such as drifters, blocked the surface above the nets and mines. Specialist unpowered Boom (Defence) Vessels were towed to their stations by tug. In the high winds of the Channel they hoisted staysails on their single masts. By illuminating the barrage with their four searchlights (they had onboard engines to power generators and winches) they forced submarines to dive into the minefields. These craft were numbered rather than named. Vessels intended specifically for East Coast anchorages (Cromarty, Granton and the Humber) were designated BD rather than BV and had single guns and only a single searchlight, atop the pilot house. All had lightship-type hulls. Typical length (overall) was 100ft. The BV and BD were in a single numerical series running up to *BD 60* (of which *BD 40, 44* and *53–60* were cancelled in December 1918). The series included fourteen BV (*BV 1–10, BV 17–18* and *BV 41–42*), of which *BV 1* was launched on 12 November 1917. Those not discarded in 1923–4 survived into the Second World War. The specially-designed Boom Vessels and Boom Defence vessels supplemented numerous trawlers and drifters which tended booms from which anti-submarine nets were suspended. At the end of the war, 125 such craft were assigned to Scapa Flow alone. The boom defence force began with a few old sloops and gunboats assigned in August 1914. (Author's collection)

Nieuport (French). Once the enemy had been shaken by this attack, Bacon planned to land three divisions, which would link up with the advancing British ground force and turn the German flank. The army was interested and Field Marshal Haig ordered more detailed studies. The problem was the advance beyond the beach, as at Gallipoli. The British would be advancing on a very narrow front and the Germans could rush in reserves. Moreover, it would be necessary to rush through the town so as to hold it from outside attack. Any Germans in the town could hold up an advance and shelling the town would only create worse obstacles and better protection for surviving enemy troops. Before anything could be done, the Germans built the Knocke Battery, which could shell the jetties at Ostend, making the operation impossible after February 1916.

Zeebrugge and Ostend were so important that the Admiralty and army GHQ remained interested in an amphibious attack. The decision was to postpone any landing until an advance up the Flanders coast had shaken the Germans. Late in 1916 Bacon proposed what he called the Great Landing on the Belgian coast.[44]

The only feasible landing place was the foreshore outside Ostend. Bacon chose the area to the west because it was covered by a seawall 30ft high, hence would seem to the Germans an unlikely place. He understood that the element of surprise was key. The area to the east was rejected because sea communication would be difficult unless the batteries were silenced or the army advanced from Nieuport. The seawall sloped up at a 30° angle and was topped by an overhanging buttress 3ft high, of semi-circular coping stone facing the landing area. Bacon thought the Germans, armed with machine guns, would think it impregnable; but he also thought they would not imagine the effect of a heavy smoke screen his force could create.

To Bacon, the lesson of Gallipoli was that it was too dangerous to land large numbers of men in small numbers in open boats. He envisaged a landing pier, which could be moved into position by ships alongside. That would still leave the problem of getting the troops onto the piers. His next idea was to have the troops ride the piers, which would be moved into position by his monitors. To provide enough draught, the piers would have to be 300 yds long,

The other important Narrow Sea of the First World War was the Adriatic. In contrast to the southern part of the North Sea, the main naval bases of both principal combatants, Italy and Austria-Hungary, were relatively close together. Neither made much use of her main fleet, but each sought to tip the balance of seapower by destroying the other's battleships in harbour. For example, the Italians credited Austrian sabotage with the destruction of the battleships *Leonardo da Vinci* and *Benedetto Brin*. For their part the Italians developed special attack craft with which they penetrated the main Austrian base at Pola, sinking the Austrian *Viribus Unitis* (an Italian motor torpedo boat sank her sister *Szent Istvan*). Both countries built substantial fast light forces suited to raiding the enemy's coast and his coastal shipping. All of this was in addition to the Austrian submarine force, based at Pola inside the Adriatic, but passing through the Straits of Otranto to operate in the Mediterranean (the parallel to German attacks on the Dover Barrage was Austrian attacks against the barrage across the Straits of Otranto). The large Italian destroyer *Carlo Mirabello* completed in August 1916 exemplified Italian interest in fast powerful light warships intended to contest control of the Adriatic. The post-war French Navy focussed on the destroyer war in the North Sea as the model for a possible future naval war against Italy, its idea being that ships such as this one would be used against vital French trade in the Eastern Mediterranean. (Maurizio Brescia)

but he could save 100 yds by having the monitors push instead of being lashed alongside. Two monitors would propel a pier using half their power to push it. Careful photo analysis revealed the slope of the beach, so Bacon calculated that each pier had to draw no more than 18 inches at its landward end and 9ft at its seaward end (so the monitors could stay afloat while pushing). To do that, each pier had to be 550ft long. This was a 2500-ton ship. DNC assigned the design to Charles Lillicrap, who eventually became DNC himself. Building several such ships would strain British shipbuilding resources, so Bacon needed the support of the First Sea Lord.

He got it; first Admiral Jackson and then his successor Jellicoe supported the project. It was agreed that work would not start until the army GHQ in France felt reasonably certain that the army would advance in Flanders. Built at Chatham, the prototype pontoon was tested in the Swin Channel at the entrance to the Thames in March 1917. Once it had succeeded, two more were ordered. Each pontoon was designed to carry three tanks at its forward end; they would spearhead the attack. Special fittings were designed to allow the tanks to climb the seawall and by 1 June they had been demonstrated successfully on a test section (which turned out to be steeper than the actual seawall). The pontoon had also demonstrated the ability to carry the tanks.

Bacon was enthusiastic and he pointed out that both his six monitors and the army division involved were essentially expendable in a high-risk high-payoff venture. To keep the operation secret, all the naval crews involved were sequestered beginning in July. By September weather and the time at which dawn broke began to make the operation difficult. The hope of linking up with the army died because the army was blocked at Passchendaele. Bacon suggested simply seizing a stretch of the Belgian coast, destroying the defending guns and allowing the navy to land its own heavy guns, but the army vetoed the idea. Then the possibility of executing the operation by moonlight was raised, so the operation stayed alive until 15 October, when it was abandoned until 1918.

The plan envisaged landing 13,750 men, three tanks and twelve artillery pieces at Middelkerke, on the Flemish coast, protected from German artillery by smoke. Would it have worked? The British thought the Germans had only two brigades on the coast, but in fact they had nearly a division and a half, including reserves. However, the British would have had a lot of firepower, in the form of the monitors and the tanks.[45] Moreover, they would have had considerable mobility along the seawall, much better than the Germans would have had inland.

Narrow seas were well-suited to fast motor boats. The Royal Italian Navy built numerous motor torpedo boats called MAS. Initially that meant *Motobarca Armata SVAN*, indicating an armed motor launch from the initial builder (*Societa Veneziana Automobili Nautiche*); later it meant *Motobarca Anti-Sommergibile*, anti-submarine motor launch as well as *Motobarca Armata Silurante*, torpedo-armed motor launch and later *Motoscafo Anti-Sommergibile*. The MAS series included Elco motor launches of the type the Royal Navy designated MLs and some MAS were armed with depth charges rather than torpedoes. They also functioned as minelayers. The two prototypes were laid down in 1915 and ran trials between November 1915 and December 1916. Torpedo boat MAS were MAS 1– 62, MAS 91– 102, MAS 158– 175, MAS 203– 232, MAS 319– 326 and MAS 397– 422 (total 156, of which three were cancelled). MAS 423–438 were cancelled at the end of the war. MAS 9 penetrated the Austrian naval base (Trieste) on the night of 9 December 1917, sinking the pre-dreadnought *Wien*. This was essentially the attack the Harwich Force planned against the Schillig Roads, using CMBs. MAS 15, shown here, sank the Austrian battleship *Szent Istvan* off Premuda on 10 June 1918. Her companion boat MAS 21 hit the battleship *Tegethoff* but the torpedo failed to explode. Built by SVAN, MAS 15 was powered by two-shaft Isotta-Frascini petrol engines (total 450bhp) plus two-shaft Rognini electric motors (10hp) for silent operation. She attained 24.8 knots on her July 1916 trials. The guns shown are 6.5mm machine guns, probably US-supplied Colts; some craft of this type also had a single 3pdr (47mm) forward (typically as an alternative to the torpedoes, but sometimes in addition to them). MAS 15 survives at the Museo del Vittoriano in Rome. (E Bagnasco collection via M Brescia)

Bacon also developed plans to block Zeebrugge and Ostend, but he had no chance to execute them. He was summarily fired late in 1917. The new Admiralty Plans Division, headed by Rear Admiral Roger Keyes, began to consider purely naval methods of blocking Zeebrugge and Ostend. The division began work on 3 November and presented a draft to the Admiralty Board on 3 December.[46] Keyes would soon succeed Admiral Bacon at the Dover Patrol, hence would have the opportunity to execute the plan he had helped develop. Keyes estimated that the Flanders submarines were responsible for a quarter of all shipping losses. His plan would also remove the threat of surface attack, as yet unrealised but very real. Ultimately it envisaged sinking blockships at both Zeebrugge and Ostend.

By this time the barrage immediately off the Flanders coast had been abandoned in favour of a mine and net barrage extending across the Straits of Dover from the Downs to Dunkirk.[47] Mines and nets were vulnerable to gales and to tides in the Channel, but it was clear that some way had to be found to block the entrance of the Channel to U-boats. A new Channel Barrage Committee was formed on 17 November and chaired by Keyes, who had led the British submarine service at the beginning of the war. Keyes and his committee recommended laying deep minefields into which submarines would be forced to dive by trawler and drifter patrols equipped with flares, backed by destroyers using searchlights.[48] In January 1918 Keyes

replaced Bacon as commander of the Dover Patrol. If anything, he was even more determined to wipe out the German base. The Germans found the new barrier so effective that they stopped sending submarines through the Straits. The extra time needed for the trip around the north of Scotland reduced time on patrol and thus was a valuable contribution to the anti-submarine war. The barrage sank four U-boats during January 1918 alone; during 1914–17 the Germans had lost a total of two U-boats in the Channel. The Flanders U-boat commander demanded an attack against the barrier.

During the autumn of 1917 the surface force of the Flanders base was worn down, so that even when it became clear that the threat of a British attack had eased, it was impossible to return to offensive operations. For a time, too, five of the destroyers returned to the High Seas Fleet for Operation 'Albion', the attack on the Åland Islands off Finland (they returned to Flanders in November 1917). Also, the air component of the Flanders force was no longer able to beat off air raids, so that in the first months of 1918 it became impossible to keep destroyers in Zeebrugge harbour. Ships had to be moved into the Bruges canal every night. However, German destroyers from Zeebrugge managed to shell Yarmouth on the night of 14 January, even though Keyes had warning and was at sea in strength (for a minelaying operation). This was again proof that even powerful British surface forces were ineffective at night (in this case, the British and German forces never came into contact).

In February, von Schröder personally asked Scheer to attack the mine barrier; Scheer sent a destroyer flotilla. Apparently the British were unaware that it was coming. Standing orders on the barrier were that in the event of a destroyer attack the drifters and trawlers would fire green flares and flee. The German destroyers crippled a paddle sweeper so quickly that she could not launch her flare and others in the patrol took the sound of gunfire to indicate that a U-boat was being attacked. This was much the complacency that had made for an effective attack in October 1916. In one case two French torpedo boats saw the German destroyers but assumed they were British. Despite the recent raids, no one seems to have been awake to the possibility of an additional raid. At Dover, Keyes did not realise that something was wrong until he heard unusually sustained gunfire. His countermeasures were too late. The Germans sank a trawler and seven drifters and badly damaged a paddle sweeper, a trawler and five more drifters. The raid succeeded, but it had no lasting effect and von Schröder did not ask for more help from the High Seas Fleet until September.

Keyes carried out his attacks on Zeebrugge (23 April 1918) and Ostend (9 May). The attacks were heroic and, as Keyes expected, costly. He did succeed in placing blockships in both harbours, but not exactly as intended. Zeebrugge was largely blocked, but Ostend was not. The canal from Bruges to Zeebrugge was partly blocked: it could still be used by UB-boats and by the small 'A'-class torpedo boats, but not by destroyers. Some of the dredgers needed to clear the canal had been destroyed in the attack. It proved possible to dredge a channel around the blockships, so that on 14 May four destroyers managed to pass at high water. Ostend was entirely usable, but, as noted, it was considered vulnerable to air attack. Chief of the Admiralstab von Holtzendorff considered the attack a major German defeat, although publicly (and to the Kaiser) it was portrayed as a victory. Keyes felt that his partial success justified trying again, but the Admiralty turned him down.

The Germans certainly learned that neither Ostend nor Zeebrugge was really safe, so they pulled their ships back into Bruges, confident that they could run out through the canal. However, during a 28 May air attack a bomb hit the caisson in the canal, disabling it. Just as repairs were completed, a monitor hit the caisson on 9 June, completely destroying the new gate. It proved difficult to remove and for the rest of June the canal was blocked, all the Flanders destroyers and submarines confined behind it to the basins at Bruges. By this time the Dover Barrage had made the Flanders submarine base far less useful and there was little interest in using Flanders destroyers offensively in the southern North Sea. Moreover, by this time British air attacks against the Flanders base were proving effective against both submarines and destroyers. Heavy new minefields off the Flanders coast made it necessary for minesweepers to escort all submarines to sea and that swallowed any remaining offensive potential enjoyed by the Flanders force. For example, on 27 August an entire destroyer flotilla was needed to escort one submarine to sea.[49]

The Germans were finally compelled to evacuate the 'Triangle' as the German army fell back after the failure of its 1918 offensive. Late in September von Schröder was told that the army could no longer hold the coast and that he was to prepare to leave. He finally did so in October, the Flanders flotillas being officially dissolved on 14 October.

Far more than in more open waters, the fight over the southern part of the North Sea involved combined operations not only of different types of warships, but also of different arms: naval forces, the land forces which held Flanders (and which tried to seize it back) and air forces. The latter began mainly as reconnaissance assets and as spotters for indirect artillery fire by both the British monitors and the heavy German guns on the Belgian coast, fighters seeking to prevent one side or the other from spotting effectively. By 1917–18 the British were able to bomb effectively, seriously damaging or sinking submarines and surface units.

There were important implications for other countries contemplating coastal naval warfare. The Flanders operation apparently became the basis for Soviet naval command and control.[50] From the outset the Germans saw Flanders as an all-arms operation based on a central command ashore. Their first step on seizing the Flanders coast was to set up a radio station. The reconnaissance arm consisted of the surface force and, to some extent, German seaplanes based in Flanders. Scouting required a geographical reference: in 1918 some German seaplanes had possibly the world's first radio aid to air navigation (using directional W/T). Without the navaid, positions after long flights were accurate only to within 15 miles. As of June 1918 this system was proven but still experimental. A post-war British attempt to understand MarineKorps Flandern was frustrated because the Germans destroyed their command and control equipment, publications and bunkers before abandoning the Flanders coast.[51]

As an alternative to the barrage off the Flemish coast, Bacon tried to attack the German force at source by using his monitors to shell Zeebrugge and Ostend. To do that he had to neutralise the defending German shore batteries. An early attempt to silence them with shellfire failed, much as shellfire had failed to neutralise some of the shore batteries at Gallipoli. During 1917 the Dover Patrol leaned to cloak its monitors in smoke screens. Because their targets were fixed and because they had air spotting, they could still fire effectively as long as they had effective reference points offshore. Those were provided in the form of towers sunk in the shallow water. This harassing fire was not particularly effective and Bacon (and later his successor Keyes) became interested in more dramatic attacks.

MAS 7 (Lieutenant Gennaro Pagano di Melito) displays her hard-chine hull form at Brindisi in the summer of 1916. Note the torpedo-dropping gear for 45cm weapons, which was standard for MAS torpedo boats. The Royal Navy had rejected this type of gear on the grounds that it could not be used at high speed. The ships in the background are, from left to right, the armoured cruisers *Pisa* and *San Giorgio*. At right is the salvage ship *Anteo* recovering the hulk of the battleship *Benedetto Brin*, sunk by sabotage on 27 September 1915. (E. Bagnasco collection via M. Brescia)

The 'E' class was an enlarged 'D' with side-by-side bow tubes (instead of the over-and-under configuration of a 'D'), two broadside tubes and more powerful diesels. The low bow made these submarines wet even in mild weather, as this pre-war photograph of *E 7* shows. This photograph does not show the topside rudder. (Perkins via Naval Institute Collection)

CHAPTER 11
Submarines

PRACTICAL SUBMARINES EXISTED BY 1900, but they were limited to harbours and then to coastal areas. To achieve greater range (and, incidentally, higher surface speed) required reliable, efficient internal-combustion engines, which became available from about 1905 onwards. In 1914 all navies had long-range submarines, but they were only beginning to understand their potential. They could not effectively attack commerce under the universally-accepted Prize Rules, which required that a raider examine a ship and protect its passengers and crew before sinking it. Navies became interested in submarines as elements of, or adjuncts to, fleets. For example, several navies, including the Royal Navy, the German navy and the US Navy, were interested in tactics which would lead an opposing fleet over a submarine trap. Submarines were also the only craft capable of imposing a close blockade on an enemy fleet in the face of his own mines, torpedo boats and submarines. If anything, pre-1914 navies seem to have exaggerated the ease with which submarines could find and

attack fast warships in the open ocean.

Submarines were relatively immobile when submerged and whether surfaced or submerged they could not see very far. They had to wait for targets in places they were likely to pass. That meant, for example, the areas immediately to seaward of the entrances and exits of fleet bases and major ports and the focal areas identified many years earlier as likely hunting grounds for commerce raiders. Once in the open sea, a naval force could consider itself reasonably safe from submarine attack, although that was not always the case. Conversely, a submarine was unlikely to encounter targets while transiting from base to a patrol area where it might expect to encounter targets.

Although submarines were equipped during the war with hydrophones, they were not good enough to support an attack conducted entirely on the basis of sound information. A submarine might be difficult to find in the open, but she could not attack without using her periscope. At the very least, a ship sighting a periscope might speed up or turn away; a submerged submarine was quite slow. Torpedo attack created further dangers for the submarine. All First World War torpedoes were propelled by air (in many cases, heated and even turned into steam), which left a visible wake, a warning of imminent attack, but for a fast escort such as a destroyer it was also an arrow pointing back at the firing submarine. Both periscope and array were very fleeting indicators, so there was a premium on quick reaction, particularly to an indicator some distance away. Hence the great interest on the Allied side in depth-charge throwers and various howitzers and charge-throwing guns.

With the 'D' class, the Royal Navy began building 'oversea submarines' capable of working on the far side of the North Sea, in the teeth of German local defences. This class introduced external ('saddle') ballast tanks, which left more volume inside the hull, but also made for poor streamlining. *D 1* shows her saddle tanks and also her W/T antennas, with characteristic Royal Navy spreaders to form cylindrical arrays. *D 4* of this class had the first British submarine deck gun, a short 12pdr.

Before 1914 increasing torpedo range attracted great naval attention and much affected the tactics of capital ships and of destroyers. However, submarines typically fired single shots from close range. Before the war, British doctrine was to fire from 500 yds and it was presumably typical. Firing was complicated enough that it was difficult or impossible to fire spreads. As the submarine fired, the weight represented by the torpedo was ejected and the air ejecting the torpedo created a visible air bubble. The submarine had to take on balancing water quickly enough to avoid broaching. It was also difficult to shift rapidly from target to target. A submarine might be very effective against one target at a time, but unable to take advantage of a mass of targets suddenly presented, as in a convoy.

To hit a moving target, the shooter has to solve a triangle, the sides of which represent his own speed, the target's speed and the torpedo's speed. The solution is to aim the torpedo so that it leads the target just enough to hit. Aim is in terms of the angle between the torpedo course and the target course. The faster (or shorter) the target, the more acute the problem. Unfortunately the submarine could not directly measure either the target speed or its course. Both had to be estimated based on a quick glance through the periscope. The purpose of much First World War naval camouflage was not to hide a ship so much as to prevent a U-boat commander from accurately estimating either key quantity. That applied to dazzle painting and also to false bow waves.

The submarine's need to show a periscope, perhaps repeatedly, as she prepared to attack explains why it was assumed by both the British and the Germans at the outbreak of war that a destroyer screen would be an effective means of shielding capital ships.[1] Given limited underwater speed, a submarine had to get into a position ahead of a fast target. Typically it had to be within 'limiting lines of approach' defined by the ratio of torpedo and target speeds (and by submarine submerged speed). To the extent that a destroyer spotting a periscope could run down the submarine, she could keep that submarine out of the attack area ahead of the moving ships. At the outbreak of war the British had thought through a means of destroying submarines occupying the limiting lines of approach. The Germans apparently thought that the presence of destroyers *without* anti-submarine weapons was enough; *Krieg zur See* makes it clear that that in 1914 the High Seas Fleet relied heavily on destroyers as anti-submarine ships despite their toothlessness. It might be imagined that a shallowly-submerged submarine which had just exposed its periscope was in danger of being rammed, but lightly-built destroyers had at least as much to fear until they were fitted with reinforced bows.

All submarines of this era were propelled underwater by batteries, which were charged by diesel (sometimes petrol) engines on the surface. Submarines were not designed to run their engines while submerged, although there were attempts to devise means of doing so. For example, some British submariners tried to run while awash with an open hatch, using cloths to keep most water out of the largely-submerged submarine. Submerged endurance was limited, typically less than 24 hours and speed was also very limited. A submarine could make good a substantial distance only when running on her engines, on the surface. She would also run her engines whenever out of sight of potential attackers. It helped that the submarine had a low silhouette which could not be seen at any great distance and that coal-fuelled surface ships generally created smoke which could be seen well over the horizon, either as warning (to dive) or as indication that a target was nearby. The periscope offered a raised vantage point which was not very visible at any distance. Moreover, a submarine had to find its quarry. It could hunt most effectively near a base or a port or in the sort of focal area which had been defined in studies of trade protection. It followed that formations had to be protected mainly either when they emerged from (or returned to) their bases, or when they were near enemy bases on blockade duty.

Any kind of co-ordination between submarines and a central authority depended on W/T, but a small submarine could not initially support a massive transmitter-receiver. The Royal Navy's preferred solution to long-range control of submarines was to use a surface ship, from which orders could be sent over shorter range to surfaced submarines (in 1914 there was no means of contacting a submerged submarine by W/T, although there were crude underwater sound signals). During the Scarborough Raid, Commodore (S) Roger Keyes was on board the destroyer *Firedrake*, which was in W/T contact with the Admiralty via Yarmouth. He contacted his surfaced submarines via shorter-range W/T. In this way he tried to control a patrol line he had formed off the Dutch coast, on what he hoped was the escape route of the German battlecruisers (he wanted permission from the Admiralty to move the patrol line). On the other hand, by December 1914 the Royal Navy had submarines positioned off the German coast as pickets more than as attackers and it appears to have received current W/T reports from them.

The Royal Navy

Admiral Fisher was an early advocate of submarines, initially as a means of coast defence. As submarine engines improved, however, he became interested in using them further afield. Submarines were an important element of his 'flotilla defence', which initially applied mainly to the British coast and then became an argument that the entire North Sea would probably become untenable for conventional fleets in wartime. He therefore became intensely interested in 'oversea' submarines capable of operating off the German coast. The first such craft were the 'D' class, followed by the 'E' class which was the standard British First World War submarine.

All of this was less purposeful than might be imagined. Initially Vickers developed a series of single-hull submarines from the Holland boats it had built under license ('A', 'B' and 'C' classes). The company, which had an Admiralty monopoly on submarine construction until 1910, determined which improvements it could add in successive classes. Like contemporary foreign submarines, all were powered by petrol engines, whose fuel created poisonous (and intoxicating) vapour liable to explosion. The 'B' and 'C' classes were the first to be considered ocean-going, but that did not suggest the endurance to cross the North Sea.

The succeeding 'D' class (1906–7 programme) was the first DNC submarine design, Vickers developing its details (for a time it was to have been built by Pembroke Royal Dockyard).[2] It turned out to be the first overseas submarine, but it is not clear how much that role was taken into account by DNC, hence to what if any extent the 'D' class reflected Fisher's personal evolving vision of future North Sea warfare.[3] The design was produced about May 1905 as an alternative to a modified version of the current 'B' class, which DNC called C2. Initially the main feature of both designs was increased reserve buoyancy, 'D' having saddle tanks and C2 having ballast tanks atop the pressure hull. The object was to improve seakeeping. The French and others had already shown that by moving ballast tanks outside the hull a submarine could gain considerable reserve buoyancy (sea-keeping) and that virtue was unquestioned. The 'D' design was chosen over C2 at a 23 June 1905 meeting of the Submarine Design Committee, which included Controller, DNC, Engineer in Chief, Naval Assistant to First Sea Lord (and also former Inspecting Captain of Submarines) Captain Bacon and Inspecting Captain of Submarine Captain Lees. It seems to have been accepted at the outset that this submarine should be considerably larger than earlier ones; C2 was still smaller than French 450-tonners. The Committee opted for the larger submarine with better seakeeping, using saddle tanks. They

Earlier submarines, relegated to coast defence at the outbreak of war, proved useful as a means of attacking U-boats in the waters around Britain. This is *C 9*. The men standing on the superstructure give some idea of her small size. She also had very limited internal volume due to her single-hull configuration. Four of this class operated in the Baltic. They were scuttled in Helsingfors Bay in April 1918 when the Russian Revolution made further operation impossible.

The 'E' class was the wartime workhorse of the Royal Navy submarine service. This is *E 20*, probably upon completion in August 1915. During the war, British submarines typically had their names painted on their superstructures; pre-war photographs typically show pennant numbers instead. The gun is a 6in howitzer. Note the ship-like 'plough' bow (introduced in *E 19*) for better seakeeping. Initial units had no guns, but experience in the Sea of Marmara (Dardanelles) showed that they were needed. Malta Dockyard installed a 12pdr on board *E 11* and a 4in on board *E 12*. Some North Sea boats were given high-angle 3in or 12pdr guns in 1916–17. Some boats operating in the Sea of Marmara carried spare torpedoes lashed to the casing. 'E' class minelayers carried their mines in tubes in the ballast tanks instead of the usual beam torpedo tubes.

Although nearly at the end of the 'E' series, *E 55* was built by Denny to the original design, its bow poorly adapted to seakeeping. She did not have the topside rudder eliminated after the initial boats in the series.

As with battleships, cruisers and destroyers, in 1914 the Royal Navy took over submarine contracts with foreign navies. *E 26* had been ordered from Beardmore for the Turkish navy. These pre-launch photographs show the broad saddle tank of an 'E'-class submarine but not the unusual beam torpedo tubes (the bow photo shows one of the two bow tubes). The stern view (which shows the cap for the single stern tube) is dated 23 August 1915.

offered some protection to the pressure hull, which was somewhat better shaped for diving and for steering in a horizontal plane and they made for less hull depth, which meant that the submarine had a lower, hence less visible, silhouette on the surface.[4] Both alternative designs invested much of the additional size in greatly increased battery capacity (212 rather than 159 cells) for greater underwater speed and endurance. Armament was doubled, fuel stowage was doubled and both designs featured twin screws. Enlarged hulls provided accommodation for relief personnel, so the submarines could remain longer at sea. There was no discussion of how much longer at sea a submarine had to stay to achieve sufficient performance to operate on an enemy's coast rather than off the British coast.

There was some reluctance to accept the increased size and cost in ships which had to be built in large numbers and there was scepticism that simply carrying extra personnel would allow a larger submarine to remain at sea for longer than the usual three days in fine weather and less in bad weather. At the meeting both Bacon and E-in-C (A J Durston) raised the possibility of using a heavier-oil engine. The Royal Navy had been interested in such engines for some time, but as yet no satisfactory engine had been built and tested. Now a diesel was available and it would be tested on board the earlier submarine *A 13*. It required about 50 per cent more volume than an equivalent petrol engine, but its fuel had only about half the energy content of petrol, hence would make for a slower submarine. Another possibility was a heavy-oil engine that Vickers was developing.[5]

None of this made the new design an immediate favourite. Third Sea Lord (Admiral Jackson) agreed with other members of the Committee that the navy should continue building the current standard coastal boats ('B'/'C'-class) while developing the much more expensive 'D' design. DNI (in effect chief of naval staff) Captain Ottley agreed: should the Royal Navy build something

which cost as much as a destroyer but had less than half its speed, a third of its radius of action and 'incomparably worse sea-keeping powers'? That seemed to depend on whether it could be towed at high speed, perhaps by a battle squadron. Fisher agreed to keep building 'B'-class submarines so as to limit costs.

In November, however, Bacon suggested building a 'D'-class prototype, presumably reflecting Admiral Fisher's current wishes. He cited a French newspaper report to the effect that Britain currently led the world in submarines conceived to attack, given their size and general seaworthiness. At this point, to Bacon, 'overseas' still apparently meant France. The British lead might soon be lost, as French 1905 and 1906 programmes totalled thirty-six 400-ton submarines, which outclassed the British 'B'/'C' boats. 'I cannot express too strongly that I feel sure the time has arrived for a further increase in size, speed, radius of action and armament.' That had been his reason for suggesting the 'D' design in the first place. The new (1906–7) Estimates provided for one experimental submarine and he wanted it to be the prototype 'D' boat. Inspecting Captain of Submarines Lees agreed, as without the new submarine 'we shall be left helplessly behind the French'.

It was by no means obvious that the Royal Navy would keep building expensive 'D' class submarines. In April and May 1906 Vickers offered three single-hull designs for what it assumed would be the next ('E) class. All were enlarged versions of the 'B'/'C' class. DNC rejected them; the new 'D' design offered too great an advantage, in the form of increased armament, speed, comfort and radius of action. DNC was also interested in trying an alternative to Vickers' preferred single-hull designs. Apparently the objections voiced so strongly the previous year had gone, but nothing in the surviving Cover shows a shift towards a strategy of forward-deploying submarines. The Committee on Submarine Design formally approved the 'D' design on 13 July 1906 and DNC submitted it to the Board on 7 August 1906. That day it received

The 'L' class was in effect a stretched 'E' without the beam tubes and with a gun on a raised mounting to reflect wartime lessons. The torpedo battery was four 21in bow tubes rather than the four (later five) 18in of an 'E'. *L 2* is shown. Later units had their 4in guns on a raised platform forward of the bridge.

the Board Stamp. By that time 10ft had been added to the submarine's length and estimated submerged displacement was 580 tons, compared to about 320 tons for the last of the 'C' class, The new submarine was powered by a pair of four-cycle six-cylinder diesels. A second large submarine was included in the 1908–9 programme (the gap allowed for completion and trials of *D 1*) and in July 1909 another six were included in the 1909–10 programme,[6] the first in which the earlier coastal type was abandoned.[7] As had been predicted, the more expensive 'D' could not be built in the same numbers as earlier submarines. The 1910–11 and 1911–12 programmes were six 'D'-size submarines each; the 1912–13 and 1913–14 programmes were larger, but many of the submarines ordered were experimental.

As early as January 1905, much impressed by submarine performance in exercises, Fisher pointed out that a submarine might be used as part of a blockade on an enemy's coast.[8] As with much other new technology, he overrated the 'D' class, but a November 1908 memo shows that he clearly understood he now had a new kind of weapon.[9] He credited the newest submarine ('D' class) with the ability to operate for up to two months at a time, far beyond what any other kind of warship could do.[10] Attempts to develop an effective means of ASW had all failed. He concluded that the submarine was the offensive torpedo craft of the future, replacing the destroyer, because unlike a destroyer it could attack

equally well by day or night (submarines were already being called 'day torpedo boats' because conventional torpedo boats were effective only at night). Given the new capability, it was essential to develop some antidote to submarines equivalent to the destroyer as an antidote to torpedo boats. What Fisher did not write, perhaps because it was obvious to him, was that such an antidote had to be a submarine lying off an enemy's submarine base, just as the early destroyers were intended to lie off enemy torpedo boat bases, waiting for enemy submarines to emerge and then running them down. Enemy submarines near base would be running on the surface in order to make good any distance to their patrol areas. A British submarine on submerged patrol would have to surface and run them down at maximum speed before submerging to attack. There was no hope, at this point, of attacking a submerged enemy submarine. To some extent Fisher's paper was prompted by news that, for the first time, the Germans were spending the sort of money on U-boats that the British were already spending on their submarines. A British officer had managed to get aboard the German-built *U 3*, which was delivered by sea (albeit with escort) from its builders to Pola (Fisher wrote that a British submarine could have made the trip without any escort).

British practice was to aim the submarine at its target and it seemed that the 'D' class was the longest which could easily be manoeuvred that way.[11] The British rejected angled firing (which

The later version of the 'L' class was the final development of the oversea submarine series begun with the 'D' class in 1908. *L 55* is shown, newly completed, in 1919. She was armed with six 21in torpedo tubes and two 4in guns (at either end of her sail).

The pre-war Royal Navy ordered several submarines to foreign designs to gain experience with the double hulls which it hoped would make for higher surface speed. *W 2* was based on the French Schneider-Laubeuf design. She was completed in May 1915.

was used abroad) on the ground that it required a very accurate range (the torpedo does not turn immediately onto the desired course as it leaves the tube, so the shooter has to take the straight run into account). However, experiments had shown that even without the bar used on board fast ships, a torpedo could be fired from a broadside tube at moderate speed. It turned out that by adding $2\frac{1}{2}$ft to the beam a broadside tube could be incorporated into an enlarged 'D' class submarine. The resulting 'E' design was 15ft longer than a 'D', displacing another 180 tons (it had 24 per cent more reserve buoyancy). The first two submarines of the new type were initially considered the last of the earlier class: *D 9* and *D 10*. They were soon redesignated *E 1* and *E 2*. Six were ordered, plus the Australian *AE 1* and *AE 2*.

These submarines were clearly considered a stop-gap. British submarine officers considered the saddle-tank 'E' class limited. It could not, for example, be driven faster than 15 knots on the surface without the danger of inadvertently diving. That precluded developing it into a fast submarine capable of working with the fleet, an idea already circulating. The fully double-hull French and Italian submarines, with much greater surface buoyancy, could be driven at higher speeds and thus could make use of any considerable advance in engine design. There was also a feeling that Vickers had been too conservative and that foreign designs might be better. DNC produced three new designs in 1911 for the 1911–12 programme: an Improved 'E' and two others based on French and Italian practice.[12] The Improved 'E' was a lengthened version of the

When war broke out, the Royal Navy ordered twenty submarines to the US Navy's 'H' class design. The Vickers 'H' class was an improved, lengthened version with 21in rather than 18in torpedo tubes. These submarines proved useful in coastal waters and, after the war, for training. The Second World War 'U' class was conceived as a replacement. This is *H 28*, probably on completion in June 1918.

The point of double-hull design was to provide a submarine with a ship-shaped outer hull for good surface performance. The first major application of this idea was the 'J' class, referred to as a 'Reaper' in its Ship's Cover (no explanation is given there). The 'J' shared the underwater hull form of the 'K' class, but not the power needed for really high speed. The 'Reaper' designation suggests that they were intended to 'reap' what patrol submarines off the German coast 'sowed' in the form of reports of German warships coming out of Wilhelmshaven. *J 5* is shown in drydock. The raised and flared bow was introduced because the free-flooding bow initially brought the bow down in a seaway, badly slowing the boats. (Allan C Green via State Library of Victoria)

existing 'E' class design, which officers considered inferior to the two foreign designs.[13] DNC was unwilling to order any of the large new designs, as they were too experimental.[14]

In September 1910 a new Inspecting Captain, Roger Keyes, replaced Captain S S Hall, who in turn had succeeded Bacon. Hall saw little point in continued improvement, because in his view the key to submarine effectiveness was the commander, the second consideration being reliability.[15] It would be best to fasten on a successful design (the 'E' class) than to seek higher performance. He did, however, support the 1000-ton enlarged 'E' without a bow tube and he commented early in 1911 that a 1000-ton submarine with two good guns would 'form a most interesting comparison with a destroyer', which, incidentally, would also fire her torpedoes

on her broadside.[16] Controller (Jellicoe) was much interested in a 'submarine destroyer', which seems to have meant a submarine fast enough to run down any enemy submarine seen leaving port. Keyes rejected further saddle-tank submarines on the ground that they could never evolve into the sort of fast submarine Jellicoe wanted.[17]

Thus, the Royal Navy still wanted to try something other than the saddle-tank 'E' class. Representatives of DNC, E-in-C and Inspecting Captain of Submarines visited both Laurenti in Italy and Schneider in France. They were much impressed by the former and much less by the latter. Both had the desired high surface buoyancy (60 and 40 per cent, respectively), but the French Schneider boats were considered too long, too slow and outdated overall (among other things, they carried some of their torpedoes externally). Under the 1911–12 programme DNC ordered a Laurenti boat from Scotts (*S 1*) in addition to five repeat 'E' class.[18] The high surface buoyancy of *S 1* influenced later British designs. By the time the British officers had visited Schneider and Laurenti, the US Electric Boat company, which had designed the first British submarines, was also offering a fast submarine, which Keyes described as a compromise between the two European concepts.

After the officers visited Laurenti and Laubeuf, First Lord Winston Churchill ordered a new submarine conference, which met in February 1912.[19] It divided future submarines into oversea and coastal types. The oversea submarine was essentially Jellicoe's submarine destroyer, with high surface speed (20 knots) and high burst underwater speed, to displace about 1000 tons (as in the abortive large 'E'), with two bow tubes, four beam tubes and one stern tube. Diving time should be no more than three minutes. Later the 'oversea' submarine was described as a ship-shaped double-hull craft fast enough to accompany a battle fleet and capable of keeping the sea in all weather (in 1914 that was taken as 20 knots). By 1914 the Germans and the French were thought to be building such submarines, which could more easily achieve high speeds because they did not have to accommodate broadside torpedo tubes. Yet the British considered such tubes essential. The report specifically rejected any development of the 'E' class. Successful foreign alternatives were the Laubeuf, Laurenti, Krupp and Electric Boat submarines. It was assumed that diesel engine power could be increased sufficiently to provide the desired speed. A large prototype oversea submarine should be built as soon as possible.

A 'J' class submarine operating with the Grand Fleet. (Dr David Stevens, SPC-A)

For pre-war tacticians in many navies, the great goal in submarine development was the fleet submarine, which should be fast enough to work with the battle fleet. The serious problems manifested by the British 'K' class have obscured the reality that nearly all the major navies (the Russians may have been the sole exception) were interested in such submarines. All agreed that only steam power offered any hope of achieving the desired speed. In the 1980s a British submarine engineer pointed out that steam was still the only way to achieve high speed – and that the success of nuclear submarines (which have steam plants) proved the point. *K 6* is shown as completed.

It was Vickers' *Nautilus*, which turned out to be much larger than expected (Vickers also designed the coastal 'V' class conceived by the committee). She had even greater surface buoyancy than the Laurenti submarine (800 tons on 1270 tons surfaced) and a complete double hull (Laubeuf type). However, she did not match the desired surface speed; she was limited to 17 knots. She did have the very long surface radius of action of 5300nm. The 1912–13 programme added five repeat 'E' class submarines, the coastal prototype *V 1* and Armstrong's *W 1* and *W 2*, which were Laubeuf submarines designed for Greece. The considerable size of the programme – eleven submarines rather than the six of recent years – reflected Churchill's interest in submarines, which was probably due mostly to that of Fisher, his mentor.

The Vickers *Nautilus* design could not meet the oversea submarine requirement, even though Vickers was thought to have more experience with diesels than any other British firm. For the next year's programme the Admiralty turned to Laurenti, which guaranteed 18 knots for its *Swordfish*, but cautioned that it might not make the guaranteed power. Keyes asked the obvious question, which was whether the alternative, a steam turbine, would solve the problem. Scott had already designed a turbine installation which seemed attractive. The Royal Navy was having trouble with the diesels of the 'D' and 'E' classes and it mistrusted more powerful ones. At the same time it was reported that the Germans had been unable to complete many of their submarines due to engine problems and that the French were reverting to steam turbines in their large submarines. The *Swordfish* was ordered with a steam turbine, on the theory that if it succeeded, the desired fast submarine could surely be built.

Fisher had argued that submarines would make the North Sea too hot for battle fleets, but many officers, including Fisher's acolyte Admiral Jellicoe, disagreed. He wrote that, once the submarines had done their best and had probably been sunk, the battle fleets would come out and fight.[20] War experience showed that submarines found it difficult to locate cruising fleets, even when they were organised (by the Germans) into patrol lines. The war did create a few choke points at sea, in the form of gaps in minefields and in shallows near the Dogger Bank, but for the most part warships were endangered only near their bases, where submarines could wait for them.

Navies, including the Royal Navy, became interested in how a submarine working with a fleet could be used during or immediately after a fleet action. Both the Royal Navy and the German navy experimented with 'submarine traps' during their last pre-war exercises, the idea being to deploy submarines in advance so that the enemy fleet could be led over them. Given a limited submarine force, the idea implied that the submarines in question should be fast enough to work with the fleet.

On this basis, some time in 1913 a third type was added: the 'ocean' submarine which would work with a fleet. First Lord Winston Churchill defined it in a 20 August 1913 memo, although the idea probably came earlier: 'the Ocean Submarine is a decisive weapon of battle and as such must count in partial substitution of battleship strength'.[21] In Churchill's memo, the 'ocean' submarine

High speed meant high surface speed and a low bow made for poor seakeeping. *K 3* is shown off Scapa Flow on 4 December 1917 at 20 knots in Sea State 3. This class introduced a fully-enclosed bridge structure, which provided protection against this sort of sea. Note the high masts for good W/T performance.

It did not help that these submarines were given a powerful gun armament on deck. *K 3* shows her two 4in guns and one 3in high-angle gun (closest to the bridge); note how much spray she threw up even in a moderate sea.

had 24-knot speed. The idea of substitution was significant: when he wrote his memo Churchill was having real problems selling his 1914–15 programme. The governing Liberals expected to fight an election in 1915 and they badly wanted to do so on the basis that they had increased social spending without increasing taxes. It seemed likely that the single largest item of defence spending, the naval budget, would be cut. Churchill was looking for ways out, including persuading the Canadians to pay for new battleships. In fact the large 1914–15 budget was approved with its four battleships, but by that time Churchill was interested in buying submarines and other torpedo craft rather than battleships. He continued to explore such options in the spring of 1914. In 1913, then, DNC designed a large 'ocean' submarine. It was deferred while *Nautilus* and *Swordfish* were built. *Nautilus* was seen as a prototype very large submarine and *Swordfish* as test submarine for a British steam plant.

Aside from the two experimental submarines, the only oversea submarines in the 1913–14 programme were two repeat 'E' class. They and the 'Ds' were Keyes' only submarines capable of oversea patrols, the 'E' class much preferable to the 'D' (which should be relegated to coastal work as soon as possible).[22] At this point Keyes' possible oversea submarine roles were (i) blockade and (ii) work

with a battle or cruiser squadron.[23] Everything else in the 1913–14 programme was the new coastal type, albeit somewhat larger than expected: Scotts' *S 2* and *S 3*; Vickers' *V 2*, *V 3* and *V 4*; and Armstrong's *W 3* and *W 4*. The Vickers monopoly having expired, a DNC-designed coastal submarine (F 1) was ordered from Chatham.

The British programme was discussed at a conference in First Lord's room on 9 December 1913.[24] British policy was to revive the previously projected close blockade of the German fleet, but this time by submarines which could survive in waters near the German coast.[25] This idea had been discussed for some time. The rub was insufficient numbers; eventually a goal of four flotillas, each of twelve overseas submarines, was set.[26] The standing requirement for coastal submarines was reaffirmed, but as yet there was no agreed number of coastal submarines.

The conference discussed DNC's design for Churchill's 24-knot 'ocean' submarine.[27] DNC showed great confidence in the design and commented that even if it failed as a submarine it would be a formidable surface torpedo ship like the old torpedo ram *Polyphemus* (Churchill would soon become interested in a new *Polyphemus*-like ship). Churchill repeated his earlier view that, scouted for by fast cruisers, such a submarine could overtake and

The cure for the wet bow was a big 'swan bow', shown on *K 16* in a post-war photo. The gun battery was relocated to the raised deck abaft the bridge. A new open bridge was built atop the earlier enclosed one to clear the line of sight over the raised bow.

By the end of the war, submarines were being armed with depth charges so that they could react quickly to diving U-boats. *K 22* sported a depth-charge mortar at the after end of her gun deck, with her 3in high-angle gun between her stacks. Her forward stack is tilted in preparation for diving. The gun between it and the bridge is her 4in.

work around an enemy surface force. That was much the way post-First World War navies such as the Imperial Japanese Navy planned to use their big cruiser submarines. Keyes saw no insurmountable problem, but he pointed out just how great a leap the new submarine would be. It would displace three times as much as an 'E' and would be nearly twice as long, which would complicate diving control. Its much greater reserve buoyancy would require it to take on far more water when diving. Its steam plant would have to be shut down and cooled and it would produce three times the power of the experimental *Swordfish*. The *Nautilus* would provide experience in handling so large a submarine and the *Swordfish* would show how her steam plant should be operated. Churchill did not want to delay building repeat ships until the first had been tested, but Keyes extracted an agreement not to proceed until *Nautilus* had been tested. A second *Swordfish*, but not a repeat *Nautilus*, was therefore included in the 1914–15 programme.

Keyes still much preferred double-hull to saddle-hull submarines. He was attracted by a Vickers proposal for what amounted to a double-hull 'E' class submarine, the 'G' class. Compared to an 'E' class submarine, it cost considerably more but offered somewhat higher speed (given in 1913 as 15.5 knots rather than 13.5 knots) and more torpedo tubes (one bow tube, two broadside tubes and two stern tubes rather than one bow, two broadside and one stern tube; and the bow tube in the new design was 21in rather than 18in).[28]

At the end of the December 1913 conference, one double-hulled 'E' class submarine replaced one of the planned coastals, so that the 1914–15 submarine programme stood at two Vickers double-hull 'E' class, one Dockyard-built double-hull 'E', seven coastals and the repeat *Swordfish*. Not long after the conference, Second Sea Lord (Admiral Jellicoe) wrote to Churchill that the programme made him uneasy. He had understood that the programme of coastal submarines could not be changed, but he feared that the coastals were being bought in quantity because of a false impression that they could somehow be used for oversea work. Third Sea Lord agreed with him. Churchill reviewed the situation a few days later and decided to recast the 1914–15

programme. He would eliminate the repeat *Swordfish* and buy the maximum number of double-hull 'Es' as he could without breaching contracts.[29] That was not too difficult legally because five of the coastal submarines were being built by Chatham Royal Dockyard, which was not constrained by any commercial contract. Chatham received the orders for the five oversea submarines in June 1914. Thus the final programme consisted of seven of a new Admiralty Improved 'E' ('G') class and, despite the conclusions drawn in December 1913, two more coastal submarines (*F 2* and *F 3*).[30]

Churchill also considered adding more submarines in place of one of the four battleships of the 1914–15 programme.[31] In May 1914 he apparently told Fisher that First Sea Lord Battenberg approved the idea, but that Jellicoe (already Grand Fleet C-in-C designate disagreed strongly.[32] Fisher accepted Jellicoe's arguments that any such plan would destroy the attempt to convince the Canadians to provide battleships (an ultimately-doomed plan, but that was not yet obvious), it would shatter the battleship standard that the Royal Navy used to justify its building programme and it might fail because it would be difficult to get the submarines in the first place. He wrote, however, that he believed (wrongly) that Tirpitz was now surreptitiously increasing German submarine strength, so at any cost the British must accelerate their own programme. In July, Churchill sent First Sea Lord Battenberg a proposed revised 1914–15 programme in which fifteen submarines were substituted for one of the battleships.[33]

The expanded 1914–15 programme was a problem, because Vickers was still the main submarine builder. It was also already failing to meet delivery schedules. Chatham had never built a large submarine and further capacity would take time to come on stream. Vickers was also an export builder and in the wake of the Balkan Wars both Greece and Turkey were anxious to buy ships, including submarines. In February 1914 it seemed likely that Greece would try to buy four to six 'E' class submarines (in fact it was Turkey which ordered two).[34] Vickers apparently received a Greek order, but it was cancelled.[35]

By November 1914, many of the submarines under construction were badly delayed.[36] Among the first tasks put to newly-returned First Sea Lord Admiral Fisher was to accelerate submarine production. Churchill asked for twenty more submarines. Fisher did much more: he created a massive new programme. He ordered twenty small coastal submarines from Bethlehem Steel in the United States ('H' class). They were not what the Royal Navy wanted, but they were more or less immediately available (although in fact diplomatic problems connected with American neutrality slowed delivery).

Most of the programme was inevitably repeat 'E' class submarines, because the iron rule of such mobilisation is to keep building what is already being built.[37] Investigation showed that an 'E'-class submarine could be built faster than a 'G, so new orders were for 'Es' (an order for eight 'G' class submarines had been approved in September, but not placed, probably due to congestion in the yards). Fisher created his large a programme by bringing in many more builders. Aside from the H class, the programme consisted entirely of medium-speed oversea submarines: *G 8–G 15* (*G 15* was cancelled 20 April 1915) and *E 19* to *E 56*, of which *E 27* and *E 28* were cancelled but work on *E 27* was resumed in 1915. Six submarines were completed as minelayers (*E 24, E 34, E 41, E 45, E 46* and *E 51*).

Interest in the big 'ocean' submarine survived. Of the two test submarines, *Nautilus* was launched in December 1914 but not accepted until October 1917. Presumably she demonstrated that a long submarine was controllable. She also introduced a new 1850bhp 12-cylinder Vickers engine; the engine of the 'E' class developed only 850bhp. She was never fully operational. *Swordfish* was launched in March 1916 and completed in July. In theory she tested a prototype steam plant, but by the time she was complete the decision had already been made to build the 24-knot steam submarine. However, in designing the steam plant for this submarine Scotts met and solved many of the problems inherent in the larger and more powerful (10,000shp vs 4,000shp) 24-knot submarine. They included developing central control capable of shutting down the many openings a steam submarine required, so that she could dive reasonably quickly. Having proven the underwater steam concept and not being any faster than a conventional diesel submarine, *Swordfish* was converted into a surface patrol vessel less than a year after completion.

Late in 1914, then, the 'ocean' design was in hand but the two prototypes considered necessary to test its features had not been completed. Late in 1914 it was reported (incorrectly) that the Germans had some 22-knot submarines in service.[38] Fisher decided to build some fast submarines, in effect the 'submarine destroyers' of earlier interest. At this point the steam plant was not yet ready, so the only option was diesel power. The big new engine planned for *Nautilus* also not yet having been proven, Vickers offered to expand the eight-cylinder engine of the 'E' class to twelve, for about 1200bhp. To further increase power, a third propeller shaft was provided. The submarine was designed around its engines, a particularly efficient hull form being chosen. All of these compromises precluded reaching 22 knots, but a speed of 19.5 to 20 knots was quoted (which actually considerably exceeded German performance) and in practice this submarine could reach 19.5 knots. Six were ordered for the Royal Navy in January 1915, followed by a seventh specifically for the RAN (*J 7*).

Jellicoe badly wanted submarines to support the Grand Fleet during a fleet action. He was well aware of the pre-war 24-knot fleet

The Royal Navy explored submarines' potential to a greater extent than any other. Its 'M' class were submarine 'monitors', but their 12in guns were really an alternative to torpedo tubes in an era of relatively unreliable torpedoes. This photograph was taken soon after the war.

submarine and he seems to have been the reason the 'K' class was built.[39] The dates of the drawings suggest that he made his request about March 1915. The existing Admiralty design was chosen over an alternative offered by Vickers.[40] As a cover, ships were referred to as flotilla leaders and later as 'K Class Flotilla Leaders'.[41] The first two (*K 3* and *K 4*) were ordered from Vickers in June 1915, followed by others up to *K 14* in August. Three more were ordered in February 1916. *K 3* made 23.84 knots on trial despite being at greater than designed displacement, due to some flooded tanks. The 'Ks' were much longer than previous British submarines and it seems unfortunate that no experience was gained with the big

Diesels offered submarines, or at least U-boats, endurance unimagined before the war. As an indication of the sort of effective endurance with which U-boats were credited in 1914, when Scapa Flow was found unsafe due to a lack of submarine obstructions, the Grand Fleet was temporarily based on the West Coast of Scotland and on the Northern Irish coast, which were considered beyond U-boat range. Visiting Newport, Rhode Island on 7 October 1916, *U 53* demonstrated much greater range. Note the US cruiser in the background. Her rated endurance was 9000nm at 8 knots, compared to 7600nm for the last pre-war class (*U 19*). She was a Mobilisation type U-boat with four torpedo tubes, two forward and two aft and a vertical stem rather than the sharply raked one adopted later. Commissioned on 22 April 1916, she survived the war.

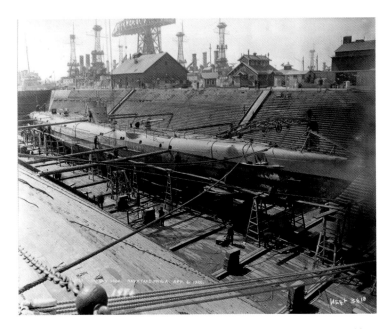

The main ocean-going German submarine was the 'Mobilisation' type. *U 111*, launched in September 1917, was turned over to the US Navy. She is shown at the Philadelphia Navy Yard on 6 April 1920. This dry dock view shows the double-hull (ship-shaped outer hull) design adopted by the Germans. Note the heavy gun battery: one 10.5cm/45 and one 8.8cm/30 aft. The torpedo battery was four tubes forward and two aft. Note the sharply raked bow, for open-ocean seagoing, which contrasts with the vertical bow of *U 53*.

Nautilus before they were built. Given great length and very little reserve buoyancy in the bow, they could easily dive steeply, so that parts of the hull could quickly get below the designed diving depth of 200ft. The original low bow also made for poor performance in a seaway. One was lost when not all of the openings were closed as intended. The main problem of the 'K' class, however, was tactical. Despite intense interest in using submarines as part of the fleet, little had been done to ensure that the fast 'K' class did not become entangled with surface units, which would always tend to shoot first and ask questions later when confronted with unknown submarines. Both during the First World War and later, the ability to distinguish friendly from enemy submarines was notoriously poor. That, more than anything else, made the sort of fleet support operations widely discussed pre-war impossible.[42] The great demonstration of the problem was the 'battle of May Island', when two were sunk by collision, one with another 'K'-class submarine.[43]

From a more technical point of view, the 'Ks' did what was expected of them: they could and did keep up with the fleet. In September 1918 two of them actually overtook the Grand Fleet, but at that time it was hove-to in a gale.[44] To achieve the high desired speed the designers had to use a very long, inherently unmanoeuvrable, hull and the low freeboard of the 'K' class (otherwise an important submarine virtue, since it helped the submarine evade detection even when surfaced) made it difficult for friendly surface ships to see. For its part the Royal Navy continued to see the virtue of submarines which could co-operate tactically with a surface force, as indeed did other navies. The Royal Navy continued to operate the improved *K 26* until she was discarded in 1931 due to the limits imposed by the 1930 London Naval Treaty on total submarine tonnage. As an indication of contemporary views, the US Navy showed considerable interest in

fleet-speed steam submarines in 1917–20.

Having asked for submarines which could keep up with the Grand Fleet, on 24 July 1915 Jellicoe asked that a flotilla of the existing slower submarines be provided. He knew that they could not keep up with his fleet, but he already planned to rendezvous at sea with the Harwich Force and he could do the same with submarines based in the Tyne. Pending supply of fast enough submarines, he would make do with groups of three 'E' or similar type, with one destroyer to escort each three. The Admiralty told Jellicoe that submarines were in too short supply, but that his request would be reconsidered when more were in service.[45] Jellicoe visited the Admiralty to press his case and in November he was rewarded with twelve 'E' and 'G' class submarines of the 11th Flotilla, to be based at Blyth. He was also promised 'J' and 'K' class submarines when they became available. In November he was told that, since the 'E' class submarines were too slow, he would be getting 'Js' and 'Ks' when they became available. Grand Fleet Battle Orders were revised to include supporting submarines. Each Grand Fleet submarine was to be given one of the new long-range torpedoes because it seemed likely that a submarine operating with the cruiser (scouting) line or in a flank position might be able to make a 'browning' shot before getting into range to fire the usual close-range submarine torpedoes.[46]

Submarine co-operation with the fleet required long-range W/T, meaning the powerful Poulsen set. As of February 1916 the Grand Fleet had none, but it was decided that the 'Js' and 'Ks', which would all be assigned to the fleet, should have the new sets. As soon as the six 'Js' and the four *Talisman* class destroyers assigned to work with them had been fitted, the fleet flagship *Iron Duke* and the flagships of the dreadnought battle squadrons and then of the Battlecruiser Fleet and the 2nd Cruiser Squadron (his scouts) would be fitted, in that order. Poulsen equipment was particularly wanted because in the past submarines off the Norwegian coast had been unable to receive even the highest-power signals from Scapa. Ultimately the Admiralty approved a high-power shore set instead of one on board a fleet unit, presumably because it would be less likely to give away the position of the fleet.[47]

The bridge of *U 111*, photographed at Philadelphia Navy Yard on 8 April 1920. US officers who crossed the Atlantic aboard the surrendered U-boats were surprised at how dry they were and at how well their diesels ran.

U 117 was a cruiser minelayer surrendered to the US Navy. Unlike the small UC-boats, she had dry mine stowage in the form of tubes with conveyer belts to carry the mines aft to be dropped. This is her mine stowage.

Given the experience of a year of war, a Submarine Development Committee met in 1915.[48] To the existing three types (including the new fleet submarine) it proposed to add three more: a cruiser submarine, a minelayer and a monitor. The cruiser was a long-range submarine with a heavy gun armament (two 5.5in), conceived as a stretched version of the 'E' class powered by the new engines of the 'J' class. It became the 'L' class. The minelayer would be an adapted 'E' class submarine. The idea of the monitor seems to have been that existing torpedoes were not proving reliable enough. A heavy shell could travel further and more accurately – and reliably. Three repeat 'K' class submarines (*K 18, K 19* and *K 20*) were reordered as monitors ('M' class) and a fourth added. All were renamed in a new 'M' series on 25 June 1918.[49]

Of the submarine committee's projects, only the cruiser submarine produced much. The first two 'L' class submarines were ordered as *E 57* and *E 58*, then redesignated because this was different enough to be considered a new class. After the series of 'K' class orders in August 1915, the next series of submarine orders came in February 1916: four 'K' class (one, *K 18*, soon reordered as a monitor) and the two stretched and otherwise modified 'E' class. Seven more submarines were ordered in May (a second monitor and *L 3–L 8*) and three more in August (two monitors and *L 9*). By this time production of 'E' class submarines was nearly complete, so some industrial capacity was available.

In October 1916 the Admiralty wrote to Jellicoe that a 'very substantial' new programme of submarine construction was imminent, although he should be aware that no such programme could begin without interfering with the construction of surface ships which were also urgently needed. It was hoped that about twenty-five more submarines of the 'E', 'G' and 'K' classes would become available on 1 April 1917.[50] The letter to Jellicoe reflects orders for twenty-five L class submarines in December 1916: *L 10–L 35. L 50–L 55* were ordered in January/February 1917 and *L 56–L 74* (nearly all later cancelled) in April 1917.[51] There were also repeat orders for the much smaller 'H' class.

The 'L' class of 1916 was not the 1000-ton super-'E' class offered in 1912. It had four bow tubes (double the bow armament of an E) and more powerful engines. From *L 9* on, the bow tubes were 21in and minelayers omitted beam tubes. An 'L' was about 50ft longer than an E with a pressure hull of 7in greater diameter, with a new stern form (chisel-shaped, as in an 'H'). Submarines with 21in tubes gained another 7ft 6in in length. The *L 50* class was further modified to increase bow firepower to six 21in tubes (there were no longer any broadside tubes), as in post-war submarines.[52]

By the end of 1916 the British considered a German submarine offensive imminent. Submarines and mines were their most effective ASW weapons. Beatty complained in January 1917 that of eighty-six submarines in British waters on 28 December 1916, only ten were in forward positions where they could sink U-boats: one on patrol off the Maas, five off Terschelling in the North Sea and four patrolling off Horns Reef and the Skaggerak. The rest were reserved for defence of the British Isles (and also for support of the Grand Fleet). Beatty called for total reorganisation, which would provide at least forty submarines for offensive action.[53] The catch was that under winter conditions a submarine might well fail to spot a U-boat until it was very close. Beatty's submarine commander wrote in January 1917 that although submarines were not primarily intended to fight each other, but 'if surface targets are not available, the submarine can be employed to advantage on this service. Under favourable conditions a submarine can deliberately attack and destroy an enemy submarine which is unaware of its presence. This is a man to man fight as both submarines start on the surface and the one that observes the other first has all the advantage . . . our submarine officers have had more experience than the Germans and should come off well'. He did not think that submarines on this service should do so submerged. At this point oversea submarines (now called patrol submarines and including

The success of 'merchant U-boats' demonstrated to the Germans that they could build submarines capable of sustained operation on the far side of the Atlantic. *U 151* is shown at Cherbourg in 1920 alongside the old French steam submarines *Thermidor* and *Fructidor* (note their single stacks and the 75mm gun visible on board one of them). *U 151* was to have been named *Oldenburg* as a commercial submarine, but was completed in July 1917 as a U-cruiser. Her broad (unhydrodynamic) hull is evidence of her merchant ship origin. Rated range was 25,000nm at 5.5 knots. (Robert W Neeser via US Navy Historical and Heritage Command)

the small 'H' and 'V' class units) were mainly being used to watch the Heligoland Bight for German warships going to sea or returning. In addition to watching German waters for U-boats, the substantial force of coastal submarines retained in Home waters on anti-invasion duty could deal with U-boats in their own hunting areas. Some of the proposed coastal ASW patrols were soon begun.

Under these circumstances it was natural to design a specialised ASW submarine, the 'R' class.[54] These submarines were to lie in ambush. If the U-boat came towards the 'R'-boat, she could fire a heavy torpedo salvo. She was also given a high submerged speed so that she could close with a target seen at a distance. Since she could not catch up with a U-boat seen going away, the design incorporated a 4in gun for surface fire (later 'L' class submarines had two 4in guns for much the same reason). It does not appear that any 'R' class submarine had a 4in gun as completed. DNC's March 1917 proposal was rejected, but later in the year Commodore (S) suggested that the design be completed and it was approved by the Board later in 1917. Twelve were approved at a 2 October 1917 Admiralty conference (ordered in December), of which two were cancelled on 28 August 1919.[55] The initial design called for four 18in bow tubes and a submerged speed of 13.5–14 knots (11–12 knots on the surface) using 'H' class machinery. As built they had six bow tubes, a submerged speed of 15 knots and a surface speed of 9.5–10 knots with one rather than two 'H'-class diesels. They were slightly smaller than the later 'H' class (410 tons vs 438 tons surfaced). Unlike the patrol or oversea submarines they reverted to the single-hull design of the earliest British submarines. The most striking feature was the sensitive combination of five hydrophones, which it was claimed made it possible to approach an enemy to firing position without using the periscope.[56]

Compared to German submarines, at the end of the war the British considered theirs better, with one essential exception: engines. In 1914 the British hoped to test alternative engines in their 'G' class, but once war began they had to standardise on the Vickers diesels of the 'E' class. The only important wartime development was to add cylinders so as to gain more power. The 'E'-class diesel itself was an eight-cylinder version of the six-cylinder engine, the first British naval diesel, in the 'D' class. The larger engine in the 'J', 'K', 'L' and 'M' classes was a twelve-cylinder version of the same engine. It was reliable enough for wartime service, but it paled in comparison with the four-stroke MAN engines used by the Germans. A German engine delivered three times the power in the same weight and it required far less maintenance. The US Navy, which came to admire the British submarines alongside which its own served, copied the German engine after the war. US submarine designer E S Land, later Chief of the Bureau of Construction and Repair and then chief of the Maritime Administration, said immediately after the war that 'boat for boat I consider the L 50 class of the British design to be the equal if not the superior of the U-boat. If the engines of the two were traded, the British boat would completely outclass the German boat. The British boats are better designs so far as the design of submarines is concerned.'[57]

The German Navy[68]

Tirpitz famously had little time for submarines. He said that he did not want to finance experiments, but it also seems fair to say that he was interested in a visible fleet and no matter how effective,

By the end of the war, the Germans were placing very powerful guns on board U-boats. In 1918 *U 155* was rearmed with two 15cm/40 guns from the old battleship *Zähringen*, one of which is shown. To meet such powerful weapons, the British planned to introduce a 5.5in gun specifically to arm merchant ships. The war ended before it entered production. She was on display in London after being surrendered on 24 November 1918. *U 155* was unusual in that initially she had only external torpedo tubes, which could not be reloaded while she was submerged.

submarines did not contribute to the prestige value of the Imperial Navy. Tirpitz also had no use for coast defence, because his entire programme was intended to move his navy away from small coast-defence ships towards large blue-water capital ships. Thus, unlike the Royal Navy, he also had no interest in coastal submarines. In 1914 his U-boats were by far the longest-legged German warships, but not so much because they were intended for long-distance service; it was just that diesels were so efficient. As a consequence, the Germans were able to deploy U-boats to the Mediterranean in 1915, with real impact on the Gallipoli campaign. The same U-boats were most prominently used in the submarine war against British and Allied trade.

Initially, like surface torpedo boats, German submarines were managed by the Torpedo Inspectorate (TI), but in December 1913 a separate U-Boat Inspectorate (UI) was created. It was responsible for U-boat design and training and for operational doctrine. As the branch with technical expertise, the UI (and the TI before it) set characteristics and evaluated designs. It developed designs for submarines built by the Imperial navy yards, initially the Danzig yard. However, in the fractured German system, the UI could not control U-boat operations. It was up to the Navy Office (which, until 1916, meant Tirpitz) to decide whether and how many U-boats to build in any given year. Moreover, the Navy Law system encouraged a rigid long-term approach to both funding and numbers, despite the contradiction between the two as ships developed. The absolute priority Tirpitz assigned to capital ships presumably drastically limited spending on subsidiary types such as submarines; U-boats benefitted in that they were so inexpensive that their construction did not seriously impact that of the larger ships.

The contradiction between technological development and rigid funding shows in the 1912–14 programmes. There was enough money in 1912 to order eleven U-boats (*U 31–41*) from a single builder, Krupp. That was the first year of a new Navy Law extending through 1917. Presumably it seemed wise to front-load U-boat construction when capital ship costs were escalating. The consequence was much smaller projected programmes for successive years. The habit of long-range planning shows both in pre-war and in early wartime thinking. The goal of seventy U-boats proposed in 1912 was to have been met in 1919, the end year for the 1912 Navy Law. When the UI proposed a large programme in 1915, it looked toward completion about 1924. It is not clear whether anyone involved realised how absurd that was. Some conversations between Tirpitz and other high command officers in 1914–15 indicated a belief that the war begun in 1914 would end in a compromise peace, after which Germany would fight a greater war against England for what Tirpitz always called 'world power'. Until at least October 1918 the view at the top seems to have been that the war would end in some sort of armistice, to be resumed later and that U-boats would then be an effective offensive arm, or at the least a deterrent to hold back Allied peace demands.

German policy for the use of U-boats varied considerably after 1914. However, submarines could not be built very rapidly; the record for full-size submarines, set in 1915–16, was eleven months. There was an initial burst of construction orders upon mobilisation in August 1914, but given the assumption that the war would be short, nothing followed until February 1915. By that time it was generally accepted that the war would last at least past the autumn. The Germans had announced unrestricted submarine warfare, but they knew that they had nothing like the force required to execute it. There had been little or no planning for such a campaign during the autumn of 1914 and no effort to design U-boats which could be built more quickly in larger numbers. Nor had there been any equivalent to Fisher's dramatic expansion of the British submarine-building base. Probably the worst problem was diesels; MAN could produce no more than a pair (for one U-boat) per month. Expanding production meant adding many diesel producers, some of which must have been considerably better than others.

Given the inherent constraints of construction, the U-boats ordered in the spring of 1915 became available in the spring of 1916, just as the Germans found themselves pulling back from unrestricted submarine warfare under largely US pressure. Under those circumstances the most effective way for U-boats to attack British shipping was to lay mines, but when programmes were framed in 1915 torpedo or gun attack was more effective than minelaying. When the U-boats were ordered to adhere to the Prize Rules (stopping and examining merchant ships and placing passengers and crew in boats before sinking them), the UI tried to design armoured and heavily-gunned U-cruisers, the construction of which would have interfered with that of more conventional U-boats.

Also, until well into 1917 U-boats were by no means the highest German naval priority. Much more of the effort went to capital ships, both the remaining battleships and battlecruisers of the pre-war programme and no fewer than seven battlecruisers ordered automatically to replace large cruisers and battlecruisers lost during the war. The UI was only one hungry mouth among many demanding new ships. When it finally did receive priority in 1917, it was far too late, because the first fruits of the new programme were not at sea until 1918, when the anti-shipping war was being lost due to convoy operations and also to improved means of hunting U-boats. The Germans still thought that they could win the

U-boat war; as in 1945, morale remained high. It is not clear whether the increased numbers (but not new technology) which would have been available in 1919 would have won. By that time new Allied programmes would also have been far more effective, given massive US destroyer and merchant shipbuilding and a considerable expansion of air ASW.

U-boats were designed both by Germania (Krupp's shipbuilding arm) and by the Imperial Navy (as supervised by the UI). Pre-war relations between Krupp Germania and the TI were complicated by Krupp's willingness to export submarines. German policy in general was to prevent export of designs the navy was using, so that when MAN began to make four-cycle diesels for the German navy it generally exported far less reliable two-cycle ones (as the pre-war US Navy learned to its cost).

After the success of the *Forelle*, a Krupp boat built for Russia, Tirpitz approved two submarines in 1904: the Krupp (Germania)-built *U 1* and the navy-designed and built *U 2* (Project 7). *U 1* was based on Krupp's design for the export *Karp* class for Russia. Both Germania and the official designers developed alternative designs from then on.[59] Unlike contemporary foreign submarines, both *U 1* and *U 2* were powered by engines burning paraffin (kerosene) rather than petrol.[60] In 1907 the TI turned down a Krupp design for an enlarged *U 1* because the company was selling two ships of this type to Austria-Hungary, the only close German ally. Norway bought a similar submarine as *Kobben*. It did not help that Krupp's submarine designer, d'Equivilley, was a foreigner (in 1907 he was replaced by Hans Techel, a German). Soon after d'Equivilley left Krupp received its second contract, for *U 5–U 8* (*U 3* and *U 4* were built by the German navy at its Danzig yard). These were Germania-designed substantial twin-screw submarines with two bow and two stern tubes. They had gyro-compasses, an important feature in a boat filled with metal which precluded the use of a

Specially-designed U-cruisers like *U 140*, shown after surrender to the US Navy, were considerably more efficient (and much faster) than the ex-merchant U-boats. Rated surface speed was 15 knots and endurance was 17,750nm at 8 knots. The guns were two 15cm/45.

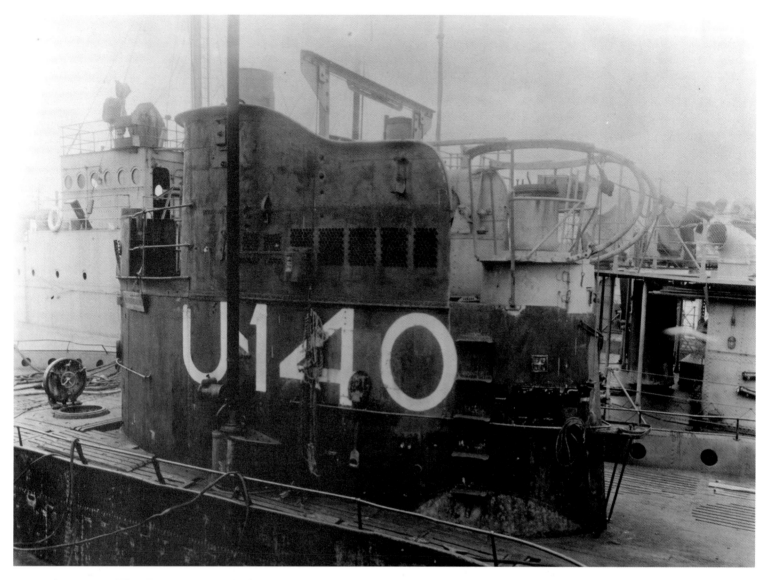

The bridge of *U 140*, with an Eagle Boat in the background.

magnetic compass. The German navy built four similar submarines (*U 9–U 12*) and these eight 500-ton U-boats were the first true seagoing U-boats. Aside from relative inefficiency, paraffin created very visible white smoke. The pre-war German navy found that a much more expensive form of paraffin minimised the smoke and reserves were earmarked for wartime use only.

In 1910 the navy ran exercises in which several of the new U-boats tried to operate together, the TI later stating that unless some form of effective underwater communication was developed, such operations were too dangerous. The accounts in *Krieg zur See* show in some detail how boats were allocated separate patrol areas, although given the limits of navigation at the time it is difficult to see how this practice could have succeeded, as sometimes the sectors were quite narrow. The official history also gives examples of submarines which completely lost their bearings so that they barely recognised where they were near the British coast.

As in the Royal Navy, the most important pre-war machinery development was the adoption of diesel power. Krupp had installed diesels in the Russian *Karp* even before the Körting engine was ordered. The leading builder, which became the supplier to the German navy, was MAN (Maschinenfabrik Augsbert-Nürnberg). Its initial proposals were rejected first as too heavy and also because of long delivery time. In 1907 MAN offered a 300bhp six-cylinder engine (note that at this time Vickers was offering 600bhp in the

six-cylinder engine for the 'D' class). A prototype was ordered in 1908. Germania began building its own diesels in 1906 and, as in the United Kingdom, there was interest in the Italian FIAT engine. In 1908 the TI asked for proposals for an 850bhp engine (450 rpm). The last Körting engines, in *U 17–U 18*, developed 350bhp each.[61] *U 17* seems to have been a turning point, since her rated endurance was far greater than that of her predecessors: 6700nm at 8 knots rather than 2100nm at 15 knots. The two figures are probably equivalent (displacement and power did not change), but the much greater figure given for *U 17* suggests long- rather than short-range operations. This submarine was designed soon after the first tactical trials were completed in 1910–11.

The TI had hoped for some time to shift to diesel power in a larger submarine, but it would not do so until a powerful yet light enough diesel had run for six days without interruption. MAN produced the first test engine in August 1910, after two years of development of a four-stroke engine. Germania experienced problems with its two-stroke engine, but ran a successful test in June 1911; the engine was installed in the submarine *Atropo* for Italy. Other engines ordered from FIAT, MAN (Nuremberg) and Körting all failed. MAN's four-stroke engine was quieter than Germania's two-stroke type and used less fuel (190g/BHP/hr vs

220g/BHP/hr), but it suffered more from torsional stress in its crankshaft, which was understood to be a serious problem (the solution was generally to add heavy weights to move the resonant frequency away from that produced by the engine). The first diesel U-boats were *U 19–U 22*, assigned to the navy yard at Danzig, powered by MAN engines. In effect *U 19* was the prototype of pre-war U-boats, displacing 650 tons with an endurance of 7600nm at 8 knots. Germania received a contract for *U 23–U 26*, to be powered by its two-stroke engine; another four MAN-powered boats were ordered from Danzig (*U 27–U 30*). It turned out that the decision to buy the Germania diesels had been premature. From here on MAN four-stroke engines were dominant, but Germania engines continued to be bought.[62] The 1912 programme included another eleven Germania boats, *U 31–U 41*. As with the battle fleet, the Navy Laws provided only limited financing. In June 1912 plans were announced for further U-boat construction: three in 1913, three in 1914, four in 1915, five in 1916 and six each year between 1917 and 1919, with experimental boats (FIAT engine and caustic-soda closed-cycle propulsion) planned for 1920.

In 1912 UI proposed a deployment (and force growth) plan combining a defensive line around the Heligoland Bight and offensive operations in the North Sea. It required a total of seventy U-boats, which were to be completed by 1919.[63] When war broke out *U 31* class submarines were being launched (the last was *U 41*, launched on 10 October 1914). These submarines were armed with two bow and two stern torpedo tubes and they typically carried six torpedoes (later 9–10 torpedoes in some). The last pre-war orders were for *U 43–U 45* (Project 25).[64] The navy's mobilisation plan called for 17 duplicates of the latest (*U 41* [Krupp] and *U 43*) design, of which *U 46–U 50* were ordered from the navy yard at Danzig on 7 August. The remaining twelve were called the Mobilisation (Ms) type. Germania got the next six (*U 51–U 56*) and after protracted negotiation Weser, which had been experimenting with caustic-soda steam propulsion, received a contract for *U 57–U 62*, which duplicated the much earlier *U 27*.[65] These were all twin-screw submarines and diesels (one per shaft) were probably the production bottleneck. The U-boats were all assigned to the High Seas Fleet and they were based with it at Wilhelmshaven on the North Sea. Like the British, the Germans saw submarines as a valuable adjunct to a battle fleet. Co-operation with the surface fleet was first demonstrated in the German 1913 exercises and U-boat capability impressed the fleet command.

Soon after the outbreak of war UI was asked for a design of a small submarine which could be in service before the expected short war ended.[66] By late 1914 two classes of such submarines were being ordered, mainly for use from the new German base in Flanders. From there they could easily reach British coastal waters. The UB design was chosen in September 1914 and the first fifteen ordered in October, the first boat (*UB 1*) being built in a hundred days.[67] Initial numbers were kept small so that lessons learned in their operation could be applied to later units. Given intense pre-war German interest in minelaying, work also went ahead on a long-range minelayer, the design of which (Project 38) was completed on 5 January 1915. The project was designated UE because it was ordered under War Contract E. Like the UB- and UC-boats, UE was conceived for quick production, with a single low-powered diesel. Like the earlier small submarines, this one was intended for completion before the end of the war, which in January 1915 was not expected to last past the autumn. That

For the US Navy the greatest war prize was surely German diesels, which grossly outperformed anything in US or British service. *U 140* was powered by two ten-cylinder MAN four-stroke engines plus two six-cylinder battery-charging engines. The post-war US Navy copied the MAN diesel engine at the New York Navy Yard and installed its version on board many 'S' class submarines. Under the provisions of the Versailles Treaty, the Germans were not permitted to export military materiel, so there was no question of license production. US naval intelligence noted angrily that the Japanese had no such scruples (their initial long-range submarines were based on German designs) and within a few years the US Navy was considering buying German naval equipment. This photograph shows the engine room of *U 140*.

calculation may have taken the initial unrestricted submarine campaign into account. UI planned on building ten by the end of 1915, but initially only four were ordered (*U 71–U 74*).

By mid-February it seems to have been accepted that the war would continue, even though the effects of the U-boat campaign had not yet been felt. The UI was authorised to let a new round of orders. It designed a larger torpedo-armed version of UE which it called UF, but that mass-production U-boat was rejected by the Navy Office in favour of the current standard Mobilisation type. At the same time six more UE were ordered (*U 75–U 80*). The new Mobilisation boats were simplified for quicker production, but only three out of the initially projected six (*U 63–U 65*) were ordered (March 1915).[68] Their eleven-month construction time was a German First World War record.[69]

Germany opened the first unrestricted submarine campaign with a limited fleet; on 1 April 1915 there were only twenty-seven operational ocean-going U-boats. Only boats already under construction could participate; the UI estimated that as late as 1 July 1916 it would have only forty, counting likely losses. At the time, it was estimated that a full blockade of the United Kingdom would require forty-eight U-boats equivalent to the Mobilisation type. To that had to be added twelve for the Baltic and twelve for the High Seas Fleet, under the direct command of the High Seas Fleet U-boat commander (FdU). Given likely wastage, the UI estimated that another thirty-two U-boats would be needed.

The UI presumably knew that it had no chance at all of a crash programme, so it couched its April 1915 proposal for a greatly-expanded U-boat in terms of a target date of 1924. Experience to date showed that U-boats needed higher surface speed and greater endurance at sea (including better habitability), which meant larger engines and greater unit cost. To replace the Mobilisation type, the TI looked back at a Project 31 design begun in 1913 as an alternative to the closed-cycle steam submarine it was then building. In its current incarnation it would be powered by new-generation 1500bhp MAN and Germania engines.[70] The TI planned forty-six such boats, the first six (*U 81–U 86*) to be delivered as quickly as possible, the rest at the rate of one per month. Because these boats required new design effort, it was quicker to continue building Mobilisation boats (Project 25) to a modified design with four rather than two bow torpedo tubes than to switch designs. In May 1915 the UI asked for five more Mobilisation boats on an immediate basis, later increased to six: *U 87–U 92*. These submarines began a rolling programme of new Mobilisation type construction (with gradual improvements) in five- or six-boat batches.[71] A parallel programme developed improved coastal U-boats (UB II and UC II [Project 41] classes). Project 41 in particular extended these boats beyond the North Sea; one of the design requirements was that it be able to reach Austro-Hungarian bases. The failure of the spring 1915 offensive and of the initial U-boat campaign made it clear by the summer of 1915 that the war would last at least another year, so follow-up contracts for improved coastal U-boats were let.

Project 31 was abandoned, but not the search for greater endurance and performance. A new Mobilisation design was developed: Project 42. It grew from about 760 tons to 1200 tons in a single jump. To achieve the desired high surface speed, the two main diesels (1650bhp to 1750bhp) were supplemented by two battery-charging diesels (450bhp each), so that the entire power of the main engines could be devoted to surface power. Project 43 was considered a U-cruiser (10,000nm range at 8 knots) and was given a 10.5cm gun so that it could, if necessary, comply with the Prize Rules and attack on the surface. The design was presented to the Navy Office in December 1915. After a series of delays, the first contracts were let in May 1916. Meanwhile a new smaller Mobilisation U-boat design (Project 43) was also completed. One of its supposed virtues was that it could introduce a new builder to the greater complexity to be expected of Project 43.

Projects 42 and 43 were too large for the mass production needed to support a new U-boat campaign. In April 1915 the UI had called for a simplified 600 ton type. With unrestricted submarine warfare renewed (as it turned out, briefly) early in 1916, the project became more urgent. The new design (UB III [Project 44]) was based not on the Mobilisation boats but rather on the smaller UC II minelayer, its mine shafts replaced by four torpedo tubes with two reloads. The engines were more powerful than those of a UC II, but still far short of the expensive ones in a Mobilisation boat or in the new types. Since engines were the great bottleneck in production, in April 1916 the UI ordered enough for twenty-four submarines; boats were ordered the next month (*UB 48–UB 71*).[72] The first units were delivered in the summer of 1917.

In February 1916 the Admiralstab submitted a plan for unrestricted submarine warfare against Britain to the Kaiser. This was considerably more ambitious than the UI plan laid out in 1915. The Admiralstab envisaged twenty-seven U-boat operating areas (stations) around the British Isles; to occupy them would require 170 ocean-going boats (taking losses into account) based on the Heligoland Bight. Another twenty would be required for operations

with the High Seas Fleet and to patrol the Baltic. With a 10 per cent reserve, that made 209 ocean U-boats. Another thirty UB-boats (improved type) would be used both to keep British minelayers and submarines out of the Heligoland Bight (so U-boats could get in and out). Twenty-five more would protect the coast and operate out of Flanders.[73] Other requirements were minelaying against England (fifty-four large and seventeen small U-boats), minelaying against Russia (ten large and twenty small boats), Baltic operations (other than patrolling the newly-conquered eastern territories) and Mediterranean torpedo and mine operations (thirty-five ocean-going torpedo U-boats, eleven small torpedo U-boats, ten ocean-going minelayers and six small minelayers). The totals were 270 large and ninety-six small torpedo U-boats and seventy-four ocean-going and forty-three small minelayers. This must have been breathtaking. Even the UI, in stating a big long-range programme in April 1915, had been content with 154 ocean-going torpedo U-boats and another forty-six minelayers and coastal boats. The reality was worse: as of 1 January 1916 U-boats built and building amounted to seventy-five ocean-going torpedo U-boats, forty-four small torpedo U-boats, ten ocean-going minelayers and four small minelayers. The requirement was so far beyond capability and the resources so thin, that the calculation had no impact, except as an indication of what the Germans actually thought an unrestricted campaign required.

Early in 1916 the UI designed a longer-range minelayer (Project 44) based partly on its new ocean U-boat (Project 43), but with mine stowage adapted from the earlier and much smaller Project 38 minelayer. Submerged range was less than that of a Mobilisation U-boat because the mines took up space which would otherwise have gone for fuel. In April 1916 the UI and the Navy Office laid out contracts for delivery in 1917. The UI decided to stop building Mobilisation boats (the last of which would be delivered in the summer of 1917), shifting to the new types. There was sufficient capacity for twenty-four Project 42, but instead the UI planned twelve Project 42 (*U 127–U 138*) and ten Project 45 minelayers (*U 117–U 126*).[74] Unfortunately it was soon evident that the big new U-boats would take longer to build than expected, leaving a three-month gap in deliveries between the summer and autumn of 1917. With two or three large U-boats being lost each month, the UI decided to let an immediate contract for twelve more Mobilisation boats (*U 105–U 114*). The initial twenty-four UB IIIs (*UB 48–UB 71*) were ordered for delivery in the first quarter of 1917. With the contracts for the Mobilisation boats and the big U-boats let, the only remaining capacity was for UB IIIs, so *UB 72–UB 87* were ordered in September 1916.[75]

While all this was happening, the Germans' second attempt at unrestricted U-boat warfare was collapsing due to US pressure after an April 1916 incident. The Prize Rules were reinstated. Since the presence of so many warships in the Channel and the North Sea made that dangerous, interest turned to more distant waters. The Admiralstab asked the TI to design a U-cruiser capable of fighting an armed merchant ship, which up to that point had been an antidote to any U-boat operating on the surface. Although the trade campaign soon collapsed altogether (U-boats were reassigned to support the High Seas Fleet directly), the project survived, since it was reasonable to assume that operations under the Prize Rules would soon resume. In May 1916 the Admiralstab asked the UI to design and built a big long-range high-performance U-boat: Project 46. As usual, the problem was to provide enough power. MAN was

At the other end of the scale, the Germans built small submarines of the UB series, initially to operate out of the new base in Flanders. The next series were ocean-going submarines well suited to the North Sea. *UB 88* is shown at Mare Island on 23 September 1919. Submarines of this type operated extensively in the Mediterranean.

sketching a 3000bhp diesel, but for the time being the designers had to make do with the current 1650–1750bhp type (there could be no question of steam power, as in the British 'K' boats); surface speed was only 14–15 knots. Range was 12,000nm at 10 knots. In August the UI awarded contracts for three U-cruisers (*U 139–U 141*).[76] In October, when the order was given to resume trade warfare under the Prize Rules, the Navy Office wanted more U-cruisers, so it asked how many could be completed by the spring of 1918. The UI ordered nine more: *U 142–U 150* to a slightly modified design (Project 46a).[77] Construction of some of the Mobilisation boats was deferred in favour of the new U-cruisers.[78] British intelligence became aware of this project; in the autumn of 1916 Admiral Jellicoe and others wrote about the expected extension of the U-boat war to North and probably to South America.

The UI was also interested in something with better protection, which it called Project P (Panzer, armoured): Project 47. In June 1916 it sketched such a submarine, which would require the projected 3000bhp engines.[79] Compared to Project 46, which was already expensive, Project 47 would have cost twice as much, with twice the crew and slightly greater surface endurance. Project 47 was probably offered during the autumn of 1916 to High Seas Fleet commander Admiral Scheer. After Jutland and particularly after his August 1916 sortie, he became convinced that he wanted fast powerful U-boats to provide direct support, in much the way Jellicoe had demanded the 'K' boats more than a year earlier. Project 47 was still more or less alive in May 1917, but by then the UI was also interested in something smaller but much faster: Project 50 (K44, the K presumably indicating a cruiser [kreuzer]). Just like the British 'K'boat, it needed steam power to achieve high surface performance.[80] One boat was ordered under War Contract AA (February 1918) as *UD 1*, but at the end of the war it had not been laid down, overtaken by the priorities set by the unrestricted submarine campaign.

However, in the autumn of 1916 orders were issued for resumed trade warfare, this time under the Prize Rules. As initial steps *U 63–U 65* were given greater fuel capacity, the *U 71* class minelayers were provisionally ordered converted to torpedo

submarines and all ocean-going U-boats were ordered armed with 10.5cm rather than 8.8cm guns. The big Project 45 minelayers would have one 15cm gun in place of the earlier pair of 10.5cm weapons. Ultimately the campaign should employ longer-range U-boats. In 1916 the Germans already had some experience in that direction, with a group of cargo-carrying U-boats built specially to evade the British blockade. One of them, *Deutschland*, made two highly-publicised (and commercially successful) visits to the United States. A sister-ship, *Bremen*, was already complete (she was lost on her first trip) and six more planned. With the shift to Prize Rules warfare, necessarily in distant waters, the big cargo U-boats became attractive as potential U-cruisers, which could be armed with 15cm guns. In December 1916 four cargo U-boats were taken over as *U 151–U 154*. Once unrestricted submarine warfare was resumed, the other three were taken over as *U 155–U 157*.

Within a few months the Kaiser agreed to resume unrestricted submarine warfare. Now smaller U-boats were once again very well worthwhile. From UI's point of view the important point about the new campaign was that it was personally supported by chief of the army high command (OHL) Field Marshal von Hindenburg. In January 1917 von Hindenburg and his chief of staff General Erich Ludendorff in effect controlled German industry in support of the land war. Their strong support of the U-boat campaign, which they sometimes called Germany's 'last card', caused them to send an officer to UI in Kiel in January 1917 specifically to ask its problems and to agree on solutions in terms of making material and labour available. UI convinced the OHL to approve immediate contracts for more U-boats: twenty-five UB IIIs for the middle of 1917, plus another ten UB IIIs and twenty-eight Mobilisation boats by the middle of 1918 and another seventy boats of various types by the end of 1918. At this point the Navy Office did not want to order any boats which might be completed after the beginning of 1918, on the ground that they would overburden the navy budget. In effect its new connection with OHL gave UI an end-run around the Navy Office which up to that point had run German naval shipbuilding. The overburdening most likely referred to the Navy Office's hopes of completing capital ships.

The UI almost immediately began ordering UB IIIs, replacement UC IIIs and a few Mobilisation boats and U-cruisers.[81] Production was slowed by crippling shortages of raw materials (which can be attributed to the British blockade) and to severe labour shortages (partly due the demands of the army for ever more men). Given the OHL connection, in July 1917 the Navy Office asked the War Office to give the submarine programme priority over all others. In exchange it finally had to cut its surface ship programme, transferring all skilled workers to U-boat construction.[82] This step unfortunately roughly coincided with the beginning of the convoy operations which made U-boats far less effective.

Once U-boats were given the highest priority, ninety-five more of existing designs were ordered: thirty-seven UB III, thirty-nine UC III, ten U-cruisers and nine Mobilisation type boats.[83] All were scheduled for completion between the summer of 1918 and January 1919. In hopes of increasing production, in the autumn of 1917 UI designed a new 364-ton single hull boat (UF, Project 48a) specifically for the Flanders Flotilla, in effect a replacement for UB III.[84] Due to previous construction and to limited losses due to ineffective anti-submarine warfare, the U-boat force peaked in October 1917 at 140 units. By that time the convoy system and other anti-submarine measures were becoming effective. Moreover, the number of U-boats in commission was several times the number active at any one time.[85]

Scheer was not convinced that the U-boats were losing. By the late autumn of 1917 the Admiralstab finally had executive authority over all naval forces and in November Scheer pressed its chief to create a U-boat Office directly under his operations directorate. Scheer believed that the Estimates Department in particular was holding back orders for sufficient U-boats. In November 1917 its head expected that the navy would receive eighteen U-cruisers and sixty other U-boats during 1919, a figure he considered adequate. Almost everyone else present disagreed. By this time sixty-three submarines had been lost in 1917, so it seemed likely that another 102 would be lost in 1918. The proposed programme would not even replace them, even though U-boats might be Germany's only effective offensive weapons. The UI thought that yard capacity was 118 submarines, including twenty-two U-cruisers. However, instead of a single U-cruiser, three UB III or four UC III or five UF-type submarines could be built. Another twenty-four single-hull UF-boats could be built (the Head of Estimates disagreed).

This argument brought in OHL, because it might be possible to increase production if the army could release labour. Ludendorff pointed out that he was finding it difficult to replace his own losses. By this time, moreover, Russia was in turmoil and Ludendorff was probably beginning to think about a new 'last card', the massive Western Front offensive he launched in April 1918. That required not only troops but also new munitions, for which he had to allocate the same labour the navy wanted to build U-boats. The autumn programme was finally set on 17 December 1917: 120 units, consisting of thirty-six UB IIIs, thirty-four UC IIIs, twenty UFs, twelve Mobilisation boats and eighteen U-cruisers.

The Russian collapse made it possible to shift some Baltic yards to submarine construction. Scheer's U-boat Office came into existence in December 1917 and the following January it began awarding contracts for a big UF programme, as that was the simplest type to build.[86] Efforts to subcontract were finally proving effective. However, the demoralisation of German society traceable to the blockade was also having an effect. Workers were refusing overtime. Strikes and absenteeism were increasing. The summer 1918 influenza epidemic was particularly damaging because of the workers' inadequate diet. Labour was also being stretched. For example, the UI estimated that 185,000 riveter worker-days were needed during 1918 at Germania, but only 145,000 were available. One yard offered to increase production by a third if they build only one type of boat and went to full day and night shifts – if only they could get 3000 to 4000 more workers.

Meanwhile, with the extension of convoys it seemed that U-boats would have to work further afield, beyond the range even of Project 46a. An enlarged version (3000 tons) would be able to steam 20,000nm at 8 knots and thus could reach the Gulf of Mexico and even Brazil. A new programme was proposed in May 1918: two 3000-ton U-cruisers, six modified Project 42, thirty-six Mobilisation boats, fifty UB IIIs, thirty-five UC IIIs and thirty UFs. It is somewhat surprising that both UB III and the similar UF were to be bought. Formal requirements set by the new U-boat office in June 1918 were: forty-four UB IIIs (War Contract AB), forty UC IIIs (War Contract AC), forty-eight Mobilisation boats (War Contract AD), sixteen large Mobilisation boats (Project 42a: War Contract AE) and forty-four UFs (War Contract AF).

Once the Spring Offensive failed in August 1918, the U-boat war seemed even more important. The U-boat office looked for ways to increase production. One option (small programme) was to draft 15,000 workers to achieve a 25 per cent increase in production at all yards. A second (the large plan) was to draft 50,000 workers for a 70 per cent increase in production in eighteen months. A third was to transfer all contracts for minor warships (torpedo boats, minesweepers and armed trawlers) to yards in occupied territories, freeing all Reich yards to build submarines. Yet another possibility was to use Austrian yards, whose capacity was thought to be thirty-seven UB IIIs. It might be possible to double the current rate of 12.7 U-boats per month by the end of 1919. On 30 August the requirement to achieve the 25 per cent increase was immediate drafting of 20,000 skilled workers as of 1 October, to be followed by another 30,000. Another 70,000 were wanted later. On this basis the U-boat Office expected to increase the planned delivery of fifty-four large and 133 smaller U-boats between October 1918 and the end of 1919 to seventy-four large and 188 smaller ones, with even more possible if the 70,000 men could be made available. As the situation on the Western Front deteriorated, it became more difficult for the army to release men, or to limit its demands for fresh men.

On 11 August 1918 Admiral Scheer became head of the Admiralstab, which now meant that he was head of the whole navy. He considered the U-boat campaign paramount; in his eyes it was the only offensive arm left to Germany. The Large Programme became the Scheer Programme. Scheer pressed Ludendorff for the men the U-boat Office wanted. The army had bled badly in the failed offensive and the subsequent retreat and it badly needed new men. For his part Scheer considered the 'small' building programme inadequate in the face of improved Allied ASW as well as new Allied merchant ship construction. He decided to limit the number of distinct types and he pressed for American-style mass production, which would bring in many firms outside the traditional shipbuilding business. To keep sinking more ships than the enemy could build, Scheer needed a lot more U-boats. His goal was to increase the monthly total from 12.7 to 16 in the fourth quarter of 1918, to 20 in the first quarter of 1919, to 25 in the second quarter, to 30 in the third and to a steady 36 from the fourth onward. Even if this was possible, Scheer faced a considerable crew shortage and a fuel-oil shortage.

As late as early October 1918, it seemed that Germany might be able to stabilise the Western Front. The Germans would be able to shorten their front and they might be able to release men to the

U-boat industry by mid-November. For a time Hindenburg and Ludendorff imagined a new stand-off on land in which the U-boat offensive provided Germany with the necessary leverage to force an acceptable settlement. Plans were therefore drafted for a 1919 programme. It seemed that enough UF had been ordered, so the UI designed an enlarged version (UG, Project 51), with better surface performance.[87] C-in-C U-Boats wanted a new minelayer, so the UI developed what it called Type I. The Mediterranean commander liked the UB III as exactly what he needed, so he wanted more of them (other officers considered UB III obsolete). Ultimately, in early October, the types favoured were the large Mobilisation boat (Project 42a), the Mobilisation type, UG, UC III and a large minelayer of unspecified type (fifteen to be built). The ratio of the other types was to be 1:2.5:4:1.5, actual numbers depending on industrial capacity. On 29 October 1918 the Admiralstab announced that all surface ships to be completed after the beginning of July 1919 were to be cancelled in favour of maximum U-boat production. By that time the main competitor with Scheer's programme was a plan to produce 1000 tanks beginning in November 1918, which would have cut U-boat production by about 30 per cent by mid-January 1919. There was, however, insufficient fuel for the tanks.

By this time the situation was beginning to crumble. None of the big 1919 programmes every came close to fruition. By November 1918 Germany was short of resources. Fuel that was too scarce to run tanks was also too scarce to run aircraft and it was probably scarce because heavier oils, on which submarines ran, were also scarce. The Western Front might be stabilised, but elsewhere around Germany allies were defecting and the German army would have had to cover the frontiers around the country. The slight manpower surplus Scheer imagined for November 1918 would have been much more than wiped out. Even had the High Sea Fleet not mutinied, it seems that the blockade had badly undermined German society, so that the kind of intensive effort on which Scheer relied would have been impossible.

For anyone looking ahead to a new U-boat war, the lesson was obvious: the Germans had started too late and had taken far too long to get their priorities straight. The whole idea of defeating Britain by sinking merchant ships might or might not have worked, but the campaigns of 1915–16 had given the British far too much time to understand the problem. That the British had failed to adopt convoy tactics earlier had made it possible for the Germans to mount a third campaign in 1917, again with insufficient forces. Remarkably, the Germans began the Second World War with another very small U-boat force, although this time it had effective ways of dealing with convoys.

The UC series were the minelayer equivalents to the UBs. *UC 97* (UC III type) is shown visiting Toronto on 10 June 1919 during a post-war bond-selling tour of the Great Lakes. The object under her conning tower is a torpedo tube; her fore end was occupied by minelaying tubes. She also had a torpedo tube right aft. The gun was a 10.5cm/45. Alongside the submarine is a fleet tug. (RCN)

By 1917–18, smoke screens seemed to be the best way to prevent U-boats from seeing ships in convoy, hence the best way to prevent attacks. This smoke-screened convoy was photographed from the air in June 1918.

CHAPTER 12

Protecting Trade: The U-Boat War

U-BOATS CHANGED THE GAME of trade protection. The mechanisms developed to track and find raiders still worked and code-breaking made it even easier to locate U-boats – but only to locate them approximately. Unfortunately during the First World War there was no reliable means of locating and then killing a submerged submarine. Nor was there a means of systematically re-routing merchant ships. On the other hand, convoy was once again a practicable proposition, because a U-boat, particularly when submerged, was so fragile. Small, inexpensive ships could be effective escorts.

There is always a balance between hunting submarines and protecting their targets. The goal of anti-submarine warfare might be stated either as protecting the targets or as destroying the submarines, but the First World War shows that the two are hardly equivalent. At the end of the war, unlike the situation in 1945, most U-boats still existed and their crews did not regard war patrols as suicidal. However, the U-boat offensive had failed and sinkings of merchant ships were declining as more escorts entered service.

During the war, as noted previously, the Germans shifted back and forth between unrestricted submarine warfare (sinking on sight) and observance of the classic rules of trade warfare (stop, examine, protect passengers and crew). The classic rules did not favour U-boats, because surfaced submarines were inherently vulnerable. If the target merchant ship was armed, she had a fair chance of sinking a surfaced U-boat lying-to while some of her officers examined papers. In 1915 the Royal Navy commissioned its first 'Q-ships', warships disguised as merchant ships specifically to act as U-boat traps. Aside from their ability to sink U-boats

which stopped them, the advent of Q-ships would inevitably force the Germans to choose between following the classic blockade policy or sinking ships on sight. The latter policy would cause them to attack and kill neutrals and that in turn might tip the largest of the neutrals, the United States, into the war. It is not clear from surviving documents whether anyone at the Admiralty considered this aspect of Q-ship operations.

U-boats carried limited numbers of torpedoes, which were not entirely reliable. Even with shoot-on-sight orders, a U-boat commander might prefer to attack merchant ships with his deck gun or even with standard scuttling charges, which they carried. A Q-ship which could withstand some damage might still be effective under such circumstances. For example, a U-boat might surface and close with a merchant ship she had torpedoed but left afloat. When the Germans sent cruiser submarines across the Atlantic in 1918, the US Navy fitted out Q-ships on the theory that U-boat commanders would be even more reluctant to expend scarce torpedoes when they had no nearby base.

British successes in radio intelligence extended to U-boats as much as to the German surface fleet. The British were aware of roughly where the U-boats were, at least in the Atlantic and in the North Sea. However, rough location was never enough, because existing means of detection were not nearly good enough to convert such information into attacks against submarines. Intelligence often was good enough to protect shipping by ordering evasion. For example, evasion limited losses among major British liners early in the war (*Lusitania* was warned about the U-boat which sank her, but her master did not realise how serious the warning was and its code-breaking basis could not be disclosed to him). Even the dispersion ordered at the outbreak of war, before code-breaking intelligence became available, could help. On the Germans' side, once, however, British codes were compromised, advisory messages became dangerous.[1] Attempts to use evasive routing in the Mediterranean in 1917–18 generally failed, possibly because the orders were chosen from among a limited repertory of routes. It is not clear to what extent, if any, the Admiralty was able to order evasion in something like real time in response to intelligence, as it typically did during the Second World War.

The anti-submarine campaign was extremely frustrating. Even in 1918, with enormous effort invested in it, the Germans were completing submarines at least as rapidly as they were being sunk. The main success was that the U-boats were sinking fewer and fewer merchant ships. The great fear was that as the U-boat force grew, the Germans would become more effective against convoys. Given greater numbers, the Germans had a better chance of intercepting convoys in coastal and focal areas, unless hunting became so much more effective that U-boats could not operate there (as they could not in the next war).

In modern terms, First World War ASW operations split into five different options, which are much the ones available both in the Second World War and during the Cold War. One was self-defence for merchant ships. A second was to attack U-boats where they were known to be: at their bases: attack at source. A third was to attack U-boats in transit between base and patrol area. That might mean hunting U-boats, or laying minefields in areas they had to pass, or using submarines to ambush them. Mines were particularly effective because during the First World War no submarine had any way of detecting them. She might try to transit a known deep minefield on the surface, but that would expose her to attack (which would force her to dive into the mines and take her chances). This type of threat was apparently uniquely demoralising. A fourth was to hunt U-boats down. That might mean patrolling areas to keep U-boats out (they would be hunted if they appeared), or trying to destroy U-boats whose approximate position was indicated in some way, e.g. by sinkings ('flaming data' in later parlance) or sightings or intelligence.[2] The fifth was to deal with U-

As long as U-boats approached their victims on the surface, they could be dealt with by guns on board merchant ships. The Ellerman & Bucknall liner *City of Karachi* shows her stern gun, as well as the dazzle painting intended to make it difficult for a U-boat to hit her with a torpedo. At least in theory, the gun and the dazzle paint were complementary, as a U-boat unable to make a torpedo attack would use her gun on the surface, hence be vulnerable to the ship's own gun. (Allan C Green via State Library of Victoria)

Q-ships were converted from merchant ships and also from the new sloops and P-boats. The total of about 180 included twelve brigs (sailing ships) in the Mediterranean and at least one X-lighter. HMS *Harebell* was one of thirty-four modified 'Flower' class sloops (designated convoy sloops) built to resemble a specific small merchant ship. She is shown in 1921, with her heavy gun armament exposed. By the summer of 1917 U-boat commanders were so suspicious that they rarely approached ships on the surface, relying mainly on torpedoes. The Q-ship force was reduced but not eliminated.

In effect a Q-ship (Special Service Ship) was an extreme version of an armed merchant ship, a decoy intended specifically to destroy a U-boat compelled to attack on the surface. The object was to entice a U-boat into effective range. To that end Q-ships were often fitted to absorb torpedo hits and their crews included 'panic parties' which would visibly (and slowly) abandon ship while the engine room crew and the gunners remained on board. In effect Q-ships made it risky for German submarines to obey international law by stopping and examining merchant ships before taking further action. The alternative, to sink merchant ships on sight, infuriated Americans and thus made it more likely that the United States would enter the war on the Allied side. Built in 1901, HMS *Baralong* was one of the first Q-ships. She was armed with three concealed 12pdrs, the small gun right aft being mounted to give the impression that she was a defensively armed merchant ship. She sank *U 27* in August 1915 and *U 41* that September. In the August incident, *Baralong* (Commander Godfrey Herbert) came alongside the steamer *Nicosian*, which was under attack by a U-boat. At the time *Baralong* was flying the American flag as part of her deceptive rig. Out of sight of the U-boat, she hoisted the White Ensign and cleared for action. As the U-boat sank, her crew tried to scramble on board the *Nicosian* rather than surrender; *Baralong*'s crew shot them down. A few Germans managed to get below and the *Baralong*'s crew found them and shot them. The Germans claimed the incident was an atrocity and the action drew publicity as the '*Baralong* incident'. After Mediterranean service, *Baralong/Wyandra* was returned to civilian service in November 1916. She had been built in 1901. In the background is the hospital ship *Carisbrook Castle*. (Dr David Stevens, SPC-A)

boats when they attacked: convoy. In the First World War, convoy was much more a way to protect the U-boats' targets than a way of destroying the U-boats themselves.

Self-Defence

During the First World War, both the Royal Navy and allied navies devoted considerable effort to arming merchant ships, initially with guns but also with ASW weapons such as depth charges and, in the case of the Royal Navy, with anti-submarine howitzers. The initial logic of gun armament was that a U-boat was much like the lightly-armed commerce raiders the initial defensively armed merchantman programme was intended to counter. In February 1915 fifty 12pdrs were allocated to coastal vessels considered vulnerable to U-boat attack, priority going to ships of at least 1000 GRT and a speed of less than 13 knots, which were constantly at sea in the English or Irish Channels and not visiting neutral ports (keeping in mind the previous year's problem with the Americans). Half of them were to be Admiralty Chartered Colliers and Store Carriers running between the East and West Coasts and France (and possibly Spain), the other half to be local coastal traders. The first ships to be armed were chartered colliers, to be armed on arrival at the Tyne and at Cardiff. By April 1915, fifty-eight ships had been inspected and were considered suitable for arming. Of this total, forty-eight ships had been armed, and three more were being armed. As more guns became available, more ships were armed: by 10 May 1915, 115 had been armed, nine ships were in hand for arming and another fifteen had been earmarked, a total of 139 ships (plus *Atalanta*, which was captured by a U-boat). In many cases, guns were taken from other ships.[3]

In April 1915, it was decided that one 4.7in gun would be mounted right aft on board some of the larger classes of merchant ships engaged in overseas trade.[4] Because the number of such guns was limited, outward-bound ships steaming through the Mediterranean transferred their guns on the outward-bound voyage to ships on the homeward-bound voyage. Initially the transfer was done at Gibraltar, the idea being that the U-boat threat was confined to the area around the British Isles. As the threat extended to the Mediterranean, the transfer point was moved to Port Said. A fixed number of guns was assigned to each shipping line. Later the transfer system was extended to the South Atlantic, transfer points being Halifax, Sierra Leone and Capetown. On 2 November 1918 there were a total of 4203 defensively-armed British merchant ships. Another 1684 had been sunk, making a total of 5887 ships fitted.[5]

Masters of British ships certainly considered defensive guns valuable, to the point that those sailing from neutral ports sometimes mounted dummy wooden guns. SS *Nicosian*, which was so fitted, was attacked by a submarine, which sheered off out of gun range for more than half an hour before closing to attack with gunfire. That gave the Q-ship *Baralong* sufficient time to reach the *Nicosian*, probably saving the ship (and sinking the U-boat). Between 1 January 1916 and 25 January 1917, 310 defensively armed merchant ships were attacked. Of those, 236 escaped. Another sixty-two were torpedoed without warning and twelve sunk by U-boat gunfire. During the same period, 302 unarmed merchant ships were attacked, of which sixty seven escaped. Of the remainder, thirty were torpedoed without warning and another 205 were sunk by gunfire and also by scuttling charges.[6]

Once a submarine spotted her target, she had to set up a torpedo solution. That required that she correctly estimate target speed and course. A zig-zagging ship could ruin such a solution, so

Thornycroft built the small *Hyderabad* specifically as a Q-ship ('decoy tramp'). She was the only ship designed and built specifically for this purpose. Thornycroft proposed a ship based on a shallow-draught steamer (so that torpedoes would pass beneath her) but with the appearance of an ordinary tramp. The company used the lines of the pre-war *St. Patrick*, a coastal tunnel-stern passenger ferry built for Trinidad in 1913 (*Hyderabad* was considerably longer). Her above-water appearance was that of a General Steam Navigation Company ship at half-draught. Draught was initially to have been 4ft, but was later reduced to 3ft 8in; she displaced 595 tons light (624 fully loaded). Projected armament consisted of two 4in concealed in the forecastle and two 4in in the poop plus two 'aerial torpedo guns', a Thornycroft invention which never entered service, plus four torpedo tubes. She was armed with one 4in, two 12pdr and one 1½ pdr plus two 18in torpedo tubes and four bomb throwers (presumably depth charge throwers). All guns except the 1½ pdr were concealed, the 12pdrs being on tilting mountings. *Hyderabad* was launched on 27 August 1917 and delivered on 24 September. She was named after the Nizam of Hyderabad, who financed construction. In March 1919 she was converted into a command and depot ship for CMBs used against the Bolsheviks at Murmansk and in 1920 she was sold to become a fruit carrier.

long as the zig-zag pattern was sufficiently complicated that the U-boat commander could not detect it and cancel it out in his calculation. By 1916 the Royal Navy often linked zig-zagging, which was introduced about 1915, with defensive armament. The expectation seems to have been that a U-boat would be unable to torpedo a fast zig-zagging ship. She would have to surface and use her gun and in that case an armed merchant ship could fire back.[7] Even limited damage might cripple the U-boat. The threat of such damage might drive off a U-boat. This linkage explains the enormous effort to provide merchant ships with guns, even after the Germans resumed unrestricted submarine warfare in 1917.[8] The records of the programme show, sadly, that often armed ships were sunk. However, the protection of merchant shipping was always a matter of averages. If, over time, the U-boats were destroyed, that would be enough. In reality armed merchant ships failed to sink U-boats at all, so that the guns were much more a matter of keeping up morale.

It was also possible to paint a ship in such a way that her course was difficult to estimate visually: dazzle-painting (later some escorts and merchant ships were deliberately arranged to make it difficult to estimated their course). Because the submarine depended so heavily on visual cues, by 1918 there was intense interest in smoke generators. There was also interest in ways of reducing the visibility of funnel smoke. Thornycroft developed a

water device to damp smoke, claiming that it reduced visibility from 20 miles to 10. That would dramatically reduce a U-boat's chance of detecting its target.

Attack at Source

In the North Sea and the Atlantic, U-boats were divided between a High Seas Fleet force in German waters and a Flanders Flotilla based at Zeebrugge. As long as the High Seas Fleet existed and presented a credible threat, an attack against its U-boats was unlikely. If an attack cost too many modern ships, the U-boats might be blocked but the High Seas Fleet would be released to prey even more effectively on shipping. With the entry of the United States into the war, the Allies had such an advantage in modern warships that risky operations became much more attractive. There was also renewed interest in a direct attack on the High Seas Fleet in harbour, which again would have made direct attack on submarine bases and building yards possible. British operations against the High Seas Fleet could be considered integral with the submarine war.

The US Navy became interested in air attacks against German U-boat bases and building yards. As the war ended it was beginning to build up the land-based air force which would be required. By that time the RNAS had been absorbed into the new RAF and it is not clear to what extent the British (who had long-range heavy bombers) shared the US Navy's faith in its ability to bomb out German facilities. Official documents of this period describe the potential of air attacks in much the terms which might have been used just before the Second World War – but the means of attack, including bomb sights, were far more primitive and attacks would have been far less effective. The base in Flanders was not covered by the High Seas Fleet; attempts to neutralise Zeebrugge and Ostend, culminating in the heroic 1918 raids, were intended as ASW measures.[9]

Attack in Transit

A U-boat had finite seagoing endurance. At the very least, the mine-net barrage across the Straits of Dover forced U-boats to pass the long way around northern Scotland. That passage, which had to be made largely at night, consumed time which the U-boat might otherwise have spent productively on patrol. This wartime experience helped convince the German naval command that in any future war Germany should seize bases on the Atlantic, at least in Norway.

Other mine barriers were intended to keep U-boats out of important areas. The most impressive was the Northern Barrage extending from Norway to the Shetlands, the object being to confine U-boats to the North Sea. A barrier across the deep Strait of Otranto was intended to keep U-boats based at Pola from entering the Mediterranean. Both the Dover and the Otranto barriers were prosecuted largely by small ASW craft and they were subject to attack by surface forces. The Dover Barrage was raided by German destroyers based in Zeebrugge, which the Germans saw primarily as a submarine support force. The Otranto Barrage was raided by the Austrians. Their battleship *Szent Istvan* was sunk (by an Italian motor torpedo boat) *en route* to one such attempt.

Closer in, the U-boat routes through the Heligoland Bight could be mined. The British had no effective mines at the beginning

One anti-submarine strategy was to attack U-boats in transit. Submarines were the best means of doing so, because they could stalk U-boats proceeding on the surface in supposedly safe areas. Given their very limited underwater endurance, U-boats had to spend much of their time surfaced. Similar arguments applied to U-boat operating areas, which is why the British and their US allies based submarines in the Irish Sea in 1918. The Royal Navy developed a specialised anti-submarine submarine, the R-class. *R 7* is shown.

Convoy turned out to be the most effective way to protect merchant ships. Here Convoy HG 85 passes up the Irish Sea, 30 June 1918. This convoy left Gibraltar for the West Coast of the United Kingdom, comprising ships for Liverpool, Manchester, Barrow and the Clyde. Note that most of the ships are not dazzle-painted. Dazzle was a means of confusing a U-boat commander trying to estimate his target's course and speed, but in a convoy both were obvious enough not to be worth concealing. This photograph was taken from an air escort and only one escorting ship is visible. The uneven lines of ships testify to Royal Navy official scepticism that merchant officers could keep station in convoys. In contrast to Second World War practice, the convoy is organised in lines abreast rather than in columns.

of the war, but by 1917–18 they had exactly what they needed and they used huge numbers in the Bight. They also laid deep minefields around the British Isles, in places U-boats normally patrolled submerged. The US Navy much preferred the idea of a distant (hence unsweepable) mine blockade, as in its view anything the Royal Navy laid in the Bight was quickly swept up because it could not be patrolled. One British rejoinder was that the North Sea barrage still had to be patrolled, to keep U-boats from evading mines by passing through on the surface. The sheer length of the barrier demanded a huge patrol force.[10] In 1918 the Royal Navy pioneered magnetic and acoustic mines, both intended to destroy U-boats; it laid magnetic mines off Zeebrugge.

In theory, mine barriers limited U-boat operating areas and thus made hunting more effective. Hunting in turn required destroyers which would otherwise have operated with the Grand Fleet or with convoys. Again, there was a trade-off between hunting and convoy escort and the need to maintain the Grand Fleet to deal with possible German surface operations.

Another approach was to limit the mobility of the submarines. Even more than their Second World War successors, First World

Convoys could and did manoeuvre together, as this photograph attests.

War submarines had limited underwater endurance, running on batteries. To make good any substantial distance they had to run on the surface. A surfaced submarine had a low silhouette, so typically she could spot a surface ship well before being spotted, long enough in advance to dive to safety. That was particularly true of any coal-fired ship, which would almost inevitably produce a column of funnel smoke. A submarine was least likely to spot another submarine and submarine vs. submarine tactics became important (see the next chapter). By 1916 the British believed that their superior hydrophones gave their submarines a considerable edge over the Germans, helping justify submarine vs submarine operations.[11]

Aircraft could spot surfaced U-boats and, in theory, bomb them, but during the First World War their weapons were ineffective against a submerging submarine. However, the very real threat of

U-boats could attack ships in convoy as they formed up (and as they dispersed to different ports). SS *Tregenna* was torpedoed while in Convoy OF 18 at 1510 on 26 December 1917. The convoy was forming after ships cleared the swept channel.

bombing caused submarines to dive upon spotting an aircraft or a blimp and that in turn drastically reduced their mobility, hence their effectiveness. A U-boat immobilised miles from a convoy could not attack it.

All of these measures were directed against U-boats in the open sea. All sank some U-boats, but the sinking rate was painfully small. All of them also reduced U-boat productivity and that was worthwhile in a war against Allied tonnage. Decoy ships (Q-Ships) fitted into this category.[12] To some extent they and guns to arm merchant ships were associated with the period of the war during which U-boats might abide by a version of the Prize Rules, hence inspect a merchant ship before sinking or releasing her. However, even during the period of unrestricted U-boat warfare, U-boat commanders had to conserve torpedoes, so they often resorted to their deck guns. Decoys had a dual role. They sank U-boats and their existence also forced U-boats to attack submerged, which in turn limited the number of ships any one U-boat could sink.

Hunting

Until mid-1917 the principal British measure for trade protection against U-boats was a massive Auxiliary Patrol of trawlers backed by destroyers. In theory they could run down U-boats, but in practice they lacked effective means of finding them. The great reality of later ASW using an effective means of detection (sonar) was that a submarine hunt tended to be protracted. It required both an effective way of holding and regaining contact (sonar) and an effective weapon (the depth charge and later ahead-throwing weapons with much better kill probability). There is no evidence in the First World War of the massive numbers of depth charges carried and employed during the next war; in December 1916 a British officer wrote that he wanted more depth charges and 'that the idea should be punched into officers' heads that each represents a round of ammunition and not the Bank of England'.[13]

Hunting, as opposed to patrol, became practical with the advent of hydrophones, by means of which a submerged submarine could usually be detected (unless it was lying silent on the bottom, or anchored underwater). By the beginning of 1918 the Royal Navy considered its hunting groups its most effective offensive ASW weapon.[14] The groups consisted of trawlers, as most of the fast ASW ships (sloops, destroyers and P-boats) had been drawn off for convoy work. The main admitted drawback of hunting was low speed.

Convoy tactics demanded large numbers of escorts. Many were US destroyers, which became available as a slightly indirect consequence of the same outbreak of unrestricted submarine warfare which made convoys necessary. The sterns in the foreground belong to USS *Warrington* (nearest) and *Walke* (alongside her), with USS *Porter* in the background, in British waters. Note how few depth charges these ships carried. In the First World War convoy was far more a means of keeping merchant ships out of the way of U-boats than of sinking them.

At the beginning of 1918, the British coast was split up into twenty-two designated coastal areas, each of which was to have its own hunting group and associated aircraft. Twelve hunting groups, each of four trawlers, had been formed. A key development was a towed hydrophone, which finally overcame noise created by the trawler's machinery (it still could not be used when the trawler was running her propeller). Hunting groups of motor launches (the US-supplied MLs) had been formed to operate in the Channel, at Portsmouth, Portland, Torquay and Newlyn and on the East coast off the Tyne. They could make 15 to 16 knots. In addition, a North Sea Hunting Force was being created, to consist of thirty-two trawlers working with half a dozen destroyers or sloops. Each group would probably consist of four trawlers and one fast ship. The fast ship might tow a kite balloon with an observer. They would operate further out to sea than the trawler and motor launch groups. The North Sea hunters would probably work designated squares; if the whole force was operating at one time 'it should be probable that 50 or 70 per cent of Atlantic enemy submarines will pass within range of one of these units at least'. All of this was rather optimistic, but it gives a fair idea of expectations at the time. The hunters were in addition to the large auxiliary patrol operating off the coast and also escorting merchant ships.[15] Because really effective hydrophones did not enter service until about the same time as convoys, it is difficult to distinguish the effect of improved hunting from the effect of convoy as a counter to U-boats. Hunting had to be scaled back in 1918 due to the desperate need for more convoy escorts, particularly to protect US troops going to France to deal with the German offensive that began in April of that year.

Convoy

Convoying trade offered three advantages. It grossly complicated the U-boats' basic task, which was to find targets in the first place. It was one thing to lurk in a busy shipping lane, waiting for individual merchant ships to pop over the horizon. It was quite another to find the sea nearly empty because ships had been concentrated into compact groups. From a distance, a convoy was not too much easier to see than an individual ship. With no easy way to detect convoys in the open sea, U-boats found themselves drawn into focal areas, where hunting forces could be concentrated. Moreover, with good intelligence as to where U-boats were (thanks to signals intelligence), the Admiralty could route convoys away from them. There were never enough U-boats at sea (as there may have been in 1942) to make evasion impossible. Moreover, naval escorts could receive and use coded Admiralty messages, hence could further Admiralty control of shipping.

Second, when an individual U-boat did locate a convoy, she could sink only a few of the convoy's ships.[16] Attacking an individual ship took time. Each torpedo had to be aimed individually at short range; U-boats did not fire salvoes because they carried too few torpedoes. In the presence of escorts, a U-boat could not pursue the convoy on the surface and she lacked the underwater endurance to keep up with even a slow convoy for very long. That left the U-boat with only a brief opportunity to attack. German practice was almost never to concentrate U-boats, because they risked attacking each other. The U-boats' problem of locating targets made attacks overwhelmingly likely in coastal rather than deep-sea areas. Concentration also made it more likely that a damaged ship would be saved. Even if a ship sank, rescue of the seamen was far more likely, raising their morale. A ship in a coastal convoy might well be beached, saving its cargo.

Third, the convoy concentrated anti-submarine forces where the U-boats were. This was often advertised as the key advantage, since it converted convoy from a defensive to an offensive strategy; the convoy became the fatal bait for U-boats. In 1917–18, however, this shift was not so obvious, because the escorts lacked the ability to detect and kill U-boats. The only effective detector of a submerged U-boat, the hydrophone, was useless if a ship was moving and the noise of a convoy would drown out U-boat sound even if the escorts were numerous enough (and fast enough) to practice 'sprint-and-drift' tactics. That left two indicators, the submarine's periscope and the track of her torpedo, beginning with

USS *Henley* was a relatively small US destroyer ('flivver') assigned to escort duty. She is shown in New York harbour. Unlike most US destroyers in European waters, she did not have her hull number painted on her hull.

The Imperial Japanese Navy contributed twelve destroyers for the Mediterranean anti-submarine campaign, of which *Sakaki* was torpedoed by the Austrian *U 27* on 11 June 1917. They made an excellent impression on the Royal Navy, but their experience seems to have had no lasting influence on the Imperial Japanese Navy itself. *Kaba* is shown in European waters.

the bubbling due to its discharge. An escort could run down the track and drop depth charges, but typically convoy escorts did not carry the mass of depth charges assigned to separate hunters. U-boats were sunk when attacking convoys, but most of them survived and most U-boat commanders had no qualms about attacking convoys.

Convoy was not, as in the Second World War, a nearly guaranteed killing-ground for U-boats. Escorts had no means of maintaining contact with an escaping U-boat, because the only detector of submerged U-boats, the hydrophone, could not be used while engines were running. That limitation explains why destroyers and other ships assigned to convoy escort duty were not heavily armed with depth charges: they had no hope of maintaining contact and attacking again and again. Nor was that the idea. It was more important for the convoy to keep moving, having driven off an attack. Only at the end of the war did the US Navy develop array hydrophones (MV) which promised to be useful from a moving escort and they were never tested in that role.

The Second World War was different because sonar (Asdic) made it possible for a moving escort to keep contact with a U-boat, attacking again and again until it was sunk. Even so, before the outbreak of the next war the Admiralty had to reckon with a lack of escorts. It initially expected that U-boats would attack singly, as in the First World War, so even a single Asdic escort could drive off an attacker, and similarly separate hunting groups would also kill most U-boats; with Asdic they would be far more efficient. Once the Germans began using multi-boat wolf-packs, the idea of driving off a lone attacker died and convoy escorts multiplied. Now the convoys did become killing grounds.

The success of convoy operations explained the change in German tactics. In January 1918 the U-boat commanded by Karl Dönitz was sunk during a convoy attack in the Mediterranean. He commented not that such attacks were inevitably dangerous, but that creating convoys made it difficult to find targets and also made it impossible to sink many of them in the available time. The tactics he evolved between wars emphasised finding convoys (code-breaking and patrol lines) and concentrating enough U-boats to get results.

Although convoy largely stopped losses of merchant ships, it did not necessarily destroy U-boats. In addition to threatening the merchant fleet, U-boats could and did threaten the Grand Fleet

and other vital naval units. Successful U-boat attacks against the Grand Fleet would have opened unacceptable possibilities, such as German surface attacks on trade (which might well have been much more effective than U-boat attacks, as some convoy raids showed) and even an invasion of the United Kingdom (an important issue in British eyes, but apparently never in German thinking).

Whether convoy is necessarily the best way to counter submarines depends on several factors, such as the enemy's ability to find ships and convoys at sea and the cost of escorts sufficiently powerful to deal with the attackers. For example, during the Cold War the Soviets fielded both an effective means of ocean surveillance (including satellites) and numerous nuclear and high-performance conventional submarines. Western navies had to face the fact that adequate escorts were so expensive that they could not be had in large numbers. The US Navy also pointed out that the submarines were not the whole problem: the Soviets also had a large naval air force which the escorts could not resist. If the Soviet submarines were like the Kaiser's U-boats, the Soviet Naval Aviation bombers with their stand-off missiles were like the High Seas Fleet. The situation was worse, because it was not at all clear that escorts had the slightest chance of finding or stopping a nuclear submarine firing homing torpedoes from the noise under a convoy, something inconceivable in the First World War.

The Admiralty and convoy

The Royal Navy had operated convoys in earlier wars, generally to the disgust of shipowners who thought that unescorted ships could get to their destinations much more quickly and economically (and who dismissed the chance that they would never get anywhere, due to raiders). It seems likely that by late 1916 the Admiralty thought it had a better answer, analogous to the technique it had already successfully used against surface raiders. It could determine the locations of the submarines by means of two rather secret sources,

The Admiralty view was that convoy and hunting were complementary operations. Because the only available underwater sensor, the hydrophone, was virtually useless at any speed, convoy escorts typically could not maintain contact with a U-boat until they destroyed her. The implicit argument was that unless U-boats were destroyed in numbers, the Germans might ultimately find some way of overwhelming convoy escorts – like the Second World War wolf-packs. Trawlers were used both as escorts (particularly for coastal convoys) and as hunters, in groups. HMS *John Cope* was an Admiralty *Strath* class trawler, completed at the end of the war (she was delivered on 19 November 1918). The gun was a 12pdr. In this photo she lacks the usual heavy depth-charge battery.

code-breaking and radio direction-finding. Analogous information had sufficed to solve the surface raider problem in 1914–15. Hunters could be vectored out on the basis of the location data. While the raiders were being run down, merchant ships could be told how to evade them. U-boats were not very mobile, so evasion should be easier than in the case of cruisers.

The reality was that evasion was sufficient protection for large numbers of separate ships only if the raider threat could be contained quickly by hunting. It was one thing for a cruiser vectored to an approximate location to spot the smoke of a raider over the horizon. It was another for a destroyer a mile from a submerged U-boat to have no way whatever of finding it, short of seeing its periscope pop up, or the track of its torpedo. This disconnect seems not to have been obvious. It is not clear how many of those involved realised that hunting without any adequate underwater sensor was unlikely to work. When Admiral Jellicoe admitted his frustration, he was saying that everything had been arranged to favour the strategy he and others had carefully developed – which was failing. He kept hoping that the intense effort to solve the location problem would make the rest of the system work.

Another problem was undue faith in the value of zig-zagging as a means of protecting merchant ships. Zig-zagging seemed to be a way of neutralising the U-boat's torpedo armament and forcing her to use her gun on the surface, where an armed merchant ship could beat her off. For example, in December 1916 Director of the Trade Department Cap Richard Webb wrote that convoy would not be of much use to a defensively armed merchant ship providing she zig-zagged properly (i.e., without taking up a predictable course). Smoke screens would soon further complicate the task of a submarine operating on the surface.[17] Director of the A/S Division agreed: 'differences of speed, loss of safety afforded by zig-zagging and the inevitable tendency of Merchant Ships to straggle at night

when under convoy, are some of the reasons against an organised system of convoy'. Another note on the file explained that there were not enough ships suitable for escort duty: 'the shortage of destroyers would not admit of their doing this work and would fall to inferior substitutes . . . If we had enough destroyers, they could be usefully employed on convoy duty in home waters and the Mediterranean'.

By 1916, everyone in a decision-making role in the Admiralty was badly overworked. It may have been enough that convoy had been abandoned in the past after careful study. No one is likely to have had time to go back to the arguments of the 1870s. Later critics were generally unaware of the extent of that study or of its logic, or for that matter of later trade-protection measures. The Admiralty had given up on convoys so long ago that no one had thought through how they should be organised or operated. Moreover, tacticians like Jellicoe were not at all happy with the implications of 'browning' shots against capital ships in close company. If capital ships in close order could be hit, what would a submarine do to a convoy of merchant ships?

Officers who had not been close to Admiralty policy-making and trade protection thinking could see the likely virtues of convoy much more clearly. That is probably why Admiral Beatty, never a staff man, became a supporter while Jellicoe, who had been intimately connected with pre-war thinking, emphatically did not.

By late 1916 the anti-submarine outlook was grim enough for a special conference to be called.[18] Chief of Staff Admiral Oliver gave a stunning commentary. One proposal on the table was to appoint a flag officer to handle ASW; Oliver thought that pointless unless the officer was given operational control of British forces. He also doubted that new ASW weapons would have much effect. The auxiliary patrol might have defeated the enemy's earlier close submarine blockade, but now he had many more U-boats (Oliver incorrectly thought 400 of them). By sending his submarines further afield, he could dissipate British forces and then quickly reconcentrate in coastal waters. The enemy coastal attack had not been broken; he was still operating off the East Coast, in the Channel and its approaches and in the Irish Sea. Jellicoe did not want to give up destroyers for ASW, arguing that they would be 'mostly a defensive measure'. Oliver wrote that they had never been

In 1918 the Admiralty was building specialised 'Kil' class hunters (which it considered fast trawlers and designated patrol gunboats). HMS *Kilour* shows her deliberately confusing profile (identically raked bow and stern, superstructure symmetrical around the single vertical funnel and a single mast, so that her course could not be estimated through a periscope).

Hunters were expected to keep attacking until they killed their U-boat quarry. This is the long high-capacity depth-charge rail of the 'Kil' class patrol gunboat HMS *Kilgobnet*.

used in a systematic offensive. 'If it can be shown that new dispositions are not possible, we must suffer our losses with such complacency as we can command', but there were real options.

Oliver saw evidence that convoy worked. Individually valuable ships, such as troopships, were already being convoyed – protected directly. The question was whether the mass of shipping should be protected in that way.[19] If the opponents of convoy were right, the escorts provided for troopships and other valuable vessels would not have given them much additional security. In reality they had proved very effective. 'Millions of troops have been carried in safety and enormous sums in specie'. Escorted ships were very rarely attacked. When they were, the submarine did not sink the whole group, even when it amounted to very few ships. An attack on two ships escorted by a French destroyer netted only one. A U-boat which encountered Italian destroyers escorting troops attacked one of the destroyers. It and the destroyer were both lost, the other destroyer rescuing survivors from the U-boat. 'If the system of escorting is given up and the loss of troopships resulted it would be very difficult to justify ourselves in abandoning a plan which has been eminently successful for two years.'

In the wake of the conference, a separate Anti-Submarine Division of the War Staff was created on 18 December 1916. It superseded the earlier (Anti) Submarine Committee. The new division would control the movements of all vessels of the auxiliary patrol (except minesweepers) and of all other vessels permanently employed in anti-submarine work, as well as the work of the Auxiliary Patrol Branch (which procured the craft). It was also responsible for materiel, including development and training (formerly under the Submarine Committee). Among other things, it intensified work on hydrophones, whose technology came to be called A/S after the name of the division. The ultimate result was active sonar, which the British called Asdic – A/S-dic (to make it

pronounceable). Initial roles, according to the 16 December 1916 memo setting up the new Division, included not only the tactics to be followed by merchant ships but also 'convoy of merchantmen' and 'trade routes and diversion of trade'. The Division would receive all reports of submarine sightings and all reports of attacks on shipping.

By late 1916 other voices had been raised in favour of convoying, with proposals as to how convoys might be organised.[20] Buried in the objections was the experience of lengthy warfare against the Board of Trade, which had resisted all attempts to impose naval control of shipping in any form. A January 1917 response to proposals from the Battle Cruiser Force, which included various forms of convoy, was that 'convoy is a difficult question, which is being examined'.[21]

To a limited extent the Royal Navy was already operating three kinds of convoy. In July 1916 it began convoying trade from Holland to England, not so much against the submarine threat as against the threat of German destroyers based at Zeebrugge. That happened to coincide with the suspension of unrestricted submarine warfare by the Germans. The Dutch operation was called a controlled sailing, the idea being that British warships would be close enough to the merchant ships to beat off attacks, but not so close that some of them would lose their neutral status. When the Norwegians suffered severe shipping losses in November, a similar system was proposed. The Trade Division opposed any form of convoy and proposed setting up a protected lane between the Shetlands and Norway, but Chief of Staff Admiral Oliver pointed out that such a lane would require at least twenty ships always at sea.[22] The alternative was Dutch-style controlled sailings, ships assembling and crossing on prearranged days. Despite misgivings as to allowing neutral ships to follow the same routes as British ships, on 3 December Admiral Beatty submitted proposals that the Norwegian ships be met by British armed trawlers at a set rendezvous at sea 130 miles from the Norwegian coast and 50 miles from Lerwick. Eastbound traffic would be escorted 50 miles from Lerwick in daylight and then the rest of the way in darkness, reaching the Norwegian coast at dawn. Traffic from Norway would travel the 130 miles in darkness and reach a rendezvous 50 miles from Lerwick at dawn. That began the Norwegian Convoy operation.

A convoy system to protect the French coal trade was created to deal with German attacks, which began in September 1916. As a shortage of coal in France became acute, the French asked for a system of controlled sailings, which were actually convoys. Quite aside from sinkings, ships were often detained in harbours because a submarine was reported nearby. That in itself drastically reduced coal shipments.[23] Over the sixty-three days between 29 October and 31 December 1916, traffic of unarmed vessels running from Dover to Bay ports was held up for twenty-eight days (of armed vessels, for fourteen days). Overall, the mere presence of submarines had created a blockade effective 30 to 40 per cent of the time. At a 2 January 1917 conference, Commander Vanvier French Navy, representing the French naval chief of staff, presented a convoy plan based on an estimate that about 800 colliers (half of them neutral) had sailed from English ports to France in November. He proposed three separate sets of convoys. The Admiralty did not want to use the word 'convoy' because of its implications for neutrals; instead it used the phrase 'controlled sailings'. Whatever the Admiralty's views of convoy in general, it could not refuse the French. At the least their idea had to be tried.

A detailed British plan was drawn up by Commander Reginald Henderson and approved by First Sea Lord Jellicoe on 25 January. The first convoy sailed from Mount's Bay to Brest on 10 February 1917.[24] Henderson, who later became Third Sea Lord in the 1930s (and was responsible for, among other things, the armoured flight deck carrier) was significant because he became an important proponent of convoy operations.

Late in 1916 many in the Admiralty thought that zig-zagging was an effective protection against submarine attack. However, it was no defence against a surface raider. By late 1916 the Germans had three of them at sea. Convoy was a reasonable defence, because one ocean escort would have a good chance of dealing with such a threat. Early in December 1916 Admiral Jellicoe became interested in this possibility and he asked that the subject be reviewed. The Trade Division produced figures showing that on a particular day (4 January 1917) 128 ships were *en route* from Halifax and elsewhere in North America to the United Kingdom, France and the Mediterranean.[25] Another 122 were in North American ports. During December an average of thirty-three British ships were at sea in the North Atlantic. Estimated monthly sailings from the main Atlantic ports (Halifax, Boston, New York, Philadelphia, Norfolk and Baltimore) were 180 to the United Kingdom and sixty-two each to France and the Mediterranean. These figures, much more than later ones, clearly defined the problem. Somewhat later, when the Admiralty was resisting introducing convoy, the problem was considerably exaggerated by using statistics showing thousands of port calls per month.[26] Jellicoe's query suggests that the statistics cited were never particularly relevant.

During the period between late 1916 and April 1917 the Admiralty repeatedly rejected calls to convoy most or all merchant ships. It made several arguments.[27] One was that a convoy was more visible than an individual merchant ship, hence would invite attack. It was considered preferable to sail valuable ships singly, each with her own escort. When the subject was reviewed at the end of 1916, the objection was that the number of escorts needed could not be provided. At the time it seemed that only destroyers were suitable. Detaching sufficient destroyers to screen convoys would immobilise the Grand Fleet and thus open the British to even worse kinds of attack. Initially it was argued that a convoy might need as many as one escort per ship escorted. As described in 1917–18, a twenty-ship convoy required eight to ten escorts. It later became apparent that something far less expensive than a destroyer could be a useful escort. In addition to sloops and the like, the British mounted a programme to arm merchant ships as escorts (not just for self-defence).

A second was that merchant ship masters would be unable to keep station, particularly at night, hence would endanger each other. It would be difficult to group ships of comparable speed. Unlike warships, merchant ships typically steamed in the open ocean at constant speed, so their masters and engineers were unused to the frequent changes of speed needed to keep station. Moreover, by operating in close formation merchant ships would have to give up the considerable advantage of zig-zagging. This may have been a matter of naval prejudice against merchant mariners with whom they did not have close association, particu- larly once the pre-war naval reserve officers in the merchant fleet had been drawn off into the Royal Navy. In practice, transatlantic convoys spent most of their time in the open ocean where U-boat attacks were unlikely and where the ships of a convoy could practice formation steaming relatively safely.

Merchant ships were the other side of the anti-submarine equation: the Germans would lose the tonnage war if the Allies could built merchant ships faster than they could be sunk. Both Britain and the United States carried out large emergency shipbuilding programmes. At its first meeting in December 1916 the Merchant Shipbuilding Advisory Committee adopted standardised production in principle. *War Aconite* was a 400ft Type A standard ship built by W Doxford and Sons, completed in 1918 (*War Shamrock*, the first of this type, was completed in August 1917). War standard construction deliberately eliminated all but one topmast, to complicate any attempt to estimate a ship's course. The single mast could telescope down. Note the raised pilot house with an open bridge atop it, adopted to make station-keeping easier in a convoy. In contrast to typical merchant ship practice, the crew was accommodated in the poop rather than in the forecastle (note the scuttles there). That would reduce casualties if the ship were mined. The prominent pipe emerging from the ship's funnel was used to divert smoke so as to eliminate the visible vertical smoke column a ship normally made (this was a Yarrow device). Some Type A ships were completed as Type AO tankers. This ship was sunk by a U-boat on 3 March 1943 as *Trefusis*. (Allan C Green via State Library of Victoria)

A third was that convoy would cost ship capacity, because ships would be delayed in sailing and in reaching port to suit convoy schedules. This argument turned out to be specious. Current practice, which was not working, was to hold ships in harbour if a submarine was known to be nearby. The Ministry of Shipping found that the loss of carrying capacity due to this practice was enormous, comparable to the capacity lost to submarine attack. To some extent the port congestion argument was sometimes justified on the basis of figures on port visits, which were misleading because coastal trading ships were included as equivalent to ocean traffic. It is not clear how seriously this argument was advanced, given the figures on Atlantic traffic which Admiral Jellicoe already had.

A fourth was that a convoy was an ideal target for a 'browning' torpedo attack, of the sort that preoccupied the Royal Navy before and during the war. In fact by this time no one had used 'browning' tactics successfully (torpedoes were too inaccurate at long range). Captured German tactical handbooks showed that, rather than encouraging long-range shots, the Germans warned against wasting valuable torpedoes. U-boat commanders closed in before firing. The Germans did not become interested in long-range anti- convoy shots until the Second World War, when they deployed pattern-running torpedoes.

A fifth, raised during the review of convoy in January 1917, was that convoys would have to assemble in the open sea, placing a heavy burden on navigation. Such assembly would also present a U-boat with an attractive target, as ships milled about until all had joined. Such assembly at sea was connected with the absence of a

suitable assembly port (it is not clear why Halifax and Bermuda were not considered sufficient, as they were both used successfully before the United States entered the Second World War). US entry into the war ended the problem, as US ports were used. It also seemed that convoys would suffer increased losses in coastal (pilotage) waters from mines since, presumably, the swept channels were too narrow for convoys.

The French convoy project seems to have been crucial, because it demonstrated what convoy could do and because it created an advocate within the navy in Commander Henderson. He seems to have told Maurice Hankey, the Secretary of the War Cabinet, about it. Hankey later wrote that in February 1917 he kept looking at daily figures of sinkings, becoming more and more depressed. On 11 February he wrote a memo describing a convoy system. It seems almost certain that this was the result of Henderson's comments to him, but in his memoir *The Supreme Command* he does not say so (he may have felt that to credit Henderson, who was alive when the memoir was written but not when it was published, would be to damage his reputation, since he had gone far outside official channels to talk to Hankey). In any case, Hankey in turn interested new Prime Minister Lloyd George, who assembled First Lord Carson, First Sea Lord Jellicoe and Director of Anti-Submarine Division Duff for breakfast on 13 February.[28]

Hankey recalled that they admitted they were already convoying transports and agreed to inquire about the results of a big experimental convoy of eight transports from Australia (which does not figure in the Technical History of convoy). He lacked the information to defeat the usual counter-arguments. He recalls that Prime Minister Lloyd George agreed with him, but could not drive the matter through. For the next two months, Lloyd George was intensely concerned with the Nivelle Offensive in France.

It appears that the outcome of the breakfast was that on 23 February 1917 Jellicoe held an Admiralty conference on the practicality of convoy.[29] Ten masters of merchant ships were invited. Jellicoe first pointed out that station-keeping would be essential. The ideal formation was line abreast, with an escort on either beam, because a submarine would feel limited to attacking the wing ships

because she might be run down if she tried to attack the centre of the formation. Alternative formations would be line ahead and two divisions in line ahead. He also raised the possibility of 'browning' shots. Any straggler would be liable to attack. Jellicoe asked whether eight merchant ships differing in speed by about 2 knots could keep station $2\frac{1}{2}$ cables (500 yds) apart in two columns 5 cables (1000 yds) apart going down the Channel. The masters considered this impossible; those left (not having gone into the navy) in the Merchant Marine were not reliable enough. One master, who had been in a twelve-ship convoy between Alexandrovsk and Archangel (presumably organised by the Russian Navy), said that station-keeping was quite impossible. No convoy could maintain formation at night without lights. With current low-quality coal it would be difficult for a ship to maintain constant speed. It might be possible for two ships to keep station, but not even for three to do so. The assembled masters told Jellicoe that they would prefer to sail alone.

A note appended in February 1919 pointed out that the group assembled was hardly representative, because the meeting was called so urgently and because two of the masters, who arrived late, were barred from attending.[30] Five commanded coasting vessels, a community which vehemently rejected convoying as late as the summer of 1918. Two of the remaining four were masters of ocean-going vessels, both recently torpedoed (one under escort of a destroyer, the other an Admiralty Collier). Most did not 'represent the better and most intelligent type of British Master Mariners'. The writer suggested that, had the meeting included a fair number of masters of large ocean-going liners and freighters, the conclusions would have been rather different and, he was sure, would have supported convoy unanimously.

In April 1917 the situation seemed desperate. Of every four ships that left the United Kingdom, only three returned. The Germans claimed that at this rate the United Kingdom would be defeated by August; the British Ministry of Shipping thought that by October shipping would be inadequate to meet minimum demands.[31] Although the United States had entered the war, without adequate shipping US troops and materiel could not be brought to bear against the Germans. Every proposed measure other than

The US Navy's contribution to U-boat hunting (as opposed to convoy) was a massive fleet of small sub-chasers. They worked in groups of three, two using directional hydrophones to fix the target, the third making a depth-charge run. Communication was by radio-telephone rather than the wireless telegraph used by most warships. The sub-chaser programme was inspired by the motor launches built by Elco for the Royal Navy and the US Navy's view was that they were too small for their open-water job. However, after the war final U-boat force commander Captain Andreas Michelsen wrote that once their listening devices were ready for service, the sub-chasers were more effective than their British and French counterparts owing to their speed and sea-keeping qualities (their crews might have disagreed: they rolled badly and were too small for the seas they often encountered). In March 1918 the Allied Naval Council recommended that the first thirty-six sub-chasers go to Corfu to support the Otranto Barrage. After some debate, in April 1918 it was decided to base the next thirty-six at Plymouth and the next thirty-six after that at Queenstown in Ireland. Later it was decided to double both forces and the repair ship *Hannibal* was sent to Queenstown to support the force there. Neither force seems to have grown beyond the original thirty-six boats. Queenstown ultimately supported six divisions (six boats each) based at Queenstown, one division each operating out of Queenstown, Berehaven and Holyhead, plus two in reserve. Plans to base divisions at Waterford and Milford Haven were not implemented before the end of the war. Another eighteen, originally meant for Plymouth, were based at Brest. At the end of the war, after the Austrian surrender precluded access to Austrian naval bases, German U-boats tried to get home via the Straits of Gibraltar. Seven (of a group of nine) sub-chasers *en route* to Europe via the Azores were redirected to Gibraltar to help stop them. The US Navy considered that there was good evidence that they destroyed one U-boat (presumably *U 34*). This late-war photograph shows sub-chasers in the Azores, the stopping-off place *en route* to European waters. The boats in the foreground (*SC 223, 330, 180, 363, 331* and *353*) were among those deployed to Gibraltar. By the end of the war, a total of 135 sub-chasers were in European waters. (Chris Cavas)

convoy had failed and with the entry of the United States into the war numerous potential escorts became available. The new Ministry of Shipping controlled all British merchant ships, hence could order ships to sail in convoy. On 26 April Director Anti-Submarine Division formally called for convoys. All vessels slower than 15 knots sailing between the North and South Atlantic and the United Kingdom should be convoyed. Surface warships would escort the convoys to ocean meeting points where they would be handed over to anti-submarine escorts. First Sea Lord Admiral Jellicoe approved the proposal the next day. The first trial convoy left Gibraltar on 10 May and the first trial convoy from the United States left Newport News on 24 May. Both were considered entirely successful and the convoy system soon began full operation. It dramatically reduced losses to U-boats. By the end of October 1917, ninety-nine homeward convoys brought 1502 ships to the United Kingdom, only ten of which were lost before the convoys dispersed.

The convoy system was expanded again and again to cover areas U-boats attacked where merchant ships were not protected. For example, initially convoys dispersed off the British coast so that ships could go to various ports. U-boats attacked them; ocean convoys were continued up to the ports. Coastal convoys had to be formed (against bitter opposition by many traders). Some of them were quite large, but there was no appreciation in the First World War of the 'law of large convoys' discovered during the next war, which showed that very large convoys were more efficient than small ones – they were no easier for U-boats to find and they required fewer escorts per escorted ship.

When the United States entered the war on 6 April 1917, President Wilson compared the rational strategy of convoy with the current British hunting strategy, which he called 'hunting around the farm' for hornets rather than concentrating forces where they were. His representative Admiral Sims pressed for convoy as the ideal offensive ASW measure. However, as late as May 1917 US official naval opinion was opposed to convoy.[32]

Exactly when and how the Admiralty changed course is a ticklish issue. After the war Lloyd George claimed that he personally forced a recalcitrant Admiralty to accept the convoy strategy which won the shipping war (in effect the first battle of the Atlantic). On 25 April the War Cabinet voted for the Prime Minister to investigate the entire ASW question. The next day Duff submitted his Minute proposing convoy. It is not at all clear that he was aware of the War Cabinet decision. On 29 April Hankey wrote in his diary that he was depressed over the U-boat offensive and he spent the morning dictating a long memo to Lloyd George, apparently unaware that Jellicoe had already approved convoy. Lloyd George had already planned to visit the Admiralty on 30 April; when he got there he learned that convoy was no longer an issue, but he pressed for other changes, including the appointment of Sir Eric Geddes as Controller. Commander Henderson became the Royal Navy's convoy expert. He apparently wrote the convoy volumes of the post-war *Technical History* series. Having adopted convoy, the Admiralty did not abandon hunting. Considerable surface forces, which might otherwise have been added to convoy escorts (for example in the poorly-escorted Mediterranean), were retained in large hunting groups. How irrational was that?

Convoy dramatically reduced the rate of sinkings but it did not kill U-boats at a high rate. A US officer observed that U-boat commanders did not seem to fear attacking convoys; they merely enjoyed very little success in doing so. If the Germans ever had enough U-boats and if they could co-ordinate well enough, a convoy might turn from a haven for merchant ships into a tasty meal for a pack of U-boats. Ultimately the only ways to prevent that were either to destroy U-boats closer to their bases (at or near source, in later terms) or to find and kill them in their hunting areas. Many critics of hunting did not take into account how well British signals intelligence worked. The gap was in converting its information (and other reports), which was inevitably approximate, into a dead U-boat. In 1918 it must have seemed that masses of ships using hydrophones, which were now becoming effective and also using increasingly effective anti-submarine weapons, had a real chance of killing enough U-boats to hold back the threat of effective anti-convoy tactics.

Convoy escort was possible only because relatively weak ships could attack and kill submarines. If something attacking a convoy could destroy its ships rapidly enough and if it could keep up with the convoy, the convoy was converted from refuge to disaster. In 1917 two fast German minelayer-cruisers, *Brummer* and *Bremse*, attacked a convoy *en route* to Norway. They sank the escorting destroyers and then all of the merchant ships. A second raid using destroyers was also successful. A much larger fleet attack against a Scandinavian convoy was aborted only because inept German intelligence thought a convoy was at sea when it was not.

These German operations showed that convoy was effective only so long as the German surface fleet was neutralised by the Grand Fleet and other British efforts. In September 1918 the US Navy's planning group in London asked what would happen if the Germans decided to send battlecruisers on a raid into the Atlantic. What, if anything, would or could stop them? It would not do to weaken the Grand Fleet, so the US Navy based three battleships at Berehaven in Ireland and earmarked another four on the US Atlantic coast for possible duty (they were ultimately to move to Halifax). The plan was to reinforce the ocean escorts of convoys, particularly those supporting the US Army in France, with single dreadnought battleships. These were not the ones assigned to the Grand Fleet. A co-ordinated plan (designated BCR) was announced by the Admiralty and the Navy Department on 4 November 1918. Renewed efforts were made to convince the Japanese to lend the Allies their four *Kongo* class battlecruisers, at that time the only battlecruisers in the world not

already spoken for.[33] The Germans seem never to have considered such a raid, perhaps because they could not see how the ships would survive after reaching the Atlantic (some of the US planners imagined that they might run through the Mediterranean to a haven in Turkey).

Convoy in action

The Germans adapted their tactics to convoy operations. By 1918 U-boats were sometimes attacking in pairs, although never in threes. A paired attack gave a better chance of sinking many of the ships in convoy (in a 1918 summary of anti-convoy tactics, the Admiralty pointed out that whichever U-boat fired first often provided enough warning for the convoy to evade the second U-boat).[34] After the war, U-boat force commander Captain Andreas Michelsen observed that U-boat commanders acting together would be less likely to admit that the mass of escorts cowed them; they would not want to pull back in sight of their comrades.[35] Multiple attacks might have required some form of real-time control. Due to the limitations of existing W/T, it could not be exercised from a great distance. Early in April 1917, as the unrestricted U-boat campaign developed (but before convoys), U-boat force commander Captain Hermann Bauer proposed equipping one of the large U-boats as a radio command ship, to operate in the southwestern approaches to the British Isles.[36] The Admiralstab was uninterested and the idea died; the earmarked U-boat was assigned to independent patrol in the Azores.

Initial Allied ideas of German attack tactics were based more on analysis than on detailed intelligence.[37] It was known that the ideal position was ahead of the convoy, within the limiting lines of approach ('danger angle'). The U-boat might attack either from between two columns of the convoy or from the flank, but 'whatever he does, once he has committed himself to one form of attack he cannot subsequently change his mind. To be successful, the final stages of an attack must be made at slow speed, otherwise there is a very good chance of his periscope being given away by the feather and even if not depth-charged or rammed, his attack will probably be frustrated'. For an attack between the columns, the U-boat would approach at slow speed or let the convoy overtake it. When about a mile ahead, the U-boat would turn at right angles to the course of the convoy, so as to be between the columns when the convoy passed over it. Judging by sound or timing, it would come up to periscope depth so as to fire (the U-boat commander might 'possibly bring off the double event by using his stern tubes'). If the approach was miscalculated, or if the commander's nerve failed, he might try a browning shot (in fact such shots were forbidden; this was a remnant of earlier British thinking). As for gyro shots, it was known that the Germans could angle their torpedoes by as much as 90°, but there was no record of their having done so on board their submarines. Angling made for less accurate shots and a sharply-angled torpedo could not keep depth very well while turning, so it might broach and give its position away. About a year later the Admiralty accepted that U-boats would not take 'browning' shots, but assumed that they might angle their torpedoes (which was never done).

Once he had fired all the torpedoes he could without undue risk, the U-boat commander would take his boat as deep as possible to avoid depth charges and sweeps. Without any reason to go slow, he could use full helm and speed to get away from the last position in which he might have been spotted. He would use his

The Type B standard ship *War Magpie* went further towards eliminating verticals which would give away a ship's course. Her kingposts could be folded down at sea, her funnel was cut down and her single mast was stepped dead amidships. She was completed by Doxford in 1918 and was wrecked (as the Japanese *Kobryu Maru*) on 10 March 1928. Type A was a single deck (in each hold) ship, Type B a two-decker. Both had the same capacity, 5030 GRT. Both displaced 11,375 tons loaded. (Allan C Green via State Library of Victoria)

hydrophones to be sure that he was clear of the convoy, waiting until it was hull-down over the horizon before surfacing. If conditions were favourable, he might surface and run ahead beyond the convoy's horizon to reattack.

The U-boat had to approach at slow speed because it had to conserve battery capacity for post-attack escape. Given limited battery capacity, it is not clear how many, if any, attack-reattack cycles any U-boat could execute. The same 1917 analysis pointed out that in an hour a U-boat could cover 7nm on a sprint and drift (showing a periscope) basis. That too would run down her battery charge. If the U-boat commander expected to be hunted after he attacked, he would be particularly anxious not to run his battery down beforehand, for example, in a high-speed rush towards a convoy.[38]

Up to a point, bad weather favoured the submarine, since she could proceed at greater average speed for a short time, not limited by the feather a periscope would create. However, if conditions became much worse (probably sea state 6 to 8), there was a critical depth above which the submarine lost control and might suddenly shoot to the surface. It might take 5 to 10 minutes to force her back underwater. The critical depth generally exceeded periscope depth and without the use of a periscope the submarine could not attack. Under these circumstances U-boats typically dived to 60 to 80ft and went dead slow, about 1.5 knots. The U-boat would then feel little motion and her crew could rest.

Occasionally U-boats lost trim and popped to the surface even in good weather. During an attack on a Mediterranean convoy on 4 October 1918, *UB 68* accidentally surfaced after firing a torpedo (she did not compensate quickly enough for the weight discharged). She was spotted by a freighter, which opened fire and hit her twice. Although she submerged at once, she had been damaged badly enough that she had to come back to the surface before sinking. She was the last U-boat sunk in a Mediterranean convoy action.

The Germans created a dummy convoy against which U-boat commanders at the Submarine School at Kiel could practice their attacks. The U-boat's problem was to determine the approximate course of the convoy without being seen. Typically the convoy was spotted by the columns of smoke of the ships, which could be seen beyond the horizon. U-boats could also detect a distant convoy by

its sound, using their hydrophones. Hydrophones could best be used only at a considerable distance, because a ship made relatively little propeller noise dead ahead. A U-boat could therefore place herself in position to be rammed, thinking that she was actually far from her target. Under ideal sound conditions, the U-boat would presumably approach on the surface using sound, but stop her approach before the ships themselves could be seen. She would proceed slowly on the surface, taking a series of bearings every 10 to 15 minutes to determine the course and speed of the convoy. If the convoy was zig-zagging, the U-boat might take at least an hour and perhaps two hours, to definitely determine the mean course of the convoy from beyond the horizon. The U-boat would then close the convoy on a course 45° from the mean course of the convoy, seeing to reach a point about a mile ahead of the convoy on its mean course. She would dive as soon as there was danger of being seen (in average visibility, when the funnels could be made out distinctly over the horizon).

Once in position, the U-boat would move towards the convoy at low speed, counting on the onward rush of the convoy to carry it into range. That placed her in a favourable attack position whether the convoy continued on the same zig-zag leg or turned onto the other leg. The U-boat typically used the leading wing ship of the convoy as a mark to get into position, but generally attacked the second or a later ship in that line. Having fired a torpedo, the U-boat would if possible pass down the space between two columns of the convoy at periscope depth, turning at right angles to the columns to deliver bow and then stern shots at ships in both columns. Alternatively, she could continue down the columns and deliver two angled shots (at 90°).[39]

All of this meant that denying the approach from ahead might well save the convoy from attack. A convoy needed to keep a sharp lookout in the mean direction it was going, its zig-zag pattern had to vary and on sighting a submarine close to or on the track of a torpedo, the convoy had to alter course together at once to force the U-boat to dive.

Note that to close with the convoy the U-boat had to approach on the surface, diving only once it might be spotted by the convoy. It followed that a blimp or kite balloon above the convoy, which extended the horizon, would much complicate the U-boat's task and probably cause it to break off. That made blimps, which had the endurance to remain aloft above slow-moving convoys, valuable ASW assets.

Because convoys were not effective killing grounds, at least in theory a U-boat commander who encountered one could take time to choose his targets. If he was unlikely to sink more than one or two ships in a convoy, he might as well select larger ships. The British observed in the late summer of 1918 that U-boats were doing exactly that.[40] The percentage of ships over 6000 tons attacked increased from 12.2 per cent in the first quarter of 1918 to 21.1 per cent in August; the per cent of such ships among sinkings rose from 7.4 per cent to 25.9 per cent of the total in August. The compensating reduction came almost entirely from ships of under 4000 tons. In the first quarter of 1918 they accounted for 68.3 per cent of attacks, but in August they were down to 57.7 per cent. This was not due to a change in the distribution of ships of various sizes sailing (there was a slight increase in very large ships of over 10,000 tons). It was not clear whether the U-boats were sinking larger merchant ships because they were becoming more efficient or whether the circumstances favoured

Although conventional standard ships could be built remarkably fast, production could be improved further by fabricating portions of a ship at inland bridge-building and engine makers and assembling them at a new specially laid out yard. To this end all frames were made straight and ships' sides vertical (bilges were cut off at a 45° angle). The hull had a hard chine and the stern was cut off flat. There was no sheer between the masts. Turbine (rather than the usual reciprocating) power was planned, with watertube boilers, for easy transportation from distant plants. These ships were called N (national) ships. Eleven ships of N1 design and sixty-six of N design were ordered, most from conventional builders. The only special yard was an eight-berth plant at Haverton Hill (which built the N1 design), approved late in 1917. *War Courage* (built by Armstrong Whitworth, completed in October 1918) is shown. Note her mast stepped against her funnel, to make course estimation difficult and the scuttles at her stern for her crew. She was sunk by a U-boat on 16 October 1943 under the name *Essex Lane*.(Allan C Green via State Library of Victoria)

them. Sinkings were also occurring further from land. To deal with such attacks, convoy escorts would have to cover their charges further out to sea, but there were not enough suitable escorts (destroyers); also 'their radius of action and sea-keeping qualities were not all that could be desired'. The best alternative was the Patrol Gunboat ('Kil' class), though it was necessarily less effective attacking U-boats because it was so much slower. The US Navy was to be asked for help in the form of either Patrol Gunboats or something better.[41]

The German U-boat command had no means of ocean surveillance. However, from time to time it obtained intelligence indicating standing routes. In April 1918 papers from the US freighter *Lake Michigan* indicated that convoys of fast ships from the United States dispersed after ships passed the Fastnet or St. George's Channel. Early in May five U-boats were concentrated in the area between the Lizard and northern France. This was not a combined attack on a convoy, but rather an attempt to saturate an area through which ships were expected to pass without escorts. The operation failed. One U-boat made contact with two convoys but failed to attack (on his return, her CO was ordered to U-Boat School to study convoy attack procedure). A second detected the fast liner *Olympic*, which she could not attack or evade (by diving) in time; the liner rammed her and sank her. The radioed assignment of a third to attack *Olympic* tipped off the British and HMS *D 4* torpedoed her. The other two achieved nothing.[42]

It did not help that the British could read messages the Germans sent to co-ordinate U-boats. In January 1918 two big U-boats (*U 156* and *U 157*) communicated with each other and with the control station at Nauen. *U 156* signalled that the rendezvous had been compromised. When she arrived there, a British

submarine fired three torpedoes at her. Fortunately two missed and the third failed to explode. An early May rendezvous was less successful. *U 62* arranged a meeting with *U 153*, using a new code the Germans thought unbreakable. *U 154* picked up the message and also came to the rendezvous, to be greeted by a British submarine which sank her. Arriving slightly late, *U 153* warned off *U 62* and both survived. When they got home, the Admiralstab refused to believe that its new code had been compromised, but the orders given to the British submarine prove that it had been.

Convoy was always advertised as an offensive strategy, but through 1918 there was considerable evidence that convoy escort commanders considered it enough to drive off submarines they detected. The situation was bad enough to prompt vigorous memos from US Force Commander Vice Admiral Sims and also to cause the Admiralty to convene a conference on the subject on 28 May 1918.[43] The Royal Navy and the US Navy planning divisions issued a joint memo describing the situation. As an example of current defensive thinking, they published an after-action report. A destroyer zig-zagging ahead of a convoy spotted an oil streak which was recognisably a submarine wake. The destroyer ran in and dropped a single depth charge set for 100ft. Fresh oil was seen, so the destroyer dropped another single charge. Now strongly smelling oil and bubbles were seen, so a third depth charge was dropped. When the ship passed over that spot at slow speed, much strongly smelling oil was seen. 'As the convoy was now at a safe distance away (10 to 12 miles) and as there would be very little change of the submarine renewing the attack . . . I decided to rejoin the convoy.' The Escort Commander approved. He did not understand what had to be done and had been approved in the General Estimate of the Situation approved by the Allied Naval Council: 'we must assure ourselves that on every occasion of contact with a submarine the maximum tactical use shall be made of that contact'.[44] The destroyer commander should not have abandoned the scene of the attack without having obtained a decision, 'although every indication should have led these officers to be satisfied with nothing less'. The best method of defending a convoy was to destroy any submarines found nearby. The convoy had to be seen as a submarine trap. The mission of protecting the convoy should be secondary to the mission of destroying U-boats.

For example, in open water, if a submarine were sighted ahead of a convoy in position to attack, up to 4 miles away, at least half the escorts should attack, using up a large proportion of their depth charges if the submarine left any definite trace. The destroyers had no means of detecting the submarine once it dived, but they could pepper its likely course with depth charges, on the assumption that, having fired at the convoy, the U-boat would probably turn away and run off at an average speed of 6 knots. Given the great number of depth charges now carried and the supposed deterioration of enemy morale, it might be possible to change escort formation in favour of offensive action. The wing escorts could be stationed further astern and one escort could follow the convoy, zig-zagging. Systematic offensive tactics should be developed.

About this time the Admiral at Milford Haven reported that although there had been several attacks on convoys, offensive tactics had produced no tangible results. He wanted more escorts concentrated around the quarters and the rear of the convoy, the route a submarine running down the columns would have to take after attacking.

As late as September 1918 the Admiralty made a clear

distinction between convoy as a means of controlling losses to U-boats and other methods, such as hunting, which would more likely destroy U-boats. Escorts' reactions just were not effective enough and the escorts were more likely simply to drive off U-boats – which might often be enough. Reports on offensive escort tactics continued to be produced through the autumn of 1918.[45]

Ominously, by August 1918 it seemed that the steady fall in tonnage lost to U-boats had bottomed out over the past four or five months. The total tonnage (British and foreign) of all sizes sunk by enemy action was about 265,000 tons in each month from April on. In home waters, ships were still being sunk mostly within 50 miles of shore (all sinkings in January, 86.9 per cent in July), but the U-boats were beginning to work further offshore (13.1 per cent of sinkings in July were more than 50 miles from shore; the trend towards sinkings this far out apparently began in April, with a jump from 2.3 per cent to 10.3 per cent).

In September 1918 the Admiralty reported to the War Cabinet that the ASW situation was deteriorating because increasing demands for convoy escorts had forced it to scale back hunting and to avoid forming new hunting groups.[46] The Royal Navy thought that the German U-boat force hit its low-water mark in May 1918, when the Dover Barrage and patrols across the Straits of Dover were most effective. At about the same time the Germans mounted their final offensive in France and it became urgent to bring more American troops across. The Royal Navy had to scrap its hunting plans, the ships involved being shifted to patrol and convoy escort. As a consequence, although the troops were successfully brought across, fewer U-boats were sunk. The Admiralty was also aware that the Germans were stepping up their efforts to build more U-boats.

Moreover, the Germans were now operating U-boats on both sides of the Atlantic, forcing the US Navy to keep some of its ASW force on the US East Coast. That further reduced the submarine-killing (as opposed to shipping-protection) effort. Moreover, the new U-boats had heavier guns, so better transatlantic escort ships were needed. Merchant ships needed more powerful guns (an Admiralty memo cited an SOS which simply read 'gun outranged'). The convoy system was stabilising losses, but it was not killing enough U-boats and as the U-boat fleet grew it would probably sink more ships. The Admiralty estimated that 160 U-boats were available and that by the end of 1918, even at the most favourable rate of sinking U-boats, there would be 180, more than the Germans had ever had before. The convoy strategy consider-ably reduced the productivity of each U-boat, but it could not destroy enough of them. The situation is 'not one free from anxiety – an anxiety which my Colleagues in the Cabinet may overlook in a way which is impossible in land warfare'.

In fact the Admiralty, which was usually well-informed about the U-boat situation, was more pessimistic than it need have been. During 1918, for the first time in the war, the Germans lost more U-boats than they completed, so that on 11 November they had 134 operational compared to 142 on 1 January.[47] In 1918 convoy escorts sank ten U-boats, compared to eighteen by hunters.[48] Another eighteen were mined. Six were torpedoed, presumably all by submarines. In 1917, convoy escorts sank six U-boats, compared to eight by patrols and hunters – the hunters were only beginning to be organised. Patrols had accounted for ten U-boats in 1915–16. During that same period submarines sank five U-boats and in 1917 they sank seven more, for a total of at least eighteen sunk by submarines. Mines accounted for ten U-boats in 1915–16,

The United States began a huge emergency shipbuilding programme upon entering the war in 1917. It included the creation of several fabricated-ship yards, the largest of which was at Hog Island (American International Shipbuilding Co.), just outside Philadelphia. *Schenectady*, shown here, exemplifies the yard's Design 1022 cargo ships, with the absolutely flat sheer and largely parallel hull sides characteristic of fabricated ships. Bows were vertical, but there was no attempt to provide a vertical stern to confuse a U-boat commander. The US Shipping Board listed its designs in a 1000 series, so this was the 22nd design. The yard called it Type A. Capacity was 7500 DWT (390 x 54 x 27.5ft) and it was turbine-powered. All 110 ships of this contract were completed. Other fabricated cargo ship designs were Nos. 1023 (Submarine Boat Corp main yard at Newark): 154 built, 116 of them for the Shipping Board, thirty-two of 150 ships cancelled]; 5075 tons DWT and 1025 (Harriman Type Merchant Shipbuilding Co., 9000 DWT, sixty-two built, six cancelled, forty of them at Harriman, Pennsylvania). *Schenectady* (Yard No. 511) was completed in May 1919. (Dr Stephen P Roberts)

despite the poor performance of British mines and for twenty in 1917: a total of at least forty-eight through the war. All of these figures may be incomplete, because a total of nineteen U-boats were lost to unknown causes during the war.

It seems that the Royal Navy concluded from its First World War experience that in a future war it would again have to combine convoy with hunting. In the inter-war period the Royal Navy assumed that a convoy would have a limited escort intended mainly to drive off single attacking submarines. Escort numbers would be limited partly due to the mass scrapping of destroyers demanded under the London Naval Treaty of 1930.[49] The service also planned to form hunting groups, the theory clearly being that with the advent of sonar (Asdic) a submarine located by signals intelligence could be run down and sunk. Some destroyers were given very heavy depth charge batteries specifically so that they could form hunting formations. Wolf-pack attacks on convoys changed the situation. Convoy escorts had to be strengthened, using corvettes which had been intended for coastal operations (but were available in sufficient numbers). Since U-boats could no longer simply be driven off, convoys became the killing ground for them. The very different reality of the Second World War should not colour evaluation of First World War tactics and force allocation.

The Supply Side of the Equation

The other side of the anti-U-boat war, or rather the war against the German anti-shipping offensive, was to preserve and build up Allied

shipping stock, or rather Allied shipping capacity, which was not necessarily the same thing. If ships could be built faster than they could be sunk, the German campaign would be frustrated. The numbers involved were huge. British losses alone during 1917 amounted to about 3.7 million gross tons: 1195 ships. The British lost 1.2 million tons (396) ships in 1916, which was much worse than 1915 (854,000 tons, 277 ships).[50] Even that was only about two-thirds of what the German navy had promised before the campaign. The capacity of a large freighter was 5000 to 8000 gross tons, so to make up for the losses about 460 large freighters had to be built. Overall, at the end of 1917 Great Britain, France and Italy had 18 million tons of shipping, compared to 24.5 million pre-war and 5.5 million were in direct war service. During 1917 the British, who had the largest shipbuilding capacity in the world, launched 1.16 million tons, not enough to replace losses the previous year and total 1917 production outside Germany and her allies was only 1.688 million tons. It was estimated that the Allies had to move 32 million tons per year. If a ship averaged four round trips, the Allies needed at a minimum eight million tons of shipping outside military requirements. More round trips could make up for a smaller shipping pool. Conversely, anything which caused ships to wait in port reduced shipping efficiency, hence ramp up the total needed.

The pinch in shipping affected strategy. Given free use of the sea, the Allies could carry out peripheral operations like the one at Gallipoli. If any of those operations succeeded, it would enormously increase the burden on the Germans. In 1917 substantial British and French land forces were in place in Salonika, from which, it was hoped, they might eventually advance into Serbia and then into Austria-Hungary. They were sustained by sea. Similarly, the Italian army facing the Austrians lived off supplies carried to Italy by sea, because the country could not sustain them by itself. The situation in the spring of 1917 was so bad that it would soon no longer be possible to maintain the force in Salonika, which in turn was keeping Greece neutral and pro-Allied. Greece in turn helped keep the Germans and the Turks out of the Mediterranean and thus helped preserve an essential Allied line of maritime communications.

By December 1916 the British recognised that the shipping situation was becoming grim, so they appointed a Shipping Controller with wide powers. He began an emergency shipbuilding

Design 1024 was Hog Island's Type B troopship (8000 tons DWT, 437 x 58 x 36ft). Of seventy ships ordered, fifty-eight were cancelled. This fabricated design was superseded by the conventional Designs 1029 (the '535 trooper', after its overall length (13,000 DWT, of which ten were built for the Shipping Board – three cancelled) and six to the same design after the war for private companies and 1095 (the '502 trooper', of which thirteen were ordered, but six were completed to Design 1029). *Cantigny* (Yard No. 670) was the second of the series, completed in August 1920 for the US Army and sold as in 1925 to become a civilian passenger-cargo ship.

programme.[51] The situation was exacerbated by the drastic decline in British merchant shipbuilding during the war, as the Admiralty took over most British shipbuilding capacity. That applied not only to new construction but also to repairs of existing ships.[52] For example, it designed important combatants such as sloops to merchant standards specifically to make use of the large pre-war merchant shipbuilding base. In April 1916 the Board of Trade, which was responsible for shipping, stated that naval orders had effectively crowded out merchant ship construction. That is why, for example, an incomplete liner ordered for Italy was available on the slip for completion as the aircraft carrier *Argus* in 1918. Merchant ships were ordered abroad, but foreign yards could not match British capacity.

The new merchant ship programme emphasised foreign orders because they did not compete with the Admiralty for British ship-building capacity.[53] After several false starts, the solution adopted in May 1917 was to make the Admiralty responsible for both naval *and* merchant shipbuilding, so that a single agency could decide how to balance the two. Trade-offs were not obvious: for example, was it better to build destroyers and other craft intended to neutralise U-boats, or to build more merchant ships to replace those the U-boats sank? Some decisions had already been made. In March 1917 three of the four new *Hood* class battlecruisers were suspended specifically to free capacity for merchant shipbuilding.[54] In May Prime Minister Lloyd George took the unprecedented step of making a civilian, Sir Eric Geddes, Controller (in effect Third Sea Lord), with the new responsibility. Geddes was famous for his efficiency in solving the problem of supply railways behind the lines in France.

The two key factors in British shipbuilding were steel and

labour; the country already had the largest shipbuilding plant in the world. By 1917 both were in short supply. When Lord Kitchener recruited his 'new armies' in 1915–16, he refused to cut back recruiting to leave men in industries supporting the war effort, despite pleas by other Ministers. He also refused to set an upper limit on the size of his army. The Royal Navy fought back, gaining measures which prohibited men in key trades from joining the army; in 1915 it accounted for 80 per cent of all men prohibited from joining the army. Once a draft was instituted at the beginning of 1916, the Royal Navy argued that heavy shipbuilding work could not be done by women, so that shipyard workers had to be exempt. It managed to resist calls in 1917–18 to release men from industry for the army in France, for example during the emergency due to the German attack in April 1918. The Admiralty also had to fight for steel allocation and also for industrial capacity (for example, the mushrooming army needed many more heavy guns). For all of these reasons the Admiralty was far better placed than the new Ministry of Shipping to press forward with a massive commercial shipbuilding and ship repair programme. Presumably Lloyd George doubted that it would do that unless a civilian was placed in charge.

Ideas as to what should be built shifted from time to time. In March 1917 the Admiralty advised the Shipping Controller to build small (about 2000-ton) ships.[55] It argued that the damage a U-boat could do was limited by the number of torpedoes available on a given trade route; by the percentage of hits; and by the average tonnage of ships sunk. Even a large merchant ship could be sunk by the same torpedo it took to sink a small one, but the less a torpedo bought, the less net damage a given U-boat force could inflict. This particular analysis discounted the fact that the effort to build a ship was not proportional to tonnage and smaller ships required disproportionately large crews.

The first standardised ships were ordered some time early in 1917.[56] They were improved to make them less vulnerable to submarine attack. When the standard designs were being developed, convoy lay in the future. It seemed that ship speed was key to survival: a ship making over 12 knots was more immune to attack

than a slower one.[57] British policy was therefore to accept a trial or design speed of 11.5 knots (sea speed about 10 knots) for most ships, but to seek a sea speed of about 13.5 knots if ships of 450ft length could be quickly and economically built (their 450ft F1 and F2 designs, their largest and fastest, had a rated speed of 13 knots). The British hoped that many shipowners would be interested in such fast ships for 'special trade requirements'. The main survivability feature was an added bulkhead, enabling a ship to survive the flooding of any single hold or compartment or two compartments amidships. In effect they were adding as many bulkheads as possible without losing cargo capacity. It proved impossible, however, to design a 450ft ship to a two-compartment standard. The bulkheads were also strengthened. Shaft tunnels were blocked at the engine room so that a ship could not flood through them and suction pipes to compartments were given non-return valves, so that the sea could not simply run up through them. In the 450-foot standard ships engine and boiler rooms were separated by a cross-bunker.[57] By this time there was intense interest in complicating U-boat fire control by making it difficult to decide a ship's course. Like the roughly contemporary 'Kil' class gunboats and '24 Class' sloops, the new standard ships were designed with only one mast and funnel, as close together as possible; the usual derricks fore and aft were designed to fold down. However, unlike the US 'Hog Islanders', all the standard ships had conventional counter sterns easily distinguished from their bows.

In July 1917 Geddes set an annual goal of 4.6 million tons, including 3.1 million tons of merchant ships, about six times the amount completed in 1916. Merchant shipbuilding was to be accelerated gradually over the next 18 months: 1.566 million tons in all in 1917 and 2.3 million in 1918.[58] There was some difficulty in providing sufficient labour, as the increase Geddes obtained went mostly to repairs. There were no large transfers of labour from naval to merchant construction until October 1918. Part of the increase in completions in 1917–18 was achieved by completing ships already on the slips. Geddes failed to meet his targets by 25 per cent in 1917 and by 67 per cent in 1918 (the latter was 16 per

The seaplane tender USS *Wright* was begun as Hog Island Yard No 680 and completed in 1922. This 2 February 1924 photograph shows her vertical stem and stern, adopted to make it difficult to judge her course. The non-fabricated transports also had this feature. Of the Type B series, *Argonne* served the US Navy as a transport (AP 4), a submarine tender (AS 10) and a miscellaneous auxiliary (AG 31); *Chaumont* was a transport and later a hospital ship (AP 5 and then AH 10); *St. Mihiel* was a wartime transport (AP 32, acquired 1941); and *Chateau Thierry* was an army transport and then a wartime navy transport (AP 31, 1941).

The outbreak of war in 1914 swept the German merchant fleet, the world's second largest, from the sea. Ships in neutral ports were laid up so that they would not be captured by the Royal Navy; many ships at sea were captured, to enlarge the British merchant fleet and to compensate for German depredations. SS *Diyatalawa* was the former German *Rapenfels*, taken as a prize by HMS *Espiegle* on 8 August 1914 and taken over by the Admiralty in 1915. (Allan C Green via State Library of Victoria)

cent below a minimum level set by Geddes in 1917). These failures occasioned some sharp criticism, some of it focussed on the Admiralty's apparent extravagance in warship construction.[59] However, by 1918 the United States was deploying enormous ship-building resources and the convoy system was dramatically reducing shipping losses. In effect the decision to accelerate merchant shipbuilding over naval building paralleled the decision to introduce convoy (shipping protection) in place of the previous emphasis on hunting down U-boats.

Geddes' relative failure to accelerate British merchant ship-building did not matter in the long run, because the United States was able to create a massive wartime merchant shipbuilding industry. This was very much what the United States did again in the Second World War and many key individuals of the later era had extensive First World War experience. President Franklin D Roosevelt had served as Assistant Secretary of the Navy, in charge of procurement: he knew what American industry could do. The Maritime Commission which built the flood of the Second World War ships was the direct descendant of the US Shipping Board of the previous war.

In 1917 the United States was the greatest industrial nation in the world, but it had only a small merchant fleet and shipbuilding (aside from warships) was very limited. Thus, for example, German estimates of the Allies' ability to make good shipping losses emphasised British industrial capacity. Probably no one outside the United States had any idea that American mass-production techniques could or would be applied to shipbuilding. Soon after the US Congress passed the massive 1916 naval construction bill it also passed an Act establishing a US Shipping Board intended to promote a revived US merchant fleet.[60] Some in Congress surely associated the big projected fleet with protection of a doctrine of 'freedom of the seas' opposed to the British blockade of Germany. Ironically, it turned out that the main effort of the Shipping Board was to manage the US mass production programme directed at Germany. The Act which set up the Shipping Board authorised it to set up one or more corporations to build ships. Once war began, the Shipping Board requisitioned US shipyards to ensure that all

output went to the United States. The Emergency Fleet Corporation commandeered all steel ships of over 2500 deadweight tons building in US yards, a total of 431, many of which were British emergency orders placed by the Shipping Controller.[61]

When the United States entered the war, the US Government assumed that its contribution to the Allies would be an enormous army. It quickly became apparent that the army could not be transported to Europe unless its ships survived and that there was insufficient existing shipping. On this basis the United States Shipping Board Emergency Fleet Corporation was incorporated on 16 April 1917. Its two General Managers were George W Goethals, who had supervised construction of the Panama Canal, and Washington L Capps, a former Chief Constructor of the US Navy. An Emergency Shipping Act (18 June 1917) authorised the President to order such ships and material as he might deem necessary during the war. By that time the major existing yards had already accepted navy contracts amounting to about 75 per cent of their capacity. Those orders were, moreover, largely for the destroyers and submarines deemed essential to win the anti-submarine war (capital ship and cruiser construction was largely suspended, so there was little or no slack to expand construction of US merchant ships.

The size of the programme was set by the rate of sinkings the Germans had achieved. At the outset it was assumed that they would sink as much as 800,000 tons of US ships. Like other crash programmes, this one was somewhat wasteful and it attracted a post-war Congressional investigation. The Select Committee of the House of Representatives concluded that 'the accomplishments in the number of ships constructed, the tonnage secured and the time within which the ships were completed and delivered constitute the most remarkable achievement in ship building that the world has ever seen'. The full programme was 2368 ships (13.6 million deadweight tons), of which 1056 (5.7 million deadweight tons) were delivered before the Armistice.[62] That included 1725 steel ships (770 delivered), 629 wooden ships (236 delivered) and fourteen concrete ships (none delivered). It was understood that the wooden and concrete ships would have no commercial value after the war, but they did contribute valuable tonnage for wartime use (1.7 million tons of wooden ships planned, 1 million tons delivered by the Armistice).

Because the United States had so little shipbuilding capacity when it entered the war, the Emergency Fleet Corporation found itself building and manning shipyards, in some cases in effect building the villages in which the workers would live and running buses and trolleys to get them to work.[63] It even created its own guard and police force to protect the yards. At its peak, the Emergency Fleet Corporation was spending $4 million each day. The shipbuilding work force expanded from about 50,000 to about 530,000.[64]

By the end of the war, the United States was outbuilding Great Britain. A table produced for post-war Congressional testimony showed Great Britain producing 2.4 million deadweight tons in 1918, compared to 4.5 million for the United States. The figures for 1915 were one million tons in Great Britain (due to a shift in capacity to the Admiralty) vs. 250,000 in the United States. In 1917, before the emergency programme delivered any ships, the British delivered 1.8 million deadweight tons vs 1.5 million in the United States. However, at the end of the war the US shipping industry, which had been weak before the war, collapsed into much its pre-war state and most of the new ships were laid up. In addition to ships it built in the United States, the Fleet Corporation contracted for ships in China (four ships at Kiangnan Dock and Engineering, Shanghai) and in Japan (thirty ships, total 245,000 DWT, plus fifteen built or building which were purchased). The shipping board also chartered neutral ships.

Where possible the Emergency Fleet Corporation simplified the designs of the ships it requisitioned. For new construction it turned to a well-known naval architect, Theodore Ferris, who designed a new kind of fabricated steel ship suited to mass production.[65] Initially the American Bridge Corp fabricated the parallel midbodies of two ships; it limited itself to this straight part of the hull. That amounted to 60 per cent of the weight of the ship. After the first two ships, that increased to 70 per cent. Ultimately bridge shops contracted for 85 per cent of the hull and even built some of the complex curved parts. Extension to 100 per cent was impractical because bridge shops lacked the necessary equipment, such as sufficient furnaces to bend frames and bevel angles. Ships were designed without sheer and with absolutely flat sides. They had specifically military features.[66]

The new kind of ship could best built at a new kind of yard. The Emergency Fleet Corporation built four of these agency yards, which together accounted for a quarter of the steel ship contract programme: Hog Island (American International Shipbuilding Corp.), Bristol (Merchant Shipbuilding Corp.), Newark (Submarine Boat Corp.) and Wilmington (Carolina Shipbuilding Co). Their total of ninety-four ways could build more tonnage than any country had produced before 1918. They were, in effect, earlier versions of the Kaiser yard which mass-produced Liberty ships and escort carriers during the Second World War and presumably they inspired the later project.

Hog Island near Philadelphia was the largest and by far the most famous, with fifty slips. The current Philadelphia International Airport occupies its former site. While fifty ships were being built on the slips, another twenty-eight could be fitted out at the yard's piers. The yard built 7500 DWT freighters ('A' ships) and 8800 DWT troop transports ('B' Ships). Plans called for 110 freighters and seventy transports, but fifty-eight of the transports were cancelled at the Armistice. The first ship *Quistconck* was laid down in the half-complete yard on 12 February 1918. At its height the yard laid a keel every 5$\frac{1}{2}$ days. During FY21, its last in operation, it delivered thirty-one ships, including transports (one of which became the seaplane tender *Wright*; others were delivered to the US Army). The last of the freighters was completed on 21 January 1921. At its peak, the yard employed 34,049 men, but because it was an assembly facility it actually employed many more at other plants. Fabricated steel came from west of Kansas City and from as far north as Montreal. The yard's products became well known as 'Hog Islanders', with their turbine engines and their distinctive profiles. The other agency yards were similar but smaller.[67]

The Emergency Fleet Corporation also ordered wooden ships, because lumber, but not steel, initially seemed to be available in great quantity. The Pacific Coast yards completed most of the wooden ships, the Atlantic and Gulf yards not doing as well. The argument in favour of wood was revived twenty years later when the US Navy ordered wooden sub-chasers and wooden minesweepers on the theory that wood was easier to work, required fewer specialised workers and could be handled more easily. The reality was that wooden shipbuilding was not nearly as widespread

as might be imagined, either in 1917 or in 1940 and that it involved considerable skills which had to be developed. In the First World War case, the wood ships were clearly of no post-war commercial value and the Emergency Fleet Corporation was much criticised for the programme.[68]

As it was, when the crisis came in the spring of 1918, enough ships had been built to transport 125,000 men per month, but many more were needed. The minimum was 250,000 per month and that was exceeded by trading off freight for troop capacity. President Wilson personally approved the programme, which sent 300,000 men in July 1918. About half the US troops were carried to France on board foreign ships. Fleet Corporation President Hurley later wrote that, had the war continued another year the army in France could not have been completely fed and supplied by US-built ships.[69]

Another factor in Allied shipping was the mass of German and Austro-Hungarian shipping interned in US ports since 1914. Crews on board tried unsuccessfully to sabotage these ships once the United States entered the war and the ships became available to the Allies. The roughly 1.7 million tons involved was roughly equivalent to what the Germans sank in the first three months of their campaign.

There was interest in building torpedo-resistant ('unsinkable') ships, to the extent that a conference on the subject assembled in London on 10 August 1917.[70] With their small merchant fleets, the French and the Italians were very interested in modifying existing ships to make them more survivable.[71] The British view was that they could not afford to make ships unsinkable; the only practicable form of protection was to prevent ships from being hit in the first place.

Entry of the United States into the war immediately provided the Allies with considerable ex-German merchant tonnage, which helped compensate for the U-boats' depredations. The transport *Leviathan*, formerly the German *Vaterland*, one of three *Imperator* class liners, at the time the largest in the world (upon launch in 1913 she was the largest passenger ship in the world; only her near-sister *Bismarck* was larger). On the outbreak of war she was in New York. With no safe way of reaching home, she was laid up, to be seized by the US Shipping Board on 6 April 1917 and turned over to the US Navy. She was designated SP-1326 and renamed *Leviathan* on 6 September 1917. She is shown after the end of the war, painted grey rather than her wartime dazzle, bringing US troops home. Decommissioned 29 October 1919, turned over to US Shipping Board, then operated post-war by US Lines. The seaplane is an HS-1. (US Naval Institute Collection)

The US submarine *K-5* (not at all related to British 'K' boats) displays two standard US hydrophones on her foredeck. The foremost is a K-tube, showing three rubber 'rats'. Between it and the conning tower is a C-tube, with rubber balls at its ends to detect sound.

CHAPTER 13

Anti-Submarine Warfare: Tactics and Technology

Because they relied so heavily on blockade as a means of neutralising enemy fleets, the British early became unhappily aware of the threat of submarines. Before 1914 the Royal Navy seems to have been the only one to take anti-submarine warfare at all seriously. It concentrated on attempts to neutralise the threat of submarines against its major warships. That meant preventing (mainly deterring) submarines from getting within attack range. The British were soon aware that a submarine attacking a moving formation had to approach from ahead, within an area defined by 'limiting lines of approach'. The faster the formation, the narrower the lines of approach. The faster the force (compared to the attacker), the narrower the approach area. A 15-knot force facing a 6-knot submarine needed protection over a $^{3}/_{4}$-mile line ahead of it. A block athwart the approach area was effective only for a relatively short column of ships, because a submarine outside the limiting lines of approach could work around the block and attack further down a long column.

Both the British and the Germans seem to have assumed that submarines would be deterred by the presence of destroyers, which could ram them when they were at periscope depth. Submariners sometimes pointed out that often the destroyers failed to see their periscopes, hence were no threat at all and that in any case they could be torpedoed. War experience showed both that the submariners were right that they often approached unseen and that they were wrong that destroyers were easy torpedo targets. A fast manoeuvring destroyer was a difficult target, particularly if its look-outs could easily spot the visible wake of a torpedo. Ideally the submarine had to fire from short range, but it took some time (*i.e.*, running distance) for a torpedo to rise to the shallow depth of a destroyer's hull.[1] Destroyers were successfully torpedoed, but not often.

289

Mines

Mines were effective because, like a surface ship, a submarine could not detect them. Once the British had effective mines, in 1917, they laid very large numbers as an ASW measure, including deep fields into which they hoped surface ASW forces would compel U-boats to dive. Because a submarine could not simply evade mines as she could hope to evade surface forces, they were considered particularly effective against crews' morale. It is impossible to say whether this was so, because after 1918 it became important politically for the Germans to claim that the morale of the U-boats had never been broken. Post-war US attempts to evaluate the effect of the Northern Barrage on the U-boats seem to have been unsuccessful. ASW mining is discussed in Chapter 15.

Nets

Allied to mines were nets, which could detect submerged submarines or detect and destroy them using mines in the nets. One form was a fixed obstruction, as off Zeebrugge or in the Straits of Dover. Soon after the outbreak of war the British and the French tried to block the Straits of Dover with a mine and net barrage, but it was not very successful. It could not be anchored effectively against the strong tide and the weather (particularly winter storms), so that it was rarely complete and the debris from it endangered shipping. A net-and-mine barrage off Zeebrugge was also relatively ineffective.[2] It was impossible to emplace nets across the other important submarine choke point, the Straits of Otranto at the mouth of the Adriatic, because it was too deep (in 1918, however, there were plans to mine it).

Nets could also be deployed by fishing craft. As in fishing, there were two alternatives. A trawler towed a net which might engulf the submarine, as it would a school of fish. A drifter lay above a net into which a submarine, again like fish, might swim. In both cases the net bore indicator buoys and it might also contain contact mines. That made a trawler a hunter, to some extent. For example, by the spring of 1915 numerous Royal Navy trawlers were towing floating nets buoyed by Kapock balls and later by glass floats. They bore indicator buoys and contact mines. The nets with their mines were laid on the ebb tide north of the straits, the trawler and her nets drifting down until they reached the level of Folkestone, where they were hauled in so that the trawler could go back up the Channel to drift down again.

Groups of drifters could create a net barrier across a narrow strait, typically Dover or Otranto at the mouth of the Adriatic.[3] Nets typically bore indicator buoys. A submarine would foul a net and thus indicate its presence. If nets were arranged in lines and if the lines were complete enough, a series of indications indicated passage of a submarine and depth charges could be dropped on it. Nets could also be mined. The net idea recalled fishing by drifter, so drifters were typically used to lay and watch nets, both in the Dover Straits and in the Straits of Otranto.

Net operations required large numbers, because no single trawler or drifter covered a large area. That in turn meant that the individual craft were small and effectively defenceless against attack by destroyers or cruisers. Thus the Zeebrugge destroyers successfully raided the Dover barrage at least twice, the Austrians successfully raided the Otranto barrage and the Germans and Turks raided drifters (presumably operating a barrage) off the Turkish Straits in 1918. Each time they sank

An experimental installation on a British 'Large America' flying boat late in the war shows a standard PDH hydrophone (A); the aircraft fuselage gives a sense of scale.

some of the small craft trailing nets, but they never inflicted enough damage to prevent the barrage from reforming immediately afterwards. On the other hand, none of the barrages was very effective until late in the war, when the Straits of Dover were finally closed to U-boats.

Detection

There seems to have been little or no interest in acoustics before 1914, so it could be assumed that submarines would rely on their periscopes. A short periscope exposure might well be the only warning of a submarine attack (about 1910 British submariners pointed out that it might well not be seen at all, so that the first indication of attack might be an exploding torpedo). Periscopes became the aim point for counter-attack. The other pre-1914 means of detection was a sweep (described below in connection with weapons) which might register contact with a submarine. Sweeps were attractive as a means of ensuring that the path of a ship or a squadron was clear, but they could not be used to search any considerable area and they proved ineffective.

During the pre-war decade Reginald Fessenden in the United States developed underwater acoustic signalling on a commercial basis, forming the Submarine Signal Co. to market his system.[4] Various navies adopted it (during the war the Grand Fleet used it as an alternative to wireless). That naturally led to interest in

A standard British late-war towed 'Single Eel' hydrophone slung vertically (at right) on the cab of the blimp *SSZ 49*. Towed hydrophones were isolated from the noise of the towing vessel and they could be used at very low (drifting) speeds, but not at normal operating speeds. Ships so equipped could hunt U-boats using 'sprint and drift' tactics, listening while drifting. Unfortunately a U-boat could hear the hunter slowing down to listen and for five to seven minutes (normal listening time) she could turn off her motors entirely, briefly becoming silent. Active sonar, which was being developed by the end of the war, solved this problem by making it possible for a ship moving at considerable speed to detect a submerged submarine. The limitations of 'sprint and drift' explain why moving convoy escorts usually were not effective hunters.

acoustics (listening) as a means of submarine detection, but pre-war tests were unsuccessful.

In 1914 the United States had a large developing electronics industry with products such as telephones, phonographs and movie equipment. It also had experts led by Edison and Fessenden. They offered an enormous potential for rapid wartime development. Once the Germans declared unrestricted submarine warfare, hence the break with the United States, the US Navy created a Special Board on Submarine Devices.[5] The public face of the Special Board was a Naval Consulting Board chaired by Thomas A Edison. President Wilson also convened a National Research Council. During the war the Special Board developed

detection devices which were soon considered superior to those which the British and the French already had, so that by 1918 they were in widespread Allied service. In a war in which US forces were typically armed by the Allies, this was a major case in which US assistance counted heavily well before the end of the war. In 1918 most other kinds of US industrial assistance were only beginning to accelerate.

Initial British work on submarine detection was supported by the Submarine Committee and taken over by the Anti-Submarine Division (ASD) of the Admiralty when it was formed in December 1916. The Admiralty's Board of Invention and Research (BIR) began working on the same subject when it was formed in July 1915 by new First Lord A J Balfour. Thus in 1917 there were multiple separate centres of British acoustic research: Parkeston Quay (BIR), Hawkcraig (ASD), Portland (ASD), Cardiff (ASD) and Portsmouth (ASD), all working on both acoustics and electro-magnetic detection. Other centres dealt with anti-submarine weapons.

By mid-1915 the British were systematically considering a wide variety of possibilities. Experiments with magnetic, optical and thermal (IR) methods were all tried and abandoned as impractical, although experiments with visual detection from aircraft continued well into the war. Magnetic detection later revived in the form of detection loops.[6] That left acoustics as the main method of detecting a submerged submarine. The great problem was how a ship could move and yet listen.[7]

All operational wartime acoustic devices were hydrophones, passive devices listening at audible (sonic) frequencies. All ultimately relied on the listener's ear to distinguish the complex sound of a submarine from surrounding sounds.[8] The simplest hydrophone was an empty vessel with a tube leading to the listener's ear. Sound in the water could be heard through the tube. The US version had a rubber receiver in the form of a nipple; the alternative was the metal 'Broca'. The 'Broca' was more sensitive, the nipple more faithful in reproducing the sound in the water. Another form, used by the Royal Navy, used a microphone or magnetophone and a headset. It could be connected to a plate in a ship's hull.

It was also possible to make hydrophones directional. Narrowing (in effect) the beam heard by the hydrophone eliminated a great deal of background noise. When the beam was pointed at a submarine, its noise was much easier to distinguish. For example, US tests made in August 1917 showed that the range of a typical hydrophone (in this case a C-tube) doubled when it was made directional. On the other hand, an operator using such a sensor could listen in only one direction at a time and it took time to recognise the sound of a submarine. That made an omni-directional hydrophone more attractive as a search (patrol) device, a directional one more valuable for attack. The noise of the ship also mattered; in the same trial, the range of a microphone increased six-fold when it was moved away from a ship. Combining the two would make a considerable difference. Tests on board a destroyer showed that 'a destroyer's hull is like a sounding board'. To US researchers, that suggested that the best detector would be a towed fish housing a directional receiver.

Human listening using two ears (binaural) is directional, so separate connections could be made to an operator's ears. He could find direction by rotating his device so that all sound was eliminated. Microphones were directional to some extent. It was possible to screen one hydrophone from another, so that, unless the submarine was centred between them, it would produce more sound in one than in the other. That was tried with plates on either side of a drifter or a submarine, but in that case the entire ship had to be turned to search. Probably the most important wartime technique was to rotate an array of hydrophones electrically using compensating lines (the Germans called them 'electric water' when applying this method to U-boat hydrophones). By applying different delays to the different hydrophones it was possible to point an array in different directions – a technique now used in sonars. The United States went furthest in this direction with blister hydrophones for destroyers.[9]

The French Walser device used a different approach, an array of Broca receivers delivering sound waves to a reflector which focussed them and carried them to the listener's ear via a flexible tube. The reflector was turned to turn the beam of the device.[10] The crucial French contribution seems to have been their superior electronic amplifier, which had been developed for the Walser gear.[11] The British adopted it late in 1917.

Virtually all the wartime sonic devices were effective only from a stopped or very slowly-moving ship. Thus they were irrelevant to convoy operations. They were very relevant to barrage work and to sprint-and-drift hunting. The enormous effort expended on such devices continued after convoy was well established and well demonstrated, because hunting was the main means of destroying many U-boats in contested waters. It was probably seen as the only way to exploit increasingly effective intelligence (and aircraft sightings) to destroy, rather than evade, U-boats.

British work on anti-submarine hydrophones was due largely to the efforts of Commander C P Ryan RN, formerly a wireless specialist and then employed by Marconi. He returned to active service on the outbreak of war and in the autumn of 1914 began working on submarine detection by hydrophone. He attracted official support early in 1915 and was given the drifter *Tarlair* for sea trials. He set up base at Hawkcraig, which became the main British A/S detection establishment. In February 1915 the Admiralty decided to establish with a coastal chain of non-directional hydrophones set about 1^1/$_2$ miles apart at a depth of 50 to 100 fathoms. Which hydrophones picked up a submarine gave the approximate direction. The success of this chain led Ryan to propose an acoustic ('magnetophone') mine, which was almost ready at the end of the war.

Ryan's non-directional coastal hydrophone was then installed on board ships as the 'drifter' or Portable General Service (PGS) set, which was lowered over the side. Beginning late in 1915, 4534 were made, production continuing to the end of the war. In 1916 Hawkcraig developed a Portable Directional Hydrophone (PDH). It entered service in 1917 in two versions, Mk I (844 made) and Mk II (2586 made). By April 1917, about fifty Mk IIs were in service and on 22 May the Admiralty ordered 1500 of each of the two types. Trials showed that P-boats were particularly well-suited to listening, because their shallow draught made them relatively safe from torpedoes and they were fast enough to overtake submerged submarines while pausing at intervals to listen (sprint and drift). By February 1918 the consensus was apparently that these overboard devices were good in a smooth sea but practically useless as soon as there were waves. The British agreed that they were much inferior to the US C-tube.

PDH was less sensitive overall than PGS, but directionality made it more valuable. It employed two diaphragms on a ring-shaped body, responding to sound approaching each plate broadside-on.

The PGS idea was attractive for submarines, which could have a plate on either side of the hull. The first thirty installations were ordered in April 1916, fittings beginning the following year. The Mk IV version had a diaphragm acoustically isolated from the hull. In addition to sets for submarines, 499 were made for surface ships. They were considered the best of the wartime British hydrophones. In the trawler version, the plates followed the contour of the hull but the microphones were placed vertically inside the hull.

An alternative 'shark fin' version (854 made through February 1918) had its hydrophones in streamlined bodies outside the hull. Shark fins were abandoned in favour of fish (see below). Even in January 1918 a US Navy Captain noted that the Shark Fin was 'considered of so little value that they were only listened to as a matter of curiosity and at no time seriously considered or used . . . The impossibility of obtaining definite direction with the Shark Fin accounts for their being so little used'.

The British Submarine Signal Co., which made underwater sound signalling devices pre-war (as a subsidiary of Fessenden's US company), developed a towed (fish) hydrophone, the Nash (after its inventor).[12] It was usable only when underway (drifting with engines stopped, at up to 10 knots) or anchored in a tideway so that it could stream. Otherwise the fish would assume a vertical position. The microphone became ineffective when the sound was very close in, hence the fish was ineffective at very close range. A US evaluation (February 1918) was that the fish was very effective for closing in on a U-boat from a considerable distance, but it was not so useful for the final attack due to its position 150ft abaft the towing ship and the difficulty of quickly turning the ship.[13]

Its single bi-directional hydrophone, employing a microphone, was rotated by a motor controlled by the towing ship. In its final version the Nash Fish also contained a uni-directional hydrophone, which could also be rotated. A U-boat running at 4 or 5 knots could be detected at three miles, perhaps somewhat more when the trawler was drifting. A P-boat could be heard easily at 350 yds from a trawler making 3 to 5 knots. Sound direction could be determined within 5 to 10°.

After a January 1918 test in the Channel aboard trawlers, US Navy Captain Leigh (seconded by the Special Board) commented that in a sea, the fish outranged the US SC C-tube, but its cable did not operate in a moderately heavy sea, creating excessive vibration which ultimately ruined the cable. It had to be recovered after waves ran 4 to 5ft high. On the average it took 7 men about eight minutes to get it overboard and 12 to 20 minutes for the fish to fill with water and be ready. Recovery took 6 to 10 minutes. It worked well from an anchored ship, as it was stabilised by tidal currents. However, at slack water the fish could tip into a vertical position, staying that way for 1^1/$_2$ to 2 hours in mid-Channel. The fish proved unable to find the direction of more than one sound at a time. The fish weighed 1200lbs and its cable was its weak point. Initially it vibrated so badly that it lasted only up to three hours; by February 1918 that had increased to 60 to 80 hours. After successful trials the Nash Fish was accepted in October 1917. The Admiralty ordered 136 and for a time planned a total of 360. Nash Fish were the preferred sensors on board hunting trawlers.

In 1918 the US Navy's Special Board saw the Nash Fish and other towed bodies as a means of providing all ships with listening equipment for, among other things, navigation (using underwater beacons then in service). It turned out that the machinery noise of large ships swamped whatever a fish could pick up. In his April

1918 summary of listening equipment, Vice Admiral William Sims, commanding US naval forces in Europe, listed fish among devices useless unless a ship was stopped.

Captain Ryan at Hawkcraig developed his own small fish, only 18in long and 3in in diameter, which was called the 'rubber eel'.[14] Ryan tried various fillings, but ended up using water (most of the eels free-flooded). It was typically towed 100 to 200 yds abaft a ship, 20 to 30ft down. At 8 knots maximum range was about four miles (8000 yds). At that speed the disturbed water created by the propellers screened the device from sound from ahead, but above 10 knots propeller noise limited range to about $1^1/_2$ miles. Ryan saw the rubber covering as a filter which kept out flow noise but admitted the noise of U-boat engines. Typically two non-directional eels were towed in tandem, a compensator on board the towing ship forming a directional beam.

Ryan's more sophisticated towed 'porpoise' entered production in September 1918, thirty-one out of 100 ordered being delivered. The wooden fish was 5ft long and 12in in diameter, containing a single unidirectional PDH Mk II hydrophone rotated by a small electric motor. Compared to a Nash Fish, the Porpoise offered longer range and good directional indication up to 6 knots. The British view was that it was better than the Nash for a single-ship (sprint and drift) hunt, but that the Nash was better for two-ship hunts. The war ended before a fish containing a US K-tube, developed at Shadon by the Lancashire Anti-Submarine Committee, could enter production. All of this was aside from extensive work on shore hydrophones, the Admiralty creating a Hydrophone Service (the US Navy had an analogous organisation). Both navies placed listening devices on harbour floors and on board light ships. Hydrophones were widely installed on board Royal Navy and US submarines.

Although the US Navy did not begin work on listening devices until the country entered the war, the United States enjoyed a considerable advantage in the enormous effort already applied to sound technology by Bell, to gramophones (phonographs) by Edison and to underwater signalling by the Submarine Signal Company. It, GE and Western Electric (the industrial arm of the Bell Telephone System) pooled their efforts at Nahant and the US Navy opened a Naval Experimental Station at New London.[15] Initial meetings between US, British and French scientists were held in late May through early July 1917. The Anglo-French scientific mission helped convince the navy to finance a second experimental station at New London. Within a few months US hydrophones were in service in all three navies.

The Special Board issued its initial report to Secretary of the Navy Josephus Daniels in July 1917, as a basis for the US ASW programme. Having met the Anglo-French mission and already having US listening devices under development, the Board urged Daniels to order 500 simple sound and direction indicators at once for patrol vessels, to be put into service as soon as possible to train personnel. When a satisfactory device became available, all patrol vessels in service should have it. For the moment, the Board recommended that the relevant Bureau (Steam Engineering) buy a large number of Fessenden's sound detection and direction-finding devices to equip US and Allied destroyers (and also merchant ships, to help them evade attack). At this time Fessenden was advocating a very low frequency (1 to 5 Hz) receiver which he hoped would detect the hull vibrations of submarines. Nahant was originally built specifically for this project. The report of the Anglo-French mission

US 'L' class submarines at Berehaven in 1918 show their hydrophones. That on the left has a C-tube on her deck. On the right, AL-1 (US submarines were prefixed 'A' to avoid confusion with the British 'L'-class) shows three fixed hydrophones. The beam they created could be rotated using an internal wire array, a technique the Germans also developed for U-boats. The gun is a 3in/23 on a retractable mount (when housed, it looked like a short vertical mast). The battleship in the background was assigned to Berehaven to help deal with the perceived threat of a German battlecruiser raid in the Atlantic, an issue raised by the US Navy's Operations Committee in London.

singled it out as pointless. Presumably the 500 simple detectors became the C-tubes which were soon under development.

When it visited in mid-1917, the Anglo-French mission considered current US developments well behind current European practice. Equipment received in the UK for tests in the autumn of 1917 was considered somewhat immature. For example, the SC tube was excellent at short range and would have been useful in the final chase of the submarine – but it was difficult to handle underway. The K-tube seemed inferior to the 'drifter' set and to a new British towed 'eel' hydrophone. However, when an American mission visited England late in 1917 it felt the opposite. The British apparently agreed. Given detailed drawings of the US listening gear, they planned to place it in mass production.[16] That included K-tube Compensators and the Pierce Trailing Wire device. A British submarine was being fitted with a US C-tube for use through the top of her hull. Other American gear would be installed immediately on board trawlers. The US mission also planned to investigate the possibilities of quieting destroyers and P-boats, though that seemed to offer little potential.[17]

The first US listening device was the C-tube, various forms of which were under test by August 1917. The C-tube was derived from a Colladon-Sturm device (whence probably its name) perfected in 1913 by Broca.[18] It consisted of a pair of air-filled rubber receivers (globes), set nearly 5ft apart, each leading to one of the operator's ears. The operator rotated the array to find the direction of the sound he was receiving. Tests showed that putting a C-tube over the side, rather than running it through an opening in the hull, greatly increased the noise of water slapping against the hull and thus reduced range by as much as two-thirds. Once the new devices had been installed on board three sub-chasers (SC 6, SC 19 and SC 21), it was possible to conduct a simulated hunt (6 October 1917) against the test submarine G 1. The weather was so rough that a third of those on board the sub-chasers were seasick. The boats rolled so badly that their rails went under and there was considerable fog. The sub-chasers were arranged in line abreast, about 3/4 of a mile apart, the flagship in the centre. After an hour, the submarine surfaced about 400 yds from the starboard bow of the flagship. The chase was considered successful. One lesson was that each chaser should have two overboard hydrophones, one on each side, because conditions on the windward side were very poor owing to water noise against the side of the ship. Those on the lee side worked properly. *SC 6* had a through-hull installation.

Installation of C-tubes on board the new sub-chasers was approved in October 1917, the device being renamed the SC-C-tube. In initial tests it was simply put over the side, but the preferred installation was a tube through the hull. Tests showed that it could detect submarines as soon as the sub-chaser slowed to 1.5 knots. In an April 1918 summary of ASW devices, Admiral Sims described the SC Tube as useful when stopped, when drifting, or when moving slowly with engines stopped.[19] The instrument was simple and sturdy and never got out of order, but it suffered interference from water noises and excessive motion of the listening ship and it was not suited to rough weather. The cycle from signalling to stop engines to restarting after listening was about two minutes (sprint and drift operation). An SC C-tube could determine the direction of a sound within less than 5°. Depending on the sea state and the speed of the listening vessel, the SC-tube could detect a U-boat making 0.6 knots at 500 to 700 yds, one making 2 knots at 1200 to 2500 yds and one making 4 knots at 2000 to 4000 yds.

In September 1917 GE and Submarine Signal developed a non-directional non-resonant hydrophone which they mounted in a watertight rubber enclosure, with a rubber diaphragm. Because it looked like one, it was called a Rat; several subsequent US arrays were built out of Rats. The first was the K-tube, a directional array of three Rats at the vertices of an equilateral triangle. The listening beam was turned by a compensator. The main developmental problem, not completely solved even in January 1918, seems to have been the compensator, which had to add up the inputs of the three receivers without distorting them. In an early test, it managed to detect shipping beyond the horizon, when only stack smoke could be seen. Both the C-tube and the K-tube could distinguish one among several ships, but the K-tube was better. Compared to the C-tube, a K-tube seemed almost immune to water noise. It and the C-tube became standard US wartime equipment. The K-tube was also developed as a drifter set and as a harbour-floor submarine detector (initially tested in Boston harbour).

To Admiral Sims the K-tube, like the C-tube, was rugged and reliable and it was limited to drifting, coasting with engines stopped, or anchored in a tideway. It could determine the direction of a sound (except one close in) within 5 to 10°. The listening cycle took one to two minutes for a K-tube in an internal tank (five to eight for the overboard version). Unlike the C-tube, a K-tube was not affected by water noises in rough weather, except for tank installations. The three tubes offered greater gain and therefore greater range: 2500 to 3000 yds on a U-boat making 0.6 knots, 8000 to 10,000 yds on a 2-knot U-boat and 15,000 to 20,000 yds on a 4-knot U-boat. In April 1918 there was as yet no towed version.

Once the new US devices were available in European waters, the Royal Navy conducted comparative trials. In January 1918 three trawlers operating in the Channel (*Andrew King*, *Kunishi* and *James Bentole*) operated for eight days with SC C-tubes, C-tubes

(presumably the over-the-side type), K-tubes and Nash Fish.[20] The trawlers operated in several ways. One was a slow-speed running patrol. By the end all the fish were dead due to cable failures, but the SC-tubes were still intact. Fish located a total of forty-five ships, compared to sixty-seven by SC C-tubes before the fish died; fish picked up fifteen sounds missed by SC C-tubes. A second was a drifting patrol (about two miles apart, drifting with the current and tide for 10 to 12 hours) to create a barrier or to wait for a stopped ('balancing') submarine to reveal itself by getting underway. Fish were useless in this case. A third was anchored patrol, either to set up fixed sentries on a barrier or to wait for a bottomed submarine. K-tubes gave good directionality except at slack water (due to the tide). K-tube and C-tube range was much greater than that of the fish and both offered much better resolution (of one sound from another).

In these tests K-tubes were effective in any sea in which a trawler could chase submarines. It was free of water (background) noise and tests showed that it could detect a surface ship at more than 20 miles; at 12 miles or less engine rhythms could be heard distinctly (at greater ranges the pulsating sound was replaced by a high-pitched continuous roar whose direction could be measured). The SC C-tube seemed better adapted to calm weather, in which it could detect a surface ship at 8 to 10 miles, determining direction within about 5°. A moderate sea reduced range to about 4 to 6 miles. When the trawler was pitching so badly that the bow was rising and falling 6 to 8ft (when it was too rough for the towed fish), the SC C-tube was still serviceable. In quiet weather the SC-tube was useable (with a P-boat 1 1/2 miles away) at half speed. The C- and K-tubes could locate three or four ships simultaneously, even if one was considerably fainter than the others. Compared to the SC C-tube, the over-the-side C-tube was usable only when the ship was stopped and when the tide was running at less than a knot. However, it could be used up to the point at which waves were breaking over the ship's gunwale. Although no better than an SC C-tube, it offered convenience because it was on deck, so K-tube operators used C-tubes to investigate sounds they picked up, so that they could estimate ranges.

No British device had a range comparable to that of the K-tube; the British considered it a very useful adjunct to patrols and suggested that in towed form it could replace the Nash Fish. The US mission supplied the Admiralty's Board on Invention and Research, which was managing ASW development, with the best description it could make of a possible towed K-tube, using work on towed bodies by the Special Board's Dr Coolidge to date. It did not expect a towed K-tube to be any better than the Nash Fish in withstanding the shock of a depth charge explosion or in its close-in effectiveness (like the fish, it used a microphone).

The January 1918 tests confirmed the importance of bridge-to-bridge radio telephones to co-ordinate a final attack against a submarine. The trawlers also had US-style direction bearing indicators, the big arrows often visible atop the bridges of sub-chasers. They were not used because the trawlers in the experiment never got close enough to a U-boat, but it was clear that the angles indicated could quickly be read with an accuracy of 5° or less. Similarly, US-style position plotting was not used, as it was needed only for the final attack, but it was clear that it had to be mechanised for quick action.

Early in 1918 the Admiralty decided to fit fifty C-tubes to P-boats and sloops which were to work with the trawlers of the new

The US Navy became interested in linear arrays of hydrophones because it appeared that they could be used even by a moving ship. This MV-series array is shown on board the transport *Von Steuben*, 26 February 1919. Similar arrays were installed on board destroyers. They offered the best hope to date that ships could hunt effectively while moving, hence that convoy escorts could usefully deal with attacking U-boats. There was no expectation that so noisy a ship as the transport should listen for U-boats or even for torpedoes, but the array made it possible for her to detect underwater signals, such as those from lightships off ports. The array was mounted in the ship's bow. Below the bow, to the left and below the blister covering the array, can be seen the triangular fitting for 'Burney gear' (paravanes).

hunting groups. Its own engineer officers had concluded that these ships could be adequately silenced. Late in 1917 trials had been conducted in the Mediterranean with HMS *Colne* and HMS *Acorn* to determine whether all machinery in both oil- and coal-burning destroyers could be stopped for long enough to obtain a bearing using a portable directional hydrophone without damaging the machinery, yet retaining enough power to attain 15 knots within a few minutes of starting up. The target was a motor launch. In each case engines were stopped and ordered astern to lose way, the hydrophone was put in the water, a bearing was obtained and the engines restarted.

In the case of *Colne*, it took 45 seconds to put the hydrophone down, another 2 minutes 30 seconds to get a bearing and the circulator was started in 5 minutes total. All engines except the circulator could be kept stopped for 15 minutes. The circulator was stopped for 5 minutes, run for 5 minutes and stopped again for 5 minutes in several cycles without heating the condenser unduly. *Acorn* took a minute to get her hydrophone down and another 2 minutes 10 seconds to get a bearing; she restarted her engines 4 minutes 30 seconds after shutdown. On one occasion all engines except the circulator were stopped for 24 minutes. Time to stop all engines was about a minute.

To Sims, this was very important, because although trawlers and sub-chasers might hunt effectively in the Channel, it took destroyers to operate further out to sea. He also concluded that C- and K-tubes could and should be installed on board US destroyers

for sprint- and-drift operation. He did not realise that the Special Board would soon be able to offer hydrophones a destroyer could use while underway.

Meanwhile the Special Board became interested in towed devices, which could be installed easily. There was no question of operating them from a moving ship, as they were not shielded from the noise of main machinery. Presumably they were insulated from the noise of auxiliaries. In March 1918 the only towed listening device in service was the British Nash Fish, which could detect a submarine at about four miles (8000 yds). It could do better if fitted with an amplifier. It could determine the direction of a sound within 3 to 10°. The fish could be towed at any reasonable speed.

The Special Board really hoped that a fish of some kind could work while being towed by a moving ship, although that never seems to have been practical. The Board tested American towed devices in March 1918:

1. Nash Fish with three Rats (Seaphones): it was considered as good for range and quietness as the original, but much simpler, as the amplifier and most of the leads were eliminated. There was some difficulty telling from which side sound came. A similar fish had been tried abroad. Rats were rubber housings around microphones, 3ft long and 5in in diameter at the widest end, with balancing tails to keep them from spinning in the water.

2. Electrostatic Eel (Professor Pierce at New London): a promising device, with greater range than the others and good directivity, but as of April 1918 it was considered rather complicated, in that it used amplifiers. The Special Board hoped they could later be eliminated. Some problems had been encountered with the cable (cross-talk among the elements of the eel). In its service form (C-1) the Eel contained twelve microphones spaced 12in apart inside a flexible rubber tube about 13ft long (4in in diameter) fitted with a balance tail and a streamlined nose through which the leads from the microphones were carried to an electrical compensator, six to each of the operator's ears. The Eel or Snake (as the British knew it) was later designated U3. It was typically towed at a depth of 100ft. Two eels could be towed in tandem to obtain more accurate bearings.[21] Combining two Eels some distance apart with an MV-tube made it possible to triangulate a submarine.

3. OS-tube ('dinosaur'), a spreader with three rats (in effect a towed K-tube) trailed in the form of a 4ft equilateral triangle, was under test at Nahant. It had many advantages: it was rugged, readings could be taken quickly and it probably had a better range than either form of the Nash Fish. However, bearings were inaccurate and it was unstable under tow except at one speed. As of April 1918 the GE representatives (Dr Coolidge, Dr Langmuir and Mr Eveleth) were planning to adopt the towing body Dr Coolidge was already using in experiments at Key West to the three rubber fish. In December 1918 the OS-tube, towed at the end of a 500–600ft cable, was considered the best current U3 towed listening device for long-range work.[22]

For the moment, none of the towed devices was satisfactory, because none could be used in a chase.

The US Navy hoped that it could go beyond hunting to providing convoy escorts – destroyers – with equipment they could operate while underway. The size of the programme shows how important it was. It began late in December 1917 with tests of different devices on board the destroyer USS *Aylwin*.

At this time Professor Fessenden, a founder of the Nahant experimental station, was heavily promoting his low-frequency receiving oscillator, which he had originally developed to receive the signals of his company's submarine bells. The *Aylwin* test demonstrated three alternatives, each at least equal in range at all speeds and much simpler to install, maintain and operate. Each was also considerably lighter and much less expensive. Fessenden did not accept defeat.[23] His four-oscillator array was installed on board the destroyer *Colhoun* by July 1918.[24] With the ship lying-to, a 5-knot submarine could be heard $2^{1}/_{2}$ miles away, but when the submarine was astern its noise was blanked out by the ship's engines and auxiliaries. Operators could tell roughly when the submarine passed from one quadrant to another, but they could do no better unless it was within 800 to 1000 yds. With the ship lying-to, a K-tube (D-2 tube) could hear a submarine about $1^{1}/_{2}$ miles away, but at 10 knots turbine sounds overwhelmed it.

The best detector was the MV Tube (Multiple Unit Variable Compensated Acoustic Tubes, also called the Mason Device and the Wisconsin Device and, in one November 1917 report, MF). It may have been inspired by the French Walser device, in the sense that both used multiple receivers to form a moveable beam (using a reflector in the French case). MV arrays were built using both acoustic and electrical compensators, in the latter case with microphones instead of rubber nipples. The simplest form, MF, was a double rotating hydrophone with a narrow focussed beam. The head of the New London group considered it the best rotating hydrophone developed by the Americans during the First World War. It was tested on board *SC 254* late in 1917, on a through-hull basis like an SC C-tube. It was unanimously much preferred to the SC C-Tube and it was being made for further installation in both single- and double-tube forms. The single-beam MB (multiple unit beam compensated, with eight rubber receivers for each of the user's ears) could use the same hull castings and interior fittings as the SC C-Tube. It was developed as a seaplane listening device. At the end of 1918 the MB was part of standard sub-chaser equipment, mounted on the side of the hull opposite the SC C-tube. It had slightly less range than an SC C-Tube, but its selectivity (due to its narrow beam) was better for overcoming background noise or for distinguishing one sound source among several.

As tested on *Aylwin* in January 1918, MV was not yet suitable for mass installation; an improved standardised form was being built for a later test. For example, until nearly the end of the tests it suffered from a leaky acoustic valve. Once that was fixed, the MV showed its great superiority. However, just how test results should be interpreted depended on the observer. In February 1918 the ship's CO clearly preferred the Fessenden oscillator, which he saw as a good source of general bearing (within 4 points – 45°). Compared to the Mason Apparatus (MV), the oscillator offered better performance with all engines running. MV had the edge with main engines stopped. The oscillator was more reliable, no surprise since it used well-tested components.

The alternative to MV was the 'S' Tube 4-spot (Mason four-spot receiver) installation. It was simple, easily made and could be quickly and inexpensively installed. It employed four acoustic leads, each ending in a Broca, with a rotary compensator. Until the MV was repaired, it appeared that the 4-S was as good for range

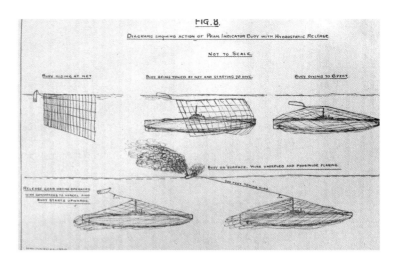

Indicator nets were important for wartime ASW. they were tried as early as the 1904 Royal Navy manoeuvres and the Royal Navy's (Anti-) Submarine Committee began formally considering the use of nets as early as February 1911. It dismissed them, but the idea was revived in May 1914. One was made for a test, with explosive charges in its foot. This was the beginning of the indicator net. In an 8 December 1914 test, the submarine C 25 was completely fouled by a net in the Firth of Forth. The submarine commander reported that the net was invisible through his periscope, so he could not evade it. By January 1915, four firms were making indicator nets and another 100 had been approached. By the end of the war 120,000 nets (6000 miles) had been made. All were 100 yds long and sections could be joined together. Standard depths were 30ft, 60ft, 84ft and 120ft (a few were 180ft deep), with 12ft mesh (10 x 12ft in 30ft deep nets). The upper edge of the net was typically supported in the water by standard fisherman's 5in glass balls. The net could be moored, or allowed to drift, or towed by (or near) a drifter. A drifter could readily carry twelve sections of net in her fish hold. As the name implied, such nets were conceived to indicate the presence of a submarine, so that accompanying ships could attack. This drawing from a wartime handbook (1916) shows a net attached to a standard pram (indicator) buoy, which would be drawn down by a submarine fouling the net. On being drawn down, the buoy would release its 300ft mooring line and return to the surface, the friction of the wire igniting its visible phosphide charge to indicate that the net had been fouled. In mid-February 1915 the idea of combining mines with indicator nets was proposed and an electro-contact (EC) mine designed, using plungers. By the end of 1916, about 15,000 such mines had been made.

and direction. While the more complex MV was further developed, in January 1918 the Special Board recommended that the 'S' tube (or 4-S) be installed in the oil tanks of all active destroyers.[25] One hundred were soon ordered. A prototype was installed on board the destroyer *Caldwell* in February 1918.[26]

Further tests conducted in April 1918 on board the destroyer *Jouett* heavily favoured the MV over the 4-S.[27] This time the MV consisted of four 5ft lines strapped to the ship's side to form a single line, with connections every 5ft to a compensator. A planned simplified compensator would be connected to lengthened units (to avoid splitting the array at hull frames). The destroyer operated at stop to twenty knots, the target submarine (*G 2*) at 7 knots down to 1.5 knots. With the destroyer running at 14 knots and the submarine at 7, she could be detected and her bearing measured out to 1900 yds, with an average error of 6°. With the destroyer at 7 to 12 knots and the submarine at 6, effective range was 1200 yds (average error 10°). Even with the submarine at 1.5 knots and the destroyer at 7 knots, the submarine was picked up at 800 to 1000 yds. The Board added that *G 2* was exceptionally quiet. A sub-chaser lying dead in the water had been unable to hear her at 1000 yds when she was running at 1.5 knots. The rival 4-S was next best, better than the alternative K-tube (Delta tube) in one of the ship's tanks. It worked even when the oil tanks were not full and when the ship was rolling.

On 10 June 1918 CNO approved fitting MV (at that time with twelve air tubes) to all destroyers; it was ordered installed on board all of those under construction. Many existing ships were also fitted.[28] This initial series the same kind of nipple-type rubber receivers as in the original K-tube, mounted in a line on an inertia plate which shielded them from a ship's own noise. Their outboard cover was a thin metal blister. Acoustic leads from the nipples were led into the ship and their phases adjusted by a compensator to form a steerable beam. An alternative form of MV used microphones, electric leads and amplifiers. At the end of the war the standard version was MV-16. As a submarine detector, it completely outclassed the Fessenden oscillator (which was still being tested) and the K-tube in a tank. At that time an electrical MV was about to be installed on board the large transport *von Steuben* for tests.

Meanwhile, many destroyers in European waters had K-tubes (called Delta Tubes for this purpose) in their tanks, but they proved useless when the ship was underway and not very useful as listening devices when she was stopped. In November 1918 Admiral Sims recommended that such installations stop in favour of MV tubes, particularly the electric version of MV. He considered that the MV 'embodies the best physical principles of any listening device, so far known, for use on vessels underway'.[29] Failures to date (he cited the destroyer *Murray*) were due to faulty construction or installation. The MV was particularly liked because it had selectivity, so it could be used by a convoy escort.

Array listening equipment was more than an anti-submarine device. Because it could be used while a ship was moving, it could usefully detect surface ships despite fog. Admiral Sims reported in December 1918 that the destroyer *Parker* had avoided collision during fog by using her array. Listening equipment could also be used to aid navigation. Given the variety of installations in service at the end of the war, CNO asked for standardisation tests. In January, the MV-8 on board USS *Walke* was compared with MV-16 on board USS *Evans* and USS *Lamberton*. Tests were somewhat compromised by a destroyer steaming on a parallel course. A submarine bell at the Ambrose Light Vessel could be distinctly heard by destroyers running at 18 knots. At 10 knots, with the noise maker at 10 knots, effective range was 3000 yds. With the noise maker (another destroyer) at 20 knots, range was 4500 yds. Drifting at an average of 10 knots, the noise maker (at 20 knots) could be heard at 6000 yds.

Development continued, so that in July 1919 the US Navy's experimental station recommended installation of an array of twenty-four spot microphones in the peak tank of a destroyer (USS *Bernadou* was chosen). An alternative was an MV-16 in the forward trimming tank (USS *Breckenridge* was chosen in July 1919). Both arrays were installed at Philadelphia Navy Yard.

The alternative to listening, tried extensively during the war but not operational at its end, was echo detection – sonar (Asdic).[30] The advantage of this approach was that the ping sent out could easily be distinguished from other sounds. Alternative techniques were to use short-wavelength sound above audible frequencies

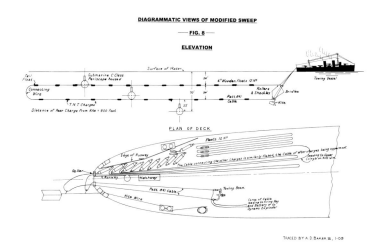

At the outbreak of war the only Royal Navy anti-submarine weapon in service was the Single Sweep shown here. Several hundred Modified Sweeps were made; by 1917 they were used almost exclusively by slow vessels such as trawlers and sloops. It was considered very efficient, but was unpopular due to its bulkiness and inconvenience. (A D Baker III)

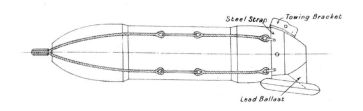

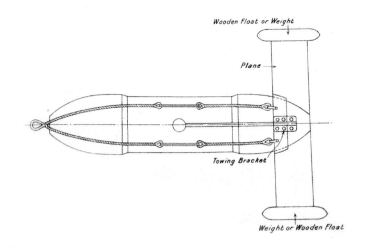

The Single Towed Charge was intended as a simple weapon which could be towed at an adjustable depth and bearing abaft a trawler or other small craft. It consisted of two Modified Sweep Charges fitted to tow at a set depth, one on each quarter of a trawler. At the same speed it could be considered about 60 per cent as efficient as a Modified Sweep. Construction of the first eighteen, for trawlers, was approved in January 1916, a provisional handbook being prepared in May. The charge proved satisfactory in service, so another fifty sets were ordered in October for trawlers with no other type of sweep. It was not as efficient as the Modified Sweep used by destroyers, but it was considered superior in bad weather given its simplicity and its small drag. During the war about 1000 ships were fitted with this type of sweep.

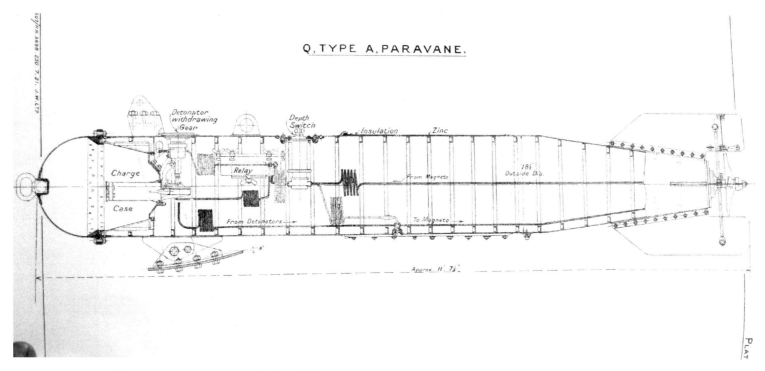

Q, TYPE A, PARAVANE.

(supersonics), audible sound (sonics) and explosions.[31] In 1916 Dr Paul Langevin, a well-known French physicist, sent a signal 3km and detected the reflection of a large iron plate 100m away, using a 100 kHz signal. His transmitter was a condenser. The BIR in England took up this work in August 1916, trying alternatives to the French work to avoid duplication. Both Langevin and the principal British investigator Dr R W Boyle used quartz crystals; both during and after the war the US Navy preferred Rochelle crystals. In each case, the key was piezo-electricity: the crystal converted electricity into an oscillation and vice versa. The British work apparently lapsed after 1916, because in February 1918 the US mission to England reported that the Board on Invention and Research was just about to take up Langevin's idea that a beam of high-frequency sound could be used to detect a stopped submarine. By that time a quartz transmitter, eight-stage amplifier and nine-stage amplifier had received echoes from a ship 1000 yds away. The 15 to 20° wide beam was powerful enough to produce an unpleasant sensation in a hand held nearby and to kill fish.

Initially the key to echo detection was an amplifier to process the weak signal from the crystal. The French led because they had the best electronic amplifiers (a technology in which the United States was also ahead at the time). By 1918 Boyle was using compressed sheets of quartz and an eight-tube amplifier. He enclosed the quartz transducer in a streamlined water-filled dome under a ship's keel, so that however the ship moved, the quartz was surrounded by still water. It worked better than expected, offering a range of about 1000 yds on a submarine, submerged or surfaced, or on a small surface ship. This was possible at 7 knots, the highest speed of the available experimental vessel. A bottomed submarine could be detected at 400 to 700 yds in 25 fathoms (140ft).

By the autumn of 1917 the US Navy was also working on supersonics for echo detection, a group at San Pedro generating the signals. This group was also working on detecting sub-audible (very low frequency) submarine sounds. The US Navy dropped nearly all of its passive sonic devices post-war in favour of what it called supersonics and later sonar. French experiments in active detection continued after the war, but with only limited success; the French

The High Speed Submarine Sweep was the original 'Burney Sweep' using his paravane, a towed body which could be set to ride at a set depth and angle from the towing ship. It was developed into a High Speed Mine Sweep (HSMS) and into the High Speed Combined (i.e., anti-mine and anti-submarine) Sweep. This is the anti-submarine paravane (Q Type A) with explosive head. Like the other towed charges, it was detonated on command from the towing ship. These paravanes did not prove successful.

seem to have been surprised when the British revealed Asdic to them in 1939.

Silencing

Sensitivity made it possible to hear a U-boat at a much greater range, but a sensitive receiver could also hear too much self-noise. Among the earliest points made by the US Special Board was that self-noise was the main problem in detection.[32] In new ships, all auxiliaries should be sound-insulated from a ship's hull; all blowers, pumps, etc. should be silent-running; and provision should be made to secure all equipment and fittings so that they would not move in a seaway. Existing ships should be refitted to make them quieter. The Board pointed out that noise both reduced the effectiveness of the ship's listening devices and betrayed her presence to a U-boat.

If silencing running machinery was impractical, it could be shut down temporarily, the hunter operating in what would later be called 'sprint and drift' mode, shifting rapidly between silent drifting operation and the sprint towards the submarine's estimated position before she could move very far. In 1917 the new petrol-powered sub-chasers were particularly well adapted to such operation, because their engines could be shut down quickly and restarted. Converted yachts had limited low-powered auxiliaries which could also be shut down completely. Destroyers were a different story. Steam-powered ships could not shut down auxiliaries, such as pumps which ran their boilers, and then rapidly re-start. Tests on the destroyer *Aylwin* showed that the main source of noise was reciprocating machinery; turbines and electric motors were relatively quiet.[33] The Board recommended installing quiet pumps in new-construction destroyers not yet laid down. In July 1918 the Board was supporting a proposal to eliminate most of the noise produced by existing machinery by rebalancing it.

The US submarine *L-10* was used for tests, the object being both to make her a particularly effective listening ship and to measure effective listening ranges against her. As was often later discovered, the problems were not the obvious ones. Sources of noise were loose and vibrating stanchions and lifelines; radio masts and aerial (of negligible effect, however, at low speed); the chain of the deck anchor; gear in deck lockers; loose flaps over openings in the superstructure; blowing and flooding tanks when trimming down and maintaining depth at very low speed; the gyro compass (impractical to remove); and the muffler exhaust when on the surface. The Special Board then eliminated these sources one by one, for example by removing stanchions and life lines and securing the anchor chain in the chain locker.

Another approach was to insulate a hydrophone from self-noise by towing it, like a modern towed array. On this basis in February 1918 the British abandoned a programme to fit all trawlers with hull hydrophones in favour of one to fit many (not all) trawlers with towed 'fish' hydrophones.

In 1917–18 the British were experimenting with both water-jet propulsion (on board two trawlers) and with bubble screens to block the noise of the propellers from a hull hydrophone further forward. In 1918 two *Strath* class trawlers were fitted with water-jet propulsors in place of their conventional (loud) engines.[34]

Non-acoustics

During the war, the British experimented with both magnetic detection and what would later be called underwater electric potential (UEP).[35] Although magnetic detection offered only a short range, it proved useful in the form of wire indicator loops laid on the sea bottom (to detect the presence of a submarine directly above) and as a triggering mechanism for magnetic mines. Notes on indicator loops in the December 1918 summary report of the Admiralty Board on Invention and Research (BIR) indicate that the idea was first advanced in a September 1915 letter describing experiments carried out by Professor Crichton Mitchell in the Firth of Forth that July; he could detect ships using a loop on the bottom. During 1917 Parkeston Quay experimented with signalling between ships and a loop in Harwich Harbour. The loops could also detect ships and they soon became the basis of 'search apparatus'. The loops proved sensitive, although in some cases they picked up disturbances from nearby trolley lines. The loops were also sensitive to variations in the earth's magnetic field, but both forms of interference could be balanced out. The experiments were described in the September and November 1917 editions of the ASD *Monthly Notes* and loops soon entered service both in the United Kingdom and in the United States. Loops were also used to fire controlled ASW mines. Both in the UK and in the US electromagnetic methods were proposed for search by ships, but they did not reach the test stage. Another possibility was to detect the UEP produced by the rotating propeller of a submarine or ship, at the frequency of the propeller blades. Detection was by towed electrodes. In very early tests, a boat could pick up a trawler several hundred yards away and a bottom array could pick up a torpedo boat at 500 to 600 yds. UEP was tested as a mine sensor during the Second World War and it became important in the 1960s.

Yet another technique (Search Apparatus) detected currents in

Submarines were fleeting targets. Aside from hydrophones, they were usually detected when they showed their periscopes (which they had to do in order to attack) or from the wakes of their torpedoes. The British Lance Bomb, shown here being thrown, was conceived early in the war as a way of dealing with a sudden nearby sighting, or with a submarine a ship had just narrowly missed ramming. In effect it was an anti-submarine harpoon. It was a 7lb TNT charge mounted on a broomstick for easy throwing out to 30 or 35ft. The fuze was designed to detonate only on hitting a solid object, not when hitting the water. Early trials showed that it would seriously damage the outer hull of a submarine and possibly even the inner hull. Its handbook recommended using at least two charges to ensure the destruction of the target. The project began in November 1914 as a proposed motor boat weapon. It seemed that, given their speed, the boats had a fair chance of getting close to a submarine. Initial trials were carried out in January 1915, using a 5lb charge. By February 1915, 1000 were on order and enough TNT for 6500 was being obtained. In March it was proposed to double the order and by mid-April Lance Bombs had been sent to all bases at which Indicator Net drifters were stationed. In a September 1915 test against the old submarine A 2, a Lance Bomb dropped from 3ft above water (with the submarine deck 10ft below the surface) destroyed the superstructure within a radius of about 4ft, caused the hull to bulge up about 15 inches over a 3ft radius. Although plates were not broken, seams and rivets were started and internal frames cracked. Instructions issued in March 1915 called for a ready-use supply of four. By 1917 the Lance Bomb had been dismissed as of little practical value. In 1915 there were also hand changes consisting of three or more 9oz discs of guncotton, with a detonator and safety fuze. A 40-yd line was to be attached, with a weight at the free end. One man would throw the charge, the other pulling on the line to move the charge into contact with the target

the sea arising from the submarine itself between electrodes towed by the hunter, fed by a generator aboard it. A Mk III version fielded in limited numbers used two towed electrodes, detecting current generated by the submarine, which had both intermittent and non-intermittent components (VF and CF). Mk IV, which was also fielded, relied only on CF and was somewhat limited because its readings were disturbed whenever the boat turned (Mk V largely solved that problem, using three electrodes). Effective range was 100ft, whether or not the submarine was moving. It was considered the best available short-range detector. This technique was also proposed as the triggering mechanism for an explosive paravane.

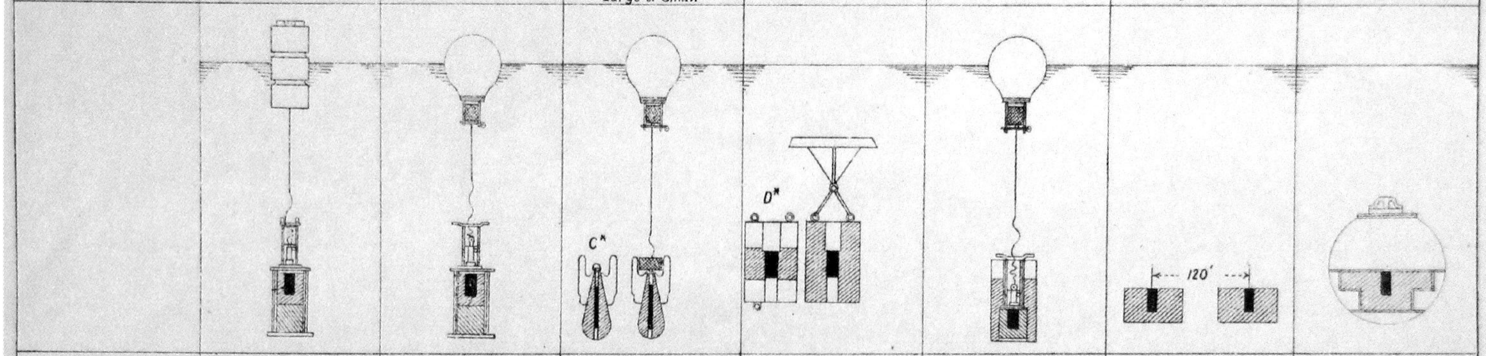

Type	A	B	C & C* Large or Small	D & D*	E	Egerton	Cruiser Mine
Charge	G.C.	G C	T.N.T. or Amatol	T.N.T. or Amatol	T.N.T or Amatol / G.C.	T.N.T	G.C
Weight	32½ lbs	32½ lbs.	65 lbs or 35 lbs.	D 300 lbs D* 120 lbs	100 lbs / 16¼ lbs.	Total 150 lbs.	250 lbs
Primer	G.C. 2¼ lbs	G.C. 2¼ lbs.	Tetryl 12 ozs	G.C. 2¼ lbs	G.C. 2¼ lbs.	G.C. each 2¼ lbs	G.C. 2¼ lbs.
Total Wt. of Explosive	34¾ lbs.	34¾ lbs.	65¾ lbs or 35¾ lbs.	D 302¼ lbs. D* 122¼ lbs.	118½ lbs.	154½ lbs.	252¼ lbs.
Danger spheres in feet showing Submarine to same scale.	20'	20'	20'	70' / 140'	70'	55' / 55'	100'
Danger Volume in C.Ft.	4200	4200	50,000 or 4200	D 1,437,000 D* 180,000	179,600	65,400 / 65,400	589,000
Depths arranged to Fire at	40 Ft	40 or 80	C 40 or 80 C* 50	40 or 80	40 or 80	Probable Max^m - 50 but depends on speed	45
Total weight of Charge & Float	210 lbs.	170	90	D 430 D* 250	220	200	1,150
-Ve Buoyancy of Charge	80 lbs	80	50	200	50		50
Rate of Sinking			10 F.S.	D 5 F.S. to 40' with Parachute D 8 F.S. to 80' without Parachute D* 5 F.S. without Parachute	5 F.S.		7-8 F.S.
How operated	Mechanically	Mechanically	C Mechanically C* Hydrostatically	Hydrostatically	Mechanically	Electrically	Hydrostatically
Special Features				Primer Safety Gear		Electrically Fitted	

Beginning in the summer of 1917, the US Navy's Special Board developed the Pierce Trailing Wire as an essential adjunct to listening devices. The wire would register a metal object it brushed; in effect it was the sensor of the special ASW mine (used in the Northern Barrage) without the mine. It was considered essential as a means of detecting and locating bottomed submarines, which could hide from listeners because they were silent.[36]

By 1915 the Royal Navy was beginning to deploy depth charges, initially described as mines intended to fire on reaching a set depth. Development began with a December 1914 request by Admiral Jellicoe. Some Service Mk II mines were converted and issued as 'cruiser mines' set to fire automatically at 45ft depth. Type C was a converted 65lb bomb, part of a project to develop an ASW bomb for aircraft; test examples were ordered in January 1915. It had a 20ft hydrostatic fuze and a contact fuze. Other 65lb bombs were adapted using pull-out fuzes employed pending development of the preferred hydrostatic fuze: the charge was connected to a float, going off when the wire was pulled from it as it sank. Several guncotton charges were fitted with the same type of fuze, pending development of a permanent type (Types A, B and E). The ultimate depth charge, Type D, was conceived from the outset with a charge of 300lb of Amatol and a hydrostatic fuze. By June 1915 *Vernon* had a two-setting hydrostatic fuze and by the end of August an order for 1000 Type D had been approved. In October a smaller 120lb charge was approved, for use by smaller or slower craft (it became Type D*). Distribution of Type D charges began in January 1916. Type G was an even smaller charge (45lbs TNT); Type F was a bomb from a 3.5in howitzer. Wartime experience showed that the supposed lethal radius of depth charges had been badly overstated. The Egerton depth charge consisted of two Modified Sweep charges which could be quickly let go; when the electric cable became taut, it fired them. Total Royal Navy depth charge expenditure reported from June 1917 to the end of the war was 16,451, out of 74,441 depth charges issued beginning in January 1916.

Weapons

Admiralty trials (proposed on 29 December 1903) conducted between 8 and 18 March 1904 showed that the mere threat of a submarine off a blockaded port would force ships to manoeuvre at high speed to avoid torpedo attack. A few simple weapons had been offered: a hand charge, a towing charge, an indicator net and a lasso net. The towing charge was fitted with a grapnel intended to foul the submarine's periscope and to be set off by a firing key on board the destroyer armed with it. The umpires pointed out that the trials would have been even more depressing had they been less artificial. Destroyers were tempting targets: they had to stop, often within 400 yds of a submarine, to use their grapnels.

Given trials experience, a Captain Ogilvy proposed an explosive sweep (in a 9 June 1905 report). It became the basis of the first major British anti-submarine weapon: an explosive charge in a depth-keeping kite. It would explode on contact with anything it fouled, which might be a periscope or even a submarine. The sweep was tested on board torpedo boats in January 1906, in a version fired electrically when contact was indicated. Like contemporary mine sweeps, this one was towed by pairs of boats. Unfortunately its drag was such that sweep speed was limited to 6 knots. However, the sweep was interesting enough that by 1909 work was proceeding on a high-speed sweep which a destroyer could tow. Further submarine exercises, including work with a battle fleet, were conducted in June and July 1909.

A Submarine Committee was formed in March 1910. It included submariners, who could evaluate potential countermeasures. The Committee called for trials of the high-speed sweep on board a 'Tribal' or 'River' class destroyer. It also wanted to know whether a destroyer spotting a periscope 500 yds away could torpedo the submarine under it. The Committee also suggested that observers in a balloon or dirigible might see submerged submarines, much as sea-birds spotted their fish prey from aloft.

A destroyer towing a sweep could detect and attack any submarine over which it passed. A screen of destroyers could protect a column of heavy ships by blocking the approach area ahead of it. HMS *Vernon* designed a sweep employing two cables separated vertically by 30ft, to cover the full range of likely submarine depth. An explosive charge would be run down the sweep when it snagged a submarine. Trials of a sweep towed by a pair of torpedo gunboats began in May 1910. The destroyers *Maori* and *Crusader* were given strengthened decks and special winches for high-speed (17-knot) trials, towing a sweep together. The results were unhappy. Fitted to submerge automatically, the old submarine *A 1* passed over or simply parted the sweep.

The next step, proposed by the Committee in March 1911, was a towed charge which would be carried into any object which fouled the sweep. It was used effectively against *A 1* by the destroyer *Crusader* in July 1911. On 27 October 1911 the Admiralty approved fitting the charges to two destroyers in each of the four fleet flotillas. The Committee hoped that a screen of fast ships three to four miles ahead of a group of surface ships could effectively screen it. Screening diagrams produced in 1911–12 were much like those of a later era, the idea of limiting lines of approach being the same. Clearly a submarine could evade the screen, but in that case it would not be able to attack the ships being protected. An attacking submarine would have to show her periscope. A submarine not doing so would be blinded at a critical moment and would risk being rammed by one of the ships in the main body. Submarines approaching from ahead would find it difficult to estimate the speed of the fleet, but would have to do so in order to attack. Even pickets without sweeps would deter submarines.

A Modified Single Sweep tested by HMS *Seagull* in June 1912 had upper and lower wires, the latter carrying nine 80lb charges, so that instead of being dangerous (to the submarine) only at one end, the sweep could damage a submarine wherever it was fouled. It covered a much larger area than the Single Sweep: a vertical area 300 yds long by 48ft deep (and a submarine would have to dive to 70ft to clear the lower wire). An electrical signal was generated whenever either wire was fouled. Given the signal, an operator on the towing vessel triggered the charges. In July 1913 it was decided to fit the Modified Sweep for trials in four light cruisers, six mine-sweeping former torpedo gunboats and two destroyers. Commodore (S) considered the Modified Sweep an 'unpleasant menace to a Submarine approaching at an angle to the course of the vessel towing [it] and it is superior to anything which has been suggested in that its operation does not depend on the Submarine being sighted'. Meanwhile all the Single Sweeps were placed on board destroyers of the 4th Flotilla. The main attempted pre-war improvement in the sweep was an attempt to detect a submarine over which (or near which) it passed without fouling it. In 1911 the Submarine Committee tried electric and magnetic detectors without success.

The sweeps defined pre-war ASW tactics. During the 1913 manoeuvres, the Blue fleet tried experimental tactics.[37] The fleet was preceded by a double screen of destroyers, the forward one four to five miles ahead in line abreast, the destroyers five cables (1000 yds) apart, the inner screen in an irregular line abreast, 1500

Depth-charging required that the attacker fill an area with explosions. At the least, she had to do more than roll charges off her stern. That became more urgent as submarines demonstrated their agility, so in June 1917 trials with a depth-charge thrower (in effect a miniature howitzer) were ordered. This was the Thornycroft depth-charge thrower. Range was fixed at 40 yds. Installation was ordered in August 1917, two such throwers being added to the depth-charge battery (four charges) of torpedo craft. These paired throwers were on board a US destroyer in European waters. The Royal Navy continued to use Thornycroft throwers in the Second World War.

to 2500 yds ahead of the fleet. The fleet ran at high speed. Its cruisers altered course every 15 minutes, always being two points off the course to be made good. The fleet flagship *Neptune* and the 1st Battle Squadron used the screen and high speed when approaching Perth on the morning of 27 July in smooth weather. Despite the precautions, *D 6* surfaced 1500 yds from the rear battleship, presumably having attacked. It was not clear to what extent the screen had handicapped her. *Collingwood* was successfully attacked off the Swaarte Bank while steaming at 10.5 knots. In describing these trials, Home Fleet C-in-C Admiral Callaghan commented that explosive sweeps did not seem to be the answer, because their efficacy depended on the number of screening vessels. He 'did not know of any case during the manoeuvres where, when a ship was attacked by a submarine, the submarine could have been herself attacked by a destroyer with single sweep in time to be of any use'.

Remarks by Commodore (S) Roger Keyes were even less comforting. He found ships' commanders, with some notable exceptions, very vague about submarine capabilities and methods of attack and of evading counter-attack, 'judging by the claims made against submarines and the manner in which the claims of the latter were often ignored and over-ruled'. Keyes was well aware of his submarines' limitations, of their low submerged speed, the risk they ran while surfaced and their very limited full-speed radius when submerged. But if it was conceded that their torpedoes ran straight, they could deliver a high percentage of successful attacks. In his view, during the manoeuvres submarines 'took practically all the risks they would be called upon to take in time of war. Ships altered course frequently at high speed, destroyers and light cruisers rushed full speed at the submarines who, thanks to the training they have received during the last year, have learnt that there is nothing to fear from light draught vessels. The vitals of submarines are at all times below the keels of destroyers and those of later classes under the keels of light cruisers.' It was practically impossible for a light-draught ship to run down or damage any part of a submarine other than her periscope and a few degrees of 'down' helm would take even an extended periscope out of danger. Although diving under a battleship was not so attractive, submarines often saved themselves by doing so. During the manoeuvre, *D 2* deliberately dived to 60 or 70ft on hearing battleship propellers, having passed through two destroyer screens. A submarine needed sufficient additional depth to dive (10 fathoms for a small submarine, 12 fathoms for a larger one), but given that she could dive to 60 to 70ft in under a minute.

It seemed to Keyes that the only danger his submarines had not been subjected to during the manoeuvres was gunfire while surfaced; but he doubted that a destroyer rushing a submarine at high speed could sink her in two minutes, as her vitals were all under water and her conning tower was so small a target. Even so, a conning tower seen on the surface during the manoeuvres sufficed to count a submarine as out of action. Keyes entirely discounted the popular idea of firing at an exposed periscope, despite claims of success against dummy periscopes. He also pointed out that unless its feather was seen, a visible periscope gave no idea of a submarine's course. Submarine commanders already knew how to show their periscopes intermittently.

Keyes later pointed out that in the exercise *D 8* was not much bothered by the destroyer screen, but that was partly to unusual water conditions. The propellers of the battle fleet could be heard at an abnormal distance. The CO of the submarine thought that the battleships had altered course and were about to pass over him. He dove to 60 to 70ft to avoid them. The plot he was maintaining was actually correct; had he trusted it, he would have come up in position to attack the first or second ship after passing under the screen. Instead, he waited until he was clear of the last ship and came up in a position to attack her from 600 yd range (based on his periscope scale).

Many officers imagined that a submarine had to surface to fire torpedoes; on more than one occasion a submarine was counted out of action when she surfaced to claim a hit. Those involved rarely realised that the submarine was firing at a considerable deflection to hit a fast ship and that it took her about a minute to surface, so that she was not seen in anything like the relative position from which she had fired. The worst thing about the manoeuvres was that no torpedoes were fired, so success or failure was a matter of opinion. Surely in at least one manoeuvre the submarines should fire torpedoes, even thought that would deplete stocks. Admiral of Patrols de Robeck generally agreed with Keyes, particularly as to the way umpires had so often ruled out torpedo hits.

Keyes pointed to the mechanics of submarine approach and attack as keys to successful defence (not, however, to the destruction of the submarine). Once submerged, a submarine had very limited speed and it had to get close to its target. Above all, the approach had to be based on a reasonably good estimate of the target's course and speed. Anything which ruined that estimate would save the target. Keyes' formula was to keep the submarine down, limiting its mobility and also limiting its vision to that of its periscope. To do that, he proposed that a formation be preceded by a line of cruisers and destroyers at maximum visual distance. A submarine encountering the line would dive to avoid being destroyed by gunfire. If visibility was really good, it might be

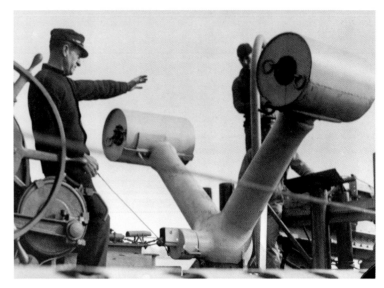

The US Navy replaced Thornycroft throwers with 'Y-guns', in which a single charge launched two depth charges simultaneously. A single Y-gun weighed considerably less than two Thornycroft throwers, but it required clear space across a ship's deck. That was no problem when a ship had a single Y-gun, but few ships had enough space for two of them.

essential to provide a second line. These scouting lines would cover a broad front. The formation behind the scouting line would be line abreast (ships as close together as possible), changing course as often as possible at high speed. The least valuable ships should be on the flanks, each of which would protected by about four destroyers about 1000 yds off, covering the danger angle from submarine attack. Given their broadside tubes, British submarines passing between ships still had good chance of hitting as they passed, but continual zig-zagging (together) by the ships would seriously hamper them. No submarine limited to bow and stern tubes (as the Germans were) could easily manoeuvre between lines of ships close enough together. Some foreign submarines had revolving deck tubes, but Keyes doubted that they were effective and he also considered angling (as practiced abroad) ineffective.

In Keyes' view, single line ahead was the worst possible formation to adopt in the presence of submarines, as it offered them the longest possible target. Even if a destroyer screen blocked the head of the line, the submarine would still be able to work around it to hit ships further down the line. He did appreciate the concept of limiting lines of approach: the faster the formation and the broader on the beam the submarine, the more difficult it would be for her to attack the leading ship or ships. It followed that a screen across the bow of a formation could protect only a few ships. Moreover, the longer the torpedo range, the broader the protected area – the greater the number of destroyers – had to be, to keep the targets out of torpedo range. During the First World War, both Admiral Jellicoe and his German counterparts used destroyer screens across the heads of formations and generally they had to assign a destroyer screen to each of several battle squadrons. That in turn greatly increased the minimum number of destroyers the fleet had to take to sea and to keep there.

All of the experiments were conducted in daylight. British submarines had been successful in night attacks against blockading destroyers in the 1904 manoeuvres, but the single-hull submarines with limited reserve buoyancy were considered very vulnerable to accidental ramming. As a consequence, they were not permitted to operate at night in peacetime manoeuvres, although undoubtedly they would often attack at night in war. That worked two ways. During the 1913 manoeuvres submarines were immune from attack at night, giving them invaluable rest. Keyes wrote that a submarine which spent a long and anxious day blockading an enemy port by day would probably be unfit for work that night, when her crew badly needed to rest. Keyes felt that his conclusions would be modified should the modified sweep prove successful, as it could be deployed particularly effectively by flanking destroyers.

Summarising a variety of comments, Admiral of Patrols de Robeck observed that 'high speed and alteration of course by the Fleet must be its means of salvation once the enemy's submarines are in touch with it'. He thought that smoke, particularly if it could be made to lie low on the sea, would be a valuable means of blinding a submarine relying on its periscope. In mid-September C-in-C Home Fleets Admiral Callaghan circulated the comments to his major subordinates and to C-in-C Mediterranean and Admiral of Patrols.

On 5 May 1914 the Submarine Committee proposed that patrol flotillas of destroyers be fitted with the Modified Sweep on a priority basis, to screen the fleet when it was most vulnerable, approaching or leaving its bases.[38] Once more sweeps were produced, they could be installed on board the fleet's destroyers. By the eve of war (as reported on 6 July 1914), the destroyers *Goshawk* and *Lizard* had both been fitted with the Modified Sweep. At the outbreak of war arrangements were made to fit the Modified Sweep to destroyers at Chatham and to trawlers at Lowestoft and to provide fifty sets of equipment at each of Portsmouth, Devonport and Chatham. A few days later a Commander Superintending Modified Sweep (CSMS) was appointed. His staff gradually grew and on 8 December 1914 it became the Submarine Attack Committee (SAC), which survived (albeit renamed) until the formation of an Anti-Submarine Division in the Admiralty in December 1915. Trawlers should be trained in the use of the modified sweep and detailed to form a constant patrol across the approaches of principal ports to keep submarines out. This was the basis of the Auxiliary Patrol set up after war broke out.

Mining should be revived as a defensive measure, using some reliable form of EC (Electric Contact) and mechanical contact mines to block entrances to harbours. It might be possible to devise mines which could be floated and retracted at will, so that channels could be changed back and forth as desired. That might be expensive, but it would be worthwhile.

'In the future when aircraft accompany a fleet, they may possibly be able by scouting ahead to so harry submarines that the latter will never successfully attack, but this is a degree of perfection still very far from attainment'. It only became really practical well after the First World War, when regular anti-submarine air patrols were typically mounted either by catapult-fired floatplanes or by carrier aircraft. Like Keyes' screen ahead of a fleet, such patrols kept submarines out of the limiting lines of approach in front of and to the sides of a fast-moving formation.

The Committee considered the danger zones to be within 60 miles of the enemy's coast and within 100 miles of the British coast, at places such as approaches to bases and to coaling ports. The open sea would be far safer. It suggested other ASW measures: British submarines lurking off an enemy's bases (or cued by patrolling aircraft in British coastal areas) and scouring areas with fast motor craft to force submarines to dive and thus to use up their

reserves of battery power. The Committee also pointed out that 'damage may be done to a submarine by bursting high explosive shell of large calibre in her vicinity and it may therefore be worth firing even the largest guns for this purpose'. This was the essence of the depth charge.

For Keyes the clearest implication of the report was that the best way to attack a hostile submarine was to catch it on the surface and torpedo it. He also observed that the advent of the submarine had revived defensive mining. Just a few years earlier Admiral Fisher and other had used the existence of *British* submarines to justify eliminating defensive mining as an anti-invasion measure. Keyes was also careful not to overplay the submarine's immunity.

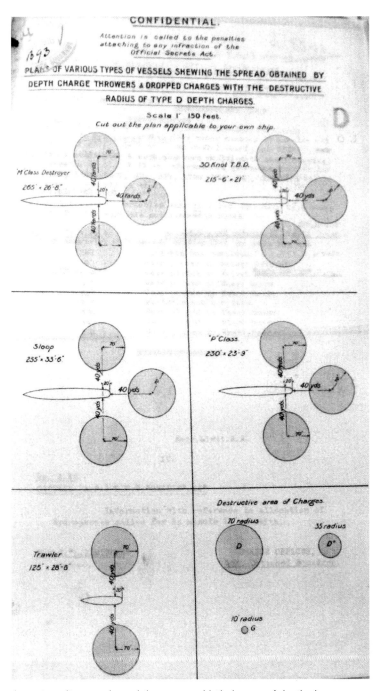

A wartime diagram showed the supposed lethal areas of depth charges dropped by various types of ships. There was no attempt to create the elaborate 'sandwich' patterns of explosions common in Second World War ASW. Depth charges launched abeam were from Thornycroft throwers.

Those with submarine experience 'were not inclined to exaggerate their powers and are quite alive to their limitations and to the great risks they will run of being caught on the surface at night, in a half-light, or in hazy weather and rammed or destroyed by gunfire before they can dive. Casualties in this connection are bound to be heavy in war, particularly among those carrying out the blockade of an enemy's ports.'

Keyes also pointed out that the submariners' ability to get a high percentage of hits would not equate to massive damage to the enemy until there were many more British submarines. Any one submarine would enjoy only a few opportunities; the submarine menace to the enemy might be more moral than real, particularly on the high seas or at a distance from a base. That was not to denigrate the moral effect of a constant threat of attack. Keyes felt that the Germans understood as much. Unlike the British, they did not rely on submarines to defend their harbours. Instead, they spent the whole of their submarine appropriation, which was about that of the Royal Navy, on oversea submarines.[39]

War revealed some good news for the defence. Destroyers turned out to be far more difficult targets than expected, particularly if they were manoeuvring rapidly at high speed. Even when fired at a shallow depth (20ft) a torpedo took some time (distance) to come to its set depth. Because the submarine had to fire at short range to hope to hit a manoeuvring destroyer, the torpedo generally could not come to the proper shallow depth in time. The British experienced this problem and they had reason to think that the Germans were in much the same position, since their torpedoes used the same depth-keeping technology. Worse, when the submarine fired, it created a very visible air discharge, which a lookout would see. This was a much easier proposition than searching for a periscope in rough water.[40] A submarine on patrol, unaware of the presence of a hostile submarine, was a much easier target than a destroyer manoeuvring at speed.

The Modified Sweep was both complex to make and difficult to stream, so once war broke out the fleet proposed single-charge alternatives, still towed. The Harwich Force developed the 'Egerton Depth Charge', consisting of two Single Modified Sweep charges which could be let go quickly at the end of their electrical cable. When it tautened, they were fired automatically. It armed thirty-five destroyers and some light cruisers. The next step was a charge towed at an angle to a ship's course, sweeping out a wider path. This Modified Single Sweep charge (Single Towed Charge) was tested on the orders of Captain (D) 7th Flotilla. Tests showed that the charge body used in the Modified Single Sweep was unstable at destroyer speeds, so this weapon was issued only to trawlers.

When war broke out the only existing anti-submarine weapon was the sweep in various forms. It was good enough for Admiral Jellicoe to see his destroyers (which were fitted with sweeps) as an essential means of screening his battleships as they left base. He needed enough destroyers to screen each battle squadron as it sortied, but he did not see a need to maintain the screen once the fleet was well out to sea. Jellicoe cited the need for screens as a basis for demanding more destroyers to work with the Grand Fleet.

The sweep offered defensive capability. A simplified sweep, which could be towed at an angle, materialised as the High Speed Submarine Sweep, using the explosive-laden (240lb) Paravane Type Q and it entered service in 1917. The paravane carried its explosive down and away from the ship's wake in a controllable way. Typically a ship towed a Q Mk IV dead astern at a depth set

A British fleet destroyer shows her limited depth-charge armament: two charges on a centreline track and four more on slides (one of the after port slides is empty). The canvas-covered shape is a paravane crane, with a second crane on the other side. These 'M' class destroyers could not have accommodated throwers except by sacrificing either their after guns or some torpedo tubes and thus substantially reducing their ability to deal with surface threats – including surfaced submarines. Destroyers assigned to hunting groups had much heavier depth-charge batteries at a cost in surface firepower.

by the length of cable (down to 200ft, which was considered deep for a submarine). A Q Mk III was towed off to one side at a set depth of 100ft. Each could be exploded by contact, by tension as the electric tow line snagged, or by command from the ship. The paravane could be towed continuously at 20 knots and for short periods at 25 knots. It was light and easily handled and it was safe when stowed aboard a ship. It did not inhibit manoeuvres by the towing ship and it was considered more effective than any other

Hunters had considerably heavier depth-charge batteries. This is the quarterdeck of a sloop in a fish hydrophone division. On each side is a long depth-charge track. Between them are four Thornycroft throwers. The single paravane visible aft was an anti-submarine version with an explosive head.

sweep. The sweep was considered complementary to depth charges. It was generally described as an offensive weapon to attack a submarine in a known position, e.g. one caught in an indicator net (trawlers also had a version of the paravane). However, it could also be used to screen a moving force from ahead. Explosive sweeps survived the war in both the French and the Italian navies (the British abandoned the sweep in favour of depth charges). In theory the sweep could also be used to search for a submarine, but it was unlikely to be effective, because it swept out only a narrow path.

Once war began, it became clear that submarines had to be hunted. At the very least, there had to be weapons which could be used whenever a submarine showed itself, however fleetingly. That required some sort of underwater detector. In 1914 navies and merchant marines already used underwater sound for signalling. The obvious next step was to use it to detect submarines. The Royal Navy began work on hydrophones (passive sonar) by November 1914.

Vernon began work on depth charges after a 7 December 1914 request from Admiral Jellicoe for an ASW mine. To meet urgent demand, some Service Mk II mines were modified into what amounted to depth charges (they were called 'cruiser mines'). At first they were triggered by lines attached to floats. When the charge sank to the intended depth, the line from the float was expected to pull out of the charge body, triggering it. Once hydrostatic fuzes became available about 1916, the earlier charges were modified with them. The Germans and the Austrians used pull-out lines throughout the war. Charges were initially set to 80ft, but during 1917 it became clear that deeper settings were needed and a new depth-charge pistol could be set at 50, 100, 150, or 200ft.

Standard depth charges were rolled off a ship's stern, but there was also interest in throwers which could place a charge at a distance. A thrower could react to a submarine spotted (by, say, the track of her torpedo or her periscope) at a distance. DNO later wrote that the Anti-Submarine Committee had been interested in bomb-throwers even before the war, but that ranges were too short to be worthwhile.

The idea of a bomb-thrower or aimable howitzer was revived in the latter part of 1916, possibly as a direct result of a suggestion made late in October 1916 by Admiral Jellicoe.[41] The resulting Sutton Armstrong 3.5in 200lb stick-bomb thrower, thirty of which were ordered in December 1916, was the first purely naval weapon of this type. Successful range and accuracy trials on 28 April 1917 led to orders for fifty more; eighty-two had been delivered by November 1918.

Early in 1917 all three major British armament firms were asked for designs. The army was asked whether an existing trench mortar might be adapted to naval use. Twelve army 5in howitzers were sent to Elswick early in March 1917 and their mountings adapted for naval use. This design, whose shell was too light, led to a widely-produced 7.5in weapon. It was the first howitzer adapted to throw bombs at submerged submarines to enter service. Orders for 750 Vickers 7.5in howitzers were placed in March 1917, followed by another 250 in May, of which the first fifty were to be smoothbores (bomb-throwers) and the rest rifled. Both types used the same non-recoil mounting and fired the same 100lb projectile with a $43\frac{1}{2}$lb burster. The projectile was the heaviest that could be man-handled. By November 1918, 933 of these howitzers had been delivered, plus forty-eight bomb-throwers. Seven of the howitzers were allocated to the French and US navies. Of the howitzers, 660 were no board defensively-armed merchant ships (DAMS) and another 170 on board auxiliary patrol ships, plus six on board sloops and special service vessels. Of the bomb-throwers, eighteen were on board DAMS and nineteen on board auxiliary patrol ships. None of either type was on board conventional British warships.

The 100lb shell was not powerful enough, so work began on larger-calibre weapons, a 10in bomb-thrower and an 11in howitzer. At the end of March 1917, 210 Vickers-designed 11in howitzers were ordered, distributed among the three firms. A total of 107 had been delivered by the end of the war, of which twenty were on board British warships and another thirty-two on board armed merchant cruisers (AMCs). The 10in bomb-thrower was designed by Vickers after successful tests of a 9.5in Thornycroft bomb-thrower. A total of 750 was ordered in July 1917, but production proved so difficult that in April 1918, 350 bomb-throwers were cancelled and re-ordered elsewhere. Of ninety-four delivered by the beginning of November 1918, eighty-four were on board DAMS. None was on board a commissioned British warship.

The allocation of the howitzers and bomb-throwers suggests that they were considered exclusively as a means of snap attack against submarines which suddenly revealed themselves. In about August 1918 Captain F C Dreyer, who was then DGD, advocated mounting two howitzers on board each capital ship, on the forecastle, to deal with pop-up submarine targets. However, Admiral Beatty, commanding the Grand Fleet, rejected the idea in favour of strengthening the screening force; no howitzers were mounted on board British capital ships.

These howitzers and throwers were apart from the 9.5in depth-charge thrower developed by Thornycroft and installed on board destroyers beginning in 1917. It had a much shorter range (40 yds). The installation on board the 'L' class destroyer *Linnet* was typical: one thrower on each side, on a 50° bearing abaft the beam, 124ft from the chute in the stern. This ship was tested in June 1917, dropping three charges simultaneously from throwers and chute. The Royal Navy retained the Thornycroft thrower in the inter-war period and into the Second World War.

Overall, no one seems to have imagined how many charges it would take to destroy a submarine. Thus the first formal scale of fitting, promulgated by the Admiralty on 8 April 1916, was two Type D charges in chutes, one to have a hydraulic (i.e., remote) release and one manual on all destroyers not fitted with the High Speed Sweep or Modified Sweep (but those fitted for minesweeping would have only a single Type D charge with hydraulic release). All cruisers and light cruisers in Home and Mediterranean waters and all flotilla leaders (except *Abdiel*) would be similarly fitted. Older destroyers unsuited to carrying Type D charges, as well as torpedo boats in home and Mediterranean waters would carry Type C★ charges in tilting trays. The armament of two Type D or D★ remained standard until mid-June 1917, by which time it was clear that U-boats could take survive more depth-charging. The standard for sloops (and then all torpedo craft) was increased to four charges. Formal depth-charge battle practice began in December 1917. Two throwers (termed howitzers), each carrying a single charge (range 40 yds) were added beginning in August 1917. This was the same device used between wars and during the Second World War (a 1924 proposal for an alternative thrower failed). The installation on board the *Linnet* was typical, with a thrower on each side, on a 50° bearing abaft the beam, 124ft from the chute in the stern (she was tested in June 1917, dropping three charges simultaneously from throwers and chute). The six-charge outfit was inadequate, particularly after ships were fitted with listening devices.

During 1918 all destroyers, P-boats and sloops outside the North Sea and Dover Patrol areas were given thirty to fifty depth charges, sometimes at the cost of guns. The ships modified were probably the ones with fish hydrophones. They were carried on rails and in reload racks at throwers. The *Acasta* class destroyer *Cockatrice* was typical. As refitted with the heavy depth-charge battery, she was tested on 28 February 1918. She had a three-charge reload rack alongside each depth-charge thrower. She also had a twenty-charge rail, the aftermost of which was held in a hydraulically-released trap, with a hand-worked trap through which only one charge at a time rolled. The destroyers *Christopher* and *Ambuscade* had been similarly equipped. 'L' and 'M' class destroyers surrendered their after gun and platform and their after torpedo tubes and all sweeps (the 'K' class surrendered both tubes). HMS *Lookout* carried fifty charges: four throwers, two chutes (thirty charges) and four spares on deck.

Another possibility was a bomb which could be fired from a standard destroyer gun to attack a submarine seen diving (or revealed by her periscope). A stick bomb fired from a 12pdr was tested on 27 June 1918. The 200lb bomb flew 305 yds at 30° elevation, the gun requiring no modification. DNO planned to supply these bombs to all destroyers or other craft operating against submarines. Trawlers and old destroyers mounted these guns. The normal outfit was four bombs per ship. At this time seventy-six destroyers armed with 12pdrs were engaged in ASW: eleven in Irish Sea Hunting Flotillas, twenty-six in 7th Flotilla (Immingham), three at Lowestoft, one at Portland, thirteen at Portsmouth, eight at Dover, three at Devonport, six in the North Channel and six in the Thames. In addition, eight 'Rivers' and four coastal torpedo boats armed with 12pdrs were engaged in ASW in the Mediterranean. Another 430 trawlers operated in home waters, with ninety more abroad. In July 1918 a similar bomb was successfully tested from standard 4in destroyer guns. A Mk IV gun could project a 356lb bomb to 200 yds at 20° elevation (270 yds at 30°); the more powerful Mk V could project a 456lb bomb to 205 yds.

Submarine-hunting flotillas also needed thrown bombs, but they could not easily accommodate the howitzers. Early in 1918 they were assigned received instead 3.5in stick-bomb throwers, which projected a 200lb bomb. The design was modified to reduce deck stress and also to take an alternative 350lb bomb. This stick bomb was later (June 1918) allocated to merchant ships as a quick-reaction weapon. To this end another 1000 (of an improved design) were ordered, of which 500 were to be begun as soon as the new design was ready. All were cancelled at the Armistice. That left 630 stick bombs on order, of which eighty-two had been delivered. Of those, thirty-five were on board auxiliary patrol vessels and eighteen aboard sloops and special service vessels (Q-ships).

The wartime US Navy adopted the British Type D depth charge but not the howitzers and bomb-throwers. It already had a 50lb depth charge (Mk I) using a float and lanyard pull-out. The pre-war US Navy was aware of the smallest British depth charges but not the big Type D, which it adopted (with a different pistol) as its Mk II. British depth charges were provided to US ships in European waters when they arrived and through the war the two navies exchanged depth charges to maintain sufficient numbers. The US Navy's Bureau of Ordnance ordered 10,000 Mk IIs in the summer of 1917 and another 20,000 in January 1918; the British agreed to provide another 15,000 Type D. The small US order was based on limited British use (typically 125 to 150 per month). In April 1918 Admiral Sims pointed out that opportunities for attacks against U-boats were so few that maximum advantage should be taken of each: many more depth charges should be used each time. In contrast to British destroyers working with convoys, US destroyers should carry more depth charges. That was practical because most US destroyers were so much larger than their British equivalents.

The US Bureau of Ordnance developed its own depth-charge thrower, the Y-gun. It fired two charges at a time, one to either beam, using a single impulse charge. Range (to each side) was 40 yds with a 1lb impulse charge, 98 yds with 2lbs. Loading machines were provided to train crews to load in as little as 6 to 10 seconds. A ship so equipped, carrying fifty depth charges, could cover an area 200 yds wide and 1100 yds long with a single barrage. US patrol craft carried British Thornycroft projectors (howitzers) until they could be supplied with the Y-gun. In mid-1918 plans called for equipping all destroyers and some yachts with either one Y-gun and two Thornycrofts or two Y-guns.

In February 1918 ships were ordered to carry at least six 300lb charges, which was the maximum that could safely be carried. Destroyers on anti-submarine duties should carry fifty charges each, sub-chasers twelve, yachts eight to twelve, other escorts twenty-four, cruisers twenty-four, gunboats twelve to twenty-four, transports four and ships on overseas naval transport duty four. No depth charges were assigned to battleships because they would have few opportunities to use them and because escorting destroyers would generally be present. As a result, the total allowance for US naval forces in Europe in September 1918 was 5095 depth charges. The rate of expenditure reached nearly 1000 per month at Base 6 (Queenstown) and over that at Base 7 (Brest), so reserve supplies had to be set up.

In May 1918, given reports of armour in U-boats, BuOrd designed a 600lb depth charge, which offered slightly greater destructive radius (90ft) and a depth setting of 250ft. It was intended not to replace the 300lb charge, but to be used only when

Quite separate from depth-charge throwers were longer-range howitzers whose bombs would explode at a depth of about 30ft – at periscope depth. They were quick-reaction weapons to deal with sudden sightings of a submerged submarine (i.e., of her periscope) or of a diving submarine (a big bomb exploding near even a surfaced submarine would do considerable damage). The idea of a bomb thrower was raised as early as March 1915 and at an August 1915 conference it was decided that minimum range should be 500 yds. In February 1916 the Ministry of Munitions was asked to produce two bomb throwers with 1000 yd range, one firing a 100lb and the other a 200lb bomb. Official drawings were reviewed in April and both howitzers fired proof shots in July. Firing strains were limited enough that they could be mounted on trawlers. At the beginning of December 1916 thirty 3.5in 200lb stick bomb howitzers were ordered. Not long afterward there was interest in a howitzer with variable range and twelve army 5in howitzers were adapted for use afloat. Their shells were too small to be useful, but they demonstrated that a howitzer could be mounted on board ships. Early in March 1917, 750 Vickers 7.5in howitzers, of the type shown, were ordered, with another 250 in May. As of November 1917 deliveries amounted to 933 howitzers and forty-eight x 7.5in bomb-throwers. There were also eighty-two of the earlier 3.5in stick-bomb throwers, fifty of which were ordered early in 1918 specifically to arm submarine-hunting flotillas, firing 350lb as well as 200lb bombs. Another 1000, specifically to arm merchant ships, were ordered in June 1918 but cancelled at the Armistice.

the U-boat had definitely been located. US destroyers were ultimately fitted with one or two stern racks containing twenty or even forty charges. Dropping speed was set by the need to avoid countermining (sympathetic explosion of one charge by another).

The US Navy also used the flat-nose or non-ricochet anti-submarine shell which several European navies had already adopted. By December 1917 such shells were available in 3in, 4in, 5in and 6in calibre and had been issued to all ships which might meet submarines. As in the Royal Navy, guns were attractive because they could fire instantly, whereas depth charges required a ship to turn and run over the presumed U-boat position, giving the U-boat time to evade. The US equivalent to the British howitzers was the 8in howitzer Mk VII. It never entered service. In July 1918 Admiral Sims asked the Bureau of Ordnance to develop an equivalent to the British stick bomb, to carry at least 250lb of TNT, with a range of up to 200 yds, to be fired by 3in and 4in guns. Sims also wanted a 'marker shell' which could indicate where a submarine had just been spotted or had just dived, as a focal point for counter-attack. The indicator should last 5 to 10 minutes. Both requests came too late to result in weapons.

In the spring of 1917 the Royal Navy experimented with circling torpedoes (describing roughly a 200 yd circle at 21 knots). About 120 torpedoes were modified. They were issued to about thirty destroyers and torpedo boats on escort duties. In 1917 some convoy escorts in the Mediterranean were provided with kite balloons, the hope being that an observer aloft could spot even submerged submarines in that very clear sea.

Because submarines had to see their targets in order to attack them, smoke screens became ASW weapons. Initial tests were conducted in February 1918 aboard HMS *Garland*, which screened a simulated two-ship convoy consisting of USS *Vestal* and HMS *Gleaner*. In a force 4–5 wind, a pure white screen 120ft high and 1000 yds long soon developed, turning black and then back to white. It was considered quite satisfactory. Smoke was created using a tank of more than 6 tons of sulphuric acid, so special safety precautions were needed (one trial early in March 1918 acid wore away ship's paint and charred nearby coil matting).

A late 1918 list of destroyer anti-submarine equipment for the 2nd (Northern Ireland) and 4th (Devonport) Flotillas showed several variants. The basic version for a 'K', 'L' or 'M' class destroyer was twenty-four charges in place of the after gun and sweep gear on one side: twelve on a single rail, two throwers with two charges, four per thrower in trays, two in chutes (one hydraulic, one hand). Ships carrying kite balloons surrendered their after twin torpedo tubes (both single tubes in the 'K' class). Ships carrying smoke plants had only ten charges (four in chutes at the stern [two hydraulic, two hand], two in throwers, two spares in chocks). 'K' class destroyers surrendered the after gun, all torpedo tubes and all sweep gear (sweep gear on only one side in the 'L' and 'M' classes).

Air ASW

From the beginning of the war, there were hopes that aircraft could spot and attack submarines. The Germans seem to have had some limited success in seeing submerged submarines, probably by using special anti-glare glasses. All aircraft could spot surfaced submarines. Like surface ships, they were potential threats, so U-boats dived when they saw aircraft. Unlike surface ships, aircraft could appear suddenly. Since submarines could make good considerable distances only on the surface, the presence of aircraft could in effect immobilise them, whether or not the aircraft could actually attack. In 1917, at the outset of the unrestricted U-boat campaign, there were few sky-search periscopes, so a submarine commander who crash-dived to evade attack could not know whether the aircraft or airship had left the area.[42] To some extent he might hear an aircraft, but that was uncertain. As an indication of the potential of air operations, even though they were not conducting systematic patrols, during the first six months of 1917, British aircraft sighted sixty-nine U-boats in home waters.[43]

Proposals to use aircraft against submarines predated the war.[44] The first for a specialised anti-submarine aircraft seems to have been Admiral Fisher's February 1915 proposal for a non-rigid airship, later called a blimp (see Chapter 14 for details of this programme). These aircraft proved extremely important because, unlike aircraft, they could stay with a convoy. They also offered very long endurance patrol, typically up to 24 hours.

Early in the war the Admiralty expected to rely on seaplanes for long-endurance work. It split the class into large and small types, both twin-engine Curtiss aircraft called Americas because the smaller of the two (H 4) was conceived for a 1914 transatlantic flight. The Large America was the Curtiss H 12. Both proved underpowered.[45] They were greatly improved by Commander J C Porte of the Felixstowe naval air station, the result being the Felixstowe in various versions. Later, when the Germans began to use their own seaplanes to attack shipping, a requirement for a seaplane fighter was framed. The Germans posed a particular problem because they could land on the sea to await Large Americas in the certainty that they could take off again.

In April 1917 the Royal Navy established a 'spider-web' patrol system by its new Large America seaplanes in the North Sea Each could carry two 230lb bombs.[46] This was the heavier of the two standard bombs then in service, the other being a 100lb. Later it was argued that neither bomb was big enough (the Kangaroo was designed for a 525-pounder), although a 114lb bomb with a quarter-second delay (detonating 26ft under water) dropped from

a French airship accidentally sank a British submarine. Many wartime attacks failed due to poor aiming (particularly if the submarine crash-dived before bombs could be released) and to fuzing errors.[47] On the other hand, if the attacker flew too low, it could be destroyed by the explosions of its own bombs. A low-flying aircraft spotting a submarine had to climb to safe altitude before dropping its weapon and that might take long enough for the submarine to escape. Despite the massive air effort, only one U-boat was sunk unassisted by bombing.[48] The main contribution of aircraft was to immobilise U-boats.

Given wartime experience, during 1917 the Admiralty laid out requirements for both landplanes and seaplanes for ASW. That year a squadron of HP 100 heavy bombers was successfully based on the East Coast of England and land-based Farman and Sopwith aircraft were used successfully against submarines in the Aegean and the Adriatic. On this basis the first specification was drawn up for a specialist ASW aircraft, which appeared as the Blackburn Kangaroo. Requirements for both land and sea planes included silenced engine and propeller. One squadron of these aircraft was converted from the seaplanes previously used and based on the East Coast. The Kangaroo was very well liked, but the Armistice cut production short.

In 1917 the British began to install portable non-directional hydrophones on board their seaplanes.[49] The hope was that they could execute sprint-and-drift operations, the sprint being a leap into the air. A seaplane might, for example, listen every five or six miles. A U-boat could generally hear surface hunters and could hide by bottoming. However, it was unlikely to hear aircraft, even if one was sitting on the surface listening. Experiments were extended to bi-directional hydrophones early in 1918 and an installation designed for the Large America. However, by the time the hydrophones had been issued and crews trained, it was autumn and the weather had turned. Group commanders were reluctant to risk their few serviceable Large Americas, particularly as they often could not take off in any sea state. Hydrophones were also trailed from blimps.[50] The US Navy was also interested in seaplane hydrophones, apparently independently of the British.[51]

Early in 1918 the British established a unified policy for air ASW, dividing it into four different types of operation.[52] Each air station was to have its own W/T specifically to connect patrolling aircraft (so that pouncers could be sent to attack as needed) and a system of D/F stations was to be set up. Large numbers of aircraft were involved.[53] This policy was still being implemented at the end of the war.

1. Coastal areas. An Air Group was formed for each coastal area. Patrols were to be established 15 to 20 miles to seaward, both to force U-boats down and to assist in escort work when weather barred airships. In 1918 U-boats frustrated by convoy operations were increasingly moving into these areas. Because U-boat commanders felt compelled to dive whenever any kind of aircraft was cited, the British set up what was later called a 'scarecrow' patrol using surplus DH 6 trainers. The patrol was a bluff, in that the aircraft could carry only a 100lb bomb and even that at the expense of a second crewman.

2. Barrages. As far as possible, aircraft were to patrol the barrages, one important role being to force U-boats to dive into deep minefields.

3. Deep sea areas (convoy areas). Airships would work with surface ships, both as convoy escorts and with hunting groups. Further to seaward, seaplanes would carry out sweeps (such as the 'spider-web'), escort convoys and (see below) use hydrophones. Further out to sea, the air contribution would be by kite balloons operated by the seaborne forces.

4. Direct attack on enemy bases, which early in 1918 meant the 'Triangle' in Flanders. The object was to mount continuous attacks so as to neutralise the bases. In addition, lighters were built, each capable of carrying a Large America. The expectation was that the seaplanes could take off from the lighters when they were towed at sufficient speed by destroyers. In this way attack aircraft could be brought within range of German submarine bases and other objectives. The US Navy became interested in this project, ordering its own 'sea sleds' for the purpose.

More than other naval weapons, aircraft offered the possibility of attacking at source even in areas the enemy dominated. For example, the British repeatedly bombed Zeebrugge and the rest of the 'Triangle', forcing the Germans to build concrete U-boat shelters as early as 1915. The Italians bombed Fiume, where small U-boats brought by rail from Germany were assembled.

When the United States entered the war, the US Navy formed a Northern Bombing Group specifically to attack the 'Triangle'. It consisted of a Day Group manned by Marines and a Night Group manned by Navy personnel, using British DH 4 and DH 9A day bombers and large Italian Caproni Ca 5 night bombers. The Germans were evacuating Flanders by the time the Day Group was ready and the Night Group made only one raid.

Submarine ASW

In mid-1917, U-boats were sighted more often by British submarines on patrol than by any other patrol craft. Using submarines against U-boats had two advantages. First, submarines were the only Allied warships which could survive close to enemy submarine bases. They could, therefore, have a chance of sinking U-boats in transit to their patrol areas. Second, like aircraft overhead, Allied submarines operating in German patrol areas could force U-boats to submerge during the day, hence could immobilise them. Unlike an aircraft overhead, a submerged submarine in a patrol area presented a constant threat, because the U-boat was unlikely to see her before she attacked. A report of the interrogation of prisoners from *UC 38* stated that several of them 'gave clear evidence of the fear inspired by the possible presence of enemy submarines submerged when they themselves were on the surface . . . the apprehension of it constitutes a seriously demoralising influence'.

The only drawback to submerged patrol was limited sight range using a periscope. Some accounts of the prospect for submarine vs submarine operation therefore assumed that both submarines would begin surfaced, the contest being to see which could dive before the other fired. Throughout the war British submarines operated in U-boat transit areas, because those were also the areas through which the High Seas Fleet had to come if it sortied. In 1917–18 the British added patrols in U-boat patrol areas, supplemented in 1918 by US 'L'-class submarines (designated 'AL' class to avoid confusion with the British 'L' class).

None of this made a U-boat an easy target. Because its radio masts were usually not up, its course was difficult to estimate. It was short and its speed was also difficult to estimate. It was difficult to set torpedo depth. In mid-1917 a British submarine reported firing four torpedoes at 600 yds, missing with all of them. This was the rule rather than the exception.[54]

Up to the end of 1915, British submarine operations against U-boats were confined to the North Sea, orders being to attack any enemy ship, including any submarine, sighted.[55] Thus in January 1917 a U-boat was practically immune from attack by British submarines once clear of the German coast or the Straits of Dover. British submarine deployment was essential defensive, but with the advent of unrestricted U-boat warfare that changed radically. Initially most British merchant ships were unarmed, so that Germans economised on torpedoes and often attacked on the surface, making U-boats good targets for British submarines. A new flotilla was organised at Queenstown, to attack U-boats passing down the west coast of Ireland *en route* to the southern trade-route approaches to the United Kingdom. It gradually grew to six 'E' class, six 'D' class and two 'H' class. The Admiralty was reluctant to place its submarines on the trade routes, not least because of danger from its own patrol vessels, particularly while the submarine was passing to its patrol station. The existing method of routing was another problem. Once a route had been chosen, it took 10 to 14 days to change, during which time ships might be confined to port. Routes were stopped as soon as a submarine was sighted and a British submarine might easily be mistaken for a U-boat. In April 1917 the flotilla was split, the more modern 'E' and 'H' class boats going to Lough Swilly and the 'Ds' to Killybegs. Submarines were then assigned fixed patrol lines clear of surface patrols. They operated under Admiralty control, the Admiralty being able to keep ASW forces from attacking them based on various reports. During the transfer to Lough Swilly, *E 54* sank *U 81* on 1 May 1917. It was the first success by a British submarine in her patrol area, outside of sinkings by submarines working with decoy ships. Between May and September 1917, the Lough Swilly flotilla made thirteen contacts and three attacks.

Meanwhile some of the small 'C' class submarines assigned to coast defence were formed into a new flotilla at Harwich specifically to operate against U-boats on passage through the North Sea south of the line between Yarmouth and Texel. Coast defence had, it turned out, made many of the officers stale, but the submarines soon reported numerous contacts. In April 1917 *C 7* torpedoed *UC 68* in a night attack. A third ASW area was opened north of Scotland in March 1917, using 'G' and 'E' class submarines. Their first success was the sinking of *UC 43* by *G 13* on 10 March 1917. This flotilla was transferred to Scapa in April, three small 'C' class submarines being added during the summer. This type of warfare was dangerous, however: on 19 July *U 52* sank *C 34*.

As the Atlantic convoy system developed, successful attacks on Atlantic shipping became rarer, so the U-boats concentrated on the Irish Sea and the Channel. The Lough Swilly flotilla moved to Berehaven and new patrol areas were set up in the approaches to the Channel and the St. George's Channel (the southern entrance to the Irish Sea). New patrol areas were also set up for the Killybegs flotilla north of Ireland. On her first patrol there, *D 7* sank *U 45* (12 September).

Initially it seemed that the crowded Channel was ill-suited to such operations, but patrols were established in May 1917, given the success of the 'C' class in the southern North Sea. The first contact (17 May) had to be broken off when a British seaplane unaware of the submarine patrols arrived. On the night of 1 November *E 52* sank *UC 63* while surfaced, keeping his target, which suddenly appeared, silhouetted in the moonlight. On 3 November *C 15* sank *UC 65* even though the German commander had spotted the British submarine's periscope as she dived to attack. He was homeward bound and apparently sure he could evade a torpedo.

During the winter of 1917–18 U-boat activity in the Irish Sea, previously rare, became intense, so British submarine patrols were set up in the southern part. The Killybegs flotilla moved to Campeltown to cover the northern part of the Irish Sea. Patrol craft but not merchant ships were informed of the submarine patrol lines: on a dark night in March 1918 *H 5* was rammed and sunk with all hands. The US flotilla arrived at Queenstown (it later moved to Berehaven) on 27 January 1918.

As the Dover Barrage strengthened, German submarines increasingly came out of the Kattegat (the Danish Straits) rather than out of the Heligoland Bight, whence the High Seas Fleet might emerge. Thus submarine patrols which in the past might have dealt with either U-boats or with the High Seas Fleet now had to deal with one or the other. In January-June 1918 on average 7 submarines were on Grand Fleet Observation Patrol to watch for the High Seas Fleet. Others were on ASW patrol, typically 2 to 2.5 north of Ireland; 1.6 in the Irish Sea; 1.1 (US submarines) in the southern Irish Sea and its approaches and 2.7 in the English Channel and the Western Approaches (these were also anti-raider patrols), a total of about ten submarines.

In October a new flotilla (ten 'H' class, two 'R' class) was formed to attack U-boats emerging from the Kattegat and heading for the open ocean across the northern part of the North Sea. Apart from the 'Rs', none of these submarines was specifically designed for ASW. In September and October 1918, the first two 'R' class (*R 7* and *R 8*) carried out patrols north of Ireland and in the Irish Sea. On the one occasion on which one of them encountered a surfaced U-boat, she approached to within 2500 yds, 3 points on the enemy's bow submerged and prepared to make a low-speed (*i.e.*, quiet) final approach. The attack was ruined by the approach of a steamship, which caused the U-boat to dive. No one envisaged an attack on a submerged U-boat (which was, however, carried out successfully in 1945 by HMS *Venturer*). The new flotilla barely had time to carry out an operation before the U-boats concentrated again off the East Coast of Scotland, presumably in preparation for the abortive final High Seas Fleet sortie. By this time the flotilla operating in the southern North Sea had been reinforced with new 'L' class submarines, one of which, *L 12*, sank *UB 90* on 13 October. On 28 October *G 2* sank *U 78* in a night attack. Gibraltar was also an important operating area, reinforced against German cruiser submarines late in 1917. On 11 May 1918 *E 35* sighted *U 154*, which was apparently waiting to communicate with another U-boat, sinking her.

This list is all the more impressive because it omits sinkings by patrolling British submarines in 1915–16 as well as U-boats sunk by submarines working with decoy ships. In 1919 the British counted eighteen U-boats sunk by their submarines, beginning with *U 40* sunk by *C 24* on 23 June 1915. Another seven were hit but not sunk. At the end of the war, submarines seemed to be the single best antidote to other submarines, at least as long as the enemy's submarines were operating in relatively well-defined areas. British operations revealed the main problems, which were how to avoid encounters with friendly surface and air patrols and with other friendly submarines. Thus much of the official account of submarine vs submarine operations is taken up by the development of recognition signals (IFF), including special deck markings and special sound signals. Aircraft and hunting groups were particular threats.

Navigation emerged as a major issue, because patrol lines had to be defined so that submarines did not attack each other. Navigation could be sufficiently precise only near visible landmarks. For anything else, patrol areas had to be widely separated, reducing the chance of contact. This problem would not be solved until the advent of electronic aids to navigation more than twenty years later.

In May 1917 US Submarine Force Commander Captain J K Robison proposed a US parallel to the 'R' class, of which he was aware.[56] To date submarines had been the most effective ASW weapons because of their invisibility. By September the British were operating about fifteen submarines against U-boats – but the British were also operating more than a thousand surface craft, including destroyers.

It was later pointed out that, because they were so quiet, submerged submarines could listen while moving, whereas surface ships found that difficult except when drifting. Robison wanted a submarine with very high underwater speed and the greatest possible number of bow torpedo tubes which could be fired simultaneously (the Sperry Co. was then working on a 14in electric torpedo) and a gun arranged so that it could be fired as soon as the submarine submerged. Robison thought the 'R' class less effective in this role than the new 850-ton 'S' class submarines under construction, which were rated at an impressive 12.25 knots submerged (one-hour rate). He thought the British were using a special 14in anti-submarine torpedo (it was actually the old 14in weapon, with a short range, which had been installed on board many ships as a stop-gap).[57] Robison headed his paper 'plan to blockade enemy coast by use of submarines', and later added that he thought a fixed minefield could force U-boats to operate on the surface where they would be exposed to attack. Nothing came of Robison's plan, partly because by January 1918 there was no spare industrial capacity for either new torpedoes (which might not be developed for years) or for new submarines. The US Navy (and the Royal Navy) had to wait about thirty years to develop submarine anti-submarine tactics, this time against submerged submarines.

Hunting Tactics

Hunting was an essential complement to convoy, but it was difficult or impossible until the advent of directional hydrophones, beginning with the Nash Fish. Before late 1917, trawlers were organised as patrols, but from late 1917 the Royal Navy used special hunting groups. Hunting could exploit the mass of U-boat location data provided by signal intelligence as well as radio D/F stations, shore listening stations, aircraft patrols and distress calls from sinking ships (flaming data). Alternatively hunters could operate on patrol, either an anchored patrol, a drifting patrol, or a running patrol. An anchored patrol created a fixed barrier line, hopefully athwart the path of a submarine. It was impractical in a rough sea, ships could not get underway instantly and it lost a

It was soon clear that something more powerful was wanted; at the end of March 1917, 210 x 11in howitzers, of the Vickers type shown, were ordered from Vickers, Coventry and Elswick. There was also a Thornycroft design for a 9.5in bomb-thrower, which Vickers developed into a 10in bomb thrower and Elswick offered a 13.5in howitzer (one ordered in April 1917 for trials).

submarine drifting near the bottom. At slack water for about an hour directional capability vanished because devices did not retain their steady headings. A drifting patrol line shifted with the current, or around an area in which a U-boat was believed to be drifting. It could be used in deep water where a submarine had been seen to submerge. It offered the enemy no warning, since the drifting ships made no noise at all. Ships in the group could determine relative bearings and ranges by listening for periodic tapping on hulls. It was, however, difficult to maintain position and unless a buoy were anchored as a reference, the patrol might slip away from the assumed U-boat position. Even though they were not being used, engines had to be kept warmed-up.

A running patrol could be used to search a large area, or ahead of a convoy. This was a spring-and-drift operation, ships in the patrol periodically shutting down to listen and then restarting. That made timing essential, so that all ships would shut down simultaneously. A fast supporting unit such as a destroyer had to be far enough back that its own noise did not swamp out the submarines, yet close enough to pounce once the submarine was localised. The ideal formation was line abreast, the distance between them set by

likely detection range. That also set the intervals between listening: the longer the sound radius, the longer the intervals. A running patrol could cover a large area, but its noise alerted the U-boat.

Once a patrol located a U-boat, it switched to pursuit tactics. The wording of the US notes on hunting by sound are much the same as those of the Second World War ASW handbooks: 'once contact with a submarine has been made, nothing but bad weather should be accepted as legitimate reason for losing contact'. Because this was still the era of passive sound, pursuit, like search, was by sprint-and-drift. Silent (drift) intervals had to be chosen so that the submarine would not get away before the hunters could catch up and also so that the hunters would not overrun it. Tactics would be chosen on the basis of a plot kept by the leader of the hunting group. It would take two or more hunters to provide good location. Since the submarine could hear the hunters' propellers stop and start as they drifted and then sprinted, it could try to synchronize its propellers with theirs, running only when they did. To defeat that, one of the hunters could start engines somewhat after the others. Hunters could estimate the speed of the target submarine by (propeller) blade count, but typical U-boat speed submerged was 4 knots (maximum speed, 10 knots, could be sustained for only an hour, so it would not be used except if the U-boat had a chance of escaping).

All of this was much simpler for a hunter powered by internal combustion engines, such as a US sub-chaser or a British motor launch (ML) than for a steam-powered trawler, because internal-combustion engines could be shut down and restarted considerably

311

more quickly (note, however, that in 1917 the British showed that destroyers could manage a four- or five-minute cycle of shutdown and restart). British work on silent propulsion (jet and later bubble screen) was intended to make it possible to track a submarine continuously, without having to shut down to listen. Trawlers so powered were intended to carry a heavy depth-charge load.

Hunting tactics favoured amiable, relatively long-range ASW weapons rather than depth charges, not least because to drop depth charges required a final rush towards the U-boat which inevitably alerted it just as listening became difficult or impossible. In the First World War destroyers and sloops often did have just such weapons, but the smaller sub-chasers and trawlers did not.[58] This was the same logic which favoured ahead-throwing weapons in the Second World War; it is surprising in retrospect that the idea did not carry through.

The US Navy seems to have been a particularly strong advocate of hunting tactics as an essential complement to convoy *not* as an alternative. It was very much in character that the Special Board's mission to England (November 1917–January 1918) pressed for immediate assignment of numerous sub-chasers for the Channel (for hunting) and for construction of no fewer than 600 special hunters. The Royal Navy conducted the first hunting experiments using directional hydrophones in January 1917, using five motor launches with bi-directional hydrophones.[59] Results were promising, but showed the need for a training school for officers. The Admiralty wanted a direction-finder which would work at 5 knots. Standard US procedure was to form units of three hunters working together as permanent units, well enough armed to deal with a surfaced U-boat and capable both of attacking a submerged U-boat they located and of preventing a U-boat for surfacing and escaping due to her superior speed. These requirements shaped the Eagle Boat, which began as an attempt to develop a suitable hunter. At the least, one of the three units should be powerful and fast enough to cope with a surfaced U-boat. The US sub-chasers, which certainly were equipped and trained as hunters, were not powerfully enough armed for that, with their 3in/23 guns. In theory, pairs of hunters could triangulate a submerged submarine. A third hunter could run over the spot and drop depth charges. Aimable ASW weapons became useful as hydrophones improved and became more directional, but sub-chasers and trawlers were too small to accommodate them. Sub-chaser equipment for hunting included large arrows atop their superstructures so that each member of the group could indicate the direction to the target U-boat as well as bridge to bridge radio telephones for quick co-ordination. A chaser had to be able to receive information from its base (W/T range 100 miles) and to exchange information with others in its group (R/T range 5 miles and a directional arrow atop the bridge, as in a sub-chaser). It also needed a plotting room to make sense of the directional information it developed and received.

Hydrophones were not enough, because the U-boat might rest on the bottom (down to 30 or 35 fathoms) or anchor submerged, in either case making little or no noise. It could also balance (neutrally buoyant) in the water while stopped, particularly on a density layer. The hunters therefore needed some additional means of detection, typically a trailing wire or wires which could detect the steel in the U-boat's hull.

Early in 1918 the British were beginning to use hunting groups of four trawlers plus a P-boat (pouncer), but they were limited by the slow speed of the trawlers, the fish (insufficiently directional), poor communication between ships and a lack of training on the

part of the fishermen forming the crews of the trawlers. At the very least, they needed a fast pouncer to exploit information from the slow trawlers. A hunt by three trawlers and a P-boat using US equipment was apparently more successful.[60] To the Special Board's mission, that was proof that the hunting concept could finally work, after the failed efforts of 1917. The US mission promoted hunting by helping create a school to train signalmen in the use of special rapid signals (to co-ordinate hunters) and also to train listeners. The US Navy installed radio-telephones on its sub-chasers for quick bridge-to-bridge communication. Once listening devices suited to P-boats and destroyers could be produced, hunting groups could be reduced to three units: two listening trawlers and a pouncing destroyer or P-boat.

The US mission (meaning the Special Board) envisaged both patrol (running, drifting, or anchored) and the chase itself. That meant a C-tube (range 1 to 3 miles), which was adequate in anything but rough weather; a K-tube (10 to 30 mile range) for anchored or drifting patrol; a towed K-tube (under development at Nahant); and the Pierce device to locate a bottomed submarine. Weapons should be one 4in/50 to equal or outrange U-boat guns, twenty 300lb or heavier depth charges and a depth-charge thrower capable of reaching 1000 yds with a 100lb charge. To be seaworthy enough, the hunters should be at least 200ft long, preferably built of steel and capable of 22 to 24 knots. They might use mixed steam and internal combustion propulsion, as the latter could be stopped and started promptly. In that case, speed on internal combustion engine should be at least 12 knots. The US Navy could not quite produce masses of convoy escorts (destroyers) and hunters, but it did order 100 hunters (plus twelve for Italy).

A hunt conducted by British 'K' class destroyers in April 1918 illustrates contemporary tactics.[61] The flotilla consisted of HMS *Cockatrice*, *Christopher* and *Ambuscade*, each of which had a Nash Fish and a heavy depth-charge battery including two throwers (*Ambuscade* was not present during this hunt). *Cockatrice* found that the best towing speed was 10 knots; her No. 1 fish lasted over 100 hours, the tail and fin finally breaking when it was taken aboard hurriedly at night. Fish varied in sensitivity from ship to ship. They picked up steamers over the horizon. The fish was used only with engines stopped and underway only when coasting. All auxiliaries were also shut down, although sometimes it was necessary to keep water flowing through the condenser. *Cockatrice* listened for a minute and a half to three minutes at a time, coasting at 6 down to 2 knots. Both ships managed this cycle of starting and stopping for six days without problems. Typically it took 20 minutes from the order 'out fish stations' to completion; in took about 6 minutes to get the fish back on board. Fish range on a slow-moving (2 knots) U-boat was about a mile, compared to 6 to 8 miles on a fast surface craft. The two destroyers communicated by buzzer radio rather than by radio-telephone.

Ships formed a triangle at visibility interval, since cross-bearings were essential for an attack. The second in command constantly plotted the course of his ship and the bearings. If sound ceased, a buoy was dropped as the basis of an immediate attack. A second drifting buoy indicated the likely drift of the U-boat (the stationary buoy had a red flag, the drifter two flags; at night lamps were used). Starting from the mark buoy, the attacker manoeuvred at 10 to 15 knots with helm hard over, dropping charges every 15 seconds until the circle was completed. Then she stopped while the other ship listened. The process was repeated on the other side of

At the end of May 1918 one of the hunting flotillas reported that it expected better results if it could project a depth charge to 150 yds rather than the 40 yds of the Thornycroft thrower. In February the possibility of firing stick bombs from standard guns had already been considered and this time the desired range was shorter. The 3.5in stick bomb, suitably modified, was modified for use in a 12pdr gun. As soon as the 12pdr trials succeeded, a 4in gun was tested with a 350lb bomb (270 yds range) and then with a 500lb bomb (305 yds range). The 4.7in gun could throw a 600lb bomb to 270 yds. Trials also showed that after a few such rounds (twenty 12pdr, ten 4.7in) had been fired the gun was no longer safe for firing conventional shell. The stickbombs were in the experimental stage at the end of the war. This is a 12pdr, a standard trawler gun.

the buoy. If nothing was heard, depth charges were dropped every few minutes on different courses for two hours, to keep up the tension on board the U-boat, either to force her to the surface or to get underway again and thus again give herself away by her noise. This was done with the regular listening routine, stopping to listen every half hour. Any ship which sighted the U-boat on the surface fired a Very pistol, green for 'I have sighted submarine on surface to starboard', red if to port.

This required enormous numbers of depth charges, far beyond what any convoy escort could or would carry. At the time of the hunt, that meant 150 charges and the goal was to carry 200. During the attack made on 28 April, *Cockatrice* used forty-nine charges and *Christopher* thirty. The belief of CO of *Cockatrice* was that if charges were constantly dropped in a two square mile area after the main attack, the effect would be intolerable, the U-boat being forced either to the surface or to run and thus reveal itself. If certain that he was within 200 yds of a bottomed submarine, the CO would drop four charges at once, two from the rails and one from each thrower, every 16 seconds, with the destroyer running a straight course. If uncertain of the position, the destroyer followed a curved path, dropping a charge every 15 seconds. At one point *Christopher* was ordered to take in her fish and run ten miles ahead, creeping back towards *Cockatrice*, which had heard a noise, albeit faintly. Shortly after it was lost altogether, depth charge and gun fire were heard, indicating an attack elsewhere in the area.

One night at 20.00 both destroyers heard a noise, so it was possible to take cross-bearings and begin a chase. The sound suddenly stopped at 21.20 and a calcium buoy was dropped to mark the spot as the basis for an attack. *Cockatrice* dropped sixteen charges, but nothing more was heard and both ships listened again. *Cockatrice* then began dropping charges every few minutes for the next two hours. About 02.00 a reciprocating (diesel) engine was heard, indicating a surfaced U-boat. It vanished (submerged) and the hunt resumed. Both ships again heard faint sounds at about 04.00. A buoy was dropped and the attack resumed, *Christopher* dropping charges this time. No further sounds were heard until 09.00, when a loud sound indicated an approaching convoy. A blimp was sent out to help, but the U-boat was never found again and the two destroyers returned to port. The conclusion was that the U-boat had not been hit, but that he had been badly shaken. For the time, expending a total of seventy-nine depth charges was a lot, but it paled into insignificance by Second World War standards.

German ASW[62]

The Germans were much affected by British submarine operations, both in the North Sea and in the Baltic. In the North Sea, successive High Seas Fleet commanders were much exercised by the threat of British submarine attack, as British submarines were frequently reported in the Heligoland Bight and in the German Bight. In the Baltic, British submarines were considered the major threat to the key trade, particularly in iron ore, with Sweden. Unlike the British, the Germans had a far smaller commercial fleet on which to draw for ASW craft: up to October 1915, for example, there were only 311 German trawlers. Both for minesweeping and for ASW they drew on their old torpedo boats. In the North Sea early in the war the torpedo boat minesweepers were also used to sweep for submarines, using the same equipment. On 7 April 1916 the Germans ran their first iron ore convoy from Sweden to Schwinemünde. This operation continued three times each week to the end of the war. Another convoy system operated (also tri-weekly) along the route Danzig–Pillau–Memel–Libau.

By the autumn of 1916 the Germans, like the British, were using over-the-side hydrophones, in their case using microphones and telephone headsets. This was the UGE (Unterwassergerauschemfänger – underwater sound receiver) or 'flying' hydrophone. UGE was directional in the sense that it was binaural. In theory a ship could find the direction of a sound by listening and turning until the operator thought he was receiving the same sound level in both ears. That made for a lengthy listening cycle, with a typical total listening time of five to ten minutes. UGE was presumably the same set used at this time on board U-boats. The U-boat sets were tuned to a relatively high frequency (700 Hz in the case of UC-boat hydrophones examined at that time) in order to eliminate background noise, the long listening period presumably being needed because the narrow-band sound was relatively weak. UGE could be used only when not only the engines of the listening boat but also of all other boats in its group were stopped. In addition to shipboard use, UGE was employed in the western entrance to the Baltic. Later the Germans also had the SS (Schwimmschalle – swimming shell), a body suspended from a towing buoy, carrying a disk with a microphone on either side. SS was intended for towing at 10 to 12 knots, but (as the British found with fish) it was limited both by flow noise and by machinery noise. It is not clear whether the Germans tried to use it while coasting.

The Baltic organisation late in 1916 was a single flotilla for both minesweeping and ASW, led by the destroyer *S 167*, whose force included seaplanes at Arcona and Stralsund. A submarine hunt employed both seaplanes and surface ships. The dedicated ASW element of the force was the 1st 'S' Half-flotilla, led by the destroyer *S 142*. It consisted of three groups of trawlers (twelve each, three with W/T), each led by an old torpedo boat (later

replaced by an 'A' boat). Trawler groups, one or sometimes two of which were at sea at any one time, searched for submarines by towing a large net. The other half-flotilla was minesweepers whose ASW weapons were towed (kite) and depth charges. They were also the weapons of fleet destroyers. Motor boats armed with depth charges were also attached to the 2nd Half-flotilla. The organisation was formed in November 1915 and it did not become operational until the end of the following April. It generally reacted to reports of submarine activity and ice in the Baltic made it possible to lay up and repair ships between late December and April.[63]

Surface ships had no ASW weapons at all until the first depth charges were issued in June 1915 (Carbonit began work on a depth charge during the winter of 1914). Charges were in general use by June 1916. This 200lb C/15 used a pull-out line to detonate it; it was far bulkier than the corresponding British depth-charge, but the charge was only 50kg (110lbs) and it had a 50 per cent dud rate. As of late 1916 maximum known depth charge depth was 33 fathoms (198ft). Typically two men were needed to lift a single depth charge. As of 1916 a minesweeping trawler typically carried four, one in a chute on either quarter (they do not seem to have been carried by the specially-built minesweepers). The other two were stowed upright. Destroyers and torpedo boats typically carried six. They were apparently not carried if the destroyers were carrying mines. The Germans disliked the C/15 and they produced only 2256 of them.

The Germans also developed two explosive sweeps, the Sprenganker (Explosive Anchor) and the U Bootsdrachen (UD). The Sprenganker was a grappling hook on a wire between two trawlers or sweepers 50m apart, held down to a depth as great as 30m by a kite. It was analogous to pre-war British ASW sweeps; when the grappling hook met an obstruction, it pulled a line down which a charge slid from the deck of one of the towing ships. The device was in effect an elaboration of the standard German mine sweep. It was used only during 1916, when the better UD was in short supply.

The operational version of the kite was UD15, a 200lb charge on a 300ft line held down to up to 80ft by a kite.[64] It could be towed at 6 to 21 knots. The kite was about 4ft long and 2ft across. The charge fired automatically when the kite struck an obstruction. The kite was the main weapon of destroyers screening fleet units. Unfortunately the kite limited destroyer speed. Maximum speed when putting a kite out was 6 knots and maximum with kite trailed was 21 knots. Kite depth could be adjusted while in the water, but at no more than 10 knots and a ship hauling in a kite was limited to 4 knots. German destroyer instructions suggest that kites were preferred to depth charges.[65]

Groups of trawlers typically towed kits in line abreast (close order), led by a torpedo boat which also towed a kite; sometimes two groups towed kites together. Like the British towed charge, the kite was considered a means of searching for a submarine already reported in a particular place. The preferred tactic was a line-abreast search in an expanding spiral. Although in theory an effective way of attacking a submarine once seen, the technique was ineffective; a kite accounted only for the Russian submarine *Bars* (21 May 1917).

Airships were provided with anti-submarine bombs beginning in October 1914 (they seem to have been ineffective). During the war, there was a widespread belief that the Germans had been far more successful than the Allies in finding means of seeing submerged objects from the air, presumably using filtered glasses. Although they did not sink any submarines, German air ASW patrols impressed British submariners and, as with U-boats, helped limit their mobility by forcing them down.

Like the British, the Germans saw nets as a means of containing submarines. The Jade (off Kiel) was closed to submarines by a net reaching down to the bottom, patrolled above. During 1915 orders were placed for 65nm of nets, though the fleet resisted deploying them in the open sea, where they might constrict German U-boat operations. Nets up to 1000m long, which could be towed or dropped around a submarine, became available about the end of 1915. The first were seven nets laid in the western Baltic on 26 October 1914; early in 1915 they were replaced by new nets with indicators and four more places were mined. The limited effect of these nets is indicated by the British report that before Jutland, the only German anti-submarine net definitely reported was a single line moored at the southern entrance to the Sound, doubled after Jutland. Because the water was shallow, the net could extend all the way to the bottom. It was watched by patrol craft. Like the British, the Germans found their nets torn up by currents and weather. Their post-war conclusion was that nets were useless except for harbour defence. The only submarine caught in a German net was *E 19*, off Bornholm on 2 October 1915; she broke free, having once been forced to the surface and ineffectively fired upon.

The towed net was 2000m (6600ft) long (four 500m panels) and 25m (about 80ft) deep, consisting of sections joined together. The top was typically one to two meters below the surface. A net was towed by a pair of trawlers steaming nearly in line ahead, making about 1.5 knots (their normal speed was 7 to 8 knots). As of 1916 there were no indicator buoys; that the net had trapped a submarine was indicated only by increased weight on the tow.

Eventually the nets carried indicators (flares), which unfortunately ignited under fire or while the nets were being handled. Initially the hope was that the trawlers could manoeuvre to catch a submarine in their net, as trawlers would catch fish, but that was dismissed as impractical. It was succeeded by a line-abreast formation, followed by a line of attack craft, but a submarine could escape between the two formations. Ultimately the Germans adopted a formation of two lines alternating nets and gaps, but none of these tactics seems to have worked.

Up to February 1915 the chief anti-submarine weapon, offensive and defensive, was a special mine, of which 3000 had been issued in the Baltic (where the Russians also had a considerable submarine fleet) and another 1500 in the North Sea. These mines were not in very large-scale production until 1916. The Germans also laid their standard contact mines across suspected submarine routes.[66] In addition, during 1915 the Germans began to lay indicator loops on a cable running from Nordenny to Helgoland to Eidermünde. Anything passing over was indicated to the shore station (SMP, Schiffsmeldpost, ships reporting post), but without any indication of where along the loop system it was.

As with the Allies, German and Austrian submarines sometimes torpedoed submarines, though usually not when on specifically ASW patrol operations. In all, German and Austrian submarines sank five British, two Italian and two French submarines; their attackers included one U-boat and two Austrian submarines on specifically ASW patrol.

Although the Germans had a depth charge (with a pull-out rather than hydrostatic fuze), they relied mainly on towed charges, which they called kites. This kite from the surrendered destroyer *G-102* was photographed at Norfolk Navy Yard, 27 April 1921.

The mass of 110ft wooden sub-chasers was the first evidence of the impact of US mass production on the anti-submarine war. Sub-chasers are shown at Norfolk Navy Yard, 2 April 1918. (Chris Cavas)

CHAPTER 14
The Anti-Submarine Armada

NTI-SUBMARINE WARFARE IS ultimately about numbers. In The First World War detection range was short (to vanishing), so it took very large numbers of ships to hunt submarines. Once convoy was adopted, it took large numbers to provide sufficient escorts. For the Royal Navy, most of the types which fought the U-boat war began as units of Admiral Fisher's massive new construction programme. It is not clear to what extent any of them was conceived specifically for the Baltic. Their mere existence was crucial, because they provided prototypes for massive wartime building programmes. The principal types were the 'Flower' class sloop, the 'Kil' class patrol vessel, the '24 Class' sloop, the P-boat and the Z-Whaler, the last being the least important (and least successful).

'Flower' Class[1]

The 'Flowers' began as direct replacements for the torpedo gunboats converted before the war as fleet sweepers, and on 7 September 1908 Rear Admiral Callaghan, who was then President of the Mining Committee, laid out a specification for them.[2] He wanted a speed of 16 knots, a displacement of about 600 tons and a single caged propeller (to avoid underwater obstructions). The radius of action was to be 1200nm. DNC produced a series of sketch designs with maximum speeds of 15 to 17 knots. The largest, design D, would displace 900 tons.[3] Limited draught was a particular design problem, because all experience with tugs showed that it would be a great disadvantage, the pull on the tow rope interfering greatly with the tug's ability to use its rudder to manoeuvre. It did not help that the towing hawsers had to be at the stern. Normally that would not present any problems, but the ropes and kites of the sweep gear might become entangled with an underwater obstruction. In that case the pivoting point of the ship would move aft towards the point of attachment of the hawser, which was practically over the rudder and the rudder would no longer control the ship. Twin screws would help enormously, even though they could not readily be caged like a single screw. The design showed sufficient coal to steam 1200nm at 12 knots. No provision was made for equal steaming using oil, as that would have made for a much larger ship. Nor did the design include any armament, although DNC was sure it would be required. An undated paper, which seems to have been associated with the 1908 project, called for a total of eighteen ships: six for the Home Fleet, six for the Channel Fleet and six for the Atlantic Fleet.[4]

Nothing happened immediately, because other projects had higher priority and the torpedo gunboats were good enough for a time. However, Callaghan, who was now Home Fleet C-in-C, revived the project in 1913. He wanted a sweeper capable of 21 knots (18 knots cruising speed) with enough firepower to deal with

HMS *Foxglove* was a 'Flower' class sloop built to merchant ship standards (she resembled a small merchant ship). She was part of the initial series, armed with 12pdrs. These ships were conceived partly for minesweeping, hence the sweep gallows right aft. Note also the tug-type arch across the quarterdeck for towing.

a destroyer on equal terms. A staff paper cut the speed to 17 knots to keep the sweeper as small (and inexpensive) as possible, since it would run considerable risks. The converted gunboats were ageing (they were about 20 years old), slow, had had too little endurance, had worn-out armament and lacked wireless (only one was fitted as of 1913).[5]

Again, nothing happened immediately, but the project was revived in January 1914, it being accepted that replacements for the torpedo gunboats should be built under the 1915–16 and later programmes. The higher speed (18/21 knots) was revived, as was the requirement that armament be the equal of that of a destroyer, or at least capable of engaging one. Design details were settled at an 18 February 1914 conference attended by Third Sea Lord (Rear Admiral E F B Charlton) and his Naval Assistant, by DNC (actually his representative J H Narbeth) and by ICMS (Captain R M Harbord).[6] In order to reduce costs, an alternative 16-knot design was to be prepared. The ship would have a destroyer W/T set (Type 4) and a bow mine catcher, her forward part specially compartmented to protect against any mine she set off. DNC produced a sketch design of the 16-knot ship on 25 April and a machinery design ordered. Minor changes included moving the mast forward and fitting a crow's nest from which the ship could be conned in the vicinity of mines (as they might be visible from above). As he developed the design, DNC found that the weights he had to put into the ship made it difficult to hold down her size. The alternative was to convert an existing commercial ship; on 5 September, with the country at war and new construction not available nearly quickly enough, First Lord Winston Churchill asked for a list of suitable ships (to be provided by Director of Transport).

Once war broke out, small ships were wanted for wider purposes. Minutes dated 22 September 1914 were submitted to Fourth Sea Lord concerning 'Small Ships for Patrolling, Hunting Submarines and Sweeping'.[7] Admiral Oliver, who was then Director of the Intelligence Department, wrote that it was already clear that a large number of fast seaworthy vessels were needed. In a few months the need would be at least as great, because many

destroyers would be out of action due at the least to wear and tear during the winter. Yachts and trawlers were hardly fast enough to hunt submarines. Surely it would be possible to build a number of small fast vessels within four or five months. They could be based on the existing fleet sweeper design, but they would need a speed of about 20 knots. Gun armament should be a 12pdr 12 cwt gun fore and aft and two or three 3pdrs or 6pdrs in the waist. They could stand up to poorly-armed German destroyers, which typically had only two 15pdrs and four machine guns. The new ships would have no torpedo armament and they would be fitted for sweeping. They should be fitted for the current anti-submarine weapon, the towing charge, they should be turbine-powered and they should be well subdivided. About fifty would be required. 'When the time comes for attacking the German Fleet in the Baltic should they not come out and have to be dug out before the end of the War, the need for large numbers of armed sweeping vessels capable of putting up a fight with destroyers will be very great.' Oliver had been involved in the earlier programme; he remembered that as Naval Assistant to the First Sea Lord in 1909 he had proposed replacements for the torpedo gunboats. The idea got as far as having plans and estimates prepared to build two as a start, but they were dropped from the sketch estimates in 1909 or 1910; DNC probably still had the plans. Oliver mentioned that Captain Greatorex (Naval Assistant to Third Sea Lord) had worked a long time on fleet sweepers (as described above) 'and knows more about it than I do'.

Director of Operations Division Admiral Leveson fully concurred with Oliver 'as the *necessity* for these are more and more evident'. Chief of (War) Staff Admiral Sturdee went further: 'the lack of efficient subsidiary vessels is very evident . . . The whole question requires early consideration as the War looks as if it may be prolonged for some time'.

DNC provided the 1908 sketch and also a preliminary design for the more recent 16-knot sweeper informally considered at a conference presided over by Third Sea Lord, but the arrangements shown were *not* concurred in by him (italics in original). Somewhat

The later 'Flower' class sloop HMS *Cornflower* is shown in tropical livery (white hull, buff upperworks) at Gibraltar, January 1928. Armament was a pair of 4.7in guns. By this time sloops were valued as, in effect, small colonial cruisers rather than as anti-submarine escorts or as minesweepers. As such they became the basis for the post-war sloop programme.

The '24 Class' sloops incorporated late-war ideas on confusing U-boat commanders as to ships' course and speed: more or less identical bow and stern, superstructure split into identical blocks, funnel dead amidships and only a single mast. This is HMS *Orby*.

later (mid-October) DNC pointed out that the machinery for the 16-knot sweeper might have to be operated by civilian ratings, hence that it might be wise to use merchant marine type machinery.[8] Through October the design for the 16-knot sweeper was elaborated, the object being to produce the least expensive ship possible so that it could be built in the greatest possible number. On this basis 16 knots was the highest possible speed. Third Sea Lord Admiral Tudor pointed out that a 20-knot ship, which Oliver wanted, was an entirely different proposition: she would be about 300ft long and the cost would roughly treble. The complement would also grow considerably. The main impact of Oliver's proposal was that instead of being simply a fleet sweeper, the new ship was multi-purpose: she would be suitable for minesweeping, for towing the modified sweep, for patrol, for general fleet auxiliary purposes and for anti-submarine work. Special features included fittings for explosive sweeps to attack submarines and a strong sharp forefoot for ramming them.

Initially Churchill attacked the proposal to build forty of the new fleet sweepers. He pointed out that each would cost as much as a small submarine, but could easily be destroyed by a torpedo boat. They would be valuable enough to be worth attacking and too expensive to be built in large numbers.[9] Churchill wrote that the British Isles 'teem with nondescript small vessels' which the navy should use instead of the new ships. He particularly pressed for trawlers as the obvious and immediate resource, to be supplemented with small yachts and other vessels.

Oliver (now Chief of Staff) replied a few weeks later (in a paper sent to First Sea Lord) that 'there are no more fast small merchant vessels available for sweeping or patrolling'.[10] Trawlers could not sweep at more than 7 knots, hence were useless to sweep ahead of a fleet. 'We are very short of destroyers and these vessels will answer many of the purposes of destroyers.' The Royal Navy would be no better off for destroyers in 1915, as the Germans were building as

hard as they could, having turned the large Blohm & Voss yard at Hamburg over to destroyer construction, to supplement the three earlier destroyer yards. Germany was also building numerous small craft in addition to destroyers and submarines, 'and we must have something to meet them with'. Oliver added that 'we must have numbers of small vessels of good speed to meet the German submarines next year'. In another paper dated 2 November, Third Sea Lord Admiral Tudor pointed out that combining the two functions of fleet sweeping and anti-submarine would 'meet the two menaces which hamper, restrict and wear out the Fleet to an intolerable extent. No other type of vessel can do this as effectively'. The new ships should never have to face attack by enemy torpedo boats or destroyers 'because they are as the "Filet Fish" to the "Shark" and therefore as a rule under parental protection'. None of the warships Churchill mentioned could deal with mines. Finally, the new ships had the considerable advantage that they did not require trained ratings, other than gunners; they would be manned from the merchant fleet.

Combining functions made sense. In 1914 the main fleet anti-submarine weapon was a modified sweep which destroyers could tow ahead of a fleet unit to keep submarines out of its path. Similarly, fleet sweepers were intended to work ahead of a fleet unit to clear its path of mines. The Grand Fleet used its sweepers for that purpose, but a unit of destroyers had to be assigned to sweep each Battle Squadron out of its base. It was assumed, reasonably, that submarines intending to attack the fleet would be waiting near the bases, because they were unlikely to find fast ships in the open sea. Thus the ships with modified sweeps did not have to accompany the fleet once it left base; they were part of its local defence. Nor did they need destroyer speed. By this time Admiral Jellicoe was already demanding more destroyers specifically for anti-submarine screening (modified sweeping, at this time). Anti-submarine operation was distinguished from modified sweeping because it was an attempt to find and kill submarines rather than a means of keeping them out of the way of specific ships.

Auxiliary services listed in November 1914 included boarding merchant vessels, towing targets, picking up torpedoes after they had been fired for practice, carrying stores to large ships and trans-

'P-boats' were conceived as fast (if shorter-range) alternatives to the sloop. *P 32* is shown. Note the two torpedo tubes on her stern.

ferring liberty men (from ship to shore) with their baggage, 'and any duties carried out by gun vessels and sloops'. As auxiliaries to the large ships, they would relieve destroyers.

When the design was reviewed in mid-October, it seemed possible that, given bonuses, some firms could complete ships within nine months. They would be built to merchant marine standards (Lloyd's survey) and bids would be invited only from firms which did not build warships. That decision was soon reversed, because some of the warship-builders also built merchant ships and could be expected to produce hulls and machinery very quickly.[11]

The first twelve ships were approved in November 1914.[12] Not long afterwards another twenty-four were under consideration.[13] All of these ships were to have been armed with two 3in anti-aircraft guns, but as these were not likely to be available in time, two 12pdr 18 cwt guns (on new high-angle mountings), which were also going on board the new monitors, were substituted. Ships also two 3pdr Hotchkiss QF anti-aircraft guns. The first twenty-four ships had 12pdrs. The next forty-eight had 4in or 4.7in guns instead (fifty rounds per gun compared to 200 rounds per 12pdr).[14] Installation of 4in guns was approved for all sloops and that required stiffening and added about 20 tons. By 1917, some ships with 4in or 4.7in guns had a 12pdr in addition to the two 3pdr anti-aircraft guns.

Admiral Oliver apparently chose the 'sloop' designation for these ships.[15] They received 'Flower' names. Despite their fine lines, they proved excellent seaboats. Twelve of them, caught in an extremely violent hurricane off the southwest coast of Ireland, came though unscathed.[16] However, in service they pitched badly, increasing their effective draught. The screw was shallow, hence often came out of the water and raced badly. Even in moderate weather a racing propeller considerably reduced speed. The turning circle was considered quite large. Even so, the fleet liked them very much and in spite of their small size, they turned out to be quite tough.[17]

Only early units had bow protection against mines.[18] The sloops were widely used and they suffered such considerable weight growth in service (up to 200 tons) that in September 1918 DNC considered bulging some of them to recover stability. Before or after ships were completed, four depth charges were typically added. The addition of four depth-charge throwers was approved for all sloops (those in sweeping flotillas received two). Sloops for

the Northern Patrol were given twenty depth charges for their throwers and also fittings for towing kite balloons. They were also given forty depth charges on rails. Some sloops had their sweep gallows removed when depth-charge rails were fitted. Some Mediterranean sloops were given high speed mine sweeps or combined sweeps. Some sloops had single-ship French Sweeps in place of the two-ship British 'A' Sweep.

There was early interest in a new fast sloop. In February 1915 a third series of twelve sloops was planned. On 9 February Admiral Oliver asked Third Sea Lord to review the sloop design to achieve higher speed with a shallower draught. DNC prepared a sketch design of a twin-screw shallow-draught sloop.[19] The newer German submarines reportedly had a higher surface speed (18 knots) than previously thought (this was not actually the case). At the same time AMS (Admiral Mine Sweeping) was anxious to get shallower-draught fleet sweepers. Given the higher speed of the German submarines, it would also be desirable for fleet sweepers to be faster, as the fleet itself would have to cruise at higher speed. All of these criteria pointed to a longer ship with twin screws and water-tube (naval) boilers. DNC considered the combination of shallow draught and high speed difficult, so he turned to his model tank for tests of a new hull form.[20] DNC's report proposed substituting geared turbines for the fast-running reciprocating engines of the sloops and to fix length at 320ft overall, accepting the best combination of draught and speed without exceeding that length. That implied a draught of about $8\frac{1}{2}$ft and a displacement of about 1100 tons to achieve $19\frac{1}{2}$ knots on 3000hp. Boilers and turbines would be of destroyer type, but the hull might be built to merchant ship standards (British Corporation Registry supervision).[21] To go further (to greater length for higher speed) would mean unacceptable sacrifice of strength and sea-keeping.

Substituting oil fuel for coal would reduce both fuel weight (by 25 to 30 tons, 2in of draught) and complement (by six, since furnaces would not have to be stoked). DNC cautioned that nearby explosions could cause the ship to leak oil fuel or even to burn and

A 'Z-Whaler', the only unsuccessful anti-submarine craft of the Fisher programme. The name *Meg* painted on her bow identifies her as *Z 1*, launched 29 May 1915. She was renamed *Zedwhale* in January 1915. The gun was a short submarine-type 12pdr; by 1916 she also had a high-angle 6pdr.

that it might be difficult to provide oil for the twelve ships. He therefore provided a design for a coal-fuelled sloop, with provision to substitute oil.

To provide sufficient hull strength, the ship was built up amidships, the officers being accommodated near the bridge and the ratings aft. No crew member would have to sleep forward, where there was the greatest danger of mine or submarine attack. The general design of the ship 'invites comparison with a merchant vessel and in order to increase the similarity it is proposed to fit two masts, with a slight rake and a counter stern. This arrangement will increase the chance of the vessel approaching more closely to the enemy before her identity is discovered'. For good performance in moderate weather the hull was given good sheer and flare forward, but DNC cautioned that in bad weather the ship would not be a good seaboat. She would drift more noticeably and be tossed about considerably more than a sloop, hence would be unable to maintain high speed, whereas the sloops would maintain their somewhat lower speed. In bad weather it might be difficult to use stern gallows for sweeping. The merchant-ship style hull envisaged had a shelter (flying) deck amidships and the design showed sweep handling arrangements on it.

Admiral Oliver accepted that this would be worse than the existing sloop: more expensive, longer to build (probably nine months) and needing skilled naval engine room ratings. It would also be a worse sea-keeper. On 19 February he recommended that twelve repeat sloops be ordered. First Lord Churchill agreed. At the test tank at Haslar, R E Froude kept working on the project, but on 2 March DNC wrote him that work could stop, because it was doubtful that the ship would be built.

That was probably not quite the end of the story. Watson seems to have conceived an alternative way to get 20 knots with 8ft draught and good sea-keeping – and also a deceptive silhouette – in the P-boat described below. The connection was never made in the documents which have survived and indeed the P-boat Cover reveals nothing about the origins of the design. However, the match between the two in their demands for speed and draught does not seem coincidental.[22]

The first twelve ships went to the Grand Fleet, to free destroyers he needed for fleet operations. Jellicoe liked them, but considered them too slow. On 11 May 1915 he wrote that he had visited HMS *Foxglove* after trials and that her sea speed probably

would not exceed 15 knots when loaded. He understood that twelve more were on order. Surely their speed could be increased to at least 18 knots; however he would prefer eight 20-knot ships to twelve 18-knot ships. He also considered twin screws very desirable 'as the large single screw is apt to foul the sweep'. In June, Jellicoe pointed to the submarine danger, which demanded a fleet speed of 15 to 16 knots, which was impossible due to the slow speed of his sweepers. Sweep gear could not stand more than 14 knots. Jellicoe wanted either eight sweepers capable of 16 knots or eight mine-bumpers (presumably something like the German Sperrbrechers) with that speed.

Two British trawlers escort a laden War Standard freighter (probably Type A or B) in British waters. The upper trawler (pendant number 1505 painted on her bow) is HMS *Viernoe*, a trawler requisitioned in 1915 for minesweeping and later employed as a patrol vessel and local escort. Note that the kingposts have been folded down to deny a U-boat commander information as to the ship's course (at sea only the mast abaft the funnel would be up, and it was as close as possible to amidships). Note that only one of the two guns aft has been mounted; throughout the war there was a considerable shortage of guns to arm merchant ships. Local escorts were generally provided for ships which had left convoys for particular ports. *Viernoe* survived to serve with the Royal Canadian Navy in the Second World War. (RCN)

DNC pointed back to the rejection of a design for a fast sloop only a few months back.[23] The twelve 'Flowers' just ordered could not be altered for higher speed. To achieve 18 to 20 knots would entail radical redesign. Moreover, it was impossible to sweep at a speed above 12 to 14 knots in any case. DNC also recalled that he has been asked specifically for a single-screw design, as twin screws were said to be likely to foul the sweep (they would project much further than a single screw). The best that DNC could offer Jellicoe was a modified version of the Patrol Boat (P-boat, see below), twenty-four of which had just been ordered. The 20 extra tons involved would reduce speed to about 19.5 knots and the minelaying gear now proposed would have to be given up. The alternative to buying more P-boats fitted for sweeping would be to fit destroyers.[24]

Early in July, Jellicoe was still pressing for a fast sloop and DNC still had to dissuade him. The necessary change would defeat the main advantages of the sloop: moderate cost, quick construction, engines suited to a small and unskilled crew and non-interference with other Admiralty programmes – like the destroyers Jellicoe craved. DNC described a variety of ships, including a 25-knot destroyer. It would cost two-thirds as much as a modern 'M' class destroyer and building time might be protracted because all suitable firms were busy building real destroyers. To Third Sea Lord, there was no point in a further type intermediate between sloop and 'M' class destroyer. It took destroyer performance to make sub-hunting safe without support against a German surface raid; 25-knot destroyers 'would fall prey to almost anything the Germans liked to send out; they could not escape'. Policy, then, as stated by First Sea Lord, was to build 'M' class destroyers, which were useful both as fighting ships and as submarine hunters. Continue the sloop programme without radical redesign. Test the Patrol Vessel (P-boat) and also the patrol boats from the United States (the Elco boats) when they arrive (probably in August). If the boats proved suitable for winter work, few additional craft would probably be needed (by this time 500 were on order).[25] Presumably convinced that sloops were the best he could get, on 18 July 1915 Jellicoe wrote to Admiral Jackson (Fisher's successor) that had had just told Prime Minister Asquith that another sixty-five should be laid down on an urgent basis. He certainly wanted another thirty and ten for Rosyth.[26]

Interest in faster sloops did not die. Late in 1915 Admiral Bayly submitted a report on future ASW ships. DNC commented that a point of departure was being reached: a choice had to be made between a fast ship with good draught and good seakeeping capable of maintaining speed in a seaway and a shallower-draught ship optimized for mine sweeping rather than for submarine hunting, in which seakeeping had to be sacrificed for shallow draught.[27] The sloop might make a good starting point for the latter type. If given twin screws, water-tube boilers, oil fuel (to hold down complement) and a draught of 12ft, a modified sloop might make 19 knots. It might also be more heavily armed. DNC suggested that such a ship might be very useful if (a) the submarine moved out into the ocean when the Germans introduced larger submarines or (b) if the war required a closer blockade of the German coast.

The proposals amounted to considerable redesign, but in January 1916 it was suggested that the power of the most recent twelve sloops, which had just been ordered, should be increased to 2700hp (i.e., increased by a third). E-in-C pointed out late in January that this would be impossible without enlarging the

The 'Kil' class patrol gunboat *Kildangan* as built, showing her unusual bow and stern configuration.

machinery compartments and thus increasing size and draught. That in turn would badly delay construction of these important vessels. A more modest change would give 2500hp for six hours (maximum 2700hp).[28]

By May 1916 Jellicoe himself was writing that 'the policy of building fleet sweepers of high speed is not sound. They would be inferior cruisers or scouts'.[29] It would be preferable to adapt cruisers or destroyers. By this time, however, with the advent of paravanes, Jellicoe could be far more confident that his fleet could pass through a minefield unharmed. Sweepers were now a back-up

Kilmun was the last 'Kil' class gunboat. She was completed in February 1920, as a cable vessel rather than an escort, but she retained her characteristic bow and stern, her bow distinguishable by its cable reel. She was photographed in 1938. The Royal Navy sold her in September 1946 and she was wrecked in January 1950.

against problems such as the loss of a paravane or its fitting at sea. Whether destroyer sweeping was practicable depended on whether the paravane, then in an early stage, would be satisfactory. Otherwise sweeping destroyers would have to use the awkward two-ship 'A' Sweep. At about the same time, however, Captain Charles Hopkins was visiting Scapa to review fleet sweeping practices and a new method of fleet sweeping, which would require some fast new sweepers, was being proposed.[30] When the US Navy brought its 'Bird' class sweepers to European waters in 1917, DNC considered the 'Flowers' far superior.[31]

Convoy Sloops

Even during the unrestricted U-boat campaigns, U-boats often approached their targets on the surface. Their commanders were always told to conserve torpedoes, so they tried to sink some merchant ships with gunfire or even with scuttling charges. They could avoid obviously armed merchant ships, but not ships with disguised armament, which the British called Q ships. Many were converted merchant ships, but the Royal Navy also converted existing sloops and P-boats (see below). The first decoys were deployed in 1914 and up to the end of the war there were probably a total of about 215.[32] Operations continued after the Germans adopted sink-on-sight tactics, the hope being that a U-boat would be compelled to approach a ship she had torpedoed but not sunk (due to floatation material on board the Q-ship), hence would become vulnerable. Several Q-ships sank without seeing the U-boats which attacked them.

Sloops proved effective against U-boats off the south coast of Ireland and in the Irish Sea; typically submarines dived before coming into range of their 12pdr guns. Captain Webb of the Trade

Division suggested that some be modified to resemble merchant ships, in hopes that U-boats would come within gun range.[33] A conference was presided over by DNE; Captain Carpendale attended on behalf of C-in-C Queenstown. Six ships then under construction were ordered converted, *Begonia* (already completed as a sloop) becoming prototype. The six sloops had been ordered on 23 January 1916 as part of a twelve-ship programme, the other six going to France.[34] The cover designation was Convoy Sloop. Of thirty-four Convoy Sloops later ordered as such, one was allotted to France (*Andromede*).

DNC pointed out that conversion was difficult because a sloop had a much larger complement than a merchant ship of similar size, because it had a much more powerful engine, hence needed many more engine-room personnel. It became clear that it was pointless to try to make the vessels resemble larger merchant ships. Instead, type ships were selected, preferably built by the same yard which was building the Convoy Sloop. Masts, funnels, awnings, boats and other structures had to be arranged accordingly. Visiting Queenstown, the captain of the submarine *K 5* thought that several convoy sloops had well decks so short that they would arouse suspicion. In fact there were several existing ships which had just the same sort of well decks. The constructors could not copy a larger ship because it would be obvious at once that the convoy sloops were miniatures. The captain also thought that many of the Q ships were kept too trim and smart. They also had unusually fine lines which might show up in good light. By November 1916 there was enough experience to show that the pseudo-merchant ships seemed real enough to U-boat commanders.

Begonia was completed as a sloop and then converted into a convoy sloop armed with four 12pdr 12 cwt guns, two in the forward well deck and two aft. She was followed by six ships converted while building (the first was *Tamarisk*) in which the after 12pdrs were replaced by one on the poop. Disguising it was difficult but considered well worthwhile. *Heather*, the last of the first group of six, was completed on 19 October 1916.

At least some ships (e.g. *Candytuft*) had underwater torpedo tubes. By the end of the programme, the typical armament was two

4in and two 12pdr plus, in many cases, a howitzer throwing a bomb. Four ships had twin 18in revolving torpedo tubes (*Bryony*, *Candytuft*, *Ceanothus* and *Chrysanthemum*). Others had depth-charge throwers (four each). A planned battery of four 4in for six ships ordered in January 1917 seems not to have been installed. More exotic weapons were also adopted, such as a floating anti-submarine mine device (three mines [40lb charge, total 100lbs] and 50 fathoms of line connecting them, plus a drogue, the connecting lines buoyed by fishing floats). The mines were to be used in connection with a smoke device.

Begonia was lost ramming *U 151* in the Mediterranean. *Arbutus*, *Bergamot*, *Salvia* and *Tulip* were also torpedoed as Q-ships; others were sunk after reverting to normal escort roles. *Candytuft* was torpedoed but managed to beach herself. On 23 January 1918 the Admiralty ordered the Convoy Sloops and 'P' type Special Service Boats (PC-Boats) no longer be employed as decoys; instead they would operate in the normal way, their armament no longer concealed.[35] Some became surveying ships after the war.

The '24 Class'

A new programme for twenty-four more anti-submarine sloops brought forth a new design dated 16 August 1917. They were originally conceived as the final group of sloops, turned over to DCAS (Deputy Controller for Auxiliary Shipbuilding, later Director of Auxiliary Vessels [DAV]) rather than DNC. The class name ('24 Class') was adopted at a 21 August 1917 meeting attended by Third Sea Lord, Controller, DNC and DCAS. When the ships emerged, DNC suggested that the class name did not convey enough to the fleet; he proposed in October 1918 that they be called Patrol Sloops, to distinguish them from the sloops. They corresponded to the fast trawlers now known as Patrol Gun Boats ('Kil' class, see below). The original sloops would be called Single Screw Sloops and the decoy ships (see above) would remain Convoy Sloops.

Like the 'Flowers', these ships would be built in merchant shipyards. DCAS rather than DNC would be in charge of the

The US Electric Boat Co. (ELCO) built large numbers of wooden motor launches (MLs) for the Royal Navy, beginning with fifty 75-footers ordered on 9 April 1915 by Admiral Fisher. Another 500 were ordered on 8 June 1915; they were slightly larger (80-footers). All were assembled by Canadian Vickers in Montreal, then shipped as deck cargo, four to a freighter. The contract called for delivery of the first twenty-five boats by 30 November 1915 and the next 200 by 31 May 1916, with fifty per month after that, the last to be delivered by 3 November 1916. Another thirty (*ML 551–ML 580*) were ordered in July 1917. The motor launches made a considerable impression as inshore warships, for roles such as submarine patrol, minelaying, smoke-making (for example, in support of Dover Patrol monitors) and inshore minesweeping. At least eighty-two six-boat inshore motor launch patrol units (numbered 500–581) were formed. In effect the motor launches replaced the civilian motor boats the Royal Navy took over earlier in the war. Their good seakeeping qualities encouraged use in place of some of the early patrol trawlers. The original armament was an army-type 13pdr gun, but they were diverted to arm merchant ships and the motor launches armed with the 3pdr shown here. Forty Royal Navy motor launches (ML 114-548 series) were sold to France, which gave them V (vedette) designations (V.1 to V.40). The French ordered another twelve (V.62 to V.73) from Canadian Vickers for delivery in May 1918, but even the first four did not arrive until after the Armistice. ELCO also built this type of boat for the Royal Italian Navy: *MAS 63– MAS 90* (twenty-eight), *MAS 103– MAS 114* (twelve), *MAS 253– MAS 302* (fifty) and *MAS 377– MAS 396* (twenty), a total of 110 boats. They were called the MAS 'C' type. Italian yards built *MAS 303–MAS 317* (fifteen) and *MAS 327–MAS 376* (fifty) to a modified design. Another fifty ELCO type boats were planned for construction in Italian yards, but only the first thirty were ordered and they were cancelled. Russia received nine 75-footers (*MT 10-18*). The success of the motor launches inspired the US 110ft sub-chaser project. *ML 260* is shown carrying mines. (Dr David Stevens, SPC-A)

design (DNC would furnish him with full information on previous sloops). A sketch marked to show that it 'embodied latest suggestions for anti-submarine expedients' and signed by DNC E T D'Eyncourt showed a ship with identical raked bow and stern profiles and with a single stack and mast as close to each other and to amidships, as possible (the funnel was exactly amidships).[36] To further confuse a submariner, in half the ships the mast would be before the funnel and in half it would be abaft the funnel. The ship would have nearly identical blocks of superstructure fore and aft, so that a submarine commander could not be sure of her direction and, because of the single funnel and mast, of her heading. To make it impossible to measure rate of change (presumably of bearing), there were no prominent features at the ends of the ship. Armament as shown was four 4in guns, all on the centreline, two at the ends (forecastle and poop) and two on fore and aft extensions of the midships superstructure. If desired, each pair of 4in guns could be replaced by a 6in gun. The main point about the arrangement was that it was fully symmetrical fore and aft. Provision had been made for depth charges, but not for howitzers, throwers or torpedo tubes, any of which might replace some of the guns shown in the sketch. Machinery would match that of current sloops, which could make 17 knots.

Ships were ordered between December 1916 and April 1917, presumably initially as 'Flowers'. Ten were completed early enough in 1918 to serve in sloop flotillas at Granton and Gibraltar. As completed, they had vertical steam and stern and two rather than four 4in guns, but heavy depth-charge batteries including in some cases a prominent long depth-charge rail aft. Of the twenty-four ordered, the last two were cancelled on 3 December 1918.[37]

Patrol Boats (P-boats)

The origins of the P-boat are obscure (but note the likely connection, discussed above, with the abortive fast twin-screw sloop of February 1915). The DNC history of wartime design cites the need for more and more destroyers in the early months of the war, which inspired attempts at substitution. One was clearly the sloop. Early in April 1915 DNC proposed a highly-manoeuvrable ship with a powerful armament, moderate speed and low visibility.[38] To reduce visibility, the ship was given the appearance of a surfaced steam submarine. Another explanation advanced in 1915, when DNC was heading off demands for a fast sloop, was that the new ship had been designed specifically for sea-keeping, the idea being that, like the submarine it resembled, it could shrug off heavy weather, presenting little obstruction to the sea.[39] The new ship (Patrol Boat) was conceived largely as an anti-submarine craft and to that end it was provided with a hardened ram bow. DNC later said that the Patrol Boat had been designed for light mild steel construction, which could be undertaken by non-specialist firms. However, DNC's disappointed comment on bids submitted was that in effect the Patrol Boat was a destroyer built out of less expensive material (mild rather than high tensile steel). He considered the bids too high. Like the sloops, the P-boats were built to merchant standards (e.g., Lloyd's survey).

The initial order covered twenty-four ships, which were numbered *P 11* to *P 34* because P 1 to P 10 had been allocated as pendant numbers for major warships. After successful trials, another thirty were ordered (*P 35* to *P 64*), but ten of them were completed as Q-ships called PC-boats (*PC 42–44, 51, 55, 56* and *60–63*). Further PCs were ordered in 1917.[40]

DNC submitted drawings and particulars to the Sea Lords on 28 April 1915 but, unusually, his description of the new design is not included in the Cover. Second Sea Lord limited himself to cautioning against anything that would make the ships more complex. Churchill wanted the new ships to be convertible to lay

Petrol engines were dangerous. *ML 219* is shown wrecked on the Rhine at Cologne, 13 May 1919, while taking on fuel. The steel shoe on her bow was added so that she could ram U-boats. (Dr David Stevens, SPC-A)

mines 'on a special occasion'. The projected armament included ten mines, but they were dropped because the freeboard was so low that they would be difficult to lay. A later requirement for fittings for thirty mines was also abandoned, partly because the type of mine was not defined. The new project coincided roughly with Jellicoe's push for higher sloop speed and he was offered minesweeping Patrol Boats as a possible solution (see above).[41] The Cover includes a drawing of a minesweeping installation for a P-boat.

By mid-April 1915 the design had been worked out to the point where E-in-C was submitting weight and centre of gravity for the projected 3500hp machinery. At the same time DNC knew that planned armament was one 4in gun, one 2pdr pom-pom anti-aircraft gun and two fixed 14in torpedo tubes – half the gun armament of a sloop. By this time, too, dimensions had been fixed: 220 to 230ft x 23ft 6in x 8ft, 580 tons (the Legend showed 230ft x 23ft 6in x 8ft and 575 tons). The ship would have twin screws driven by geared turbines and would burn oil fuel. They would have a searchlight and wireless. Depth charges were coming into widespread service as the later ships of the initial series entered service. Initially they had two and later four, depth charges; later two throwers were added, with two spare charges (total eight). Reports from sea favoured a second 4in gun and provision was made to add it. There was also interest in replacing the two fixed torpedo tubes with a single revolving 18in tube, but it was decided to replace all torpedo tubes with more depth charges. Designed full speed was 20 knots, but on trial 22 knots was achieved at 4000hp (3800hp designed power). In August 1915 DNC produced an outline design for what he called a 125ft vedette boat (patrol boat) capable of 23 to 24 knots on 2500hp twin-screw machinery.[42] Displacement would have been 120 tons and armament one 4in or two 12pdr plus depth charges and mine sweeps.

Z-Whalers

On 16 March 1915 Admiral Fisher wrote to Jellicoe that 100 new small craft had just been ordered of three classes – small whalers (the Z-Whalers), big whalers and £60,000 vessels (sloops), *more or less dictated to us by the capacity of unemployed shipbuild-ing facilities to proceed with the work at once and the speeds vary from 13 to 17 knots. The small whaler costing £4000 and only going 11 knots catches more whales than the big whaler of 15 knots, because ever so much more handy and turns on her heel, so in the whaling industry they've given up big whalers for small ones after an exhaustive trial. A submarine is 'very much like a whale.' (Shakespeare, in* Hamlet*) Turn on her quick and harpoon her with a bomb!*[43]

Non-rigid airships (blimps) were an essential element of British ASW, initially as patrol craft. Admiral Fisher thought them the ideal submarine hunters, though they were more valuable for their ability to spot U-boats than for attacks. This is *SSP 4*, an improved version of the original Submarine Scout (SS). (Philip Jarrett)

At just about this time the British were experimenting with a 'lance-bomb', which much resembled a harpoon with a high explosive head. There is no indication that Fisher's 'big trawlers' were ever bought and the number of trawlers bought at this time does not correspond in any way to his figure. Nor did Fisher ever include the 'big trawlers' in his compilations of ships ordered under his tenure at the Admiralty.

In mid-March 1915 Fisher verbally ordered fifteen whalers from Smith's Dock; at that point they were part of a project for a large number of ships to replace destroyers on anti-submarine patrol. He planned 100 of them, but it turned out that sloops could be obtained more easily and also that to keep up with German submarines and to keep the sea in any weather something of sloop size was needed.[44]

On 19 March Third Sea Lord proposed to confirm that order and also to buy four existing whalers (hence Fisher's reference to nineteen of them). DNC explained that 'a certain number of slower vessels with good manoeuvring characteristics might be useful for convoying the slower merchant ships', for which purpose the 12 knot whalers would be suitable. 'These are of special type and though they lack the high speed their extreme handiness should enable them to deal with submarines at close quarters.'[45] This may be the earliest surviving mention of convoy tactics in British First World War papers. It is in striking contrast to the later rejection of convoying as an ASW tactic.

Fisher's published letters of this period do *not* refer to convoy as a rationale for buying whalers; convoy (as in 'convoy sloops') may have been a euphemism for decoying submarines. Thus on 17 June Third Sea Lord wrote that 'as the sole intention of construct-ing these vessels to make them resemble Whalers, I am not clear who is responsible for permitting the design to depart so widely from this intention, causing considerable delay and expense to put it right'.[46]

On 22 March Churchill approved both the new whalers and the purchase of existing ones 'subject to it being established that the torpedo launches from America [actually the Motor Launches, which were not armed with torpedoes] will fulfil the tactical object in view, I am quite ready to affirm their being ordered'. Eight days later the builder, Smith's Dock, sent DNC a summary of its outline design for its Ships 641–655.[47] The only fixed armament was one 12pdr gun on a submarine (S2) mounting. The Admiralty told Smith's Dock that the principal factors governing the general design were (1) rapid manoeuvring, (2) minimum draught to escape mines and torpedoes, (3) maximum speed within the dimensions, (4) bow built for ramming submarines, (5) raised main deck forward for a 12pdr and (6) six watertight bulkheads and a watertight lower deck abaft the machinery, for maximum safety.[48]

No further whalers were built and no more were bought until 1917. By the time the whalers were complete, the anti-submarine harpoon had been discredited and the depth charge was not yet ready. A whaler could not tow an anti-submarine sweep and it was not fast enough to run down a surfaced submarine; the submarine had to come to it. Unlike a trawler, a whaler could not deploy a heavy net. The fifteen whalers survived in British service, but they were clearly a dead end.[49]

Trawlers and Drifters

In 1914 Britain was a great fishing power, so on the outbreak of war the Admiralty had access to a large fleet of trawlers which could be converted into sweepers (see Chapter 15) and into low-speed anti-submarine and patrol craft. Before the war a large force of trawlers was earmarked specifically for minesweeping. The Admiralty bought six trawlers for training, four in April 1909 and two in 1910. Another was bought in May 1914, followed by four in July 1914, mainly for subsidiary duties such as target-towing. Two more trawlers were bought for survey work, but fitted for sweeping. Further purchases were for minesweeping: another in October (plus two more bought some time in 1914, presumably after war broke out).[50] Once war broke out all Admiralty trawlers were used for sweeping and patrol.

Ten trawlers (the 'Military Class', although they were in three groups) were bought on the stocks, six by order of 11 December 1914 and four by order of 14 April 1915. Nine assorted British-built Portuguese trawlers were bought in September 1915. All were apparently used for auxiliary patrol work.

In 1915 it was mainly the Auxiliary Patrol trawlers, with associated yachts, which sought U-boats in areas off the British coast. Jellicoe complained that the system was pointless.[51] The trawlers were under-armed compared to U-boats and some of them had not yet been armed at all.[52] Others could fire on only one side. Few had W/T, so it was difficult or impossible to concentrate a hunting patrol once one trawler spotted a U-boat. Even then, given their low speed, the trawlers often could not concentrate quickly enough. As yet there was no shore organisation to turn disparate reports into indications of where a U-boat might be, let alone signal that information to the senior officer of a patrol group offshore. As the war continued, all of these issues except speed were addressed.

All the trawlers were armed and the 6pdrs on board early ones were replaced by 12pdrs which really could damage a U-boat. The shore command and control system was created and more and more trawlers were fitted with W/T. Speed alone could not be addressed without building considerably larger ships.

Numerous British trawlers were taken up for the Auxiliary Patrol and by the summer of 1915 there were fears that the British fishing industry was being unduly damaged.[53] By mid-1916 it seemed that further requisitions were unacceptable for that reason. All ships fit for Admiralty service had, apparently, already been requisitioned. As of September 1916 the Admiralty had requisitioned 1300 out of about 1800 trawlers in existence in 1914. New construction since then had amounted to only 240 and 102 trawlers had been lost.[54] On 18 August 1916 Fourth Sea Lord held a conference with representatives of the major trawling ports (Hull, Grimsby and Aberdeen) to ask for recommendations as to the type of trawler which would have good commercial value post-war and the builders best suited to provide working drawings. A higher-level Admiralty conference (26 September 1916) formally decided to buy large numbers of new trawlers, which could easily be sold off post-war. Finally a conference of the Admiralty technical departments (11 October 1916) recommended three types. Each was already being built by a major trawler builder.

The Admiralty chose Cochrane's *Mersey* (138$\frac{1}{2}$ft long), Hall Russell's *Strath* (115ft long) and Smith's Dock's *Castle* (125ft long). The *Mersey* type usually worked pre-war on the White Sea and Iceland fisheries out of Hull and Grimsby, but such ships could even reach the coast of Morocco and the banks of Newfoundland. The *Castle* type, mostly built for Castle Steam Trawlers Ltd of Swansea, was a slightly smaller version of the Mersey, for home waters, but also capable of foreign service. The smallest of the three, the *Strath* type, was primarily for home waters. It was built mainly for the 'Strath' Steam Trawling and Fishing Co Ltd of Aberdeen. Designed speeds were, respectively, 11, 10 and 10.5 knots, hence clearly below that of any surfaced submarine. The main Admiralty modifications were to add a magazine and shell-room in the fish-hold, accommodation for more men (four in a *Mersey*, three in the others) in the fish-hold and a gun platform, plus depth-charge chutes and stands, kite racks and towed-charge gear.

The earlier hired trawlers had their 6pdr (and later 12pdr) guns over their engine casings, or over their fish-holds, or in the bow. The new ones all had 12pdr 12 cwt guns (often on high-angle mountings) over their engine casings. However, in July 1918 it was decided on the basis of experience that a bow position was better and builders were offered to fit two gun platforms, one in the bow and one over the engine casing aft. Guns were mounted in the bow position, but could be remounted aft if desired. There was also interest in mounting a heavier gun, presumably because U-boats were more heavily armed: in April 1918 experimental bow mountings were ordered for the *Mersey* class trawler *Thomas Jago* and for the *Castle* class trawler *Giovanni Guinti*. Trials were successful.

Trawler armament reflected the development of ASW weapons. Trawlers initially had a single set of towed charges, although many were completed without it. Fitting of these charges was stopped in January 1918, because by then depth charges were considered far more effective. The new trawlers appeared as depth charges were being deployed; each had one D★ type charge in a

Once convoy was introduced, long-endurance airships were clearly ideal escorts, at least in British waters. This blimp is an SS Zero. At the end of the war the Royal Navy had a total of 103 airships in commission: four rigids (*R 23, R 25, R 29* and *R 31*), six long-range North Sea blimps (*NS 4, NS 6, NS 7, NS 8, NS 11* and *NS 12* with *NS 14–NS 18* in reserve]), fourteen coastal (*C* 1–C* 10* and *C 2, C 4, C 5A* and *C 14A*), nine SS (*SS 14A, SS 28A, SS 29, SS 30A, SS 31A, SS 35, SS 36, SS 37A* and *SS 39A*), three SSP (*SSP 1, SSP 5* and *SSP 6*), ten SST (*SST 1–SST 4, SST 7, SST 8–SST 12*) and fifty-four SSZ (*SSZ 1, SSZ 3, SSZ 4, SSZ 6, SSZ 8, SSZ 9, SSZ 11, SSZ 12, SSZ 14, SSZ 16, SSZ 18, SSZ 19, SSZ 20, SSZ 27–SSZ 34, SSZ 36, SSZ 37, SSZ 39–SSZ 48, SSZ 50, SSZ 52, SSZ 53, SSZ 55, SSZ 57– SSZ 67, SSZ 69* and *SSZ 72–SSZ 76*, plus *SSZ 68* and *SSZ 70* being re-erected in Eastern Mediterranean]), plus the sole SSE (*SSE 2*) and the ancient No. 6 Parseval. (Philip Jarrett)

stern chute plus four smaller G type charges in racks on the upper deck aft. In May 1917 it was decided to add a second D★ charge and in June 1918 the battery was increased to four D★ charges in two double rails.

In October 1917 trawlers were ordered fitted with either the Shark Fin (*Castle* and *Strath* classes) or Plate hydrophones (*Mersey* class), but fittings were discontinued in January 1918. Presumably self-noise was too great. In April 1918 a project was approved to equip two *Strath*s (*George Ireland* and *Henry Jennings*) with silent propulsion in the form of centrifugal pumps for jet propulsion. The other way of isolating a hydrophone from the trawler was to tow it. In November 1917 it was decided to form a special force of 120 to 140 trawlers equipped with fish (towed) hydrophones, including ninety-six ships under construction. The whole force was to be completed by March 1918. Equipment included two depth-charge throwers. A silent cabinet was installed for the hydrophone listener (in a *Strath*, the wheelhouse had to be moved forward to provide space). Because so much work was involved, the number of new ships was cut to sixty-nine, the rest being trawlers already in commission. Standard trawl fittings were considered suitable for minesweeping gear, except that early trawlers needed racks aft for 9ft kites (the use of these kites was discontinued in February 1918). Several trawlers were fitted for minelaying. One trawler in three was given W/T, but all the *Mersey*s were equipped because they were the largest trawlers and hence most suitable. The rest of the W/T trawlers were *Castle*s; all had $\frac{1}{2}$ kW sets and their mizzen masts raised to hold the aerial 50 to 60ft above water. The required dynamo was installed in the engine room.

The overall programme envisaged in 1916 was 500 trawlers to

The Coastal (C type) blimp was the step above a Submarine Scout (SS), offering greater range. Here one overflies a light cruiser. It is recognisable by its unusual envelope.

	Strath	Castle	Mersey	
Delivered by 11.11.18	80	127	69	285
Delivered unarmed as M/S	14	18	8	40
Completed as Fishing V.	46	52	35	133
Cancelled	18	20	44	82[55]
Total	167	217	156	540

be completed by the end of 1918, about twenty-one per month. The maximum capacity of the eight specialist trawler firms was about 200 per year, seventeen per month. The Admiralty immediately began to strengthen these firms, for example by re-stocking their labour (in the words of the DNC history) and by giving them priorities for materials second only to the warship yards. Their situation was simplified to some extent by decisions to accept substitutes for scarce material such as copper. However, service needs for manpower made the labour situation difficult. The Admiralty brought another twenty-four firms into the trawler programme in hopes of reaching production targets. For the first ten months of 1917 output averaged only fourteen trawlers per month, but that increased to twenty-three and twenty-four in November and December and the rate for 1918 would have been twenty-five to twenty-six per month on that basis. However, in July 1917 a new class of Patrol Gunboats ('Kil' class, see below) was ordered from five of the trawler-builders, with priority over trawlers. Output fell to fourteen per month during 1918.

As part of the 500-trawler programme, in October 1916 the decision was made to order 250 trawlers and all the leading builders were informed at the end of the month that their full output was being requisitioned. As for trawlers on order for private use, only those on which at least one instalment had been paid could be completed, in that case as quickly as possible to clear the way for the big Admiralty programme. Of 112 trawlers on order at the time, instalments had been paid on sixty-nine, the Admiralty taking over the remaining forty-three as part of its standard-design programme despite their non-standard designs. Orders for standard types were placed as quickly as possible from November 1916 onwards. This was the 'November programme'. In 1917 the War Cabinet formally approved extension to 500 trawlers, all to be completed by the end of 1918.[55]

Later in 1917 it was pointed out that steam drifters could be used as minesweepers, so fifty trawler orders were cancelled in favour of 115 drifters. That cut the programme to 450 trawlers as of July 1917. Later in 1917 another 60 drifters were approved, so that the programme called for 400 trawlers and 175 drifters. In 1918 the War Cabinet approved a further programme, to be completed by the end of 1919, for 140 trawlers and 160 drifters, for a total of 540 trawlers and 335 drifters.

The total of 540 amounted to:

In addition the Royal Canadian Navy ordered two classes of Canadian-designed trawlers in January 1917. The Royal Navy then decided to order standard trawlers and drifters from Canadian yards to supplement home protection, with the understanding that they might be needed in Canadian waters as the Germans deployed longer-range submarines. The January 1917 programme amounted to thirty-six Castle class and 100 standard wooden drifters, arrangements being made by the Canadian government. In July another twenty-four Castles were ordered. Nine modified (wood and steel) Castle class were ordered in India in 1917, but completed only after the war and six were bought in March 1917 as minesweepers (supplementing two tugs used up to that point).

British warships took twenty-seven German trawlers as prizes in the North Sea. Another seventeen British-built Russian trawlers were reported seized in the White Sea on 3 August 1918 (some were apparently handed over by the White Russians) to form the Axe class. Six had been built during the war by Smith's Dock and one by Cochrane.

At the Armistice, all trawlers nearing completion or due for delivery before the end of 1918 were to ordered completed as unarmed minesweepers for post-war mine clearance. The 133 others under construction were completed as fishing vessels, 104 of them being sold by the Director of Contracts. All not yet laid down were cancelled, except those whose cancellation would cause serious unemployment or dislocation.

Trawlers pull their nets through the water to pick up schools of fish. Drifters lower their nets into the water, picking up fish which swim into them. They therefore needed less power and were smaller than trawlers and less expensive. They had smaller crews, typically ten rather than fifteen. At the outbreak of war the Admiralty had no drifters, but soon it was requisitioning them for, among other things, minesweeping and anti-submarine patrol, as well as fleet auxiliary functions otherwise undertaken by trawlers. Because they were smaller than trawlers, drifters could be built by more firms. By 1917 drifters were proving effective minesweepers.

When the trawler programme was reviewed in March 1917, it was suggested that shifting some of it to drifters would relieve some of the yards. Despite initial opposition, in April 1917 First Sea Lord Admiral Jellicoe approved the idea and, as noted, 115 drifters replaced fifty trawlers in the programme. The plan was to build both steel and wood drifters. A design by A. Hall & Co. of Aberdeen (Ocean type) was chosen for the steel drifter and one by J. Chambers Ltd. for the wood drifter. In each case the design firm became 'parent' for the others building its design. The standard trawler W/T set was installed in selected steel trawlers. Armament was initially one 6pdr in the bow and two Type D depth charges (later increased to four, as instructed in May 1918), plus two smaller G type depth charges. As with the trawlers, fitting of Shark's Fin hydrophones was approved in October 1917 and discontinued in January 1918. The drifters had about half the power of the trawlers and designed speed was 9 knots.

As with the trawlers, firms were told to give Admiralty drifters absolute precedence. Orders were placed in May 1917, for completion by 1 May 1918. Of forty-two drifters then under construction, twelve were taken over by the Admiralty. In theory the seven main builders could have built many more than the required ten per month, but shortages of labour and material and the pressure of other work (including repairs) delayed matters so badly that as of the end of April only nine had been completed, with another thirty-four launched. The Admiralty approached sixty-four other firms and nine of them received orders for a total of twenty drifters. By May 1918, a total of thirty firms were involved in the programme; during the last five months up to the Armistice, output averaged nearly fourteen per month. At the Armistice, eighty-four had been completed and handed over. Another sixty-eight were cancelled, thirty-four were completed for minesweeping and 105 were completed as fishing craft.

'Kil' Class (Patrol Gun Boats)

The trawlers were slow and they had not been designed for anti-submarine warfare. In mid-1917 the Admiralty raised a requirement for a fast anti-submarine ship of roughly trawler size, but not intended for fishing. It was conceived as an escort, with greater sea-keeping capability and greater endurance. Six trawler-builders submitted designs and Smith's Dock won. Orders were placed with all six firms beginning in July 1917 and financial approval for all eighty-five and priority over trawlers, was given in November 1917. Some trawlers were cancelled to make way for the programme.[56] The following year trawler priority was revived and on 2 March 1918 thirty were ordered cancelled. Four of the builders sent their material to Smith's Dock, so that it alone could keep building the fast ships. On 16 July 1918 Smith's Dock had cancelled contracts relocated to it for twenty-one ships. Final cancellation of thirty ships then building at Smith's Dock was announced on 6 December 1918. At least eleven ships were fitted as minesweepers.

An interesting feature of the design was the attempt to frustrate an attempt by a U-boat commander to estimate the ship's course. To that end bow and stern were made as similar as possible. The ship had two apparently identical superstructure blocks flanking a funnel dead amidships, with a single mast which could be either before or abaft the funnel. This idea was later applied to the '24 Class' sloops described above. The 'super trawlers' were called 'fast trawlers' until 18 January 1918 and then Patrol Gun Boats. All were given 'Kil' names, hence were described as the 'Kil' class. In 1939 Smith's Dock representatives pointed to this design as the corvette of the First World War (like the earlier ship, the 'Flower' class corvette was conceived as a step above a trawler).[57]

Motor Launches

One of Admiral Fisher's early successes was to buy warships in the United States. They included fifty big motor launches built by Elco (Electric Boat); after Fisher left office another 500 were bought through Canadian Vickers in June and another thirty in July 1917. The initial units were 75ft long, the later ones 80ft long. They are significant here mainly because they seemed to be an alternative to deeper-sea patrol craft, the hope being that U-boats would be forced to operate inshore. They could carry depth charges and they

The Royal Navy used flying boats for anti-submarine patrols, initially US-designed Curtiss 'Americas' (so named because the prototype had been designed for an abortive 1914 transatlantic flight). Captain E C Bass acquired British manufacturing rights in 1912. Invalided out of the Royal Navy, J C Porte became interested in flying one of these craft across the Atlantic. When war broke out, two imported Curtiss boats were impressed and Porte convinced Commodore Murray Sueter, head of the RNAS, to buy these aircraft from Curtiss. The original H.4 was known as a 'Small America' once the fifty larger H.12 ('Large America') entered service. Once the United States entered the war, collaboration between the Royal Navy and the US Navy produced the even larger H.16 shown here in January 1922.

were fitted with hydrophones. Some were used for inshore minesweeping.

Airships

No account of ASW craft would be complete without the mass of naval airships, most of them non-rigids (blimps), beginning with Admiral Fisher's prototype Submarine Scout of 1915. That year Fisher wrote Admiral Jellicoe that at last he had hit on a 'submarine destroyer', meaning his airship, which would be begun that day (28 February) and completed in three weeks to begin work over the Dover Strait. It would cost less than a tenth as much as a sloop (£5000).[58] This *SS 2* became the prototype for about 200 wartime non-rigid airships.

By 1915 the RNAS was the sole British service using and developing airships, so the navy already had experienced personnel.[59] The navy already had rigid and non-rigid airships, but not small ones suited to quick production. It was already accepted that airships might be uniquely suited to ASW, both because a submarine could not torpedo them and because under some conditions an observer aloft could see a submerged submarine (and also mines). That turned out to be much truer of the Mediterranean than of the North Sea.

When Admiral Fisher called for instant creation of a small scout airship, it was not too difficult to improvise, combining the envelope of the small Willows No 2 (*HMA 2*) and the fuselage of a BE 2c. It ran successful trials within five weeks. Fisher wanted a crew of two, a speed of 40 to 50 knots, W/T, eight hours endurance and 160lbs of bombs. The most important requirement was quick production. Fifty were ordered after successful trials, fifty-four being built (*SS 1* to *SS 49*, but there were also *SS 28a, SS 30a, SS 37a, SS 39a* and *SS 42a*). As of March 1916, of forty required, twenty-six were on hand and another eighteen were on order.[60] The SS was further developed into the SSP (patrol), SSZ (zero, because initially they had a zero prefix, as in SS.01) and SST (twin, for twin engines).[61]

At Felixstowe, Porte, brought back to the Royal Navy at the outbreak of war (and Wing Commander at its end), developed a better hull for the Curtiss flying boats the Royal Navy was buying. His first production type was the Felixstowe (for his air station) F2A. The first aircraft were delivered in November 1917; by the end of the war a year later, there were six F2A squadrons, with another forming. There were also five squadrons of the related F3, plus six independent Flights attached to the Grand Fleet for reconnaissance. These units were all in addition to training formations. (Philip Jarrett)

A larger Coastal (C) class (170,000ft^3 compared to the 70,000ft^3 of the SS) was intended to mount a longer-range patrol, for example between Margate and Dunkirk. It had a tri-lobe envelope (less streamlined than that of an SS) based on that of the French *Astra Torres*. Compared to an SS, a C had a larger bomb load and, like the later rigids, it had a gun position on top of its envelope. The car was designed around an Avro 504 fuselage with fore and aft skids. Production was *C 1* to *C 27* and then the improved *C*1* to *C*10*. In 1916, twenty-eight Coastals and six improved Coastals were on order.

The next step up, an improved C type, was an attempt to achieve something like rigid airship performance in the sort of semi-rigid which was being built successfully. It was seen as a stop-gap while the desired fleet rigids were built. This was the North Sea (NS) class, with two 250hp Rolls-Royce engines (later two 240hp Fiats in some). The main requirements were endurance, reliability, ample fuel and crew comfort. That meant providing for a relief crew. For the first time in a non-rigid, the engines were in a power unit separate from the crew's car. Endurance was spectacular: in the summer of 1917 one set a British record of 49 hours 22 minutes and after the Armistice one managed 101 hours in the air. Two of these airships, *NS 7* and *NS 8*, escorted the German fleet to surrender at Scapa Flow. The first was delivered in February 1917, the last in March 1919. Production amounted to *NS 1* to *NS 16* (but there was no *NS 13* or *NS 15*). *NS 14* was sold to the United States.

By April 1917, however, the non-rigids were in some disfavour, perhaps because their endurance was not so important as their vulnerability to enemy aircraft. That month a writer in the airship department emphasised the British rigid airship programme, but claimed that most senior naval officers would prefer two Large America flying boats to one Coastal and one Large America to an SS; at this time more than 176 Large Americas were on order.[62] Appended to this paper was one giving a very different point of view: that due to their superior speed, endurance, independence of surface craft, the power to vary their airspeed and their superior facilities for observation and signalling, airships were superior to heavier than air craft as fleet lookouts, for patrols and for supporting convoys against submarines. They were unsuited to close reconnaissance due to their inherent vulnerability. Kite balloons were an inadequate substitute. For convoy operations the writer considered Coastals 'very valuable for convoy and local patrol and infinitely preferable to the Large America providing they are secure from attack by enemy aircraft'.

The key difference between the two papers is probably their dates – the second was dated 17 July, after convoy had been introduced, which meant after it really mattered that an airship could keep station above a slow convoy. In April 1918 the Admiralty wrote the Air Ministry that it wanted to retain the North Sea type until it had a good enough rigid to work with the fleet. For local patrols, it wanted to concentrate on the SS Twin, discarding the C class as it wore out.[63]

The projected further programme at the end of the war was revised from twelve NS and twenty C* to six NS and 10 C and 115 SS Twin because the rigids were finally successful and also because the smaller blimps were considered so useful for convoy work.[64]

The US Ships

The apparent success of the motor launches helped convince the US Navy to buy 110-ft subchasers when it entered the war. At that point there was no real understanding of what submarine chasing or hunting might entail, but the subchasers were large enough and contemporary sensors small enough, that they proved adaptable. It was soon clear that they were not large enough or fast enough. In May 1917 the General Board asked whether something intermediate between the sub-chaser and the destroyer was needed. It argued that the destroyer was 'so far as can now be seen, the best form of submarine chaser', its only defect being that with 4in guns it could not face huge new U-boats armed, it was understood, with three 5.9in guns (an exaggeration). It seemed to the General Board that ideally the United States should continue building destroyers, but without torpedo tubes and with a heavier gun battery (four 5in guns). Meanwhile construction of fully-equipped destroyers should continue.

In July the new Special Board reported that destroyers were best for hunting down and destroying submarines owing to their speed, seaworthiness, habitability, reliability and endurance.[65] It endorsed Secretary Daniels' decision to order another fifty destroyers and proposed building 150 to 200 more of a new standardised simplified type (Daniels agreed). Standardisation would make it possible to order machinery and auxiliaries on a mass-production basis. The US Navy was already building fifty new 'flush decker' destroyers approved under the big 1916 programme, of which twenty had been laid down immediately under the FY17 programme. The Special Board wanted all the new destroyers equipped with a sound-detecting device suitable for use while the destroyer was steaming, which it hoped to develop. In fact no such device existed even in rudimentary form until well into 1918. Note that the call for destroyers did *not* connect them with convoy operations, which turned out to be their single vital ASW role.

For its part the General Board, which normally advised the Secretary on the building programme, pointed out in July 1917 that a new design would entail considerable delay. It would take thirty months for production of a new type, however simplified, to exceed the numbers of the type already building and for the first eighteen months the existing type could be had in greater numbers than any new type. The desired 200-destroyer programme would have to supersede all other naval construction and the government might have to take over the five major shipyards (Newport News, New York Shipbuilding, Cramp's, Fore River and the Union Iron Works), with all that entailed. The Board pressed for construction of the existing type, although to speed production the 35-knot contract speed guarantee might be relaxed to 30 knots. Another fifty destroyers (total 100, including the 1916 ships) could be ordered for completion by January 1919. All of these ships should have 5in guns. Secretary Daniels agreed, rejecting a private August 1917 proposal for a 16-knot 156ft steel subchaser.

In a more elaborate version of its recommendations, the Special Board added that the British had felt compelled to build a special type of ship specifically for anti-submarine work (it is not clear what it had in mind, as it was two years since the P-boat and sloop programmes; all British destroyers were conventional general-purpose ships). By this time the Navy Department had reviewed the priority of various ship types, placing sub-chasers first, destroyers second, scout cruisers (to deal with raiders) third and submarines fourth. They were followed by battleships (soon to be demoted); the new battlecruisers came last of fourteen types. The Board recognised that merchant ship construction was integral to the ASW campaign and it called explicitly for close co-ordination between the Navy and the Emergency Fleet Corporation. Probably construction of large warships would have to be sacrificed, as it was. Only battleships already under construction would be finished.

The initial reaction to General Board rejection of the 200-destroyer programme was that instead of assigning these ships to conventional shipyards, these 'submarine destroyers', like some of the Emergency Fleet Corporation merchant ships, should be fabricated, their parts produced across the country. As of 19 July 1917, sixty-six destroyers were building and their builders could

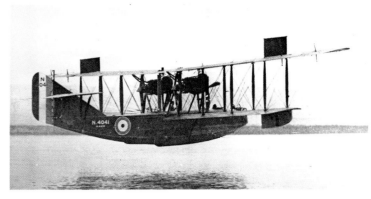

Porte's F5 was the culmination of his work and probably the best wartime seaplane design. It was just too late to see service. The prototype was built late in 1917 and was adopted as an RNAS (rather than simply a Felixstowe) project in March 1918. Large-scale production was planned, in Britain, in the United States and at Malta. US orders amounted to sixty from Curtiss, fifty from Canadian Aeroplanes and 480 from the Naval Aircraft Factory at the Philadelphia Navy Yard; most were cancelled. The Liberty-powered F5L version became the only foreign type adopted after the war by the US Navy. The US version was armed with a Davis 6pdr recoilless gun in the bow. (Philip Jarrett)

take another fifty contracts for completion by January 1919. OpNav recommended building another 200, but it did not want a new design; it suggested repeating the earlier 750-ton 'flivvers' (the current type displaced 1150 tons) on an assembly-line basis. The Technical Bureaus said that 200 more fleet destroyers could be built by devoting the five largest shipyards exclusively to this project. To OpNav the flivvers offered a slower but more reliable ship. Although the General Board wanted 5in guns, it would be easier to obtain the 4in/50s originally planned for the 'flush deckers'. They seemed adequate against U-boats. The recommendation was to let contracts for fifty more fleet destroyers plus 150 standardised 'submarine destroyers', some of which would be built

In addition to self-propelled airships and aircraft, the Royal Navy used numerous kite balloons towed by ships. Here one accompanies the destroyer Onslow. The first Royal Navy use of kite balloons was at the Dardanelles, the merchant ship Manica being converted to support them. A Kite Balloon Service was formed in March 1915 specifically to support anti-submarine operations, but by 1918 there were also thirty kite balloons with the Grand Fleet.

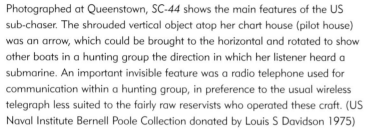

Photographed at Queenstown, SC-44 shows the main features of the US sub-chaser. The shrouded vertical object atop her chart house (pilot house) was an arrow, which could be brought to the horizontal and rotated to show other boats in a hunting group the direction in which her listener heard a submarine. An important invisible feature was a radio telephone used for communication within a hunting group, in preference to the usual wireless telegraph less suited to the fairly raw reservists who operated these craft. (US Naval Institute Bernell Poole Collection donated by Louis S Davidson 1975)

The iron law of mobilisation is that you build what you have been building – or else suffer brutal and unpredictable delays. In 1917 the US Navy was well aware that its big new destroyers were not particularly well-adapted to anti-submarine warfare and the Royal Navy advised it to build specialised ships. The navy leadership also realised that numbers were much more important than particular capabilities, so it ordered as many standard destroyers as it could get. The *Wickes* class destroyer USS *Fairfax* (DD 93) is shown running builders' trials off Mare Island Navy Yard, 21 May 1918, at 25 knots, deliberately making smoke as she would to protect a convoy. There were two detail designs, one by Bath Ironworks (as in this ship) and one by Bethlehem Steel. The Bath-design destroyers were built by all yards other than those operated by Bethlehem Steel. They enjoyed greater endurance and were popularly known as the 'Liberty' type. Compared to many of her sisters, she lacked the usual baffles (venturi) around the base of her bridge and the plating under the waist 4in gun; her 4in guns were all shielded. The small shrouded gun just abaft the forward 4in gun is the ineffectual 3in/23 anti-aircraft weapon, substituted for the original pair of 1pdrs when the latter were diverted to arm small craft. The main concession to the new anti-submarine role was to add fuel tankage in follow-on *Clemson* class destroyers (which were completed too late for the war). Another concession was to accept ships even though adequate numbers of torpedoes were not available; in 1918 most twelve-tube US destroyers had only six of them filled. *Fairfax* was transferred to the Royal Navy in 1940. For the US Navy, the war programme produced far more destroyers than the fleet needed, so many of them were laid up after no more than two years of service.

on an assembly line basis.[66] The CNO cabled his representative in Europe Admiral Sims asking what he wanted as characteristics of a 'submarine destroyer'.

The Royal Navy pointed out that the existing destroyer, designed for fleet work, was unnecessarily large. Plans were drawn in August 1917 for a smaller (850-ton) destroyer which might be considered a First World War destroyer escort. The programme unravelled because it turned out to be much faster simply to duplicate the current design, as the General Board had said Instead of the new design, the US Navy ordered 156 *Clemson* class destroyers, of which six were cancelled in 1919.

By late 1917 it must have been obvious that the new destroyers would be used mainly as convoy escorts, as all the US destroyers sent to Europe had been. The Special Board felt that it had solved enough of the detection problem to think that it would be largely solved by the spring of 1918. Sound could be detected 10 miles away and its direction determined. Dragging and magnetic methods made it possible to detect a bottomed, hence silent, submarine. These solutions could not be applied to the sub-chasers, but the Board argued that a large number of sub-chasers suited to the new detectors and placed in service in the summer of 1918, might solve the U-boat problem. At the Board meeting on 26 October it was clear that the Board did not have the technical or manufacturing advice needed to determine whether that was feasible, so they called a meeting in New York two days later with outside experts, including some from the US Navy.[67]

The key point was that none of the Board's detectors was effective from a moving ship. Sprint-and-drift tactics were inescapable and they ruled out the one substantial ASW ship, the destroyer. Destroyers could not stop and start their main engines quickly and (it seemed) they could not shut down their noisy auxiliaries at all. Destroyers were inherently noisy: one could locate a noise source 1000 yds away, but she could be located from 2500

yds. Moreover, current practice forbade a destroyer from stopping in the submarine zone because they might be torpedoed (a boat drawing only 7ft would be reasonably immune, as torpedoes were typically set for 15ft). Existing sub-chasers were limited to calm weather. That was the fault of their hulls and engines, not their listening gear. Any fleet of new-model ASW craft had to be able to operate in rough water.

The suggested solution was a 175ft 20-knot ship, displacing 200 tons (about twice as much as a sub-chaser), with 1800–2000hp engines (1300–1400hp for 18 knots). Higher speed was justified by a recent report of a surfaced U-boat escaping at 16 knots. For sprint-and-drift, the new ship should be powered by petrol or diesel, not steam, engines. Such a craft might accommodate a 5in gun sufficient to answer the new U-boats (but convoy crews preferred the 4in/50). According to a naval officer at the meeting,

In 1917 US shipbuilding capacity was fully committed. The Emergency Shipbuilding Corporation resorted to new yards and to fabricated ships; for its big sub-chasers the navy ultimately went to Henry Ford and his car-builders. The resulting Eagle Boats had the same awkward flat lines as the new freighters, but they were adequate. As with many other big US industrial programmes, they reached service too late for the war, but they give some idea of the added resources the Allies would have had if the war had continued into 1919. *Eagle 58* is shown in April 1925.

assuming a listening range of two miles, a thousand such craft could make the North Sea impassable to German submarines. A new drifter set released by a stationary ship might increase detection range to 10 to 12 miles.

Captain F H Schofield of OpNav pointed out that the three proposed methods of dealing with submarines were to seize their bases, to mine them in, or to deal with them in the open sea. The last broke down into defensive (convoy) and offensive (hunting) methods. Schofield argued that the defensive approach was to the advantage of the enemy, because the U-boat's crew knew that it was safe whenever it was not attacking a convoy. That had to be a major morale advantage. Knowing that they were subject to attack day and night would make a considerable difference. That argument in itself would justify an ocean-going chaser. It could be the ears of destroyers. Even fifty hunting groups (three ships each) could, it was thought, cut merchant ship losses in half if they were currently operating.

One other consideration was that no new programme could interfere with the large ongoing destroyer programme. That meant not using existing yards. The country still had plenty of steel capacity and steel was being produced faster than the yards could use it. One of those at the meeting suggested using the facilities of the Pullman Co., which made railway carriages, to build hulls.

The new ship was tentatively named the Liberty Magnetic Boat, to be approximately 175 to 200ft long, 24ft beam and 7ft 6in draught, with a reliable speed of at least 15 knots in ordinary weather (18 was favoured), driven by a diesel or semi-diesel engine (approximately 1200 to 1400hp). It should be designed for sprint-and-drift operation, 3 to 5 minutes running and 1 to 3 minutes stopped. Minimum crew would be fifty. The principal offensive weapons would be machine guns and depth charges, backed by one 4in or 5in gun. The Board pressed its case in November. The project moved fast; on 1 December the General Board circulated comments, based on a preliminary design C&R had already prepared for a 200 x 24 x 6$\frac{1}{2}$-ft, 475-ton ship capable of 20 to 21

knots. The Special Board wanted 250 built by May 1918 and a total of 1000 that year.

The General Board had collected considerable information about listening devices. Great progress had been made, but the level of development did not warrant a huge new programme. Clearly such devices were important and experiments should continue while existing listening devices were produced to equip US and Allied patrol craft. The key point the General Board made, however, was that much more needed to be tried with destroyers before they were abandoned as hunters. The General Board referred specifically to the K- and SC-C Tubes and to the Trailing Wire Device. It may have been aware that at just that time the Special Board was beginning to attack the problem of listening from a moving destroyer.

Even if the General Board could not endorse the Special Board's massive programme, it agreed that the proposed ship would fill the ongoing need for better patrol vessels. It reluctantly rejected the Special Board plan (which would cost about $500 million, which might better be spent otherwise) and it doubted that organisation and labour were available for even a more limited programme. The effort required to create the 150-destroyer programme suggested that shipbuilding had reached its limit. The navy's own experts doubted that a thousand ships approaching destroyer size could be built without interfering with existing urgent programmes. Surely either the destroyer or the merchant ship programmes would suffer. The much simpler sub-chaser programme had been difficult enough. Two other programmes which could deploy listening devices deserved mention: submarines (ninety-six building) and flying boats. As for propulsion, there was no capacity for further steam plants and diesels had not been sufficiently standardised (the US submarine diesel programme was proving less than successful). What would power all those big new sub-chasers?

In wartime, OpNav trumped the General Board and it favoured the project. Thus in December CNO endorsed the idea and sent rough characteristics to the Bureaus of Construction & Repair (C&R) and Steam Engineering. He envisaged a 200-footer with a sustained full speed of 18 knots (cruising speed 10 knots) armed with one 3in/50 and one 3in anti-aircraft gun. He also emphasised the need for sprint-and-drift. Tentative plans were in CNO's hands by mid-January. On the other hand, the Special Board never got its thousand boats. Instead, Ford Motor Co. received an order for one hundred of them in an echo of the earlier idea of mass-producing the new type. They were turbine-powered, which made it somewhat questionable that they could execute the favoured sprint-and-drift tactics. BuOrd protested that they were not fast enough to run down some large U-boats on the surface, but even then they would be a useful patrol ship. Probably it could be built fastest by not insisting on the highest possible speed.

Not surprisingly, the large new sub-chaser featured prominently in the January 1918 report of the Special Board mission to England, this time as a 200-footer. After the first 100 had been ordered, the Special Board pressed OpNav for more. The Italian government ordered another twelve, of which the fifth ship, every tenth ship and the 112th ship were earmarked for transfer. This contract and that for all but sixty Eagle boats, was cancelled at the end of the war.

The destroyer leader *Abdiel* was converted into a minelayer while under construction specifically to lay tactical minefields. Her capacity was eighty mines. *Abdiel*'s sister-ship HMS *Gabriel* is shown, with a canvas screen aft to prevent observers from seeing whether she had mines on board.

CHAPTER 15
Mine Warfare

THE RUSSO-JAPANESE WAR demonstrated the value of offensive mine warfare. Before the war only Germany and Russia were enthusiastic proponents of mine warfare. During the war, a single Japanese mine sank the Russian flagship *Petropavlovsk* (13 April 1904) and killed Admiral Makarov, the only effective Russian naval commander. A Russian minefield sank two of the six Japanese battleships on one day, 15 May 1904.[1] Both navies used mines extensively, both in enemy territorial waters and further offshore. Numerous mines broke their moorings and were recovered. The war also demonstrated that there was no existing method of quickly clearing mines. The textbook methods were countermining, sweeping, dragging and creeping, but all of them took time and could not be carried out under fire.[2]

A distinction was drawn between offensive and defensive mine warfare. Offensive warfare, such as that practiced by both the Japanese and the Russians, meant laying mines in an enemy's waters in hopes that his fleet would encounter them. That might mean a surprise minelaying sortie or a concerted attempt to use mines to blockade an enemy fleet. It also might mean an attempt to prevent merchant ships from using a port or a sealane. Offensive mines were necessarily relatively indiscriminate and that in turn raised legal questions about their use in non-territorial waters.[3] In 1914 it seems to have been generally agreed that any minefields

should be announced and that mines which broke loose from their moorings should be made self-neutralising within an hour. In theory this last convention limited the life of a drifting mine.

In theory, a mine offensive could bottle up an enemy fleet, but in 1914 it seems to have been generally accepted that mines could be swept (as indeed many were during the Russo-Japanese War). Unless a minefield was defended, an enemy could regain freedom of action as soon as he was aware of its presence. It seems not to have been understood generally that sweeping would be difficult and slow. The main example of a defended minefield was the Turkish field in the Dardanelles, which sank several Allied battleships. Attempts to sweep this field were frustrated by the guns which commanded it.

Defensive mining was an attempt to deny the enemy access to a port or to an anchorage. In 1903–4 the Royal Navy convinced the British Government to abandon the mine defence of ports in favour of an offshore defence by submarines (the beginning of Admiral Fisher's flotilla defence concept for the North Sea). The Admiralty argued that it would be dangerous to employ both submarines and mines and that submarines could carry coast defence considerably further to seaward. Admiral Fisher, not yet First Sea Lord, seems to have been particularly active in pressing the pro-submarine argument. At roughly the same time the Royal

The converted minelaying cruiser *Latona* is shown at Malta during the First World War. Transferred to the Mediterranean in August 1915, she was the only ship of her class to continue minelaying. She joined the converted Channel Islands ferry *Gazelle*, which laid minefields beginning in April 1915 intended to protect the fleet in the Dardanelles from Turkish submarines. The first were laid in the Gulf of Smyrna. During 1916 HMS *Angora* was transferred from the North Sea and the smaller merchant ship *Perdita* converted locally to minelaying duties. The Mediterranean ships laid large fields off the Dardanelles after Gallipoli was evacuated in January 1916, largely to bottle up the German *Goeben* and *Breslau*. One of these fields, periodically replanted, caught the German ships when they sortied in January 1918. (Dr David Stevens, SPC-A)

The first British reaction to the new importance of mines as demonstrated by the Russo-Japanese War was to convert seven obsolete *Apollo* class cruisers into minelayers. At the same time a new contact mine was developed; it was some time during the war before the Royal Navy to realise that it was less than reliable. Before that, mining policy was a matter of considerable debate. HMS *Naiad* is shown, newly converted.

Navy ceased work on defensive controlled mines for the sort of anchorage it might have improvised to support a blockade. Remote control of the mines would, in theory, have allowed friendly ships to pass safely.

Other navies continued to espouse controlled mines, particularly as an improvised defence for a forward anchorage. For example, before 1914 the main war scenario envisaged by the US Navy was defence of the Monroe Doctrine (which denied Europeans new colonies in the New World) against a European navy, most likely the Germans. The US fleet would rush down to, for example, the Caribbean to deal with the enemy incursion. It would improvise an advanced base, which would be defended by Marines ashore. The defence would include 'naval defence mines' laid by boats from the battleships.

The Russo-Japanese War dramatised an entirely different kind of offensive mine warfare, carried out by both sides using unprecedented numbers of mines. In its wake navies previously unenthusiastic about mining prepared to use it in wartime. The Royal Navy considered the use of mines on the most important lessons of the war.[4] It decided to buy a supply of 10,000 contact mines and to convert seven old *Apollo* class cruisers into minelayers.[5] It is not clear to what extent they were expected to penetrate enemy waters.

Pre-war British naval opinion opposed large-scale minelaying on the theory that it would limit the freedom of action of the fleet. Churchill absorbed the idea that blockade mining was pointless, because the enemy could always sweep up what the British laid. Mining would hinder British offensive operations such as his favoured attack on Borkum. Fisher took Jellicoe's subtler point that mining the Heligoland Bight was the best way to force the Germans to disclose their intentions by minesweeping.[6]

Minelaying was practicable in any depth of water in which a mine could float; the buoyant mine body had to support not only the contents of the mine but also the weight of its mooring chain (which is why mine operators have sometimes traded off mooring strength for more explosive content).

First World War experience showed that minelaying, particularly by submarine, could be extremely dangerous. Navigation in areas controlled by the enemy's fleet was largely by dead reckoning. However, once a field had been laid, the enemy would inevitably try to sweep it, so the field had to be refreshed. Navigational error could easily bring a minelayer into an unswept part of the previously-laid minefield. This danger made it difficult for the Royal Navy to maintain an effective mine blockade in the Heligoland Bight, even after it acquired fully-effective mines. It also made for considerable casualties among submarine minelayers on both sides (these craft were also vulnerable to explosions among mines still on board).

As it happened, the mine adopted by the Royal Navy was badly flawed, so British minelaying was ineffective until 1917.[7] However, early in the war the Royal Navy began a major effort to block the Straits of Dover against both German surface ships and submarines. This Dover Barrage employed a combination of mines and nets, the latter with mines. It was lit at night and patrolled by a variety of craft, the idea being that submarines would be forced to pass through the Straits on the surface at night. One of the unpleasant surprises of the war was that the weather in the Straits often swept away much of the barrage, requiring that it be replaced frequently. The Royal Navy also began work on minesweeping,

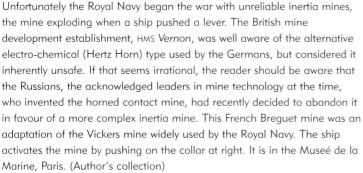

Unfortunately the Royal Navy began the war with unreliable inertia mines, the mine exploding when a ship pushed a lever. The British mine development establishment, HMS *Vernon*, was well aware of the alternative electro-chemical (Hertz Horn) type used by the Germans, but considered it inherently unsafe. If that seems irrational, the reader should be aware that the Russians, the acknowledged leaders in mine technology at the time, who invented the horned contact mine, had recently decided to abandon it in favour of a more complex inertia mine. This French Breguet mine was an adaptation of the Vickers mine widely used by the Royal Navy. The ship activates the mine by pushing on the collar at right. It is in the Museé de la Marine, Paris. (Author's collection)

Probably the most effective wartime example of German mining was the blockage of the Dardanelles, using mines like this one in the Turkish naval museum, Istanbul. Mine clearance techniques which worked well in undefended waters failed badly under fire. (Author's collection)

converting six old torpedo gunboats into sweepers and also developing a reserve trawler sweep force.

German Minelaying

The Germans and the Russians both had effective mines in 1914 and both planned to use them extensively. The Germans completed two *Nautilus* class cruiser-minelayers in 1905 and 1907, to plans begun in 1904; each could carry 200 mines. Beginning with the *Kolberg* class (1906 programme), German light cruisers were designed to carry mines, typically 120 of them. After war broke out in 1914 and the machinery being built for the Russian battlecruiser *Navarino* became available, the fast cruiser-minelayers *Brummer* and *Bremse* were designed around it; each could carry 400 mines, twice the load of the earlier pair of cruiser-minelayers and each was fast enough (rated at 28 knots) for offensive sorties into enemy-controlled waters. Beginning with the *V 1* class (1911–12

programme), many German destroyers were fitted to lay mines, although in practice only about a quarter of them carried them.[8] None of these ships was used at the outset of war because they were considered integral with the High Seas Fleet, which was ordered maintained as a 'fleet in being'. Only the two slow specially-built minelayers *Albatross* and *Nautilus* and ships taken up from trade could be used.

The most important impact of German destroyer minelaying seems to have been Admiral Jellicoe's idea that they would probably be employed tactically.[9] He repeatedly warned his fleet that if he met the Germans on opposing courses, he would avoid circling around and crossing their wake because he expected the Germans to lay mines as they steamed. This warning seems to have reflected earlier British ideas about how destroyer minelayers would be used in combat.[10] It is not clear that the pre-war Royal Navy understood how well the Germans were equipped for mine warfare.[11]

Although at the outbreak of war the Germans had numerous warships suitable for minelaying, their first operation employed the converted liner *Koningen Luise*, which was well across the North Sea before the British declared war.[12] She was seen by a trawler laying her mines on the night of 4/5 August 1914, she was reported and she was sunk by the cruiser *Amphion* – which soon hit one of the mines and sank.

The British identified two phases of German minelaying in

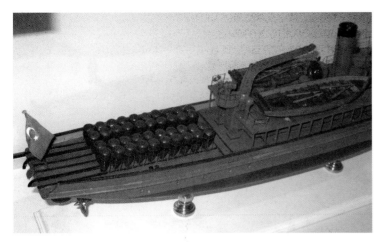

The Dardanelles fields were laid by the minelayer *Nusret*. This model is in the Turkish naval museum, Istanbul. (Author's collection)

Home Waters.[13] The first began on the outbreak of war and continued spasmodically until the beginning of 1916. The second began early in 1916 and continued to the end of the war, the last six months of 1915 marking a transition. During the first phase surface ships laid large minefields intended mainly to sink warships trying to cut off or chase a raiding squadron. However, on 7 August the Germans announced that they would mine the approaches to British ports. The British protested that mining in the open sea was illegal; eventually the Germans replied that they were laying mines as close to the coast as possible. By the time the reply had been received, about twenty neutral ships had been sunk. German surface ships laid about a thousand mines during 1914, mostly in August and October.[14]

To the British, evidence that in this first phase the Germans were more interested in sinking warships than merchant ships was their shift in 1915 to increased mooring depths and also to open-sea mining in the North Sea that spring.[15] The British believed that the Germans were soon aware that minefield locations were given away whenever a merchant ship or fishing boat of moderate draught was mined. Mooring mines deeper would minimise such

Further fast ships were soon converted into minelayers. *Abdiel* is shown alongside the light cruiser *Aurora*, at left. During 1917, eleven light cruisers and twelve destroyers were fitted as convertible minelayers. Note the canvas screens. The horned H type mines shown were fully effective. Once they became available, the Royal Navy began a massive mining campaign, principally against U-boats.

contacts, whereas deep-draught warships, particularly capital ships, would still be mined.

The end of this phase was apparently the Whiten Bank Minefield to the west of the Orkneys laid by the disguised surface raider *Moewe* between 31 December 1915 and 2 January 1916. The object was to catch the fleet in its exercise area, but the tidal set and water depth were such that mines usually dipped below the draught of the ships. The victims were the battleship *King Edward VII* and two neutral merchant ships.

The second phase was part of the larger war against shipping, consisting of small minefields laid by submarines. To the British, the fields were placed as part of a systematic attack on the tracks of merchant ships which could be fixed using landmarks ashore, light-vessels and channel buoys.

From a tactical point of view, numerous small fields laid by submarines presented a much worse minesweeping problem than a few large ones, each laid by one or two surface ships. Once the Germans gained the Belgian ports, they made Bruges a mine depot and deployed twelve UC class minelaying submarines, each armed with twelve mines in vertical tubes. They began operations in the summer of 1915. Given a limited radius of operation, they were

By 1918 the Germans had torpedo-tube mines, so they could use any U-boat as a minelayer. That allowed them to mine the Canadian and US coasts. This one, recovered off Halifax, is in the Canadian military museum in Ottawa. (Author's collection)

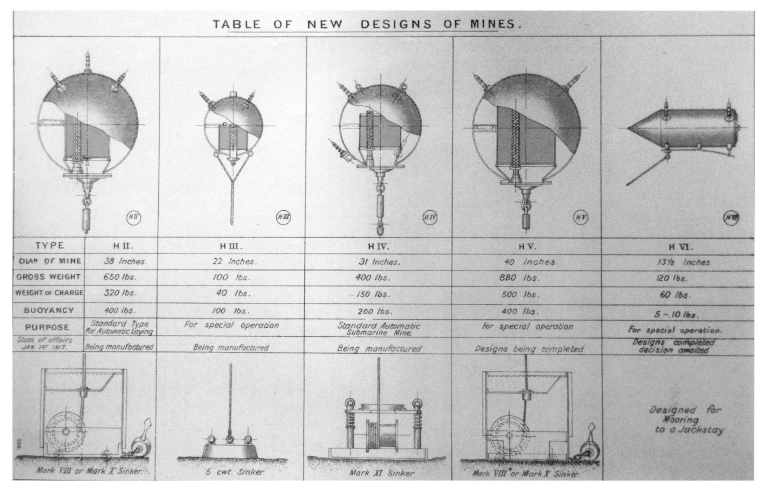

TABLE OF NEW DESIGNS OF MINES.

TYPE	H II.	H III.	H IV.	H V.	H VI.
DIAR OF MINE	38 Inches.	22 Inches.	31 Inches.	40 Inches.	13½ Inches
GROSS WEIGHT	650 lbs.	100 lbs.	400 lbs.	880 lbs.	120 lbs.
WEIGHT OF CHARGE	320 lbs.	40 lbs.	150 lbs.	500 lbs.	60 lbs.
BUOYANCY	400 lbs.	100 lbs.	200 lbs.	400 lbs.	5 – 10 lbs.
PURPOSE	Standard Type for Automatic Laying	For special operation	Standard Automatic Submarine Mine	for special operation	For special operation.
State of affairs JAN. 1ST 1917.	Being manufactured	Being manufactured	Being manufactured	Designs being completed	Designs completed decision awaited
	Mark VIII or Mark X Sinker.	5 cwt. Sinker.	Mark XI Sinker	Mark VIII or Mark X Sinker	Designed for Mooring to a Jackstay

The British horned mines which made the late-war mine offensive effective, from a contemporary diagram. The most important type was H.II. These mines came into production at roughly the same time that the Germans began their campaign of unrestricted U-boat warfare which caused the British to contemplate a much larger mining campaign against the U-boats.

confined to the approaches to the Thames Estuary, Harwich and Dover. They may have laid a field off the Belgian coast in March, but the first UC-laid mines the British encountered were off the South Foreland on 2 June 1915.[16] Initially submarines took care never to lay mines twice in the same area, for fear of being mined themselves; later in the war the Germans assumed the British would soon sweep up their fields and were willing to revisit after ten days.[17] The campaign did not become serious until August 1915. The Germans later reported that the UC-boats had laid 648 mines between Dover and Grimsby during 1915. Two of the minelaying boats were lost, one in the Harwich area and one off Lowestoft, of which one was sunk by her own mine. A third ran aground on the Dutch coast and was interned. The following year another was sunk in the Mediterranean by her own mine.[18]

During 1916 the UC boats were supplemented by large ocean-going U-boat minelayers with more sophisticated dry stowage for thirty-four to thirty-six mines. The Germans created two separate minelaying flotillas, one based on Ostend and Zeebrugge (Flanders Flotilla), the other on the Elbe (High Seas Fleet Flotilla). Given their greater radius of action, the High Seas Fleet boats were allocated all waters other than the southern area from Flamborough Head to Land's End (later extended westward).[19] As the number of minelaying U-boats increased, the British were forced to allocate more and more ships to minesweeping, reducing their patrol strength. Through 1916 the Flanders and High Seas Fleet U-boats laid a total of 195 groups of mines, mostly on the East Coast of England.

Although at this time most minefields were designed mainly to sink merchant ships, at the end of May a U-boat was sent specifically to mine the channels used by the Grand Fleet. The British Staff History associates this mining operation with the plans for the German fleet sortie which culminated in the battle of Jutland (on her homeward journey the U-boat passed through the wreckage left by the battle). This field sank HMS *Hampshire*, which was then carrying Lord Kitchener to Russia. Another U-boat laid a similar field in the Whiten Head Channel; other U-boats of the High Seas Fleet Flotilla mined the Moray Firth and the entrance to the Firth of Forth, another fleet base.[20]

In 1916 the Germans began to assist the Austrians in mine warfare, transferring some UC-boats to them. They mined both the Italian and French ports, Malta the areas which could support Dardanelles operations (including the Piraeus in Greece, Crete and Mudros), Port Said, Alexandria and also the Russian Black Sea ports.

During 1916 the Germans built minelaying submarines, both the ten large *U 71* class and additional UC-boats. They began a new mine offensive in January 1917. Before the spring the number of mines the British destroyed each month was more than double the figure of any previous record. In 1917 the total number of groups of mines laid by U-boats in British waters rose from the 195 of 1916 to 536 and the mines were more widely distributed, with as many on the south and west coasts as off the Nore or Dover.

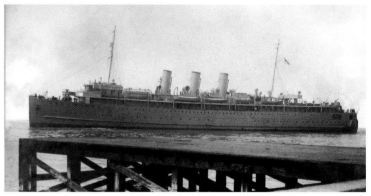

The old *Apollo* class cruisers proved inadequate, so early in 1915 six merchant ships were taken up from trade for conversion, including the two big (5934 GRT) fast (23-knot) new Canadian ferries *Princess Irene* and *Princess Margaret*. Each could carry 500 mines. Armament was two 4.7in, two 12pdr and two 6pdr high-angle guns. The merchant ships relieved the old cruisers in March 1915 and laid the first minefield in the Heligoland Bight. The new ships laid the initial field in May 1915. On 27 May *Princess Irene* blew up, probably due to a mine pistol going off as mines were prepared for laying. As she and *Princess Margaret* were considered by far the best of the conversions, this was a serious blow. The other initial merchant ship conversions were *Paris*, *Orvieto* (replaced in 1916 by the smaller *Wahine*), *Biarritz* and *Angora*, of which only *Biarritz* (23 knots) and *Paris* (25 knots) were comparably fast, but neither had even a third of the capacity of the two Canadian ships.

H-type mines on board the light cruiser *Aurora*, which had a capacity of seventy-four.

Through the year an average of one submarine-load of mines was laid every 30 hours, many of them being set shallow to sink minesweepers. In the last fortnight of April 1917 the Royal Navy was losing on average one sweeper each day. The situation was complicated by numerous mines which broke from their moorings and drifted. They included mines the Germans laid in defensive fields off the Scheldt and in the Heligoland Bight.[21]

Submarine minelayers typically laid mines on the observed track of merchant ships and then laid off to seaward, waiting for traffic to be diverted so that it could be attacked by torpedo (all the large U-minelayers and later UC-boats had torpedo tubes, whereas the original UCs lacked them).[22] British policy was to minimise the mined area so that traffic could be moved shorewards, placing mines between ships and U-boats. U-boats also laid fields in the Mediterranean during 1917, including 108 mines off Malta and many in French areas of responsibility.

The only German surface minelayer active outside home waters in 1917 was the disguised raider *Wolf*, which broke out of the North Sea in the latter part of 1916 carrying 458 mines. She began with a 25-mine field off the Cape on 16 January 1917 and another on 18 January. She also transferred twenty-five mines to one of her prizes, the steamer *Turritella*, which laid them off Aden, at the mouth of the Red Sea. *Wolf* laid further fields off Colombo (Cape Cormorin), Bombay, Australia (Cook and Bass Straits), Three King's Island in New Zealand and then a large field (110 mines) near the Andaman Islands in the South China Sea.[23]

The British found that in 1918 the German minelaying effort declined noticeably, as anti-submarine operations were destroying many of the minelayers. They had to operate in coastal waters where they were particularly exposed to air reconnaissance and to hunting flotillas and the new controlled minefields also made it difficult for the submarines to operate off headlands where there

was a concentrated traffic flow. Except for the area around Harwich (where the Flanders flotilla operated), the Germans seemed to be sparing mines for more definite objectives, such as certain important convoys (particularly to neutrals) and to the transit of American troops. The British speculated that the loss of trained U-boat personnel was probably a worse problem than the loss of submarines.

During 1918 the Flanders Flotilla concentrated mainly on particular British ports. The High Seas Flotilla had three objectives: attacks on the Dutch coast to disrupt Dutch convoys; an attack on the inner waters of the Firth of Forth, which were used by the Grand Fleet; and the creation of a huge circular barrage (43-mile radius) centred on the Bell Rock, intended specifically against the exit used by the Grand Fleet. Despite German attempts to maintain security, the British deduced the purpose and scope of the big barrage shortly after it had been completed and they proceeded to sweep it up. The big barrage seems to have been associated with German plans for a final battle against the Grand Fleet. In October 1918 the Germans assembled every non-minelaying U-boat they had available and placed them in a large square to seaward of the barrage. Their plan was for the High Seas Fleet to sortie to attract the Grand Fleet into battle. The Grand Fleet would have steamed through the combination mine and submarine trap. For their part, the Germans were never aware that their barrage had been completely swept.[24]

The Germans introduced ocean-going U-boat minelayers which brought the mine war to the other side of the Atlantic. The mined the Canadian, Portuguese, US and Sierra Leone coasts, the Portuguese coast particularly heavily (as it was accessible to the earlier type of minelaying submarine). The first mine was found off Sierra Leone on 10 April 1918, the U-boat first having shelled the Liberian coast. The first mine damage on the US coast was to a

The battleship HMS *London* was also converted into a minelayer, at Rosyth (completed 18 May 1918). She was armed with three 6in, one 4in high-angle gun and 240 mines. (Abrahams via Dr David Stevens, SPC-A)

Once the British had an effective horned contact mine in 1917, they needed large numbers of minelayers, but the mounting U-boat campaign made it impractical to convert more large merchant ships. The Royal Navy therefore turned to obsolete warships such as HMS *Amphitrite*, shown here. The large cruiser *Ariadne* was also converted. At the end of the war HMS *Euryalus* was under conversion at Hong Kong. As a minelayer, *Amphitrite* was armed with four 6in guns, one 4in high-angle gun and 354 mines. She was completed at Portsmouth, 9 August 1917.

tanker near the Overfalls Light Vessel, on 3 June 1918. The most spectacular victim was the cruiser *San Diego*. The first mines were laid off Halifax, in the approach to the swept channel, on 16 October 1918. Among other things, the overseas mine campaign forced the Royal Navy to begin building a much more global mine countermeasures force.[25]

From 1915 on the Germans laid defensive minefields off the Belgian coast, which had to be cleared by sweepers operating at night so that bombardment ships could move in. This was not too different from the experience at Gallipoli. As part of their campaign to protect their Belgian coastal bases at Zeebrugge and Ostend, the Germans tried to make the French ports of Calais and Cherbourg unusable by mining them (Dunkirk was first mined on 20 August 1915, followed by Boulogne and then by Calais on 2 September).

British Minelaying[26]

The first major British wartime minelaying effort was intended to protect the passage of troop transports to France in mid-September 1914. At first the transports were covered by patrols, on which duty the three armoured cruisers *Aboukir*, *Hogue* and *Cressy* were sunk by *U 9*. Mines then became a preferable alternative and on successive nights four of the minelaying cruisers laid 1064 mines. Much of this field had to be swept to allow access to the port of Zeebrugge, then relaid once the Germans captured that port. By the end of 1914 the Royal Navy had laid 3064 mines off Zeebrugge and in the Strait of Dover and the initial Dover barrage had sunk two U-boats (*U 5* and *U 11*).

In January 1915 the British laid their first field (440 mines) in the Heligoland Bight to block known German routes and thus to complicate German fleet operations. By the end of the year, 4538 mines had been laid in the Heligoland Bight. At the same time they kept refreshing the Dover Barrage: 4390 mines in February, protected in part by sweep obstructors called Destructors, plus another 1471 in July. At the same time deep anti-U-boat fields were laid around the British coast (1328 mines). The converted ferry *Gazelle* laid forty to fifty French Breguet mines off Turkish ports in support of the Dardanelles operation. In the following year the German Flanders Flotilla of small U-boats became a major problem; Flag Officer Flanders proposed a large minefield (the Belgian 'Zareba') to contain them. It included 5077 mines, some of them deep to destroy submerged U-boats. The barrage also included nets.

The Royal Navy became more interested in offensive minelaying, for which it needed minelayers which could penetrate enemy-controlled waters: in 1916 it commissioned its first destroyer minelayer (*Abdiel*) and its first submarine minelayers. In May 1916 *Abdiel* laid a unique tactical field off the Horns Reef intended to support a Grand Fleet operation, but the battle of Jutland intervened. This field damaged the German battleship *Ostfriesland* as she returned from the 1916 battle. During 1916 the British laid 13,280 mines in northwest European waters and additional mines in the Mediterranean.

British minelaying activity accelerated considerably during 1917, as a reliable mine (the horned H2) finally became available. Many ships were converted to lay mines, including both fast cruisers and destroyers, the old cruisers *Ariadne* and *Amphitrite* and CMBs. The Dover barrage was reinforced and measures were taken to replace mines and nets of the Belgian Zareba removed by the Germans. Coastal fields were laid around the British Isles (8609 mines on the south and east coasts) to trap U-boats in their operational areas. First Sea Lord Admiral Jellicoe proposed a U-boat barrier field in the Heligoland Bight, but the 60,000 mines

A mine is released by a motor launch, operating as an inshore minelayer. There were also minelaying trawlers.

The most spectacular and also perhaps the most controversial, minelaying operation of the war was the huge Northern Barrage, which was mainly a US Navy operation. The US Navy converted a fleet of merchant ships, including train ferries, to lay the barrage. Here the fleet is in minelaying formation, with eight ships in line abreast and two in advance waiting their turn. The British Minelaying Squadron is in the left distance. Six destroyers are visible near the horizon. The US Minelaying Squadron would steam in this formation, planting five or six lines of mines at one time, for a distance of 46 to 55 miles at 12 knots. Ships were 500 yds apart. On board the minelayers, steam winches hauled trains or fleets of twenty to forty mines each, aft to the feeding section, where they were seized by gangs of four men each and pushed into the traps at the stern from which they were released. Marker buoys were laid at the end of each field so that the squadron could later resume laying. (US Army Signal Corps via US Navy Historical and Heritage Command).

required were not available. However, the bulk of mines laid in 1917 were in the Bight (15,686 mines). Another 2573 mines were laid in the Mediterranean, plus 334 as part of a project to close the Straits of Otranto, the access between the Mediterranean and Austro-Hungarian naval bases on the Adriatic.

By this time mines were considered a primary anti-submarine weapon and their use accelerated again in 1918. An average of 6200 mines was laid each month up to October 1918. Overall, the British claimed that their mines laid in northwestern European waters definitely sank forty-three U-boats (and probably sank four more); mines also accounted for another two U-boats (one in a field across the Straits of Otranto laid by France and Italy) and three more probables.

The Royal Navy was unique during the First World War in developing non-contact (influence) mines, beginning with February 1916 trials of mines fitted with magnetophones (microphones), inspired by earlier work on submarine detection by hydrophone. At this stage the magnetophone was to have been the detector for a group of controlled mines. Magnetophone-controlled minefields were laid at Cromarty and at Scapa Flow for defence against submarines and that at Scapa (Hoxa) attacked a submarine on 12 April 1917. An alternative low-frequency acoustic sensor was tested some time before the summer of 1918 and the A attachment (acoustic sensor) for mines was ready for service at the end of the war.

A magnetic mine actually entered service. Development began in July 1917 and a concrete (i.e., non-magnetic) case was used. In September 1917 orders for 10,000 magnetic mines were placed; the mine became available in July 1918 as the 'M Sinker'. Although unreliable (in one trial, 60 per cent exploded shortly after having been laid), the M mine was laid off the Belgian coast and it seems to have accounted for several U-boats whose loss was otherwise unexplained.

In 1918 there was also a controlled L (loop) mine using a magnetic loop as a sensor for a field of controlled mines; the loop indicated that a U-boat or ship had passed overhead. The first test field was laid in December 1917 and at the Armistice a special field, controlled by towers sunk into the seabed, was being laid in the Dover Strait. By the end of the war about 100 Royal Navy ships and craft could lay mines and others were being converted.[27]

The Northern Barrage[28]

When it entered the war, the United States brought with it huge industrial resources which made it possible to propose large projects. One of the more spectacular was the Northern Barrage, a belt of mines extending from northern Scotland to Norway, to close off the Atlantic to U-boats. On 15 April 1917 (i.e., less than two weeks after the United States entered the war) the US Navy Bureau of Ordnance (BuOrd) mine section submitted a memorandum

The key to the Northern Barrage was the US Mk VI antenna mine. Extending well above and below the mine, the antennas would (at least in theory) allow the mine to destroy any U-boat passing at any safe depth. This Mk VI, photographed at Inverness, shows its characteristic wire antenna in stowed position on its left side.

proposing mine barrages to close off the North Sea and the Adriatic to U-boats. It suggested that even partially-effective barrages would be decisive. These barrages were alternatives to the existing British policy of close-in mining, which had not yet been successful (the British did not yet have a reliable mine; it would enter service later in 1917). This was an enormous project; the 250 mile North Sea barrier would require an unprecedented number of mines and it would cost $200 to $400 million, an enormous sum at the time. In May 1917 the US Navy Office of Operations (OpNav) proposed the idea to the British. It assumed that the barrier would resemble that off Dover: nets and moored and floating mines, effective at depths of 35 to 200ft, hence safe for surface ships. Patrols would deal with submarines trying to cross the barrage on the surface. Given problems maintaining the short Dover Barrage, the idea must have seemed ludicrous.[29] Moreover, minefields had to be patrolled to be effective and the barrage would absorb far too many patrol vessels.

BuOrd persisted. It conceived a new type of mine mechanism (the K-pistol) by means of which a mine could destroy a U-boat floating well above or below it. A K-mine had an antenna which floated above it (another could be suspended below). It was fired by electromagnetic action between antenna and the steel hull of a submarine which touched it (similar methods were used in trailing wire devices intended to detect bottomed U-boats). The concept was discovered in April 1917 and brought to the point at which it was worth producing in July.[30] Initially it was offered not only as a mine but also as an ASW sweep. A mine with a 300lb charge could destroy a U-boat 100ft away, so nominal antenna length was set at 100ft. An incidental advantage was that the mine could be planted deep enough to be immune to wave action.

US Atlantic Fleet commander Admiral T H Mayo pressed the project on First Sea Lord Admiral Jellicoe during his visit to England. Jellicoe in turn raised the idea at the Allied naval conference held in London on 4–5 September 1917.[31] He offered it as a preferable alternative to a closer-in barrage, one advantage being that it was so far from Germany that the Germans could not possibly sweep it. When he returned to the United States, Mayo sold the idea to OpNav. CNO Admiral Benson directed BuOrd to procure 100,000 mines. By this time the K-pistol and the mine case had been designed, but normally a new mine would have taken a year from concept to prototype, let alone to mass production. To simplify the project, BuOrd adopted a modular approach, in which components were designed so that changes in one would have minimal impact on others (in fact very few changes were needed). The anchor was based on the current British design. The first contract for K-1 pistols was let as early as 9 August 1917, with a follow-up for 90,000 more on 3 October – about a month before the barrage project was officially adopted.

The initial BuOrd proposal called for 72,000 mines to fill a 300-mile barrier, plus mines for US coast defence (say 25,000), hence for a total of 100,000 mines. This estimate was intentionally high, but it was retained. A later BuOrd proposal added 28,000 replacements and reserves to the 72,000 barrier mines. Once the Northern Barrage project had been accepted, Adriatic and Dardanelles (Aegean) barrages (15,000 mines to cover 30 miles) were projected. In July 1917 the estimated cost of 125,000 mines for all these projects was $140 million, considerably under the original estimate using more conventional mines.

To sell the project, BuOrd had to show that the huge barrage

The first British fleet sweepers were converted torpedo gunboats like HMS *Circe*, shown. Visible mine countermeasures features are the gallows on her bow for a protection device and the A-frame on her stern to handle one side of a two-ship sweep. The torpedo gunboats were backed by trawlers, which conducted most early Royal Navy sweeping. The 'Flower' class sloops were intended partly to replace the torpedo gunboats.

could be laid in a reasonable length of time. In July 1917 it estimated that the British had eighteen minelayers and that the United States could furnish another four, for a total of twenty-two, each laying 200 mines per day. With one day for reloading, this force could lay 2200 mines per day. Alternatively, forty destroyers could each lay 50 per day, for a combined total of 4200 mines per day. In the end the British furnished the mine bases but the US Navy converted the eight ships which, with the cruiser minelayers *Baltimore* and *San Francisco*, laid the mines. Minelaying began in June 1918 (the British had begun laying their own mines in March). Critical to the project was the enthusiastic support of Assistant Secretary of the Navy Franklin D Roosevelt, in charge of naval procurement (and described in contemporary US Navy correspondence as the 'go-to' man for urgent programmes).[32]

To produce so many mines, BuOrd became the first navy agency to take advantage of the huge capacity of the US auto industry. Plans initially called for producing 1000 mines per day, but that was easily exceeded. The first mines became available in March 1918, by which time production was already well underway. Meanwhile the US automobile industry became available for war production, BuOrd apparently being the first navy agency to take advantage of its huge capacity. BuOrd chose to have the elements of the mines produced separately and to assemble mines only just before they were to be laid, at British bases supporting the barrage. The bureau hoped that in this way it could maintain the secrecy of the K-pistol.

Initially the barrage was a way of keeping U-boats out of the

The Royal Navy took up many civilian paddle steamers as minesweepers. This is HMS *Mercury*, built in 1892. She was armed with two 6pdrs. this photograph was taken in Weymouth in 1917.

sea lanes from the United States to England. When the Royal Navy presented a review of the ASW war to the War Cabinet in January 1918, it added the argument that U-boat hunting was nearly impossible outside once a U-boat reached the broad waters of the Atlantic. Convoy might same merchant ships in the Atlantic, but it was essential to cut down the U-boat force.

British experience to date showed that to be effective a minefield had to consist of three lines of mines. Mines did not have to be effective below 200ft, because U-boats would not willingly dive below that. The total barrier length of 280 miles, most in water less than 300ft deep, was divided into three areas. The central (notified) area A would block both surface ships and submarines. It was deliberately limited because it affected the Grand Fleet and also neutral shipping. Area A was 56 miles wide, mines being laid 40 yds apart, with mines at two depths (total six lines of mines). That required 56,500 mines.

The flanking areas B (to the Scottish coast) and C (to Norwegian waters) employed deep mines covered by air and surface patrols, to force submarines to dive. Area B was a British responsibility. Because the mines used contact pistols, they had to be laid at multiple depths: 63ft, 96ft, 128ft, 133ft and 156ft, a total of 67,500 mines. Area C employed American mines (two depths), over a length of 60 miles (18,000 mines). The number of British mines could be substantially reduced by using the acoustic mechanism (X mechanism, early in 1918) then under development, but it was not ready in time.

By the Armistice, 56,611 US mines (and 13,652 British mines) had been laid in the Northern Barrage. Area A, originally the US portion, was complete except for 6400 mines (10 days' laying). The US Navy also laid some mines in Areas B and C, originally allocated to the Royal Navy (the British had been unable to mine down to 200ft depth, as planned). The massive projected barrier patrol force was never assembled.

After two U-boats were damaged trying to pass through Area C in July 1918, the Germans re-routed U-boats through Area B (not yet proclaimed as mined) and through Norwegian waters; eventually the Norwegians were convinced to mine their waters against such incursions. Surprise mining in Area B in September 1918 damaged two U-boats and sank another. It appeared that at least six U-boats had been sunk by the barrage and another six severely damaged. It is not clear to what extent the existence of the Barrier convinced U-boat commanders not to pass through the mined area (Admiral Sims claimed after the war that there was

evidence that some had hesitated before entering).

The Germans never understood how the mine worked. After the war, US officers in Berlin met former U-boat officers, who thought that the barrage consisted of small mines because their submarines had triggered mines well below or above them.

Russian Minelaying

In 1914 the Russians were probably the greatest proponents of mine warfare. Much of their fleet had been destroyed in the Russo-Japanese War and the replacements were not yet in service in great numbers. Even then the Russian Baltic fleet could hardly match the German High Seas Fleet. In November 1906, therefore, the Russians began to plan large mine barrages to deny the Germans access to the Gulf of Bothnia and to their capital, St Petersburg.[33] By 1914 the Russians had already laid down the world's first submarine minelayer (*Krab*), which would be completed in 1915, after the first German minelaying U-boats. The Baltic Fleet strategy approved by the Tsar in 1912 envisaged offensive minelaying off the German coast plus a defence, involving heavy minefields, of the Central Position defending the capital. In 1914 the Russians had 7000 mines in the Baltic, 4500 in the Black Sea and 4000 at Vladivostok (1000 of which were later given to the Royal Navy). The first field of 2129 mines was laid in a single day in July 1914 to protect the Central Position; later minesweepers and torpedo boats added 871 and 290 mines, respectively, to guard the flanks of the main minefield. After a German feint attack on Windau, destroyers laid 100 mines to protect that port. Later in 1914 the Russians began to lay mines off German ports to immobilise the German fleet in the Baltic, beginning with 295 mines laid in three barriers off Memel.

The Baltic Fleet laid 3648 mines in offensive barriers and 34,943 mines in defensive barriers, the latter beginning with the 2995 mines laid to protect the Central Position in 1914 (plus another 2165 in 1916 and another 4342 between May and September 1917). The Black Sea Fleet laid a total of 6385 mines in defensive fields (1750 mines off Sevastopol, 3513 off Odessa, 550 in the Kerch Straits and 572 off Batumi/Poti). Offensive mining amounted to 5238 mines in the Bosporus, 440 off Anatolia (to

The *Ascot* class paddle sweeper *Eridge* on her trials. The two cranes abeam her after funnel were intended to handle seaplanes, which it was hoped would intercept Zeppelins spotted while the ships were sweeping mines. They were never embarked.

disrupt Turkish sea traffic supporting army operations) and 1370 off Varna/Constanta.

In the Baltic, mines sank the armoured cruiser *Friedrich Carl* on 17 November 1914 and the light cruiser *Bremen* on 17 December 1915. The light cruiser *Augsburg* was mined (but not sunk) on a Russian barrier on 24/25 January 1915 and the old cruiser *Gazelle* was so badly damaged that she was towed home but not repaired. During the German attack on the Åland islands in 1917 (12 October 1917), the battleship *Bayern* was seriously damaged but not sunk by a mine. Seven of eleven German destroyers were mined and sunk during a night raid in the Baltic on 10 November 1916 (*S 57*, *S 58*, *S 59*, *V 72*, *V 75*, *V 76* and *G 90*). Other modern German destroyers mined in the Baltic were *S 31* (19 August 1915), *V 99* (17 August 1915), *V 162* (13 August 1916) and *S 64* (18 October 1917). In addition, during the British intervention in Russia, the cruiser *Cassandra* (5 December 1918) and the destroyer *Verulam* (4 September 1919) were mined. There were also lesser craft. In addition, mines seem to have claimed three U-boats (*U 26* about 31 August 1915, *U 10* about 26 May 1916 and *UC 57* about 18 November 1917). In the Black Sea, the Turkish cruiser *Medjidieh* was sunk off Odessa (3 April 1915). Mines also sank the gunboat *Berk* (2 January 1915); the smaller gunboats *Duruk Reis*, *Hizir Reis* and *Issa Reis* (all in 1915); and the submarines *UB 45*, *UC 15* and *UB 46* (1916), plus lesser craft.

British Minesweeping

Minesweeping required massive numbers of vessels, because all forms of sweeping were slow and cleared a narrow path. For the Royal Navy, the industrial effort involved produced ships some of which (sloops) turned out to be well-adapted to the anti-submarine campaign of 1917–18, including convoy work. Had these ships not been conceived for minesweeping, the numbers required for convoy would have been considerably more difficult to assemble.

The official British post-war minesweeping history dates the beginning of systematic Royal Navy sweeping experiments to 1907, as the lessons of the Russo-Japanese War were being assimilated.[34] Annual *Vernon* reports show earlier sweeping experiments, but they were generally intended to recover exercise mines. In 1907 a high-speed explosive sweep (also applied to anti-submarine work, as is explained separately) was invented. It

employed a sliding charge which could be fired electrically from a ship when it contacted a mine. It worked, but it required skilled operators and even then it was not reliable. The need for skilled operators insured that it could not be deployed in sufficient numbers in wartime.

In the summer of 1907 the new C-in-C Home Fleet Admiral Lord Beresford warned that in wartime mines might well immobilise his fleet. He doubted that small warships would be available for sweeping, so he proposed experiments with Grimsby trawlers, using their sweep gear. He hired two of them (*Andes* and *Algoma*) for experiments at Portland, using their regular fishing crews. The ordinary fishing trawl was unsuccessful, but a wire could be towed between the two, its depth controlled by a wooden water kite. It could entangle or cut the mooring wire of a mine, but unlike the explosive sweep it could not destroy the mine directly. In wartime sweeps which dragged mines were sometimes a problem and sometimes special mine dumping areas had to be designated.[35]

This sweep (initially the 'fixed wire sweep') was adopted as the 'A' Sweep, which became the wartime British standard.[36] The sweep could be extended over a width of two cables (200 yds) and towed at 5 to 6 knots. Its depth was maintained by a pair of 'water kites', one towed by each sweeper. There were initially two types, one with 2in or 2½in wire and 12ft kites and one with 1in wire and 6ft kites. Later experience showed that this tow speed could not be exceeded in practice, although the sweep itself would survive at much higher speed. It also turned out that the sweep could not be relied upon to indicate the presence of a mine, which in theory

The 'Hunts' were more conventional minesweepers intended to replace the paddlers and also to function as fleet sweepers. HMS *Cattistock* is shown running trials in May 1917, her gun not yet having been mounted.

The smallest of the purpose-built wartime sweepers were the shallow-draught tunnel sweepers built as Mesopotamian river tugs for the War Office, then taken over by the navy. Launched in September 1917, *Quadrille* was turned over to the Royal Navy (and named) that December.

might have been indicated by the strain on the wire. A dynamometer (strain indicator) was added before the war, but in practice it showed fluctuating strains when ships manoeuvred, or when they encountered heavy weather (which did not prevent sweeping). In 1916 the AMS asked Messrs. Bullivant, who made torpedo nets, to try a serrated wire which could improve the sweep's ability to cut mine moorings. It proved very successful; the Staff History of British sweeping accounted it one of the greatest technical improvements in sweeping. British sweepers used gallows rather than davits to handle their gear, because they kept the kite under better control when it was lifted out of the water.

The Royal Navy liked the 'A' Sweep for clearing minefields, but it demanded accurate station-keeping and in rough weather it often parted. Nor was it recommended for marked War Channels which were infested with wrecks. The Royal Navy also used a single-ship paravane sweep for what it called searching sweeps, to define a minefield. It did not require accurate station-keeping and because it was independent the sweeper could zig-zag at will to evade submarine attack (a pair 'A' Sweeping had to be guarded by two others).

In contrast to the 'A' Sweep, the French and Russian navies used a single-ship sweep, a ship trailing sweep wires on each side. Mechanical cutters were attached to the wires. The British designated the French sweep the 'B' Sweep and by 1917 their sweeping handbook described it as obsolete. However, when the US Navy entered the war it found the French sweep more attractive and adopted it (however, the post-war clearance of the Northern Barrage was done with 'A' Sweeps).[37] The Royal Navy later discarded the 'A' Sweep in favour of a single-ship sweep.

To provide the fleet with a mobile sweeping force, six old torpedo gunboats were converted into minesweepers (to parallel the seven old cruisers converted into minelayers). The first entered service in 1908. Conversion entailed fitting double drum steam trawler winches (typically forward of the engine room casing on the upper deck, slightly to port) and gallows for the water kite. All torpedo tubes and supporting equipment were removed. The ex-gunboats were manned on a nucleus basis and were intended to develop sweep methods and to train the reservists for the trawlers. They were worked as a flotilla in conjunction with the fleet or with a single capital ship representing the fleet. Fleet sweepers were also

exercised with minelayers, partly to arouse a healthy rivalry. The four torpedo gunboats assigned to fishery protection were also fitted for sweeping and were occasionally released from fishery protection duties for that purpose. Two other torpedo gunboats were retained at the technical schools at this time. The gunboats became a permanent part of the Home Fleet in the summer of 1912, conducting fleet exercises.[38]

Exercises by the Gunboat Flotilla showed the great advantage of high sweep speed, that sweeping was possible even in moderately bad weather, the absolute need to keep accurate station and the need for accuracy in the amount of sweep and kite wire veered.[39] It also turned out that anti-sweep devices did not work. However, pre-war exercises failed to show the need for absolutely accurate navigation and for accurate estimates of tidal effect.[40] Experiments with 'River' class destroyers showed that they would be adequate replacements for the gunboats; approval to fit sweep gear (1912) was revoked because it appeared that they would be needed for patrol work.

At the same time a trawler (sweeping) reserve was formed; during a pre-war period of strained relations, 100 were to be mobilised.[41] The policy laid down before the war was to maintain a force of fairly fast fleet sweepers for open water (in sheltered waters fleet picket boats might be used), trawlers to defend home ports and local authorities at commercial ports to be encouraged to keep their entrances free by using suitable local vessels.[42] Conferences to arrange these last arrangements proved unsuccessful. The sweeps devised to deal with mines were clearly closely related to sweeps devised to destroy submarines (described in Chapter 13). It is not altogether clear which came first.

Despite successful mobilisation of trawlers, in 1914 the Royal Navy had nothing like the minesweeping force it would soon need. The Staff History prepared in 1920 blamed that on two detrimental factors: a belief that somehow the Great Powers would come to an understanding limiting mine warfare and a belief that the appropriate counter to a minelaying campaign was patrols to find and destroy minelayers (the initial mining operation by the German *Koningen Luise* showed that this was wrong). It was also difficult to arrange peacetime co-operation with commercial and dominion authorities. The replacement of the gunboats was postponed and the claims of the patrol flotillas and the trawlers took precedence. Even so, it was clear that the Admiralty understood the importance of minesweeping. It established a Minesweeping Section in 1911 under an Inspecting Captain of Minesweeping Vessels, much as the submarine service had its own Inspecting Captain. In 1912 the Inspecting Captain came under the authority of the Admiral of Patrols. In 1914 he had the six gunboats and eighty-six trawlers, most of them assigned to specific ports. Six, which were available for reallocation by C-in-C Home Fleet, were transferred almost immediately to Scapa Flow.[43]

Shortly after the sinking of HMS *Amphion*, news from a source regarded as reliable reached the fleet that the minefield involved had been part of a much larger operation and about 29 August another fifty trawlers (in addition to the 200 already taken up) were mobilised as part of a 'special reserve'. However, no enemy mines had yet been recovered and the efficiency of the 'A' Sweep had not yet been demonstrated. Trawler crews were largely raw. It was clear that the 'A' Sweep would be slow, so a naval officer suggested instead drifter nets of the type used for fishing. A trial showed that the nets were both unreliable and dangerous.[44] Due to their low speed, drifters tended to drag mines rather than to cut their mooring wires so that they could be sunk by gunfire.

Fortunately after a sortie by the minelayer *Albatross* late in August the Germans did not lay further minefields until the end of October, providing the nascent minesweeping force time to train.[45] By 1 September, six sweepers had been lost and only thirty mines destroyed; confidence in the 'A' Sweep was nearly gone. Each trawler sunk carried with it half its crew. The situation was so bad that sweeping had been temporarily suspended in favour of aerial reconnaissance of suspected minefields.[46]

The crisis in September 1914 led to appointment of an operational commander for East Coast Minesweeping, Admiral Mine Sweeping (AMS), who also became responsible for developing and fitting mine countermeasures. He was not, however, responsible for building minesweepers. As part of the reorganisation of the Admiralty in 1917, the new post of Director of Torpedoes and Mines (DTM) was created (previously this would have been part of the organisation headed by the Director of Naval Ordnance). He now took over responsibility for mine protection and sweep gear and also for the production of sweepers. Operations and training were delegated to a Captain of Mine Sweeping (CMS) who headed a section under the Director of the Anti-Submarine Division (DASD) of the Naval Staff; later CMS became Superintendent of Minesweeping (SMS). Under a further reorganisation (October 1917) the minesweeping section became a division of the Naval Staff under a Director responsible for all sweeping in Home Waters. The rise in stature of the minesweeping function gives some idea of the increasing scope of the mine problem.

In addition to sweeps of various types (mainly the 'A' Sweep), the Royal Navy tried to spot mines from the air as early as the autumn of 1914. That turned out to be difficult in the North Sea, but it was quite successful in the Mediterranean. For example, late 1917 aircraft flying over the Gulf of Ruphani spotted suspected mines and dropped buoys so that motor launches could be directed to them. During 1918 kite (towed) balloons were used for mine spotting.[47]

By December 1914, the British minesweeping force was becoming far more competent. After the Germans laid a minefield during the Scarborough raid, a mixed force of fleet sweepers and trawlers managed to define the extent of the field (for the first time) and then clear it. The first German mine was recovered during this operation. During 1914, the Germans laid 840 mines in British waters, accounting for over fifty merchant ships and fishing boats, roughly one for every seventeen mines. Three hundred had been neutralised. Initially many in the Royal Navy saw merchant ships as, in effect, mine sentries: mining one indicated the location of a new minefield. However, losses of merchant ships were becoming less and less acceptable.

Initially the Germans laid large minefields and the British established a swept War Channel. Once the Germans began laying very small fields using submarines, it became vital to inform ships at sea when minefields were discovered. The Admiralty Signal Division began a systematic series of such messages in January 1916, using the designating letter Q. They were sent by wire to bases and by W/T from Cleethorpes, all ships being instructed to look out for such messages every two hours. The 'Q' designation later came to indicate a cleared route (a 'Q route') and that designation became standard in Allied mine countermeasures in later years ('Q' routes were, for example, to be maintained in the 1980s in US harbour areas).

Losses peaked in 1917, the German submarine mining campaign paralleling the unrestricted submarine attack campaign. Overall, the German campaign extended submarine mining well beyond the original East Coast area, so that by the summer of 1917 every part of the coasts of Great Britain and Ireland was being mined. Quite apart from making up for losses, that greater extent demanded many more sweepers. In some cases the same large trawlers could be used either to attack submarines or to sweep any mines they laid. Thus the Admiralty was forced to choose between assigning much the same ships to either sweeping or to anti-submarine work. The author of the British Staff History of minesweeping argued that the Germans expanded submarine mining specifically to force the withdrawal of anti-submarine craft and thus to help their submarine torpedo campaign. For their part the British laid out the swept war channel specifically to limit both torpedo and mine attacks by placing it in the shallowest possible water.[48]

Up to early 1917 standard British practice was to close a port whenever mines were reported, keeping it closed until it seemed certain that the entrance had been thoroughly cleared. That left merchant ships bound for the port had to stand off, making them easy targets for U-boats offshore. The British learned to reopen ports as soon as the fairway had been swept once. Once the convoy system was introduced, there could be no question of closing a port, so sweepers had to operate ahead of all inbound and outbound convoys to sweep them through the danger area. This new practice began with the Tyne paddle sweepers.

Minesweeping was finally considered effective in 1918. That year only twelve ships were sunk by mines in areas for which the Royal Navy was responsible, which made for an average of eighty-five mines laid per ship sunk, a dramatic improvement over previous figures. The British were, however, uncomfortably aware that the Dominions and overseas governments were not nearly as well-prepared for mine warfare as they were in home waters, so the offensive by minelaying

Aside from sweepers, the Royal Navy developed a form of self-defence in the form of paravanes, which towed mine-cutting cables from a ship (at the least, the cable could deflect a mine about to swing into a ship). Paravanes were produced both for warships and for merchant ship self-protection (under the cover name 'otter'). The paravane secret was given to the US Navy when it entered the war. This is a US Navy paravane. (Kadel and Herbert via US Navy Historical and Heritage Command)

The battleship *Emperor of India* displays her port paravane ready to stream. The great achievement of paravane development was that the paravane could maintain a set depth and offset from the ship. Paravanes only became obsolete when large numbers of influence mines were brought into service. Otherwise they offered ships valuable self-defence whenever they had to cross areas shallow enough to be minable.

U-cruisers could have been far more effective.

In 1914, the Royal Navy was developing a new sweeper to replace the converted torpedo gunboats, but construction had not yet been approved. First Lord Winston Churchill preferred to convert existing merchant ships and eight cross-Channel or cross-North Sea steamers were taken up, despite their deep draught, as 'auxiliary sweepers'. The first pair arrived in December 1914; one sank by collision soon after arrival. These ships were soon relegated to ferry and other services during the Gallipoli campaign. No further suitable ships were available, so Churchill reluctantly approved construction of initial 'Flower' class sloops.

It was clear in 1914 that a special shallow-draught sweeper with good seakeeping qualities was needed, ideally with a draught less than the tidal range. The Admiralty sought fast shallow-draught ships. At the end of October it seemed that a paddle excursion steamer might be ideal and the *Brighton Queen* was commissioned, the first of a large number of such ships. After trials of the first six, the Admiralty decided to take up as many as possible, while laying down further ships. Compared to a trawler, the paddler offered shallower draught ($6\frac{1}{2}$ft vs 14ft) and higher sweep speed (10 knots vs 6 knots). Over seventy paddlers were hired, average dimensions being 227 x 47 x 6ft 5in (the largest was 280 x 65 x 7ft, the smallest 177 x 48 x 12ft). It was initially imagined that the paddlers would not be good seaboats, but that was not the case. Ships were fitted with a gallows, winch, minesweeping stores, guns, ammunition and increased coal and water stowage; as fitted some could keep the sea for four to six days. The great advantage of the paddler was that she had no screw to foul the sweep or kite war, so that when an

obstruction was found she could instantly reverse. On the other hand, in rough weather it was dangerous for two of them to approach each other closely.

In May 1915 the Admiral of Minesweeping reported that the paddlers were far better than other minesweepers, so he asked for an Admiralty-built class of them. The main requirements were a sea speed of 15 knots (sweep speed 12 knots), one week endurance at sea, strengthened bows and good watertight subdivision, a small crew, wireless and draught not to exceed 7ft forward or aft. Based on reports from sea, the Ailsa-built *Glen Usk* was chosen as the basis of the Admiralty design. Larger bunkers were provided and two boilers, so that they could be placed fore and aft of the engines, for better subdivision. Shell plating was thickened and carried up to the upper deck. That greatly increased reserve buoyancy. Armament was two 12pdr 12 cwt guns. While the first batch was being built, it was decided to provide them with seaplanes so that they could maintain a patrol 70nm from the coast, to intercept Zeppelins offshore. Provision was made, but because construction was so urgent the seaplanes were never fitted. In service it turned out that even a slight heel greatly affected speed, as it lifted the paddles on one side out of the water. Ships therefore had special

Royal Navy sailors adjust a paravane.

anti-heel tanks in their sponsons. Designed speed was 15 knots, but owing to underpowering the average speed was 14 knots; sweep speed was 9 knots. The initial group comprised twenty-four ships (seventeen ordered September 1915, another four in October and three in January 1916), followed by another eight in January 1917. Five more paddle sweepers, named after sea birds, were ordered in 1918 but cancelled on 10 December. Two more may have been planned but were not ordered.

The paddlers were not entirely satisfactory, as mines could get under the paddles. Moreover, paddlers were inefficient in anything like heavy weather. Early in 1916, therefore, DNC designed a more conventional twin-screw sweeper, the 'Hunt' class, for a sweep speed of 12 knots. Because these ships were much faster than the paddlers, they were suited to Grand Fleet service and could replace the 'Flowers'. They had much the same draught as the paddlers, but were faster (16 knots, typically 17 knots on trials). They were smaller than the Admiralty paddlers (730 tons vs 810 tons, 230 x 28 x 7ft vs 245 x 58 x 6ft 9in). There was some fear that due to their shallow draught they would race their propellers in any sea, but in fact they raced less than either the gunboats or the sloops and

could easily sweep in all weather. Like the paddlers, they were armed with a pair of 12pdr guns; they also had two 2pdr pompom anti-aircraft guns.

Twenty were initially ordered. All twelve initially completed were assigned to the Grand Fleet. The first joined at Rosyth during the last month of 1916. The first repeat order was for fifty-six, but by November 1918, 131 ships were either built or building or had been ordered. On 17 December, thirty-five of them were cancelled, followed later by HMS *Bolton*.

In addition to sweepers designed by DNC Department, the Royal Navy took over a series of shallow-draught Mesopotamia. They had their screws in tunnels to minimise draught and they were given 'Dance' names. The first six were transferred in October 1917, the next four in December 1917 and the last four in April 1919. Some were transferred upon completion. Also in 1915, Elco motor launches at Dover, Harwich and the Nore were fitted for local sweeping, using special light gear. They proved fairly successful.

As the Germans mounted their major mining offensive in the spring of 1917, many of their mines were inadvertently moored at shallower than intended depths, causing such casualties to British minesweeping forces in the early part of 1917 that a large building programme had to be mounted. Until it took effect, civilian craft once more had to be taken up. By this time all available paddlers had been taken as sweepers. It proved possible to use a lighter form of 'A' Sweep, hence a lighter ship, once the serrated wire had been adopted.[49] That brought drifters back into the sweep force. German mines initially sat on the bottom until a timer released them to rise to their set depth. The British therefore became interested in bottom sweeps. During 1917 they developed an otter board bottom sweep worked by drifters. The sweeper force grew from 523 on 1 January 1917 to 643 on 1 July and then declined slightly to 631 on 1 January 1918, in each case including numerous units which might otherwise have been devoted to anti-submarine work.[50]

Late in 1914 work was underway on a bow protection mechanism. Deflecting wires towed from the forefoot were tried on board the ex-gunboat *Skipjack* and this equipment was being fitted to the new sloops. The wires were deployed using minesweeping-type kites and booms. However, it proved useless when tried on a larger scale on the battleship *Emperor of India*. Trials continued using deflecting devices. In 1915 they finally succeeded with the invention of the Burney paravane.

The paravane was a float which could maintain the far end of a wire well outboard of the ship towing it, at a suitable constant set depth. Normally a ship passed a mine rather than collide with it. Her bow wave would push the mine away, but the mine would then swing back and hit the ship. The effect of the deflector bow protection was to prevent the mine from swinging back until the ship passed. It seems to have been generally assumed that the paravane wire would cut the mine mooring, so the effectiveness of the device was often, incorrectly, assessed in terms of the number of mine moorings cut. The British came to see paravane protection not as an alternative to minesweeping, but as an invaluable complement. The usual search methods could not be used effectively against minefields laid well offshore. In some cases ships trailing paravanes were the first to discover new minefields. During 1915 paravanes were fitted to all British warships drawing more than 12ft of water.[51] A simplified paravane, given the intentionally deceptive name Otter, was supplied to some merchant ships and the steamship *Accrington* fitted as an instructional ship at Portsmouth. The success of the paravane led to another application, a high-speed sweep by means of which destroyers could detect or clear mines ahead of a fleet. Like the French 'B' Sweep, this one was streamed from either quarter, in this case held down at its inner end by a 'Tadpole' kite.[52]

Soon after the Germans began their submarine mining campaign, the senior officer of the Sheerness Torpedo School (HMS *Actaeon*), who was responsible for patrolling the Thames Estuary, introduced a new *Actaeon* sweep based on the French and Russian types. It consisted of a light wire, a small kite and a diving spar with outward thrust carrying an explosive grapnel.[53] A patrol boat such as destroyer or torpedo boat towed one from each quarter at a speed of up to or over 12 knots. When the wire hit a mine, its mooring wire slid down and hit the explosive, which parted the mooring and often also exploded the mine. The *Actaeon* sweep was considered a means of exploring a potential minefield rather than a means of clearing it. The main objections were limited spread and depth and the *Actaeon* sweep was not widely accepted until much later in the war. It had the great advantage that it was suitable for night work, because there was no need for two sweepers working together to keep station with each other.

German Minesweeping

Like the Royal Navy, the German navy created minesweeping units before the war, organising its first Minensuche (Mine-Seeking) Division in 1905. It consisted of old torpedo boats adapted for the task. These boats they were used both to detect mines and to detect submarines, their mine detection gear either in use or not. They were criticised as too slow and unable to work in a Sea State over 3 or 4. On mobilisation auxiliary divisions were formed using trawlers and drifters. They were far more seaworthy than the old torpedo boats, but they were slower and their draught was greater (as in the British case). As in the Royal Navy, pre-war calls for specialised sweepers had gone unheeded. Once war broke out in 1914, a standard tug-type 450-ton minesweeper ('M' class) was designed. The first unit, *M 1*, was commissioned on 17 July 1915.[54] At that time at least three serviceable divisions were considered necessary to open the fairways to the North Sea bases on short notice. The small new 'A' class torpedo boats were also used as sweepers.

Once the British began to mine the Heligoland Bight in earnest in 1917, more sweepers were needed, so a 170-ton shallow-water sweeper (FM-Boot, flachgehende M-Boot) was designed; sixty-six were built. Unlike the M-boats the FM-boats were not seaworthy enough for the open North Sea. The Germans also experimented with motorboats (18-ton F-boats drawing about 1m, compared to 1.7m for an FM-boat). UZ-boats conceived as sub-chasers were also used for sweeping (forty-seven built); they were the forerunners of the Second World War R-boats. Finally, most High Seas Fleet torpedo boats (destroyers) could sweep.

At the outset the Germans used a two-ship 'search sweep' (minensuchgerät) developed in 1913 by Carbonit, which also developed the navy's mines. Sweepers were 165 yds abreast, the 275 yd sweep wire being 550 yds astern.[55] The sweep was dropped at 7 knots and could be worked at 13 knots, with a maximum towing speed of 18 knots. It could be used at a depth as shallow as 39.3ft (12m), but in order to avoid false alarms when the gear touched bottom, effective minimum depth for sweeping was 50ft. At minimum depth the kite would maintain a depth of 32.1ft and mines would be swept at a depth of 27.2ft (they would still be caught if their upper edges were 22.3ft below the surface). Speed had to be reduced to 11 knots for kite depth to be changed.[56] Up to four sweepers could work abreast. The sweep was held down by a kite suspended from a float, a second kite spreading the sweep line away from the sweeper. Note that the sweep was called a search device (suchgerät). At the outset German sweep gear used a grapnel which gripped the mine underwater when it cut the mooring. In the process many mines exploded. Explosive cutters were introduced during the war.

Unlike the British, the Germans had a separate requirement for barrage breakers (sperrbrecher), which were conceived as fast and effectively unsinkable ships which could create paths through minefields by deliberately exploding mines (a testimony to the inefficiency of conventional sweeping). On the outbreak of war the German navy took up steamers from trade and ballasted them down (to trigger mines) with sand or cement ballast. They had special bow mine protection (projecting wires, not paravanes, which were called spreading boom C), but no other mine countermeasures. In 1918 a net catching gear was being tested. A list of mine countermeasures dated March 1918 included an Otter mine clearer which could be towed at 4 to 9 knots and was presumably intended as a replacement for the boom. They were considered too slow and too vulnerable, the ballast having reduced their buoyancy. The sperrbrechers seem to have been conceived particularly to lead the fleet through supposed minefields in the German Bight.

During the war the Germans developed a considerable variety of minesweeping devices, which they grouped either as mine-seeking (MS) or mine-clearing (MR), or mine-protective (self-protection) gear (G).[57] MS gear was intended for accurate mine search up to Sea State 4, route searching up to Sea State 5 and single-ship operation up to Sea State 6. SMS was rapid (Schnell) search gear for destroyers (fleet torpedo boats). MR gear was intended for use up to Sea State 4, with light or heavy kite. Sea State limits were imposed by the ability of the kite to maintain depth.

The pre-war type was probably the light kite MS (a type with 2/3 kite was used only on board mine-clearing divisions). There was also a 300m MS (300m swept path [328 yds]), which could be set to sweep mines at depths of 4 to 7.1 fathoms at a speed of 10 knots. Single-ship sweep gear was introduced during the war, initially using a grapnel. It could be towed at up to 11 knots and path width was 120 yds; depth limits were 3.3 and 8.2 fathoms. The M-boats alone had a single-ship sweep with explosive cutters, presumably similar to the French sweep.

For mine clearance there were light kite sweeps with either a fork grapnel or explosive cutters, designed to clear a 49.2 yd (45m) path at a minimum depth of 3.3 fathoms (maximum 8.5 fathoms),

at a maximum sweep speed of 8 knots. Alternatives were a light kite seeking sweep with explosive cutter (164 yd path) and a single-ship seeking sweep with explosive cutter (120 yd path). There was also a clearing sweep using a heavy kite, which could clear the widest path (328 to 546 yds [300 to 500m]).[58]

Mine-seeking flotillas typically had light MSG, MS 300 (except for the 4th Flotilla), a light MSG with grapnel, light MR with fork grapnel, light MSG with cutter and heavy MSG (with light MSG with explosive cutter planned). The mine-clearing divisions had a light MSG with 2/3 kite and light MR with fork grapnel. M-boats had single-ship sweep gear with explosive cutters. UZ-boats had light MSG. In March 1918 single-ship mine-seeking gear with grapnels was being fitted to sprerrbrechers.

The Germans may have been alone in using aircraft successfully to spot mines. Their official history is replete with examples of such searches, though clearly they were not always successful.[59]

Although the Royal Navy used a two-ship sweep to clear minefields, it fitted destroyers with single-ship paravane sweeps. They would steam ahead of battleships, using these sweeps to ensure that the immediate path ahead was clear. The paravane sweep was called the High Speed Mine Sweep. The destroyer function of keeping the path of the battleships clear of mines – and submarines – remained between the wars and into the Second World War. This is a typical destroyer paravane crane, right aft.

How do you exploit the advantages of the submarine without bringing neutrals into a war? One answer was the submarine cruiser – a submarine designed to surface and deal with merchant ships one by one. HMS *X 1* was the British version (the French built *Surcouf*). She was armed with a pair of twin 5.2in guns (the design originally called for twin 4in guns). The Naval Staff had sought permission to lay down such a submarine in 1918, but they were turned down because the project was not considered sufficiently important. The project was revived in 1920.

CHAPTER 16
Lessons for the Future

FOR THE BRITISH, THE great lesson of the First World War was that they had squandered too much of the advantage their seapower gave them. Centuries ago, Sir Francis Bacon pointed out that 'he who commands the sea can take as much or as little of the war as he likes'. The maritime character of the war offered the British choices as to how they would fight. The British Cabinet understood as much. It resisted sending the BEF to France at the outset and it sought alternatives to reinforcing the army in France. In this light, the attacks on the Dardanelles were a rational strategic move rather than a half-baked way for the Royal Navy to participate in a land war. They represented an understanding that Britain offered her allies something more than raw manpower. The combination of failure in the Dardanelles and a deteriorating situation on the Western Front ended the search for such alternatives, but it did not change the perception that no victory in the West could be decisive. That perception was reinforced by the disaster the British Army experienced on the Somme in July 1916. The British always accepted that *defeat* in the West would be a decisive defeat for France. That made it nearly impossible to withdraw the large British army once it was engaged in France.

The Royal Navy controlled the sea. At the very least it could deny the Germans access to British shores. Thus a sense that the war could not be won hardly meant that the British should surrender. Instead, the British understood that they might eventually have to accept a temporary and unsatisfactory peace, much as their forebears had accepted a brief peace with Napoleon in 1801 after the alliance the British assembled had collapsed. As in the Napoleonic War, understanding that the peace was only a truce, the British would use it to improve their position once war

inevitably resumed. The conclusion in 1916–17 was that the British position in the East – which existed thanks to the mobility granted by seapower – was much more likely to be decisive than the continuing stalemate on the Western Front.[1] The British began to move into places like Palestine and the Caucasus. This was not too different from the earlier idea that the Russians and the Eastern Front were likely to be the crux of the war. This partial strategic reorientation was possible only because the sea offered the British such flexibility. Conversely, it was badly slowed because the U-boat offensive of 1917 choked off so much shipping. Winning the war against the U-boats, or at least stopping their depredations, was a necessary condition for achieving the strategic position the British felt would ultimately decide the war.

In the autumn of 1916 the Germans also had a sense of stalemate, particularly after the failure of their offensive at Verdun. They became interested in a negotiated peace – a truce – but their demands proved unacceptable to either the British or the French. Neither felt badly enough punished to concede what the Germans demanded. When the French showed they were still willing and able to fight (by a minor offensive), Ludendorff, who by that time was effectively German dictator, conceded that no attack in the West was likely to end the war. He turned to sea power in the form of unrestricted submarine warfare, as a way out. At about the same time, for the same reason, he authorised an operation to subvert Russia: the Germans placed Lenin and other Bolsheviks on a sealed train into Russia (and provided them with funds) in hopes that they would create a revolution.

Unrestricted submarine warfare brought the United States, with its vast industrial resources and its untapped manpower, into the war. Once the United States was in the war, the British could indeed envisage a decision on the Western Front, simply because American troops and resources would so heavily tip the balance. For US resources to come to bear, however, it was essential that the German submarine campaign be defeated or at the least neutralised. That was very much a naval operation.

The Allied victory at sea was a precondition for victory over Germany and the Central Powers. HMS *Queen Elizabeth*, flagship of the Grand Fleet, is seen over the guns of USS *New York*, flagship of the 6th Battle Squadron of US ships seconded to the Grand Fleet. The great post-war question was how to blend the highly visible seapower represented by the main fleet with other forms of seapower, such as anti-submarine forces.

The inter-war Royal Navy recognised that battleships were only part of a larger kind of seapower, a lesson taught by the war but easily forgotten afterwards. It never rebuilt seven of the ten First World War battleships which it retained into the late 1920s. HMS *Royal Sovereign* is shown off Philadelphia Naval Shipyard on 14 September 1943, modified with radar and numerous anti-aircraft weapons, but otherwise not too different from when she was completed in 1916.

By late 1917 the Russians had largely collapsed, in theory freeing large German forces for one last great offensive in the West before US troops swelled the Allied armies to the point where they could no longer be defeated. US troops already in France helped stop Ludendorff's last-chance offensive. It also became clear in the spring and summer of 1918 that British Empire and other Allied troops had finally mastered combined-arms warfare, to the point where they could successfully force the Germans back. The Allied defence and then offensive in 1918 were possible only because it was possible to move so much to France by sea. Conversely, the blockade affected the German army, for example substantially reducing its mobility. By August 1918 Ludendorff had to concede that he could not mount a further large-scale offensive.

However, he did not concede defeat. In 1918, as in 1914, the power of defence was enormous. It was entirely plausible that the Germans could mount a successful defence in the West, perhaps even remaining on conquered French territory. The German army had been forced back before, only to rebound. The German General Staff envisaged a continued war in which a much larger U-boat force would regain its effectiveness and compel the Allies to accept terms. None of this happened.

British sea power was an essential element of the Allied success on the Western Front in 1918. Without it the land battles could not have been fought. In 1918 the largest army on the Western Front was that contributed by the British Empire. Every man in it came from overseas – at the least from across the Channel, but in many cases from much further away, mainly from Australia, Canada and India. Similarly, without Allied sea power, no American troops could have reached the Western Front.

In October 1918 Ludendorff broke. He told the Kaiser that the war was lost. The word got out before Ludendorff regained his nerve and recanted. German civilians had sacrificed heavily for victory and they had been told again and again that their army was winning the war. Despite some serious problems in 1917, the government had managed to qualm popular dissatisfaction. Once it

admitted disaster, all the privations and social stresses created by the blockade (coupled with the stress of supporting offensive operations) broke out. The Germans later attributed much of the revolt to soldiers and others infected by the Bolshevik virus in Russia. To the extent that was true, it was blowback from Ludendorff's own operation against Russia.

What broke Ludendorff? The answer has never been entirely clear. There was no single massive defeat in the West, but the German position in the southeast was collapsing. Once Austria-Hungary left the war, southeast Germany was open to attack. The Turkish collapse opened the Dardanelles to a massive influx of Allied forces, which could move up the Danube into the heart of Austria and southern Germany. Ludendorff needed all his troops to hold the Western Front; he had nothing left. An attack into southeast Germany ultimately meant an attack on the most sensitive part of the country, eastern Prussia. That was an intolerable threat. This aspect of the war would have been inconceivable without the flexibility British seapower bought.

The question is whether a more creative use of the enormous investment the British made in sea power would have won the war at a much lower cost in British and Empire blood. There can be no question but that the cost actually paid was enormous and that the payment badly crippled Britain (and, for that matter, France) for the next quarter-century. That terrible cost convinced statesmen in both countries that no one would welcome a repetition of the war and therefore that Hitler did not mean to fight. Surely it is one of the great questions of the twentieth century how Hitler convinced Germans, who had also suffered badly during the war (not least from the blockade) that a repeat engagement was an excellent idea.

It seems unlikely that the First World War could have been fought without the horrific losses armies suffered on both the Eastern and the Western Fronts. For a land power like France or

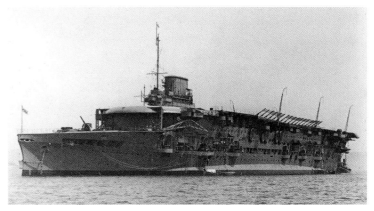

The post-war naval arms limitation treaties ended battlecruiser construction, but not the need for long-range scouts and commerce protectors (and raiders). That navies were quite willing to build largely unprotected 'treaty cruisers' shows that the lesson of the war was that fast heavy ships would do much of the fleet work, not that lack of protection would be fatal. Large lightly-protected cruisers proved extremely useful during the Second World War. HMS *Devonshire* is shown before the war.

The Royal Navy invented the aircraft carrier during the First World War and immediately after the war it was by far the world leader in this new type of warship. The rebuilt 'large light cruiser' HMS *Courageous* is shown. It was the Royal Navy which insisted at the Washington Conference that allowance be made for converting capital ships like this one into carriers. (Dr David Stevens, SPC-A)

Russia or Germany, there was no alternative. Britain was differently situated. She could have taken 'as much or as little of the war' as her Government wished. It was not foreordained that hundreds of thousands of *British* soldiers would die. The British Government failed to grasp this possibility. It did not see the implication of building Kitchener's New Armies, perhaps because at the outset no one in power (except possibly Kitchener himself) imagined that the war would last much beyond late 1914. British statesmen may have naively overrated the 'Russian steamroller' – the vast Russian army attacking from the east – as a decisive factor. They surely overrated the immediate potential of economic attack against Germany as a means of weakening their enemy.

Once the New Armies existed (without being engaged elsewhere), it was impossible for the British government to resist French demands that they should be deployed to shore up the Western Front. In the autumn of 1914, the Cabinet agreed that feeding more troops into the Western Front, where they would only 'eat barbed wire' would not produce decisive results. After the German offensive in the spring of 1915 the British had to confront a real possibility that without masses of their troops France would be overrun. Although there was talk of successful offensives after that, they were never advertised as means of winning the war; they were always tactical. It is not clear to what extent the two wartime British Governments accepted the idea that somehow defeating the German army in the West (if that were possible) would end the war.

There was never any question but that a French defeat would be a terrible outcome, but the question for the British Government should have been how terrible (or how unacceptable) and therefore how much should have been sacrificed to prevent it. British seapower made it possible to ask that question, because even the collapse of France would not have given the Germans the ability to leap the Channel into the United Kingdom – as long as the British fleet was in the way. Some pre-war advocates of a large British army (to be built up through Continental-type conscription) argued that invasion was a real threat, but they were not taken very seriously before 1914. The British war aim was the defeat of Germany, not the preservation of France. If the Germans did overrun France, but lost the war, they would have had to disgorge what they had seized. That

is just what happened in the Second World War, which in a sense was a rerun of the First World War with very different strategy.

The men who led Britain through the inter-war period and the Second World War had all experienced the First World War and they all had reason to think about its lessons. The obvious one was to try to avoid a second round, which was not too different from the pre-war idea that it was far better to deter the Germans than to fight them. What if war could not be avoided at all? What should British strategy be? Anyone in the British Government in 1939 would have echoed Prime Minister Asquith's comment in September 1914 that the fall of France would be a disaster, but this time they realised that they could not again offer a blank cheque to preclude it. Instead of Kitchener's attempt to build the biggest army he could, in 1939 the British controlled the balance between the services and other national requirements by introducing conscription and what Americans would call selective service. When France began to collapse, the British did not feed in everything they had, including their national air defence. They understood that they could not afford to.

Moreover, the British Government of the late 1930s understood that they had viable strategic choices as long as the British Isles were secure. In 1939 that meant secure from invasion and also from the 'knockout blow' then attributed (as it happened, unrealistically) to bombing. The British Government played for time in the late 1930s while British radar-controlled air defences were built. As that defensive system became effective, the British became noticeably more willing to confront the Germans – Britain was once again a defendable island, hence once again could choose her strategy.[2] As in the First World War, the remaining key issue was whether the British could maintain their link to the resources of the Empire and the world. There was a reason Winston Churchill wrote that the only aspect of the Second World War which truly frightened him was the Battle of the Atlantic – the battle to maintain that link.

In effect, British strategy in the Second World War recalled their strategy against Napoleon. British seapower made it possible to strike at the enemy's periphery. The British knew that they could not create a massive enough ground force to destroy their enemy – but they also knew that their seapower would prevent their enemy from destroying them (in the Second World War, of course, defensive

The wartime US Navy closely followed British work on aircraft carriers and it benefited from the British initiative at the Washington Naval Conference. USS *Saratoga* is shown in the early 1930s, landing her T4M bombers. Probably the most important US carrier innovation was the deck park: aircraft were parked at the bow rather than being struck below after landing. Equating deck area to aircraft capacity made for much larger air wings.

In 1939 the Royal Navy had six fleet carriers on order, many more than any other navy in the world. They were also the only carriers in the world with armoured hangars (which meant partly armoured flight decks). Three were rapidly completed, but the other three were badly delayed by the stress of other wartime work and the US Navy much outbuilt the wartime Royal Navy. HMS *Formidable*, one of the first three, is shown passing through the Sydney harbour boom in 1945. (State Library of Victoria)

airpower was a vital factor). Their enemy could not rest as long as they survived and continued to attack him. His attempts to find ways of attacking the British indirectly would inevitably create powerful enemies. The British role was to hold out and continue the fight while creating a series of alliances which would eventually destroy their enemy. That strategy worked against both Napoleon and Hitler. Once those allies came into play, the combination of British seapower and landpower would be fully effective. It might be argued that a similar strategy exercised against the Kaiser would have left Britain in a far better position post-war, perhaps a good enough one that there would not have been a second World War.

The British Government of the Second World War, particularly in the person of Winston Churchill, also understood what the First World War government badly missed: war was global and maritime. The maritime element offered possibilities a land power could not seize. The Russian steamroller really did work during the Second World War, but it was probably crucial that it was supplied by sea – which is what opening the Dardanelles was supposed to offer in the First World War. The sea offered access all around the edges of Hitler's European empire – so he had to defend all of them. When Allied deception operations were declassified, it became clear that much of the effort went into convincing Hitler that the Allies were planning to land in Norway. That was credible because maritime power offered access there. Hitler dissipated considerable strength by keeping it in Norway to oppose the notional invasion.

It is not clear that the implications of First World War experience were written down between the wars. However, the lessons of the earlier war seem obvious in any comparison of the way the British Government responded to the crises of 1914 and 1939. In neither case did the British expect war until virtually the last moment and in neither case did the British have a detailed war plan. The immense difference between 1914 and 1939 was that this time the British did not slide into an open-ended commitment to a land war in Western Europe. That was rather fortunate for the world.

The most obvious strategic lesson of the war was that it was foolhardy to allow armies and navies to plan, or to fight, separate wars. In 1914, of the powers which fought the First World War, only the British had even a tentative means of co-ordinating the services, via the Committee on Imperial Defence (CID). The CID, which included Prime Minister Asquith, did hear both sides' versions of what they thought should be done, but it imposed no agreed joint plan. Admiral Fisher maintained that the British army was 'a projectile to be fired by the Royal Navy', but he did not elaborate a plan for combined operations which might have appealed sufficiently to the pre-war British Government to impose it on the army. His hints of a Baltic operation came closest, but he was unable to sell the idea persuasively enough and the army's resistance was enough to kill the idea.

For Britain the larger pre-war reality was that the Liberal Government in office between 1906 and 1914 thought war unlikely due to the economic interdependence of the major powers. In common with other European governments, it was far more concerned with internal problems. War broke out because one or more of those governments saw it as a solution to an internal problem, not because of traditional causes such as appetite for territory. In the British case, the government saw social reforms rather than any form of external action as a way of defusing internal problems. Most members of the pre-war Liberal Government were uninterested in military issues. Given the underlying belief in economics as the determining factor and the central role of the City of London in the world economy, the pre-war British Government naturally adopted economic attack, far beyond the usual idea of blockade, as a weapon. It seems to have been the only possible answer to the question of how Britain could (or could help to) defeat Germany.

The perceived reality, that global economics would deter anyone from fighting, made war planning a relatively remote business. As a result, Prime Minister Asquith seems to have considered party politics a more immediate concern. He did not reject the army's plan to place the army in France simply because he could not afford to have his pre-war Secretary of State for War (Haldane) resign from the Cabinet. Instead, he left the plan as an army initiative unsanctioned by the Cabinet, hence rejectable if war ever became imminent. For some days after the outbreak of war he refused to send the army to France and he wrote privately that he did not want to do so. Unfortunately the lack of serious pre-war planning at the Cabinet level left Asquith and his colleagues with little or no sense of the alternatives available to them. It did not help that First Lord Winston Churchill kept pressing particular operations rather than any overall strategy and that once he was back in office Admiral Fisher tended to growl in opposition rather than explain exactly what strategy he wanted to pursue. By 1918 the British had formed the War Cabinet, a kind of civilian general staff to oversee and co-ordinate all aspects of the war. Those involved at the top in 1939 understood why that mattered. The non-military aspects were as important as the services' part.[3]

The Continental governments had army general staffs which prepared elaborate war plans, but they generally amounted to calculations which would place masses of troops in the right places to attack. The Germans in particular seem to have imagined that they could win a war in a single titanic battle which would destroy the enemy's army. By 1914 that was unrealistic: armies were far too massive and countries had far too many resources. They could and did keep fighting to the point of exhaustion. Not only did the German General Staff not take resource issues fully into account, it paid no attention at all to the maritime aspects of a world war. The extent of this blindness and the absence of any higher-level control, seem to have been inconceivable to the British.

The disaster of the First World War led various countries to try to co-ordinate land and maritime factors in future war planning. This was in and is an intractable problem, because land and naval warfare are so different that their exponents find it difficult to speak a common language. The British went furthest with their Committee of Imperial Defence and a Joint Chiefs of Staff

A key wartime problem, insufficiently appreciated before the war, was how to find an enemy fleet in the vastness of even the North Sea. At the end of the war, both the Royal Navy and the US Navy were interested in rigid airships as a solution, but the new Royal Air Force dropped the idea. The US rigid airship *Los Angeles* is shown moored to its tender, the converted tanker *Patoka* on 13 September 1926. The tender offered mobility.

Because it controlled its own aircraft, the US Navy could use them creatively. The Washington and London Naval Treaties drastically limited the number of aircraft carriers, hence fleet aircraft. The Royal Navy needed more than could be accommodated on board its carriers, so it planned to use battleship and cruiser catapults to launch strike aircraft. The US Navy became interested in large seaplanes, whose tenders were not limited by treaty. For a time it envisaged a seaplane bomber force (which is why the Second World War seaplanes were PBs, not P – patrol – aircraft). This possibility was not open to the Royal Navy, because the separate RAF controlled seaplanes, which it sometimes saw as an alternative to more conventional forms of seapower (however, some RAF commanders, e.g. in the Far East, considered their seaplanes the eyes of the surface fleet). Without long-range seaplane support, the inter-war Royal Navy emphasised long-range carrier-based reconnaissance and signals intelligence. The US seaplane tender *Albemarle* is shown on 30 December 1943, with a Catalina (PBY) patrol bomber on her quarterdeck.

Committee. The United States formed a Joint Navy-Army Board charged with war planning. The Joint Board signed off on various versions of the national plan for dealing with Japan, although they were primarily naval plans. For both countries, through much of the inter-war period the primary future war scenario was a war with Japan, which was necessarily naval. Allied victory in World War II was very largely a matter of understanding how to use land and sea power together.

The Germans created what looked like a joint staff, the OKW (Oberkommando der Wehrmacht), but in practice it was ineffective. That the Japanese completely failed to co-ordinate their services is well known. It was a leading cause of their disasters, beginning with the army's attack on China without any thought that there might have been a Western naval response. Perhaps that should have been expected of an army educated by the pre-1914 Germans, who also lacked interest in maritime issues or in the associated economic ones.

A review of war planning during the Cold War offers some additional insight into British options in the First World War. In some ways the NATO situation opposite the Soviet Union and the Warsaw Pact recalled the situation in 1914. Most NATO effort was concentrated on the Central Front, which was not too different in concept from the Western Front of the First World War. To most in NATO, the role of navies, if there were one, was to support resupply of NATO armies fighting a desperate battle on the Central Front against massed Soviet ground forces (this of course assumed that the Soviets did not win instantly and that the war did not turn nuclear). Beginning in 1979, the US Navy suggested a different way of looking at a NATO War, which it called the Maritime Strategy. Given the dominant role of the US Navy among Western navies at the time, it is not too far-fetched to see the Maritime Strategy as a much-modernised version of the strategy the Royal Navy might have offered in 1914. The US idea was maritime, not naval – it was a way to exploit NATO's maritime advantages and the geography of the situation.

The idea was to exploit Soviet sensitivities to, at the least, cause the Soviets to hold large ground forces back from any advance into Western Europe. The Soviets were much impressed by US amphibious capabilities, which meant that any threat to, say, Leningrad (St Petersburg) would be taken seriously. The seaward flanks of any advancing Soviet land force would be also be vulnerable and sensitive. Operations in such places were open to exactly the same objections that Admiral Fisher's Baltic project encountered. They were, to put it mildly, high-risk. The fleet could not readily be risked as long as the enemy's fleet was intact, because the loss of the fleet would be disastrous to a sea power. US naval strategists agreed; their first move would have been to trigger a decisive naval battle which they expected to win. By the late 1970s it seemed that new technology made that possible and through the 1980s enormous effort was expended to develop the relevant tactics and to push the relevant technology. In this case the Soviet fleet to be destroyed consisted mainly of long-range anti-ship bombers and submarines and the expected battle area was the Norwegian Sea.

As before 1914, the issue was how to force the Soviets to accept battle. The British had hoped to trigger a battle by blocking German access to the North Sea. As the Maritime Strategy developed, the US Navy expectation was that the Soviets would find it intolerable that US strike carriers loaded with attack bombers would come within attacking range of their most valuable naval assets, their ballistic missile submarine bases. The only remotely comparable First World War equivalent would have been an amphibious attack against the islands near Wilhelmshaven and that was raised but rejected as far too dangerous. Victory in the Norwegian Sea would have released the US fleet to carry out risky

Seapower is inherently global; British naval strategists always thought on a global scale. This British *Edgar* class cruiser, after the war at Batumi on the Black Sea in present-day Georgia, was part of the British strategic shift towards the East.

The Royal Navy took the wartime lessons of mine and submarine attack very seriously. The Royal Indian Navy sloop *Hindustan* was a modified version of the British *Hastings* class. She was conceived primarily as a peacetime gunboat and wartime minesweeper, a direct replacement for wartime-built 'Flowers'. When she was designed, it was assumed that the large surviving force of old destroyers would be used for anti-submarine warfare. In 1929, as it approached the London Naval Conference, the Royal Navy proposed to accept a sharp reduction in destroyer numbers only if submarines were banned. It was unpleasantly surprised that the British Government offered the reduction without the ban. With the London Naval Treaty in force, the Royal Navy scrambled to build sloops capable of anti-submarine operations, at the least as convoy escorts. (Allan C Green via State Library of Victoria)

but very rewarding operations on the flank of any Soviet advance and also in the sensitive Baltic.

The 1970s–1980s equivalent of the Russian steamroller was China, which had been hostile to the Soviets for years. The mere existence of the large Chinese army forced the Soviets to deploy about a quarter of their ground and tactical air forces to remote areas of Asia, where they cost a great deal more to maintain than in the Western Soviet Union. The US rapprochement with China made the Soviets even more aware of what might strike them if their forces were held down in a protracted European war. No one could force the Chinese into such a war. However, the presence of a powerful US Pacific Fleet would certainly suggest that Chinese involvement could not be ruled out – the US fleet could provide a Chinese attack force with the support it needed. By executing some particular strikes, the US Pacific Fleet could strongly suggest that just such an offensive was imminent. At the very least, the Soviets would find it difficult to transfer anything out of the Far East to fight in Europe.

The US Navy fought hard for this approach to war. When the Soviet Union collapsed the issue was still contentious. Looking back at 1914, we can and should ask whether something more like the Maritime Strategy would have been a better way for the United Kingdom to have prosecuted the war. It might not have been better, in the short run, for the French – but in 1914 Herbert Asquith was Prime Minister of the United Kingdom, not of some Anglo-French conglomerate. Ultimately seapower is about national goals and national sovereignty, because deployed ships are not tied to particular foreign territory the way deployed armies are. For an army, deployment usually entails an agreement with a host country, which has its own interests. Withdrawal of that army also requires agreement. Ships come and go as their navy pleases.

Would the Maritime Strategy have kept the Soviets at bay? No one knew, but the US Navy pointed out that the strategy embodied a valuable deterrent. It reminded the Soviets that even if their army reached the Channel, the war would not be over. Their vast empire was filled with hostile, unstable populations, many of them accessible around the periphery of the Soviet Union. Ultimately the US Navy's argument was that a better analogy to a big European war against the Soviets might well be 1940 rather than 1914. Disaster on land would be bad but not fatal. Disaster at sea would have been fatal.

After 1918 every major navy studied the First World War, just as all of them had studied the Russo-Japanese War a few years earlier. It was not that any of them imagined it would refight Jutland, but rather that it was the first test of so much new technology, working in combination rather than (as in exercises) in isolation. There were enough surprises to keep all the major navies busy over the next twenty years. Jutland showed what it took to control a massive all-arms fleet spread out well beyond the vision of its commander. Jellicoe's experience showed that even a primitive plot offered enough situational awareness to dominate the battle. That Scheer spent the battle trying to extricate himself meant that he knew that he had lost. In retrospect it seems clear that with better British shells (and better magazine practices) – with what the British had well before the end of the war – the battle would have been a rout. The British and their Allies – the Americans, the French, the Italians and the Japanese – all learned how to use plotting to give a fleet commander a view of a battle spread out far beyond his eyes.[4] Plotting was also key to combining different arms. It finally made night action something more than a mad scramble, although it still had serious limits. It made Matapan and Savo Island possible; the US disasters in the Solomons demonstrated its limits. Only the Germans seem not to have understood this lesson. Did their post-war mythology, which transformed Jutland from bare survival into triumph, preclude questions about their lack of situational awareness?

Many in the Royal Navy saw the disappointing outcome of Jutland as a demonstration that their service had throttled aggressiveness and initiative. It seems arguable that the requirements imposed by the sheer size of the Grand Fleet were much more to blame, but certainly the post-war Royal Navy emphasised the need to be individually aggressive and always to take the initiative. With fleet forces much smaller in 1939 than in 1914 (not least because the battle fleet was always split between Home and Mediterranean Fleets), there was much less need for the rigidity imposed by the Grand Fleet Battle Orders. Incidentally, if sheer mass was the deciding factor in whether or not ships should adhere rigidly to rules, it should be no surprise that the much less numerous wartime Battlecruiser Fleet (or Force) had much more flexible instructions. Individual initiative and aggressiveness certainly stood the Royal Navy in excellent stead in the next war. The inter-war US Navy, which maintained a single massive battle fleet, seems to have operated more like the First World War Royal Navy. That had all sorts of implications for centralised command and control, which were naturally opposed to individual initiative.

The war in the North Sea demonstrated what should have been (but was not) obvious before the war: it was nearly impossible for two fleets to find each other in even a fairly narrow sea. The war revealed two solutions of this ocean surveillance problem: code-breaking and aerial reconnaissance, rigid airships such as Zeppelins having proven themselves. Another possibility was submarine reconnaissance of the enemy's bases, although that gave little information as to where the enemy was going beyond port. This surveillance problem received little public notice after the war, but navies understood it. British allies also gained insight into the kind of operational control the wartime Admiralty had exercised and some of them created equivalents. The Italian Supermarina is a clear case in point.

Jutland did not really show that long-range hits would penetrate armour decks and destroy ships, but that message – initially a means of avoiding the real explanation – was widely accepted. It was one reason post-war capital ship designs generally featured heavy deck armour. The US and Imperial Japanese Navies in particular understood that long-range fire really could be devastating and between wars they worked hard to achieve it. The Royal Navy, which had created the idea that long-range fire was a new and terrible threat, did not develop it for much of the inter-war period, so that by the early 1930s one of its major tactical problems was how to close with a Japanese battle line which grossly outranged its own. The British (and the US Navy) were unaware that the Japanese had learned another wartime lesson, that a speed edge over the enemy was well worthwhile. During the inter-war period the Japanese spent a fortune rebuilding their battleships with, among other things, considerably higher speed. However, it was the British *Warspite* which made the longest-range hit in battleship history, in 1940.

The Royal Australian Navy modified *Grimsby* class sloop *Warrego* was a product of the post London Naval Treaty programme. In place of the single 4in anti-aircraft gun of the past *Grimsby* was armed with two 4.7in guns: destroyer weapons considered effective against armed merchant cruisers and surfaced submarines. These ships could be fitted with Asdic (sonar) and depth-charge throwers could replace their sweep winch. *Warrego* was one of the second pair of Australian ships, which had a twin 4in high-angle gun forward in place of the single 4.7in and a single 4in high-angle gun aft (in wartime it was replaced by a twin mounting). The change in weapons responded to the threat of air attack against convoys, even before the confrontation with Italy over Ethiopia. *Warrego* is shown in 1949, with a 40mm Bofors gun in place of the pre-war 12pdr in 'B' position and with a combination of British (Type 285 gunnery) and US (SC air-search) radars. This design was the basis of the very successful wartime sloops. (Allan C Green via State Library of Victoria)

Before 1914 the Royal Navy well understood that seapower was much more than battleships, or even a post-battleship main fleet. The German official history commented that in 1914 the Royal Navy exploited the full spectrum of seapower while the Germans were fixated on a major surface battle. This broader outlook shaped the post-war Royal Navy. For example, the Royal Navy spent less on battleship modernisation than the other major navies – but a lot more on vital areas such as anti-submarine warfare, mine countermeasures and other forms of trade protection. The great wartime gap in British naval capability was in anti-aircraft capacity, but other navies did not do much better and the Royal Navy certainly invested heavily in this area between wars. In 1939 major British warships were far more heavily armed with anti-aircraft guns than their foreign counterparts. The work it financed and the experience it accumulated between wars, made it possible for the Royal Navy to maintain free use of the sea – to survive – when Britain stood alone against Hitler in 1940. Certainly more could have been done – but no other navy did anything remotely like what the Royal Navy did, despite the financial problems of the 1930s.

Every navy realised that aircraft were an important new element of seapower. The British were so aware of its importance that at the Washington Conference in 1921 they fought successfully for a large tonnage allowance for what were then experimental aircraft carriers. Without that allowance, neither the US Navy nor the Imperial Japanese Navy would have had the substantial naval air arms each had in 1941. An understanding of the potential of air power at sea also shows in the clause of the Washington Naval Treaty which allowed each power to convert capital ships into carriers. That is often considered nothing more than an economy measure, but it is difficult to see how much money was saved by converting enormous battlecruisers, which were less than half built in the US and Japanese cases, into the largest warships in the world, let alone the cost of operating them later on. Without the ships, with their large capacity, neither navy would have invested enough in aircraft development to field the forces which contested the Pacific in 1942. Proof may be found in the far less impressive aircraft the French navy fielded on its single less capable carrier.

The Royal Navy maintained a large carrier force despite straitened post-1918 finances. Its carrier force suffered badly in two ways. First, because it had built a substantial carrier force before other navies (and before much experience had been accumulated), the Royal Navy's total carrier capacity was smaller than that of the US and Japanese fleets. Second was the effect of transferring naval aircraft to the Royal Air Force in 1918 – a move the Admiralty stoutly resisted, but could not reverse until 1939. Quite aside from the strong RAF preference for land-based strategic bombing over tactical (including naval) aviation, the shift to the RAF prevented the Royal Navy from building up a corps of senior naval aviators who could have provided it with a deep understanding of the potential of and requirement for fleet aviation. The Admiralty certainly remained air-minded: in 1939 the Royal Navy had a much larger carrier-building programme than any other.[5]

After the First World War both the Royal Navy and the US Navy considered Japan the most likely future enemy. Both sought to apply the lessons of the naval war just fought. When Admiral Jellicoe toured the empire in 1919 to develop a new strategy, he

envisaged a new version of what Ballard had conceived in 1907: a fleet with an unreachable base supporting a distant blockade. As in 1907, he imagined that the enemy would find the fleet's presence intolerable, so he would come out to fight. Once the enemy fleet had been destroyed, the blockade could tighten. In this case, the base was Singapore. The assumptions were reasonable until the Japanese occupied French Indo-China in 1941 and gained effective control of Thailand. The geography was not nearly as favourable as in 1907, because although the British could block trade from the south and the west, they could not easily block it from the east (the United States and South America).

The British could not base a fleet at Singapore in peacetime. It lacked industrial infrastructure, as well as facilities for crews to enjoy when ships were in port. The British war plan called for the Mediterranean Fleet to proceed to Singapore to face the Japanese. While that was going on, they needed some way to hold off the Japanese, who might be planning to invade British Empire territory. For that, the British initially looked back at another wartime experience. In 1914 it took enormous forces to track down a few German raiders, such as the famous *Emden*. In 1920 Rear Admiral Frederic C Dreyer, Jellicoe's assistant on his Empire tour, suggested that a few big British cruisers infesting Japanese trade routes might attract enough attention to paralyse the Japanese until the main fleet turned up.[6] Later the delaying role was largely transferred to large submarines based in the Far East (they were transferred to European waters once war broke out in 1939). The surface-ship idea raised in 1920 was echoed in 1941, when Winston Churchill, who had experienced the *Emden* and other chases in 1914 as First Lord, sent the *Prince of Wales* and *Repulse* to the Far East. It was their misfortune that formation commander Rear Admiral Tom Philips decided to disrupt the Japanese landings in Malaya and thus placed himself squarely within the area Japanese naval air reconnaissance was covering.

To the US Navy, at first the right analogy for war against Japan was the U-boat war which had so badly damaged the British. Japan depended far more than Britain on overseas supply. However, the US Navy also looked to its own wartime experience: a German-style submarine war might well bring neutrals into the war on the wrong side. The fear was that US submarines would be sinking British merchant ships. Few in the United States seem to have realised that to the British Japan was also the most likely enemy. Only after the Second World War broke out did the political (and strategic) situation change to make unrestricted submarine warfare a viable proposition again. Meanwhile, the lesson seemed to be that Japanese trade must be choked by a British-style surface blockade. To make that work, the US Navy had to neutralise the Japanese battle fleet and to seize islands near Japan from which a blockade could be mounted. That was the content of War Plan Orange. It began with alternative ways to bring the US battle fleet into position to fight a decisive battle, the basic requirement before the blockade could be imposed (Japanese war planning concentrated on the decisive battle). By the late 1920s there were questions as to whether a blockade would be enough. The 1929 version of War Plan Orange included basing bombers on the seized islands to burn down Japanese cities. Does that sound familiar?

Then there was the Allied blockade itself. How effective had it been? After the war it was credited with having brought down the Germans. The official British blockade history (completed in 1937, but not published until after the Second World War) argued that the key damage had been to German society, in effect exacerbating the tensions which had brought on the war in the first place. To the Germans, the blockade was a convenient explanation for collapse, as it did not place the blame on the army general staff and therefore on the ruling Establishment. Hitler often cited the 'hunger blockade' both as an example of Allied inhumanity and as an explanation for the need to conquer the East. To many on the Allied side, the success of the blockade suggested that there had been an alternative to the horror of the Western Front, which is surely the enduring image of the First World War.

It is not clear how the post-war Germans read the experience of naval war in 1914–18. Until 1933 their navy was too constricted by the Versailles Treaty to have much potential at all, even when it built the unconventional 'pocket battleships'. Initially the Germans seem to have assumed that in any future war they would be limited to classic cruiser warfare against trade. It seems significant in retrospect that the official history of the cruiser trade war was written by Captain Erich Raeder, who soon became navy chief.

The Germans did manage to evade the Versailles Treaty prohibition of continued submarine development, but it was one thing to build secret prototypes for foreign navies and another to decide the proper balance between surface and underwater forces. Hitler's rise to power removed the restrictions, but it also imposed the sort of personal rule the Kaiser had enjoyed. Hitler certainly had not spent his years working for power learning about naval strategy or pondering the naval lessons of the First World War. His approach was probably influenced most powerfully by Tirpitz's effective pre-1914 navalist propaganda, particularly his emphasis on capital ships. Thus the great bulk of German pre-1939 naval resources were spent on exactly the sort of heavy ships which bought nothing in 1914–18. The German naval staff did develop a more sophisticated idea of how they might be used, for blue-water raiding, but there seems not to have been any serious attempt to convince Hitler to concentrate instead on building U-boats to attack British commerce. Only Hitler's U-boat commander, Admiral Dönitz, had spent his time thinking about how to counter the successful convoy strategy introduced in 1917. Once he had enough U-boats, in 1942–3, his wolf pack tactics worked – but only for a time. Allied countermeasures peaked not long after U-boat numbers in the Atlantic peaked. Had much larger numbers of U-boats been available earlier, the situation might have been rather different.

For the two big Mediterranean navies, neither Jutland nor the big U-boat war seemed to represent the future. In the 1920s both the French and the Italians looked to the short sharp fights in the North Sea and in the Adriatic. The French believed that the Italians would use their fast light forces to intercept vital French Mediterranean trade and they concentrated on building their own fast forces to deal with the Italians. Both navies recognised that their battle fleets were not worth heavy new investment. As in the North Sea, they would probably spend most of any future war deterring each other from coming out. The situation changed with the advent of fast battleships, beginning with the French *Dunkerque*s, which could work with the fast light forces (the French began building such ships not to deal with the Italians but with the Germans' 'pocket battleships').

A century later, the most striking tactical or technical feature of the First World War was the Royal Navy's very successful beginning of what we now call situational awareness warfare or network-centric warfare, in the way it used code-breaking for ocean surveillance and in Admiral Jellicoe's use of plotting. We use satellites, drones, computers and data links, but we are doing the same things and experience from the First World War can help show us what we need.

The greater naval lesson of the First World War is how using – or not using – the sea determined the outcome. Success at sea was certainly a necessary condition for Allied victory, but it seems that the war would have had a very different shape had the British, the pre-eminent seapower, used their power differently. In an age in which sea travel is so often a means of entertainment, it is easy to forget that the sea still carries almost everything *but* people. It is still the fastest way to move heavy ground forces. The vital geographic fact of the sea is that coasts are somehow closer to other coasts than they are to the interiors of countries and continents. The sea – and the fact that navies maintain good order at sea – is why globalisation – probably the single most important current reality and the basis of our prosperity – works.

Gallipoli was the beginning, not the end, of assaults on defended shores. Both the Royal Navy and the US Navy saw Gallipoli as a demonstration that a properly-prepared landing would probably succeed. The British concluded that given the sheer length of the European shore, defences could not be everywhere: surely the mobility of seapower could be exploited to attack somewhere only lightly defended. Hence the enormous importance of the deception operation to limit German defences at the chosen beaches in Normandy. The US Marines had to seize small islands; they could not hope to evade defences. In this sense their Second World War II operations were very much analogous to those mounted at Gallipoli. Here US Marines land in the Marshalls in 1944. The boats are 50ft LCMs designed to carry troops and vehicles; '937' on the left is an LCT, a larger landing craft intended to land medium tanks. One of the big differences from Gallipoli was the tanks visible here, which could advance despite machine-gun fire. Another was the conscious decision to limit the size of the landing craft (and to increase their numbers) so that it was impossible for the defenders to overwhelm them using concentrated fire.

Notes

Introduction

1. After the First World War, Admiralty and fleet papers were collected to form the basis for the official history. They form the ADM 137 series (about 5000 entries) in the Public Record Office (The National Archive of the UK), most but not all of which are British official documents. A few are German and even fewer are Austrian, often in the original language. Most of the British official histories, for example of minesweeping, are in the ADM 186 series (formerly Confidential Books); it also includes many handbooks of various types. Other First World War records are in the ADM 1 (Admiralty dockets) and ADM 116 (Admiralty cases, meaning collected papers) series and a few are outside these series. Other papers are held by the Naval Historical Branch in Portsmouth and the Covers in the National Maritime Museum Brass Foundry out-station at Woolwich Arsenal include many documents referring to policy decisions. In some cases US papers in the National Archives include important British material.

2. The ADM 167 series. Pre-1917 books exist, but they are useless except as rosters of the Board.

3. When Arthur J Marder, the pre-eminent historian of the First World War Royal Navy, arrived in London to begin research on what became his history of the pre-war Royal Navy, *The Anatomy of British Seapower*, the Admiralty still retained all of its historical files and only those from 1885 and before had been opened under the existing fifty-year rule (later relaxed to thirty years and recently to twenty). Marder's considerable achievement was to convince the Admiralty Librarian to allow him access to documents, apparently mainly Admiralty printed papers, as recent as 1904. He did not realise that access had been strictly controlled. The relevant file (ADM 176/207 – an Admiralty case held outside the usual ADM 116 series) was released a few years ago. In November 1935 Marder's request for access to post-1885 papers was rejected altogether on the ground that the Admiralty would reap no special advantage by releasing them to him. Marder later provided a list of specific subjects. In September 1938 he was specifically denied access to his Subjects 4 (commerce protection in the event of war), 10 (naval aspects of the Anglo-Japanese Alliance of 1902), 14 (naval war plans, particularly blockade policy, against France and Russia) and 21 (Admiralty concern over the Balearics – Port Mahon), the implication being that more than forty years later the Admiralty still considered them sensitive. The Anglo-Japanese issue was clearly sensitive because the Admiralty considered Japan the likeliest enemy and the Balearics figured in the ongoing Spanish Civil War. Trade protection was interesting both because so many writers (wrongly) assumed that the Admiralty had not been interested in it and because the cost of the cruisers needed for trade protection was a driving force in Admiralty and therefore British government policy around and after the turn of the twentieth century, probably even the reason for the alliance with Japan. Because he was denied access to the mass of papers on the subject (now mostly at the Naval Historical Branch), Marder accepted published and personal claims that the Admiralty had neglected trade protection in the decades before 1914, which was emphatically not the case. The blockade aspect of naval war plans was also sensitive, because it involved the changing role of underwater weapons, as understood at the turn of the twentieth century. The Admiralty put Marder off by citing the sheer volume of papers that would have to be sifted in order to meet his requirements. Later in 1938 the Admiralty Librarian was specifically told not to show Marder any papers concerning policy (few now seem to remain). They included the First Sea Lord's Minute of 15 June 1892 (not reproduced in the file), which presumably referred to the effort to build support for the 1893 supplement to the 1889 Naval Defence Act. In reviewing Marder's manuscript in 1940, the Admiralty was particularly anxious that Marder *not* write that he had had access to most of the relevant papers for 1885–1905. What is interesting in this story is just what the Admiralty considered sensitive.

4. Marder relied heavily on papers left by many key officers (and reminiscences) as a substitute for closed official papers. His references to Admiralty manuscripts are often to the answers generated to specific questions by the staff of the Naval Historical Branch. Because no one on that staff had already done extensive research on the topics which interested Marder, no one could have suggested further questions, even had they been allowed to do so (apparently they were not so encouraged).

5. *Krieg zur See* is very nearly without footnotes and there is no way to be sure that its representations of either pre-war plans or wartime thinking are unbiased and accurate. It was published as German nationalism (ultimately Nazism) grew and some of its assessments may well have been shaped to make wartime naval leaders with preferred post-war politics look aggressive and therefore attractive. Thus the account of Jutland is used to justify Tirpitz' policies and Scheer is clearly the only heroic High Seas Fleet commander. The seven North Sea volumes provide an excruciatingly detailed account of all (even minor) naval operations in the North Sea, in most cases correlating German records with the initial volumes of the British official history. The full series amounts to seven North Sea (Nordsee) volumes (six of them translated by the Admiralty, carrying the story to the spring of 1917), three Baltic volumes (of which the two translated by the Admiralty complete the story only to 1915; the third volume carries the story to the end of the war), three cruiser warfare volumes (the first written in 1928 by Captain Erich Raeder, the future Kriegsmarine commander-in-chief), two volumes on the war in Turkish waters (the first on the Mediterranean Division, the second on the

Dardanelles and related matters), one volume on the East Asian cruiser squadron (commanded by Graf Spee), one volume on the war in the German colonies (in two parts), five volumes on the U-boat war against trade (of which Volumes 4 and 5, which covered 1917–18, were not published until after the Second World War) and a volume on wartime surface warships. This combination is far more massive than the unclassified British official history, but to some extent it combines the roles of published official history and staff history. It also incorporates considerable editorial comment on command decisions and on tactics. I have used the translations of volumes of *Krieg zur See* produced by the Admiralty (except as noted, page number references are to those volumes, not to the German originals). These volumes are held by NHB and most of the translations were published in the inter-war issues of the navy's *Monthly Intelligence Report* held by NHB and, except for a few years, PRO. Other navies also translated the German history; the US Navy Library holds the Italian versions of some volumes, as well as some English translations produced by ONI. The final volumes of the North Sea, Baltic and U-boat series were not published until the 1960s and therefore they were not translated by the Admiralty (reportedly copies published during the Second World War were not distributed and were mostly destroyed). The US Navy Library holds the final North Sea and Baltic volumes, but not the two final U-boat volumes.

Chapter 1. A Maritime War

1. For an excellent account of the interaction between banks, customer and ship designers, see David Topliss, 'The Brazilian Dreadnoughts 1904–1914' in *Warship International* No 3 (1988). Dr Topliss took his degree in history after studying economics. At the time of his early death, Dr Topliss, who was then in charge of the Brass Foundry, was working on a book about the warship export market, the 1988 article being his main legacy.

2. For this writer, the great symbol of small government is to be found in surviving films of Britain during the 1914 crisis: the Prime Minister arrives at a meeting *in a taxi* (he is seen paying the driver).

3. As an example of the way capital markets think, about 2000 the author participated in a US Navy-sponsored discussion of globalisation and its consequences. Someone thought to ask a major Wall Street firm about its vision of the future, including the prospect of various wars. After all, Wall Street put its money where its mouth was – as the City did before (and after) 1914. The view on Wall Street was that the consequences of even a small war were so bad economically that war was nearly obsolete.

4. The best-known is Norman Angell's *The Great Illusion*, first published in the United Kingdom in November 1909 as *Europe's Optical Illusion* and then reprinted as *The Great Illusion* in 1910. By 1914 it had sold two million copies. The *Daily Mail* called it 'the most discussed book in years'. Angell later said that he got the idea of the prohibitive financial consequences of war from *The Meaning of Money*, by Hatley Withers, the financial editor of *The Times*. Angell received the Nobel Peace Prize in 1933. In his book on First World War economic warfare, *Planning for Armageddon: British Economic Warfare and the First World War* (Harvard University Press, 2012), Nicholas A Lambert cites many other such prophets. For example, in April 1910 secretary of the Liverpool Stock Exchange Edgar Crammond concluded that the catastrophic effect of war would guarantee the peace. The President of the Institute of Bankers (a director of the Bank of England) pointed out that unfortunately the decision for war does not rest with the mercantile community. This paper was brought to the attention of the Prime Minister and of the CID. Perhaps the earliest such book was Ivan Bloch's massive analysis of the changing character of war, initially published in French in 1898 as *La Guerre Future*. Bloch, a Polish banker and railway financier, was a Russian delegate to the 1899 Hague Peace Conference, where he met Admiral Fisher. Six months later an abridged version of his book appeared as *Is War Now Impossible?*, with a preface by W T Stead, the journalist who had worked with Fisher to put the Royal Navy's case for modernisation in 1884–5. Bloch's work, which predicted the sustained mass warfare of 1914–18, was widely read in Europe, but, as might be expected, it had no impact on European armies. Britain was anomalous, as its army was the weakest in Europe and had the least influence on government policy.

5. Lord Hankey, The *Supreme Command 1914-18* (London: George Allen & Unwin, 1961), I, p 136.

6. Lambert, *Planning for Armageddon*, argues that initially two of the six divisions earmarked for the British Expeditionary Force were kept home due to fear of instability, but it had also been argued that this was due to fear of invasion, the Territorials being untrained.

7. The only major departure from the navy's belief in blockade seems to have come during the short tenure of Admiral A K Wilson as First Sea Lord in 1910–11. Wilson argued that the Germans could use neutral ports to evade any blockade. That can be taken as a reference to an emerging Admiralty position that a wider economic attack, which would deny British ships to German cargoes, might well be effective.

8. Lambert, *Planning for Armageddon*, describes a drawn-out fight over the validity of the navy's statistics showing German vulnerability.

9. As understood by the British about 1911, Rotterdam was second only to Hamburg as a centre of German trade. About 20 per cent of their seaborne trade passed up the Rhine through Rotterdam, including two-thirds of iron ore imports and half of imported grain. No other neutral port had the necessary infrastructure. The Admiralty argued that Rotterdam and Antwerp were so tightly integrated into the German economy that they should be considered German ports. Admiral Bethell told the CID subcommittee in 1911 that the Admiralty would grasp the slightest pretext to close these ports to transoceanic traffic. By this time the War Office (army) understood that the Germans would almost certainly attack France through Belgium, leaving only Rotterdam. The Admiralty would have liked to blockade Rotterdam at the outset of a war, but the Foreign Office argued successfully that it was in British interest to keep Holland neutral. That was so much the case that the British found themselves running convoys between Holland and England in 1916.

10. Fisher's insistence that war plans were secret was tied up to some extent with both his assumption of operational (rather than strategic) control as First Sea Lord using W/T and also his feud with Admiral Charles Beresford. When Beresford became C-in-C Channel Fleet, Fisher provided him with war orders but not with war plans. Beresford protested that he needed something more in order to train his force; Fisher replied that he would find out what he needed to know when he needed it. British war planning documents for fleet commanders exist prior to 1906 and after 1912, but the only documents produced between those dates were Fisher's elaborate printed version of alternatives. There is some question as to how seriously most of them should be taken, as they were partly a means of beating back Beresford and his supporters.

11. Austria-Hungary provides perhaps the most painful case in point. In 1913 the Austrians discovered that their chief war planner, Colonel Redl, had been a Russian spy for years. Even though they knew that the Russians had their war plan, they could not change it quickly enough to have any alternative available in 1914. Replanning railway movements was just too complex.

12. Churchill's comments on proposed British army deployments (he wanted the army to deploy to Belgium so that it would be on the Germans' flanks) survive as ADM 116/3474, '1911-Crisis: Miscellaneous Memoranda and Correspondence Between Cabinet Ministers'. These documents show, incidentally, that as of 1911 the British were aware that the Germans were likely to deploy through Belgium; General Wilson thought that would force the British to declare war.

13. Roy Jenkins, *Churchill* (London: Macmillan, 2001) writes that Asquith came to realise that Churchill was not well suited to the Home Office. The incidents were the 'battle of Sidney Street' after a serious outbreak at Tonypandy in the Rhondda, both being followed by over-enthusiastic reaction to a Merseyside strike. Jenkins wrote that many regarded Churchill as too trigger-happy after Sidney Street, but that Tonypandy unfairly caused intense resentment in the Labour Party, affecting events in 1940. When offered promotion in February 1910, Churchill had asked for either the Admiralty or the Home Office, in that order, and was given the Home Office at an unusually young age.

14. A J P Taylor, *The Struggle for Mastery in Europe 1848–1918* (Oxford University Press, 1954), p 67, points out the particular hostility of the Junkers in eastern Prussia – the basis of the Prussian army officer corps and of much of its administration – to German nationalism, meaning to the idea that Germany was defined by a popular movement, rather than from above by the Kaiser.

15. V R Berghahn, *Germany and the Approach of War* (New York: St Martin's Press, second edition, 1993), p 22. Bismarck relied on assumed powers during the 'gap' after the diet was dissolved, the idea being that he would seek retroactive approval for spending.

16. Berghahn, *Germany and the Approach of War*, p 27, cites a 1907 German General Staff study on 'fighting in insurgent towns' and studies by some local commanders of how they would deal with insurgency, including plans to arrest Reichstag deputies and others considered subversive. Prussia (and later the Empire) had an 1851 State of Siege Act under which local military commanders were empowered to take over in the event of internal disorder as well as war. They and their superiors were empowered to decide when such intervention was appropriate. If a state of siege were announced, all civil liberties would be suspended, censorship enforced and all of those considered subversive arrested.

17. For an account of this 'Zabern affair' see Jack Beatty, *The Lost History of 1914: How the Great War Was Not Inevitable* (London: Bloomsbury, 2012), pp 20–36. In this case the lost possibility was that, had the Reichstag pushed further, for example rejecting that year's budget, the Kaiser and the General Staff might well have resorted to the often-discussed *Staatstreich*. In that case there would have been no point in triggering a war to win over German voters.

18. This point is repeatedly made by Berghahn in his *Germany and the Approach of War in 1914*. There was considerable sentiment in the army and its general staff for a pre-emptive war against France in 1905–6, on the ground that defeat in the Russo-Japanese War and the subsequent 1905 revolution had so weakened the Russians that they could not effectively support the French. To that end the 1905–6 crisis in Morocco was precipitated specifically to induce the French to declare war; but with British support the French managed to avoid this trap.

19. Fritz Fischer, *War of Illusions: German Policies from 1911 to 1914* (New York: Norton, 1975), p 463, as seen by Dr Wilhelm Muelon, a member of the Krupp board. Fischer cites a number of German claims that the war was preventive, that the Entente planned to attack at some point in the next two years. That having been disproven, Fischer explores other possible German motives. However, if the point of prevention was

internal German politics, the claims of preventive war make sense.

20. Even in 1870, the Germans almost found themselves fighting a drawn-out war when the Commune in Paris refused to comply with the surrender of the French field army. The Germans had to besiege Paris. Their task was simplified in that the Paris Commune was trying to promote a revolution against the French state which had surrendered, hence was also opposed by the post-surrender French army (with results which embittered post-1870 French politics).

21. The reader may object that in 1940, fighting a massive French army, the Germans did exactly that: they triumphed rapidly. Had the British not remained in the war, it would have been over in June 1940. The difference was that in 1914 the Germans could not move fast enough to envelop the French army, which was moving on interior lines. Nor did they have the command and control advantages which made it possible for them to outpace French command and control decisively in 1940.

22. ADM 116/3474, note by Director of Military Operations General Henry Wilson, who had presented the army's war plan at the 1911 meeting.

23. Berghahn, *Germany and the Approach of War*, p 38, describes the domestic factors involved, assuming that they were responsible. He points out that the big industrialists were particularly receptive because in 1895–6 they were just recovering from a world depression which had begun in 1873 and they did not want to suffer similarly again. Tirpitz' guaranteed future building programme was extremely attractive to them. Krupp founded and financed the German Navy League. Berghahn cites numerous comments by Tirpitz explaining how his projected fleet could defeat the Royal Navy and thus be a threat which could force the British to offer Germany 'fair treatment' (as opposed to high tariffs). However, these papers were for the Kaiser, who was disposed to dislike the British. '

24. Patrick J Kelly, *Tirpitz and the Imperial German Navy* (Bloomington: Indiana State University, 2011), pp 108–10. The document was initially issued on 28 November 1895. Tirpitz was then asked officially to comment on it.

25. Kelly, *Tirpitz and the Imperial German Navy*, pp 131–2.

26. For this campaign, see Ruddock F Mackay, *Fisher of Kilverstone* (Oxford: Clarendon Press, 1973), pp 177–82.

27. Translated versions are in the Admiralty *Monthly Intelligence Report*, in PRO and in NHB, beginning with No. 12, 15 April 1920. The series begins in August 1914.

28. As described in a letter from a US Navy officer assigned to the Allied Control Commission, copy in OpNav Undersea Warfare Division records.

29. Translated extracts from 'Why the German Revolutionary Movement Emanated from the Fleet', in *Monthly Intelligence Review* No. 7, 15 November 1919, ADM 223/807.

30. After the war Admiral von Hollweg described the cruise as grossly irresponsible in a review of Admiral Scheer's memoirs translated for *Monthly Intelligence Reports* in 1919.

31. In 1964, discussing whether to fight North Vietnam after a Viet Cong attack on some Americans in South Vietnam, a US official remarked that crises were like trolley cars; if you missed one, another would soon come along (this particular one was missed). It is difficult not to see 1914 in a similar light.

32. In 1870 Prussian Chancellor Bismarck manoeuvred French Emperor Napoleon III into declaring war on him, so that in theory he was the offended party, even though it is generally accepted that he was also the architect of that war.

33. In particular the French lacked heavy artillery, although in their '75' they had an excellent rapid-fire medium gun.

34. The French Foreign Ministry was reading German diplomatic codes at this time and the British had sufficient contacts in Constantinople for their Foreign Office to be aware of the developing German intrigue with the Turks. Neither considered this information relevant to naval operations, so it was never communicated to the navies. A French researcher at their Higher Naval School discovered this lost opportunity in the 1920s. The lesson, which seems to have been learned both in the United Kingdom and in France, was that naval staffs should receive diplomatic information as well as purely naval data, such as ship positions. In the British case, the wartime naval code-breakers handled diplomatic as well as naval traffic and later code-breaking was handled on an all-service (including diplomatic) basis. I am grateful to Alexandre Sheldon-Dupleix, of the naval staff of the *Service Historique de Défense*, for this insight.

35. Sean McMeekin, *The Russian Origins of the First World War* (Cambridge: Harvard University Press [Belknap], 2011), pp 25–9.

36. Sean McMeekin, *The Berlin-Baghdad Express: The Ottoman Empire and German's Bid for World Power* (Cambridge, Mass.: Harvard University Press, 2010)

37. The Turkish Caliph was, at least in theory, the spiritual chief of all Sunni Muslims. In 1914 the British Empire had more Muslim subjects than any other country.

38. The context was a proposal, mooted during a Cabinet inquiry into the army budget, that the army be reshaped as a small expeditionary force to be deployed by the navy. The army certainly became interested in expeditionary operations, but on a much larger scale.

39. Fisher's friend and biographer Admiral R H Bacon described a crucial 18 November 1909 CID meeting. In the course of a crisis over Morocco, the French government had demanded that the British deploy 120,000 troops to the French border to deter the

Germans. Fisher confirmed that he could provide the necessary transport. When pressed for further comment, he said that he had 'nothing else to say that anyone present would want to hear'. When Prime Minister Asquith pressed him, he said that the Germans would stop at nothing to destroy that force and would do so, 'Continental armies being what they are'. The army should be restricted to sudden descents on the coast, the recovery of Heligoland and the garrisoning of Antwerp. Fisher then pointed to the ten mile stretch on the Pomeranian coast near Berlin. Were the army to seize and entrench there, a million Germans would find occupation; 'but to despatch British troops to the front in a Continental war would be an act of suicidal idiocy arising from the distorted view of war produced by Mr. Haldane's speeches and childish arrangements for training Terriers [the Territorial Army]. After war broke out . . . the British Army should be administered as an annex to the Navy and that the present follies should be abandoned'. Asquith adjourned the meeting but presumably remembered Fisher's comment. Admiral Sir R H Bacon, *The Life of Lord Fisher of Kilverstone* (London: Hodder and Stoughton, 1929), II, pp 182–3.

40. The British were aware of German thinking. In commenting for Winston Churchill on a note by *Times* military correspondent C A Repington, DNI Captain G A Ballard wrote on 20 April 1912 that 'there is evidence to show that it is quite possible that it is the intention of the Germans to act at first on the defensive, in the hope that we shall expose our ships in close blockading operations which will afford them opportunities for torpedo attacks, until they can reduce us to something approaching equality. Their elaborate and expensive system of coast defence is a fairly clear indication of the ideas which find acceptance in responsible quarters, mistaken though they may be. And even their latest destroyers are of small displacement and radius of action as compared to our own and correspondingly less fitted for offensive operations'. Repington had correctly guessed British policy as to close or open blockade; 'it is of the utmost importance not to let our general policy as regards blockade become generally known, or even known outside the War Staff'. Repington had asked the 'assistance' of Naval Opinion; in Ballard's view it was appropriate that 'a knowledge of Admiralty policy on the major points of the subject is confined to a very few officers within the Admiralty and to a small number of selected Admirals'. *Churchill* Companion Pt 3, 1534-1535 (Repington's paper is not reproduced).

41. Field Marshal Lord Roberts was the strongest advocate of this view. Randolph S Churchill, *Winston S. Churchill* II, Companion Pt 3 1911-1914 (London: Heinemann, 1969) includes several of Roberts' 1912 letters. In a 25 January 1912 letter (pp 1500–1) Roberts argued that the usual figure of a possible 70,000-man German attack was purely hypothetical, arising from his own statement that 70,000 was the least the Germans would use to invade the United Kingdom. He argued that the Germans would surely land many more men. He also argued that the projected six-division Expeditionary Force was ludicrously small in view of the size of Continental armies.

42. Thus a 12 August 1914 telegram from First Lord Winston Churchill to Jellicoe, warning him that the 'silence and inertia' of the High Seas Fleet (which really was silence and gross inertia) might indicate that a serious enterprise was afoot; Churchill enjoined Jellicoe to conduct cruiser sweeps to detect the Germans should they come out for a landing. A Temple Patterson (ed), *The Jellicoe Papers* Vol I (Navy Records Society, 1964), p 49.

43. Patterson (ed), *Jellicoe Papers*, I, pp 86–8, dated 12 November 1914. Churchill wrote that the shipping at Hamburg would suffice for a quarter of a million men, 'and there is no doubt that their shipping has been specially fitted with all appliances necessary for the transport and speedy embarkation of an army'.

44. Comment in the Admiralty's *Monthly Intelligence Review* when the translation of the German account of this operation was published.

45. This may have been the first British wartime use of signals intelligence. According to *Krieg zur See*, Nordsee 2, during the morning of 31 August call-signs were intercepted which indicated that the battleships *Pommern* and *Brauenschweig* were at sea, hence that evacuation had to be hurried. This turned out to be a false alarm.

46. According to *Krieg zur See*, Nordsee 2, on 16 September the Admiralstab wired C-in-C High Seas Fleet that the British were transporting a large force to Ostend and that it was of the utmost importance to the army to hinder this operation; a submarine should be ordered to attack 'in spite of difficult conditions of navigation'. Commander Southern Force (RN) was aware of this threat and he planned a destroyer screen to operate with the armoured cruisers on patrol (*Aboukir*, *Hogue* and *Cressy*) to cover the transports. Initially that was impossible due to the short steep sea set by a gale, which it was thought would also make submarine operation impossible. The cruisers had recently moved position and there was reason to think that the enemy would be concentrating further north. Admiral Tyrwhitt soon took a destroyer force to sea. Three U-boats were deployed, of which *U 9* (Lieutenant Commander Otto Weddigen) managed to get to her patrol area despite the weather. When the wind died down he found himself within close range of the cruisers, which he sank. The destroyers were still in port due to the gale just ended. This was not quite the example of mindless ignorance of the submarine threat which is often described; it was more an unlucky example of underestimation of the submarine's ability to ride out weather which would keep a destroyer in port. According to the German account, *U 9* did not have an easy time. Violent motion knocked out her gyro-compass, forcing her commander to fall back on navigating by soundings and then landfalls (the compass was restarted and recovered as the boat was able to steam with the sea). Even then the weather was bad: lying on the bottom in 13½ fathoms (81ft) she still felt the motion of the sea and had to surface and come into the wind, fighting the sea and exhausting the crew. She first saw ships when it was still dark, with Force 5 winds; she had to dive when they were within 1000 yds. She then proceeded at 8 fathom depth, apparently not using her periscope, until dawn. When she then surfaced, the cruisers were in sight (they were probably the ships seen the night

before) and *U 9* attacked them in sequence. She fired five torpedoes:. First she fired one bow tube at one of the cruisers, then (35 minutes later) both bow tubes (having reloaded No. 2) at a second, then both stern tubes (25 minutes later) at the third (torpedoes set to turn 180°). Having used up his torpedoes, Weddigen had none left for any transports he might find, so he turned for home. For the British the main impact of Weddigen's attack was that slow heavy ships should no longer be employed in the North Sea and the Channel.

47. *Krieg zur See*, Nordsee 2 makes this point strongly: the Grand Fleet moved south in response to the threat to the transports, but no one at the top of the Imperial Navy seems to have understood what that could mean. The German history argues that this did *not* indicate a lack of will to fight under favourable conditions on the part of either the Fleet Commander (von Ingenohl) or the Admiralstab itself. It states that, under the influence of Chief of the Naval Cabinet Admiral von Müller Admiralstab chief Admiral von Pohl (who would replace von Ingenohl) adhered to the Chancellor's view that the fleet had to be preserved as a bargaining chip at the end of the war.

48. This idea died when the German General Staff refused to dilute its planned attack on France sufficiently to provide the forces for Denmark.

49. According to *Krieg zur See*, Nordsee 1, the root idea of all German naval war planning before the war was an attack by the British, with Germany on the defensive. That caused difficulties, because as the 1914 crisis deepened the navy was told that Germany might be fighting only France and Russia, with the British attitude uncertain. The Admiralstab concluded that even then forces had to be concentrated in the West, its chief task the protection of overseas shipping, which was essential to restore economic life from the destruction of a war on land. This is less than credible. The history quotes chief of the Admiralstab Admiral von Pohl, writing on 25 July: if Great Britain remained neutral, in spite of important duties in the North Sea, Russia should be finished off first. That makes sense; the Admiralstab argued that it would be essential to keep the British out of the war and to do that anything that would irritate the British should be avoided (Admiralty translation in NHB, p 20). Only in the Baltic could an appreciable success be achieved and insufficient forces there might lead to failure. At this time the planned concentration in the North Sea left only a weak force of older ships in the Baltic. Other senior naval officers disagreed with von Pohl. In theory the completion of the Kiel Canal made it possible to transfer ships quickly between the Baltic and the North Sea, but no large battleships had yet made this passage (with a reduced coal load, the *Kaiserin* made the passage on 25 July). According to *Krieg zur See*, once the British had mobilised their fleet, the proposed concentration in the Baltic had to be cancelled in favour of the earlier planned concentration of German ships in the North Sea, as nothing less would have been prudent. The German fleet adopted its planned war organisation.

50. For example, in 1912 the British naval attaché reported in May 1912 the Danes, who seemed well informed about German thinking, said that in wartime the British fleet would be concentrated off Norderney. Report in Backhouse Papers, NHB.

51. *Krieg zur See*, Nordsee 1, p 75 (Admiralty translation, NHB).

52. Kelly, *Tirpitz and the Imperial German Navy*, p 289 mentions a pamphlet published in the autumn of 1907 by retired Vice Admiral Carl Galster advocating a cruiser and U-boat programme (for commerce warfare and Kleinkrieg) instead of the Tirpitz battleship programme. He was willing to accept the need for a battle fleet, but considered that against an opponent as strong as England only Kleinkrieg was possible. Only the Socialists were interested and at this time they were in a distinct minority.

53. The great gap was ocean surveillance: without it, no kleinkrieg force could easily find and attack enemy warships. One of the major surprises of the British 1913 Manoeuvres was that there were none of the expected night destroyer attacks, because the destroyers never found any targets at night. Even a narrow sea can be quite wide. Before 1914 no one seems to have realised just how difficult – and how vital – ocean surveillance could be.

54. *Krieg zur See*, Nordsee 1, p 89.

55. *Krieg zur See*, Nordsee 1, p 90. The author argues that, had the Admiralstab looked clearly at the implications of distant blockade, it could have guessed British policy: (i) attack Germany economically by suppressing foreign trade and communication; (ii) protect troop transports; (iii) bring the German fleet to action if circumstances are favourable. The reference to the Heligoland Bight obsession is the German official author's. He assumes, incorrectly, that the British treated the possibility of invasion similarly. The author also points out that Tirpitz and his Navy Office had failed to build light cruisers and destroyers with sufficient range to break a distant blockade. A comment on the failure of the High Seas Fleet to take offensive action in the summer of 1914 (Nordsee 1, p 130) credits its destroyers with an endurance of two days and two nights; assuming a cruising speed of 15 knots and allowing 30 per cent of fuel for use in action, they could steam out only 250nm from their fleet base. The official history (p 92) quotes a January 1918 memo by Admiral von Ingenohl, High Seas Fleet commander in 1914: 'before the war the whole training of our Fleet, our tactics, manoeuvres and to some extent even our shipbuilding policy and even certain constructional details (for instance, the small radius of action of a large number of our destroyers) were based on the hypothesis that a decisive action would take place in, or very close to, the German Bight, on the assumption that the British would organise a near blockade of the German Bight with their superior Fleet, in order to cut off our overseas supplies and at the same time force our Fleet to take up the strictest defensive and to accept action. It is true that in the years immediately preceding the war there arose now and again doubts and hesitations prompted by sundry expressions of opinion in articles written by British experts; it was asked whether the enemy would still adhere to this procedure or if he would perhaps content himself with the blocking of the

Channel and the line Scotland-Norway. *However, these doubts were always dissipated by the observation that a blockade of that kind would never be recognised by Neutral States, the USA in particular* (italics in *Krieg zur See* translation)... even if the British did endeavour at first to get on without a blockade, they would soon find that they could neither cripple the activities of our Fleet, particularly of our minelayers, etc., nor cut off our overseas supplies without a near blockade of our North Sea coast. In our manoeuvres in May 1914, Vice Admiral Scheer, the Senior Officer of the side representing the enemy, wrote in his report that, in his opinion, British prestige would not permit of their foregoing the blockade or closer patrol of the German Bight'.

56. As quoted in *Krieg zur See*, Nordsee 1, from von Ingenohl's memo of January 1918, previously cited (but quoted in a later part of the book). The official report attached less importance to submarines. In the peacetime manoeuvre, U-boats were forced to show their periscopes frequently in order both to manoeuvre and to attack and particularly to avoid accidents. In wartime U-boat commanders would feel constrained to use their periscopes much less often. Moreover, ships would be alert, so they would more often evade torpedoes. Ships in manoeuvres also suffered from limitations on the speed and course of ships and escorts could remain closer than in peacetime exercises. It would be difficult for a U-boat to hit a ship and her escorts zig-zagging at high speed and it would be extremely difficult for a submarine to penetrate a screen unobserved to get into position to attack the main body.

57. *Krieg zur See*, Nordsee 1 frequently refers to destroyer screens against submarines, but it is not clear what weapons were envisaged. The descriptions of the two August 1914 sorties include the use of guns against submarines which briefly appeared, to little avail. *Krieg zur See* added that in 1914 nothing was known of anti-submarine weapons: depth charges (the Germans adopted the Austrian one in 1915), anti-submarine mines, nets and means of detecting submerged submarines.

58. According to *Krieg zur See*, Nordsee 1, German war diaries revealed that the movements of heavy ships were strongly influenced by fear of submarines. The German history claims much the same effect on British movements. The first report of a British submarine in the Heligoland Bight came a few hours after war broke out. Light cruisers on patrol were immediately withdrawn, the destroyer defence was reinforced and the Senior Officer of Scouting Forces was ordered to have the German (Heligoland) Bight swept by the Mine-Seeking Divisions using their sweep gear. Nothing came of these sweeps, but British submarines were certainly seen further offshore, beginning with one sighted by a fishing boat about 100nm WNW of Heligoland on 5 August. The light cruiser *Hela* was torpedoed on 13 September 1914 in an area the fleet had used for an exercise the previous day.

59. *Krieg zur See*, Nordsee 1, p 79. *Krieg zur See*, Nordsee 1, p 78 emphasises the difference between the order to keep the fleet home while executing kleinkrieg and the Admiralstab's insistence that kleinkrieg would be preparatory to fighting a fleet action on better terms. It criticises the staff for not laying sufficient emphasis on the basic principle of employing the fleet, particularly its heavy ships, more actively to even the odds. Given the political imperative to treat the battle fleet as a 'fleet in being', it was nearly impossible for any fleet commander to do otherwise. *Krieg zur See* generally ignores the fragmented character of the German command system, the Admiralstab being advisory only.

60. The German estimate of British intentions is given in *Krieg zur See*, Nordsee 1, pp 81–9.

61. *Krieg zur See*, Nordsee 1, p 123. The official history shows the claim the German General Staff wanted the transports spared so that the British troops could be dealt with on land is nonsense.

62. *Krieg zur See*, Nordsee I. Before the submarine operation failed, the fleet command thought that the transport of troops to France would occupy the British 2nd and 3rd Fleets and also some of the light forces of the 1st Fleet (Home Fleet), perhaps creating the desired opportunity to bring the Home Fleet to action on even terms. This idea was then abandoned because reports of enemy operations and intentions were clearly unreliable (Nordsee I, p 129).

63. *Krieg zur See*, Nordsee 1 argued that the scale of defence needlessly exhausted ships which should have been kept ready for a fleet sortie. On 5 August the defence comprised outer and inner picket lines, each held by one destroyer flotilla (twenty ships), radii being 35 and 25nm around Elbe Lightship I. Submarines operated between the two lines, at a radius of 29nm. One light cruiser was stationed behind each of the right and left flanks of the defence, with a third off Heligoland harbour. In addition, a cruiser and a flotilla were at instant readiness in the Weser and three flotillas were in the estuary. Inside the lines, the anti-submarine force was initially an additional destroyer flotilla, soon relieved by a minesweeping division (once the 3rd Minesweeping Division at Cuxhaven was ready. Until September, there was no mine defence, as it was thought that would hamper German forces in the expected decisive surface battle in this area. Given the strain picket duty imposed, the submarine line was almost immediately abandoned, most of the boats being released for offensive duty (some were retained in Heligoland, but were not to leave harbour until an enemy had been sighted).

64. *Krieg zur See* explains the smaller calibre of German cruiser guns on the basis of the fleet's preference for larger numbers; between 1909 and 1912 the fleet demanded that a light cruiser be able to repel a simultaneous night attack by two destroyers on each side. Meanwhile there was pressure to replace the 4.1in (10.5cm) gun with the 5.9in (15cm). In the summer of 1911 that was deferred to the summer of 1912, when it was adopted. The Germans also expected that in most cases battlecruisers would be backing their light cruisers, so that their lighter main batteries would be balanced by the much heavier ones of the battlecruisers. Similar considerations applied to torpedo boats (destroyers). In a day battle the destroyers would be covered by battleship and cruiser fire as they approached their targets; their own gun calibre would not be as important as the number of torpedoes. The navy rejected the greater displacement required to mount heavier guns on the ground that it would reduce handiness; it also argued that a larger boat would not be as effective during a night attack. *Krieg zur See* offers no rationale for the poorer speed of the German destroyers, but does comment that Heligoland in effect demonstrated that the single-purpose German destroyer, optimized for night and massed torpedo attacks, might be unable to survive a fight with British destroyers.

65. German hits on British destroyers were ineffective. At least two German HE shells failed to explode after passing through the bows and funnel of a British destroyer. *Krieg zur See* was quick to add that the British had even more such cases. That was not too surprising, as shells were fuzed to explode after penetrating thicker plating.

66. According to *Krieg zur See*, the problem was an inability to concentrate fire on one of several approaching destroyers. It claims that German adoption of electrical bearing indicators (Richtungsanlagen) for cruisers was inspired by this battle. They permitted a gunnery officer to bring all available guns automatically onto one target. Note that although the German phrase was often translated as director control, it was something simpler.

67. As described in *Krieg zur See*, Nordsee 2 (the history to November 1914). *Glory* was already near Halifax. Now three of her sisters were sent: *Albion* to Gibraltar, *Canopus* to Cape Verde and *Ocean* to Queenstown to replace *Illustrious*, which became guardship at the new Grand Fleet anchorage, Loch Ewe. Comments in *Krieg zur See* suggest that the Germans did not understand the key significance of coal stocks, as the similar measure taken in the Falklands is derided. The defence of coal stocks had been a key anti-raider measure in British thinking as early as the 1880s. Obviously there were many other stocks of steaming coal, but most of them were British-owned, hence could be denied to the Germans in neutral ports. A small raider could seize colliers and coal at sea, but that was impossible for even a small fleet of larger ships.

68. ADM 137/2708, pp 301ff (PD. 065).

69. The Japanese were promised the German Pacific islands, which became the League of Nations Mandates so important in US inter-war planning.

Chapter 2. Resources

1. According to Lambert, *Planning for Armageddon*, the first Cabinet meeting on war finance was not held until 15 December 1914 and the first item to be considered was a Russian request for a £100 million loan (which exceeded the total British peacetime military budget and equalled one-seventh of the British national debt) for munitions and the plant to produce it. Among other requests, the Romanians wanted £12 million and threatened to go to the Germans if they did not get it.

2. Kitchener is quoted in Michael and Eleanor Brock (eds), *H.H. Asquith Letters to Venetia Stanley* (Oxford University Press, 1982), p 420.

3. This is Lambert's view, in his *Planning for Armageddon*.

4. Nicholas Tracy, *Attack on Maritime Trade* (University of Toronto Press, 1991), p 129. He highlights the effect *on Britain* of the economic attack against Germany. The scholar he quotes is Kathleen Burk.

5. Lambert, *Planning for Armageddon*. He quotes a paper by Maynard Keynes which was circulated at the 28 January War Council which approved the Dardanelles operation. For Keynes, the only operation worth undertaking was to storm the Dardanelles. Lord Hankey, who was secretary to the War Council, described its discussions leading up to the Gallipoli operation in his memoir *The Supreme Command 1914-18* (written before the Second World War and suppressed until then). Balfour pressed two issues, the need for wheat and the need to repair Russian finances. The Council favoured an attack on the Dardanelles because it would 'cut the Turkish army in two; put Constantinople under our control; give us the advantage of having the Russian wheat; and enable Russia to resume exports ... It would also open a passage to the Danube. It was difficult to imagine a more helpful operation'. Asquith's letters to Venetia Stanley reveal that a Committee on Food Prices was formed on 20 January (he was chairman). According to his 22 January 1915 letter (Brock (eds), *Asquith's Letters to Venetia Stanley*, p 390) 'There is no doubt that we are at last beginning to feel the pinch of war in reference to food prices, mainly because all the German ships which used to carry food are captured or interned and the Admiralty has commandeered for transport etc over 1000 of our own. Further, the Australian crop has failed and the Russian (which is a very good one) is shut up, until we can get hold of Constantinople and open the Black Sea'.

6. In August 1914 the Grand Fleet alone had 1560 pieces of artillery, compared to 476 field guns (and no heavy siege artillery) in the BEF. Jon Tetsuro Sumida, 'Forging the Trident: British Naval Industrial Logistics, 1914-1918' in John A Lynn (ed), *Feeding Mars: Essays on Logistics and Resource Mobilisation in Western Warfare from the Middle Ages to the Present* (Boulder: Westview, 1993). Revised version courtesy of the author.

7. Operations Committee Minutes, 27 September 1917, ADM 116/3148. The Committee was initially chaired by First Lord Sir Eric Geddes and later by First Sea Lord Admiral Weymss. It seems to have been the executive committee for Admiralty materiel decisions in 1917–18. This volume effectively ends on 30 September 1918. However, ADM 137/834 Operations Committee Minutes and Memoranda, extends to the end of 1918.

8. DCNS pointed out that to provide two 'K' class flotillas (ten each), six 'K' class should be ordered, so the number of *L 50*s was cut to sixteen.

9. The proposal was to complete seven of the leaders under construction by the end of 1918, then one per quarter. That would retard six leaders. The rate of destroyer

completions was to be reduced from 7.5 per month to four per month after 1 January 1919, provided the United States could complete and commission sixteen per month for eight months. US destroyers could take over definite and independent duties from British ships. At this time 116 destroyers were under construction and eighty would be slowed (3.5 per month). All work on three 'M' class submarines would be stopped at once. The 'L' (fifty-one) and 'H' (eleven) class submarines now building for completion by 1 January 1919 would be continued, the rest being slowed to two per month, with priority given the 'L' class. Work on 'R' and 'K' class submarines would continue as before. Notes indicated that the 'M' class 'have no important operational value'. The rate of trawler completion could be reduced from $12\frac{1}{2}$ to eight per month from 1 July 1919, provided the US could complete and commission $4\frac{1}{2}$ per month (drifters, however, were not considered suited to US construction). Minesweeper completions would be reduced from six to three per month after 1 January 1919, provided the US could complete and commission three per month. At this time 116 were on order and fifty would be affected by retardation. An appended table compared the British destroyer force as of 31 December 1918 (total 404 ships) with the required establishment (498). That included 111 (123 required) for the Grand Fleet, fifty-seven (fifty-seven) for Dover and Harwich, twelve (twelve) minelayers, 105 (135) escorts, fifty-seven (sixty-seven) in hunting flotillas, twenty-one (fifty-seven) in local flotillas and none (six) at Halifax. Data from Appendix to 27 August 1918 Operations Committee Minutes, ADM 116/3148.

10. Requirements from Appendix to 27 August 1918 Operations Committee Minutes, ADM 137/834.

11. This was probably the '24 Class' sloop.

12. On the basis of past experience, trawler casualties were not fewer than six per month (seventy-two for 1919) and eighty were obsolete or approaching obsolescence. The projected establishment as of 1 January 1919 was 1312, against a desired 1410, the increase of ninety-eight being needed to supplement currently inadequate patrol and escort forces. The required total of new trawlers was then 250. Perhaps as many as 100 would be released from minesweeping duties by the arrival of fast 'Hunt' class sweepers. Projected British construction in 1919 was ninety-six trawlers, so the United States was asked for fifty-four, which should if possible be on 'fast gunboat i.e., Kil class. lines'. As with the destroyers, the US trawlers should operate in their own units. The 1918 list of requirements shows the expected numbers in hunting units as of 31 December 1918: sixty-four in Northern Patrol, sixty-four in Southern Patrol and thirty-nine in the Otranto Patrol, plus 951 in UK Home Waters, 166 in the Mediterranean and twenty-eight in other waters. Requested increases were eighty-two in Home Waters, fourteen in Mediterranean and two in other waters. The US minesweeper programme was a total of forty-five ships (three per month), for completion by 1 April 1920 or earlier. About two minesweepers were lost each month, for a total of thirty up to 1 April 1920. The estimated establishment as of 1 January 1919 was 152, the objective being 210; the British planned to match the rate of US construction. US sweepers were to take over particular Canadian and Mediterranean areas. The British accepted that they would have to be built on US lines, but hoped that they would burn coal rather than oil 'with a view to safety when mined and in order to save oil tonnage'.

13. ADM 116/1349. This was part of a 17 January 1918 plea to keep enough men available for shipbuilding. *Anson* was justified on the ground that the British battlecruiser force was too weak, with seven proper battlecruisers (only three of which were equal to the German ships) and the two lightly-armoured *Renown*s, with *Hood* due to complete in 1919. The Admiralty claimed that the Germans were building fourteen light cruisers, compared to eleven British light cruisers of the 1918 programme; the eight proposed were all that could be built, as completing *Anson* would cut one. Destroyer and leader numbers were predicated on expected losses; the Germans were thought to be building thirty-six destroyers. Submarine numbers were required to maintain the current output. An appended table showed a current British destroyer strength of 371, with sixty-nine US destroyers and 193 German. At the end of 1918 there would be 465 British destroyers and 137 US destroyers compared to 211 German and at the end of 1919, 526 British, 144 US and 232 German destroyers. Estimated destroyer losses to the end of 1919 were thirty-seven British, ten US and twenty German. The British hoped that by 1919 the Germans would have lost 150 U-boats, leaving them with 279.

14. Data from the Admiralty's September 1918 paper for the War Cabinet in ADM 137/834.

15. Jellicoe tried to limit capital ships to no more than four days for docking and urgent repairs, a remarkably short time compared with peacetime standards. However, frequent sustained steaming caused machinery problems which took much longer to repair. Four battleships were out of service for as long as three weeks each between August and December 1914 due to condenser problems. Boiler repairs to the two latest light cruisers took two to three months. As more ships joined the Grand Fleet, Jellicoe was able to permit three- to four-week refits. Overall, the wartime rate of refit and repair was ten times that in peacetime, seriously draining overall shipbuilding resources. Jon Tetsuro Sumida, 'Sustaining Neptune: British Naval Operational Logistics, 1914-1918', *Journal of Military History* (July 1993). Revised version courtesy of the author.

16. In mid-July 1914 the Royal Navy had 146,000 active personnel, but by mid-August, with the fleet mobilised, it had over 200,000. At the end of the war the Royal Navy had over 400,000 personnel. The Grand Fleet accounted for 52,000 men in August 1914 and nearly 76,000 at the end of the war. Sumida, 'Sustaining Neptune'.

17. Patterson (ed), *Jellicoe Papers* I, p 15, quoted from his post-war autobiographical manuscript.

18. From another item in Patterson (ed), *Jellicoe Papers*, I, p 20, it appears that this visit was made in June 1910.

19. This was, however, a low-speed evolution, the battleship towing the destroyer and passing a hose along the tow cable. It was not the higher-speed side-by-side technique developed between wars by the US Navy.

20. The main pre-war sources were the United States and Russia. Under the deal struck with Persia (Iran), the Admiralty had access to the Persian oil fields and by 1917 they provided about 15 per cent of its supply. Sumida, 'Supplying Neptune'.

21. Sumida, 'Supplying Neptune', based on an 18 July 1915 Admiralty document on requirements for Welsh coal.

22. Sumida, 'Supplying Neptune'.

23. War Staff paper, 17 September 1917, enclosed in January 1918 ASW report to War Cabinet, ADM 116/1349.

24. ADM 116/1349. Presumably the idea was that the ships already existed. The destroyers or sloops should make at least 18 knots, with five or six days' endurance at that speed, armed with not less than two 4in guns, four depth-charge throwers and a high-speed submarine sweep, with very good seakeeping qualities. The trawlers should make at least 11 knots, not less than 250 tons (for seakeeping), armed with one 4in gun, two depth charges and one deep sweep. Both types should burn coal. Of the sub-chasers, forty were wanted for the Mediterranean, twenty for the West Indies and twenty for the Canadian coast, all fitted for mine sweeping as well as ASW. The request seems to have been included in a Naval Staff paper dated 17 September 1917.

Chapter 3. Blockade, Trade Warfare and Economic Attack

1. A merchant anywhere in the world could accept a bill 'on London' in exchange for goods which would later be received by a buyer. The bank holding the bill accepted various risks, such as that the cargo would not arrive at its destination. Thus the credit system was intimately bound up with the shipping insurance industry – which was also cantered in London, at Lloyd's. As with other systems of (in effect) paper money, the whole system depended on the confidence of all concerned. Lambert, *Planning for Armageddon*, p 111, quoting a 25 March 1908 RUSI paper by the leading British statistical economist of the day, Sir Robert Giffen KGB FRS. His research was inspired by observation of the effect of the US financial panic of 1907, which caused the collapse of US internal and external trade. Giffen's immediate argument was that an outbreak of war would cause a panic and that the British government had to have reserves in place to overcome it.

2. Tracy, *Attack on Maritime Trade*, pp 93–4 points out that the Union ships caught only a small percentage of blockade-runners; in 1865 only 16.7 per cent of steam blockade runners but 71.1 per cent of sail blockade-runners. Profits from cotton smuggled out of the Confederacy bought 600,000 stands of arms. The Union forces connived at smuggling to New York, partly because the city's economy depended heavily on its role as the main trans-shipment centre for cotton. Economic cost *to the blockader* figured prominently in the history of the First World War blockade.

3. The text of the Declaration of London shows just how slippery this definition was. 'The question whether a blockade is effective is a matter of fact ... A blockade, to be binding, must be effective – that is to say, it must be maintained by a force sufficient really to prevent access to the enemy coastline'. Nowhere does the Declaration explain how leaky a blockade had to be to be declared ineffective. Text in Nicholas Tracy (ed), *Sea Power and the Control of Trade: Belligerent Rights from the Russian War to the Beira Patrol, 1854- 1970* (London: Navy Records Society, 2005), pp 136–7.

4. Lambert, *Planning for Armageddon*, p 29.

5. Lambert, *Planning for Armageddon*, based on 1904 CID papers.

6. Lambert, *Planning for Armageddon*. Note that Bacon placed the conference in 1909 and claimed that Fisher used it to press his Baltic strategy. The Baltic strategy does not figure at all in Lambert's account

7. Asquith laid out his principles in a 2 August 1914 letter to Venetia Stanley: (1) we are under no obligation to give military help to France or Russia; (2) despatch of the expeditionary force is out of the question and would serve no object; (3) we mustn't forget the ties created by our long-standing and intimate friendship with France; (4) it is against British interests that France should be wiped out as a Great Power; (5) we cannot allow Germany to use the Channel as a hostile base; (6) we have obligations to Belgium to prevent her being utilised and absorbed by Germany. Brock (eds), *Asquith Letters to Venetia Stanley*, p 146. Of the principles, (4) was the classic British insistence on a balance of power on the Continent and (5) and (6) were to prevent invasion. His opposition to sending the BEF to France was partly due to the strong opposition felt by a majority in the Cabinet. Many Liberals refused even to consider what should be done with the BEF. They were shocked by the German invasion of Belgium. Asquith commented in a 4 August letter that the German invasion simplified matters for him.

8. Lambert, *Planning for Armageddon*, p 129. He takes the qualifier 'by naval force alone' to indicate that a more complete economic attack would be needed to achieve quick results. That would involve unprecedented controls on service industries, particularly banking.

9. Tracy (ed), *Sea Power and the Control of Trade*, pp 121ff.

10. From a précis of Hankey's remarks by CID Secretary Sir Charles Ottley, 17 February 1911, in Tracy (ed), *Sea Power and the Control of Trade*, pp 154–5.

11. According to Ottley, Hankey proposed putting off the announcement until the Royal Navy had defeated the German fleet and thus had achieved such preponderance that neutrals would not feel they could object. Ottley considered Hankey's views unrealistic. It would be a violent reversal of existing British policy. He also doubted that it would

make much difference in wartime whether or not the British Government ratified the Declaration of London.

12. Distant blockade was tricky because blockade referred to specific ports. Under the Declaration of London a blockader could not bar access to neutral ports or coasts. A ship which had broken the blockade was subject to capture as long as a blockader pursued her. Announcing that ships in a wide swath of the North Sea were part of a blockade broadened that provision considerably.

13. The issue was raised in a 3 July 1911 open letter to Asquith, signed by 138 admirals; Tracy (ed), *Sea Power and the Control of Trade*, p 123. They argued that the navy clearly did not have enough cruisers to protect trade. To some extent the letter can also be seen as a reaction to Admiral Fisher's dramatic change in trade protection strategy away from occupation of focal areas and towards interception of raiders.

14. September 1913 letter to Prime Minister Asquith, enclosing a 21 August 1913 memo on trade protection. *Churchill* Companion Pt 3, pp 1770–1.

15. Matthew S Seligmann, *The Royal Navy and the German Threat 1901–1914: Admiralty Plans to Protect British Trade in a War Against Germany* (Oxford University Press, 2012), p 137.

16. Admiralty Technical History (TH 13), *Defensive Armament of Merchant Ships* (Technical History Section, August 1919), RN Historical Branch. In January 1914 White Star strengthened the poop deck of the liner *Brittanic* to receive a single 6in gun and Cunard fitted some ships trading with the United States. The ships in the programme all had 4.7in guns.

17. As recounted in the first volume of the *Krieg zur See* series on cruiser warfare. German shipping companies and the German Home Office objected to placing ammunition on board in peacetime. Before the war the German navy considered a speed of at least 20 knots necessary for a converted liner and 17 knots a bare minimum for a ship beginning her operations outside home waters (the liner had to be faster to break out past the expected British close blockade). In 1916, however, the Germans adopted the alternative of using slower disguised cruisers not readily recognisable as warships. (e.g. *Moewe* and *Wolf*)

18. The pre-war list, by line, was White Star (to Australasia): *Cufic, Runic, Tropic, Zealandic, Medi, Afric* and *Suevic*; Royal Mail (to River Plate): *Aragon, Amazon, Deseado, Desna, Asturias, Demerara, Darro, Drina* and *Alcantara*; FHA Line (to River Plate): *Rosorina, La Correntina, El Uraguayo, La Negra* and *El Paraguayo*; G. Thompson & Co. (to Australasia): *Themistocles, Demosthenes* and *Euripedes*; Wilson Line (to USA): *Francisco, Idaho* and *Colorado*; NZS Co. (to Australasia): *Rotorua* and *Hororata*; Federal Steam Navigation (to Australasia): *Wiltshire* and *Shropshire*; Shaw, Savill, *Albion* (to Australasia): *Tainui* and *Pakeba*; and Turnbull, Martin, Co. (to Australasia): *Argyllshire*. The Admiralty History does not list the additional ships envisaged in August 1914. The extra ten were: Allan Line: *Grampian* and *Scotian*; Canadian Pacific Railway: *Montreal, Manitoba* and *Montezuma*; White Star: *Arabic, Adriatic* and *Baltic*; and International Navigation Co.: *Haverford* and *Merion*. The three disarmed ships were those of the Wilson Line.

19. The Declaration was signed in November 1909. It should have come to a vote in 1909, but that year there was a constitutional crisis when the House of Lords rejected Chancellor Lloyd George's 'People's Budget'. The crisis was resolved the following year.

20. Lambert, *Planning for Armageddon*, p 204.

21. A C Bell, *A History of the Blockade of Germany and of the countries associated with her in the Great War: Austria-Hungary, Bulgaria and Turkey 1914-1918* (CID Historical Section, 1937 for official use only , published by HMSO, 1961). German provisions to resist economic attack are summarised on pp 192ff. The Germans called economic attack the third front of a war.

22. Bell, *History of the Blockade of Germany*, p 194, sees the Schlieffen Plan not so much as an attempt to win in a short war, as an attempt to preclude a dreaded long war. Schlieffen's predecessor von Moltke the Elder had warned that Germany might face a seven- or even a thirty-year war.

23. Germany was slowly splitting into two almost separate economic units. The manufacturing areas in the west were fed via Holland and the Rhine. The more agricultural areas in the east sent their surplus to Russia and industrial Bohemia (now the Czech Republic) rather than to the west.

24. According to Bell, *History of the Blockade of Germany*, work on such studies was suspended during the Hague and London conferences, the Declaration of London being seen as a satisfactory guarantee against economic attack. Even after the British failed to ratify the Declaration, the Germans took it as effective international law, protecting them, although clearly Tirpitz disagreed. The results of new studies (one from the General Staff, one from a Dr Fröhlich) were circulated within the German government in November 1911. Bell associates the new studies with panic over the Agadir crisis that year. It appears from Bell's account that the Germans did not take into account possible attack through the credit market.

25. Bell, *History of the Blockade of Germany*, p 196. The commission rejected the public demand for economic mobilisation directed by an economic general staff.

26. Bell, *History of the Blockade of Germany*, pp 196–8.

27. The initial application for reflagging, which was casually accepted, came from Chile. It later emerged that some of the ships, which had retained their German crews, replenished Graf Spee's cruiser squadron when it appeared on the Chilean coast.

28. Tracy (ed), *Sea Power and the Control of Trade*, p 126.

29. This announcement is in Tracy (ed), *Sea Power and the Control of Trade*, p 177.

30. Bell, *History of the Blockade of Germany*, p 567.

31. I am indebted to Dr Stephen Prince, head of NHB, for this example.

32. Bell, *History of the Blockade of Germany*, pp 568–70. Maximum prices for staples were first set in December 1915 and in nearly all cases they rose substantially within a year. Between December 1915 and December 1916, for example, the maximum allowable price of a dozen eggs rose by 52 per cent to 357 per cent above the July 1914 price. The equivalent rise for lard was 315 per cent, for pork 249 per cent and for beef 170 per cent.

33. Conclusion drawn by Bell, *History of the Blockade of Germany*, p 674, based on German statements.

34. Bell, *History of the Blockade of Germany*, p 686. The exception was quality clothing.

35. Tracy, *Attack on Maritime Trade*, p 129.

36. As quoted in Tracy, *Attack on Maritime Trade*, p 144.

37. Bell, *History of the Blockade of Germany*, p 203, based partly on the German official history.

38. Correspondence quoted by Bell, *History of the Blockade of Germany*, pp 206–7.

39. Tirpitz also argued that, since Fisher had just replaced Battenberg as First Sea Lord, the Grand Fleet would probably soon mount an attack, so U-boats assigned to the High Seas Fleet should not be detached at this time for the trade warfare campaign. In December 1914 he wanted to wait until the Flanders U-boats were available in the autumn of 1915.

40. Bell, *History of the Blockade of Germany*, p 211.

41. In January the highest authorities outside the government, plus the professor of political science, the professor of law and five other dignitaries of the University of Berlin signed a paper advocating the submarine offensive; it went to the Chancellor as well as to von Pohl and von Ingenohl. They thought that the current economic problems would soon be overcome, but only temporarily. Recovery could only be made permanent by breaking the British blockade. To do this they advocated a co-ordinated attack by airships against London and by submarines against trade.

42. Bell, *History of the Blockade of Germany*, p 212, based on Zimmermann's post-war recollection of a meeting at which Bethmann-Hollweg and, among others, General von Falkenhayn, were present. No minutes were taken. When Admiral Bachmann relieved von Pohl as chief of the Admiralstab the day after the meeting, he was astounded that the order for the submarine campaign had already been prepared, though the Kaiser had not yet signed it. Bell states that von Pohl made sure his assurance would not be questioned by other high naval officers and he did not take Tirpitz into his confidence.

43. According to Bell, *History of the Blockade of Germany*, pp 599–600, this was because in September, under the prize rules, the Flanders U-boat commanders managed to sink 82,000 tons of shipping. Their commander thought that on this basis he could persuade Scheer that a campaign embodying the prize rules would be worthwhile. The success of the Flanders flotilla led to the 6 October order that submarines in home waters were to concentrate on trade warfare (but under the prize rules). Scheer accepted the order as a preliminary to unrestricted submarine warfare. According to Bell, had the results of this short campaign been presented honestly, the Germans would have realised that they could cause the British considerable harm without risking American entry into the war. No comparison between prize-rule and unrestricted submarine warfare was ever presented to either the Chancellor or to Hindenburg and Ludendorff. In September Ludendorff told the Admiralstab that he favoured unrestricted submarine warfare and, according to Bell, that he thought it a great pity that the civil authorities had been given any say in the matter. Surely this was a purely military matter.

44. *Krieg zur See*, Nordsee 6 is explicit about the relationship between the situation in the East and German willingness to risk bringing further powers into the war. Bell, *History of the Blockade of Germany*, p 599, regards this reasoning as somewhat absurd, since it was the most distant of dangers. He sees the August meeting as the point at which it was decided definitely that unrestricted submarine warfare would be resumed. Apparently the decision was to await the defeat of Romania.

45. Lance E Davis and Stanley L Engerman, *Naval Blockades in Peace and War: An Economic History Since 1750* (Cambridge University Press, 2006), pp 174–6 analyse this claim, which they trace to Prof Dr Hermann Levy, who specialised in British agriculture. He wrote that British grain stocks amounted to only $6\frac{1}{2}$ to 17 weeks, so that the British relied on continuous supply. It seemed to follow that if imports were cut off when the stock was lowest, there would be an immediate panic in England, followed by a shortage so bad that the war could not go on. In the summer of 1916 Levy reported that overseas harvests had been poor, meaning that there was no surplus of North American wheat. It followed that the British would rely on more distant supplies, e.g. from South America and India, hence that each British freighter would carry much less wheat per month (because it would be making much longer voyages). That would further stretch the limited pool of British shipping. Most of Levy's data turned out to be wrong and even some German politicians pointed out some of the gaps in his reasoning.

46. Davis and Engerman, *Naval Blockades in Peace and War*, p 176.

47. Ludendorff's claim that the Admiralstab paper did not influence him and Scheer's refusal to predict results within some fixed period, make it difficult to credit the explanation that the Germans expected to win in six months, before any US troops could reach Europe. Bell, *History of the Blockade of Germany*, suggests something far

simpler. He sees Ludendorff's published memoir as clear evidence of a very narrow military outlook, focussed on Europe alone. In that case the 15 December 1916 French counter-attack at Verdun really could have convinced him that the Germans were in deep trouble on the Western Front and that only some radical step could save them.

48. *Krieg zur See*, Nordsee 6, pp 230–1.

49. Davis and Engerman, *Naval Blockades in Peace and War*, cite a July 1916 Output of Beer Restriction Bill which saved 150,000 tons of imports annually; the creation of a Royal Commission on Wheat Supplies in October 1916; compulsory changes in the way flour was made to increase supplies (creating 'war bread') by Order in Council of 20 November 1916 and the creation of a Food Controller to buy food abroad and control its distribution in the United Kingdom. A Food Production Department was set up in the Board of Agriculture. It increased domestic wheat production by 60 per cent between 1916 and 1918. Measures were also taken to use merchant ships more efficiently; a Ministry of Shipping was formed in December 1916 to control all British merchant ships. In effect it added tonnage to replace what was being sunk. The Ministry was also responsible, initially, for new construction (but that role was taken over by the Admiralty). Later an Allied Maritime Transport Council (organised in December 1917) co-ordinated all Allied-flag shipping.

50. Tracy, *Attack on Maritime Trade*, p 139.

Chapter 4. Expectations versus Reality

1. Pre-war issues of *Jane's Fighting Ships* generally included silhouettes of the major fast liners alongside warships in each national section. The Royal Navy became interested in using armed liners as auxiliary warships as early as the 1870s and it subsidised such liners as *Lusitania* and *Acquitania*. In the process it learned just how vulnerable such ships were. When war came, the Royal Navy mobilised a considerable force of armed merchant cruisers, whose superior seakeeping made them useful in enforcing the Northern Patrol element of the blockade of Germany. The Germans arranged to have minor warships on foreign stations and obsolete warships employed as station ships available to arm their own large merchant ships, but the results were very limited. Only six ships were taken over. The newest was *Cap Trafalgar*, a 23,640-ton liner which had been launched in March 1914. At Buenos Aires on the outbreak of war, she was armed by the obsolete gunboat *Eber*, which steamed from German Southwest Africa and then interned herself in Bahia. *Cap Trafalgar* was commissioned on 31 August and on 14 September she was intercepted and sunk by the British armed merchant cruiser *Carmania*, a considerably older (and much better-armed) former Cunard liner. *Vineta* (ex *Cap Polonio*) was a new liner launched in March 1914. She was never commissioned, apparently because she was not considered fast enough. The much older near-sisters *Kaiser Wilhelm der Grosse* and *Kronprinz Wilhelm* were also taken over. They were the fastest of the pre-war German liners converted into cruisers, at 22.5 knots. *Kaiser Wilhelm der Grosse* was in Germany when war broke out and was commissioned on 2 August 1914. She operated in the northern and mid-Atlantic. She scuttled herself when caught by HMS *Highflyer* while coaling off Africa on 26 August 1916. By that time she had captured all of three ships (10,683 GRT). Her near-sister was in New York on the outbreak of war; she was armed at sea by the light cruiser *Karlsruhe*, but received no ammunition for her heaviest guns. Nevertheless, she managed to capture eleven ships (33,423 GRT). She operated with Graf Spee's squadron for a time. She was forced to put into the United States, where she was interned, on 26 April 1915 and was later taken over as a US troopship. Two slower ships in the Far East were taken over and armed: *Prinz Eitel Friedrich* and *Cormoran*. On mobilisation the former was sent to Kaioutchao where she was armed with guns from the obsolete gunboats *Luchs* and *Tiger*. She operated for a time with Graf Spee and was the most successful of the lot (fifteen ships, 60,522 GRT). Once she ran out of coal, she was forced to intern herself in the United States, 26 April 1915. *Cormoran* was a prize taken by the cruiser *Emden* on 4 August 1914 and then armed at Tsingtao with the guns and personnel of the old gunboat *Cormoran*. She was interned at Guam on 13 December 1914 after running out of coal and provisions.

2. For details, see the author's *British Cruisers of the Victorian Era* (Barnsley: Seaforth Publishing, 2012), much of which is based on the Trade Protection file held by NHB.

3. Budget figures from Jon Tetsuro Sumida, *In Defence of Naval Supremacy: Finance, Technology and British Naval Policy 1889-1914* (London: Unwin Hyman, 1989), Tables 1 and 3. The *Cressy* class, the first British armoured cruisers, cost 36 per cent more than their protected cruiser predecessors of similar size; the next (*Drake*) class cost 32 per cent more again. The French were clearly well aware of the effect of building armoured cruisers; their 1897–8 programme sacrificed battleships to add armoured cruisers. Figures from Sumida, *In Defence of Naval Supremacy*, pp 19–20. A graph on p 21 shows that whereas first-class cruisers built in 1889–96 cost *in toto* about a third as much as the battleships of that period, first-class cruisers (mostly armoured) of 1897–1904 cost nearly as much as the battleships, despite the drastic attempt to cut cost by building inferior 'County' class armoured cruisers. Sumida points out that the big cruisers also demanded much more manpower, a problem Admiral Fisher's fleet reforms were intended to address. It was also necessary to add barracks and docks, particularly as the cruisers were much longer than battleships of similar displacement.

4. Taylor, *Struggle for Mastery in Europe*, pp 376–8. Taylor sees the proposal as directed against Russia in the context of Russian seizure of Port Arthur, which revealed British inability to back the Chinese. Port Arthur gave the Russians a cruiser base outside the Sea of Japan, with a wide (hence difficult to block) exit to the Pacific. Imanuel Geiss, *German Foreign Policy 1871-1914* (London: Routledge & Keegan Paul, 1976), p 85, notes that in November 1899 (after the attempt at alliance had died) German Foreign Secretary von Bulow was relieved that 'nobody in Britain really knows how anti-British German public opinion is'. On 29 March 1898 British Colonial Secretary Austen Chamberlain, acting for the Prime Minister Lord Salisbury, who was ill, told the

German ambassador that the British wanted to revise their policy of non-alignment and that they wanted above all alliance with Germany, because frictions with Germany were only secondary. According to Geiss, in the British Cabinet only Chamberlain and Chancellor of the Exchequer Balfour believed in the move towards Germany. They were exactly the ones who realised what the cruiser problem was doing to British finances and to her Empire. According to Geiss, the Germans feared that the British wanted them to fight the Russians. According to Geiss, the British had already approached Japan and the United States.

5. Initial very secret (presumably in the Merchant Navy Code) advice was for British shipping to steer course parallel to and from 30 to 150 miles away from their regular tracks, trying to fill their bunkers with enough fuel so that they did not have to coal on passage. They should try to pass through areas where traffic was most congested (i.e., focal areas) at night and to use neutral territorial waters when possible. Ships were to pass this message visually to any British ships they encountered. ADM 137/987, 'Policy: Various', 1914, p 337, repeated in modified form on p 386.

6. The Backhouse Papers (NHB) include a brief proposal by Captain Frederic Dreyer, dated 4 May 1914, to use plotting boards both to track the approach to the enemy fleet and to support divisional tactics. Document courtesy of Dr Jon Tetsuro Sumida. ADM 116/2090 is an early post-war compilation of descriptions of different approaches to plotting. ADM 1/8662/109 describes early post-war standardised action plotting arrangements for battleships and cruisers. According to the Admiralty *Handbook of Plotting* (CB 3039, August 1936, in NARA II ONI collection RG 38), the earlier practice of maintaining a chart of the situation on a navigational chart became unsatisfactory with the advent of radio and fast ships, so during the First World War two separate charts were maintained, one navigational and the other showing the tactical situation, for the fleet commander. Neither was satisfactory and plotting really became practical only with the advent of automatic devices such as the mechanical plotting table (ARL Table). They were being tested by 1930.

7. See the author's *Network-Centric Warfare: How Navies Learned to Fight Smarter in Three World Wars* (Annapolis: Naval Institute Press, 2008).

8. Printed rules, as used by the Royal Naval College, in the Backhouse Papers, NHB. One *Hercules* could neutralise another in 22 minutes at 7000 yds, but in 50.7 minutes at 10,000 – figures somewhat more optimistic for gunfire than those Jellicoe used in notes for his 1912 manoeuvres. Unfortunately the more detailed figures Jellicoe used (printed as a Home Fleet memorandum) have not come to light; the PZ instructions in the preserved pre-Grand Fleet Home Fleet Orders do not include the 'knock-out' tables. Jellicoe's estimate is in ADM 1/8268, the report of the January 1912 tactical ("P.Z.") and strategic exercises by the Second Division of the Home Fleet, the only pre-war exercises for which such a package has survived. Objects included experiments with divisional tactics, communications and the use of fast divisions by an inferior fleet.

9. An undated version of Jellicoe's war orders (probably 1912) is in Patterson (ed), *Jellicoe Papers* I, pp 23–5. They describe divisional tactics and the offensive use of destroyers. These orders are probably modified versions of Callaghan's, which have not survived. Despite later claims that there were no written fleet battle orders before 1913, it seems likely that fleet commanders had been issuing them in memorandum form for many years; for example there are references to Fisher's fleet memoranda. Without earlier orders, it is impossible to say how Jellicoe's differed from those of the past.

10. The October 1913 instructions are given in 'Naval Tactical Notes Vol I', OU 6183, ADM 186/80, issued 1929.

11. Callaghan's memo HF.0184 of 18 March 1914 in Backhouse Papers, NHB, argues that the Germans will not use theirs as independent hunters because they were unlikely to find anything (as in the 1913 manoeuvres). His diagram showed two flotillas, one either flank of the fleet in cruising formation (columns) so that they could deploy at the ends of the line. Callaghan expected 40 per cent hits in a 'browning' attack against ships in close order, say $2^1/_2$ cables apart because if a ship was 200 yds long, the total space was 500 yds, so two-fifths of space was ships.

12. Churchill's printed Minutes include one to Second Sea Lord and DNO dated 26 August 1913, asking for a demonstration 'in the near future' of 'a squadron of at least 4 ships firing torpedoes at a similar squadron at the longer ranges. I am told that the torpedo practice of battleships is very far below the standard which obtains in submarines; and, further, that the danger to both sides of reciprocal exchanges of torpedoes when the lines are within effective range is greatly exaggerated. I wish to test this firstly by experience . . . the least possible warning should be given to the ships which are to fire. Each ship should fire several torpedoes; and the conditions of the work should be arranged so as to correspond as closely as possible to those which would arise in a fleet action where the lines had closed to within effective torpedo range' (Churchill Minutes I, p 259, NHB). Churchill's Minutes were apparently collected and printed as reference material when he began writing *The World Crisis* (alternatively, they may have been printed for the Dardanelles Committee).

13. Admiralty *Gunnery Manual* (23 December 1915 edition, superseding the 1911 edition) Vol III, pp 17–18. The section seems to have been slipped in without revising earlier sections which in effect warned against some of the new techniques.

14. That is not surprising. Because the new medium-range technique went nowhere (at least for major units), it did not figure in memories of fleet development. It is unlikely that anyone writing after Jutland wanted to say that the Royal Navy, which found itself fighting at longer ranges, had developed an effective way to fire at shorter ones.

15. Captain Henry G. Thursfield, 'Development of Tactics in the Grand Fleet: Three Lectures', delivered Feb. 2, 3, 7, 1922, in Thursfield papers, THU 107, National Maritime Museum, Greenwich.

16. Jellicoe's August 1914 battle orders are in Patterson (ed), *Jellicoe Papers* I, pp 52–62, with the ranges given on p 59.

17. Patterson (ed), *Jellicoe Papers* I, p 63.

18. A paper on this topic is in the Backhouse Papers, NHB. The August 1914 Grand Fleet Battle Orders state that the case of fleets on opposite courses is to be described later.

19. Lieutenant R A R Plunkett (later Admiral Lord Drax), *Modern Naval Tactics* (Admiralty, 1910), NHB. The reference to regular turns to throw off enemy gunnery is from p 52.

20. NID report 973, dated December 1914 (ADM 137/4799).

21. May's compilation of exercise data, issued on 19 September 1911, is in NHB. ADM 1/8120 is a parallel discussion of destroyer integration into the fleet, with comments by various subsidiary fleet commanders.

22. Comments are from Admiral Jellicoe's 'War Orders and Dispositions . . . prepared when in command of 2nd Division, Home Fleet,' but they seem to be his version of Callaghan's orders. Item 18, Patterson (ed), *Jellicoe Papers* I. Much the same points were made during a discussion of the 1912–13 destroyers ('L' class) in the autumn of 1912.

23. NARA RG 38 ONI series E-2-d Register 09/572 of 1909–14.

24. May's report is in ADM 1/8051. His account of the tactical implications (not in the PRO report), printed for fleet use, is in the NHB Library (copy courtesy of Dr Jon Tetsuro Sumida).

25. Conduct of a Fleet in Action: C-in-C's Instructions – HF.04 Memo dated 14 March 1914. Fleet Memos 1914 from Backhouse papers in NHB.

26. Based on C-in-C High Seas Fleet, 'Very Secret Tactical Order No. 1: Hints for Battle', dated 29 September 1914, in NHB PG Box 634, SL 3078. The same document is in NID 979, ADM 186/17 (January 1915) and PRO also has a copy of the January 1914 version published for the Royal Navy in October 1914. The NHB copy is in typescript, but the wording is identical to that of the printed 1915 version.

27. This manoeuvre was described in paragraph 103 of the German fleet signal book (on the first page of the manoeuvring section). This is in the set of German tactical orders in ADM 186/17, the draught Manoeuvring Orders being dated 3 February 1914. A draft set of Signals in Action had not yet been issued. The signals were separate from the German Tactical Orders, which in this collection were ID. 979, O.X.O., dated January 1915. They included Tactical Order No. 1, Hints for Battle. This document included the note that the 4th Battle Squadron (pre-dreadnoughts) should take up a position on the disengaged beam of the battle line so that it could intervene or assist on its own initiative. The battlecruisers would be designated the 'Fast Division'. Once the fleets were engaged, its duty would be to fire torpedoes at the head of the enemy line while engaging the advanced fast fighting forces of the enemy (i.e., British battlecruisers at the head of the British line) with gunfire. The best position would be about 4 points before the beam from the head of the enemy line.

28. In 1914 the 1st Battle Squadron was the *Nassau* and *Helgoland* class dreadnoughts (with reciprocating engines); the 2nd Battle Squadron was the *Deutschland* class pre-dreadnoughts, the last before the dreadnoughts); the 3rd was the turbine dreadnoughts of the *Kaiser* and *König* classes. The fleet flagship *Friedrich der Grosse* was separate, in contrast with British practice which made it part of a battle squadron. Tactical organisation of the High Seas Fleet in 1914, ADM 137/4715. By 1918, the 3rd Battle Squadron had been split into a five-ship squadron (*Bayern* and *König* class) and a five-ship 4th Battle Squadron (*Kaiser* class including *Friedrich der Grosse*, Baden now being fleet flagship). No pre-dreadnoughts were any longer associated with the fleet. Revised organisation from notes in *German Navy Tactical Orders* 1920, NHB.

29. ADM 137/2018, Grand Fleet Orders and Memoranda Aug–Dec 1914, p 116.

30. Patterson (ed), *Jellicoe Papers* I, p 75.

31. ADM 137/2018, pp 225–6, notes by Paymaster Hugh Miller on interrogation of a German lieutenant, distributed 3 December 1914 by Jellicoe.

32. Patterson (ed), *Jellicoe Papers* II, p 49, revision of Grand Fleet Battle Orders September 1916.

33. Tactical Orders for the High Seas Fleet War Edition, NHB Box PG 634. The numbered Tactical Orders, with their dates, were: (1) Method of screening the Fleet when under way of 9 April 1918; (2) Destroyer submarine screen of 10 February 1918; (3) Recognition Signals during Night Action of 19 October 1918; (4) Enemy Recognition Signals of 25 June 1915; (5) Conduct against Submarines of 25 June 1915; (6) Attack signals for TBDs in day action of 11 June 1915; (7) Depth adjustment of mines of 17 September 1914; (8) W/T Duties of Scouting Groups of 2 November 1917; (9) Rules for conduct of Fleet Flagship of 14 July 1914; (10) Report on Distribution of Fire of 19 July 1914; (11) Aircraft Division of 23 July 1918 (actually notes on the capabilities and characteristics of various fleet aircraft, including reconnaissance endurance 300nm, fighting reconnaissance endurance 240–300nm, long-range reconnaissance endurance 550nm. and 'Giants' endurance 750nm; all large reconnaissance and Giants had W/T with a range of about 150nm, using a hanging aerial 80 m long and the Giants could transmit on the Fleet Wave range over 450nm); (12) General Statement on naval airships of 5 July 1918 (*L 50* and high-altitude *L70* types); (13) Reconnaissance and screening by Airships of 13 September 1918; (14) Records during War of 6 October 1918; (15) Signals when attacking submarines with depth charges of 21 November 1918 (as written, but clearly wrong); (16) Employment of 2nd Battle Squadron of 10 May 1916; (17) Aerial escort service of 1 April 1918; (18) Conduct of fleet during night destroyer attacks of 24 May 1916; (19) Rapid mine searching gear (no date); (20) Reinforcement of 1st Scouting Group (Battlecruisers) by Battleships of 13 August 1916; (21) Cruising station of flotilla cruisers of 12 September 1916; (22) 3rd and 4th Battle Squadrons of 8 November 1916; (23) Conduct in submarine areas of 10 February 1918; (24) Approach formation of 1 March 1917. All of these were very brief items, typically one or two pages compared to the fourteen pages of 'Hints for Battle'. Originally Tactical Order No. 15 (2 August 1914) was Orders for conduct after an action ending shortly before nightfall, which discussed whether battleships should be held back during the night to keep them out of the way of hostile destroyer attacks. These orders were printed up by the Admiralty as CB 1548 (April 1920), *German Navy Tactical Orders*, but the typescript includes notes on Jutland. NHB.

34. German and British night recognition signals are described in the 1920 collection of German tactical orders (CB 1548, NHB). The British data are dated 25 June 1915.

35. This section benefitted greatly from the material on the Royal Navy Radio Museum (HMS *Collingwood*) website, which includes the texts of the W/T Appendices to the annual *Vernon* reports from 1900 through 1913. Unfortunately it does not reproduce the secret W/T Appendices for 1914–18. The site also includes other important Royal Navy radio documents. It seems to be the closest approach to a history of Royal Navy radio taking technology into account.

36. Policy set in 1905 was for all ships above destroyer size to be fitted with W/T, with destroyers and lesser craft under consideration. The following year thirty-nine destroyers ('River' and ocean-going classes) were ordered fitted.

37. The Type system, superseding an earlier Mark system, was introduced in 1910, the first sets being Type 1 (Mk II: high power ship set for cruisers and battleships), Type 2 (Mk I*: 14 kW set for surface ships larger than destroyers, low-power shore stations), Type 3 (1 kW short-range set, initially for 5nm range; by 1913 redesignated the battleship auxiliary set), Type 4 (1 kW destroyer set), Type 5 (portable), Type 6 (harbour defence set), Type 7 (high power installation for Horsea/Cleethorpes) and Type 8 (Malta high power set). The first submarine installation was Type 'X' on *B 5*, a modified Type 4 destroyer set. Sets introduced in 1913 were Type 9 (cruiser auxiliary set) and Type 10 (submarine set, modified Type X; twenty-six RN submarines and two Australian 'AE' class fitted before the outbreak of war). On the eve of war a submarine set (Type 11) and an aircraft set (Type 12) were introduced. Wartime sets were: Type 13 ('after-action' set used if main sets were destroyed), Type 14 (3 kW Poulsen set, originally in *Europa*, later in submarines; *Europa* later had a prototype 14 kW set), Type 15 (3 kW Poulsen destroyer set, supplemented by Type 4), Type 16 (3 kW auxiliary capital ship set), Type 18 (25 kW arc set, 1916 for shore stations, capital ships and cruisers), Type 19 (Poulsen set at Horsea, operational 1914), Type 20 (Bermuda and Jamaica stations, 1915, spark sets), Type 21 (strategic CW stations, guaranteed range 1000nm at 1300m). There were three major wartime tube radios: Type 31 (co-ordination of fire by two or more ships using tubes to multiply frequencies), Type 32 (auxiliary to Type 14 submarine set) and Type 33 (auxiliary to Type 9 cruiser set). The first (post-war) generation of long-range tube sets was Type 36 (10 kW for large ships, tested 1921), Type 37 (destroyers) and Type 38 (submarines). There were separate designations for receivers.

38. *Vernon* Annual Report for 1906, It included three major fleet exercises carried out when the three fleets met off Lagos in February. Exercise I represented a division of each fleet watching a common enemy (HMS *Exmouth*), 40 miles away. Every half hour *Exmouth* made a signal and each watcher simultaneously tried to communicate with her own fleet. The watchers in turn received orders through a line of cruisers. Exercise II tested interference (jamming), an inner division closing with *Exmouth*, the main bodies being 40 miles away. *Exmouth* and battleships in company with her jammed. In Exercise III, *Exmouth* tried to evade and jam watchers with other ships at eight-mile intervals to transmit information. In all, thirty-nine signals were sent, of which the Channel Fleet correctly received eleven, the Mediterranean Fleet thirteen and the Atlantic Fleet only on. A further strategic exercise (IV) in which the Channel Fleet tried to bring one of the others to battle before they could unite. To do that it used a new frequency (F tune, 3000ft). One important lesson was that it was possible to use the new frequency while completely tuning out the A and B tunes used by the two other fleets. The Channel Fleet was therefore able to jam both A and B tunes. The wash-up conference (1 March 1906) concluded that ships should communicate on only a single frequency rather than the combination of two previously used. The conference also recommended adoption of a roof aerial instead of the existing fourfold type. Using a roof (distributed horizontal wire array) made it possible to stay the gaff from which antennas were slung.

39. The 1907 *Vernon* report contains the report of a W/T Conference held at *Vernon* on 31 October 1907. It cautioned that special cipher should be limited to messages absolutely to be kept secret, all other signals being made in Service code (a means of limiting the length of messages, but not secure). The means of automatically enciphering and deciphering was to be 'on the typewriter principle'. The exercise that year showed that the Service code could be used very rapidly by anyone familiar with it, but that a ciphered message often was not attended to until after it became useless. It was recommended that a special war signal book be prepared, although it would become useless if it fell into enemy hands. Therefore the Supplementary Signal Code should not be issued to destroyers (which might well be lost near enemy shores), which should simply encipher their messages. A crypto machine called the Teletyper was tested in 1912, operating by transposing letters (the cover name was chosen so that manufacturers of parts of the machine would not know its purpose). It consisted of two standard typewriters side by side, with a common roller controlled by the left-hand typewriter. Depressing a key on the left hand typewriter sent an electrical signal to a 'magic box' which was electrically linked to the right-hand keyboard, so that depressing a letter on the left printed that letter and also the appropriate transposed letter on the right. A

keycard in the 'magic box' set the connections. One sheet of paper provided eight different codes, obtained by turning the card 90° and turning it over. Twelve were ordered for initial trials. It was rejected on the ground that a transposition code was easily broken. *Vernon* proposed an internal means of changing the transposition after every letter had been transposed, but it was abandoned as unreliable. The encryption machine was apparently intended to solve a problem demonstrated by 1911 Home Fleet tests: a hundred-word message took thirty-five minutes to code and twenty-five to decode. Transmission (ten minutes) was half as fast as for an uncoded message, presumably because the receiver could not use the natural redundancy of language to overcome transmission errors. The process was far too slow for emergency tactical purposes. Experiments in 1914 with a coding machine (probably the Teletypewriter) failed. Admiral Jellicoe defined a series of fixed four-letter signals for wireless transmission. The 1911 and later Home Fleet W/T Orders include 'Organisation of a Coding Branch' on board ships as distinct from signallers, with two coders to stand each watch. ADM 116/1665. Instructions for the use of cipher, code and plain language were included in *Grand Fleet W/T Memoranda* dated 1 December 1916 (ADM 116/1664).

40. ADM 186/682, *Wireless Instructions* 1915 (CB.0121). The group system seems first to have been laid out in 1912; it can be found in the printed 1913 Home Fleet W/T instructions in ADM 116/1665.

41. These were the frequencies adopted about 1903: Tune A, Tune B and the two alternatives for Tune C.

42. It was said to produce a damped wave, because the burst of energy into the antenna (aerial, in British parlance) was brief and soon died out. The shorter a burst of energy, the wider the range of frequencies it represents.

43. All of this is from a modern perspective, not the way the inventors of early wireless systems wrote. It avoids numerous technicalities such as the difficult problem of feeding wireless energy from transmitter to antenna. Initially the aerial was connected directly to the spark gap (the Royal Navy called that the 'plain' system). The result was a highly-damped wave (a 'whipcrack' in American parlance). The wavelength was the natural wavelength of the aerial. About 1903 an alternative 'oscillator method' appeared (it became standard in the Royal Navy about 1907). Instead of feeding a spark directly into the antenna, the transmitter was linked to the antenna by induction (a receiver was linked to an antenna in a similar way). Because the transmitter was an oscillator, the wave was not as sharply damped as that of the 'plain' system (*i.e.*, was not as broadband), although it was still a short burst of power. Induction coupling had a limited frequency range, so it provided a degree of tuning. The rival Marconi and Slaby-Arco systems differed in the technique they used for coupling, but both were roughly equivalent. In a typical system shown in the *Vernon* report for 1904 (p 22, in this case the US deForest system), a motor-generator supplied power through a transformer to a circuit containing the sending key. This circuit was linked by an inductance to a circuit containing a condenser, which fed into the spark gap proper. The spark gap was linked to an oscillator, a wire helix. That helix was linked inductively to the antenna. The oscillator converted the broad-band sparks into slightly narrower-band signals. Later in 1906 *Vernon* was able to receive signals from HMS *Furious* despite jamming due to HMS *Culver* six miles away, due to the 'high note' (modulation) inserted into the sparks produced by HMS *Furious*. Such high notes also made signals more recognisable despite atmospherics.

44. The frequency is more or less pure because any interruption or imposed signal, which is necessary to transmit information, mixes in other frequencies in small amounts.

45. That would be a heterodyne receiver, a type common in radios, which produces its own continuous-wave signal and 'beats' it against the received signal. Hence early references to Poulsen sets include references to special receivers. As of 1914, Poulsen receivers had been installed on board the battleship *Marlborough* and the cruiser *Defence*. The latter received signals at a range of 1100nm. ASWE History, ADM 220/2448.

46. ADM 1/8403/430 dated 17 November 1914. Director of Operations Division Admiral Oliver ordered *Europa* fitted with a Poulsen set during a machinery refit. She was the second long-range W/T ship, much wanted to improve Atlantic communications. *Vindictive* was the first such linking ship, described as 'a wireless asset of great importance', albeit limited because no other ship had similar equipment. She could communicate with Horsea at up to 1200nm range and *Defence* (which had a Poulsen receiver) could receive from her at a similar distance. On 12 November it was proposed that *Europa* and *Argonaut* or *Amphitrite* be similarly fitted (it is not clear which ship if any was fitted). A diagram showed that with a Poulsen set (on a cruiser) at Fayal or off Cape St. Vincent, Horsea and Gibraltar could link to each other and to ships half way to America. To the south, a link ship could connect with Ascension and Cape Horn. At this time Poulsen stations were being built at Jamaica and Ascension, but the cruisers would be ready first.

47. The Poulsen transmitter created an electric arc (in a gas) oscillating (Poulsen called it 'singing') between two carbon poles. It could not be keyed on and off, but superimposing another signal slightly shifted its frequency. The oscillator fed the aerial through a tuned circuit, the resonant frequency of which was determined by factors such as the length of the coil in it. That made it possible to signal, by sending the signal through one tuned circuit or another. When the Morse key was not pressed, the signal passed through one circuit; when it was pressed, through another. In one example, the difference was whether the signal went through one coil or two (1700 vs 1600m 176.5 vs 187.5 kHz.). The alternatives were called 'back' ('back wave') and 'front' ('front wave'), receivers being tuned to the 'front wave'. A receiver tuned to the back wave would hear an incoherent version of Morse Code. Within a few years the back wave was eliminated altogether. In effect the Poulsen was the first application of Frequency Shift Keying, the frequency indicating the information. The curator of the RN Radio

Museum web site points out that the Poulsen was the only example of a true continuous wave (CW) transmitter, even though the term CW was later applied to all dot-and-dash transmitters, as an alternative to voice. The arc was conceived to support voice (telephony), but in 1909 the Royal Navy decided to abandon that and stick with Morse to avoid mistakes in recognising spoken letter and words with similar sounds.

48. The most important type of vacuum tube (triode) consists of a grid between a hot cathode and a cold anode (collector). Electrons boil off the cathode and travel to the anode, but the field created by the current in the grid controls how strong the current between cathode and anode is. Thus the relatively powerful current between cathode and anode can be made to reflect changes in the current in the grid. The output of one tube could go into another, or even back into the grid. In this way a vacuum-tube circuit could be made to resonate at a desired frequency, creating a continuous-wave transmitter. Because the grid current controls the flow of the main current in the tube, the British term a vacuum tube a valve. The great problem in tubes is the heat they necessarily generate (radar transmitter tubes are typically water-cooled).

49. The 1908 tube was used in a tuner; it lit up when exposed to a high-frequency discharge. It could also be used to indicate when an aerial was not radiating. In 1909 Marconi was using tubes for reception (sparks for transmission) at its long-range station at Clifden, Ireland, described in that year's *Vernon* report.

50. The post-war set of *Technical Histories* (TH) does not include a W/T history, but does include (as TH 41) an account of the development of (a) The Model MN Eight-Valve Amplifier; (b) a CW Receiver; and (c) Tube experiments conducted in 1915–19.

51. Vice Admiral Sir Arthur Hezlet, *Electronics and Sea Power* (New York: Stein and Day, 1975), p 107. Tubes were also used in a herodyne circuit, but not for transmission, because they were considered too fragile. Hezlet may have referred to a 1916 project for a tube amplifier considered 'essential for the furtherance of several W/T developments by HMS *Vernon*, which were in an experimental stage'. There was already a Model L tube receiver, which was needed, it appears, for reception by submarines at periscope depth. The British were trying a French three-tube amplifier for submarine reception. Most of TH 41 is a monograph describing the theory and practice of vacuum tubes.

52. There was no equivalent to the simpler more or less vertical whips used by the US Navy (but not the Royal Navy) during the Second World War, because wavelengths were far too long. Whips operated at HF (high frequency: roughly 1–30 MHz, meaning a wavelength of 10 to 300m), the operators accepting low efficiency in return for clearing the sky arcs of anti-aircraft guns. Marconi's first antenna was a vertical wire – a whip.

53. Coherers were initially used to ink a moving tape rather than to feed headphones. By 1904 they had been replaced in British service by magnetic detectors. At that time the US Navy was using an electrolytic detector. In 1904 typical British W/T performance was ten to fifteen words/min (wpm), but de Forest (who provided US Navy sets) achieved thirty in trials. The Royal Navy adopted crystal detectors in 1909. They became popular after the First World War in home radios, the user moving a wire (the 'cat's whisker') over the surface of the crystal to find the signal. This was the first solid-state device to be used in electronics, although no one then understood how it worked.

54. The Home Fleet W/T instructions included an article on Fleet Manoeuvring by W/T in its 1913 edition. Ships would use the vocabulary in the Fleet Signal Book, but with letters indicated by radio rather than by flags. A special 'flag sign' would precede each letter representing an alphabetical flag, to distinguish it from a letter indicating a procedure. Pendants would be preceded by a pendant sign. The technique seems to have been experimental, since an appended note pasted to the page requires all ships to keep rough records of all signals made and to be able to state course and order of the fleet at any instant. ADM 116/1665 (Article XVI). Grand Fleet W/T orders (ADM 116/1663) contain much more elaborate instructions for manoeuvring by W/T dated 1915, superseding those dated 24 December 1914 (not included).

55. ADM 137/2027, *Post-Jutland Committees Pt 1*, pp 373ff.

56. By the end of the war, the MBT W/T direction-finding set was standard. It equipped HMAS *Australia* and HMS *Barham, Courageous, Lion, Queen Elizabeth, Princess Royal, Campania, Alsatian* (AMC) and *Orvieto* (AMC). In the AMCs the direction-finder was installed for rendezvous purposes. A table of performance data showed HMAS *Australia* achieving 2° accuracy (but not reliably), much depending on the operator. Only comparative bearings could be relied upon. To avoid interference, the D/F system had to work on a frequency well separated from that of the ship's main antenna. A difference of 200m was needed near S wave. The ship had two sets, one for Q and U waves and one for P to T waves. Her antenna was 85ft high, with a base of 40ft, placed unsymmetrically between the foremost and second funnels, very close to the main W/T feeder. The peak of the array was supported by the ship's main aerial (actually, by the horizontal part of her aerial array). *Lion* reported an effective range of 300 miles, using a symmetrical array between her second and after funnels, 25ft high, with a 50ft base. *Queen Elizabeth* had a symmetrical array between her funnels, offering roughly 5° accuracy (range was not given). *Princess Royal* (which claimed 400 to 500nm range by day on Q wave and 5° accuracy with a skilled operator) had a symmetrical array over Q turret, about 30ft high, with a 45ft base. Errors were blamed on her lack of a gyro compass (presumably in her W/T office). *Courageous* (which claimed 3° accuracy out to 500nm) had a symmetrical array abaft her funnel, 66ft high, with a 48ft base. *Barham* (which claimed a range as great as 1000nm) had a symmetrical array 75ft high, with a 66ft base, suspended from the triatic between her fore topmast and her main top, close to her funnel. All of these installations used fixed vertical wire antennas and a rotating receiving coil, the operator deciding when he could hear the signal. The Grand Fleet also tested a French rotating-frame set intended for use ashore on trucks and in 1919 a more

suitable rotating loop antenna was being made. *Annual Report of Signal School 1917* (issued 1919), CB 1523 (ADM 186/753), pp 86–7.

57. Telefunken (Gesellschaft für drahtlose Telegraphie) was a monopoly formed by the merger of Braun-Siemens and Arco-Slaby. In 1905 it claimed to have fitted 450 stations, including eighty shipboard ones and about a dozen shore stations for the German navy. According to the 1905 *Vernon* annual report, Telefunken claimed that it had installed as many, if not more, stations than all others combined. The US Navy was using Telefunken systems extensively and they were erecting one in New Orleans with a 360-mile range to communicate with twenty-three of their other stations up the coast.

58. Patrick Beesly, *Room 40: British Naval Intelligence 1914-18* (London: Hamish Hamilton, 1982), pp 30–1 comments that the Germans fell into the trap of using their W/T excessively because their transmitters were so good, better even than they realised (meaning that the British were intercepting their signals at extraordinary ranges, even when the Germans turned down the power to cut range). Using 800m signals, their big land station at Nauen could reach the Mediterranean, the Adriatic, the United States, Southwest Africa and even China. U-boat transmission (400m) extended over several hundred miles rather than, as supposed pre-war, fifty or sixty miles. Doubtless some of the British successes at long range were due to the adoption of vacuum-tube amplifiers developed from 1916 on.

59. In 1916 the British obtained and translated the German 1913 W/T regulations, which were still in force (July 1916: CB 0233, in NHB compilation, *German Naval Warfare: Translations of Instructions Regarding Tactics, Torpedo Firing, W/T, etc 1914-1918*). In contrast to contemporary British W/T instructions, it shows no emphasis on W/T silence or on intercepting enemy communications (it does discuss jamming enemy communications).

60. ADM 186/793, CB 1516(D), *Reports on Interned German Vessels: Pt IV, Wireless Telegraphy Installations* (June 1919). There is no indication of a separate report on radio telephone installations.

61. For example, Article XXVIII of Grand Fleet W/T instructions, issued on 21 September 1911, called for signals from all foreign ships and shore stations to be intercepted unless ship was told off by a W/T guard ship (i.e., unless other ships were already doing so). ADM 116/1665, *Grand Fleet Signal Orders* (up to 1917). A special log was to be kept; 'much useful information with regard to foreign methods of W/T signalling can be obtained by careful and systematic interception'. An Admiralty letter had recently been issued explaining how analysis was to be organised. Pre-war *Vernon* annual W/T reports include comments on intercepts as measures of foreign capability and progress.

62. M (merchant ship method) was for a warship to simulate a merchant ship, among other things by running her alternators dead slow so as to create unmusical notes similar to pure spark transmissions; the NC (numerical call) method would avoid the use of known call signs; the F method permitted ships to answer while obscuring any connection with the relevant message; and the I (Indirect) method would be employed by ships at bases and by shore stations when transmitting to ships when the ships were not answering calls or messages. Ships were not to re-transmit by radio, but if necessary to pass the message to its intended recipient using visual signalling. Instructions issued 27 December 1915 in ADM 116/1663.

63. Beesly, *Room 40*, p 5.

64. *Krieg zur See*, Nordsee 3, p 126 points out that although the British might have obtained the keys to German codes from the stranded *Magdeburg*, it was also possible that they might simply have broken the codes on the basis of intercepts and analysis, 'as the German coding system was by no means inviolable according to present 1922. ideas'. The Germans later broke British codes in this way. Beesly, *Room 40*, pp 22–3 describes the SKM (which was sometimes called the SB). It provided a three-letter code for each phrase, plus equivalents to letter which might have to be spelled out. Because obsolete phrases had never been edited out, by 1914 it had grown to a massive 34,304 groups. Because it was so massive, it could not easily be replaced and it remained in force as late as May 1917. Remarkably, the SKM remained in force for more than two years after the inquiry into the loss of the light cruiser established that it might well have been recovered by the Russians. Without alternate groups for each phrase, it offered opportunities for Room 40 to solve the keys used to super-encipher the text. Orders to change key were made by wireless and often not all ships had the new key, so that the same message was sometimes sent in both old and new keys.

65. According to Beesly, *Room 40*, p 27, the VB was the best of the German codes, intended for attaches and some embassies, consulates and agents abroad, as well as warships overseas (all by cable) and, with special super-encipherment, for flag officers. It was a 100,000-group code using five-digit groups with a particularly good potential for super-encipherment. Although not very significant in the war at sea, it was extremely useful because it enabled Room 40 to read German diplomatic traffic, particularly that between Berlin and Madrid and Berlin and Washington.

66. Hope's collection of notes survives as ADM 137/4685 and ADM 137/4686. After the First World War Room 40 (ID 25) produced its own history of wartime German naval operations under the title 'A Contribution to The History of German Naval Warfare 1914-1918 in Three Volumes'. Marked 'Most Secret', it is HW 7/1, 2 and 3.

67. Patterson (ed), *Jellicoe Papers* I, p 181, in Document 158, a letter from Jellicoe to the Secretary of the Admiralty, 14 August 1915.

68. Beesly, *Room 40*, p 145.

69. Beesly, *Room 40*, p 274.

70. Beesly, *Room 40*, p 277 describes various tips that Room 40 should have been able to assemble into a viable prediction. One reason for the 17 October debacle was a serious delay in passing on intelligence which should have alerted Admiral Beatty to what was happening. He speculates that the episode reinforced Lloyd George's determination to get rid of both Admiral Jellicoe and Admiral Oliver, who as Chief of Operations was responsible for passing messages to the fleet. Beesly does not give details of Room 40's information about the December destroyer raid.

71. Beesly, *Room 40*, pp 283–9. By this time the Germans were finally trying to take reasonable security measures, changing keys every seven to ten days (Room 40 now needed two or three days to crack them). They were also using low-powered transmitters, which were more difficult to intercept fully and accurately. For this operation, Scheer imposed not only full wireless silence, he issued all orders, even to minesweepers, in writing. Necessary wireless orders were passed by transmitting single code phrases ('catch-words'). There were hints, but they were ambiguous. The worst failure was that the submarine *J 6*, on picket duty in the Heligoland Bight, mistook the High Seas Fleet for a British formation.

72. Beesly, *Room 40*, p 32. The operation is described in detail by Hilmar-Detlaf Brückner, 'Germany's First Cryptanalysis on the Western Front: Decrypting British and French Naval Ciphers in World War I', in *Crytologia* (June 2005). According to Brückner, Roubaix had two Heavy W/T Stations, a Fortress W/T Station at Lille and a Motor Car W/T station, of which the expected ranges of the heavy stations were 125 to 250km and of the fixed fortress station up to 1000km. I am indebted to Dr Josef Straczek for this article. Beesly's comments on German code-breaking are taken largely from a 1934 official paper by Kkpt Gustav Kleikamp, *Der Einfluss der Funkaufklarung auf die Seekriegsfuhring in der Nordsee 1914-1918* ('The Influence of Radio Intelligence on Naval Command in the North Sea 1914-1918'), which was presumably originally written for classified official use. Kleikamp was particularly disgusted that it took three years for the Germans to recognise their radio vulnerability.

73. This message (with its source) is mentioned in *Krieg zur See*, Nordsee 4, p 10.

74. Beesly, *Room 40*, p 32 also mentions centres at Libau for the Baltic and at Pola for the Mediterranean.

75. *Krieg zur See*, Nordsee 5, p 20. References in the 1915 volume suggest strongly that no messages, other than those sent in plain language, were then being read.

76. Brückner speculates that much of Roubaix' success could be traced to the rapid expansion of the Royal Navy and particularly its auxiliary services, whose officers cannot have received much training in coding and therefore had to be given simple ones.

77. According to Brückner, the volume of signals dwarfed that handled by Room 40. Between August and November 1917 Roubaix handled 29,189 messages, whereas Beesly records that through the whole war Room 40 dealt with about 20,000 German messages (nearly all of which it broke). The success rate achieved by Roubaix is not recorded and most of the messages it handled were low-level.

78. Beesly, *Room 40*, p 33, quoting Kleikamp.

79. The purchase of the first German naval airship was correctly reported in 1912, with rumoured purchases of two more and press reports that airship sheds were to be built at Kiel, Hamburg, Wilhelmshaven and Emden. Submission by Captain Hugh Watson, naval attaché, 21 October 1912: Note on German manoeuvres 1912, in Backhouse Papers, NHB.

80. The Royal Naval Air Service had previously raided Friedrichshafen from Belfort in France (21 November 1914), nearly destroying *L 7* as she neared completion. Douglas H Robinson, *The Zeppelin in Combat: A History of the German Naval Airship Division 1912-1918* (London: Foulis, 1962), p 43. A British naval pilot flying from Antwerp the day before it fell destroyed the army's *Z IX* in her shed at Dusseldorf on 8 October 1914.

81. The steamer *Santa Elena* completed conversion in mid-December 1917; she carried four seaplanes. The light cruiser *Stuttgart* was to have been the second aircraft mothership: *Krieg zur See*, Nordsee 7, p 174. Santa Elena does not figure in Gröner's compendium of German warships, but the *Stuttgart* conversion does: it entailed adding a hangar with a flat deck on top and clearing the quarterdeck to take a seaplane which could be handled by a crane. The ship was rebuilt between February and May 1918 (she re-entered service on 16 May 1918). Gröner lists the incomplete Italian liner *Ausonia* as the first German ship earmarked as a carrier. Unlike the seaplane carriers, she had a flying-off deck forward and a landing deck aft. Conversion was stopped by the Armistice. The *Ausonia* design seems to have been developed from a 1917 proposal to rebuild the armoured cruiser *Roon* with a flat deck aft. According to R D Layman, *Naval Aviation in the First World War: Its Impact and Influence* (London: Chatham Publishing, 1996), p 41, as Baltic commander Prince Henry (Heinrich) of Prussia (the Kaiser's brother) ordered the first embarkation of an aircraft on a German cruiser, *Friedrich Carl*, to reconnoitre the Russian coast. The prince was an early aviator. Layman credits him with the first German aerial torpedo operations and also with the first German aerial minelaying operation. The German July 1918 notes on air operations credited battlecruisers and sperrbrechers with two aircraft each and light cruisers one. In each case aircraft were slung out and retrieved after landing on the sea.

82. Based on an account of German wartime aeronautics in *Marine Rundschau* (March 1928 issue) as translated by ONI: RG 38 ONI series A-1-g Register 15461. Note that despite its title this article and others on German naval aeronautics were limited to airships. The Imperial Navy had an Airship Division. These data were supplemented by RG 38 ONI 'German Naval Dirigibles' (1921) A-1-p Register 9602, based partly on notes provided by the British Control Commission enforcing the Versailles Treaty. The

British had good information on German airship construction because they intercepted the W/T messages sent when airships left their sheds for initial trial flights.

83. According to Layman, *Naval Aviation*, initially Admiral Tirpitz resisted investment; he later justified his resistance on the grounds that, as a seaman, he was too aware of the vagaries of weather, which would limit airship reconnaissance. Prince Henry of Prussia, the Kaiser's brother, became an aviator and managed to reverse Tirpitz. According to Robinson, *The Zeppelin in Combat*, pp 20–1, Tirpitz changed his mind in 1911 in response to pressure from the Kaiser and from public opinion, but more in response to a threat by the Zeppelin company that without an order it would sell a ship to the British. The contract for *L 1* was placed on 24 April 1912. Tirpitz demanded a larger ship than the standard type Zeppelin wanted to sell (25,000m³ vs 20,000m³). *L 1* was completed on 25 September 1912 and first flew on 7 October 1912 (22,500m³, 518ft 2in long and 48ft 6in in diameter). On 13 October she took off for a flight lasting more than thirty hours. On 18 January 1913 the Kaiser approved a five-year programme envisaging two squadrons of Zeppelins (each of four operational and one spare airships). The first was *L 2*, a modified type with increased capacity but with engines too close to the gas bags. *L 3* was delivered on 11 May 1914.

84. Based on Zeppelin war diaries, Robinson, *Zeppelin in Combat*, p 40, states that on the outbreak of war the naval airships were subordinated to Admiral Hipper, who commanded the First Scouting Group (battlecruisers) of the High Seas Fleet. Initially *L 3* was assigned to patrol the inner destroyer line in the Heligoland Bight, making two cruises during the first week of the war. Her first flight under full war conditions was an 11 August reconnaissance of the Dutch coast out to a distance of 170 miles in response to reports of British minelayers. On 17 August she was assigned to reconnoitre the Skaggerak in response to a report that the British were operating there. She was also sent out during the battle of Heligoland Bight, but only glimpsed the retiring British force (and was fired on by German destroyers). On 19 October *L 5* reconnoitred to within 60 miles of Great Yarmouth without seeing British ships, encouraging von Ingenohl to execute the Yarmouth raid. As an example of the limitations of Zeppelin reconnaissance in bad weather, *L 4* passed close to the Harwich Force on 25 October when it attempted an abortive carrier strike. There was apparently no Zeppelin support for the Scarborough Raid in December 1914, but *L 5* and *L 6* did take off in an attempt to find the Harwich Force as it executed the Cuxhaven Raid on 25 December. *L 6* tried but failed to hit the carrier *Empress* with a single bomb.

85. Airship size was measured in cubic meters (m³) of hydrogen volume. The *L 3* class measured 22,500m³ (payload 8700kg). The successor *L 9* of 1915 measured 25,000m³; the next class (*L 10–L 19*) measured 32,000m³ (payload 15,600 kg). They were followed by *L 20–L 25* (35800m³, payload 17,800kg), *L 30–L 42* (no *L 26* to *L 29*: 55,000m³, payload 30,000 kg), *L 43–L 52* (55,800m³, payload 39,000kg), *L 53–65* (56,000m³, payload 40,000 kg, commissioned late 1917–early 1918; *L 71* was in service on 10 August 1918, *L 72* only after the Armistice). *L 57* and *L 59* were a special high-lift type (68,500m³, payload 52,000kg) with a maximum altitude of 6850m compared to 6000–6500m for the *L 53* class, 5500m for the *L 43* class and 4000m for the *L 30* class (the maximum for the *L 3* class was 2500m). *L 70* was a new type embodying wartime lessons, capable of climbing to 7000m. *L 59* made an extraordinary round trip to East Africa. She was a 55,000m³ ship lengthened 30m to accommodate cargo (her sister *L 57* burned while on trials). She was recalled by W/T because East Africa had already been evacuated, so she flew back to Jamboli in Bulgaria after a 96-hour, 7000km flight. The final Zeppelins were *L 70* (62,200m³, payload 47,000kg) and *L 71* and *L 72* (62,200m³, payload 49,000kg). There were apparently no *L 66–69*. Schütte-Lanz airships were *SL 3* and *SL 4* (32,400m³, payload 13,400kg) of 1914–15; *SL 6*, *SL 8* and *SL 9* (35,000m³, payload 20,000kg); and *SL 20* and *SL 22* (56,000m³, payload 35,500kg). There were also three Parseval (PL) semi-rigids used only in the Baltic and one M-ship (M-4, 19,500m³, 7000kg). Data from the *Marine Rundschau* article, which was presumably based on German records. According to Robinson, *Zeppelin in Combat*, p 35, the jump in size to the *L 10* class was due to the fact that at the outbreak of war Zeppelin was building an enlarged airliner (*LZ 26*) for DELAG, the Zeppelin airline. *L 9* was of this type. *L 10* was an enlarged version offered by Zeppelin soon after the outbreak of war. Schütte-Lanz was already building a very large airship, which it sold to the army in May 1914; it received a navy contract for three airships (*SL 3*, *SL 4* and *SL 6*, presumably part of the navy's mobilisation programme). They were disliked for their fragile wood structure. At the end of the war the firm switched to metal, but too late to complete any airships before the Armistice.

86. *Krieg zur See*, Nordsee 4, p 108, arguing that in 1915 the German fleet was closer to equality with the British than its commander realised.

87. This *PL 6* was used pre-war for advertising by the Stollwerck Chocolate Company. A second Parseval, *PL 19*, was one of four building under a British Admiralty contract. The only other navy Parseval was *PL 25*, ordered by the army. None was considered satisfactory. Robinson, *Zeppelin in Combat*, pp 36–7.

88. Initial Admiralstab and Navy Office proposals preceded those for the U-boat campaign. They were opposed on the ground that few airships were in service and all were essential for reconnaissance. Thus proposals made in September and October were postponed. When the idea was revived in December, it fell afoul of Chancellor Bethmann-Hollweg's view that London should be spared. Admiralstab chief von Pohl (soon to command the High Seas Fleet) considered London and the military establishments further down the Thames the chief objectives in the campaign of terror which would soon include the U-boats. He also argued that the British would surely repeat their Christmas Day carrier air raid on the Zeppelins in their sheds. With its long nights, winter was the best time for an attack. A German deputation pressing the government to open the U-boat campaign linked it with a Zeppelin campaign. On 9 January the Kaiser approved an attack, but he barred any attack on London itself; bombs were to be

dropped only on dockyards, arsenals and other military establishments. No one seems to have realised that bombs could not possibly be aimed that precisely. After delays due to bad weather, the first raid was carried out by two Zeppelins (one had to turn back) on the night of 19/20 January 1915. They attacked Great Yarmouth, a target justified by the presence of coast defences. *L 3* dropped six 110lb HE bombs and seven incendiary bombs from 4900ft. *L 4* missed the target and attacked a town from which anti-aircraft guns had fired at her; she dropped seven 110lb bombs. The Royal Navy saw Zeppelins as an extension of the coastal threat from German warships, hence as its responsibility. It armed warships in the approaches to London with anti-aircraft guns and it also placed guns on board submarines which it hoped could suddenly surface and, in effect, ambush Zeppelins.

89. Robinson, *Zeppelin in Combat*, p 81. The Zeppelin was soon forced up and out of visual touch by British light cruiser fire. The observation that only four British battle-cruisers could be seen encouraged the Germans to think they had sunk HMS *Tiger*.

90. Tactical Order No. 12 in the collection of wartime German tactical orders, NHB.

91. Stephen W Roskill, *Documents Relating to the Naval Air Service 1908 - 1918* (Navy Records Society, 1969), p 7.

92. Roskill, *Naval Air Service*, pp 45–1.

93. In January 1912, in addition to aircraft orders, Royal Navy Chief of Staff Admiral Troubridge called for the purchase of two non-rigid Zodiac (or Astra) airships, one from the manufacturer and one from Vickers (under license), for training. He also thought *Mayfly* should be reassembled for ground training and as a target simulating a Zeppelin. The CID suggested that the Royal Aircraft Factory build a non-rigid 'Gamma' type airship, of the type the army already had, for the navy; it was suited to training and to coastal scouting, but not to the 'larger naval strategical requirements', meaning long-range fleet scouting. In this sense the 'Gamma' was the forebear of SS 1. A 'Willows' airship which happened to be on the market should also be purchased (Roskill, *Naval Air Service*, p 53). By this time the navy was also buying a French Astra airship (*Astra Torres*). It later negotiated for rights to the German Parseval non-rigid (one of which flew from Germany to Sheerness and back).

94. Roskill, *Naval Air Service*, pp 87–107. Of the Parsevals, one had a capacity of 500,000ft³ and three of 300,000ft³.

95. According to the British Airship Trust web-site, the Vickers design (*HMA 9*) was based on technology revealed when German Army Zeppelin *Z IV* landed accidentally in France on 3 April 1913. Design work began on 9 April and the order was placed on 10 June. The order was cancelled on 12 March 1915 on the grounds that the war would probably end before the airship could be delivered, but it was reinstated in June and *HMA 9* left her shed on 16 November 1916, the first British rigid airship to fly. Of the many missing numbers, a 1913 chart reproduced in Roskill, *Naval Air Service* shows all non-rigids except for *HMA 9*: *HMA 2* was the Willows non-rigid, *HMA 3* was the Astra-Torres, *HMA 4–HMA 7* were Parsevals, *HMA 9* was the big Vickers rigid, *HMA 10–HMA 11* were the Armstrong Forlanis, *HMA 12* was the projected third Armstrong Forlani, *HMA 16* was the second Astra and *HMA 17–HMA 20* were Royal Aircraft Factory non-rigids. The Forlanis were semi-rigids.

96. Drawings of a stretched version of *HMA 9* were approved in October 1915 and three rigid airships (Nos. 23–25: '23 Class') ordered from Beardmore, Armstrong, Shorts and Vickers (which was delayed by work to complete *HMA 9*; *HMA 23* was completed 23 August 1917). By December plans called for sixteen airships of this type. Five were ordered in January 1916 (Nos. 26–30), but only *HMA 26* (designated *R* (for Rigid) *26*) was completed. These airships had a gun platform on top for a 2pdr and two Lewis guns, from then on a standard feature of British rigid airships. The other four were reordered to a modified 23X design, but *R 28* and *R 30* were later cancelled to concentrate on a new *R 33* class based on technology revealed when Zeppelin *L 33* was brought down relatively undamaged in North Essex. Five of these modified Zeppelins were ordered (*R 33–R 37*). In August 1917 the Admiralty proposed extending the order to a total of sixteen (to *R 48*) and cancelling *R 28*, work on which had not yet begun. *R 31* and *R 32* were derived from Schütte-Lanz technology, which paralleled Zeppelin's. *R 31* flew in July 1918 and was commissioned on 6 November, the last British airship of the First World War. As of the Armistice, *R 32* to *R 40* were to be completed, followed by one each year to keep the builders alive. The programme was soon heavily cut. Some of these data are from Roskill, *Naval Air Service*, p 531, quoting the Admiralty submission to the War Cabinet, 30 August 1917.

97. Roskill, *Naval Air Service*, p 319 reproduces a paper indicating that Flight Commander H A Williamson RNAS, who was invalided home from the Dardanelles to the supply side of the Naval Air Department, stated in 1915 that his own experience proved to him that the future of naval aviation lay with wheeled aircraft capable of taking off from *and landing onto* ships. To that end he conceived a primitive form of arrester gear and produced a crude model of a carrier with a flush flight deck and an island. He showed it to Captain Sueter, who in turn showed it to Naval Constructor J H Narbeth. An alternative put forward by Lieutenant Commander Gerard Holmes RNVR (also in DNC Department) had a completely flush deck, smoke being directed under it. This design was adopted for the carrier *Argus*. Williamson's contribution was recognised post-war by the Royal Commission on Awards to Inventors.

98. Roskill, *Naval Air Service*, p 327, dated 26 February 1916. In the list, raiding targets ashore (including ships in harbour) came fifth and attacking enemy ships at sea came eighth and last. Sueter pointed out that only four carriers were large enough: *Campania*, *Ben-my-Chree*, *Ark Royal* and *Vindex*, but *Ark Royal* was too slow, *Ben-my-Chree* had no hangar forward (hence could launch only one aircraft over her bows before stopping to move aircraft around) and *Vindex* was too small, hence could fly off only two scouts

before stopping. Sueter pointed out that it would be best to arrange a ship so that an aircraft could fly off and return aboard, citing the recent experiments.

99. Roskill, *Naval Air Service*, p 460.

100. Roskill, *Naval Air Service*, p 470.

101. ADM 137/1938, p 137, preface to a description of present policy on aircraft in ships, September 1917.

Chapter 5. The Fleets
1. ADM 116/900B.

2. Andrew Lambert, 'The German North Sea Islands, the Kiel Canal and the Danish Narrows in Royal Navy Thinking and Planning, 1905-1918', in Michael Epkenhans and Gerhard P Gross eds), *The Danish Straits and German Naval Power 1905-1918* (Potsdam: Militärgechichtliches Forchungsamt, 2010). Lambert cites a December 1905 CID study of a possible war against Germany, with France as ally. It featured fleet operations in the Baltic including seizure of islands from which a later assault on the north German coast, threatening Berlin, could be mounted. This operation was particularly interesting in the event of a stalemate in the West, the German front against France. Lambert, *Planning for Armageddon*, sees the CID study as an attempt to extend naval planning beyond a mobilisation plan. It was conducted by an unofficial 'preparedness group' consisting of CID Secretary Colonel (Ret) Clarke, DNI Captain Ottley, General French (who would command the BEF in 1914) and Lord Esher, an important figure in British defence thinking at this time. The project for an amphibious operation was abandoned because there were not enough troops and the French would not make up the numbers.

3. ADM 1/8997, a memoir Ballard wrote in 1933. In 1905 Ballard, who had won two RUSI gold medals for papers on strategy, because war plans deputy to DNI Captain Charles Ottley. Since Naval Intelligence was in effect the Admiralty war staff, that made him chief war planner. Maurice Hankey was Secretary of this planning cell. Hankey, *Supreme Command* I, p 40 gives the background. Fisher formed a committee on war plans some time in November 1906, having decided while on vacation to begin formal war planning against Germany. Work began at the Naval War College at Portsmouth that December. As chairman, Ballard worked with a gunnery expert and a mine warfare expert. Fisher saw Ballard every week or two in London. The project took about four months and produced a sixty-page report, among whose conclusions was that the Germans were very vulnerable to economic attack (e.g., the distant blockade). Alternatives were a close blockade and a Baltic landing operation such as Fisher later proposed. Those in on the secret and therefore peripherally involved were DNI Captain Ottley (soon to join the Committee of Imperial Defence) and new head of the Naval War College Captain Slade. The product is probably part of the massive war plans file Fisher soon produced and (in part) brandished to prove that, contrary to charges raised by Admiral Beresford, he really was conducting formal war planning. The larger file is ADM 116/1043B, marked 'War Plans 1907-1908'. It includes a very wide variety of planning documents, even one for a war against Germany and the United States.

4. In discussing the War Plans after the 1913 manoeuvres, Admiral Callaghan commented that 'we must not expose ourselves at a critical time to attack like that delivered by the Japanese on Port Arthur 'which, we now know, had it been followed up vigorously, would have ended in the destruction of the demoralised Russian fleet; the Germans would not be likely to make such a mistake'. Backhouse Papers, NHB.

5. Wegener was outraged that the Germans had allowed the North Sea to be blocked. He argued that the emphasis should always have been on attacking British sea lines of communication and to that end the Germans should have occupied Norway to provide bases on the Atlantic. This criticism in turn infuriated many German officers, such as Captain (later Grand Admiral) Erich Raeder, the Second World War naval chief and a classmate. The 1929 book was a compilation of three staff papers Wegener wrote in 1915 under the signature of his superior Admiral Lans. The first was a February 1915 reaction to the perceived failure at Dogger Bank the previous month. Wegener's book was republished in English as *The Naval Strategy of the World War* (Annapolis: Naval Institute Press, 1989). For an analysis of his thinking and its impact, see Commander. Kenneth P Hansen, RCN, 'Raeder vs. Wegener: Conflict in German Naval Strategy', *Naval War College Review* (Autumn 2005).

6. Nicholas A Lambert, *Sir John Fisher's Naval Revolution* (Columbia: University of South Carolina Press, 1999), p 203.

7. ADM 116/866B, collected naval staff papers, p 284 (item 25), 'Observation Force in North Sea: Remarks on War orders for, in connection with lessons of 1912 Manoeuvres', dated 16 September 1912.

8. Even in 1918, typical W/T range under good conditions was only about 150 miles. A few submarines, intended specifically to watch the German fleet, had long-range Poulsen transmitters, a point made in the post-war British study of submarine vs. submarine operations to explain why particular submarines were assigned to the Heligoland Bight in 1917–18. Ballard wrote that no plan for close blockade would be worth considering until suitable submarines had been built in sufficient quantity, 'although our existing 'D' and 'E' classes might be usefully employed in advanced positions'.

9. Ballard made the interesting point that large-scale mining in the open sea presented no legal problem as long as the mines were not intended for blockade; the Germans had led the opposition at the last conference on international law to British proposals to limit minelaying to the territorial waters of belligerents.

10. ADM 116/866B, collected naval staff papers, p 294 begins an unsigned account (probably by Ballard) of the anti-invasion part of the 1912 manoeuvres. They were the first to evaluate invasion since the Clacton military manoeuvres of 1905, which had tested only what was needed for disembarkation, primarily to support British offensive plans. This time the enemy Blue Fleet could choose invasion among possible objectives. Under the rules, it succeeded, since it was left undisturbed in Filey Bay for four hours in fine weather. A battle squadron and submarines of the defending fleet actually spotted the attackers while they were (in theory) landing troops, but the commander of the battle squadron mis-calculated the positions and movements of other battle squadrons and took no action by himself. On the other hand, because the defending force was weakened so as to provide an attacking force, its reconnaissance was badly weakened. The invasion force was smaller and less recognisable than a real one, because no large merchant ships had been hired for the exercise. That confused the watching submarines, some of which sighted the attacking force far to the north but did not realise they were an invasion force. The only indication was a special flag flown by the notionally escorting battleships. Defence was also complicated by the need to provide the attackers with a base somewhere which 'would not alarm the Foreign Office', so part of the British coast was used, depriving the patrol flotillas of the use of the Humber, the most centrally located base and the nearest to Filey Bay. This analysis added that the sheer distance from Germany would make the passage more difficult for the troops, but that the increasing size and speed of German liners would simplify an invasion operation – except that submarines defending the British coast would find it easier to hit fewer targets, none of them particularly survivable. The mid-North Sea patrol was complicated by foggy conditions in the western part of that sea (the east was clear).

11. As described, for example, by Jellicoe in an autobiographical note in Patterson (ed), *Jellicoe Papers* I, p 29.

12. ADM 116/3130, a report submitted by Admiral Callaghan (C-in-C Home Fleet) on 28 August 1913.

13. ADM 137/818, 'Home Fleet & Detached Squadrons: War Orders Oct 1913 to July 1914'. It repeated Ballard's earlier comment that his strategy was modelled on the one which led to successful battles in the Anglo-Dutch Wars. This file contains war orders as modified several times, but their content did not really change. The wording here is from the first set of orders, as changed in ink. Callaghan commented on the orders and the file includes the Board's reactions dated January 1914. They included instructions that he was to keep his ships 70 per cent coaled at all times, so that they could sortie instantly; this figure was based on analysis of Japanese operations during the Russo-Japanese War. The tentative War Plan issued on 26 November 1912 (ADM 116/3412) matches the October 1913 plan. It is not clear whether it was the first to be issued in this form.

14. In a December 1913 memo, in ADM 137/818, the writer (probably Ballard, according to a pencil note) pointed out some problems which his favoured mines might solve. Initial War Orders (ADM 137/818, p. 460) to the minelaying squadron envisaged the Dover Straits minefield.

15. The War Orders included Organisation for War. The Grand Fleet commander was C-in-C Home Fleets. He had three Battle Squadrons (1st, 2nd, 3rd) plus the *Duncan* class of 6th Battle Squadron, all with attached ships (and might be joined by 4th, which otherwise might be used independently); he had the 1st Battle Cruiser Squadron; six cruiser squadrons (2nd, 3rd, 6th, 7th and 1st and 2nd Light Cruiser Squadrons; 5th and 8th Cruiser Squadrons were crossed out; in January 1914 this was cut to 2nd, 3rd and 6th plus 1st Light Cruiser Squadron), four destroyer flotillas (1st, 2nd, 3rd, 4th and 6th when ready) and one submarine flotilla (8th). The 8th Flotilla ('D' class) was earmarked for offensive action either in the Heligoland Bight or the Kattegat, whichever seemed more useful. The 10th and 11th Cruiser Squadrons were assigned to the Northern Blockade (cut to 10th in January 1914). A later document in the same package placed one destroyer flotilla (6th) and two submarine flotillas (3rd and 4th) at Dover to establish a cordon from South Godwin Buoy to French territorial waters off Calais, as the southern end of the blockade zone. C-in-C Coast Patrols was the Admiral of Patrols, with eight light cruisers (ex-Scouts), four destroyer flotillas (6th, 7th, 8th, 9th) and four submarine flotillas (3rd, 4th, 6th and 7th). The Channel Fleet consisted of three Battle Squadrons (5th, 7th, 8th) with attached ships; 12th Cruiser Squadron (to intercept German merchant ships in the Channel; supplemented by 7th Cruiser Squadron in January 1914); minelayers and sweepers (minelayers were controlled directly by the Admiralty). A crossed-out paragraph stated that the minelayers would mine the enemy's coast near his naval ports, covered by cruisers. An Atlantic Squadron (commanded by Admiral commanding 4th Cruiser Squadron) would cover Atlantic trade routes with 4th and 5th Cruiser Squadrons (9th and 11th added in January 1914), the Cadet Cruisers and 9th Cruiser Squadron. Finally there were local defence forces at The Nore (Nore Flotilla and 5th Submarine Flotilla), Portsmouth (Portsmouth Flotilla and 2nd Submarine Flotilla), Plymouth (Plymouth Flotilla and 1st Submarine Flotilla) and Rosyth (so new it was added in ink: commanded by SNO Coast of Scotland, with the Rosyth Flotilla). When the German fleet reached a particular level of readiness, the Battle Squadrons would be placed out of reach of surprise attack (the words 'along the south and west coasts of Great Britain' were crossed out, as plans shifted to placing the fleet at Scapa). Actual movement to Scapa Flow was to be carried out during the period of 'strained relations' in which the political situation made it possible that war might break out. The deployment to Scapa was written in ink, replacing a probable movement to a port on the west coast. All of this was apart from forces abroad. When the War Plan was revised in June 1914, numbered cruiser squadrons were merged into cruiser *forces* designated by letter.

16. For details, see the author's *Network-Centric Warfare*.

17. ADM 1/7736. The proposals were submitted on 10 November 1904 and approved on 21 November, Admiral Fisher having concurred on 12 November.

18. ADM 1/7880, 23 October 1906.

19. 'The Home Fleet', undated print (marked MSS 252/12/26) in Robinson Papers I (RNM). A later paper in this series states that the Home Fleet would not attain its full development until May 1908.

20. The Channel Fleet now had all eight *King Edward VII* class battleships, which had not been in service a year earlier. Fisher maintained that no foreign power had any ship comparable to the *King Edward VII* class in commission in Home waters.

21. Up to January 1909 the Navy List did not show the Home Fleet, because it consisted of ships in reserve. However, the January 1910 list showed the Home Fleet but no Channel Fleet. The distinction between the third and fourth divisions was in the strength of their nucleus crews. Later they became the Second and Third Fleets.

22. However, Fisher pressed exactly this idea in the context of Mediterranean dispositions at a 4 July CID meeting (minutes in ADM 116/3493, *Strategical Situation in Mediterranean*, 1912. He argued, first, that the current Mediterranean battle squadron sufficed, because an adequate flotilla of destroyers and submarines based at Malta could make it impossible for any battleship to move in the Mediterranean. Asked whether submarines would also make the North Sea unsafe for battleships, he agreed and said that the fleet would be off the North Coast of Scotland or outside the Straits of Dover. 'If the German fleet came out it would be attacked by submarines and destroyers, if it came out far enough it would then have to fight our battle fleet'. Churchill said that the Board of Admiralty 'did not entirely accept Lord Fisher's views on submarines. They did not think that they could deny the open waters of the Mediterranean to battleships . . . the Mediterranean might become very precarious as a trade route'.

23. ADM 116/3493 is largely devoted to a 4 July 1912 CID meeting to discuss proposed changes in fleet disposition loosely connected to the previous November's approach to the French to go into more detailed arrangements for supporting the British in the Channel in the event of war. At that time the French had only torpedo boats, destroyers and submarines in the Channel and the idea was that they would help block it against the enemy (as they did when war broke out in 1914, supplementing this force with cruisers). The Mediterranean drawdown had begun as early as 1904. The 4 July meeting followed a May 1912 CID meeting at Malta to inspect the Mediterranean Station and try to reach some conclusions about naval forces there.

24. At the CID meeting, Churchill's predecessor Reginald McKenna explained that during his tenure neither the Austrian nor the Italian fleet had been of much account; the strength of the Mediterranean Fleet had been fixed to deal with any fleet smaller than the French. When the Austrian dreadnoughts were announced, the plan was to send the eight *King Edward VII*s to the Mediterranean. They alone would not have been equal to the Austrians, but with the Atlantic Fleet (as a swing fleet) the superiority would have been crushing. At that time a combination of the Austrians and the Italians was 'not more than a remote risk'.

25. ADM 116/3099, *Mediterranean: Consideration of Situation in 1912.* Churchill asked for the consequences if (i) France is our ally and (ii) if we have no ally. He also wanted to know what could be done at Gibraltar to control the straits if the fleet were withdrawn and similarly to cover the Canal with dispositions at Alexandria. The reply to criticism that the Mediterranean Fleet was in the eyes of Europeans the symbol and measure of British power was (a) that the international situation between Britain and Germany was 'to all intents and purposes a state of war without present violence; (b) it was therefore vital to rearrange British naval forces; and (c) such preponderance must also be adequate to stir up the lesser maritime North Sea countries to positive concerted action, or at the least impose upon them a benevolent neutrality. The typed paper describing brilliant German diplomacy is unsigned, but it seems to include some of Churchill's signed comments, so I have attributed it to Churchill.

26. The Secretariat paper (in ADM 116/3099) reviewed the troubled history of the Triple Alliance. When it was concluded, England confronted France and Russia. Although England did not join the Triple Alliance directed against France and Russia, she leaned towards co-operation with its members. At that time the German partners were Spain and Italy. When the growth of Anglo-German friction made it clear that England might one day fight Germany, Spain dropped out of the Triple Alliance; neither she nor Italy could welcome a war against an Anglo-French combination. Despite strong national feelings to the contrary, Spain drew closer to France, thus remaining in touch with England. Italy could not afford to leave the Triple Alliance, but 'made it clear that in a war between France and Germany and still more in a war between England and Germany, she would not consider herself bound to fight by Germany's side'. The somewhat ambiguous position of Italy 'has been a factor in the overall balance of power in Europe well calculated to serve the maintenance of peace and therefore eminently favourable to British interests'. The fear was that 'recent events in Tripolitania Libya. ', meaning the Italian conquest of territory on the Egyptian border, would tighten Italian bonds with the Triple Alliance because 'with military forces engaged overseas, she will more than ever be at Austria's mercy'. However, the same engagement would open her to maritime pressure.

27. ADM 116/3493, CID minutes 4 July 1912, p 15.

28. A discussion before the CID on 4 July 1912 (in ADM 116/3493) mentioned instead HMS *New Zealand* and HMS *Indomitable.* Of ten British battlecruisers, *Australia* was unavailable because she was RAN flagship. That left nine against five Germans, so detaching two was acceptable. Mediterranean strategy had last been reviewed in 1909, when it seemed that Italy was far less susceptible to the Triple Alliance. The previous Board (under McKenna, who had been succeeded by Churchill in 1911) had planned to send HMS *Indomitable* to China, but that idea had now been scrapped.

29. The talks are described in a note date-stamped 16 September 1936 (but dated 29 August 1911) in ADM 116/3109, *France – Co-operation with in War.* The conversations were held at the Admiralty, between First Lord McKenna, First Sea Lord Admiral Fisher and the French naval attaché, who was acting on verbal instructions of the French Minister of Marine. The talks were reopened on 24 August 1911 on the initiative of the French Ambassador. This time the participants were First Sea Lord Admiral A K Wilson and Captain Mercier de Lostende, who had taken part in the 1908 negotiations. Two of the conventions agreed in 1908 were accepted again and Wilson wanted radical changes in a third. In September 1911 a French wireless expert was sent over with an interpreter to provide the British with the French signal code. On several occasions French Foreign Minister Cambon said that he had avoided a written agreement because the French Admiralty 'knew themselves to be surrounded by spies in the pay of Germany and on several occasions they had proof of important leakage on the most secret questions, so. they were therefore opposed on principle to anything in writing'.

30. Report of interview with Admiral Foué de Lapeyrere, 31 January 1913, in ADM 116/3109.

31. The navy's organisational history, as recounted in Kelly, *Tirpitz and the Imperial German Navy*, reflects the Kaiser's desire to make his navy personal. As founded in 1871, the Imperial Navy was run, like the Royal Navy, by an Admiralty. Its chief was its commander. He also dealt with the Reichstag, which supplied funds. Once he became Kaiser in 1888, Wilhelm II abolished the Admiralty in favour of a three-part organisation he considered analogous to that of the army: a Naval Cabinet (Marinekabinett, MK) to handle personnel, a Staatsekretar (State Secretary) of the Navy Office (RMA: Reichs Marine Amt, i.e., Navy Department) to deal with the Reichstag and an Oberkommando (OK) to command the navy and run it. The Staatsekretar might be considered analogous to a US Secretary of the Navy, but he was a commissioned officer. According to Kelly, the Kaiser considered anyone who had to deal with the Reichstag 'tainted' by that contact with the elected masses. Although in theory the OK and Staatsekretar were complementary, in practice they often collided. On 14 March 1899 the Kaiser dissolved the OK. Its staff became a new Admiralstab, which amounted to war planners without responsibility for the building programme and also without command responsibility. The Admiralstab was also responsible for gathering intelligence and for allocating ships to foreign stations. There would no longer be an overall fleet chief equivalent to the British First Sea Lord; in effect the Kaiser took on that role. The key operational commanders and the Admiralstab all reported directly to him. At that time they were the Chief of the First Fleet, the Chiefs of the North Sea and Baltic Stations, the Chief of the Overseas Squadron and the Chief of the Training Inspectorate. The RMA under Tirpitz was responsible for the building programme.

32. To Kelly, *Tirpitz and the Imperial German Navy*, p 163, the total disconnect between army and navy war planning can be traced to the Kaiser's insistence that he would not name a supreme naval commander in peacetime, leaving that choice to the outbreak of war. Tirpitz imagined that he would be given the wartime post, but in fact it was never filled. This was not the post of High Seas Fleet commander; it would have been analogous to the British post of First Sea Lord.

33. Tirpitz hoped that once war broke out he would be made supreme naval leader. *Krieg zur See*, Nordsee 2, 126, gives an account sympathetic to Tirpitz: on 29 July 1914 he sent a letter via Admiral Müller (naval cabinet) proposing that he fuse the Admiralstab with Tirpitz' Navy Office (Navy Department) under a single head with comprehensive powers, ending the dual system of administration the Kaiser had earlier adopted. Naturally Tirpitz nominated himself. The Kaiser preferred not to act, but he also retained Tirpitz as head of the Navy Office. According to Kelly, *Tirpitz and the Imperial German Navy*, p 378, by this time the Kaiser distrusted Tirpitz, who had constantly threatened to resign in order to force him to approve Tirpitz' programmes. He was also heartily disliked by both the fleet and the Admiralstab, who felt that he been too ready to sacrifice readiness for his building programme. There seems to have been particular enmity between Tirpitz and von Ingenohl and the Tirpitz and von Pohl papers published after the war in translation in the Royal Navy's *Monthly Intelligence Review* for 1919–20 show deep enmity between Tirpitz and von Pohl.

34. *Krieg zur See*, Nordsee 2, p 128 blamed the Kaiser's order that ships not be risked on the 'very influential' chief of the Naval Cabinet while complaining that only Tirpitz (at that time in the Reichstag and an energetic navy supporter) could have commanded the navy. *Krieg zur See* repeatedly asserts that von Müller blocked any representations made by officers on the spot, but it also states that after the losses at Heligoland Bight none of them could be expected to risk his neck by advocating action. *Krieg zur See*, Nordsee 2, p 131 quotes a 7 October letter from von Müller to Albert Ballin, director-general of the Hamburg-America Line, that it would be a gross military and political error to seek an action 'only in order to bring the Fleet into evidence as an instrument of war'. This was in connection with Ballin's argument that the British might be willing to make peace if they suffered reverses only on land and did not lose much of their fleet; in the face of serious naval losses, they would 'break out into uncontrollable fury' because so much of their power depended on the Royal Navy. Ballin also argued that, because they were wedded to the balance of power, the British were the only one of the three allied powers that would gain nothing by crippling Germany, because that would only create a new pre-eminent Continental power which would have to be faced. Von Müller considered Ballin overoptimistic about what would bring the British to a conference table. *Krieg zur See* quoted the exchange to show that von Müller was grossly cynical about the navy's pressure to be allowed to fight.

35. W R van Auken, on board USS *Massachusetts*, reporting 16 July 1911 (NARA RG 38 ONI Series R-3-c Register No. 1178): 'The German Navy is a smooth water navy. The discipline is splendid from a spectacular point of view. Attention is concentrated upon drills to attain smartness rather than excellence in gunnery. They over estimate their power in efficiency in believing they are better than any other navy. They have carried

the secretive spirit so far that they do not appreciate that other navies have equally good or better schemes. Their Engineer Officers are most efficient and unjustly considered the inferiors of line officers'. He added that 'the enlisted men . . . consider their discipline very strict but are led to believe that such is necessary in order to have what they believe are the most efficient ships in the world. They are taught to carry out orders implicitly and to take no initiative; they believe their officers to be perfect though at times grumble at the rigid discipline . . . in the absence of their officers they are at a loss as to what to do without detailed orders . . . they think the discipline in the US Navy to be too lax . . . Yet many of them feel they would like to be free, become American citizens and enlist in the US Navy . . . The whole idea seems to be that the Kaiser is the greatest man alive; the ships the greatest built; . . . and to prevent dissension, no newspapers are allowed among the crew.'

36. Translated extracts from 'Why the German Revolutionary Movement Emanated from the Fleet', in *Monthly Intelligence Review* No. 7, 15 November 1919, ADM 223/807. He mentioned serious problems among Engineer and Warrant officers, who were considered socially inferior to deck personnel. He cited a secret memo sent to the Kaiser on 14 January 1913 by Admiral von Holtzendorf after seven years as C-in-C of the High Seas Fleet. The fleet was badly undermanned , hence overworked. Persius cited the monotony of life on board the idle wartime High Seas Fleet, 'the crowded quarters, the crews did not live ashore, as some later claimed, the constant drill and especially the blind rage of Prussian militarism – i.e., the lack of understanding of the soul of the ordinary seaman, the ignoring of personality and the stifling of the spirit, humiliating treatment, frequent punishments of excessive severity for the smallest faults, the completely illusory right of complaint, etc . . . To this must be added the constantly deteriorating quality of their food, while in the Admirals', Captains' and Officers' messes there was an almost universal superabundance and much too frequent drinking bouts were organised.' Persius cites a 7 November 1915 secret order urging naval officers to treat their subordinates better. Persius was the most widely published pre-war and wartime naval commentator, appearing frequently in *Nauticus*, the German equivalent of *Brassey's Naval Annual*. Persius' comments were echoed by those of former Warrant Officer E Alboldt, who testified in 1928 for the Reichstag committee on the causes of the German collapse. The US Office of Naval Intelligence considered his material so valuable that it had the whole lengthy transcript translated (RG 38 ONI Series F-6-g Register 24191, NARA).

Chapter 6. The Chessboard – Naval Geography

1. Drydocking was a frequent necessity, as ships rapidly accumulated marine growth which would drastically reduce their speed. Paints which do not require docking more than once in (say) three years are a very recent development. Ships also had to resort to dockyards frequently to have their condensers repaired, which also required access to the underwater hull (condenser inlets and outlets).

2. *Krieg zur See* refers to limited destroyer endurance, which also limited unit cost. Limited endurance was probably inevitable given the German decision to use coal fuel and the poor quality of German coal. In this connection *Krieg zur See*, Nordsee 1, 71 refers to the limited radius of German destroyers as a limitation on the endurance of the High Seas Fleet on the ground that the fleet had to have a destroyer anti-submarine screen; but the German navy did not develop anti-submarine weapons pre-war and it seems unlikely that its destroyers could have operated as an effective screen. The first German depth charge appeared only in 1915 (the British did see destroyers as an anti-submarine screen, but that was because of their pre-war work on destroyer sweeps). *Krieg zur See* does not mention the pre-war idea of using destroyers to deliver torpedo fire as during a daylight engagement.

3. There were also commercial ports on the North Sea: Hamburg (inland on the Elbe), Bremen, Cuxhaven and Bremerhaven on the Weser. None of them was a naval base, but the western end of the Kiel Canal (the Kaiser Wilhelm II Canal) met the Elbe below Hamburg.

4. These points are made in *Krieg zur See*, Nordsee 1, p 74 (Admiralty translation, NHB).

5. The alliance probably had a mainly naval origin. About 1900 the British government decided that it badly needed an ally, probably because the two-power standard and the need for a large fleet of armoured cruisers (see below) was less and less affordable. The two candidate allies were Germany and Japan. At this time the likely enemies were France and Russia, which were allies. Each of the two possible partners would reduce pressure from one of the enemy allies. The Germans offered an alliance on such coercive terms that the British backed off. Japan proved much more interested, because a British alliance offered valuable deterrence against Russia's ally France. By 1900 the Japanese were already embroiled with Russia over Korea, which Japan had conquered in the Sino-Japanese War of 1894–5. A settlement imposed at the end of the war denied Japan this territory, leaving Russia dominant in the Far East. From a British naval perspective, the alliance with Japan balanced Russian power in the Far East and so considerably reduced the British fleet that had to be stationed there. The situation changed after Japanese victory over Russia in 1904–5 and also after the British shifted their attention to Germany.

Chapter 7. Fleets in Battle

1. *Krieg zur See*, Nordsee 2, translation in *Monthly Intelligence Report* of 15 October 1923.

2. According to *Krieg zur See*, Nordsee 2, the need to set up U-boat reconnaissance helps explain why only *U 9* was available in the Channel to attack the troopships there.

3. Behncke was Acting Chief since von Pohl was at General Headquarters with Tirpitz, von Müller and the Kaiser.

4. This supposed technological superiority is a frequent theme in *Krieg zur See*, one of whose aims was to justify the pre-war Tirpitz building programme. No memorandum of von Pohl's is quoted. After the war the Germans made much of the supposed superiority of their AP shells and their fire control, for example in contact with the US Navy's Bureau of Ordnance in 1921.

5. Much depended on how the war order was read. In the view reflected in *Krieg zur See*, Nordsee 2 (published in 1922), the point was that action was to be avoided *unless conditions were favourable*, with the emphasis on setting up favourable conditions. Von Pohl emphasised the other clause and he clearly doubted that conditions would ever be favourable. To *Krieg zur See*, his comments on the September 1914 plan were the first time that the idea surfaced that action was to be avoided altogether, though that was clearly Chancellor Bethmann-Hollweg's view.

6. Based on von Ingenohl's January 1918 paper on the attitude and activities of the High Seas Fleet during the first six months of war, quoted extensively in *Krieg zur See*, Nordsee 1 and 2.

7. According to *Krieg zur See*, Nordsee 2, he assumed that the British would attack only at full strength, whereas he might well have ships under repair or in the Baltic. This was a perfect mirror image of Jellicoe's fear that the Germans would come out at full strength while he was at average strength due to refits and repairs. Neither side seems to have had the slightest ability to sense the readiness of the other.

8. For the moment, Tirpitz did not want to fight until Turkey had entered the war and the main issue on the Western Front had been decided. *Krieg zur See*, Nordsee 2, 114.

9. Von Pohl also met with Scouting Force commander Rear Admiral Scheer, whose battlecruisers would go out. *Krieg zur See*, Nordsee 2 reports a 1920 interview with Scheer (pp 120–1), which gave a very different view of von Pohl's message. In particular Scheer had no idea of the restrictions which had been added to the war order and he thought the restrictions had been added by von Ingenohl rather than at GHQ. Then and in 1916 (when he was Fleet C-in-C) Scheer and von Pohl agreed that a battle in the German Bight fought in reply to a British challenge, should be avoided; the British must be prodded to come out and fight (presumably under disadvantageous conditions).

10. According to *Krieg zur See*, Nordsee 2, p 123, the Kaiser never signed the order, but the chief of his naval cabinet Admiral von Müller told von Pohl not to press the point, as everything had been approved at an Imperial Audience. The order was forwarded to von Ingenohl on 4 October 1914.

11. *Krieg zur See*, Nordsee 2, p 242 adds that the mines were also intended to sink the three ex-Brazilian monitors the Royal Navy was then using to support the army in Flanders. Their shallow draught had frustrated attempts by U-boats and the German army was demanding their destruction. The four *S.116* class destroyers involved carried twelve mines each; *Krieg zur See* speculates that forty-eight mines were hardly enough. Initially the battlecruisers were to have been sent to the Dogger Bank in distant support, but one developed turbine trouble and this part of the operation was abandoned.

12. *Krieg zur See*, Nordsee 2, p 242 observes that despite all German precautions the British were aware of the operation and they assigned a strong force to intercept and destroy the minelayers. That raises the question of whether signals intelligence was involved. *Krieg zur See* notes that at this time operations orders were generally circulated fairly widely in written form before an operation.

13. *Krieg zur See*, Nordsee 2, p 325. This account claims that there was no other stated reason for the bombardment, although there was also some hope that the appearance of a powerful German force so close to the Thames Estuary would destroy British morale.. Scouting Force commander Admiral Hipper was one of the main proponents of this operation.

14. As in many other First World War operations, the problem of co-operation between surface ships and submarines was ignored. When Hipper's force approached on its way home, *U 21* recognised him and surfaced as required, but *U 14* prepared to attack, recognising a German cruiser just in time.

15. Air reconnaissance was precluded by strong easterly winds blowing for some days prior to the operation and by fog on the day of the operation. A few seaplanes took off, but saw only German ships.

16. As he turned home, Hipper reported that one British light cruiser (which turned out to be HMS *Undaunted*) was shadowing him at long range and he saw many columns of smoke on the horizon (*Undaunted* was withdrawn with Tyrwhitt's other ships as it became clear how powerful Hipper's force was). The withdrawal of the shadowing cruiser killed any chance of intercepting Hipper. The cruiser was on Hipper's return route, but von Ingenohl did not think that he needed cover from the main body, so he turned for home. He turned out to be correct; the only heavy British ships in the area were five pre-dreadnoughts, only one of which was at two hours' readiness. During the raid, only the British battlecruisers and some light cruisers were on the East Coast, concentrated further north at Cromarty. The three ships Hipper encountered were assigned to the Yarmouth Patrol and they were minesweeping off the port. Three British overseas submarines (*E 10*, *D 3* and *D 5*), which were just leaving Gorleston for the Skaggerak and Kattegat tried but failed to intercept Hipper and *D 5* sank after hitting a drifting (probably British) mine. Commodore Tyrwhitt ordered two light cruisers to concentrate off Smiths Knoll and he prepared to take another light cruiser and destroyers across to Terschelling to cut off Hipper's retreat. The old East Coast battleships were also alerted. It is not clear whether Hipper was being shadowed at all, although the Germans did pick up numerous British W/T signals clearly associated with the raid.

17. War diary of Captain Hahn (*Von der Tann*), quoted in *Krieg zur See*, Nordsee 2, pp 366–7.

18. *Krieg zur See*, Nordsee 3, pp 27–30.

19. *Krieg zur See*, Nordsee 2, p 30, quoting his War Diary entry dated 12 November, before the operation.

20. *Krieg zur See*, Nordsee 3 quotes a report that British newspaper experts agreed that the High Seas Fleet was about to attack the British coast, because with the Baltic icing over the German Baltic Fleet would become available to reinforce the North Sea Fleet. The 'extensive preparations' carried out in Kiel and Hamburg since the outbreak of war were thought to be nearing completion. Von Ingenohl speculated that somehow the telegrams between him and GHQ (or something else) had betrayed the operation. He ordered a particular code, which he thought had been compromised, changed. The Admiralstab doubted that the British newspaper report represented a leak, only a natural deduction from the Yarmouth raid. Apparently von Ingenohl was propelled into action by a report by Naval Attaché Captain Boy-Ed in New York that the British were preparing to attack. The new raid was justified as a spoiling attack. The Admiralstab also thought that the despatch of British battlecruisers to the South Atlantic to deal with Graf Spee's squadron had evened the odds (there were even reports that battle squadrons had been sent). The Admiralstab pressed for a wholesale mine attack on the British bases: the Thames Estuary, the Firth of Forth and Cromarty Firth.

21. This and other comments made by von Ingenohl are from his 23 December 1914 report, published in translation in in *Monthly Intelligence Report* No 27, 18 July 1921 (ADM 223/809). This was Operation 'XX' (roman numerals, not letters).

22. The Germans made their signal at 1:15pm and the Admiralty sent it to Warrender and Beatty at 2:43pm.

23. *Krieg zur See*, Nordsee 3, p 134 reads the British official history as indicating that the Admiralty had no idea that von Ingenohl was at sea. He was observed 70 to 80 miles off Wilhelmshaven by British submarines, but the Admiralty concluded that he was going out, not back. That assumes that von Ingenohl's message to Hipper was not intercepted. On the basis of this mis-perception, Jellicoe concentrated the entire Grand Fleet. As a result he was able to carry out important fleet battle practices.

24. Throughout the war, Beatty suffered from the ineptitude of his Flag Lieutenant (flag signaller) Ralph Seymour, to whom he was inexplicably loyal. Cynics may trace Beatty's survival after Scarborough to his personal friendship with First Lord Winston Churchill.

25. *Krieg zur See*, Nordsee 2, p 232, commenting on von Ingenohl's reaction to the report that the British cruiser *Hawke* had been sunk – and a major opportunity lost.

26. *Krieg zur See*, Nordsee 3, p 140.

27. *Krieg zur See*, Nordsee 3, pp 140–5 quotes the War Diary of Captain Sölken of the battleship *Pommern* to this effect, as typical of the views of the fleet. The author of *Krieg zur See* is extremely critical of von Ingenohl for his caution and he uses War Diary entries to show that the fleet understood better.

28. *Krieg zur See*, Nordsee 3, p 157. At this time the German 1st and 3rd Battle Squadrons were in the Jade, the 2nd and 4th in the Elbe specifically to defend its estuary. Complete blockage was considered unlikely due to the strong tidal currents and navigational problems. However, information seemed so definite that the Germans took defensive measures, such as strengthening their pickets and extending their defensive minefield in the German Bight.

29. *Krieg zur See*, Nordsee 3 repeatedly cites the experience of the Falklands to show that older warships could not match modern ones. However, the older ships fighting at the Falklands were armoured cruisers, whereas the older ones in the Channel Fleet were pre-dreadnought battleships. Later in the war the Russian pre-dreadnought *Slava* put up a good performance against German dreadnoughts in the Ösel Island campaign.

30. Grand Fleet Orders and Memoranda for January–June 1915 (ADM 137/2019) includes a report of long-range practice carried out on 24 December 1914 (p 27). Most ships fired at ranges of 17,000 yds down to 15,000 yds against a fixed target (an island). In several cases battle range was more than 1000 yds off and in others between 600 and 1000 yds off. At such ranges even a 400 yd bracket was not wide enough to ensure quickly crossing or straddling the target. Ships tried to turn while firing; those with directors were delayed while making a two-point turn. Analysis of firing by *Iron Duke* showed 'how slow the average rangetaker is to detect an alteration in rate, the rangefinder curve in both her runs continuing on the original slope for a considerable period after the turn; this has been frequently found previously'. Many ships suffered from bad director laying and the rate of fire of director ships was generally too slow. Only two ships, *Orion* and *Erin*, hit with their first salvoes. One implication was that individually-laid guns might often do better than those under director control. A great deal of ammunition would be wasted until the fleet closed the range.

31. This memo was requested on 27 December and delivered by von Pohl and Bethmann-Hollweg at a 9 January audience.

32. The issue of German destroyer endurance arises frequently in *Krieg zur See*, which argues that it had been badly underestimated before the war; British destroyers actually carried less fuel (the author is apparently unaware of the much greater thermal content of their oil fuel and also of the inferiority of German steaming coal). Apparently German destroyers practiced coaling at sea in pre-war exercises.

33. The operation could not be postponed for more than a few days because soon the moon would enter its second, brighter, phase. It was therefore moved ahead to the next new moon, in February. Plans for that operation seem to have envisaged Scarborough-style battlecruiser support, so *Von der Tann* was ordered into dockyard for a twelve-day refit to prepare her for it. She was therefore unable to go on the Dogger Bank operation.

34. Like Jellicoe, von Ingenohl was much exercised by the reduction in maximum fleet strength due to the need for repairs. In January 1915 he wrote that generally one battleship of each (eight-ship) squadron, one large cruiser (battlecruiser or armoured cruiser) and one modern and one older light cruiser was always in dockyard hands, allowing each ship six weeks annually for repairs. That was the peacetime standard, but in wartime ships were kept in a high state of readiness, frequently getting up steam, which affected their boilers. Two flotillas were almost always in dockyard, one for repairs lasting three to four weeks, the other to clean boilers. If an additional half-flotilla was assigned to Zeebrugge (as was then planned), he would have only 3½ flotillas for offensives and for frequent necessary runs out to the outer German Bight. About half the U-boats were always under overhaul. This was aside from training, which could not be undertaken in the Bight due to the British submarine threat. With few exceptions, the 1st and 3rd Battle Squadrons and the destroyers (except the 9th Flotilla) had no opportunities for torpedo firing between the outbreak of war and January 1915; some new ships carried out no practices at all. The same could be said of day and night gunnery practice. Squadron exercises were also essential and they could be conducted only in the Baltic. *Krieg zur See*, Nordsee 3, pp 244–5. Von Ingenohl wrote that he could time his repairs and training so that he whole fleet was ready for a planned offensive – but not an unplanned defensive – operation. This was much the same as Jellicoe's frequent complaint that the Germans could pick their day, when he would face their peak force with his average force.

35. Admiral Hipper's report on the Dogger Bank action was reprinted in the *Monthly Intelligence Report* for 15 August 1921 (ADM 223/809).

36. According to the German account in *Krieg zur See*, *Blücher* was doomed by the first hit, which struck the ammunition gangway running a third of the way along her centreline. She immediately began to burn, the shell having ignited thirty-five to forty 8.2in cartridges. Flash penetrated the two forward wing turrets, which also began to burn. The hit also generated poisonous gas, which spread through voice pipes and ventilation shafts into the central gangway, the conning tower and the rest of the ship. All fire-control and order-transmission gear and steering gear was immediately put out of action. Splinters penetrated the main steam pipes of No. 3 boiler room, slowing the ship to 17 knots. According to the German account, the ship was ultimately hit by 70 to 100 heavy shells and seven torpedoes. *Blücher* lasted three hours under this punishment.

37. According to *Krieg zur See*, Nordsee 3, p 272, a single 13.5in shell passed through the turret armour of 'D' turret at a junction of two plates and exploded inside. The hot splinters it produced in the barbette penetrated the working chamber and ignited main charges and front charges in the hoist. Flash passed up and down, setting fire to further charges lying on the turret turntable and on or near the lower hoists. Only charges in cases not yet opened did not ignite. Those caught in 'D' turret tried to escape into the neighbouring 'C' turret; to do so they had to open the bulkhead door dividing the two, letting the fire and flash into the neighbouring turret and hoist. The reference to charges in cases not yet opened is not clear, in that the Germans placed all their cartridges in metal cartridge cases, which were not removed (there is some question about the smaller forward charges). A later paragraph claims that main cartridges, even in open cases, did not ignite; the main charges were the ones definitely in metal cartridge cases. The open cases were presumably protective outer packing cases. The ship was saved by flooding her magazines and presumably the reserve buoyancy represented by her forecastle kept her afloat with all that water on board. The fire and flash instantly killed 159 men in the two turrets.

38. *Seydlitz* took only two such hits. The second struck the belt armour abreast the forefunnel and had little effect. Like *Seydlitz*, *Derfflinger* was hit only once and in this case damage was limited: a hit (presumably underwater) abreast the fourth boiler room forced the 3in plates inwards and caused flooding; the boiler room had to be pumped out. She ship was also lightly damaged by shorts. *Derfflinger* was ready for sea again on 17 February, less than a month after the battle; *Seydlitz* was ready on 1 April.

39. She was hit twice, one hit starting a spectacular (but irrelevant) fire in one of her boats, which was destroyed. This was the fire the Germans interpreted as her destruction.

40. Beatty letter to Jellicoe, item 107 in Patterson (ed), *Jellicoe Papers* I.

41. With Beatty out of the battle on board *Lion*, command devolved to Admiral Moore. By the time the fight with *Blücher* was over and Moore could return to the chase, Hipper's ships were 12 miles away and Moore's edge in speed was so small that he expected to require two hours to catch up. By that time he would be only 80 miles from Heligoland and the battle would bring him closer still – and a lot closer to the High Seas Fleet, which the British thought was in distant support of Hipper. A British submarine had already signalled that the High Seas Fleet had left harbour.

42. Beatty to Jellicoe, item 107 in Patterson (ed), *Jellicoe Papers* I.

43. This was not *Lion*. *Krieg zur See*, Nordsee 3, p 293. *L 5*, which was still over the scene of the battle, was asked how many battlecruisers she could see; she answered that there were four (*Lion* was out of sight), which seemed to confirm the feeling in the fleet. At this time the Germans were considering ordering destroyers to find and attack the British battlecruisers. Von Ingenohl rejected the idea because some of the flotillas involved were too slow and also because he wanted to retain them as an anti-submarine screen. He also doubted the destroyers could catch up with the retiring enemy force. The destroyer idea does help explain Admiral Moore's reluctance to pursue Hipper. The Germans did retain some hope that U-boats could be set in place to attack the British as they steamed home, but they accomplished nothing.

44. *Krieg zur See*, Nordsee 4, p 94, quoting Vice Admiral von Lens (1st Battle Squadron); Tirpitz called his memo 'poison for the fleet'.

45. According to *Krieg zur See*, Nordsee 4, p 103, von Pohl explained his views at a 23 March Wilhelmshaven conference of admirals, captains and senior officers of flotillas and half-flotillas, all present being much depressed.

46. The fleet steamed out on a northwest course at 15 knots, turned to the northeast and an hour later began to steam home. According to *Krieg zur See*, this sortie was so limited that there was virtually no hope of encountering the enemy. Presumably it was intended to raise the fleet's confidence after so much inactivity and also to familiarise it with the battle formation.

47. *Krieg zur See*, Nordsee 4, pp 120–3.

48. *Krieg zur See*, Nordsee 4, p 159. After the sortie Scouting Group commander Admiral Hipper wanted all new airships stationed in the German Bight instead of in Belgium. In that case every air raid against England would also be a long-range reconnaissance operation, perhaps of decisive value to the fleet. His advice was disregarded.

49. His reasoning, as given in *Krieg zur See*, Nordsee 4, p 222 was that if these ships were destroyed the High Seas Fleet would lose prestige and 'the nation would lose faith in the Fleet Command'. The Germans had already lost the minelayer *Königen Luise* and the half-flotilla of old destroyer-minelayers, as well as the cruiser *Blücher* and two torpedo boats off the North Hinder, all of which losses von Pohl cited.

50. Text in *Krieg zur See*, Nordsee 4, p 224. The text also refers to a W/T direction-finding station at Norddeich, which worked on the strong British signals detected that evening. The station at Heligoland intercepted signals but did not D/F them. The Grand Fleet was indeed at sea on an intercepting course. *Krieg zur See* argues that von Pohl could indeed have given battle on favourable terms (using the new German minefield), had his airship reconnaissance been effective. 'An astonishing fact is that during their advance the enemy actually became aware of the Dogger Bank minefield and even as early as April they had expected 'on the strength of a report' that mines would be laid there'.

51. The fleet proposals were first that all torpedo boats (destroyers) should have sweep gear and second that the fleet should be provided with fast sperrbrechers – more or less mine proof ships which could precede the fleet. Existing sperrbrechers were merchant ships, but they were not fast enough to work with the fleet.

52. In the case of the 29 May sortie, the 3rd Sperrbrecher Group proceeded from the Outer Jade light vessel to test the planned route of the fleet, as it had already done on 26 May. An hour before this group reached the Norderney gap, the battlecruisers and light cruisers of the Scouting Groups sailed, followed two hours later by the main body of the High Seas Fleet. The Scouting Groups and the two fastest torpedo boat flotillas were to scout 30 to 60 miles ahead of the main body. In case of contact, they were to drive any enemy force into the main body. *Krieg zur See*, Nordsee 4, pp 293–4.

53. *Krieg zur See*, Nordsee 4, p 292. Once von Pohl was at sea, the Admiralstab informed him from intercepted British W/T that simultaneously with his sortie British auxiliary patrol forces had been withdrawn and naval commands warned to keep in good communication with each other. The author of *Krieg zur See* observes that by this time it was clear that the British were aware of all major operations and that the German naval command was therefore naturally 'uneasy'. However, no one could imagine any means by which the British were gaining this information. The Germans assumed that the problem was espionage; there was, according to *Krieg zur See*, no attempt to search *German* W/T traffic. In this case the key message was probably the detailed order to the 3rd Sperrbrecher Group to search a particular area. It should also have been noted that, as reported by the airships, the British had sent out no patrols other than submarines. The German naval command (presumably von Pohl) took that report as an indication that the British would accept battle only in their own waters and were not at all inclined to send portions of their fleet into the German Bight where they might be snapped up. In reality the Grand Fleet sailed on 29 May, preceded by the battlecruisers. They were in position to intercept in the event the High Seas Fleet was heading for a coastal raid. As the German fleet returned, the battlecruiser *Moltke* narrowly avoided a torpedo from a British submarine. The Germans thought their torpedo boats precluded any second attack. An hour later they intercepted a loud British W/T signal (1000m wave), which they assumed was the submarine's contact report. Another British submarine nearly torpedoed one of the two U-boats sent out ahead of the High Seas Fleet as part of this operation.

54. This was not a very successful operation. *U 14* and *U 40* were both sunk. *U 17* sank three merchant ships, but no warships (she attacked, but failed to hit, the armoured cruiser *Argyll*). *U 38* torpedoed, but did not sink, the armoured cruiser *Roxburgh* (she was hit in her bow). *U 6* attacked, but failed to hit, the light cruiser *Nottingham*. *U 32* apparently achieved nothing at all.

55. Particular improvements mentioned in *Krieg zur See*, Nordsee 4 were the German form of director firing ('bearing indicators'), additional oil-firing in boilers and repair of propeller shaft bearings (which had suffered as ships lay in the muddy waters of the Jade and the Elbe). Director firing was to be complete on board *Moltke*, *Von der Tann* and *Grosser Kurfürst* by mid-June, after which *Friedrich der Grosse* and *Ostfriesland* were to be taken in hand. The German form of director firing was limited to aiming all of a ship's guns at an indicated target, as the other important object of British director firing, to compensate for a ship's roll, was taken care of by a gyro at the gun.

56. According to *Krieg zur See*, Nordsee 4, p 492, of the flotillas assigned to the High Seas Fleet, $2^{1}/2$ to 3 were always unavailable due to repairs, boiler-cleaning and the exchange of older for newer boats. Even when all were available, they were just enough to provide sufficient anti-submarine screens. At best von Pohl had fifty to fifty-five boats available, of which at least three flotillas (thirty-three) were required to screen three battle squadrons. Another $1^{1}/2$ to 2 flotillas (fifteen to twenty boats) were needed for the Scouting Squadrons operating ahead of the fleet. That would leave, at most, one boat for

each of the six cruisers screening the main fleet from surface torpedo attack. One this basis, to surrender even one flotilla to the Baltic would immobilise the High Seas Fleet. Note that *Krieg zur See* never discusses the offensive use planned for High Seas Fleet destroyers.

57. One was at the disposal of the officer commanding the scouting force, operating near his flagship; a second went out to the Skaggerak; the others operated NW, WNW and W of Heligoland out as far as possible. This was in marked contrast to earlier practice, in which all the attached airships stayed close to the fleet. The planned reconnaissance around Heligoland failed because of the squally southwest wind.

58. The German official history drily comments that von Pohl's decision to break off did not meet with universal approval and therefore his reasoning, recounted here, was written down in detail. The Kaiser had given blanket approval to North Sea operations, appreciating that they involved some risk, but he specifically ordered that the fleet not risk heavy losses by fighting the whole Grand Fleet and von Pohl commented that had he waited to break off until he sighted the British fleet he would incur considerable losses. He would also incur considerably greater loss of morale.

59. ADM 137/2019, pp 334–7. A further exercise (ordered 10 July 1915) concentrated on (i) representing some possible German torpedo attacks and (ii) attacks when the enemy fleet turned away to gain an advantageous torpedo position or to retire towards his base. ADM 137/2020, pp 64–9

60. ADM 137/2020, pp 48–9. The next item in the file is an account of a war game played on board HMS *Benbow* to test tactics.

61. ADM 137/2021, p 141.

62. ADM 137/1898, section on battlecruisers. In fact *Derfflinger* was commissioned on 1 September 1914 but clearly was not ready for Dogger Bank; *Lützow* was commissioned on 8 August 1915 (but was barely ready for Jutland) and *Hindenburg*, the last German battlecruiser completed, was commissioned on 10 May 1917.

63. ADM 137/1898 contains a rough calculation. Substitution would cost 1500 tons, equivalent to an increase of 15in in draught and the loss of about a foot of metacentric height, which would be sustainable in broad-beam German ships. There was no attempt to calculate the loss of speed involved. This was one up on an assumption Beatty and Jellicoe made late in 1914 that *Derfflinger* was armed with 14in guns (ADM 137/995, 207). The Germans made errors of their own. They thought they had sunk HMS *Tiger* at Dogger Bank, so when another ship turned up at Jutland they assumed it was a direct replacement, armed with 15in rather than 13.5in guns. Comments by Austrian naval attaché after Jutland, who was correctly sceptical.

64. This appears to have been the extent of Jellicoe's acceptance of divisional tactics: the fast division could apply pressure on the wing or some other part of the enemy's fleet, making up for the inflexibility of line-ahead tactics. This comment is from the account of Jutland in *Krieg zur See*, written by the officer who was navigator on board *Von der Tann* during the battle, hence aware of tactical issues.

65. Hipper's gunnery report dated 4 July 1916 is in ADM 137/1644, *Jutland: Later Reports, 1916* , pp 130–6. 'The fire of the English battlecruisers resulted in no serious damage to our battlecruisers. As the shots seldom fell near our ships, a definite opinion with regard to their spread could not be arrived at in this squadron. On the other hand, the fire of the ships of the *Malaya* class [*Queen Elizabeth*s] and later of the main enemy fleet created an excellent impression.'

66. The first such operation was scheduled for 6 February, but it failed because of bad weather: the airships could not go up and the seas were too heavy.

67. The Royal Navy was deploying ships with anti-aircraft guns to attack (not defend against) airships.

68. A 12 May 1916 conference at Rosyth chaired by First Lord Balfour concluded that the Firth of Forth (i.e., Rosyth) should be developed urgently as the sole fleet base, both for the Grand Fleet and for the Battlecruiser Fleet. Jellicoe urged that Scapa be retained as a secondary base, both because it was much superior for exercises but also because it was a base for the 10th Cruiser Squadron (enforcing the blockade) and for forces supporting it. It was also proposed that 12in gun battleships be organised into a 4th Battle Squadron based permanently either in the Humber or further south. All of the changes were to be carried out before the winter of 1916–17. Jellicoe once again opposed attaching the 5th Battle Squadron to Beatty's Battlecruiser Fleet.

69. Tyrwhitt's light cruisers and destroyers escorted the carrier *Vindex*, with the British battlecruisers in support. The operation was nearly aborted when torpedoes were reported near the cruiser *Cleopatra*. No German submarine was nearby; the German official history speculates that it was a British submarine on station, unaware that she had encountered a British force. The air attack was unsuccessful.

70. One of the British destroyers was mined. She was being towed back at low speed, screened by most of Tyrwhitt's force and, at a distance, by Beatty's battlecruisers. The German official historian notes that Scheer bungled his instructions to his surface fleet: he wanted it to pursue the British aggressively until dark, but his signal was read as an instruction to turn back. *Krieg zur See*, Nordsee 5, noted as German text p 85.

71. According to *Krieg zur See*, Nordsee 5, German text p 116, the argument was that the Grand Fleet would probably not penetrate the German Bight because the British minefields just outside would greatly interfere with its movements. An attack could only be mounted by fast divisions appearing at dawn from the north or west or both to shell the islands or to support another air raid against the airship sheds or else perhaps attack the Kiel (Kaiser Wilhelm) Canal. The bulk of the Grand Fleet would be outside the German Bight, in support.

72. *Krieg zur See*, Nordsee 5, noted as German text p 135.

73. The aircraft were all floatplanes. Only the carrier *Campania* could launch a landplane (which she could not recover). She was not involved in this operation (the carriers were *Vindex* and *Engadine*).

74. He placed submarines off Scapa, the Moray Firth, the Firth of Forth, the Humber and north of Terschelling on the Dutch coast. Submarines of the Flanders Flotilla were to operate off the Thames and others were to mine British ports. When the operation was postponed, additional submarines were assigned to the area in which the British fleet usually assembled (as the Germans understood it). It happened that these submarines left their stations before the Grand Fleet passed through exactly the area involved. According to *Krieg zur See*, Nordsee 5, the British became aware of the U-boats and hunted them intensively, much reducing the threat they represented. *Krieg zur See* also comments that some U-boats were assigned operating sectors so narrow that they were likely to come into conflict with each other.

75. The 23 April 1916 order for this Operation 'XX' is in ADM 137/2021 pp 501–3. The plan would be executed on or after 1 May 1916. A second more detailed version dated 30 April is on pp 533–6 and 545–6. Another memo (pp 624–8) dated 29 May described Operation 'M', a sweep into the Skaggerak still including *Abdiel* but not the air raid.

76. The entire Grand Fleet was at sea $2^1/2$ hours before the first German ships left port. Forces were to rendezvous in the North Sea. They included the ships at Scapa as well as Beatty's force from Rosyth and ships from Cromarty.

77. The southern forces could deal with either another battlecruiser raid or with the initial stage of an invasion, the latter often being given as the reason they were not sent out to Jellicoe. The Harwich Force was too small to make much difference in a fleet action.

78. In a 26 April 1915 letter (G.01679/1915) Jellicoe warned of serious consequences unless the rate of fire was increased once the range had been found, based on the experiences of the Falklands and of the Dogger Bank. German survivors of the Falklands had said that it was much easier to fire at a slow-firing ship than at a rapidly-firing one, as rapid enemy fire produced splashes and smoke which made gunnery difficult. Jellicoe quoted two current Grand Fleet orders, A.80 and A.109. The first stressed the need for rapid fire. The second pointed out that actions thus far in the war had shown the importance of (i) quickly opening fire, (ii) rapid fire and (iii) shorts as opposed to 'overs'. A ship which did not start firing quickly enough could be smothered by her enemies. Even if she missed at first she would slow enemy fire. 'Shorts' were not merely valuable for fire control, their splashes helped confuse the enemy. Jellicoe felt that such facts had not been sufficiently impressed on fire-control officers. Document courtesy of Dr Nicholas A Lambert.

79. As was evident in a television documentary. I am grateful to Laurence Burr, who produced the documentary, for this information.

80. When the United States entered the war, the Admiralty provided a package of its contemporary papers on lessons of Jutland (specifically the battlecruiser losses). It survives in the RG 38 series of ONI papers in NARA (F-6-f Register No. 9231), dated 20 September 1917. The package included full battle damage reports for HMS *Southampton*, *Lion*, *Princess Royal*, *Warspite* and *Tiger*. An associated blueprint, copies of which are in several US files (including those of the General Board) summarised all battle damage at Jutland. Evidence of lax procedures included testimony of the surviving Gunnery Commander of HMS *Invincible*, given eight days after the battle, upon which initial precautions were based. In a letter (S.01960/1916) on p 4 of the file, Jellicoe admitted that the procedure (drill) in force at the time of Jutland 'was to keep all cages and waiting positions loaded and the magazine doors open and all the evidence seems to show that if a turret was pierced by a shell which exploded inside it, the magazine was almost certain to blow up'. Jellicoe prefaced this with the remarkable comment that he concurred with Beatty that 'there is no evidence that, in the ships lost, the precautions essential to the safety of cordite charges, *as we then knew them*, were neglected'. He observed that although fourteen German ships had been sunk by gunfire to date, none had blown up, but of nine British losses to gunfire, six had blown up. On 26 October Tudor wrote that 'there is little doubt in my mind that in the great anxiety to attain a rapid rate of fire, the ordinary precautions for safety of cordite cartridges have been gradually relaxed, until at least the best of the enemy's shells has proved the danger of what was being done'. Remedies had been enforced and the fleet was now safe. In a 16 December 1916 letter in the package, Third Sea Lord Admiral Tudor (soon to go to the China Fleet, having censured Beatty for lax [suicidal] magazine procedure and then having denied doing so) noted that the Germans were using a different propellant ('a modified cordite, but rather more modified than ours') and that their last quarter charge was 'contained in a brass cylinder for obturation sealing the breech. and that the remaining quarters are "believed" to be enclosed in light metal cases which are consumed in the gun'. Beatty suggested that in some cases nose-fused HE (Lyddite) shells had exploded sympathetically, which might explain an explosion as the mined HMS *Audacious* sank (an explanation which might absolve him of the fatal magazine sin). As Jellicoe's successor, Beatty was perfectly placed to send a 22 December letter absolving his predecessor. The US package reproduces part of the more extensive file in PRO: ADM 1/8463/176.

81. DNO's 3 August 1916 comments are in the package provided to the US Navy in 1917. He was convinced that the problem was not the instability of British propellant but instead the grossly unsafe magazine practices. What mattered was not the nature of the propellant but the way it was protected. Beatty had contrasted the survival of the German *Seydlitz*. DNO Captain Murray Singer observed that (going by a report on the *Goeben*) the Germans kept charges in ready racks in their turrets, which was why *Seydlitz* burned so visibly at Dogger Bank. Because they were protected, they would not pass the fire to the magazine (this was incorrect). He thought that, having suffered at Dogger Bank, as the British had not, the Germans had probably adopted new safety procedures. In fact the new procedures were minor and nearly irrelevant. DNO confirmed that in their 11in guns the Germans used only encased charges. He noted that Beatty imagined that cordite ignited in the open would explode, but that was not true; it would burn and produce gas. Charges set afire in HMS *Lion* burned without exploding, but produced a flash which went down the trunk (the nearest vent), igniting some charges in the handling room *en route*. Had the magazine been open and lids off the powder cases the magazine would have blown up. In the case of *Lion*, the shell burst did not ignite the charges (they were ignited 20 minutes later) and it was impossible to say either why they ignited or why charges in the handling room were not sent down once the turret had been hit (all gear in the working chamber was still intact). In a parallel letter, DNC quoted a 1914 gunnery report (G.15134/14) to the effect that a good supply of ammunition near the gun and in ammunition passages, was most essential and that the risk of fires had to be accepted; this view was corrected by Gunnery Order G.043-5 of 1 February 1915 after the battles of Coronel and the Falklands. To him, the fact that the charges in *Lion*'s turret, hoists and working chamber were not sent back into the protection of the magazine before the doors were closed indicated the nearly casual manner in which loose cordite was regarded on board British ships at the time. Beatty pointed to destroyers sunk without exploding as proof that powder should be in metal cartridge cases (as in QF guns), but DNC observed that light cruisers, which used bag charges, had been heavily damaged without blowing up.

82. DNC's 7 October letter is in the package provided to the US Navy in 1917. Beatty had argued that either British construction was at fault, or that British ammunition was faulty. DNO handled the second argument, DNC the first (note that Beatty avoided the leadership issue of encouraging or at least allowing suicidal magazine practices).

83. DNC Memorandum S.02136/1916 of 19 December 1916, extract in Staff History, *Home Waters Pt VII* (Appendix A). This was published in October 1927.

84. ADM 137/2021, Grand Fleet Orders and Memoranda, p.630.

85. See the author's *Naval Firepower* (Barnsley: Seaforth Publishing, 2007) for details of the Dreyer and Argo systems and their logic. The Argo Clock made it possible for a ship to manoeuvre while firing and that might have made Beatty's battlecruisers significantly less vulnerable. It would not have made any difference in trying to hit the zig-zagging German ships. The Argo Clock was the ancestor of the analogue computers adopted by all navies after the First World War (its relationship to the US Ford Rangekeeper was somewhat complex).

86. It is certainly true that British shells often failed to penetrate and then explode, but they did plenty of damage when they hit, as witness the near-destruction of SMS *Seydlitz*. It may be fairer to say that given the actual rather low hitting rates at Jutland, it was almost impossible to sink ships, the British battlecruisers and the cruiser *Defence* being lost only because of incredibly bad magazine practices. In the case of *Defence*, the fatal defect was an ammunition passage between her end magazines; when one exploded, the passage was a powder train to the other. Had only one magazine exploded, the ship might have survived, the amount of explosive being much smaller than in a battlecruiser. Second World War experience suggested that a magazine hit on a cruiser might not be fatal because the explosion would burst the hull and let in water, releasing gas which would otherwise cause a much larger explosion. For the fuze issue, see Ian Macallum's two articles on 'The Riddle of the Shells' in *Warship 2002–3*, and *2004*.

87. This and the argument for superior armour-piercing quality were important post-war to Germans trying to sell shell and fire control capability. After the war, the Germans promoted their shells and fire control system to the US Navy on this basis; the US ONI file (RG 38 NARA) contains a detailed report by Commander W R Furlong (later Chief of the Bureau of Ordnance) of a visit to Germany to learn about both. Arthur J Marder, *From the Dreadnought to Scapa Flow III: Jutland and After* (Oxford University Press, 1978), pp 196–200 thoroughly debunks the claim of German gunnery, showing that the German figures include numerous hits on ships dead in the water at close range and exclude what must have been numerous major-calibre hits on German capital ships such as *Derfflinger* and *Lützow*.

88. The magazine problem is dealt with obliquely in many places, such as Marder, *Jutland and After*, pp 208–14, but not the connection with magazine overloading and with tactics entailing a low rate of hitting at long range. Accounts typically emphasise the role of flash rather than the effect of systematically creating a powder train from turret to magazine. The first more complete analysis seems to have been Nicholas A Lambert, '"Our Bloody Ships" or "Our Bloody System"? Jutland and the Loss of the Battle Cruisers, 1916', in *Journal of Military History*, 62, No 1 (January 1998). The extent to which both Beatty and Jellicoe sought alternative reasons (amounting to excuses) for the disaster is clear in the file sent to the US Navy in 1917.

89. She was hit by the disabled light cruiser *Wiesbaden*, not by the expected mass destroyer attack. Damage was analysed by D K Brown, *The Grand Fleet: Warship Design and Development 1906- 1922* (London: Chatham Publishing, 1999), p 162. The torpedo hit about 25ft below the waterline outboard of the 6in magazine abaft 'B' 13.5in magazine. Side plating and framing were destroyed over a length of 28ft and badly distorted over more than twice that length (70ft). The diesel generator near the hit was destroyed. A watertight door into the bunkers failed and the forward transverse bulkhead also opened, allowing water into the forward boiler room, putting out four and then all six boilers there. However, the 6in magazine bulkhead about 25ft inboard was not affected. Overall, damage was much more extensive than that predicted on the basis of pre-war experiments using 280lb wet guncotton warheads. Even after the hit, the ship was able to maintain her position in line at 17 knots, firing 162 rounds of 13.5in.

Probably due to worsening weather, flooding rapidly increased during the night after the battle, but the ship managed to reach port under her own power. Repairs took six weeks.

90. Damage to *Marlborough* could be compared with the mine damage which sank the earlier but similar *Audacious* on 27 October 1914. The main difference seems to have been that in the earlier case the mine exploded just forward of the after transverse engine room bulkhead, so the space which could be flooded (the port engine room) was both larger and further off-centre than in the case of *Marlborough*. Counterflooding brought the ship back to nearly an even keel (from a 10–15° list) but it also brought her lower in the water and she began to flood progressively through the many openings in her structure, which could not be closed off. Her starboard engine room flooded, followed by the remaining (centreline) engine room. The final catastrophic flooding came when she was so low in the water that the sea washed over her quarterdeck, carrying away ventilators and pouring down. Brown argues that damage control was poor; presumably the ship could have been saved despite the damage. It is not clear to what extent lessons learned from the loss of *Audacious* helped save HMS *Marlborough*. The standard German mine at the outbreak of war carried a charge of either 170 or 230lb of wet guncotton. The standard torpedo (G6) carried a 357lb warhead, but probably only about half of that was explosive.

91. ADM 137/2021, p 660.

92. Jellicoe should have known better, because on 1 June First Sea Lord wrote him that intercepts showed that *Lützow* had been sunk, the cruiser *Elbing* sunk, the cruisers *Rostock* and *Stettin* damaged and several destroyers were missing. He added that *Derfflinger, Moltke, Ostfriesland, Oldenburg, Seydlitz, Nassau* and *König* had been badly damaged. 'I think they were completely surprised and never expected to meet anything, but they got out of it somehow' – not a bad summary of the battle. Patterson (ed), *Jellicoe Papers* I, p 268.

93. ADM 137/1645, *Grand Fleet: Post-Jutland Changes 1916*, copy of document courtesy of Dr David Stevens, RANHB. Jellicoe's letter to the Admiralty listing conclusions is apparently the only surviving evidence of this conference.

94. On 25 August 1916 Beatty wrote that he understood that three or four of the fastest and newest German battleships 'are believed to be attached' to the 1st Scouting Group (the battlecruisers). This information was entirely false.

95. DNC was to consider increasing the height of main belt armour by a foot and using weight saved by thinning the side armour above that to thicken deck protection and also to provide an armoured bulkhead 20ft inboard of the top of the main belt specifically to catch fragments of German shells burst by the thin upper side armour. Similarly, the upper part of the anti-torpedo bulkhead inboard of oil tanks should be thickened. Deck armour in the *Repulse* and *Glorious* classes would be thickened. Arrangements to keep flash from reaching magazines were also discussed: the best was Third Sea Lord's proposal that only one quarter charge be in the air lock at any one time.

96. Assistant Director of Torpedoes, who was responsible, found that installation in a 'G' class submarine (the type assigned in 1916 to the Grand Fleet) was possible and the Board decided to fit all six such submarines of the 11th Flotilla at once. Installation on board all other 'G' class submarines and, if possible, all 'E' class was 'considered to be a matter of the first importance'.

97. Jellicoe not only deployed across the path of the German fleet, he did so in such a way that he enjoyed the advantage of better light, so that the oncoming Germans could barely distinguish the British battleships apart from their muzzle flashes.

98. According to Marder, *Jutland and After*, pp 132–3, one of the surprises of the battle was that the German torpedo tracks were so visible. Jellicoe later wrote that he ordered ships to turn away partly because he thought (due to information from DNI) that tracks would not be visible.

99. *Gunnery Progress 1914-1918* (Admiralty Gunnery Division, June 1919), p 15.

100. This is clear from the reports of the Shell Committee which developed the new-generation armour-piercing shells. They had to be hardened more effectively than their predecessors, filled with insensitive explosive and provided with appropriate delay fuzes. The pre-Jutland shells were too sensitive and too often broke up when they hit armour. After the battle, one of Beatty's excuses for the poor performance of his battlecruisers was that shells (which had been developed during Jellicoe's tenure as Third Sea Lord, ending in 1910) were defective. Jellicoe had actually tried to change the shell requirements, but his successor had not pressed the project. The 1917 and 1918 reports of the Shell Committee are in ADM 186/169. British doctrine was to open fire with high explosive shells, the bursts of which would be visible aids to spotting.

101. Description in Marder, *Jutland and After*, p 219. These exercises were carried out by a ship's navigator, action plotting officer and signal officer. That these were harbour exercises may explain why plotting at Jutland was often ineffective due to navigational errors. After Jutland the fleet plotted in terms of distance and bearing from the flagship, not in absolute navigational terms. This comment forms the beginning of the post-war (1923) file on standardised tactical plotting arrangements, ADM 116/2090.

102. See, for example, Marder, *Jutland and After*, pp 217–24.

103. Scheer and other Germans certainly radioed enough information, as is evident in the account by Beesly, *Room 40*, pp 159–62. The German signals were quickly broken and at least some of their contents passed to Jellicoe by the Operations Division. Exactly how much was passed and what Jellicoe did with what he received, are controversial. To Beesly it is difficult to see why Director of Operations Admiral Oliver did not take into account the mass of information already available when he drafted a signal to Jellicoe at 1.48am on 1 June. Jellicoe considered this omission inexplicable and after the war he felt

that the Naval Staff was leaving him to take the blame by concealing its own egregious error (Marder, *Jutland and After*, p 175). In order to maintain secrecy, all signals to Jellicoe were summaries of information and they sometimes did not reflect the full content of the intelligence.

104. Appendix B of Naval Staff Monograph Vol XVII, *Home Waters to November 1916*, p 246.

105. ADM 137/2022, p 26, comments on a fleet exercise.

106. Report of Austrian Naval Attaché, NHB Box 633, document courtesy of Dr David Stevens, RANHB.

107. According to the Austrian attaché, Scheer said simply that 'those who make a study of this engagement will be very puzzled as to my object in advancing thus against the wall of British ships. The fact is that I had no particular object. I made the first advance because I had a feeling that I ought to endeavour to assist the *Wiesbaden* and because the situation ahead was quite obscure to me, for I saw nothing of the *Lützow* and received no W/T reports. I soon saw, however, that the leading ships were coming under an overwhelming fire and that I could not risk the fleet on the *Wiesbaden*'s account. When I noticed that the British pressure had quite ceased and that the fleet remained intact in my hands, I turned back, under the impression that the action could not end this way and that I ought to seek contact with the enemy again.' The Austrian attaché was not amused and German Admiral von Trotha 'said jokingly that, if an Admiral brought about such a situation at a war game or in manoeuvres, he would never be entrusted with another command'.

108. *The battle of Jutland (German Official Account)* (O.U. 5359, 1 May 1926), a British official translation of parts of *Krieg zur See*, Nordsee 5, p 112. Document from NHB, copy courtesy of Dr. David Stevens, RANHB.

109. German account of Jutland, footnote on p 114.

110. An enemy bearing abaft the beam would run towards torpedoes fired at it by the enemy battle line.

111. *Krieg zur See*, Nordsee 6, pp 33–5. The argument in favour of a new U-boat campaign against British commerce was in a 4 July 1916 note to the Kaiser. Chief of the Naval Cabinet Admiral von Müller wrote to Scheer on 23 June, saying that although to Scheer the alternatives seemed to be simply all or nothing, matters were more complicated; the Germans were being obliged by the Americans to pull back, though 'raging inwardly'. Von Müller wrote that he personally favoured a ruthless U-boat campaign. He added that the current conflict between the United States and Mexico (currently involving US Army action south of the border), the 'growing embitterment' of neutrals over the British blockade, increasing prospects for the 1916 harvest and German successes on both fronts, all were 'rungs on the ladder leading to such a use unrestricted warfare. of our submarines, without their employment constituting an uncertain political adventure'.

112. *Krieg zur See* took pains to argue that Jutland was a great German victory (in Nordsee 5) and that it proved the wisdom of Tirpitz' building programme. These were such sensitive points in post-war Germany that it is difficult to take any official comments on them at face value. Unless they were accepted, it would be difficult or impossible for the post-war German navy to gain acceptance.

113. Of the other badly-damaged ships, *Ostfriesland* (mined on the way back) was ready on 12 July, *Grosser Kurfürst* on 19 July, *Markgraf* on 19 July, *König* on 22 July, *Moltke* on 20 July, *Von der Tann* on 31 July and *Derfflinger* on 15 September.

114. In May the MarineKorps Flanders reported that heavy British patrols by monitors, destroyers and trawlers were making it difficult to remove the net and mine barrage laid off Ostend and Zeebrugge on 24 April; the torpedo boats could raid the British offshore force and thus open the bases for more extensive submarine operations. After that had been done, the torpedo boats would return to the Heligoland Bight. Scheer provided his most powerful (2nd) flotilla, which was transferred on 7–8 June, while the High Seas Fleet was still repairing the damage inflicted at Jutland. It returned after two months, in time for the August operation.

115. The author of *Krieg zur See* notes that Scheer sent an order similar to that he issued before steaming out to the battle of Jutland: 'Gg 2750/0 takes place today', which was comparable to '31 May Gg. 2490', hence could be recognised by British intelligence. The British did not publish any of the German signals traffic on which they based their decision to send the Grand Fleet to sea. If the British did base their action on this sort of evidence, it suggests that even in 1916 (when most historians consider it primitive) the Admiralty intelligence organisation was quite sophisticated in its interpretation of otherwise obscure German signals. The Germans do not seem to have created anything like a comparable integrated view of British operations via their signal traffic.

116. *Nottingham* was sunk by three torpedoes, but initially Jellicoe did not know whether she had been torpedoed or mined. HMS *Dublin*, which was nearby, did see a torpedo track. Jellicoe had already witnessed an unsuccessful attack on HMS *Royalist*, from which he transferred to his fleet flagship HMS *Iron Duke*.

117. According to *Krieg zur See*, U 53 successfully shadowed the British main body for a considerable time on 19 August, operating at high speed on the surface and observing the smoke made by the fleet. Not all of her W/T reports got through. One of the German airships, *L 31*, also kept in touch with the British fleet. Neither unit seems to have reported very frequently; Jellicoe thought, however, that Scheer knew exactly where his fleet was. It is not clear from *Krieg zur See* why Scheer's submarine commander was not on board his flagship, in personal contact with him. It appears that Jellicoe was not supplied with decrypts of the shadowing messages. *Krieg zur See*, Nordsee 6, p 92

comments that the submarine's messages were far better than those from the airships, on which Scheer placed such reliance.

118. The sequence of events as reported in *Krieg zur See*, Nordsee 6 is that *Nottingham* was attacked at 7am and 7.24am on 19 August; Jellicoe received the report at 8am and gave the order to retire at 8.05am. He had received the D/F position of *Westfalen*, an indication of the position of the High Seas Fleet, at 6.45am. Scheer received the signal intelligence report from Neumünster at 9.45am and the airship report that the British main body had been spotted at 10.50am (the airship referred to the main body as already supposedly spotted by *U 53*). Meanwhile, Jellicoe had turned back to the south at 10am, no more German submarines having been spotted. Jellicoe received the second D/F report, giving the current German position, at 1.30pm (it was timed an hour and 30 minutes previously). Scheer received the signal intelligence report (of HMS *Aurora*) at 3.40pm; it in effect ruined his faith in his airship reconnaissance. He ordered the turn home at 5.12pm, having made the decision to break off at 4.30pm. However, note that at 3.30pm the Admiralty informed Jellicoe that Scheer had turned back at 1.30pm. At 5pm the Admiralty informed Jellicoe that at 3.45pm the High Seas Fleet had been standing 75 miles northeast of the Humber. Jellicoe turned home, but also informed Tyrwhitt that the High Seas Fleet would probably return to base via the Dutch coast (Terschelling).

119. The tabulation in *Krieg zur See*, Nordsee 6, p 71 shows twenty-nine Grand Fleet battleships to eighteen German; six battlecruisers to two German; five armoured cruisers with the Grand Fleet (none with the German fleet), twenty vs eleven light cruisers and twenty-six vs twenty-four submarines; but seventy-five British vs. ninety-three German destroyers/torpedo boats.

120. In a 24 August 1916 letter to First Sea Lord (in ADM 137/1645, p 120), Jellicoe laid out what he considered minimum screening requirements: twelve to screen an eight-ship battle squadron; eight to screen a five-ship battle squadron (*Queen Elizabeth*s), two to screen an armoured cruiser, one to screen a light cruiser, twelve to screen a battlecruiser squadron and two each for the carriers *Campania* and *Engadine*. The Germans would consider his minimum too few, as indicated by the numbers they took to sea with the High Seas Fleet. On this basis, Jellicoe wanted sixty-one destroyers for the force at Scapa or Cromarty and twenty-six for the Rosyth force, a total of eighty-seven; he had fifty-five and thirty-one, respectively, including flotilla and half-flotilla leaders. Refits would cut the Scapa force by eight ships and escort duties would take another two, leaving forty-five. Figures for Rosyth were six ships under refit, leaving twenty-five. Only Rosyth had nearly enough destroyers by Jellicoe's reckoning.

121. The Admiralty approved a total of ninety-two destroyers and eight leaders for the Grand Fleet, of which eighty and eight were currently available. Allowing for no losses, the full strength could be reached in December. However, the five Mediterranean light cruisers, particularly those in the Adriatic, were 'equally if not more entitled' to screening and the Admiralty hoped to send them a half-flotilla for that purpose. The need to escort troopships was increasing and minesweepers had to be protected. It was nearly impossible to provide enough destroyers for those duties. Destroyers could screen light cruisers only in fine weather (in anything else they were a hindrance) and First Sea Lord suggested substituting a large flotilla leader under those circumstances. At this time the Royal Navy was building rigid airships which it hoped could replace cruisers as fleet scouts in good weather. First Sea Lord added that 'it cannot be overlooked that the C-in-C Jellicoe. lays great stress on the injury the enemy can inflict on our forces in the North Sea, but offers no suggestion as to the employment of his forces to inflict similar losses on the enemy. It is also to be noted that practically all large movements of the Fleet have to be initiated by the Admiralty...we should welcome any suggestions from him . . . with the object of inflicting similar injury to the enemy'. ADM 137/1645, pp 126–7. A later version of this letter added further calls on the Admiralty for destroyers to serve outside the Grand Fleet.

122. The policy was agreed in a meeting between Jellicoe and Chief of War Staff Admiral Oliver on board HMS *Iron Duke*, on 13 September 1916. Jellicoe was willing to risk mine damage in areas which could be reconnoitred by submarines with long-range W/T, but until he had enough destroyers to screen against U-boats he would not go south of the Dogger Bank. Oliver told Jellicoe that the Admiralty had informed the War Committee that the fleet could not interfere with a raid on the British coast for the first 28 hours. Jellicoe thought that more constant cruiser patrols in the North Sea would deter the Germans from raiding, because they might be sighted at sea and also because 'it was very desirable that it should not appear to the Germans that the presence of our fleet in the North Sea always coincided with the departure of their own fleet from its home bases'. That is, it was essential that the Germans not realise that the Grand Fleet was acting on intelligence of High Seas Fleet operations. ADM 137/1645, pp 311–12. Jellicoe also feared that the Germans could simply bring his fleet into mines and U-boats while their own Zeppelin reconnaissance protected them from fleet contact.

123. War diary entry by Lieutenant-Commander Michelsen, assistant torpedo force commander, in *Krieg zur See*, Nordsee 6, p 105. Michelsen was U-boat chief during the unrestricted submarine warfare of 1917–18.

124. The U-boats were arranged in lines across the enemy's probable line of approach. As the German fleet moved, the lines were moved and apparently the U-boats were able to follow on the surface. This policy replaced the previous one in which U-boats had been stationed off the enemy's bases. These submarines were ineffective if the enemy was already at sea. That *U 53* had managed to shadow the Grand Fleet was also noteworthy. He wanted a faster U-boat, which would find it easier to shadow enemy surface forces.

125. According to *Krieg zur See*, Nordsee 6, p 159 the deputy commander of the torpedo forces present decided that if he changed plans and attacked the convoy, his

return home would be delayed, the flotillas standing near Terschelling Bank lightship at 7am the next morning. He considered that this change would 'bring the undertaking . . . into some sort of conflict with the basic order of the Fleet Command'. *Krieg zur See* justifies this on the basis of uncertainty concerning the convoy.

126. *Kronprinz* was ready on 6 December 1916, *Grosser Kurfürst* on 10 February 1917.

127. *Krieg zur See*, Nordsee 6, p 208. The author cites excessive tactical rigidity, which the British addressed after Jutland and the undue subservience of subordinate captains.

128. According to *Krieg zur See*, the route to this decision was circuitous. The Admiralstab proposed to mine the convoy route. Clearance would open British sweeping forces to attack far from British bases, so the sweepers would have to be backed up by more powerful forces and there was a prospect of fleet action on favourable terms. Scheer and von Schröder argued that these mines would limit their own forces. Better to use German surface forces directly against the convoys.

129. According to *Krieg zur See*, Nordsee 6, p 331, 'in view of the latest news of the enemy', which may mean information that the Grand Fleet was confined to the north. However, 'news' also translated as the German 'nachrichten', which means reports, perhaps by intercepts.

130. This was not due to some perception that German signals were insecure; if the British received word any time before the High Seas Fleet left the Outer Jade (e.g., by submarine scout), the trap could be sprung.

131. *Krieg zur See*, Nordsee 6, pp 334–5.

132. According to Mark D Karau, '*Wielding the Dagger': The MarineKorps Flandern and the German War Effort, 1914-1918* (Westport: Praeger, 2003), p 145, on 25 May Flanders commander Admiral von Schröder received a memo from Scheer predicting an Allied attack late in May or early in June. On the basis of traffic analysis von Schröder already thought that the British force opposite him had been reinforced, so he assumed that an operation was imminent. The British War Council was considering the attack on Flanders at just this time.

133. *Krieg zur See*, Nordsee 7, p 43.

134. Later in 1917 the Admiralstab considered sending cruisers beyond the British Isles to attack shipping from the United States, or to attack shipping near the Azores. It realised that the cruisers would have to be fuelled at sea, a difficult proposition. Eventually the Admiralstab proposed sending out a tanker with 1500 tons of oil on board. Although nothing came of this discussion, it points to later German interest in tanker support for raiders breaking out past the British Isles, as in the Second World War. *Krieg zur See*, Nordsee 7, p 89.

135. Two minesweeping flotillas were covered by the battlecruiser *Derfflinger* and the battleships *Rheinland, Nassau, König Albert* and *Kaiserin* plus light cruisers (with aircraft on board) and destroyers.

136. The advanced force consisted of a battlecruiser squadron (*Lion, Princess Royal, Tiger, Repulse* and *New Zealand*) with a destroyer force led by a light cruiser, a cruiser squadron consisting of *Glorious, Courageous* and four destroyers and two light cruiser squadrons. The force in distant support consisted of six battleships and eleven destroyers.

137. *Krieg zur See*, Nordsee 7, p 218 describes security measures. Information was restricted to the fewest possible officers and essential orders for reconnaissance and for mine clearance limited as far as possible and wireless particularly limited. *Krieg zur See*, Nordsee 7, p 221 speculates that on 22–23 April British attention was concentrated on the Zeebrugge raid, but that seems unlikely. The raid having been mounted, the High Seas Fleet sortie could be seen as a reaction rather than as a raid against the Scandinavian convoy.

138. Patterson (ed), *Jellicoe Papers* II, p50. Revised Battle-Cruiser Orders (31 August 1916) are in Brian Ranft (ed), *The Beatty Papers* I (1902–1918) (Navy Records Society, 1989), pp 370ff (the passage on torpedo attack is on p 371).

139. Patterson (ed), *Jellicoe Papers* II, p 59.

140. In his 1 January 1918 destroyer instructions (*Beatty Papers* I, p 477) Beatty wrote that the longest known range of a German torpedo was 13,000 yds at 25 knots, so it was reasonable to imagine that the latest weapons would make 15,000 yds at this speed.

141. Ranft (ed), *Beatty Papers* I, p 457.

142. *Krieg zur See*, Nordsee 7, pp 340–1.

143. *Krieg zur See*, Nordsee 7, p 337.

144. Aside from U-boats, the force would have consisted of four capital ship groups (five ships each), two light cruiser groups (four each), eight torpedo boat (destroyer) flotillas and six airships. However, the order of battle (for the end of October 1918) in *Krieg zur See*, Nordsee 7, pp 344–5 shows three battle squadrons plus the fleet flagship *Baden* (consisting of, respectively, seven, five and five ships), three scouting groups (one consisting of the five battlecruisers, one of eight light cruisers and one of six light cruisers), seven destroyer flotillas (mostly understrength), twenty-five U-boats and seven airships.

145. The attack on the Flanders coast would be carried out by the light cruisers *Graudenz, Karlsruhe* and *Nürnberg* and a torpedo boat flotilla. That on the Thames Estuary would be carried out by the light cruisers *Königsberg, Cöln, Dresden* and *Pillau* and a half-flotilla of torpedo boats.

146. ADM 137/2089, p 7, 13 July 1915, submission by Commodore Tyrwhitt of a

proposal by Lieutenant C C B Hampden (HMS *Lookout*), Surgeon Probationer G F V Anson (HMS *Lookout*) and Sub-Lieutenant Bremner (HMS *Laertes*). The submission states that the idea had already been the subject of a War College Essay. The writers suggested either purpose-built boats or commandeered racing hydroplanes (they named six [*Maple Leaf IV*, *Ursula* and four *Miranda*s], all of which had achieved over 40 knots while racing). The writers preferred the latter, as plenty of such craft were lying idle. They assumed the boats would be armed, like ships' picket boats, with 14in torpedoes.

147. David Lyon, manuscript *Thorneycroft List*, Brass Foundry. The boat ran trials on 25 April 1916 and was delivered on 8 May. She made 39.73 knots on one run. Another twelve boats were ordered in January 1916 (*CMB 2–CMB 13*). *CMB 13* seems to have been an experimental 40-footer with experimental semi-submerged propellers (thrust line on the waterline), but the number was also used for *CMB 10* when she ran trials. Of these boats, *CMB 1* was lost in action off Ostend on 19 June 1917, *CMB 8* was sunk on 29 September 1917 to avoid capture and *CMB 11* was lost after a collision on 2 November 1917. The first loss explains why the total under Dover command was twelve rather than thirteen as of September 1917; the others explain why one of the Dover boats was not converted into a DCB as planned (see below). Three of the original CMBs were converted to DCBs (Distant Controlled Boats) and were replaced by new 40-footers. Four more were ordered from Thorneycroft specifically to be carried by HMS *Diamond* (total ten) solely for overseas operations. (ADM 137/2085, p 580). Construction of another eighteen was ordered 'hastened', with at least six sets of spare engines, to ensure that the Harwich Force would have a full complement of twelve CMBs (two could be carried by each of its six light cruisers). These were presumably *CMB 40–CMB 61* (twenty-two: the eighteen plus the four, with the extra three not clearly accounted for). The next unit after *CMB 61* was delivered as *DCB 5* rather than as a CMB (Thorneycroft Yard No. 1657, MB 1256, delivered 22 October 1918). Further 40-footers were *CMB 112* (experimental boat) and *CMB 121–CMB 123*. Of this last series, Thorneycroft Yard No. 1692 was delivered on 28 July 1919 (for Thorneycroft, as a stock boat, sold to Hermes before completion) and Nos. 1693–1708 were cancelled on 13 November 1918. *CMB 41* and *CMB 55* were completed by Thorneycroft and sold to the Spanish Tobacco Monopoly (*CMB 44* was sold to Thorneycroft for this service in January 1921). MB 1571 was not completed for the Royal Navy; it is not clear what her CMB number would have been (*CMB 112* was MB 1632). Sixteen more *CMB 121* type were cancelled (MB 1693–MB 1708). A further 40-footer (MB 1571) was not completed as a CMB.

148. ADM 137/2085, p 523 is the 19 August 1916 report of CMB commander Captain H Lyns RN. His crews had been trained, Commodore (T) had conducted trials with light cruisers and four CMBs had visited Lowestoft armed with depth charges (as requested by Admiralty Letter dated 20 June). As an alternative to torpedo and depth charges, each boat could lay one submarine-type torpedo tube (S 1) mine. The boats had demonstrated a radius of action of 225nm and an average speed of 30 knots (full speed loaded was 35 knots and full speed light was 38 knots). Each boat carried one 18in Mk 8 torpedo, with a range of 1500 yds at a maximum speed of 41 knots (29 knots for 3500 yds). Minimum water depth to launch a torpedo with high-speed setting (due to its initial dive during the first 100 yds) was 30ft . The high speed setting had to be used with net cutters to attack ships anchored with their torpedo nets out. At this time each of Commodore (T)'s six light cruisers was fitted to carry two CMBs, so any two of the light cruisers could be used for the projected attack. The operation order was drafted some time prior to 25 August, as a later paper in this file refers to a revised draft of that date. At this time the Harwich Force consisted of six light cruisers and twelve 'L' class destroyers. The operations order (with rationale) is on pp 531–9.

149. As noted in ADM 137/1646 *Grand Fleet Policy: Special Papers, 1915-1918*, pp 280–1. 'Before any new attempt is made a reconnaissance from the air is necessary because the Germans now know about the Coastal Motor Boats' (13 September 1917).

150. ADM 203/88, a lecture on CMBs, but the date, given as March, was actually April. Only one destroyer was sunk: *G 88*.

151. ADM 116/1479, *Coastal Motor Boats*.

152. *CMB 14* (ordered 2 May 1916, just after *CMB 1* ran trials) was the prototype 55-footer. By September 1917, more had been approved, four of which were complete: *CMB 15–CMB 39* (twenty-five) and *CMB 62–CMB 99* (thirty-seven). These numbers do not tally with the statement that as of September 1917 a total of fifty-six had been ordered, of which four were complete. However, in November 1917 another twelve were approved, including part of the final series of *CMB 113–CMB 120* (eight boats). That presumably included the last few of the *CMB 62* series. Of the last series, *CMB 118* and *CMB 119* were delivered in 1922. Eleven more were cancelled (MB 1536–MB 1562 series). The limiting factor in production was engines. On 1 September 1917 there were enough engines for twenty-one more 55-footers, each with two engines, or for a few more with single engines. At this time twenty-seven boats had Thorneycroft 250hp engines, twenty-five had 275hp Green engines and four, allotted to Dover, had 450hp Sunbeams. There were enough 450hp Green engines for eight boats (four were eventually used). Data for hull numbers beyond *CMB 15* are from Lyon's list, supplemented by F J Dittmar and J J College, *British Warships 1914-1919* (London: Ian Allan, 1972), pp 137–40. According to Lyon, *CMB 24* and beyond were Thorneycroft hull numbers 1551–1600, all 55-footers. The 55- and 70-footers had suffixes indicating engine type.

153. *CMB 9* was converted into a prototype Distant Controlled (i.e., remote-controlled) Boat (*DCB 1*) in 1918 (redesignated July 1918). *CMB 13* became *DCB 2* in July 1918, as did *CMB 3* (*DCB 3*). The other two DCBs were never designated as CMBs (ex MB 1143 and 1256, all CMBs having alternative MB designations). Originally four new 40-footers were to have replaced four Dover 40-footers converted into DCBs, but presumably MB 1143 (*DCB 4*) was a new hull ordered as a DCB to leave a CMB

unconverted. The DCB project was both very secret and very urgent. *DCB 5* was an additional hull ordered in 1918.

154. Undated Plans Division paper in ADM 137/1646 p 283, probably September 1917.

155. Operation 'GL', sketch description in ADM 137/2085, p 569. By this time the light cruiser *Diamond* had been fitted with three sets of davits, so she could take all six. The mine risk was less for one than for three ships, but *Diamond* was considerably slower than the oil-burning Harwich cruisers. This time there was some question as to whether being slung in davits for a long time would throw CMBs out of alignment.

156. They were the four Harwich Force cruisers *Canterbury*, *Cleopatra*, *Concord* and *Conquest* plus four additional ships: *Curacoa*, *Centaur*, *Coventry* and *Curlew*, plus *Diamond* with her six CMBs. Plans Division proposal, ADM 137/1646, p 306. The second series of ships are marked 'to be fitted', with 'now reported ready' typed in. Plans Division proposed to have light cruisers tow 55-footers (two per cruiser), thus solving the CMB carrier problem. Tyrwhitt considered the Plans Division scheme quite feasible (note dated 9 June 1918).

157. Operation order issued by the Admiralty to Tyrwhitt, 22 June 1918, in ADM 137/2085, p 590. All enemy ships were to be attacked, the CMBs not rejecting torpedo craft, minesweepers, or patrol craft in hopes of finding something larger.

158. Tyrwhitt was particularly impressed by Camel pilot Lieutenant Culley; as far as he knew this was only the second successful Camel take-off from a lighter. 'He made his attack, to all intents and purposes in the open, as there were few clouds to take cover in and he single handed successfully attacked and destroyed a Zeppelin in a most gallant and businesslike manner'.

159. The 70-footers were designed in November 1917 (ordered January 1918) specifically to lay magnetic mines ('M-Sinkers') off German bases on the Belgian coast. The initial plan seems to have been to form a unit of twelve. *CMB 100–CMB 104* were 70-footers, another seven (*CMB 105–CMB 111*) being cancelled.

160. Roskill, *Naval Air Service*, p 434, is a 20 December 1916 memo by Sueter on the current state of torpedo bombers and their potential. The first torpedo seaplane, a Short 184, had been tested successfully in October. The design of the Cuckoo land-plane torpedo bomber was being developed.

161. Roskill, *Naval Air Service*, p 536.

162. Roskill, *Naval Air Service*, p 478, a 2 May 1917 Admiralty letter announcing that the Germans were using large seaplanes to attack shipping, having struck near Ramsgate and sunk a ship near the Shipwash Light Vessel. The torpedo bomber was typically accompanied by a second aircraft.

163. ADM 137/1938, *Operations Proposed But Not Carried Out*, p 103. Beatty presented his elaborate paper as a supplement to and continuation of, papers submitted in August on future mining policy and on the naval offensive. They raised the aerial torpedo attack idea in less detailed terms. According to Layman, *Naval Aviation in the First World War*, p 192, Beatty's proposal was an elaboration of a proposal by Captain (later Rear Admiral) Herbert W Richmond and Flight Commander Frederick Rutland (who flew a floatplane from HMS *Engadine* at Jutland). Layman states that Beatty's scheme was developed independently of (and later than) an Admiralty project for a mass attack, but the 23 September Admiralty memo on air policy suggests that was not the case.

164. As evidenced by the memo on 'Policy of Aircraft Carried in Ships' (25 September 1917) sent to Beatty in reply to his proposal.

165. ADM 137/1938, Admiralty reply to Beatty, pp 142–3, 'Alternate Proposal for 200 Torpedo Carrying Aeroplanes'. The Admiralty later pointed out that it was over forty cruisers short for convoy work, hence that it was almost certain that the 10th Cruiser Squadron would be needed for that purpose. Experimental work with catapults had not progressed sufficiently. It was impossible to alter the design of the Cuckoo or of the torpedo and also impossible to accelerate deliveries. The 100 Cuckoos were to be delivered between March and July 1918.

166. Roskill, *Naval Air Service*, p 546.

167. The Beatty letter is in Roskill, *Naval Air Service*, p 684; p 680 is a protest to the Air Ministry (8 July 1918) listing requirements to be met by 30 June 1919 compared to the Air Ministry offers for deliveries through 30 September 1919. Against a required 234 torpedo bombers the offer was 126.

168. I am grateful to Commander David Hobbs RN (Ret), formerly curator of the Fleet Air Arm Museum, for showing me this remarkable card, which he has used in lectures about the history of British naval aviation.

Chapter 8. Capital Ships

1. For more details of British dreadnoughts and battlecruisers, see the author's forthcoming book on *British Capital Ships*. For details of British cruiser and destroyer development of this period, keyed to changing British policy, strategy and tactics, see the author's *British Cruisers: Two World Wars and After* (Barnsley: Seaforth Publishing, 2011) and *British Destroyers: From Earliest Days to the Second World War* (Barnsley: Seaforth Publishing, 2009). There does not appear to be any German-language (or other) account of German cruiser and destroyer development keyed to German policy or tactical documents. It does not seem worthwhile to go in detail into British development without such comparison. Comparison is, however, possible for submarines and it is provided in a later chapter.

2. ADM 1/7736.

3. The *Cressys* had the same side armour as *Canopus* class battleships and their creator, DNC Sir William White, told the Board that they could fight battleships. See the author's *British Cruisers of the Victorian Era* for details. The key was the new lightweight armour technology. The comment that armoured cruisers could fight second-class battleships, hence might be countable as battleships, is in ADM 1/7736, the discussion of fleet distribution including First Lord Selborne's comments.

4. The other two first-generation battlecruisers, *Australia* and *New Zealand*, were built as part of a 1909 Admiralty scheme to promote trade protection groups called 'fleet units', which in an emergency could coalesce into a Pacific Fleet.

5. 'When we designed the *Queen Elizabeths*, we were deliberately trying to get rid of the battlecruiser type and to break them, the Germans, of it. We ought to wait at least another year to let the experiment have its full force . . . the speed and power of the *Queen Elizabeths* . . . is sufficient to protect the battle fleet against any turning movement by German battlecruisers.' Minute to Third Sea Lord, 27 October 1912.

6. Minute to Third Sea Lord, 11 March 1914, asking how much it would cost for the 1914–15 ship to be redesigned to match the speed of HMS *Tiger*, a reduction to 11in belt armour being acceptable. 'I think it is essential that this ship should be as fast as anything now projected'. Churchill *Minutes* in NHB. For the 1913–14 programme of five capital ships, the initial proposals were for one improved *Tiger* (eight 15in, improved anti-torpedo battery) and four slower *Iron Dukes* with ten 13.5in or 15in guns. Other alternatives were given in a Minute to Third Sea Lord, 27 October 1912, Churchill *Minutes*, NHB – see note 11 below.

7. The August 1914 British handbook of world navies, *War Vessels and Aircraft: British and Foreign (Pt II: Quarterly Return)*, gave three speeds for each ship: design, trial and seagoing. The battlecruiser *Seydlitz* was credited with a design speed of 26.5 knots, a trial speed of 26.75 knots and a seagoing speed of 23.7 knots. She was the fastest of the lot (p 90). The new *Derfflinger* was credited with a design speed of 26.5 knots, although in November 1914 Admiral Fisher would demand 32 knots for the new *Repulse* class in order to match what he thought would be her 29-knot speed. The British battlecruisers were only slightly faster. The fastest, *Queen Mary*, was credited with a sea speed of 25.2 knots (design speed 28 knots); the first battlecruiser *Invincible* was credited with a sea speed of 23.2 knots (design speed 25 knots, like a *Queen Elizabeth*). Dreadnought battleships (design speed 21 knots) were generally credited with a sea speed of about 19 knots. The fastest pre-dreadnoughts were credited with 18 knots. The August 1914 book is the earliest edition of in the Admiralty Library (NHB), but it probably was not the first (it is marked, 'Previous Returns to be Destroyed'). Pt I, which is more widely available, is a register of ship and aircraft stations. The same seagoing speeds are given in the German Navy handbook issued in August 1914 (*Germany: War Vessels*, NID 896, NHB), but *Derfflinger* is credited with a sea speed of 23.5 knots. Her sister *Lützow* is credited with a possible design speed of 28 knots rather than the 26.5 knots of her sister. Detailed notes show that *Seydlitz* had sustained 26.75 knots for six hours and that seagoing speed meant sustained speed at roughly two-thirds power (in this case, 43,100shp rather than the design figure of 63,000shp. On trials the ship made 89,738shp and sustained 73,923shp for six hours. The notes in the preface do not define seagoing speed or power. In 1914 *Seydlitz* seems to have been the latest German battlecruiser for which full information was available. *Krieg zur See*, Nordsee 4, p 149 mentions some of the problems of coal fuel in connection with an April 1915 minelaying operation. The very dusty coal used by the fleet caused showers of sparks, which made ships far more visible at night and it also left so much clinker (which blocked fires) that 'only the utmost exertions of the stokehold personnel and very high air pressure' made it possible for cruisers to maintain 22 knots. *Ostfriesland* class battleships found it difficult to maintain 17 knots despite good coal and nearly full bunkers, because it was difficult to move coal from the bunkers quickly enough and also because boiler fire bar area was too small. Because bunkers had been arranged for protection more than for efficient steaming, by the time they had been reduced from 2500 to 2300 tons, seamen had to be sent below to move coal from side (protective) bunkers. This was particularly ironic, because the Germans resisted shifting to oil fuel precisely because they considered coal effective side (anti-torpedo) protection. That most coal was more for protection than for steaming presumably reflects Tirpitz' idea that the decisive battle had to be fought within 100 miles or less of the fleet base at Heligoland. The situation in the battlecruisers was similar.

8. In an 18 June 1916 confidential despatch to the Admiralty, Jellicoe observed that the official quarterly return of British and foreign war vessels credited the *Kaiser* and *König* classes with a design speed of 20.5 knots. He had always expected that they might reach 22 knots for a short time, but during the whole battle the *Queen Elizabeths* (which he called 25-knot ships, although they were actually capable of no more than 23.5 knots, if that) had failed to close with them. That 'unpleasant surprise' would have considerable impact on future operations. Patterson (ed), *Jellicoe Papers* I, pp 285–6.

9. This appears in the Admiralty file on the financing of the 1912–13 programme (ADM 116/1294B). This file makes no mention of the increased size and cost of the new ships. Churchill circulated the text of the new German Navy Law with a memo dated 14 February 1912. The nominal size of the German target fleet did not increase very much: forty-one battleships, twenty battlecruisers and forty small cruisers instead of thirty-eight battleships, twenty battlecruisers and thirty-eight small cruisers but 'in fact there is a remarkable expansion'. The Germans would immediately build three new battleships and fully man five others, four of which had previously counted only on paper, by bringing home three large cruisers from abroad and by providing crews for four others previously counted only in the material reserve. Thus they would increase the number of large armoured ships immediately available in full commission from twenty-one to thirty-six. 'The new scale of the fleet organised in five battle squadrons, each attended by a battlecruiser squadron, complete with small cruisers and auxiliaries and attended by flotillas of destroyers and submarines, of which nearly four-fifths will be maintained in full permanent commission, is extremely formidable'. This analysis completely undercut proposals to solve the naval arms competition by slightly modifying the German building plan. Ironically, the Germans themselves had provided the text of the modified Navy Law in advance of submitting it to the Reichstag. When the final text of the law was received, it showed a slightly larger increase in personnel and plans for seventy-two submarines (but slightly fewer surface torpedo craft). Provision for four large cruisers abroad would not be changed (but the Germans actually had only two on active foreign service and authorised foreign strength was eight). Churchill circulated a memo to this effect to the Cabinet on 19 April 1912. The only effect of a mission to Germany by Lord Haldane, an attempt to end the building rate, was that the Germans would buy two rather than three extra battleships during 1912–17, hardly a significant change given the massive change in readiness.

10. Unfortunately the surviving documents explaining pre-First World War building programmes are generally those provided to the Cabinet or to Parliament explaining what would be needed to maintain the desired or agreed standard of strength. They are advocacy papers intended to win political arguments, not internal analytic ones. Hence it is impossible to say what analysis lay behind them. The Admiralty papers on finances (which are not available for the period before 1912) do show that by that time the Treasury and others were strongly opposing the building programme and Churchill's Minutes show that he was considering alternatives to the full projected programme. The CID-approved standard was a 60 per cent margin. At times the Germans offered a 2:3 margin, which was 50 per cent over their own strength. The need for a declared margin in the North Sea was always complicated by the need to maintain strength elsewhere, particularly in the Mediterranean. Also, it was often pointed out that the Germans could act at a moment of their own choice, which would catch the British at their *average* moment, with some ships unavailable because of refits and boiler cleaning.

11. On 17 June 1912 Churchill noted in a Minute on buying armour that the battleship programme for the next five years had been set at four, five, four, four and four. The four for 1912–13 did not include HMS *Malaya*, a gift from the Federated Malay States. The first of the four-ship years was 1914–15. Churchill Minutes as printed for the Dardanelles Committee, Vol I, 1911–13, NHB. A Churchill Minute dated 27 October 1912 laid out alternatives for the 1913–14 programme, which ultimately included the five *Royal Sovereign* class battleships. The alternatives were: (a) *Tiger* (but with armour superior to *Seydlitz*) and four repeat *Iron Dukes*; (b) *Tiger* (as improved) plus four *Iron Dukes* with 15in rather than 13.5in guns; or (c) four *Queen Elizabeths* or (d) two improved *Tiger* and two repeat *Iron Dukes* or (e) one improved *Tiger* and three *Queen Elizabeths* or (f) Two improved *Tigers* and two improved *Iron Dukes* with 15in guns. Programmes (a), (c) and (d) all left additional money for smaller ships. Churchill considered the best alternatives (a) and (c), of which he was inclined to prefer (c) because it simplified the 1913–14 programme into (1) the fast capital ship for all purposes; (2) the fast light cruiser to destroy torpedo craft and for all scouting; (3) destroyers and (4) submarines. 'There are two classes of vessels now being built by the Germans, to which no answer was made in our programme of 1912–13 and which this new programme also ignores, viz., the 30-knot battlecruiser and the 6000-ton small cruiser. On 29 October (pp 119–120), in connection with the increased cost of the *Queen Elizabeths*, Churchill wrote to the Chancellor of the Exchequer that it had been proposed by the previous Board that the 1912–13 programme consist of three battleships and one battlecruiser. He wanted the planned price of the 1913–14 battleship, rather than the lower one of the 1910-11 ship, to be the basis for comparison with the projected higher cost of the new ship, which was more expensive than either a battleship or a battlecruiser. He had explained the increased cost in a letter sent on 12 July (now lost). Nothing in the set of Minutes explains how Churchill was persuaded to substitute five slow battleships for four fast ones in 1913–14. A Minute dated 17 January 1913 observes that if battleship speed drops back to the previous standard, it would be satisfactory to use coal rather than oil fuel; Churchill requested a Legend showing how the latest ships (*Royal Sovereign* class) could be made coal-fired with auxiliary oil spray (as First Sea Lord, Fisher reversed this decision). The printed Minutes for 1911–13 include no reference at all to the dramatic change Churchill made to the 1912–13 Programme to create the *Queen Elizabeth* class. It is clear from the printed Minutes (January 1914) that the 1914–15 programme was heavily modified to fill a gap created by the collapse of Canadian plans to build three battleships in 1914–15. The 1914–15 programme definitely consisted of four battleships and it was decided that in order to accelerate construction the two dockyard ships would be repeat *Royal Sovereign* class. It seems likely that the initial version of the programme called for three repeat *Queen Elizabeths* and one repeat *Royal Sovereign*, but nothing in Churchill's Minutes makes that clear.

12. The Admiralty file on the financing of the 1914–15 programme is ADM 116/3152. Much of the file is Churchill's resistance to the Treasury based on the approved 60 per cent margin over the Germans. His Minute dated 1 June 1914 asks DNO for the saving to be had if, as DNO proposed, one of the repeat *Royal Sovereign* class battleships were replaced by submarines. This suggests a shift in which a group of submarines might be considered a viable substitute for a battleship in comparisons of naval strength, since up to this point the number of battleships was set by the need to achieve the 60 per cent margin over the Germans. In a slightly later note to Third Sea Lord (11 June) Churchill asked for the effect of substituting six torpedo cruisers (a type he personally favoured) for the projected repeat *Queen Elizabeth* class battleship *Agincourt*. The *Royal Sovereign* and *Agincourt* were relatively easy to cancel because they were being built in Royal Dockyards rather than under contract (however, in his fight against the Treasury, Churchill used potential disruption at the Royal Dockyards as an argument against any cancellation in the 1914–15 programme).

13. Churchill's speech to the House of Commons on 17 March 1914 held out hope that

the Canadians would reverse course, but by then the Canadians clearly had no interest in proceeding. The Estimates showed a reduction in cruiser and destroyer construction compared to previous years' figures. Data on the proposed programme from contemporary British newspaper accounts in US ONI Register O-6-c No. 3746, RG 38, NARA. There was speculation that Churchill might be planning to submit a Supplementary Estimate later in the year, a tactic he had previously used. Churchill's naval Minutes include one to First Sea Lord and Chief of Staff on the disappointing Canadian situation; Churchill asks for the consequences of either a year's delay in the Canadian battleship programme or complete abandonment. At this point he was hoping for three Canadian ships and he proposed to form an Imperial Squadron to be based at Gibraltar, to consist of the *New Zealand*, *Malaya* and the three Canadians, the whole squadron capable of 23 knots. He wanted to show the Canadians that such a squadron, so centrally based, could range widely over the Atlantic as well as the Mediterranean and the North Sea. It would have been a return to the Atlantic Fleet as a 'swing' squadron. The memorandum is dated 17 January 1913. NHB. On 14 January 1914, having received news from Canada that nothing could be done that year to build the promised three Canadian dreadnoughts, Churchill minuted First Sea Lord that he had decided to accelerate the capital ships of the 1914–15 programme in order to maintain the previously declared British programme despite the Canadian delay. He wrote that he had asked Third Sea Lord (Controller) to make proposals to accelerate construction of the two contract battleships of the 1914–15 programme so that they could be completed before the end of the second quarter of 1916. To that end they would be made repeat *Royal Sovereign* class, providing seven of the squadron of eight such ships which was desired. The additional expense involved would be met partly be readjusting the first instalments in the programme and partly by a slight reduction in it. This acceleration would make it possible to maintain six modern capital ships (dreadnoughts or *Lord Nelsons*) in the Mediterranean up to the end of the first quarter of 1917 without sacrificing the desired 50 per cent edge over the Germans in home waters. Churchill Minutes printed for the Dardanelles Committee, vol II, pp 7–8 (NHB). Churchill also referred to a *Royal Sovereign* class battleship to be built at Plymouth. That brought the total programme to three *Royal Sovereigns* and one repeat *Queen Elizabeth*. Additional costs would be balanced by dropping two light cruisers and some projected torpedo boats. Later Minutes offered other alternatives. Note that in a 19 January 1914 Minute Churchill referred to three Canadian ships in 1913–14 and two, as proposed, in 1914–15. On 24 January he asked Director of Intelligence Division (DID) for the latest possible completion date of two of the 1914–15 battleships (if the first two were completed in September 1916) which would maintain the desired 60 per cent edge over the Germans. At this point he was planning three ships in 1915–16, five in 1916–17 and four in 1917–18. In January 1914, Churchill was still trying to convince the Canadians. In a 30 January Minute he asked the Admiralty Secretary to show how much the Canadians, as evidenced in their speeches, had relied on the Admiralty statement that there was an emergency. Opponents of the plan had challenged the statement; Churchill clearly hoped that he could demonstrate that they were wrong.

14. The Cover for the 1914 Battleships does not mention the cancellations. The *Queen Elizabeth* class battleship (*Agincourt*) and one of the repeat *Royal Sovereigns* (*Resistance*) were to have been built in Royal Dockyards (Devonport and Portsmouth, respectively). Tenders for the other two repeat *Royal Sovereigns* were provisionally accepted from Palmers and Fairfield about 22 May. The Legend for these ships received the Board Stamp on 13 May 1914.

15. Letters to Churchill and Jellicoe quoted by Mackay, *Fisher of Kilverstone*, p 474.

16. The 1914 Battleship Cover gives the date for the first ten plates of the keel of HMS *Repulse* as 30 November 1914, but Woolard's Constructor's Notebook dates initial calculations to 19 December, when he began with a lengthened *Indefatigable* hull (630 x 80 x 36.5ft). DNC Notebook 111/II, Brass Foundry. That suggests that plans initially were to restart the ship as the battleship originally designed. Woolard estimated that the new ship would displace 21,000 tons and that she would be armed with four 15in guns. Armour would generally follow that of *Indefatigable*. There is no reference in Woolard's notes to a decision to follow up with what amounted to the *Courageous* design. After completing these calculations he tried an entirely new ship, 720 x 86 x 27ft (26,500 tons), apparently with the same battery. Further calculations, dated 20 December, envisaged three twin 15in turrets. Woolard reported a 24,750-ton ship (720 x 88 x 27ft) to DNC. It seems to have been chosen for development. At this stage the ship would have had twenty-five 4in secondary guns and two torpedo tubes (ten, later fourteen, torpedoes). Further calculation brought the ship to 26,000 tons. DNC sent for his senior battleship designer, E L Attwood, on 21 December and gave him figures derived from Woolard's: 750 x 83/90 x 27ft , 25,000 to 26,000 tons, two twin 15in forward, one aft, one torpedo room forward, twenty 4in guns, with a long high flared-out bow and 111,000shp (as in *Tiger*, but with oil fuel). Nowhere in the notebooks or in the Cover is there an explanation for the choice of 4in secondary guns. By 26 December speed had been set at 32 knots and there were twenty-five 4in 'automatic guns – range 14,000 yds, 30° elevation'. Meanwhile the 'large light cruisers' were being designed with 90,000shp powerplants, so Attwood's notebook includes a new (unfortunately undated) sketch design for a 750 x 90 x 24ft ship with the 'cruiser' powerplant. It would have made 30 knots rather than 32 knots. Armament would have been either three twin 15in B (18in) guns arranged as in *Repulse*, or that ship's three twin 15in. Attwood also observed that a ship using the light cruiser machinery could carry four twin 15in guns on a length of 800ft (31,105 tons). She would make about 29.5 knots.

17. ADM 137/1080, pp 136–40.

18. Tudor included the battlecruiser *Salamis*, ordered pre-war by Greece, in the German total, 'if guns can be found for her'. They never were and the incomplete ship became the subject of lengthy lawsuits after the war. Her American-made guns ended up on board British monitors. Of the planned German ships, the battleship *Ersatz Worth* (*Baden*) was laid down on 19 February 1914; her earliest possible date of completion was December 1915 (the actual date of commissioning was 14 March 1917). Battleship T (*Bayern*) was laid down in September 1913; the earliest probable date of completion was also December 1915 (actual date: 15 July 1916). *Ersatz Kaiser Friedrich III* (*Sachsen*) was believed not to have been laid down before the war, having been ordered only on 23 May 1914, so she could not be completed in 1915. In fact she was never completed, work stopping nine months before she could have been. The fourth ship of the class, *Württemberg* (*Ersatz Kaiser Wilhelm II*), was not included in the forecast (she was laid down in 1915). Of the battlecruisers, it was assumed that *Lützow* would be completed in April 1915 (actually commissioned 8 August 1915). Her sister *Ersatz Hertha* (*Hindenburg*) was laid down 9 June 1913 and as yet there was no evidence that she had been launched, although when laid down she had been scheduled for launch in March 1915 (she was actually launched on 1 August 1915); the earliest possible date of completion was September or October 1915, but the actual date of commissioning was 10 May 1917. None of the later German battlecruisers ever entered service. The only one known in 1915 was *Ersatz Victoria Louise* (*Mackensen*), which had not been laid down by the outbreak of war. She was launched on 21 April 1917 and was stopped about fifteen months from completion.

19. That is the date of the first sheet in the Cover, a request for a provisional complement for a 735ft 17,800 ton ship armed with four 15in guns in two turrets, with sixteen 4in guns (twelve in triple mountings) and with two submerged torpedo tubes, with a 90,000shp powerplant. Folio 6 in the Cover is DNC's submission (dated February 1915) of a sketch design to Third Sea Lord, 'in accordance with First Sea Lord's instructions'. Speed had been laid down as 32 knots, as in *Renown* and *Repulse* 'as modified'. Design requirements were high speed, heavy guns and light draught. The accompanying Legend was dated 28 January 1915. A note dated 24 January from Fisher to First Lord (Churchill) informs him that 'in accordance with your wishes' it has been arranged this morning with Elswick (Armstrong) and Harland & Wolff of Belfast to build these two ships '*within the year*'. Sir E T d'Eyncourt's design notebook in the National Maritime Museum shows the *Courageous* design submitted on 28 January 1915 and notes that Furious had a different underwater form.

20. The Cover does contain correspondence concerning the 5.5in secondary armament. The first reference to the 15in B gun is in an armament statement dated 6 October 1916. The *Furious* Legend, dated 1915, is in the second Cover, together with the usual summary of calculations.

21. ADM 137/1013 ('Intelligence 1914').

22. ADM 137/1080, Intelligence January–June 1915, pp 101–13, file on German ships armed with 15in guns.

23. The 2 April 1915 report was signed by Third Sea Lord (Rear Admiral Tudor), Chief of Staff (Rear Admiral H F Oliver), DNO (Captain Murry Singer), Engineer in Chief and representatives of DNC and DID.

24. Unfortunately there is no record of Admiralty Board discussions or decisions before 1917, so the point at which the capital ships were introduced into the 1915–16 programme cannot be identified. Laying before the Cabinet the planned 1915–16 programme in December 1914, Churchill made a point of the battleship cancellations in 1914–15 and the absence of battleships in the planned 1915–16 programme. Had there been no cancellations, the programme for each of the two years would have included four battleships. Instead, three (two Turkish, one Chilean) had been bought, five ships (including the two *Repulses*) costing about half as much as eight would have cost pre-war. CAB 37/122.

25. Attwood's notes on the new design are dated 25 October 1915 (p 52 of his Notebook 11). DNC proposed about 750 x 101 (92-23 at the waterline) x 22ft for a displacement of 29,000 tons; armament would be eight 15in and twelve 5in, the latter all in the bow. The 5in 60pdr gun existed only as a design, but the British had 5.5in guns and mountings which had been manufactured for a planned Greek programme (they armed the light cruisers *Birkenhead* and *Chester*). A paper in the *Courageous* class Cover, signed by Fisher (dated 9 May 1915), explains why this weapon was considered superior to both the 6in and the 4in guns, proposing it for *Furious*. The same gun was adopted for HMS *Hood* and also for the carrier *Hermes*. For a time the Royal Navy considered it as a replacement for 6in secondary guns, but instead it adopted a powered 6in mounting for the post-war battleships. It is not clear why DNC adopted an unusually shallow draught, but by this time the British were very interested in torpedo protection, which required greater beam. Great length offered high speed for a given horsepower and on a given displacement increased length and beam would be balanced by reduced draught. The 7800 tons of armour included tube protection against torpedoes. The ship would have four underwater torpedo tubes, as in the *Royal Sovereign* class. Speed would be 25 to 26 knots on 90,000shp. Machinery would be as light as possible, with three-quarters of the boilers of the small-tube type and geared turbines. Attwood scaled hull structural weights from the 'large light cruisers' *Glorious* and *Furious*, but assumed heavier machinery (3200 tons compared to an estimated 2600 tons in *Furious*, producing the same power). Initially estimated armour weight was 7800 tons, compared to about 4700 tons in *Renown* as then estimated. More detailed estimates showed 9417 tons or even 9613 tons, which was to be cut to 9150 tons. This included an 11in belt amidships, with 3in forward and aft and 4in and 6in bulkheads forward. Barbette armour would be 10in maximum. In December the design was ordered recast with 60,000shp engines (as in a light cruiser) on a length of 735ft and a maximum beam of 90ft. She was still expected to make 25 to 26 knots. This ship became Design A in a new series: 760 x 104 x $23\frac{1}{2}$ ($23\frac{1}{2}$ deep) ft , 31,000 tons, 75,000shp, 26.5 to 27 knots. B was the slower alternative (25 knots, as in *Queen Elizabeth*): 750 x 90 x $25\frac{1}{2}$ ($28\frac{1}{2}$ deep) ft , 29,500 tons, 60,000shp for 25 knots.

26. Tudor's typed note, dated 6 January 1916, is in Attwood's Notebook 11, p 83. Alternative C.1 is a 22-knot ship with *full* bulge protection (Tudor's emphasis). C.2 was a 22-knot ship no longer than a *Queen Elizabeth* with *best* possible bulge protection on the dimensions. Tudor also wanted a ship of beam and draught as in Design A, but of 22 knots speed, with length much reduced so that she could fit in floating docks, not only in the three graving docks or locks. Attwood's first shot was a 40,000shp ship (power as *Royal Sovereign* class), 600 x 104 x 23½ft (25,000 tons) capable of 22.5 knots. Ultimately C1 was 660 x 104 x 23½ft , 27,600 tons; C2 was 610 x 100 x 24¾ft, 26,250 tons. There is no record of what was submitted to the Board, but Attwood's notebook includes a Board Decision dated 26 January 1916. The designs considered were to be submitted to C-in-C (Jellicoe) for his views. The Board requested a modified A design with the same beam, draught, armour and armament, speed as *Queen Elizabeth*, but to be shortened as much as possible. With the submission the Board wanted the overall length and a list of docks capable of taking the ship. This became Design D: 710 x 104 x 23½ (26½ deep)ft, 65,000shp for 25.5 knots. At this point it seemed likely that Design D would actually be built: the note indicates that a Cover was to be opened. Sir E T d'Eyncourt's design notebook in the National Maritime Museum describes these as designs for a 'New (Experimental) Battleship', submitted November 1915 (A) and January 1916 (B. C1 and C2). The battlecruiser alternatives, which became HMS *Hood*, were submitted in March 1916.

27. A typed copy of Jellicoe's remarks is pasted onto pages 103–5 of Attwood's notebook 11.

28. In fact *Hindenburg* was the last battlecruiser the Germans would complete during the war and she had the same 12in guns as her two predecessors. The ships Jellicoe listed would have had a new 14in gun, considerably inferior to the British 15in weapon.

29. Attwood's initial notes are dated 15 February 1916. Alternative batteries were (1) eight 15in, (2) four 15in B, (3) six 15in B and (4) eight 15in B, all to have 30° elevation. Attwood estimated that 120,000shp would give 30 knots and he wrote out an initial Legend for a 38,300-ton ship whose armament weight was based on that of the earlier Design D. Estimated dimensions were 835 x 104 x 26ft. Attwood submitted a profile and weights (for a 38,500-tonner) on 17 February. The next page shows alternatives for 30, 30.5 and 32 knots. For 32 knots and eight 15in B guns, Attwood needed 160,000shp and a hull 810 (860ft overall) x 104 x 26 (29½ deep) ft displacing 36,000 tons. This series of estimates was not sent in.

30. As evidenced by a table of the A to D series pasted into Attwood's notebook *after* his calculations of the battlecruiser design.

31. The name appears on the page in Attwood's notebook immediately after Jellicoe's remarks, in connection with estimates for a 35-knot ship (*Hood* is given as 810ft x 36,500 tons).

32. This was Design 3 of six alternatives, all of which had secondary batteries of twelve 5.5in guns and two submerged torpedo tubes. All had small tube boilers and forced draft, alternatives being wide vs. narrow boiler rooms. No. 3 had wide boiler rooms and 15in rather than 15in B guns: 810 x 104 x 26 (29½ deep) ft , displacing 36,500 tons; on 160,000shp she would make 32 knots. She could be docked at Rosyth, Portsmouth and Liverpool, but not in the floating docks (of the six, only the 710ft Design 4 could be). No. 3 had full bulge protection with crush tubes. A table of protection weights for 'Battle-Cruiser Design 1915–16' in Attwood's notebook shows an 8in waterline belt amidships (5in forward, 4in aft) with a 5in upper strake, well short of what Jellicoe wanted. Attwood's notebook also shows a 'new battlecruiser design' of March 1916, which was presumably a redesigned version of No.3.

33. ADM 1/8470/236.

34. Axel Greissmer, *Linienschiffe der Kaiserlichen Marine 1906-1918: Konstruktionen zwichen Rustugnskonkurrenz und Flottengesetz* (Bonn: Bernard & Graefe, 1999). The Kaiser's personal requests run though the book, which is based mainly on primary German sources.

35. The *Lord Nelson* Cover includes Design B4, with twelve 10in and no other guns larger than 12pdrs, displacing 15,800 tons. The set of Legends involved is not dated. A later Design E (Legend dated 29 November 1902) also had twelve 10in guns. All of the many other designs in the Cover are for mixed batteries of 12in and 9.2in guns. The *Lord Nelson* design had been settled for some time by the beginning of 1905 and the attaché report seems to have been a muddled reference to Fisher's desire for a single-calibre main battery and his preference (abandoned by them) for 10in guns.

36. This time the maximum unit cost was set at 31 million Marks. The constructors proposed a maximum beam of 23.8m (formally set on 4 March) and a speed of 19 knots, later reduced to 18.5.

37. Design c would have displaced 16,000 tons. In design c3, two more 17cm guns were added (the citadel was lengthened by 5m and length grew to 134m); displacement grew by 300 tons. Detail improvements increased beam to 25 m and required 20,000ihp. Then a 35mm torpedo bulkhead was added (17,000 tons, 32.7 million). The next step was Design F (18,000 tons), with a 26m beam and a length of 133m (torpedo bulkhead 3.5m rather than 3m from the outer hull). It would cost 35.2 million.

38. Axel Greissmer, *Grosse Kreuzer der Kaiserlichen Marine 1906-1918: Konstruktionen und Entwurfe in Zeichen des Tirpitz-Planes* (Bonn: Bernard & Graefe, 1996), p 14, comparing Tirpitz' ships with the large British armoured cruisers of the *Duke of Edinburgh*, *Warrior* and *Minotaur* classes built under the 1902–3 to 1904–5 Estimates. According to Greissmer, the cruisers *Yorck* and *Roon*, which were designed to reach 22 knots, failed to do so, partly because their length was limited by the size of the docks at Wilhelmshaven. To worsen the situation, tests at Meppen of a model of the waterline protection of the earlier cruiser *Prinz Heinrich* (100mm belt) showed that she was vulnerable to medium-calibre rapid-fire guns. Later cruisers had 150mm side armour. For his 1905 programme Tirpitz felt compelled to build larger more expensive cruisers: Cruisers C and D, which became *Scharnhorst* and *Gniesenau*. They were somewhat more expensive than their predecessor: budget documents showed 17.97 million Marks for *Yorck*, but 19.17 million for *Scharnhorst* and 18.75 million for *Gniesenau*, the latter figures being exceeded. This was still well below the cost of a contemporary battleship (*Deutschland* cost 24.5 million). The new ships introduced a uniform main battery (eight 21cm/40 in two twin turrets and four casemates) backed by six 15cm/40 and the usual 8.8cm anti-torpedo battery. Side armour was increased and design speed was increased to 22.5 knots. To get the additional speed, waterline length was increased from 127.3 to 143.8m and designed power from 19,000 to 26,000ihp. On trial both ships exceeded 23.5 knots.

39. Greissmer, *Grosse Kreuzer*, p 16, refers to a 25 May 1904 meeting.

40. Tirpitz asked for sketch designs on 4 March 1905 so that he could show them to the Kaiser on the 18th. This was well before there was any news of the *Invincible*s. Sketch A was a *Scharnhorst* with two more 15cm guns (total eight); B had twelve 21cm in double turrets, the sort of armament then being discussed for the *Nassau*s, plus the eight 15cm/40. The two alternatives were later redesignated E1 and E2 because they applied to 'cruiser E', the 1906 ship. Both designs showed the new 21cm/45 instead of the 21cm/40 of earlier German armoured cruisers. In E1 designed power was increased to 30,000ihp to increase speed to 23.5 knots; displacement increased to 12,700 tons. E2 displaced 13,600 tons, even though the designers sacrificed 1000ihp and half a knot. In E2 belt thickness amidships was increased from 150mm to 180mm. Estimated cost was battleship-like: about 23 million for E1 (compared to the actual cost of *Scharnhorst*, about 20.3 million) and 25.6 million for E2. The additional twin turrets accounted for much of the cost growth in E2. Tirpitz was unhappy with the cost of E2, so he asked for another design (E3) with the two end twin turrets but with six 21cm in casemates and with the increased belt armour of E2. With E2 machinery, this somewhat smaller ship would have made 23.3 knots. Cost fell back to roughly that of E1 (the initial estimate was 24 million). From Tirpitz' point of view, the Kaiser showed an unfortunate tendency to see these ships as future standard capital ships. Tirpitz now tried another alternative which revived the hexagonal turret arrangement, but with single rather than twin turrets (not casemates) on the sides (E5). He traded the weight of the 21cm guns for more (ten) 15cm/40, the result being slightly smaller and less expensive than E2. E5 paralleled the contemporary 15,700-ton project for a 28cm capital ship with two twin and four single turrets (Design C). For a time it appeared that it would be developed into Cruiser E and detail changes were made, for example to provide somewhat higher speed (30,000ihp engines).

41. Initially the 24cm guns would have been arranged as in E5. The alternative was a version of E2 with ten 15cm/45 or /40. The gun was a projected 24cm/45, not the 24cm/40 actually mounted on board German battleships. Nothing happened at the time, but the idea was revived later.

42. This E6 design (May 1905) began a cycle of what amounted to improved *Scharnhorst*s. The 17cm/45 was a new gun: German battleships had a 17cm/40). E7 was similar but less expensive (23.7 rather than 24.7 million), having sacrificed some speed. The final design in this group was E8 (design ordered 2 June), which reverted to 15cm medium guns but had two twin and two single 21cm turrets on the broadside. She would have displaced 13,400 tons and cost 23.7 million. The E-series designs had unusually powerful anti-torpedo batteries of twenty 8.8cm guns (*Scharnhorst* had eighteen). Compared to E3 and E5, E6 was 500 tons heavier and had 3000 more ihp, to give her a speed of 23.5 knots. She would have been too long overall for the Kiel Canal. None of these designs was developed in further detail. E5 had been prepared for the Kaiser's approval and it was developed in detail, up to September 1905.

43. The new series of designs began with E9 (11 September 1905): 14,400 tons, six twin 21cm turret, eight 15cm/40, about 30,000ihp for about 23.3 knots, at a price of 25.5 million. Belt armour would have been 180mm amidships, tapering to 160mm fore and aft, the fore and aft sections a considerable improvement on earlier designs. E10 and E11 were alternative versions offered at the same time, E10 with six rather than eight 15cm guns and E11 with 32,000ihp for 23.5 knots (15,000 tons, 26.2 million). Compared to the others, E11 offered increased separation between the beam turrets to reduce the effect of a lucky hit. By this time the Germans were well aware of the impact of underwater weapons during the Russo-Japanese War, so E11 had both a torpedo bulkhead and better internal subdivision. A developed version of the design, E15, was ready on 26 September. It had the original eight 15cm guns, still 40 calibres long. Power increased to up to 32,000ihp to maintain a speed of 23.5 knots. The final design dated 12 June 1907 showed a displacement of 15,700 tons and a speed of about 24 knots (32,000 to 34,000ihp). The final sketch was dated 21 September 1907. Estimated cost was 27.5 million.

44. The designs were E17 to E23, executed between September 1905 and March 1906, with six or eight 24cm/45 guns. Displacement would have been 15,200 to 15,900 tons. The first in the series, E17, would have been armed with six 24cm (twins on the centreline, one single on each beam) and twelve 15cm/40 (possibly 45 calibre in E21). E21 differed from the others in having eight of her 15cm gun in twin mounts fore and aft of the beam twin 21cm guns. The last in the series (E22 and E23 of March 1906) would have had two single turrets on each beam and eight 15cm/45, the secondary guns of the German dreadnoughts. E23 had the 15cm guns in twin turrets of their own between the two single 24cm on the beam. Estimated cost of the 15,200-ton E17 was 26.5 million; the 15,800-ton eight-gun E21 (March 1906) would have cost 28.83 million. Greissmer does not give estimated costs for E22 and E23.

45. Greissmer, *Grosse Kreuzer*, which is based on Tirpitz' Navy Department records.

46. Kelly, *Tirpitz*, p 269.

47. Greissmer, *Grosse Kreuzer*, p 43.

48. For Greissmer, the indirect reply of the Navy Department was a 24-page article in the July 1906 *Marine Rundschau*, 'The Armoured Cruiser as Standard. Fleet Type', by Korvettenkapitän (Lieutenant Commander) Vollerthun of the News Bureau (i.e., Tirpitz' own naval propaganda office).

49. Greissmer, *Grosse Kreuzer*, p 45.

50. The smallest, Scheme 1, was expected to produce 33,000ihp (36,000 on trials), for a speed of 23 knots (23.5 on trial). She would have carried her guns in a hexagon arrangement, but with single turrets on the beam and she would have displaced 19,500 tons, which was slightly more than the 1906 battleship. Cost would have been 35.1 million. The belt amidships would have been 260mm thick. The other designs in the series had twin wing turrets and in one of them (Scheme 2, 34.8 million) power was increased to 35,000ihp (39,000ihp on trial), for a trial speed of 24 knots. While the first four schemes were being produced, chief of the construction department Vice Admiral von Eickstedt proposed sacrificing one of the 28cm turrets to reduce displacement (and cost), replacing the 15cm medium battery with 17cm guns. Mounting all the 28cm guns on the centreline would preserve the six-gun broadside. Tirpitz rejected the idea on the ground that building a ship with fewer guns *and* less powerful ones than the *Invincibles* would be unacceptable. A slightly later Scheme 5 offered a rather different armament arrangement, with two turrets on the centreline (on the same level) aft and two single wing turrets abaft the forward single turret on the centreline. That gave a seven-gun broadside. In effect it was von Eickstedt's ship with single wing turrets. This 19,600-ton ship also had the more powerful machinery; it was expected to cost 35.3 million. Both Scheme 1 and Scheme 5 were further elaborated a few days after having been submitted. Project 2a (25 September) offered greater power (34,000ihp and 38,000 on trial, or 38,000shp turbines capable of 42,000shp on trial). On turbines she could make 24 knots (24.5 knots on trial). Tirpitz showed the last three sketch designs (1a, 2a and 5) to the Kaiser on 28 September 1906, the Kaiser choosing 2a. It was further elaborated in October as Scheme 2b, which had its wing turrets spaced out along its length (*en echelon*) so that each could fire on the opposite beam, for a full eight-gun broadside. This change may have been inspired by a newspaper report that the *Invincible*s had their turrets *en echelon* for this purpose. In fact they could not easily fire cross-deck. A further Scheme 2b1 (8 November 1906) introduced turbines, which offered 36,000shp (40,000shp on trial), for estimated speeds of 24 knots (24.5 knots on trial). Scheme 2c1 (1 February 1907) offered slightly more powerful turbines (43,000shp on trial). Ultimately rated power was increased to 39,000shp. The smaller *Invincible*s were rated at 41,000shp and 25 knots. Note that German figures are in metric horsepower and do not quite match English figures. Belt armour was thickened to 250mm (9.8in); the *Invincibles* had the same 6in belts as earlier British armoured cruisers. However, the second-generation British battlecruisers (*Lion* and successors) had belt armour nearly as thick (9in, which was 229mm). Tirpitz chose the faster alternative design because he still thought of the ship as a cruiser. Greissmer gives no estimated costs for 2b1 and 2c1. The total cost of Cruiser F was 36.66 million, compared to 27.66 million for the previous year's Cruiser E (*Blücher*) and 18.75 million for Cruiser C (*Scharnhorst*), the ship bought the year before.

51. Scheme (Entwurf) 1 was the up-gunned *Nassau*. Scheme 8 had the *Nassau* class battery (twelve 11in/45), but the after two were superfiring, the rest being mounted pairwise on the forecastle deck. In Scheme 9, three of five 12in turrets were on the same level on the centreline, with two more superfiring aft. Finally, Scheme 10 was arranged like HMS *Dreadnought*. Tirpitz ended up with a modified *Nassau* with a 320mm belt (instead of 300mm) and 12in guns. He decided to stay with reciprocating engines rather than the turbines his constructors proposed. He seems to have been particularly determined not to lead the pack in gun calibre (an increase from 45 to 50 calibres was acceptable, however). In May his constructors offered new alternatives. The original twelve-gun turbine design would have cost 44–44.5 million Marks. A 21,500 to 22,000-ton ship armed with ten such guns (presumably Design 9) would cost 26.5 to 27 million Marks. At this point the twelve-gun ship was expected to cost 27.5 to 28 million Marks. Discussion of the various sketch schemes continued through at least May 1907, sketches being grouped as either A (six turrets) or B (five turrets). Thus Scheme 12 (A) showed the usual hexagonal arrangement, but with a somewhat taller barbette for No. 1 turret. Scheme 14 (A) was termed 'American, because it had two superfiring turrets forward. It also had two wing turrets and two centreline turrets aft (on the same level). Scheme 16 (series B) had two forward turrets side by side on a forecastle, the other three turrets being in line (between forefunnel and after funnel, between after funnel and mainmast and abaft the mainmast). Of other Series B designs, Scheme 16 was in effect a modified Scheme 9, 17 was the *Dreadnought* arrangement and 18 was entirely new. It had one twin turret fore and aft, the other three turrets set amidships in a diagonal arrangement. The designers liked 12 and 16, both of which had potential for further development. Tirpitz stood pat and the enlarged *Nassau* was built. It was based on Scheme 13, the most striking difference between sketch and ship being that the sketch showed Russian-style narrow cage masts (as in the *Imperator Pavel I* class).

52. Greissmer, *Grosse Kreuzer*, p 69, but presumably this idea originated with the W office, in correspondence which has been lost.

53. Details of alternative designs, which Greissmer gives for the other battlecruisers, seem to have been lost. The design presented to the Kaiser was 2i. No alternatives seem to have been offered. To Greissmer, *Grosse Kreuzer*, p 65, the choice of 2i seems to have been connected with the Kaiser's knowledge of the Brazilian *Minas Gerais* class, then building in the United Kingdom, with superfiring turrets fore and aft plus wing turrets. That seems to have justified (to the Kaiser) the adoption of superfiring turrets aft. However, it is not clear just when details of the Brazilian ships became public and the Germans were also inspired by the US Navy's adoption of superfiring turrets at about this time.

54. A memo to this effect was dated 22 March 1908, resulting in Design 5, an improved Cruiser F. Eliminating the superfiring turret aft shortened the citadel by about 7.2m. Displacement would be reduced to 22,600 tons and about 1.5 million Marks would be saved. Tirpitz rejected the idea; he saw Cruiser G as a way station towards a more heavily armed Cruiser H, to be built under the 1910 programme.

55. Greissmer, *Grosse Kreuzer*, p 73.

56. Scheme I was H with the additional armour. II added a forecastle for extra buoyancy and was expected to cost 1.2 million more than H (0.2 million more than I). These ships would have displaced 23,700 and 23,900 tons, respectively. III was the alternative with eight 30.5cm guns arranged as in *Von der Tann*, displacing 24,000 tons (no cost was given). In these designs the slopes of the armoured deck were thickened from 30mm to 50mm. The thicker side armour was introduced in Scheme IIc, 24,700 tons, dated variously 8 October and 25 November 1909. The final version, IIe, was approved on 27 January 1910. Output was increased to 52,000shp to maintain speed; design displacement was about 24,700 tons. *Seydlitz* cost 44.685 million: she and her near-sisters finally offered Tirpitz the fiscal stability he badly needed. The series described by Greissmer, *Grosse Kreuzer*, includes a radical departure from these designs: Scheme IV (IVe dated 7 December 1909; no Scheme III is described). It followed the centreline turret arrangement of the new British *Orion* class (and of the coming German *König* class battleships), with superfiring turrets fore and aft and a midships centreline turret. As weight compensation for the additional high turret forward, IVe had no forecastle. The midships turret took up space which might otherwise have gone to boilers, so IVe had twenty-two rather than twenty-seven boilers. The idea seems to have been rejected because it reduced end-on fire by 50 per cent. That would be particularly important in a cruiser, which might not always be firing on the broadside. Greissmer ascribes German interest in this kind of superfiring configuration to the example set by the US *Michigan* class.

57. Initially Tirpitz asked for the previous year's Scheme 14 and a *Helgoland*-type hexagon arrangement. At the beginning of June 1908 the constructors offered Schemes 1a, 1b and 1c, all with the 'American' arrangement fore and aft and a pair of wing turrets. They differed in freeboard and in the height of their 15cm guns, 1a having them at the same height as the previous class. In 1c the 15cm guns were moved out of the hull into a deckhouse amidships. This deckhouse carried the two wing turrets and the superfiring turrets at the ends rose above it. A sketch shows that it did retain four 8.8cm anti-torpedo guns in hull casemates forward of No. 1 turret. This ship would have displaced 24,500 tons, about 2500 tons more than its predecessor (1a would have displaced 23,600 tons). This was too rich for Tirpitz; it might be built under the next programme (1910–11), but not in 1909–10, when he had to save some money. Surely something could be done to cut it down.

58. They had superimposed turrets fore or aft (Schemes 8–12) or two turrets forward side by side and the other three amidships (Schemes 12 and 14) or all amidships (Schemes 13 and 16). There were also two more, Schemes 8a and 16a, arranged like the earlier Scheme 1c, with its six turrets: one turret forward, two on the broadside and two superfiring aft. In Scheme 16a the two midships turrets were arranged on a diagonal so that either could fire across the deck over a limited arc. That gave Scheme 16a the same broadside as Scheme 1c at much less cost. In this scheme the midships deckhouse of Scheme 1c was extended to the bow, No.1 turret in effect being eliminated.

59. In connection with the somewhat convoluted history of the *Queen Elizabeth* class (as the Germans understood it), Greissmer, *Linienschiffe*, p 139 reports that in the spring of 1911 Krupp proposed arming the new *König*s with 35.6cm guns like those the US Navy had just adopted. The Germans traced the British 15in choice to a reaction to the US *Texas* class, which introduced 14in guns in the US Navy.

60. Scheme 1 (September 1910) was essentially the Scheme III offered for *Seydlitz*. Scheme 2, offered at the same time, was a new design with a forecastle and four turrets on the centreline. It introduced a new feature, sheer from Turret 'B' to the bow. In Scheme 3 (also September 1910) the sheer was brought further aft and the secondary battery was brought above the hull so that it could fire in rough weather. Scheme 1 would have displaced 25,000 tons; Scheme 3 would have displaced about 25,600 tons. Scheme 4 (25 September 1910) was a developed version of Scheme 3. Scheme 1 was apparently first offered in May 1910, the all-centreline version first being offered a month later. There were minor improvements. In mid-March 1911 the constructors offered Scheme 4b and Scheme 5. Scheme 4b was Scheme 4 (the 1911 ship) with about 400 tons of additional displacement, which bought improved torpedo tubes and a new version of the 15cm mounting. The ship was lengthened forward by 3m. Scheme 5 added freeboard to restore casemate height lost due to the greater displacement of Scheme 4. It also added improved casemate deck protection. Bow armour was eliminated to increase freeboard forward. Both versions had a new boiler arrangement with twenty-two rather than twenty-seven boilers. There was interest in reducing metacentric height (from the 2.7 to 2.9m of Schemes 4b and 5) to 1.6 to 1.8m to slow their roll, for better gunnery, by reducing beam by 2m, but that was not done, because it would also reduce survivability against underwater hits. Instead the Imperial Navy tried anti-roll tanks. They also had their price: they lengthened the citadel by 3m and added 300 tons (without the roll-damping water in the tanks). The estimated price of a Cruiser K with anti-roll tanks was 49.55 million. An improved Scheme 5d, without anti-roll tanks, was offered to the Kaiser on 24 June.

61. Kelly, *Tirpitz and the Imperial German Navy*, pp 326–43.

62. According to Greissmer, *Linienschiffe*, p 135.

63. The 1914 ship was *Ersatz Kaiser Friedrich III* (*Sachsen*); the 1915 ship was *Ersatz Kaiser Wilhelm II* (*Württemberg*). As Krupp-Germania was too busy to bid on the 1913 ships, it was promised a 1914 ship with its diesel engine on the centre shaft. As of the end of September 1913 the estimated price of a ship without armament and armour was 21.2 million with the diesel and 20.3 million with the alternative of two main turbines and a smaller turbine on the centre shaft. Both figures were later somewhat reduced. Compared to the earlier ships, *Sachsen* was somewhat longer (by 2.4m on the waterline) and had a heavier torpedo battery and other improvements. When Germany mobilised on 1 August 1914 Tirpitz ordered that *Sachsen* be a repeat *Baden* with three turbines and minimum changes. *Württemberg* was apparently to have had a diesel engine. The 1916 and 1917 ships appear in a table of German dreadnoughts in Greissmer, *Linienschiffe*, p 169: *Ersatz Kaiser Wilhelm der Grosse* in 1916 and *Ersatz Kaiser Barbarossa* in 1917. Another ship, *Ersatz Kaiser Karl der Grosse*, was dropped from the 1912 Navy Law.

64. Greissmer, *Linienschiffe*, p 136, calls this the Kaiser's 'Lieblingsobjekt', his 'love object'. Presumably this would have been a battlecruiser-speed ship with battleship armament, something Tirpitz would consider entirely unaffordable. The context was the 1911–12 discussion of what became the *Baden* class.

65. On 5 December 1911 the general (naval intelligence) department offered a memo on a possible change from the 1911–12 design. It wanted more 15cm guns (eighteen rather than fourteen) and a higher design speed (28 knots rather than 27.5 knots). The higher speed was clearly attainable: *Moltke* made 28.4 knots on trial, far above her designed speed of 25.25 knots. The most spectacular improvement was substitution of the new 60cm H type torpedo for the 1906 model 50cm Type G of earlier ships. This substitution was also made in the 1913 battleship. The desired increase in 15cm guns was rejected. However, the turrets were all equipped with the same 8m rangefinder then being installed in the 1913 battleships (*Baden* class). *Hindenburg* cost 46.4 million, compared to 47.1 million for *Lützow*.

66. Greissmer, *Linienschiffe*, also describes other foreign programmes in detail, but it is not clear to what extent they affected modifications to the 1914–15 German battleships.

67. Greissmer, *Grosse Kreuzer*, does not mention any physical limit, but in 1916 discussions of post-Jutland possibilities German constructors referred to limits on length imposed by locks at Wilhelmshaven.

68. Beginning with the fourth ship of the class and continuing to the next (*Ersatz Yorck*) class, ships would have four completely independent sets of machinery, including two cruising turbines geared to the outer shafts.

69. From 'German Official Documents Relating to the Development of Warship Design 1916-1918' in *Monthly Intelligence Report* No. 23, 15 March 1921 (in ADM 223/809). These translated memoranda, including marginal notes by the Kaiser, were concluded in No. 24, 15 April 1921 (in the same file). These seem to have been the same memoranda as those published in German in Friedrich Forstmeier and Siegfried Breyer, *Deutsche Grosskampfschiffe 1915- 1918: Sonderausgabe die Entwicklung der Typenfrage im Ersten Weltkrieg* (Bonn: Bernard & Graefe, 2001 reprint of 1970 book).

70. According to a 19 June 1917 letter from von Capelle to Scheer, the fifty-round idea was first proposed on 24 July 1916 by CO 3rd Battle Squadron and then endorsed by Scheer. Von Capelle pointed out two objections. One was that battlecruisers would be wanted for post-war foreign service and they might be far from any base. He recalled that ships based at Tsingtao had always carried as much secondary battery ammunition as they could accommodate. The other was that in view of increased torpedo range and the disappearance of the 8.8cm guns, the 15cm gun was now the anti-torpedo weapon and it would often be firing at such long ranges that it would expend considerable ammunition. It appeared that the British were providing either the same or more ammunition to their secondary guns as previously. Von Capelle also observed that the British allowed less space and weight per round. A marginal note suggested a compromise: by the time 100 rounds per gun had been expended, probably the main battery ammunition had been exhausted, so 100 rounds per 15cm gun would be enough. The battlecruiser commander Hipper agreed with Scheer that in no engagement to date had so much secondary ammunition been exhausted that a third would have made a difference, but that was due to the limited opportunity for secondary-battery fire due to very long ranges; future engagements might be very different. Rapid fire could expend ammunition very quickly. Given a gain of only three tons per gun, he could hardly approve the proposal.

71. Two alternatives were offered on 11 January 1917. Scheme I was essentially a *Mackensen* hull with draught increased by 0.3m to 8.7m, adding 1350 tons. Machinery was not changed, so the extra displacement cost a quarter-knot (27.75 knots rather than 28 knots). Changes to armour were based on a November 1916 analysis: the after armour deck was thickened by 20mm (to 100–70mm) and the decks over magazines thickened from 3mm0 to 50mm. Side armour had to be reduced to 250mm to compensate for this weight and also for the weight of the heavier guns. Scheme II was a redesign with an enlarged hull, 2400 tons heavier than *Mackensen*. The additional 1050 tons (compared to I) bought better protection, for example of the machinery and magazines against deck hits (60mm over magazines). The middle part of the barbettes was 180mm rather than 150mm thick, the upper part 300mm thick. The citadel was lengthened. A modified Scheme II was chosen. Among the improvements to Schemes I and II, side armour amidships was restored to the 300mm of earlier designs. Power was cut to 90,000shp, for a speed of 27.75 knots. Two 15cm guns were sacrificed, for a total of twelve and there were three rather than five torpedo tubes, with twenty-four torpedoes. As described to von Capelle on 17 February 1917, the ship gained sufficient strength to support the heavier turrets by insertion of a 11.8in thick foundation. The draught remained within the set limits and the ship sacrificed half a knot. It was intended to press on as rapidly as possible with construction of the three cruisers before the first peace budget had to be presented. By this time some work had already been done on the ships as repeat *Mackensen*s and the work already done had to be scrapped and rebuilt at a cost of several million Marks.

72. On 16 October Von Capelle wrote that preparations were being made to design a fourth lock at Wilhelmshaven. It appeared that the work would take six years. Battlecruisers would be laid down three years before scheduled completion.

73. As given in the memo, 6.7in (17cm) – 10.6in (27cm) – 5.9in (15cm). According to Greissmer, *Grosse Kreuzer*, the equivalent thicknesses in the GK 6 design were 10cm–30cm–12cm.

74. Dimensions for *Ersatz Yorck*, as given by Greissmer, *Grosse Kreuzer*, were 227.8 x 30.4 x 8.7m (747.2 x 99.7 x 28.ft).

75. The memo, signed A2, is not dated. In the translated material it comes after a June 1917 letter from CO 3rd Battle Squadron of the High Seas Fleet and a February 1918 memo by A2. The assumption that A2 was in the general (Allgemeine, A) bureau of the Navy Department is this author's.

76. At the Kaiser's conference on the design (22 January 1918), Scheer said that he considered 16,400 yd range sufficient. Torpedoes had to be available both for short and for long ranges and for short-range fire the ship should have submerged tubes. Scheer argued that he could not rely entirely on torpedo craft, which might be unable to get into firing position due to an enemy's barrage fire. Alternatively, they might fire off all their torpedoes early in the action, as at Jutland. In these cases the torpedoes on board a capital ship might be valuable. A marginal note suggested that one purpose of torpedo armament was to force an enemy to fight at long range, but that is not logical given the previous German preference for short to medium ranges. The Torpedo Inspectorate clearly did not take Scheer's preference seriously. It maintained that the High Seas Fleet wanted at a minimum a range of 24,060 yds at 30 knots with a 661lb (300kg) charge. It was working on a torpedo, presumably the J-9 planned for the new ships, capable of meeting this requirement. It became clear at the meeting that these capabilities were unlikely to be used. The torpedo would need 20 minutes to reach at a target 19,685 yds (18,000m) away. Before firing another three to five minutes would be needed to calculate range and bearing for firing. Range would have to be measured accurately and for that purpose a rangefinder with a 16 to 20ft base would be needed; it was not clear where it could be mounted. The enemy could manoeuvre considerably in the 23 minutes or more between the decision to fire and the arrival of the torpedo. Why trade the permanent speed advantage of the above-water tube ship for a possible but unlikely torpedo firing advantage? For his part, Admiral Schrader (head of the construction bureau) pointed out that above-water tubes could not be sufficiently protected against heavy shellfire; their warheads and air flasks might explode if a heavy HE shell went off nearby. It might be necessary to dispense with broadside tubes altogether, retaining only a bow tube.

77. The file in the *Monthly Intelligence Review* includes the minutes of this meeting. In addition to the Kaiser, those present were the Admiral von Müller, the chief of the Naval Cabinet (in effect the Kaiser's naval aide), head of the Admiralstab von Holtzendorff, head of the Navy Department von Capelle, High Seas Fleet commander Admiral Scheer, construction department chief Vice Admiral Schrader and the Chief Constructor Dr. Bürkner. Capelle strongly emphasised that 45,000 tons was the outer limit of what could be done in the immediate future, presumably to head off any of the Kaiser's demands for major improvements.

78. In contrast to A2, Scheer held that current fire-control systems could offer effective fire even with fewer guns.

Chapter 9. Inshore Operations and an Inshore Fleet

1. In 1914 War Orders for the British China Station contemplated taking Tsingtao; no other fleet commander had similar responsibility for other German overseas territory, because Tsingtao was unique as a naval base. ADM 137/819, Foreign Stations: War Orders 1912-14, begins with a 3 July 1912 letter from C-in-C China Station to the Admiralty arguing that 'the best course to be pursued from an Empire point of view would be the reduction of Tsingtao by a combined Naval and Military expedition. Its position is a standing menace to our trade and to the peace to the Far East. It is inconceivable that, given the opportunity, Germany should not seek territorial gains in China and Tsingtao once reduced there would be no pretext for German interference in Eastern affairs'. The Admiralty replied that, once the German ships had been dealt with, 'an operation of this kind might become necessary'. War Orders dated September 1912 included only the earlier requirement to mask Tsingtao (i.e., to blockade it). In February 1913 the China C-in-C again wrote about an operation to take Tsingtao (in compliance with an October 1912 Admiralty letter not in the file) using Indian troops. Operations Division asked whether, if the German Far East ships could be dealt with in some other way, Tsingtao was worth taking at all. The final pre-war plan (12 February 1914), which included variants in the event of war against France, the United States and Russia (with Germany first [taking into account the possibility that the Netherlands would be allied to Germany]), included an attack on Tsingtao 'if events in Europe showed that the war was likely to be of long duration'. This file also includes extensive discussion (1912) of wartime co-operation with the French. Earlier War Orders did not include an attack on Tsingtao at all. ADM 116/3132, *War Orders Far East*, which includes the 1908 and 1910 War Orders for the Eastern Fleet. The 1908 version allowed for possible war against Germany, the United States, France and Japan, in that order. In the event of war against Germany, the China Squadron would bring German warships to action and mask Tsingtao; the Australia and East Indies Squadrons would paralyse German trade. The 1910 version matched the 1908 version, but mention of the Australia Squadron was deleted, as it was now the RAN. Since the alliance with Japan had been extended to 1915, war with Japan was considered improbable.

2. The Germans fortified the only usable beach in their colony, but the Japanese outflanked them by landing in Chinese territory (Lai-chau Bay near the town of Lun-kau), having reconnoitred the beach with a floatplane and with ships offshore. This was a divisional landing (18th Division) using twenty-six transports covered by thirty-two warships. According to *Krieg zur See*, the Japanese chose to land far from Tsingtao, although they could have landed in the surrounding Neutral Zone or in the German protectorate itself. Small numbers of British troops were later landed. The German troops on the beach retreated into the fortifications of Tsingtao itself, which the Japanese besieged using, among other things, heavy siege and naval guns. *Krieg zur See* volume on Colonial Operations (NHB, document courtesy Dr David Stevens RANHB).

3. ADM 137/835, covering the period November 1915 to September 1916.

4. ADM 137/452, 'Seizure of Advanced Base Sept 1914 to Apr 1915'.

5. ADM 137/452, 9, interim report headed 'Invasion Question: Seizure of Advanced Base', for First Sea Lord.

6. Answers to invasion question dated 17 March 1913.

7. Churchill to Bayly, 11 April 1913 in *Churchill* Companion Pt 3, p 1724. This was part of a larger study of possible German surprise attacks, the CID having concluded that 'if it made the difference between victory and defeat, the Germans would begin operations of war without either warning or pretext'. (Churchill to Adm Sir Henry Jackson, 18 April 1913, *Churchill* Companion pp 1725–7, in connection with a paper called 'A Time Table to A Nightmare'). One scenario had the Germans making feints so that the British army was concentrated near Harwich and the fleet between Harwich and Heligoland, while the Germans landed elsewhere.

8. *Churchill* Companion Pt 3, pp 1729–33. It did not help that in analysing the possibility of invasion the Admiralty War Staff blithely accepted that during the 46 hours the German attack force would take between despatch and arrival off the British coast the secret not only of the despatch of the expedition but also of the general hostile German intent could be kept perfectly. Churchill's critical memo is in *Churchill* Companion Pt 3, pp 1735–6.

9. The places involved were the Borns Deep in Holland, the Loeso Channel in the Kattegat (Denmark), the Kungsbacka Fjord (Sweden, in the Kattegat) and Ekersund (Norway, in the North Sea).

10. They were a modified version of the 1907 Horse Boat and a proposed motor lighter. The volume in PRO refers to plans in a separate volume, HS 552, which the author did not consult.

11. ADM 137/452 contains a comparison between Bayly's conclusions and those of the Operations Division. The significance of the Operations Division report is that the idea of the landing was clearly not Bayly's, but emanated instead from higher authority. The published Churchill Admiralty papers do not refer to this project, so it is not clear who ordered the studies.

12. A pen note on Bayly's text, probably from Churchill, dated 31 July (1914) states that three Brazilian monitors now completed in England 'can be obtained on the declaration of war . . . The use of these craft in the shallows between the islands and the shore must be considered'.

13. Patterson (ed), *Jellicoe Papers*, I, pp 40–1. The submission is not given, only parts of Jellicoe's replies to the Chief of Staff at the Admiralty. They are dated 27 July 1914.

14. This story of negligence seems somewhat odd in that Bayly's pre-war notes on anti-submarine defence of a battle force were considered important enough to survive in ADM 137/1926, a collection of miscellaneous British submarine papers. During the 1913 manoeuvres he was attacked four times by submarines: once in a moderate seaway, when no attack was expected; twice in smooth water when an attack was expected; and once in smooth water while zig-zagging as an ASW precaution. His lookouts never saw a submarine or its periscope before the submarine got within effective range, which Bayly took as 1000 yds (he doubted the submariners' claims that they could hit at longer ranges). He hoped that high speed in darkness could cloak ships near their bases, where submarines could expect them and he also hoped that specially-trained lookouts would do better. He wanted air patrols near the bases and he wanted ships to have only a single mast so that a submarine could not easily estimate a target's course. Chief of Plans pointed out that aircraft could spot submarines only in calm weather and that their noise gave a submarine plenty of time to dive. Location was pointless unless a submarine could be evaded. He doubted that even the best lookouts could stand the strain of looking for a periscope for more than a short time.

15. ADM 137/452, pp 190–1.

16. Patterson (ed), *Jellicoe Papers*, I, pp 122–3.

17. ADM 137/452, p 297. The file does *not* include any orders for this bombardment, only an evaluation dated 6 November 1914.

18. Mackay, *Fisher of Kilverstone*, p 473. Corbett's paper was delivered to Fisher on 19 December 1914. Fisher apparently never answered Corbett's question. Mackay notes that that before September 1916 Fisher's paper was not called 'The Baltic Project' but instead was 'On the possibility of using our Command of the Sea to influence more drastically the Military Situation on the Continent', hence more general than the Baltic project.

19. In his biography of Fisher, Bacon wrote that Fisher much preferred an attack on Zeebrugge to the Dardanelles operation, arguing that it would have shortened the war by a year. That would have driven the Germans back 350 miles and, in Bacon's view, 'lifted the last shadow of the threat of invasion and allowed us to concentrate in waters north of Holland. The vital point was that as far as anyone could foresee, continued occupation of Belgium meant threat of starvation in England'. As commander of the Dover Patrol Bacon would naturally have seen matters in this way, whatever Fisher thought.

20. Hankey, *Supreme Command* I, p 241, describing meetings held on 1 December 1914 and on 7 January 1915. On 7 January Asquith wrote to Venetia Stanley that 'we agreed we could not back Sir J French in is projected Ostend-Zeebrugge operation, for which he requires 55 also given as 50. more battalions and an impossible amount of artillery. Winston Churchill. pressed his scheme for acquiring a base at Borkum (which we have agreed always to speak of and if possible to think of as Sylt) – a big business, as it is heavily fortified and the necessary preparations will take till the end of March. We gave him authority for this'. Brock (eds), *Asquith Letters to Venetia Stanley*, pp 364–5.

21. The only complete account is Ian Buxton, *Big-Gun Monitors: Design, Construction and Operation 1914–1945* (Barnsley: Seaforth Publishing, 2008 second edition). Despite the title, Buxton covers the smaller 9.2in and 6in gun monitors as well as the larger ones. As he points out, there is no Cover, but the key Constructor's Notebook kept by Charles S Lillicrap survived. The initial sketch was submitted by Constructor A M Worthington by 6 November 1914. According to *DNC Records of Warship Construction 1914-1918* (NHB and Brass Foundry) 'the Monitors were designed as the outcome of the German occupation of the Belgian coast in the early stages of the war; they were required to bombard the ports on that coast which were being converted by the enemy into TBD and Submarine bases'. This is open to question because the writers of the DNC publication were far more interested in technical details than in the origins of projects.

22. Mackay, *Fisher of Kilverstone*, p 490. These craft do not figure at all in the *DNC Records of Warship Construction 1914-1918* (NHB and Brass Foundry). The Cover for these 'Beetles' or X-lighters (No. 343) is missing. Data from F J Dittmar and J J College, *British Warships 1914-1919* (London: Ian Allan, 1972), p 313. According to Brown, *Grand Fleet*, pp 152–3, the design of the X-lighters was completed in four days after an urgent requirement was levied in February 1915. Two hundred were initially ordered, the first being completed in ten weeks and half by the end of March (almost all by the end of August 1915). Brown had access to DNC records.

23. As given in the *DNC Records of Warship Construction 1914-1918* (NHB and Brass Foundry). It adds that the Falklands Battle had just shown that lightly-protected ships with long-range guns could destroy inferior enemy ships without risk to themselves. The Covers give no preliminary information at all, nor do the relevant Constructors' Notebooks (which have survived for the *Repulse* class).

24. According to Mackay, *Fisher of Kilverstone*, p 460, Fisher's copy of the relevant minutes was significantly altered in September 1916. The original stated that the issue on 3 November was to expedite the delivery of twenty submarines, which were to be built at once, but that a further large building programme had been decided on. The words 'for a special purpose' were added later. According to Mackay, minutes of the relevant conference taken by Maynard Keynes show that it was largely about submarines.

25. Bacon, *Fisher*, pp 188–9. Bacon admitted that an operation in the Baltic would have been costly, but that 'the ships used would largely have been ships built for the special purpose; they would have been cheap and with small crews and it must not be forgotten that the Germans would also have lost ships'.

26. The US Navy and Marine Corps thought much this way when they contemplated amphibious operations on the Danish and other coasts as part of the Maritime Strategy of the 1980s. In that case the risky enterprise was to have become possible with the destruction of much of the Soviet fleet, but in Fisher's case it was possible because he expected to have an expendable fleet in the Baltic.

27. This is an alternative interpretation of Fisher's failure to answer Corbett's question about how he would deal with German mines in the Baltic.

28. Mackay, *Fisher of Kilverstone*, p 468, quoting words Oliver wrote long after the war.

29. This is the list Fisher published in later years, for example in his memoirs. It is taken from Bacon, *Fisher*, II, p 284. Details are from Dittmar and College, who give dates of order. Some destroyer orders may postdate Fisher's departure in mid-May 1915. In a 15 December 1914 Minute Churchill defended the War Programme to the Cabinet, explaining how it differed from the planned 1914–15 and 1915–16 programmes. At that time it consisted of five battleships (including three purchased), six light cruisers, fifty-eight destroyers, eight flotilla leaders, fifty-five submarines, three small and eight large monitors and twelve fleet sweepers. The three small monitors were the ex-Brazilians. Two of the battleships were *Renown* and *Repulse*. The light cruisers included the ex-Greek *Birkenhead*s. The submarine figures are not consistent with the numbers ordered in November 1914. They must include the original eight units of the first war programme.

30. To complicate matters, Mackay gives different figures for destroyer orders: ten early in November, twenty-two at the end of the month, eighteen in February and twenty-two in May 1915 (an order initiated before Fisher left), a total of 72, of which two of the May order were later cancelled. The figures in the text are from Dittmar and College, *British Warships 1914-1919*.

31. This list did *not* include the six 'J' class long-range submarines ordered in January 1915 or the first two 'K' class. Both types of fast submarine seem to have been considered Grand Fleet assets, hence irrelevant to any Baltic operation. Fisher's list of ships ordered since 30 October 1914, dated 23 April 1916, showed sixty-five submarines: twenty 'H' class (from the United States), thirty-five 'E' class, six 'J' class and four 'K' class.

32. On 29 November 1914 Asquith wrote to Venetia Stanley that 'desperate efforts are being made to find some territorial formula which will bring Bulgaria and Romania into the fighting line alongside of Servia [Serbia] and Greece. It is not an easy job.' Brock (eds), *Asquith Letters to Venetia Stanley*, p 324.

33. Hankey, *Supreme Command*, II, p 280. This 28 February 1907 study was conducted during a short period in which Hankey was not Secretary to the CID. He unearthed it for circulation to the War Council when such operations were being considered in 1915. He particularly drew the attention of Churchill and Kitchener to the study, which he writes did not sway the War Council.

34. According to Hankey, *Supreme Command*, I, p 223, the British Ambassador to Turkey suggested the idea on 20 August and a few days later forwarded information. On 31 August Churchill discussed a possible attack with Secretary of State for War Lord Kitchener. On 27 August Greek Prime Minister Venizelos offered to place his resources at the disposal of the Entente. He was rejected in hopes of keeping Turkey neutral. However, the Greeks gave Rear Admiral Mark Kerr, the head of the British naval mission to Greece, their war plan against Turkey, which Kerr passed on to London. For their part, with Greece and Turkey on the verge of war, the British assured the Greeks that they would sink any Turkish ships emerging from the Dardanelles (as Asquith wrote to Venetia Stanley on 2 September). Later the King of Greece decreed that the neutrality of Bulgaria had to be guaranteed before Greece would attack Gallipoli. Churchill approached the British General Staff. Just before the breach with Turkey, the British Director of Military Operations described to Churchill the problems of a land attack. Hankey described the run-up to the Gallipoli campaign in detail as a prime example of what could happen without the effective Supreme Command he espoused. In his view the Cabinet members who formed the War Council, who had essentially no staff support, could not possibly evaluate proposed operations, particularly complicated ones like Gallipoli.

35. Paul G Halpern, *The Naval War in the Mediterranean 1914-1918* (Annapolis: Naval Institute Press, 1987), p 47 notes that as soon as the treaty was signed, the Ottoman government offered to give the Germans the new battleship *Sultan Osman I*, about to be completed in England, as soon as the British delivered her. That makes First Lord Winston Churchill's slightly later seizure of the ship much less provocative than is usually imagined. The Foreign Office still imagined that some sort of conciliation was possible, so it vetoed plans to make the former head of the British naval mission to Turkey, Admiral Limpus, commander in the Eastern Mediterranean. Unlike Admiral Carden, he was very familiar with the fortifications in the Straits.

36. Halpern, *Naval War in the Mediterranean*, p 50. The experts included Admiral Guido von Usedom, who became Ottoman Inspector-General of Coast Fortifications and Minefields.

37. On 5 December 1914 Asquith wrote to Venetia Stanley that 'His [Churchill's] volatile mind is at present set on Turkey & Bulgaria, & he wants to organise a heroic adventure against Gallipoli and the Dardanelles: to which I am altogether opposed.' Brock (eds), *Asquith Letters to Venetia Stanley*, 327. The editors add that at this stage Churchill envisaged support by a large army force, but that the troops could not be found. A large force of Australian and New Zealand troops (ANZACs) had been moved to Egypt to defend the Canal and Kitchener pointed out that it would take time to organise them for a complex operation.

38. Hankey, *Supreme Command*, I, p 243.

39. Hankey, *Supreme Command*, I, p 253. At this time most of the French generals, but not Joffre, agreed. British commander Sir John French wrote to Kitchener that he thought the deadlock on the Western Front could be broken, given sufficient troops and shells. However, he also wrote that although a German victory on the Western Front would be decisive (at least against France), no Allied victory, even one driving the Germans back to the Rhine, could be: 'ultimate victory must be sought for in the eastern theatre'. French warned that a crushing defeat of France 'would be very dangerous and embarrassing to our own safety and must be made impossible'. Presumably that meant the threat of invasion. Hankey, *Supreme Command*, I, p 261.

40. Hankey, *Supreme Command*, I, pp 244–50. Hankey's contribution was the 'Boxing Day Memorandum'. Asquith wrote to Venetia Stanley on 30 December that he had just received memos from Hankey and from Churchill which, written independently, had come to much the same conclusion: the stalemate in France could not be broken (Churchill wrote that further troops sent to France would only 'chew barbed wire' or be slaughtered in pointless attacks). Hankey proposed to attack Turkey in conjunction with the Balkan states, clearing her out of Europe. Churchill wanted 'to close the Elbe and dominate the Baltic', which meant seizing Borkum, then invading Schleswig-Holstein and then obtaining naval command of the Baltic so that the Russians could land 90 miles from Berlin'. Asquith pointed out that Churchill's plan entailed considerable problems, not least the violation of Danish neutrality, but it is interesting that at this point he was not pressing to attack the Dardanelles: Brock (eds), *Asquith Letters to Venetia Stanley*, pp 345–6. After reading the memoranda by Hankey and by Lloyd George, Churchill told Asquith that he had liked the idea of attacking Gallipoli, but had abandoned it because of the problems it presented. The direct attack on Austria from the Adriatic was ruled out due to the submarine threat in the Adriatic. An attack by Greece and Serbia via Salonika was attractive, but it would be difficult to support due to poor land communications (it was eventually carried out). Foreign Secretary Sir Edward Grey wanted an operation in the Adriatic to impress the Italians, who were edging closer to joining the Allies (they did so in April 1915).

41. Halpern, *Naval War in the Mediterranean*, p 56. This issue does not figure in either Hankey's account in *Supreme Command* I or in the Asquith letters, but it was extremely important in later French accounts quoted by Halpern.

42. Hankey, *Supreme Command*, I, p 253.

43. Hankey reports that at this time, in January 1915, Kitchener wrote to French, the British commander in France, that he had rejected the Zeebrugge operation in view both of the expected casualties (20,000, where French thought they might be 5000 to 8000). The War Council rejected the operation because it was not clear how it would help win the war. It turned out that even French army commander Joffre thought that the Russians would finish the war. He did not want to support any operation outside France, but he admitted that something might be necessary if no breakthrough was possible.

44. Hankey, *Supreme Command* I, p 320, based on Ludendorff's memoirs.

45. Brock (eds), *Asquith Letters to Venetia Stanley*, p 403. According to Hankey, Churchill persuaded Fisher to support him by appealing to his patriotism, his good comradeship, the desires of other members of the War Council and the great projects he (Fisher) was developing at the Admiralty. That might be read as a reference to future support of the Baltic project. Fisher privately commented to Hankey that coastal bombardments could be justified only if they were intended to force a decision at sea. To do that required either cutting off enemy trade or attacking on land. The army, which in Fisher's view existed mainly to help the navy, the decisive service, should therefore attack either in Flanders or at Gallipoli. Hankey commented much later that Fisher, who had confided his doubts to him, had been grossly remiss in never telling the War Council of his doubts. Neither did Admiral of the Fleet Sir A K Wilson, also a member of the navy's War Group. Fisher seems to have used Hankey as a back channel to Asquith, but he would not air his views at the War Council. The later Dardanelles Committee took both Fisher and Wilson to task for not warning the War Council and Asquith for not asking them in front of it. Fisher did get to veto a proposed separate naval operation after the army was stalemated (11 May). Fisher told Hankey that he would give his views if asked. He sometimes said that he would not oppose the operation because he felt personally loyal to Churchill, who had brought him back into office. According to Hankey, 'when Fisher first came into office in 1914. he still clung to the general ideas he had conceived in 1906 for mining and netting the German Fleet into their river harbours in the North Sea , after which he hoped that the war could be carried into the Baltic. He had obtained approval for a vast programme of naval construction designed to this end. Early in 1915 he had favoured the idea of offering military support to the Balkan States. But from the first in his heart he was bitterly opposed to the naval attack on the Dardanelles and as time went on, he began to see that the Gallipoli commitment would make so great a drain on our naval resources as to render his projects in northern waters impossible…He also maintained that it would endanger the safety of the Grand Fleet. The trouble was that he could never bring himself to the point of coming into the open and advising against the plans at the War Council'. Hankey, *Supreme Command* I, pp 312–13.

46. Formerly Conservative Prime Minister and Churchill's successor as First Lord; Balfour had been intensely interested in defence issues. Balfour was particularly impressed by the financial and wheat issues, remarking that 'it was difficult to imagine a more helpful operation'. Kitchener thought that if successful bombardment would be as good as a victory by one of his 'New Armies'. If the bombardment failed, surely the navy could simply withdraw. Hankey, *Supreme Command*, I, p 271.

47. Asquith mentioned Hankey's fears in a 13 February 1915 letter to Venetia Stanley, adding that he had 'been for some time' coming to the same conclusion and 'I think we should be able without denuding French to scrape together from Egypt, Malta & elsewhere a sufficiently large contingent. If only these heart-breaking Balkan States could be bribed or goaded into action, the trick would be done with the greatest of ease and with incalculable consequences. It is of much importance that in the course of the next month we should carry through a *decisive* [italics in original.] action somewhere and this one would do admirably for the purpose'. Brock (eds), *Asquith Letters to Venetia Stanley*, p 429.

48. Churchill found Sir John French unwilling to disgorge his troops. British hopes of forming a Balkan confederation collapsed as the Russians took huge losses, hence no longer appeared to be an effective support against Turkey – which doubtless would try to regain some of what had been lost in 1912–13. Having received a large German loan, the Bulgarians were willing to spread the story that the Russians were so short of ammunition that they could no longer maintain any offensive. In Greece, Venizelos cooled on assistance to the Allies. Both the British and the French became interested in putting troops in Salonika to encourage Greece to enter the war on their side. If that happened, Bulgaria would not join the Germans and Romania would probably enter the war on the Allied side. The idea was to announce the deployment to Veneizelos the same day that the bombardment began. Unfortunately co-ordination was poor. The bombardment was delayed until 15 February by the need to assemble minesweepers and then to 19 February by problems with the turbines of the battleship *Queen Elizabeth*. Venizelos refused to act unless the Romanians entered the war. The Near East strategy was nearly dead.

49. As described in ADM 137/452. The spotting aircraft were floatplanes and they could take off only in a flat calm. The type available typically could not fly high enough to clear all Turkish fire. Services were therefore limited.

50. Hankey, *Supreme Command* I, p 287. Hankey felt that due to their greed the Russians had destroyed one of the most promising combinations of the war. On the outbreak of war with Turkey, Foreign Secretary Gray had notified the Russians that the British Government understood that a settlement of the straits in their favour was necessary; Russian Foreign Minister Sazonov said that Russia would be content with possession of the Bosporus and the neutralisation of Constantinople. Now, early in March 1915, she wanted much more, Constantinople and the whole of the European shores of the

Bosporus, the Sea of Marmora and the Dardanelles. She also wanted parts of Asiatic Turkey to cover the straits. The British had to deal with Russian suspicions that they still wanted to thwart Russian ambitions. The situation was so serious that Opposition members were invited to the 10 March War Council meeting. Hankey helpfully found an old (pre-1907) CID paper which declared that excluding the Russians from Constantinople was *not* a vital British interest. The British told the Russians that, owing to their earlier sacrifices, their claims would be respected, but they still wanted a permanent base in the area. The favoured place was Alexandretta (present-day Iskenderun) on the north Syrian coast (now the southernmost part of the Turkish coast), but the French considered Syria their own future domain. Asquith sympathised with the Russians (as long as the fortification of the straits was forbidden), arguing that as long as the British had command of the sea, they could always block the exit from the straits. He considered Greek demands 'rather a matter of sentiment' but could see that both Bulgaria and Romania, like Russia, badly needed the access the straits provided. Brock (eds), *Asquith Letters to Venetia Stanley*, p 463 (6 March 1915).

51. According to the *Staff History of British Minesweeping*, p 24, the civilian crews would not make any appreciable attempt to sweep under fire until they had been stiffened by Active Service (regular) officers and men; by 18 March 1915 the trawlers were manned entirely by volunteers from the fleet.

52. According to Hankey, *Supreme Command* I, p 292, Fisher commented that he had always said the operation would cost twelve battleships.

53. On 18 April two *Beagle* class destroyers sweeping ahead of the battleships *Triumph* and *Majestic* came under enemy fire and increased speed to 20 knots. Their sweep behaved well, but there was no later attempt to repeat this performance in trials. The fast sweepers also had a surface sweep intended to cut the floats away from floating mines, 600 fathoms of wire rove through a roller shackle on the bight of the kite wire where it entered the water.

54. With the collapse of Turkey in 1918, the minefields in the Straits were no longer protected by guns, but they had to be swept so that, as planned, the Allied fleet could reach Constantinople. The necessary force was assembled at Mudros and sweeping began on 1 November. The scale of the force gives some idea of what would have been needed in 1915: one kite balloon ship (the gunboat *Ladybird*), five twin-screw sweepers, fourteen trawlers and three motor launches. Sweeping was complicated by the shallow settings of some of the mines. By 12 November, 184 British and French and 424 enemy mines had been removed at the cost of one trawler; a patrol yacht, possibly outside the buoyed channel, was later sunk. The twin screw sweepers had only just joined the force and their high speed proved valuable. Data from the *Staff History of British Minesweeping*.

55. According to the editors of Asquith's letters to Venetia Stanley, Hankey wrote in his diary for 19 March 1915 that 'on the first day proposal was made I warned P.M. [Asquith] , Lord K[itchener], Chief of Staff, L[loyd] George and Balfour that Fleet could not effect passage without troops and that all naval officers thought so'. Brock (eds), *Asquith Letters to Venetia Stanley*, pp 373–4. At least in their published version, the letters contain very few direct references to the Gallipoli operation.

56. Hamilton reported at once to Kitchener that ships could not force the straits because 'every night the Turks under German direction repair their fortifications: both coasts bristle with howitzers and field guns (outside the forts) in concealed emplacements; and the channel is sown with complicated & constantly renewed mine-fields'. Brock (eds), *Asquith Letters to Venetia Stanley*, p 488 (18 March 1915). According to Hankey, Kitchener's instructions to Hamilton were that should the navy fail to force the straits, he was to build up a sufficient force to do so. On this basis the instructions issued on 13 March were the key step leading up to the landings. This instruction was not discussed with or even communicated to the War Council, but the idea of a landing assault had been in the background for some time. Hankey was apprehensive because the operation had not been thought through. For example, there had been no detailed consideration of what sort of artillery support was needed. Hamilton was thinking tactically, but those preparing the expedition in London should have been more thorough. By 19 March Hankey was asking whether the operation would be a seize or a coup de main; he thought that the fleeting opportunity for the latter had gone. He was aware, at least retrospectively, that much depended on the choice of the landing place. 'A fortnight lost at this end in careful diagnosis and examination of the problem may save months in carrying out the operation'. Neither Kitchener nor Churchill was interested. Hankey, *Supreme Command* I, pp 291–4.

57. Churchill thought de Robeck had lost his nerve; he told Asquith on 24 April (and Asquith agreed) 'that the ships, as soon as the weather clears and the aeroplanes can detect the conditions of the forts and the positions of the concealed guns, ought to make another push and I hope this will be done'. Brock (eds), *Asquith Letters to Venetia Stanley*, p 506 (24 April 1915). Fisher apparently prevented Churchill from ordering de Robeck to attack again; he was only able to ask why he had 'altered his intention of renewing the attack as soon as the weather is favourable'. Fisher was asserting his position as professional head of the Navy and presumably Churchill had lost some of his power due to the failure of the earlier attack.

58. Hankey, *Supreme Command* I, p 303.

59. Halpern, *Naval War in the Mediterranean*, p 69; on the outbreak of war Romania, which was neutral, stopped allowing transit of munitions. Halpern recounts several desperate measures considered by the Germans, including a run to Smyrna by the Austrian cruiser *Novarra*. However, Michael Forrest, *The Defence of the Dardanelles: From Bombards to Battleships* (Barnsley: Pen and Sword, 2012), p 138 gives quantities of heavy shells and actual expenditures on 18 March, in his view showing that the Turks had plenty of ammunition with which to oppose a second naval attempt (unfortunately he does not give his source). Forrest does give extensive details of the fortifications. In his view, the key change after 3 November was much more extensive mining of the Narrows, five lines instead of the two initially there. Until 15 August there were only two lines and in Forrest's view the Mediterranean Fleet had a real chance of forcing the Dardanelles in what amounted to hot pursuit of *Goeben* and *Breslau*. Presumably the Foreign Office would have taken a dim view of such action. A few ships would have been lost, but most would have made it to Constantinople. Immediately after the 3 November bombardment there was still a chance, particularly as the Turkish gunners were initially shell-shocked. Mobile howitzers and two additional lines of mines were soon added. British shelling did damage the forts and their guns and in some cases guns were neutralised temporarily by dirt thrown up by near-misses. Shelling also had enormous psychological impact. However, nothing the ships did affected the smaller mobile guns which made sweeping difficult.

60. ADM 116/1348 (Case 5863 Vol I), *War Plans and Policy 1914-1918*. Arguments laid out in a 23 August 1915 memo 'for Balfour' (with indecipherable signature, but probably from Churchill) in ADM 116/1348. It emphasises the gravity of the situation and the severe likely consequences of withdrawal: 'The scale, the dangers and *the importance of the operation* italics added. have increased beyond all expectation'. This is followed by a detailed proposal for step-by-step operations.

61. As a young Royal Marine, Hankey had experimented with a small landing force, so he knew something of amphibious operations. Robertson, the Chief of Staff to French, described the Dardanelles landing 'as the stiffest operation anyone could take'. Hankey himself was very anxious. Asquith wanted to get Hamilton to send him 'a considered view of the prospects' before going any further. Brock (eds), *Asquith Letters to Venetia Stanley*, p 535 (7 April 1915). After a 6 April meeting with Asquith, Churchill and Kitchener to discuss the land attack, Hankey remarked that 'none of them appeared to me in the least to realise the extreme difficulties of the operation. Hamilton's plan seems to me fraught with the possibility of an appalling military disaster, if the Turks can fight at all. When I suggested that even the operation of landing would be one of extraordinary difficulty, Churchill merely remarked that he could not see that there was any difficulty at all'. Italy was about to enter the war. If the British and French delayed their attack, they might be able to convince Greece and possibly even Bulgaria to join the war against Turkey in combination with Italy. These countries might carry out a great combined attack on Constantinople, obviating the hazardous landing. According to Hankey, Asquith said no; after all this talk we must go through with it. Hankey thought that the best reason to delay; if something had to be done, it would be better to do something else, such as attack Haifa in the rear of Turkish army invading Egypt. He asked Admiral Richmond to gain Fisher's support. Churchill was furious, but Asquith agreed to postpone the attack until the question of Italian co-operation had been decided. Hankey, *Supreme Command* I, p 300. Italy denounced the Triple Alliance on 4 May and signed a naval convention with Britain and France on 10 May.

62. ADM 116/1348.

63. Robin Prior, *Gallipoli: The End of the Myth* (New Haven: Yale University, 2009) is adamant that it would not have, but many others have argued the opposite. Prior's account of the potential advantages of winning in Gallipoli omit the most important of all, that it would have opened the key water route to Russia, changing the situation on the Eastern Front.

64. The clearest indication is that the submarines were not taken into account in Churchill's August 1915 exhortation to renew the naval attack, which did take into account the possibility that naval gunfire would disrupt the Bulair road. For an extended account of the submarine campaign, see Victor Rudenko, *Gallipoli: Attack from the Sea* (New Haven: Yale University Press, 2008), which gives details of the numerous sinkings, particularly by E-class submarines.

65. HMS *Queen Elizabeth* was withdrawn with the appearance of the U-boats in the Eastern Mediterranean. In effect her 15in guns were replaced by those aboard monitors, whose bulges gave them near-immunity to torpedo attack. *U 21* sank the battleships *Triumph* (25 May 1915) and *Majestic* (27 May 1915). A Turkish torpedo boat sank the battleship *Goliath* (15 May 1915).

66. Hankey, *Supreme Command* I, p 321.

67. The mine argument may reflect experience with British mines, whose moorings were notoriously unreliable. The German mines used by the Turks had no such problem. Keyes' argument is in Paul G Halpern (ed), *The Keyes Papers* (Navy Records Society, 1979), I, 188 (proposal dated 17 August 1915). Keyes made the point that the August landings had achieved complete surprise, but even so the Turks had fought effectively, which to him meant that the ground war was stalemated. He also wrote that 'from more than on source it has been stated that the enemy were on the verge of being defeated' by the 18 March naval attack, 'until the unlucky accidents robbed the Navy of its chances of victory'. Keyes thought the situation was now easier, as an attack would probably surprise the enemy and many of his small guns had probably been moved. The monitors could engage the forts more effectively, the air service was a lot better (for spotting) and the sweepers were now efficient. He acknowledged the submarines, but pointed out that supplies could still be towed along the shore in shallow water or convoyed by destroyers, 'the usual method of transportation'. However, if three or four ships could get into the Marmara with six to eight destroyers this squadron would, with submarines, suffice to completely dominate that sea. This is not too different from the argument Churchill made a few days later in ADM 116/1348. Admiral de Robeck disagreed that 'we never got to tackling the real mine field & I do not think our sweepers are capable of clearing it under gun fire!' and that 'the naval failure has been due to starting on bad information & underestimating the enemy's powers of defence from the very start!' Above all, 'what are 3 or 4 ships to do in Marmora. Is Constantinople to be bombarded & trust to

surrender of Turks? A very doubtful matter'. Keyes and Godfrey submitted a more elaborate plan on 13 September (p. 194), which de Robeck rejected. When he sent Keyes back to report to First Sea Lord Admiral Sir Henry B Jackson, de Robeck noted that Keyes was very anxious to get his views before the Admiral, in the context of which he would provide a great deal of information about the Dardanelles, but that his plan would be disastrous; 'the Turks would not lay down their arms if we bombarded Constantinople . . . They have several months supply on the peninsula'. However, de Robeck also thought the Turks were war-weary and getting short of ammunition, so 'we are getting nearer the end than by making mad & heroic efforts that cannot bring about a final result!' Very soon, however, Bulgaria was letting German ammunition through to Turkey.

68. Halpern (ed), *Keyes Papers* I, p 268.

69. Initially High Seas Fleet inactivity was seen as likely cover for an invasion, given the absence of ocean surveillance in the North Sea. See, for example, Patterson (ed), *Jellicoe Papers* I, p 49, in which Jellicoe writes that he 'cannot wholly exclude the chance of an attempt at landing during the week on a large scale by High Seas Fleet. Extraordinary silence and inertia of enemy may be prelude to serious enterprise'. Later there was the spectre of all the shipping immobilised by the British blockade, sufficient, it was thought, for 250,000 troops. ADM 137/966, 'Anti-Invasion 2', is a thick volume of papers devoted entirely to means of disabling East Coast ports in 1914–15, as is ADM 137/967, 'Anti-Invasion 3', which is devoted to Thames and South Coast ports.

70. The report is in ADM 137/835. The 1 January 1916 conference, chaired by Adm of the Fleet Sir A K Wilson, sought to determine the largest force the enemy might be expected (i) to transport to British shores and (ii) succeed in landing before the operation was interrupted by the navy. To avoid underestimating the threat, the conference assumed that enemy numbers would be limited only by transports. Recent experience (transport to France and, presumably, overseas) was that it took 6 GRT to transport each man, so the million tons available to the Germans equated to 170,000 men (a CID estimate of the largest force that could be embarked with artillery, etc., was 135,000). In November 1915 the army's Director of Military Operations (DMO) estimated that the Germans could assemble a force of 50,000 to 100,000 infantry at any time they were not mounting a major operation. The conference translated that as a ten-division threat. DMO added that he was not at all confident that the British would know about such an operation even at the point at which it embarked. In the instructions to be followed in the event of an invasion, the CID maximum estimate became a minimum enemy force.

71. In a test landing at Clacton in 1904, about 12,500 men, 2500 horses, 55 guns and 320 vehicles were landed from ten transports, six ships being cleared in an average of under 20 hours and four more averaging under 28 hours. It seemed that this underestimated what could be done in wartime, when safety precautions would be relaxed.

Chapter 10. The Battle of the Narrow Seas

1. Karau, '*Wielding the Dagger*', p 3. *Krieg zur See*, Nordsee 2, p 151 credits Tirpitz as probably the first to realise the extreme importance of Flanders 'as regards Germany's position at sea and her military, politic and economic future'. Bruges was connected by canals to both Ostend and Zeebrugge. The canal to Ostend was dug in the seventeenth century and then deepened and widened, so that in 1914 it could take destroyers and submarines but not larger vessels. The harbour of Zeebrugge and the Zeebrugge-Bruges canal were begun in 1895 and opened in 1907. The harbour was created by building a curved 2500 yd long breakwater (mole), with a quay 1500 yds long on its inner side. To prevent silting up, a 300 yd gap was left in the mole. In 1914 the average depth of water in the harbour was about 23ft at low water (but the harbour silted up considerably during the war). Before the war the mole was fitted with railway lines and cranes. Locks at Zeebrugge were over 150 yds long, the water at the entrance being 20ft deep at low water. These locks could therefore handle ships up to light cruiser size. From the locks a straight six-mile canal extends to Bruges. At the Zeebrugge end were interconnected basins. The Zeebrugge and Ostend canals were interconnected by a cross-canal running through Bruges. Yet another canal (navigable by destroyers at light draught) connected Bruges with Ghent, the latter being connected to Antwerp by the Scheldt, which was under Dutch control. The MarineKorps frequently proposed widening the canal between Bruges, Ghent and Antwerp to take destroyers and submarines. In 1914–15 it was generally imagined that the war would end before this work could be completed and later resources were not available. However, small submarines and minelayers ('A' boats) were built in Antwerp and sent by canal to Bruges so that they did not have to make the seaward trip around Flanders. Details from *Krieg zur See*, Nordsee 2.

2. *Krieg zur See*, Nordsee 2, p 151 argues that the Flanders project, of which the MarineKorps was an integral part, was due to Tirpitz' concentration on Great Britain as the ultimate enemy. The Germans would sooner or later be using the Belgian harbours, but Tirpitz wanted the navy to establish itself firmly on the Flanders coast as a guarantee that Germany would concentrate on fighting England. Presumably he feared that otherwise the harbours would be given away casually in a peace settlement.

3. Tirpitz first formally proposed creation of a MarineDivision in a 23 August 1914 telegram to Berlin which claimed that the project had already been approved by the Naval Cabinet (meaning the Kaiser, via Admiral von Müller). The 20,000 men would be taken first from naval battalions (i.e. marines), then from seaman artillery and then filled out by naval detachments. As in the United Kingdom, the major bases all supported naval battalions, in this case 3000 men at Kiel and 4500 at Wilhelmshaven, which would be filled out by the reserve detachments at Kiel (1000) and Wilhelmshaven (2000). The North Sea station commander (Wilhelmshaven) was willing to provide as much as was desired, but the Baltic station commander (Kiel) was unwilling to weaken his defences, presumably because he would not enjoy much fleet support with the fleet concentrated in the North Sea. Even so, the division included 1400 seamen artillery

from Kiel and 3000 from Wilhelmshaven. All personnel involved would be replaced in naval barracks by reservists. Associated with them would be minelayers (small torpedo boats would not be needed). Liège was a candidate initial station and then possibly Antwerp, if it was captured. Artillery to protect the positions might be taken from naval fortresses or perhaps from ships. Command was given to retired Admiral Ludwig von Schröder. During discussion of the role of the new organisation (24/25 August) Tirpitz wired from GHQ (Coblenz) to the Acting Head of the Admiralstab that 'the draft organisation must . . . be framed primarily with a view to offensives against the British coast'. *Krieg zur See* admits that formation of a naval division fighting alongside the army was also attractive as a way of showing that the navy was really participating in the war. At this time the Navy Office was considering various possible employments for its mass of idle reservists, even their wholesale incorporation in the army. Another possibility was to send them to Turkey to supplement the personnel already there. Tirpitz' idea of using the MarineDivision (later MarineKorps) specifically to secure the naval position he wanted in Belgium contrasts with the Admiralty's decision to form a Naval Division to be incorporated in the British army, without any direct naval role. The army was less than pleased, but it soon asked whether the MarineDivision was ready, assuming that it would act as an occupation force for the Belgian coast rather than fight in the field, where it might interfere with the army. The army envisaged a division organised like one of its own, under army orders. Tirpitz was strongly opposed: he wanted troops to support his vision of naval warfare from coastal positions. To that end he sought to shape the establishing order the Kaiser would sign. Von Schröder suggested that initially the division might be placed under army orders, but that once it was established on the coast it should come directly under the Kaiser's orders, like other naval units.

4. *Krieg zur See*, Nordsee 2, pp 360–1. The Germans felt that minesweeping would be simplified by the great variation in water depth between high and low tide, as a mine viable at low tide would be deeply submerged at high tide.

5. Karau, '*Wielding the Dagger*', p 10, but he refers to a single radio station, not the six listed by *Krieg zur See*. The assumption that control was to be based on air reconnaissance is the present author's, but note that even for events in 1914 *Krieg zur See* constantly refers to German air reconnaissance by both Zeppelins and aircraft.

6. Karau, '*Wielding the Dagger*', p 16. It has also been suggested that the Belgians resisted the destruction of these ports, Antwerp already having been destroyed.

7. Kurnau, '*Wielding the Dagger*', pp 39–40. These points are *not* made in *Krieg zur See*. On 9 November 1914 *U 12* became the first German submarine to use the 'Triangle'.

8. After von Schröder was refused his cruiser, he asked for two *Siegfried* class coast defence ships, but they too were refused due to difficulties in bringing them around from the Heligoland Bight. *Krieg zur See*, Nordsee 6, p 259.

9. Karau, '*Wielding the Dagger*', p 45: according to a 22 January telegram, twenty large and twenty-eight small submarines, a half-flotilla of destroyers and twenty-four small torpedo boats.

10. Because these craft were not part of the High Seas Fleet, Tirpitz could assign them to Zeebrugge on his own initiative (aside from the Kaiser, there was no overall naval commander to decide whether or not to do so). Presumably the design work was also begun on Tirpitz' initiative, well before Zeebrugge was in German hands: the design of the UB-class began on 18 August 1914 and that of the UC-class in September 1914. These boats were sometimes described as coast defence weapons which would free the ocean-going U-boats for open-sea operations. The first orders were placed on 15 October and 23 November, respectively. Note that the UB-class design was begun before the MarineDivision was formed. In addition to boats assigned to Flanders, UB- and UC-boats were deployed on the German coast and to Pola (the main Austro-Hungarian naval base) and to Constantinople.

11. On average the UB-boats required 10 days between launch and completion. They went under their own power to Ghent and then by floating dock through shallow canals to Bruges (20 hours). They ran torpedo trials in the canal at Bruges and sea trials took another week. After the first eight went by canal, the rest went via the open sea, being delayed for months by bad weather. Thus the second batch did not arrive in Flanders until 20 December 1915 (had they gone by canal, they would have been ready on 1 August). These boats displaced 128 tons and were armed with two torpedo tubes (one torpedo each) and a 5.5cm gun. Surface speed was 6.5 knots, using a 60hp engine originally intended for a ship's boat. It seems to have been sufficient even against the strong tidal stream in the area. Typically boats did a three-day protective patrol, followed by five-days' rest and then by a five-day offensive patrol, which might extend as far as Harwich or Le Havre. The minelayers (UC series) typically carried out one minelaying sortie per week in the area between the Humber and Portsmouth. *Krieg zur See*, Nordsee 4, pp 196–7. According to *Krieg zur See*, the 'A' class torpedo boats were initially intended only for minesweeping. Typical displacement was 136 tons and speed was 19 knots; armament was the same two 17.7in torpedo tubes as in a UB-boat, with the same two torpedoes, plus the same 5.5cm gun.

12. *Krieg zur See*, Nordsee 4, pp 8–9.

13. Karau, '*Wielding the Dagger*', p 49, quoting Admiral Scheer's post-war memoirs. More typically the relatively small size of the Flanders force is associated with a large fraction of overall sinkings (generally given as 25 per cent) to explain the urgency of blocking Zeebrugge.

14. Karau, '*Wielding the Dagger*', p 34, citing a 1914 memo on the use of the aircraft.

15. According to *Krieg zur See*, Nordsee 4, p 192, a German seaplane flying from Flanders used her W/T in the air for the first time on 9 July 1915. *Krieg zur See* describes

numerous bombing attacks made by the Flanders aircraft during 1915, but they were using 10kg bombs, which cannot have had much effect.

16. It seems that initially the alarm was raised not by the Admiralty but by the Foreign Office and the War Office, in the persons of Sir Edward Grey and Haldane, as reported by Asquith in a letter dated 23 October 1914. In Cabinet Winston Churchill derided their fears that Ostend would become a German submarine base, saying that he could have it quickly shelled into ruins and made uninhabitable. By this time the Royal Navy was already shelling Flanders.

17. Attacks began on 17 October (two days after Ostend fell) and continued through 9 November, then resumed between 21 and 26 November and continued off and on through the winter of 1914–15. The MarineKorps began planning heavy gun emplacements to deal with such bombardments (and with landings) in October 1914.

18. In a letter dated 6 January 1915 Asquith described French's memo on an attack on Zeebrugge and Ostend, for which he wanted fifty battalions 'and a quite impossible supply of artillery and ammunition'. At this time French wanted Kitchener's 'New Army' broken up battalion by battalion to strengthen his own force, a project Secretary of State for War Kitchener absolutely rejected. A day later Asquith wrote that the Cabinet had decided against the Zeebrugge project and in favour of Churchill's project to seize a base at Borkum – 'a big business, as it is heavily fortified and the necessary preparations will take till near the end of March'. A few days later French was complaining that the French wanted him to reoccupy the 'Ypres salient' to release their own troops for offensive operations . He could not do this and also carry out the Zeebrugge-Ostend operation, which he preferred, unless he received at least the fifty more battalions he wanted. Brock (eds), *Asquith Letters to Venetia Stanley*, p 362.

19. The British lost much of their initial highly-trained army during 1914. Secretary of State Lord Kitchener raised a New Army, which the British expected would be ready to fight in 1916 or 1917. The French bitterly opposed any withdrawal of troops from the Western Front to fight elsewhere. Canada, Australia and New Zealand contributed large numbers of troops, but early in 1915 they were still fairly raw. Thus the Australia-New Zealand (ANZAC) troops were considered effective against the Turks but not the Germans. Any plan to attack in Flanders required considerable reinforcement of the British army there, which is why the views of its commander Gen Sir John French were significant.

20. Von Pohl was particularly intent on limiting the loss of torpedo boats (destroyers) to Zeebrugge and after the experience of the 7th Half-Flotilla he could cite particular problems. According to *Krieg zur See*, he also argued that it was dangerous to get submarines through the Hoofden, the area between the Norfolk and Suffolk coast and the coast of Holland *en route* to Zeebrugge and that torpedo boats could not be sent without an escort. A fleet operation covering that movement would be observed by the enemy. Von Pohl also argued that submarines were better than surface minelayers and that minelaying itself was difficult because without lights the positions of mines could not be fixed. Von Pohl also argued that one half-flotilla of torpedo boats was not enough; to be effective, Zeebrugge would need at least two of the best torpedo boat flotillas, the loss of which would seriously reduce the capability of the High Seas Fleet.

21. Von Pohl's successor as Admiralstab chief, Admiral Bachmann, telegraphed von Pohl that he would submit the question to the Kaiser, mentioning that Tirpitz also supported the transfer of the half-flotilla to Flanders. That infuriated von Pohl, who had spent the previous six months with Tirpitz at the Kaiser's GHQ in Coblenz. He rejected Tirpitz as a purely military expert; 'after six months association with him I gained the conviction that his views on military and tactical matters are so confused that he must not be allowed to have any influence on the employment of naval forces...At the beginning of the war I had hoped to benefit by his advice and it was His Majesty's express wish that I should do so, but with the course of time I found it impossible to accept his views, as they always involved risking the Fleet'. *Krieg zur See*, Nordsee 4, pp 44–5.

22. Von Schroder's 12 April 1915 request for these ships is quoted in *Krieg zur See*, Nordsee 6, p 259.

23. Karau, '*Wielding the Dagger*', pp 55–6. The boats became available as new destroyers were delivered. Von Schröder considered three a bare minimum. They fought their first, inconclusive, action against British destroyers on 20 April. Slightly later they tried and failed to prevent the British from laying a mine-net anti-submarine barrage off Zeebrugge; they represented far too weak a force to fight the massed Dover Patrol.

24. *Krieg zur See*, Nordsee 6 also stresses the contribution of aircraft stationed in Flanders, although at this point they cannot have been very effective in attack. They were, however, necessary for reconnaissance of the waters beyond the barriers (*Krieg zur See* calls the patrol by radio-equipped aircraft 'decisive' in the fight against the barrage).

25. *Krieg zur See*, Nordsee 6, p 271 dates von Schröder's plea to 20 May, but does not make the transfer of the full flotilla a direct consequence.

26. According to *Krieg zur See*, Nordsee 6, passing through the Thornton Ridge, a gap so shallow that submarines could not pass through it submerged.

27. Karau, '*Wielding the Dagger*', p 75, notes the decision but does not give any rationale. Nor does *Krieg zur See*, which generally lionizes Scheer and emphasises his offensive-mindedness.

28. This traffic was considered important partly because Dutch food exported to England was denied to Germany; the convoys in effect supported the blockade of Germany.

29. *Krieg zur See* describes careful arrangements to keep different groups of destroyers in separate operating areas so that they could not attack each other at night (similar arrangements were made for U-boat patrol areas). Such arrangements raised navigational issues which *Krieg zur See* does not address.

30. Karau, '*Wielding the Dagger*', pp 73–5.

31. Karau, '*Wielding the Dagger*', p 80; note that neither had the power to force Scheer to give up any destroyers, although they could influence the assignment of new ones.

32. One of the flotillas returned to the High Seas Fleet during the night of 2/3 November but the other remained with the Flanders force until the end of that month. Another High Seas Fleet flotilla was transferred temporarily on 22 January, the Flanders Destroyer Flotilla returning home for refit. British signals intelligence picked up this operation and the Harwich Force was sent out to intercept the German destroyers. It was reinforced with destroyers from Dover. The German destroyers all survived, albeit several were seriously damaged. The Harwich Force lost the destroyer *Simoom*, so badly damaged that she had to be scuttled.

33. *Krieg zur See*, Nordsee 6 does *not* suggest any possibility that by forcing the Royal Navy to reinforce the Dover Patrol and the Harwich Force the destroyers in Flanders might draw down the destroyer force of the Grand Fleet and so perhaps immobilise it. That is clearly what Jellicoe feared at this time.

34. Therefore, according to Karau, '*Wielding the Dagger*', p 84, the Germans announced that the operation had been conducted by High Seas Fleet destroyers operating from the German Bight.

35. Karau, '*Wielding the Dagger*', p 86. Bacon wrote that he had advance notice; Karau was sceptical, given the failure to intercept the German destroyers.

36. Karau, '*Wielding the Dagger*', p 154. At about the same time the Asquith government fell and Lloyd George became Prime Minister. He much favoured an offensive in Italy against Austria-Hungary; for him France and Flanders were killing far too many men for far too little return. As Lloyd George enjoyed too little support for his strategy, he turned to a French plan advanced by General Nivelle. When Nivelle's offensive collapsed and the French army mutinied, the British had to undertake some offensive in France to keep the Germans from crushing what was left of the French army. Haig now returned to the Flanders plan, supported by Jellicoe.

37. It is not clear how Jellicoe's statement should be taken. In several contexts he claimed that without some solution to current problems (generally ASW) the war could not be continued. It is sometimes suggested that he felt that he could not get the resources he needed unless he made this kind of case; otherwise the army would starve the navy. It is also true that Jellicoe had always been a pessimist and that by the spring of 1917 he was also quite tired. By June, Lloyd George was saying that he could not stand Jellicoe's pessimism; better to find someone who would propose solutions rather than predict disaster. According to Karau, Jellicoe was impressed with the threat of German destroyers, but underestimated the number of submarines in Flanders by two-thirds. In June Jellicoe stated that it was pointless to plan for the summer of 1918 because unless the British took the Flanders coast they would lose before then.

38. These six (i.e., just over a half-flotilla) fresh destroyers came from the Baltic. Von Schröder was informed on 6 February that they would soon be transferred. They arrived in company with more of the short-range torpedo boats ('A II' class) which were used for local defence and minesweeping.

39. Data from Paul Köppen, *Krieg zur See, Die Uberwasserstreitkrafte und ihr Technik* (Berlin: Mittler, 1930), the German official account of surface warship development. This book includes comparative data on British warships. The account of the LM-boats is on pp 186–90.

40. According to Karau, '*Wielding the Dagger*', p 149 initially von Schroder was promised the first eight *S 113* class (oversized destroyers), for delivery to him between August 1917 and April 1918, but then Scheer volunteered to send a half-flotilla of conventional destroyers and von Schroder had to agree that the first eleven of the new large destroyers would go to the High Seas Fleet. Karau does not associate the unusual design of the *S 113* class with the needs of the Flanders force. In the event, only two of these ships were ever completed (and only one during the war, the other being completed for transfer as a war prize).

41. There was no question but that sustained bombardment could wipe out both facilities and the ships; the Japanese had done exactly that to the Russians in Port Arthur during the Russo-Japanese War. Karau, '*Wielding the Dagger*', pp 124–5, describes German expectations, on the eve of the submarine offensive, of a British operation which would include a landing in the Netherlands. The result was combined German army-navy planning (for the first time) for the defence of the Flanders bases. Presumably the army command agreed because the army had agreed that the U-boat offensive was a national priority and because the loss of the Flanders bases would seriously reduce its effectiveness. Measures taken at this time included reinforcement of the air component of the Flanders force. On 11 April the Kaiser authorised creation of a third Marine Division for the MarineKorps Flandern.

42. Dover Patrol files in ADM 137 include proposals for a combined military and naval landing on the Belgian Coast in April – August 1916 (file 46/26) and proposals for a landing on the Belgian Coast in August 1917 (file 46/27). Although both files are extensive, they provide details rather than any overall account of what was planned. According to Karau, '*Wielding the Dagger*', p 154, after the French vetoed a projected 1915 attack into Flanders, they agreed to one in 1916. It was abandoned in favour of the attack on the Somme, which was intended to relieve pressure on the French at Verdun. On 25 July 1917 the Dover Patrol laid a mine and net barrier specifically to shield the planned landing (which was to have taken place two weeks later) from interference from

Zeebrugge. A cycle of minelaying and German minesweeping followed.

43. Admiral Sir R H Bacon, *The Dover Patrol 1915-1917* (London: Hutchinson, n.d.), I, p 215.

44. Bacon, *Dover Patrol*, I, p 228. In the one-volume version of the book, Bacon describes his concept for what amounted to an LST, a modified merchant ship carrying tanks behind bow doors and beaching to unload them. This concept is not described in the earlier two-volume version. It seems remarkable in retrospect that Bacon's widely-read book apparently had no effect whatever on the development of the LST during the Second World War, to judge by surviving primary sources.

45. Karau, '*Wielding the Dagger*', p 161, argues against Bacon's chances.

46. In his account of the Dover Patrol, Bacon is quite bitter about his dismissal, arguing that had he been consulted much of the amateurishness which marred Keyes' raid would have been avoided. He considered the blockship concept pointless, as it was easy to clear a wide-enough channel for a small submarine to pass a blockship, however well placed it was.

47. According to *Krieg zur See*, the employment of the slow monitors, which backed up the patrol force outside the barrage, had been given up as too dangerous. On 10 October 1916 the Admiralty decided to shift to the barrage further south, which was 27 miles long.

48. Typically the barrier was patrolled by fourteen trawlers burning flares, sixty drifters and four motor launches backed by searchlight units: four old destroyers or patrol boats and two paddle sweepers. In support were one large monitor and six to eight destroyers. During the day a monitor and five destroyers operated off the Flanders coast.

49. Karau, '*Wielding the Dagger*', p 223.

50. I am indebted to David C Isby for this idea. Robert W Herrick, *Soviet Naval Strategy: Fifty Years of Theory and Practice* (Annapolis: Naval Institute Press, 1968), pp 13–14 quotes early Soviet experts on the needs of a small navy. In *Morskoi Sbornik* in September 1923, for example, Professor M Petrov argued that the two greatest require-ments were an offensive concept and exceptionally complete intelligence – which amounts to local ocean surveillance. In the August 1925 issue Iu. Rall argued for exploitation of First World War experience – 'tactics of limited engagement, active defence, resolution of a series of specific tasks stemming from conditions of a given theatre'. Only the German operations in Flanders seem to fit all of these terms. On 31 October 1926 the US attaché at Riga (there was as yet no Moscow embassy) reported that the 1926 Soviet war plan called for the two Baltic battleships to form a strongpoint at Kronstadt from which submarines, torpedo boats and destroyers would sortie to the mouth of the Gulf of Finland to engage invaders. Much the same tactics were practised in the 1927 manoeuvres, which also envisaged coastal minefields covered by the battleships or by shore batteries. Again, this was much what had been done in Flanders.

51. The two-volume report is PRO ADM 239/27. The British made no such studies of any other German coast defence systems.

Chapter 11. Submarines

1. For example, in connection with the Yarmouth Raid (November 1914), *Krieg zur See*, Nordsee 2, p 336 describes the High Seas Fleet cruising formation: two battle squadrons in line ahead, with the flagship between them, light cruisers ahead and on either beam at extreme visibility and destroyer zigzagging ahead as a submarine screen in two lines abreast, one two miles and the other five miles ahead, the boats being spaced two miles apart. 'Enemy submarines were thus unable to approach.' In this case one of the destroyers reported two torpedo tracks in quick succession – which was apparently no great surprise. The destroyers had no ASW weapons whatever, so exactly what they were to do if they spotted a periscope is not clear.

2. The 'D' class generated the first substantial submarine Cover (No. 212). A design report was submitted to DNC on 18 May 1905. This was a true Admiralty design, its hull form tested at the experimental tank at Haslar.

3. In January 1904 Bacon, who was then Inspecting Captain, credited himself with forcing Vickers to develop new submarine designs with better performance, including increased endurance. He had been responsible for the requirements levied on Vickers. Bacon minute in correspondence on assigning a constructor to assist the Inspecting Captain, in effect the origin of the 'D' class, Document 41 in Nicholas A Lambert (ed), *The Submarine Service 1914 - 1918* (Navy Records Society, 2011).

4. The notes in the Cover describe the two options as C2 and D.

5. Bacon commented that 'the question of air economy should be considered with the engine design, as it may have an important bearing on submerged running'. That suggests he had something like a snorkel in mind. The 'D' design was sized for the existing 12-cylinder petrol engine. There was room for increased height and breadth but not length.

6. More 'D' class submarines would have been ordered in 1908–9, but *D 1* had not yet run full trials (she was not accepted until September 1909). Hence the continued 'C' class orders.

7. Until that time the 'C' class was being built in considerable quantity: the 1906–7 programme comprised *D 1* and seven 'C' class (one of them built at Chatham Royal Dockyard instead of by Vickers, providing the Royal Navy with a second source of submarines); the 1907–8 programme was entirely the 'C' class (twelve submarines) and the 1908–9 programme was *D 2* plus the last eight 'C' class, a total of thirty-eight 'C' class having been built.

8. Fisher to Prime Minister A J Balfour, 24 January 1905, Document 57 in Lambert

(ed), *The Submarine Service*. At this point Fisher claimed an effective radius of action of 500 miles, which could be increased by towing. He was already writing about how submarines made close blockade impossible, but he had not yet made the leap to longer-range submarines operating independently off an enemy's coast.

9. Lambert (ed), *The Submarine Service*, Document 66, draft memorandum.

10. Inspecting Captain of Submarines Roger Keyes reported in August 1910 that during the recent manoeuvres *D 1* had operated continuously for thirty days, but on her return she still had enough oil for a 400-mile run. He pointed out that her heavy oil engines were scarcely out the experimental stage and she was missing a blade of one propeller, yet she performed extremely well. Document 68 in Lambert (ed), *The Submarine Service*. Other tests showed that submarines could be vectored to targets well out in the North Sea.

11. 'Development of British Submarines', a printed paper enclosed in a report submitted by Commodore (S) dated 3 November 1914, in ADM 137/2067, Volume I of Commodore S War Records.

12. According to the printed paper in Commodore (S) records, the 'French' design was copied from a Laubeuf design 'which had passed through DNC hands in connection with a Chilean order in which he was interested' (DNC was Sir Tennyson d'Eyncourt, who had worked for Armstrong) and the 'Italian' design was based on one advertised by Laurenti.

13. The 'E' class began as the smaller (800 tons: 'D' Mod X) of two alternative upgraded 'D' class submarines, the larger ('D' Mod Y) displacing 1000 tons. Lambert (ed), *The Submarine Service*, p 169. As of February 1911 Inspecting Captain S S Hall favoured the larger of the two, on the ground that the smaller one did not realise its potential for sea-keeping. He clearly considered broadside torpedo tubes the best armament for such a large submarine, since he recommended eliminating the bow tubes altogether to gain space for better accommodation: Document 76 in Lambert (ed), *The Submarine Service*. The design actually submitted had bow and stern tubes and four beam tubes, as did the alternative pseudo-Laurenti and Schneider designs. The version of Mod Y brought up again in 1911 featured reduced engine and battery power and increased surface buoyancy. Approval of any of the designs required new engines, a French Carrels 2400bhp engine having been chosen tentatively by DNC the previous year. As of September 1911 it was producing only 1500bhp. Without some alternative, that was enough to kill the big submarines for the 1911 programme: Document 77 in Lambert (ed), *The Submarine Service*.

14. The officers sent were constructor H G Williams (DNC's submarine designer), Engineer-Commander H Garwood (E-in-C's submarine engine expert) and Commander P Addison (Keyes' chief of staff 1910–13). According to the print in Commodore (S)' file, however, Keyes (Document 80 in Lambert (ed), *The Submarine Service*) killed the alternatives by saying that they would be too difficult to build in England because there was so little space between inner and outer plating. Keyes considered the 'E' the largest practicable saddle-tank submarine, so he approved the repeat 'E' class. At that point Laurenti offered to sell the Royal Navy a submarine. The three officers went out with no obligation to buy, but they unanimously recommended the submarine. Scotts was willing to build a boat subject to the condition that it would not be paid for if it was not accepted.

15. Hall made this point in a 17 February 1914 letter he sent to Fisher attacking Keyes. Document 104 in Lambert (ed), *The Submarine Service*.

16. Letter to Controller, 7 February 1911, Document 76 in Lambert (ed), *The Submarine Service*. In Lambert's view, Hall was replaced by Keyes in September 1910 because of his opposition to the fast submarine concept (in Lambert's view, the fleet submarine, but comments of Keyes which he quotes suggest that this was the 'submarine destroyer' discussed earlier by Fisher and Jellicoe). Document 80 in Lambert (ed), *The Submarine Service*.

17. Document 80 in Lambert (ed), *The Submarine Service*.

18. At this time Vickers had a monopoly on British submarine-building (to DNC designs incorporating the Holland patents), subject only to submarines built by the navy at its Royal Dockyards (i.e., Chatham). This monopoly did not affect submarines to non-DNC designs. The Vickers contract required two years' notice, which was given on 31 March 1911. Under this arrangement the Royal Navy was already permitted to buy submarines of foreign design.

19. Its report dated 29 February 1912 is Document 81 in Lambert (ed), *The Submarine Service*. The committee hoped that on a surfaced displacement between 250 and 300 tons the coastal submarine might attain 14 knots surfaced, with a radius of action of 1200nm. They would have two bow and, if possible, one stern tube. The Vickers 'V' and the Admiralty 'F' class, intended to meet this requirement, had little impact on wartime British operations and so are not further discussed here.

20. Jellicoe (as Controller) notes on Fisher's April 1909 memo, Document 67 in Lambert (ed), *The Submarine Service*.

20. Document 92 in Lambert (ed), *The Submarine Service*. Churchill described an Ocean Submarine Flotilla, which he considered a Commodore's command 'equal as a decisive fighting unit to a first-class battleship or battlecruiser'. It would comprise three or four submarines and two fast light cruisers, one of which would serve as depot and the other as scout for the submarines, with three or four seaplanes. Four Submarine Squadrons might be created for general service in the North Sea and Mediterranean, based on harbours deep enough that the submarines could get to sea submerged, hence covert. Cromarty, Gibraltar and Malta all fulfilled this condition. It is not clear how squadrons would have corresponded to flotillas and it seems that Churchill meant that

a flotilla/squadron could be equated to a battle squadron. On 30 August (Document 93 in Lambert [ed], *The Submarine Service*) Churchill wrote to Fisher that 'if the submarine is to be a partial substitute for battleship strength or battleship predominance and not merely a substitute for destroyers, it must possess a strategic speed which will enable it to effectively to overhaul or circumvent a battle fleet, so that it can come into action without fail and be counted on as a decisive weapon. If this speed can be attained at the present time or in the immediate future by any other path except by those of size and steam, I should be delighted to learn it.' The file of miscellaneous British wartime submarine documents (ADM 137/1926) contains 6 August notes of ASW lessons of the 1913 manoeuvres by Home Fleet C-in-C Admiral Callaghan, including the question, on p. 415 of the file, 'to what extent is it feasible for submarines to accompany a fleet to sea?' Commodore (S) Keyes considered it perfectly feasible for 'E' class submarines to accompany a fleet to sea, but it was not clear how they would be brought into touch with an enemy attempting to avoid battle. He did think that submarines by their presence might induce an enemy to turn into the arms of the battle fleet. It would be wise to try that in an exercise.

22. Document 91 in Lambert (ed), *The Submarine Service*, Keyes' 15 August 1913 memo on submarine functions. This paper answered a Minute from Churchill.

23. In the autumn of 1913 Keyes' title was changed from Inspecting Captain to Commodore (S), to emphasise his operational role.

24. Document 99 in Lambert (ed), *The Submarine Service*.

25. Keyes argued that until there were enough submarines they could not be assigned to an early standing blockade force, because they would risk being mined or even being torpedoed by enemy submarines when on the surface. His reasoning (in the same words, with the emphasis on not sending submarines right *into* the Heligoland Bight) can be found in his 21 August 1913 remarks on the 1913 manoeuvres (ADM 137/1926 p 428). He thought a reasonable operating cycle would be three days on blockade, three on passage there and back and six resting and making good defects, in which case a quarter of a submarine force (actually somewhat less, to allow for refits) would be on station at any one time.

26. According to the April 1914 print in Commodore (S) papers, the conference was called to discuss the fact that the Germans were spending about as much on submarines but only on oversea types, so they had more of those than the Royal Navy. The text in Lambert (ed), *The Submarine Service* shows that the conference was a much more general review of British submarine policy, beginning with Keyes' insistence that even the coastal submarines have good seagoing capability, capable of keeping the sea in all weather in the North Sea for two or three days at a time. The Laurenti design and its Vickers and Admiralty derivatives ('V' and 'F' classes) was recommended as the smallest available double-hull submarine, the type favoured by submarine officers. It was considerably smaller than a 'D'. The text of the committee report (printed as an appendix and also in Lambert (ed), *The Submarine Service*) stresses the need for habitability but does not mention co-operation with the fleet.

27. Bizarrely, DNC d'Eyncourt's design notebook in the NMM does not describe the 1913 design, or indeed many other DNC submarine designs. The sole exceptions are the submarine monitor (*K 18*, later *M 1*), the 'L' class and a submarine cruiser (*L 50*) based on it. Haslar reports in PRO include tests of a new submarine design (form UX) dated May 1913 and follow-on tests of form UY in June. Tests of varied bow forms were reported in October. Model experiments to date on the 1913 submarine were summarised in a July 1914 note, showing that the project was very much alive at that time. The chapter on submarines in the DNC history of warship construction 1914–18 (NHB) states that the 1913 design would have displaced 1700 tons and would have been 338ft long. The design was revived in 1915 and modified. The 18in tubes were replaced by 21in tubes, a twin revolving set added in the superstructure and an 800bhp battery-charging diesel generator added. In this form surface displacement was 1980 tons. This design and the big 'J' class used model UR, originally a light cruiser hull form, which Brown, *Grand Fleet*, p 125 describes as the best ever tested for its speed-length ratio.

28. The 1914 print in Commodore (S) records reverses this account, which is based on a 1913 memo by Keyes. According to the print, some submarine officers suggested to Vickers that it design a double-hull submarine with the same armament, engines, etc. as an 'E' class submarine, but with a flat upper deck, more reserve buoyancy and good habitability. It was known as the 'Vickers double hull "E"'. Third Sea Lord directed DNC to design a similar ship. It displaced less, with a partial double hull and had one 21in torpedo tube aft instead of two 18in. It would also be less expensive. According to the 1914 paper, this Admiralty Improved E Class design was being offered by Vickers, Scott's and Armstrong and could be considered the standard oversea type. The 1914 print includes a copy of the 1912 Submarine Committee report.

29. Document 101 in Lambert (ed), *The Submarine Service*, date given as 25 December 1914 but clearly 1913. In this paper Churchill also ordered the one Admiralty and four Vickers coastals be treated as overseas boats, with letter designations ('F' and 'V'). Churchill also ordered design of a new coastal boat, to cost less than £50,000, but the war intervened before anything happened.

30. Five were ordered from Chatham Royal Dockyard. Two were ordered from Armstrong, which could now tender thanks to the end of the Vickers monopoly. None was ordered from Vickers, which was building other submarines.

31. Document 102 in Lambert (ed), *The Submarine Service* is a 22 January query to Third Sea Lord: what is the latest date on which fourteen submarines ordered in place of the battleship to be built at Plymouth could be ordered and yet be ready when the battleship would be completed, in 1917? If the submarines could be completed quickly enough, they could be pushed into the 1915–16 budget and the cost of one of the four 1914–15 battleships saved.

32. Fisher to Jellicoe, Document 106 in Lambert (ed), *The Submarine Service*.

33. Document 109 in Lambert (ed), *The Submarine Service*, dated 12 July 1914. The submarines replaced the battleship *Resistance* with fifteen Improved 'E' class and the battleship *Agincourt* was replaced by six torpedo cruisers of a new type. Four *Calliope* class cruisers would replace ten planned destroyers. Alternatively, the destroyers could be replaced by four flotilla leaders and four more Improved 'E' class submarines. This change was to be brought before the Board as soon as possible.

34. Document 103 in Lambert (ed), *The Submarine Service*, a February 1914 memo by Keyes on the difficulty of increasing submarine production.

35. The Greek naval programme was awarded to a French firm, which formed an Anglo-French syndicate to build the ships. For example, the Greeks were to receive a French *Bretagne* class battleship. The programme included two British-built light cruisers and four 'M'-class destroyers.

36. Soon after war broke out Churchill asked for an emergency destroyer and submarine building programme. Third Sea Lord Admiral Tudor replied the next day (11 August) that any programme would be limited by Vickers' diesel output. The Admiralty had tried to use the 'G' class programme to introduce alternative engines, but that project died when war broke out. Tudor thought that the maximum would be twelve Improved 'E' class, of which eight could be ordered immediately and another four at the end of the year. Two of them would probably be powered by FIAT engines built by Scotts. Although an emergency destroyer programme was soon put in hand, no submarines were ordered. Documents 130–133 in Lambert (ed), *The Submarine Service*. Agreeing with Tudor, Fisher considered engines the bottleneck; he proposed to ensure delivery of twenty submarines by ordering twenty-five sets of engines. He assumed that some would be delayed by the need to make good defects in castings, etc.

37. Dittmar and College, *British Warships 1914-1919*, p 85, describes the 'E' class as the hardest-working of all British submarines, with a loss rate of about 50 per cent. Vickers slightly modified the design for *E 9–E 11*, but Chatham reverted to the original one with its *E 12–E 13* and all but Vickers built the later boats to the *E 12* design. Fisher's initial twenty submarines comprised six from Vickers, two each from Armstrong, Beardmore and Yarrow and one each from John Brown, Laird, Palmers, Scott, Swan Hunter, Thorneycroft and White. Of these, the two from Beardmore were the Turkish boats taken over. Six of the seven single-boat firms soon claimed that they could build two boats as quickly as one, so the twenty-boat programme grew to twenty-six. Churchill apparently thought the eight offered by Tudor had already been ordered under the War Programme. They must have been the last eight 'G' class, approved but not yet ordered. In December 1914 Director of Dockyards offered a 42-boat 'G'-class programme to be executed by Royal Dockyards: twelve at Portsmouth, twelve at Devonport, twelve at Chatham and six at Pembroke. (Document 138 in Lambert (ed), *The Submarine Service*). In January 1915 Churchill vetoed the programme, as seventy-seven submarines were already under construction. He saw no tactical argument for more submarines, although he could accept the argument that Portsmouth and Devonport should gain some submarine-building experience, perhaps by building two 'G' class each (that was not done).

38. A N Harrison, *The Development of H.M. Submarines: From Holland No. 1 (1901) to Porpoise (1930)* (BR 3043, January 1979). Harrison was a long-time submarine designer and he based his book on notes he took from official design files in 1928–39, when he was involved in submarine refits. As an argument against steam at this point, Harrison mentions an attempted crash dive by the French submarine *Archimede* when in company with British 'E'-class submarines. A beam sea struck her funnel; it took 20 minutes to clear it so that it could be lowered.

39. Unfortunately, aside from the comment in several official places that the Grand Fleet rather than the Submarine Service was responsible for the 'K' class, no document showing Jellicoe's request for this submarine has surfaced. The 'K' class cover (353) lacks policy information. It begins with a 3 May 1915 statement that the design has been approved as submitted by DNC and Commodore (S); DNC, E-in-C and DEE must meet and decide all necessary details regarding machinery etc. DNC D'Eyncourt had submitted a drawing on 31 April 1915. Drawings were sent to Vickers on 4 May 1915.

40. According to Harrison, *The Development of H.M. Submarines*, 8.2, Vickers was designing the 'J' class 'and tried to anticipate the next step'. According to the chapter in the DNC 1914–18 history of warship design, Vickers submitted its design on 15 April 1915 (it does not appear in the Cover). The company offered a 280 x 28 x 23 (depth)ft submarine (2000 tons), geared turbines producing 14,000shp for 23 knots on two wing shafts, with diesel on a centre shaft, with four bow and four broadside tubes, all 18in and one 4in gun. The 1913 DNC design was preferred because it was faster on a smaller shp. The most important change was to use 18in rather than 21in tubes because as yet there was no satisfactory design for a 21in broadside tube and the project was urgent.

41. In the Cover, which does not give any design background.

42. This problem also killed off US Cold War attempts at direct support by nuclear submarines for carrier battle groups. The US *Los Angeles* class was designed specifically for this role, which is why it had the first NTDS (situational-awareness) installations in US submarines.

43. *K 1* was sunk after having been disabled by collision with a sister-ship off the Danish coast in November 1917 and *K 13* was lost on trials when a remotely-controlled intake failed to shut (she was salvaged and renamed *K 22*). There were also post-war losses. This is not the record of a horribly unsafe class, as the 'K'-boats are usually described.

44. In February 1918 Beatty wrote to the Admiralty that over the past year experience had shown him that the 'K' class was an important adjunct to the Grand Fleet, as 'their speed and seagoing qualities enable them to conform to Fleet movements and tactical requirements; in consequence they may be confidently expected to arrive at the scene of action at the right time; moreover their speed admits of their being employed to cut off an enemy's retreat at a strategic point. These are great advantages and cannot be over-estimated.' Since Jutland British tacticians had been wrestling with the problem Scheer posed when he withdrew his fleet: should the Grand Fleet follow. The 'K'-boats offered a solution, in that they could get in behind a retreating High Seas Fleet. Beatty wanted four laid down. The objective should be two ten-boat flotillas (so that eight would be available at any time). They would be in addition to the 'special "K" class' ('M' class). ADM 137/1926, p 203. In fact six new K-boats were ordered (*K 23–K 28*), but all but *K 23* were cancelled on 26 November 1918. The additional orders were presumably intended to make up for the three losses. *K 23* was completed after the war. After cancellation, an order was issued on 31 December 1918 to take the frames of *K 24*, *K 25* and *K 28* to Chatham for completion, but that project too was cancelled. Brown, *Grand Fleet*, p 127 comments that, had the 'K'-boats been completed only slightly earlier, they would have been available at Jutland and the verdict on the class might be rather different.

45. ADM 137/1926, general submarine service records for 1914–18, p 40. Jellicoe specified two rendezvous positions, noting that his speed of advance was 17 knots and that of the submarines 13 knots. Basing the submarines on the Tyne would bring them 180nm from a rendezvous 260nm from Scapa, so it would take them 14 hours (and the fleet 16 hours) to get there. Two other rendezvous were specified. In a November 1915 letter to the Admiralty, Jellicoe wrote that he understood that current plans called for submarines to try to ambush the High Seas Fleet on its way back to harbour, but he much preferred to use submarines during an action. He thought that attacks by German submarines during an action 'might conceivably be so heavy as to turn the balance of gun power in favour of the Germans'.

46. Jellicoe to Admiralty after discussion with Commodore (S) S S Hall, 3 February 1916 in ADM 137/1926, p 56. At this time the 11th Flotilla was to consist of six 'G' and six 'J' class (it had included 'D', 'E' and 'H class submarines). Once they were ready, the fourteen 'K' class plus the six 'Gs' and six 'Js' would form the Grand Fleet Submarine Flotillas. Jellicoe proposed that the flotilla at Scapa should consist of the first eight 'K' class, the others being assigned to the Battlecruiser Fleet at Rosyth.

47. W/T was an issue through the war, because submarines were ideal scouts in enemy-controlled waters, but without effective W/T they could not report. A report by Captain (S) of 10th Submarine Flotilla dated February 1918 gives the then-current situation (ADM 137/1926, p 208). Submarines had Type 14 sets. Under good weather and with aerials properly insulated, they could be heard at 350 to 400nm range – all the way across the North Sea. In moderate weather, if the aerial and feeder were not enveloped in spray but dampness hampered performance, range was about 250nm. If the aerial and feeder were enveloped in spray, the arc could be put out. Using 'arc steadying circuits' a submarine might be heard at 150nm. If the aerial insulation was badly enough damaged by moisture in its deck tube, performance might be ruined altogether until the mast was dried out. These figures applied to a submarine with two masts and a large aerial. A submarine with one mast and an inverted-V aerial would lose about 100nm under good conditions and 50nm under moderate ones. It followed that the big masts were needed by the long-range Grand Fleet submarines. Under some circumstances submarines would be out of range of both the Grand Fleet flagship and their parent ship, so linking ships would have to be used. An aerial raised by a kite would be more efficient than one slung between masts and would also be cut down quickly for a crash dive (but it could also be sighted).

48. Brown, *Grand Fleet*, p 124. I have been unable to find its report. Members were Third Sea Lord Admiral Tudor, Chief of Staff Admiral Oliver, DNC, DNO, Commodore (S) and A W Johns, DNC's submarine designer.

49. Brown, *Grand Fleet*, p 130 writes that there were two alternative designs, one with a 7.5in and one with a 12in gun, the latter taken from an old pre-dreadnought (there was also an abortive design featuring a new gun). The concept was due to Commodore (S) Hall, who said that a 12in gun could overcome the limitations of torpedo attack. The gun might be likened to later attempts to use anti-ship missiles in place of torpedoes. Despite the initial use of 'K' designations, these ships were entirely different from the 'K' class. Note that they, but not the 'Ks', were included in D'Eyncourt's design notebook in the NMM. The monitor Legend was signed by DNC on 1 June 1916 and the Board Stamp was affixed on 13 June 1916. The same dates apparently apply to the 'L' class.

50. ADM 137/1926, p 89.

51. It is not clear why the numbers *L 36–L 49* were not used.

52. The d'Eyncourt notebook in NMM shows *L 50* as a Cruiser Submarine, with the word Cruiser lightly crossed out. The battery is given as two (later one 5.5in) guns and four (later six) 21in torpedo tubes, with one 3in anti aircraft gun added in the final version. The design is dated 1916. The earlier 'L' class is credited with one 3in HA 20 cwt guns, four 18in bow tubes and two 18in broadside tubes.

53. ADM 137/1926, pp 93–4, 3 January 1917.

54. Account based on Harrison, *Development of H.M. Submarines*.

56. Notes of the conference are Folio 4 in the Cover (292); they indicate that initially the submarines were to have had two 4in guns as well as the six bow tubes.

56. Brown, *Grand Fleet*, p 129 points out that unfortunately on the only occasion an 'R' made an attack, the torpedo failed.

57. Brown, *Grand Fleet*, p 135, quoting Land.

58. This account is largely based on Eberhard Rossler, *The U-Boat: The Evolution and Technical History of German Submarines* (London: Arms and Armour Press, 1981). Rössler based his account on German records, but as he points out the technical records of German submarine design were largely destroyed after the First World War to keep them out of Allied hands. That left policy documents and the written accounts of various German submarine designers. I have also made use of Gröner.

59. German navy submarine designs had project numbers. It is not clear whether missing numbers in the series referred to surface warships or to rejected submarine projects. *U 2* was Project 7; *U 3/4* were Project 12; *U 17/18* were Project 20; the *U 43* Mobilisation class was Project 25; the *U 71* class minelayers (UE series) were Project 38; the *U 81* Mobilisation class was Projects 25 (*U 158*, *U 159*) and 43 (*U 115*, *U 116*, *U 263–U 276*); the *U 117* class cruiser minelayers were Project 45; the *U 127* class cruiser submarines were Project 42; the *U 213* class were Project 42A; the *U 139* class cruiser submarines were Project 46; Project 47 was an abortive armoured U-cruiser; the UD1 armoured U-cruiser was Project 50; the *UB 1* class was Project 34; the *UB 18* (UB II) class was Project 39; the *UB 48* class (UB III) was Project 44; the *UC 1* class was Project 34; the *UC 16* class (UC II) was Project 41; the *UC 80* class (UC III) was Project 41A; the abortive UF 1 class was Project 48a; and the abortive UG 1 class was Project 51A. The Second World War Type II was based on UF; Type VII was based on UG and on UB III.

60. *U 1* had a Körting engine. *U 2* was to have used one built by Daimler-Benz. Daimler-Benz encountered problems and by the time its engine was satisfactory, the navy had adopted diesels. *U 2* had the Körting engine instead. She was modified to take the Daimler-Benz engine, but there were problems and she never entered service.

61. Körting produced two engines: a six-cylinder 220–260bhp unit and an eight-cylinder 310–345bhp unit, at 550rpm. These were 1910 figures. Weight/power ratio was 24kg/bhp. From *U 5* on, submarines used two engines in tandem on each shaft to provide sufficient power. These engines could not reverse. They manoeuvred on their motors, using battery power.

62. According to Rossler, *The U-Boat*, p 28, the torsional problem seems to have worked in Gemania's favour, until its engine proved unreliable. Germania also offered to bore out its cylinders to achieve 925bhp at 430rpm. It helped MAN that its engines were already demonstrating their reliability and that they had boosted power to 1100bhp in *U 27* and *U 28*. This exceeded what the British were achieving in their 'E' class.

63. The defence of the Heligoland Bight required thirty-six boats, on the theory that at any one time twelve should be disposed around a 30-mile radius, five miles apart. They should be relieved daily, which required another twelve and a reserve of twelve in Wilhelmshaven. That made for twelve-boat flotillas. An additional flotilla would be held as a war reserve at Kiel. Another twelve boats would patrol the approaches to Kiel (one in the Little Belt, three in the Great Belt and the Fehmarn Belt, with four for reliefs and four as material reserve). Another flotilla, at Emden, would be available for offensive operations in the North Sea. Typically one U-boat in six was under repair at any one time, so another ten were required as a material reserve.

64. *U 42* was ordered from Laurenti, but not delivered due to the outbreak of war. Of the three planned 1913 boats, *U 43–U 44* were ordered on time, but *U 45* was not ordered until June 1914. The three 1914 boats should have been *U 46–U 48*, but they were ordered under the mobilisation plan.

65. The initial mobilisation U-boats were ordered under War Contract A. *U 42* was the odd submarine out. In 1912 the Imperial Navy ordered her from Fiat in Italy for comparison with domestic designs, much as the British ordered several foreign submarines at about the same time. She was taken over by the Italian navy at the outbreak of war, becoming the Italian submarine *Balilla*.

66. According to Rössler, *The U-Boat*, on 18 August the RMA asked the U-boat Inspectorate (UI) to develop a design for a U-boat which could be operational before the envisaged short war ended. The UI considered the project feasible, but only if it delayed construction of large U-boats. It therefore rejected the idea (25 August). However, on 11 September a member of the UI proposed a small minelaying boat for use off the French coast. The Navy Office (Tirpitz) then asked about a pure electric minelayer, which turned out to be the 80-ton Project 32, with one torpedo tube. The UI thought it could be built in four months, but that it would hardly be worthwhile. By this time Tirpitz was personally interested in operations from the Flanders 'Triangle', so the project received support. On 14 September the UI was asked for a small rail-transportable U-boat and the Navy Office approved its Project 34, for a 125-ton boat using a 60bhp Körting diesel. Construction of fifteen of these UB-boats was approved on 15 October, the first boats being ordered on 15 October. The programme included two spare boats, *UB 16* and *UB 17*. Despite UI disapproval, on 17 October the Navy Office ordered two experimental Project 35a minelayers (UC-boats); contracts were awarded on 17 November. This project included a special UC-120 mine. The UA designation applied to one submarine building for Norway at the outbreak of war and taken over (later designated *UA 28*). The Germans also took over *U 66–U 70*, which had been building for Austria-Hungary, under War Contract D and for a time they were designated UD. However, that designation was later used for U-cruisers designs (but the submarines themselves were in the main U series). UE was the *U 71* class. UF and UG were separate designations for late-war U-boats, which were not completed.

67. Both the UB I (*UB 1–UB 17*) and the UB II (*UB 18–UB 47*) classes were ordered under War Contract B, the second to be issued. The UC I (*UC 1–UC 15*) and the initial UC II (*UC 16–UB 33*) classes were ordered under the next War Contract C. Although there were no re-orders for UB IIs, there were further orders for UC IIs under War

Contract H (*UC 34–UC 79*).

68. This was presumably War Contract D, all the other War Contracts being accounted for.

69. Rössler, *The U-Boat*, does not associate these orders with the decision to begin unrestricted U-boat warfare, although his comment that it was associated with the understanding that the war was likely to continue suggests as much; that perception triggered the U-boat campaign. The missing numbers *U 66–U 70* were applied to four U-boats building for Austria-Hungary and taken over at the outbreak of war.

70. Project 31 was a considerable departure from past practice, with two side by side cylindrical pressure hulls joined by pressure-tight passageways. That greatly increased battery capacity, so that submerged endurance at 5 knots was 120nm vs 90nm for *U 43* (Project 25). With more deck space, a Project 31 boat could accommodate a twin deck tube. Using the planned 1500bhp diesels, it could reach 18.5 knots on the surface. Further lengthening would increase surface speed to 19 knots. The new diesels were first tested on board *U 19* and *U 26*. Project 31a was a version with equivalent Germania diesels. The design was completed in August 1914. Nothing was done at the time and when Project 31 was reviewed in June 1915, Project 31 was dropped in favour of a new more conventional (single pressure hull) Project 42 Mobilisation design.

71. The *U 81* class Mobilisation U-boats were ordered under War Contracts F (*U 81–U 92*), G (*U 93–U 104*), K (*U 105–U 116*), R (*U 158–U 172*), Y (*U 201–U 212*) and AD (*U 229–U 276*). *U 115* introducing design improvements such as a 20 per cent increase in endurance. *U 167* was the last to be completed. From *U 87* on, submarines had one 10.5cm rather than two 8.8cm guns. The original design incorporated a vertical bow, but beginning with *U 81* boats had sharply-raked bows. Given engine production problems, it proved impossible to adopt new 1200bhp MAN and Germania engines for all of these boats; they had to use what was available. Note the gap between K and R, which was filled by U-cruisers and UB IIIs. Originally War Contract F (1915) was to have covered a torpedo version of the *U 71* class minelayer, six of which were planned; approval was granted on 27 February 1915. The *U 81* class was built instead. Of the ships above, *U 115–U 116* were the prototype Project 43 boats.

72. War Contract J.

73. Rossler, *The U-Boat*, p 65 gives numbers. Coast protection required six UB-boats, the four stations between Dover and Calais would require thirteen and the two at the eastern end of the Channel would require six boats.

74. War Contract L: *U 117–U 126* for the minelayers and War Contract M: *U 127–U 138* for the Project 42 torpedo U-boats. The large Project 127 submarines were described as U-ships rather than U-boats.

75. War Contract O, the progression from J to O indicating how rapidly contracting was running at this time. Further boats were ordered under War Contract O (*UB 72–UB 87*), War Contract Q (*UB 88–UB 132*), War Contract T (*UB 133–UB 169*), War Contract W (*UB 170–UB 205*) and War Contract AB (*UB 206–UB 249*). The last unit completed in wartime was *UB 149* (*UB 155* was completed for surrender to France). The UC III class was ordered under War Contract S (*UC 80–UC 118*), War Contract V (*UC 118–UC 152*) and War Contract AC (*UC 153–UC 192*). The last unit completed was *UC 105*. Note the apparent pairing of some War Contracts for UB III and UC III class submarines (S and T, V and W, AB and AC).

76. War Contract N (*U 139–U 150*). These boats had two 5.9in guns and one charging engine in addition to their two main diesels. They had 90mm total thickness over the control room (60mm protection inside the hull). As in large submarines from Project 42 on, diving depth increased to 75m from the previous standard of 50m (Project 43 was 50m). War Contract N may not have covered *U 143–U 150*, which would presumably be War Contract P.

77. The submarines involved were *UB 133–UB 169* (War Contract T), *UC 80–UC 118* (War Contract S), U-cruisers *U 173–U 182* (War Contract U) and *U 164–U 172*. The repeat Mobilisation U-boats were part of War Contract R.

78. The deferred Mobilisation boats were *U 111–U 114*. According to Rossler, *The U-Boat*, p 73, in a burst of optimism the head of the Navy Office wavered at this point; the war might be won before 1918, so it might be time to go back to building battleships. He wanted to cut the new order to three U-cruisers, but the Admiralstab stood its ground and the contracts were let in November 1916.

79. According to Rossler, *The U-Boat*, p 73, this would have been a three-shaft boat with two 3000bhp main diesels and two 1750bhp battery-charging diesels. On the surface the two outer shafts would have been driven by the main engines, the centre shaft by an electric motor running off the battery and thus indirectly off the charging engines (which is why they were so powerful). Uniquely among German submarines, this one featured two broadside torpedo tubes. Gun armament would have been four 15cm guns with shields. Surface speed would have been 15 knots.

80. The Germans had assumed that it would be difficult to dispose of the heat of a boiler as a submarine submerged. The British already knew that was not the case and the Germans discovered as much when a steam launch sank in Kiel harbour but did not burst its boiler in the process. Still cautious, the Germans planned to use 'diving boilers' with water jackets, providing steam to four 6000shp steam turbines. The hull would have been a stretched version of Project 46a and surfaced speed would have been 25 knots.

81. In February, War Contract Q (*UB 88–UB 132*) and War Contract R (*U 158–U 159*, modified for longer range). War Contract R also covered *U 160–U 162* (February 1917). To make up for losses in UC II class minelayers, a modified UC III (Project 41a) was ordered at the end of June (War Contract S: *UC 80–UC 118*), together with more

UB IIIs (War Contract T: *UB 133–UB 169*), U-cruisers (War Contract U: Project 46a: *U 173–U 182*) and Mobilisation boats (*U 164–U 172*). U-cruisers *U 183–U 200* were built under War Contract Z). The last big U-boats were the 'U-ships' of the abortive *U 213* class (War Contract AE: *U 213–U 228*).

82. U-boats took priority over capital ships and all other surface combatants except torpedo boats (destroyers). Only the cruiser *Cöln* and Schichau torpedo boats were spared.

83. The submarines involved were *UB 133–UB 169* (War Contract T), *UC 80–UC 118* (War Contract S), U-cruisers *U 173–U 182* (War Contract U), and *U 164–U 172*. The repeat Mobilisation U-boats were part of War Contract R.

84. The UF class were ordered under War Contracts X (*UF 1–UF 48*) and AF (*UF 49–UF 92*), but none was launched (some were broken up on the slip).

85. After the war retired Captain. Ludwig Persius sharply criticised the two decisions to begin unrestricted submarine warfare, in each case with insufficient numbers of submarines. He claimed that only 12 per cent of nominally active submarines were at sea as of January 1917. At that time 30 per cent were in harbour, 38 per cent were running trials and 20 per cent were unserviceable or worn out. In April 1917, 129 U-boats were on active service and in April 1918, 128. Translated extracts from 'Why the German Revolutionary Movement Emanated from the Fleet', in *Monthly Intelligence Review* No. 7, 15 November 1919, ADM 223/807.

86. Four new yards were involved. Contracts awarded on 28 January 1918 were for *UF 21–UF 48*. It was estimated that five more U-boats could now be delivered each month beginning at the start of 1919.

87. *UG 1–UG 101* were projected but not ordered.

Chapter 12. Protecting Trade: The U-Boat War

1. Beesly in *Room 40* recounts such an instance on pp 95–6. On 27 March 1915 the British analysts of Room 40 decrypted a broadcast from the German naval transmitter at Neunmünster which revealed that the Germans were reading the British Merchant Navy Code, in which merchant ships received instructions, including those for evasion. Chief of Staff Admiral Oliver, who received the decrypts, immediately signalled various forces that 'wireless messages should not be made to merchant vessels giving them directions as to routes. It only informs German submarines where to look for them'. Signals should be given visually or not at all. This message did not get to Queenstown, which continued to use the compromised code.

2. ADM 137/1211, p. 164, file marked 'Anti-Submarine Measures: Remarks by C-in-C HF Home Fleets, i.e., Grand Fleet. – Conference on Question'.

3. A 3 April 1915 Minute ordered all 12pdr guns assigned to Monitors, Fleet Sweepers and River Gunboats, other than the six accelerated Monitors (to be ready in May), surrendered. Other ships which would be laid up before most of these ships commissioned would surrender their 12pdrs for them. Ships on the North American station would surrender some of their anti-torpedo (boat) guns. Ships undergoing long refits (*Drake*, *King Alfred*, *Sutlej*, *Duncan*) would surrender light guns. The defensively armed ships each surrendered one 4.7in gun. For details of guns used on board merchant ships, see the author's *Naval Weapons of World War I* (Barnsley: Seaforth Publishing, 2012).

4. As of July 1915, fifty-two 4.7in guns were allotted to ships trading to the Mediterranean. Another seventy-six such guns were permanently mounted, eight in colliers and fifty-nine in meat-carrying ships trading to and from Argentina, Australia and New Zealand (i.e., the extension of the pre-war DAM programme). Another fifty-one 12pdr 12 cwt and forty-one 12pdr 8 cwt guns were on board coastal vessels, twenty-two 12pdr were mounted in collier transports and twelve 12pdr were mounted in transports with military stores.

5. All data on defensive armament is from the Technical History of defensive armament for merchant ships (RN Historical Branch).

6. 'The Atlantic Convoy System 1917-1918', p 7.

7. Merchant ship masters who met with Admiral Jellicoe in February 1917 told him that they were confident that, if armed, they could survive in the face of U-boats. The connection between zig-zagging and guns is the author's, but it is difficult to find any other explanation for continuing faith in guns. By 1918 merchant ships were also being given depth charges and throwers such as howitzers. The war history published by the US Navy's Bureau of Ordnance recounted a long fight between an armed merchant ship and a U-boat, unfortunately ending with the loss of the merchant ship.

8. At about this time a standard 5.5in gun, considerably more powerful than previous merchant ship weapons, was entering production. It was considered necessary to counter the more powerful deck guns being mounted on board newer U-Boats. In September 1918 the Admiralty complained that taking men 20 and 21 years old from ordnance plants into the army had slowed this programme by six months. Ships without guns had to be convoyed on the out-bound trip as well as on the inbound, which the Admiralty estimated would cost about 10 per cent in available capacity. Admiralty Memorandum for the War Cabinet, 'Some Important Aspects of the Naval Situation and Submarine Campaign', September 1918 in ADM 137/834.

9. Late in November 1916, for example, CO HMS *Canterbury*, writing about possible anti-submarine ideas: 'Zeebrugge must go. It should never have been allowed to remain a thorn in our side and its existence is the greatest blot to the Navy that has occurred during this War: and it is being run for all it is worth by our enemies to lower our Navy in the eyes of the whole world. Would we have sat down and allowed the Germans to do the same with Calais? No. Then why allow them to do what they like with Zeebrugge, Ostend and Nieuport?' ADM 137/1211, p 284.

10 . In the January 1918 War Cabinet paper in ADM 116/1349, a total of at least thirty-two destroyers or sloops and 128 trawlers constantly on duty, requiring in turn a total force of ninety-six destroyers or sloops and 256 trawlers. A light cruiser force was needed to drive off raiders. The need for light cruisers to support the barrage may explain why the Scout cruisers had a high priority in US naval planning in 1917.

11. ADM 137/1211, p 174, comment on a plan for submarine patrol on Scandinavian trade routes submitted by C-in-C Rosyth Admiral Hamilton, 7 November 1916. This comment appears in many other places at about this time. The plan died because it entailed withdrawing many of the Home Fleet (Grand Fleet) submarines.

12. They were also called Special Service Ships. In January 1918 the Royal Navy had eighteen steamships, ten sailing ships and twenty-seven fishing smacks and trawlers acting as decoys, according to the January 1918 War Cabinet paper in ADM 116/1349. According to Dittmar and College, *British Warships 1914-1919*, the Royal Navy operated about 215 decoys in all, including the specially-designed standard merchant ship *Hyderabad*, the 'Convoy Sloops', and the PC version of the P-boat. Even the lighter *X.22* served as a decoy. Some decoy trawlers worked with C-class submarines, the idea being that she could destroy the U-boat attacking the trawler. According to Gröner, *German Warships*, II, U-boats sunk by Q-ships were: *U 23* (by submarine working with the Q-ship, 20 July 1915), *U 27* (19 August 1915), *U 36* (24 July 1915), *U 41* (24 September 1915), *U 68* (22 March 1916), *U 83* (17 February 1917), *U 85* (12 March 1917), *UB 13* (24 April 1916), *UB 19* (30 November 1916), *UB 37* (14 January 1917), *UB 42* (14 January 1917) and *UC 72* (20 August 1917). Dittmar and College list twenty of the merchant ship conversions as sunk by U-boats, plus five Convoy Sloops, some serving as conventional warships.

13. ADM 137/1211, p 296, in a centralised patrol concept proposed by CO HMS *Miranda*. He pointed out that U-boats tended to attack merchant traffic at focal areas. The cited Drake and Nelson for the enduring principles of trade warfare, which were certainly still valid in 1916: without ocean surveillance (which neither they nor the U-boats had) there were only three places for raiders to find and attack deep sea traffic: at its starting point (unlikely in this case), at its arrival place 'in this case they are escorted once they arrive at the patrol line', and at the converging point which 'I understand is the point at which most of our traffic has been lost'.

14. Collection of Papers for the War Cabinet, 18 January 1918 in ADM 116/1349, 'War Operations and Policy'.

15. The January 1918 War Cabinet report on ASW (ADM 116/1349) gives an idea of the huge numbers involved. It gives numbers in UK waters and abroad (in parentheses) as of 1 August 1917, which were not too different from those on 1 January 1918: fifty-two (seventeen) yachts, 951 (213) trawlers, fifteen whalers, 343 (132) motor launches, 775 (152) net drifters, 194 other drifters, sixty-five motor drifters, three (seven) motor boats, ninety-four paddle sweepers, (nine) patrol paddlers for boom defence, 119 (four) trawlers for boom defence and 179 (two) drifters and other boom defence vessels. Trawler wastage (due to enemy action and to wearing out) was about ten per month.

16. Even bunching ships without escorts could help. Late in 1916 several officers of the Battle Cruiser Force suggested compelling ships to travel in groups (the size varied between three or four and four to six), of which at least two should be armed. ADM 137/1211, p 316.

17. ADM 137/1211, referring to rejection of a convoy proposal.

18. ADM 137/1211, 'Policy: Anti-Submarine, 1916 July-Dec;' the account of the 3 November conference is pp 148–71.

19. For example, ADM 137/1097, the July–December 1915 compendium of papers on anti-submarine warfare, includes at its end a précis of a 27 July 1915 paper by the Captain in charge at Falmouth, suggesting an improved system of escorts for convoys in the Channel, as 'at present escorts are apt to miss their convoys owing to either party being out of its reckoning, to darkness, or to arrivals at rendezvous at wrong times. Nearly all casualties have taken place in Mid-Channel track'. From mid-1915 through March 1917 specially valuable ships were brought to specific rendezvous to meet escorts, or at least to follow a patrolled route. This procedure worked, but it could not be extended to many ships. Between July 1915 and the end of March 1917 the special procedures covered 1256 ships, of which fourteen were sunk before reaching port (six of them during the week after the Germans began their unrestricted submarine campaign). The 'special route' procedure was then extended to all Government cargo 'of national importance'. Once inside a specified triangle, ships were protected by patrolling destroyers, sloops and trawlers. That was not very effective, because typically only twenty ships were available in a 10,000 square mile triangle. Between the end of March 1917 and the end of June, that applied to 890 ships, of which sixty-three were sunk.

20. ADM 137/1211 includes a 19 December 1916 proposal by CO HMS *Marksman*, with detailed explanation of how an escort might be organised (p 270 of this file). The reply to one of them was that 'the question of convoy has frequently been gone into, but experience so far has not justified its existence outside the Mediterranean. SNO Malta has raised the question of convoy in the Eastern Mediterranean, but by means of further supply of guns, added to arrangements now coming into place to divert still more ships round the Cape I hope that very shortly no unarmed vessels will enter the Mediterranean.'

21. ADM 137/1211, p 358, One of the proponents, Captain Plunkett Drax, also called for more complete naval control of shipping near ports; the answer by Director A/S Division (19 January 1917) was that 'the Merchant Service has been carefully organised to a far greater extent than Captain Plunkett Drax is aware of'.

22. Naval Staff Monograph, *Home Waters Pt VII*, pp 159–60.

23. Naval Staff Monograph, *Home Waters Pt VII*, pp 243–4. This 'was not only one of the first important measures taken against the submarines, but served as a preliminary step towards the subsequent introduction of convoy'.

24. According to 'The Atlantic Convoy System 1917-1918', p 10, the French convoys, which were escorted by armed trawlers, were intended to protect against gun attack, but by April 1917 it was clear that they were also effective against submarines. Ships sailed in loose order, hence did not have to meet tight standards for station-keeping. The success of the operation was unexpected. Admiralty Technical History 20, June 1920, 'Miscellaneous Convoys' recounts the intense pressure from the French during the latter part of 1916 and early January 1917. The first 'A' crossing was apparently in February 1917. Ships sometimes joined the convoys. Thus the total number of ships convoyed on this route was 10,585, including 299 others. Of these, losses due to enemy action amounted to thirty-five, plus three wrecks. The total of ships convoyed was the total number of ship trips. A set of totals by month begins in March 1917. The four routes (A, B, C, D) involved a total of 39,352 ships, of which fifty-three were lost (0.14 per cent). Naval Staff Monograph, *Home Waters Pt VIII* (CB 917Q), May 1933, pp 30–3.

25. Naval Staff Monograph (Historical), *Home Waters Pt VII: From June 1916 to November 1916* (CB 917(P), October 1927, p 240.

26. According to 'The Atlantic Convoy System 1917-1918', p 4, weekly returns of numbers of ships entering and leaving United Kingdom ports and also returns showing available shipping were intentionally misleading to show both friends and enemies that the submarine war was not succeeding (published figures also included unsuccessful submarine attacks). To do so, they showed the arrival and departure of all ships of all nationalities of over 100 tons, but statistics on sinkings were limited to British ships and then divided into those over and under 1600 tons gross. Weekly arrivals for the week ending 22 April 1917 were given as 2585 and sailings as 2621, but only about twenty ships arrived each day from the North and South Atlantic, including ships for northern French ports. At the same time forty ocean-going ships of over 1600 gross tons were sunk: forty out of 140. Another fifteen ships of under 1600 gross tons were sunk. The published figure was, then, that losses amounted to fifty-five ships out of 2585. Another distortion was due to the statement of total tonnage available, because it included tonnage used by the services, hence not available for carrying essential supplies from overseas. On 30 April 1917 available tonnage, including prizes, was 3534 ships totalling 15,800,000 gross tons (ships over 1600 gross tons), of which 721 were passenger ships (4.5 million tons). Of the ships listed, 1125 were on navy or army service. A round trip to the nearest foreign source of supply, North America, took 60 days.

27. Most of these arguments can be found in the Admiralty's 'Remarks on Submarine Warfare' (CB ...), issued in January 1917, evidently partly in response to pressure to form convoys. Arguments and counter-arguments are summarised in Admiralty Technical History 14, 'The Atlantic Convoy System 1917-1918' (October, 1919).

28. Hankey, *Supreme Command* II, pp 648–9.

29. ADM 137/2753, 'Policy: Convoy'.

30. ADM 137/2753, apparently before the Historical Branch filed the conference report. The original, signed by a Captain RNR (name not clear), who was apparently Statistical Information Officer (SIO), is dated 10 February 1919.

31. 'The Atlantic Convoy System 1917-1918', p 9.

32. 'The Atlantic Convoy System 1917-1918', p 4, quotes the US Navy Department (presumably OpNav): 'The Navy Department does not consider it advisable to attempt the character of convoy outlined by the British . . . In large groups of ships under convoy fog, gales, inexperience of personnel and general tension on merchant vessels make the hazards of the attempt great and the probability of a scattering of the convoy very strong. The Navy Department suggests instead sending vessels, as an experiment, in groups of four of equal speed, each group convoyed by two destroyers.'

33. Jellicoe had tried to obtain them in 1917 to make up for a perceived imminent German battlecruiser edge. In 1918 the Japanese did contribute destroyers to escort Mediterranean convoys and they made an excellent impression on the British. The price of this assistance, which was not widely known at the time, was British support for Japanese retention of formerly German Pacific islands post-war. For Jellicoe's 1917 attempt to obtain the battlecruisers, see Patterson (ed), *Jellicoe Papers* II, pp 184–9.

34. 'German Methods of Attacking Convoys' (M.014601/18 of 23 September 1918) in ADM 137/2655, a compendium of 1918 convoy papers, including protection by a continuous smoke screen and offensive action against submarines attacking convoys. This paper is the source of the dummy convoy and of the tactics described here. However, the idea of passing between the columns of a convoy also appears in the 1917 Admiralty pamphlet on convoy, issued in September 1917. The 1918 tactics are from a 'reliable source', presumably collated interrogations and perhaps German documents, translations of which have not apparently survived.

35. Captain Michelsen was the second and last overall U-boat commander (neither he nor his predecessor had authority over the Flanders U-boats or boats on foreign stations, however). His remarks are from the ONI translation of his *U-Bootskrieg 1914-1918* published in 1925.

36. As described in Volume IV of the official history of the U-boat war against commerce. The command boat would have been *U 155* (ex-*Deutschland*). The idea was described in guarded terms in a December 1930 article in *Marine Rundschau*. Admiral Spindler, who wrote the official history, described the way the radio command ship could use enemy radio signals to discern the approach and course of important convoys

and the presence of enemy escort forces, but that was probably hindsight, since in April 1917 there were no convoys or escorts. The radio ship might have been able to steer U-boats away from hunting groups. Bauer was also an early exponent of multi-U-boat operations. Bauer observed Dönitz's wolf-pack exercises in 1936, but Dönitz was apparently unaware of his ideas up to that time. Bauer was removed from his command about two months after making his radio U-boat proposal, but that may have been no more than normal rotation. He had been the first overall U-boat commander (Führer der U-Boote), having served since 1914. Philip K Lundeberg, 'The German Naval Critique of the U-Boat Campaign 1915-1918', in *Military Affairs* (Fall 1963), document courtesy A D Baker III.

37. 'Remarks on Submarine Tactics Against Convoys', December 1917 (ONI Publication 21, copy of CB 620 prepared by Admiralty Naval Staff Anti-Submarine Division), in NARA RG 38 ONI series.

38. The British authors of the 1917 convoy pamphlet noted that although complete records of surface trials and battery capacity had been obtained (presumably from sunken U-boats), no definite information on underwater speed had been recovered. However, judging from the lines of U-boat hulls and from the many external fittings added despite the way they added to resistance, it seemed that the Germans were not aiming at high underwater speed, for which qualities such as surface speed and armament and even underwater endurance would have to be sacrificed.

39. Other Admiralty papers denied that German U-boats ever angled their torpedoes, for various technical reasons; it is not clear whether the 90° option was included in German orders.

40. ADM 137/834, paper appended to 27 August 1918 Minutes of Admiralty Operations Committee.

41. Director of Plans was to produce the necessary paper, to be submitted to US Assistant Secretary of the Navy Franklin D Roosevelt, but it is not clear that it was ever delivered.

42. Paul G Halpern, *A Naval History of World War I* (Annapolis: Naval Institute Press, 1994), p 427 puts the five U-boats in the context of a large concentration of eight U-boats in an area through which nine convoys would pass. The Admiralty diverted a Gibraltar convoy (HG.73), though one of the U-boats sank a ship dispersed from that convoy (but escorted by a pair of trawlers). Another sank two ships in convoys. Halpern's account differs from Grant in that he had access to the 1918 volume of the German official history, which was not published until 1966; he therefore knew the full extent of the May 1918 U-boat operation. Note that there was no attempt to co-ordinate attacks; each U-boat had its own operating area, as in earlier U-boat operations.

43. Minutes in ADM 137/2708, *Plans Division War Records March -May 1918*, p 257 (marked 292 in crayon).

44. These words show that the new policy was of US origin. According to US officers the Admiralty Plans Division had little impact and was supported mainly by the Planning Section the US Navy had set up in London. Writing an 'estimate of the situation' was a planning technique developed by the US Naval War College and not normally used by the Royal Navy.

45. ADM 137/2655 contains a 10 October 1918 report by Captain (D) of 4th Flotilla on 'Offensive Action Against Submarines Attacking Convoys' in response to a 30 August 1918 Admiralty letter. By that time the proportion of escorts expected to take part in offensive action was at least half. By this time elaborate diagrams had been prepared showing how to saturate the likely path of a submarine once it had revealed itself.

46. ADM 137/834, p 289. This was partly an argument against the scaling-back of warship production and of other Admiralty priorities. Among the points raised were the unsatisfactory organisation (under the French) in the Mediterranean; according to the memorandum, the reorganisation carried out early in 1918 halved losses. This memo also complained that the new RAF was shortchanging ASW: ASW air squadrons asked for to serve around the British Isles had been reduced by 42 per cent and total naval aircraft requirements by 27 per cent.

47. Robert M Grant, *U-Boats Destroyed: The Effect of Anti-Submarine Warfare 1914-1918* (Penzance: Periscope Publishing, 2002 reprint of 1964 publication), p 140. Grant did not have access to the last volume of the official German history (published in 1966), but is generally considered the best source on First World War U-boat losses.

48. Based on a chart of U-boat losses by causes in Grant, *U-Boats Destroyed*, p 160. Grant does not distinguish patrols from hunters.

49. The Royal Navy proposed that the British offer a limit on total destroyer tonnage if the treaty banned submarines, but discovered to its unhappy surprise that the British Government offered the limit without any quid pro quo. The immediate reaction was to order sloops adapted specifically as ASW escorts, but they could not be built in sufficient numbers to provide escorts on a First World War scale. The hunting strategy was an inescapable consequence; there were too few escorts, given the demands of the fleets. British ASW handbooks of the 1930s explain hunting tactics.

50. Figures taken from a table produced by the Planning Board, US Emergency Fleet Corporation, for post-war testimony by its general manager (RG 32, NARA II). In 1918, with a convoy system operating, British losses were 1.69 million tons (534 ships). These figures do not include Allied shipping.

51. The programme is described in W H Mitchell and L A Sawyer, *British Standard Ships of World War I* (Wartime Standard Ships Vol 3) (Liverpool: Sea Breezes, 1968). Unfortunately they provide no information as to when ships were either designed,

authorised or ordered.

52. Sumida, 'Forging the Trident', notes that although there were eight times as many merchant ships as warships (including auxiliaries) in 1916, many more warships than merchant ships were docked for refits. He argues that the non-building or deactivation (due to needed repair not being done) of British merchant shipping between August 1914 and February 1917 was almost equal to the tonnage sunk by U-boats during 1917. In February 1917, 330,000 tons were under repair. Many ships damaged by submarines required major repairs. In 1918 three million tons of British merchant ships required major overhaul. Even major overhaul and repair cost less steel and labour than replacement construction. During 1917–18 the available merchant ship tonnage was considerably increased through repairs. The number of men engaged in merchant ship maintenance doubled between July 1917 and April 1918.

53. All ships on order in the US other than the completed *War Sword* were requisitioned when the United States entered the war. That amounted to 159 steel ships and 2 wooden ships.

54. Sumida, 'Forging the Trident', suggests that the Royal Navy took over the merchant ship programme specifically to protect remaining parts of its warship programme from the demands of the War Office and the Ministry of Munitions. According to Hankey, *Supreme Command*, II, p 644, the Admiralty programme as understood early in 1917 would have reduced merchant shipbuilding by 500,000 tons. The decision to cancel the three *Hood*s and other ships was coupled with one to order forty large merchant ships in the United States and also to build ships in Japan and 'British Columbia model' wooden ships in Canada and in the United Kingdom. According to Edward N Hurley (wartime chairman of the US Shipping Board), *Bridge to France* (Philadelphia: Lippincott, 1927), p 44 (quoting Lloyd George), British Prime Minister Lloyd George was personally responsible for the British wood ship programme, arguing that even by making a single voyage such ships might make a crucial contribution.

55. BIR report summarised in US Special (ASW) Board report, September 1917. No ships of this size were built. However, the C type was noticeably smaller than the initial standard ships of A and B types: 3000 GRT (5050 DWT) compared to 5030 GRT and 8175 or 8075 DWT for an A or B ship. The D ship was even smaller, but it was a specialised collier. The E was a larger ship (4400 GRT and 7020 DWT) and the F (6440 DWT, 10795 GRT) and G (8000 GRT, 10,800 DWT) were much larger. The G type seems to have been the modern fast type the British referred to in the August 1917 inter-Allied conference on building unsinkable merchant ships. According to Mitchell and Sawyer, it was conceived specifically to replace meat-carriers. Of twenty-nine ordered, only one (*War Icarus*) had been completed by the Armistice. H was a smaller ship (2800 GRT, 3860 DWT) requested late in the war. J was slightly larger (4600 GRT, 7250 DWT). In addition, there was a fabricated N design, to be assembled entirely from flat plates in a special 'national' yard (6150 GRT, 10500 DWT). Of three tanker designs, AO and BO were converted from A and B types, but Z was specially designed. The largest and fastest of the dry-cargo types were G1 and G2, single- and twin-screw 13-knotters. All others were rated at 10.5 (H) to 12 knots (F and F1). There were also five coaster designs (C1 and C4 through C7).

56. In the United States through the Cunard company and also in Canada, China (Shanghai), Japan and Hong Kong. B and C type ships were built in Hong Kong and the C type in Shanghai, but otherwise ships built abroad were to individual designs. They included wooden ships built in Canada and the United States. Excluding orders in the United States, 821 ships were ordered and 416 completed during the war. Another 279 were sold before completion, the rest being cancelled. Fourteen ships were sunk during the war. The ships of this programme could be distinguished by their 'War' names.

57. British logic of survivability and merchant ship design is taken from proceedings of an August 1917 Allied conference on merchant ships designed to resist torpedo attack, in folder C-84-40 to C-84-48 of Classified records of US Chief of Naval Operations (RG 38), NARA.

58. Presumably these were actual tonnages, whereas merchant ship tonnage is usually expressed in gross registered tonnage, which is an approximate measure of capacity or ship volume. Comparisons are complicated by different definitions of merchant ship tonnage. *Gross Net Tonnage* is a measure of ship *volume* used partly to calculate fees. *Deadweight* is the tonnage the ship transports. Although in principle they measure much the same thing, in practice the two figures differ. An example was given in post-war Congressional testimony by Vice President Ackerson of the US Emergency Fleet Corporation (RG 32, NARA II). A typical modern freighter displacing 13,350 tons (the measurement used for warships) would have a deadweight (carrying capacity) tonnage of 10,000, a gross register tonnage (GRT) of 6000 and a net tonnage of 4000. Both net and gross tonnage are measures of volume, net excluding certain legal deductions. The Germans typically described their sinkings in GRT rather than deadweight terms. Total British wartime losses are given as either 7.7 million gross tons (2456 ships). Figures as high as nine million tons, are sometimes quoted. Warship tonnage is displacement, the actual weight of the ship.

59. In April 1918 Churchill, who was then Minister of Munitions, contrasted his success in producing munitions with the Admiralty's failure to produce merchant ships. A J Balfour, who succeeded Churchill as First Lord, charged that the light cruisers and monitors ordered in 1914–15 were 'naval luxuries'. Sumida, 'Forging the Trident' estimated that during the last two years of the war fleet units not involved in the anti-submarine war accounted for 45 per cent of total tonnage laid down. Much of it was justified on the basis of grossly inflated estimates of German construction, but on the other hand it could be argued that by backing up convoy escorts the Grand Fleet made an important if indirect contribution to the anti-submarine war.

60. Hurley, *Bridge to France*, p 21, points out that the declaration of war in 1914 in itself dramatically reduced available tonnage. About six million tons of German and Austro-Hungarian shipping suddenly became unavailable, together with one million tons of Russian and French shipping. Much of the world's largest merchant fleet (British) was diverted to wartime requirements. The United States was plunged into a severe economic crisis, partly because it became nearly impossible to export goods which otherwise have travelled in foreign ships (the crisis was also due to a financial panic which set in as the crisis of July 1914 developed). The first Congressional reaction was to pass the Shipping Act of 1914 (18 August), which made it possible to transfer any foreign-flag ship to US registry to replace lost carrying capacity (the British saw this as a means of evading the shipping control they were trying to exercise). In March 1915 Congress repealed penalties on foreign-built ships owned by Americans; US consular officials were enabled to issue provisional certificates of registry to ships bought abroad by US citizens. Up to 30 June 1915, 148 ships (half a million GRT) were registered. However, US shipbuilding declined, as it was easier to acquire foreign (interned) tonnage. As of the end of FY 15 (ending 30 June 1915), it was a third less than for the previous fiscal year and less than for any of the sixteen preceding years. The Shipping Act was introduced in Congress in May 1916.

61. According to Hurley, *Bridge to France*, p 28, nearly all were still at the contract and material ordering stage; they were not actual hulls. The Emergency Fleet Corporation had to create a construction division to build the ships. In at least one case, that of the *War Sword*, the ship had been paid for completely before the requisition order and she was allowed to leave as a British ship. Hurley, *Bridge to France*, p 33 later saw the requisition order as primarily a means of keeping tonnage prices from exploding and also of beginning the mobilisation of US economic resources.

62. According to Hurley, *Bridge to France*, p 39, the original building programme was: 431 requisitioned steel ships (3,056,008 DWT), 1741 contract steel ships (11,914,670 DWT), 1017 contract wooden ships (3,052,200 DWT), fifty contract composite (wood and steel) ships (175,000 DWT) and forty-three contract concrete ships (302,000 DWT). According to Hurley, *Bridge to France*, p 106, the Shipping Board built and delivered 533 ships in 1918 and 1180 in 1919; the discrepancies with other figures suggest that these were deliveries in the relevant Fiscal Years ending 30 June.

63. In 1917 the United States had thirty-seven yards (142 slips) building steel ships and twenty-four yards (seventy-three slips) building wooden ships, in each case of more than 3000 tons. Shipyards built from April 1917 on were: thirty-three for steel ships of over 3600 deadweight tons (247 slips), sixty-one for wooden ships of over 3000 deadweight tons (223 slips) and seventeen yards for tugs and barges (forty-seven slips). Existing yards were encouraged to expand. The corporation also had to build dredges and dry docks.

64. According to Hurley, *Bridge to France*, p 2, at the end of the war there were 350,000 shipyard employees, backed by another 180,000 in 553 mills, factories, etc. supplying engines, boilers and materials. The Shipping Board also trained 42,000 merchant ship officers and seamen. Page references to Hurley are to the retyped version currently on the Internet, not to the original. This history is based partly on papers in RG 32, NARA II, which were assembled for the post-war Congressional Hearings on the programme. Figures for total deliveries are in the package collected for testimony by Commander John L Ackerson, who by 1918 was Vice President in charge of ship construction, having begun in 1916 as Assistant to the General Manager (he had been a naval constructor before that).

65. Hurley, *Bridge to France*, p 40. Ferris had to resign (to become a consultant to the Corporation) in 1918, after a Congressional committee objected to the agreement under which he had been allowed to continue his private practice. His successor as head of the Department of Naval Architecture and Marine Engineering of the Emergency Fleet Corporation was Daniel H Cox, another naval architect. Hurley points out that during the winter of 1912, when there was a sudden demand for oil tankers, the engineering managers of the Chester Shipbuilding Co and the Merchant Shipbuilding Co (C P M Jack and Max Willemstyn) decided that they could convert ordinary freighters into tankers using tanks built and tested ashore; Hurley considered this the beginning of the fabricated-ship idea. Vice President Henry R Sutphen of the Submarine Boat Corp (Electric Boat) told General Goethals, while he was General Manager of the Emergency Fleet Corp, that he could save enormous time and money by using bridge and tank shops to build components for assembly. Hurley recalls that the engineers at Hog Island pointed to Jack and Willemsteyn as the pioneers in the process.

66. They are indicated in a 28 December 1918 order to shipyards to eliminate them. They included lookout stations (gun and elevated); gun platforms with ammunition stowage, a rudimentary fire-control system and arrangements to accommodate naval armed guards (the US Navy provided these personnel); depth-charge stowage; hinged and telescopic derrick and signal masts (so that they could be folded to make it difficult to estimate a ship's course); staggered masts (for the same purpose); 5- and 30-ton derricks; shorter smoke stacks; additional life rafts; extra watertight bulkheads (including frames to take an extra bulkhead); deep tanks to carry water ballast or fuel oil as cargo; a searchlight; signal lights; convoy lights (masthead and stern); bridge control of visible lights; master radio control; smoke boxes; a bridge engine indicator; and a revolution counter in the chart house (for convoy manoeuvring).

67. The Bristol, Pa., yard had twelve slips for 9000-ton ships. The original contract was for sixty freighters, of which twenty were cancelled; the last ship was delivered on 28 February 1921. The Newark Bay Yard had twenty-eight slips and a contract for 5000-ton ships (it laid down its first ship on 20 December 1917). It completed all of the planned 150 ships, of which the Submarine Boat Corp kept thirty-two after they were cancelled. Data from Hurley, *Bridge to France*, p 65. He does not give details of the Wilmington yard, but notes that nine smaller yards (total fifty slips) also fabricated ships. Elsewhere Hurley mentions the Federal Yard (twelve slips, 9600-ton freighters) and the Southwestern Shipbuilding Co. (six slips, 8800-ton ships).

68. Contracts were let for 703 wooden ships, of which 203 were cancelled at the end of the war. Of the others, 323 were completed, seventy-three lost and forty-four sold. In 1922 surviving wood ships were declared obsolete, 256 of them being sold. Of the ships completed, 265 carried wartime cargoes overseas. Composite ships (wood stiffened by steel) were more difficult to build and the first was not delivered until 28 August 1918. According to Hurley, *Bridge to France*, p 45, the concrete ship, which no one in the Shipping Board or the Fleet Corporation liked, was pushed by Senator McCumber, who argued that cast concrete buildings were typically put up astonishingly quickly, so that hundreds of ships could be built using concrete poured into moulds. On the other hand, a concrete ship needed steel reinforcements amounting to a third as much steel as an equivalent steel ship and concrete seemed too rigid to withstand the vibration of a ship's engine. Advocates of concrete construction built the freighter *Faith* in San Francisco and she successfully carried cargoes abroad. A design error made her unsafe when unloaded; ultimately she foundered off the southern coast. As of 1917, a few concrete barges had been built in Europe. Congress forced the issue with a special $50 million supplemental appropriation. The concrete ship returned in the Second World War Maritime Commission programme.

69. Hurley, *Bridge to France*, pp 88–9. After June 1918 the Fleet Corporation could not keep up with the army's constantly-growing demands to support a sixty-, eighty-, or hundred-division programme (2.5, 3.35, or 4.3 million men) by 31 July 1919. The sixty-division army required five million DWT, which was about the most the Fleet Corporation could provide (but total deliveries in April 1919 after large cancellations were 4.5 million DWT). Hurley estimated that the eighty-division requirement could have been met after June 1919, but that the hundred-division requirement was entirely impossible. The army adopted the eighty-division programme, but cargo shipments lagged considerably. For example, eighty divisions required 1,082,500 tons in November 1918, but only 823,382 tons were shipped and that was considerably more than in previous months. Shipments would have caught up during 1919. That the deficit was largely due to General Pershing's demand for 250,000 tons of construction material each month explains why it was not crippling. The British had to be asked for 1.2 million tons on a temporary basis.

70. Proceedings in folder C-84-40 to C-84-48 in Classified records of US Chief of Naval Operations (RG 38), NARA, as forwarded by Force Commander (Admiral Sims) to the Secretary of the Navy, 27 February 1918; Admiral Sims had already forwarded a summary. The Chairman was Third Sea Lord Admiral Halsey, with DNC attending; delegates came from France, Italy, Japan, Russia and the United States (Naval Constructor L C McBride of the Preliminary Design section of the Bureau of Construction and Repair). The Italian delegation included Major Pugliese, who developed the cylindrical anti-torpedo system used in later Italian battleships (it was originally conceived for torpedo-resistant merchant ships).

71. French delegate Captain de Marguerye said that, were time and cost of no concern, it might be possible to provide ships with external protection. As it was, the French had developed satisfactory internal protection ('stuffing') and were applying it to the 12,000-ton passenger ship *Latetia* as well as to two large passenger ships and to two old cruisers which were to be used as troop transports. They were considering fitting ships steaming between France and Algeria, all these ships amounting to about 26,000 tons. In addition, the twenty patrol boats now building were all to have internal protection. As yet none of the ships involved had been torpedoed, so the technique had not been tested. 'Stuffing' meant filling empty spaces between beams and frames and also excess machinery spaces with water-excluding material. The French had been experimenting with cork, special cement, etc. The patrol boats had internal bulkheads to stop splinters. The Italians thought they had a viable technique of composite bulging which would protect a ship against a torpedo, or even against two hitting in the same place. US delegate McBride said that the first series of emergency ships was conventional, but that the design of follow-on ships was currently under consideration. 'My own impression is that they are laying great stress on speed and size of ships – the opinion being that a speed of 14 knots was necessary. The question of placing boilers well above the waterline (on deck) and engines amidships is also being considered.' US work on liquid-layer protection for warships led to the conclusion that complete protection would be impractical for merchant ships, though it might be possible to provide a liquid screen.

Chapter 13. Anti-Submarine Warfare: Tactics and Technology

1. Lambert (ed), *The Submarine Service*, Document 128, Keyes (Commodore (S)) to Chief of War Staff Oliver, 1 November 1914, on early war lessons (item 5).

2. *Krieg zur See*, Nordsee 4, pp 205–6 quotes a disparaging 27 December 1915 letter from the commander of the Flanders U-boats. He decided to ignore the mines laid off the Flanders coast, on the theory that otherwise his boats would never get to sea. His boats had sunk hundreds of them with rifle fire (British mine moorings were not yet adequate). To limit the mine danger, his boats proceeded on the surface as far as possible, diving only when necessary and then lying on the bottom and listening by hydrophone to be sure that they were safe to proceed. Nearly all of his boats had been caught in nets, but they had been able to surface and cut their way out. As a result, they had no problem passing between Dover and Calais, despite the presence of a massive net barrage. He found British destroyers and aircraft entirely ineffective. The Germans described the trawlers' drifter nets as 300ft long and 30 to 115ft in depth; each trawler carried ten of them.

3. The Otranto barrage was described by HRM the Prince of Udine at the Navy Department, 29 June 1917, as the US Navy tried to develop ASW measures of its own. (RG 38 ONI series, U-1-j Register 8286-E). The drifter technique was the forerunner of modern upward-looking bottom arrays which indicate the course of a submarine as

it passes over them.

4. For example, a US Navy report dated 16 April 1908 described British experiments with submarine-to-submarine and surface ship-to-submarine signalling (ONI RG 38 series in NARA: P-10-a Register 08-290). Royal Navy tests of submarine signalling were described in a series of reports in 1906-7 (ONI RG 38 series: P-10-a Register 07 - 54). The file includes extracts from the Admiralty trials report dated October 1906. Test communication ranges were up to 16 miles. It also includes a January 1907 brochure printed by the Submarine Signal Company.

5. A 3 April 1919 Planning Committee report to CNO on the need to train hydrophone officers and listeners places the beginning of the Board in February 1917 and points to hydrophone development as the first priority. NARA RG 38 OpNav confidential files 1917-1919, folder C-26-208 to 26-211. Development took time. An Anglo-French naval scientific mission visiting the United States between 19 May and 9 July 1917 found little of material significance, but its report 'was strongly of opinion that the organisation of the scientific resources of the American nation . . . should produce results at an early date of great value'. US resources existed 'to an extent at present quite unobtainable in England or France'. According to the report, by this time the Americans had reached the point the British and French had reached a year or eighteen months ago (i.e., about January or June 1916), although many of them thought they were already ahead. Lengthy conferences changed the US view and, according to the report, saved considerable time. In this sense US devices may be considered as having evolved from the British and French devices at the design stage in mid-1917. ADM 116/1430. Unless otherwise indicated, information about US developments is from the weekly progress reports of the Special Board in confidential OpNavy files (1917-1919), C26 series, NARA RG 38.

6. BIR Report, 31 December 1916 (in ADM 116/1430). US files include an extensive description of a loop laid off Norfolk.

7. Attempts to solve the problem may be the origin of the often-derided sea lion experiments. An account of BIR work reported 9 January 1917 (in the US September 1917 Special Board report) includes 'experiments with seals and sea-lions showed their ears more sensitive than microphones and that they could hear apparently as well at 9 knots as at rest' – what would now be called an attempt to learn how to improve equipment based on natural examples.

8. It appeared at this time that a submarine had no definite frequency, hence its sound could not be recognised automatically. The idea of a signature with definite frequency components lay far in the future. As there was no single frequency characteristic of a submarine, there was no point in making a detector resonant at one frequency. That would have been a way of screening out background noise.

9. According to the December 1918 BIR report, the advantage of this approach was that it could use a number of non-resonant (hence accurate) receivers both to gain sufficient sound strength and to screen out background noise.

10. In developed form the Walser employed two 'sound lenses' (blisters) on each side of the ship, 3ft and 4ft in diameter, made of steel, each carrying numerous diaphragms and thus resembling a fly's eye. Sound was focused inside the ship by a trumpet-like device connected to the listener's ears. The focussing effect of the lenses eliminated much extraneous noise. An operator could find the bearing of a submarine within about 5° and he could also determine when his ship was directly above a submarine. Walser claimed that his device could be used at 5 knots and that in good weather it could detect a 3-knot submarine at 800 to 2000m. Later he said that at 7 knots a trawler using the Walser device could detect a 3.5-knot submarine at 500m and that at 11 knots a sloop could do the same. In an October 1917 tracking experiment a submarine ran past a ship equipped with a Walser device at 4 knots. The ship also made 4 knots while manoeuvring to point at the submarine, sprinting at 8 knots between observations. By the end of the test the trawler had gained on the submarine, although it not caught up. The French found this encouraging, but US observers were discouraged; they had done better in July 1917 with the US 'C' tube. The French Navy liked the Walser because it could be used by a moving ship; by November 1917 it equipped fifteen ships, including small auxiliary cruisers, trawlers, sloops and ASW scouts. As of January 1918 about fifty were being made.

11. According to a March 1918 US report on vacuum tubes (valves) and amplifiers, French tubes were generally superior to British at that time. A noise, such as the bubbler in the tank which was barely audible on the HF side of the French or the British army set was very loud on the LF side of the French set. The French amplifier could be used on the HF side for microphones and on the LF side for magnetophones, whereas the British army set could only be used for the former, since audibility with the latter was poor. NARA RG 38 ONI series, P-10-f Register 9644C.

12. This project may have begun with a directional hydrophone towed at 10 knots inside a water-filled torpedo-shaped container (it worked but at reduced range). BIR report dated 17 July 1917, reported in the September 1917 report of the US Special Board.

13. February 1918 report in P-10-f Register 9644C.

14. Willem Hackmann, *Seek and Strike: Sonar, Anti-Submarine Warfare and the Royal Navy 1914-54* (London: HMSO, 1984), pp 61–3.

15. Nahant was initially intended to test Fessenden's theory that submarine hull vibrations (1 to 5 Hz) could be detected at great distances and converted into audible signals, extraneous noise being filtered out. This project failed. As of May 1917 General Electric, Western Electric (the industrial arm of Bell Telegraph and Telephone) and Submarine Signal Co. were all working on ASW under the National Research Council, using the experimental station at Nahant near Boston. The scientific mission helped convince the navy to finance a second experimental station at New London.

16. As noted, for example, in a January 1918 report by C E Eveleth (Eveleth Report, 19 January 1918), a member of the Nahant group who was part of a Special Service Party headed by Captain R H Leigh USN (Assistant Chief of the Bureau of Steam Engineering) which presented current US developments to the Admiralty. Confidential OpNav files in RG 38, folder C-26-118 to 26-120, NARA. Hackmann, *Seek and Strike*, p 59 cites more sceptical British reports, but also reports that the measured range of a K-tube was at least 16 miles. The British never developed any equivalent to the MV device.

17. Eveleth Report. Little hope was held out, since a submarine could easily stop when the destroyer or P-boat stopped to listen and 'these boats are not suited for continued listening when drifting'.

18. Hackmann, *Seek and Strike*, p 56.

19. Enclosure to extract from Sims' general report to Navy Dept dated 5 April 1918, issued to all US naval vessels in European waters. NARA RG 38 Opnav confidential papers 1917-19, folder C–28-99. The formal set of notes on hunting, from which this was taken, is NARA RG 38 ONI series P-10-f Register 9664-D.

20. Report dated 9 January 1918 by Captain Leigh in P-10-f Register 9644C.

21. Some details are from Hackmann, *Seek and Strike*, p 58.

22. ONI *Antisubmarine Information*, 1 December 1918, booklet in NWC archive.

23. For example, an 11 March 1918 report to Sims of a hunt in the Channel by *Aylwin* and trawlers reiterated the lesson that the Fessenden oscillator was useful only at short range and that there were better alternatives. NARA RG 38 OpNav confidential files 1917-19, folder C-26-118 to 26-120. In answer to Fessenden's claim that with his oscillators *Aylwin* could do good work as a 'courser', i.e., running down and attacking U-boats whose approximate position had been determined by a line of sub-chasers or trawlers, Commander E C S Parker USN of the Special Board wrote on 10 April 1918 that 'in comparison with the precision of attack attainable with co-operating motor driven chasers, her offensive operations would be analogous to those which might be carried out on a dark night by a race horse against a muskrat'. NARA RG 38 OpNav confidential files 1917-19, folder C-26-121. He was responding to Fessenden's 8 March 1918 paper arguing that the functions of locating a U-boat and attacking it ought to be separated.

24. 8 July 1918 memo from Special Board in RG 38 OpNav confidential papers 1917-19 folder C-26-99. The oscillators were mounted in oil tanks beneath the crew quarters forward of the bridge (Frames 25–31). The receiver was in the sound-proof booth above the chart house. In addition, a K-tube was in the tank between bulkheads 12 and 15, the three rats being hung in a sound-insulating mounting.

25. The *Aylwin* test report, dated 5 January 1918, is in NARA RG 38 OpNav confidential papers 1917-19, folder C-26-99. Other devices were the Western Electric Magnetophone, the Western Electric Microphone, the K Tube (in an oil tank), the MV tube, the four-spot receiver (S Tube), the Pierce Magnetophone (B-M Device: four Broca magnetophones located similarly to the four Fessenden oscillators) and the Bridgman Geophones (Multi-Unit Geophones, i.e., low-frequency phones). Note the variety of equipment. The four Fessenden oscillators, each in its own oil tank, were connected to a switching device, filters and amplifiers at a receiving station. The Western Electric phones were connected in adjacent pairs, each with a two-stage amplifier leading to one phone of a headset for binaural reception (the beam was turned using a compensator). The 'S' receiver used four rubber receivers in pairs (as in C- and K-tubes) connected by air to a four-spot compensator and an acoustic switch. The switch made it possible to use different pairs binaurally and the compensator rotated the receiving beam. It turned out that the Fesseden installation could do no better than determine the quadrant of the submarine.

26. NARA RG 38 ONI series, P-10-f Register 9644-E. Trials in March showed that the directions of sounds on the beam (20 to 150° on each side) could be measured fairly accurately. It was not satisfactory for weak or confused sounds. Maximum range on a submerged submarine was about 900 yds and that was exceptional; at times the 4-S failed to detect a submarine 100 yds away. Most important, the 4-S was useless unless the ship's engines were stopped. On the other hand, it could detect a large steamship when both destroyer and steamer were running at 20 knots somewhat less than a mile away. This was less than encouraging, but there were at least a few more installations (e.g., USS *Lawson* by August 1918).

27. Summary report of tests, 18 April 1918, in NARA RG 38 OpNav confidential papers 1917-1919, folder C-26-64 to C-26-64/20.

28. For example, on 27 July New York Navy Yard was ordered to outfit the destroyers *Perkins*, *Walke*, *Preble*, *Bailey* and *Bagley*. Paper in NARA RG 38 OpNav confidential 1917-19 files, folder C 26-64 to C 26-64/20. Contractors were to do as much of the work as possible on board new destroyers.

29. Force Commander to OpNav, 4 November 1918, in NARA RG 38 Opnav confidential papers 1917-19, folder C-26-64 to 26-64/20. *Murray*, which had been commissioned on 21 August 1918, had both an MV 8 and a Delta tube (in her peak tank) and her CO reported in October 1918 that neither was satisfactory. The compensator was wired from an obsolete blueprint, hence was non-directional and the Delta tube suffered serious water noises in the tank. Many ships had entirely untrained listeners, so Sims circulated special *Notes on Listening Devices*. They cautioned that a destroyer was a difficult listening platform because it was inherently noisy due to its all-steel structure and its numerous auxiliaries, all of which had to be shut down for best listening.

Destroyers also rolled and pitched badly in moderate seas. 'On rough days therefore results both as to ease of listening and ranges are going to be *totally different* from those obtained on good days'. Due to the location and method of suspension of the K-rats in K-tubes, the best results would be obtained with the Drifter type, the next best with the Boom type and the worst with the Tank type. It was also better than the usual submarine signal receiver for receiving oscillator signals. Sims doubted that a destroyer using a K-tube could hear a submarine against the noise of a convoy. However, a destroyer 4 or 5 miles ahead of a convoy might hear a submarine making high speed to close the convoy.

30. The word Asdics appears as the current term for supersonic echo-ranging in the 31 December 1918 BIR report, p 16. Supersonics was sound above 20 kHz. Objectives at the time were both secret signalling and echo location. The report by Dr R W Boyle, who was then developing Asdic, includes a historical section mentioning that a British Patent was issued for supersonic signalling and echo location in the wake of the *Titanic* disaster. Nothing came of it. French work began in March 1915.

31. In 1918 the British were experimenting with explosive echo-ranging as a means of determining the location of ships, for example for shore bombardment. After the war it was used to determine the range of ships beyond the horizon, the ship sending a radio signal at the same time that an explosion was set off. Explosive echo-ranging (EER) became a sonar technique in the 1950s. Work on sonics began only shortly before the Armistice, using a Fessenden oscillator and a hydrophone receiver; it ended when the experimenter, Mr. G. H. Nash, left Admiralty service in December 1918. Nash had argued that using a narrow beam for direction was a disadvantage of any supersonic technique. He was right to the extent that 'searchlight' sonar proved to be a poor search device but excelled in maintaining contact with a submarine once it was detected. Nash also hoped for much greater range, based on experience with underwater signalling, perhaps as much as 10 miles.

32. Special Board to OpNav, 20 August 1917, in RG 38 classified OpNav files, folder C-26-28 to 26-40, NARA.

33. This is much the conclusion modern machinery designers have reached: gas turbines are a lot quieter than diesels. In 1917, the Special Board found that most of the noise made by the big reciprocating pumps was caused by the sudden starting and stopping of the water at the beginning and end of each stroke. It could be reduced by installing air chambers on the discharge side, but new ships should have turbine-driven rotary pumps.

34. BIR final report, 31 December 1918, in ADM 116/1430, pp 28–30. The principal investigator for BIR was Major Gill of the Royal Engineers. Both he and Thorneycroft concluded early in 1917 that silent propulsion was best achieved using hydraulic or waterjet propulsion. He submitted proposals to BIR several times in 1917 and his idea was finally approved in March 1918 for installation in two *Strath* type trawlers. Experiments to develop design data were carried out between March and July 1918, extended to larger ships between July and the end of the year. Work on the bubble screen began earlier and in May 1918 the recently-formed Lancashire Anti-Submarine Committee began work on the subject, installing a bubble screen on board a Motor Launch and then the steel trawler *Leonora*, in both cases successfully. Other investigators worked on insulating the propeller from engine noises, electric propulsion and specially-designed quiet propellers. The bubble screen did not enter service at the time (Asdic could make do with a reasonably quiet conventional propeller, as it turned out) but it was rediscovered after the Second World War.

35. BIR final report, December 1918, ADM 116/1430.

36. According to the 3 September 1917 report of the Special Board (folder C-26-28 to 26-40 in RG 38 Opnav confidential file 1917-19, NARA) a trailing wire could detect a submarine 10ft away. The Special Board also tried magnetic coils, but they were considered inferior. The wire was first installed on board a sub-chaser for trials in September 1917.

37. ADM 137/1926, p 415.

38. ADM 137/1926, p 460.

39. This comment had already fed into the December 1913 review of the British submarine building programme described in Chapter 11.

40. ADM 137/1926, p 475, Keyes comments dated 28 September 1914. During the war the British worked hard to develop a means of invisible (torpedo) discharge. Keyes also warned that well-defined patrols were easy prey, which can be read as a prediction of the sinking of the armoured cruisers *Aboukir*, *Cressy* and *Hogue*. Jellicoe circulated Keyes' comments under date of 2 October 1914.

41. Patterson (ed), *Jellicoe Papers*, II, pp 88–92 is a long memorandum sent on 29 October 1916 by Jellicoe to First Lord A J Balfour, generally an admission of frustration. It includes as its item 10 a suggestion recently made by Lieutenant C D Burney (inventor of the paravane) to use howitzers designed to throw a series of bombs to cover the probable track of a submarine whose periscope had been seen. The bombs should be depth charges powerful enough to damage a submarine they straddled. Jellicoe added that experience with howitzers and trench mortars suggested that the idea was feasible, if the effect of a rolling platform could be eliminated. Jellicoe considered the idea important enough to press forward energetically. This was the only materiel proposal in Jellicoe's memorandum. Probably its most important suggestion was to form a special ASW committee, which became the Admiralty Anti-Submarine Division.

42. Layman, *Naval Aviation*, p 81, in connection with the 'scarecrow' patrols, wrote that none of the U-boats had sky-search periscopes. However, according to the Technical History, in 1917 a few U-boats had altiscopes (sky-search periscopes) and in 1918 most had them. The British found that fast aircraft could still be effective even if the U-boat had an altiscope.

43. According to Layman, *Naval Aviation*, p 86, during the first quarter of 1918 British aircraft sighted 202 submarines (138 in home waters) and made 125 attacks (101 in home waters). Through the war the French made 246 attacks, all but sixteen in 1917–18. The US Navy made a total of thirty-two attacks.

44. Layman, *Naval Aviation*, p 79, quotes a March 1912 proposal by Lt Hugh Williamson, a submarine officer who had just qualified as an aviator, for a long-endurance ASW aircraft carrying what may have been the first depth charge to be proposed: a bomb whose time (i.e., depth) fuze would be activated upon hitting the water.

45. According to the Technical History, the Large America could not be flown for long in bad weather, because their controls were too heavy; they were difficult and expensive to house; and after a few weeks they became waterlogged to the point where they could not take off fully loaded. Even when powerful enough engines became available, the housing problem and the lack of pilots could not be solved, so that much of the seaplane work was left to much smaller Short and Sopwith Baby seaplanes.

46. The spider-web was famous after the war. It was a specific counter to the Zeebrugge U-boats operating in the southern North Sea. Layman, *Naval Aviation*, p 82 quotes a description: it covered a rough octagon 60nm across, aircraft flying along its radial arms and along chords joining the arms, ten, twenty and thirty miles from the centre. NARA RG 38 ONI files include Admiralty Air Dept. Pamphlet 29, *Methods of Carrying Out Anti-Submarine Patrols* (7 November 1917) as A-1-z Register 9879. It includes various patrol patterns, including the 'spider web'. Felixstowe operated only Large Americas on 'spider web' ('circular') patrols. Operations were complicated by the presence of British submarines, the positions of which were obtained the night before, patrols being arranged to clear them. The Felixstowe seaplanes typically patrolled at 1000ft but attacked at 800ft or below. When a submarine was sighted, the whole crew was warned. The pilot, who was observing, got into the front cockpit, fusing the bombs as he got in. The W/T operator got ready to make the recognition signal (IFF) and, if there was time, wound up the aerial. The pilot at the controls opened up to full speed, diving towards bombing altitude. The Felixstowe instructions were that the aircraft should keep on course and speed even if the U-boat dove, because a large bomb near a submerged submarine was considered more effective than the same bomb as close to a surfaced submarine. Aircraft typically bombed from 800 to 600ft at 85 knots. All bombs were dropped in one run. The recognition signal was made 2 miles from the submarine and if possible repeated. A Large America carried four 100lb or two 230lb bombs, two being preferable to four. The assumed destructive radius of one bomb was 30ft, the bombs being dropped 80ft apart (average U-boat length was taken as 240ft). Effective target area was 300 x 140ft, allowing for a turn by the U-boat.

47. Bombs were typically set to explode with a $2\frac{1}{2}$-second delay after hitting the water, equivalent to 80ft depth. Interrogation of prisoners and other information indicated that German U-boat commanders split into two groups. A minority sought to escape over the explosion by staying at periscope depth. A majority went deep (180ft).

48. Layman, *Naval Aviation*, p 86, noting that British claims were winnowed from as many as 100 to six in the RAF official history (1934) and then to one by Robert M Grant, Gröner, *German Warships 1815-1945*, lists only *UB 32* (29 September 1917), but also lists several for which the cause of loss is unknown. The Technical History of 1918 air operations lists *UC 49* (31 May 1918), *UC 70* (28 August 1918), *UB 83* (10 September 1918) and *UB 115* (29 September 1918). These were not all unassisted; *UB 49* was sighted and bombed by a DH 6 while attacking a convoy, then depth-charged by surface craft, then attacked twice by a Sopwith Baby and then by an obsolete FE 2B two-seat fighter (two 230lb bombs) and then by HMS *Locust*; she was sunk either by the destroyer or by the FE 2B. *UC 70* was attacked by a Kangaroo (530lb bomb) and then depth-charged on the spot indicated by oil and bubbles by HMS *Ouse*. *UB 83* was spotted by a kite balloon flown by HMS *Ophelia*, which was conned into position and killed the submarine by depth-charging. *UB 115* was bombed by airship *R 29*, which saw oil rising to the surface. She dropped a calcium flare to indicate the position to HMS *Ouse*, which made a co-ordinated attack with HMS *Star* and three trawlers. In addition, Russian bombing sank *UB 7* (October 1916). At the end of the war the US Office of Naval Intelligence credited *UC 1* (24 July 1917), *UB 20* (20 July 1917), *UB 32* (18 August 1917), *UC 72* (22 September 1917), *UC 6* (28 September 1917), *UC 49* (31 May 1918) and *UC 70* (28 August 1918) to US Navy air attacks. Gröner credited *UB 20*, *UC 1* and *UC 6* to mines, *UC 49* to depth charges (on 8 August 1918), *UC 70* to gunfire from British monitors and *UC 72* to a Q-Ship. The ONI list is from RG 38 ONI series, A-1-z Register No. 11412, NARA.

49. Technical History 7 (July 1919), *The Anti-Submarine Division of the Naval Staff December 1916 - November 1918*, NHB. According to this history, the idea of using hydrophones from aircraft first presented itself in the Aegean during the spring of 1917, as it seemed conditions there during the summer would be ideal. It was first tried in July 1917 from a Short seaplane, lowered from one float. Neither the Mk I non-directional nor the Mk II bi-directional hydrophone was entirely suitable. Attempts to use a Portable General Service Hydrophone failed because every time it was used nearby destroyers drowned out any submarine noise. Experiments resumed at Westgate Air Station using a non-directional Portable General Service Hydrophone on a floatplane, but it was soon clear that a directional hydrophone (the type used in the Nash Fish) was needed. A first trial was made in a Large America seaplane on 7 May 1918 off the Nore. Ultimately several Large Americas and floatplanes were fitted.

50. British experiments with airships began in the latter part of 1917, the airship remaining aloft while using the hydrophone. The Nash Fish, the eel, the directional snake and the K-tube were all tried. In March-April 1918 trials with single Nash Fish were carried out, followed by trials in July with a C-class blimp with both a Snake and a K-tube, the latter being very promising. The C-class blimp effectively hovered 200ft

above the water, which was running a heavy swell. The bearing of an approaching ship was measured to within 20° by an untrained observer. The 'rubber eel' was also tested successfully at this time. The eel was adopted and sets ordered for all SSZ blimps ('Zero Airships').

51. As early as September 1917 the US Special Board tested an R-class (small) floatplane with a C-tube, but it was too lightly-built to land in any sea greater than 3ft . The January 1918 US ASW mission to England recommended installing hydrophones (C-tubes) on board US seaplanes. British aircraft and airships often saw U-boats, but lost them when they submerged. A seaplane could maintain contact with a hydrophone until a hunting group could arrive.

52. Technical Histories, *Aircraft v. Submarine: Submarine Campaign*, 1918 (TH 4: March 1919), NHB. Presumably 1918 was chosen because that April 1918 British naval aircraft were absorbed into the new RAF. None of the Technical Histories deals with air ASW before 1918.

53. According to the Technical History and excluding Dunkirk and the Mediterranean (which were not limited to ASW), requirements and actual numbers were:

	Seaplanes	Land Planes
1918 programme estimate D of P Nov 1917	525	66
Revised 1918 programme	459	726
Operational 1 January 1918	291	23
Operational 9 November 1918	285	272

The difference between requirements and reality reflected the competition for most types of aircraft with the army and the Independent Bombing Force. The US Naval Air Service reduced British requirements by taking over Killinghome on the Irish coast (but these stations had hardly begun to operate at the end of the war).

54. Comments by Admiral Jellicoe at the Allied ASW conference in September 1917, at which time the Northern Barrage was first publicly proposed, in ADM 1/8934.

55. Technical History TH 1, *Submarine v. Submarine* (March 1919), NHB.

56. RG 38 NARA Opnav Confidential files 1917-19, folder C-26-102 to 26-106.

57. The history of wartime use of this weapon is difficult to trace because it was the one torpedo so obsolete that it was not included in *Vernon*'s accounts of wartime development; no separate technical history of British torpedoes was compiled after the First World War.

58. US Navy instructions on hunting using sound (February 1918) had the three sub-chasers of a group close in while 100 yds apart in line abeam. The centre ship would drop the first depth charge 100 yds short of the estimated U-boat position, dropping later charges as soon as the charge before exploded (listeners were warned of the effect of depth-charge blasts on them). The flanking ships would drop their first depth charges 50 yds beyond the first one dropped by the centre ship, the charges forming a pattern intended to catch the U-boat no matter how it turned. The instructions do not mention Y-guns, which made it possible for a single hunter to fire a wider pattern.

59. Report of sub-committee of BIR in the 14 September 1917 report of the US Special Committee, RG 38 OpNav confidential files 1917-19, folder C-26-55 to 26-63, NARA. The report of the sub-chaser experiment was given on 9 January 1917.

60. Eveleth Report. Eveleth described a hunt in the English Channel, using tactics which had not yet been successful. Given his knowledge of contemporary US listening devices, he considered the British types ineffective. Everleth was surprised that the British were not undertaking offensive ASW operations, as their trawlers and drifters were too slow. As an experiment, US devices (not specified) were installed on board three trawlers backed by a P-boat; Eveleth believed that the P-boat sank the U-boat they thought they found, but the water was too deep and the current too strong for a diver to go down to confirm the kill. Initially the British rejected the US device in favour of the Nash Fish, but by the end of the hunt all the fish were out of commission but the US devices were still 'in perfect working condition and were considered by the hydrophone officers on the trawlers superior to the Fish. While certain minor officials of the Admiralty are alive to the situation, none of them have personally been out with the devices on hunting patrols and there is no one today in authority who appears to have a grasp of the problem of hunting submarines as one which can be and must be solved. The Admiralty have ordered a considerable quantity of this American material but their plans today do not extend beyond improving the situation in the English Channel and hoping that something may be done in the Mediterranean. They still plan to carry out offensive operations by means of ten knot trawlers'.

61. Account by Lieutenant j.g. G G Dominick, USNRF, 30 April 1918, in NARA RG 38 OpNav confidential files 1917-19, folder C26-159 to 26-170. Dominick wrote that he knew of no US instrument which could operate while coasting at 6 knots, but he seems not to have been familiar with the MV. He found the fish inferior in many ways to the Mason (MV) and the K-tube.

62. This section relies heavily on Dwight R Messimer, *Find and Destroy: Antisubmarine Warfare in World War I* (Annapolis: Naval Institute Press, 2001) and comments in *Krieg zur See* (Nordsee volumes).

63. ADM 186/376, 'German Anti-Submarine Methods' (CB 1263), November 1916. Despite its date, this pamphlet is likely to be accurate because it reflected the experience of the British submarines in the Baltic.

64. Messimer, *Find and Destroy*, p 223 gives this 80ft depth and comments that the

Germans considered it too shallow, but the British 1916 note on German ASW gives a maximum known depth of 22 fathoms (176ft).

65. German destroyer ASW instructions dated 10 February 1918 (Tactical Order No. 3) in *German Navy Tactical Orders* 1920 (CB 1548), NHB.

66. Messimer, *Find and Destroy*, p 218 notes that total losses in German-controlled areas were six Russian and ten British submarines, mostly probably to mines (but that is not at all certain). All losses to mines appear to have been due to full-size rather than U-mines.

Chapter 14. The Anti-Submarine Armada

1. This account is based mainly on the Cover at the Brass Foundry (351).

2. Folio 5, M.01201/08, meaning that this sketch was produced in 1908. The ship would be 220ft long. Draught was not to exceed 10ft and beam would be 25 to 30ft as required for stability. Continuous speed would be 15 knots (2000hp); at full speed 3000hp would be required. The requirements given to DNC (Folio 5 is his Minute) were 16 knots on 600 tons, for which lightweight fast-running machinery would be required. DNC proposed vertical reciprocating rather than turbine engines for a ship which would take a variable tow. On this basis he could offer a 14-knot ship on 600 tons (15 knots maximum). To achieve a cruising speed of 16 knots, DNC would need 750 to 900 tons, depending on the conditions under which that speed should be attained.

3. Folio 8 of Cover 351.

4. A précis prepared for Third Sea Lord Admiral Tudor in November 1914 dated the original Admiralty committee report as 16 November 1908. C-in-C Home Fleet concurred on 28 August 1909 and asked that a class of minesweepers be included in next year's Estimates. Third Sea Lord considered that impossible, but suggested reconsidering in time for the 1911–12 Estimates (First Sea Lord Fisher concurred). On 29 April 1910 C-in-C Home Fleet again forwarded a request for sweepers, but Director of Military Branch (D of M) disagreed and Third Sea Lord and First Sea Lord backed him up (M.0566/10). However, on 18 November 1910 ICMS submitted a report on the Moray Firth exercises which made the provision of new sweepers an urgent matter. No decision on this paper (M.01527/10) could be traced. In 1911 it was decided to fit destroyers for fleet sweeping (M.01440/11), but the idea was abandoned in February 1913. This project apparently precluded interest in new fleet sweepers. On 3 September 1913 C-in-C Home Fleets (Admiral Callaghan) reported that there were insufficient fleet sweepers and ICMS called for at least twenty-six at the outbreak of a war. On being relieved in March 1914, ICMS urged provision of more fleet sweepers. The first conference on a design was held in Third Sea Lord's room on 18 February 1914. The précis, prepared by ICMS, in Folio 105 is dated 1 October 1914. It responded to a request Admiral Tudor made dated 30 September 1914.

5. Requirements laid out in M.01517/13, Folio 1 of the Cover. This paper is undated. The Folio does not include Callaghan's request.

6. The project was approved by First Sea Lord Admiral Battenberg. on 29 January 1914 and the conference was called by Third Sea Lord. (Folio 15). Folio 13 is a calculation sheet dated 3 March 1914, the new ship being 180 x 30 x 10ft (805 tons) and capable of 16 knots. A 15 May paper requests horsepower for 21 knots for an alternative ship 270 x 29 x 10ft (1200 tons).

7. Folio 37 of Cover 351, S.0575/14.

8. DNC described the 16-knot design ('New *Seagull*') in a paper attached to his 16 October 1914 comment on machinery: it was 220ft (pp) x 27ft x 9ft 6in (mean), 750 tons and 1500ihp (reciprocating engine), with a very fine underwater form to achieve the desired speed on a small power. Subdivision was unusually complete, the boiler and engine rooms each being divided in two. That required extra engine-room personnel (six men). The ship had a clipper bow and a stiff bowsprit, for handling the bow mine-catcher (trials with different mine-catchers aka 'bow protection'. were then underway). A DNC memo dated 3 December substituted a vertical bow with a catcher as approved for HMS *Sharpshooter*; it would simplify construction. Like the converted torpedo gunboats, the ship had a gallows aft. There was deck space for four sweep kites. A light bulwark was carried around the upper deck; otherwise the ship resembled the torpedo gunboat HMS *Seagull*. She had two masts, each with a derrick for handling buoys, sinkers, etc. Small steadying sails would help keep the ship's head or stern on to the sea in the event of engine damage (as the ship had only one screw). This rig made for a convenient W/T arrangement, with the W/T office near the bridge and the CO's cabin. The armament was two 3in anti-aircraft guns rather than the two 12pdr previously contemplated (later the 12pdrs were reinstated). Magazines would be above water and right aft to minimise the risk in the event the ship was mined. Unlike previous designs, this one did not provide for 50 per cent maximum power over continuous power. If the ship were built to merchant standards (Lloyd's survey), with heavier merchant ship type machinery, she would be substantially larger, but cost per ton and per ihp would be less. A 19 October 1914 conference decided that merchant service engines and boilers (Scotch boilers, 1800ihp engines) would be used. Radius of action was to be extended to 2000nm at 10 knots and 16 hours at full power. Engines and boilers would not be protected and the ship would have a single screw. DNC thought he could have a design ready to submit for tenders in four days. That left the key questions: how many were needed and what roles should they have? Roles listed were mine sweeping; anti-submarine using the modified sweep; patrol; and other fleet auxiliary purposes. Somewhat later the modified sweep role was separated from the anti-submarine role. Forty were proposed. A note to the compass department requesting details of compasses required mentioned that 'it had been approved to proceed with the utmost despatch' with a number of these new fleet sweepers. It turned out that the desired endurance (2400nm) required considerably more coal and (as DNC had mentioned)

the shift to Lloyd's survey and merchant marine standards also enlarged the ship, so that she grew to 1150 tons, 1800ihp and 250 x 32 x 11ft (extreme draught 12ft rather than the 10ft desired). The paper giving these data was not dated. In the 3 December memo ordering the vertical bow, DNC pointed out that twin screws had many advantages, but that he was bound by the Board decision for a single screw. Late in 1914 endurance was set at 2000nm at 10 knots plus two hours at full speed. A Legend dated 19 December 1914 showed a displacement of 1200 tons (250ft pp, 261ft 6in on the waterline, 262ft overall x 33ft x 10ft 6in forward and 11ft 6in aft, with a freeboard of 16ft 6in forward; on 1800ihp the shp was to make 16 knots. Coal stowage was 130 tons normal and 250 tons maximum. Armament was given as two 3in high-angle guns (100 rounds each).

9. Dated 21 October 1914, page 7 in Folio 105 of Cover 351, which begins with Oliver's 17 November paper. None would be ready until July 1915, by which time the Royal Navy would have a large new light surface force: sixteen *Arethusas*, six leaders and twenty to twenty-five 'M' class destroyers, which Churchill characterised as 'almost little cruisers from their size, speed, sea-keeping qualities, gun and torpedo armament'. He thought the fleet he had listed unequalled in keeping the sea swept clear of enemy light surface craft. He admitted that it needed to be supplemented by large numbers of small craft – but 300 or 400, not forty or fifty, 'of the lowest value consistent with seaworthiness' for sweeping, picket and patrol.

10. S.0753/14, Folio 105 in Cover 351. This 17 November 1914 paper was signed by Oliver as Chief of Staff.

11. E-in-C suggested adding Cammell Laird, Fairfield, Palmers and Denny and possibly Swan Hunter. DNC added John Brown, because its very successful light cross-Channel steamers seemed to him closest to the proposed sweeper. Harland & Wolff was invited to bid but decided to concentrate instead on monitors. Ultimately thirty firms were contacted and six tendered, most of them not currently building warships. Initially it was assumed that ships could be completed in nine months, but Admiral Oliver, who conceived them, considered that estimate very long. He pointed out that trawlers were built in batches in three months. These ships were not more than twice the size; if sufficient pressure were exerted, surely they could be completed in four months.

12. G.01832/14 (Folio 96 in Cover 351) of 17 December 1914 (about orders for guns) states that construction of 12 ships was decided at the Board meeting that day. However, the 12-ship order is mentioned in a 24 November 1914 note to possible contractors (Folio 71 in Cover 351), the first six to be completed in four months and the second six in six months from date of order. These completion dates were as instructed by First Lord Winston Churchill.

13. The first batch of twelve were ordered on 1 January 1915, followed by twelve more on 12 January 1915. Another twelve were ordered on 4 May 1915 (*Azalea* class) to a slightly modified design, with two 4in or 4.7in guns instead of 12pdrs and steering gear below decks instead of on the weather deck. A slightly larger (40 tons more, 5ft longer, 17 knots rather than 16 knots) *Arabis* class was ordered: nine on 6 July 1915, twenty-one on 15 July 1915, six on 25 July 1915 and twelve on 23 January 1916, six of them for the French navy (two more were ordered for France on 23 September 1916). A 21 February 1916 paper in Cover 351A mentions that 'as approved on other papers' the last of a group of six sloops is to be transferred to France. It would be the ship built by Swan Hunter at the Neptune Yard, Walker. Ships were built in nineteen to twenty-one weeks from the date of order. French sloops had 5.5in guns in place of the British 4in guns, hence needed not only different magazines but also considerable structural alteration. The ninth French ship *Andromede*, was a convoy sloop (decoy ship).

14. The idea of a heavier gun armament was first raised in August 1915 (G.03469/15, Folio 6 of Cover 351B) for both armed boarding vessels and minesweepers, because of experience with the heavily-armed German *Meteor*, which attacked the armed boarding steamer *King Orry*. It was also suggested that 14in torpedo tubes be taken from old torpedo boats. Unfortunately 4in guns were in very short supply. New sloops were armed with old 4.7in guns. DNO proposed in September 1917 that nine sloops have these guns replaced by modern 4in guns: *Camellia*, *Crocus*, *Delphinium*, *Godetia*, *Gentian*, *Gladiolus*, *Linnet*, *Myosotis* and *Myrtle* (Cover 151A, Folio 63, sheet dated 13 September 1917).

15. Mackay, *Fisher of Kilverstone*, p 490 quotes a 30 December 1914 memo by Oliver proposing twelve ships and calling them sloops, but as shown in the Cover, this date cannot be correct and the quoted content of the memo seems to conflate many of the papers in the Cover.

16. Cover 351A, Folio 91, comments on reports from sloops of the 1st Flotilla as to experiences in the gale of 12 November 1915, which DNC considered 'makes a new record for the seaworthiness of small fine-ended vessels in bad weather'. A heavy easterly swell combined with a high sea from the north to create a heavy confused sea. Although the ships were built on very fine lines to achieve high speed (for their size) with small horsepower, they achieved a high degree of seaworthiness by having a forecastle with a good flare and by avoiding tumblehome amidships and aft to the greatest possible extent, 'and by a carefully preserved balance of the qualities of the design as a whole'.

17. Cover 351A includes an extensive description (Folio 57) of damage which HMS *Myosotis* survived in the autumn of 1917 when she was torpedoed right aft. Fifty feet of her stern was blown off and the after 4in guns blown from its pedestal, its deck turned up. The framing, plating, bulkheads and decks extending another 20ft were distorted and crumpled 'to an extraordinary degree'. The loss of the after end of the ship was credited to a secondary explosion of sweep charges due to the torpedo explosion. Although the report did not mention whipping (which was probably not known at the time), whipping seems to have caused separate damage at the fore end of the well deck, near the bridge, where side plating buckled. A paper (Folio 61) on the French sloops of the 'Flower' class mentioned that *Rigel* was lost in the Mediterranean after having been torpedoed twice (at 09.00 and 14.00) and then towed until 22.00, after 'carrying on a good fight with a submarine'. Her CO demonstrated his faith in the type by immediately applying for command of a similar ship.

18. According to the DNC history, this *Skipjack* type bow protection was difficult to use and did not completely eliminate the danger, so it was abandoned in later units.

19. These papers are all in the Cover for the Z-Whalers (342). This was apparently actually a file of miscellaneous designs (the twin-screw sloop had no connection whatever to the Z-Whaler).

20. Before ordering the model test, DNC cautioned Third Sea Lord that it would be difficult to achieve 20 knots with shallow draught, presumably because propeller diameter would have to be limited and propellers shallow. On 13 February 1915 DNC wrote Froude at Haslar that a design had been prepared for a shallow-draught 20-knot ship. He wanted Froude to run a model for a 1000-ton ship (300 x 31 x 8ft) with a forefoot carried straight down (i.e., for ramming a submarine). Good manoeuvring power was essential and the very shallow draught made that difficult, so DNC wanted Froude to try various options, such as twin rudders. The report was written by A W Watson, who designed the slightly later P-boats – which met the 20-knot and 8ft draught requirements. The hull form was based on that of the *Chao Ho*, a British-built Chinese cruiser. Froude found that he would need 1256ehp to make 19 knots, 1542ehp to make 20 knots and 1943ehp to make 21 knots, all at 992 tons. A Scheme of Complement was titled 'New *Seagull*'.

21. DNC planned to design the hull in sufficient detail, with sufficiently detailed specifications, that it would not be necessary to go to a Registration Society (e.g., Lloyd's) to ensure that a ship would be satisfactory. The civilian overseers mentioned would replace the usual Admiralty overseers. Specifications would be based on those of a 'C' class light cruiser, with details based on those of the torpedo gunboats *Jason* and *Halcyon*. The Legend was dated 19 February 1915. The ship would displace 1100 tons and it would be 310ft (pp) x 32ft x 8ft 6in (fore and aft), with a freeboard of 13ft forward and 10ft aft. Coal capacity would be 250 tons, as in a sloop; substituting oil would reduce that to 200 tons. Planned armament matched that of a sloop, which was then two 3in anti-aircraft guns with 100 rounds each.

22. After the material on the fast sloop, the Cover abruptly shifted to undated calculations for a 600-ton twin-screw ship with 1800shp turbines, capable of 17 knots. The next entry is for twin-screw steamer for Lake Tanganyika (but this designation is in quotes in places) in answer to Chief of Staff minutes dated 3 and 11 February 1916. Apparently it was hoped that the craft could be built in England, disassembled and then bolted together, but DNC cautioned that anything this large would have to be riveted together in a kind of shipyard at the Lake. He offered a 150–160 x 24 x 7¾ft ship with a deep load displacement of 370 to 400 tons; twin-screw reciprocating engines (600ihp) would drive it at 12 knots and it would burn oil fuel, to limit its crew. Armament would be one 4in and one 12pdr. This was not the 600-tonner and the drawing in the Cover makes it obvious that it had no relationship with the 'Dance' class minesweeper later developed for Mesopotamia. It was not apparently ever built (DNC cited press reports which made it less likely that the craft was needed).

23. Cover 351C, Folio 164, with Third Sea Lord's letter to DNC accepting his conclusions. DNC's comments were dated 21 May 1915. Third Sea Lord Admiral Tudor wrote on 25 May that he proposed to inform Jellicoe of the characteristics of the new Patrol Boats and to tell him that if neither they nor the sloops met his requirements, he would have to use destroyers. The entire point of the sloop and patrol boat programmes had been to set those ships free to work with the Grand Fleet. A somewhat stiffer letter sent on 4 June is in this Folio. DNC later pointed out that some 16 knot sloops were touching 17 knots on trial (*Sunflower* did 17.5), so it was reasonable to expect some of the new 17 knots sloops to approach 18, which was the sort of speed Jellicoe wanted.

24. DNC did realise that he had to offer a viable possibility, so at the end of June 1915 he produced a sketch design of a sloop modified to produce 3000ihp (18 to 18.5 knots). It would necessarily have twin screws. Draught would be reduced from 11ft to 8ft. The ship would have to have naval-type watertube boilers to save weight. She could probably be built in seven rather than five months and she would cost £18,000 more than a sloop.

25. An appended table compared the current sloop (£65,000), the new patrol boat (P-boat: £80,000), a notional 25-knot destroyer (£110,000 minimum), an 'M' class destroyer (£165,000 minimum) and a new-design 18 to 18.5-knot sloop (£83,000). The new sloop, with a 3000ihp engine (rather than 2200ihp) would take 7 rather than 4½ to 6 months to build. The P-boat was credited with 20 knots. Admiral A K Wilson commented that if the American boats proved sufficiently seaworthy to operate in the approaches to the English and Irish Channels they would be the best vessels for submarine hunting and nothing more would have to be built for that purpose. He considered the sloops too slow for that work, but agreed that it would be impractical to make them faster. Another paper in the docket, prepared for First Sea Lord, questioned Jellicoe's assumptions. If the battle fleet were to steam at 16 knots, sweepers working ahead of it would have to steam at 18 knots or more, to allow for the drag of their sweeps. Jellicoe was asking for only eight fast sweepers, which could handle only a very narrow channel. If the fleet zig-zagged, it would need a much wider channel and if it did not, the submarine threat would much exceed any mine threat. It might be entirely impractical to clear the track of the fleet in advance. The huge outlay required for 20-knot sweepers would not be warranted. The idea of the 25-knot destroyer instead of the sloop seems to have come from Admiral Oliver, who suggested that the sloop was becoming so large that she was too good a torpedo target to be useful against submarines; the 25-knot destroyer would be half her size.

26. Patterson (ed), *Jellicoe Papers*, I, p 173.

27. Cover 351B, Folio 97. Handwritten comments by Narbeth, who was designing sloops, were dated 12 November (without a year). Narbeth commented that with two 2000hp engines and three watertube boilers, a 135- ton ship would make about 19 knots (a 1200-ton ship would have to be lengthened only 10ft). Cost would rise from the present £70,000 to £98,000.

28. Cover 351C, Folio 4, 28 January 1916. These were twelve ships, six of which were ordered for the French government.

29. Cover 351C, Folio 164, comments on submission by Captain in Charge, Fleet Minesweepers dated 21 March 1916 (remarks dated 30 May 1916).

30. Cover 351C, Folio 204, marked 'not to be circulated'. The system would comprise *Fleet Searchers* to lead the line at high speed, well ahead of the fighting ships, to locate minefields; *Mine Clearers* (on a protracted basis); *Channel Searchers* or track sweepers to maintain tracks and routes into the approaches to bases; and trawlers for purely local sweeping. The new type was the Fleet Searcher, with a speed advantage over the fleet (say 24 knots trial speed), to search at up to 21 knots using paravanes (neither the 'A' sweep or any variation would likely be useful at such a speed). Fleet searchers might be made redundant if self-protection by paravane proved successful. Fleet sweeper commander Captain L G Preston thought that possibility so remote that the fleet would always need searchers. Ideally draught would not exceed 10ft. The ships might also be used as a submarine screen or for patrol. Armament would probably be two 4in high-angle guns. They might also be used for minelaying, to carry thirty mines. If they were to be used for patrol, they might also have a torpedo tube on deck (Admiral Madden considered the torpedo tube essential). Destroyers could be used, but that seemed undesirable because they had too little fuel capacity to stay with the fleet, they could not keep the sea in all weather and they were urgently required for other work. Twelve ships would always accompany the fleet and to have that many ready at all times, eighteen should be built. It was understood that Jellicoe agreed with this idea. In the end, the new ships were not designed or built; destroyers with high-speed sweeps took over the fleet search function.

31. Folio 56, Cover 351A. The analysis was written by Chief Constructor (not DNC) Gard. He considered the US sweepers to be essentially twin-screw Ocean Tugs, designed primarily for that role and as such superior to high-powered Admiralty twin-screw ocean tugs of the *Rover* class. They were well divided, but that was vitiated by fitting watertight doors. They burned oil fuel only, which was a serious fire risk: oil was carried fore and aft. Typically that was exactly where sloops suffered torpedo and mine damage. An explosion at one end would throw flaming oil over the ship. Mounting the two 3in guns abreast forward of the bridge gave a much narrower arc of fire than mounting them on the centreline, as on the sloops. Accommodation was very well arranged, but less elaborate than in the Royal Navy. Gard was working on the basis of plans supplied in December 1917 by Stanley Goodall, who was then attached to the US Bureau of Construction and Repair. Goodall thought the 'Bird' design should be compared with the 'Hunt' class twin-screw sweeper in British service. Of thirty-six on order, twenty-four had been laid down. Goodall had heard of a desire that the remaining ships be special-purpose minesweepers like the 'Hunts' rather than multi-purpose ships. An appended paper, probably by Goodall, reported that the 'Birds' were conceived for post-war use as tugs and also to carry twenty-four mines on portable rails. They were being built to commercial standards (American Bureau of Shipping). The machinery was triple expansion. Kites for sweeping were stowed below deck. Goodall did not point out that the US Navy had adopted the single-ship French sweep rather than the 'A' Sweep favoured by the Royal Navy. Note that there was no ASW function.

32. Dittmar and College, *British Warships 1914-1919*, p 126.

33. Statement by DNC as to Production of Convoy Sloops, Cover 381, Folio 193.

34. Orders are shown in a table on the inside cover of Cover 381. Four orders were involved: 7th (23 January 1916: six French and six altered to Convoy Sloops when nearing completion); 8th (two ships for French government, 23 February 1916); 9th (fourteen ships, all built as Convoy Sloops, but one *Andromeda*. for the French government; six ordered 26 December 1916, six on 6 January 1917 and two on 13 January 1917); and 10th (twenty ships, All Convoy Sloops, but of several types, all ordered 21 February 1917). Convoy Sloops were *Begonia* (prototype), six *Aubretia* class and thirty-three *Begonia* class, but the latter varied considerably. According to the Cover, of the second series of fourteen, *Convolvus* and *Eglantine* were similar, but all others differed in profile, etc. and in armament. Of the final order for twenty, except for *Gardenia*, *Gilia* and *Harebell*, all ships were sisters to commercial ships built by their respective firms. *Sweetbriar* and *Tuberose* were similar; *Coreopsis*, *Cowslip* and *Dianthus* were similar; *Marjoram* and Mistletoe were similar; and *Gardenia* and *Gilea* were similar. *Gardenia* and *Harebell* were new types.

35. Cover 381, Folio 170, M.017617/18. The order came into effect in March. At that time some of the Convoy Sloops were still under construction.

36. Sketch in Cover 351A. The associated file, dated 21 August 1917, was Folio 89. The Legend compared the new design with the sloop *Nasturtium*. Both had the same length between perpendiculars, but due to the raked bow and stern the new ship was 281ft 3in overall, compared to 267ft 6in for the earlier sloop. She was also beamier (35ft vs. 33ft 6in), but she had the same draught and about the same displacement (1290 vs 1280 tons). Armament was given as four 4in and two AA machine guns, compared to two 4.7in and two 3pdr AA guns. Both had $1^1/_2$in HTS plating over their magazines.

37. Details in the Sloop Cover are sketchy because DNC was not involved beyond producing the initial sketch. The design was the responsibility of DCAS. According to Brown, *Grand Fleet*, p 140, they were bad seaboats and heavy rollers. The sloops long outlived them in post-war service. Brown points out that DNC records deliberately did not describe DCAS projects (Covers were DNC's records).

38. DNC *Records of Warship Construction 1914-1918*, Brass Foundry.

39. Brown, *Grand Fleet*, p 141 credits their designer A W Watson with the idea of reducing visibility by using a very low freeboard (6ft 3in amidships). Very shallow draught (8ft) gave them some immunity from torpedoes. The submarine-like appearance was fostered by the small superstructure and funnel. Brown credits Watson with the idea that seas washing over the low deck would reduce roll and pitch and reports from sea were favourable (the main complaint was that the anchors threw up spray). On trials, *P 24* turned rapidly and was not wet going astern, because the spoon-shaped stern lifted. When running into a head sea, the ship did not pitch and the low after deck was dry. All of this must have been in DNC records, because the Cover is nearly empty.

40. *P 11* to *P 34* were ordered in May 1915. Following successful trials, *P 35* to *P 40* were ordered in February 1916, *P 41* to *P 54* in March 1916, *P 55* to *P 62* in April and May 1916 and *P 63* and *P 64* in June 1916. According to Dittmar and College, *British Warships*, p 99, PC conversions of these ships were ordered in December 1916. *PC 65* to *PC 70* were ordered in January 1917 and *PC 71* to *PC 74* in June 1917. Like the Convoy Sloops, the PCs were withdrawn from decoy service in March 1918.

41. Cover 351C, Folio 164, DNC comments dated 9 July 1915 on Jellicoe's renewed pressure for a fast minesweeper. Unfortunately none of this background material is in the P-Boat Cover.

42. This design is described in the d'Eyncourt notebook in NMM; there is no sketch. It is item 51 in the book. Dimensions were given as 125 x 14 x 5ft, with freeboard at the bow of 7ft 6in and 4ft 9in aft. Deep draught was given as 5ft 3in. Radius of action would have been 1200nm at 10 knots, or 280nm at full speed. The design book also gives particulars of the P-boat (item 36), of the single-screw sloop (item 37) and of the whaler (item 38, described as a Smiths Dock design). It does not include the abortive twin-screw sloop.

43. Arthur J Marder (ed), *Fear God and Dread Nought: the correspondence of Admiral of the Fleet Lord Fisher of Kilverstone* (London: Jonathan Cape, 1952–9) III, p 165. Fisher generally claimed that he had ordered nineteen small whalers (Z-whalers). At this time thirty-six sloops had been ordered, leaving forty-five 'big whalers'. These ships do not figure in Fisher's accounts of his 612-ship building programme and they do not correspond to know numbers of trawlers purchased at the time. The day before Fisher wrote Jellicoe that it was interesting that he (Jellicoe) was pressing for less expensive ships to replace destroyers, when 48 hours before he had ordered a hundred 'glorified whalers' of 15 knots speed, with a gun and a searchlight and crew of twenty men, to be built in six weeks.

44. ADM 137/1097, 'Anti-Submarine, Auxiliary Patrol', July- December 1915, folio on Whalers initiated by Director of Stores, 29 May 1915. This paper dated 2 August 1915 is pp 270–2. The paper hints at the originally planned decoy role; 'it is not considered possible for alterations of any kind to be carried out to make these vessels look like Whalers (and not Warships) at close distances'. Virtues were a good speed (14 knots and 13 knots could be relied upon), very good manoeuvring qualities and could turn very quickly. They had a searchlight and Type 4 W/T and were armed with a 12pdr forward and a 3pdr aft and with a ram bow. Against that, they had a limited radius of action and a large complement for their accommodation. One was turned over to a Commander Charcot, but he did not find her 'suitable for the duty on which it has been proposed to employ them'.

45. Z-Whaler Cover (347), Folio 1 in the section on whalers, CP 05934/15, dated 19 March. The new whalers were expected to cost , 10,000 each, the existing ones bought in Norway about £7000 each. Dittmar and College, *British Warships 1914-1919*, p 219 shows two whalers bought in January 1915 and another four, presumably the ones Fisher had in mind, purchased in April 1915. Six more were obtained in 1917. In addition, two were hired in January 1915 (one later bought) and three German whalers were seized in South Africa at the outbreak of war. The whalers bought in April 1915 served in East Africa. Papers in the Cover indicate that whalers were still being bought in Norway in July 1915, so the April date may be wrong. The initial offer of Norwegian whalers was apparently made in mid- November 1914 by Messrs. Salveson & Co. of Leith for *Herpia* and *Ramna*. They were leased rather than bought, though *Ramna* was bought in January 1915. A slightly later offer covered the whalers *Macquaui*, *Skeem* and *Sprout* (some of these names were difficult to read), but the other ships bought in January 1915 were *Barrowby* and *Norvegia*.

46. Cover 347, Folio 45, comment on paper submitted by Superintendent of Contract Work (SCW), CF 06356/15. The mast had to be cut down from 60 to 48ft (the higher mast had been chosen to make W/T more effective) and the funnel from 34 to 18ft .

47. Dimensions were 125 x 25 x $12^1/_2$ (moulded depth, not draught) ft and displacement fully loaded was given as 370 tons. The bottom of the large propeller projected about 6in below the keel. The stem, presumably strengthened for ramming, was the same as that in the trawlers (Nos. 596 and 599–603) recently delivered to the Admiralty. This is Folio 3 of the Whaler part of Cover 347. Important changes from standard practice were the larger complement and electric power for lighting (including a searchlight and destroyer-type W/T).

48. Smith's Dock letter to Admiralty 4 June 1915 summarising their side of a meeting with SCW on 18 May, pointing out their promise to complete ships within three months. Given the Admiralty requirements, draught was less than usual in whalers and that gave the ships greater manoeuvrability. Smith's Dock traced its expertise in whaler design to the experience gained by its general manager Mr. Reed whaling off South

Africa. The company used ordinary steel in order to complete the ships as quickly as possible. It adopted the White-Forster boiler to minimise machinery weight. It tried for better speed than the 12 knots promised at the 15 March Admiralty conference at which the ships were defined and the ships were expected to make nearly 13 knots for a short time (in fact Z.6, HMS *Bullwhale*, made 14.09 knots on trial in September 1915). That raised the cost of machinery. A variety of special features, none of which would be required of a commercial whaler, explained why the proposed price of the Z-whalers was about £30,000, which was six times the initial Admiralty estimate. Folio 72 in Cover 347. Based on trials, expected endurance was 1300nm at 10 knots.

49. Brown, *Grand Fleet*, p 142, writes that the project died because the whalers had poorer seakeeping than trawlers. That is the explanation given by Dittmar and College, *British Warships*, p 218. The Cover provides no account of seakeeping; it ends with the trials of the first ships.

50. Data on Admiralty purchases and other acquisitions from Dittmar and College, *British Warships*, pp 153–78. DNC's history of *Admiralty Trawlers and Drifters 1916-1921* is in ADM 1/8597/1. It is *not* in the compiled DNC warship construction history in the Brass Foundry and in NHB.

51. Patterson (ed), *Jellicoe Papers*, I, pp 159–60, letter to the Secretary of the Admiralty dated 17 May 1915.

52. Trawlers and drifters competed with merchant ships for the miscellany of guns arriving in England. For example, a paper in ADM 137/1097 (G.03345/1915 stamped 6 August 1915) lists guns available at various ports. All trawlers at Lowestoft, Devonport, Sheerness and Pembroke had been armed. At Harwich, eight guns and mountings had been sent for the eight 'smoke' trawlers. At Portsmouth, the twelve unarmed trawlers were to be given Japanese-supplied 3pdrs, which were hardly impressive. A decision was needed as to the priority to be accorded drifters, minesweeping trawlers, minelaying trawlers (for home minefields) and for supplying a second 12pdr to yachts which currently had only one. Most of the trawlers came under AMS (Admiral Mine Sweeping), who listed trawlers at Lowestoft with 3pdrs. Only one of the Nore Trawler Sweepers (*Javelin*) had a gun (6pdr). All of the White Sea sweeper trawlers were armed (one 12pdr each). AMS proposed that one out of every seven trawler sweepers at Lowestoft, one out of every six at Grimsby and one out of every four at South Shields be armed with one 6pdr or 12pdr as soon as possible as an anti-submarine gun. If the same gun could conveniently be used against either submarines or aircraft, he proposed 6pdrs on high-angle mountings 'as aircraft sometimes molest sweepers'. At other bases (not under AMS) he proposed arming one officer in every sweeping group (an officer's ship) with 6 or 12pdr (or 6pdr in HA mounting), except if the ship were stationed on North, West, or South West coasts. Ultimately one ship in four should be armed. At this time there were seventy-eight sweeping trawlers at Lowestoft, twenty-five at The Nore, twelve at Dover, thirty-two at the Humber, twelve at the Tyne, twenty-one at Granton, eight at Peterhead, eighteen at Cromarty and fifteen in the Orkneys (a total of 221), plus twenty-four drifters at Lowestoft (all working independently, hence all to be armed), plus the paddle sweepers.

53. ADM 137/1097 includes a 17 August 1915 paper, M.06308/1915 (p 281), stating that the Admiralty was considering the issue. It used trawlers for mine sweeping, auxiliary patrol and harbour defence, in that order and its needs had not yet been satisfied. It was willing to offer some relief, perhaps by substituting older trawlers for the newer ones recently taken to support boom defence of ports. The larger trawlers thus released were considered more valuable because they landed a greater tonnage of fish and also because they went to Iceland for their catch and supplied most of the fish for the 'poor man's market'.

54. That the Germans believed that British and even neutral trawlers in the North Sea were betraying their operations is evident throughout the Nordsee volumes of *Krieg zur See* (they refused to imagine that signals intelligence was the culprit). At least some senior British officers had much the same idea of German trawler operations. On 16 July 1915 Jellicoe wrote Beatty that he feared that he would not be allowed to sink all German trawlers at sight (which was prohibited by various conventions of international law, unless the trawlers were carrying out military operations). In his opinion all German trawlers were carrying out such operations, 'and there is no time to ask questions. We are still trying to make war with gloves on'. Patterson (ed), *Jellicoe Papers* I, p 172.

55. It is not entirely clear from the DNC history whether the 500 trawlers were envisaged from the outset.

56. For example, sixteen *Castle* class trawlers were cancelled so that Smith's Dock could build gunboats (Admiralty hull numbers 3800 - 3815). Dittmar and College, *British Warships*, p 101. Similar cancellations affected the other firms, but figures are not given.

57. Brown points out this parallel in *Grand Fleet*, p 143.

58. Marder (ed), *Fear God and Dread Nought*, III, p 161.

59. Roskill, *Naval Air Service*, pp 133.

60. Figures for March 1916 from a report on naval air service in Roskill, *Naval Air Service*, pp 309–15. Production SS airships had a different envelope with two rather than one ballonets inside. Most SS were delivered in 1915–16, the last in October 1917. Some were modified after delivery with cars made of Farman aircraft bodies. Transfers: ten to Italy, four to France and four to the American Expeditionary Force.

61. Details of airship completions are from the Airship Trust website. Other data are from the Admiralty Technical History of Air ASW. SS capacity was 70,000ft^3. The first SSZ (75,000ft^3) was delivered in September 1916, the last (*SS 77*) being delivered in January 1919. This was by far the most numerous type. It had the same 75hp engine as the SS class and endurance was 17 hours at full speed. The first SSP (Pusher) flew in January 1917, six being built (*SSP 1–SSP 6*). They were delivered between January and June 1917, powered by either the 75hp Rolls-Royce engine of the original SS or by a 100hp Green engine. Endurance was 24 hours at half throttle. SST was a larger airship (125,000 ft^3 rather than 75,000ft^3) powered by two 100hp Sunbeam or 75hp Rolls-Royce engines. Endurance at full speed was 17 hours, compared to 12 for an SS. Thirteen were built (*SST 1–SST 14*, but no *SST 13*). Three were transferred to the United States. Effective performance as given in the Admiralty Technical History: SS-Z, with three men in tandem (W/T operator in front, pilot and engineer; two 350lb bombs, endurance 8 hours. A C could carry four 100lb bombs. C* capacity was 210,000ft^3. NS capacity was 360,000ft^3, with a crew of ten. By way of comparison, *R 31*'s capacity was 1,553,000ft^3 and it had five engines. Some data are from a May 1918 US Navy Scientific Attaché report in NARA RG 38 confidential files 1917-19 folder C-26-188 to 26-202. The attaché thought that given the early failure of Zeppelins most of the British were reluctant to develop rigid airships. They concentrated on semi-rigids, which had a rigid keel under the usual gas bag. In one flight with an NS, it was possible to see the disturbance made by a submerged British submarine two miles away. The attaché thought that combining airships with hunting units would make the latter 50 per cent stronger.

62. ADM 137/1953, Airships: Correspondence in Grand Fleet files, p 261. The paper was unsigned. The opposing paper begins on p 262. It is signed by R S Seymour, 17 July 1917.

63. Roskill, *Naval Air Service*, p 663.

64. From the Technical History. It does not give the convoy rationale, but it is difficult to see any other in the large order for SS Twins.

65. NARA RG 38 confidential OpNav papers 1917-19 folder C-26-20 to 26-24.

66. Unsigned Navy Department memo, 19 July 1917, following several memos signed by McKean. NARA RG 38 confidential OpNav papers 1917-19 folder C-26-20 to 26-24.

67. Minutes of 27 October 1917 meeting in NARA RG 38 confidential papers 1917-19 folder C-26-91.

Chapter 15. Mine Warfare

1. This was a single fifty-mine barrier laid by the minelayer *Amur* after a week of observations of the movements of the Japanese ships, which always followed exactly the same path. The battleships sunk were *Hatsuse* and *Yashima*. *Vernon* considered the standard Russian M1898 horned mine the first modern contact mine. It suffered from an unreliable safety device (to arm it only after it entered the water); the minelayer *Yenisei* was destroyed by her own mines during the Russo-Japanese War. As early as 1905, many Russian mine officers favoured an alternative means of detonating mines and the Russian M1912 mine used an inertia mechanism rather than Hertz horns. Russian experience may explain *Vernon's* distaste for electric mine pistols.

2. Lecture by Commander Roy C Smith USN at the School of Submarine Defence, Fort Totten, 1 July 1908, in NWC Archives (code XMIG). He pointed out that ever since the end of the Russo-Japanese War (1906) the Russians had been raising mines off Vladivostok; they hoped to be finished by the end of the summer of 1908. To Smith, the usual methods had made sense only before the advent of searchlights and rapid-fire guns and against fields of limited area close to forts. Attacking boats would sound their way in and sweep and drag for mines or for their control cables, or they would countermine a suitable channel. Smith thought that the last time this had been done was at Santiago, Cuba in 1898; 'the Japanese never attempted to attack the mine field at Port Arthur and if any people are capable of accomplishing such hazardous undertakings it is they'. As for Santiago, it was known that the entrance to the harbour was mined and there was supposed information as to mine locations. In places the channel was only 125 yds wide. That was why Lieutenant Hobson tried to block it by scuttling the collier *Merrimac* (he failed because she did not sink until she had drifted into the wide part of the channel – an unfortunate foretaste of what happened at Zeebrugge twenty years later). The minefields were well covered by artillery and riflemen. With the Spanish fleet destroyed, it seemed that a US fleet forcing the mines could cause the city to surrender. The collier *Lebanon* brought down a countermining outfit from the Torpedo Station at Newport, consisting of mines each containing 500lbs of guncotton, which were to be laid in the minefield by an open launch towed by a steam launch and detonated electrically. The plan called for assembling the entire naval force off the harbour entrance during the night, two auxiliary gunboats going in initially towing the countermining launches. Each of two parties consisted of a ship's steam launch towing an open launch, the whole being brought up by a ship's cutter carrying one end of the control cable and a firing battery, to ensure that all the countermines exploded at the same time. The two lines of countermines were to be 180ft apart, because the lines of Spanish mines had that separation. Once the mines exploded, the US battleships, which would have been shelling Spanish positions from offshore, would rush the harbour following the gunboats. In fact Santiago fell just before the attack was scheduled. Smith's account highlights how cumbersome the countermine method was, as the circuit had to be assembled completely before any of the countermines could be laid. Smith thought the plan had a chance of success. Mines actually found after the Spanish surrender were seven controlled and nine contact mines, all in poor condition and probably inoperable. Three controlled mines had been exploded when the *Merrimac* entered, probably in a failed attempt to fire all of them simultaneously. An up-to-date minefield would be much larger, with much more numerous mines, in much better condition, covered by picket boats, searchlights and shore batteries and possibly also shore-launched torpedoes and submarines. Smith emphasised that no one knew how to sweep mines, although he reported that the Royal Navy had a sweep suitable for the shoal waters of the North Sea or the Baltic. He emphasised the problem posed by mines defending a harbour, where

sweepers would be faced by active defences (he though the Royal Navy assumed that it would face mines strewn in open water, hence undefended). Countermining was less and less attractive because mines were less and less liable to sympathetic detonation. However, Smith apparently saw it as the only available alternative in the face of serious defences. His lecture seems to have been typical of naval views at the time.

3. Article II of the 1907 Hague Convention barred the use of automatic contact mines off an enemy coast solely to intercept civilian traffic, but it contained a military exigency clause which effectively negated it. In 1914 the British official view was that general shipping warnings should be issued prior to laying a minefield.

4. According to an ONI file, 'Notes on Foreign Long-Range Torpedoes and Mine Sweeping, British Navy', dated 1912, in NWC Archives (code XMIO). The torpedo part of the file was dated 30 October 1912. At this time the US Navy had a very close relationship with the Royal Navy and its perceptions were reasonably accurate. The British considered mines a threat to a fleet as long as it was in soundings (depths) permitting minelaying. The US writer pointed out that given the increased draught of modern capital ships, a fleet might have only a limited number of routes out of a chosen anchorage. The US report described the 'A' Sweep accurately, the water kites having been observed from a boat passing the converted sweeper gunboats *Speedwell* and *Gossamer*. It also described their self-protection device, a horizontal spar carried far enough ahead of the stem that a mine fouling it would not sink the ship. As drawn in the report, the device consisted of a bow boom from which a pair of angled spars were suspended, carrying a third, horizontal, spar between them. The NWC Archive also contains a typed 'Foreign Manual on Mine Sweeping 1912' (Code XMIO), which is almost certainly the Royal Navy's manual of that date (some of its language duplicates that of the later minesweeping Staff History, which used the British manual as one of its sources). This manual mentions the rapid explosive sweep the Royal Navy tried, which was replaced by the 'fixed wire sweep'. The plates were replaced by hand sketches, suggesting that a US officer was allowed to borrow a copy of the manual but not allowed to reproduce it directly.

5. In March 1903 the Royal Navy cancelled development of non-controlled mines because no successful type had emerged (*Vernon*, the mine developers, considered the German and Russian horned mines too unsafe for those laying them). Early experience during the Russo-Japanese War convinced the Admiralty to reverse this policy; the Naval Service Mk I pistol was adopted in 1905 and 1000 mines ordered that year (they became available in 1907). Each cruiser could carry 100 mines, with a maximum speed of 17 knots. The British choice may have been influenced by the success of the standard Japanese mine, which used an inertia mechanism (when struck, the mine casing moved more than the heavy brass knob inside). According to Mackay, *Fisher of Kilverstone*, p 377, a committee on mines assembled at Fisher's instruction in May 1905 concluded that the navy needed 10,000 contact mines, of which 3000 should be laid against the Germans in the North Sea, off the mounts of the Elbe, Weser and Jade. He quotes CID Minutes to this effect. The figure of 10,000 was still valid in 1906. In 1914, about 4000 spherical mines were in stock. By January 1908, arguing against 'invasionists', Fisher rejected the argument that the Germans could paralyse the Royal Navy in war by mining it in. He said that the navy knew how to neutralise mines but it was a 'deep secret' (according to the proceedings of the committee on invasion, 27 January 1908). That year, in connection with mine and torpedo manoeuvres, he wrote to Admiral Beresford that the Channel could easily be cleared of mines.

6. Mackay, *Fisher of Kilverstone*, p 475.

7. *Vernon*, which developed British mines, regarded mechanical mechanisms as inherently safer than the Hertz electric horns used by the Germans and the Russians (by 1914 the Russians also preferred an inertia mechanism to the electric horn). The initial British Mk II inertia pistol had to be cocked before it was laid. That made it too easy to trigger. After a field was laid in Lough Swilly in 1912, the mines could not immediately be recovered due to weather and once they were recovered it turned out that many had already fired, due to the swell. Work on a Mk III cocked-spring pistol therefore began in 1913; it used two arms extending across the top of the mine. When a ship bumped the mine, the arms rotated. The result was too sensitive; it probably caused the loss of the minelayer *Princess Irene* in 1915. A Mk IV pistol entered service in July 1915. At the outbreak of war, most pistols were the over-sensitive Mk IIs. The Royal Navy also bought the Vickers Elia mine, which also had an inertia pistol. In addition to pistol problems, the standard British mines also suffered from sinker and mooring problems. Unfortunately the problems of the British mines did not become evident before trials were conducted in 1916. On the outbreak of war, the Royal Navy had about 4000 mines and sinkers. Maximum production of both the standard naval mine and the Elia was ordered in July 1915, but in the autumn of 1915 problems with the Elia caused the planned output to be cut from the 1000 per week to which Vickers was building to 250 per week. In December 1915 projected total weekly mine output (service plus Vickers) was cut to 1200. *Vernon* later claimed that although a German horned mine had been recovered about April 1915, there had been no attempt to copy it because it was thought that all the problems of the service mine had been cured. However, in February 1916 it was approved to fit 500 of the new submarine-laid mines with German-type Hertz horns. Then bumping tests were ordered of service mines fitted with horns and in December 1916 the first horned (H) mines were ordered in quantity. Orders for 10,000 H II and 7000 H IV were recommended in January 1917; parallel orders for service and Elia mines, intended as insurance against the failure of the H mines, were later cancelled.

8. According to Gröner, *German Warships 1815-1945*, I, the *V 1* class could carry eighteen mines (*V 1–V 6, G 7– G 12, S 13–24*). Destroyers of the next *V 25* class (1913–15 programmes and Mobilisation programme: *V 25–V 30, S 31–S 36, G 37–G 42, V 43–V 46, V 43–V 48, S 49–S 66, V 67–V 84, G 85–G 95*) were credited with twenty-four mines. The *G 96* class (1916 and 1917 Mobilisation types: *G 96, V 125–V 130, S*

131–*S 139, V 140–V 144, H 145–H 147, G 148–G 150, WW 151, S 152–S 157, V 158–V 165, H 166–H 169*) could carry twenty-four mines (forty in the 'G' type). The final design in this series (*V 170* or 1918 Mobilisation class: *V 170–V 177, S 178–S 185, H 186–H 202, V 203–V 210, S 211–S 223*) could each accommodate forty mines. The large *B 97* class destroyers taken over from a Russian order (*B 97–B 98, V 99–V 100, B 109–G 112*) could each carry twenty-four mines, as could the large *G 101* class destroyers taken over from an Argentine order (*G 101–G 104*). The larger *S 113* class (*S 113–S 115, V 116–V 118, G 119–G 121, B 122–B 124*) could each carry forty mines. The missing numbers in this list are *V 105– V 108*, which were torpedo boats taken over from a Dutch pre-war order; they did not carry mines. In the absence of a German destroyer history based on internal documents, it is impossible to say how important or unimportant the provision of mine carrying capacity was.

9. Jellicoe repeatedly mentioned this idea in messages to his commanders, often claiming that he had special secret information confirming a German policy of laying mines ahead of a pursuing fleet. The July 1916 British handbook on German submarines and naval weapons (CB 1182A, in NHB) includes an account of German mining policy as then understood. Surface minelayers would harass British trade routes and the movements of the fleets. They would also lay mines in connection with a pre-arranged operations plan, e.g. in the path a fleet would have to take to engage the German fleet. Submarine minelayers would lay small groups of mines off ports. Warship minelayers rated a much more elaborate description. They might lay mines tactically during a fleet or cruiser action, or they might lay them as part of an operation such as the bombardment of Scarborough. Instances of every case *except* the tactical one had occurred, but the tactical possibility rated further discussion. Since it was known that certain light cruisers and a large number of destroyers were fitted to carry considerable numbers of mines, the use of moored mines during a fleet or cruiser action or by escaping cruisers 'may therefore be expected whenever opportunity admits'. This section also claimed that German mines were 'of excellent workmanship' and therefore expensive, 'but it is doubtful if their efficiency is appreciably greater than that of the British types now (November 1st, 1915) in use' – doubtless reflecting *Vernon*'s continued rejection of horned mines. According to the Staff History of British wartime minesweeping, during the Scarborough raid (3 November 1914) the cruiser *Stralsund* laid a minefield which sank the submarine *D 5*, which was trying to cut off the enemy force as it retired. The cruiser *Kolberg* laid another field (100 mines) as part of the Scarborough raid on 16 December.

10. The British became interested in drifting mines laid by destroyers because the Japanese used them successfully during the Russo-Japanese War, a fact revealed to a Lieutenant Niell RN on detachment to the Imperial Japanese Navy in 1908-9. He considered it so important that he convinced the naval attaché in Japan to report it immediately (Niell's and the attaché's 11 August 1909 reports are in Destroyer Foreign Cover, Folio 95). Considerable enthusiasm was generated, officers often failing to distinguish between moored and drifting mines. Thus in December 1912 the Director of the Operations Division (Rear Admiral G A Ballard) claimed that during the Russo-Japanese War drifting mines sank three battleships as well as lesser vessels, not realising that he was actually referring to moored mines laid tactically. Recent tactical exercises (PZs) included mine laying by destroyer flotillas assigned to the battle fleet. On one occasion battleships of the opposing side ran into the mines and on another an enveloping movement was frustrated when destroyers out of range ahead were seen dropping mines across the intended path. As for the danger to friendly ships, 'it is a very rare thing in PZ exercises for ships to re-traverse the same water twice over'. Chief of (War) Staff E C T Troubridge strongly supported a drifting mine programme. Moored mines laid off the enemy coast might be quite useful, but minelayers would generally be 'a gift to the enemy' if they came close offshore. Destroyers alone were fast enough to lay mines in enemy-controlled waters, but their capacity was so limited that they would be better employed laying drifting mines. DNO suggested that beginning with the 1913–14 flotilla all destroyers should be fitted to lay mines. It was decided (1912) that four of the 1911–12 programme destroyers (*Paragon, Porpoise, Unity* and *Victor*) would each carry fifteen mines of a new design. In future programmes 20 per cent of destroyers would be fitted to lay moored mines. There was some question of exactly how the mines were to be used, so in December 1912 First Sea Lord Battenberg decided that the policy should remain in abeyance; possibly the destroyers involved would be completed without mines. However, at an April 1913 meeting it was decided that all destroyers of the 'River 'and later classes would be fitted to carry four mines on their upper deck. In fact no destroyer-layable mines were in service in 1914. However, 'L' class destroyers apparently retained mine rails into 1915 (according to the *Mining Manual* issued in 1923, removal of mine rails, which would accommodate four Elia mines each) was authorised only in November 1915.

11. The NID book *Germany: War Vessels 1914* (issued in August: NID 806, NHB) includes tables of German guns and ballistics, but nothing on underwater weapons. Tables of cruiser data do include mine capacity, crediting the old cruisers *Thetis* and *Arcona* with 300 and 400 mines, respectively (Groener I does not mention any mining capacity). It had been reported in 1912 and 1913 that these ships were being (or would be) modified for minelaying. The old cruiser *Berlin* was similarly reported being modified as a minelayer, the number of mines not specified (she actually carried eighty U-mines [ASW mines] in 1915–16). Such modifications would have been broadly equivalent to the minelaying conversions of the British *Apollo* class, undertaken some years earlier. Of modern cruisers, the data tables credited only *Strassburg* and her sisters *Magdeburg, Breslau* and *Stralsund* (100 mines each), but notes in the main text added (correctly) that the *Kolberg* class 'were believed to carry mines'. That applied similarly to the *Magdeburg* class (reported to carry 100 mines each) and to *Pillau* and *Graudenz*, taken over from a Russian order in 1914 ('fitted for rails for about 200 mines' [actually 120]). Of the two specially-built minelayers, *Nautilus* was credited with 200 mines and her near-sister *Albatross* with 600. The data tables did not show any mines on board

destroyers. However, according to the main text, a large number of destroyers were understood to have been fitted for minelaying, including several of the series *S 138–S 161*, one at least of the series *G 174–V 185* and several (reportedly six each) of the series *V 186–G 197*, *V 1–G 12* and *S 13–S 24*. Several had their sterns cut away and mine rails fitted. Another report had some of the *G 192–G 197* series fitted with a plate aft to accommodate six mines, but it did not show up in photographs. Later destroyers had special provision for stowing mines on board; earlier boats (*S 138–V 161* series) reportedly discharged their mines at Cuxhaven after mining exercises. Several had been seen carrying twelve mines each (six on each side, between the funnels). *Koningen Luise* was listed as the only merchant ship earmarked as an auxiliary minelayer.

12. *Koningen Luise* was a new ship (completed 1913) commissioned as an Auxiliary Minelayer B on 3 August 1914. She carried 200 mines. Although the two specially-built minelayers could each carry 400 mines, they could lay only 200 at a time and the Germans did not want to risk them near the British coast until the nights grew darker and German reconnaissance could reveal the pattern of British patrols. The German mobilisation plan, as described in *Krieg zur See*, Nordsee 1, p 95, included six auxiliary minelayers, three for the North Sea and three for the Baltic; three more were added early in the first year of the war. Average speed was 13 to 14 knots; they carried between 150 and 200 mines. The only two of superior speed were the train ferries *Deutschland* and *Preussen* (Sassnitz-Trellsborg ferry service), each of which could carry 400 mines. They could not be employed in the North Sea because of their inferior seakeeping qualities. That left *Koningen Luise*, which began fitting out at Cuxhaven on 1 August and was completed in about 12 hours; she left Wilhelmshaven Roads for the Ems on 4 August. Due to the uncertain situation, she was completed without the planned two 8.8cm guns and when she left had on board only two 3.7cm cannon. She was designated Auxiliary Cruiser B and, according to the German official history, she was ordered to sea upon the outbreak of war (the auxiliary cruisers were designated by letter: *Victoria Louise* was A, *Berlin* was C and *Kaiser Wilhelm der Grosse* was D). Cruiser D was also sent out at this time. Neither was escorted as far as the presumed line of British (close) blockade, a failure the author of *Krieg zur See* attributes to the order to keep the fleet in harbour. The railway ferry *Preussen*, which was considerably larger than *Koningen Luise*, was commissioned on 5 August 1914 as a North Sea minelayer, but she saw no service. The larger railway ferry *Deutschland* was commissioned on 4 August as an auxiliary minelayer for the Baltic. These were apparently the only auxiliary minelayers intended to operate offensively. In addition were two unplanned merchant conversions. The former Norddeutscher Lloyd liner Berlin was converted to a minelayer/auxiliary cruiser (the earlier minelayers had been virtually unarmed) and commissioned on 28 September 1914. Her first mission was to lay mines, capture British fishing vessels and raid trade. One of her mines sank the battleship *Audacious*. On approaching a British freighter, her captain decided that his ship had been recognised and he thought he did not have enough coal to return to Germany; he interned his ship at Trondheim on 18 November 1914. The interned British merchant ship *Vienna* was taken over as the auxiliary minelayer *Meteor*. She made two minelaying sorties near the British Isles, on the second of which (9 August 1915) she was caught by British cruisers and scuttled herself. Further German auxiliary minelayers were intended only to lay defensive minefields.

13. Naval Staff, *History of British Minesweeping in the War* (CB 1553, December 1920, NHB).

14. During 1914–15 Germans surface ships laid 3001 mines, according to the 1920 British Minesweeping Staff History. The first was the 5 August minefield laid by *Koningen Luise* in the Southwold area (about 180 mines, number uncertain because she was sunk at sea). On 26 August *Albatross* laid 200 in the Humber Approach while her near-sister *Nautilus* laid 194 in the Tyne Approach. On 26 October, *Berlin* laid 200 off Tory Island (this was the field which sank HMS *Audacious*). On 3 November the light cruiser *Stralsund* laid 130 mines in a zig-zag pattern near Smiths Knoll. On 16 December the cruiser *Kolberg* laid 100 mines off Scarborough during the German raid, for a 1914 total of 1004 (elsewhere the history claims that only 850 mines were laid in 1914). All of these mines were moored to float at depths of 2m or 2.5m (in one case, maximum depth was 3.5m).

15. In the spring of 1915 German surface ships mined both the Eastern Dogger Bank (480 mines in two lines of 240 each) and the Swarte Bank (360 mines), the mines being moored to float at, respectively, depths of 5m and 4.5m. A field (281 mines) was laid North of Terschelling in September 1915 specifically to damage the Harwich Force (it was revealed by a chart captured in 1917). Hence its mines were set to float at shallower depths, 2.5m to 4m. They did not damage, even though the Harwich force often passed through the field. The British concluded that the mines had been mis-set. Once they knew about the field, they swept part of it in 1918. On 7 August a field of 374 mines was laid in the approach to the Moray Firth by the minelayer *Meteor*, the mines set to float at depths between 4 and 6 m. On 31 December a field of 252 mines was laid west of the Orkneys, to float at depths between 4m and 4.5m. There was also a field (250 mines) laid in the White Sea, specifically to catch merchant ships (hence the mines were set to float at 2m depth). According to the British Staff History, it was successful 'to some extent', but it was largely cleared by the winter weather. It was discovered when a British merchant ship was mined on 13 June 1915 when approaching Archangel. Six trawlers were sent from Lowestoft to sweep this field (two more were later added). The British found out about the Dogger Bank minefield soon after it was laid and they assumed that it was intended to catch any British force pursuing German battlecruisers as they had after the Dogger Bank battle. The British therefore assumed that the field was a seaward protection to the line between the Elbe and Scapa Flow and accordingly they secretly declared a dangerous zone to their fleet. Fleet sweepers explored the assumed line and found nothing, but on 20 March some mines were destroyed. A further sweep found nothing, but on 20 May a Norwegian tanker was mined and efforts were redoubled because the minefield was likely to restrict the freedom of action of the Grand Fleet. At the same time it was considered essential that the Germans not discover that the British were aware of their minefield. Ultimately the minefield was ineffective, as it claimed no British warships, but according to the British Staff History it considerably stimulated work both on sweeping and on ship self-protection.

16. The author of the British Staff History noted that German submarines often ran trials in the Hoofden and speculated that the initial field was a practical experiment, the mines being laid in the area occupied by British ships shelling the Flanders coast.

17. As speculated by the author of the British Staff History. CMS suggested early in 1917 that the British could turn this confidence against the Germans by leaving some selected areas uncleared. That could not be done until the end of 1917, when traffic control was tight enough to keep merchant ships out of the uncleared areas. At the same time protective minefields were laid off Portsmouth, Beachy Head, Portland, Plymouth and Penzance. Navigational lights were kept burning, but some lightships had their lights dimmed and they were moved slightly. It was expected that each minelayer would make full use of the navigational aids available in the form of these lights. The Germans suffered a large percentage of their losses in these areas. Each of the early UC-boats had six minelaying tubes, each of which carried two mines. Initially UC-boats laid their mines in groups of two or three, but after a time they laid all twelve, so that minesweepers would seek mines in a group until all twelve had been neutralised.

18. According to the British Staff History, victims were three destroyers, five transports or supply ships, one hospital ship, twenty-four merchant ships, two Trinity House vessels (lighthouse service vessels), twenty-four neutral merchant ships, ten fishing boats, fifteen minesweepers and nine patrol trawlers or drifters.

19. According to the Staff History, the German records of the High Seas Fleet flotilla were more accurate than those of the Flanders Flotilla.

20. After the war, much was made of supposed German spy activity which had betrayed Kitchener. The Staff History shows clearly that the mines were laid away from their intended positions. On the other hand, it identifies the Moray Firth fields specifically with an attempt to mine the battleship *Marlborough* on passage from the Tyne (where she was repaired after Jutland) to Cromarty.

21. According to the Staff History, p 45, the post-war German statement gave a total of 10,237 mines laid in British Home waters during the war, of which the Royal Navy swept 8316 before the Armistice. Another 2384 floating mines were sunk off the British coast, but many of them probably did not come from fields laid in British waters. The author of the Staff History considered German mine moorings much more reliable than British, except in the last three months of the war, after the British had conducted numerous experiments.

22. *U 71* class minelayers had two bow tubes and four torpedoes. UC IIs had three tubes, two at the bow and one aft. They also had a raised bow, which lengthened each of the mine tubes so that it could accommodate three rather than two mines.

23. According to the minesweeping Staff History, *Wolf*'s minefields were discovered because a captive on board, a British merchant ship master, threw bottles overboard from time to time giving details of the ship's activities. One of them was picked up by natives in Toli-Toli in the Celebes (Netherlands East Indies) on 9 December 1917. Eventually it reached the British consul-general in Batavia (now Jakarta), who informed C-in-C China. A second bottle, thrown off during the ship's return to Germany, was found off the Norwegian coast was dated 10 February 1918. It revealed the final 110-mine field, but the writer was unsure of its position (he did not realise how far north *Wolf* had gone). The Aden mines were swept by small local tugs using 6ft kites and 2in wire, crewed by Somalis with a few British naval ratings.

24. As proof, the Staff History cited an incident immediately after the Armistice. The light cruiser *Kolberg*, carrying a German Admiral, was ordered to meet C-in-C Grand Fleet off the Firth of Forth. The rendezvous was provided only as the cruiser neared the British coast. She arrived late, the apology being that she had had to steam southward around the barrage of 340 German mines laid in equidistant groups – all of which had been swept.

25. In 1918 the British Mediterranean sweep force was based at Gibraltar (four drifters), Malta (four light paddlers, nine trawlers and eight motor launches), Alexandria (seven trawlers), Port Said (five light paddlers), Mudros (seven trawlers), Saloniki (seven trawlers), Trebuki (two trawlers), Syria (two Greek tugs and one trawler), Suda Bay (two trawlers), the Doro Channel (two trawlers) and the Thermia Channel (two trawlers). The force in Sierra Leone was two whalers and four drifters. At Simonstown in South Africa (the Cape base) were four whalers. On the North America and West Indies station there were units at St Johns in Newfoundland (six trawlers), at Sydney-Cape Breton (four trawlers), at Halifax (eight trawlers), at Kingstown in Jamaica (five drifters), at Barbados (two local vessels), at St. Lucia (two local vessels) and at Trinidad (seven motor launches). Australia and New Zealand had a few (unspecified) local craft. On the East Indies station were units at Aden (six local tugs etc), Colombo (six trawlers), Bombay (six local vessels), Karachi (two local vessels), Madras (three local vessels), Calcutta (two local vessels) and Rangoon (four steam launches). On the China station there were units at Penang (six steam launches), Singapore (six steam launches) and Hong Kong (five local vessels).

26. Notes on British First World War minelaying operations are based on the introductory section of the Naval Staff History, *British Mining Operations 1939-1945* (BR 1736(56)(1)). A *History of British Minefields* produced after the First World War was not available (it is referenced in the 1924 *Mining Manual*, CB 1592 (of which Vol III is in NARA II).

27. Figures for 1918 are given in the 1924 *Mining Manual*. In the list which follows, numbers in parentheses are ships being converted at the end of the war. Not included in the list are ships lost (the old cruiser *Ariadne*, one trawler and two 'E' class submarines) and ships converted for minelaying but discarded during the war. The list was: six (three) converted merchantmen, two (one) old warships (the obsolete battleship *London* and the cruisers *Ariadne* and *Amphitrite*, of which *Ariadne* was lost), eleven light cruisers (fitted 1917, of which only *Royalist* and *Blanche* laid appreciable numbers), thirty destroyers and leaders, sixteen trawlers, 0 (four) shallow-draught tunnel vessels, fifteen (ten) CMBs (40ft and 55ft type), 0 (two) large CMBs (70ft type), eighteen motor launches, one (two) motor lighters, four 'E' class submarines, two (six) 'L' class submarines and six (two) paddlers (for controlled L minefields). Of the destroyers, the 20th Flotilla, led by *Abdiel*, laid considerable numbers of mines. Trawlers were used mainly in the Dover area. Of the motor launches, six were converted to lay French Breguet mines in the Mediterranean. The motor lighters (*X/149* and two others) were converted in 1917 and 1918 specifically for use in the Thames Estuary (thirty-eight mines each). This list does not include the 'large light cruiser' *Courageous*, fitted in 1917 to carry 220 mines, but never used as a minelayer.

28. Navy Department Office of Naval Records and Library Publication No. 2, *The Northern Barrage and Other Mining Activities* (Washington: GPO, 1920). British January 1918 comments are from ADM 116/1349.

29. William N Still, Jr., *Crisis at Sea: The United States Navy in European Waters in World War I* (University Press of Florida, 2006), p 427 makes it clear that at the outbreak of war opinion in the United States strongly favoured creating some sort of North Sea barrier, whereas the British and Admiral Sims roundly rejected what was offered. Secretary of the Navy Daniels kept pursuing the idea and as early as 11 April Admiral de Chair, who had commanded the Northern Patrol, told the Admiralty that the Americans were strongly committed. The British apparently saw the idea as typical American grandiosity, untempered by realistic war experience. Still also records opposition by CNO Benson as late as November 1917.

30. It was described to OpNav in an 18 July 1917 letter.

31. The printed report of the conference is in ADM 1/8934. The first item on the agenda was a possible close offensive in German waters, given the accession of a large number of older ships from the United States. Item 2 was the alternative, 'a mine or net barrage in German waters or further afield'. Jellicoe proposed two alternatives, (a) an efficient mine barrage which would completely shut in the North Sea, requiring 100,000 mines (not available for some time) and (b) a barrage of mine nets (impractical). Jellicoe stressed the limited success of minelaying to date (but he thought the U-boats were being compelled to use Dutch territorial waters due to mining of the Heligoland Bight). The British were about to lay large numbers of the new H mines, but they could not produce the required 100,000 quickly enough. The problem was whether to lay them as they were produced, or to wait until there were enough for the full barrage. He much preferred the latter. The conference decided that (a) could not be undertaken until an adequate supply of mines of a satisfactory type was assured. At no point was the new US mine discussed. The US and Italian representatives undertook to consider how far they could supply the necessary personnel to assemble a large stock of mines. The conference also considered an offensive in the Adriatic against enemy submarine bases and assistance by Allied fleets to protect traffic in the White Sea against submarines. According to Still, *Crisis at Sea*, p 429, before the meeting the Admiralty War Staff offered tentative approval, if the United States provided the mines. That may have been nothing more than an attempt at conciliate to convince the Americans to provide more assistance. The British formally accepted the US proposal in October 1917 after the Cabinet approved it on 23 October. At this conference Jellicoe announced that with improvements in hydrophones it was possible to hunt effectively, using a trawler flotilla in the North Sea working with destroyers and kite balloons towed by sloops. He planned to use thirty-two trawlers, about four sloops and eight destroyers, for which purpose some trawlers had to be withdrawn from patrols.

32. The post-war official history of the barrage emphasises Mr. Roosevelt's crucial role in supporting the general idea of a barrage. Still, *Crisis at Sea*, p 428 notes that although Roosevelt certainly did not originate the idea (as some claimed), he made it happen. Rear Admiral Frederick Harris, Chief of the Bureau of Yards and Docks and a strong exponent, wrote later that without Roosevelt, the barrage would never have happened. The Bureau prepared the sketches the designer of the K-pistol (Commander Fullinwider) used to sell the project to Roosevelt. One of Roosevelt's biographers considered the project Roosevelt's single greatest wartime achievement.

33. N Dogoroff, 'Naval Mining Operations (A Russian View)', translation published in the October–November 1930 *Monthly Information Bulletin* of ONI, from the NWC Archives. No source is given, but it was probably the historical magazine published at that time in Russian by ex-Tsarist naval officers. Dogoroff wrote in the article that during the war he had supervised the minelaying operations of the *Rurik* off the German coast. In 1907 special mining depots were established at Kronstadt, Sevastopol and Vladivostok, to serve the three fleets; floating depots were established on the mine transports *Amur*, *Yenesei* and *Volya* in the Baltic, the *Roog* and *Doonai* in the Black Sea and the *Mongoogai* in Vladivostok. Beginning in 1908 special mining officers were commissioned to run the mining service. The chief of naval forces was made chief of the mining service. The next step was creation of a minelaying squadron. From this time on, fleet manoeuvres always included minelayers and minelaying operations were carried out with the entire fleet. The concept was to compel the enemy to conduct the battle over them. In the event of an enemy breakthrough, the fleet would retreat, laying mines as it ran towards a second line of minefields protected by the fire of shore batteries. When war broke out, the Russians expected that the Germans would soon appear before Kronstadt, so they immediately laid their planned initial line of minefields.

According to Dogoroff, the Black Sea Fleet commander did not belief in minefields, hence did not block the entrances to the Black Sea after the *Goeben* and *Breslau* got to Turkey. Had he done so, the ships would not have been able to bombard Sevastopol, the act which brought Turkey definitely into the war. Ironically, once they did enter the Black Sea, they sank the minelayer *Prut* with 750 mines on board. The ONI translator added that Dogoroff failed to mention that at Sevastopol *Goeben* passed over a field of controlled mines whose current happened to be switched off.

34. As described in the standard British minesweeping handbook (which was reprinted by the US Navy), the sweeps on either quarter were towed from a central 6ft kite (towed by the sweeper) which controlled its depth. The outer end of each sweep was held down by a 12ft towing spar with fins. Since the spars had a tendency to dive and also to push outwards, they were suspended from rectangular hydroplaning floats, the rudders on which kept the spars out on the quarter. Cutters were attached to the sweep wire close to the towing spars. The 1917 British *Handbook of Minesweeping* added that there were two types: a 150-fathom sweep using a 7ft float, for trawlers, paddlers, twin-screw minesweepers and light paddlers (spread 220 yds at 6 knots); and a 100-fathom sweep with a 5ft sweep, for destroyers, drifters and motor launches (spread 100 yds at 15 knots and 140 yds at 6 knots). At that time the sweep was normally fitted with a cutter, into which mine moorings would slide. At night an explosive grapnel (2^1/4lb service primer of dried guncotton) might be used instead. The explosion of the grapnel would part the mine mooring and destroy the mine (otherwise it would float to the surface unseen).

35. The 1912 version of the Royal Navy's sweep manual (as held by the US Naval War College) gives the advantages of the new sweep as simplicity, safety and no need for special torpedo officers and ratings. Against that, when caught a mine had to be separately dealt with and it might come to the surface and float free. To the author of the handbook, this was not so great a problem as it might appear, since the sweep would probably fire the mine. Any mine which fulfilled the requirements of the 1907 Hague Treaty would self-neutralise when it broke its mooring – an unrealistically optimistic view. The manual listed different employments for sweepers: an internal sweep for the internal waters of defended ports; an external sweep for those ports using torpedo boats (to be relieved by trawlers before or shortly after the outbreak of war); fleet sweepers (torpedo gunboats) for more open waters (distinguished from the local flotillas of torpedo boats and hired trawlers); and picket boats and steam pinnaces carried by all battleships and first class cruisers, which were suited to sweeping a short channel for a fleet to pass through when more specialised sweepers were not available. Under standard conditions gunboats were expected to sweep 400 yds apart at 12 knots, trawlers 400 yds apart at 9 knots, torpedo boats 300 yds apart at 10 knots, steam launches (harbour service craft, etc) 200 yds apart at 7 knots and picket boats (45ft and above) 150 yds apart at 7 knots. Torpedo gunboats had swept successfully under very favourable conditions as much as 3^1/2 cables (700 yds) apart. To go to 10 knots, they had to run their engines with revolutions for 14 knots and the kites ran 6 or 8ft shallower. Normally kites had to run at a depth of 6 fathoms (36ft). It was better to sweep against than with the current, especially if it had a strength of over 2 knots.

36. According to the Staff History, the 'A' Sweep destroyed over 30,000 mines during and after the war; the Germans later claimed that they had laid 34,700, so this must have been the great bulk of the mines countered.

37. The US Navy built tug-type 'Bird' class sweepers. The British liked their seakeeping qualities, but commented that their draught (11ft or 12ft) was too deep for wartime sweeping.

38. Examples given in the Staff History were sweeping and marking (buoying) a fairway for the fleet to follow; keeping the entrance to a fleet base clear; searching ahead of a moving fleet (warning of mines); and working as a submarine screen ahead of a fleet, then proceeding ahead and sweeping and buoying an entrance to the base.

39. According to the 1912 Royal Navy handbook (as held by the US Naval War College), the fleet would normally be preceded by three pairs of sweepers in line ahead. On catching a mine the leading pair of sweepers hoisted a signal or fired a gun, then turned together 4 points (45°) to port or starboard (as chosen by the senior officer of the pair) and after about 4 minutes on this course they could slip the sweep, releasing the mine. The mine position would then be buoyed. The pair would then return to station 4 cables (800 yds) ahead of the fleet and resume sweeping. The next (centre) pair would meanwhile proceed on course until they were 10 cables (2000 yds) ahead of the fleet, then reducing speed to 7 knots (sweeping speed). The rear pair would continue to keep station 3 cables (600 yds) astern of the former centre pair. The fleet would reduce its speed to 7 knots by signal until all the sweepers were again in station with their sweeps out. The fleet would resume normal speed once the sweepers had all signalled that they were ready. Similar procedures would be followed if the other pairs caught mines. Alternative formations had also been tested. The handbook also described the use of trawlers as sweepers, noting that six of the largest type had been bought in 1909. Their normal maximum speed was about 9 knots, but maximum sweep speed was 6 knots. The normal crew was nine. This handbook included a chapter on buoyage of war channels and destruction of swept-up mines.

40. According to the Staff History, this problem had been revealed by a 1910 exercise by Admiralty trawlers which tried to sweep the war exit channel from the Nore to the Tongue Lightship. During the first part of the war channels were sometimes incompletely swept due to inaccurate navigation by sweepers and the Admiralty found itself setting up a special minesweeping school during the latter part of the war.

41. The first skipper of the RNR(T) signed on in February 1911. Plans were later enlarged to 142 reserve trawlers, on the theory that a third would not be available for mobilisation. In fact on mobilisation there were only enough crews for ninety-four trawlers. At the Armistice the RNR(T) consisted of 39,000 officers and men; about a

quarter were employed on minesweeping. It was soon realised that, however large the reserve, there would be an appreciable delay before trawlers could be mobilised and that they would be unavailable for peacetime training. In 1909 eight trawlers were bought from their owners. The issue was considered urgent enough not to wait for the next year's Estimates. They were the peacetime training boats, but they could not operate as a flotilla because a pair had to be assigned to each major fishing port where reservists were to be trained. The mobilisation ports were Aberdeen, Granton, North Shields, Hull, Grimsby, Milford and Fleetwood. Each was assigned a mobilising officer; by 8 August 1914, 96 hired trawlers had been mobilised.

42. The picket boat option was impractical; they lacked the power to use an 'A' Sweep. This option was never exercised during the war.

43. Only five of the original gunboats were available, one being under refit; the sixth was a fishery protection ship (the other three fishery protection ships were retained at Lowestoft). Of the seventy-four trawlers immediately available, twenty were assigned to the Firth of Forth and six of these went to Scapa. Another twelve were 'detachable', to make up numbers as needed until the full 100 were available. This is from a table on p.8 of the Staff History. In addition, there were two naval trawlers at each of the Home (naval) Ports. Hopper barges at Home Ports were to be relieved by trawlers. By 10 August another 100 'special reserve' trawlers were ordered commissioned; all of them were being fitted out at Lowestoft (at the rate of six per day) by 21 August. Lowestoft was organised as a full naval base.

44. The Staff History reports the loss of two minesweeping trawlers in the Tyne Section on 27 August as a further incentive to try an alternative. A flotilla of drifters led by the gunboat *Speedy* left Lowestoft on 1 September. The gunboat and the drifters *Eyrie* and *Linsdell* were all mined and sunk.

45. This sortie, incidentally, illustrated the navigation problem. Until the Germans provided mining charts after the Armistice, the British had no way of knowing exactly where they were trying to lay mines. The British found a line of mines off the Tyne, laid by *Albatross* (escorted by the cruiser *Stuttgart*) on 26 August. The chart showed a zigzag running from Souter Point to Blyth, four to eight miles from the coast, but they were actually laid considerably farther to seaward. A field off the Humber was laid more accurately; it consisted of two short four-mile lines and was particularly destructive of fishing vessels.

46. An Admiral, East Coast Minesweeping (AMS) was appointed. Rear Admiral E F B Charlton had no previous sweeping experience. One of his first acts was to fly over the Humber minefield; he found that mines could not be spotted in the thick water and shoal conditions. He also realised that the deep draught of the trawlers was a serious problem; they would have to work at high tide, or when the tide was so strong that the mines would dip. Moreover, the weather was about to become too bad for intensive minesweeping. Policy therefore changed from an attempt to clear the supposed large minefield to keeping an East Coast war channel open, buoyed for day use only.

47. According to the Staff History, French sardine boats with 3ft draught (compared to 6ft for motor launches) proved particularly useful. They could tow kite balloons and they worked with the specialised kite balloon vessels.

48. The Staff History quotes the April 1917 minesweeping statement. A submarine with torpedoes and long-range guns can see targets about six miles away, but the same size submarine can spread her mines sparsely over three miles in one direction. Thus the submarine can strike further with her torpedoes, but the closer she is to land, the less effectively she can use them. The shallower the water, moreover, the better chance of saving a ship and the less the loss of life. Moreover, shipping is more easily controlled and patrols can be more concentrated using shore lookouts. The swept channel allowed the British, not the submarines, to choose the area of action. When there were outlying shoals, the Germans never attempted torpedo attacks at all. Hence the enormous volume of mining in such areas. In 1917 the British began to lay defensive minefields to protect the war channel along the Yorkshire coast, supplying the protection offered by shoals further south. There was some question as to the value of a war channel without seaward protection, as it concentrated U-boat targets. According to the minesweeping Staff History, the war channel was retained even when not protected because it much simplified minesweeping and concentrated patrols on a definite line of water near the coast. It was therefore retained through the war and extended north to May Island, for the Norwegian convoys, in the latter part of 1917.

49. According to the Staff History, upwards of thirty smaller paddlers, ten small tugs built by the War Office for Mesopotamia, eighteen Scotch motor drifters and numerous ordinary drifters were taken up. At the same time 100 'Hunts' and 300 drifters were ordered. It was decided that when the 'Hunts' and the Admiralty drifters became available and the requirements of various areas settled, they would as far as possible replace heavy-draught trawlers, freeing the latter for anti-submarine work.

50. Table in the Staff History, p 45. It distinguished between fast sweepers – sloops, gunboats, twin screw and paddle sweepers – and slow sweepers – trawlers, drifters and motor launches. The number of fast sweepers grew from 93 to 112 to 122 on 1 January 1918, despite losses. The number of slow sweepers grew from 430 to 531 on 1 July 1917, then fell to 509 on 1 January 1918. Heavy losses during 1917 included deeper-draught trawlers used to sweep a danger area or sink moored mines seen awash before motor launches re-swept the area at low tide.

51. According to the Staff History, shallower-draught ships were not suitable because it was impossible to find a suitable towing point in a small fast ship squatting by the stern; because it was difficult to work a paravane in a small craft; because a shallow-running paravane wire would be more liable to make contact with the mine itself than with its mooring, hence trigger the mine; because of the serious effect on speed; and because the constant starting and stopping of a minesweeper would make the device ineffective.

52. This sweep is described in the 1917 Royal Navy *Handbook of Minesweeping* (CB 0378). A US Navy copy is in the ONI collection in RG 38 (NARA) as Register No. 10574 U-4-a. US sweep manuals issued in 1917 were copies of this and related British manuals. The *Handbook* was issued on 29 May 1917, superseding CB 62 of 1914. This file includes Addendum No. 1 of 1918 (CB 0378A), which appears already to have been inserted into the original 1917 book. Although it could be towed at a higher speed than any other existing sweep, there was no means of ensuring that the paravanes were working accurately, so there was no way to be sure that the sweep was deep enough. It was therefore considered unsatisfactory for clearing a minefield. Sweep was about 120 yds. Each sweep wire was held down by a 'C' Type Paravane and there was an additional Depressor paravane towed right astern of the ship to hold down the fore ends of the sweep wires. Typical sweep depth was 45ft. Each paravane carried a cutter, which was considered good for two or three mine moorings. According to the Handbook, maximum towing speed was 26 knots. Trials showed that a destroyer could turn 16 points (180°) with helm 10° over without interfering in any way with the depth keeping or total spread of the sweep (ships had even turned with 20° helm).

53. British ships already had a standard (Service) explosive sweep. The *Annual Report of the Torpedo School* (HMS *Vernon*) for 1905 includes a description of the Japanese method of minesweeping, which was considered similar to that used by the Russians. Two light surface vessels towed a buoyed surface line between them. From it was suspended a deeper line carrying grapnels intended to seize mooring cables. The mines thus seized were towed into shallow water and dumped there. Trailers suspended from both cables kept the grapnel line roughly below the surface line. This might well be seen as the basis for British sweeps. The 1906 report described trials of a rapid explosive sweep proposed by Captain Ogilvy, suitable for torpedo boats and destroyers. Trials in the Mediterranean using fleet boats at Malta showed that the kites used with the sweep worked very well and were easy to handle; that the wire carried away too easily; that more practice was needed with the drum used to handle the wire; and that boats had to turn very carefully to avoid fouling the sweep. The experiments were generally satisfactory, but much more practice was required. The *Vernon* report stated that the usual quarterly practice with the Service explosive sweep would be suspended in ships supplied with the new rapid explosive sweep.

54. A modified 1915 design was adopted for boats after *M 27* and a second modified 1916 design after *M 57*. The 1918 version was adapted as a U-boat flotilla leader for the Mediterranean and for groups of U-cruisers. The highest First World War number was *M 176*, but many were cancelled at the end of the war: *M 141–M 143*, *M 148–M 149*, *M 153–M 156*, *M 159–M 176*. A few others were not completed. Planned U-boat tenders, none of which was completed, were *UT 1–UT 7*. There were also shallow-draught sweepers (Flachgehende Minensuchboote, FM), *FM 1–FM 66*. The first was completed in July 1918. Some are listed as having been rejected by the navy before completion.

55. Technical details from ADM 186/428, *German Navy (Torpedoes, Mines, etc.)* (CB 1182 W), March 1919.

56. Sweep depth data from Tactical Order 19, 'A possible application of the rapid mine searching gear ahead of the Fleet when under way', undated, in the collection of wartime Tactical Orders published by the Royal Navy as *German Navy Tactical Orders April 1920 (CB 1548)*, NHB. These data do not quite tally with those in the March 1918 list. It probably corresponded to the light kite MS gear which was credited with sweep widths of either 109 or 164 yds and minimum and maximum sweep speeds of 7 and 11 knots, with minimum sweep depth 3.3 fathoms (19.8ft) and maximum depths of, respectively, 7.3 and 6.3 fathoms.

57. 'Summary of Mine-Seeking and Sweeping Gear and Their Employment', 10 March 1918, in the collection of wartime Tactical Orders published by the Royal Navy as *German Navy Tactical Orders April 1920 (CB 1548)*, NHB.

58. This sweep width seems excessive and it may reflect an incorrect translation of metres (in the original) into yards. If the figures are in feet, the sweep width becomes 100 to 166m. The table of which ships had which devices does not list the MR series at all.

59. ADM 137/1211, 'Policy: Anti-Submarine July-December 1916' includes a discussion of a partly successful French experiment to see whether their submarines could hide from aerial detection and, conversely, to see whether mines and submerged submarines could be seen from the air. Given reports of German success in mine-hunting from the air, the British liaison officer reported that the French had concluded that the Germans were using some kind of filter (he did not know what sort, but it was probably a polarising filter). The report was dated 15 August 1916 (p 20 of the file).

Chapter 16. Lessons for the Future

1. This argument is developed in Brock Millman, *Pessimism and British War Policy 1916-1918* (London: Frank Cass, 2001). Millman points out that at the end of 1916 British war aims were still undetermined, hence the British Government could not tell what a satisfactory end to the war might mean. The army argued that the Germans might be led to offer a tolerable peace if they were badly enough hammered on the Western Front, but that was hardly a set of war aims. The navy wanted more but did not have definite war aims – which was reasonable, since the war had begun as a reaction to the German attack. The new Prime Minister Lloyd George was inclined to seek peace, but only if a grand strategy could be formulated to determine just what conditions the British should set. In Millman's view, by late 1916 the civilians in the government considered victory most unlikely and the disasters of 1917 reinforced that view. These disasters were both the dramatic loss of shipping and the indecisive battle in Flanders, ultimately undertaken to prevent the collapse of the Western Front in the wake of the big French army mutiny.

2. Wesley K Wark, *The Ultimate Enemy: British Intelligence and Nazi Germany 1933-1939* (Cornell University Press, 1985) points out that the British became more optimistic about January 1939 even though data showed that the Germans were better-armed than they had been. He does not observe that by January 1939 the evolving British national air defence system was about to become operational, making a knockout blow impossible (in British minds). In fact the knockout blow was never a reality before the nuclear age.

3. The need for and the advantages of, such a staff are the theme of Sir Maurice Hankey's memoir *The Supreme Command 1914-1918*.

4. For the development and later evolution of such situational awareness, see the present author's *Network-Centric Warfare*.

5. For the impact of inter-war decisions, some of them attributable to the RAF, see the author's *British Carrier Aviation: The Evolution of the Ships and Their Aircraft* (London: Conway Maritime Press, 1989). For example, in 1931 the Royal Navy became aware that the US Navy was using deck parks. British adoption of this practice would roughly have doubled the capacity of each British carrier. The problem was acute for the navy because British carriers designed during the First World War had unusually small hangars (later, the policy against deck parks severely limited the capacity of the armoured carriers). The Air Ministry refused to increase the number of aircraft allowed per carrier because it expected that a new arms limitation treaty would apply to aircraft. In that case the RAF land-based force would have to pay a penalty for any increase in fleet aircraft. Apparently no one thought to reverse policy once it became obvious that the arms control agreement would never be signed. Because the Royal Navy did not adopt deck parks, yet badly wanted a large air striking force, in the 1930s it planned to place catapult-launched strike aircraft on board battleships and cruisers. That in turn set the take-off speed of a loaded torpedo bomber at 60 knots, the end speed of the standard catapult – which shaped the performance of the aircraft involved, the Fairey Swordfish. The Royal Navy adopted US-style deck parks during the Second World War. Without them, it could never have accommodated the necessary combination of strike aircraft and fighters on board its fleet carriers.

6. For details of Dreyer's argument, see this author's *British Cruisers: Two World Wars and After*. The parallel with Churchill's 1941 decision to send the two capital ships is striking; he apparently thought that, hiding within the thousands of islands of what is now Indonesia, they would absorb considerable Japanese effort. The Japanese certainly took them seriously as a threat to their invasion of Malaya, as is evident in their accounts of the operation to destroy the two ships.

Sources

1. Primary Sources Not Referenced in the Text

ADM 1/8460/149 Gunnery Information from Jutland
ADM 116/1670 Grand Fleet Secret Orders 1915–18
ADM 116/1672 Grand Fleet Secret Orders 1915–17
ADM 137/260 Home Fleet Orders Pre-war
ADM 137/265 Grand Fleet Secret Orders
ADM 137/288 Grand Fleet Battle Orders 1914–15
ADM 137/289 Grand Fleet Battle Orders 1916–18
ADM 137/469 Grand Fleet Operations Orders 1914–15
ADM 137/470 Grand Fleet Operations Orders 1916–17
ADM 137/471 Grand Fleet Operations Orders 1917–18
ADM 137/473 Grand Fleet Tactics 1917
ADM 137/500 Staff Papers 1915–17
ADM 137/511 Staff Appreciations 1917–18
ADM 137/834 Operations Committee Minutes and Memoranda 1917–18
ADM 137/965 Policy: Anti-Invasion I, 1914
ADM 137/968 Policy: ASW 1914
ADM 137/969 Policy: Armed Merchant Cruisers 1914
ADM 137/987 Policy 1914 (I)
ADM 137/988 Policy 1914 (II)
ADM 137/995 Grand Fleet Policy 1914
ADM 137/1054 Policy Jan–June 1915
ADM 137/1073 Grand Fleet Policy Jan–June 1915
ADM 137/1089 Dardanelles various papers Jan–April 1915
ADM 137/1090 Dardanelles various papers May and June 1915
ADM 137/1097 ASW Policy July–Dec 1915
ADM 137/1098 Policy July–Dec 1915
ADM 137/1103 Grand Fleet Policy July–Dec 1915
ADM 137/1143 Dardanelles Despatch of Vessels July–Dec 1915
ADM 137/1144 Dardanelles Various July–Dec 1915
ADM 137/1145 Dardanelles Various Sep–Oct 1915
ADM 137/1146 Dardanelles Various Nov 1915–Jan 1916
ADM 137/1159 Policy Jan–Feb 1916
ADM 137/1161 Policy May–June 1916
ADM 137/1165 Grand Fleet Various Papers Jan–May 1916
ADM 137/1207 Grand Fleet Various Papers June–Dec 1916
ADM 137/1211 ASW Policy July–Dec 1916
ADM 137/1216 Policy July–Dec 1916
ADM 137/1243 Dover Patrol: German Raid 26 Oct 1916 etc
ADM 137/1329 Policy IV of 1917
ADM 137/1330 Policy V of 1917
ADM 137/1331 Policy VI of 1917
ADM 137/1332 Policy VII of 1917
ADM 137/1333 Policy VIII of 1917
ADM 137/1334 Policy IX of 1917
ADM 137/1541 Policy I of 1918
ADM 137/1542 Policy II of 1918
ADM 137/1543 Policy III of 1918
ADM 137/1544 Policy IV of 1918
ADM 137/1545 Policy V of 1918
ADM 137/1546 Policy VI of 1918
ADM 137/1547 Policy VII of 1918

ADM 137/1548 Policy VIII of 1918
ADM 137/1643 Jutland. Additional Papers
ADM 137/1644 Jutland – Later Reports (German Report on Jutland)
ADM 137/1645 Post-Jutland Changes 1916
ADM 137/1646 Grand Fleet Special Papers 1915–18
ADM 137/1926 Grand Fleet Submarines General including ASW
ADM 137/1927 Grand Fleet ASW (including Bomb Lance)
ADM 137/1929 Grand Fleet ASW Weapons (Mainly Depth Charges)
ADM 137/1931 Grand Fleet Decoys (Q-Ships)
ADM 137/1932 Grand Fleet Defense Against Submarine Attacks
ADM 137/1936 Grand Fleet Strategy
ADM 137/1943 Grand Fleet Miscellaneous Battles 1914 (including Heligoland)
ADM 137/2018 – 2026 Grand Fleet Orders and Memos not for General Circulation
ADM 137/2027 Grand Fleet Post-Jutland Committees Pt 1
ADM 137/2028 Grand Fleet Post-Jutland Committees Pt 2
ADM 137/2029 Grand Fleet Post-Jutland Committees Pt 3
ADM 137/2078–2093 Harwich Force
ADM 137/2094–2103 Dover Patrol
ADM 137/2129–2135 Battle Cruiser Force Records, with Battle Orders in 2135
ADM 137/4052 Grand Fleet Orders including Gun and Torpedo
ADM 137/4055 Grand Fleet Battle Instructions 1918
ADM 137/4173 ASW Equipment
ADM 137/4313 German W/T instructions (translated)
ADM 137/4715 German High Seas Fleet organization 1914
ADM 186/429 *The German Admiralty's Views on Unrestricted Submarine Warfare* (translation of a German document in the possession of a German staff officer with the Turkish army; published by the British as CB 01381A, April 1919)
ADM 186/564 Miscellaneous technical data on U-boats (CB 1489 and CB 1406)
ADM 275/22 *Review of German Cruiser Warfare 1914–1918* (1940: OU 6337(40))
HW 7/1 through /3: W F Clarke and Frank Birch, *A Contribution to the History of German Naval Warfare 1914–1918*. Vol I (HW 7/1) is *The Fleet in Action*; Vol II (HW 7/2) is *The Fleet in Being* (in effect a complete ship list), and Vol III is miscellaneous notes including a list of publications held by Room 40. Birch prefaces the series with the comment that this is actually what happened, because Room 40 knew what the Germans were doing. For a time Vol I was to have been published as a CB, but that was rejected in the 1920s partly because of potential embarrassment to the Admiralty: if it knew so much, why was it not so successful? There was also fear that information in the volumes would contribute to the acrimony over Jutland and other actions.

2. Ships' Covers

Z-Whalers (Cover 342)
'Flower' Class Sloops (Covers 351 through 351F)
Paddle Sweepers (Cover 355)
Convoy Sloops (Covers 381 and 381A)

Note that the P-class Cover had very little content. Nor were the relevant submarine covers useful for policy or design information.

3. Printed Official Sources

Royal Navy Documents:

BR 1736(56)(1), Naval Staff History: *British Mining Operations 1939–1945* (1973; includes First World War material)

BR 3043: *The Development of HM Submarines From Holland No.1 (1901) to Porpoise* (1930) (January 1979. by A N Harrison)

British Naval Staff Monographs (Fleet Issue)

Vol I: Coronel, German cruisers in Pacific, Falklands, *Goeben* and *Breslau*

Vol II: East Africa to July 1916, Cameroons 1914

Vol III: Passage of Expeditionary Force 1914; Patrol Flotillas at Outbreak of War; Heligoland; Operations vs Raids on Northeast Coast; Dogger Bank

Vol IV: Operations in Mesopotamia and the Persian Gulf

Vol V: Eastern Squadrons 1914

Vol VI: Dover Command Vol I

Vol VII: Tenth Cruiser Squadron I, Baltic 1914

Vol VIII: Mediterranean 1914–15

Vol IX: Atlantic Ocean 1914–15 including Coronel and Falklands (Atlantic I and II)

Vol X: Home Waters I (to 27 Aug 1914)

Vol XI: Home Waters II, Sept and Oct 1914

Vol XII: Home Waters III, Nov 1914 to Jan 1915

Vol XIII: Home Waters IV, Feb to July 1915

Vol XIV: Home Waters V, July to Oct 1915

Vol XV: Home Waters VI, Oct 1915 to May 1916

Vol XVI: Lowestoft Raid, 24–25 April 1916

Vol XVII: Home Waters VII, June – Nov 1916

Vol XVIII: Home Waters VIII, Dec 1916 – Apr 1917

Vol XIX: Home Waters IX, May – July 1917

Tenth Cruiser Squadron Under Command of Admiral de Chair, 1914–1916 (ADM 186/609)

Zeebrugge and Ostend Operations (printed report: ADM 137/3894)

Operations off the East Coast of Great Britain 1914–1918 (1940: OU 6354(40), ADM 275/23)

German Navy **Krieg zur See** *series:*

Firle, Rudolf (ed), *Ostsee* v. 1 (Outbreak of war to mid-March 1915) (Berlin: Mittler, 1920) (note: third volume, ed. by Ernst Freiherr von Gagern, was published in Frankfurt in 1964; it covers 1916–18)

Groos, Otto (ed) (with contributions by Walter Gladisch), *Der Krieg in der Nordsee* (Berlin: Mittler, 1920–65 in 7 vols, of which vols 1–6 were translated by the Royal Navy and Vol 7 was published only in German, after the war, in Frankfort-am-Main)

Koppen, Paul (ed), *Die Überwasserstreitkräfte und ihre Technik* (Berlin: Mittler, 1930)

Mantey, Eberhard von (ed), *Kreuzerkrieg* v. 3 (*Die Deutschen Hilfskreuzer* [Auxiliary Cruisers])

Raeder, Erich (ed), *Kreuzerkrieg* Vol 1 (Berlin: Mittler, 1922) and Vol 2 (Berlin: Mittler, 1923) (Raeder became navy chief in 1928)

Spindler, Arno (ed), *Der Handelskrieg mit U-Booten* (Berlin: Mittler, 1932–66 in 5 volumes, of which vols 1–3 [to February 1917] were available, including English translations in the British Monthly Intelligence Report; Vol 4 [Feb–Dec 1917] was published in 1941 and in facsimile postwar, and Vol 5 [1918] in 1966)

US Navy Documents:

Publication No. 2, *The Northern Barrage and Other Mining Activities* (Washington: GPO, 1920)

US Navy Bureau of Ordnance, *Navy Ordnance Activities: World War 1917–18* (Washington: GPO, 1920)

4. Printed Unofficial Publications

Bacon, Reginald, *The Life of Lord Fisher of Kilverstone* (London: Hodder & Stoughton, 1929)

_____, *The Dover Patrol 1915-1917* (London: Hutchinson, 1919; there is a single-volume 1932 version featuring a proposal for what amounts to a proto-LST, which is not in the 1919 version)

Beatty, Jack, *The Lost History of 1914: How the Great War Was Not Inevitable* (London: Bloomsbury, 2012)

Beesly, Patrick, *Room 40: British Naval Intelligence 1914-18* (London: Hamilton, 1982)

Bell, A C, *A History of the Blockade of Germany and of the countries associated with her in the great war: Austria-Hungary, Bulgaria, and Turkey 1914-1918* (originally for the Historical Section, Committee of Imperial Defence, 1937, reprinted by HMSO, 1961)

Berghahn, V R, *Germany and the Approach of War in 1914* (New York: St. Martin's Press, 1993 [second edition])

Black, Nicholas, *The British Naval Staff in the First World War* (Woodbridge: Boydell Press, 2009)

Brock, Michael and Eleanor (eds), *H.H. Asquith Letters to Venetia Stanley* (Oxford University Press, 1982)

Brown, D K, *The Grand Fleet: Warship Design and Development 1906-1922* (London: Chatham Publishing, 1999)

Buxton, Ian, *Big Gun Monitors: Design, Construction, and Operations 1914-1945* (Barnsley: Seaforth Publishing, 2008 [second edition])

Cain, P J, and A G Hopkins, *British Imperialism 1688-2000* (London: Longman, 2002 [second edition])

Chesneau, Roger, and Eugene M Kolesnik (eds). *Conway's All the World's Fighting Ships 1860-1905* (London: Conway Maritime Press, 1979)

Churchill, Randolph S (ed), *Winston S. Churchill Companion Volume II Pt 3, 1911–1914* (edited documents: London, Heinemann, 1969)

Davis, Lance E, and Stanley L Engerman, *Naval Blockades in Peace and War: An Economic History Since 1750* (Cambridge University Press, 2006)

Dittmar, F J, and J J College, *British Warships 1914-1919* (London: Ian Allan, 1972)

Epkenhans, Michael, and Gerhard P Gross (eds), *The Danish Straits and German Naval Power 1905-1918* (Potsdam: Militärgechichtliches Forchungsamt, 2010)

Fischer, Fritz, *War of Illusions: German Policies from 1911 to 1914* (New York: Norton, 1975)

Forrest, Michael, *The Defence of the Dardanelles: From Bombards to Battleships* (Barnsley: Pen and Sword, 2012)

Fraccaroli, Aldo, *Italian Warships of World War I* (London: Ian Allan, 1970)

Forstmeier, Friedrich, and Siegfried Breyer, *Deutsche Grosskampfschiffe 1915-1918: Sonderausgabe die Entwicklung der Typenfrage im Ersten Weltkrieg* (Bonn: Bernard & Graefe, 2001 reprint of 1970 book)

Friedman, Norman, *U.S. Small Combatants: An Illustrated Design History* (Annapolis: Naval Institute Press, 1987 [includes sub-chasers and First World War motor launches])

_____, *British Carrier Aviation: The Evolution of the Ships and Their Aircraft* (London: Conway Maritime Press, 1988)

_____, *Naval Firepower: Battleship Guns and Gunnery in the Dreadnought Era* (Barnsley: Seaforth Publishing, 2007)

_____, *British Destroyers: From Earliest Days to the Second World War* (Barnsley: Seaforth Publishing, 2009)

_____, *Network-Centric Warfare: How Navies Learned to Fight Smarter in Three World Wars* (Annapolis, Naval Institute Press, 2009)

_____, *British Cruisers: Two World Wars and After* (Barnsley: Seaforth Publishing, 2010)

_____, *Naval Weapons of World War I* (Barnsley: Seaforth Publishing, 2011)

_____, *British Cruisers of the Victorian Era* (Barnsley: Seaforth Publishing, 2012)

Fromkin, David, *Europe's Last Summer: Who Started the Great War in 1914?* (New York: Knopf, 2004)

Gardiner, Robert (ed), *Conway's All the World's Fighting Ships 1906-1921* (London: Conway, 1985)

Geiss, Immanuel, *German Foreign Policy 1871-1914* (London: Routledge & Kegan Paul, 1976)

Gemzell, Carl-Axel, *Organization, Conflict, and Innovation: A Study of German Naval Strategic Planning 1888-1940* (Lund: Esselte Studium, 1973)

Gordon, Andrew, *The Rules of the Game: Jutland and British Naval Command* (Annapolis: Naval Institute Press, 1996)

Grant, Robert M, *U-Boats Destroyed: The Effect of Anti-Submarine Warfare 1914-18* (London: Putnam, 1964)

Greissmer, Axel, *Grosse Kreuzer der Kaiserlichen Marine 1906-1918 (Konstruktionen und Entwurfe in Zeichen des Tirpitz-Planes)* (Bonn: Bernard & Graefe, 1996)

_____, *Linienschiffe der Kaiserlichen Marine 1906-1918: Konstruktion zwischen Rüstungskonkorrenz und Flottengesetz* (Bonn: Bernard & Graefe, 1999)

Gröner, Erich, *German Warships 1815-1945* (London: Conway Maritime Press, 2 vols, 1990 and 1991)

Hackmann, Willem, *Seek & Strike: Sonar, anti-submarine warfare, and the Royal Navy 1914-54* (London: HMSO, 1984)

Halpern, Paul G (ed), *The Keyes Papers Vol I (1914-1918)* (London: Navy Records Society, 1979)

_____, *The Naval War in the Mediterranean 1914-1918* (Annapolis: Naval Institute Press, 1987

_____, *A Naval History of World War I* (Annapolis: Naval Institute Press, 1994))

Hankey, Maurice P A, *The Supreme Command 1914-1918* (London: Allen and Unwin, 1961)

Herrick, Robert W, *Soviet Naval Strategy: Fifty Years of Theory and Practice* (Annapolis: Naval Institute Press, 1968)

Herrman, David G, *The Arming of Europe and the Making of the First World War* (Princeton University Press, 1996)

Herwig, Holger H, *The German Naval Officer Corps: A Social and Political History 1890 - 1918* (Oxford University Press, 1973)

_____, *'Luxury Fleet:' The German Imperial Navy 1888-1918* (London: Allen & Unwin, 1980)

Hezlet, Arthur, *Electronics and Sea Power* (New York: Stein and Day, 1975)

Jenkins, Roy, *Churchill* (London: Pan, 2001)

Hobbs, David, *British Aircraft Carriers: Design, Development, and Service Histories* (Barnsley: Seaforth Publishing, 2013)

Hurley, Edward N, *Bridge to France* (Philadelphia: Lippincott, 1927)

Karau, Mark D, *'Wielding the Dagger:' The MarineKorps Flandern and the German War Effort, 1914-1918* (Westport: Praeger, 2003)

Kelly, Patrick J. *Tirpitz and the Imperial German Navy* (Bloomington: Indiana University Press, 2011)

Labayle-Couhat, Jean, *French Warships of World War I* (London: Ian Allan, 1974)

Lambert, Nicholas A, *Sir John Fisher's Naval Revolution* (Columbia: University of South Carolina, 1999)

_____ (ed), *The Submarine Service 1900-1918* (Ashgate: Navy Records Society, 2001)

_____, *Planning for Armageddon: British Economic Warfare and the First World War* (Harvard University Press, 2012)

Layman, R D, *Naval Aviation in the First World War: Its Impact and Influence* (London: Chatham Publishing, 1996)

Lumby, E W R, *Policy and Operations in the Mediterranean 1912-14* (London: Navy Records Society, 1970 [includes *Goeben* operation, providing insights into Admiralty control])

Lynn, John A (ed), *Feeding Mars: Essays on Logistics and Resource Mobilization in Western Warfare from the Middle Ages to the Present* (Boulder: Westview, 1993)

Mackay, Ruddock F, *Fisher of Kilverstone* (Oxford University Press, 1973)

Marder, Arthur J (ed), *Fear God and Dread Nought: the correspondence of Admiral of the Fleet Lord Fisher of Kilverstone* (London: Jonathan Cape, 3 vols, 1952–9)

_____, *From the Dreadnought to Scapa Flow* (Oxford University Press, 5 vols: 1961, 1965, 1966, 1969, 1970 [second edition of Jutland volume 1978]; Vol 2 is outbreak of war to Jutland, Vol 3 is Jutland, Vol 4 is the crisis of 1917)

McMeekin, Sean, *The Berlin-Baghdad Express: the Ottoman Empire and Germany's Bid for World Power* (Cambridge: Harvard University Press, 2010)

_____, *The Russian Origins of the First World War* (Cambridge, Mass: Harvard University Press, 2011)

Messimer, Dwight R, *Find and Destroy: Antisubmarine Warfare in World War I* (Annapolis: Naval Institute Press, 2001)

Millman, Brock, *Pessimism and British War Policy 1916-1918* (London: Frank Cass, 2001)

Mitchell, W H, and L A Sawyer, *Wartime Standard Ships Vol 3: British Standard Ships of World War I* (Liverpool: Sea Breezes, 1968)

Nowarra, Heinz J, *Marine Aircraft of the 1914-1918 War* (Letchworth: Harleyford, 1966)

Osborne, Eric W, *Britain's Economic Blockade of Germany 1914-1919* (London: Frank Cass, 2004)

Osborne, Richard, Harry Spong, and Tom Grover, *Armed Merchant Cruisers 1878-1945* (Windsor: World Ship Society, 2007)

Patterson, A Temple (ed), *The Jellicoe Papers* (London: Navy Records Society, 1966 and 1968)

Prior, Robin, *Gallipoli: The End of the Myth* (New Haven: Yale University Press, 2009)

Ranft, Brian, *The Beatty Papers Vol I (1902-1918)* (London: Navy Records Society, 1989)

Robinson, Douglas H, *The Zeppelin in Combat: A History of the German Naval Airship Division 1912-1918* (London: Foulis, 1962)

Roskill, Stephen W (ed), *The Naval Air Service Vol. I: 1908-1918* (London: Navy Records Society, 1969)

Rössler, Eberhard, *The U-Boat: The Evolution and Technical History of German Submarines* (London: Arms and Armour Press, 1981)

Rudenko, Victor, *Gallipoli: Attack From the Sea* (New Haven: Yale University Press, 2008)

Seligmann, Matthew S, *The Royal Navy and the German Threat 1901-1914: Admiralty Plans to Protect British Trade in a War Against Germany* (Oxford University Press, 2012)

Siney, Marion C, *The Allied Blockade of Germany 1914-1916* (Westport: Greenwood, 1973 [reprint of 1957 book published by University of Michigan])

Steinberg, Jonathan, *Yesterday's Deterrent: Tirpitz and the Birth of the German Battle Fleet* (New York: Macmillan, 1965)

Stevenson, David, *With Our Backs to the Wall: Victory and Defeat in 1918* (London: Allan Lane, 2011)

Still, William N Jr., *Crisis at Sea: The United States Navy in European Waters in World War I* (Gainesville: University Press of Florida, 2006)

Sumida, Jon Tetsuro, *In Defence of Naval Supremacy: Finance, Technology, and British Naval Policy 1889-1914* (Boston: Unwin Hyman, 1989)

Taylor, A J P, *The Struggle for Mastery in Europe 1848-1918* (Oxford University Press, 1954)

Tracy, Nicholas, *Attack on Maritime Trade* (University of Toronto Press, 1991)

_____, *Sea Power and the Control of Trade: Belligerent Rights from the Russian War to the Beira Patrol 1854-1970* (Ashgate: Navy Records Society, 2005)

Wark, Wesley K, *The Ultimate Enemy: British Intelligence and Nazi Germany 1933-1939* (Cornell University Press, 1985)

Wegener, Wolfgang (ed. by Holger H Herwig), *The Naval Strategy of the World War* (Annapolis: Naval Institute, 1989)

Index